THE TRANSFORMATION OF MODERN EUROPE

Volume two

EUROPE AND THE MODERN WORLD

*Europe's political, economic, social, and intellectual problems and the changes
they have brought to the modern world from 1800 to 1954*

SCOTT, FORESMAN AND COMPANY

Chicago, Atlanta, Dallas, New York, San Francisco

THE

TRANSFORMATION

OF

MODERN EUROPE

LOUIS GOTTSCHALK *The University of Chicago*

DONALD LACH *The University of Chicago*

PREFACE

WE HAVE chosen the title of this work—*Europe and the Modern World*—with a special and deliberate purpose. Many teachers of history have been saying, in speeches and articles, that we should broaden the study of European history, that we should give students a more meaningful grasp of the part played by Europe's past in the development of our present civilization, that we should mark more clearly the interplay between Europe and the rest of the world, that we should examine the history of European culture more searchingly for a possible key to a future world culture. We have used phrases like "Atlantic community," "living past," "civilization in transit," "transatlantic influences" and "expansion of Europe" until they have begun to look familiar, even shopworn. And yet little has been done in our history textbooks to give such phrases a context. This book is an attempt to live up to our own and others' pronunciamentos along these lines.

Historians of modern European history have frequently been content to concentrate upon events in Europe to the neglect of their world setting and of their impact upon non-European peoples. We have rejected this approach. Taking "Europe" as a phenomenon transcending its geographical boundaries, we have tried to tell the story of the modern European heritage and to trace its ramifications wherever they lead. This approach has meant, for one thing, giving special attention to the contacts of Europe with America and Asia, and of America and Asia with Europe, though always from the point of view of the development—the advances, the stand-stills, and the retreats—of European civilization. It has meant being equally concerned with a broad definition of history; our study is directed toward "Europe" as a rich cultural concept rather than as a place on a map.

v

In spite of national boundaries, linguistic barriers, and local differences, Europe is after all fairly uniformly Caucasoid in race, Indo-European in language, Christian in religion; most of Europe has had similar, related, or overlapping experiences that together form a common background and provide a common fund of achievements. We have attempted to relate the story of that common background and that common fund. We believe that students have a particular need for an understanding of that story—an appreciation of the long-term trends, the interacting contemporaneous forces, the lasting human problems, and the enduring achievements of European civilization as an organic whole, as against a chronicle of the merely political developments within the separate nations. And so, while endeavoring to make national-political developments clear, we have given as much if not more attention to the economic, social, and intellectual phases, and we have made a special effort to organize our story on a European rather than a national scale.

Throughout this work, we have proceeded from a central thesis. We are convinced that the last five centuries have revealed an increasing awareness of the interdependence of the world. This awareness has grown into a firm conviction in the period covered in this volume—a conviction that spells alarm for some and hope for others. We do not prognosticate that "One World" is therefore bound to come; perhaps annihilation or degeneration will come before oneness. But the possibility of world unity seems to us greater in the twentieth century than it was in the fifteenth and, barring catastrophe, now looks more real than the possibility of permanent disunity. We hold that conviction because, not fully persuaded by some recent philosophies of history, we see in the past of mankind no inescapable morphology that dictates the rise, maturity, and decay of unaffiliated civilizations. On the contrary, despite the current animosities and dangers we feel that all contemporary civilizations tend more and more toward affiliation and that the continuous accumulation of scientific knowledge and the steady mastery of the forces of nature leave some room still to hope for a gradually merging and improving world.

As conscientious historians, however, we are also obliged to record and develop a parallel central theme—that in the race between progress and catastrophe, catastrophe has kept pace and may yet be the winner. The slow accumulation of man's knowledge may eventually provide a satisfying outcome to man's painful struggle toward the fulfillment of his aspirations for freedom, justice, prosperity, self-expression, and peace. But that struggle has regularly run parallel with man's tireless quest for power—the conflict between person and person, party and party, class and class, nation and nation, region and region, each seeking to accomplish its own ever-widening purposes. Knowledge, of course, may be used for uncommendable ends, and aspirations may be manipulated and corrupted toward disaster. Power itself may be checked or counterbalanced and may be used to promote the accumulation of knowledge and the fulfillment of aspirations. While we have attempted to give particular attention to the constant interaction between man's achievements and aspirations on the one hand and his quest for power on the other, we cannot, of course, pretend to know whether man's incomplete knowledge and unfulfilled aspirations will become the instruments of power for ultimate good or ultimate evil.

As long as man strives, says Goethe, he must err. It does not lie within our province, as it lay within the poet's, to decide whether Faust or Mephisto will triumph in the end. In consequence, we have not tried to propose or to dispose; we have tried only to expose. But the reader will probably guess where our sympathies lie. He will probably discern, too, from our last chapter that, even if contemporary man can avoid destruction, we dare suggest no quick and easy solution of age-old problems, no sure realization of enduring aspirations. We do suggest, however, that, given time, man may well look upon his past record, for all its blots and blunders, as a source of hope for a better future. Yet, as we go to press with this volume, an old expression takes on a new meaning: Time is of the essence.

ACKNOWLEDGMENTS

Critical Reading

A s WE STATED in the first volume, in a work of this kind, in which all areas of the world and all aspects of culture are proper subjects of discussion, no author or set of authors can hope to be wholly competent throughout, and for that reason we have sought and have been graciously granted the editorial assistance of a number of specialists. Alastair Taylor, formerly of the University of Southern California and the United Nations, assisted us in the writing of the first chapter on the history of the Western Hemisphere. To Mary Herrick Porter and to Dr. Frederick Sternthal we are indebted for much of the groundwork and research that has gone into a large part of this volume. The sections dealing with art have greatly benefited from the criticisms of Professor Ulrich A. Middeldorf, of the University of Chicago, and Mr. David Watson, of Denison University, and the sections dealing with music from the criticisms of Professor Otto Gombosi, of Harvard University. Professor Hill Shine, of the University of Kentucky, helped us improve the style in general as well as those parts of the book that deal with literature. Professor Henry Guerlac, of Cornell University, checked the discussions of science and technology, and Professor Alexander Kolin, of the University of Chicago, strengthened a particularly difficult passage in nuclear physics. Professor Richard P. McKeon, of the University of Chicago, examined the paragraphs dealing with the history of thought. Professor William T. Hutchinson, of the University of Chicago, went carefully over the chapters dealing with American history. Professor Herbert Heaton, of the University of Minnesota, tightened up the discussion of economic affairs. Professor Hans Kohn, of the College of the City of New York, made numerous helpful criticisms on all parts of the book. Professor Chester W. New, of McMaster University, took most extraordinary pains with the parts dealing with British history. Several of these people have made suggestions beyond the realm of their specialties. If because of pedagogical and space considerations we were not always able to follow their advice, we are no less grateful for their painstaking and expert cooperation, and we absolve them from all blame for whatever weaknesses this book despite the truly valiant efforts of all of them may yet retain.

Maps

THE MAPS in this volume have been prepared especially for *The Transformation of Modern Europe* by R. M. Chapin, Jr., Vincent Puglisi, and Jere Donovan. The task of translating often complicated and occasionally inaccurate atlas materials into simple storytelling maps has been carried out by Elizabeth Coleman Creed.

Illustrations

THE AUTHORS are indebted to David Watson for the planning and realization of the illustration program.

TABLE OF CONTENTS

LIST OF MAPS

THE ILLUSTRATIONS FOR *The Transformation of Modern Europe* have been selected with two purposes in mind. In the first place, the authors and editors have intended to provide, as is often done in history textbooks, a selection from contemporary artists, illustrating not merely their style and talents but also their interpretation of events and their portraits of prominent persons. In addition, a studied attempt has been made to depict objects and customs, sometimes of extraordinary significance, sometimes of everyday life, in direct association with their setting in the text. Reproductions of political cartoons, costumes, architecture, means of transportation, mechanical and scientific phenomena, and the like (nearly always from contemporaneous sources) have been presented in order to give a better-rounded picture of the tastes, manners, institutions, and opinions of the periods under discussion. The illustrations are thus planned as an integral part of the story presented in this volume and not merely as a decorative supplement.

A list of the illustrations (with acknowledgments) will be found on pages 1034-1035.

Part one

Introduction: The European heritage around 1800

Chapter one: Legitimacy or revolution?

THE AFTERMATH
OF THE
FRENCH REVOLUTION

Introduction

THE EUROPEAN

HERITAGE

AROUND 1800

THE STUDY of history is a study of both continuity and change; things either remain the same in the course of time or they become different. At the beginning of the nineteenth century many things, of course, were different from those that are familiar to us today. If some fabled slumberer had gone to sleep in Columbus' day and had waked around 1800, his astonishment would probably have been less than if he had gone to sleep in 1800 and waked only in the present day. For greater changes—in outward appearances, at least—have taken place in the last century and a half than in the preceding three centuries. In order to understand a Rip Van Winkle's astonishment on waking in the middle of the twentieth century—and thus to form some idea of the changes with which this volume will deal—we must first attempt to form some picture of the world that he would have found at the beginning of the nineteenth century. Later (in Chapter 16) we shall deal with some problems of human affairs that in the course of time have not fundamentally changed.

One hundred and fifty years ago the peoples of the world were far more interdependent than they had been around 1500, though far less aware of and far less dependent upon one another than they are today. By 1800, the inhabited continents had already developed close mutual ties, and it was constantly becoming harder to think of the globe as divided into wholly self-contained or isolated units. Commercial, intellectual, and sometimes political ties bound Europe more closely than ever before to the non-European world, and this change the peoples of the world usually recognized. They were less likely to be aware that the Americas, Asia, and Africa were on the threshold of a new technological and imperialist era in which European contacts would increasingly help to determine the destinies of other continents. Bonds which had once not existed at all or had remained loose and unnoticed would now be tightened as other parts of the world, whether civilized or uncivilized, would feel the mounting impact of the European way of life upon their own.

The major continental peoples of the world nevertheless were to retain most of the characteristics peculiar to them at the beginning of the nineteenth century. And yet, while differing significantly from each other, the several continents and their national and cultural subdivisions had already lost many of their unique qualities during the three centuries before 1800. "The expansion of Europe"—the spread of European people and European culture throughout the world—had promoted a constantly increasing interchange, interaction, imitation, and interdependence. In the century and a half after 1800 this interaction (or, as the anthropologists might call it, mutual acculturation) accelerated, and today social changes occurring in widely separated parts of the globe may quickly make a perceptible difference in the daily life of most of us.

A closer examination of the world in 1800 will reveal the ways in which it compared and contrasted with the world of 1500 and with that of the 1950's. In 1500 no European had gone around the world. By 1800 the globe had been circled several times. In 1500 a European who knew of America (and there were a few) would most probably have thought of Europe as lying between Asia and America, the outlying continents being as yet unable to communicate with each other. By 1800 he knew that he could, and he sometimes did, go across the Atlantic to America and then continue across the Pacific to Asia and overland back home. If he had done so, he might have found some marks of European influence almost anywhere and would, upon his return, have been able to detect, perhaps better than before, many marks of non-European influence in his homeland. Let us go on such a supposed journey.

EUROPE AT THE BEGINNING

OF THE NINETEENTH CENTURY

WHILE maps of the European continent have been available for nearly all periods of history, a strict definition of Europe as a geographical or political unit has never been easy. Its geopolitical base was the ancient Roman Empire (which, however, also included areas outside of Europe) and the territories indirectly under Roman influence, such as the Teutonic countries of the north. It comprised the Indo-European, Caucasian, and, eventually, Christian peoples whom today we loosely call "the white race"— loosely, because the Whites were not exclusively found in Europe, and today some Europeans are not white. The Holy Roman Empire, theoretically the successor to the Roman Empire, in the Middle Ages claimed universal jurisdiction, but it never managed to exert practical control over certain outlying nations like Spain or England. Nor did the Roman Catholic (i.e., universal) Church wholly succeed in welding the diverse states and peoples of either medieval or modern Europe into an integrated spiritual empire. Not only was Catholicism divided between a Roman Catholic Church in the west and an Orthodox Eastern Church in the east, but Moslems, Jews, and heretics always eluded the jurisdiction of both Christian churches, and in the sixteenth century a series of Protestant churches arose to fragment Christianity still more. Never having existed as a political or spiritual unit, Europe was nevertheless bound together by cultural affiliations and a way of life, an ethos, that derived its main characteristics from its Hebrew, Greek, Roman, and Christian heritages. These heritages persisted throughout the centuries despite local, provincial, dynastic, and eventually national differences, and gave to the concept "Europe" a meaning that the common derivation of most European languages and the white complexion of nearly all Europeans would have failed to give it.

The political geography of the European continent EUROPE MAY be conventionally defined as that part of the Eurasiatic land mass which extends from Scandinavia to Sicily and from Ireland to the Ural Mountains. Christian though it remained in almost all its sweep in 1800, Europe contained in its southeastern portion the continuing, though declining, Moslem empire of the Ottoman Turks. Furthermore, the sea-bound nations of Europe by 1800 had carried their culture westward across the Atlantic to America. For contemporaries, however, as for the nineteenth-century German historian Leopold von Ranke (page 69), the heartland of European culture continued to be the community of the Latin and Germanic nations of the west and center. The Slavic peoples of the east, most of whom had never come directly under Roman influence and had adopted Orthodox rather than Catholic Christianity, were often considered, and were likely to consider themselves, as somehow outside of Europe and separate from other Europeans. This attitude, though far from justified, made an important difference in their outlook, then as now.

In the three centuries before 1800, the center of political gravity shifted from southern to northern Europe. Dominant until the seventeenth century, Spain and Portugal, sometimes in close alignment, were replaced as the preponderant European powers by France. But France was not left to enjoy her continental supremacy unchallenged. The northern countries of England, Sweden, and Holland took part in the development of the overseas world after 1600 and increasingly acted as an effective check upon French expansion on the Continent. England remained a great power, but Holland's and Sweden's strength notably diminished in the next century. In the eighteenth century the power center moved further eastward and northward with 5 the establishment of a strong Prussia and a vast Russia, both of which had grown at the expense of less fortunate neighbors such as Sweden and Poland. At the end of the eighteenth century five European nations—England, France, Austria, Prussia, and Russia—were numbered among the great powers. They lived in a delicately balanced equilibrium that could be easily tipped by shifts in alliances or changes in economic or military strength. Poland had disappeared; the Holy Roman Empire was but an impressive shadow; Turkey, Portugal, Spain, Holland, and Sweden were second-rate powers; and several other countries came following after in size or military importance or political strength, though not necessarily in cultural significance.

The decline
of rural predominance

FROM 1500 to the advent of Napoleon in 1799, the inhabitants of the European continent, like the various cultural groups of the world at large, had become more aware of each other than ever before. Although people in all countries still lived close to the land, cities had boomed in size and importance. Trade and industry, once mainly local and limited, had in England largely replaced agriculture as moving forces in the economy and in all countries were more active and more extensive. Even the farmer, whether freeman or serf, had had to adjust his traditional methods to new crops needed outside his village and new tools brought into his village over roads that extended farther and in more directions than before. New ways of doing his daily work had helped to free the isolated farmer and the urban artisan somewhat from slavish imitation of the practices of the past. And as his methods of work changed, the European worker, in the country as well as in the city, had become more receptive to change in general. Expansion of outlook brought to him challenging if disturbing experiences with the new, the strange, and the unexpected.

The rise
of the middle class

THE EXPANSION of trade and industry tended to raise the banker, the merchant, and the manufacturer, economically at least, to the level of the landed nobility. Though averse to accepting the man in business as a social equal, the aristocracy were forced to accord him greater recognition as his wealth and influence grew. Striving to stand above the aristocracy, and often in conflict with them, the crowned heads of Europe had at first encouraged and worked with the middle-class groups. But, while willing to accept the protection of royal authority, industrialists, merchants, and investors had become increasingly impatient with royal restrictions upon business enterprise and called for greater freedom of trade. Hence the alliance between king and middle class had in the eighteenth century run upon evil days. As the aristocracy declined in power and as the bourgeoisie became more and more independent and dangerous, the king and the aristocracy had been thrown together out of a mutual fear of middle-class strength.

The growing tendency of the middle class to oppose the traditional limitations upon their economic activities made them less willing to tolerate inferior social and political status. In western Europe especially, they found occasion to demand greater political equality with the aristocracy. In business they began to insist upon the principle of laissez faire (literally, "let alone"). Some of them wanted the government to interfere with them as little as possible but also wanted more power in government affairs, if for no other reason than to keep the government out of their affairs. For such middle-class militants laissez faire was coming to mean less government in business and more business in government. In the mid-eighteenth century several great classics, written by a school of French economists known as the Physiocrats and by the Scottish economist Adam Smith, upheld their point of view.

Experimentalism and the "scientific revolution"

ADVANCES in trade and industry had been made possible in part by parallel developments since 1500 in science and technology. An empirical, secular research spirit, though it emerged only slowly and with numerous setbacks, had freed scientists and technicians to a considerable degree from the theories, prepossessions, and practices of the past and had led them in the direction of unbiased experimentation. Lacking precise research instruments, they had had to develop observing and reckoning devices such as the microscope and logarithms, the pendulum clock, the chemical balance, and the calculus. While devising new instruments and mathematical processes they had also worked out new techniques of experimentation and a suitable methodology. By 1800, the principles of the modern scientific method, involving mathematics, minute measurements, experimentation, generalization, and prediction, had won wide acceptance as a practical way of detaching and systematizing what had once been the secrets of nature. Galileo Galilei and Sir Isaac Newton had been among the foremost figures in this "scientific revolution."

The ascendency of secular thought

NOR WAS the scientist alone in his concern to formulate new methods for ascertaining the truth about the physical universe and man's place in it. Since the schism in western Christianity brought about by the religious revolution of the sixteenth century (the Reformation), the church had lost much of its power to persuade men to accept the old beliefs, and many had found various reasons for doubting some of them. Refusing to regard the revealed knowledge of the churches and the venerated insights of scholastic philosophers as final, and often returning, under the impact of the Renaissance, to the pagan thought of Greece and Rome, the thinkers of early modern times sought to formulate new and independent philosophical systems. They tried in a definite context to describe, evaluate, and define the nature of reality, the relation of mind to matter, and the place of God in a secularized world.

7

Since these philosophers found it hard to accept each other's explanations of these eternal problems, conflicting schools arose. The thought of René Descartes was particularly influential in and after the seventeenth century. Descartes worked out a system which asserted that rational doubt was the beginning of all knowledge. Although he employed experiment as well as reason, Descartes based his philosophic method on mathematical deduction from "clear, distinct, and adequate ideas," or, since their truth is not determined by experience, "innate ideas."

The Cartesian school was most directly challenged by the empirical school, or empiricists, led by John Locke and David Hume, principally on the question of "innate ideas." Holding that the senses and experience are the source of reason, Locke led his and later generations of thinkers to focus upon that knowledge which is attainable by the exercise of the reason reflecting upon the perceptions of the senses alone. Empiricists and rationalists alike, though generally religious men, sought secular explanations of problems once answered by revelation and the persuasions of theologians. Although frequently at odds with each other, the philosophers were united in their purpose to separate the treatment of philosophic problems that require only the senses and reason from the problems of theology that depend on revelation.

Rationalism in political and social matters

THE Age of Enlightenment (c. 1685-1789) derived its character and direction from the teachings of these scientists and philosophers. Its disciples of the mid-eighteenth century are frequently called Voltaireans because of the recognized leadership of Voltaire among them. In setting the tone in literature and the arts, the restrained classical tradition with its emphasis upon regularity and symmetry shared honors with the equally balanced but lavish and ornamental baroque, which made its appeal to old rich and new rich alike. In government, emphasis was laid upon the rational organization and direction of the state by the paternalistic ruler and his trained administrative bureaucracy. Hence the Age of Enlightenment tended also to be the age of the so-called "enlightened despot." The Voltaireans, or *philosophes,* preached that the universe of human affairs had a "natural order" no less ascertainable than the order in the material universe, and that it was the business of the enlightened government to discover and apply the laws of that natural order. Movements for reform of the law codes, schemes for the preservation of international peace, proposals to ease poverty through philanthropy, and attempts to abolish ancient abuses by the application of "the laws of nature" came in rapid succession—in part as outgrowths of the expanding belief in the ability of reasonable human beings to solve social problems voluntarily by introducing a better "natural" order into society. Even in the established churches a tendency to give rational explanations of miracles, the Resurrection, and the existence of God was not unknown.

Romanticism
as a challenge to rationalism

SIDE BY side with the Enlightenment there developed a tendency that is sometimes thought of as a countermovement. It was later to be called "romanticism." Reacting against the regularity of classical and baroque art forms, "rococo" artists of the early eighteenth century had stressed irregularity, innovation, and ornateness for their own sake. In the latter half of the century writers began to rebel against the rationalist's emphasis upon a materialistic, determined reason and his stifling of emotion and instinct, and they recoiled from the dreary doctrine that men have no inner sense of God and of morality. One of the fathers of romanticism, Jean-Jacques Rousseau, in particular pointed out that neither the five senses nor human reason provided satisfactory answers to problems of right and wrong and would not unaided lead to the betterment of mankind. Immanuel Kant, founder of a school of German idealists (i.e., philosophers who sought the foundations of science and morality in principles above the mind rather than in ideas based on experience), likewise described the limitations of "pure" reason, and differentiated carefully between the various applications and levels of human cognition, allowing room for faith and an innate sense of morality. Religious leaders, particularly John Wesley, the founder of Methodism, deplored the attention paid by the established churches to mere rationalism and stressed the need of the emotional appeal in repentance and of personal faith for salvation. By 1800, this "Romantic Movement," with its emphasis upon the emotions and inward convictions, bade fair to become the dominant persuasion of European artists and intellectuals. But the rationalist spirit, reinforced by recent scientific and industrial trends, remained strong and persistent.

Revolution
and revolt as a tradition

"ENLIGHTENMENT" was not the only trend of the past to succumb by 1800 to more dynamic movements. Through the political history of Europe from the Renaissance (and before) to the end of the eighteenth century (and beyond) runs a tradition of protest against vested, official injustice. The Reformation with the Protestant break from the authority of the Roman Catholic Church was a widespread revolutionary attack upon established institutions and practices. The century and more of religious wars that followed manifested and contributed to the growing lack of respect for traditional religious authority; and because church and state were closely bound together, the traditional political authority shared in the disrespect. In the seventeenth century numerous revolts flamed up against the kings or their agents, and at least two important monarchs were killed by their subjects for motives that involved an inseparable web of religious and political rationalizations. Shocked by such attacks, amenable to the numerous demands of their subjects for reform and for a greater role in government, and subscribing to the current concepts of enlight- 9 ened government, the rulers of the eighteenth century, as already indicated, usually sought to head off revolt by voluntarily rectifying the more patent evils and by paying a close, patriarchal attention to the business of government.

The failure of "enlightened despotism"

WHILE FAIRLY successful in some countries, the system of "enlightened despotism" failed to work effectively in France. Though the leading nation of Europe, France under its last Bourbon monarchs suffered from continual war, inefficient administration, outworn social discriminations, and incompetent or overreaching royal authority. To be sure, France's kings and wealthier classes patronized the arts and sciences, with Paris as the center of artistic and intellectual advance, and France also began to undergo rapid change along the lines sometimes described as the "Industrial Revolution." Her political life, however, remained virtually static and unrevised—an absolute monarchy—for most of the eighteenth century. Systematic reform was not undertaken, despite demands from all classes of society, until the 1770's and 1780's, and the reforms that were then attempted generally met with marked opposition from the vested interests and privileged classes. Not content to accept limited reform from above, which would probably have meant the preservation of the absolute monarchy without vital concessions to either aristocracy or middle class, each group of society called for its own greater participation in determining the nation's welfare. Finally, bowing to imminent bankruptcy and public pressure, King Louis XVI agreed to convoke the Estates General in 1789.

The triumph of the middle class in France

THE Estates General, though seeming to presage a cooperative and peaceful solution to France's problems, brought in its wake the great French Revolution. Within a few years France transformed itself from an absolute monarchy to a middle-class republic. In the process the French overturned many of the revered social, economic, and religious institutions of the Old Regime, and substituted for them new ones based upon—or at least rationalized by—the revolutionary principles of "Liberty, Equality, and Fraternity."

Politically, the French Revolution partly substituted a parliamentary government for absolutism, and at the same time gave to political organizations a recognized place in the choice of certain officials. The principle of special privilege by virtue of birth or royal selection was in good measure superseded by the principle of equality of opportunity regardless of social class. Feudal survivals, both political and economic, largely disappeared as the elective principle was substituted for the hereditary in government, as more power in local affairs was concentrated in the hands of the central authority, and as many administrative overlappings and anachronisms were swept away with the uniform reorganization of government.

10   Though the pendulum of revolution swung wildly for a period, in the

early decades of the nineteenth century French politics reached a point of relative stability that marked a triumph for the middle class. The prestige and the power of the crown, the aristocracy, and the church had meanwhile been diminished by executions, confiscations, and the distribution of their land and other properties. The Revolution passed on much of their wealth to businessmen and the well-to-do peasantry. It prohibited workingmen's associations and disenfranchised the poor, while resanctifying the new pattern of private property and opening nearly all doors to the middle class. Careers, in the phrase generally attributed to Napoleon Bonaparte, were made "open to men of talent," or at least more open than when they had been largely monopolized by the privileged classes, although high office was still more readily available to those who had wealth and leisure than to those who had not.

The rise of popular nationalism

THE EMERGENCE of the middle class as the ascendant political power marked a victory in the struggle to replace the concept of royal sovereignty with that of popular sovereignty. Royalty lost out, for example, when the church lost out. Before the Revolution, philanthropy, vital statistics, and education in France had been largely in the hands of a clergy in alliance with the monarch. The temporary disestablishment of the Roman Catholic Church by the Revolution brought into being a system of secular social agencies, supported by the state and supervised by state officials with a view to serving the purposes of the state. Civil and secular education, philanthropy, and vital statistics meant a wider separation of the citizen from the church and made less necessary the old alliance of the state with the church. Thus the system of public education, politically oriented, replaced the old system of church education, religiously oriented. The new state schools inaugurated a program of training for good citizenship rather than good Christianity, and even when the church was reëstablished, the secular, civic educational system managed to survive.

In the course of the French Revolution good citizenship meant loyalty to the new regime, particularly since the monarchs of Europe, fearing the spread of revolution, endeavored to divide the French people from their republican leaders. To resist foreign encroachments and to raise a citizen-army, the French Republic elaborated the principle of the nation-in-arms, or universal military service. In the process of defending, and eventually of spreading, the Revolution, the Republic gave new meaning to the concept of patriotism. Patriotism was no longer mere loyalty to one's native heath or to one's liege lord. The concept of "blood and soil" took on a wider meaning. Frenchmen were brothers and France was their soil; they owed that allegiance to each other which once they had owed to their king because *they* were the state, because *they* were the sovereign. The concept of popular sovereignty carried with it the concept of popular solidarity, or nationalism—the belief that "people" and "nation," "citizen" and "patriot" are synonymous. 11

It was a concept hostile both to the Christian doctrine of the brotherhood of man regardless of national origin and to the rational and cosmopolitan spirit of the eighteenth century, but we shall find it flourishing and growing stronger in the course of ensuing generations.

The spread
of revolutionary doctrine

THE FRENCH Revolution had in part been inspired by the American Revolution (pages 17-18) and was itself "for export." Revolutionary sympathies were widespread in other parts of Europe, and leaders soon appeared who sought to impress upon their compatriots the need for fundamental changes along the lines being worked out in America and France. This revolutionary sentiment had a dual effect. It encouraged French patriots to think of their revolution as a mission or a crusade, and it roused the anxiety of crowned heads outside France about their own safety. As the French Revolution swung farther and farther to the left, the position of Louis XVI became more and more precarious. In response to the pleas of the French monarch for help, and in the hope of securing their own positions, the other monarchs of Europe lined up solidly to resist revolutionary change and to check, if possible, the swirling political currents that threatened to engulf them all. For the second time in modern history, an international ferment from a common source roused peoples all over Europe. The first time had been the Reformation, when their resentment was directed against their churches. Now it was directed against their rulers.

The rise
of Bonaparte and Bonapartism

WE, WHO in our own time have been exposed to revolutionary ferment originating in Russia, will find striking though imprecise parallels in the movement that over a century earlier emanated from France. Though the European powers twice directed military interventions against revolutionary France before 1800, they failed to check the growth and spread of revolution. Ringed by a series of puppet republics, revolutionary France with its mass armies was victorious, although not decisively triumphant, after almost a decade of continuous war. In the meantime, however, the character of the revolution within France had been considerably modified by internal readjustments and external pressures. Once relatively free of social privilege and relatively secure from invasion and defeat, the French tired of successive changes and continuous violence. Their crusade for liberty at home and abroad lost its glamor and they began to seek order and stability. New threats of defeat from abroad and of instability at home led to the quest for the great leader who would bring peace out of war and order out of chaos. They found him in Napoleon Bonaparte.

By 1800 the Revolution was well on the way to being disciplined, and Bonaparte had outclassed all rivals. It was, or quickly became, his purpose to tame the Revolution without destroying its gains completely. He hoped thereby to bring an end to domestic strife and at the same time to organize France for continental conquests beyond anything thitherto conceived of, thus making his own glory great at home and weakening the enemies of France (and therefore of himself) abroad. The glory of France, the revolutionary crusade, and the personality of Napoleon Bonaparte quickly became hard to distinguish from one another. At the dawn of the nineteenth century Bonaparte's revolutionary France, and the principles for which it seemed to stand, symbolized the wave of the future for many of the peoples of European extraction, whether in Europe itself or in the Americas across the seas. The intense nationalism that many peoples of the world were soon to cultivate was to arise to a considerable extent as a reaction, sometimes direct, sometimes indirect, to Bonaparte and Bonapartism.

THE AMERICAS AT THE BEGINNING
OF THE NINETEENTH CENTURY

THE VOYAGES of exploration at the end of the fifteenth century, particularly those of Christopher Columbus, brought the states of Europe located on the Atlantic seaboard into distant touch with the Western Hemisphere. Explorers and adventurers from Spain and Portugal took the lead in opening the new area, exploiting their superior technology and equipment to overcome the resistance of the natives. The other seaboard countries of Europe only slowly followed suit, but by the seventeenth century the English, the French, the Dutch, the Swedes, and the Danes had also entered the race for colonial empire in the New World.

The Iberians in the New World

USING Mexico City as their continental headquarters, the Spanish sent expeditions north and south to claim new lands, to search for silver and gold, or to hunt slaves. The Portuguese centered their activities around Bahia in Brazil. Despite unusual hardships, the Iberians managed gradually to establish and retain control over the Americas south of the Rio Grande. In colonizing Latin America the Iberians encountered numerous difficulties. They were handicapped by small numbers and limited resources, the territories they sought to win were vast, and the natives were hostile. The rugged topography and the uncertain climate also seriously complicated their problems of settlement and administration. Appalling distances by land and sea separated the pioneers from their homelands; and frequently shortsighted policies of the home government made their situation extremely hard and sometimes alarming. Their troubles multiplied when the northern Europeans, particularly the English and the French, began to encroach upon their holdings.

The modification
of Iberian culture in America

BY THE END of the first century of colonization huge imperial tracts, about twenty times the size of the mother countries, had come under Spain's and Portugal's control. For sixty years (1580-1640) the two Iberian kingdoms loosely united their holdings in Latin America and elsewhere, but then they separated again. Dominant everywhere except in Brazil and certain western areas of Central and South America, the Spaniards sought to exploit their New World possessions for the purpose of increasing the wealth and security of Spain itself. Commerce was almost entirely limited to direct trade between Spain and the colonies until 1700. After 1713, the British forced the Spanish to permit them to compete on a limited basis for the commerce of the Spanish empire in America. In the colonies the Spanish settlers controlled economic, social, and political affairs, though they freely intermarried with Indians and Negroes. Having acquired immense estates, the Spanish aristocracy worked them by means of enslaved Indians and Negroes. As in Spain, the Roman Catholic clergy enjoyed special privileges and determined the religious, intellectual, and cultural destinies of New Spain. Nevertheless, the Spaniards were unable to prevent the persistence of native customs and institutions in the New World, where red, black, and white men together formed a new culture. In its language and in its metropolitan aspects at least this culture was superficially Spanish (or, in Brazil, Portuguese). But it was the culture of a variegated society, with the Iberian contributions, especially in the rural districts, modified significantly by admixtures or survivals of non-European elements.

New Spain
around the year 1800

THOUGH the revolutions in the British colonies of North America and in Europe at the close of the eighteenth century made exciting news, the Spanish colonies remained loyal to their rulers overseas, and in any case too weak to rebel against them. Spain's power declined steadily in Europe after the sixteenth century, though the eighteenth century marked a partial "comeback"; and the growing strength of Great Britain meanwhile forced the Bourbon rulers at Madrid to watch carefully for insurgency in the New World out of fear of an alliance of discontented elements in the Spanish colonies with the English. Consequently a Spanish government that made few reforms at home granted to its American subjects several concessions that could not be used to compromise Spain's sovereignty. Through a policy of strict administrative supervision in conjunction with local reform, the Spanish managed to retain their grip upon New Spain until the nineteenth century. The Portuguese in Brazil, even after they ceased to be subject to Spanish control in 1640, followed similar policies with similar results.

14

The French in North America

WHILE THE Spanish successfully fought off most efforts by other powers to invade the Americas south of the Rio Grande, the French painfully staked out a claim for themselves in the basin of the St. Lawrence River in North America. At last the founding of Quebec in 1608 crowned almost a century of French enterprise in the northern waters. Slowly extending up the St. Lawrence and Ottawa valleys to the Great Lakes, New France was colonized mainly during the reign of "the Grand Monarch," Louis XIV. Trappers and missionaries explored the Great Lakes, and by 1682 Sieur de La Salle descended the Mississippi River and named the newly discovered Mississippi regions "Louisiana" in honor of his king. By the beginning of the eighteenth century, France claimed a continental empire in America second in size only to that of Spain.

Like the Spanish, the French pioneers were sparsely settled over a vast and largely uncharted wilderness. As in New Spain, lands were not open for the first pioneer to claim but remained in the hands of the king and the aristocracy. From Quebec and Montreal the Catholic Church dominated the religious and intellectual life of New France through the ubiquitous parish priest. Though the life of the Canadians was a rigorous one, a native French-American culture had begun to develop by the end of the seventeenth century. With the founding of New Orleans in 1717 a white, French-speaking, Catholic civilization extended in a thin line of settlements from the St. Lawrence to the Gulf of Mexico, defying the wilderness, the Indians, and rival Europeans.

The ousting of the French from North America

IN THE Mississippi Valley, the French settlers were especially few, and there the French ran the greatest risk from hostile Indians and equally hostile British settlers. Widely scattered, the French colonists found it hard to resist alone but quickly learned that they could expect little help from the mother country. In Europe, the French held their own in the numerous wars of the eighteenth century and in the land fighting even won new laurels, but in the colonies, whether in America or India (page 21), the British outmaneuvered them. In the course of the world-wide Seven Years' War (1756-1763) the French in America, despite determined resistance, were overwhelmed by numerically superior naval and military forces from both England and the English-American colonies. The resulting diplomatic arrangement divided France's empire on the North American continent between her Spanish ally and her English enemy. New Orleans and Louisiana west of the Mississippi went to Spain, while Canada and the holdings east of the Mississippi fell to Great Britain. Of the Americas France retained only some islands, including the sugar-producing French West Indies, and French Guiana. Thus by 1800 France had lost her largest possessions in America; what were left were insular or isolated areas; and she had to be content to exert her influence upon North America's future growth through diplomatic and cultural channels.

The British colonies in the Western Hemisphere

THROUGH THE acquisitions of 1763, both in America and in Asia, Great Britain outstripped Spain and France as the foremost colonial power. Since their astonishing defeat of the Spanish Armada in 1588, the British had progressively profited from their maritime strength. The relative proximity of the British Isles to North America enabled explorers sailing under his English majesty's auspices, as well as independent British pioneers, to stake out claims in the areas that today are the eastern seaboard states of the United States. Unlike the French and the Spanish, the British went to America in fairly large numbers. Hard times, bad crops, and religious constraint impelled many British subjects to seek new homes and a freer life in the unknown wilderness of America; and the government and the joint-stock companies for the exploitation of the colonies encouraged them to go. Those who went to America in search of religious freedom did not always extend that freedom to others even from the same country, and they had little in common with those who went in search of wealth. Hence, the several seventeenth-century British settlements on the eastern coast of North America—widely scattered, relatively isolated, and generally friendly—were sometimes hostile to each other. Moreover, the Dutch at New Amsterdam (later New York) constituted a potential menace to the British settlements.

The ousting of the Dutch from North America

WITH THE passage of time, however, the British settlements spotted from Virginia to New England became increasingly interdependent and cooperative. Before the end of the seventeenth century, economic and cultural cohesiveness began to appear as the English-speaking colonies shared in common achievements, interests, and dangers. This increase in solidarity helped in 1664 to effect, among other enterprises, the conquest of New Amsterdam by the British. The capture of this Dutch stronghold removed a geographical hurdle to direct communication between the British colonies and forced the Dutch to withdraw from the North American continent. In the Western Hemisphere, the Dutch were thenceforth isolated in the West Indies and Guiana— approximately, as indicated above, a century before a similar fate overtook the French.

The growth of the spirit of independence

AS THE Anglo-American colonists learned to work together more closely, and as the danger from other European settlements diminished, the colonists began to identify themselves with America rather than with Europe. Cooperation produced self-

16

reliance on the one hand and aversion to direction from abroad on the other. An open frontier permitted resolute men to go and try new social and political departures in a brand-new settlement whenever their neighbors in an older one objected. Meanwhile economic interests flourished under a policy of "salutary neglect" from the theoretically mercantilist government in London. Distances that required weeks and sometimes months for sailing vessels to overcome also helped to inspire a sharp desire for independence and local autonomy. Mounting American aspirations for separate institutions, however, ran directly counter to the growing concern in Great Britain for closer attachment of the colonies to the British economy, and for their closer association with the motherland's political system. The ensuing clash of aspirations and interests culminated in the third quarter of the eighteenth century in war and revolution.

The United States in the revolutionary tradition

OUT OF this struggle emerged a new nation, the United States of America. This nation was the first colonial area to achieve independence from its European masters, although it did so with the armed help of the French, the Spanish, and the Dutch and with the good will of other European nations that had reason to fear or to envy the preëminence of the British empire. In the nationalist and liberal revolts of the following centuries the American example was to serve as an inspiration on numerous occasions when a philosophical rationale for revolt, a constitution based on the rights of man and the separation of powers, or a system of federal government was under consideration.

The achievement of political independence by the United States after 1776 did not mean that America had withdrawn from the European tradition. On the contrary, despite the influence of a new environment and the constant need to readjust to advancing frontiers, it could readily be seen in 1800 that America had not severed—and perhaps could not sever—her spiritual and intellectual ties with Europe. The Anglo-American colonies in fact acted in keeping with their European heritage in revolting against Great Britain. They had brought their own Bibles with them in their baggage, and they remained deeply imbued with the spirit of the Greek and Latin classics that were part of the post-Renaissance gentleman's intellectual paraphernalia. They were conscious also of the Reformation's effect on the diversity of religions, achieved in some places at the cost of bloody revolt. Moreover, the colonists, as British subjects, had been exposed to—sometimes victimized by—the subsequent revolutions of the seventeenth century, and had adapted the lessons of British history—of the British Civil War, the Bill of Rights, and the Glorious Revolution—to their own needs. And in America no less than in Europe, traditional institutions and values had been called into question by rational philosophy and empirical science. Thus a long chain of deeds and thought anent the higher justice led the American colonists to believe that when they   17 revolted, they were acting to preserve what was rightfully theirs—whether in religion and philosophy or in British law and the economic order.

American indebtedness to the European heritage

THE AMERICAN movement for self-determination and reform derived genuine inspiration, rhetorical backing, and the solace of precedent from European traditions and thought even as the colonies were cutting loose from the imperial ties of Great Britain. The discussions preceding the Declaration of Independence in 1776, and the Declaration itself, made frequent use of the idiom of the natural rights philosophy then prevalent in European and American intellectual circles. In the domestic conflicts that followed upon the split from Great Britain, the numerous appeals to justice frequently were couched in language reminiscent of the English Bill of Rights of 1689. After victory had been assured, despite the readjustments required by political independence, the Americans still stood directly in the European intellectual stream, their economy was still tied to Europe's economy, and they still found themselves enmeshed in Europe's diplomatic complexities. When the constitution of 1789 was finally worked out, and the present federal state was brought into existence, it reflected in part—and perhaps in greater part—the American's own practical experiences on the frontier, but it was also made up of elements abstracted from the Judeo-Christian Bible, the Greco-Roman philosophers, Roman, canon, and English common law, Renaissance attitudes, Reformation schismatism, and Enlightenment rationalism, and it re-echoed the revolts that through the ages had dotted the European's quest for the right. A Bill of Rights was quickly appended to the new constitution, almost exactly one century after the adoption of such a document in England and within a year of the adoption of a similar one in France.

The New Europe across the Atlantic

BY THE DAWN of the nineteenth century, then, the New World was partly independent of Europe but largely dependent upon it still. The inhabitants of the Western Hemisphere, to be sure, had been freed by the frontier and at the same time conditioned by it; and American Indians and African slaves had contributed substantially to the fabric of the new society. Yet the American continued to live within the cultural tradition of Europe. In the Americas south of the Rio Grande Iberian languages, customs, religious institutions, and political practices formed at least an outward veneer in the rural areas and dominated the urban areas, and at the same time gave Latin America a cultural homogeneity that is still one of the most striking of its assets. North of the Rio Grande the European cultural influence, though more varied, was likewise apparent. Canada remained a British colony but with an important portion of its population of French descent and stubbornly determined to remain French-speaking and Catholic. South of Canada and east of the Mississippi, the independent

United States of America, essentially British in background, had already begun to receive significant numbers of immigrants, and "the melting pot" was in the making. In Louisiana and west of the Mississippi, a three-cornered struggle of Americans, French, and Spanish was well under way for control of the undeveloped and little known empire of wilderness, prairie, and mountains that stretched to the Pacific Ocean. In 1800, many of the major aspects of American culture, north and south of the Rio Grande, had been etched in rough outline, though the future was to bring some changes even in its basic pattern. Fundamentally, however, wherever the white man had reached, the Americas at the beginning of the nineteenth century appeared to be a European cultural province—a new Europe across the Atlantic.

ASIA AND EASTERN EUROPE

AROUND THE 1800'S

ALTHOUGH Spanish vessels since the sixteenth century had regularly carried men and goods from America to Asia, the Pacific Ocean remained in 1800 an effective barrier between the two continents. American Indians had almost certainly migrated, millennia before Columbus, from Asia to America across the Bering Straits. Yet there seems to have been no consciousness among the peoples of either continent about fellow-Mongoloids on the opposite side of the Pacific Ocean. It remained for the enterprising, aggressive Europeans with their superior ships and skill in navigation to explore and exploit the overwhelming reaches of Asia and Oceania, and to awaken Asia and America as well as Europe to one another's existence.

The opening of the sea routes to Asia

UNTIL THE seventeenth century the peoples of eastern and southern Asia and of the islands off the mainland regarded the Pacific Ocean and the neighboring seas as an almost impenetrable protective expanse. True, a few daring adventurers, pirates, and other Europeans bent on trade, conquest, or missionary effort had already appeared in Asia from across the Pacific, and they had already destroyed the independence of some of the local chiefs in the East Indies and the Philippine Islands. But they rarely came to the continent in numbers large enough to indicate that the waterways to eastern Asia might someday become a major route for the invasion of all of Asia. In 1800 still, as in ages past, Chinese, Japanese, Indians, and other Asiatic peoples oriented their daily lives and their national policies toward the great land mass of continental Asia, turning their backs on a seemingly infinite and friendly sea.

From today's vantage point it appears obvious that the Asiatics were blind to have remained so long indifferent to the future importance of the sea routes. Beginning with Vasco da Gama's voyages in the fifteenth century, 19

Europeans had appeared in the islands and in the cities along the coastal rim of southern and eastern Asia, and had established a chain of trading posts and mission stations stretching from Goa in India to Macao off the southern coast of China. It was by using these outposts as strategic footholds that they had been able to take control of the Philippines and East Indies.

The closure of Japan to Westerners

THE EUROPEANS even sought, with striking initial effects though without lasting success, to establish themselves in Japan. In the sixteenth century, Portuguese traders and Jesuit missionaries began to move swiftly and successfully into Japan. Stunned by their rapid progress, and well aware of how the profit motive and missionary zeal had worked together in the East Indies to destroy the native princes' power, the Japanese rulers of the Tokugawa shogunate (1603-1867) expelled the Westerners, condemned their religion, and forbade them access to Japan's shores. Thus, by swift and decisive counter-measures, the Japanese in the seventeenth century sealed their islands against the Westerners and thereby preserved their ancient civilization from serious contamination by western influences until the nineteenth century.

The imperturbability of the Middle Kingdom

THOUGH no less aware than the Japanese of the role of trade and missionary activity in Europe's imperial progress, the great continental countries of Asia—India and China—exhibited less fear of the Westerners on their shores. China especially had long been accustomed to receiving tributary missions and respectful if adventurous visitors from surrounding areas. To have responded with less dignity to the appearance of the "long-nosed barbarians" from Europe would have been quite out of harmony with the confidence of the Chinese in themselves and in their place as the dominant political and cultural people of eastern Asia for almost two thousand years. The Chinese emperors initially ignored the activities of the Westerners and later severely limited them when they became too bold to be ignored. Secure in their assumption of superiority, the Chinese accorded but slight attention to the Westerners' pretensions to treatment as equals. For the Middle Kingdom, as the Chinese called their country, the Westerner was not yet of major concern at the close of the eighteenth century; a greater danger seemed more likely to lie upon the land routes of the north and west than upon the sea routes of the south and east.

The penetration of India by Europeans

LIKE THE Chinese emperors, the rulers of the Indian states, even after the first Europeans had set foot on India's soil, continued to look upon central and western Asia, from which past invasions had come, as the areas from which their future security might most likely be threatened. Unlike China, India had no strong central authority through which to deal with the Europeans who came sailing to her seaport towns. Divided internally over religious and political questions, the peoples of India had been unable to maintain control of the Westerners. Taking full advantage of India's internal dissensions, the western traders and missionaries successfully made their way into the subcontinent's interior. Since, however, they proceeded circumspectly and at times even had entirely commendable motives, the Europeans had managed on most occasions to allay all fear of their intentions. In fact, Hindu and Moslem rulers in India, preoccupied as they were by domestic problems, sometimes sought from the Jesuit missionaries advice in political matters as well as information on western learning.

Before long, the Europeans consolidated their commercial, territorial, and cultural gains in India. By the eighteenth century, the trading companies of England and France had staked off extensive spheres of influence. In the course of the world-wide wars which characterized the eighteenth century, the British gradually extended their interests, in India as in America, at the expense of other Europeans and of natives alike. In the Seven Years' War, the British defeated the French in India as elsewhere, and became thereby the arbiters of India's future. Later, British successes in India offset the failure in North America and encouraged the British to build that enormous empire which in the nineteenth century was to be the most impressive symbol and citadel of European predominance in Asia.

*China
in the eyes of Europeans*
ALTHOUGH the Spanish in the Philippines, the Portuguese and the Dutch in the East Indies and southern Asia, and the British in India advanced their national colors quickly and effectively during the seventeenth and eighteenth centuries, the Westerners who sought to extend their commercial interests in China had only qualified concessions to report. Permitted to trade at Canton only under strict regulation, western merchants did not succeed as well either financially or politically in China as in India, though they had better luck than in Japan. The Jesuits, however, had greater success in carrying out their spiritual mission. They penetrated to Peking and to the heart of the Chinese Empire. Respected and admired for their learning, they were able to exert a marked influence upon the Chinese imperial court. Moreover, their reports to Europe of the Middle Kingdom constituted the most valuable and reliable source available in the West of information regarding the high achievements of Chinese civilization and thought. Western philosophers and theologians in the seventeenth and eighteenth centuries seriously studied and were obviously impressed by Chinese writers like Confucius and Mencius. Chinese art, gardens, jade, lacquer work, cloisonné, and porcelain were avidly collected and imitated. The Chinese system of government aroused curiosity and admiration.

The advance
of Russia into Asia

DESPITE the Europeans' growing cultural contacts with China, they failed to establish effective political relations. Unified under the Romanovs in the early seventeenth century and reaching to China across the land routes of Asia, the Russian state was the first non-Asiatic power to conclude a treaty with the Middle Kingdom on the basis of equality. The Treaty of Nerchinsk of 1689 was concluded when Peter the Great was czar of Russia. It established equal relations and defined roughly the boundaries between the two countries. Thereafter Russian influence, political and cultural, grew conspicuously at Peking. In the eighteenth century, although western European traders and missionaries lost many of the privileges granted to them earlier, the Russians continued to live and work at Peking, and their trade with China expanded. Other Russians meanwhile explored the maritime territories of northeastern Asia and the northern Pacific region. By the early nineteenth century they had crossed to Alaska and moved down the Pacific coast of North America, rousing fear in the new American republic of Russian designs upon the Western Hemisphere.

Russia now loomed like a colossus on three continents, stretching across northeastern Europe to northeastern Asia and northwestern America. Inevitably "the Colossus of the North" began increasingly to exert pressure in all directions. As already intimated, under Peter the Great, Russian expansion was particularly vigorous. Russia moved into northeastern Asia and began to seek new commercial contacts in central and western Asia. Peter sought a maritime outlet on the Amur River, which emptied into the strait connecting the Sea of Japan with the Sea of Okhotsk, at the same time that he reached out on the Baltic Sea and sought also to find an ice-free port on the Black Sea. Though Peter and his successors prospered in their Baltic and Chinese programs, they encountered heavy resistance in their designs upon the Black Sea. The reason for this comparative failure is to be sought in the peculiar international status of the Ottoman Empire.

The rise
of Ottoman predominance

IN 1800, the dominant power in southwestern Asia and southeastern Europe was the Ottoman state. Moslem by faith, the Ottoman Turks had taken over the Mohammedan empire in the latter half of the fifteenth century and with it the surviving Arabic culture. Their capture of Constantinople in 1453 had made them the masters of Christian Byzantium and had placed them menacingly across the routes that linked Europe, Africa, and Asia together. By the sixteenth century they had gained a manifest preëminence in the Mediterranean Sea from Asia Minor to the Nile Basin and across northern Africa to the Atlantic Ocean. By the time of their famous sultan Suleiman the Magnificent (1520-1566), the Mediterranean had practically become a Turkish lake. By the end of the sixteenth century the shores of the Black Sea also were acquired, so that when

Russia began in the next century to move southward the czars were confronted by entrenched settlements that could count upon the support of a large and well-trained Turkish army.

Religious disunion within the Ottoman Empire

THE TURKS had many enemies among the other Moslem groups of southern Asia. The shahs of Persia fought bitterly against the extension of Ottoman hegemony eastward and were frequently supported by the Moslems of India. Though Suleiman had pushed eastward to the shores of the Dead Sea, the Turks were never able to consolidate and pacify the peoples of the Mesopotamian valley. Time after time these peoples rebelled against Turkish overlordship and received aid in their revolts from the outside. Though the Turkish sultans had assumed the religious office of Commander of the Faithful, the Moslems of western Asia, like the Christians of western Europe, placing sovereign independence above religious obligation, rent the Moslem world asunder. Sectarian strife and political disloyalties among its Moslem subjects proved a constant source of weakness to the Ottoman Empire in its eastern reaches.

To the west, the Porte (as the Turkish government was called) was faced simultaneously by the problem of assimilating and controlling the Christians and Moslems of eastern Europe. After numerous Christians had been enslaved, and the cities of Danubian Europe to the gates of Vienna had been ravaged, the Turks managed in the sixteenth century to establish and maintain a fair degree of control and order in southeastern Europe. Nor did they feel obliged to ensure their own power by eliminating the Christians mercilessly. The Christian "slaves of the Porte" were often taken into the army or government, and as servants of the Ottoman state sometimes became eminent soldiers and statesmen. Many Christians found the opportunities under the Ottomans so attractive that they willingly renounced Christianity to become followers of the Prophet of Allah. In an era when persecution of minority religious groups was common elsewhere in Europe, the Turks granted toleration also to the many loyal Greek Orthodox Christians and the scattered Jews within the Ottoman Empire.

Ups and downs of Turkey before the eighteenth century

THE RELIGIOUS problem was but one, and not always the most divisive, factor in the disharmony that prevailed within the far-flung Ottoman Empire. Until the eighteenth century constant commercial and naval wars with the powerful Republic of Venice, sporadic hostilities with Spain, and the recurrent prospect of a Christian crusade also contributed to the insecurity of the Porte. Within their African possessions, moreover, the Turks, faced with fairly common sectarian rivalries, had to contend at all times with the especially vehement resentment and independent action of the tribal chieftains. In the seventeenth century, when Turkey was already confronted east and west by a multitude of complex domestic and foreign problems, Russia loomed up as a new threat to Ottoman control.

Since the Porte had isolated itself, it now had nowhere to turn for support against its own recalcitrant vassals. Though the French kings had earlier made an alliance with the Turks, and Louis XIV proved momentarily willing to do so again, little could be expected from that quarter. Fortunately for the Porte, the powers of western and central Europe were locked in battle during most of the seventeenth century, while the Romanovs were preoccupied with consolidating and expanding their own empire in Russia. Thus, if the sultan got no aid from Europe, neither did his fractious subjects. Left to their own devices until the last quarter of the century, the Turks experienced a short revival of prosperity and order, and even renewed the offensive, marching once more to the walls of Vienna and retreating only in the face of a Holy League of Christian powers.

The origin
of the Eastern Question

WITH THE accession of Peter the Great, the Turks found themselves on the defensive. Russian pressure upon the Ottoman state soon began to be felt in the Black Sea area, the Danube Valley, and the Balkan Peninsula. There lay the access to the Straits (the Dardanelles, the Sea of Marmara and the Bosporus), which separated Europe from Asia and offered an outlet for Russia to the Mediterranean. By the beginning of the eighteenth century the struggle between these two titanic empires began in western Asia and eastern Europe, and therewith the Eastern Question—the problem of whether and how to partition the Turkish empire among the powers—became a constant source of irritation in the international body politic.

Not until the eighteenth century did the Turk begin to give way slowly before repeated assaults from without and within his dominions. As Turkish weakness became more and more evident, the objectives of Russia in the Danube Valley and the Straits became better defined. The western European powers, however, and particularly Great Britain, having ambitions of their own in the eastern Mediterranean, began to view Russian ambitions with misgivings. Fear that the Russians might succeed in their transparent designs prompted the British to inaugurate their policy of befriending the Turk as "the sick man of Europe" who had to be nursed back to health in order to keep the Russian bear from swallowing him limb by strategic limb.

The disappearance
of Poland as a sovereign state

THOUGH chagrined by the attitude of the western Europeans, Russia continued to push southwestward throughout the eighteenth century. Profiting somewhat from the divisions among the western powers both in Europe and in the overseas colonies, the Russians made steady progress in their drive against the Ottoman holdings. At the end of the century their westward march ran into further

24

complications in the crumbling of the Kingdom of Poland. In former days Poland had been one of the largest and most powerful states of eastern Europe, and in the glorious reign of John Sobieski it was a Polish army that had driven the Turks in 1683 from the walls of Vienna. Poland now found herself unable to build a strong domestic regime even though her need was pressing, since she was surrounded by a set of grasping neighbors in Sweden, Russia, Prussia, and Austria.

The Russian rulers quickly tied the future of Poland into their program of westward expansion, and the Polish Question became a bone of contention among the powers of central and northern Europe. The unhappy country was torn by a feudal aristocracy who jealously treasured their power against an elective king and readily broke into factions as foreign rulers electioneered to put their own puppets on the Polish throne. Poland's tottering became the principal cause of unbalance in the arrangement of power among her neighbors. Finally the Polish Question was resolved—for the rest of the eighteenth century at least—by a compromise in which the Poles had almost no voice. By three separate treaties of partition the Polish lands were divided among Austria, Prussia, and Russia, who then all but turned on Sweden. In 1795 the Polish state ceased temporarily to exist as an independent political unit.

*Russia's special position
by the Peace of Kuchuk Kainarji*

PARTITION of weak neighbors was not uncommon in the eighteenth century. The Russians and the Austrians contemplated partitioning the Ottoman Empire also, but the British stood firmly against such a step, since it was detrimental to their own interests to have the Russians replace the Turks in the eastern Mediterranean. Far removed from the scene, other western European powers had no desire for a formal partition of Turkey. Largely as a result of the support from western Europe, the Turks were able to resist the Russians with some degree of success. Nevertheless, by the Treaty of Kuchuk Kainarji (1774) Russia got significant advantages. She widened her control of the northern coast of the Black Sea. Russian merchant vessels also won the freedom of Ottoman waters, including the Straits. By these concessions the "Colossus of the North" obtained a "window on the south" and direct access to the Mediterranean Sea. Finally, the czar was recognized as protector of all Orthodox Eastern Christians within the Ottoman Empire—a provision designed to be used opportunely in the future as a pretext to interfere in the domestic affairs of the Turkish state.

*Anglo-Russian rivalry
in the Near and the Far East*

FROM THE viewpoint of 1800, the developments of the previous three centuries in Asia had been the outcome of a one-way imperialism and a two-way cultural interchange. Imperialism had been marked particularly by the opening of India and southern Asia to the western Europeans. Yet the onward march of European empire-building seemed stopped by the closure of Japan to western traders and missionaries and by the ability of the Chinese Empire to permit relations with west Europeans and Russians alike only on its own terms. Asia's future, however, was to be more largely determined by what was happening in Europe than by what was happening in Asia—by the unification of Russia as the Eurasiatic colossus, by the steady decline of the Ottoman Empire in Europe, and by the full bloom of the imperial impulse in Great Britain, France, and nations not yet fully grown like the United States and Germany. The dynamic elements in this composite picture in 1800 appeared to be the British, who were pushing into the Asiatic continent from the south, and the Russians, who had begun to move southward toward the Chinese and the Ottoman empires. Unable for a while to exert pressure upon the Middle Kingdom, the czars confined their activities largely to their westward drive while striving to maintain good political and commercial relations in the East. The East at the end of the eighteenth century appeared relatively stable, for the great French Revolution kept the western powers more fully occupied elsewhere.

B Y THE dawn of the nineteenth century, the globetrotter would have found that the entire world had come into touch with the western Europeans. In America, Asia, and Africa, missionaries, merchants, and adventurers from Europe had left indelible, though sometimes only shallow, impressions. Where resistance to their penetration had been weak or badly organized, the Europeans had quickly staked out valuable commercial and strategic holdings. Where resistance had been strong, they had either been excluded completely, as in Japan, or had had to acquiesce to the limitations imposed upon their activities, as in China. Nevertheless, by 1800, almost the whole of the Western Hemisphere, some of the insular regions of Asia, and large parts of India had fallen under their domination. Only in the Americas, however, had they managed to build up great colonial empires in their own images, and there these empires had already begun to collapse. In Asia, their successes were inevitably limited by the vast numbers and the higher degree of culture and sophistication of the native peoples. Yet they had made a beginning, and their empires were to grow piece by piece. Not until the twentieth century would the imperialistic edifices that the European countries had begun in Asia almost five hundred years earlier start to crumble, and then the Europeans would find the spirit of 1776 and 1789 and the new technology sometimes turned against them in the name of a new spirit that was to develop from the revolutions of the nineteenth and twentieth centuries.

In Europe itself, the events of the three centuries before 1800 had altered the fabric of life. Europe was ceasing to be leisurely, to live close to the soil, or to be dominated by a landed aristocracy. Large-scale and world-wide com-

26

merce and industry were coming to the fore. Land, spices, jewels, gold, and souls convertible to Christianity were still objectives of overseas expansion, but so now were numerous other products like coffee, rubber, cotton, furs, tobacco, sugar, rum, ivory, rice, silk, tea, and opium; and markets for home products, backward areas to exploit and in which to invest money profitably, and new cultures to discover were fast becoming incentives for a more dynamic imperialism. The formidable growth of the British empire and the expansion of Russia in Europe and Asia seemed around 1800 to be the major political developments, matched overseas only by the independence and patent vitality of the new United States of America. Moreover, the revolutionary spirit of 1776 and 1789 and the first of the great technological innovations loosely called the "Industrial Revolution" had become dominating forces of life in some parts of western Europe and of America. Nevertheless, Russia almost entirely and Spain, Germany, and other countries largely remained aloof from the principles of 1789 and the political and economic currents lapping the area now called the Atlantic community; and reform in the aloof countries, when it came at all, was to come at first by royal grant rather than by popular initiative. Yet Russia, neither wholly European nor wholly Asiatic, had become a vital factor in the life of Europe and Asia and a mighty force for the western powers to reckon with in their diplomatic and overseas programs. And the German states, despite the efforts (which we shall soon examine) of Napoleon Bonaparte to dominate them, were to continue to stand —weak, despite the individual strength of some of them, and disunited—between the great empires east and west of them until they too could be united into a mighty empire. Great Britain was to remain the center of commerce, industry, and liberalism throughout the nineteenth century, and was also to build the largest empire.

14th-16th centuries	The Renaissance
15th-16th centuries	The Ottoman Empire rises
15th-17th centuries	The great discoveries and the Commercial Revolution
16th-18th centuries	European peoples and their culture spread throughout the world
16th-18th centuries	Center of political gravity shifts from southern to northern Europe
16th-18th centuries	Principles of modern scientific method emerge and win wide acceptance
16th century	Iberians colonize Latin America
c. 1517-1648	The Reformation, Counter Reformation, and religious wars
1519-1522	First circumnavigation of the globe
1520-1566	Suleiman the Magnificent
17th-18th centuries	Russia becomes the "Colossus of the North"
17th century	British oust Dutch from North America
17th century	Sea routes to Asia opened
1564-1642	Galileo Galilei
1596-1650	René Descartes
1608	Founding of Quebec crowns century of French endeavor in New World
1640	Japan closed to all Europeans but the Dutch
1683	Turkish advance in Europe halted at Vienna
1632-1704	John Locke
1642-1727	Sir Isaac Newton
1643-1715	Louis XIV, the "Grand Monarch," reigns in France
1682-1725	Peter the Great is czar of Russia
Early 18th century	English and French trading companies acquire extensive spheres of influence in India
18th century	Great Britain outstrips France and rivals Spain as foremost colonial power
18th century	Cultural contacts with China grow
1685-1789	The Age of Enlightenment and the philosopher
1694-1778	Voltaire
1723-1790	Adam Smith
1724-1804	Immanuel Kant
1740-1786	Frederick the Great reigns in Prussia
c. 1750-1789	The spirit of independence triumphs in Britain's American colonies, and a federal republic emerges
1769	Watt first patents his steam engine
1789-1799	The French Revolution
1799	Napoleon Bonaparte becomes virtual dictator of France

Chapter one

LEGITIMACY OR

REVOLUTION?

A_T THE dawn of the nineteenth century, the old order in Europe was crumbling under a rain of stunning blows. Not the least telling of them was aimed at the old religious faiths. No longer was the church in its various forms the unchallenged authority it once had been in spiritual, ethical, and religious questions. In the preceding centuries a lay body of knowledge and principles had gradually accumulated and had acquired respectability, undermining the veneration once unhesitatingly granted to ecclesiastical authority, but in the process no universally acceptable doctrine had been produced as a substitute.

On the contrary, the ordered dictums of the rationalists and empiricists of the Enlightenment were themselves now viewed with increasing skepticism by informed minds everywhere. The eighteenth-century belief in the inevitability of human progress and the eighteenth-century confidence regarding nature and human nature had begun to appear naïve to a generation whose accepted ideals and customs had been rudely shaken by the violence of the French Revolution. The initial enthusiasm for the Revolution had been dampened by the excesses of both its advocates and its adversaries in purges, lynchings, and terror; by the instability of the reforms it effected, because some thought they went too far and others thought they did not go far enough; and by doubts that what was gained for liberty was worth what it cost in disorder and the destruction of ancient values.

Moreover, ferocious wars had emerged in part from the effort of revolutionary crusaders to spread the blessings of the Revolution and from the effort of shocked counterrevolutionaries to contain the Revolution. France, now a sovereign people in arms, had badly shaken the old balance of dynastic powers as an effective method for maintaining international equilibrium. Sev- 31 eral contemporary observers were profoundly disturbed not only by the social and economic changes wrought by the French Revolution but also by the disquieting implications of the ruthless destruction of ancient states like Poland and Venice through partition by revolutionaries and counterrevolutionaries alike.

In every sphere of life the sensitive and informed had been obliged to realize, sometimes reluctantly, that the dawn of the nineteenth century marked something a great deal more upsetting than a mere change of dating on the Christian calendar. It meant the beginning of a new search, in Europe and beyond, for leaders who either would apply the revolutionary principles that justified continued change of the old order in an undiminished quest for a better one or would dare to exert authority sufficient to preserve the more tried and acceptable institutions of the past in order to avoid worse. Napoleon Bonaparte, for a while at least, seemed to be a person who was prepared to do both—to apply revolutionary principles at the same time that he exerted a conservative authority.

THE ACHIEVEMENTS
OF NAPOLEON BONAPARTE

ALTHOUGH Bonaparte has frequently been reviled as an unscrupulous dictator and conqueror, his regime may also be looked upon as an effort to provide a synthesis of the old and the new for the war-weary and revolution-weary Europe of his day. When he became master of France in 1799, his new charge had undergone a decade of social, economic, and political turmoil in the course of which it had helped to impart to Europe a widely held conviction that "the source of all authority resides essentially in the nation" (as the French Declaration of Rights of 1789 had stated) and that "Liberty, Equality, and Fraternity" were objectives for which one should fight, bleed, and die. But in the course of that decade France had also imparted, along with notions of popular sovereignty and the hope of a freer and better world, an atmosphere of uncertainty, instability, and fear such as Europe had not known since the close of the religious wars in 1648. The initial success of Bonaparte's triumphs at home and abroad derived not alone from his undeniable personal qualities, his carefully nurtured reputation, and the strength of his following, but just as much from the inability of his rivals and enemies to prescribe better remedies for the patent social, economic, and political illnesses of the times. Though Napoleon was ultimately to forget his principles, as even those who are not conquerors often do, and to act rather out of considerations of expediency, he forced both peoples and rulers of Europe either to adhere to his system or else, in order to survive his onslaughts, to modify the old order and make place for the aspirations embodied in the principles of 1789, whether they liked those principles or not.

The reorganization
of the French government

ALTHOUGH absorbed for the first three years of his rule by the problem of making France's military position secure and strong, Bonaparte planned for the reconstruction of France from the outset. With the achievement in 1802 of the first general truce in ten years, he proceeded to round out the reforms earlier initiated and to inaugurate a series of new measures designed to increase the efficiency of France's governmental machinery. He reorganized the system of local government in order to prevent internal disorders and to center firmly in his own hands the guide lines of power. A similar centralization of the fiscal administration extended his control to the economic life of France. In overhauling the educational structure he again invoked the principle of centralization; and in reëstablishing the disrupted relationship of the church with the state he proposed to make certain that the church would, as an obedient dependent, cooperate with the state in upholding his own concept of morals, law, and order. Most important, he completed the codification of French law begun during the revolutionary era, and thereby enshrined in lasting legal respectability many of the changes wrought by the Revolution. Through such reforms Bonaparte made government more uniform and, apparently at least, more efficient. Where individual liberties and human rights, however, stood in the way of centralized and ordered government, they were likely to be subordinated.

The apogee
of the Napoleonic empire

THE STRAINED peace won in 1802 ended slightly more than a year later when an insecure England again declared war upon the enterprising republic of France. Though hostilities did not spread immediately to the Continent, each side did what diplomatic and military damage it could to the other. Bonaparte meanwhile took advantage of the popular desire that he strengthen his position at home by having himself proclaimed Emperor Napoleon in 1804 and king of Italy in 1805. That step, capping a series of measures that the other emperors of Europe considered arrogant and menacing, led to a renewed coalition of England, Russia, Austria, and, when it was already too late, Prussia.

Unable to attack England directly, the French proceeded first to dispose of her partners. After quick victories over Austria and Prussia, the Grand Army of Emperor Napoleon had only the armies of the czar to face. Napoleon dissolved the obsolete Holy Roman Empire, establishing in its place a satellite Confederation of the Rhine, and then in 1806 drove the Russians out of most of Germany. Needing time to consolidate his victories, he agreed to a truce with the czar, and in 1807 at Tilsit he arranged a good bargain. He was given a free hand in western Europe to expand his "Continental Sys- 33 tem" designed to build up France's economic hegemony and to destroy Britain's, while Russia received a conditional guarantee of freedom of action in eastern Europe and western Asia. Moreover, Russia pledged herself to a policy of cooperation with the new French order in western Europe. The Colossus of the North seemed about to divide the world with the new colossus of the west.

European resistance
to the Empire of the French

AFTER HIS success at Tilsit, Napoleon continued his economic blockade of England, and with still more earnestness. He demanded closer cooperation from the conquered nations of the Continent, including Russia; but he now ran afoul of a kind of underground resistance in the occupied countries. Having come announced as a liberator, he had sometimes stirred deeply liberal and nationalistic sentiments that ran counter to his own intentions. While they had been generally loyal to their native absolutist systems, the peoples of Europe, and of central Europe in particular, showed hostility to a foreign authoritarian rule. Hence Napoleon's efforts to control the continental nationalities in the interests of France proved less successful than his wars against the princes.

Bonaparte's problems were complicated further by Britain's determination to attack France from its beachhead in the Iberian Peninsula. Equally determined to prevent the Iberian bases from being exploited against him, the French emperor expended numerous troops and valuable resources in a vain attempt to drive the English into the sea and to hold the Spanish in thrall.

A contemporary anti-imperial cartoon shows Napoleon's stilts, one in Russia, the other in Spain, breaking under the weight of distance and defeat.

Though he succeeded once (to use an anachronism) in "dunkirking" the English, they returned, and the Spanish "sore" continued to "run" (the figure is his own) throughout the rest of his career as emperor. Here again he underestimated the venom that his brand of order was certain to rouse among a proud and resentful people.

Despite serious trouble in Spain from 1808 on, Napoleon's "star" seemed to ascend higher and higher until 1812. In the interim, French soldiers and their cohorts became masters of the Continent from Königsberg in East Prussia to Madrid in Spain, from the seaport of Hamburg at the mouth of the Elbe to that of Reggio at the toe of the Italian peninsula. The Austrian emperor as well as the pope at Rome were defeated by the "little corporal" from Corsica, and Bonaparte's relatives sat upon some of the oldest and most respected thrones in Europe. Statesmen, scholars, musicians, poets, and artists were inspired by the figure and the monumental achievements of Napoleon and France. And yet several of them feared and condemned—and on occasion found the courage to denounce—the brutalities and injustices committed in the name of conquest, glory, and liberation.

The downfall of the Empire of the French

THE FRENCH, too, began to weary of the costs of Napoleon's victories. The belief became prevalent that Napoleon's aims no longer coincided with the welfare of France and that he was sacrificing his country's liberties, wealth, and manhood to his personal desire for power and glory. A number of the French leaders, like the shrewd ex-bishop Charles Maurice de Talleyrand-Périgord, began to conspire at home and abroad against their emperor. Thus, at the height of Napoleon's power, the cracks in his edifice began to appear. Napoleon's allies, whom he had sometimes coerced into his system, and his own people, whose wishes he generally consulted only that he might manipulate them better, soon were dragging their heels as he urged them to venture farther and farther.

Profiting from Napoleon's preoccupation with these problems, England sought an alliance with Russia, the only other European power that had never capitulated to him, and girded herself for a showdown. Angered by what he considered the duplicity of "the shifty Byzantine," and reasoning, somewhat like Adolf Hitler over a century later, that he must knock out Russia before he dared to settle with England, the French emperor in 1812 embarked upon his storied campaign against Russia, until then his ally. Although at first victorious, Napoleon's army suffered so cruelly that it was forced into a catastrophic retreat from which it never effectively recovered.

Nevertheless, two more years of notable diplomacy and classical campaigning were required before the continental powers and England were able to push the French forces back across their own frontiers and make Napoleon a virtual prisoner on his island-empire of Elba in the Mediterranean Sea. Napoleon soon escaped from Elba and returned to France in 1815 for a dramatic "Hundred Days," but his hastily mustered forces were defeated decisively at Waterloo in 1815, and he was again taken captive. This time the fallen emperor was outlawed and entrusted to the British for safekeeping; and he spent his last embittered years as dictator only of memoirs on the remote and otherwise undistinguished island of St. Helena, off the African coast.

Europe's heritage
from the Napoleonic regime

EUROPE AND in particular France, however, never lost the Napoleonic imprint. For France, Bonaparte had modified, stabilized, and institutionalized many of the more significant legal, religious, political, and economic changes hammered out in the heat of the French Revolution. For the rest of Europe his very effort to impose an authoritarian regime, even though it sometimes embodied a deep felt need for reform, had frequently hastened the ripening of a strong nationalist resistance. Despite Napoleon's defeat, the aspirations of the French Revolution toward "Liberty, Equality, and Fraternity" continued to inspire loyalty throughout the world. "Liberty" and "Equality" remained the slogans of the forces of liberalism, and the cry of "Fraternity" was converted into a demand for national unity. Nowhere were they more loudly heard than in such nations as Italy and Germany, where unity had seemed only an idle dream before Napoleon had temporarily united large parts of them under his own domination. The short experience with popular constitutions and the green memory of successful resistance to a foreign conqueror gave solidarity to radical movements aimed, in the name of liberty and equality, at deep alterations of the social and economic order.

Patriotic fervor, after the meteoric career of Napoleon as savior or Antichrist among the peoples of Egypt, the Levant, and Europe as far east as Moscow, was less prone than ever before to be satisfied with gracious concessions voluntarily made by paternalistic rulers. Even when the peoples of Europe rallied again around their ancient dynasties, they did not forget that it was the fury of their national spirit that had helped tame the French imperial eagle. Hence nationalism and the liberal sentiment were not imprisoned with Napoleon on St. Helena. They were to survive, even to prosper, and to constitute in the nineteenth and twentieth centuries two of the most powerful spiritual forces at work in a turbulent world.

For the time being, however, the suppression of the outlawed usurper, "the son of the Revolution," was a victory for "legitimacy," for the status quo of pre-revolutionary days. The rulers of Europe rather than their more radical subjects seemed victorious, and they again had their inning to work out their own solutions of the unending problem of preserving order without prohibiting change.

"LEGITIMACY" OR "LEGAL CRIME"
IN EUROPE

H.M.S. *Northumberland* had hardly turned her nose toward the island of St. Helena with the captive Napoleon Bonaparte aboard when the emperor's former enemies began to fight among themselves. As long as the French emperor stood as a threat to national independence, divergent groups in the various countries had temporarily submerged their differences and united their forces against a common foe. After the defeat of France and the Corsican, many of the unresolved differences of the past remained to be fought out. Despite the discrediting of revolutionary France and the cause of liberalism, the ruling groups in Europe could not expect to maintain their ascendancy without serious challenge. Percy Bysshe Shelley, perhaps the most radical among the great poets of the day, expressed the liberals' sentiments in his ode, "Feelings of a Republican on the Fall of Bonaparte":

> ...I know
> Too late, since thou and France are in the dust,
> That Virtue owns a more eternal foe
> Than Force or Fraud: old Custom, legal Crime,
> And bloody Faith the foulest birth of Time.

"Legitimacy"
in the postwar settlements

TO THOSE who shared Shelley's sentiments Napoleon's fall had not made way for liberty. The postwar settlements meant a prosaic restoration of the pre-revolutionary ruling houses, the "legitimate" dynasts, to their thrones, and at least a partial revival of the suspect practices and principles of the Old Regime. Nevertheless, impressed by the dangers of recurrent revolutionary upheavals, the statesmen of Europe were generally too realistic to pretend that the changes brought by the Revolutionary and Napoleonic programs could be completely obliterated, and they were content with compromises between the old and the new. Their compromises leaned, however, toward conservativism and aimed at containing the revolutionary spirit everywhere and at controlling France in particular as the potential center of a revolutionary tornado.

In the First Treaty of Paris of 1814, France, the defeated nation, was required to return to her frontiers of 1792, before her revolutionary armies began their triumphal processions through Europe. Thus France was restored to her "legitimate" size. Since the French statesman Talleyrand had convinced the victorious powers that they should not require the entire French nation to suffer for the misdeeds of the Revolutionaries and Napoleon, the peace arrangements were not entirely unfavorable to France. For example, in the overseas world France regained most of her former insular possessions. Although an occupation of France was undertaken by the anti-Napoleonic allies, the victors subscribed to Talleyrand's belief that the newly restored government must not become identified with defeat and weakness. On the contrary, the restoration of the Bourbon rulers must be celebrated in France and Europe as a victory of legitimacy and stability over revolution and instability.

The restoration of the Bourbons in France

IN FRANCE, the "legitimate" house of Bourbon was restored in the person of Louis XVIII, brother of the beheaded king, Louis XVI. Returning, as contemporary wits put it, "in the baggage train of the allies," the new king was in no position, even had he been so disposed, to set the clock back to pre-revolutionary times. On the contrary, he returned to France from an unhappy exile in England in a flexible, conciliatory mood. After his arrival in Paris, as king "by the grace of God" he presented the Royal Charter of 1814 to the French people. Drafted as a constitution, it obligingly "granted" to the French as a noble gesture most of the civil rights won by blood and sacrifice during the Revolutionary and Napoleonic eras. In another way the Charter bowed to the inevitable by affirming the inviolability of private property—an astute and necessary concession to those who had profited by the confiscations of the Revolution and who might in the future be expected to resist the new regime unless it consented to protect their interests.

Talleyrand at the Congress of Vienna

THE FRENCH armies had ridden roughshod over much of Europe and had toppled many venerable thrones, and it soon became clear that a congress of the powers would have to be called to work out the numerous territorial and diplomatic problems resulting from twenty-six years of almost uninterrupted revolution and warfare. The locale of the new congress was to be Vienna, the capital of Austria, then next to Paris the most magnificent of continental cities. The seat of the Habsburgs, one of the most ancient and revered of the European dynasties, Vienna thus became in the nineteenth century a symbol for "legitimacy" and reaction. The decisions taken in the old city on the banks of the blue Danube were hailed by princes as triumphs for ancient principles and the established order, and were reviled by liberals as "legal Crime."

Even before Napoleon's final defeat, Talleyrand had been in communication with the Austrian minister of foreign affairs, Prince Clemens von Metternich. In his discussions with Metternich, Talleyrand insisted that the European powers possessed at least one objective in common with those "good Frenchmen" who were opposed to Napoleon. That common objective was "legitimacy"—to restore the European monarchs, to reëstablish as far as possible the institutions of the pre-revolutionary era, and to realign international frontiers and diplomatic engagements so as to prevent the revival of the revolutionary spirit. In a letter to Louis XVIII, Talleyrand, once a revolutionary hero, commented regarding his activities at Vienna:

> We showed that the principle of legitimacy must be held sacred in the interest of the people themselves, because legitimate Governments can alone be strong and durable, whereas illegitimate Governments, relying upon force only, fall to pieces the moment that support fails them, and then the people are delivered over to a succession of revolutions of which no one can foresee the end.

Castlereagh
as British spokesman at Vienna

TALLEYRAND'S contentions received a sympathetic hearing in Vienna and other capitals. Lord Castlereagh, the British minister for foreign affairs, was prepared to agree with the argument that "legitimacy" meant peace and that revolution meant unremitting disorder. The Russian czar, Alexander I, who had a mystical streak in his personality, was also convinced of the need for forming a united front against the disturbers of order and of bringing the monarchs of Europe together as brother rulers. Although the Prussians enjoyed perhaps the strongest tradition of enlightened government among the victorious continental powers, their representative, Prince Hardenberg, followed Metternich's lead with but few reservations. To the liberals of Europe these men were the major perpetrators of "legal Crime."

Taking a benign attitude toward continental problems, Castlereagh posed as a sort of impartial arbitrator at the Congress of Vienna. England's major concern was to help restore the balance of power and, as she had tried several times in the past, to insure the Low Countries against French aggression. For compensation, Great Britain was content in 1815 to receive strategic overseas territories that would not materially affect the balance of power in Europe. Peace on the Continent, control of the sea lanes, and large chunks of the colonial world seemed sufficient advantages to the emissary of the leading industrial and commercial nation of the world.

Metternich
and the new balance of power

METTERNICH had his own reasons for championing "legitimacy." He hoped that it would produce the international settlement best designed to aid Austria in the solution of her complex domestic problems. Having inherited an unwieldy empire of many peoples of diverse backgrounds, the Habsburg emperor, Francis I, profoundly dreaded the rising demands for national freedom and autonomy. The Habsburg government was determined that the principles of nationalism 39 and liberalism so dangerous to heterogeneous Austria be fought and defeated wherever they might appear.

It was part of Metternich's policy also not to force France into the dust. More than a French revival Metternich feared the expanding influence of Russia and the growing intimacy between the rulers of Russia and Prussia. Thus, Austria like Britain directed its attention to a reëstablishment of the power equilibrium of former times, which meant a loose, Austrian-dominated confederation of German states holding off the Russians to the east while the Atlantic powers balanced each other to the west. Austria could hold her place in the Germanies only if the struggle were won against the liberals with their frightening demands for nationalism and the rights of man. Standing in the center, Metternich could hope by persuasive diplomacy to balance the other powers' demands against each other and keep their rulers' attention directed to the necessity for cooperation against unrest and revolt, which the liberal spirit forecast.

Alexander I
and the aspirations of Russia

THE ENIGMA of the Congress of Vienna was Czar Alexander, whom Metternich looked upon as "the madman of the north." Early in his reign he had been hailed as a reformer, and for a time he had been an admirer of Napoleon. One of Alexander's most intimate advisers commented of his paradoxical nature: "He would gladly have agreed that every one should be free, if every one had freely done only what he [Alexander] wished." Castlereagh also recognized the idealistic qualities of the czar, but felt that at Vienna he was "suspicious and undecided." Alexander's pronouncements, although sometimes extremely autocratic, were usually couched in phrases testifying to his concern for the "good of humanity."

The czar, however, rarely permitted his social conscience to interfere with his political aims. As he understood it, Bonaparte had been overcome by the crowned heads of Europe leading drilled professional armies. His words in behalf of humanity notwithstanding, he never quite grasped the fact that the armies which had conquered Bonaparte were infected by the very germs of nationalism that had infected France in the eighteenth century and, despite bitter opposition, had fused the French people into a popular unity thitherto extremely rare. Alexander, therefore, had little hesitation in entering into arrangements by which sovereignty was shifted and boundary lines were redrawn without attention to the wishes of the peoples affected.

Containing France
and strengthening Austria

DESPITE the prevailing hardheadedness at Vienna, territorial rearrangements presented particularly knotty problems to the conferees. In his anxiety that Austria maintain a balanced position between Russia and France, Metternich advocated a plan to prevent future French aggression by the erection of a geopolitical barrier running through the Rhine area from the Netherlands in the northwest to Sardinia in the southeast. The Rhineland, German in language but deeply influenced by French institutions and predominantly Catholic, was divided between Prussia and Bavaria. Belgium (the former Austrian Netherlands) and the United Provinces were united into a single state under the Dutch house of Orange, to form a northern bulwark. The German Confederation under Austrian leadership was to hold the center. The southern anchor was fixed in Switzerland, which was reconstituted as an independent and neutralized confederation of twenty-two cantons, and the neighboring Sardinia, which, under the Italian house of Savoy, was reinforced by receiving control over the recently independent Republic of Genoa. As compensation for the loss of the Austrian Netherlands, the rest of northern Italy, including another recently independent republic, Venice, was placed under Habsburg jurisdiction (for when it suited the conferees they found it possible to overlook the principle of "legitimacy"). Thus, by strengthening the states bordering on France and by backing them up with a rejuvenated Austria, the statesmen hoped to contain France without disturbing fundamentally the European balance of power.

And the Habsburgs of Austria, humiliated by defeat in four successive wars with France before the final victory over Napoleon, won handsome indemnity for their losses in battle and sacrifices of territory. Besides being restored to whatever they had lost of their "legitimate" domains in Austria, Hungary, Bohemia, Lombardy, Galicia (except Cracow), and the Tyrol, the Habsburgs received Venetia in northern Italy, the Illyrian provinces on the east coast of the Adriatic Sea, and the former archbishopric of Salzburg. Thus, as compensation for giving up the distant possession of Belgium and the city of Cracow, Austria received nearby holdings that better enabled her to consolidate her dominions and to function with less effort and greater administrative effectiveness. In the new German Confederation the Habsburgs also regained their traditional position of supremacy.

Creation
of the German Confederation

THE VIENNA negotiations conceived the German Confederation as the successor to the Confederation of the Rhine, which had been the Napoleonic substitute for the Holy Roman Empire. Composed of thirty-nine states, the Confederation was intended mainly as a defensive alliance of German rulers to enable them to withstand invasions such as had come from France and Russia in the past. Although the cooperating rulers were theoretically of equal rank, the Confederation was dominated throughout the first decades of its existence by Metternich and Austria. Prussia, the only other major nation in the Confederation, at times appeared to the smaller states as a possible counterbalance to Austria, but no serious challenge to Austrian supremacy was, in fact, 41 forthcoming until Metternich and his German system collapsed before the onslaughts of Austrian revolutionaries in 1848.

Poland and Saxony
in the new balance of power

IN THE effort to untangle the German problem, the most baffling knot confronting the Congress of Vienna had to be brusquely cut rather than painstakingly unraveled. It involved strands that were tied to the future of Poland, Saxony, and the entire European balance of power. Among the states that Napoleon had freely made and unmade, he had established an independent Polish state called the Duchy of Warsaw, and Alexander now wished to make it a "free" Poland under his own rulership. Since most of the proposed free Poland was "legitimate" Prussian territory (the rest being Austrian), it was considered expedient to compensate Prussia for her loss at the expense of her weaker neighbors. Alexander thought it only just that this compensation should be at the expense of Saxony, whose ruler, also duke of Warsaw, had made the mistake

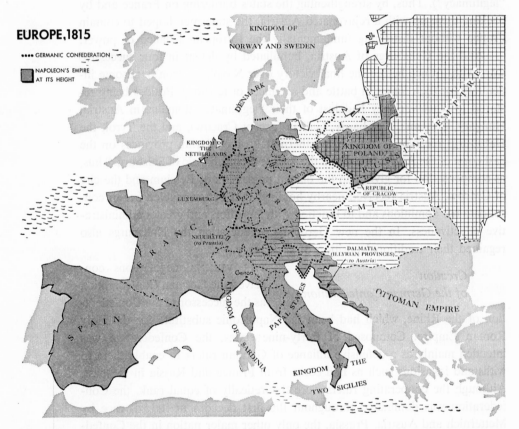

EUROPE, 1815

•••• GERMANIC CONFEDERATION

NAPOLEON'S EMPIRE
AT ITS HEIGHT

KINGDOM OF
NORWAY AND SWEDEN

DENMARK

KINGDOM OF
THE
NETHERLANDS

LUXEMBURG

KINGDOM OF
POLAND

REPUBLIC
OF CRACOW

E—M—P—I—R—E

DALMATIA
(ILLYRIAN PROVINCES)
to Austria

NEUCHÂTEL
(to Prussia)

Genoa

FRANCE

SPAIN

KINGDOM OF SARDINIA

PAPAL STATES

OTTOMAN EMPIRE

KINGDOM OF THE
TWO SICILIES

In a series of treaties culminating in the Final Act of the Congress of Vienna in 1815, the system of conquests and alliances built by Revolutionary and Napoleonic France evaporated. Austria, Prussia, and Russia appropriated sizable spoils (note corresponding hatchings). France, Spain, several Italian states, and other conquests were restored to their former rulers. The resulting map of Europe remained basic until the wars of the 1850's and 1860's.

of remaining loyal to Napoleon too long and whose lands were occupied by the Russians. Prussia was ready to exchange its Poles for Saxons, and the Prussian delegation supported the czar's scheme.

There was good reason, however, to fear that the aggrandizement of Prussia at Saxony's expense would result in a German, and hence a general European, disequilibrium. Already suspicious of Alexander's aims in the Near East, Castlereagh and Metternich joined forces to oppose him in Poland, and a dangerous impasse developed among the victorious powers. Talleyrand, supported by Spain and the smaller powers, took the opportunity to inject his country's influence into the discussions. With Castlereagh's assent he proposed a reduction in the size of the Poland to be placed under Russian tutelage, thereby diminishing Prussia's Polish losses, and a correspondingly diminished compensation to Prussia (only about two fifths of the Saxon state). The French diplomat's suggestion was accepted, with the consequence that, having had the decisive voice in a crisis, France began once again to play an important part in the councils of Europe.

This Polish-Saxon solution marked the fourth time that Poland was partitioned among her neighbors. Part of Prussian Poland was restored to Prussia. Cracow was created a Polish republic under Austrian supervision, and the other boundaries of Austrian Galicia were rectified in favor of Austria. The remainder of the former Duchy of Warsaw—often called "Congress Poland," to distinguish it from the areas that had been annexed by Russia in the first three partitions of Poland—became a kingdom in personal union with Russia. The constitution that Alexander granted it was generally hailed as liberal.

Waterloo and the Second Treaty of Paris

ALTHOUGH Napoleon's return from Elba in 1815 required the powers for the Hundred Days to turn their major attention to the war effort again, the Congress of Vienna continued its deliberations without serious interruption. While the British Wellington and the Prussian Blücher took the field against Napoleon, the congress incorporated its decisions in a Final Act, and it was formally accepted even before the allies crushed Napoleon at Waterloo. Napoleon's defeat meant his second abdication and a second restoration of the Bourbons. Since the Congress of Vienna by that time had dispersed, a new treaty with the French was negotiated at Paris.

The Second Treaty of Paris was sterner than the first. It was now somewhat more difficult to pretend that the French, who had hailed Bonaparte's return with undisguised enthusiasm, were fundamentally opposed to the imperial program of glory and conquest. In addition to suffering a few small territorial losses, the French were required to pay the unprecedented indemnity of 700,000,000 francs and to bear the costs of an army of occupation to prevent new disorders. That the peace arrangements were no more severe was

43

probably due to Castlereagh's insistence that moderation was the best guarantee of future peace.

British supremacy
in the overseas world

AS MENTIONED earlier, Britain was most concerned to reëstablish the power balance in Europe, claiming no continental prizes for herself and guarding against too generous concessions to any other power. In the overseas world, however, England received handsome compensation, acquiring naval and commercial bases strategic to the holding and extension of her far-flung possessions and interests. The Union Jack was hoisted over areas that had formerly belonged to the French, the Dutch, or others in the West Indies, Cape Colony, Malta, Ceylon, Helgoland, and Mauritius. England emerged with the choicest spoils in the colonial and maritime world from the wars that, with but one brief truce, she had fought from 1793 to 1814, and her leading rivals for empire were, temporarily at least, forced out of the centuries-old contest for superiority on the seas and overseas.

Religious revival
and the Holy Alliance

THE DELIBERATIONS of the powers that presided over the redistribution of the Napoleonic empire were not restricted entirely to secular matters. Closely related to the problems of the peace was the future status of religion. Like the secular rulers, Pope Pius VII returned to his domain. His realm, however, was not temporal alone, and he almost at once revived the once strong Jesuit order as a now much needed special agency of papal authority. "Legitimacy" needed a restoration of the religious faith and practices of the past, for revolution and religious liberalism, both enemies of established faiths, had advanced hand in hand. Accordingly, the statesmen at Vienna had assigned an honored position to religion. Czar Alexander was particularly impelled by his own mystical temperament and by the millennial teachings of his friend Baroness von Krüdener. In his zeal to effect a religious and political reconciliation, Alexander induced Europe's rulers to join with him in a Holy Alliance, which bound its members to treat each other as Christian brethren and their subjects as beloved children. That way, he thought, would come peace and well-being after a generation of war and upheaval. Nearly all the Christian crowned heads of Europe signed it, with the notable exception of the pope and the king of England.

Castlereagh
and the Quadruple Alliance

ANTICIPATING that few of the signers would take the Holy Alliance seriously, Castlereagh insisted upon more realistic collective action of the four great powers to preserve the peace. Austria, Prussia, Russia, and Britain transformed their wartime alliance into a peacetime concert pointed expressly at France and designed to maintain the Vienna accord. By acting together as a Quadruple Alliance

44

in diplomatic and military affairs, the victorious powers proposed to maintain the system of "legitimacy." Their success was to be notable. The subsequent practice of meeting in international congresses to resolve diplomatic crises before rather than after wars broke out came to be called the "Concert of Europe." Since it was employed especially by a victorious and contented Britain to promote her pacific policy and to make the period from 1815 to 1914 a century of well-balanced power, the nineteenth century is often called the age of the "Pax Britannica."

STABILITY
BY REPRESSION (1815-1820)

THE NEW era in Europe began auspiciously. For the first few years after the Treaty of Vienna, statesmen and intellectuals were prone to believe that preserving the Vienna settlement would provide a successful means of preventing domestic or foreign wars, and governments assumed that paternalistic reform would provide all the liberty their peoples wanted and would do away with all inclination to revolt. Europe, it was thought, placed stability and the opportunity to develop economically above such high-sounding aspirations as "Liberty, Equality, and Fraternity."

British reaction to the Vienna settlements

UPON HIS return to London, Lord Castlereagh was greeted as a hero by conservatives and as a malefactor by liberals. Though the old-line Tories, devoted to the status quo, held power in England until 1822, the British government and people were not content to accept the continental version of legitimacy without qualifications. Being inclined to think of Britain as the homeland of civil liberty and free enterprise, and having struggled successfully against the principle of divine right of kings since the seventeenth century, the British refused to become a party to that principle as embodied in the Holy Alliance. They nevertheless supported the Vienna arrangements and the Quadruple Alliance as a promise of continued peace and order in Europe without intending to be trapped into any of Alexander's "sublime mysticism and nonsense."

Industrial development and labor problems in Britain

TO BRITAIN peace and stability meant a clear opportunity to promote her special economic advantages. In a world where agriculture was still the major form of production, Britain had recently won a marked lead in the mechanization of industry. That lead gave her an industrial preponderance that, together with her naval and colonial superiority, lifted her influence in international affairs. At home, technical advance also produced striking changes in everyday life. The growth of the factory brought with it a swarm of new social, economic, and cultural problems. The movement of workers toward the factory towns helped to make urban centers larger and more complicated. As families migrated from the countryside to the city, they gave up the narrow margin of economic independence which living on the land had sometimes made possible for cottagers, small farmers, and domestic laborers. Industrialism tied the material welfare of the worker to the success or failure of a business about whose direction he had little or nothing to say. With the spread of the factory, thousands of workers gradually lost whatever freedom the exacting demands of farming had once permitted. For a time, to be sure, the real wages of the workingman in the new industrial towns tended to rise and he was probably economically better off than his country cousin, but specialized tasks, fixed hours, and slum conditions left him a mere cog on a great economic wheel whose total operation and objectives were hidden from his view; and he quickly learned to be more articulate about his destitution than his country cousin.

Urbanization and an inadequate food supply

THE MOVEMENT toward the cities brought overcrowding and disease. Nevertheless, the food supply increased because new technological developments brought improvements in farming, canning, and transportation; and medical, hospital, and sanitation facilities, poor though they still were in our terms, became more readily available. Hence the death rate was gradually reduced and (although the birth rate also tended downward until 1840) the total population increased.

The rapid increase in population led, however, to an expanding demand for food. The pressure upon the food supply, although not severe until a later date, had been intensified by the prolonged war, Napoleon's Continental System, and the protective tariff policy of the Tory regime. The Tories, usually representative of the landed interests, feared that the return of peace and the reopening of the normal channels of commerce would result in competition with foreign grains and a drastic cut in the price of foodstuffs and of other agricultural commodities that had long been scarce. To protect their home market they passed a Corn Law in 1815 that practically excluded foreign breadstuffs from Britain.

The "Industrial Revolution" as a source of domestic problems

IN PROTECTING the agricultural interests from possible losses, the Tory government worked a hardship upon other economic and social groups. Those to suffer most were the workingmen and their families. England's industrial capitalists, too, were well aware of the economic effects of the Corn Laws and were opposed to high tariffs advocated by the landed interests. Each group sought allies among the rest of the population. The industrialists supported the poor in their hostility to the Corn Laws, and the landed interests supported the factory workers in their struggle for better working conditions and shorter hours of labor.

46

The leadership in the demand for better factory conditions came, however, from humanitarians and religious figures. The innovations effected by the so-called "Industrial Revolution" tended to upset all calculations that social stability might result from the restoration of political "legitimacy" on the Continent.

Romanticism in British arts and letters

FOR QUITE other reasons sometimes, English poets and artists participated in their own way in the unrest of the working classes, giving rise to the Romantic Movement in England. The word *romanticism* has many different connotations and is variously described by various contemporaries and later scholars. One characteristic, however, which was fairly common to the post-Napoleonic romantics was their deep attachment to nature. Theirs was not the cold, orderly, material nature of the eighteenth-century *philosophes* from which a rational system of human affairs could be derived but rather an ardent, variable, colorful, irregular nature toward which the poet or the artist might feel an emotional and reverent warmth, a close communion as with the Deity. In this nature he sought refuge from the meannesses, the errors, the uniformity, and the arrogance of the man-made universe.

This romanticism was a reaction against the philosophy that had worshiped regularity and reason in human affairs only to bring on, as the romantics saw it, revolutionary violence and aggressive war. Still, for all the disillusioning failure to right the world, the expansive forces that had found expression in the French Revolution had released poets like Samuel Taylor Coleridge and William Wordsworth from the approved forms and ideals of the eighteenth century and now led them to seek less conventional esthetic and spiritual norms. These "Lake School" poets and the famous trio of younger poets, Lord Byron, Shelley, and John Keats, rebelling against the materialism and rationalism of the earlier "Age of Reason," united in their praise of human emotions and inner feelings. A simple devotion to home and hearth, a detailed appreciation of nature's bounty and splendor, a profound but untheological reverence for the divine, and, in some like Shelley and Byron, an intense hatred of political injustice became the marks of the English Romantic Movement in poetry.

Several painters of this era, too, fell under the spell of romanticism. John Constable and J. M. W. Turner put upon their canvases the landscapes that nature had provided as their models, depicting the lights and hues of the outdoors with picturesqueness and personal affection, and William Blake gave to his paintings and engravings a poetic and mystical afflatus. The academic tradition in art nevertheless continued to be upheld by the Royal Academy, whose preferences were generally accepted by artists and critics alike. Sir Thomas Lawrence was especially distinguished and worthily carried on the splendid tradition of English portraiture. In the arts, conflict between the

"The Complaint of Job," an engraving by William Blake.

old standards and the newer spirit was much less rampant than in literature, economics and politics.

The course
of the British reform movement

FACED BY a difficult postwar situation, the Tory government of Lord Liverpool determined to uphold the status quo. The "rotten borough" system by which rich patrons, usually nobles, controlled the choice of about two fifths of the House of Commons, had for a century or so guaranteed that no government in office would lose an election. The continual call for change only persuaded the old-line Tories to resist change the more—particularly the demand for a more popular franchise. This demand was loudly expressed in the writings of Jeremy Bentham, recognized leader of the Utilitarians (a school that emphasized "public utility" rather than "natural right" as the source of political good), and of William Cobbett, a radical journalist. Wider representation in the House of Commons was repeatedly advocated as one of the preliminary steps most essential to the achievement of economic and social well-being. Public demonstrations by working people in the new industrial cities also let the government know of the workers' sense of grievance. The humanitarian efforts of philanthropists like Robert Owen to better labor conditions, to promote cooperatives among consumers and producers, and to provide stricter regulation of factory conditions failed to produce the immediate and pronounced relief that the times demanded.

48   A bad harvest coincided with a short industrial depression in 1819. In

St. Peter's Field in Manchester a mass meeting was called to petition Parliament for parliamentary reform and repeal of the Corn Laws. Whether the local magistrates were frightened or angry, they interfered with the meeting, and in the resulting disorder the Manchester Yeomanry, made up of untrained upper-class civilians, charged the crowd. Around six hundred were wounded and eleven were killed in a massacre that came to be called England's "Peterloo." The government blamed the demonstrators rather than the Yeomanry for the disaster and put through Parliament a series of repressive measures known as the Six Acts. Meetings for military drill were forbidden, seditious libel was made more severely punishable, freedom of the press was restricted in such a way as to hamper workingmen's publications, and regulations governing public meetings became harder to evade. Though strong voices were raised in protest against the Six Acts, the government was saved for the time being by the public indignation over an abortive plot ("the Cato Street Conspiracy") to kill the responsible cabinet leaders.

Continental reactions to the settlements of Vienna

ON THE Continent, the years between Waterloo and Peterloo were even more decidedly years of triumph for the system of "legitimacy." Like England's, the continental governments were determined to prevent the resurgence of the revolutionary spirit and hoped to preserve order through repression. Unlike England, the continental countries were not yet undergoing profound industrial and social change and, except for France, had little tradition of insurrection. Hence, the restored governments found for a while no serious opposition, though they were quick to repress what opposition they did find.

Political reaction under the Bourbons in France

DESPITE King Louis XVIII's Royal Charter, France moved gradually away from constitutional monarchy toward a more transparent absolutism. Led by the king's brother, the Comte d'Artois, the restored aristocrats and clergy exerted continuous pressure in a reactionary direction, hoping to undo the changes brought by the Revolution. The push toward reaction was not at first seriously challenged. A few liberal reformers under Lafayette were more dramatic than effective, and a group of more moderate liberals, contemptuously labeled the Doctrinaires, who believed that history taught the wisdom of strict adherence to the spirit of limited government in the Charter, were certainly less dramatic and only slightly more effective. The lack of success of the liberal efforts can be accounted for at least in part by the fact that Frenchmen before 1830 had built no great industrial empires and so France's middle class did not yet boast any great captains of industry who could provide the proponents of limited government with political prestige and financial support. For a decade after the promulgation of the Charter absolutism threatened to carry off an almost uncontested victory.

*Conservatism
among the French intellectuals*

IN FRANCE, the Romantic Movement met the same kind of conservative opposition as it met in England. While Théodore Géricault and young Eugène Delacroix led a trend in painting away from the preference for smooth surfaces, classical lines, and statuesque poses of the Revolutionary period, the classical tradition was still largely acceptable to J. A. Dominique Ingres. France's sculptors and architects for the most part also continued to work in the classical vein, contributing significantly to the survival of interest in the Napoleonic era by completing projects undertaken upon the emperor's direction. In literature the influence of a restored Catholicism was perhaps all the more clear because of its recent exile and martyrdom. Journalists, historians, novelists, and critics wrote with approval of the Catholic creed and with great reverence for the Middle Ages, which the *philosophes* of the Age of Reason had condemned as an age of obscurantism. The neo-medievalists, like the philosophers Joseph de Maistre and Louis de Bonald and the novelist-statesman François René

*"Arab
Attacked by
a Lion,"
a drawing by
Eugène Delacroix.*

de Chateaubriand, blamed the Revolution and the concomitant disordered state of society upon the unreligious, materialistic, divisive character of "enlightened" thought, and pled for an orderly and moral society under recognized authority with a respected tradition. As in the Napoleonic era, meanwhile, the intellectual disciplines that were free of direct political implications made great advances. In the biological sciences, Georges Cuvier and Étienne Geoffroy Saint-Hilaire made particularly significant contributions although Cuvier opposed the theory that the higher forms of animals had evolved from the lower.

The success of Louis XVIII's foreign policy

THE FRENCH romantics were more closely tied to their religion and institutions, which they had nearly lost, than the English to theirs, which had not been successfully threatened since the seventeenth century. Though both the French and the English romantics referred frequently to a glorified past, they had vastly different backgrounds from which to derive either authority for national traditions or inspiration for daring innovations. In France traditional authority won some support because of the cheap but impressive successes of Louis XVIII's foreign policy. Once viewed with suspicion by the other powers as the disturber of European equilibrium, France under the Restoration became one of the stabilizing forces of Europe. As fear of a revolutionary revival diminished, France was admitted in 1818 into the highest international councils on a basis of equality. The armies of occupation were withdrawn and France was invited to membership in the Quadruple Alliance (which thereupon became a Quintuple Alliance). "Legitimatized" France now caused less concern to the continental powers than industrialized England.

Nationalism and liberalism in Austria

CENTRAL Europe had as yet known neither the popular revolution nor the "Industrial Revolution." Such political and social change as it had undergone had been the work of enlightened hereditary rulers. Through "legitimacy," Metternich, now the dominant figure in central Europe, hoped to preserve the wide Habsburg interests from succumbing to the pressures of the subject nationalities for self-government and of liberals for reform. Nationalistic agitation among the Austrian-dominated Italians, Bohemians, Poles, Hungarians, and South Slavs jeopardized the peace and safety of the hereditary Habsburg realm; and in the newly constituted German Confederation, which Metternich controlled indirectly, the greatest danger to his program came from liberal aspirations. German liberals, whether from the north or the south German states, hoped to free their political, economic, and social institutions from aristocratic and princely control and from the supervision of Austria, and to a certain extent they could count on the support of the non-German minorities in the Habsburg empire.

*Prussia's role
in Germany and Europe*

OF ALL the German states, Prussia was looked to most hopefully by German nationalists and liberals. Through demonstrations in the universities, numerous addresses and pamphlets, and patriotic student organizations such as the *Burschenschaften,* liberal agitators drove home the idea that the peoples of Germany would willingly follow Prussian leadership toward union and freedom. As the leading economic power in Germany, Prussia was certainly the state best equipped to assume such a role. Her commercial self-interest, as interpreted by the economic theorist Friedrich List, seemed to dictate an anti-Austrian policy and the remodeling of the Confederation into a free-trade area.

In fact Prussia in 1818 began the organization of a *Zollverein* (customs union) with the neighboring German states. This independent economic policy was undertaken primarily because of the pressure exerted upon the government by growing industrial, commercial, and banking interests in Prussia's Rhenish and Silesian territories. Prussia's promotion of the *Zollverein* was resisted at first by a truncated Saxony and a suspicious Austria, but, supported by the expanding economy of the leading north German state, it quickly achieved success in northern Germany. Though initiated as a strictly economic program with the primary purpose of removing the barriers to trade among the states bordering on the Hohenzollern realm, the *Zollverein* gave Prussia a significant strategic advantage in the race for leadership in the movement toward the political unification of Germany.

King Frederick William III preferred, however, to steer clear of the less traveled lanes of political liberalism and German unification. Politically, Prussia continued to collaborate with Austria and Russia—so much so that in the minds of most observers, contemporary and since, the Holy Alliance came to be identified incorrectly with the cooperation of Prussia, Russia, and Austria in a program of repressing liberalism. This popularly conceived "Holy Alliance" had considerably more real cohesion than the formal Holy Alliance of 1815. Believing that peace and order could best be maintained by the "Congress system," Prussia consistently acted in concert with the other two eastern powers to smother European liberal movements.

*The suppression
of German liberalism*

MOREOVER, Frederick William III regularly endorsed Metternich's policy of muffling opponents of the status quo in Germany. Between 1818 and 1820 a series of repressive measures went into force inside the Confederation. The most effective of these were the Carlsbad Decrees, which established a notorious censorship of the press and a meticulous "supervision" of the universities. At Mainz a special tribunal was created to deal with liberal agitators. In 1820, Metternich got the small German states to agree that the federal government might intervene to preserve order in states not able to maintain internal peace by their own efforts. Thus, as in Britain and France, the German rulers, preferring order to freedom, sought to preserve domestic peace by stifling innovation.

Innovations
in German letters and music

WHILE THE "Holy Alliance" engaged in vigorous repression, some writers and musicians of central Europe nevertheless produced works that favored national or liberal ideals, whether so intended or not, without incurring the wrath of the political authorities. In Germany, the intellectuals' interest in national origins grew while practical projects for achieving national unification were being banned. Ludwig Tieck and the brothers Jakob and Wilhelm Grimm collected old folk stories, poems, and fairy tales. This folklore provided the Grimms and others with a major source for the serious investigation of the history of the German language and its relationship to other languages. Their investigations gave impetus not only to the disciplines of comparative philology and comparative literature but also to a great national pride in the purity of the German tongue.

Related to the study of language as a key to national origins was the growing interest in historical and prehistorical antiquity. The scholarly study of history was stimulated by the use of surviving objects and logical deduction as a check on and supplement to literary testimony and tradition. Barthold Georg Niebuhr brought archeological inferences into his *Roman History,* begun in 1811. Georg Wilhelm Hegel began his courses in philosophy at Berlin in 1818, designed to show that "The World Spirit" worked itself out through the historical process and would lead ultimately to a modern, orderly state like Prussia, where law and freedom (avoiding the potential antipathy between them) would be welded together.

In music, too, it was possible to work in a new spirit without running the danger of political reprisal. The great German romantic composers, like Carl Maria von Weber, the later Ludwig van Beethoven, and Franz Schubert concentrated their attention upon dramatic orchestrations and lyrical brilliance, seeking to give voice to human moods and emotions, at times with disregard of the forms that the prestige of the older masters had rendered classic. Vienna was at the time second only to Paris as the musical capital of the world, and the greatest virtuosos of the day, such as the Italian violinist Nicolò Paganini, the Polish pianist Frédéric François Chopin, and the Hungarian pianist Franz Liszt, sooner or later sought the approval of the cultivated Viennese audiences, which were generally cosmopolitan in their musical taste.

Revival
of autocracy in Russia

IN RUSSIA the trend after 1815 away from reform and toward autocratic institutions was still more pronounced than in central Europe. Though the serfs of the Baltic provinces were freed by 1816, these "new peasants," granted freedom without land— 53 which might easily mean only freedom to starve, excited the czar's fear of domestic upheaval by their protests and uprisings. These disorders and his jealously guarded prestige in the so-called "Holy Alliance" induced Alexander I to halt all efforts at reform. After 1818 he became notoriously reactionary, reinstituting a censorship of the press and a stricter surveillance of the universities.

By 1820, despite the defiance of the older themes and forms that the Romantic Movement sometimes brought with it, the prevailing spirit in Europe was conservative. The "Holy Alliance" seemed to have triumphed in its intention to preserve an ordered, legitimate, and unswerving status quo.

REVOLTS IN EUROPE

AND AMERICA (1820-1823)

A FEW BOLD spirits continued to believe in the inevitability of freedom's victory. In 1820, Shelley wrote several poems on "Liberty." In one of these he prophesied:

> From billow and mountain and exhalation
> The sunlight is darted through vapour and blast;
> From spirit to spirit, from nation to nation,
> From city to hamlet thy dawning is cast,—
> And tyrants and slaves are like shadows of night
> In the van of the morning light.

His prophecy was not entirely false. Held in check for two decades either by a French conqueror or by restored legitimists, the revolutionary flood rose again in 1820. This time, however, it avoided the big powers and wreaked its greatest damage on some lesser European countries and in Latin America. In the larger countries the legitimate governments continued vigorously to enforce their antiliberal and antinational decrees and to dam revolt elsewhere.

*Dissatisfaction
with the Bourbons of Spain*

THE FIRST of a series of widely scattered insurrections occurred in Spain. Spanish liberals had been outraged by the refusal of the restored Bourbon monarch, Ferdinand VII, to abide by the liberal Constitution of 1812, drawn up during his exile while Spain was fighting off the invading Bonapartes. Backed by a good part of the army, they were now ready to overturn the Bourbon dynasty, if necessary, to preserve their constitution. The violence of their demands upon Ferdinand prompted immediate attention from the Concert of Europe. It also met with a quite different response from the Spanish colonies across the Atlantic.

There, during the Napoleonic period, the representatives of the Bourbon king had had to rule without recourse to a Madrid dominated by a Bonaparte, and the spirit of independence and self-reliance which had developed at that time still survived. Armies sent out from Spain to quell the Spanish colonies met with marked success in the years immediately following Ferdinand's restoration. In 1820, however, a revolt in Spain, begun by soldiers protesting against being sent to America to fight, brought at first a respite and then victory to the Spanish colonial rebels. In Spain the insurgents, making Ferdinand VII a virtual prisoner, extracted from him a promise to respect the Constitution of 1812.

*Spread
of revolt in southern Europe*

IT SOON became clear that the continental spirit of revolt was far from exhausted. Once the revolutionary signal was sounded in Spain, it reverberated throughout southern and eastern Europe. The Portuguese quickly followed the Spanish in raising the flag of insurrection, and amidst the ensuing complications Brazil established its independence of Portugal. Italian patriots considered the occasion opportune. The post-Napoleonic settlements had restored Italy (with some exceptions) to its old "legitimate" rulers. Hence Italy was once again merely "a geographical expression," divided among a number of sovereign states all more or less under Austrian tutelage and each anxious to undo the work of the Napoleonic regime. The liberals, organized into secret societies, of which the foremost were the Carbonari (Charcoal-Burners), kept fresh the memory of the recent interlude when Italy had been nearly united—under French domination, to be sure, but with constitutional regimes that looked like the essence of liberty when compared with the current Austrian hegemony. The example of revolt in Spain and Portugal was welcomed by the Italian liberals. The reactionary Bourbon ruler of Naples found himself face to face with an indignant populace demanding constitutional reform, and King Victor Emmanuel of Sardinia, who was reluctant to show any sympathy for the Neapolitans, was forced by his outraged subjects to abdicate. These essentially liberal revolts were followed in 1821 by nationalistic uprisings in Greece against the rule of the Ottoman Turk.

*The policy
of concerted intervention*

THE PROPONENTS of the status quo in Europe quickly recognized the need for positive action, and Metternich and his cohorts rapidly converted their *cordon sanitaire* into militant action against the liberal contagion. At the conference of the Quintuple Alliance at Troppau in 1820, the members of the so-called "Holy Alliance" (Russia, Austria, and Prussia) committed themselves explicitly to a protocol announcing their intention to intervene in any state having "undergone a change of government due to revolution." Because of its own revolutionary background and its people's sympathy with the revolted countries, England 55 was in no position to commit itself to such a policy, and France also hesitated. England protested, but France gave the Troppau protocol its approval, and from that moment England ceased to act fully as a member of the Quintuple Alliance. In 1821 the five powers met again at Laibach in company with some of the rulers of the Italian states. At this conference, despite English protests, it was decided to dispatch Austrian troops to Naples to quell revolt and to restore the Bourbon king to his "legitimate" powers. The work of the liberals in Naples and Piedmont was quickly undone, reaction was once more enthroned, and the Carbonari went into exile or underground.

The riddle of how to deal with Greece

THOUGH the eastern powers were determined to halt the liberal revolts, the proper course of action to take in connection with the Greek rebellion presented some difficulties. No matter how unwelcome to the "legitimate" rulers, the national and liberal impulses released by the French Revolution had stirred the Christian subjects of the Ottoman Empire to hope for their own liberation and independence. While many among the Christian minorities pinned their hopes for release from the sultan's control upon the great powers, it soon became apparent that the legitimate and Christian rulers of western Europe were caught in a dilemma. If they acknowledged the Porte as the legitimate government in the Ottoman domains (as they had so far done), they could not commit themselves wholeheartedly to support a revolt against it. On the other hand, if they did not acknowledge the Porte as the legitimate government in the Ottoman domains, then they would be giving a diplomatic advantage to Russia that none of the other powers would willingly give. For Russia was by an old treaty (page 25) the recognized protector of the sultan's Christian subjects and might welcome the disintegration of the neighboring Turkish empire as a good excuse to take up this obligation. The Greeks, like the Russians, were Orthodox Christians, and Russia had its own ambitions to serve in promoting the decline of the Ottoman Empire.

Czar Alexander thus found himself in a peculiar position. He sincerely advocated a strong alliance of European princes to preserve the status quo, but he was at the same time under considerable pressure at home to aid the Christians of Greece against their Moslem overlords. He was frankly under Metternich's influence; yet he would have to look to Russia's interests in the eastern Mediterranean area if the Austrians, as he feared they might, took advantage of their intervention in Italy to establish themselves more firmly there. Reassured by Metternich and prevailed upon by Castlereagh, Alexander decided to refrain from open intervention in favor of the Greeks in order to preserve the united front of the "legitimate" powers against revolution. He was, however, willing to overlook his "legitimate" scruples to the extent of giving secret encouragement to the Greek patriots.

*Britain
as an advocate of revolt*

THE CONTINENTAL revolts were greeted in liberal circles in England with loud acclaim. Byron went off to die in the Greek cause. Shelley published his lyrical drama *Hellas* in 1822 depicting the independence of Greece and the disruption of the sultan's realm as the dawning of an age of universal love and freedom. In several other poems he celebrated the Spanish and Neapolitan revolutions, as in his "Ode to Liberty":

> England yet sleeps: was she not called of old?
> Spain calls her now, as with its thrilling thunder
> Vesuvius wakens Aetna, and the cold
> Snow-crags by its reply are cloven in sunder.

Nor was it only poets who showed enthusiasm for the Spanish revolts. Stirred by the prospects of Latin-American markets, British commercial and industrial interests wanted to encourage the independence movements in the New World as a means of ending Spain's tight economic control. In the face of rising continental tariff barriers against the influx of cheap manufactured goods from the factories of England, trade with the New World had become particularly important to the British. The liberal and business interests won a victory in 1822 when the suicide of the distraught Castlereagh permitted the

A poster issued by the French government depicting the capture of the fortress of Trocadero from the "brigands" of Spain. The slogan on the defenders' flag, "Constitution or death," refers to the Constitution of 1812.

dominant position on Liverpool's cabinet to pass to George Canning, a "liberal Tory."

Intervention in Spain
on behalf of "legitimacy"

AS "THE workshop of the world," Great Britain was at the opposite pole from the agricultural countries of eastern Europe. England now broke definitely with her former continental partners. When a congress of the powers met in the northern Italian city of Verona in 1822, the English openly resisted a proposal to employ the French army to crush the Spanish revolt. In the following year, nevertheless, the congress decided to permit the French Bourbon to offer a "relief force" to the Spanish Bourbon. The revolution in Spain was quickly crushed, Ferdinand VII restored the Bourbon absolutism, and the Constitution of 1812 was discarded. The reaction in Spain encouraged the Lisbon government to revise the recently granted Portuguese constitution in the direction of absolutism. The victory of "legitimacy" in Europe led Britain and the United States to fear that an intervention in the New World would follow.

REPUBLICANISM AND INDEPENDENCE

IN THE AMERICAS

SINCE THE declaration of the independence of the United States in 1776, theorists and commentators, liberal and conservative, had looked to the Western Hemisphere for examples of the effectiveness or ineffectiveness of republican institutions. The American experiment had helped to translate republicanism from the realm of theory to that of action. In republican France at the turn of the century, though part of the time the two republics were at sword's point, republicans had strengthened their rhetoric by glowing references to the ideals and the heroes of the United States. In Poland, Holland, Italy, Switzerland, and wherever republican governments had taken unsteady root, the revolutionaries had sought aid and inspiration chiefly from France but also in the example of the United States. Still more in Latin America, as sentiments for independence mounted, the example of the North American republic served as an inspiration, a precedent, and a model.

Beginnings
of the Spanish-American revolts

AS ALREADY indicated, revolution had flared up in Latin America in 1808. Napoleon's invasion of the Iberian Peninsula and the establishment of a French-dominated regime at Madrid had given the Spanish colonies their opportunity to strike for independence even while upholding loyally the rights of the Bourbon dynasty. Refusing to recognize the regime of the Bonapartes, the colonists formed provisional governments of their own and opened their ports to the commerce of the world. When, however, Ferdinand VII returned to his throne at Madrid, all his colonies with the exception of Argentina were once more returned to the fold, and their ports were virtually closed to trade outside the Spanish possessions. As in Europe, so in the New World "legitimacy" seemed triumphant.

But in the Western Hemisphere the triumph was shorter than in Europe. The colonial revolutionaries after 1815 turned upon the hereditary Spanish ruler. While King Ferdinand tried ruthlessly to weed out the revolutionary elements from Spain, Latin-American insurgents, after some initial setbacks, launched increasingly more effective attacks upon royalist armies. José de San Martin freed most of the southern provinces of South America from Spanish control. In the northern sectors of the continent, particularly in the valley of the Orinoco River, Simón Bolívar consolidated the revolutionary activities of divergent groups in preparation for a final drive. In Central America and Mexico the revolutionary spirit also rose again, and all of Spanish America was in full revolt even before the uprisings in Spain stirred the Concert of Europe to take measures to prop up Ferdinand's regime.

Sale of Florida to the United States

MEANWHILE popular sympathy in the United States for the revolutionaries of Latin America had crystallized. Conscious of the weakness of the restored Bourbons in Spain, the North Americans had taken an aggressive stand in Florida, still a Spanish possession. General Andrew Jackson in 1817 had led an American punitive expedition into Spanish territory to pacify the turbulent Seminole and Creek Indians, who had been harassing American border settlements. Fearing that the United States might decide to seize Florida unceremoniously, the Spanish in 1819 agreed to work out a new settlement. Florida was sold outright to the North American republic, and all lands east of the Mississippi were ceded to the United States. In return the American government agreed to adjust the claims of American citizens incurred by Spain during the Napoleonic wars to the extent of $5,000,000 and to relinquish whatever titles to Texas might have been derived from the Louisiana Purchase of 1803.

The mutual interests of the United States and Britain

IN THE course of the negotiations with Spain, the United States discovered the extent of Britain's interest in the future of the Spanish colonies. The War of 1812 between Great Britain and the United States and the burning of Washington by British invaders was still fresh in American minds, and American sentiment toward England in some quarters was bitter. Nevertheless, relations with Britain had improved after the war, and in 1817 the two countries worked out the Rush-Bagot agreement establishing permanent peace between the United States and Canada. A convention of the following year set up an international boundary between the United States and Canada that has been unfortified ever since. Spain's tottering position in the New World, however, led the 59

United States and Great Britain to suspect one another's purposes in Central and South America for a time.

The eventuality proved that American and British interests in that area coincided. The outbreak of revolution in Spain in 1820 was viewed, as we have seen, with equal elation, though for different reasons, by British liberals and commercial interests. American business groups, too, welcomed the opportunity to trade freely with Latin America. Though the administration of President James Monroe (1817-1825) was under considerable pressure to recognize the self-declared republics to the south, the president feared that premature recognition might involve the United States in hostilities with Spain. The outbreak of civil war in Spain increased American readiness to cooperate with the Latin-American states. The government at Washington, however, out of fear now of becoming involved with the champions of Spain in the Concert of Europe, moved with caution.

Pronouncement of the Monroe Doctrine — UNDER THE "liberal Tory" influence of Canning, positive opposition to the Troppau program developed in Britain. Canning not only obtained from France an engagement not to support intervention in Latin America but also proposed that the United States and Great Britain issue a joint declaration against the use of force to resubjugate the former Spanish colonies. President Monroe for a moment contemplated such a joint action, but finally, under the persuasion of John Quincy Adams, his secretary of state, he resolved to pursue an independent course. This decision put Britain in the same category as other European powers with regard to future American policy in the Western Hemisphere and, at the same time, left Monroe free to rebuke Russia, which was still engaged in colonizing American territory on the west coast.

Monroe formally enunciated this policy in his annual presidential message to Congress in 1823, and it became known as the Monroe Doctrine. In this declaration Monroe proclaimed that "the American continents...are henceforth not to be considered as subjects for future colonization by any European powers." Asserting that the American states had never interfered, and would not interfere, "in the wars of the European powers" or with their "existing colonies or dependencies," Monroe indicated that he expected a reciprocal forbearance from the European states: "We should consider any attempt on their part to extend their system to any portion of this hemisphere as dangerous to our peace and safety." The proclamation also announced bluntly to Spain and Russia that their efforts to regain lost claims or to stake out new ones in the Western Hemisphere would be viewed as "the manifestation of an unfriendly disposition toward the United States."

The cooperation of the two English-speaking countries prevented the "Holy Alliance" from calling a conference or taking other steps to determine the course of events in the New World. Thus the New World, in which the great empire-building states of Europe had established their first great overseas colonies, was closed to them, and they found themselves obliged to look for other worlds to conquer—to Asia, Oceania, and Africa. The American areas, except for the few remaining dependencies on the mainland and in the West Indies, became a congeries of sovereign republics, European in culture but proudly aware of their separate national aspirations.

COMPETITION
FOR EMPIRE IN ASIA

THE WHITE men's contacts with the countries of Asia before 1800 had been largely limited to trade, missions, and the annexation of garrison outposts. Though the struggle for control of Asia's trade had gone on for almost three centuries, no decisive victory had been won by any of the European states until the eighteenth century. Then, as a result of a long series of colonial wars, Great Britain gained control of India and became paramount in the China trade. The Spanish, Portuguese, Dutch, French, and Russians, nevertheless, continued to hold on to important posts in Asia and showed no signs of ceding their share of its trade or territory. The industrialization of Europe in the nineteenth century heightened the competition among the European empires, for, in addition to making still bolder the grab for Asia's raw materials, it intensified the race for Asia's teeming millions as customers.

Britain's displacement of the Dutch east of India
AT THE beginning of the nineteenth century, the British began to push eastward from India into Malaysia and Oceania. The death struggle with Napoleon in Europe markedly accelerated their progress in these areas. After having fallen under the control of France at home, the Dutch, formerly masters of the East Indies, were turned out of their colonies by the British. Dutch Ceylon, too, fell into British hands. In the peace negotiations of 1814-1815 the British agreed, in order to win Dutch cooperation with Castlereagh's and Metternich's program for containing France on the Continent, to restore the Indies to the Dutch. The British, however, retained posts considered strategic for the control of the major sea routes. They kept Malta, Cape Colony, Ceylon, and Mauritius, and after 1815 sought similar outposts in Far Eastern waters. The ambition to dominate the most direct route to the Far East was finally realized in 1819 when the British acquired Singapore, a small island off the tip of the Malay Peninsula. There followed a series of Anglo-Dutch negotiations which eventuated in a general settlement (1824-1825). By its provisions Great Britain permitted the Dutch to retain almost exclusive control over the East Indies and, in return, the Dutch agreed to surrender Malacca and not to oppose Britain's advance into the southeastern portion of the Asiatic continent. The 61

sea routes to eastern Asia continued to be dominated by the British, strategically posted at Singapore and Malacca. Of the once vast Dutch empire all that remained were the Dutch East Indies and the Dutch West Indies.

*Britain's war
with Burma (1824-1826)*

ON THE Asiatic continent, the British pursued after 1815 an ever more aggressive policy. Secure in its position in India, the quasi-sovereign British East India Company moved into Burma and the Malay Peninsula. A dispute with Burma over control of Assam, a state lying between western Burma and Bengal, the British center of power, resulted in a clash. The war lasted for two years, but in the end the Burmese were forced to abandon their claims to Assam and to cede the Tenasserim coast on the Malay Peninsula to the British East India Company. This victory gave the British a more secure hold in southeastern Asia and reduced Burma to a tiny, landlocked state, almost at the mercy of the British East India Company.

*The decline
of the East India Company*

SO FAR the British East India Company had acted as the spearhead of the British movement eastward. Nevertheless, its position as the dominant force in Britain's Asiatic affairs had been gradually weakening. Unable to penetrate into China effectively, the company's agents had markedly lost prestige. This defeat in China was particularly serious because it followed a half-century of growing discontent at home with the company's conduct of affairs in India. As a culmination of several rocking scandals, the government canceled the company's monopoly of the India trade in 1813.

Appreciating the enormous potentialities of the China trade, the British made a serious effort to win formal recognition from the self-centered Chinese rulers. In the hope of obtaining equal treatment for British nationals in China and of establishing a regular diplomatic exchange with the Celestial Empire, Lord Amherst in 1816 went to China as a semi-official representative. Like his predecessors, Lord Amherst refused to acknowledge the Chinese emperor's superiority by performing the kotow and so accomplished nothing substantial to improve Anglo-Chinese relations. Nevertheless, the British by their victories in neighboring lands advanced toward China by sea and by land, and traders and missionaries called for a more vigorous governmental policy in China and for an end to the monopoly of the East India Company in the China trade. Liberals at home, and many in the Orient, advocated free trade in the China area under government protection. The traders of other nations, particularly the newly arrived Americans, whose trade was unregulated, appeared to be faring better than the British. But the European effort to crack the hard shell of China was to be frustrated until the war of 1839-1842 (pages 271-273).

Within India itself, meanwhile, the British were encountering serious administrative difficulties. The bellicose Mahrattas of central India violently opposed the British efforts to bring them under the Bengal government. By 1828, nevertheless, the Mahrattas, along with most of India, had been pacified. Lord William Bentinck, the governor general, then inaugurated a program of enlightened reform (page 297).

*The advance
of the Russians in Asia*

AFTER THE settlement of 1824-1825, the British had no further cause to worry over embroilments with the Dutch. The Spanish, the Portuguese, and the Americans were too weak to constitute serious threats, and France had but recently been forced by the Napoleonic debacle to watch Britain assume uncontested supremacy in the non-European world. By 1830, it had become clear that only Russia would be a fit antagonist for Britain in Asia.

While the British had been hopping from victory to victory in southern Asia, the Russians had been pushing steadily overland into northeastern Asia and beyond that into the regions of the northern Pacific. By moving into Alaska and then southward down the Pacific coast of North America, the Russians aroused the fears of the British in Canada and of the North American republic, which was simultaneously creeping across the prairies and mountains toward the Pacific Ocean. By annexing the coasts on both sides of the Bering Sea as well as the intervening islands, the Russians also keyed up the suspicions of natives and foreigners alike in Japan. The Dutch, who were the only western traders permitted to call upon Japan, took care to warn the

A drawing, made in the early 1820's, of Irkutsk, the central city of Russia's Siberian empire. The architecture is that of an earlier Russia; Irkutsk shows little of the western influence apparent at the time in St. Petersburg or in Moscow.

Nipponese that the Russians were approaching from the north and the British from the south. The better informed Japanese were constrained to realize that their hard-won isolation would sooner or later become impossible to preserve. Moreover, the British in India and the Russians in Central Asia were soon to clash, as we will see, in Afghanistan and Tibet.

THE LIBERAL MOVEMENT
IN EUROPE AND AMERICA (1823-1830)

By the time of Napoleon's death in 1821, some of the sharp hate and bitterness bequeathed to Europe by the violence of the Revolutionary and the Napoleonic era had begun to wear smooth and thin. The passions and biases of the men who had marched against the tricolor and Napoleon were as a rule neither so vindictive nor so influential now as they had been a few years earlier. The problems of the Restoration, besides, had called into prominence some new personalities and new ideas. Though many of the old divisions still cut deep into international, national, and even family groupings, the quest for peace, order, and fortune had softened the fighting spirit evoked on both sides by the old challenge of "Liberty, Equality, and Fraternity." For the rising generation political issues were complicated by a desire to share in the fruits of the industrial and technological changes that were

A contemporary caricature of Charles X breaking his teeth on the hard nut of the Constitutional Charter of France.

already well advanced in Britain and were beginning to be familiar on the Continent.

*Reaction
in France under Charles X*

UNDER THE easygoing, politic, and obese Louis XVIII, France had achieved both a fair degree of internal stability through a policy of tempered repression and a high degree of international respectability through a policy of tactful "legitimacy." By 1823 the Bourbon ruler of France had become one of the most reliable supports in Metternich's political edifice. But the accession of the ultraroyalist Charles X (the former Comte d'Artois) in 1824 seemed to presage a dangerous extension of reaction. Charles believed in the alliance of the throne with the altar and sought a close association with the more conservative clergy. At the same time he frankly favored the former *émigrés,* the men who had fled France during the Revolution, and showed hostility to the rising middle class. Hence the liberals criticized his regime with mounting fervor throughout the twenties. Charles' reply was to put through measures restricting freedom of expression, the franchise, and the middle-class National Guard. While being thus pushed toward the Old Regime by its king, France was beginning to feel the effects of the nineteenth-century "Industrial Revolution." Tugged in opposite directions, French society developed deep cleavages between those who felt the Charter was for the king to interpret as he saw fit and those who saw in it a set of fundamental principles that not even the king could violate.

*The development
of French "romantic socialism"*

THE AUTARKICAL principles of Napoleon and the growth of industry in France gave rise to several schools of thought that placed great emphasis upon the role of industry in French society. Led by the Comte de Saint-Simon, one of these schools got well under way in 1825 with the publication of his book, *The New Christianity.* The new dispensation called for adjusting the state to the emerging social pattern by placing politico-economic power in the hands of scholars, scientists, and engineers, who presumably would work like good Christians for the abolition of poverty rather than for private profit. The followers of Charles Fourier, the author of *The New Industrial World* (1829), also advocated a planned "socialism" (a word that was just beginning to appear). Like Robert Owen in England, Fourier proposed a high degree of social control over economic activity and the establishment of cooperative communities. Fourier called such communities "phalanxes" and their cooperative dwellings "phalansteries." In a society where the unbridled quest for fortune was still rewarding, schemes of social amelioration and warnings about the evils of free enterprise met with only limited approval even from the working class, and as socialistic programs grew in number, even the socialists of one school generally viewed other socialists as impractical and utopian. No "scientific" school had yet developed.

Revolt and repression in Russia

THOUGH not exposed directly to the main stream of liberal and socialist thought, Russian intellectuals were no less divided than those of western Europe. Their divergencies arose not only from varying estimations of the ideas and values of western Europe but also from different understandings of Russia's traditions and institutions. One group, called "Westerners," had little sympathy with Romanov autocracy and the isolation of Russia. Among this group at the time was Alexander Pushkin, whose greatest work of this period was a moving story of usurpation and rebellion, *Boris Godunov* (written in 1825). The "Westerners" were opposed by the "Slavophiles," who believed in the superiority of the Slavs and of Russian institutions and were highly contemptuous of western practices and ideas. The Westerners called for liberal reform; the Slavophiles, like some of the historians and philosophers of contemporary Germany, warned against the dangers that might come from the importation of foreign political convictions.

As already indicated, Czar Alexander wavered in his own mind between the two sides of this conflict. Upon his death, the imperial crown by virtue of a secret family agreement passed to Nicholas, the younger of his two brothers, who was known as a reactionary. Alexander's older brother, Constantine, who had voluntarily renounced the throne, was, however, the preferred candidate of the Westerners. Confusion over the succession arose in December 1825, and a group of liberal conspirators instigated a mutiny at St. Petersburg with the intention of forcing the government to submit the question to a national representative assembly. Having no program or recognized leaders, the "Decembrist forces" were quickly overwhelmed by Nicholas, and the chief conspirators were either executed or exiled.

Thus, the reign of Nicholas (1825-1855) began with a signal defeat for the Western movement and victory for autocracy and Slavophilism. No longer could there be any doubt, either inside or outside Russia, where the czar stood on the question of reform. Dedicated to the maintenance of the royal prerogative, Nicholas instituted an internal "police regime" and a policy of "official nationalism." In foreign relations he lined up regularly with the forces fighting liberalism except where such a policy might conflict with what he conceived to be the basic national interests of Russia.

Nicholas I in the Greek War of Independence

SUCH AN exception occurred when Nicholas encouraged revolt in the Balkans against Turkey as a part of his program of westward expansion. In the Near East, the imminence of conflict between Russia, the greatest land power of the early nineteenth century, and Britain, the greatest sea power, kept the European diplomats who were interested in preserving the Vienna settlement in a constant dither. The Ottoman Empire continued to present obstacles to the effective cooperation of the Concert of Europe. Czar Alexander, we have seen, had been unwilling to defy his western colleagues, and during Alexander's lifetime, the ostensible preference for "legitimacy" had prevailed. Nicholas, having assured himself of the throne only by suppressing an uprising in his own domain, at first looked with profound disapproval upon every revolt against established authority. Nevertheless, Orthodox, conservative, and imperialistic groups in Russia exerted pressure upon him to support the Greek revolt and other incipient uprisings against the Porte. Nicholas, without a great display of reluctance, yielded to this pressure, and Russia openly went to war to help the Greeks attain their independence (1829). The attempts of the other powers to restrict Russia's pro-Greek activities were frustrated, largely by the sympathy of their own people with the Greek cause but also by the indiscreet defiance of the Turks. By the Treaty of Adrianople not only was Greek independence assured, but also the autonomy of the Rumanian provinces and of Serbia was affirmed. Together with Montenegro, which had long been independent, all these Balkan states looked to Russia for protection.

The collapse
of the Quintuple Alliance

RUSSIA'S collaboration with Greek rebellion, coming soon after England's collaboration with Latin-American rebellion, made clear for all to behold the breakdown of the Vienna coalition and the collapse of the Troppau program of united action

THE BALKANS IN 1829

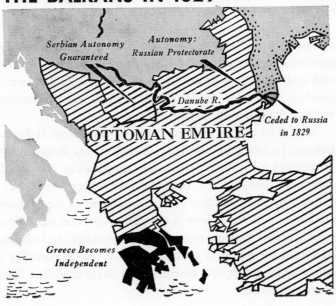

This map shows the results for the Balkans of the treaty of 1829 by which Greece was acknowledged independent, Serbia and the Rumanian provinces were granted autonomy, and Russia was allowed to strengthen her control of the Danube. The map does not show the gains Russia made in the Caucasus area.

Serbian Autonomy Guaranteed

Autonomy: Russian Protectorate

Danube R.

OTTOMAN EMPIRE

Ceded to Russia in 1829

Greece Becomes Independent

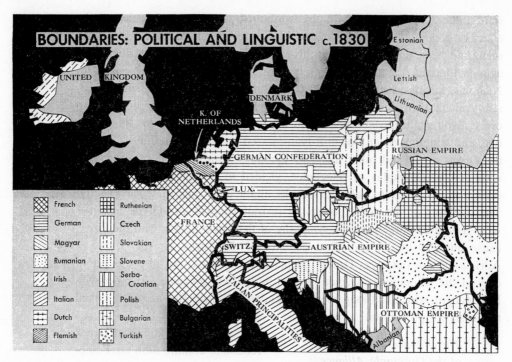

BOUNDARIES: POLITICAL AND LINGUISTIC c. 1830

Key:

☒ French	⊞ Ruthenian
≡ German	⫴ Czech
◺ Magyar	⊞ Slovakian
⋮ Rumanian	⦙⦙⦙ Slovene
⧄ Irish	⦚ Serbo-Croatian
⧄ Italian	⊞ Polish
⊞ Dutch	⊞ Bulgarian
⧄ Flemish	∴ Turkish

Superimposed on this linguistic map of Europe (as of 1911, but holding largely true for the preceding century) are the political boundaries drawn by the peacemakers of Vienna in 1815. It is easy to see where linguistic complications would become a source of political conflict. Note especially the linguistic conglomerations of the Austrian, Russian, and Ottoman Empires, and of Switzerland, the Netherlands, and Ireland. Note also the political disunity of the German-speaking and the Italian-speaking peoples. For the sake of clarity, this map does not attempt to show all the political affiliations or linguistic groups of Europe, but only the major ones in the areas of greatest heterogeneity, although English and the Scandinavian languages, as well as Estonian, Lettish, Lithuanian, Albanians and those shown in the key, are distinct linguistic groupings.

against domestic revolt. Thus, by 1830 England's political and economic interests in the Americas and Russia's interests in the Near East had conflicted with their concern over disturbing the status quo. The concern for the status quo had proved the weaker in the conflict, and its weakness did not augur well for the future of "legitimacy."

The chief centers of unrest of this period were in France and in central Europe. In Germany and Italy liberalism was bound up with the problem of national unification. It was not always clear that the German national movement should, could, or would follow liberal lines, but the German liberals continued, even after several indications to the contrary, to believe that the house of Hohenzollern in the person of Frederick William III of Prussia would provide the best answer to their problem. In Italy, the liberal Charles Albert, of the house of Savoy, cousin of the conservative monarch of Sardinia and Piedmont, was emerging as a likely candidate to become ruler of a united peninsula.

68

Berlin
as an intellectual center

IN GERMANY the northern *Zollverein* was steadily acquiring new members and influence. That was not the only reason, however, why Prussia was slowly becoming the great hope of German liberals and nationalists. In the early decades of the nineteenth century, Berlin was steadily overtaking Vienna as the intellectual center of Germany. Historians, philologists, chemists, and philosophers of international reputation lectured, wrote, and experimented at the new University of Berlin (founded 1809). Hegel continued as professor of philosophy at Berlin from 1818 until his death in 1831, and his answer for the ageless conflict between the individual and the state fitted exactly into the new picture of Prussia's future. Unlike many of his French contemporaries, Hegel looked to history rather than to reason for understanding of the divine purpose and, as explained above, believed that the state, particularly the Prussian state, was a moral, historical entity and that by conforming with it the individual achieved "freedom." A young historian named Leopold von Ranke joined the Berlin faculty in 1825. He combined a careful, "scientific" combing of contemporary sources for historical data and an interest in many different kinds of historical themes in many different places with a belief that the power struggle was the most important theme of history and that the German peoples were outstanding participants in that struggle. Friedrich Karl von Savigny taught law at Berlin at the same time, and in a monumental history of Roman law in the Middle Ages preached the dependence of each people's institutions on its own folk character and warned the Germans against importing the unsettling French ideas of "natural" law. Arthur Schopenhauer's pessimistic philosophy, premised upon a universal and ceaselessly conflicting "will-to-live," was not well received in Berlin.

Discontent
among the minorities of Austria

THE BRIGHTENING glow of Prussia on the northern horizon did not pass unobserved in Vienna. Emperor Francis and Metternich felt obliged, however, to avoid competition for popularity and to maintain strict adherence to the program of "legitimacy," counting upon being able to play off the various popular groups against each other. Afraid that concessions would lead to the disintegration of their seething empire, the rulers in Vienna found no better answer for discontent than repression. But beneath the lid of repression national aspirations continued to simmer, building up an explosive pressure. In Bohemia the Czechs demanded cultural autonomy in an effort to free themselves from at least the petty tyranny of the German language and schooling. In Hungary Magyar patriots protested the continued use of Latin in the schools, courts, and diets. Italian patriots like the novelist Alessandro Manzoni in his *Betrothed Lovers* (1825-1826) and the composer Gioacchino Antonio Rossini in the operas *Barber of Seville* (1816) and *William Tell* (1829) subtly preached liberalism and called for cultural and political independence of Austrian-dominated Italy. The Carbonari and other secret societies continued to plot the overturn of the local governments and the ousting of the hated *Tedeschi* (Germans). To this rising clamor the Austrian government turned a deaf ear, continuing its policy of repression and thus evoking unintentionally but efficaciously a violent effort to overthrow the Habsburg regime.

Humanitarianism
and industrialism in England

LIBERALISM made its greatest advances in the twenties in Britain and America. Always opposed to involvement with continental reactionaries, the British liberals had welcomed the events that led to a break with the conservative European concert. The new industrial society was no less pleased with the "liberal Tory" program inaugurated in domestic affairs by the home secretary, Robert Peel. Reforms in the criminal code, prisons, and police administration kept the government's program abreast of the humanitarian spirit, which exhibited itself also in a popular antislavery movement.

The growth of reform and humanitarian activity was in part a reflection of an unparalleled expansion of industry and trade in England. At the close of the eighteenth and the beginning of the nineteenth century, advances in manufacture, distribution, and communication had been more rapid than at any earlier time in England or in any other part of the contemporary world. Some of the most striking features of this advance were due to the improvement of the steam engine. The harnessing of a steam-driven wheel to ships introduced the steamboat, and putting some steam-driven wheels ahead of coaches introduced the steam train and ushered in the railway age. Faster locomotion on water and on land speeded up industrialization by providing quicker means of transportation for raw materials and finished products. The earlier introduction of the railway in England widened the technological gap between England and the Continent, already conspicuous because of the fuller development of the factory system in England, and placed the "tight little isle" definitely in the lead in the competition for commercial and industrial supremacy.

Utilitarianism
and the idea of laissez faire

ECONOMIC prosperity helped to further the program of social reform of the Utilitarians. Accepting the predominance of the middle class as their starting point, these philosophical liberals expounded a doctrine congenial to contemporary proponents of laissez faire. With "the greatest happiness of the greatest number" as their avowed aim, the Utilitarians held that its realization would best come about through unregulated competition and the strict avoidance by the state of interference in business, social, or individual affairs. A natural harmony would result from the autonomous clash of individual interests. The state's functions were held to be not economic betterment but rather the promotion of gradual political reform and a long-term program of secular education. Though the Utilitarians formed only a small party in Parliament—the Philosophical Radicals—their intellectual attitudes were reflected in concrete measures reducing the restrictive powers of government. In 1824 Parliament repealed the Combination Acts, thereby granting labor the right to organize, but riots and strikes during a subsequent depression (1825-1826) brought about new antistrike legislation. In 1828, the Corn Law of 1815 was revised so as to lower the tariff wall against importation of foreign grains in times of scarcity. A greater degree of freedom was also won by religious minorities. First the dissenters (i.e., Protestants of denominations other than the Church of England), who had previously been enabled to hold public office only by special acts of indemnity by Parliament, and then the Catholics, who had been kept out of office, were befriended by the repeal of their disabilities.

The victory
of Jacksonianism in America

IN THE United States, too, the decade of the twenties was marked by a lively demand for reform. The enunciation of the Monroe Doctrine in 1823 placed the United States in the forefront of the defenders of liberalism and republicanism in a world still dominated by the spirit of the "Holy Alliance." In the presidential campaign of 1824, however, many Americans, particularly in the less tradition-bound West, evinced great concern that their country's domestic policy was far from democratic. The election of John Quincy Adams of New England was hotly disputed. The frontiersmen felt that they had too little to say about governmental policies in Washington and that their welfare was subordinated to the vested interests of the East. The failure of Adams to win a majority in the electoral college over the candidates of the West, Henry Clay and Andrew Jackson, and the necessity of making the final choice in the House of Representatives convinced them that they had been cheated out of the electoral victory by a "corrupt bargain."

Like many popular beliefs, western indignation over eastern dominance was composed of a mixture of truth and fiction. Westerners and Easterners alike rarely comprehended in the mid-twenties that an industrial acceleration had produced a new working class and was beginning to open a deep divergence of interests between the commercial and the industrial groupings in New England. Several states had by this time abolished property qualifications for voting and had made the choice of presidential electors a decision of the voters rather than of the state legislatures. Further broadening of the electorate between 1824 and 1828 helped Jackson's cause immeasurably. More new voters went to the polls in 1828 than the total number who had voted in 1824, and most of them cast their ballots for Jackson. Political lines were slashed by the common interests of the frontiersmen and the newly enfranchised urban workers, both of whom felt the need for a representative of 71 the average man to rule in Washington. With the help of the agricultural South, which opposed the high tariff policy of the Adams administration, Jackson defeated Adams.

Though conservatives feared that Jackson's election would bring with it "mobocracy," Jackson's reforms were to prove neither so violent nor so far-reaching as some of his enemies feared and some of his friends hoped. The "Age of Jackson" was to parallel the Bourgeois Monarchy of Louis Philippe in France and the English developments after the passing of the Great Reform of 1832.

Independence
and separatism in Latin America
IN LATIN America most of the former Spanish colonies, as well as French Haiti and Portuguese Brazil, established their independence in the 1820's and were recognized as sovereign countries by the United States and Britain, though not by Spain until much later. The high degree of cooperation among the various sections of South and Central America that had prevailed during the wars of independence disappeared with the realization of sovereignty, and disruptive tendencies became more and more familiar. Various plans to establish one vast Latin-American federation quickly fell through. In fact, some of the larger republics—Brazil, Argentina, Mexico, Colombia—began to break up. An attempt by "The Liberator" Simón Bolívar to bring about Pan-American solidarity led to a fruitless congress at Panama in 1826, and Pan-Americanism remained a dead issue until the close of the century.

The end of Iberian control in the New World was not followed by the adoption of the liberal institutions intended by several revolutionary leaders. Wealth remained generally in the hands of the Whites. The Catholic Church continued to oppose religious freedom and secular education, and to exert a conservative influence upon a population which was approximately three quarters Indian or Mestizo (mixed breed). Military leaders, generally Whites or Mestizos, began fighting among themselves for control of the newly emancipated states. Thus was ushered in an age of dictators, which in some areas of Latin America has not yet come to an end. Many contemporaries, especially in Europe, derived from the American experience the lesson that republicanism might mean discord and dictatorship rather than liberalism and democracy.

THE REVOLUTIONS OF 1830

THOUGH most of the European powers still felt a common responsibility for maintaining the balance of power, wide differences had arisen among them by 1830 as to the problems growing out of the surge of liberalism and nationalism. While Metternich refused to ease his repressions in the Habsburg lands, the Prussian customs union tended to encourage liberal aspirations for the unification of Germany. In Russia strict repression seemed to have suffocated an incipient liberal movement, but in France liberalism seemed too old and tough to kill by similar treatment. Continental liberals derived encouragement from the persistence of the liberal spirit in France, England, and the United States, and from the cracks beginning to appear in the wall of "legitimacy."

*Agitation
for liberal reform in France*

KING CHARLES X of France announced in 1829: "I would rather saw wood than be a king of the English type." It was not long before he was sent off to saw wood. The ground in France, well prepared by a revolutionary tradition, had been carefully seeded in the twenties by the development of a liberal school of romantics. The plays of Victor Hugo or the novels of Alexandre Dumas were now as likely to be aimed at royalist reaction as at the classical rules of art. Classicists and ultraroyalists were equally outraged by Hector Berlioz, whose music departed from accepted musical patterns, and by Rossini, now living in Paris, whose operas exploited the liberal themes of political defiance and individual freedom. Conservative and academic efforts to suppress the often flamboyant liberal romantics served to fan their smouldering hostility to a colorless, stodgy regime, and they rallied around glamorous survivors of a more revolutionary age—men like Lafayette and Benjamin Constant, a novelist who was also a political figure—as well as younger leaders like the journalist and historian Adolphe Thiers, who had written a friendly history of the French Revolution. The number of liberals elected to the Chamber of Deputies grew.

*The "July Revolution"
against the Bourbons of France*

CHARLES X sought to check the alarming victories of the liberals at the polls by a series of repressive royal edicts euphemistically called "ordinances." These "July Ordinances" of 1830 dissolved a newly elected Chamber of Deputies, interfered with the freedom of the press, modified the existing electoral laws, and called for an election of new deputies. Charging that the king had violated the Charter, newspapermen like Thiers, followed by workers in the printing shops, who feared at least temporary unemployment, fired the population of Paris to action.

The consequent "July Revolution" was sudden but decisive. Joined by workers, republicans, and other malcontents, the insurgents after less than three days of barricade fighting forced the king to abdicate in favor of his grandson, the Duc de Chambord. Lafayette, now leader of the more popular element among the insurgents, was unwilling to accept any Bourbon at all but was also fearful that an elective republic was not appropriate for France. He induced the victors of the barricades to retain the hereditary monarchy but in the form of a more flexible dynasty than the Bourbons. The new

"King of the French" (a title intended to imply popular consent) was Louis Philippe, head of the Orléans family, which had a long record of insurrection behind it.

The creation
of the "July Monarchy"

THE NEW monarch was required to accept a significantly revised Charter. It increased the number of qualified voters. It reintroduced the tricolor as the official flag. All implications that the king ruled by divine right were stricken from the Charter and with them the power of the monarch to issue exceptional ordinances for the safety of the state. The elective Chamber of Deputies was given authority to initiate legislation. Catholicism lost recognition as the state religion but was acknowledged to be the faith to which most of the French adhered. France now had, in a phrase attributed to Lafayette," a throne surrounded by republican institutions." It was a bourgeois monarchy, much like that which Louis XVI had been obliged to accept in 1791. The major spoils of the July Revolution, though it had been fought out by the lower-class elements of the Paris populace, went to the new industrial and financial classes that had been gaining stature steadily during the fifteen years of the Bourbon Restoration.

Separation
of Belgium and Holland

THE JULY Revolution in France set off a chain of liberal and nationalist outbreaks in other countries of Europe. The recently created state of the United Netherlands, an artifice of the Congress of Vienna, was torn by nationalistic revolts the next August. United by no effort of their own to the Dutch, the self-reliant and Catholic Belgians had felt annoyed at their subordination to the Protestant, Dutch-nationalist regime of King William I. Moreover Belgium, long a center of industry, felt that its interests were being sacrificed to those of commercial and agricultural Holland. The eastern powers, Austria, Prussia, and Russia, would have been willing to repress the Belgian revolt as a dangerous violation of the Vienna settlement, but they were embroiled with revolutionary repercussions nearer home, and, besides, Britain, where Wellington was now prime minister, and France, now governed by Louis Philippe, were so plainly opposed to interference that the "Holy Alliance" preferred to do nothing to prevent the Belgian secession. The Dutch government was reluctant either to make the compromises that would have kept the Belgians loyal or to risk a war. In 1831, therefore, a liberal monarchy was inaugurated in Belgium, which became for the first time an independent and united nation.

The failure
of the Polish revolt

THE REVOLT that absorbed the attention of the eastern powers broke out in Poland in November 1830. Alexander I's relatively enlightened rule of Congress Poland had ended with his death, and Czar Nicholas I had extended his police regime there.

The Polish army, when it heard that it might be sent to quell the revolution in Belgium, mutinied in Warsaw. Internal divisions among the Polish revolutionaries, however, prevented effective cooperation in a common program. In 1831 a Russian army recaptured Warsaw. The czar took pitiless revenge, and until the twentieth century, Russian Poland was administered as a frontier province of Russia.

The failure of the anti-Habsburg revolts

METTERNICH'S Austria, too, caught the fever. In northern Italy particularly, hopes ran high that the era of freedom had arrived. Local dukes were ousted and even the subjects of the pope rebelled. Like the Poles, the Italians looked for help from abroad—particularly from France—but in vain. Louis Philippe was primarily preoccupied with national prosperity and security, and gave his support to the Party of Resistance (the conservatives) rather than the Party of Movement, which advocated at least financial and moral aid to foreign revolutions. Austrian armies overwhelmed the revolts with dispatch and drove their leaders into exile. Among them were Giuseppe Mazzini and Louis Napoleon Bonaparte. The world was to hear again from these two young men.

Revolt and reaction in Switzerland and the Germanies

THE REVOLTS spread to Switzerland and the German states but took the form of relatively feeble demonstrations and riots. In general, the German and the Swiss insurgents called for political reform calculated to permit greater participation in gov-

POLAND REPARTITIONED

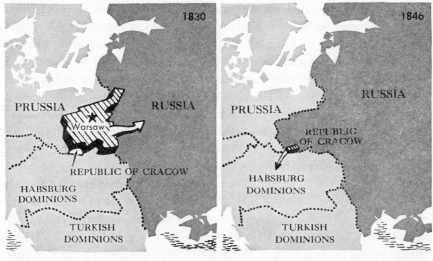

The Polish Revolution of 1830 against Russia collapsed with the capture of Warsaw, and the "Congress Kingdom of Poland" set up at Vienna in 1815 became a mere border province of Russia. The little Republic of Cracow created by the Congress of Vienna remained the last toehold for Polish nationalists, but after a revolt in the Polish areas of Austria and Prussia fomented from Cracow, Prussia and Russia agreed to the absorption of Cracow in 1846 by Austria (page 121).

A German cartoon of 1836, "A Study for Actors," satirizes the nouveau riche banker, fat and pompous, ostentatiously carrying a wallet bulging with money.

ernment by the expanding middle class. They met with some success in some of the Swiss cantons and a few German principalities, particularly in Brunswick, Hesse-Cassel, and Saxony. In the Rhineland, enthusiasm for German unity led to a demonstration at a "National Festival" held at Hambach in 1832. This Hambach Festival gave Metternich a good reason for swiftly checking further manifestations. The now badly frightened German rulers joined him in the issuance of a repressive federal ordinance known as the "Six Acts." These acts reinforced the Carlsbad Decrees and, though political disorder was not completely quieted until 1835, they muzzled the liberal and national movements in the Germanies for a decade or more.

The victory of parliamentary reform in England

THOUGH Britain escaped an open outbreak in the 1830's, the reform movement reached a climax that is sometimes loosely referred to as a revolution. Upon the death of King George IV and the beginning of William IV's reign in 1830, a general election was held whose outcome left small doubt of the strong public feeling for reform. Wellington nevertheless announced himself against reform and resigned. The Whigs then came in under Lord Grey. Committed to extending Parliament's representative character, the Whigs undertook a program designed to

76

weaken the grip of the landowners upon the House of Commons. In 1831, the government proposed a Reform Bill intended to redistribute parliamentary seats on a more equitable basis and to extend the right of voting to a larger section of the population by requiring a uniform qualification for the franchise (a payment of an annual rental of ten pounds). Though the House of Lords sought to defeat the bill, Grey and his supporters garnered enough strength from all classes, acting not only out of principle or self-interest but also out of fear of revolt spreading from the Continent to Britain, to maneuver the Lords into a reluctant acceptance of the "Great Reform."

The new political forces, now led by men who had once been friendly to the French Revolution, became stronger. The Great Reform Bill of 1832 almost doubled the number of Britain's eligible voters, and was but the first of several reforms of the franchise in the nineteenth century. Still, only about 800,000 had the right to vote after 1832; about thirty times that number lived in the British Isles. The rest could not be permanently denied. The Reform Bill broke the rotten-borough system and gave control of Parliament to the electorate. The middle class, though by no means fully enfranchised, gained especially by the transfer of seats from the small overrepresented boroughs to the new underrepresented industrial cities.

THE GAINS of the middle class in 1830 were limited to western Europe and were not uncontested even there. Nevertheless, they indicated that the struggle between the bourgeoisie and the landed aristocracy would be a keener social issue in the near future than it had been in the past, even though bourgeois class-consciousness was still somewhat obscured by the alliance of the urban middle class with the workers in the quest for liberal reform and national entity. The Vienna system, which had sought, in the general longing for order, to return to the principles and practices of the past, had not yet failed, but it had left little room for the forces of liberalism and nationalism that had grown to maturity in the years of the French Revolution and Napoleon and that would acquire new strength from the processes of industrialization and urbanization. The statesmen of the Restoration and the Metternich era, worn out by constant revolution and war, had understandably sought order and peace, but their well-laid plans met defeat from their inability to provide a satisfactory means of peaceful change. The tradition of the French Revolution and the impact of the new industrial technology left no room for a static concept of society. If change could not come by peaceful means, it was bound to come nonetheless.

The revolutions of 1830 made still clearer what some might have discerned before—that opposition to bourgeois control of European life would come not alone from the aristocracy but eventually, too, from the growing industrial working classes. Too few, badly led, and inarticulate in 1830, workingmen died on the barricades but earned no decisive voice in the new governments, even when they were successful. They were, however, to increase swiftly in numbers and strength throughout the rest of the nineteenth century as the "Industrial Revolution" spread throughout western Europe and thence to the rest of the world. They would not always be content to fight without receiving an appropriate share of the prize.

Nor was "legitimacy" completely played out after 1830. Despite occasional revolutions and diplomatic crises, the era was a relatively stable one. Greece, France, and Belgium were the only European countries that had undergone dynastic change since the Congress of Vienna. Though Britain pursued an increasingly independent course in international affairs, she was content to initiate no changes in the European equilibrium and to act as a balance in the swings of power on the Continent. For their part the rulers of central and eastern Europe continued to cooperate earnestly in their effort to maintain the system of "legitimacy." In response to the changes taking place in western Europe and to the entente that seemed to have developed between England and France, the autocrats of Russia, Austria, and Prussia crystallized their informal alliance by the formal Convention of Münchengrätz (1833). This agreement reaffirmed their determination to uphold the status quo in the Balkans and Poland. Moreover, in the spirit of Troppau, they invited other monarchs to request their help in case of domestic revolt.

The Convention of Münchengrätz formally divided Europe into two ideological camps. In 1830, it was the western camp, the one that had the Dutch, the English, the American, and the French revolutions in its background, which advocated change and a new order in society. The rulers of the countries that had so far resisted popular revolution made up the other camp. England, by virtue of its geographical position and its leadership in the "Industrial Revolution," spearheaded the activities of the western powers in Europe and America. Situated in the center of the Atlantic basin, which her navy controlled almost unchallenged, England dominated throughout the century the industrial, social, political, and ideological life of the countries surrounding the Atlantic Ocean, where the Pax Britannica was almost synonymous both with peace and with productivity and prosperity. "Sterling" (originally an English coin) became the international standard of value, and the British navy helped to enforce the Pax Britannica the world over.

In eastern Europe, Asia, and Africa, the shopkeepers of the Atlantic nations were often viewed with aristocratic contempt or with open hostility. Nevertheless, unable to compete effectively with the industrialized areas, the merely agricultural lands of the world were to be slowly forced into a more or less dependent status. Though they sought to resist the encroachments of the maritime and industrial countries, the less technological peoples were eventually obliged to borrow the cash or the technicians, or to bow before the superior armaments, of the shopkeeping nations.

1749-1832	Johann Wolfgang von Goethe
c. 1769-1830	Height of the "Industrial Revolution" in England
1770-1827	Ludwig van Beethoven
1771-1858	Robert Owen
1798	Wordsworth and Coleridge publish *Lyrical Ballads,* the introduction of which states the principles of romanticism in literature
1802	Napoleon achieves first general European peace in ten years
1804	Napoleon proclaims himself emperor
1806	Holy Roman Empire dissolved and Confederation of the Rhine established
1808	Revolts begin in Latin America
1812	Napoleon defeated in campaign against Russia
1813	End of British East India Company's monopoly of India trade
1814	First Treaty of Paris
1814-1815	The Congress of Vienna
1815	Napoleon's "Hundred Days" (March 20-June 28)
1815	Second Treaty of Paris
1815	Formation of the Holy and the Quadruple Alliances
1817	Jeremy Bentham's *Catechism of Parliamentary Reform*
1818-1831	Hegel's career as professor at the University of Berlin
1819	"Peterloo" massacre
1820-1823	Revolt in Spain
1821	Beginning of the rebellion of Greece against Turkish rule
1823	Proclamation of the Monroe Doctrine
1824	Parliament repeals Combination Acts
1824-1826	Britain's war with Burma
1825	Comte de Saint-Simon's *The New Christianity*
1825	Alexander Pushkin writes *Boris Godunov*
1825	"Decembrist" revolt quashed in Russia
1828	Electoral victory of Jacksonianism in America
1829	Greece formally achieves independence in Treaty of Adrianople
1829	Charles Fourier's *The New Industrial World*
1829	Rossini's *William Tell*
c. 1830	Collapse of the Quintuple Alliance becomes obvious
1830	"July Revolution" ousts Charles x and Louis Philippe becomes "king of the French"
1830-1831	Polish revolt
1831	Holland and Belguim separated
1832	Great Reform Bill
1833	Russia, Austria, and Prussia strengthen their informal alliance by Convention of Münchengrätz

Part two

Chapter two: Revolution and counterrevolution

Chapter three: From Empire to Empire

Chapter four: Unification and emancipation in America

Chapter five: Europeanization and imperialism in Asia

THE TELESCOPING

THE QUEST FOR
CONSTITUTIONS
AND NATIONAL UNITY
1830-1871

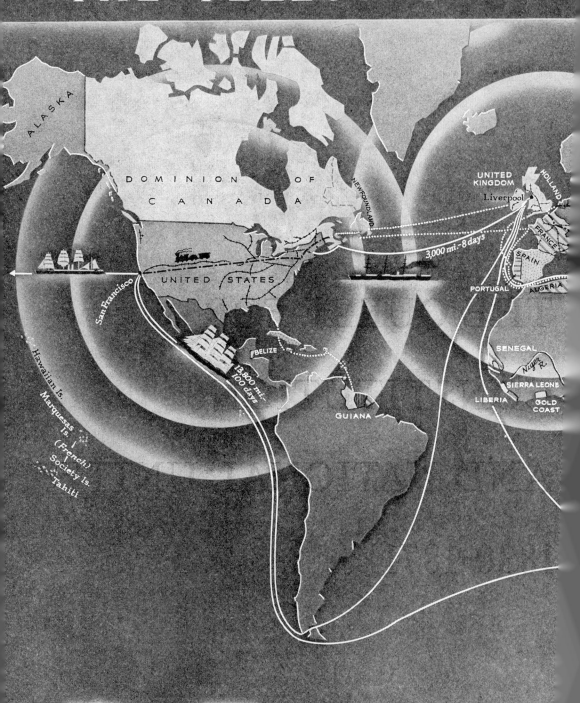

ALASKA

DOMINION OF CANADA

NEWFOUNDLAND

UNITED KINGDOM

HOLLAND

Liverpool

FRANCE

SPAIN

PORTUGAL

ALGERIA

3,000 mi. - 8 days

UNITED STATES

San Francisco

Hawaiian Is.

Marquesas Is.

(French)

Society Is.

Tahiti

BELIZE

13,800 mi. -
100 days

GUIANA

SENEGAL

Niger R.

SIERRA LEONE

LIBERIA

GOLD COAST

Telegraph   Cable   Railroads

WORLDS, 1871

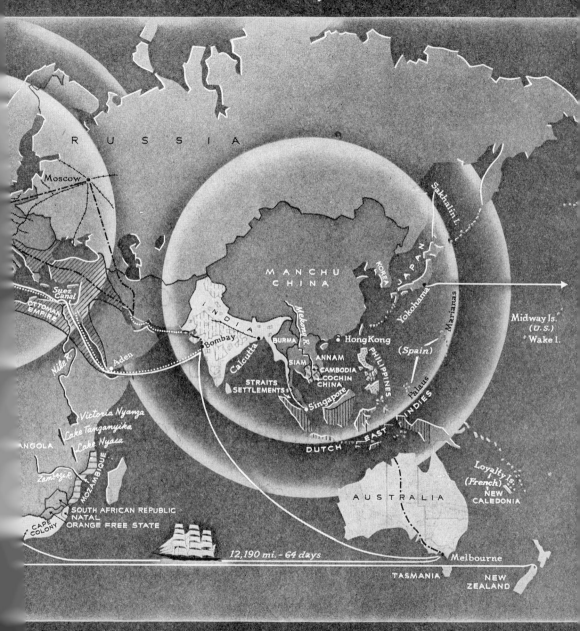

By 1871 Europe, the East, and the Americas, once virtually three separate worlds, were drawing ever closer. Millions of Europeans were migrating to the Americas and the British colonies. Great Britain continued to strengthen her control over India, Australia, and New Zealand and the routes thereto. France since 1830 had established herself in North Africa, Indochina, and various Pacific island groups. Holland, Spain, and Portugal held on to remnants of their empires. Manchu China had been forcibly opened to foreign commerce, and among other outright cessions, had surrendered Hong Kong to Britain. Improved transporation and communication were telescoping the continents into one interdependent world.

Chapter two

REVOLUTION AND
COUNTERREVOLUTION
1830-1850

For the decade that followed the settlements of the 1830's, it looked as though the "spirit of 1789" had lost its youthful explosiveness and had matured into a set of sedate principles. The word *gradualism* became good usage around 1835. All but a minority of active revolutionaries hoped that the long years of revolution, war, and reaction might be followed by an era of enduring peace and steady progress.

But the "revolutionary tradition" with its triumphs and failures, its blood and thunder, its hopes and disillusionments, had not wholly lost its appeal. The French Revolution had imbedded the ideal of "Liberty, Equality, and Fraternity" into the aspirations of peoples in many parts of Europe. The discontents which had given rise to upheaval in 1789 persisted or had been restored in several regions, particularly in central and eastern Europe, and were underlined now by the new conditions and ideas brought by the beginnings of industrialization in western Europe.

Somewhere around the year 1830 the battle between revolution and reaction, without ceasing, was clearly lost by both sides, and no blueprint of conservatism or of utopia appeared any longer to be acceptable by fiat for all of Europe. Before the year 1830 Europe had been essentially dynastic, aristocratic, agrarian, and Christian. As the century moved on, western Europe became, step by irregular step, increasingly nationalistic, democratic, industrial, imperialistic, and skeptical. This trend, which was perceptible even before 1830, appeared more pronounced in the years between 1830 and 1848.

Eastern Europe—essentially Greek Orthodox and Slavic, and uncontaminated by the radical impulses of the French Revolution or the "Industrial Revolution"—remained more than ever quiescent under the heavy surveillance 85 of the czar and the sultan. Even the radical outbursts of 1848-1849, destined to shake western and central Europe to its foundations, were to leave eastern Europe relatively undisturbed.

BRITAIN AND HER EMPIRE

AFTER THE REFORM BILL (1832-1840)

OF THE western states, Britain continued to be the most advanced, both industrially and politically. Here the "Industrial Revolution" had come earlier and, uninterrupted by the French Revolution, had advanced further than on the Continent; and here political change was more commonly associated with public order and governmental design than on the Continent.

Political reform and humanitarian programs

THE REFORM BILL of 1832 rapidly brought in its wake several other reforms. A set of measures extended representative government to the local level—notably the Scottish Burgh Act of 1833 and the Municipal Corporations Act of 1835. Rural government, however, remained for another fifty years in the hands of the justices of the peace, accentuating the growing differences between town and country.

By measures taken between 1833 and 1838 Negro slavery was abolished in the British empire. Britain thereby became the first government formally to emancipate the slave. This reform stemmed chiefly from humanitarian considerations and religious convictions. Though monetary compensation was arranged for former masters, emancipation was violently opposed by the planters in the West Indies. In South Africa, recently conquered from Holland, abolition was accepted willingly at first, but it later was to create grave problems between the British rulers and the Boers, or Dutch settlers.

The Factory Act of 1833 was likewise suggested by humanitarian scruples. It permitted children of nine to thirteen no more than forty-eight hours of work per week and children of thirteen to eighteen no more than sixty-nine, and forbade employment of children under nine except in silk mills and mines. The most important of its features—a frank departure from free-enterprise principles—was the appointment of government inspectors to keep mill owners and needy or irresponsible parents from evading the law.

The Poor Law of 1834 was, like the Factory Act, an attempt to relieve the lot of the unfortunate by government aid, but at the same time it deferred to laissez-faire attitudes on individual enterprise. A system of poor relief already existed in the so-called "Speenhamland Act." This "Act" was not in reality the work of Parliament but a scheme first adopted by the little town of Speenhamland and afterwards widely imitated by other localities. It had been implicitly approved by Parliament, however, in 1796. By the

Speenhamland plan, the local authorities supplemented a laborer's wages on a scale that slid up or down with the price of bread and the size of his family. It was now found that this escalator system of relief often encouraged laziness, destroyed self-respect, and induced employers to keep wages low. Accordingly the Poor Law of 1834 removed the allowances supplementing low wages provided by the Speenhamland plan and placed applicants for relief, except some among those actually employed, in new-style workhouses. Whether or not these workhouses were deliberately made unattractive, the act did discourage willful pauperism, and it provided an important precedent in the centralization of the administration of local affairs in Britain.

With the rise of industry and the decline of agriculture, the fabric of British institutions was slowly becoming bourgeois where before it had been aristocratic. Still the landed interests remained entrenched behind the high customs duties on breadstuffs imposed by the Corn Laws. After the Napoleonic wars the Corn Laws had been introduced to prevent a drop in war prices by reducing competition from foreign-grown wheat in years of good harvest. Though prices of breadstuffs nevertheless tended to fall below war prices, in the famine year 1839 they were high, and the Anti-Corn-Law League was founded to marshal the forces of the new era (especially the manufacturers) against this bulwark of aristocratic wealth.

Changes in transportation and communication THE MOST significant industrial change of the decade in Britain was the rapid development of transportation by steam railway. By 1840 Britain had laid eight hundred miles of track; in the next decade the tempo of railroad building was to rise even more sharply. Other means of travel were also expanding. In 1839 regular steamship service between English ports and Alexandria, Egypt, was established by the Peninsular and Oriental Line, to connect by a short overland

Steamships of types similar to the British vessel shown here began regular ocean service in the late 1830's and the early 1840's. Though powered by steam-driven paddle wheels, they also carried sails to supplement the power of their engines.

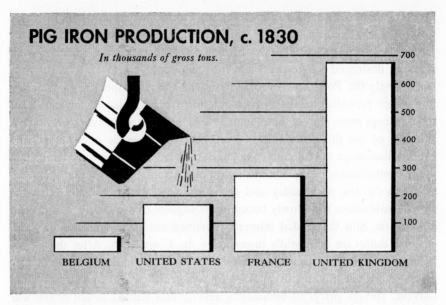

PIG IRON PRODUCTION, c. 1830

In thousands of gross tons.

700
600
500
400
300
200
100

BELGIUM   UNITED STATES   FRANCE   UNITED KINGDOM

By the 1830's the United Kingdom's industrial lead was overwhelming, as this chart of pig iron production shows. France was beginning to become industrialized; Belgium was advancing industrially to a surprising degree since she was small and less well endowed with the necessary coal and iron resources. The United States was only beginning to get its stride.

route with ships coming up the Red Sea from India. In 1840 the Cunard Line was established to provide regular service across the Atlantic. The sailing vessel was not displaced, however, since the small steamships with inefficient engines were hampered by the huge amounts of coal needed for long overseas voyages; and the mid-century was to become the great age of the fast clipper ships.

The new methods of transportation increased the rate of social change. New areas were opened up to economic exploitation and contact with the rest of the world. Products could be drawn faster and in larger quantities by long strings of cars; even the early railroad train covered the run of the stagecoach in one fifth the time. Demand for coal, iron, steel, and machinery was enormously increased. Steamships made overseas freight deliveries more predictable and cheaper since "sailings," as their departures are still called, and arrivals were not so dependent on the vagaries of weather.

As distances and costs shrank, exchange of thoughts as well as of goods was enormously stepped up. A sharp reduction in 1836 of the stamp tax lowered the cost of newspaper publishing so markedly that illicit (and usually radical) journals disappeared; and although the full development of the cheap daily had to await rapid printing and the quantity production of pulp paper in the last decades of the century, the circulation of English newspapers increased from 39,000,000 in 1836 to 122,000,000 in 1854. The introduction in 1840 of the penny post and the founding in 1851 by Julius Reuter of the first extensive news-transmitting agency made the communication of ideas and news still easier.

Protests
by political organizations

THE NEW machines and methods wrought conspicuous social changes: production increased, laborers drifted toward the cities, the population grew, and the working classes were afforded bad housing. Real wages increased until 1850, but protests against the plight of the laborer began to appear in the 1830's. A Grand National Consolidated Trades Union was formed briefly in 1834 under the spell of Robert Owen's enthusiasm, but his vague socialistic program was not enough to make it cohesive or enduring. It lasted less than a year.

A severe depression that began in 1836 gave rise to a movement known as Chartism, which emphasized political action as the basis for social and economic change. In 1838 a six-point "People's Charter" was drafted, demanding universal manhood suffrage, annual parliaments, voting by ballot (instead of openly), payment of members of Parliament, abolition of property qualifications for membership in Parliament, and equal electoral districts. By achieving these six points the Chartists hoped to get for the working classes a share in the political power recently extended to the middle classes by the Reform Bill of 1832, and then through political action to better their economic lot. A Chartists' petition, for which they claimed three million signatures, was first presented to Parliament in 1839 but was rejected. Thereupon the movement for a time lost much of its momentum, but the Chartists remained active throughout the 1840's and were to reflect in England the agitation that on the Continent brought about the revolutionary movement of 1848-1849 (pages 124-138). Though only in part a workers' movement, Chartism became significant as an ancestor of later socialist trends in England. All but one of the Charter's six points (annual parliaments) are today respected parts of English law.

Carlyle
as a critic of his times

A MORE conservative protest against the bourgeois era came from the pen of the Scotsman Thomas Carlyle. In a sometimes savage prose he decried the evil effects of industrialization, the extravagances of the wealthy, the misery of the poor, the disregard of spiritual values, and the general materialism of the age, and preached a gospel of duty, work, education, emigration, and cooperation between capital and labor. Made uneasy by social change and distrustful of laissez faire and the common man, he nevertheless shared the confidence of some contemporary German philosophers and of the French St. Simonians that obsolete cultures died only to be replaced by vigorous ones. Progress, he held, thus was highly probable, and had been achieved in the past under the guidance of inspired leaders. These views were expressed in many lectures and writings. Among his several historical works his *History of the French Revolution* (1837) was perhaps the most partisan and certainly the most popular. In it he dramatically portrayed the Revolution as a great social cataclysm resulting from the unmet need for enlightened leadership.

The Oxford Movement and the Anglican Church

ANOTHER FORM of protest against indifference to spiritual values came with the formation in 1833 of a religious group known as the Oxford Movement. Under the leadership of John Henry Newman and other intellectuals at Oxford, this group sought to restore within the Anglican Church the spirit and beliefs of early Christianity. In the 1830's their sermons and *Tracts for the Times* (whence the name Tractarians, by which the group also became known) provoked a widespread controversy over matters of church history and religious interpretation. The Oxford Movement became "High Church"— close to Catholicism in many points of doctrine and ritual. Their opponents within the Church of England became "Low Church"; and the liberal Anglicans who sought to steer a course between the two extremes became "Broad Church." The three views are found today in the Anglican Church

An illustration, "The Last Cab-driver," by the English black and white artist, George Cruik-shank, which appeared in the first edition of Charles Dickens' Sketches by Boz.

and are also reflected in the Episcopalian Church in America. In the 1840's the Oxford Movement was to lose much of its momentum by the outright conversion of Newman and others to Roman Catholicism.

*Dickens
and humanitarian literary protest*

THE YEAR of the founding of the Oxford Movement also saw the first of a series of humorous *Sketches by Boz*, whose author was identified shortly thereafter as Charles Dickens. Dickens rapidly became the most popular of English novelists. His novels captivated his readers by their exuberant humor and exaggerated pathos, and their crowds of characters—lovable and amusing eccentrics, dastardly villains, pure and long-suffering women and children—dashed off with the exaggeration of caricature but at the same time full-bodied and familiar. Himself the son of a poor man who had at one time been imprisoned for debt, Dickens painted a sometimes sentimentalized but always recognizable picture of the lower middle class and the seamy side of life in London and its back-country. He wrote at first to amuse, but soon devoted his pen to pointing out the injustices and hardships of the poor—dread conditions in the workhouse and the debtors' prison, cruelty and dishonesty of masters in private schools, victimization of innocents by swindlers and unscrupulous lawyers. His was a protest not so much against the new conditions brought by industrialization as against evils of longer standing.

*The accession
of Queen Victoria*

IN 1837 the young and appealing Queen Victoria ascended the British throne. A people who had regarded her less virtuous and more reactionary predecessors with something less than love learned gradually to associate her with the ideals of the new bourgeois era. Her private life was exemplary, and in her role as monarch, although she occasionally took bold and independent action and gave careful attention to important matters, she adapted herself to the trend toward government by Parliament. As her long reign (1837-1901) wore on, she was to become the epitome of a prosperous, peaceful, and eminently respectable upper-class culture. Since the throne of Hanover could not be occupied by a woman, Victoria's uncle became king of Hanover. After 123 years of union, the two realms were at last separated, leaving England freer to follow her own interests and views without direct involvement in continental politics.

*Lord Durham
and the British empire*

IN TIME, Victoria was to become the symbol of the new British Empire. But her reign began with little hint of this development. The revolt of the American colonies upon reaching maturity had led some Englishmen to question whether colonies were worth the trouble and expense of their upkeep when they were young and dependent. Moreover, the old mercantilist view of colonies as sources of raw materials and markets for finished products tended to give way to the laissez-faire doctrine that trade flourished best in a peaceful world free of tariff barriers and navigation laws. In this climate of opinion the problem of the future of Canada was raised by a rebellion in 1837 (page 218). Lord Durham, a man of unusual insight, was sent out as governor general of Canada to deal with the rebellion. In his *Report on the Affairs of British North America* (1839), Durham fell in with those who held that greater freedom for colonials was the proper cure of colonial discontent. He recommended that responsible government be granted Canada. This radical step was not explicitly included in the Union Act of 1840, but after gradual development in practice it became fully established when Lord Elgin was governor (1847-1854). Many considered it the beginning of the parting of the ways; in actuality, as we shall see, it was a happy solution of Canada's contemporary difficulties and became a precedent for later dealings with Canada and other colonies. Durham's *Report* thus was a keystone in the liberalization of British colonial policy, whereby the Empire is preserved even though its component parts receive independence.

Another development that was destined to draw the colonies closer to the homeland also began in the thirties. This was the emigration movement popularized by Gibbon Wakefield, who had accompanied Lord Durham to Canada. Wakefield saw in emigration the answer to England's overpopulation and the consequent wretchedness of the working classes. He proposed that colonial lands be sold rather than given away and that the proceeds be used to pay emigrants' fares. The South Australia Company, of which he was manager, colonized South Australia according to his plan. Durham was one of the outstanding figures of the day to give him support. Without official approval and against the known rivalry of the French, Wakefield sponsored a group of settlers that later made New Zealand a British colony (page 266).

Foreign policy: peace and balance of power

THE DESIRE for a peaceful Europe was reflected in British foreign policy during the thirties. In 1839 the status of Belgium, which had only recently acquired independence of Holland, was settled by an international treaty by which the five great powers—England, France, Austria, Prussia, and Russia—mutually guaranteed its perpetual neutrality, agreeing not to invade Belgium or to involve it in belligerent activity. France carefully cultivated British friendship in order to secure a balance of power on the Continent against the three eastern powers. Between Victorian England and the France of the "bourgeois monarch," Louis Philippe, there grew up an *entente cordiale*—a friendly understanding— to offset the mutual cooperation that the rulers of Austria, Prussia, and Russia had pledged at Münchengrätz. The Duke of Wellington was perhaps correct when he called this entente "a cardboard alliance," but it kept France in check and it seemed to balance the more liberal western powers against the more conservative eastern ones. In Spain and Portugal, for example, where struggles between conservatives and constitutionalists persisted (page 123), the weight of Great Britain was thrown on the side of peace and the liberal forces. In the Far East, however (Chapter 5), limited war served business interests better than liberal principles or peaceful submission to trade regulations.

APPARENT STABILITY

IN WESTERN EUROPE (1830-1840)

THE FRENCH Bourgeois Monarchy established in 1830 was a compromise phase of the complicated seesaw battle between royalism and republicanism that characterized the century following the great Revolution of 1789. The so-called "July Monarchy" had no tradition of gradual evolution behind it, and it was plagued from the beginning by opposition from extremists of both Left and Right.

The instability of the July Monarchy

LOUIS PHILIPPE'S position was, in fact, rather precarious for the better part of the decade. Fearful of the revolutionary contagion that might spread from France and infect the less immune among their own peoples, the rulers of other continental countries were not so well disposed as England to make friends with the new regime. Within France the king had the support of a bourgeois group known as the Constitutionalists, but even these were divided. The party of *résistance* thought that the constitution of 1830 had gone far enough, that French institutions should remain exactly as they were, and that France should keep out of all foreign quarrels. Its best-known exponent was the famous Protestant historian François Guizot. The party of *mouvement,* with such leaders as General Lafayette, veteran of many revolutions, and Adolphe Thiers, an energetic young historian and journalist, favored constitutional changes in the direction of democracy and open aid to liberal movements in other countries. During the 1830's Louis Philippe drew his ministries from one, the other, or both parties, in a series of shifts that gave little chance for a consistent program.

Opposed to Louis Philippe were the Legitimists (or Bourbonists) and Bonapartists on the one hand and the Republicans on the other, all of whom staged insurrections or attempted coups during the decade. A bloody insurrection broke out among the silk workers of Lyons in 1831, and another in 1834. Discontented with political as well as economic conditions, the insurgents in 1831 voiced the slogan: "Live working or die fighting!" These uprisings had repercussions in such cities as Paris and Marseilles. In 1832 the Legitimists inspired abortive uprisings in the west and south of France on behalf of the child they called King Henry v. In the same year Republicans in Paris provoked an insurrection, which, with a little more luck, might 93 have become another Paris revolution. In 1836 at Strassburg and again in 1840 at Boulogne, Louis Napoleon, nephew of Napoleon I and the Bonapartist candidate for the throne, attempted premature uprisings. Several attempts on the life of the king were made. A radical named Fieschi plotted to kill him by means of twenty-four guns rigged to fire simultaneously but killed forty other people. Until 1835 all parties agitated openly in the press. Louis Philippe was caricatured by such eminent artists as Honoré Daumier in the radical journal *Le Charivari* and other publications.

The government, forced to occupy itself with measures for its very existence, in the 1830's was distinguished more for its repressive policies than for its reforms. Repression came to a head, after the second Lyons insurrection and the Fieschi attempt, with the enactment in 1835 of the September Laws. The laws simplified the trials of conspirators and silenced all newspapers but those with the wealthiest backing (which proved, however, to be mainly Legitimist). Though greatly resented, these measures effectively muzzled the Republicans for a time.

Bourgeois aspects
of the reign of Louis Philippe

LOUIS PHILIPPE, nevertheless, did in some measure earn his title of *"le roi bourgeois."* Economic policies were geared to bourgeois interests. New industries were encouraged and their growth was fostered by protective tariffs against competition from more advanced nations, especially Belgium and England. New roads and canals were built. Court society, widely shunned now by the old aristocracy, was opened to the wealthy tradesmen Louis Philippe affected to represent. Perhaps the most important legislation of the decade was the Primary Education Law sponsored by Guizot. Requiring the establishment of at least one primary school in each commune, it was a serious attempt to organize education on a national scale, following and, in a way, surpassing the Revolutionary precedent of a secular, government-supported, lay school-system.

In foreign affairs Louis Philippe followed a policy of peace at any price. He suspected that any aggressive act on his part might be regarded as revolutionary and would be opposed by the whole of Metternichian Europe; and this consideration was reinforced by his tenderness for his bourgeois supporters, who would have had to bear the financial brunt of war. Instead of engaging in a brilliant foreign policy of his own, he catered indirectly to the French love of national glory. Napoleon's remains were brought to Paris in 1840 amid much ceremony and enthusiasm. The Arch of Triumph begun under the Empire was finally completed and, within sight of it, on the Place de la Concorde, where the guillotine once had stood, an obelisk from Egypt was raised as a reminder of France's stake in North Africa. It was hoped that freshening the memory of the great Empire would redound to Louis Philippe's own popularity. It was actually to encourage a flood of nostalgic writings on the career of Napoleon Bonaparte by surviving generals and ministers of the great emperor as well as by younger historians. Perhaps the most significant of these works was Thiers' *History of the Consulate and the Empire* (20 volumes, 1840-1855), which threw into vivid contrast the dash and enterprise of the Empire with the drab mediocrity of the Bourgeois Monarchy. The revival of the Napoleonic legend contributed in the end to Louis Philippe's fall and to the meteoric rise of Louis Napoleon as his successor. To offset charges of spiritlessness, Louis Philippe intermittently carried on the conquest of Algeria, begun by the tottering Bourbons in 1830 when a French representative was hit with a fly swatter by the dey of Algiers.

*Some differences
between England and France*

IN THE 1830's France was only beginning to revive or to adopt the industrial techniques and vast organization that were now common in England. In a few industries, such as spinning in Alsace, manufacturing was carried on under the factory system. Mining and metallurgy were also conducted on a large scale in a few places. Outside these industries, factories employing one hundred or more workers were rare. The putting-out system was still the common form of manufacture; the individual or family enterprise was still the rule in many trades; the business corporation was fairly rare; railroad building had not begun; and the waterways were defective. In the rural areas the French Revolution had continued, and in some ways had hastened, the process that had made France a land of small peasant proprietors.

*Louis Blanc
and the "national workshop"*

SAINT-SIMONIANISM and Fourierism continued to set the tone for French socialists, some of them more radical than their masters in their condemnation of private property. Secret republican societies grew up often tinged with a mystical socialism. In 1839 Louis Blanc, who was in the next decade to become the chief spokesman of the working classes, published his *Organization of Labor,* in which he argued that the spirit of competition, the cornerstone of laissez faire, inevitably led to monopoly. In order to avoid that evil he proposed the establishment of factories and offices operated by associations of workingmen—later known as "national workshops"—for which capital was to be provided by the state. The associations were to operate on the principle "from each according to his ability, to each according to his need."

*Liberalism,
ultramontanism, and Gallicanism*

THE CHURCH was early thrust into the realm of social and political discussion, largely by the philanthropy of Antoine Frédéric Ozanam. Ozanam was interested in bringing the church of his day peacefully into line with the new social conditions. In the 1830's he organized the Society of St. Vincent de Paul, a Catholic 95 charitable organization devoted to helping the poor, which has since become active on a world-wide scale. As a professor at the Sorbonne during the forties he developed, through studying the role of the church in civilizing the medieval barbarians, the idea of a comparable role for religion in the new industrial era. His example directed the efforts of several prominent churchmen toward the achievement of a church that would lead Christianity to liberty.

A number of prominent Catholics began to preach that the lot of the oppressed was a charge of the church and looked toward Rome to lead the way to a free society. They advocated a liberal ultramontanism, or, in other words, leadership "from beyond the mountains" in the struggle for liberty within France, and held that the church must be free of the state in order to achieve liberal Christian goals. The most energetic figure in this movement was Félicité Robert de Lamennais, who in the earlier years of the century had joined in the conservative Catholic revival. Gradually Lamennais departed from political conservatism and came to believe in popular sovereignty. In 1830 he founded the newspaper *L'Avenir (The Future)* with the motto "God and Liberty." He aroused both enthusiasm among those who looked to the altar rather than to the throne for guidance and opposition from those who believed in a tightly organized "Gallican" church. Lamennais and his disciples sought the approval of Rome for their marriage of liberty with Catholicism. But Pope Gregory XVI, in no uncertain terms, in the encyclical *Mirari vos* (1832) specifically repudiated the separation of church and state. Lamennais, enduring excommunication, became an extreme democrat and a professed non-Christian, but his leading disciples did not follow him into heresy.

The heyday of French romanticism

IN THIS decade French romanticism throve. Styles and subject matter, of course, varied. Some of France's novelists and poets, living, as was said of one of the most illustrious of them, Alfred de Vigny, "in an ivory tower," escaped into an idealized past or gave vent to their inward emotions rather than to indignation over the contemporary scene. The romantic novelist Aurore Dupin, better known by her pen name of George Sand, personally espoused with fervor the various "causes" of the thirties, such as socialism and Lamennais' ultramontanism, and was involved intellectually or amorously with many of the most famous literary and artistic figures of her time, among them the composer Chopin. Yet the burden of her early novels, drawn directly and freely from her own experience, was a romantic message: love is a divine instinct and it is a woman's duty to follow her heart. Her social novels were to come later.

Alfred de Musset, whose brief and tragic love for George Sand often found expression in the writings of both, became famous as a romantic poet of melancholy and passion, perhaps even more famous in his own day as a dramatist, and perhaps most famous as a frustrated and debauched artist. By cleverly uniting classic form and romantic theme in his dramas, Musset made the quarrel between the two schools seem irrelevant. He was particularly successful in adapting a Shakespearean manner to the romantic drama. His works sometimes dealt with the theme of struggle between the man of affairs and the poet.

Victor Hugo continued to dominate the Romantic Movement as poet, dramatist, and novelist. Four volumes of lyric poetry and several plays came from his prolific pen in the 1830's. In this period he also produced the first of his more significant novels, *The Hunchback of Notre Dame*. It is a melodramatic tale—set in the somewhat imaginative medieval surroundings of a great cathedral—of the love of a gypsy dancer, a corrupt archdeacon who denounces her as a witch, and a hunchbacked bellringer who gives her sanctuary in the cathedral. Here Hugo began to show the characteristics of his later novels—his literary career spanned a fifty-year period—for he touched upon social problems such as misplaced power and the plight of the poor in lengthy passages studded with theatrical characters, perfervid periods, and heroic climaxes.

Alexandre Dumas shares with Hugo the honor of being one of the French writers whose works are as popular abroad as at home. *The Three Musketeers* (1844) and *The Count of Monte Cristo* (1844) are part of the library of adventure in any language. In the 1830's Dumas was more preoccupied with the drama, producing more than twenty plays before 1845. His enormous output was made possible in part by extensive collaboration with other writers. He wrote largely to make money and to amuse, borrowing his characters from the romantic past and concerning himself almost exclusively with narrative, of which he was a master.

Théophile Gautier, though likewise preferring to ignore the social problems of his own day, was a writer of a different sort. As leader of a group of extravagant romantics, he dramatized their rebellion by outlandish dress, including a flaming red waistcoat and long, flowing hair. But his literary style, while full of learned allusion and imagery, is polished and restrained. He believed that literature should be purely an artistic medium and scorned the "goitrous cretins" who used it as a vehicle for social criticism or political propaganda. He was among the first to make a cult of "art for art's sake": "I know that there are some who prefer...bread for the body to that for the soul....They deserve to be economists in this world and also in the next." His poetry was carefully fashioned and dedicated to beauty in art and nature. Nevertheless, his best-known work, *Mademoiselle de Maupin* (1835), is a novel in which the problem of moral decay is analyzed.

*Beginnings
of realism: Balzac and Stendhal*

AKIN TO the romantics in many ways but at the same time a forerunner of later French realism was Honoré de Balzac. In an oration at Balzac's funeral in 1850 Hugo said that his departed friend's work was characterized by "observation *and* imagination." The imagination may not have been wholly romantic or the observation wholly realistic; but the combination was not yet common among novelists. Balzac's masterpiece was *The Human Comedy,* a long series of novels intended to give a complete, accurate, and detailed picture of contemporary society—a natural history of humankind such as Geoffroy Saint-Hilaire was writing for the animal kingdom. In spite of systematic literary industry—sometimes sixteen hours a day and more—the project remained incomplete at his death in 1850. Nevertheless it is a gigantic work of over a hundred stories, crowded with brilliantly drawn characters—more than three thousand of them—typical of the age of the Bourgeois Monarchy.

Another French novelist of the thirties considered a precursor of realism was Henri Beyle, who wrote under the pen name of Stendhal. His novels, notably *The Red and the Black* (1830), were carefully constructed psychological studies set in a contemporary environment. They were not widely known in his time but had great influence on such later realists as Émile Zola.

A pen and ink study made in 1840 by Gavarni (pseudonym of the satirical artist Guillaume Sulpice Chevalier) of the French novelist Honoré de Balzac.

Stendhal himself asserted that he would be understood only in 1900, a prophecy of extraordinary accuracy.

Romanticism in art: the Barbizon school

EUGENE DELACROIX (page 50) was the closest counterpart in French art of Victor Hugo in French literature—the recognized master. In the 1830's in Morocco, Delacroix acquired a new and exotic subject matter. Romanticism in art was exhibited less through imaginative and emotional expression than through a worship of nature, but here too the element of rebellion was less against social injustice than against academic standards and stodginess. In the 1830's a number of young artists developed a new approach to landscape painting by working outdoors directly from nature instead of constructing their scenes artificially in the studio, as was the approved practice. Centering their work in the village of Barbizon near Paris, they came to be known as the Barbizon school. Though their painting was an offshoot of romanticism, they produced little in common with the exciting canvases of such romantics as Delacroix; their quiet, restrained landscapes were painted with a painstaking realism. In the thirties and forties they had some difficulty in gaining the acceptance of patrons and critics; after 1850, when the temper of the times turned toward realism, they were better received (page 166).

Paris as a center of romanticism in music

PARISIAN MUSICAL taste of the period brought forth a form of musical expression that is generally regarded as typically romantic. This was the so-called "grand opera," for which Gioacchino Antonio Rossini's *William Tell* (page 70) had set the standard. The French grand opera had a plot usually based on romanticized history rather than on realistic fiction and sometimes had a liberal political slant. It was typically cast in five acts, with ballets in the second and fourth. Emotion, color, size, and spectacle were essential ingredients. The master developer of this operatic form was the German-born Jakob Meyerbeer, who, like Rossini, had gravitated to Paris, which was then the musical center of Europe. His colorful, melodious *Robert le Diable* (1831) and *Les Huguenots* (1836) were immensely successful. Another outlander, the Italian Gaetano Donizetti, was at this time trying to impress Paris, but his operas were not well received there in spite of the smashing success of his *Lucia di Lammermoor* (1835) in his own country.

Hector Berlioz also tried his hand at grand opera. But his *Benvenuto Cellini,* first performed in 1837, was hissed off the Parisian stage. Too radical for the general public, Berlioz nevertheless had his admirers among musicians, who recognized his talent. The virtuoso Nicolò Paganini, on hearing Berlioz' *Fantastic Symphony* and its sequel *Return to Life* in 1832, remarked, "You begin where the others have ended." The German composer Robert Schumann (page 104) and the Hungarian Liszt (page 168) were also admirers of Berlioz and did much to popularize his work in central Europe in the 1840's. Berlioz' chief contributions were a new emphasis on descriptive, or "program," music and a mastery of orchestration, through which he secured bizarre and often startling effects. He envisaged orchestras of several hundred pieces. In his program music Berlioz sought to portray not only aural sounds and visual scenes but even mental and emotional states. In orchestration his achievements were passed on to others through a manual of instrumentation embodying his own studies of orchestral instruments.

Outside of opera the musical darling of Paris was the Polish-born Frédéric Chopin, who settled in Paris in 1831. Here he delighted intimate audiences with the amazing virtuosity of his pianoforte performances. As a composer he gave to the short piano piece a place among the major arts. His nocturnes, études, and preludes are graceful, poignant, and romantic; and his polonaises and mazurkas celebrated the Polish dance in a manner that anticipated the musical nationalism of the later nineteenth century.

Liberalism
in some smaller western countries

SIMILAR developments in politics, society, and the arts were contemporaneously taking place in other western countries free of the Metternich system. Generally, constitutional questions continued in the forefront of politics, and in some countries—notably Belgium and Holland—the advent of industrialism brought problems and prosperity similar to those in England. In Switzerland the post-Napoleonic period became known as the "era of regeneration." In 1832 the seven cantons that had liberalized their constitutions formed the Siebener Concordat (Concordat of the Seven) for mutual defense. The conservative rural cantons replied by forming the League of Sarnen. The liberal cantons now adopted a more aggressive program, called the Baden Articles, favoring a stronger central government through which they could impose on the conservative (usually Catholic) cantons their program of freedom of worship, secular education, and a lay state. The resistance of the Catholic cantons was in the next decade to lead to open conflict.

STABILITY IN CENTRAL
AND EASTERN EUROPE (1830-1840)

IN CENTRAL and eastern Europe political stability was due to the relative weakness of the liberal and national movements and the strength of the repressive forces. In Russia in particular, liberalism and nationalism were faint voices heard only through a heavy curtain of censorship. In the Germanies and Italy, liberalism and nationalism were indigenous and highly articulate movements, but their adherents were as yet few and weak and the power of reaction was strong.

*The Metternich system
and repression in the Germanies*

THE GERMANIES in the 1830's were still dominated by Metternich. He controlled Austria directly, Prussia by persuasion, and the Germanic Confederation through its diet of princely representatives, who were chiefly interested in maintaining the thrones and prerogatives of their petty rulers. In 1833 the last eddy of the revolutions of 1830 produced an ill-prepared *Putsch* by students, Polish refugees, and nationalists to abolish the diet in Frankfurt. Though easily quelled, the uprising was made the excuse for further measures of repression. Trial of those indicted for conspiracy even within the separate states was placed on a federal instead of a local level. About eighteen hundred arrests involved innocent as well as guilty persons, and by 1836 the Berlin court alone had condemned two hundred and four students.

Still, liberalism and nationalism were not stamped out. In the thirties open protest was the province mainly of students and professors in the universities. As industrialism was only beginning to penetrate central Europe, the middle class, mainstay of liberalism in the west, was made up mostly of farmers, master craftsmen, and professional people, who were primarily interested in keeping things as they were. No large segment of the population had been sufficiently upset by changing conditions to wish things to be other than they were.

*Beginnings
of German political parties*

IN THE later thirties, however, this situation began to change. As the Prussian *Zollverein* expanded, commerce, freed of customs hazards, grew enormously and industry was greatly stimulated. The first German railroad was opened in 1835, and soon the laying of hundreds of miles of track further encouraged trade and industry. With these changes came inevitable shifts in social classes; the bourgeoisie increased in numbers and wealth, and the workers' class, though still small, grew larger.

These shifts in social status were reflected in the beginnings of clear-cut political party alignments. A conservative party made its appearance, drawn from the feudal aristocracy such as the Junkers of Prussia, from an element among the rising aristocracy of wealth who sought to emulate the older feudal aristocracy, from judicial and military officialdom, and from the orthodox church—Protestant in the north and Catholic in the south. The philosopher Hegel was the rallying point of a group of Prussian conservatives. The liberals tended to divide into several incipient parties. Believers in reform of the existing system were numerous among the new aristocracy of wealth; they formed the party of *Reichspatriotismus,* advocating a unified Germany under a progressive constitution. Professor Friedrich Christoph Dahlmann, whose *Politics* outlined a typically bourgeois constitutional monarchy, was a leader of this group.

**German literature and
the "Young Germany" movement**

BELIEVERS IN revolution, disillusioned by the failures of 1830, were persuaded that reform was impossible without the overthrow of the existing system; they were strengthened by the small but growing proletariat. Representative of this group was a coterie of writers known as "Young Germany." Repudiating the mysticism and *sensibilité* of the romantics, they regarded themselves as the hard core of a great European movement for freedom which would liberate all oppressed peoples and sweep away the privileges and injustices remaining from past ages. Among its leaders were some of the outstanding literary figures of the day, who were diverted from literature as pure art to political polemics. They wrote to persuade a public rather than to express subjective emotions. In Germany this was an age of journalism rather than of pure romanticism.

Perhaps most typical of the Young German literary movement was Karl Gutzkow, an earnest young writer whose novel *Wally, the Skeptic* (1835) because of its attack upon marriage and religion earned him the wrath of the German Diet and three months' imprisonment. Leader of Young Germany in its rebellion against literary romanticism, in its preoccupation with politics; and in its debunking of convention, Gutzkow wrote satirical novels and dramas whose timeliness in their own day has made them irrelevant and largely forgotten in ours.

Heinrich Heine, well remembered today for his sentimental verse, much of which was set to music by romantic composers, was less typical of the Young German movement. Embracing the expressiveness and *sensibilité* of romanticism, he avoided its excesses by a rational outlook and a satirical wit, and completely repudiated its medievalism as representing reaction and authoritarianism. In 1831 he moved to Paris, hoping that the July Revolution was the millennium of which young liberals everywhere dreamed and that he would find a social acceptance which his Jewish ancestry had sometimes denied him in Germany. There he wrote for both French and German journals, until in 1835 his writings and those of the other Young German writers were banned by the German Diet. Paris remained Heine's home until his death in 1856.

Ludwig Börne, like Heine of Jewish ancestry, also sought in the Paris of the July Revolution the liberal utopia of which Young Germany dreamed. There he spent the seven remaining years of his life, during which he wrote his trenchant satirical *Letters from Paris,* which became famous in the annals of Young Germany.

**Prussia
and Austria in the thirties**

IN PRUSSIA, while these new political alignments were forming, discontent with the existing regime was rarely overt. Frederick William III, for all his despotic tendencies, retained to the end of his reign a popularity based on efficient administration and earnest concern for the welfare of Prussia. It was a period of economic growth, owing in part to the *Zollverein*'s loosening of trade barriers (page 52), in part to the gradual adoption of new industrial techniques, and in part to the inauguration of new industries.

In Austria, Ferdinand succeeded Francis in 1835. Francis' will admonished his successor to "rule, and change nothing," and the censorship and espionage of the Metternich system were retained—if anything, more virulent than before. But even here western technology was cautiously introduced, and internal customs barriers began to be obliterated. Industrialism was to spread in the next decade and to combine explosively with the forces of separatism already lively in the Habsburg empire.

Science and liberalism in the German universities

WHILE THE Metternich system throughout the Germanies stifled free expression in the realm of political thought, nevertheless scientific investigation, apparently free from the stigma of political radicalism, flourished. In the 1830's the German scientist Friedrich Wöhler carried on his investigations, corroborating his earlier discovery that organic matter was formed of the same chemical elements as inorganic matter. His work was confirmed by that of Justus von Liebig, who experimented not only with animal but also with plant chemistry and chemical fertilizer. Liebig set up at the University of Giessen a teaching laboratory to which students flocked in large numbers in order to take direct part in chemical experiments. In 1838 the botanist Matthias Jakob Schleiden and in 1839 the physiologist Theodor Schwann added further to the knowledge of living matter by proving that the cell is the structural and also the functional basis of both vegetable and animal matter. Their work was made possible by the marked improvement of the microscopic lens during the 1830's. The decade also produced significant discoveries in physics that will be examined later. German universities, already made famous by Hegel and Ranke in the humanities, began attracting students from all over the world in the natural sciences; and despite all Metternich could do, the students did not always subscribe to the status quo.

Strauss and the critical spirit in theology

THE SPIRIT of inquiry flourishing in the German universities prompted the biblical criticism of David Friedrich Strauss. His *Life of Jesus* (1835) attempted to show that the Gospel accounts of the life of Christ were not literal contemporary accounts but rather creations of early Christian followers. Since it explained away the divine and the miraculous, the work called forth a storm of opposition from orthodox believers. Translated into English by the novelist George Eliot in 1846, it aroused a similar sensation in England. Strauss also examined early Christian doctrines from a similar critical angle in his *Christian Doctrines* (1840-1841).

**Romantic music
in the Germanies**

ONLY IN MUSIC did German romanticism continue to flourish uncompromised by political themes. The innovations of Berlioz and Chopin were championed in *Die neue Zeitschrift für Musik,* a periodical that made its first appearance in 1834, edited by Robert Schumann. It had a wide influence in forming musical taste in Germany and was helpful in making that country more receptive to the "new" music than such established centers as Paris. Schumann himself became famous as a composer of descriptive music for the piano, in which he attempted to express literary or pictorial ideas in musical form. He also composed in all the major orchestral forms, wrote many songs, among them settings of poems by Goethe, Heine, Byron, and Burns. Along with the composer-conductor Felix Mendelssohn and the brilliant piano virtuoso Franz Liszt, Schumann brought central Europe into rivalry with Paris for European musical leadership.

**The growth
of nationalism in Italy**

FOR THE Italian states, as for the Germanies, the 1830's were a period of defeat and repression. Austrian-dominated rulers kept Italy a parcel of disunited states and did their best to exorcise liberalism and nationalism. But their very policies gave rise to a remarkably strong organization called Young Italy. Its founder (1831) was the young political exile Giuseppe Mazzini. From France and Switzerland this fiery republican inspired and directed an organization that by 1833 numbered sixty thousand members sworn to the cause of Italian independence and, above all, of Italian unity. They considered themselves a part of a movement for Young Europe. "The tree of liberty," said Mazzini, in words reminiscent of the sentiments of Thomas Jefferson, "does not fructify unless it is planted by the hands of citizens and rendered fertile by the blood of citizens and guarded by the swords of citizens."

Mazzini perceived that the uprisings of 1820 and 1830 had been local, uncoordinated attempts. Italians, he felt, must be taught to think in national terms—not only to free Italy from foreign rule and to unite its various parts into a single Italian nation but also to merge it as a willing member into a free and united Europe. His banner, which bore on one side the slogan "Unity and Independence," bore on the other "Liberty, Equality, and Humanity" ("Fraternity" now smacked more of national rivalry than international brotherhood). Around it rallied thousands of fervent youths, whose ardor was not always equaled by political shrewdness. Attempts at revolt were usually sad failures. But Mazzini, insisting that "ideas grow quickly when watered with the blood of martyrs," turned even failures into propaganda assets. Fiery Young Italy became the inspiration of similar liberal-national movements throughout Europe, such as the much milder Young Germany movement that we have already observed.

*Autocratic reform
in the Russian Empire*

LIBERALISM, ascendant in the west and persistent in central Europe, was scarcely discernible in the easternmost of Europe's empires. The Russian czar Nicholas was regarded in legitimist circles as the leading autocrat of Europe. In keeping with the spirit of the Münchengrätz agreement, Francis, Metternich's sovereign, had admonished his successor Ferdinand to do nothing without Nicholas' advice. During Nicholas' reign censorship was so tight that, according to one official, more books were censored than were published in the course of a year. Nicholas himself suggested to Pushkin that he remodel *Boris Godunov,* his harrowing drama of royal murder and rebellion, into a kind of innocuous novel "after the manner of Walter Scott." Nicholas' secret police and harsh treatment of political dissenters became proverbial in the annals of autocratic repression.

Yet repression was a measure of liberalism's power to frighten the defenders of the Old Regime. And indirectly liberalism became responsible for a number of reforms in autocratic Russia. Nicholas, though his outlook was stringently limited by his devotion to "autocracy, orthodoxy, and patriotism," was nevertheless honestly interested in the welfare of Russia. Though he executed or exiled to Siberia the Decembrist conspirators (page 66), he made a careful study of their liberal demands and adopted those that fitted within the framework of autocracy.

Most significant of Nicholas' reforms were measures relating to the lot of the serfs. During the extraordinary westernizing activities of Peter the Great, these peasants, who once had been, at least theoretically, a free element in the Russian rural community, had been depressed to a status barely distinguishable from slavery, and no great revolutionary movement had been permitted to infect their minds with notions of liberty. Nicholas' measures to better their position were mild: he forbade their sale to purchasers having insufficient land to support them (1827); he prohibited the separation of families by sale (1833); and throughout his reign he attempted to prevent landholders from exploiting their serfs. His measures, however, only nibbled at the edges of the problem, leaving complete emancipation to future decades.

Other measures resulted from the reaction to the Decembrist movement. The codification of Russian law was completed in 1832. The work of Mikhail Speranski, an old liberal minister of Alexander, it effected none of the needed changes in contemporary practices but made law public in a systematized form. Financial reform also grew out of the effort to counteract Decembrist complaints. In 1839 the paper ruble, issued in quantity by Alexander to finance his wars, was stabilized and backed by a gold reserve, ending inflation and the currency confusion.

The only institution imported directly from the west in the thirties was the railroad. The first Russian railroad was a royal commuters' track, opened in 1837, between St. Petersburg and Tsarskoye Selo. Construction of a railroad between St. Petersburg and Moscow was begun by the government in 1842. One of the technical advisers in the building of this railroad was Major George Washington Whistler, an American engineer, husband of the lady who was to become famous as "Whistler's Mother." Russian railroad tracks were built on a gauge that was different from that used in the countries to the west so that to this day it is necessary to change trains at the Russian border. Whether so intended or not, this difference in gauge has diminished the degree of cooperation with the west that railroads might otherwise have made possible.

Thought and art under Russian censorship

NICHOLAS' POLICY of censorship was stifling to intellectual life. Only those thinkers and artists flourished whose politics were approved by Nicholas or who stayed out of politics altogether. Pushkin, who had been implicated in the Decembrist revolt, turned away from liberalism after its failure, and his writing turned to protest against rebellion. In his *Captain's Daughter* (1836) he prayed: "God save us from seeing a Russian revolt, meaningless and merciless! Those who are plotting impossible violent changes in Russia are either young and do not know our people, or are hard-hearted men who do not care a straw about their own lives or those of other people." Nevertheless, the love letter of Tatiana to the hero of his *Eugene Onegin* (1833), perhaps Pushkin's greatest single piece of poetry, was a product of this period.

In 1837, at the age of thirty-seven, Pushkin was killed in a duel over personal affairs. This tragedy occasioned a brilliant indictment in verse of the society that had allowed such a crime ("On the Death of the Poet"). Its author was a rising young Byron-inspired poet, Mikhail Yurevich Lermontov. For this outburst, the poet was sent in exile to the Caucasus. His subsequent works continued to castigate the low level of Russian life until he, like Pushkin, was killed in a duel. During Lermontov's lifetime only one short collection of his poems was published (1840), mutilated by the censor.

Somewhat luckier at evading Russian censorship was Nikolai Gogol, though he satirized the Russian bureaucracy and the institution of serfdom. His comedy *The Inspector General* (1836) portrayed the stupidities and corruption of provincial officialdom. The plot of his masterpiece, the novel *Dead Souls* (1842), centered around the traffic in serfs, revealing the pettiness of Russian rural life with a realism rare in literature of the day and which in his last years, as a religious penitent, he regretted.

As elsewhere, music, not yet regarded as readily adaptable to the expression of dangerous ideas, escaped censorship. Mikhail Ivanovich Glinka set many of Pushkin's poems to music and composed a great many other songs. Although he had studied in Berlin, he developed a distinctively Russian type of music in which the Russian folk song formed an important element.

*International crises
in the Near East (1833-1840)*

IN INTERNATIONAL as in domestic affairs the thirties were a relatively peaceful decade. The few conflicts that arose were on the periphery of Europe. The French involvement in Algeria and the British troubles in the Far East did not ruffle the diplomatic calm. Only in the Near East did antagonism threaten to upset the balance of power.

Here a local dispute between Turkey and Egypt almost became a major war. When in the 1820's the sultan had tried to reduce the rebellious Greeks to subjection, he had called upon his vassal Mohammed Ali, viceroy of Egypt. After Greek independence was won, the Turkish sultan and his Egyptian viceroy began to fight over the reward that Mohammed Ali should receive. Their dispute was temporarily settled in 1833. Mohammed Ali, however, continued his machinations to build a Near Eastern empire of his own, independent of the sultan. In this he was encouraged by France, which hoped to bring Egypt once more, as in the days of Napoleon, under French influence. Russia, fearful lest any other great power control the Turkish waters, uncharacteristically became a defender of the Porte, and England, viewing with alarm any extension of French power along the trade routes to the East, also supported the sultan.

Then in 1839 hostilities again broke out between the sultan and his rebellious vassal, and threatened to end in victory for Mohammed Ali. All five of the European powers, anxious to prevent an international tug of war, entered the diplomatic arena. In a collective note to the sultan, they asserted their determination to have a voice in the settlement. Concerted action broke down, however, when France, where the nationalist firebrand Thiers was momentarily minister of foreign affairs, supported the Egyptian pasha and prepared to play a lone hand against a general settlement of the Eastern Question. The other four powers, in the Treaty of London (1840), pledged their support to the sultan.

Had the French insisted on their position, a general European war might have resulted, but Louis Philippe's peace-at-any-price policy prevailed. He dismissed Thiers, and active European participation in the quarrel was confined to a few British actions in Syria. Finally Mohammed Ali was forced to abandon Syria in return for the recognition of his hereditary rule in Egypt. Egypt thus acquired limited autonomy within the Ottoman Empire, but no one could tell when it might fall under the domination of one of the great Mediterranean powers.

In 1841 the five great powers further underlined their interests in preserving peace within the decadent Ottoman Empire. They concluded the Straits Convention. By closing the Bosporous and the Dardanelles to all foreign warships in peacetime, the powers hoped to extend to the Near East the principle of neutralization that they had recently applied to Belgium 107 (page 92). The preservation of the Entente Cordiale of France and England, which thus was able to cooperate with and to counterbalance the Münchengrätz combination of Austria, Prussia, and Russia, seemed to augur the continued success of the Concert of Europe.

THE SPREAD
OF SOCIAL CONSCIOUSNESS (1840-1848)

IN THE early 1840's, the pace and intensity of the developments that had characterized the preceding decade were stepped up. England became more than ever the industrial leader of Europe, and the model and hope of the liberal movement on the Continent. The railroad, which was still regarded as too uncertain a risk for private enterprise, spread rapidly in western Europe. The "Industrial Revolution" began to take hold on the Continent, bringing the problems, along with the advantages, of the factory system. Economic change contributed to a ripple of socialist theories and activities that at the same time reinforced and challenged the swelling liberal and national movements.

Social awareness in English literature

THE HUMANITARIAN novel fathered by Dickens had a great vogue in the 1840's. The young Tory leader Benjamin Disraeli wrote several such novels, of which *Coningsby* and *Sybil* are best known. The first criticized both parties for their indifference to the workers, and the second portrayed the disparity between rich and poor. Charles Kingsley, in *Yeast* and *Alton Locke,* described the decay of the English country districts and the misery of industrial areas. He was among the prime movers of the Christian Socialist movement in England, dedicated to amelioration of the lot of the poor. Elizabeth Gaskell wrote in *Mary Barton* of industrial conflicts from her observation of industrial conditions in Manchester. Dickens continued to produce novels filled with memorable characters and overdrawn and ludicrous situations while pointing an accusing finger at everyday injustices.

An impetus to the vogue of the novel came from the literary journals, in which many novels were serialized before publication in book form. Much of Dickens' work first appeared in this way. William Makepeace Thackeray, already well-known for the serialized views of his character Mr. J. C. Yellowplush (1838), was one of the earliest contributors to the satirical, social-minded weekly *Punch, or the London Charivari,* which made its first appearance in 1841. Thackeray continued to produce satires on recent and contemporary society, rising topmost in the literary scale with *Vanity Fair* (1848), in which the ups and downs of the unscrupulous social climber

Becky Sharp and the steadfast simplicity of the awkward officer William Dobbin served as a foil for the delineation of various pompous and self-righteous characters of pre-Victorian society.

Two outstanding English novelists of the forties were sisters, each of whom is best remembered for one novel. Charlotte Brontë's *Jane Eyre* (1847) and Emily Brontë's *Wuthering Heights* (1848) fit the romantic pattern in their expression of sentiment and passion, but their attention to characterization and atmosphere places them in the newer school of realism. Their characters, caught in situations which they could not master, seldom acted heroically or even admirably.

Poetry too was a medium for the expression of the twinges of the social conscience. The decade could boast some of the best works of Alfred Tennyson, Elizabeth Barrett, and Robert Browning, whom Elizabeth Barrett married in 1846. Browning's psychological and moral studies and keen dramatic sense had already won recognition in literary circles, but the general public found his poetry obscure and difficult. His contemporaries were less obscure. Tennyson's narrative poem *Locksley Hall* (1842) set forth a rosy dream of the future, and Elizabeth Barrett published in 1843 *The Cry of the Children,* a heart-rending protest against child labor.

Whig history and English neo-liberalism

THE GROWING reading public was also treated to history in the grand literary manner. Thomas Babington Macaulay, a poet of no mean reputation, devoted his literary skill also to his *Critical and Historical Essays* (1843) and *History of England* (1849-1861). His clear and occasionally biased re-creation of the color and spirit of the late seventeenth century contrasted with the studied detachment being developed in the writing of history on the Continent by Ranke and his followers. His ardent defense of Whiggish principles contrasted with the biting criticism of his older contemporary Carlyle.

The laissez-faire philosophy by which most nineteenth-century Britons lived was given a new twist with the publication in 1848 of John Stuart Mill's *Political Economy*. Rigidly trained in classical economics by his father, James Mill, the younger Mill nevertheless did not accept his father's teachings unquestioningly. In *Political Economy* he posited a new utilitarianism—the theory that while production is governed by unalterable economic laws, distribution is subject to human or social control, and that through better distribution of the world's stores greater good can be spread to a greater number. Laissez faire, he contended, generally worked well, but many circumstances warranted the interference of government. Thus, he came close to being a precursor of socialism. Nevertheless, Mill was a great believer in individual freedom and in democracy as the form of government most likely to assure good government.

*Scientific
advance in England*

IN THE PRACTICAL air of Victorian England scientific experiment flourished. Michael Faraday, already famous as the discoverer of benzene, in 1831 also discovered the phenomenon of electromagnetic induction and engaged in experiments on the nature and production of electrical currents that were later to make possible the invention of the dynamo. In 1843 James Prescott Joule announced his conviction that the production of a given amount of mechanical work always produces the same amount of heat, and proceeded to prove his point with a long series of researches.

*Art and taste
in early Victorian England*

IN THIS ERA, that combination of manners, morals, literature, and art known as Victorianism was beginning to be discernible. The term implies a generalization that, like most efforts to characterize a historical period by a single word, overemphasizes some things and disregards others. Dominated socially as well as politically by the middle class, the Victorian climate is sometimes said to have been essentially bourgeois in spirit—prudish, pious, earnest, common-sense, hard-working, and sentimental. It exalted the church, the home, and the family, subordinated wife to husband, and, while banning sex from polite conversation, believed unspokenly in the double bed and the large family. It tended to identify material achievement with general welfare, was convinced of the inevitability of progress, and took for granted the superiority of Britain and all things British.

Mass production and the cultivation of hard sense at the expense of sensibility fostered a decline in taste. Rows of identical boxlike houses appeared in the city suburbs, the parlors (when the inhabitants could afford parlors) of each box outfitted in mahogany, wine-colored plush, and horsehair furniture. The Gothic Revival, which in the days of Walter Scott had dotted the countryside with medieval castles, was now carried with enthusiasm into churches and public buildings. The elaborately Gothic Houses of Parliament were built early in Victoria's reign. Old churches were "restored" and new churches built with a technical fidelity to Gothic styles that bespoke the Victorian passion for correctness and respectability and perhaps also an unconscious quest in a changing world for some anchor to vanishing traditions.

Other arts also suffered. English music could boast no great names or achievements in this era when on the Continent music was flourishing as rarely before. Paintings were apt to be judged by the amount of work expended in their creation rather than by artistic value. Turner, now an elderly man, was still considered so radical in his innovations in color and composition that when a young and unknown writer, John Ruskin, wrote in Turner's defense in 1843 (*Modern Painters,* Volume I), he brought forth a storm of abuse from critics and even from painters.

*Repeal
of the English Corn Laws*

ENGLAND took the lead in bringing her laws into conformity with the demands of the new industrial society. The first step was the work partly of the Anti-Corn-Law League, which after only a brief career proved able to marshal fairly solid support from the middle class and some from the working class behind the demand for repeal of the Corn Laws. The League contended that food prices were high because of the tariffs on foreign breadstuffs. Many British manufacturers hoped by repeal to reduce prices and thus make less necessary a rise of wages. In addition, it was in the interest of British manufacturers, since their early start in the race toward industrialism enabled them to underprice foreign competition, to remove import and export duties everywhere, and they were willing that Britain should set the example.

Under the leadership of the Manchester textile manufacturers Richard Cobden and John Bright, a "peripatetic political university" was organized to propagandize the interested groups. Cobden was elected to Parliament in 1841 to lead the fight for "untaxing the poor man's loaf." Arguments in favor of repeal poured from political platforms, daily papers, and House of Commons benches. The indigent farm hand was brought to public meetings to testify against the protective tariff: "I be protected and I be starving." As many as a million pamphlets a year were distributed during this highly organized, morally fervid, and generously financed attack.

Under this barrage the landed interests could no longer hold their own. Prime Minister Robert Peel, leader of the Tories (now called Conservatives), though pledged to protect the Corn Laws, was himself converted. When in the summer of 1845 a blight ruined the Irish potato crop and a month of rain ruined the English grain harvest, the doom of the Corn Laws was sealed. They were repealed the following summer, the loss in revenue being made up by an income tax. In the next few years other duties on farm produce, raw materials, and manufactured goods were eliminated, and England became and long remained essentially the free-trade nation envisioned by the classical economists.

Free trade was a step of far-reaching significance. It permitted countries better adapted to agricultural pursuits to sell their produce to Britain in return for finished articles such as Britain was able to produce most economically. It brought cheaper bread to the numerous poor and cheaper raw materials and wider markets for finished goods to the manufacturers. In the course of time, it made British agriculture less profitable while it made industry more so. Thus, as time went on, Britain was to become a manufacturing country dependent on imports for its food supply. The new arrangement worked very well as long as Britain held the lead in industrialization over the rest of the world. But when other countries learned from England to compete successfully in manufacture and commerce, and when,

111

in the twentieth century, wars and other "abnormal" complications were to interfere with the automatic operation of "natural" economic laws, Britain was to regret her high degree of specialization and her freedom from tariff barriers.

More immediately, the repeal of the Corn Laws brought a change in English politics. The Conservative Party was so badly split between Peelites and Protectionists over Peel's "betrayal" that it was unable to put up a united front against the Whigs, who regained power. Peel was discredited and the brilliant young Disraeli climbed to Conservative leadership of the House of Commons.

A period
of British prosperity

AFTER THE REPEAL of the Corn Laws, an era of improved economic conditions ensued. Due partly to repeal and pro-business policies, it came also as a result of rapid railroad building, characteristic of the forties in England and elsewhere, and the growth of steamship service. Furthermore, shortly after the first experimental line using the Morse telegraph (page 221) was built in America, a line was strung in England, making possible almost instantaneous transmission of news. With these improvements in transportation, travel, and communication, trade, freed of customs duties, expanded rapidly. England became for a few decades the economic center of the entire world. Laborers and landlords partook with manufacturers in the expanding prosperity. Increased food supplies, better wages, and greater employment alleviated the lot of many working men, while the landlord, though now unsupported by the Corn Laws, profited from the increased demand for food and wool from a better paid working class. The Factory Act of 1847—the most important of a series—was indicative of a growing attention to improvement of labor conditions. In Ireland, however, where the population shrank by death and emigration from 8,500,000 in 1845 to 6,500,000 in 1851, and where 3,000,000 people in 1847 were being fed by government rations, discontent was widespread. After the famine of 1845 the Young Ireland movement for independence won many adherents.

The ups and downs of prosperity brought a renewed interest in workingmen's associations. Trade unionism revived around 1845 after a ten-year slump; and in 1844 twenty-eight poor men calling themselves the Rochdale Equitable Pioneers opened a cooperative store from which the largest and most successful cooperative movement in England was to grow. The Rochdale cooperative, though it entertained dreams of an eventually self-sufficient community, limited itself at first to the modest business of retailing, refunding its surplus earnings to members in proportion to their purchases. Sound business practices and modest aims were to enable it later to branch gradually into wholesaling, manufacturing, banking, and other large-scale cooperative enterprises. It was to become the model of cooperative and mutual societies all over the world.

Industrialism
and railroads on the Continent

THE 1840's were, on the Continent as in England, the great age of railroad building. By 1850, except for gaps totaling about fifty miles, the traveler could ride from the North Sea to the Adriatic on the German railroad systems, and several thousand miles of the present-day French railroad network had been laid down. In most countries governments either built the railroad lines themselves or encouraged and subsidized private investors to do so. The manufacture of track and rolling stock and the operation of the railroad trains created an enormous demand for coal and iron. These industries burgeoned in Germany and Belgium, as they had in England, and to a lesser extent in France. Practically all industries felt a general stimulus through the increased railroad freight facilities. Prosperity was no longer obliged to keep pace with the water mill and the horse and wagon. Factories no longer needed to hug the streams for power or to rise in the midst of their natural resources. They could go where labor was available and cheap, counting on the railroads to bring them their coal and raw materials and to deliver their finished products.

Problems
attendant upon industrialization

THE PROBLEMS as well as the advantages of industrialization now began to become more pronounced. The cities were overcrowded, working conditions were bad, small business found competition with big business difficult, and the worker's living had become dependent on a daily wage that might disappear overnight in hard times. The condition of the factory laborer, the artisan, and the shopkeeper, contrasting with the increasing wealth of the manufacturers, impelled the lower classes to look with favor upon those who preached republicanism, socialism, and trade unionism. Discontent was directed sometimes against the manufacturers, expressing itself in demonstrations and strikes for better working conditions and more pay. Often it took the form of protests against a system of government and society that allowed such conditions. When the workers' ill will was aimed at conservative governments, they might find an ally in middle-class liberals, also discontented with the political organization though less eager to modify the economic structure.

French literature
as social propaganda

THE GROWING demand for social reform was reflected in French literature of the forties. Much that had seemed individual and fantastic in the Romantic Movement was being patently deflected toward consciously political and social pamphleteering. George Sand turned from novels of personal emancipation to novels of social significance, which she produced at an amazing rate. Alphonse de Lamartine   113 neglected poetry in favor of politics and history, becoming increasingly republican in his views. Hugo, temporarily abandoning belles-lettres for oratory, pleaded in the Chamber of Peers the cause of the Poles and other oppressed. Class conflict found its way into *The Human Comedy* of Balzac, who called himself "doctor in social sciences." The historian Jules Michelet, while writing his nineteen-volume *History of France,* gave controversial lectures at the Collège de France in which romantic nationalism, proletarian sympathies, and anticlericalism were neatly intermingled. Auguste Comte, having completed his six-volume presentation of positivism in the social sciences in his *Course of Positive Philosophy* (1830-1842), now turned to his *System of Positive Polity.* In it, on the basis of his sociological principles, he was to set forth (1851-1854) a reorganization of society that was to appear even to his disciples as mystical.

Continental advocates of the "socialist" philosophy

IN CONTRAST to the advocates of free trade in England, continental reformers usually proposed a prominent role for the state in the achievement of economic justice. It was becoming more and more apparent, they argued, that free competition did not work automatically, as the classical economists claimed, to produce the greatest good for the greatest number. Society must therefore assume direction of enterprise, if the social welfare were to be attained. A significant characteristic of "socialists" during this period in all countries was their devotion to cooperative ideas (or "mutualism")—from little utopias to great producers' unions. They were apt to be pacifists, ardently opposed to violence as a means of achieving their millenniums. Few of them as yet entertained the concept of class struggle that was to dominate later socialist thought.

Some leaders among the French socialists

IN FRANCE this socialist movement was particularly strong. Paris, in fact, became a mecca for radical thinkers who had fled or had been exiled from their own countries because of their radicalism, although occasionally they were exiled in turn from France and had to flee to England, Belgium, or Holland.

Louis Blanc now became the most powerful figure in the French socialist movement. The five volumes of his *History of Ten Years* (1841-1844) criticized the first decade of Louis Philippe's reign and focused a pitiless glare upon the political and social evils of his day. In 1847 he joined the staff of the extreme leftist newspaper *La Réforme,* where he advocated universal suffrage as a prerequisite to more sweeping social change.

Étienne Cabet also attracted a host of followers. His *Voyage to Icaria* (1840) pictured a model community in which all trade was in the hands of the government, which supervised work and education as well. Cabet's ideas

114

Comfortable by his fireside, Cabet, in this caricature from the French periodical L'Illustration, is content not to carry out his voyage to Icaria. He did, however, join his colony in America in 1849.

were largely borrowed from other socialists, particularly from the Owenites, with whom he had come in contact during an exile in England. Several Icarian cooperative experiments were attempted in America during the nineteenth century, but ultimately, like the Owenite communities, they foundered.

Proudhon
and "philosophical anarchism"

AT THE OPPOSITE extreme in his view of the state was Pierre Joseph Proudhon, one of the few social philosophers of the period actually to come from the ranks of the working class. Though he agreed, to the delight of contemporary socialists, that private property was theft, unlike them he was suspicious of government altogether, and particularly popular government. He advocated the establishment of a cooperative bank on a national basis that would give credit without charging interest. By thus eliminating the exploitative aspect of capital, he expected to promote the exchange of products on the basis of their cost in labor alone. The economic system he contended, would then supersede the political system, and true mutualism would be established. Proudhon's distrust of the liberal-national state led him to advocate a federal system for France to replace the elective, centralized authority, and this idea was to influence the later Communard movement (page 203).

Karl Marx
and the Communist Manifesto

THOUGH IN PARIS only briefly (1844), a German student of economics, Karl Marx, came in contact with the most advanced French socialist thought. Expelled from France, he continued in Brussels the development of the theme of his studies

115

—that historical materialism is the basis of economic, political, and cultural institutions. This theme was subsequently summarized by Marx's collaborator, Friedrich Engels: "The causes of all social changes and political revolutions are to be sought, not in men's brains, not in Man's better insight into eternal truth and justice but in changes in the modes of production and exchange. They are to be sought not in the philosophy but in the economics of each particular epoch."

Before meeting Marx, Engels had written a book entitled *Conditions of the Working Class in England* (1844), pointing up the misery of the factory laborer in the new industrial system. Marx, descendant of a long line of rabbis, and Engels, son of a prosperous German businessman, curiously enough made a lifelong team. Active in proletarian movements in Brussels, they both joined the secret Communist League, the first militant socialist movement organized on an international scale. For this organization they wrote the *Communist Manifesto* in 1848.

This document sounded the tocsin for revolution through class struggle: "Workers of the world, unite!" Adapting the Hegelian dialectic of thesis-antithesis-synthesis to the resolution of man's problems, the *Manifesto* asserted: "The history of all hitherto existing society is the history of class struggles....Oppressor and oppressed...carried on an uninterrupted...fight that each time ended either in a revolutionary reconstitution of society at large or in the common ruin of the contending classes....Society...is more and more splitting up into two great hostile camps...Bourgeoisie and Proletariat." The oppressed proletariat were called upon to unite to wrest political control and all capital from the oppressing bourgeoisie and thus assure that control of the instruments of production would be centered in the proletarian state. The authors of the *Communist Manifesto* intended it to be the signal for a great revolution. For this it was too late and too soon—too late because the revolution had begun before it could be published, too soon because the proletariat of the world were not disposed to unite.

GROWTH OF LIBERAL
AND NATIONAL MOVEMENTS (1840-1848)

THE BOURGEOISIE were less concerned with economic inequality and injustice than with what they considered the unjust distribution of political power. Their discontent assumed two forms, usually intimately related—a demand for constitutional reform in the direction of greater bourgeois representation and a demand for nationhood based on ethnic solidarity rather than on obsolete dynastic claims. This bourgeois movement was particularly strong in France, Germany, Austria, and Italy.

DISCONTENT IN France grew steadily after 1840. Shortly upon the dismissal of Thiers, Guizot became minister of foreign affairs and remained thereafter the dominant force in Louis Philippe's regime. The years of vacillating policy were followed by a period of firm immobility. To Louis Philippe and his chief minister the political system of France, though temporarily marred by the corruption and speculation attendant upon rapid economic expansion, was fundamentally sound. Guizot's political opponents pretended that his slogan to counteract all complaints about political and social injustice was *"Enrichissez-vous"* ("Get rich"), and he did in fact once expound some such philosophy in a public address.

The French political system was eminently suited to manipulation by the judicious granting of favors, a practice used by Guizot to assure himself a parliamentary majority. It had the unfortunate effect of blinding both Guizot and the king to the true sentiment of the country at large. Surrounded by "yes-men," they were lulled into a false sense of security at the same time

Honoré Daumier, in L'Illustration, *caricatures a French communist writer. He writes, "It is a pleasure to share with one's brothers. Because the rich are my brothers, I wish to share with them."*

that the growing reform movement was denied peaceful expression through the legislature. Hence a highly explosive situation developed.

Hardly any group in France by the mid-forties was in accord with the king. Legitimists still plotted on behalf of the Bourbon pretender. Even one-time supporters of Louis Philippe were alienated by his timid foreign policy, his domestic stand-pattism, and his mounting pretensions to power. A small but active group of republicans under Lamartine's leadership propagandized for political democracy. Another group of republicans, sometimes called the "Social Democrats," carried on a campaign for economic justice, in Blanc's newspaper *La Réforme*. Many bourgeois liberals and liberal Catholics, among them former followers of Lamennais, wanted only to effect moderate change and extension of the franchise without overthrowing the monarchy. The first volumes of Thiers' *Consulate and Empire* appeared in time to remind readers of the painful contrast between Louis Philippe's peace-at-any-price and Napoleon's domination of Europe; and Lamartine's *History of the Girondins* (1847), with at least as much rhetorical flourish as historical truth, painted the Girondin orators as heroic missionaries of republican virtue. A rising tide of patriotic sentiment, encouraged by the revival of Revolutionary and Napoleonic legends, opposed Louis Philippe's foreign policy and his subservience to England. Even the final conquest of Algeria (1847) did not satisfy the patriots' yearning for France's former glory.

When in 1846-1847 a period of temporary depression occurred, the situation became fraught with peril for *le roi bourgeois,* little though he realized it. By 1847 the opposition had crystallized around electoral and parliamentary reform, in an effort to enlarge the number of qualified electors, now no more than 240,000. When in that year two separate proposals were turned down by the corrupt and subservient parliament, the most active reform groups began openly to mobilize sentiment in the country at large. Since the police would not give licenses for political rallies, a number of gatherings in the guise of "banquets" were held in Paris and other large cities, at which plans for reform were explained and popular feeling was kept stirred to an intense pitch.

The reform movement and nationalism in the Germanies

IN THE GERMANIES liberals rallied around the cause of national unity. The Near Eastern crisis of 1840 aroused fears in Germany that France would direct her reawakened patriotism against German territory. These fears provided inspiration for the patriotic songs *Die Wacht am Rhein* (1840) and *Deutschland Über Alles* (1841). The first gave voice to the devotion of Germans to the "Fatherland," and the second coupled German prestige with "unity and justice and freedom." The ideas of the Saint-Simonians, Fourier, and Cabet were funneled into Germany through Young German writers, and the word "socialist" began to appear in German publications around 1840. As yet unchanneled by political organization, socialism nevertheless quickened the revolutionary spirit in Germany. Friedrich List, developing a Hamiltonian protective theory that he had acquired in America, published his *National System of Political Economy* (1841) and began two years later to edit the *Zollvereinblatt,* a sheet devoted to promoting the ideas of national tariffs and union.

*Science
in the German universities*

LIBERALS LOOKED more than ever to university professors for leadership as German and Austrian universities continued to gain in prestige. When the new king of Hanover in 1837 canceled the constitution, seven professors of Göttingen, among them the historian F. C. Dahlmann and the philologist Jakob Grimm, protested and were banished. Several outstanding scientists added to the luster of the universities. The Prussian astronomer Johann Gottfried Galle discovered the planet Neptune in 1846, in the location predicted by other scientists, thus impressing contemporaries with the power of theoretical science to predict. The botanist Hugo von Mohl and others studied and described the place of protoplasm in cellular structure. Most significant of the German scientific developments of the forties was Hermann von Helmholtz' formulation of the law of the conservation of energy in 1847, though its truth and significance were but slowly appreciated. The antiseptic methods of Ignaz Philipp Semmelweis, a Hungarian physician practicing in Vienna, reduced spectacularly the death rate among his own patients from puerperal, or childbed, fever (the contagiousness of which had been described in Boston in 1843 by Oliver Wendell Holmes), but fellow obstetricians refused to recognize his contribution and drove him out.

*The liberal movement
in Prussia of the 1840's*

IN PRUSSIA the year 1840 marked the accession of Frederick William IV. The new king was known to have artistic talents, to believe in political freedom, and to favor national unity; and liberals and nationalists expected great things of him. He started out by granting amnesty to prominent political prisoners, by permitting Jakob Grimm, exiled from Hanover, and his inseparable brother Wilhelm to become professors at Berlin, and by softening the censorship of the press. Liberals were soon disappointed, however, to find that Frederick William's aim was to play the role of a Biblical patriarch. He proposed to conserve the landlord-dominated estates and to promote German unity through a revived Holy Roman Empire. He spurned modern innovations like political constitutions. "No written sheet of paper," he announced, "shall ever thrust itself like a second providence between the Lord God in heaven and this land."

The liberal-national movement, relatively quiescent during the last years of Frederick William III, burst forth under the new monarch. Professional and scholarly societies took up the cry. The new king met the clamor with half-measures. In 1842 representatives of the provincial assemblies were called together in Berlin but they were given no power and they accomplished nothing. Five years later, when the king wanted funds for railroad building, he summoned a United Landtag, a diet consisting of all the provincial assemblies. It too was a failure. The delegates could not wrest a constitution from the king, and the king could not wheedle from them the funds for his railroad. The Landtag had commanded widespread interest throughout Europe, and the London *Times,* which had nearly forty thousand subscribers and was perhaps the most influential newspaper in Europe, had sent a special correspondent to cover the meetings. Local events were now known abroad shortly after they happened, and the disappointment at the Landtag's failure was general.

*Liberalism
in Austria and Hungary*

IN THE AUSTRIAN Empire, disaffection developed on several different national levels. Liberalism and nationalism, rigorously excluded from Austrian publications, crept in by way of foreign journals and pamphlets, and flourished in the universities and among city intellectuals. In Hungary Louis Kossuth gained wide publicity through his editorship of the first political journal to be founded in that country (1841). Though the Austrian government eventually severed his connection with the paper, he continued to gain popularity by his vigorous advocacy of complete independence for Hungary and abolition of surviving feudal practices. Some Hungarian liberals, regarding Kossuth's demands as too radical, adhered to a more moderate reform movement under the leadership of Ferencz Deak. Nevertheless, the liberal movement remained cohesive enough to agree on a ten-point program of reform. Most important of the ten points were responsible government, popular representation, religious freedom, freedom of public meeting, abolition of serfdom, and equality before the law. In the Hungarian diet of 1847 "The Ten Points" were adopted by the lower house but met with opposition in the upper, dominated by the greater nobility.

Nationalism was not always allied with liberalism. As the desire for Hungarian national autonomy grew, with it grew the hope for a strong and large Hungarian nation. Hence arose a paradox in the Hungarian nationalist movement. Though the Hungarians wished to be independent of Austria, they were prepared to deny to their own subject peoples, who outnumbered them, any large share of national privilege or identity. The large Slavic minorities within Hungary, for their part, resented the continued extension of the Magyar language at the expense of their native tongues, and the persistent slighting of their local institutions and customs. Among Serbs, Croats, and Rumanians strong nationalist sentiments developed in resistance to the "Magyarization" policies of the Hungarian patriots. Even the substitution in 1844 of Magyar for Latin as the official language of the Hungarian diet raised doubts and fears in some quarters.

The disappearance of the Republic of Cracow

THE FREE REPUBLIC of Cracow, created by the Congress of Vienna, was all that remained to symbolize the once haughty sovereign power of Poland. It had become a hotbed of Polish conspirators seeking to reunite the fragments of Poland that by four earlier partitions had been distributed among Prussia, Russia, and Austria. Revolt broke out in the Polish areas of Austria and Prussia in 1846, but it was easily suppressed; and Austria, with the consent of Prussia and Russia, put an end to the independence of Cracow by annexing the former free state (see map, page 75). Even in this miniature rehearsal of the drama that was fast approaching, the Austrian government was able to play one group of Slavs, the Ruthenian peasants, against another, their Polish landlords, and thus to find in national aspirations a weapon that could be turned against the aspirants.

Nationalism and Pan-Slavism in Bohemia

IN BOHEMIA, whose national tradition was in some respects remarkably like Hungary's, a liberal-national movement grew correspondingly articulate during the 1840's. Here too the diet displayed an unaccustomed vigor in resistance to the dictates of the central government, and popular sentiment grew for Bohemian autonomy within the empire. The movement gained emotional color and appeal through a Czech literary and historical revival led by the historian Frantisek Palacky, who in 1836 published (in German) the first volume of his *History of Bohemia,* reminding his compatriots of the glorious culture they had enjoyed before the Habsburg regime in Bohemia began. Subsequent volumes, despite the efforts of the Austrian censorship, continued to appear until in 1867 Palacky reached (in Volume V) the day in 1526 when Bohemia lost its independence. A Czech translation with a meaningful change of title, *The History of the Czech Nation,* was published between 1848 and 1876. Many Bohemians looked sentimentally to Russia and a union of the Slavic peoples for escape from their domination by the Austrians. Thus an intense interest in Pan-Slavism, or the unity of the Slavic peoples, arose—and not only in Bohemia—among the peoples speaking the Slavic languages.

Weakness of the Austrian government

IN THE MIDST of all these complex currents and crosscurrents Emperor Ferdinand continued his policy of "rule, and change nothing." He himself was incompetent. One of his high officials said of him, "He does not understand a single word of what is put before him, and he is always ready to sign whatever he is presented with." His two ablest ministers—Metternich and Count Franz Anton Kolow-rat, the latter of whom made a pretense of being a liberal—were scarcely on speaking terms, and the various councils of which his government was composed could seldom cooperate satisfactorily. Thus as the centrifugal forces of nationalism grew stronger, the central government grew weaker.

The Risorgimento in the states of Italy

IN ITALY, too, the sentiment against Austrian autocracy and the domination of the hated *Tedeschi* grew stronger. Mazzini's Young Italy movement made enormous strides as a propaganda force. Certain conservative voices also took up the cry for independence but propounded schemes that were less republican and violent than Mazzini's. One such scheme was that of Vincenzo Gioberti, a philosopher-priest who wrote, like Mazzini, from exile. He felt that a united and independent Italy was impossible to achieve peacefully and proposed a federation of Italian states in the monarchical-aristocratic tradition under the headship of the pope. Massimo d'Azeglio was another opponent of the Mazzinian program of violence in the name of a humanitarian nationalism; he placed his faith in the king of Sardinia rather than in the pope as leader of an independence movement.

Thus began in the 1840's the movement known as the Risorgimento—the Resurrection. No longer was the Italian movement for freedom confined to conspiratorial republicans. It was espoused by eminent clericals and royalists. It was reinforced by the growth of the bourgeoisie in the northern centers, where the "Industrial Revolution" and the first railroad tracks were beginning to foster a desire for national markets and prestige. The full flood of popular opinion was behind it.

Hopes were raised when Pius IX, elected pope in 1846, inaugurated his reign with several forward-looking measures. Gioberti's dream of a liberal, nationalist pope to unite Italy seemed on the point of realization. Influenced by these great expectations, King Charles Albert of Sardinia, hitherto known as "King Wobble" because of his vacillation between liberalism and conservatism, granted in 1847 a series of reforms to his own kingdom, and wrote, "If Providence sends us a war of Italian independence I will...place myself at the head of an army...." And thus he lent substance to the royalist D'Azeglio's dream of an Italy united under the stalwart house of Savoy.

The Risorgimento, it seemed, now had its leaders as well as its program. In the ferment of expectation a revolution was touched off in restive Sicily in January 1848. It spread quickly to the mainland, where, amid shouts of *"Viva Pio Nono"* ("Long live Pius IX"), revolutionists wrested from the king a liberal constitution. Leopold of Tuscany, under pressure of the same general unrest, granted Tuscany a constitution in February. News of revolution in Paris was soon to spur the spirit of Risorgimento further.

**The Carlist wars
and the Spanish marriages**

IN SPAIN, since the death of Ferdinand VII in 1833 a civil war (the first of a series that came to be known as the Carlist wars) had been going on intermittently. On the one side were the Conservatives, including the clericals and the particularists in the provinces, who rallied around Carlos, Ferdinand's brother, claiming that a woman could not legally rule the whole of Spain, no matter what her status in certain provinces might be. Arrayed against them were the Progressists and Moderates, led by some liberal and opportunist elements in the army, who recognized Ferdinand's three-year-old daughter Isabella as their rightful queen, with her mother, Queen Christina, as regent. Obliged to make common cause with the liberals, Christina granted several significant constitutional concessions. In 1839 the Carlist movement temporarily collapsed with a convention between the opposing generals; and in 1840 Christina, fleeing the country, left the regency as a prize to be contended for by several generals. In 1843 Isabella, though only thirteen years old, was declared of age. The Moderate general, Ramón María Narváez, at the head of a coalition representing all shades of opinion, soon became the real ruler of Spain. In 1845 Narváez granted a constitution which contained several liberal provisions, but unofficially he was dictator of Spain until 1846 and at several intervals thereafter.

France and England had meanwhile preserved their Entente Cordiale by cautious cooperation in Spain's domestic complications. In 1846, however, Queen Isabella was married off to an old roué known to be incapable of fathering heirs to the throne, while her younger sister, next in line for the throne, married the youngest son of Louis Philippe, thus threatening once more to unite France and Spain in a Bourbon family alliance. Violating the spirit of earlier international agreements, the two marriages proved the very small rock on which the uneasy Anglo-French entente foundered. English public opinion now looked with less than sympathy on Louis Philippe's accumulating domestic complications.

**Other liberal
and national movements**

IN THE LESSER states of Europe liberalism and nationalism also shaped political events. In Sweden, where the erstwhile Jacobin general Bernadotte had become crown prince in 1810, he had developed into a reactionary absolutist. During his long reign as King Charles XIV (1818-1844), he had aroused the resistance of the Swedish estates. Under his successor Oscar, liberal opposition grew and gained some concessions softening the censorship. The quest for national freedom on the part of dominated minorities also entered the Swedish scene with the formation of a Young Norway party.

In Switzerland, the quarrel between liberal and conservative cantons had   123 steadily grown more serious. In 1845 the seven Catholic cantons formed the Sonderbund (Separatist League) to defend themselves against the growing agitation for national centralization, which they feared would leave them a minority in a tight federation dominated by the Protestant cantons. Two years later the diet, controlled by the liberal cantons, ordered the Sonderbund dissolved. The Catholic cantons refused, and civil war began. It ended within a few weeks with the defeat of the Sonderbund.

General tension throughout most of Europe　THE YEARS 1846-1847 were in many parts of Europe a period of economic hardship. The great Irish famine of the 1840's was only the first of a series of disasters. Poor harvests provided too scant a food supply for Europe's rapidly increasing population. A lull in commerce and manufacturing resulted, affecting especially the newer industrial regions. The factory owners suffered business losses; the working people faced unemployment, want, and even starvation. Economic conditions now reinforced political and social conditions to produce an atmosphere favorable to violence.

THE REVOLUTIONARY
SUCCESSES OF 1848

BY 1848 THE liberal-national movement, although focused on individual nations, was in a sense a European movement. Events anywhere were watched eagerly by liberals everywhere, and a blow for liberty in one country strengthened hope and determination in all. Disorder and armed conflict were already going on in Italy, Switzerland, and elsewhere when in February 1848 a great piece of news for liberals was spread quickly by telegraph, railroad, and daily press.

The end of the "July Monarchy"　DEAF TO PUBLIC opinion, Louis Philippe had believed that even the organized "banqueteering" of 1847 represented the efforts of only a small number of dissatisfied politicians. Nevertheless, he had been concerned enough to declare these banquets illegal, and he took steps to prevent a gala banquet planned for February 22, 1848. As their reply, the leaders of the opposition published a general denunciation of the government. In accordance with the king's orders, the banquet was not held, but a crowd, consisting mostly of students and laborers, gathered, more or less out of curiosity, at the appointed place. Excitement mounted, feeding on itself, and barricades appeared in the streets during the night.

Again, as frequently before, the decision between preservation and collapse depended more upon the regime's ability to defend itself than upon the strength of its attackers. The weakness of Louis Philippe became clear the following day when the king ordered the National Guard to quell the demonstration. To his surprise his orders met with defiance and cries of "Down with Guizot!" and "Long live Reform!" The disaffection of the National Guard at last convinced the king. He accepted Guizot's resignation and agreed to grant reforms. It was too late. Shots fired in defense of Guizot's residence inflamed the crowds and turned demonstration into riot that hourly increased in violence. Finally on February 24 Louis Philippe abdicated, leaving the throne to his nine-year-old grandson, the Count of Paris.

The fighting had been done mostly by workers and students, who were usually republicans. They seized the occasion for themselves. Although the Duchess of Orléans, popular mother of the young count, almost succeeded in having the Chamber of Deputies acknowledge her son as the new king, a group of right-wing republicans in the Chamber, aided by a mob, overawed the deputies, some of whom fled, and obliged them to proclaim a provisional government. Simultaneously a group of left-wing republicans in the City Hall of Paris also proclaimed a republic. The two groups then fused, and members of each were given places in the provisional government. Most prominent of the right-wing republicans was the poet-deputy Lamartine; most prominent of the left-wing republicans was the journalist Louis Blanc.

Revolution in the Austrian domains

THE NEWS SPREAD rapidly all over Europe and opened the stopcocks on pent-up emotions in a score of places. In the Hungarian diet on March 3 Louis Kossuth made an inflammatory speech in which he likened the Austrian system to a charnel house whence "a pestilential breath passes over us paralysing our senses and deadening our national spirit." The diet thereupon drew up an address to the emperor demanding a constitution. Kossuth's speech circulated openly in Vienna in spite of censorship, and soon a crowd gathered—mainly students and workingmen, as in Paris—and rioting began. Shots were fired, barricades went up, the imperial palace and the Austrian Diet were invaded. On March 13 Metternich offered to assume responsibility for the collapse of order and to resign. Glad of a scapegoat, the emperor accepted the offer, and the minister who had dominated central Europe for thirty-three years and whose name had come to signify an era and a system of government, followed Louis Philippe to exile in England, a victim of the national spirit he had tried so long to repress.

The downfall of Metternich signaled the end of his system. In Hungary the diet speedily enacted the Ten Points, which now became known as "the March Laws." Hungary thereby became practically an independent nation again, with its own responsible government, its own foreign office and ambassadors, its own national army and flag. The only connection with Austria

REVOLUTIONS OF 1848

KINGDOM OF
SWEDEN AND NORWAY

DENMARK

HOLLAND
Constitution of 1848

IRELAND

ENGLAND

'Chartist
Petition'

Constitution of 1850

PRUSSIA

Posen

HESSE-
CASSEL

SAXONY

FRANCE

Heidelberg
Committee

Frankfurt
Parliament

Stuttgart
Rump Parliament

BOHEMIA

Cracow

SWITZERLAND

AUSTRIAN EMPIRE

VENETIA

HUNGARY

K. OF
SARDINIA

LOMBARDY

CROATIA

CENTRAL
ITALIAN DUCHIES

PAPAL
STATES

KINGDOM OF THE
TWO SICILIES

that the March Laws required was allegiance to the Hungarian king, who at
the same time was emperor of Austria. The imperial government, under the
stress of revolution nearer home in Vienna, was forced to acknowledge the
Hungarian *fait accompli*. Bohemia likewise demanded and received from the
emperor the status of autonomy within the empire. Ferdinand in April promulgated a constitution for the whole of Austria except for Hungary, which
was now self-governing, and Bohemia, where a constitutional assembly was
being convoked. The Austrian liberals, however, found that the new constitution made too few concessions and they continued their agitation. In
May the emperor fled to the more temperate political climate of Innsbruck.

126 In June a Pan-Slav Congress met in Prague under Czech leadership, with

The Republic of Cracow had already lost its independence as a result of revolutionary activity in 1846 (see map, page 75), civil war had broken out in Switzerland, disorder was rocking Naples and Sicily, and the ruler of Tuscany in central Italy had been forced to grant a new liberal constitution when, in late February 1848, the French king was toppled from his throne. Open discontent traveled quickly throughout Europe. In some cases, the revolutionaries asked little more than measures of reform (Great Britain, Holland, Sweden, Denmark, Prussia, and Switzerland). Self-appointed German nationalists met at Heidelberg and took the first steps to create a National Assembly that met later at Frankfurt in an unsuccessful attempt to write a liberal constitution for all of Germany. In Italy, the king of Sardinia put himself at the head of Italian troops for a united Italian effort against Austria, which was obliged simultaneously to face revolt in Bohemia, Hungary, and elsewhere.

Palacky as president, to see what could be done to promote cooperation among the Slavic peoples of Austria.

Revolution and war of liberation in Italy

IN ITALY, we have seen, disorder had begun even before the news of the February uprising in France. Upon learning of the overthrow of Louis Philippe, Charles Albert of Sardinia early in March granted his subjects a liberal constitution. The popular Pope Pius IX, not to be outdone by his royal competitor, instituted a constitutional, parliamentary system for the Papal States. When news of the March revolution in Vienna reached Italy, it brought a lift to the hearts of nationalists. In the Austrian territories of Lombardy and Venetia, Italians rose against the hated *Tedeschi*. A revolt known as "the Five Days of Milan" (March 18-22) drove the Austrian troops from Lombardy. Before the Five Days were over the Venetians, too, had thrown out their Austrian garrisons and had proclaimed a republic. Under the veteran marshal Count Joseph Radetzky, the Austrian army retired to the Quadrilateral, a famous line of fortresses in northeastern Italy, and stayed on the defensive. Emboldened by these daring steps toward the independence of Italy, and unwilling to defy the patriotic clamor among his own people, Charles Albert declared war on Austria (March 22). His forces were quickly joined by detachments sent by the freshly inspired governments of the Papal States, Tuscany, Naples, Lombardy, and Venetia.

The Berlin revolt for constitution and unification

THE OVERTHROW of Metternich was a signal for action well beyond the limits of the Austrian Empire. In Berlin the excitement of Paris and Vienna was duplicated. Crowds of agitators composed mainly of students and workers demanded a constitution for Prussia. Accidental shots led to rioting, barricades, and civil war. Frederick William IV, still enamored of his role as patriarch, chose not to resist the popular demands. He donned the black, red, and gold colors of the German revolutionary movement and placed himself melodramatically at the head of the movement that he had for the last eight years been staving off. He convoked an assembly to draw up a constitution for Prussia, and he issued a proclamation in favor of German unification.

127

Liberalism and nationalism within the German Confederation THE REVOLUTIONARIES' success proved contagious. In many of the smaller German states constitutions were demanded and granted without great violence. The diet of the Confederation, yielding to the irresistible fervor, tried to change itself hastily into a liberal parliament by modernizing its organization, repealing its repressive legislation, and adopting the red, black, and gold flag.

But the nationalists of the Germanies were not to be satisfied with a mere face-saving of the old and inefficient diet. Early in March a group of self-appointed patriots had met without official sanction at Heidelberg and had appointed a committee to call delegates from all over Germany to form a *Vorparliament* (pre-parliament). The outstanding figure in this movement was Baron Heinrich von Gagern. This *Vorparliament,* made up largely of professors and men of letters, met at Frankfurt at the end of March and in turn drew up its own plans for a national assembly to draft a constitution for the whole of Germany. The delegates to this constituent assembly were to be elected by direct popular vote, each to represent 55,000 people.

The Frankfurt Parliament convened in May. The product of an unsanctioned popular movement, it nevertheless met with no opposition from existing governments, which were too overwhelmed by the events of March to protest. The rival—and legal—diet of the Confederation even lent it a certain official approval by sending greetings. Gagern was elected its president, and hope ran high for the achievement of a true German nation with a liberal government. Its distinguished personnel of lawyers, professors, judges, and businessmen augured a brilliant beginning for a united Germany.

Repercussions in the smaller countries THE REVOLUTIONARY contagion of March 1848 spread to the lesser capitals of Europe also. Riots in Copenhagen forced the Danish king to sanction plans for a popularly drafted constitution. Duly drawn up in the fall of 1848 and promulgated in 1849, the new constitution made Denmark a limited monarchy in which the king shared power with an assembly representing the upper and middle classes. In Holland delayed repercussions of the revolution of February-March produced a new constitution in October, under which the legislature was made more representative and the ministers were made more responsible. In Stockholm, riots—sometimes directed against Jewish shopkeepers—forced the government to promise a more liberal constitution. Almost alone of all the western and central European countries, Belgium, profiting from its earlier liberal government, avoided the upsets of 1848, encountering only one minor display of revolutionary disorder. Switzerland's Federal Constitution of 1848 resulted from the outcome of the Sonderbund War of 1847 and brought about lasting peace among the cantons.

Demonstrations
in Ireland and England

EVEN THE United Kingdom was not immune. The Young Ireland movement staged a rebellion in Tipperary in July 1848, but it was easily quelled. In England itself the last Chartist petition was presented to Parliament. This time the Chartists claimed to have nearly 6,000,000 signatures. They planned a big parade to present the petition to Parliament, and the government, becoming frightened, swore in nearly 200,000 special constables to preserve order, putting them under the command of the Duke of Wellington. The crisis was not without its touch of irony: one of Wellington's special constables was Louis Napoleon Bonaparte, who happened to be living in London, having two years before stolen out of the French jail in which he had been imprisoned for an attempted Bonapartist coup. Rain and half-hearted leaders induced the Chartists to call off their parade and send their petition to Parliament by cab. Upon examination it turned out to have fewer than 2,000,000 signatures, and some of them like "Queen Victoria" and "Pugnose" were obviously fictitious. The exposure put an end to the active Chartist movement.

THE FAILURE OF THE LIBERAL-NATIONAL

MOVEMENT (1848-1850)

THE SPRING of 1848 seemed to justify the fairest hopes of the bourgeois liberals. In the *Communist Manifesto,* published shortly after the February uprising, Marx and Engels even thought that the dictatorship of the proletariat might be close at hand. Might not the workers of the world unite to throw off their chains?

The temporary nature
of the republican alliance

WHILE THE Continent in the spring of 1848 shook under the triumphant surge of liberalism and nationalism, the Parisian incident that had brought the initial triumph was running its own course. In Paris the crying need was not to sweep away relics of medievalism and establish liberal institutions for the first time, or to expel an alien ruling people, or to unite divided peoples of the same nationality. The issue was the perhaps more complex one of how radical the new French republic was going to be. The spirit of compromise manifested in the first fusion of right-wing republicans and left-wing republicans (page 125) continued in evidence for a time, especially through the efforts of Lamartine. But good intentions were not strong enough to overcome the differences between them. The right wing, now known as the Republicans, favored *political* reform by the introduction of universal suffrage. The left wing, now known as the Socialists, wanted a *social* and *economic* transforma-   **129**

tion as well. Conciliatory attitudes rapidly gave way, and conflicting groups sparred for advantage.

*National workshops
and the Workers' Commission*

IN THE FIRST days of its existence the provisional government was placed under great pressure from the Paris populace, which was most articulately in favor of the left-wing program. Under its influence the moderates consented to the establishment of national workshops and a Workers' Commission. Blanc was made head of the Commission, with the workingman Alexandre Martin Albert, another Socialist member of the provisional government, as his second in command. They were given imposing offices at the Luxemburg Palace with moderate colleagues who were less impressed than they with the importance of their mission. Meanwhile Lamartine became the dominant figure in the provisional government.

The national workshops were intended by the Socialists to be a realization of the plans outlined in Blanc's *Organization of Labor* (page 95). In one of its earliest decrees the new government, under radical pressure, had declared its intention to "guarantee the existence of workers by means of labor" and to "assure work to all citizens." But the moderates soon diverted these experimental measures to their own ends. The management of the national workshops was sometimes entrusted to men who had little sympathy with the Socialists and who used their posts to discredit Blanc's idea—and, by implication, Blanc himself—among the workers. The Parisian unemployed, steadily growing in numbers because the revolution had disrupted production in many factories, were put to such make-work tasks as carrying dirt from one end of the Champ-de-Mars to the other and back again. This was a far cry from the workshop as conceived by Blanc, in which cooperatively employed men were to work productively in the skills in which they had been trained.

130

AS DIVERGENCES between moderates and radicals grew, each group became more suspicious of the other, and their animosities were reflected in the populace at large. Threatening, noisy demonstrations by Paris workers in March and April achieved little more than to raise a general alarm—a property-owner's "Great Fear." Had not the *Communist Manifesto* said, "A specter is haunting Europe—the specter of Communism"?

In this atmosphere the provisional government arranged for the election of a National Assembly to draw up a new constitution for the Second Republic. The delegates were to be chosen by universal male suffrage, and Lamartine took serious measures to prevent violence at the polls. The result was an extraordinarily large turnout of voters who obviously now preferred order to change. The Socialists suffered a crushing defeat. The Republicans won a large majority, and even the Orleanists outnumbered the followers of Louis Blanc.

Finding themselves practically impotent in the government, the Socialists took to direct action. The immediate occasion for an uprising came with the news that an attempted revolt in Poland had been pitilessly crushed by Prussian troops early in May. Lamartine, as minister of foreign affairs, refused to do anything to help the Poles. On May 15, amidst cries of "Vive la Pologne!" a crowd of workers entered the Constituent Assembly and attempted to overturn the government. They took control of the Chamber for five and one-half hours but were finally driven out by Lamartine and the loyal elements of the National Guard.

The moderates' response to the attempted coup was rapid and severe. They immediately suppressed the Workers' Commission, and in consequence, on June 21, abolished the national workshops. At that time the workshops employed over 100,000. The Assembly required the young men to go into the army and the others to go into the provinces to work on railroad embankments. The response was a prompt defiance. On June 23 barri-

The Italian sketches on these pages satirize the political sympathies current in the turbulent year of 1848. On page 130, the Chartist, the Bonapartist; here, the humanitarian, the Republican.

cades appeared once more in the working-class districts. Frightened but determined, the National Assembly made the Republican minister of war, General Louis Eugène Cavaignac, temporary dictator to deal with the emergency.

Cavaignac was no Louis Philippe, and besides he could count on his soldiers. He did not wait to be attacked. With 50,000 men he began the bloodiest street fighting Paris had yet seen. Notorious in history as the "June Days," the insurrection was quelled only after four days of bitter fighting (June 23-26). The insurgents were cornered only after about 10,000 had been killed or wounded and somewhat more had been taken prisoner. Eventually, in addition to those who were shot as rebels, around 4000 were sent to the penal colonies. Even the Jacobin Reign of Terror of 1793-1794 seemed mild in comparison to Cavaignac's dictatorship.

The June Days marked the emergence of open class warfare, an acknowledged breach between parliamentary liberals and revolutionary socialists, who had hitherto fought side by side to overthrow the forces of autocracy. As the bourgeoisie climbed to power, the working classes moved into opposition. Each party grew ever more deeply suspicious of the other; and the mounting suspicion inspired moderates, conservatives, and the peasantry with an unutterable dread of communism, while it rendered the socialists and workingmen more receptive to the class-war philosophy of Karl Marx. More immediately, it compromised the future of the Second Republic.

*The end
of the liberal dream*

IN THE SPRING of 1848, in almost every capital city of central and western Europe a new constitution was being drafted, fundamental rights of citizens were being guaranteed, censorship and political repression were being proscribed, and liberals could look forward confidently to a future framed by their own handiwork. In a few short months the liberal dream vanished. Much the same kind of conflict between the forces of order and the forces of change as had occurred in Paris by June 1848 took place also in the other capitals of Europe.

*Bohemia
returned to imperial control*

THE FIRST setback came in the Austrian domains even before the June Days of Paris. In Bohemia the Czechs were a majority and the Germans a minority. The two nationalities had cooperated in March to wrest concessions from Austria, but they soon began to quarrel over Bohemia's relation to the new Germany that, it was believed, was being created at Frankfurt. The Germans wanted Bohemia included in the new nation; the Czechs feared their own nationality might be thus engulfed. At the same time the Czechs heartily supported the Pan-Slav Congress that in June began its meetings at Prague, and in appearing ready to become absorbed in an Austro-Slav confederation, they gave the

Germans some grounds for concern. Pan-Germanism and Pan-Slavism thus crippled effective cooperation among the Bohemian liberals.

The imperial governor of Bohemia was Prince Windischgrätz, who as a loyal Austrian cared little for either ism. The mounting Czech excitement led to an attack upon his palace in which his wife was shot dead. Continuing disorders provided him with an opportunity to leave Prague with his troops and camp on the neighboring hills. He bombarded the city all the night of June 16-17 and returned in the morning to assume control. Martial law was declared, and the Bohemian revolution ended somewhat in the same manner as the June Days in Paris were to end a week later.

Sardinia defeated and Lombardy recovered

IN THE FOLLOWING month Austrian military strength and the lack of cohesion among the Italian states turned the tide in Italy also in favor of Austria. The ardor of Charles Albert's allies began to wear off quite early, since they were easily frightened by Austrian protests and the excesses of the revolutionaries. Pope Pius IX, declaring that he could not fight against the Catholic Austrians and that war was no way to win Italian unity, withdrew his contingent in April. In May, Neapolitan troops were also withdrawn when, recovering from his first alarm, King Ferdinand II crushed the revolution in Naples. Left alone with his Piedmontese forces, Charles Albert, after an elating victory at Goito on May 30, was badly defeated at Custozza on July 25. In August he signed an armistice, and Austria occupied Lombardy once more.

Civil war in Hungary and defeat of the Vienna liberals

THE NEXT Austrian successes came in Hungary. The Hungarian liberals, having achieved practical independence from Austria, were determined to weld a unified nation by denying the very existence of dissidence. Only one language, one nationality, and one set of institutions would be allowed. To the demands of their subject peoples for an autonomous position within Hungary similar to the Hungarian position within the Austrian Empire, the Magyars turned deaf ears.

As in Bohemia, these nationalistic differences provided the imperial government its opportunity. In Croatia, where rebellion against Magyarization was particularly intense, the Austrian emperor appointed a Croatian colonel, Count Joseph Jellachich, governor. Jellachich inflamed the Croatians' hatreds and stiffened their resistance to the Magyars in every way he could. At first, when liberal concessions seemed the best way to handle the revolutionary crisis, the imperial court had frowned upon Jellachich's defiance of Hungary, but after Windischgrätz' and Radetzky's victories, the court became bolder. In September the emperor authorized Jellachich to attack Hungary with Croatian forces; in October he declared the Hungarian diet dissolved. Among the Hungarians the fiery Kossuth took the position of leadership away

133

from the more conciliatory Deak and determined to resist the imperial onslaught.

At this juncture the liberals in Vienna arose in support of their fellow liberals in Hungary. Soldiers being sent to the front mutinied at the railway station. Barricades rose again, and the minister of war was murdered. In July the emperor had convoked a constituent assembly. Now, in order to offset the control of the radicals in the assembly, the court adjourned it to the provincial town of Kremsier. The radicals nevertheless refused to move, and they assumed control of the city. They found an able military defender in a Polish refugee officer named Josef Bem. The emperor called on Windisch-grätz to duplicate his performance at Prague, and Vienna in turn was bombarded into surrender on October 31. Meanwhile Jellachich defeated a Hungarian army coming to relieve the Viennese rebels.

*The strategy
of Prince Schwarzenberg*

A CALCULATING statesman of the Metternich school, Prince Felix Schwarzenberg, now became head of the government at Vienna, and under him the imperial position was reconsolidated. The government again controlled Vienna, Bohemia, and part of Italy. Negotiations were going forward for a final settlement with Charles Albert, and the general trend of events elsewhere in Italy was favorable to Austria. Only the Hungarian situation remained out of control.

Schwarzenberg's strategy was first to render the whole Hungarian movement illegal. He persuaded the weak Emperor Ferdinand to abdicate in favor of his nephew, the eighteen-year-old Francis Joseph, by-passing the claims of the old emperor's brother, father of the new emperor. The promises made to Hungary in the spring, Schwarzenberg reasoned, were not binding upon Francis Joseph. The government then prepared to throw all its military weight against the Hungarian rebels. And thus matters stood in the Austrian Empire at the end of 1848.

*The stifling
of the revolution in Prussia*

THE COURSE of events in France and Austria encouraged Frederick William IV of Prussia to adopt a less vacillating policy. Frederick William had made a certain show of going along with the liberal movement and had never lost his authority or popularity to the same degree as the Austrian emperor. On the other hand, the assembly engaged in drawing up a new constitution for Prussia had grown more and more radical and lost the support of the moderate liberals. Most important, the king had the loyal and efficient Prussian army to fall back on, and, when the moment seemed propitious, he did not hesitate to make a show of force. He dismissed the constituent assembly in December 1848 and thereby ended the Prussian revolution. In keeping with his paternalistic inclinations, Frederick William immediately granted to his people a constitution which was so liberal that, as he said, it made his stomach ache.

134

It turned out, however (page 145), to be more liberal in form than in substance.

The troubled career of the Frankfurt Parliament

MEANWHILE THE Frankfurt Parliament pursued the task of creating a liberal, united Germany. Throughout the summer and fall of 1848 they deliberated, argued, and theorized over such questions as (1) the form of the government—whether monarchy or republic, (2) the degree of authority to be vested in the proposed federal state, (3) the dispute between "Great Germans" (*Grossdeutsch*) and "Little Germans" (*Kleindeutsch*)—whether to include Austria with her non-German territories, without her non-German territories, or not at all, (4) the headship of the new German state—whether Austrian or Prussian, and (5) the extent of cultural autonomy to permit the non-German minorities.

As the Parliament debated these mooted questions, international events took the final decision out of its hands. It quickly revealed itself as at least as nationalistic as it was liberal. The Prussian army with the approval of many deputies suppressed a revolt in Posen, where the people were Polish and the government German; and at the request of the Parliament another Prussian army went to war to prevent the Danish king from disregarding the claims to autonomy of Schleswig-Holstein, where the people were German and the government Danish. Meanwhile the collapse of the radicals in France, Bohemia, Italy, Austria, and Prussia changed the climate of Europe from liberalism to reaction. When the Frankfurt deputies finally produced a constitution in the spring of 1849, they were to find that their golden opportunity to create a "Big Germany" had passed them by. Schwarzenberg, repudiating a liberal federal constitution drawn up by the Austrian constituent assembly at Kremsier, had dissolved it and in March had issued one of his own. It reëstablished the old Austrian Empire, making it, if anything, more highly centralized than before. Schwarzenberg in effect thereby declared that Austria was not to be considered as separable into German and non-German territories. When the Frankfurt Constitution was completed three weeks later, it was found to favor a *Kleindeutsch* policy, Austria being left out of the proposed German Empire. It also provided a bill of rights and a federal state under a hereditary emperor, with an elective two-house legislature, a responsible ministry, and a supreme court. The imperial crown was offered to Frederick William IV.

But that monarch, once more securely in power at home, declared that he would accept the new distinction only if it were conferred by the consent of the other rulers of Germany. He would not lower himself "to pick up a crown out of the gutter." Thereupon the whole movement collapsed. Austria withdrew her representatives from Frankfurt. When protest rebellions broke out in Saxony and some of the smaller states, Prussian troops suppressed

135

them with great severity. Soon other large states recalled their deputies, and Gagern resigned the presidency. The Parliament then passed into the hands of the more bitter and stubborn elements. It moved to Stuttgart, attempted an insurrection, and was closed in June by the government of Württemberg. The disappointment and the civil tumult had added many fugitives to the growing stream of German emigrants to the United States—"The Forty-Eighters."

Reaction and Bonapartism in France

WHILE LIBERALISM thus grew cold and weary in its involvements with nationalism in central Europe, the trend in France was not dissimilar. The June Days were followed by a severe repression under the temporary dictator Cavaignac. Insurgents were condemned to death or to exile in Algeria. Louis Blanc, though he had had no part in the insurrection, was obliged to flee, like Metternich and Louis Philippe, to a haven in England. Censorship was restored; clubs were placed under surveillance.

In an atmosphere thick with reaction the drafting of the constitution of the Second Republic was completed. The new constitution, based on "the Family, Work, Property, and Public Order" as well as "Liberty, Equality, and Fraternity," set up a moderate republic. Its legislature and its president were to be elected by universal suffrage. The president, chosen for a term of four years, was not permitted to succeed himself.

Meanwhile a new sun had begun to dazzle Frenchmen who scanned the political sky. In by-elections in June 1848 Prince Louis Napoleon Bonaparte had been chosen to the National Assembly by four departments. When he took his seat, he kept sufficiently circumspect to remain in everyone's good graces. In by-elections in September, although he was already seated, five more departments declared for him. Several developments conspired to make him look like just the right man for France. Among them were the Napoleonic legend, to which he had contributed a book or two himself, arguing that Napoleon had intended to eliminate poverty; the "Great Fear" of communism, which seemed to call for a stronger man than Lamartine though a less ruthless one than Cavaignac; the hopes of the Clericals, frightened by the excesses of the antipapal revolutionaries in Rome; the alienation of popular confidence from nearly every other conspicuous figure. Right and Left and Center had convenient and adequate reasons to vote for him. When the first elections were held in December 1848, the victorious candidate for president was Louis Napoleon. Swept into office by over five million voters (his opponents, including Cavaignac, Lamartine, and the Socialist Alexandre Auguste Ledru-Rollin, polling less than two million combined), he gave immediate evidence of the temper of his regime by appointing a ministry dominated by conservatives.

**The collapse
of the revolutions in Italy**

IN ITALY, a second effort of patriots to hang on to some of their
gains was made at the end of
1848 and the beginning of 1849. In the Papal States a republican uprising
caused the once liberal Pius IX to flee to Naples, and a Roman Republic was
proclaimed in February 1849. Under a triumvirate dominated by Mazzini,
the new republic soon became popular with the former papal subjects. Meanwhile a fresh burst of patriotism induced King Charles Albert to renew the
now unequal struggle with a triumphant Austria.

The effort was futile. Charles Albert was speedily defeated at the Battle
of Novara in March and, unwilling to continue as king, abdicated in favor
of his son Victor Emmanuel II. In June the new French president Louis
Napoleon, ignoring the constitutional proviso never to employ the forces of
the Republic "against the liberties of another people," sent an expedition to
Rome to restore the subjects of the pope to their theocratic ruler. Louis
Napoleon, who had once been a *Carbonaro* and had fought the pope's defenders in the ill-fated revolt of Rome in 1831, was now more interested
in posing as a champion of the papacy and in sharing the easy Austrian
victories in Italy. In that way he could hope to please the ultramontane and
the nationalist voters at the same time. The French forces met an unexpected
resistance from Mazzini's loyal followers led by Giuseppe Garibaldi, a colorful patriot and soldier of fortune, who like Mazzini had just returned from
exile. Only after a heroic defense followed by a month-long siege did the
Roman Republic capitulate. The Pius IX who returned to the papal throne
was now as hostile to liberal and national ideas as once he had been friendly.

The remainder of Italy was soon subdued. The grand duchy of Tuscany
was restored with Austrian aid. Sicily was recaptured by Ferdinand II of
Naples in a campaign in which he so often bombarded the Sicilian towns as
to win the name of "King Bomba." In August the Venetian Republic capitulated after a long siege and bombardment by Austrian forces. The Italian
revolution seemed to have ended in total failure. Only the Kingdom of
Sardinia retained its constitution, the "Statuto" that Charles Albert had
granted and Victor Emmanuel did not repudiate. Victor Emmanuel, by comparison with the restoration rulers of Florence, Rome, and Naples, soon
gained a somewhat unearned reputation as a heroic champion of liberty, and
the prestige of the house of Savoy grew among Italian nationalists.

**Hungary's
War of Independence (1849)**

IN KOSSUTH'S Hungary radical
republicanism still fought on,
though it was a losing fight. The
Magyars waged a determined war against the imperial forces during the first
months of 1849. Hamstrung by revolts among the Rumanians of Transylvania and by the vengefulness of the Croats, they nevertheless made an im-

pressive showing against the imperial forces. When Schwarzenberg's March constitution proclaimed a highly centralized government for all Austria including Hungary, the Hungarian government in April retorted with a declaration of independence and Louis Kossuth was declared president of the new Hungarian Republic.

This was a fatal step. An independent republic at the doorstep of Russia was not to Czar Nicholas' taste. In keeping with the Münchengrätz policy of cooperation to preserve the status quo, he offered to go to the rescue of his fellow-autocrat Francis Joseph, and in two months the fledgling republic was destroyed, its leaders in exile, and its generals hanged or shot without mercy by the Austrian general Haynau, sometimes called "Hyena." By the fall of 1849, peace was restored in the Austrian Empire. For yet a couple of years the constitution of March was to receive lip service, and after that even this slim disguise of constitutional government was to be dispensed with. Except that serfdom had at last been abolished throughout the Habsburg realms with compensation to the landlords, almost nothing but some sad lessons and some new heroes remained of the minorities' achievements of 1848-1849.

The failure
of the Prussian plan for union

MEANWHILE THE problem of what to do about the old Germanic Confederation had been left hanging. Frederick William did not object to German unification under Prussia provided it could be done by the cooperation of divine-right monarchs. He now proposed a German union of his own. His plan was to create a middle European bloc consisting of two parts, the Austrian Empire and a confederation of the remaining German states under Prussian dominance. He succeeded in getting many of the smaller German states to agree to this "Prussian Union," and in March 1850 a parliament met at Erfurt, where the Prussian proposal was accepted.

At this juncture, however, the Austrians asserted their interests. Prince Schwarzenberg made it plain that Austria would not tolerate Prussian leadership in a new German state. He demanded the restoration of the Germanic Confederation under Austrian headship, as of old. Since Austria seemed ready to go to war if necessary, and it seemed likely that Russia would support Austria, Frederick William yielded. In a Prussian-Austrian meeting known afterwards as the "humiliation of Olmütz," the representative of Frederick William agreed to the restoration of the Germanic Confederation as it had been during the pre-revolutionary era. Counterrevolution in Germany was now complete.

WHY DID A MOVEMENT so widespread and so immediately successful succumb almost as quickly as it had arisen? Were there to be only limited results from all this enthusiasm, idealism, upheaval, and loss of life? Were the forces of liberalism, nationalism, and socialism defeated once and for all, or were they to continue the struggle against the Old Regime and eventually to overthrow it?

The answers to some of these questions would be hammered out on the barricades and battlefields of Europe during the next twenty years. One thing was immediately clear, however. The revolutions had demonstrated that liberalism and nationalism were not always natural allies and that nationalism might triumph over liberalism if the two came in conflict.

The liberal movement failed also because of its own internal weaknesses. Its forces were divided. United in demolishing the old regimes, they fell apart when faced with building new ones. Almost everywhere, and most clearly in France, the alliance between the middle and the working classes, which had fashioned the force strong enough to overthrow autocracy, dissolved when its *raison d'être* was removed, and in its place appeared the bourgeois "Great Fear" of communism and the proletarian resentment of the rich. Furthermore, many petty differences arose among liberal theorists—between republicans and adherents of limited monarchy, between advocates of a qualified suffrage and advocates of universal suffrage, between proponents of laissez faire and proponents of state regulation. The very liberty of expression upon which they insisted led to divergence of opinion and to weakness of central control. Their very humanitarianism led to hesitation in the face of situations that called for force, and those who were willing to use bombs could generally overcome them.

A young Prussian Junker by the name of Otto von Bismarck, watching the speech-makers at Frankfurt with a certain contempt, was eventually to come to the conclusion that Germany's problems could better be solved by "iron and blood" (page 186). The nationalist sentiments of the disunited and subject peoples of Europe were in no way diminished by the failure of the revolutions of 1848. On the contrary, they were stimulated and aggravated by the heat of conflict and repression. But in the eyes of nationalist leaders popular liberalism had been discredited. Those for whom national unity was a greater good than liberty were forced to wonder whether the marriage of liberalism and nationalism was indissoluble, whether liberalism could not be divorced from nationalism, or at least subordinated to it. The future of nationalist movements, it seemed clear, lay not in peaceful, parliamentary methods but in toughness and force—in other words with *Realpolitik*.

The year 1848 thus became the turning point of nineteenth-century politics. Nationalism, theretofore allied with liberalism and romanticism, was to become militant and aggressive. The quest for liberty and equality was to continue a powerful movement, but its chief gains were to be made in states where national independence or unity was not the major quest. The outstanding example among those states was England. There, not only a deeply inculcated evangelical morality, as some historians have suggested, promoted   **139** the orderly quest for liberty but also the struggle for national unity and parliamentary government had in large part been won before the "Industrial Revolution" introduced new complexities.

The year 1848 was also a turning point in the history of the social movement. It marked the emergence of the class struggle both in theory, through the *Communist Manifesto,* and in practice, through the June Days in France. In succeeding decades socialism, like nationalism, was to grow less sentimental. The political alliance of the lower classes with the middle classes against the aristocracy—an alliance which had, despite marked ruptures, characterized the revolutions of that and earlier generations—was going to be abandoned now. Recognizing that the workers' strength lay in their effective solidarity, the leaders of the "fourth estate," more class-conscious perhaps than their followers and more insistent upon the "proletariat's" separate social and economic advantages, would with growing assurance proclaim that the lower classes must stand alone against the combination of the upper classes.

1791-1867	Michael Faraday
1795-1881	Thomas Carlyle
1799-1850	Honoré de Balzac
1799-1863	Eugène Delacroix
1809-1847	Felix Mendelssohn
1830	Stendhal's *The Red and the Black*
1831	Mazzini founds the Young Italy organization
1832	Parliament passes the Reform Bill
1833-1838	Negro slavery is abolished in the British empire
1833	Oxford Movement begins
1836-1848	Chartist movement
1837	Victoria ascends British throne
1837	Hector Berlioz' *Benvenuto Cellini*
1838-1839	Schleiden and Schwann prove that the cell is the structural and functional basis of both animal and vegetable matter
1839	Lord Durham's *Report on the Affairs of British North America*
1839	England, France, Austria, Prussia, and Russia mutually guarantee Belgium's perpetual neutrality
1839	Louis Blanc's *Organization of Labor*
1840-1855	Thiers' *History of the Consulate and the Empire* helps to revive the Napoleonic legend
1840-1841	Ottoman Empire is stabilized by the Treaty of London and the Straits Convention
1840	Union Act paves the way for Canada's dominion status
1840	Introduction of penny post in England
1840	Cunard Line established
1846	Pius ix (Pio Nono) elected pope
1846	Repeal of Corn Laws
1847	France completes conquest of Algeria
1848-1849	Revolts and revolution in western and central Europe
1848	John Stuart Mill's *Principles of Political Economy*
1848	Marx and Engels issue *Communist Manifesto*
1848	Abdication of Louis Philippe; establishment of Second French Republic
1848	Metternich overthrown in Austria
1848	Pan-Slav Congress meets in Prague
1848	Frankfurt Parliament
1848	Thackeray's *Vanity Fair*
1849	Hungary's war of independence
1850	Germanic Confederation restored to pre-revolutionary status
1851	Julius Reuter founds first extensive news-handling agency

Chapter three

FROM EMPIRE TO EMPIRE

Lıke the periods of reaction after 1815 and 1830, the 1850's saw on the Continent a general tightening of the controls over speech and press and a return to autocratic government. Reaction was not confined to rulers whose thrones had been threatened. Among landed aristocrats, peasantry, and bourgeoisie, socialism had ceased to be a mere chimera of impractical schemers and had become the more or less frightening "specter of Communism." Liberals too were disillusioned. As one former member of the Frankfurt Assembly put it, "The sad events of the years 1848, 1849, and 1850 completely cured me of my idealism." While idealistic Mazzinian revolutionaries continued to plot and dream in the little colony of exiles in London, their mass following dropped away. Many liberals, especially among disillusioned Germans, emigrated to the United States. Europe generally agreed with the aristocrat who said: "Let there be a time of heroes after the time of cryers and scribblers."

The "heroes" appeared, as heroes often do when large parts of the population are ready to welcome them. They were to take such different shapes as Disraeli, Bismarck, Napoleon III, and Cavour, and, as heroes sometimes will, they attempted to build great nations and empires. In so doing, they came into conflict with other great nations and empires or with each other. They met sometimes with opposition and sometimes with support in proletarian, clerical, liberal, literary, and scientific circles. Before the end of the period we are now to examine, they had changed the map of Europe, and they had helped to establish more firmly—sometimes by succeeding, sometimes by failing in their own purposes—the nationalist tone of European society and thought.

By 1850 even die-hard visionaries had to admit that the Revolution of 1848 had failed. In the United States, revolutionary leaders like the Hungarian Kossuth, the Italian Garibaldi, and the German Karl Schurz might still be welcome as noble leaders of lost causes, and republicans might venture to hope that President Louis Napoleon would make of France a worthy sister republic. But when the president of the new French Republic sent a French contingent to the defense of the Papal States, the political motivation behind his action was transparent. Whatever it might mean, it certainly did not portend devotion to the republican dogma on the part of the new Bonaparte.

Increase
of clerical influence

ONCE MORE, in many parts of the Continent, the conservative force of the established churches was to receive a new emphasis as throne and altar drew closer together in alliance against revolution. In France, Austria, and Prussia education was again turned over to the clergy. As the prochurch Thiers put it, religion is "the indispensable rectifier of the ideas of the people," or, as the antichurch Marx put it, "Religion is the opiate of the people." In Spain, Austria, and some of the smaller German states concordats were concluded with the pope in which the church secured much in the way of protection of church property and control over censorship, marriage, education, and other institutions touching the lives of its lay members.

Austria:
the Bach System

IN AUSTRIA the constitution promulgated by Schwarzenberg in 1849 was openly scrapped in 1851. Until 1860, the minister of the interior, Alexander Bach, maintained the so-called Bach System for all parts of the empire. Under this system petty bureaucrats from Vienna invaded the provinces in hordes to run the most minute affairs of districts whose languages they did not speak and of whose customs they were ignorant. The Vienna government, in an effort to stamp out the various nationalisms that had recently threatened to dissolve the empire, attempted to Germanize the non-German elements. This effort was especially notable in Hungary, where the diet and the county assemblies were suppressed, the country was divided up among the minority nationalities, and all parts were governed directly by Germans from Vienna. In general the Bach System stood for a high degree of repression and centralization. Habsburg absolutism, undisguised and rendered suspicious and uncompromising by its recent dangers, dominated the Habsburg realms 144 for an unhappy decade.

*Italy's return
to Austrian dominance*

IN ITALY the old political confusion grew worse. Lombardy and Venetia returned reluctantly to Austrian allegiance. Naples and Sicily were again ruled by their Bourbon dynasty, whose reactionary incompetence soon became proverbial. The rulers of Parma, Modena, and Tuscany either were spare Habsburg archdukes or were dominated by the Habsburgs. And the now quite reactionary Pope Pius IX again governed the Papal States, with the aid of French troops. Sardinia was the one wholly independent Italian state, and its house of Savoy was the one Italian dynasty that now made any pretense of liberalism.

*Repression
and reaction in Prussia*

IN PRUSSIA Frederick William's Constitution of 1850 was put into operation. Though it permitted the lower house of a bicameral legislature to be elected by universal manhood suffrage, voting was by a three-class system: those whose taxes together added up to a third of all the taxes chose one third of the deputies; those who paid the next third elected another third of the deputies; and all the rest of the voters (around 83 per cent) elected the remaining third. This franchise system produced—as was intended—a conservative legislature that had little power to restrain an autocratically minded king. Moreover, under Frederick William IV, elections were rigged to produce a docile legislature. Through spying and intimidation, any expression of liberalism in journals, public meetings, or even private correspondence was stifled. The Constitution of 1850 prevailed in Prussia until it was overthrown in the revolution of 1918.

*The creation
of the Second Empire*

IN FRANCE Louis Napoleon had by 1852 become as powerful as any royal autocrat in Europe, although he ruled behind the façade of a liberal constitution. His rise to power was rapid and almost unopposed. As president of the Second Republic he played along with an antirepublican legislature. When, however, the Assembly voted to restrict the suffrage to those who had lived in the same place for three years (thus eliminating the migrant worker), he acted as if he were the workers' friend. At the same time he supported the Vicomte de Falloux's program by which Catholic parochial schools obtained a wide area of expansion and the clergy were granted the right to inspect lay schools. At first he tried to have repealed the provision limiting a president to one four-year term. When he failed in that effort, he staged the famous coup d'état of December 2, 1851, deliberately planned to fall on the anniversary of the first Napoleon's coronation. He secured control of the army and the police, dissolved the Assembly, and arrested its leaders on the ground that they no longer represented the will of the people. Republican protests met with gunfire, arrest, and exile.

145

The president then submitted his action for popular approval. The plebiscite, skillfully manipulated but probably truly expressive of French popular sentiment, was overwhelmingly in his favor. It gave him the right to draw up a new constitution. He promptly did so, and the new constitution granted universal suffrage, but for a legislature whose power, like that of the legislature under the first Napoleon, was splintered. All really important functions were placed in the president's hands. The next year a second plebiscite gave equally overwhelming approval to the reëstablishment of the Napoleonic Empire. France at the moment obviously preferred order and glory to liberty, equality, and fraternity.

The theory of popular dictatorship

THE DEVICE of the plebiscite symbolized a significant difference between the autocracy of Napoleon III (as he now called himself) and that of other contemporary monarchs. The Second Empire, like the First, rested upon the consent of the governed, though the emperor was always ready, if necessary, to extract that consent by force. This relationship was an important determinant of both Napoleon's methods and his policies. He had to be popular, or at least to seem to be popular. To seem popular he suppressed all opposition—an old technique—and perfected several newer techniques to give a positive impression of popularity. One of these was the systematic manipulation of the press to give the illusion that public opinion supported him. Another was the use of universal suffrage both in electing the legislature and in periodic plebiscites held to support his policies. In elections to the Assembly the government supported official lists of candidates, and various kinds of pressure were employed to discourage opposition candidates from running or from getting votes if they did run. The seemingly democratic procedure thus produced the illusion of general approval of the emperor's policies.

In the employment of these devices, as in the concept of dictatorship by popular consent, the Second Empire foreshadowed twentieth-century totalitarianism. But the Second Empire was an incomplete totalitarianism. It was comparatively easygoing in its efforts to regiment Frenchmen and French institutions. It did not resort, as Nazism would, to dubious theories of racial superiority. Like Communism, it spoke loudly of peace, but, like Fascism, its police regime and its militarism were inefficient. Its propaganda techniques and repressive machinery were, by twentieth-century standards, rudimentary. Toward the end it even proved willing to make political concessions in order to rest upon a foundation of public approval rather than force.

The "honeymoon" of the Second Empire

FOR ABOUT eight years Napoleon managed to keep the balance of public opinion strongly in his favor. He was able to be, or to seem to be, all things to all men, by riding with uncanny insight (or by happy accident) all the currents and crosscurrents of the times. He was the friend of the church, supporting the return of education to clerical influence, defending the pope with French troops against the insurgents in the Papal States, encouraging Catholic missions, and giving government funds to Catholic churches, schools, and charities. To the revolutionists he was an ex-Carbonaro who had now become the great democrat, the direct representative of the people without the interposition of a legislature—"invoking the solemn judgment of the only sovereign that I recognize in France, the people." To the socialists he was a "Saint-Simon on horseback," a decrier of capitalism, and a friend of the workingman, who founded hospitals, asylums, and charities, distributed free medicine, established government credit institutions, improved workers' living conditions, and provided more employment and higher wages. To the property owners, especially the bourgeois and the peasant, he was the strong man, the savior of society, who held down the communist menace as his uncle had suppressed Jacobin radicalism. To patriots, tired of Louis Philippe's appeasement, his challenge of Austrian hegemony in Italy seemed to promise a new set of international trophies which could be purchased at small cost. To European monarchs he represented the restoration of authority and stability, which excused his being an upstart. They recognized him as emperor quickly, although Nicholas of Russia was careful to call him "great and good friend" instead of "my brother," as was customary among monarchs. Though some radicals and exiles, including Victor Hugo, who dubbed him "Napoléon le Petit," and Karl Marx, who attacked his coup d'état in a bitter essay (1851), refused to join the general chorus of satisfaction, at home opposition for a time was disorganized.

BOOM, WAR,
AND PANIC (1850-1857)

THE CALIFORNIA gold rush of 1849 and the Australian gold rush of 1851 combined with the intense industrialization of Europe and with systematic overseas exploitation to make the years following the Revolution of 1848 an era of easy money and great prosperity. Until the great financial crisis of 1857 the "boom" continued uninterrupted, aided by the profits of the intervening Crimean War. Even the panic of that year proved to be only a momentary disruption in the program of rapid industrial and financial expansion.

Napoleon III   ALTHOUGH he had campaigned
as a patron of industrialization   for the presidency as an anti-
capitalist, the emperor's policies were exceptionally favorable to capitalists. The Second Empire became a great age of French industrialization. Railroad mileage increased sixfold, and

The scene above shows the ceremonies celebrating the opening of the new railway station at Brest in 1865. During the Second Empire, France enormously increased her track mileage.

the horsepower of machines increased fivefold. Steamship lines were founded, canals dug, and by 1855 every prefecture in France had its telegraph office. Two government-authorized credit institutions, the Crédit Foncier, specializing in real estate mortgages, and the Crédit Mobilier, specializing in investment loans, financed this expansion. In 1854 the Crédit Foncier became a government institution. It was a boom era. Napoleon's largess was supplemented by the increased gold supply coming from Australia and California after 1850. Speculation was rife, and huge fortunes were made almost overnight. The stock of the Crédit Mobilier, issued in 1852 at a par of 500 francs, was in 1855 worth 1982 francs a share.

The working classes benefited from the general prosperity, though not to the same extent as the capitalists. In addition, the workers derived keen satisfaction from a great public works program, of which Baron Haussmann's rebuilding of Paris was the major feature. Much of the old city was torn down and rebuilt on a monumental scale. Broad avenues replaced the narrow, crooked streets that in the workers' quarters had been so easy to barricade and defend. A new water and sewer system replaced the old. The grandiose Opéra was built. And all this involved such great expenditures of money as to lead to charges of waste and corruption.

A lavish and showy court vied for the favor of the gay and beautiful Empress Eugénie, a Spanish countess whom Napoleon had married in 1853. While the old court society remained spitefully and scornfully aloof from the parvenu royalty, the bourgeoisie eagerly imitated the royal standards. A dazzled and prosperous people scarcely missed its liberties. In 1855 an international exposition in Paris glorified the technological and material progress of France and the emperor who fostered it.

Industrialization elsewhere in Europe

WESTERN Europe in general experienced a similar expansion of industrial life. Under the sober governments of the 1850's businessmen regained their confidence in a stable future and once more ventured their capital. Other countries besides France felt the stimulus of the new gold supplies from Australia and California. The expansion of credit through new banks in Austria, Germany, and elsewhere also made it easy for businessmen to get capital for new ventures. Governments found it simple to borrow money, and resorted more commonly to bonds sold directly to the public, postponing repayment if the need arose, or to loans from finance companies than to loans from the great private banking families. Napoleon III deliberately encouraged the Crédit Mobilier in order to offset the power that the Rothschilds had acquired in business and politics in the important money centers of Europe.

Government aid to business enterprise

WHILE more capital was thus becoming available, its investment was made safer by the wider application of the principle of limited liability. The French Commercial Code (1807) recognized three types of business associations—the partnership, the limited partnership, and the corporation. These kinds of business firms, together with the single-man and the family firm, were common in the western world. In the partnership, any partner was liable for the debts of his company to the limit of his fortune, and a man might be ruined in a single venture. In the other forms of business association, the extent of liability was more limited—usually by some sort of advance understanding obligating some investors more than others. The growth of banks, like the Crédit Mobilier, in corporate form stimulated the growth of new corporations, not only in banking but also in railroad and other industrial developments. Stockholders naturally tried to limit their individual obligations to creditors as much as possible. Beginning in 1855 England passed a series of laws, which were eventually copied everywhere, legally limiting the liability of the investor to the amount of his investment.

This legislation further stimulated the development of corporations, and such great, impersonal business organizations rapidly came to be a characteristic feature of industrial enterprise. Big business also typically received some sort of government aid—a subsidy, a guarantee of a certain profit, or an underwriting of interest on bonds—especially in railroad building. Thus the plutocrat was preëmpting the position of special privilege that in an earlier age had been reserved for the aristocrat.

*British leadership
in commerce and industry*

ENGLAND remained the leader in trade and industry, and continued to export not only her manufactures but her skill and her capital. British railroad contractors built many of the continental and American railroads of the early fifties, and British capital helped finance them. Britain developed the finest industrial methods. The demand for rails and other hard-metal products led to investigation of the difference between iron and steel. After it was determined that the difference lay chiefly in the relative amount of carbon, Henry Bessemer in 1856 discovered a process whereby carbon and other impurities can be removed from iron by a forced blast of hot air and a precise amount of carbon restored, thus producing a good standard steel economically. In 1866 the improved open-hearth process was invented by a naturalized Englishman, William Siemens. While in France trade unions survived despite the ancient laws that forbade them and despite police repression, English law did not prohibit, though it did severely restrict, the formation of labor associations. After 1840 the trade-union movement made real headway among the coal miners. In 1851 the Amalgamated Society of Engineers was formed, a nation-wide craft union of skilled workers with a nation-wide policy. In 1859 a carpenters' union was formed on the same model. Though the strikes that occurred in the 1850's were unsuccessful, the trade union remained a cardinal feature of the English industrial scene.

*Outbreak
of the Crimean War*

EVEN WHILE the Paris exposition was dramatizing the achievements of the Second Empire, French soldiers were fighting on the faraway Crimean Peninsula in a war in which France had no vital stake and sought only glory and prestige. The Crimean

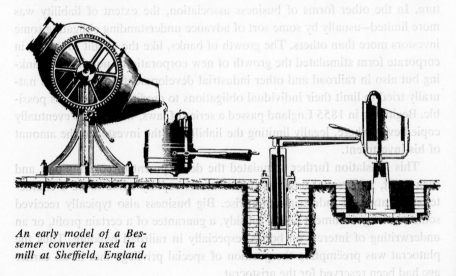

An early model of a Bessemer converter used in a mill at Sheffield, England.

War arose from a dispute between various Christian sects over control of the "holy places" in Palestine. Napoleon III championed the cause of the Roman Catholic Church, and Czar Nicholas that of the Greek Orthodox Church. The matter had presumably been settled by negotiation with the Turkish government, in whose domain the holy places were located, when the czar, convinced that Turkey was "the sick man of the East" whose heirs had better divide his property speedily, put forward a new claim. On the basis of a treaty negotiated in 1774, he insisted upon his right to protect all Greek Christians on Turkish soil. The British, anxious to preserve the integrity of the Ottoman Empire, did not believe the Turk was sick beyond recovery. The British ambassador encouraged the sultan to reject Russia's claim as a threat to Turkish sovereignty. Thereupon Russia sent troops to occupy the sultan's provinces of Moldavia and Wallachia, thus precipitating war between Russia and Turkey (1853).

The czar had figured on a localized war, but he was mistaken. Britain, anxious to prevent Russian expansion toward her route to India, and France, whose emperor was eager to clothe his new empire with military glory and to revenge the humiliation of the great Napoleon at Russia's hands, came to the sultan's aid in 1854. Nursing the hope of winning friends for a future attempt to unite the Italian states, Count Camillo di Cavour, the prime minister of Victor Emmanuel II of Sardinia, induced his sovereign too to join the western allies in 1855. Thus came the first war among the great powers of Europe in the forty years since the Congress of Vienna, as Russia found herself confronted by a coalition of Turkey, England, France, and Sardinia. It was the first European war in which mechanized warfare in the form of the steamboat, the railroad, the electric cable, and the revolver played a significant role, and it played that role almost entirely to the advantage of one side.

The fighting and its lasting results NEARLY ALL the fighting of the war took place on the Crimean Peninsula, where the key Russian fortress and naval base of Sevastopol was located. Sevastopol was besieged for eleven months, finally falling after a terrific bombardment. The warfare was notable chiefly for its exposure, after several decades of peace, of inefficiency in the participants' armies. The loss of life on both sides was appalling and mostly unnecessary. This pitiful situation was reported by William Howard Russell, the London *Times'* correspondent: "Not only are there not sufficient surgeons...not only are there no dressers and nurses...there is not even linen to make bandages." Out of the resulting indignation came the work of Florence Nightingale, who immediately organized hospitals and medical care in the Crimea for the British sick and wounded, and later (1864) became the inspiration of the International Red Cross. The Briton's admiration of his fellow countryman's soldierly qualities and his grief that

151

THE NEAR AND FAR EAST, 1853-1856

RUSSIA

Russian Pressure

Okhotsk

Nerchinsk

Nikolaevsk

UNITED
KINGDOM

Crimean War

Russian Pressure

Kiakhta

Amur R.

Petropavlovsk

FRANCE

Kuldja

MANCHU CHINA

Anglo-French
naval repulse
1854

OTTOMAN
EMPIRE

K. OF
SARDINIA

BRITISH
INDIA

Occupied by Russia
1853 and by
Austria (1854-1857)
Joint Guaranty
of Powers 1856

RUSSIAN LOSSES
BY CRIMEAN WAR

MOLDAVIA

WALLACHIA

OTTOMAN EMPIRE

Sevastopol

As the inset map shows, the military outcome of the Crimean War hinged on the allied siege of Sevastopol. The diplomatic stakes were in the Balkan and Danube areas. The peace in 1856 took from Russia part of the Dobruja (restored to the Ottoman Empire) and part of Bessarabia (given to Moldavia), thus putting the mouths of the Danube farther from Russia's grasp; set up autonomous but separate principalities in Moldavia and Wallachia under joint guaranty of the powers; declared the Black Sea neutral and the navigation of the Danube free. As the large map shows, Russia had also been exerting pressure and encountering opposition in central Asia and the Far East. (The Chinese-Russian frontier, as indicated by the broken line on this map, was not yet well defined.)

"someone had blundered" were reflected in the poet laureate Alfred Tennyson's "Charge of the Light Brigade" (1854). Out of the blunders of the war were to come far-reaching changes in Russia, as it became clear that the incompetence and corruption of Russian officials were responsible for her final defeat.

The peace conference and the Treaty of Paris (1856)

JUST AS he had planned, Napoleon III emerged from the war the leading figure of Europe. His beautified capital, Paris, was host to the peace conference, and his prestige was never greater. On the other hand, Russia was isolated. Austria and Prussia, having studiously preserved their neutrality during the war, now acted in concert with the victors to stifle Russia's urge toward the Straits. The Black Sea was declared neutral, as formerly the Straits had been, and no country was to be permitted to sail warships or maintain arsenals there. Navigation of the Danube was declared free, and Russia was pushed back from the Danube by the cession of a strip of Bessarabia to Moldavia. The Rumanian provinces of Moldavia and Wallachia, long coveted by Russia, were temporarily placed under joint guaranty of the powers, their permanent status to be determined later. The Paris treaty also formally admitted Turkey to the Concert of Europe and guaranteed her independence and territorial integrity.

The peace conference also undertook to act as an international legislative body and dealt with other matters of general interest. It issued the Declaration of Paris, abolishing privateering and limiting the rights of blockade and of capture of neutral goods by belligerents at sea. This declaration was eventually accepted formally by all the great maritime powers except the United States, which felt it did not go far enough in protecting the property of neutrals but which proved willing to adhere to it in practice. Because of Sardinia's part in the war, the conference also discussed briefly the "Italian question." Cavour's moderate presentation of the case against Austrian troops in Italy impressed his listeners, elicited expressions of sympathy from Napoleon III, and raised the prestige of Sardinia, but led to no positive action.

The decline of the idea of "legitimacy" THE CONGRESS of Paris might have seemed, at first glance, to evidence that the Concert of Europe was still operating, as it had since 1815, to preserve "legitimacy" and the European balance of power. Actually it marked a turning away from the Vienna system. Now three major powers were interested in changing the "legitimate" map of Europe: Russia, hitherto the most ardent preserver of the status quo (except in the Near East), was eager to upset the Paris settlement of the Black Sea, the Danube, and the Rumanian provinces; Prussia, despite "the humiliation of Olmütz," continued to be interested in making changes in central Europe; Napoleon III, to whom the post-Napoleonic settlement of 1815 was a standing challenge, contemplated redrawing the boundaries of Europe in a way that would make him appear the champion of the principle of nationalities. Austria, favoring the status quo, faced a potentially hostile Prussia in Germany, a potentially hostile Russia in the Near East, and a potentially hostile France in Italy; and though she might expect support from England in the effort to preserve the Ottoman Empire, she could not count on English public opinion to oppose the nationalist aspirations of the Germans and the Italians. Cooperation for the preservation of the status quo was to become hard to achieve, and the next fifteen years witnessed a rapid series of short, decisive wars among the great powers.

The question of Moldavia and Wallachia AFTER the conference, the Danubian principalities still constituted an unfinished problem. Napoleon III, as self-appointed champion of the principle of nationalities, pushed the idea of their union into a single state. He was supported by Russia and opposed by Turkey, Austria, and England. Finally the inhabitants themselves were allowed to choose. The majority voted against the union, but these plebiscites were so blatantly manipulated by the supervising Turkish officials that Napoleon refused to accept them. For a time, war threatened between France and England, but eventually both sides agreed to new plebiscites. The Rumanians were now permitted to vote for or against a deliberately loose federation in which the two provinces would have separate governments but with a central commission for common affairs. The plebiscites approved this compromise. Subsequently, however, Rumanian nationalism triumphed. Both provinces elected the same prince, Alexander Cuza, as ruler. Cuza worked skillfully toward the strengthening of common institutions, and four years later, in 1862, the powers recognized the principalities as the single nation of Rumania.

The panic and business crisis of 1857

MEANWHILE, until 1857, the era of unprecedented business expansion had continued and had produced much speculation, both healthy and fraudulent. The Crimean War had increased profits in the war industries and had raised the speculative fever. Shortly after the peace the bubble burst, panic spreading from America to Europe. The international character of the "crash" was eloquent testimony of the extent to which, even in the mid-nineteenth century, the world had become economically interdependent.

The crash also underlined the insecurity of the individual in an industrial economy. A plot of land and a man's willingness to turn a hand had once seemed sufficient to overcome economic hardship unless it was caused by the ravages of nature, but the complexities of the industrial system seemed unwilling to yield to individual effort. In times of boom a man could normally expect to profit from easy money, and in times of depression he would be lucky to escape hardship, no matter what his individual capacities might be. Industrialism appeared to spurn the individual and to breed economic instability, which in turn bred a less stable society, one susceptible to the unsettling appeal for personal or human betterment in the slogans and platforms of collective movements like nationalism and socialism.

SCIENCE, REALISM,

AND NATIONALISM (1850-1870)

THE POLITICAL reaction to the events of 1848 was only dimly paralleled in intellectual endeavor. Metaphysical speculation went out of fashion, and materialist philosophies became immensely popular. In literature and art romanticism became passé, and realism came to the fore. In music, the most cosmopolitan of the arts, a nationalist temper began to appear. In science, the urge toward the synthesis of earlier findings seemed to become stronger.

*Progress
in the laws of physics*

TWO OF THE most important laws of physics were established in these decades. The law of the conservation of energy—that energy can be neither created nor destroyed—came to be generally accepted in the 1850's. By varied experiments Hermann Helmholtz and James Prescott Joule provided further confirming data for this law. In 1852 William Thomson (later Lord Kelvin) established the law of the dissipation (or degradation) of energy, which stated that while the total of energy in nature is constant, available energy is continually decreasing through degeneration into nonusable or dissipated heat. These laws had been tentatively formulated by earlier scientists, but they now caught on and became common scientific principles.

In electrodynamics James Clerk Maxwell carried forward the work of Faraday on the nature of the electromagnetic field, translating the almost intuitive hypotheses of the nonmathematical Faraday into mathematical terms. In a series of essays between 1861 and 1873 Maxwell pointed out that light seems to travel in the fashion of electric and magnetic waves. Thus a close relationship was established between light, electricity, and magnetism. Maxwell also developed the kinetic theory of gases, ascribing the changes of direction and velocity of gas molecules, and hence the pressure that they exert, to their continual motion and collision with each other and other things. He also studied color and color blindness. Thus Maxwell contributed profoundly to the synthesis of various phenomena of physics—heat, light, mechanics, magnetism, electricity.

*The spectroscope
and spectrum analysis*

IN SOME WAYS the most important scientific invention of the period was the spectroscope, devised by two German scientists in 1859. One of them was Robert Wilhelm Bunsen, who had already invented the "Bunsen burner," which permitted the effective mixture of air and inflammable gas in the production of heat. The other scientist was G. R. Kirchhoff. Their spectroscope was an ingenious combination of a telescope and a prism, by which the characteristic spectrum, or band of colors, radiating from any substance might be studied. Since it was already known that certain elements produced certain spectra, it was now possible with the spectroscope not only to discover new chemical elements (as Bunsen and Kirchhoff did) but also to determine the elements of which heavenly bodies were composed. Thus the study of astronomy acquired a new method and purpose. The spectroscope enabled Kirchhoff to discern the so-called Fraunhofer lines in the solar spectrum and to deduce therefrom the existence of certain incandescent elements in the sun's atmosphere.

Thus in 1868 Norman Lockyer found helium in the sun before it was discovered on earth.

The periodic law of chemical elements

IN CHEMISTRY the most significant achievement of the period was also a systematizing of previous knowledge. It had earlier been learned that when chemical elements were arranged in ascending order according to their atomic weights, they tend to fall into groups of eight having similar properties. In 1869, the Russian chemist Dmitri Mendelejeff propounded the periodic law: that the properties of chemical elements are periodic functions of their atomic weight. This meant that if all the known elements were arranged according to their ascending atomic weights, they should be found to be related to one another according to their position in the table. Noting marked differences of properties in certain neighbors in his table, Mendelejeff deduced the existence of elements yet undiscovered whose absence explained the gaps in the gradual change of properties. His deduction was verified by the rapid discovery of missing elements having the chemical and physical properties that had been predicted in advance with surprising accuracy.

The physical sciences and the study of human beings

THE ADVANCING knowledge of the chemistry of organic matter, making possible the synthetic duplication of the products of nature, had disturbing implications for philosophy. Was the mystery of life or the nature of reality simply a series of chemical reactions? The materialist philosopher Ludwig Andreas Feuerbach went so far as to assert that the failure of the revolutions of 1848 was due to faulty nutrition—too many potatoes; his remedy was fewer potatoes and more beans. Physicists like Helmholtz and Maxwell studied the physics of hearing and seeing. Two German scientists, Ernst Weber and Gustav Fechner, studying similar problems from the physiological point of view, laid the foundations of an independent science of psychology. They attempted to delineate the relationships between physical stimuli and mental sensations, calling their studies "psycho-physics."

Progress in medicine and surgery

IMPROVED knowledge of physics and chemistry brought greater progress in medical science and surgery. This progress was made possible in large part by the development of pain-killing drugs to produce anesthesia (pages 233-234). In 1851 Helmholtz was able to measure the speed of the nervous impulse. Two inventions by Helmholtz (1851 and 1864) made possible the examination of the interior of the eye and the measurement of its size, permitting the perfection of the science of ophthalmology, or the physiology of the eye. Outstanding leaders in physiology of the day were Louis Pasteur and Claude Bernard. Bernard applied the experimental method to medicine and was able to shed great light upon the functions of the pancreas, the liver, and the vasomotor system. Pasteur had long been engaged in France in those bacteriological experiments with the fermentation of beer and milk and the diseases of the silkworm that were later to lead to a full-fledged germ theory of disease. In 1864 he was able to assert that bacilli caused fermentation and that they were ordinarily present in the air. England's leading surgeon, Lord Joseph Lister, quickly recognized that bacilli similarly must cause the fermentation of the blood—i.e., putrefaction. He applied (1865) carbolic acid to wounds in order to exclude the atmospheric germs. Thus began antiseptic surgery—the careful disinfecting of wounds, hands, and instruments and the general use of antiseptics—dramatically reducing the incidence of infection and the number of deaths therefrom.

Darwin's theory of natural selection A MOST influential example of scientific synthesis was Charles Darwin's theory of the origin of the various living species. Speculation on the ascent of man from lower forms of animals was as ancient as the Greeks, and the idea had found favor with some French naturalists of the late eighteenth and the early nineteenth centuries. Charles Lyell's *Principles of Geology* (1830) had demonstrated the slow development of the earth's crust, and he and other geologists had found in the rocks evidence of the affiliation of living things. Building on these foundations and upon inferences derived from Malthus' views of the struggle for existence, Darwin was able to expound a theory of the evolution of all life forms, including man, in a single more acceptable and comprehensive theory. Another English naturalist, Alfred Russell Wallace, had been reaching the same conclusions at the same time. Briefly, their thesis was that variations of physical characteristics, sometimes only minute, may occur in any species and that, in the constant fight against nature's hardships and animals of prey, those individuals survive whose variations have best adapted them to their environment. These individuals become the progenitors of offspring that in turn survive by virtue of the same characteristics or further variations of them. By this process of "natural selection" all new species, including man, have arisen from the primordial one-celled animal.

Darwin had formulated his ideas as early as 1842 but for years did not venture to publish them. Finally a time arrived when bold generalizations had become so common as to make his theory, he hoped, less shocking. With a wealth of evidence collected through years of investigation, he published it in 1859 under the title *On the Origin of Species by Means of Natural Selection*. At once it thrust into the open the none too latent controversy between science and theology, because it appeared to challenge the Biblical account of creation, to repudiate the special position of man in the universe, and to attribute to him an exclusively materialistic, or non-spiritual, origin. Among its most ardent defenders was Thomas Henry Huxley, 157 an English biologist of wide repute. On the lecture platform and in articles and books Huxley popularized the theory of evolution and, more boldly than Darwin, applied the scientific spirit to questions of religion, coming eventually to the conclusion that the idea of a moral purpose in the cosmic process was "of exclusively human manufacture." He was the first to use the word "agnosticism" to describe suspension of judgment regarding the existence and nature of God. Huxley's lively debates with pious statesmen and clergymen were renowned. Society rapidly split into two sides on the question of man's ancestry—that of the "monkeys" and that of the "angels."

While this controversy raged, Darwinism was warmly received by social philosophers like Herbert Spencer, by laissez-faire economists, who welcomed the thesis that competition in the struggle for survival was the kernel of evolutionary advance, by Marxians, who saw in the process of natural selection a buttress of their materialistic determinism, and, later on, by nationalists, who interpreted politics as a struggle for existence and survival among the fittest of the nations. In fact, so popular was the Darwinian thesis that it often lent arguments to both sides in controversies quite unrelated to biology.

Studies in heredity and eugenics

THE DARWINIAN thesis inevitably lent interest to studies of heredity. Darwin's cousin Sir Francis Galton developed in the sixties the idea that the "fit" should be encouraged to reproduce and the "unfit" restrained from reproducing, a thesis he later dubbed "eugenics" and expanded with studies of hereditary factors in genius. In the 1860's an Austrian monk named Gregor Johann Mendel developed more precise laws of heredity. Working in obscurity with the crossbreeding of garden peas, Mendel discovered that some characteristics of crossbred parent plants could be segregated for experimental purposes, could be classified as "dominant" and "recessive," and tended to reappear in successive generations in fixed ratios. Mendel's work, first published in 1866, remained almost unnoticed until the end of the century, when it was to form the basis of searching experiments in heredity.

Spencer and social evolution

THE DARWINIAN explanation of biological evolution fitted admirably into the hopeful temper of the age. That hopefulness was also expressed in the works of the English philosopher Herbert Spencer. Even before the publication of Darwin's thesis, Spencer had developed a theory of social evolution. In fact, it was from Spencer that Darwin borrowed the phrase "survival of the fittest." The Darwinian theory of natural forces working unknowingly to bring about successive changes fitted into Spencer's philosophical preferences. He equated biological evolution to social progress and elevated it to the position of a fundamental cosmic law. Evolution from the simple to the complex, from the

158

homogeneous to the heterogeneous, from the less fit to the more fit, was the essence of this great cosmic process. The perfection of the individual seemed to him the objective of biological evolution, while the objective of social evolution was a perfect society in which the individual would have free play and government would exist only for the individual's protection. In other words, Spencer's theory of social evolution was a philosophic justification of the British Utilitarians and laissez faire. His social philosophy was immensely popular in England and even more so in America.

In the sixties Spencer issued the syllabus of a work of heroic dimensions called *Synthetic Philosophy*. The project, completed in 1896 with the tenth volume, entitled *Principles of Sociology,* was an attempt to summarize and synthesize science, politics, and philosophy in terms of evolution. With its emphasis on positivism and empirical explanations, Spencer's *Synthetic Philosophy* was a remarkable expression of the confidence of the Victorian age in science and progress.

Mill's On Liberty *and Marx's* Capital IN THE same year that Darwin explained the evolution of the biological organism in his *Origin of Species,* two other epoch-making works were published. The Victorian faith in freedom of opinion found its classic expression in John Stuart Mill's *On Liberty.* Appearing in 1859 in protest against the reactionary trend of affairs on the Continent, this treatise argued the case for individual liberty— especially intellectual freedom—as the surest means to political and social progress. Free competition of ideas, Mill held, was the best determinant of truth. Individual liberty of opinion was not so much a natural right, therefore, as a "utility"—a means toward "the greatest happiness of the greatest number" —and was to be protected against even "the tyranny of the majority," "the tyranny of the prevailing opinion and feeling." Mill perceived a danger of error in conformity and convention.

For Karl Marx such conformity was part and parcel of the class struggle. Writing in exile in London, he attempted to explain the evolution of the social organism in *On the Criticism of Political Economy.* This work as subsequently reorganized and rewritten achieved fame under the title *Das Kapital.* Of the revised work Marx completed the first of three volumes in 1867; the remaining two were put together by Engels from rough manuscript, excerpts, and plans left by Marx. Here the authors expanded the materialistic interpretation of history in general and of the capitalistic system in particular that they had already outlined in the *Communist Manifesto.* As Marx interpreted history, determinism rather than liberty was the keynote. Man's way of making a living, he contended, has in all ages determined who shall rule and hence the character of all man's other institutions and attitudes. As the modes of production change, revolution produces a new dominant class, new thought patterns, 159 and new social institutions. Under the capitalist system the workingman, whose labor alone creates the value of any product, is exploited by the bourgeois capitalist, who appropriates in profits an ever-increasing part of labor's rightful share. According to Marx, capital tends to coalesce in fewer and larger productive units controlled by fewer and wealthier individuals, forcing more and more people into the proletarian class. This process drives down wages but at the same time increases proletarian solidarity. Eventually, he expected, it would reach a breaking point, when the workers would rise, take over the means of production, and establish a classless society which would own and work communally the earth's resources. Marxian propositions and predictions were respected as scientific laws by the Socialist followers of Marx.

Realism in European literature

IN AN AGE in which intellectual activities were increasingly influenced by scientific methods, positivistic thought, and utilitarian values, literature naturally showed a very considerable trend toward realism. Broad elements of realism that had appeared in the poetry of the late eighteenth century and had been elaborated in the novels of Dickens and Balzac were now developing more fully, as romanticism lost some of its novelty. Partly in reaction to romantic extravagance, partly in response to the newer empirical temper, many writers showed a preoccupation with the neighboring world and familiar people. Some of them made a conscious effort to be objective rather than subjective, descriptive rather than reflective, literal and restrained rather than moralistic and intrusive. Others, in a desire to portray human suffering under social abuse, permitted touches of sentimentalism and propaganda to color their work. In the two decades following the mid-century revolutions the realistic trend found its exponents in nearly every European language.

Dickens, Thackeray, Eliot, and their contemporaries

IN ENGLAND Dickens and Thackeray had found a worthy rival in George Eliot. Dickens was still writing sentimental but searching novels about contemporary types, who were victims of interminable law suits, or were unjustly accused, or were disinherited sons or embittered lovers. With a single departure (*A Tale of Two Cities,* 1859) into the historical novel, his stories were aimed at current social injustices. Thackeray produced in this period some of his best portrayals of the upper middle class in England and several historical novels. Mary Ann Evans, who wrote under the pseudonym of George Eliot, dealt in her novels with the personal problems of everyday people, sketched with sympathetic insight and based either upon some recollection of her own early life or placed with a master's touch in some historical setting. In some of her later novels she touched upon several important social problems: political reform, medical reform, and anti-Semitism.

Several novelists of this period fall into the lesser ranks only because the period could boast such luminaries as Dickens, Thackeray, and Eliot. Among these was another master of psychological character study, the young writer George Meredith, who began writing in the late fifties with *The Ordeal of Richard Feverel* (1859), a romance dealing with the problem of adolescent education. Charles Reade exposed the lamentable conditions in prisons, insane asylums, and trade unions through a set of piteous characters, although he is best known for a historical novel, *The Cloister and the Hearth* (1861). The "Chartist clergyman," Charles Kingsley, whose early novels were concerned with the exploitation of industrial workers and with other social problems, subsequently made a greater reputation with several historical novels and books for children. Elizabeth Gaskell continued to portray the hardships of indigent workers in novels like *North and South* (1855) but turned to genteel provincialism in *Cranford* (1853).

Browning, Tennyson,
and other mid-Victorian poets

AMONG THE British poets of this period Robert Browning well represented much of its wide learning and many of its intellectual trends. *The Ring and the Book* (1868-1869) is probably the finest and certainly the longest of his works. Each of its twelve books gives a different version of an old Roman murder case as seen by twelve different characters. Many of his shorter poems, too, reveal vigorous intellectual analysis. Often considered abstruse and difficult to understand, he was absorbed especially in the understanding of the human soul, typically casting his psychological studies in the form of dramatic monologues. His wife, Elizabeth Barrett Browning, who was a poet of note before he was, is now chiefly remembered for her *Sonnets from the Portuguese* (1850), a sequence of love poems written to her husband.

Of all the poets of mid-century England, Tennyson is usually considered most typically Victorian. Without losing any of his lyrical quality, creative imagination, emotional power, skill with metaphor, or perfection of form, in his work during this period he showed an increased interest in the problems, ideals, and conflicts of his time. *In Memoriam,* published in 1850, won popular acclaim immediately, not alone because of its obvious poetical merit but also because it gave expression to the mid-Victorian conflict of faith with the doubt that was brought on by the current positivism. Matthew Arnold, poet and critic, wrote in the 1850's poetry even more disciplined than that of Tennyson and, a little later, tightly reasoned prose, both tinged with disillusionment and with protest against modern "philistinism" (a word that he himself rendered popular).

Here again, as among the Victorian novelists, the brilliance of a group of writers who in another age might have shone among the brightest was somewhat dimmed by the first-magnitude luminaries. Foremost perhaps among the lesser lights were a group called the Pre-Raphaelites and Edward Fitz-

Gerald. FitzGerald's free translation of *The Rubáiyát of Omar Khayyám* (1859) was frankly unpuritanical and hedonistic. This un-Victorian importation at first went unnoticed, but its lyrical, epigrammatic verses lent themselves easily to quotation, and it soon became one of the most familiar poems of English literature.

Literary rebels against Victorian England

ENGLISH WRITERS of the fifties often rebelled against what they considered the mediocrity of Victorian England—the materialism, the absorption with moneymaking, the physical ugliness of an industrial culture. Carlyle had sounded the trumpet of this rebellion (pages 89-90), and he continued to attack in savage prose some of the most characteristic institutions of his age. Arnold reflected the same sentiments more gently in the closing lines of his famous poem "Dover Beach":

> And we are here as on a darkling plain
> Swept with confused alarms of struggle and flight,
> Where ignorant armies clash by night.

In *Idylls of the King* (1859-1872) Tennyson, retelling the Arthurian legend, upheld the medieval ideals of chivalry and duty for a modern world that seemed to be losing sight of its great ethical tradition.

Another rebel was Carlyle's friend John Ruskin. Ruskin's devotion to esthetic values impelled him to resist the materialistic vogue that he feared might smother the love of beauty. In the sixties his writings and lectures established him as the dictator of art in England. He expanded his ideas on the relation of art to life into a plan for reforming industrial society so as to leave room for beauty and human dignity. His schemes for the organization of labor harked back to the Middle Ages, and he believed that modern artists must recapture the moral purpose which had inspired the medieval painter.

The Rossettis and the Pre-Raphaelite Movement

AS THE leading art critic of the time, Ruskin championed a group of artistic and literary innovators known as "the Pre-Raphaelite Brotherhood." This group, organized in 1848, was the *avant-garde* of its time. Its purpose was to regain the spiritual vision that had inspired the early Italian painters and thus to free art from the sterile academicism taught in the schools. They endeavored to paint what they saw in nature without regard to conventional standards and with a deliberate effort to avoid imitation of earlier styles. Among the Pre-Raphaelite painters— notably Dante Gabriel Rossetti and John Everett Millais—minutely detailed, brilliant-colored, and realistic interpretation of nature was characteristic.

162   Rossetti was also a poet. So was his sister Christina, and his brother

"The Blessed Damozel," a painting by Dante Gabriel Rossetti.

William Michael was an art and literary critic and an editor. The father of this gifted family had fled from political reaction in Naples in the 1820's. Through the Rossettis Pre-Raphaelitism crossed into poetry. Dante Gabriel Rossetti's subjects and inspiration were romantic in their intense emotionalism and their nostalgia for the Middle Ages, but his style was disciplined by the contemporary intellectualism. The Pre-Raphaelite poets were interested in the legendary, the supernatural, the symbolic, and the sensuous.

Rossetti's art pupil, William Morris, distinguished himself rather as a poet than as a painter in the Pre-Raphaelite spirit, but he was also a novelist and a writer of political tracts. This was the period when "Gothic" architects like A. W. N. Pugin in England, and E. E. Viollet-le-Duc in France restored medieval structures or built new ones like the Houses of Parliament in the Gothic style. As a protest against the machine-made, commercialized Vic-   163 torian household articles, Morris resuscitated the dying arts and crafts of England, designing wallpaper, tapestries, furniture, and glass, and establishing his own firm to produce them with the good taste of the medieval handicraftsman.

Associated with the Pre-Raphaelites but essentially an independent rebel, was Algernon Charles Swinburne. In revolt against everything allegedly Victorian—philistinism, social conventions, religion, and political conservatism—he shocked Victorian England in the sixties with both his personal dissipations and the eroticism of his lyrics.

Persistence
of romanticism in France

IN FRANCE, where the big factory was less familiar and where industrialism's pall had cast a slighter shadow, the Romantic Movement had persisted longer than in England. Yet Hugo and his contemporaries did not escape the contemporary urge toward "social" literature. Exiled from 1852 to 1870 for his opposition to Napoleon III, Hugo wrote *Les Châtiments* in bitter condemnation of the emperor's usurpation of power—"a book written in lightning," Swinburne said. From exile also came several dramatic novels, of which the most famous is *Les Misérables* (1862), a story, laid in Napoleonic France, of the relentless pursuit by overzealous police of a guilty but worthy character. At his refuge in the Channel Islands he also wrote *Les Contemplations* (1856), upon which his reputation as France's greatest nineteenth-century lyricist chiefly depends, and the first of a three-volume poetic series (1859-1883) called *La Légende des siècles,* in which, recounting tales selected from the Bible, mythology, and history, he expounds a poetic confidence in the progress of virtue and enlightenment.

Other romantic writers too were still carrying on their work in France. In the fifties George Sand, her enthusiasm for socialism having cooled, produced, from her country retreat, village and country idylls and some tales for her grandchildren, and turned some of her novels into plays. Vigny, until his death in 1863, wrote an occasional piece from his "ivory tower," always uncompromisingly loyal to the romantic spirit but adding nothing to his glory as a poet.

Realism
in French literature

THE NEWER writers, however, wrote in an inquiring realistic spirit. Among these was Gustave Flaubert, who filled his novels of tragic love with carefully observed details at the same time that he made a studied effort to keep his own personality out of his work. His pruned and polished style—he sometimes spent weeks on a single page—made the search for exactly the right word (the *mot juste*) a common element of literary technique. In 1852 the enormously popular *La Dame aux camélias (Camille)* brought realism to the French stage. Its author was Alexandre Dumas *fils,* natural son of the romantic novelist. Several other successful plays about adultery and intrigue among the French upper classes followed it.

In the sixties several writers of nonfiction exerted great influence in setting the French intellectual tone. Ernest Renan's *Life of Jesus* (1863) aroused a storm of controversy. It was a study of Jesus as a man, not a deity, portraying him, against a background of scenes actually written in Syria, as a simple villager of incomparable soul. It was a reverent book but utterly free from supernatural implications; and in a day when those who believed in the literal interpretation of the Bible were everywhere on the defensive, Renan's historical Jesus added fuel to an already blazing controversy. Hippolyte Taine, historian and literary critic, set out to bring scientific determinism to literature and history. In his histories he sought to explain cultural events and personages in terms of heredity (*race*), environment (*milieu*), social situation (*moment*), and personality (*faculté maîtresse*). The literary critic Charles Augustin Sainte-Beuve published weekly articles about French figures, chiefly literary, both past and contemporary, that perhaps did more than any other medium to influence the contemporary Frenchman's literary tastes and preferences. Blanc and Michelet, both of whom were uncompromisingly hostile to the Empire, wrote history with the flavor of political polemic.

Realistic trends in French poetry

REALISM, historical objectivity, and the scientific attitude had an obvious effect upon French poetry. Théophile Gautier, having renounced his early flamboyant romanticism, produced his *Enamels and Cameos* (1852), in which he tried to reinstate purity of form as a primary canon of good poetry. Applying the painter's meticulous observation to poetry, he produced finely etched pictorial gems that contrasted with the subjective indulgence of the romantics. In the wake of Gautier came the Parnassians, who in the sixties began to win recognition as a school of poets. They declared war on the emotionalism of the romantics and took as their creed an objective attitude and a meticulous devotion to form. Among the Parnassians, at the beginning, perhaps the most notable was the young Paul Verlaine, but Verlaine in the 1870's was to break with the Parnassian school and to write poems marked by their simplicity and lyrical quality.

Almost a law unto himself both poetically and in private life was Charles Baudelaire, whose *Flowers of Evil* (1857) so shocked his prudish contemporaries that he, his publisher, and his printer were prosecuted for offending public morality. Reflecting the poet's dissolute, introspective, and morbid nature, these poems are nevertheless fashioned with fastidious craftsmanship and are full of carefully wrought imagery and symbolism. Baudelaire felt an affinity with Edgar Allan Poe and introduced that writer to French readers through beautiful translations.

IN FRENCH painting, too, realists made their appearance, challenging what they considered the pedantry of the schools and the stale traditions of the Academy. The leading realist painter was Gustave Courbet, who about 1850 won the attention of critics, both devastating and enthusiastic, for his earthy landscapes and studies of animals and common people. Courbet's painting along with Flaubert's *Madame Bovary* (1857) first brought the word "realism" into popular use. Courbet refused the cross of the Legion of Honor offered him by Napoleon III, and in the Communard movement of 1871 was to be responsible for the destruction of the Vendôme Monument of Napoleon I. Another realist, Honoré Daumier, was still drawing magnificent satirical cartoons for the French press, and was painting pictures that were too advanced to achieve popular recognition.

In the fifties and sixties, the Barbizon school, like the Pre-Raphaelites of England, sought to restore genuineness to painting in place of ingenuity. Spurning clever drawing and academic tricks, they attempted to put on canvas some of the emotional appeal of nature. Among the group, Camille Corot, painter of mystic and poetic landscapes, and Charles-François Daubigny, known especially for his river scenes, were the most successful during their lifetimes. Théodore Rousseau and Jean François Millet, however, were more typical of the group. Rousseau painted landscapes tinged with melancholy; Millet was the great portrayer of peasant life, in which his own life was rooted. His "Man with the Hoe" and "Angelus" have been reproduced so often as to have become commonplace, but he himself had to endure poverty and obscurity except in the final years of his life.

In the sixties another group of rebel painters began to make a stir in France. Among them were Édouard Manet and Camille Pissarro. Revolutionary both in subject matter and in technique, they had difficulty in winning public favor and their works were often excluded from the Salon. In 1863 several of them were obliged to exhibit their paintings in the Salon des Refusés (Exhibition of the Rejected) established by Napoleon III. Eventually these artists were to acquire the name of impressionists.

WHEREVER big-scale industry was penetrating, the artist, along with the writer and the musician, found himself in a new role, unless he was a brave and independent spirit. In an age of copyrights and royalties, the literary and art patron with aristocratic tastes was rare; the new society was dominated by the captain of industry, whose interests did not always include belles-lettres, whose preferences in such art as he knew frequently ran to sentimentalism and photographic realism in painting and to ostentatious borrowing from other periods in architecture, and whose musical ear was attuned mainly to lively popular melodies. The artist who formerly painted on commission now worked with an eye toward reproduction in the magazines or painted pictures that he hoped would grace the walls of a government-sponsored salon or museum, where, if the government did not buy them, some private purchaser might be captivated. The writer had to sell his manuscripts to publishers, who often felt constrained to cater to public tastes. The handicraftsman's place was taken by the machine. The artist, especially before he had won recognition, was likely to be regarded as a "bohemian," who did not quite conform to the accepted conventions; and in this bohemian world might also dwell struggling poets and musicians. Paris was the capital of this "Bohemia."

French music and the Paris Opéra

THE FORM of music that flourished best in France was the opera. Meyerbeer and Berlioz were already old men in this period, and their prime was behind them, but younger composers were taking their place. Georges Bizet, whose greatest triumph, *Carmen,* would not appear before 1875, had already achieved fame with *The Pearl Fishers,* and Charles François Gounod, whose *Ave Maria* was destined to become perhaps the best-known piece of religious music, wrote *Faust* (1859) and *Romeo and Juliet* (1867) under the Second Empire. Jacques Offenbach's light operas were the popularly favored musical creations of the period. The new Opéra, the work of the architect Charles Garnier, with its renowned staircase and Renaissance façade, became the center from which the grand boulevards of the new Paris radiated.

Music in Germany, Austria, Bohemia, and Norway

THE MUSIC capital of Europe now was Vienna, and the musical titans were to be found largely in the Germanies and the Austrian Empire. Dominant among these titans was Richard Wagner. Already admired as a composer, young Wagner became involved in the revolutionary movement of 1848-1849. Disillusioned and forced into exile in Switzerland, he wrote the great works that made him known as a musical revolutionary of the first order. Wagner devoted his life to the development of a new kind of opera, the music-drama. He sought in his operatic work to unite all the dramatic arts—music, the dance, poetry, and acting—and his many musical innovations arose from a conscious effort to achieve this objective. Wagner wrote his own librettos, striving to associate music and lyric intimately with each other and with the action of the drama. His quest for fuller expression led to the use of new harmonies and modulations, innovations sometimes unacceptable to contemporary audiences and some later critics. He used a larger orchestra than was conven-   167 tional, gave to the brass and wood-wind instruments a fuller employment than earlier masters, fitted his overtures closely to the rising of the curtain, consistently employed the leitmotif (the musical phrase identified with a particular person or sentiment), and combined voice and orchestra in new ways. Critics ridiculed him and musicians found his requirements too difficult. Nevertheless Wagner became probably the most influential composer of his century. But no one after him successfully attempted to compose opera in the new form to which Wagner had devoted his life. His influence was rather in his use of the orchestra and his new harmonic idiom. Wagner's anti-Semitism and his frequent choice of subjects from the Teutonic sagas gave to his work a nationalistic flavor that music had previously managed to avoid.

Wagner's friend, father-in-law, and champion was Franz Liszt. Famous all over Europe from childhood as a piano virtuoso, Liszt turned more and more to composition, and after 1848 he quit giving public concerts altogether. He wrote mostly for piano or for piano and orchestra. Exploiting Hungarian folk music somewhat as Wagner exploited Teutonic mythology, Liszt wrote nineteen Hungarian Rhapsodies. A devout Catholic (in 1865 he entered the Franciscan order), he also wrote several oratorios and masses. He transcribed for the piano many works written for other mediums. Through his transcriptions and as a conductor at Weimar, he helped to popularize the works of other composers and became a kind of godfather to the whole musical profession. Liszt wrote, like Wagner, for the large modern orchestra, and he developed a new form, the symphonic poem, which was to become immensely popular with modern composers, being shorter and less conventional than the formal symphony.

Contemporaneously Friedrich Smetana meant for Bohemia and Edward Grieg for Norway what Wagner meant for Germany. Smetana wrote music that was frankly nationalistic. His *Bartered Bride* (1866), a Bohemian folk opera, and "The Moldau," one of a set of six symphonic poems entitled *My Country,* became especially popular. Grieg, whose *Peer Gynt Suite* is probably his best-known composition, carried on a life-long crusade for Norwegian national music.

Realism
in Russian literature

THE REALISTIC trend in literature met with especially happy results in the hands of three recognized Russian masters, Turgenev, Dostoyevsky, and Tolstoy. Ivan Sergeyevich Turgenev is commonly believed to have been Russia's finest prose stylist. His first successful work was a series entitled *A Sportsman's Sketches* (collected in 1852), which was destined to play a part in the movement to free the Russian serfs somewhat similar to *Uncle Tom's Cabin* in the abolitionist movement of America (page 240). Turgenev freed the serfs on his own lands. In 1862 he published his most famous work, *Fathers and Sons,* in

168

which he portrayed the conflict between generations typical of Russia at that time—the conservative and devoted father and the radical, nonconformist friend of his son. The government picked up his term "nihilist" for the holders of radical ideas. In the struggle between "Westerners" and "Slavophiles" in Russia, Turgenev's influence weighed on the side of the Westerners. His novels show western influence in form and style.

Feodor Dostoyevsky considered Turgenev Frenchified and was himself a Russian chauvinist. Dostoyevsky was a master of psychological characterization, often of abnormal individuals, and portrayed with great intensity the life of intellectual and revolutionary Russians, of whom he himself was one. He was sentenced to death in 1849 along with a circle of liberal friends, but at the last moment the sentence was commuted to exile in Siberia. He spent ten years in penal servitude and in the army, became mystically interested in Christianity, the Christian mission of Russia, and the soul of the common man, and returned to write the *House of the Dead* (1861), portraying the brutality of life in the Siberian salt mines. To pay his debts he wrote *Crime and Punishment,* a psychological study of a young debt-ridden murderer and of his self-reformation. His greatest novel, *The Brothers Karamazov,* did not come until 1880. It was a remarkably effective combination of murder mystery and religious mysticism.

The third great Russian novelist of the period was Count Leo Tolstoy. His first literary work (page 182) exhibited a natural sympathy for "the people" that he held all his life, though he himself was an aristocrat. Between 1864 and 1869 his most famous novel, *War and Peace,* was published, a long panoramic work centering around Napoleon's invasion of Russia. Crowded with historical reflections and densely populated with firmly drawn Russian types, it gives a masterly picture of early nineteenth-century Russian society and probes the meaning of victory and defeat, life and death, right and wrong—problems for which Tolstoy as yet found no answer more troublesome than faith in a beneficent Providence and in the simple aspirations of the common man. Doubt and psychological difficulties were to come in succeeding decades.

Russian music and nationalism

THE AGE OF Russia's greatest novelists coincided with the age of her greatest musicians. A group of composers known as "the Five" set out deliberately to create a distinctively Russian musical literature. Three of them—Nicholas Rimsky-Korsakoff, Alexander Borodin, and Modest Moussorgsky—are well known in the west. Like Wagner and Smetana, they promoted the development of nationalism in music. Most of the five were amateur musicians having other professions, for it was difficult to make a living from music in Russia in those days. In 1862 they founded the Free School of Music devoted to the 169 development of a distinctively Russian style. Beginning in this small way in the sixties, they were to achieve their greatest successes in the latter decades of the century.

Two other Russian composers contemporary with the Five were Anton Rubinstein and Peter Illich Tchaikovsky. Both were cosmopolitan in their music; both, in fact, were unsympathetic to a musical nationalism. Rubinstein was a pianist and enhanced Russia's musical reputation abroad through his concert tours. As a composer he is best known for his piano concertos, shorter piano pieces, and songs. Tchaikovsky, who studied for a time under him, became the much greater musical figure. His highly emotional and profoundly expressive symphonies and tone poems early placed him on a par with leading western composers. Although he disapproved in principle of nationalism in music, an unmistakable Slavic and patriotic strain features some of his work.

*The music
of Giuseppe Verdi*

IN ITALY the operas of Giuseppe Verdi were adopted by the nationalist movement, whether the composer consciously intended it or not. Some of his best works appeared in the early fifties and were loudly acclaimed. Italian audiences gave political significance to innocent phrases such as *"Io ho la lingua, egli ha il pugnalo"* (meaning, by implication, "We have the culture, they have the power") in *Rigoletto,* and used the letters of Verdi's name as a patriotic wordplay standing for *"Vittorio Emmanuele Re* [King] *d' Italia."* During this period Verdi was still a young man, and some of his greatest work, as we shall see, lay in the future.

*Cosmopolitanism
in European art and science*

DESPITE THE barriers of political boundaries and language differences, and even despite the intensification of the nationalist spirit in literature and music, the triumphs of science and art were adding to the common European heritage. Tchaikovsky's *Overture 1812* or Tolstoy's *War and Peace* might remind Alexander II's Russia, humiliated by the Crimean fiasco, of the great triumph of the first Alexander over the first Napoleon, but Tchaikovsky was played and Tolstoy was read in Paris. Hugo's *Les Misérables* might indict the shallowness of middle-class morality, and Ruskin and Morris might pour scorn upon the machine-made furnishings of the middle-class home, but the middle class and other classes in all countries contained many who agreed with them. Ideas now became world property faster than before. Growing railroad networks and telegraph lines and cheaper printing had made communication easier and quicker than ever. No matter what the individual inventor or artist or his government might intend, his work soon passed beyond national boundaries, making even a neopagan Wagner, an oriental Omar Khayyám, 170   or a non-Christian Renan part of the unbroken chain of Europe's culture.

THE CRIMEAN WAR and its aftermath proved a solvent in which the prevailing autocracy of the 1850's lost its hard, crystalline character. In Russia defeat and humiliation helped to set in motion a whole series of reforms. In Austria, which had not been directly involved in the Crimean War, the postbellum financial crisis nevertheless was so severe that it resulted in renewed demands for the broadening of the base of local government. In 1858, when the Prussian king, Frederick William IV, became insane, his brother William became regent, and though by no means a liberal, William began his regency by loosening the restrictive measures that had stifled political activity in Prussia. Thus postwar developments in the three eastern conservative monarchies encouraged liberals to look hopefully forward to a "new era." But the real break in the European reaction occurred farther west, as the result of Napoleon III's interest in the Italian unification movement.

Napoleon's plan
for the map of Europe

THE POLICY of Bonapartism that Napoleon III steadfastly followed had brought him by 1858 to a seemingly creditable imitation of his uncle's eminence. He was supreme in France; he had made an impressive showing as the arbiter of Europe; his capital outshone the other cities of the Continent in brilliance. But his dreams were not yet fulfilled. Glorious as the Congress of Paris had been, the peace settlement had left practically intact the map of Europe as drawn in 1815, a piece of cartography that, to those who knew their history, was a symbol of Napoleon I's defeat. Believing or affecting to believe that his uncle had been a friend of the common people everywhere, and recognizing that the common people might more readily accept his kind of leadership than that of the ancient dynasties, Napoleon III brought his uncle's "ideals" up to date in terms of the nationalistic currents of the new age. It seems scarcely to have occurred to him until it was too late that once he began to make these ideals come true, they might get out of control. If, instead of writing a biography of Julius Caesar, he had spent his leisure hours studying the history of Austria, he might have shared Palacky's opinion that if Austria had not existed, it would have been necessary to create her. Napoleon set about to unmake Austria.

Cavour
and the expansion of Sardinia

THE NATIONALIST sentiment in Italy was still strong in spite of the failures of 1848 and 1849. Only a few stubborn revolutionaries remained faithful to the Mazzinian ideal of a republican Italy within a humanitarian world. Most patriots had become converted to a nationalist movement, directed against the provincial govern-

171

ments and against clericalism. A new organization known as the Italian National Society was formed in Paris in 1856. Led by the once republican Daniele Manin, the exiled hero of the Venetian revolt of 1848-1849, the society advocated a kingdom of Italy under Victor Emmanuel—a program vague enough to include all shades of nationalist opinion and specific enough to offer a chance of success in a pragmatic world.

By 1858 Victor Emmanuel's kingdom of Sardinia (commonly called, from its continental portion, Piedmont) was a prosperous little country. It was the only liberal state in Italy, and its ruling house had behind it the prestige of eight centuries of uninterrupted rule and of almost continuous independence since the Renaissance. It had a parliamentary government modeled on that of England, a modern railway system, a flourishing commerce and industry, and a well-equipped army. The most conspicuous architect of this progressive state was the shrewd and determined Count Cavour. Cavour had an ambitious design for Italy—or rather for Sardinia. He planned to conduct and exploit the Italian nationalist movement so as to drive out the Austrians and make Sardinia the largest and the dominant Italian state. Profiting by the lessons of earlier failures, Cavour realized that no Italian state was strong enough to achieve Italian unity by itself. His strategy was to seek a powerful European ally to help him against Austria. Hence his participation, as we have seen, in the Crimean War. This ally he now found in Napoleon III, who at the Congress of Paris had so manipulated the agenda as to permit an airing of the Italian question.

The plot against Austria by Napoleon III and Cavour
FOR SEVERAL years Napoleon had secretly held out hope of French aid to Italy, and in 1858 an attempt on his life by a disappointed Italian nationalist made him realize that his promises would not easily be forgotten. With the utmost secrecy, he approached Cavour with a plan for a solution of the Italian question. He proposed four Italian states of which a greatly enlarged Sardinia, incorporating the Austrian provinces of Lombardy and Venetia, was to be the chief. If necessary, he was prepared to undertake a Franco-Sardinian war against Austria to drive her out of Italy. France's compensation for the risks involved was to be the Piedmontese provinces of Nice and Savoy, which had been part of France in the Napoleonic period. Since both men had a taste for the histrionic, the details were arranged in hush-hush meetings at the French spa of Plombières in July 1858. The next December they were embodied in a secret treaty obliging France to go to the aid of Sardinia if Austria attacked. The marriage of the emperor's roué cousin Prince Napoleon with Victor Emmanuel's young daughter Clotilda sealed the bargain. In January Victor Emmanuel addressed the Sardinian Parliament: "With all our respect for treaties, we are not insensible to the cry of pain which rises toward us from so many parts of Italy."

172

SELDOM WAS A war more coolly
Bringing on or skillfully engineered. In order
the Franco-Austrian War to win public favor in both France
and the rest of Europe it was necessary to make Austria appear in the wrong.
The months after the Plombières meetings were spent in veiled provocation
of Austria. An Austrian law conscripting natives of Lombardy and Venetia
furnished Cavour with the opportunity he sought. He let it be known that
deserters would be given sanctuary in Piedmont, and by skillful manipulation
of the nationalist spirit, blew the matter up to the proportions of a major crisis.
In March he began to mobilize the Sardinian army. Meantime Napoleon
III, playing upon Russian resentment of Austrian neutrality in the Crimean
War, had secured Russia's benevolent neutrality by a promise that France
would look kindly on revision of the Treaty of Paris. He also let his plan for
a free and federated Italy be known.

For a time it looked as though the British desire for a peaceful settlement
by concert of the European nations would spoil everything. England proposed a peace plan so sensible that it would expose the unreasonableness of
whichever side refused it. But Cavour and Napoleon, counting on Austrian
nervousness, managed to play along for a time, and Emperor Francis Joseph,
becoming impatient at the failure of Sardinia to demobilize, ordered Austrian mobilization; and when the self-confident Cavour gave no heed to an
Austrian ultimatum demanding rapid Sardinian demobilization, Austria

Napoleon III proclaims that the Empire means peace, but Punch, *the English humorous magazine, has its doubts.*

173

sent an army into Piedmont. Austria thus became the formal aggressor; France was obliged by the terms of their treaty to go to Sardinia's aid; and another war involving great European powers was on.

The war
and the Villafranca armistice

IT PROVED to be a very short war, however. French and Piedmontese forces defeated the Austrian troops at the costly battles of Magenta and Solferino, and in six weeks drove the Austrians out of Lombardy. The sentiment for Italian unity once more erupted. Revolutions took place in Tuscany, Modena, and Parma—peaceful revolutions in which nationalists assumed control and the old rulers were exiled. Insurrection spread to the papal province of Romagna.

This self-propelling nationalism was a contingency that Napoleon had not foreseen, and it gave him pause. It also caused second thoughts in other quarters. The Prussians, though they had little love for Austria, saw no Prussian advantage in Napoleonic invasions of a neighboring German state, and they threatened to mobilize and aid Austria. The French Catholics began to feel less enthusiastic about French intervention in Italy now that it threatened to lead to disruption of the Papal States. The Italian nationalist movement bade fair to take control of Italy out of Napoleon's hands, making a strong potential enemy rather than a satellite state out of the proposed confederation. The impression persisted, too, that the bloody fields of Magenta and Solferino had made Napoleon think twice about the glories of war. Napoleon suddenly concluded with the Austrian emperor the Armistice of Villafranca (July 11, 1859). Sardinia was not even consulted, and to her the armistice represented at least a partial defeat and a betrayal. It assigned Lombardy (but not Venetia) to Piedmont but restored the rulers of Parma, Modena, Tuscany, and Romagna, and provided for an Italian confederation in which Austria as ruler of

Venetia was included. The war was over. Furious with the king for accepting these terms, Cavour resigned, convinced that his cause was lost. The Villafranca truce was formalized in the Treaty of Zurich in November 1859. The carefully manipulated war against Austria had brought only Lombardy to Piedmont, and it looked as if Italian unification had again been thwarted.

*Annexations
in central Italy*

BUT VILLAFRANCA made desperate men of the nationalists in central Italy, to whom the return of the old rulers would mean exile or worse. Everywhere patriots took up the slogan: "Italy will act for herself" (*Italia farà da se*). Roused to action, the districts in revolt voted to annex themselves to Piedmont. Cavour, taking courage once more, returned to office and began bargaining with Napoleon on the terms under which France would endorse such annexations. Napoleon, disregarding Villafranca and Zurich, made alternative suggestions: annexation of all the districts in return for the annexation of Nice and Savoy by France or annexation of part and confederation with the rest without compensation to France. Cavour unhesitatingly chose the former. A powerful north Italian state was more important to his future plans than the loss of limited territory, even though that territory included the ancestral lands of the house of Savoy and its cession made the outraged Garibaldi a foreigner in his own native city. As a gesture of respect for national consciousness and to offset foreign criticisms, Cavour, Napoleon, and the English government insisted upon the holding of plebiscites to determine the wishes of the inhabitants of the already practically annexed areas. In the Italian districts the vote was overwhelmingly in favor of annexation to Sardinia; and since Savoy had a large French-speaking population, despite charges of political

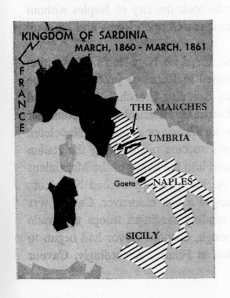

KINGDOM OF SARDINIA
MARCH, 1860 - MARCH, 1861

FRANCE

THE MARCHES

UMBRIA

Gaeta NAPLES

SICILY

The evolution of the kingdom of Sardinia into the Kingdom of Italy is traced in these maps, the hatched areas in each case representing new additions. In 1859 France and Sardinia wrested Lombardy from Austria by a skillfully contrived war marked by the bloody battles of Magenta and Solferino. Plebiscites in March 1860 in Parma, Modena, Tuscany, and the Papal State of Romagna—with annexation a foregone conclusion—were approved by France in return for the cession of Savoy and Nice. By November Garibaldi had taken Sicily and all southern Italy except Rome and Gaeta, while Sardinian troops moved south through the Papal States of the Marches and Umbria to meet him (pages 176-177). Plebiscites in favor of union with the north followed, and the Kingdom of Italy was proclaimed in March 1861. Florence became its capital in 1865. Further unification of Italy came a few years later (see map, page 192).

manipulation in Nice, all the plebiscites gave an air of righteousness to the *faits accomplis.*

**Garibaldi
and his Red Shirts**

THUS WAS completed a second stage of Italian unification, brought about by an outburst of genuine nationalist sentiments and the buying-off of foreign opposition. In less than a year Piedmont had about tripled in size, and Napoleon, not quite as he had planned, had a strong little nation on his flank. He rapidly found that this creature he had fathered had amazing powers of growth. The man chiefly responsible for this phenomenal growth was the melodramatic Garibaldi. An unrepentant believer in mass action in spite of his failure in 1849, he had been loyally serving Victor Emmanuel since the beginning of the war, putting Italian unity even above republicanism. His dislike of diplomatic niceties and his tremendous popularity made him a somewhat dangerous ally in the hazardous game Cavour was playing, but the stakes were high and worth the risks. Besides, it was desirable to divert Garibaldi from his intention of defending Nice against France.

By May 1860 Garibaldi had gathered a private army of one thousand "Red Shirts," who were ready to follow wherever he might lead. Fortunately a revolution, prepared by some nationalist agitators, broke out in Sicily and, with the connivance of Cavour, Garibaldi and his Thousand sailed to their aid. The patrolling English fleet not only failed to stop him but actually helped him to land. Rarely did corruption crumble more readily at the touch of knight-errant. The defending army of the Bourbon ruling house, twenty thousand strong, outwitted and outmaneuvered by the tiny force of Red Shirts, capitulated. In August, again without interference from the British naval patrol, the triumphant Garibaldi crossed to the mainland, where opposition melted before him. In September he took the city of Naples without a battle, and announced that he would next march upon Rome and hand all southern Italy to Victor Emmanuel.

This course was fraught with danger, for since Napoleon's intervention of 1849 French troops had been garrisoned in Rome as protectors of the pope, and, more recently, loyal Catholics, including French Legitimists, had flocked to the defense of the church and organized themselves into volunteer "Zouaves." Cavour had no desire to provoke Austria or to alienate Napoleon. Moreover, he was fearful that Garibaldi's success might swing the Italian unification movement out of his control and into the hands of the Mazzinians who had rallied to Garibaldi's banner. So he again approached Napoleon, and the two inveterate conspirators arranged a new maneuver. Cavour was to anticipate any Garibaldian coup by sending Sardinian troops to invade the Papal States, where, conveniently enough, Catholic fervor had begun to stir up dreams of a Legitimist restoration in France. Accordingly, Cavour

176

dispatched Sardinian troops, ostensibly to force the disbanding of "adventurers" but really to forestall an invasion by Garibaldi, who was still fighting in southern Italy. The Sardinian troops easily defeated the defending papal army, skirted Rome so as to avoid provocation to Napoleon, and marched south to join Garibaldi.

In October Garibaldi trounced the only remaining Neapolitan army, 40,000 strong, on the Volturno. Meanwhile the noble device of plebiscites had gone into operation, and when they were completed in November they showed that Naples, Sicily, and the papal provinces of the Marches and Umbria were overwhelmingly in favor of annexation to Piedmont. Garibaldi yielded heroically. Riding beside Victor Emmanuel, he made a triumphal entry into Naples on November 7, though the fortress of Gaeta, protected by French ships, did not surrender until the following February.

The inauguration of the Kingdom of Italy

IN MARCH 1861 the first parliament representing the unified nation proclaimed the Kingdom of Italy, which now included all of the peninsula except Venetia and Rome with its surrounding territory. The government of the new kingdom was modeled on Piedmont's liberal constitution of 1848. In April, Garibaldi attacked Cavour in the new parliament, savagely accusing him of having risked a civil war by his invasion of the Papal States. Cavour defended himself ably, but the attack aggravated his already broken health. He died in June. Mazzini meanwhile, shocked by the Machiavellian methods of Cavour and Garibaldi, and lamenting the superiority of the monarchical sword over the republican pen, mourned the perversion of his hope that humanity would take priority over the state: "I shall have no more joy in Italy; the country with its contempt for all ideals has killed the soul within me."

Efforts to make Rome the capital of the new Italy were unsuccessful for some years more. Cavour, at his death, was negotiating with Napoleon III for the withdrawal of French troops from Rome. The quest for Rome continued, for it was the historic capital of Italy and the only one acceptable to all parts of the new kingdom. While Cavour's successors patiently undertook prolonged diplomatic negotiations, Garibaldi, despite at least outward official disapproval, tried twice (1862 and 1866-1867) to take the city by force but was unsuccessful. Rome was not to become part of Italy until 1870.

The growth of opposition to Napoleon

FOR NAPOLEON III the Italian enterprise, undertaken in a quest for new laurels, had become instead the first step toward general unpopularity. By his acquisition of Nice and Savoy he had aroused the suspicion of the European powers—particularly of his erstwhile allies the British—who were at once reminded of his uncle's aggrandisements. In addition, continental monarchs were hostile because he had assisted in the overthrow of legitimate governments in Italy. Even the new kingdom itself was a dubious friend, for Napoleon had blown hot and then cold at every stage of the Italian crises, and friction over "the Roman Question" remained. At home Napoleon's effort to be all things to all men had equally disturbing consequences. The Catholics, on whom Napoleon had relied heavily for support, were alienated by the diminution of the pope's temporal power. Monarchists deplored the humiliation of former kings and dukes in Italy. Patriots were concerned over the new kingdom as a potential threat to France.

Free trade and the Cobden-Chevalier Treaty

ANOTHER GROUP of Napoleon's supporters, the financial interests, began to waver at this time. A trade treaty, amicably negotiated by Richard Cobden and Michel Chevalier in 1860, reduced French tariffs on English manufactured goods in return for lowered English tariffs on French wines. This arrangement quickly led to marked advantages for English goods, which French manufacturers resented.

Nevertheless the Cobden-Chevalier Treaty became a model for subsequent reciprocity agreements among nations. It came midway in the European free-trade movement. Since the repeal of the English Corn Laws in 1846 Europe had been moving toward free trade. The movement was slow at first, Piedmont being one of the few countries to adopt free trade in the 1850's. But after the Cobden-Chevalier Treaty, bilateral low-tariff treaties became more common. In China and Japan, for example, unilateral treaties imposed by European powers contained low-tariff provisions and most-favored-nation clauses, and new ports free to all commerce replaced the exclusive commercial areas (pages 273-277). In Europe, Prussia and the Prussian-dominated German *Zollverein* used low-tariff agreements as an inducement to the lesser German states to support her against Austria. Sweden, Belgium, Holland, and Switzerland adopted nonprotectionist policies. Napoleon III hoped, by following a liberal tariff policy, to win British support and to improve the market for French goods in Britain. He succeeded better in raising doubts among French manufacturers about his economic theories.

Beginnings of the Liberal Empire

SEEING THE conservative elements slipping away from him, Napoleon turned to the opposition parties and in a bid for their support began to liberalize his regime. In 1859 he issued an amnesty to the exiles of 1851, and many republicans returned to France. In 1860 he relaxed the restrictions on the legislature's discussions of policy and allowed debates to be published in full. In 1861, in response to protests against his fixing tariffs by treaty, he increased the financial powers of the legislature. But these measures, without winning the liberals over, allowed their opposition to become more vocal.

*France's attempt
to establish an empire in Mexico*

IN A FURTHER effort to revive imperial popularity, Napoleon turned again to the idea of military adventure outside of France—one that would win territory, economic advantage, military glory, and clerical approval. He met with considerable success in Indochina (pages 286-289). Another convenient opportunity seemed to offer itself in Mexico (pages 252-253), where an anticlerical revolutionary government had refused to pay its debts to European creditors. The preoccupation of the United States with its own Civil War made it extremely unlikely that any American government would intervene to preserve Mexican integrity. In conjunction with England and Spain, Napoleon sent troops to Mexico in 1861 to force payment of the Mexican obligations. He then revealed his more far-reaching plans—to counterbalance Anglo-Saxon America by establishing a French-controlled, Latin, and Catholic empire in Mexico under the willing Archduke Maximilian of Austria, brother of the Emperor Francis Joseph. Britain and Spain, wanting no part of such a foolhardy scheme, quickly withdrew their troops and left the French to go on alone. French troops took Mexico City in 1863 and, with the cooperation of some Mexican conservatives, placed Maximilian on the Mexican throne. It looked for a while as if Napoleon would succeed in establishing in Mexico the satellite state that had eluded him in Italy.

*Local government
granted and limited in Austria*

THE ITALIAN unification movement had important repercussions in Austria as well as in France. Besides causing a loss of prestige, Austria's war against France and Italy had brought to a head the financial crisis resulting from the Crimean War and had raised the serious danger that the Hungarians, taking advantage of the Austrian preoccupation on the Italian front, might revolt. To assure Hungarian loyalty, the Bach System was scrapped, and in its place Emperor Francis Joseph in 1860 issued a new constitution known as "the October Diploma," by which the various provinces were to be ruled largely by their own assemblies. As long as the Italian crises continued and it looked as if the Austrian armies might again become involved in a war, the imperial government seemed ready to make further concessions. When, however, Italian unification became a reality, the Austrian government repented and in a so-called "February Patent" (1861) so interpreted the October Diploma as to reduce the powers of the provincial assemblies and to strengthen those of the central government. Though less thoroughly controlled than under the Bach System, the Hungarians and other minority peoples of the Austrian Empire once more were baffled in their quest for autonomy, and it was clear that they would look upon any future international complications for the Austrian Empire as appropriate occasions to renew their demands.

*Internationalism
and interdependence*

DESPITE POLITICAL and nationalist rivalries, the spirit of international cooperation became
steadily more evident. During this period, the international fair and exposition developed into a popular institution. The famous glass hall called the
Crystal Palace created a furor at the Hyde Park Exhibitions in London in
1851 and 1854. Not to be outdone in competitive ostentation, Napoleon III
took up enthusiastically the idea of international exhibitions; and manufacturers from many countries adopted the practice of displaying their wares
and competing for medals and ribbons on lavishly laid-out grounds. The International Red Cross came into being in 1864 in direct response to the widespread horror at the bloodshed on the Solferino battlefield. Delegates from
sixteen countries meeting at Geneva agreed to the establishment and neutralization of agencies engaged in the relief of distress in wartime. Eventually the
activity of the Red Cross was extended to include relief from peacetime disaster. The rapid spread of telegraph lines throughout Europe and America led,

*Great Britain's Exhibition of 1851 offered a new approach to international amity
through the display of the arts and manufactures of all nations. Here, construction
workers are shown erecting the Crystal Palace.*

An account published in 1862 of the terrible suffering of the wounded at the battle of Solferino, shown here as defeated Austrian troops abandoned the field, led directly to the founding of International Red Cross in 1864.

after several discouraging failures, to the laying of successful submarine cables between France and England in 1851 and between Europe and America in 1866. The Telegraphic Union was formed in 1865, and ten years later became a precedent for what is still perhaps the best example of international cooperation, the Postal Union.

These international organizations made the world smaller. Railroads, telegraph lines, cables, and postal cooperation knit all the western nations together. In the 1860's the steamship came into its own; and when the Suez Canal was completed in 1869, cutting out the long voyage around Africa to the East, the nations of the East came weeks closer to the West than they had been in the eighteenth century. And as the world grew physically and psychically smaller, economically it became more and more interdependent and intellectually more and more cosmopolitan. The same instruments, however, that encouraged internationalism and cosmopolitanism were used also to tie a single people more tightly together and to propagate a growingly militant nationalism.

Alexander II and reform in Russia

RUSSIA LAY largely outside the periphery of these western movements, but Russia too was touched by them. Alexander II came to the Russian throne as the Crimean War was wearing to an inglorious end. The blundering, incompetence, and 181 corruption of Russian officials, the pricking of the illusion that Russia had the best army in Europe, and the final defeat all served to discredit the Nicholas system. The new czar was no reforming idealist, but he was an astute autocrat who recognized the responsibilities of his position. He perceived at once that Russia's humiliation was largely due to the backward character of her institutions. He lost little time in making a series of changes that perceptibly altered the most crying abuses in Russian society and government without effecting a revolution.

The most significant of these changes was the abolition of serfdom in 1861. Turgenev's *Sportsman's Sketches* had already described how the institution debased both master and servant (page 168). Tolstoy's on-the-spot stories from the Crimean front had revealed that the bravery of the Russian peasant as a soldier was no less than that of his ancestors, but the war had also made manifest the striking contrast between him and his contemporary counterpart in the French, British, and Piedmontese armies. Could it be that the westerner made a better soldier because he was a freer man?

It was not difficult for Alexander to develop his program peacefully and even with the partial cooperation of the landowners. The major stumbling block was the question of land distribution. Where the serf was still bound to the soil, the land was valueless without his labor, and at the same time he could earn no living without land. Obviously the freed serf would have to be given a bit of land; otherwise freedom would only mean starvation for him and less produce for all. But if the landlords were to provide the serfs with land free of charge, many landlords would be left in penury; and if the state were to pay for the land, a gigantic financial burden would result that the imperial treasury could ill afford after a disastrous war. Although the reform project was contemplated even before the Crimean War ended, it took until 1861 to bring it to maturity. In the end landlord, serf, and state were called upon to make sacrifices, but the landlords less than the others.

*Emancipation
of the serfs in Russia*

THE LAW abolishing serfdom took advantage of the closely knit communal organization of the Russian *mir* (village). Briefly, the law provided immediate personal freedom and with it a certain right to some land for about 22,500,000 serfs who lived on privately owned estates. The landowners were to be compensated at once with government bonds, for which the serfs were to pay in forty-nine annual installments to the government. Fortunately the Russian peasant was used to responsibility to his village organization, as well as to his landlord; and so the peasant lands were given not to the individual but to the *mir*, which parceled it out to families according to size and was made responsible for periodic redistributions. Since the members of the community were jointly responsible for their common debt, this method of allotment had the effect of binding them almost as firmly to the soil as before. They merely exchanged masters, passing from the control of a landlord to the control of a *mir,* in whose affairs, however, they had a voice. About half the cultivated land of Russia eventually was alloted thus, in pieces varying in size according to the fertility of the soil and other local conditions; the remainder was retained by the landowners.

The peasant's continued obligation to serve partly explains the static quality of Russian society in the later nineteenth century. In spite of the fact that Russia was at this time expanding her territories eastward to the Pacific Ocean (pages 289-294), no great masses migrated to the virgin Siberian lands. This immobility is in striking contrast to the rapid peopling of the American West that was going on at the same time. Nor did the Russian peasant, like the freedman of America, move rapidly to the industrial area; for years he had almost no industrial areas to move to. And though waves of emigrants left Russia for America in the ensuing decades, they came from the cities and the persecuted religious minorities rather than from the *mirs.*

At first, most of the freed serfs regarded the emancipation settlement with gratitude. In the long run, however, it proved far from satisfying. The fact that a serf now had to pay for land which formerly he had worked free was troublesome. Emancipation left him land-hungry, with neither enough land to till nor private ownership of his inadequate portion. The proprietors too were unhappy. Often they found themselves living less well than before on the income from the lands left to them after the emancipation. "Formerly," one of them said, "we kept no accounts and drank champagne; now we keep accounts and content ourselves with beer." Thus emancipation created problems that gradually piled up the raw materials of unrest.

The world-wide spread
of the emancipation movement

THE EMANCIPATION of the serfs in Russia was part of the drive toward personal freedom characteristic of the West in the nineteenth century. Two years later Abraham Lincoln issued the proclamation emancipating the slaves in certain parts of the United States without giving them any land and without compensating their former owners. In the colonial and ex-colonial world, slavery was also abolished. The British had done this in 1833-1838 (although it was not effectively applied to India until 1843) and the French in 1848; the Dutch followed suit in the Indies in 1859-1869. In South America slavery was abolished in Argentina in 1853, in Venezuela the following year, in Peru in 1856, and in Brazil between 1871 and 1888. By the end of the century slavery was officially discountenanced in all Europe and America, but it continued to survive in certain areas of Africa and Asia, and peonage (a form of involuntary servitude for the payment of debts) hung on in Mexico and other parts of Latin America.

*The reform movement
among the intelligentsia*

ANOTHER OF Alexander's reforms was the relaxation of restrictions on the communication of ideas. Travel and attendance at the universities were made easier, and the press was less heavily censored. As a result, the universities and certain newspapers and magazines became vigorous media of liberal sentiment. An especially intriguing leader of the reform movement was Alexander Herzen, who had gone into exile in 1847 and from 1857 to 1862 had edited the Socialist newspaper *Kolokol (The Bell)* from the "Free Russian Press" in London. This publication, after a few years of vain effort, succeeded in getting smuggled into Russia in large quantities. Even the czar was said to read it. Inside Russia a more radical group made its appearance, its membership drawn especially from the new university students. Its leaders reduced the logic of liberty to an absurdity by challenging existing institutions in every form. Impatient with the slowness of Alexander's reforms but unable to agree on a constructive program, they nevertheless could agree that whatever was, was wrong. It was this group that Turgenev dubbed "nihilist" (page 169). This name was subsequently applied indiscriminately to the Terrorists, who were an offspring of the Nihilist movement. They were Nihilists with a faith in the bomb as a weapon to win political and social justice. They were drawn, as were Russian radicals in general, almost exclusively from the intelligentsia, whereas in western countries reforming groups were usually made up of bourgeoisie and proletariat as well. In Russia, however, industrialization had scarcely penetrated; the whole vast country had only a few hundred miles of railroad in 1860, and the industrial classes were almost entirely lacking.

*Alexander II's
subsequent reforms*

ALTHOUGH THE reform agitation increased the government's alarm regarding radicals, at the same time it made the need for reform appear more urgent. Alexander's government complied. The system of taxation was modernized along the best western models; elementary and secondary educational opportunities were widened at state expense; tariffs were lowered. In 1863 a law regulating universities granted a high degree of academic freedom, though it did not legalize student societies, which were still frowned upon as breeders of violence. That year serfs on state and crown lands were freed upon more generous terms than the decree of 1861 had provided for privately bound serfs. In 1864 and 1870 came the very significant *zemstvo* (council) laws, which reorganized local government. Before these decrees, provincial, district, and municipal administration had rested largely in the hands of the landlords; now it was vested in local assemblies, elected and organized on a class basis. The *zemstvos* were given control of roads, health, and education,

184

but, significantly, were left without police power. Since emancipation had removed the former serf from the often strained mercy of the landlords, the system of justice was revised in 1864. Trial by jury was permitted in certain cases; a new hierarchy of courts was set up; and modern court procedure was introduced. In 1874 the army underwent a reorganization that distributed the burden of military service more equitably than before among all classes.

*Polish revolt
and the crisis of 1863-1864*

PROMISING AS these laws were, they merely titillated the liberals, who asked when "the building would be crowned"—when an elective national assembly would be called together. But the liberals were doomed to disappointment. The execution of Alexander's reforms was typically entrusted to those who wanted to limit or undo them, so that they were only partly effective. Moreover, each reform made further reform seem less urgent to the "Czar Liberator," and in his last years he became a confirmed reactionary. The reaction was due primarily to the essentially conservative temperament of Alexander II, who, though willing to rectify patent abuse, did not subscribe to the principle of reform for its own sake. His natural inclinations were bolstered not only by the growing radicalism, violence, and terror among the Russians but also by a revolution among the Poles.

Midstream in the reform movement, Alexander had relaxed the regime in Poland in an effort (1862) to correct the worst abuses and to win the support of the Poles. But his overtures only opened the door to agitation by Polish nationalists, who wanted nothing short of independence and the old Polish boundaries. An effort to silence the leading nationalists by conscripting them into the army finally produced revolt in January 1863. Most of the fighting was guerilla warfare. The Poles had no standing army, and the intervention that they had hoped for from the French emperor, avowed champion of national rights and defender of Catholics, was not forthcoming, since he was preoccupied with Mexico. On the other hand, the calculating Prussian minister-president Otto von Bismarck offered to aid the Russian government. English public opinion favored the Poles. At one point, it looked as if the Polish insurrection, adding to the tension resulting from the Schleswig-Holstein crises (page 188) might start a world conflict, putting the Prussians and the Russians into the American Civil War on the side of the Union, and the English and the French on the side of the Confederate States (pages 249-254). But in 1864 the Polish secession was suppressed locally. The defeated Poles were treated with a severity that has become legendary. All the earlier liberal concessions were withdrawn. Use of the Polish language was discountenanced. To punish the Polish nobles, whose work the insurrection had been, and to win over the Polish peasant, Polish serfs were emancipated on terms far more liberal than those of the Russian edict of 1861. Roman Catholic churches and monasteries were confiscated. The Polish episode dampened Alexander's at best lukewarm ardor for reform. Multiplying Terrorist plots, including several against his own life, practically extinguished it.

The age
of Realpolitik
AN OBSERVER of 1863—looking upon the victory of *Realpolitik* rather than of Mazzinian humanitarianism in Italy, unable to discern the weaknesses that would nevertheless soon become apparent in the reforms that in France, Austria, and Russia were concurrently being handed down from above, seeing secession forcefully suppressed by a democracy in the United States and by an autocracy in Poland, and having cause to believe that plebiscites were the rationalization rather than the grounds for the swapping of territory and peoples—might well have remembered Bismarck's words of the previous year: "Not by speeches and majority votes are the great questions of the day decided—that was the great mistake of 1848 and 1849—but by iron and blood."

"IRON," "LIBERALISM,"
AND "ERROR" (1863-1871)

THE GERMAN Confederation had long been, like Italy, an anachronism on a continent of virile national states. As in Italy, a strong movement espoused national unity and inspired several contradictory plans. As in Italy, unity was to be achieved through war and, even more than in Italy, was to be the work of a single leader working through a leading state. Provocation, trickery, and risk-taking were methods common in the unification of both countries.

The German problem
contrasted with the Italian
YET THE differences between the German and the Italian stories are perhaps even more striking than their similarities. In Germany as in Italy the main obstacle to unification was Austria. But in Germany Austria was not a feared and hated foreign power; it was the respected traditional leader of the German states. The Hohenzollerns of Prussia, unlike the House of Savoy, were relatively new challengers for hegemony, and the thought that they might be the rulers of a united German empire was still somewhat strange. Since Prussia, unlike Sardinia, was a great power, she was to resolve her difficulties not by calling in foreign aid, but by her own efforts in a series of diplomatic victories and limited wars in which one of her major concerns would be to prevent foreign intervention on her opponents' side. The Prussian dynasty made small pretense to being liberal; it counted rather upon the economic attraction of the *Zollverein* and the force of its army than on nationalist uprisings to overcome a marked separatism in some quarters, and public opinion was of secondary

importance, except as sentimental background, until the very last stages of unification. The principle of consent of the governed did not even receive the tribute of manipulated plebiscites. Prussia did not lead the German states to unity as Sardinia had led the weak states of Italy but rather imposed unity on some and maneuvered others. In the final union, because other German dynasties were also strong and particularist, Prussia, greatly enlarged, retained her identity in a federated state, whereas Sardinia merged hers in a single Italian monarchy. The new German state did not unite all Germans but deliberately excluded the largest German-dominated state—the Habsburg empire. In fact, the entire process was to be not so much a unification of Germany as an expansion of Prussia.

The effect of Italian events in Germany

IN A SENSE Cavour's war with Austria was responsible for the ultimate unification of Germany. The Italian example was contagious. Nationalism, disrespectfully buried in 1848-1850, sprang up once more in Germany. New societies were formed, and new plans for unity were hatched. The fear in 1859 that France might invade Austria, and Napoleon's subsequent annexation of Nice and Savoy, made Germans once more think of keeping watch on the Rhine. Napoleon's apparent revival of the slogan of "natural boundaries" also brought to the fore a plan for the reform of the Prussian army, and reform began in earnest with the appointment of General Albert von Roon as minister of war in December 1859. New plans for German unity were legion. They varied from a strong centralized state to a federation only slightly more cohesive than the existing Bund. Some gave Austria preponderance; some gave it to Prussia; some tried to equate the position of the two. But all were to founder on the inability to solve the Austrian-Prussian relationship and on the intransigence of Bismarck, who in 1862 was to become minister-president of Prussia and had a plan of his own. Bismarck was a Prussian Junker, an uncompromising monarchist, and a thoroughgoing advocate of *Realpolitik*. Blunt and fearless, he expounded his philosophy of politics in ringing statements that provoked admiration or consternation. He had been ambassador to St. Petersburg and then to Paris, and had taken the measure of the men he would have to deal with in both capitals.

Bismarck versus the parliament

THE PRUSSIAN army reform that Napoleon's machinations in Italy had precipitated encountered a head-on opposition. The legislature refused to appropriate the money needed for army expansion, and the ensuing deadlock induced the king to put Bismarck, previously regarded as too importunate, into the cabinet. Bismarck, as was intended, proceeded boldly with army reform, collecting taxes without the vote of parliament, applying for the current year the budget passed for the 187 preceding year, and finding technically constitutional grounds for doing so. With the danger of parliamentary explosion ever at his heels, he persuaded, cajoled, and coerced, and held steadfastly to his conviction that the crown and not a parliamentary majority should rule Prussia. There was no explosion, the army was reformed, and Bismarck was placed in position to carry out his purposes.

Crisis
in Schleswig and Holstein

A CRISIS over the little duchies of Schleswig and Holstein gave him his first opportunity for Prussian expansion. The king of Denmark was also the duke of Schleswig and of Holstein. Nationalists among the Danes wanted to make the duchies an integral part of the Danish state. But the people of the duchies were not Danish; almost all the Holsteiners and more than half the Schleswigers were German. They had no desire to be incorporated into the Danish kingdom. Their leanings were toward Germany (Holstein in fact was a part of the German Confederation), and they received support from this quarter against the Danes. The tug of war between Denmark and the duchies had led to a Danish-Prussian war in 1848-1850 (page 135) and to the compromise London Protocol of 1852, which satisfied neither side. In 1863 the king of Denmark, disregarding the London Protocol, proclaimed the incorporation of Schleswig into his kingdom. The German Confederation at once declared itself in favor of a native German claimant to the duchies, demanded contingents from the nearby German states, and sent them into the duchies.

The war
against Denmark

BISMARCK SAW in the crisis a chance for promoting his own design. On the grounds that both Denmark and the Confederation were violating the London Protocol, which Prussia and Austria were pledged to maintain, he refused to act through the Confederation. Instead he persuaded Austria to join Prussia in a joint action to restrain Denmark. The two powers sent the Danish king an ultimatum to repeal the annexation, counting on the king not to accept it (and indeed they did not allow him time enough to consider it carefully). Bismarck also encouraged the Danes in their belief that England would come to their aid, and so hardened them against appeasement. Then, with equal skill, he forestalled European intervention by persuading the international conference called at London to attempt a peaceful settlement.

On the battlefields the new army of Prussia, aided by Austrian forces, outmatched the Danish army, and the war was over in a few months. Denmark surrendered the two duchies, along with adjacent territory, to Austria and Prussia. By the Treaty of Gastein (1865), the two victors agreed that Schleswig-Holstein should be a single joint state but that Austria should administer Holstein and Prussia, Schleswig. It required no great perspicacity to grasp that this arrangement would not, and perhaps was not intended to, provide a permanent solution of the Schleswig-Holstein question, especially since Austria's Holstein was largely surrounded by Prussian territory. The Austrians accepted the arrangement chiefly because the Hungarians, once more taking advantage of the Austrian government's involvements, were, with encouragement from Bismarck, renewing their demands for political freedom.

Napoleon
and the German-Danish War

WHILE BISMARCK was thus manipulating the German situation, the self-appointed moderator of European reconstruction remained aloof in Paris. Napoleon III neither supported the duchies, as might have been expected from his nationalist principles, nor fought against Prussia, as his neighbor England suggested. Embroiled with the United States over Mexico and having failed to win any single party's undivided loyalty by his policy of offering all-things-to-all-men, he allowed events to slip beyond him, and the initiative in mapmaking passed irretrievably to Bismarck. Napoleon underestimated Bismarck and misjudged the German situation: "He has not the Liberal and revolutionary movement behind him, and so probably will lack the power to accomplish great things."

Napoleon
and the Austro-Prussian rivalry

IN FACT Napoleon had some reason to believe that he was still the umpire of Europe, since, in the rapidly approaching struggle between Austria and Prussia, both sides sought his friendship. In a meeting between Bismarck and Napoleon at Biarritz in October 1865 Napoleon, beguiled by talk of compensation for France along the Rhine, assured Bismarck of France's neutrality in case of a war between Austria and Prussia. Napoleon's policy was obvious: while the German states beat each other into exhaustion, he would profit from his neutrality. Recalling the battlefields of Magenta and Solferino, he held the Austrian army in high regard; and he underrated the Prussian army. He even gave his approval to a secret Prussian alliance with Italy, which was concluded in April 1866. It required Italy to join Prussia in any war against Austria that might break out within the next three months; in return Italy was to receive the long coveted province of Venetia from Austria. Austria also bargained with France and was finally obliged to promise, as the price of French neutrality, that she would cede Venetia to Napoleon, who would give it to Italy, no matter what the outcome of any fighting might be. Napoleon had good grounds for hoping that, win who might in Germany, the loyalty of the new Italian state would be his. But time was to show that he had squandered his only chance to forestall the creation of a unified Prussian state on the vulnerable flank of France.

Bringing on
the war with Austria

ASSURED OF French neutrality and Italian support, Bismarck lost no time in provoking a war with Austria. Always alert to mask his designs, he made a proposal for reform of the Germanic Confederation. The anticipated Austrian refusal would give him the appearance of fighting for reform, especially since his plan contained a provision for a legislative body elected by universal suffrage. To make sure that the Austrians would be provoked, he also protested the way they were running Holstein and even sent Prussian troops into that duchy. Thereupon, Austria, counting upon the sympathy of most of the other German states, persuaded the German Diet to declare war upon Prussia. Prussia immediately declared the Confederation dissolved, and the carefully prepared duel for German supremacy began.

The Seven Weeks' War
of Austria and Prussia (1866)

THE PRUSSIAN army, thoroughly modernized and highly trained, was commanded by a military genius, General Helmuth Bernhard von Moltke. A shrewd student of the blitzkrieg methods of Napoleon I, Moltke also recognized the possibilities of mechanical warfare—the telegraph, the railroad, and a new weapon, the breech-loading "needle gun," which could be loaded, lying down, four or five times as fast as the muzzle-loading weapon of the Austrian soldier, who had to stand and present a full target to his enemy. While the Prussians, poised for action, took the offensive everywhere, the Italians, even though defeated at Custozza, obliged the Austrians to divide their forces. In less than three weeks the Prussians had defeated the Austrians at Sadowa (or Königgrätz) in a tremendous and terrible battle; in another three weeks the Prussians were within sight of Vienna. By the end of July peace negotiations began, and by the end of August a treaty was signed at Prague.

The new map
of Germany and Italy

THE VICTORIOUS Bismarck now arranged the map of Germany to suit his interpretation of its historically and strategically justifiable boundaries. Austria was specifically expelled from Germany. Prussia annexed outright those states or enclaves

Prussia is shaded black throughout these maps. By 1834 (first map) the Prussian-dominated Zollverein (hatched areas) included many of the principal states in the German Confederation, to the exclusion of Austria, the dominant state in the Confederation. By 1867 all of the non-Austrian German states had joined the Zollverein. In that year (second map), after the Austrian defeat at Sadowa in the Seven Weeks' War, Prussia greatly enlarged her own holdings and also replaced the German Confederation by a new North German Confederation, from which Austria was excluded. The southern German members of the Zollverein accepted closer ties with Prussia (third map) under stress of the Franco-Prussian War (pages 199-201), and the German Empire under the king of Prussia was proclaimed in 1871. The war, touched off by diplomatic maneuvering at Ems over the Spanish succession, resulted in French defeats at Metz and Sedan, the siege and capture of Paris, and the loss of Alsace-Lorraine to the German Empire. (Though a member of the Zollverein, Luxemburg, because of her relation to the Netherlands, did not become a part of the German Empire.)

GERMAN UNIFICATION

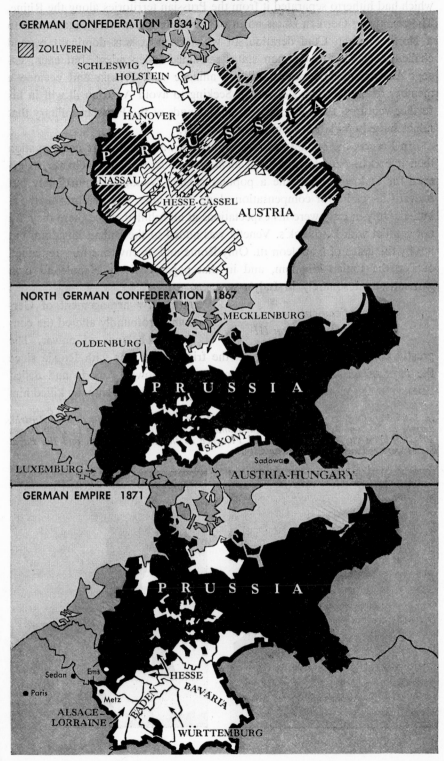

GERMAN CONFEDERATION 1834

ZOLLVEREIN

SCHLESWIG
HOLSTEIN
HANOVER
P R U S S I A
NASSAU
HESSE-CASSEL
AUSTRIA

NORTH GERMAN CONFEDERATION 1867

MECKLENBURG
OLDENBURG
P R U S S I A
SAXONY
Sadowa
LUXEMBURG
AUSTRIA-HUNGARY

GERMAN EMPIRE 1871

P R U S S I A
Sedan
Ems
Paris
HESSE
BAVARIA
Metz
BADEN
ALSACE-
LORRAINE
WÜRTTEMBURG

which had hitherto separated it from the Prussian territories along the Rhine. The remaining German states north of the Main River were organized into a North German Confederation, in which Prussia was dominant beyond challenge. The south German states remained independent, but each, except Austria, made a secret military alliance with Prussia and became a member of the German *Zollverein*. Seeking to avoid Austrian ill will in his further ventures, Bismarck resisted all demands of the Prussian military that might have humiliated Vienna unnecessarily.

In France, the collapse of Austria at Sadowa spread more consternation than it had in Austria; and *"Revanche pour Sadowa!"* ("A chance to get even for Sadowa!") became a popular slogan. Napoleon immediately put forward his claim for compensation along the Rhine, but was brusquely rebuffed. Only in Italy were his expectations at all fulfilled, since there they did not conflict with Bismarck's. Venetia was added to the Italian kingdom, but not by the grace of Napoleon III. Only Rome and its environs now remained outside the Italian kingdom, and in that papal territory Napoleon's own garrison stood squarely in Italy's way.

The predicament
of Emperor Napoleon III

THE NEW arrangement of Germany profoundly altered the continental balance of power. The greatly enlarged Prussian state, on the friendliest terms with Russia since the days of the Polish revolution, now overshadowed Austria and defied France. Suffering intermittently from the gallstones that eventually killed him

In 1866 Venetia passed to Italy as its reward for supporting Prussia against Austria, despite the Italian defeat at Custozza. Rome fell to nationalist troops in 1870 (pages 201-202). The city of Rome replaced Florence as the Italian capital, and the Papal States were reduced to the Vatican City.

192

and desperately anxious to restore his lost prestige at home and abroad, Napoleon spent the next year in trying to secure Bismarck's consent to a belated annexation along the German border—on the Rhine, in Belgium, or preferably in Luxemburg. But Bismarck, while leading him on, never went all the way, and afterwards used the correspondence in the negotiations to discredit him.

The French Empire was now in serious straits. With the close of the American Civil War, Napoleon's Mexican venture, already in grave difficulties because of native Mexican opposition, was challenged by the United States. The maintenance of French troops across the Atlantic had been a serious drain on France's military power and treasury, and war with the victorious Grand Army of the United States was out of the question. Though Maximilian's devoted wife Carlotta pled with Napoleon and the pope, and lost her mind in the process, Napoleon abruptly withdrew the French expeditionary force (1867), and the Mexican emperor, thus deserted, fell before a Mexican firing squad. Humbled in Austria and Mexico, seldom had an emperor seemed less enviable.

The Empire completely liberalized

NAPOLEON finally sought to strengthen his position at home by catering to the liberals. In 1867 he broadened the powers of the legislature by permitting the interpellation of his ministers. In 1868 he relaxed the laws restricting the press and public meetings. As with his earlier concessions, the major effect was to give the opposition more leeway rather than to win new supporters. During the later sixties, in spite of the narrow limits placed on political life by the government, republicanism had grown steadily. Strikes, legalized in 1864, had multiplied, and a trade-union movement, though completely illegal, flourished. Marxism too was penetrating France. Among the radical groups republicanism made headway, and with the removal of the censorship and of restrictions upon public meetings, its strength and activity at once increased. It found a dynamic and highly articulate leader in a young republican named Léon Gambetta, and rapidly became a real threat to the Napoleonic regime.

More moderate liberals adhered to the so-called Third Party. They were willing to retain the Empire if it were refashioned in the mold of a constitutional monarchy. Having finally learned that favoring everybody was likely to win loyalty from none, and having seen the opposition pile up nearly 3,500,000 votes (out of less than 8,000,000) in the elections of 1869, Napoleon risked his future on the Third Party. In 1869 the Legislative Body became a real lower house, though ministers were declared to be responsible to the emperor alone. In 1870, in the face of increased republican agitation, a wave of strikes, and a tremendous demonstration against the government, the constitution was completely revamped into a thoroughly liberal document.

The changes were then submitted to the people in a typical Napoleonic plebiscite and received an overwhelming approval. The new "Liberal Empire" seemed built on a broader, sounder base than the old autocratic empire. But in a few months the forces unleashed by Napoleon when he had challenged the stability of the Austrian Empire in 1859 were to topple the edifice.

Effect of the war
on Austria and Hungary

IN AUSTRIA, as in France, the Austro-Prussian war brought to a head the attempts to develop a workable governmental structure. From 1861 to 1865 the Austrian government had functioned according to the February Patent of 1861, but Hungarians refused to send delegates to the central parliament, and Hungary was ruled autocratically from Vienna. The Hungarians' overt waiting for Austrian discomfiture weakened the home front, and the empire's financial situation went from bad to worse. In 1865, in the midst of the Schleswig-Holstein crisis, the Austrian government reopened negotiations with the Hungarian political leaders. The Austrian humiliation in the Seven Weeks' War made clear to both sides the need for Hungarian cooperation if a central government were to be established strong enough to play a positive role in European affairs.

The resulting *Ausgleich* (Compromise) of 1867 set up a state unique in Europe's annals. It created a "Dual Monarchy," thenceforth called Austria-Hungary. Each of the two parts retained its own institutions and acquired its independence, but they were to have the same ruler and joint ministries of foreign affairs, war, and finance; and annually the legislature of each was to send equal "delegations" to Vienna to consider common problems. In addition, the two parts were to make a treaty regarding trade, warfare, and other spheres of common action which was to be renewed every ten years. Inside Austria the government was based on the February Patent of 1861, which gave the preponderance of political power to the German bourgeoisie. Inside Hungary the March Laws of 1848 (pages 125-126) were restored, and the preponderance of political power thereby passed to the Magyars.

The *Ausgleich* settled the relationship, however, of only one component nationality to only one other. In each part of the Dual Monarchy the strongest minority ruled over many other nationalities. The anachronism of this situation, already manifest, rapidly became more pronounced as nationalist passions grew.

Liberalism and reform
within the United Kingdom

SINCE THE LAST phases of the Crimean War, the Whigs had usually ruled England. Lord Palmerston, who was prime minister for nine years, was liberal in his foreign policy but opposed to reform at home. Some notable reforms came during the Tory ministries of Lord Derby in 1858-1859 and 1866-1868. In 1858, as the scorned Chartists had once demanded, property qualifications for members of Parliament were repealed. That year, too, after leading Jewish subjects like Lionel Rothschild and Lord Mayor of London David Salomons had been repeatedly elected to Parliament but had been prevented by the form of the prescribed oath from taking their seats, public opinion induced the reluctant Lords to compromise and permit the willing Commons to revise its oath; the Lords did not make a similar change until 1866. Various efforts to extend the franchise at first met with defeat. The growth in numbers of the working class had nevertheless outmoded the Reform Bill of 1832, with its limited franchise. In 1867, when the Conservatives again held office, Derby and Disraeli favored a wider franchise, and a Second Reform Bill passed. By lowering the tax or rental qualification for voting, it doubled the electorate, particularly among the urban workers. In the first elections under the new franchise, the Conservatives were ousted, and the Liberals (Whigs), led by the conscientious, handsome, and eloquent William Ewart Gladstone came to power.

Gladstone began a series of reforms that reflected in Britain the spirit of political change that contemporaneously characterized France, Austria, North Germany, and Russia. Prompted by growing disaffection in Ireland and by the rising Fenian Movement, he designed two acts to alleviate dissatisfaction in Ireland. The Disestablishment Act of 1869 removed, except as a voluntary organization, the established Episcopal (i.e., Anglican) Church from Ireland, where it had been supported unwillingly for centuries by a resentful Catholic population. The Irish Land Act of 1870 was intended to relieve the Irish tenant from the major evils resulting from absentee landlordism. Although it was less effective than its sponsors had hoped, it was important as the first of a series of Irish land reform measures.

Other reforms followed speedily. The Forster Education Act of 1870 established a national system of education. It was intended to bring every child in England within easy reach of a school good enough to satisfy the government inspectors. It expanded the system of public support for schools, whether run by private persons or the local school authority. It permitted no distinctively denominational instruction in the "board schools" (those governed by elected local school boards). In 1871 the legal status of trade unions (page 150) was confirmed and the security of their funds reassured in the face of recent adverse court decisions. In 1872 the ballot was made secret. The Judicature Act of 1873 united the courts of law into a simpler and more effective organization. Before Gladstone's ministry (the first of four) came to an end in 1874, he succeeded also in putting through bills affecting liberal changes in the civil service, the universities, and the army. These bills aimed at a reduction of privilege and at the application of the principles of equality of opportunity and the opening of careers to men of talent.

Liberalism, nationalism, and constitutionalism in Germany

LIBERALISM HAD become so much of a vogue in Germany and elsewhere that the notoriously antiliberal Bismarck decided to flirt with the liberals. He placed in the constitution of the North German Confederation several liberal features, notably a popularly elected legislative assembly (Reichstag). On the other hand, many liberals, in view of Bismarck's realistic achievements in unifying Germany, switched from opposing to supporting the "Iron Chancellor." The Prussian Landtag passed a "bill of indemnity" by which it appropriated the funds to pay, and thus gave retroactive approval to, the past expenditures of Bismarck's government. Those more ready to sanction the legality of Bismarck's acts among the Prussian Progressive Party and the more nationalistic, less doctrinaire liberals elsewhere hastened to join a new National Liberal Party.

Yet it could hardly be said that liberalism had triumphed in the North German Confederation. The Reichstag's effectiveness was checked by a council (Bundesrat) of representatives apportioned among member states according to a reasonable estimate of their relative importance. The king of Prussia was permanently to be president of the Confederation, and his representative, the chancellor, was responsible to him alone. Although each member state retained its own government, military power was vested in the president. In addition, in the more powerful Bundesrat, Prussia was given 17 votes out of 43, and needed only 5 more, which her prestige and power usually assured her, in order to outweigh all the others.

Growth of the labor movement

AS PART OF the liberal vogue of the 1860's, the labor movement made headway in the more industrialized areas of Europe. We have already noted the increased activity of workingmen's organizations in France (page 193) and England (page 150). In Germany, the movement began to assume significance with the formation in 1863 of a potential German labor party, the Universal German Workingmen's Association. Its founder, Ferdinand Lassalle, believed that the way to improve labor's position was through political rather than revolutionary action. He wanted to build a powerful labor association that would (1) obtain universal suffrage, (2) thereby secure control of the state, and (3) use that control to benefit the working class, particularly by means of credit and subsidies to productive enterprises owned cooperatively by the workers. After the unifying of the North German states in 1866, German industry began to forge ahead with great rapidity, thus providing increasing raw material for unionism and socialism. Lassalle's theories dominated the German labor scene until the late sixties, when a new party was founded, the German Social Democratic Party (1869), based on the Marxian doctrines of class conflict and political revolution. For the next few years the two parties fought for control of the political labor movement. Meanwhile (1868) trade unions appeared in Germany; and a law of 1870 made them legal in Austria.

Formation of the First International

THE CONSPICUOUS growth of the labor movement brought about the formation of the First International Workingmen's Association in 1864. Its early meetings provided arenas for disputes among its leaders on means and ends rather than for agreements on the common interests of labor. Gradually the socialists grew stronger, and after 1869 the chief issue was only what kind of socialism the International should stand for. On one side stood Marx, who wanted a centralized revolutionary organization, and on the other stood Mikhail Bakunin, an exiled Russian anarchist, who wanted a loose federal organization to promote local terrorism and dissolve authority everywhere. Marx eventually won, expelling Bakunin from the International in 1872. Bakunin's followers, having as anarchists lost faith in all forms of government, resorted more and more to the bomb. Their influence in Russia, where they considered the bullet a practical substitute for the ballot, was enormous. In France, because of the prestige of their leader Proudhon, the anarchists also made headway, but there they resorted more to argument than to violence.

The papal stand against some modern ideas

THE FORWARD march of liberalism, radicalism, nationalism, and the scientific temper was viewed with alarm from one very influential quarter. Pope Pius IX, who had begun his pontificate as the "pope of progress," returned to Rome from his enforced exile in 1848-1849 a confirmed conservative. By the fifties his views had become perfectly attuned to reaction. In the sixties, as unification movements succeeded and states grew more nationalist, the violent character of the change in Italy affected him directly. Nationalism was not only depriving him of his temporal power; the national state also tended to diminish clerical influence by taking over functions formerly performed by the church and by commanding emotional loyalties hitherto dedicated to the church. In action the national state was fundamentally at odds with an international church.

In the realm of ideas, too, Pius felt the ground shifting. Liberalism tended increasingly to secularism, tolerance, and religious indifference. Science was now invading the province of the church, not only claiming to be the road to pragmatic truth but even creating skepticism and agnosticism regarding the Truth of the church. And industrial development and the rapid accumulation of wealth were placing a growing emphasis on the material things in life at the expense of the spiritual.

Spurred to action by fear of a liberal movement within the church itself, Pius issued in 1864 his encyclical *Quanta Cura*, along with "A Syllabus of   197 the Principal Errors of Our Time." The "Syllabus" took the form of quotations from earlier condemnations by Pius IX of eighty propositions that were described as, in their own context at least, containing errors. Pius therein denounced not only recent theological heresies but also recent political developments. Pantheism, certain forms of rationalism, naturalism, and indifferentism were listed as errors, as well as propositions regarding socialism, communism, separation of education from the church, the historical growth of the church, the limits to be placed upon the temporal power of the pope, and the toleration in Catholic countries of other religions. The final error in the list was the belief that "the Roman Pontiff can and ought to reconcile himself to, and agree with, progress, liberalism, and contemporary civilization."

The "Syllabus" raised in many minds, including those of liberal Catholics like the historians Lord Acton of England and Ignaz Döllinger of Munich, the query whether the pope could alone speak for the church. This question had been a subject of dispute between popes and councils all during and since the Middle Ages. An important decision now favored the popes. Six years after the "Syllabus," shortly before the Italian government occupied Rome, the Vatican Council, the first ecumenical council of the church since the sixteenth century, sanctioned the dogma of papal infallibility. According to this dogma the pope, by virtue of his supreme apostolic power, when speaking *ex cathedra* (i.e., from the papal throne as the head of the church) in matters of faith and morals, is infallible. The "Syllabus" had left no doubt about where the pope stood on many "errors," and those Catholics who protested were either excommunicated, like Döllinger, or conformed, like Acton. The church, believing itself at bay between militant nationalism and materialistic liberalism, had struck back with the only weapon it had left—its claim to interpret the way of God to Man.

THE EMPIRE IS DEAD!

LONG LIVE THE EMPIRE!

For several years after the emergence of the new Rumania, Italy, Prussia, and Austria-Hungary the relations of the various countries of Europe were somewhat unsettled. Foreign policies could no longer swing on the hinges of the old status quo, the old Concert of Europe, and the old balance of power. Treaties and the diplomatic code, always delicate at best, were weaker reeds than ever in the new era of *Realpolitik,* and engagements between states seemed only snares for the unwary. Since apparently in the future each state would have to fend for itself, all cast desperately about for new alliances.

*The quest
for a new balance of power*

THE RULERS of Austria and France, feeling wronged, were naturally drawn together against the transgressor Prussia. As the governments of both countries were to a marked extent the prisoners of their internal problems—Austria of her polyglot nationalities and Napoleon of his fading popularity—they took some time to iron out details, and their relationship long remained fluid. Italy was brought into their conversations, though not very smoothly, as the presence of French troops in Rome still caused friction between her and France. Counterbalancing this grouping was a firm and friendly Russo-Prussian understanding, carried over from Russia's resentment of the Austrian attitude during the Crimean War and the Congress of Paris and from Prussia's co-operation with Russia against revolution in Poland.

*The war spirit
in France and Prussia*

BY 1870 A WAR between France and Prussia was generally conceded to be inevitable. Actually no life-and-death issue confronted the two countries. But since the Battle of Sadowa, Frenchmen had been witnessing the collapse of an age-old principle of French foreign policy. The balance of power in central Europe had been totally upset! The unexpected Prussian victory in 1866, the creation of a large and dangerous neighbor state without French consent, and the veto of French compensation in Luxemburg were all profoundly humiliating and alarming. On the Prussian side, Bismarck correctly estimated that a war against France would be welcome to most Germans and would serve as a means of driving the south German states into the Prussian fold. France began to reorganize her army. Prussia proceeded to bring the rest of the North German Confederation up to Prussian military standards. Both sides awaited only a provocative incident.

*The immediate cause
of the Franco-Prussian War*

THE INCIDENT was provided by a revolution in Spain. That country had been enduring a miserable succession of factional insurrections, civil wars, and intrigues, stemming from the revival by Don Carlos' son of his claims to the Spanish throne (page 123). In 1868, Queen Isabella II, whose profligacy united all moderate and liberal groups against her, was forced into exile, and the ensuing constituent Cortes, anxious to avoid both Carlists and republicans, cast about for a king to head the new government. Finally, and partly through the machinations of Bismarck, the crown was offered to the Hohenzollern prince Leopold. Bismarck saw in a Hohenzollern ruler of Spain a chance for an alliance that would tie up French troops on the Spanish border in case of war; and the French, looking upon the Hohenzollern candidacy as a new insult and threat, were roused to fever pitch. Peace seemed assured, however, when Leopold, 199 once of his own volition and again through his father, refused the Spanish crown.

Unfortunately, the French government was not content with a temporary victory. Spurred on by a flamboyant speech of the foreign minister, it instructed the French ambassador to demand that the Prussian king give his formal assurance that he would not approve if the offer to Leopold should be renewed. This King William politely but firmly refused to do, and from the vacation resort at Ems, where the French ambassador had followed him, he sent a dispatch to Bismarck describing their conversations.

Bismarck now did his bit to provoke an explosion. He altered the dispatch just enough to give the impression that on both sides diplomatic amenities had been shockingly violated at Ems. His distorted account, published in the press, infuriated both the Germans and the French, as Bismarck had intended it should, and gave to Paris just the pretext it was seeking.

The advance
of the Germans into France

THE FRENCH declared war on July 19, 1870, only ten members of the legislature (including Thiers and Gambetta) voting no. Contrary to expectations, France received no help from either Austria or Italy. The south German states at once joined Prussia, as Bismarck had confidently hoped. The French forces, inadequately prepared and suffering from the utmost confusion, were simply no match for Moltke's efficient military machine. One French general telegraphed: "Have arrived at Belfort. Can't find my brigade; can't find the general of the Division. What shall I do? Don't know where my regiments are." The French breech-loading rifle, the chassepot, and the new machine gun, the mitrailleuse, were superior to the Prussian needle gun, but not enough. A three-pronged German offensive steam-rollered toward France. By mid-August one of the two French armies was bottled up in Metz. On September 1 the second French army, attempting to relieve Metz, was decisively defeated in the Battle of Sedan, and on the following day, with Napoleon himself at its head, surrendered to the Germans.

The rise and defense
of the Provisional Republic

THE NEWS of the emperor's surrender could have but one result in Paris. The painstakingly erected Liberal Empire collapsed like the proverbial house of cards. Amid the wild enthusiasm of the Paris crowd, a governing committee was improvised, and the French Republic was proclaimed. This provisional government, of which Gambetta was the leading light, refused to make peace unless French territory were left intact, and spent the next months in spectacular efforts to recruit new troops.

Two German armies, having swept on from Sedan to Paris, surrounded the city with a ring of iron. Gambetta escaped from the besieged capital in a balloon and, establishing a new capital first at Tours and then at Bordeaux, conjured up relief forces in the provinces. These half-trained units tried desperately to relieve Paris but succeeded only in prolonging the war without altering the outcome. In October the surrender of Metz released more German contingents for the siege of Paris. In January, as winter and famine stalked the city, the Germans pounded it with a terrific bombardment. Mass suffering and individual heroism proved not enough, and Paris capitulated on January 28.

Completion
of German and Italian unity

WHILE THE war was in progress, Bismarck took advantage of the heightened nationalist fervor to propose to the south German states that they enter the North German Confederation. By separate agreements Bavaria, Württemberg, and Baden each consented. The enlarged German state was christened the German Empire (see map page 191). As a crowning irony, King William of Prussia, formerly president of the North German Confederation, was solemnly hailed as "German Emperor" by the confederated monarchs, their generals, and their retinues in Louis xiv's Palace of Versailles, ten days before Paris fell.

Italy too took advantage of France's desperate plight. In the hour of need French troops had been withdrawn from Rome. Italian forces immediately in-

The German emperor is led into a shuttered Paris by a diabolical Bismarck, followed by a cloud of carrion crows. A contemporary French cartoon by Félix Regamey.

A Viennese cartoonist's view in 1870 of Germany's future under the helmet of Prussian military domination.

vaded it, defeating the pope's army, and Rome was incorporated into the Kingdom of Italy (see map, page 192). Thus the plans of Bismarck for a German Empire and the plans of Cavour for a Kingdom of Italy were finally capped through the collapse of the Second Empire of the Bonapartes.

The Treaty of Frankfurt and the reaction to it in Paris

IN FEBRUARY the French elected a National Assembly, which chose the venerable Thiers as "head of the executive power." This new provisional government now sued for peace. Bismarck's terms were hard—a triumphal march in Paris, the cession of Alsace and part of Lorraine, a large indemnity, and an army of occupation pending its payment. These terms roused the bitter opposition of the Alsace-Lorrainers, who were supported by many of the Republicans. Nevertheless, the National Assembly, consisting largely of monarchists who had been elected because the countryside was defeatist and did not approve of the Republican spirit of last-ditch resistance, accepted Bismarck's terms. The German army marched into Paris on March 2 and out again on March 3. Bismarck's other terms were eventually embodied in a treaty signed at Frankfurt on May 10, but not until France had suffered a civil war.

In Paris, whose abnormal conditions had brought great secret power to the socialists led by Louis Auguste Blanqui, the peace terms were very unpopular, as was the Assembly that had agreed to them. The preponderantly conservative Assembly, having moved from Bordeaux to Versailles (an insult as well as a financial injury to Paris), was determined to keep national con-

202

trol in its own hands. The Republicans in Paris were afraid that this interim Assembly would refuse to translate into fact the Republic that had been proclaimed at Napoleon's downfall. In the post-siege atmosphere of Paris, business was still very far from normal. Many were unemployed, food was scarce, prices were high, and people ate their pets. It was not hard for radicals to exploit the discontents of the Republicans.

Civil war and the Commune of 1871
IN MARCH trouble began when the Paris National Guard seized possession of certain artillery belonging to the regular army. The Assembly sent troops into Paris to retake the guns, but they fraternized with the National Guard, and after two of their generals had been shot, they retired. The Parisians then set up a municipal council (Commune), composed of all shades of left-wing opinion from moderate republicans to anarchists. In an effort to undermine the National Assembly, the Paris Commune tried to stir up revolution in the other large cities with a view to establishing a series of communes that would eventually become the nucleus of a decentralized, federal government. This movement, sometimes called "Communist," is more correctly called "Communard"; though the spirit of the First International was present in Paris, it did not determine the Commune's program, which in fact remained uncoordinated all along.

In April and May the troops of the Assembly attacked with greater vigor, and toward the end of May finally defeated the Communard troops in bloody and savage street fighting. Much of Paris was set afire; several historical edifices including the Hôtel de Ville and the Tuileries palace were almost entirely destroyed. Hostages, including the archbishop of Paris, were shot, and in reprisal the step-by-step victorious Assembly gave no quarter. In the "Bloody Week" of May 21-28 about 20,000 were killed and about 40,000 imprisoned. Trials by court-martial continued until 1876. Over 13,000 persons were sentenced, of whom 270 were condemned to death and 7500 transported. The revolutionists were all but wiped out, and socialism was quiescent in France until the 1890's. Though the Commune in fact never became an instrument of class warfare, it assumed that character in the symbolism of both sides. The bloody denouement of 1871 was firmly linked with proletarian dictatorship in the minds of the bourgeoisie, and with relentless capitalist oppression in socialist annals. The Commune thus stamped the concept of bloody class warfare firmly into the ideological fabric of the times.

IN 1871 LITTLE was left of the Europe that had emerged from the Congress of Vienna. Four new states had appeared since 1850 (Rumania, Italy, the Dual Monarchy, and the German Empire), and the tides of constitutionalism and nationalism were submerging the traditional powers of royalty. In 1850 a   203

Concert of Europe still operated to settle international disputes; by 1871 the Concert had been undermined by national rivalries and *Realpolitik*. If peace was to be maintained, it appeared that it would have to be maintained by a new balance of power between rival alliances. In 1850 an aristocracy was still a dominant feature of European life; by 1871 in western Europe the bourgeoisie were gaining control. Before 1850 bourgeoisie and proletariat had often cooperated against the status quo; by 1871 this alliance had turned to fairly consistent enmity, since the proletariat (or at least its articulate leaders) looked upon the status quo as bourgeois. In 1850 church and state had generally cooperated to restrain radicalism; by 1871 church and state were more likely to be at loggerheads. Between 1850 and 1871 the free international exchange of goods pictured by laissez-faire economists temporarily prevailed, though only to give way in the 1870's to protectionism and economic competition between nations. Along with economic and political rivalries came competition for colonies; the relative indifference to empire prevalent before 1850 turned into active imperialist rivalry in the fifties and sixties (Chapter 5).

While political and economic institutions were thus being transformed, a comparable change was taking place in the European intellectual climate. The adoption of a wide franchise in England, France, Italy, Germany, and elsewhere before 1870 marked the end of bourgeois liberalism and the beginning of a liberalism based on universal manhood suffrage. Romanticism and the philosophic idealism of the first half-century, given body-blows by the failures of 1848, receded (without entirely vanishing) before realism and empiricism, emboldened by the rapid advance of science and industry. The materialistic determinism of Marx, *Realpolitik* as practiced by Bismarck and Cavour, and the rise of hard-headed labor movements expressed this change in attitude. In literature and art, romanticism, persistent in 1850, had by 1871 given ground to the empirical temper of the times.

The need to believe in a better world, which in an earlier age had been satisfied by religion, was now often filled through the secular creeds of progress—liberalism, nationalism, socialism, and "Social Darwinism." Advances in science and industry and the tremendous increase in material wealth seemed to bear out the conviction that society was progressing inevitably toward perfection. A few generations later one would wonder whether Cavour, Bismarck, Marx, Darwin, Wagner, and their cohorts had not led away from progress to Nazism, Fascism, Bolshevism, and crass materialism, whether technological advance had not created a Frankenstein that might in fact produce nothing but disaster. To most mid-nineteenth-century minds, however (despite popes who cried "Error!" and esthetes who hissed "Philistine!"), dialectical materialism, competition for survival among species, classes, and nations, and empirical examination of reality all pointed the same way; and no matter how hard the way, the road seemed clear and the goal certain.

1813-1883	Richard Wagner
1848	"Pre-Raphaelite Brotherhood" organized
1849-1851	Gold rushes in California and Australia
1850	Frederick William's constitution put into operation in Prussia
1850	Tennyson's *In Memoriam*
1852-1871	Second Empire of the Bonapartes
1853-1856	Crimean War
1855	England passes laws limiting liability of investor
1856	Henry Bessemer produces good steel economically
1857	International business crisis
1857	Charles Baudelaire's *Flowers of Evil*
1859-1861	The wars for the unification of Italy
1859	Karl Marx's *On the Criticism of Political Economy* (later revised as *Das Kapital*)
1859	John Stuart Mill's *On Liberty*
1859	Bunsen and Kirchhoff devise spectroscope
1859	Darwin's *On the Origin of Species by Natural Selection*
1860	Cobden-Chevalier Treaty
1861-1867	Napoleon III attempts to create a Mexican Empire
1861	Emancipation of Russian serfs by Alexander II
1862	Bismarck becomes minister-president of Prussia
1862	"The Five" contribute toward a distinctive Russian music
1863-1865	Schleswig-Holstein crisis
1863-1864	Polish revolt
1863	Ernest Renan's *Life of Jesus*
1863	Impressionists exhibit in the Salon des Refusés
1864	Pope Pius IX issues "A Syllabus of Errors"
1864	International Red Cross founded
1864	Pasteur asserts bacilli cause fermentation and are ordinarily present in air
c. 1865-1896	Herbert Spencer's *Synthetic Philosophy*
1865-1869	Tolstoy's *War and Peace*
1865-1866	Bismarck provokes and wins Seven Weeks' War
1865	Lister initiates antiseptic surgery
1866	Publication of Mendel's laws of heredity
1867	North German Confederation formed
1868-1874	First Gladstone ministry
1868	First Disraeli ministry
1870-1871	Franco-Prussian War
1871	William I proclaimed German emperor at Versailles
1871	Paris Commune defeated

Chapter four

UNIFICATION

AND EMANCIPATION

IN AMERICA

DESPITE direful auguries to the contrary, the United States after the inauguration of Andrew Jackson continued to prosper at home and to gain standing abroad, though not without some harrowing crises. Canals and railroads spread out across the land. Humanity streamed westward, constantly replenished by still greater streams from across the Atlantic, intensifying the differences between the stabler East and the brash young West. As new lands were opened up, new states found their places in a Union already precariously balanced between free-labor and slave-labor economies, until the balance was finally upset. At the same time, new industries and cities rose in the North, heightening the inequality in the distribution of wealth and economic power among the various sections of the Union. Sectionalism grew, and with it group tensions within each section. Yet, out of its accumulating resources and man power, the United States forged a new economic empire, and simultaneously its people, embracing a faith in their "manifest destiny," demanded a territorial empire as well.

All this time, an American culture was evolving. The sages of Boston and Concord converted literary and philosophical imports from Europe and the Far East into their own coinage. In Brooklyn the vibrant voice of Walt Whitman sounded a poetic call that was distinctly New World in its democratic message. In Illinois a self-tutored rail-splitter set forth his political beliefs in a style derived from the Bible, Blackstone, and the local cracker barrel. In remote California unremembered miners were finding new rhymes for "Oh! Susanna" and less quotable ditties.

During the entire period, this self-conscious culture was not so much isolationist as centripetal. In fact, it tightened some of its links with Europe— and in 1857 began the first of several attempts to lay an Atlantic cable. It   207 stretched out one hand to the Far East, while holding a loaded gun in the other. However self-reliant and self-satisfied, the American culture pattern continued to draw freely upon the world outside. New inventions, new peoples, new literary or artistic forms were eagerly borrowed from abroad, even though sometimes modified into products recognizably American.

During this period, other American areas were also creating an indigenous culture. The people of Canada were slowly groping toward mastery of the northern half of the continent, toward economic cooperation, and toward political unity. The countries south of the Rio Grande were attempting, with varying success, to work out an independent political and cultural existence. What Ralph Waldo Emerson, in an address entitled "The American Scholar," told the Phi Beta Kappa Society of Harvard College in 1837 about United States culture was becoming true of other nations of America too:

> The millions that around us are rushing into life, cannot always be fed on the sere remains of foreign harvests. Events, actions arise, that must be sung, that will sing themselves.

THE ADVANCE

OF THE COMMON MAN

THE JACKSONIANS were the heirs of the radical Jeffersonian socioeconomic philosophy. They did not hesitate, however, to make certain important modifications of their own in Jeffersonian principles in order to meet the changing times. The intellectuals who supported Jackson felt that they had a historic duty: to make government by the common people succeed in America and thus spearhead the growth of popular democracy throughout the civilized world.

*The political philosophy
of the Jacksonian Democrats*

FOR ONE thing, the Jacksonians had to make room for the new industrialism in their program. The Jeffersonians had extolled the virtues of an agricultural society, but the Jacksonians had to take cognizance of the rise of factories and mills, and recruited among the new propertyless urban laboring class, which demanded greater economic security and greater social and political recognition. The Jacksonian intellectual assigned an important role in the creation of wealth to labor. According to Martin Van Buren, one of Jackson's closest political associates, government ought to insure to the laboring classes "a full enjoyment of the fruits of their industry." To accomplish these ends, government must destroy "the blighting influence of partial legislation, monopolies, congregated wealth, and interested combinations."

Mutual interest
of Europe and America

THE JACKSONIANS looked with approval upon the successes achieved by the forces of social revolt in Europe. The Jacksonian intellectuals read the writings of French liberals; Jackson himself celebrated the Revolution of 1830 in France; Jacksonian Democrats hailed the passage of the Reform Bill in 1832 in England; and they were in sympathy with the later Chartist movement. George Bancroft, a famous historian who was one of Jackson's staunchest supporters, summed up the Jacksonian philosophy of history when he said: "It is now for the yeomanry and the mechanics to march at the head of civilization. The merchants and lawyers, that is, the moneyed interest, broke up feudalism. The day for the multitude has now dawned."

In turn, Europeans took careful note of democratic trends in America. British radicals such as William Cobbett watched the growing power of the masses in America with enthusiasm. The French political philosopher Alexis de Tocqueville, astutely evaluating Jacksonian merits and shortcomings, informed Europe in his *Democracy in America* (1835) that, for better or for worse, America had churned up the wave of the future. But not all of the travelers in America were friendly. Mrs. Frances Trollope said some harsh things about democratic customs in her *Domestic Manners of the Americans* (1832). Charles Dickens' *American Notes* (1842) reported the brutality of slavery, and the hero of *The Life and Adventures of Martin Chuzzlewit* (1843-1844) found in America not a land of opportunity but a country of merciless land swindlers.

Broadening the common
man's political power

DEMOCRACY had only recently reached down to the level of the common man in America. During the Revolution, all of the thirteen states had had some kind of property qualification for voting. Vermont, which became the fourteenth state in 1791, had allowed universal manhood suffrage. As the years passed, new states entered the Union from beyond the Alleghenies, where few wealthy or "upper-class" people lived, and these states threw out property qualifications for voting. Even in the thirteen original states, the cause of universal manhood suffrage was aided by the increase of freehold farmers and the arrival of immigrant workers, all of whom added to the pressure to remove voting barriers. Gradually, some eastern states amended their constitutions. Property requirements for voting were removed in Maryland in 1810, in Connecticut in 1818, in Massachusetts and New York in 1821 (but not in Rhode Island and New Jersey until 1842 and 1844 respectively, while adult white males were obliged to wait in Virginia until 1850 and in North Carolina until 1856).

Other restrictions upon political democracy were likewise removed during these decades. Various religious qualifications either for voting or for holding public office were abolished. Public offices were now held for shorter terms, with more rapid rotation of office. By 1828, in all the states except Delaware and South Carolina, presidential electors were chosen by the voters instead of being appointed by state legislatures. More important still, presidential electors had now lost the right to choose whom they wished and were bound to vote for the presidential candidate of their respective parties. Jackson was the first president who was chosen by an electoral process that was intended to reflect the popular preference.

Andrew Jackson as "the people's choice" THE COMING of Jackson to Washington was destined to sweep away the virtual monopoly of government that had been enjoyed until then by the country's propertied classes. For the first time, the masses had put their man into the White House, and thousands of them enthusiastically jammed Washington for the general's inauguration. What happened on that occasion confirmed the worst fears of those skeptical of popular rule. At the reception held at the White House, an excited crowd swarmed to see the president. Barrels of orange punch were upset and glasses broken as strangers stood in muddy boots on damask chairs to catch a glimpse of their man.

Andrew Jackson was the hero of the common man—and with good reason. Unlike any of his predecessors, he had been born in poverty, had been obliged to work with his own hands, and had received nothing but the rudiments of education, with the result that he always spoke an ungrammatical (though forceful) English. All this gave him great popular appeal. In addition, largely as a result of his victory over the British at New Orleans in 1815, he was a national military hero.

The personal popularity of the president had special importance in the trans-Allegheny West (which by 1830 counted roughly one-third of the population). The Westerner, less bound by tradition to his state than was customary in the original thirteen states, looked to the president for leadership and became thereby more strongly attached to the Union. Jackson, like most Westerners, believed in the right and ability of the common man to hold office and did not propose that government should remain the special privilege of eastern aristocracy. Furthermore, Jackson and his fellow Westerners chafed at the domination of their banks by eastern financiers, and they proposed to end it.

But Jackson's popularity among the masses was not confined to the West. The War of 1812 and recent protective tariffs had stimulated industrialism in the East. Textile mills had sprung up around Providence, Rhode Island, and around other centers; Lowell, Massachusetts, could count some five thousand factory workers in 1830. The factories and shipyards of New York required great numbers of workers, and to this area as well as to towns like Philadelphia and Pittsburgh, immigrants came in droves. These urban workers suffered from their lack of bargaining power, the hardship and impersonal coldness of the factory system, and their low social standing. As more and more states extended the right of franchise, workingmen became more politically conscious. At first they started movements which were less directly concerned with economic demands like collective bargaining and improved hours and wages than with free public education, abolition of imprisonment for debt, and reform of the militia system. A depression in 1828-1829, however, brought a demand for direct political action.

Innovations in government by Jackson

JACKSON immediately proceeded to meet the demands of his followers. One of his most frankly political maneuvers was the redistribution of federal offices. The obvious political advantage of distributing federal jobs among his followers was, however, not his only motive, for Jackson genuinely believed that official duties could be made "so plain and simple that men of intelligence may readily qualify themselves for their performance." Moreover, the practice of supporting political parties by a careful distribution of patronage had already been firmly established in state politics. Jackson turned hundreds of federal officeholders out of their posts. Although his political opponents greatly exaggerated the numbers involved in his sweep, this maneuver introduced the "spoils system" into national politics to a greater degree than previously.

Another innovation by Jackson was his choice of two cabinets to help him run the double business of government and patronage. The official cabinet was composed of men of varying distinction who represented various factions that had supported Jackson. But with the exception of Van Buren, his secretary of state, the president paid little attention to the members of this cabinet. Instead, he surrounded himself with certain political and personal cronies, who formed a special group known as the "kitchen cabinet." But influential though this privy council was, Jackson remained the most powerful figure in national politics.

The quarrel over tariff and nullification

JACKSON'S administration found itself faced with a grave sectional dispute. The southern planters, who favored free trade, had denounced the high tariff act of 1828 as the "tariff of abominations." Perceiving that the South was being forced progressively into a minority position by the North's increase of voters and wealth, Vice-President John C. Calhoun, of South Carolina, had set forth a considered constitutional philosophy in an essay entitled "The South Carolina Exposition" (1828). Here he argued, as Jefferson and Madison had argued before him, that the Constitution was a compact between sovereign states and that an individual state had the right to nullify an act of Congress if, speaking through an elected convention, it decided that such   211 an act was unconstitutional. But having set forth this argument of "states' rights," Calhoun urged South Carolina not to make an issue of nullification until the new administration under Jackson had had a chance to show what it intended to do about the tariff. Calhoun himself had been reëlected vice-president in 1828.

The southern planters did not have to wait long. In December 1829, it was proposed that Congress inquire into the desirability of discontinuing for a period the further survey of public lands. This proposal was at once denounced as an attempt of eastern manufacturers to restrict the growth of the western states. Naturally, the many newcomers to the West wanted the greatest possible amount of land at the cheapest possible price, while manufacturers in the East were alarmed at the rapid westward expansion, which tended to depopulate industrial centers in the East and force up the cost of labor. The southern statesmen sided with the Westerners, for, being in a minority, they hoped by an alliance with the West to defeat the protective tariff, which favored the East.

The ensuing debate lasted for several years. The issue was clear-cut: Which was to triumph, national supremacy or state sovereignty? At a public dinner in April 1830 the president gave an unequivocal answer to where he stood on this issue. Looking directly at the "nullifiers" present, he made his memorable toast: "Our Federal Union—it must be preserved." When a new tariff was finally passed in 1832, it slightly reduced the tariff rates but still upheld protectionist principles. Calhoun openly broke with Jackson, resigned as vice-president, and soon was returned to Washington as senator from South Carolina. The nullifiers in South Carolina called a state convention which passed the Ordinance of Nullification. This ordinance declared the tariff acts of 1828 and 1832 null and void, and prohibited the collection of customs duties in South Carolina after February 1, 1833. In addition, the ordinance declared that the state would secede if the federal government tried to enforce the tariffs. In response, Jackson declared: "I consider...the power to annul a law of the United States, assumed by one State, incompatible with the existence of the Union" and asked Congress for additional legislation to permit him to enforce the tariff law. Despite Calhoun's opposition, Congress passed the Force Bill, authorizing the president to use the army and navy to collect the duties. At the same time, on the initiative of "the great compromiser," Henry Clay, and with the help of Calhoun, Congress enacted in 1833 a new tariff law, which provided for a gradual reduction of the tariff until by 1842 it would reach the low level of 1816. South Carolina thereupon rescinded the Ordinance of Nullification and at the same time saved face by also declaring the Force Bill null and void. Jackson could now proudly point to the maintenance of the Union, while the South Carolinians could point with equal pride to the maintenance of state sovereignty. A crisis had been averted, but the issue had not been solved.

**The Indians
and the expansion of the West**

UNLIKE the South, the West proved ultimately justified in looking to Jackson to further its interests. Jackson, an old Indian fighter, shared the desire of the western settlers to see all the Indian tribes transferred beyond the Mississippi. During his administration ninety-four treaties were concluded with the Indians, by which they lost millions of acres and were forced to move west. The Cherokees in Georgia put up a stiff legal battle to prevent the state from annexing their lands. Although Chief Justice John Marshall upheld their position in the Supreme Court, most of them were finally dispossessed in 1838, in no small measure because of Jackson's high-handed attitude toward the Indians. Some of the Seminoles of Florida also refused to accept removal from their lands, and a war resulted that, after ten years of hard fighting, ended in 1842, when, overcome by superior forces and arms, the tribe was largely exterminated. The revolver, invented by Samuel Colt in 1836, was first used as a military weapon in the Seminole War.

**Jackson
and the development of the West**

THE LANDS acquired by treaty from the Indians became public domain. When a new state came into the Union, a small portion of the domain would be granted to it for township schools, a state university, canals or roads, and other specific purposes. But the greater amount of public domain was retained for sale by the federal government. These lands, when surveyed, would be offered at auction in large lots or, failing bidders, at low rates in smaller lots (as small as forty acres after 1832). Many western immigrants could not make the required cash outlay for land alone, and often settled down ("squatted") on unsurveyed land—running the danger of eviction once the land was surveyed. The migrants settling in the West wanted the new lands acquired from the Indians in Jackson's administration to be speedily surveyed and offered for sale to actual settlers at cost. But some residents of the older states regarded the public domain as a property to bring in income and, besides, the industrialists in the Northeast believed that low land prices encouraged migration and robbed them of an abundant labor force. Jackson's sympathies were with the settler moving west. The practice of occupying land before it was put on sale was recognized in 1830 by a law which virtually granted indemnity to those who had thus technically violated federal statute. Finally, in 1841, Congress was to pass a permanent preëmption law which gave the squatter the right to settle on a piece of land and, after its survey, to purchase it, without competitive bids, at the minimum government price. In that way the West became a land of independent farmers with large holdings compared to those of the East or of Europe.

The West had long advocated the use of federal funds to promote internal improvements. Jackson was quite willing to finance such improve- 213 ments at government expense, and his administration saw Congress appropriate four times as much for roads, rivers, and harbors as the amount expended under his predecessor. But in 1830 he vetoed a bill authorizing a federal subscription to the stock of the Maysville and Lexington (Kentucky) turnpike on the constitutional grounds that the project was entirely within the boundaries of a single state. The chief significance of this veto was that it came in a period when the steam railway was being introduced into the United States. Since 1828 several lines had begun to use the locomotive for short distances. Jackson's veto temporarily put a halt to federal participation in intrastate transportation projects. As a result, for the first decades of the railroad era, while lines were still relatively short and seldom crossed state boundaries, it fell to private capital, often foreign investors, to finance the new American railroads—in contrast with the usual European practice, and probably contrary to Jackson's preferences.

*The Second Bank
and the election of 1832*

JACKSON's dislike of big bankers became the central issue in the campaign of 1832. The question arose in connection with the rechartering of the Second Bank of the United States. The bank's advocates regarded it as the kingpin in a system of sound and stable currency; its opponents attacked it as an evil money monopoly. A bill to recharter the bank was passed by both houses, only to be vetoed by Jackson with vehemence. He denounced the bank as unconstitutional and as placing too great power in private hands, particularly the hands of eastern and foreign capitalists.

The campaign of 1832 marked the end of the system whereby the nomination of candidates for president was controlled by a small group of politicians. Hitherto presidential candidates had been chosen by the party's leaders assembled as a "Congressional caucus." An ephemeral third party, the Anti-Masons, which owed its origin to a sudden flurry of hostility to secret societies, had no representatives in Congress to form a caucus. So the Anti-Masonic Party gathered in Baltimore in 1831 and became the first national party to nominate a presidential candidate directly. The National Republicans thereupon held a similar convention, where they chose Clay, while the Democrats, also assembled in convention, pinned their hopes on Jackson. Ever since then, national parties have chosen their candidates for president and vice-president by means of a national nominating convention.

The outcome of the election of 1832 was an overwhelming personal victory for Jackson. The president, believing that he had received full public endorsement in his fight against the Second Bank of the United States, intensified his attack. The bank had four years to run before its charter expired, but Jackson hastened its doom as a federal institution by ordering the secretary of the treasury to cease using the bank or its branches as a depository for federal funds and to draw out those funds which had been already deposited. The administration now turned over the funds for deposit to twenty-three state banks—institutions whose political leanings were so agreeable to Jackson that they became known as "pet banks."

*The dispute
with France over spoliations*

JACKSON'S foreign policy centered around his successful effort to collect reparations for the damage done to American ships and sailors during the Napoleonic wars. He made satisfactory agreements in that regard with Denmark, Naples, and Spain. But one with France ran into tragicomic ramifications. When King Louis Philippe asked his Chamber of Deputies to appropriate the agreed sum of $5,000,000, some deputies, doubting the wisdom of the bargain, managed to block the appropriation. Hints in Jackson's speeches and pressure from the American minister in France did no good, and in 1834 Jackson made the French repudiation of its "solemn treaties" a major issue in his message to Congress. Sensitive of their country's honor, the French deputies thereupon voted the $5,000,000 in dispute but demanded an apology before any of it should be paid. Public pressure even obliged the king to send French naval vessels to the American coast, to dismiss the American minister, and to recall his own. Jackson, for his part, insisted that his messages to Congress were no legitimate concern of a foreign government and called for war measures. Fortunately, the English minister in Washington stepped in to mediate between the recriminating governments, and Jackson in his next message to Congress explained that he had had no "intention to menace or insult the government of France," and that it would be "vain and ridiculous" to expect "to extort from the fears of that nation what her sense of justice may deny." The honor of France was thus satisfied, and the deputies not only approved the $5,000,000 in spoliations claims but added to it the interest on those installments that had not been paid when they had fallen due. Louis Philippe thus redeemed his great popularity in the United States, and was to lose it only toward the close of his reign.

*Inflation
and the "boom" of 1835-1836*

A PHENOMENAL prosperity mushroomed suddenly during the final years of Jackson's second term. This prosperity was based largely on heavy investment, sometimes of a speculative nature. State governments and private capitalists, often foreign, undertook new projects: canals, railroads, and turnpikes. Land speculation hit a new high during 1835 and 1836, and confident Americans eagerly paid inflated prices to acquire farm lands and town property in the new West. State banks, relieved of the restraining influence of the Bank of the United States, engaged in a rapid expansion of credit, freely lending paper bank notes backed by little more than an abounding optimism. American exports and imports rose conspicuously between 1830 and 1836, and Europeans lent money and made heavy investments in America. As a result of this sudden prosperity, government revenues from customs and land sales grew to such proportions that in 1835 the entire public debt was liquidated and the Federal Treasury showed a surplus—a happy state that was to last unfortunately for only two years.

Despite the apparent good times, Jackson and his strategists perceived that the national economy was unsound. The administration took measures to restore gold to circulation and to suppress small paper notes by state banks. But these measures came too late. In 1835 and 1836, the amount of paper in circulation increased alarmingly. Inflation had taken hold; wages were rising; and an apparent prosperity reigned everywhere. The psychology of the times was epitomized in the title of a popular tract: *The Book of Wealth; in Which It Is Proved from the Bible, That It Is the Duty of Every Man to Become Rich.* Finally, Jackson took drastic action. He issued a "Specie Circular," which required federal land offices to receive only specie in payment for government lands. The effect of this action was to decrease the currency of state bank notes and to put a sharp halt to land speculation with unsound paper money.

The Panic of 1837 and the subsequent depression

NEVERTHELESS Jackson's successor, President Martin Van Buren, fell heir to a financial panic and depression not of his own making. Jackson's "Specie Circular" had tightened credit and increased the demand for specie. The money market contracted, and by May 1837, every bank in the country had been forced to suspend specie payment. To make matters worse, when the federal charter of the Second Bank of the United States had run out, the state of Pennsylvania had given it a new one. To maintain the bank, its president called in loans and tightened credit, but to no avail. In October 1837 the bank failed. Some financial houses in Britain with large investments in the United States meanwhile, becoming apprehensive, threw their American securities on the market. In order to find the money to buy up these foreign obligations, eastern banks called in loans made to western banks. The circulation of bank notes fell, and government revenues from the sale of public lands diminished. A crop failure in 1837 aggravated the plight of the now numerous unemployed. The prices of flour and other foods as well as coal and rents rose to forbidding heights. Suffering among the poor resulted in flour riots in New York, and for a time an estimated nine-tenths of the factories in the East were closed down. Work on canal and railroad projects had to be suspended; banks and businesses failed; the unemployed walked the streets; and the Federal Treasury now showed a deficit. Some of the states repudiated their debts, and the once steady flow of European credit to the United States dried up.

For five years the country underwent its first great depression. A special session of Congress undertook palliative measures. Van Buren also advocated an independent treasury. The president's plan called for the government's taking charge of its own funds in subtreasuries set up in large cities. In this way the administration hoped to safeguard the money of the federal government and prevent its use for speculative purposes. This Independent Treasury Act was passed in 1840. Though repealed by the following administration, it passed again in modified form in 1846, and remained in effect until 1913.

The Whigs
and the election of 1840

THE PANIC of 1837 cast a shadow over Van Buren's administration and ruined his chance of reëlection. The enemies of Jackson had united into a new party, drawn mostly from advocates of nullification and of a third Bank of the United States. This party, though essentially conservative, borrowed the name of "Whigs" from English political history, on the grounds that they were opponents of the tyranny of "King Andrew." The Whigs played their cards astutely. Passing over their logical choice, Henry Clay, whose conservative political and economic views were too well known to the voting masses to ensure their support, they chose the first "dark horse" candidate in American politics, old General William Henry Harrison. They made good use of the panic, slogans, and electioneering strategy to win the votes of the masses. The electoral count signified the end of Jacksonian Democracy.

A Whig lithograph for the "log cabin and hard cider" campaign of William Henry Harrison depicts the depression of 1837. A crowd gathers before the Mechanic's Bank, which has suspended specie payment. In the foreground, posters deplore prohibitive prices and the destruction of credit. Unemployment, destitution, and drunkenness are portrayed as the fruits of Democratic rule, and over the grim scene preside Jackson's hat and spectacles.

IN THE 1840's the American republic spread phenomenally. Many Americans were impelled to urge their country toward greater and greater expansion not only by the desire for land but also by a sincere conviction that the United States was intended by God to control an increasingly large portion of the Western Hemisphere. This urge brought the Americans into conflict with the British to their north and the Mexicans to their south.

Tyler as president and the split of the Whigs

ONE MONTH after his inauguration, President Harrison died, and was succeeded by his vice-president, John Tyler. The accession of Tyler nullified the strategy of the Whigs, for he had no intention of restoring the philosophy or the institutions of the Hamiltonians. Clay, who had dreamed of exerting the principal power in the administration of Harrison, now encountered unexpected difficulties. Tyler was adamant in his opposition to the creation of a new national bank and to the distribution among the states of the proceeds from public-land sales, both of which were favorite projects of Clay. These differences with Tyler brought about the resignation of Clay from the Senate and of his followers from the cabinet, and Tyler proceeded to look for support from the Democrats and dissatisfied Whigs.

Canada and the Webster-Ashburton Treaty

SINCE 1837, relations between the United States and Great Britain had been strained as a result of boundary disputes. A Canadian rebellion had broken out in 1837 (page 92), and American sympathizers, organized as "Hunters' Lodges," crossed the border to fight the British. After the brief struggle was put down, many of the rebels sought asylum in the United States, where they were hailed as martyrs of freedom. In retaliation a party of Canadian militia crossed the Niagara River into the United States, fired one American vessel, and killed one American citizen. When a Canadian named Alexander McLeod boasted in a Buffalo saloon that it was he who had killed the American, he was arrested, but the British government demanded his release on the grounds that he had acted under orders. The American expansionist mood was abetted by the increasing number of Irish Americans, who were bitterly anti-British. Many openly expressed the desire to free Canada and bring it into the Union. The tension grew when British warships off the coast of Africa stopped and searched American vessels suspected of carrying slaves.

Upon becoming secretary of state in 1841, Daniel Webster was fearful that war might break out at any moment. Fortunately the two countries were each other's best customers. Britain depended on America for cotton; the United States required British capital to finance its railroads and industrial expansion. A new ministry under Robert Peel came to power in London in 1841, and, since Peel shared Webster's pacific purposes, he sent Lord Ashburton, who was well known to be friendly to Americans, to Washington as minister. Ashburton and Webster proved clever compromisers. The old controversy over the boundary between Maine and New Brunswick was settled, with the United States receiving 7000 of the 12,000 square miles under dispute. The line between Lake Huron and the Lake of the Woods was also compromised. Webster himself was subjected to much criticism by discontented Democrats at home, who maintained that he had surrendered too much to the British. At the same time Canadians maintained that Ashburton had given away considerably more than he had received. Both governments approved the settlement, however, and the threat of war between England and the United States was temporarily removed.

Mexico
and the Texan war of independence

AMERICANS had been migrating to Texas ever since 1821, when Moses Austin was granted a patent to establish there 300 families—"honest, industrious farmers and mechanics" who should be Catholic in faith and loyal to Mexico. Similar concessions were made to other immigrant leaders—American, Mexican, English, Scottish, Irish—until most of eastern Texas had been parcelled out by the unstable Mexican government. By 1836, fully 20,000 Americans of all shades of character and degrees of affluence had settled in Texas.

Shortly a host of questions arose. Mexico was weighed down with heavy complications during the first half of the nineteenth century. Serious social and economic problems plagued its government. For example, the Indian peons wanted redress for grievances inflicted upon them by their feudal masters, and the middle class was fighting entrenched social and ecclesiastical privilege. The government, headed before 1846 in turn by an emperor, several presidents, and a dictator, was unable to populate its vast northern territories with Mexican settlers, and it was not happy at the prospect of foreigners virtually taking over the Texas territory. It resented, moreover, the violence and greed openly displayed by some of the newcomers.

The English-speaking settlers, for their part, were no more content with the situation. They wanted to keep their own language and customs. A Mexican decree passed in 1829 abolishing slavery aroused such a protest that the authorities had to make an exception of Texas. The importation of slaves, however, was forbidden. The Mexican government also took steps to expel squatters who could not show lawful deeds to their lands, and it abrogated the land contracts of those men who had not fulfilled their agreements—thereby causing a panic among land speculators.

With tension mounting daily, only an incident was needed to set off a revolt. The incident came when in 1836 President Santa Anna's government denied the Texans' petition for autonomy. Overt defiance soon led to resistance, and the Texans proclaimed their independence. Santa Anna then went north with troops, and in March a small number of Texans were exterminated in a desperate struggle waged in the Alamo, a former mission used as a fort, at San Antonio. The Texans had their revenge the next month when, under General Sam Houston, they routed the Mexican forces at San Jacinto, and captured Santa Anna himself. The Texans thirsted for the Mexican leader's life, but Houston managed to save him by compelling him to recognize the independence of Texas. The Mexican government subsequently refused to endorse Santa Anna's recognition, on the ground that it had been exacted by duress.

The question
of the annexation of Texas

THE MAJORITY of Texans now eagerly favored admission to the United States. Southern and western statesmen sympathized with them and passed resolutions calling upon Congress to admit Texas. But powerful antislavery forces opposed annexation on the grounds that the southern planters were conspiring to create new slave states out of the Texas territory. While Jackson was president, he had favored annexation but, understanding the strength of the opposition, had gone no farther than to recognize the independence of Texas before quitting office in 1837. Van Buren had likewise done nothing to intervene in Mexico, not even when a French expeditionary force occupied Veracruz and inflicted indemnities on Mexico for damages done to French property.

In 1843 Tyler appointed Calhoun secretary of state. Calhoun envisaged the expansion of the free forces into the Northwest, ultimately creating enough free states to overwhelm the South in Congress. The South would then have to yield the institution of slavery or run the risk of challenging the Union by nullification. To Calhoun, the Union's best chance for survival lay in balancing the number of potential states from free soil by the number from slave soil. In Texas the South might create perhaps five or six slave commonwealths and thus maintain the balance for some time to come. Calhoun eagerly negotiated a treaty annexing the vast region, but the Senate's northern votes defeated Calhoun's proposed treaty of annexation.

The controversy
over the Oregon boundary

MEANWHILE, a controversy over the boundary of the Oregon Territory had revived tension between the United States and Great Britain. Since the eighteenth century each country had claimed the territory west of the Continental Divide between 42° and 54°40′ latitude, although the hottest dispute was over the region lying between the Columbia River and the 49th parallel. In 1818 a compromise had been worked out, whereby the two nations had agreed to occupy the region jointly for ten years. In 1827 this agreement was revived for an indefinite period, with either party having the right to terminate it upon a year's notice. Up to about 1830 the principal interest in the region had centered upon fur trading. The British Hudson's Bay Company and the American

Fur Company, owned and operated by the German immigrant John Jacob Astor, had been the chief exploiters of the area. But the next two decades saw a remarkable American interest in colonization projects. Missionaries and travelers waxed eloquent over the beauties and economic possibilities of the wooded Pacific slope, and these accounts infected great numbers of persons back home with the "Oregon Fever." Some 400 Americans had arrived in Oregon by 1841; another 100 or so appeared the following year; and about 1000 new arrivals made their appearance in 1843. The British in the region were now outnumbered, and the American settlers no longer approved of joint occupation. The British fur traders expected an arrangement that would make the Columbia River the new dividing line, but the American expansionists were not to be denied. They began to go about shouting the slogan of "Fifty-four forty or fight!"

The elections of 1844 and the annexation of Texas

IN THE electoral campaign of 1844, the Texas and the Oregon controversies were major issues. The Whigs chose Clay as their candidate. Clay expected the Democrats to choose Van Buren as his opponent. Since Van Buren was opposed to the annexation of Texas, Clay figured that it would be good strategy to remove the problem altogether from the campaign, and he came out, too, against annexation. Just as Clay had anticipated, when the Democratic convention opened in Baltimore Van Buren appeared its most likely choice. On May 24, 1844, a group of men forty miles away, in the Supreme Court chamber in Washington, gathered around a machine invented by Samuel F. B. Morse, and listened to the clicking of the first Morse telegraph messages: "What hath God wrought!" . . . "Have you any news?" "No." . . . "Separate your words more." . . . "Oil your clock-work." . . . "Buchanan stock [James Buchanan was another possible nominee] said to be rising." . . . "Van Buren cannon in front, with a fox-tail on it." But Van Buren was not selected. The nomination went instead to James K. Polk, who campaigned on a platform calling for both the annexation of Texas and the occupation of Oregon. This combination appealed to sufficient voters to elect Polk. Tyler, also an expansionist, considered the election returns an endorsement of his own views, and he now sponsored a joint resolution of Congress for the annexation of Texas. Before he left office, he had the satisfaction of seeing it pass, and before the year was out, Texas drafted a constitution and entered the Union.

The settlement of the Oregon dispute

ON DECEMBER 27, 1845, the New York *Morning News* stated: "Unanswerable as is the demonstration of our legal title to Oregon—and the whole of Oregon, if a rood!—we have a still better title than any that can be constructed out of all these antiquated materials of old black-letter international law....And that claim is by right of our manifest destiny to overspread and to possess the whole of

EUROPE AND THE EXPANDING U. S. 1819-1867

Bought from Russia 1867

ALASKA

Disputed until 1903

NEWFOUNDLAND

WAKE IS.
First claimed by U. S. 1828

CANADA

MIDWAY IS.
Annexed 1867

*British treaty
line of 1846*

**Compromise with
Great Britain 1842**

Disputed until 1872

OREGON
TERRITORY

UNITED STATES
1819

HAWAIIAN IS.
U.S.-British-French rivalry

CUBA
*Acquisition from Spain
at issue*

**Ceded by Mexico
1848**

TEXAS
Annexed, 1845

GADSDEN PURCHASE 1853
(From Mexico)

MEXICO

**French attempt to establish
empire (1861-1867) frustrated**

Mexico City

ISTHMUS OF PANAMA
*U.S.-British rivalry over canal
and rail routes*

The 1840's were a decade of rapid continental expansion for the United States, both by compromise with Great Britain and by war with and purchase from Mexico. The discovery of gold on the newly opened west coast in 1848 heightened the importance of the Pacific approaches, and the United States was quickly involved with Great Britain over possible routes across the Isthmus of Panama. In the Hawaiian Islands the United States likewise adopted a stiffer attitude toward French and British claims. The purchase of Alaska from Russia and the occupation of the Midway Islands in 1867 helped to secure the Pacific frontier. In the Caribbean area, despite several crises, the status quo was maintained.

the continent which Providence has given us for the development of the great experiment of liberty and federative self-government entrusted to us." This mystical concept of "manifest destiny," arrogant though it may have seemed to those who did not share it, amply justified for many well-meaning Americans the expansionist activities of the 1840's. The next June, however, saw the signing of a treaty whereby the United States gave up 54°40' as the Oregon boundary without fighting. Oregon was divided by a line along the 49th parallel from the Rockies to the Strait of Georgia and thence through the Strait of Juan de Fuca to the Pacific. The compromise was a victory, incomplete though it was, of permanent American agricultural settlers over transient British fur traders. For the next thirty years, British North America was seldom free of the fear that it too would be annexed in part or as a whole.

Polk's expansionism and the war with Mexico MEANWHILE the Mexican controversy had boiled over. Mexico severed relations and recalled her minister from Washington, because, having refused to recognize the independence of Texas, she would not recognize its annexation by the United States. Though preparations for war advanced on the part of Mexico, President Polk hoped to achieve a settlement by peaceful means. In the autumn of 1845 he sent John Slidell to Mexico to try to get its government to recognize the Rio Grande rather than the Nueces River as the southern boundary of Texas and to offer besides to buy both New Mexico and California. Hostility in Mexico against the United States was so great that Slidell was not even received. Without waiting for a diplomatic agreement, Polk ordered the United States army into the disputed territory between the Nueces River and the Rio Grande. On April 24, 1846, a Mexican force crossed the Rio Grande and wiped out a detachment of American cavalry. The Mexicans insisted—and with some reason—that the Americans had invaded Mexican territory, but the skirmish gave Polk the opportunity to send a war message to Congress on May 11, stating that Mexico "has invaded our territory and shed American blood upon the American soil." Two days later, war was declared.

Opinion was divided in the United States on the justice of the war. The South and the West were enthusiastic in their support of the president. But Abraham Lincoln, then serving a term in the House of Representatives, questioned in a resolution whether the men who had been killed were in fact on soil that rightfully belonged to the United States, and he held the view that the war was "unnecessarily and unconstitutionally commenced by the President." The war was not popular in New England, and the abolitionists condemned it scathingly. Their views were summarized by James Russell Lowell in *The Biglow Papers:*

> They jest want this Californy
> So's to lug new slave-states in.

From a military standpoint, the war went well. General Zachary Taylor pushed as far south as Buena Vista, where he defeated Santa Anna in February 1847. By September Mexico City had surrendered to General Winfield Scott. American naval forces captured San Francisco, Monterey, and Los Angeles, while a force under Colonel S. W. Kearny captured Santa Fe and, pressing on into southern California, arrived to find that some American settlers had proclaimed their independence at Sonoma, and had hoisted the "Bear Flag" of the California Republic.

The war with Mexico came to an end with the Treaty of Guadalupe Hidalgo in 1848. Mexico had to accept the Rio Grande as the southern boundary of Texas and to cede New Mexico and California to the United States. In return, the United States paid Mexico $15,000,000 and assumed the claims of its citizens against Mexico up to $3,250,000. The United States acquired more than half of the territory possessed by Mexico at the time Moses Austin had received his grant of land. Yet even that acquisition did not satisfy some expansionists who wanted to annex all of Mexico. Polk resisted such advice, however, and the only additional land acquired from Mexico came in 1853 as a result of the Gadsden Purchase, whereby some 50,000 square miles were bought along the southern border of Arizona and New Mexico.

The rush for gold in California

JUST PRIOR to the signing of the treaty of peace in Mexico City, gold was discovered at Sutter's Mill in the Sacramento Valley. The news of the discovery gradually leaked out and set in motion a mighty rush from all parts of the globe. Many of the "forty-niners" perished on the way, and many more were bitterly disappointed by the small amount of gold that they were able to dig up. But if the gold rush rewarded only a comparatively few miners, it brought California rich returns. When the census was taken in 1850, the region had 92,000 inhabitants, and this figure was more than quadrupled within the next decade.

The settlement of the Utah territory

DURING THE forties, still another great western tract annexed from Mexico was filled in with settlers. In 1830, a religious leader named Joseph Smith had founded the Mormon Church in New York State. Largely because of their acceptance of polygamy, Smith and his followers were persecuted in the East. They moved west, but found no better haven. In Illinois a mob shot and killed Smith. Under Brigham Young, the Mormons decided to trek westward, where they might worship according to their beliefs. In 1847, Young reached the Great Salt Lake, and there the Mormons founded a permanent colony. Many more converts arrived and settled down in what became a model community. In 1850, as part of Clay's compromise (page 241), the region was to be erected into the territory of Utah, and Brigham Young appointed its governor.

INDUSTRIALIZATION
AND THE AMERICAN RENAISSANCE

TRAVELERS to the United States in the thirties and forties agreed that Americans were hustlers. They had even devised a "quick lunch"! Americans were also supremely self-confident. They believed in their ability to transform their growing empire into the richest and freest land in the world. Their creative drive, taking a practical turn in order to cope with a new physical environment, produced an avalanche of ingenious inventions and gadgets. Hopefulness was clearly reflected in their political and literary philosophy, though critics of materialism and industrialism were not slow to arise. To Americans, their constitution symbolized opportunity and freedom—opportunity for the individual to become a millionaire or president and freedom to enable him to seize his opportunity. In a milieu of economic abundance, political freedom, and individual mobility, no man's social status had to remain fixed by his family background. Hence social stratification in America, where the man himself counted for more than his "station in life," always was less rigid than in Europe.

The growth of American population

AMERICAN expansion was in part a result and in part a cause of a rapid increase in population. In the forty years after 1790 the census figure jumped from less than 4,000,000 to almost 13,000,000; and during the next two decades it nearly doubled again, for in 1850 the population numbered over 23,000,000. The shift in the distribution of this population is also noteworthy. In 1790, approximately 95 out of every 100 Americans lived east of the Alleghenies; by 1850 only about 55 per cent were to be found there.

The impact of immigration upon America

ANOTHER striking feature of American demography was the steady increase in immigration. In 1830, only about 400,000 people were foreign-born. In the following two decades, almost 2,500,000 immigrants came to American ports, over half of this number arriving between 1845 and 1850 alone. Except for an occasional visiting hero like Louis Kossuth, foreigners generally encountered social prejudice in various eastern areas, but for the immigrant it was more than offset by willingness to exploit his usefulness as inexpensive labor in the new factories. In the West, the immigrants were swiftly allowed to participate in politics and the benefits of the national land system. Immigrants were apt to be energetic people who had been daring enough to break home ties and leave a social setting in which they had not felt fully adjusted. By their migration they took from their old country and brought to their new an element of political and social restlessness. Thereby they added to social mobility in America. They also made it impossible for Americans to remain indifferent to events in Europe. Until the last quarter of the nineteenth century, the immigrants came chiefly from Great Britain, Ireland, and Germany, although vast numbers of Chinese flocked to the gold fields of California after mid-century.

Immigration
from England and Ireland

THE MOST easily assimilated immigrants came from England. A depression in England from about 1836 to 1843 (page 89) impelled thousands of English workers and their families to start a new life in America. Not having to learn a new language or to acquire a strange cultural tradition, these British immigrants had little difficulty in adjusting themselves to the New World, and they were readily accepted by the older inhabitants.

A great Irish migration to the United States came in the forties. Steady movement from Ireland had occurred earlier, but famine (page 112) now drove hundreds of thousands to seek their livelihood across the ocean. The misery-ridden, anti-British, Catholic Irish emigrated so rapidly that they taxed ocean transport facilities. By 1850 there were nearly a million of them in the United States. They could be cheaply employed to work in gangs on canals and railroads, to dig ditches for new gas and water mains, to carry hods of bricks for new buildings in eastern cities, or to do piecework in northern sweatshops. The Irish, drawn together by strong religious and political ties, settled in tight groups in the cities and factory villages. The Irish quarter in a town would be marked by the spires of Catholic churches and by congestion, and their political organizations became important factors in New York City, Philadelphia, Baltimore, and Boston. Their control of the Democratic society known as Tammany Hall gave the New York Irish their full share of political appointments and made the Irish policeman one of New York's lasting institutions.

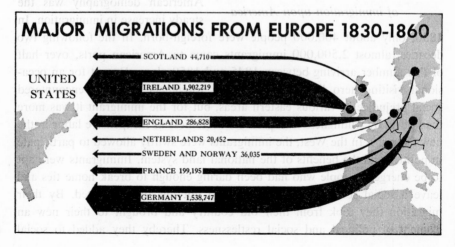

MAJOR MIGRATIONS FROM EUROPE 1830-1860

UNITED STATES

SCOTLAND 44,710
IRELAND 1,902,219
ENGLAND 286,828
NETHERLANDS 20,452
SWEDEN AND NORWAY 36,035
FRANCE 199,195
GERMANY 1,538,747

*Immigration
from the German countries*

GERMAN migration to America was also important. Prior to the American Revolution the stream had been considerable, but then it almost dried up for a time. The failure of the German revolts of the 1820's and 1830's caused a number of political radicals to leave their native land. Perhaps foremost among these was Francis Lieber, who originated the *Encyclopaedia Americana* (1829-1833), taught history and political science at South Carolina College and Columbia University, and wrote several works that are regarded as classics of American political philosophy. Other German families left because of poverty. The number of German immigrants to the United States increased greatly after the failure of the revolutions in 1848. Many of these newcomers were university graduates or skilled craftsmen, and some brought money with them. The bulk of Germans settled down in the cities or farmlands of the Ohio Valley and the Great Lakes region. They constituted an educated and artistic element in the American scene, but language and cultural preferences often tended to give them an internal coherence as well as to ostracize them from English-speaking communities.

*The factory
and urbanization*

AS THE population grew, the older cities changed and new urban centers appeared. In 1790 only six cities—New York, Philadelphia, Boston, Charleston, Newport, and Baltimore—could boast more than 8000 inhabitants, and their combined population was less than 135,000, or somewhat more than 3 per cent of the country's total population. But by 1860 there were 141 cities of over 8000 inhabitants—and they held 16 per cent of the national population.

The rise of cities was symptomatic of a profound change that had been going on in America during the first half of the century. The United States was steadily developing into a great industrial land. In 1807, there were only fifteen cotton mills in the United States, and these possessed only 8000 spindles. By 1815, some 26,000 workers were tending 130,000 spindles. The tariff of 1816 provided protection for new enterprises and did much to make the factory system a permanent feature of the American scene, especially in New England. After 1820, as transportation improvements opened up the

Political unrest, overpopulation, and the lure of economic gain were among the factors that led some 50,000,000 Europeans to emigrate between 1815 and 1914. The principal currents are shown in the map at the right. Emigration to Latin America fluctuated wildly, both in numbers and in destination. The left-hand map shows the markedly north European character of the major currents of emigration to the United States before 1860.

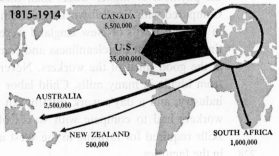

1815-1914
CANADA 5,500,000
U.S. 35,000,000
AUSTRALIA 2,500,000
NEW ZEALAND 500,000
SOUTH AFRICA 1,000,000

A contemporary drawing by William John Hennessy shows the bustle and confusion that greeted the mid-century immigrant when he arrived at the port of New York.

West, the factories in the Northeast found ever-expanding markets, and the foundations were laid for an eventual West-Northeast economic axis, whose combined industrial power would make the political subordination of the South's agricultural economy appear certain. Before the Civil War, there was little manufacturing in the South, except in Maryland and parts of Virginia. In contrast, factories had become numerous in New England, New York, New Jersey, Pennsylvania, Delaware, Ohio, Indiana, and Illinois. Although the United States still ran behind several European countries in the intensity of its industrialism, by 1850 the output of American industry was already worth over a billion dollars annually.

Working conditions in American factories

CHEAP western land sometimes provided an opportunity for native workers and immigrants to escape the city and the factory. That was why eastern factory owners resented the opening up of western lands on easy terms (page 213). Cheap land was believed to rob them of a potential labor supply and to necessitate the payment of higher wages than those paid in Europe for similar work. Compared with English working conditions of the thirties, those to be found in the mill towns of New England were good. English travelers were sometimes amazed at the cleanliness and comfort of the factories they visited and at the good spirit of the workers. Nevertheless, working conditions were far from idyllic in many mills. Child labor was prevalent all through the textile industry, and a day's work usually ran from twelve to fifteen hours. Native workers had to compete with waves of immigrants who did not have the skills required for farming in the West and were willing to take lower wages in the factories.

*The beginnings
of the American labor union*

UNIONIZATION on a limited local basis had existed as far back as 1792. That year the shoemakers of Philadelphia formed a union. Subsequently local unions of a particular trade in each large city drew together for cooperative action. In the course of time, local unions federated into national associations representing a single trade or craft. The first such federation was the National Cooperative Association of Journeymen Cordwainers, founded in 1836. Within twenty years, several major crafts instituted some kind of national organization. Workers soon came to think of the labor union rather than the political party as their medium of political power, and they attempted to bring about the combination of all existing unions in enormous regional and national federations. Such a federation, known as the General Trades' Union, was founded in 1833 in New York City, and it held frequent meetings during the next two years. It collapsed, however, in the depression following the Panic of 1837, and almost fifty years were to pass before a permanent national federation of unions came into existence.

*The revolution
in American transportation*

THE INITIAL development of a national American transportation system had come through the construction, by means of both private and public financing, of turnpikes and improved roads, of which the most outstanding was the National or Cumberland Road. By 1830, inland transportation was based principally on toll roads, toll bridges, and water facilities. Jackson's Maysville Road veto of 1830 (page 214) temporarily ended comprehensive planning of a national road system. The National Road nevertheless was extended into the heart of the Northwest through federal aid. Around 1840 it reached to Vandalia, Illinois. During those years military roads had been built in Florida.

More than ever, waterways grew in importance as routes of travel, especially since the number of steamboats was rapidly multiplying. People took steamers for the trip from Charleston to New York in preference to the land routes. Side-wheelers made good time up the Mississippi and its navigable tributaries. Impressed by the success of canals in Europe, private enterprise built short canals, one of the most important being the one that connected Philadelphia with the anthracite coal region of the Lehigh and the Lackawanna. More ambitious canals were state-financed, and were designed to connect the West with the eastern seaboard. The Erie Canal, which connected the Hudson River and Lake Erie, was completed by 1825, and it immediately proved an overwhelming success. The cost of transporting goods between the Great Lakes region and New York City was halved and the time reduced by a third. Soon the "Big Ditch" was earning annual tolls amounting to $700,000. Boom towns—Rochester, Utica, and Syracuse—sprang up along the Canal, while New York City doubled its population in a decade and

The levee at New Orleans, one of the great ports of the cotton trade, is shown just before the Civil War. Across the river lie seagoing vessels, while in the foreground are the river steamers which carried passengers and goods to St. Louis, Louisville, Cincinnati, and other river towns on the Mississippi and its tributaries.

became the country's largest city. Philadelphia, Boston, Baltimore, and other cities now feverishly began to construct canal systems so as to capture as large a share as possible of western commerce. Pennsylvania financed an ingenious combination of canal and railroad to get over the mountains between Philadelphia and Pittsburgh. Many other ventures were undertaken, so that by 1837 some 3000 miles of canals had been constructed. As we have seen, this transportation boom was an important factor in bringing the Panic of 1837, for it attracted more capital than could profitably be invested.

The steam railroad made its appearance at the height of the canal craze. The "Tom Thumb," designed by Peter Cooper, was the first steam locomotive built in America (1830). It ran thirteen miles an hour, and soon the best engineering brains were constantly improving steam locomotives and the cars which they pulled. It has been said that in the thirties, when a locomotive collided with a cow, the locomotive had to be sent to the repair shop; in the forties, the company had to pay for the cow. In 1830 there were only 23 miles of railroad in the United States. Twenty years later there were more than 9000 miles, built largely by foreign capital. By 1860, the United States government had adopted the policy of encouraging railroad construction by making land grants, and some 30,000 miles of rails had been laid down at a cost of one and a quarter billion dollars. The canals and the railroads drew the West and Northeast together, and diverted upper Mississippi Valley commerce away from New Orleans to New York and other Atlantic seaboard cities. Many Southerners noted this development with grave apprehension.

230

*The spread
of humanitarianism*

Americans were akin to the British of the Victorian age in their faith in the inevitability of human progress. To those for whom progress and prosperity were synonymous, it seemed that corrigible, individual faults rather than unyielding social conditions were the explanation of poverty. For example, in 1817 Philadelphia's charitable organizations maintained that destitution was caused by excessive drinking, individual idleness, and extravagant spending, and a year later, New York's Society for the Prevention of Pauperism added gambling, ignorance, and incontinence. Some reformers, however, recognized that poverty might also be due to misfortune, whether deserved or undeserved, and turned their attention to alleviating the distress of the physically and mentally handicapped. The Reverend Thomas Gallaudet undertook in 1817 to conduct a school for deaf-mutes at Hartford, thereby establishing the first institution to care for the physically handicapped; and in 1829 the Perkins Institute for the Education of the Blind (Boston) opened its doors. The insane began to receive more humane treatment in the thirties. They found their most outstanding and influential champion in the Quaker reformer, Dorothea Dix, who demanded before the public and legislative bodies that the care of the mentally ill be radically improved. In the years following 1841 Miss Dix won an uphill fight in several states.

Reformers also attacked the penal system and the criminal code. In time, conditions in jails and workhouses were improved materially, while such barbarous penalties of colonial days as the branding iron, whipping post, and pillory were replaced by more humane punishments like fines and imprisonment. The list of offenses carrying the death penalty was constantly being shortened, and in the forties the movement to abolish capital punishment was victorious in several states. During these years, also, imprisonment for debt (except for nonpayment of alimony) was abolished in state after state until by the time of the Civil War the system came to an end. American jails early adopted the idea of becoming reformatories as well as prisons, and soon roused the admiration of European penal reformers. Alexis de Tocqueville's reason for coming to the United States in the 1830's was to examine its penal system and institutions. He was only one of a number of observers from Prussia, France, Belgium, and England to examine the separate cell system of the Philadelphia and Auburn (New York) jails.

*Utopian attempts
in the United States*

COMMUNISTIC experiments had been made early by different religious sects in the United States, but the first decades of the nineteenth century saw the start of experiments by secular groups. Robert Owen, who had experimented with cooperative theories in his mill town of New Lanark, Scotland, founded a socialist colony at New Harmony, Indiana, in 1824. To this community Owen invited "the industrious and well disposed of all nations," and he had little trouble in recruiting hundreds. New Harmony had great difficulty in living up to its name, however, and the experiment failed. Nevertheless, it furnished the impulse to start several similar ventures.

A second series of utopian experiments was tried in the forties, this time based on the phalanx of the French philosopher Charles Fourier (page 65), whose principal American disciple was Albert Brisbane. More than thirty phalanxes were enthusiastically formed in different states. The most famous was Brook Farm. It had started out as a farm-supported literary community, to which belonged Nathaniel Hawthorne and other New England Transcendentalists (pages 235-236), but it became a Fourierist phalanx afterwards. Brook Farm could not stand the great loss it suffered in a fire in 1846, and, after it broke up in 1847, the Fourierist movement declined. Other attempts to build utopian communities had no greater success.

The improvement of educational opportunities

THE IDEA spread during the early decades of the nineteenth century that education should be universal, free of charge, compulsory, and supported by public taxation, although the fight for universal education was not won without bitter and often bigoted opposition. In the trans-Allegheny region prior to 1840, education had been provided for by specifically setting aside one section in every township for this purpose. But much of the land in the West was unoccupied, and it was difficult to get schools started—as young Abraham Lincoln learned from first-hand experience. The educational impulse was strongest in New England. Before 1820 only a few tax-supported high schools had been established in Massachusetts; several hundred were in existence by 1860. Private tuition-charging academies reached their zenith during the same period, so that by 1860 there were over 6000 of them. About 80 colleges were founded between 1830 and 1850, many the products of denominational rivalry and designed to train youth for the ministry. The founding of such colleges was by no means confined to the East; the trans-Allegheny region did everything possible to establish institutions of higher learning. One of the most interesting of the new colleges was the Oberlin Collegiate Institute in Ohio. Named after an Alsatian minister and philanthropist and founded in 1833, it quickly developed a program of higher learning on a coeducational and coracial basis and propagated a liberal theology.

Of the thousands who helped to broaden educational opportunities, two deserve special recognition. Horace Mann pioneered in Massachusetts in working out a comprehensive program of education which encompassed public elementary schools, normal schools for the training of teachers, and free libraries. Henry Barnard carried on similar work in Connecticut and Rhode Island. Both men later went to less developed parts of the country to preach the gospel of free education. Not all regions of the country enjoyed the same educational standards, but, thanks to such educators, Americans could point in 1850 to 80,000 elementary schools with more than 90,000 teachers and 3,330,000 pupils, and over 6000 secondary schools with more than 12,000 teachers and 250,000 students. Altogether, the general acceptance of the public-school system in the decades immediately preceding the Civil War was one of the most significant developments in the history of the United States.

The advance
of science in the United States

VARIOUS American scientists gained international reputations during this time. Professor Asa Gray of Harvard classified a great number of American plants, and stimulated others to carry on work in the field of botany. Gray became one of the chief exponents of the Darwinian theory in the United States. Among the other outstanding scientific figures of the period were J. J. Audubon and Louis Agassiz, both immigrants. Audubon was born in Haiti of French-Spanish parentage and had been trained in France as an artist by the famous David. He wandered through American woods and swamps, painting with an uncanny accuracy many varieties of birds in their natural settings, and combining art and ornithology in a fashion that has made him the patron saint of bird amateurs everywhere. Audubon had to look for recognition first in Europe before his genius was appreciated in America. Agassiz was a French Swiss, who, after having made notable contributions to the study of fossils and glaciers, came to the United States in 1846. As a professor of zoology at Harvard, he helped train many of America's leading scientists. One of his most important contributions was his study of Lake Superior, in which he further developed his theory of glacial epochs and movements. He also founded the first American biological station.

American surgical training at this time became less dependent upon European medical centers. In large part American medical independence was the result of the work of Philip Syng Physick at the Pennsylvania Hospital in Philadelphia. Physick died in 1837, after having made notable contributions especially in gallstone operations and orthopedics. Perhaps the greatest advances attributable to American medical men of this generation came in the use of anesthetics. In 1842 in Georgia, Dr. Crawford W. Long had successfully used ether to deaden pain, but, apparently not realizing the significance of his experiment, did not publish his results until 1849. In the meantime a Hartford dentist, Horace Wells, had experimented with nitrous oxide (laughing gas) to reduce the nightmare of tooth extraction (1844). His former student, a Boston dentist named W. T. G. Morton, acting on the advice of a distinguished European-trained chemist, C. T. Jackson, was able to improve upon Wells' discovery. He anesthetized, for the famous surgeon John C. Warren, the first patient ever put under ether for a major operation. From America the use of ether as an anesthetic spread, reducing the amount of human pain and the horror of surgery. Sir James Y. Simpson at the University of Edinburgh, Scotland, was the first to use ether as an anesthetic in childbirth but later substituted chloroform for that purpose. The greatest contemporary contribution to physiology in America came through William Beaumont's *Experiments and Observations on the Gastric Juice and the Physiology of Digestion* (1833), a report of long-time observations of the perforated stomach of a wounded man.

The quest for literary independence

IN 1837, as we have already indicated, Emerson, as the prophet and spokesman of the romantic school of American writers, announced the declaration of American literary independence. In that address, entitled "The American Scholar," he said: "Our day of dependence, our long apprenticeship to the learning of other lands, draws to a close." He thus voiced a tendency already manifest among American writers to cease imitating European letters and to study and draw their inspiration from the American scene. Emerson and his contemporaries, since they avowedly borrowed from European and oriental sources, did not cut their foreign ties thoroughly. Yet they were more explicitly and intentionally American than their predecessors. "We are the pioneers of the world," Herman Melville, who was certainly not given to shallow cheerfulness or cant, declared of the American people. "God has pre-destined, mankind expects, great things from our race; and great things we feel in our souls." Not even a naysayer like Melville could totally resist the spirit of confidence, self-reliance, and faith in American ideals that generally characterized American letters at mid-century.

New York City as a literary center

BEFORE 1830, New York City had been without challenge the literary capital of the United States. William Cullen Bryant still continued there the reputation as a poet that he had earned in Massachusetts at the age of 23 with the publication of his *Thanatopsis* (1817); and he added to it after 1825 great distinction as a journalist and editor with the New York *Evening Post*. James Fenimore Cooper, having returned to New York from France in 1833, continued his spellbinding "Leatherstocking Tales." "In every city of Europe that I visited," said Samuel F. B. Morse, "the works of Cooper were conspicuously placed in the windows of every bookshop." Cooper made the American Indian, pioneer, and sailor beloved characters throughout the world. Washington Irving, likewise having returned to New York from abroad, now turned again to American history for the subjects of some of his more important works.

After 1830 New York had to yield its preëminence to the area around Boston. But three literary figures of the next generation belonged as much to New York as to any other center. During a brief lifetime, Edgar Allan Poe, wandering between Richmond, Philadelphia, and New York, made himself one of the most creative spirits in American literature. His poetry, under the influence of Coleridge, was marked by rich imagery, melancholy, and rhythm; and, as one of the first masters of the short story, he produced prose tales which are masterpieces of the grotesque and the mysterious. Poe has always been acclaimed by the French, and it was from Paris that the American public first learned of his worth. With his introduction into France by the symbolist poets Baudelaire (page 166) and Stéphane Mallarmé, an American poet for the first time became a significant influence abroad.

Herman Melville was born and died in New York but lived some significant years as a sailor. Several of his novels and short stories were based on his own adventures on whalers and other kinds of ships. Unlike Poe, Melville stimulated reflection rather than shudders, but his works, reflecting a satiric, defeated melancholy, were no more cheerful. His most famous novel, *Moby Dick* (1851), is a story of a whaler's quest for revenge against a giant white whale that had bitten off his leg. It is sometimes considered an allegory of man's hopeless fight with evil. It has remained one of the great classics of the sea and is regarded by some as "the great American novel."

Today the reputation of Walt Whitman perhaps overshadows that of Poe or Melville. But before the Civil War, Whitman's free verse, free ideas, and free language about things regarding which Victorian America preferred a traditional restraint interfered with his recognition. Nevertheless his intensely American *Leaves of Grass* (1855) won the approval of Emerson and was destined, after the English and French poets discovered him, to move later poets to strive for freer scope both in form and in subject matter.

The development of New England Transcendentalism

AFTER 1830 one of the recognized leaders among American men of letters was William Ellery Channing, who founded New England Unitarianism. Having lived as a young man in Virginia when Jefferson was a leading intellectual light and then having entered directly into the circle of Wordsworth and Coleridge during a sojourn in England, Channing had come to advocate some of the more liberal facets of the contemporary philosophy, theology, and social thought. Under his influence, many leading Bostonians gently laid aside the old Puritan orthodoxy, and a veritable intellectual renaissance—not pagan by any means but no longer content with the Christian Trinity and with Calvinist determination —took place in New England. An impressive number of Boston elite followed Channing's intellectual leadership.

Channing was a member of Emerson's personal circle—sometimes called the "Concord group." In 1836, under Emerson's influence, some of the "Concord group" formed the Transcendental Club. Though this was only one year before Emerson declared America's literary independence, the Transcendentalists were dedicated to philosophical principles generally associated with English romanticism and German idealism, especially that of Immanuel 235

Kant. Emerson had come to know Kant largely through his admiration for Carlyle. Kant had taught that the phenomenal, or empirical, world did not limit the possibilities of knowing the truth, which might also be derived from noumenal, or ideal, sources. From Channing's humane Unitarianism to Emerson's transcendental romanticism was but a step.

Among the Transcendentalists were a number of the country's leading men and women of letters seeking a mystical answer to the problems of goodness and evil, beauty and ugliness, and the destiny of man. Henry Thoreau was one of the most fascinating of them. He spurned fame, loved the primitive, and lived the life of a staunch individualist. He resented the so-called progress of materialistic civilization, which burdens man with wars, slavery, government, taxes, and routine, and keeps him from finding philosophical peace and the eternal verities. His best-known book, *Walden* (1854), tells how he lived in the woods on eight dollars a year. Here he studied, among other things, the philosophy of ancient India, particularly the poem *Bhagavad-Gita,* "in comparison with which," he wrote, "our modern world and its literature seem puny and trivial;" and thus "the pure Walden water is mingled with the sacred water of the Ganges." Emerson too studied the translations of the Hindu philosophers and, like Thoreau, found in them a similarity to his own credo of contemplation shaped by action.

*Harvard College
as a literary center*

GENERALLY in intellectual sympathy with the Transcendentalists were several writers who, as professors or students at Harvard College, spread its reputation as a literary center. Henry Wadsworth Longfellow was the most conservative and didactic of the poets of this Harvard group. His choice of American subject matter, together with his facility in meter, soon made him a popular figure whose poems were considered respectable enough to make up most of the school child's repertory. The sonnets prefixed to his translation of Dante illustrate the depth of his culture and poetic feeling. Dr. Oliver Wendell Holmes and James Russell Lowell wrote learned essays and humorous verse, often in the local New England dialect. Holmes' "The Deacon's Masterpiece" was about the "wonderful one-hoss shay," which is commonly believed to satirize the old New England Calvinism as a perfect logical structure without a "weakest spot" and so "went to pieces all at once." His essays propounded medical truths and upheld the scientific spirit in an eloquent and attractive form. Lowell used *The Biglow Papers* to attack the imperialism and jingoism of the Mexican War, while in "A Fable for Critics" he debunked some of the literary pretensions of his contemporaries—and himself. Richard Henry Dana in *Two Years Before the Mast* (1840) wrote one of the great accounts of sea travel in the days when American clippers went around the Horn to California. The half-blind historian, William H. Prescott, pub-

236

lished vivid studies of the conquest of Mexico and Peru. Bancroft (page 209), historian of the United States, and John Lothrop Motley, historian of the Dutch, had studied historical method in Germany.

Other Boston
literary figures

OTHER men of letters lived in or around Boston. Second perhaps in popularity to Longfellow was John Greenleaf Whittier, no professor but a kindly "Quaker poet." Whittier, first roused to poetic heights by reading Robert Burns, is best remembered today for such idyllic poems as "Snowbound." As an ardent humanitarian and crusader against slavery, he wrote also "Voices of Freedom" and other poetry of a frankly abolitionist character. Nathaniel Hawthorne, for a time associated with Brook Farm and the Transcendentalists, was a brilliant story-teller, who combined good plot with deep psychological insight.

Emerson
as arbiter of letters

UNTIL his death (1882) Emerson remained the prophet and chief spokesman of the Romantic Movement in America, setting the critical standards of the mature and encouraging the neophytes. From the lecture platform, in poems, and in essays, he preached the high goals of human endeavor, the worth of individual self-reliance, and the better values of the new America, which, with all its visible limitations, had a mighty intellectual and social message, he thought, to give to the world.

American music
still largely dependent

THE MUSICAL achievements of the United States were still modest. But at least thoroughly American were the songs of Stephen C. Foster. They centered around the "minstrel show," which became both a storehouse and a source of American folklore regarding the Negro. Foster was born and lived most of his life in Pennsylvania but spent his last years in New York. The forty-niners moved west to the tune of his cheerful "Oh! Susanna" (1848), but "Swanee River" (1851), "My Old Kentucky Home" (1853), and "Old Black Joe" (1860) tugged at the heartstrings. They called up visions of the "hard times" rather than the joy in the life of the slave. The hymns of Lowell Mason, among which was "Nearer, My God, to Thee," and the piano compositions and orchestral works of Louis Moreau Gottschalk were among the rare pieces of any serious pretensions produced by Americans before the Civil War. Organized singing was common in church choirs and choral societies, the oldest of which today is the Handel and Haydn Society of Boston, founded in 1815. American music lovers, however, still had to look to Europe for talent. When in 1842 the Philharmonic Symphony Society of New York gave its first performance, it was dependent for its several conductors almost entirely, and for its music exclusively, upon European talent.

CONCESSION

OR SECESSION

B Y THE middle of the century, the United States contained two rival economic and social systems. The westward expansion of the United States favored the system of the North over that of the South, as did also the growth of industrialism, transportation facilities, and immigration from Europe. Each census return confirmed the growing fears of southern statesmen that, sooner or later, their section—which had hitherto retained predominance in the nation's government—might pass into political and economic subordination to the North. The two forms of society had worked out compromises in the past in an endeavor to permit them to live side by side in equality and peace. But changing circumstances since the Missouri Compromise had raised serious doubt whether they could continue to coexist peaceably in the same country.

Cotton
as "king" in the South

THE unpremeditated, but accelerating, conflict between the two social patterns stemmed in part from their irreconcilable labor systems. The thousands of immigrants arriving yearly in northern seaports provided a large reservoir of cheap labor for the North's surging industry. But against this free-wage system of the North, the rapid expansion of cotton culture created the demand for an ever-increasing army of plantation slaves.

At the close of the eighteenth century, as the cultivation of tobacco and rice became more unprofitable, a strong sentiment had arisen temporarily in the upper South against slavery. Cotton, however, was made profitable with Eli Whitney's invention (1793) of a mechanical gin, and, to a lesser extent, sugar culture also prospered. These two crops completely changed the southern economic system, and with it the status of the slave. Swift-mounting production and profits seemed to justify the southern boast that "cotton is king." In 1790, the United States produced only 3000 bales, or about 1,500,000 pounds of the staple. During the next seventy years production multiplied over a thousand times, and, in 1859, it reached the record figure of over 5,000,000 bales (about 2,500,000,000 pounds).

Thousands of families from some of the older southern states now shifted to the cotton belts with their slaves. In some counties in Virginia, the population decreased by half within twenty years, and houses and lands declined in value. In 1829, Jefferson's Monticello sold for only $3000, while Madison had to dispose of family servants. The cotton belt needed great numbers of slaves to work in the fields. The states of the upper South soon found it profitable to raise and sell slaves for these large plantations, the importation of slaves from Africa having been prohibited since 1808. Steady improvements in the power loom and spinning machinery increased the demand for textiles in the factories of the North and of England; and the invention of the sewing machine by Elias Howe in 1846 and its improvement by Isaac M. Singer in 1851 also increased the demand, especially for cotton cloth, and hence for slaves.

At a time, therefore, when humanitarianism was rapidly becoming a lay credo and when moral sentiment against slavery was increasing throughout the western world, the development of the "Cotton Kingdom" forced the South to run counter to prevailing attitudes, and even to reverse its own former trend. Nor was the South's position made any easier by the fact that the chief criticism of slavery came from the North and from England, whose great textile industries provided the main incentive for the spread of the cotton field and the slave market.

The hegemony
of the plantation oligarchy

NO LESS significant than the rapid growth of a cotton-and-slave economy in the lower South was the rapid concentration of wealth and power. Three or four thousand families lived on the best land, owned a majority of the slaves, and enjoyed three fourths of the yearly income. Twenty-three hundred other families could each claim one hundred or more human chattels. Two thirds of the white population of the South owned no slaves at all. Economic and political power centered in a plantation oligarchy, whose nucleus consisted of about three hundred planters, each of whom owned at least two hundred slaves. This plantation oligarchy was the most aristocratic class in America and one of the most aristocratic in the world. Its members owned sufficient land, leisure, servants, horses, and hounds for ceremonious fox hunts and maintained sumptuous mansions for open-handed hospitality. They conducted themselves as if born to military and political leadership. They had the inclination to devote themselves to public affairs, and they possessed a social and sectional solidarity that made them a power in the national political scene out of all proportion to their numbers.

The growth
of economic sectionalism

YET in reality, around 1860 southern agriculture was on the verge of a crisis. The last fertile belt of cotton land had been brought under cultivation with the expansion into Texas. Meanwhile, the inefficient method of raising cotton was taking its toll in the older sections of the South. Large fortunes had been made by exhausting the soil and then moving on to virgin lands in the West. Some far-seeing Southerners advocated a more scientific agriculture, but little was done to replenish the fertility of the older lands. While the South's spokesmen were not oblivious to the losing race which their section was waging, with few exceptions they ascribed their plight to exploitation by the North. And the North repaid them by denouncing slavery and abusing slaveholders.

The growth
of the abolition movement

SOUTHERN wrath was directed particularly against the northern abolitionists. Prior to 1830, anti-slavery sentiment had existed even in the South, and everywhere antislavery societies had advocated gradual emancipation. But a more militant abolitionism began with the appearance of William Lloyd Garrison's antislavery paper, the *Liberator,* in 1831. Breaking from what he now denounced as "the popular but pernicious doctrine of gradual emancipation," Garrison began an impassioned campaign against the "damning crime" of slavery and against slaveholders, whom he called criminals. For the next thirty years, Garrison and his followers were to preach a single gospel. They not only demanded immediate abolition but, despite the English precedent to the contrary (page 86), abolition without compensation to the slaveholders. The abolitionists found many notable supporters, including the New England orator Wendell Phillips and the poets Whittier and Lowell. In 1852, Harriet Beecher Stowe's *Uncle Tom's Cabin* dramatized the slave question so touchingly that it aroused the emotions of vast numbers on both sides. Secret organizations aided slaves to escape to Canada and other places of refuge by means of an "underground railway," in defiance of the laws regarding fugitive slaves. The abolitionist agitation was more influential in publicizing the shortcomings of slavery than in producing significant reform.

The birth of a militant abolitionism almost coincided with the most alarming slave rebellion in American history. In 1831, in Virginia, Nat Turner led a band of fellow slaves in a rebellion that ended with a few score killings and executions. The fear of slave uprisings combined with resentment of the abolitionists to increase the bitterness of slaveholders and to create greater sectional solidarity in defense of slavery. Many in the South gradually became persuaded that a patriarchal slave system was more humane and beneficent than the sweatshop industrialism of the North.

The question
of slavery in new territories

ECONOMIC sectionalism and slavery became issues requiring official attention as a result of the acquisition of new territories. The Missouri Compromise of 1820 had specified that, after the admission of Missouri, the rest of the Louisiana Territory north of 36° 30' would remain free for all time, and implied that the southern portion would be open to slavery. The political balance thus provided was threatened, however, in the forties with the annexation of the great territorial empire in the West. In 1846 David Wilmot of Pennsylvania introduced a resolution in the House declaring that "neither slavery nor involuntary servitude shall ever exist" in any territory acquired from Mexico, but the "Wilmot Proviso," though passed in the House, was defeated in the Senate.

240   The major issue in the electoral campaign of 1848 was slavery. Both

of the major parties tried to skirt it. In protest an antislavery group of Democrats broke away from the regular party organization and joined forces with other antislavery groups to form the Free Soil Party. The votes which they took away from the regular Democrats gave the presidency to the Whig Party's candidate, General Zachary Taylor, and upon his death in office, to his vice-president, Millard Fillmore.

The Whig administration was immediately confronted by the issue it had tried to avoid during the election. California petitioned for admission as a free state in 1849, and New Mexico demanded territorial government. Up to this point, the balance between free and slave states had been maintained, with fifteen of each represented in the Senate, where proposals like the Wilmot Proviso could be blocked. But the admission of California was bound to upset the old balance, and Southerners now spoke more often of the necessity of secession.

*California
and the Compromise of 1850*

THE ENSUING controversy was the occasion of one of the most memorable debates in Congressional history. It was dominated by three statesmen who had represented the people brilliantly for forty years: Calhoun, Webster, and Clay. Calhoun, too ill to deliver his speech in person, sat in the Senate on March 4, 1850, to hear it read. He declared that the Union could be saved only if agitation over slavery ceased, if the North faithfully adhered to the fugitive slave laws, if the South were granted equal rights in the new territories, and if an amendment to the Constitution were passed to guarantee sectional equilibrium. Otherwise, "let the States...agree to separate and part in peace." Webster was conciliatory; he spoke, on March 7, not "as a Massachusetts man, nor as a Northern man, but as an American." Slavery, he said, could not be solved by recrimination and violent agitation but only by compromise. But never would he agree to secession.

It was Clay's role to offer the strategy of compromise in 1850, as he had done in 1820 and 1833. He introduced a number of resolutions that, because they contained numerous proposals intended to accommodate everybody, came to be called the Omnibus Bill. After prolonged debate five of these proposals became the basis of the settlement known as the Compromise of 1850. This compromise called for the admission of California as a free state; the abolition of the slave trade—but not slavery—in the federal District of Columbia; the enactment of a more stringent fugitive slave law; the payment by the United States of the public debt owed by Texas before 1845 in return for that state's relinquishment of its claims to New Mexico; and the division of the rest of the land ceded by Mexico into the two territories of Utah and New Mexico, each with the right to eventual admission into the Union with or without slavery according to its own choice as stipulated in its own constitution. The last provision introduced into the slavery contro- 241 versy the principle of state option, or "popular sovereignty," which was soon to reveal its own peculiar dangers.

Continued tension after the Compromise of 1850
THE Compromise of 1850 was not an issue in the election of 1852, in which the Democrats' candidate, Franklin Pierce of New Hampshire, was elected. Nevertheless, the compromise was destined to be quickly broken. The northern antislavery groups refused to obey the fugitive slave law that formed part of the compromise. This statute denied an alleged fugitive trial by jury and imposed drastic penalties on those who attempted to assist him. Northern mass meetings protested against it; mobs resorted to force to rescue Negroes from the authorities. These actions bitterly antagonized the Southerners, who accused the North of deliberately violating the spirit of the compromise. Meanwhile, attempts of southern extremists in the early fifties to incite the seizure of Cuba and other Latin-American territory brought the countercharge from Northerners that the South was itself inflaming the slavery issue by seeking to enlarge its territory through imperialistic designs.

"Popular sovereignty" in Kansas and Nebraska
SECTIONAL restraint completely exploded over how to organize Kansas and Nebraska. Both areas were in the zone rendered free by the Missouri Compromise of 1820. The Pierce administration now proposed to create territories of Kansas and of Nebraska on the newer basis of popular sovereignty, which would allow each eventually to come into the Union as a free or a slave state according to its own constitutional provision. This proposal was embodied in a bill sponsored by Senator Stephen A. Douglas of Illinois. The Kansas-Nebraska Bill was evidently motivated by a sincere desire to encourage the development of a new western area; Douglas himself wished to clear the way for a northern transcontinental railroad. But it could be anticipated that the South would not consent to the development if the outcome would be only more free states. Douglas' proposal, specifically repealing the Missouri Compromise, permitted them to hope that Kansas, the farther south of the two areas, might become a slave state. Free-soil advocates, on the other hand, saw in it only an inlet for slavery where none had existed before.

The formation of the Republican Party
DOUGLAS' bill won enough votes to pass, but it immediately split the two leading national parties. The antislavery northern Whigs broke away from their organization, and the Whig Party ceased to be an effective national party. The Democratic Party was also splintered, as its free-soil members refused to accept the Kansas-Nebraska Act. Dissatisfied Whigs and Democrats in the North now sought a new party allegiance. In the political confusion, many at first joined the Know-Nothing movement, a loosely organized, secret, antiforeign, and

In this lonely frontier cabin the territorial governor, John W. Geary, faced the bitter turmoil of "bleeding Kansas."

anti-Catholic association of brief duration. But the surge toward political realignment also brought into existence a new party, which adopted the name "Republican." Many different groups joined the new party: antislavery Whigs, radical abolitionists, free-soil Democrats, and northern Know-Nothings. However diverse in origin, the members of the Republican Party were united in their opposition to the extension of slavery to the territories.

Civil war in "bleeding Kansas"

THE OPENING of Kansas to settlement was the signal for a desperate race between proslavery and antislavery forces. In April 1854, the New England Emigrant Aid Society was formed to colonize Kansas with free-soil Northerners. Proslavery forces crossed the border from Missouri, and used ruffian tactics to elect the candidates of their choice. They set up a government at Shawnee Mission, limited office-holding to proslavery men, and decreed imprisonment at hard labor for anyone claiming that slavery did not legally exist in the territory. The free-soil group held a convention in turn at Topeka, where a state constitution was drafted prohibiting slavery, and set up a state capital at Lawrence. Proslave elements staged a raid in May 1856, upon Lawrence, burning and pillaging its buildings. In retaliation, a crusading Connecticut abolitionist named John Brown led a small band to Pottawatomie Creek, where five proslavery men were murdered in cold blood.

The presidential campaign of 1856 was marked by the fierceness enkindled by "bleeding Kansas" and the slavery issue. The Democratic candidate, James Buchanan of Pennsylvania, stood by Douglas' doctrine of popular sovereignty and won. Nevertheless, the strength of the Republicans was shown by their carrying eleven northern states, besides piling up large   243 votes in several others. Civil warfare continued, however, in "bleeding Kansas."

Court invalidation of compromises on slavery

BUCHANAN's election might have augured ultimate victory for the compromising spirit reflected in the principle of popular sovereignty, if the Supreme Court at this juncture had not handed down a decision that rendered it unconstitutional. The decision concerned a Negro named Dred Scott, who had been taken by his master into the free territory of Minnesota, where slavery had been forbidden by the Missouri Compromise of 1820. When his master returned to Missouri, a slave state, Scott sued for his freedom on the grounds that residence on free soil had made him free. The lower courts held that the status of Scott had reverted to bondage on his return to slave soil. On Scott's appeal the Supreme Court, with its two northern justices dissenting, went still further and decided in 1857 that Scott had never been free, that Negro slaves were not persons but property and hence were not entitled to the rights of citizens of the United States, that Congress had no constitutional authority to abolish or prohibit property rights in any of the territories, and that hence the Missouri Compromise (and by implication the popular sovereignty provisions of the Compromise of 1850) had been unconstitutional.

The dwindling of the spirit of compromise

THIS DECISION was hailed as a triumph by the Southerners, while it brought gloom to the Republican Party. Abraham Lincoln sounded a daring note, a note that tolled the knell of compromise, when, at the Republican state convention at Springfield, Illinois, he declared " 'A house divided against itself cannot stand.' I believe this government cannot endure permanently half *slave* and half *free*." Chosen as the Republican candidate for Douglas' seat in the Senate, Lincoln challenged the "Little Giant" (Douglas was barely five feet tall) to a series of debates. Thousands of people flocked to hear the Senate's ablest debater and his opponent. In one encounter Lincoln asked Douglas to announce whether he continued to believe in his doctrine of popular sovereignty or had accepted the Dred Scott decision. Douglas' adherence to the former would wreck his political following in the South; his adherence to the latter would ruin him in the North. Douglas, still hoping for compromise, tried to adhere to both. His answer indicated acceptance of the Dred Scott decision in theory and doubt of its practical enforcement in antislave communities. It infuriated those in the South who had no more use for compromise than Lincoln had. Although Douglas was returned by Illinois as senator, his presidential chances were ruined.

There next occurred (1859) a fanatical and quixotic episode which, though relatively unimportant in itself, revealed how near the North and the

244

South had come to the verge of forceful union or forceful separation. A small band under the crusading John Brown captured the federal arsenal at Harpers Ferry in Virginia, in the hope of freeing and arming the slaves. Brown and six followers were hanged for this mad expedition. The specter of a slave uprising alarmed Virginia and the rest of the South to the point of frenzy, while the abolitionists transformed Brown into a martyr and sang of "John Brown's body" which "lies a-mouldering in the grave" while "his soul goes marching on."

The campaign of 1860 and the defeat of compromise

THE Democratic Party was badly divided when it met in April 1860 in Charleston, South Carolina, the heart of southern sectionalism. A southern faction, although the South traditionally stood for states' rights, vigorously backed a platform demanding federal protection of slavery in the territories, while the Douglas faction advocated a "nonintervention" platform designed to keep the party from splitting. When it was clear that the nonintervention faction would prevail, the Alabama delegation marched out of the convention hall, followed by others from the lower South.

The Democratic Party thereupon fatally split into Northern Democrats and Southern Democrats. The Republicans recognized their opportunity. Meeting enthusiastically in Chicago, they nominated the anticompromise Middle West debater Abraham Lincoln. They reaffirmed their party's determination to allow slavery to spread no farther. Although they appealed to northern business interests by inserting a protective tariff plank in their platform, pleased both East and West by pledging to support a transcontinental railroad, and wooed the agricultural interests by promising to enact a law giving free homesteads to settlers, the victory of the Republicans at the polls was largely due to their stressing the antislavery issue. Lincoln, the opponent of "the house divided," won the election. But it was a purely sectional victory, and from the standpoint of the total popular vote cast, Lincoln was a "minority president." The popular vote, however, also showed that 80 per cent of the electorate had balloted against secession. Even in the South, where a rival Constitutional Union Party had shown remarkable strength, the Southern Democrats had polled less than 50 per cent of the popular votes.

The creation of the Confederate States

NOW THE worst fears of the southern extremists had come true—a "black Republican" had been elected. They were swift to act. On December 20, 1860, the legislature of South Carolina, the home of nullification, unanimously declared that "the Union now subsisting between South Carolina and other States, under the name of the 'United States of America' is hereby dissolved." Before Lincoln was inaugurated, Mississippi, Florida, Alabama, Georgia, Louisiana, and 245

Texas also seceded and united with South Carolina to form the Confederate States of America. President Buchanan vacillated during these critical days, admitting that there was no constitutional right of secession but maintaining that he had no constitutional power to prevent it. Various efforts at reconciliation were put forward, but the Republicans would have nothing to do with the extension of slavery into the territories, and these efforts failed. The choice between concession or secession, which had hitherto always led to the making of compromises, no longer existed when the leadership lay, in both sections, in the hands of men who had tired of compromise. Rather than to become politically and economically subservient to a Republican North, the southern leaders preferred to secede from a Union in which they might be unable to play a dominant or even an equal role. They thought that they might be permitted to secede peacefully or after only a token resistance.

SECESSION
OR REPRESSION

WILLIAM H. Seward, who was soon to become Lincoln's secretary of state, had called the dispute between North and South "an irrepressible conflict between opposing and enduring forces." The conflict had now reached a stage where it seemed unlikely to end except in the secession or the repression of the South. The issue of war or peace hinged now not only upon whether the South would resort to arms to oust Northern forces but also upon whether the North would resist secession by a military offensive.

A political cartoon of the early days of the Civil War. The southern states, astride pigs and jackasses, are riding hard toward the precipice of secession.

*The decision
to resort to war*

WHEN Lincoln was inaugurated on March 4, 1861, he had to decide whether to allow the Confederacy to go its way unmolested, to lure it back into the Union through compromise, or to bring it back forcibly. In his inaugural address the new president appealed for a reconciliation within the framework of the Constitution. He agreed that he was bound to respect the existence of slavery in those states where it was legally established, and he promised to enforce the Fugitive Slave Act. But the Constitution, he insisted, gave no state the right to secede—and he intended to maintain the Union and "preserve, protect, and defend" the government of the United States.

Up to this time, no major act of violence had been committed by either side. The first act that could not be overlooked came on April 12 when Confederate artillery opened fire on the federal garrison of Fort Sumter in Charleston Harbor and forced its surrender. Lincoln issued a call on April 15 for 75,000 volunteers to begin the forcible repression of secession, and summoned Congress to meet in special session on July 4.

Actually, both sides expected that the conflict would be of short duration. But before the bloody fratricidal struggle came to an end, nearly 3,000,000 men had enlisted in the federal army and about 1,300,000 in the Confederate army, more than 600,000 lives had been lost, and the total cost of the war had mounted to over $10,000,000,000—or more than twice as much as it would have cost the country to purchase the freedom of all the 3,953,760 slaves recorded by the census of 1860.

*The resources
of North and South compared*

EVEN IN the South feelings were divided. The states of the upper South—Virginia, Tennessee, Arkansas, and North Carolina—had strong Unionist groups within their borders, and might have preferred to remain in the Union if their fears for southern rights could have been reassured. But Lincoln's warlike preparations removed their hesitation, and they joined the Confederacy. Tennessee, which seceded only in June 1861, was the last state to join the Confederacy. Unionist sympathy always remained high in some parts of the Confederate States. The western counties of Virginia were so opposed to secession that they seceded in their turn from the Old Dominion and were admitted to the Union as a separate state. The slave states of Delaware, Kentucky, Maryland, and Missouri, although divided in sentiment, remained with the Union. At its largest, the Confederacy contained only eleven of the forty-four states.

A comparison of the resources of the warring sections at the outbreak of hostilities shows a great disparity. Against the 22,000,000 people of the North, the South could muster only a little over 9,000,000, of whom nearly 4,000,000 were slaves. The northern railways measured about 22,000 miles as against 9000. Most of the banking and commercial houses were concentrated in the North, while New York alone manufactured goods in 1860 valued at more than twice those of the entire Confederacy. With its iron and steel resources and technical facilities, the North was able to produce almost all the war supplies which it required, while the South was always dependent to a crippling extent upon England and France for matériel. Since the North possessed the navy, it blockaded the South so as to prevent trade with Europe.

Against these advantages the South could counter with certain advantages of its own. It was a compact area and its armies could operate on inside lines. It was fighting a defensive war, for the North had to take the offensive in order to keep the Confederacy from leaving the Union. Again, since the people of the South were fighting for their independence, their already strong martial spirit was lifted further by devotion to a patriotic cause. Likewise, they won the sympathy of many abroad—even liberals like Gladstone and Acton. Indeed the South believed that Great Britain and possibly France might intervene on its behalf because their mills needed raw cotton.

The apparent success of the South until 1862

INITIAL defeats on the field of battle provided painful proof to the northern leaders that they would have to prosecute a lengthy and costly war. They soon developed what came to be a four-front strategy of offense. This involved: (1) the control of the sea and the establishment of an effective blockade of the Confederacy's ports so as to strangle it economically; (2) an eastern campaign designed to capture Richmond, the Confederacy's capital; (3) a western campaign to gain control of the Mississippi Valley and split the southern states; and (4) a diplomatic campaign whose objective was to keep Britain and other European powers from intervening in the civil conflict on the side of the Confederacy. The blockade was nearly destroyed when in March 1862 the Confederate ironclad *Merrimac* destroyed three federal frigates. But the *Merrimac* was itself checked by the northern ironclad *Monitor*. Their indecisive engagement not only signaled the failure of the South to break the blockade but served notice to the world that the day of the wooden warship was at an end. By 1863 the blockade had seriously constricted the South's economic life, and despite the successful dash of an occasional blockade runner, the Confederacy was unable to export cotton to Europe or get back all the war materials and medical supplies that it needed.

The campaign in the East was a bitter disappointment to the North for four weary years. A succession of northern generals pitted their skill and resources against a group of far superior southern strategists, who successfully defended their capital city of Richmond. The Confederates under General Robert E. Lee even invaded Maryland in 1862 in the hope of inflicting a mortal blow against the North, at that time discouraged and vulnerable. The rival armies met at Antietam on September 17, 1862. The battle was indecisive, but Lee was forced to fall back.

The interior of a heavily armored gun turret designed by Captain John Erickson for the Federal ironclad Passaic. *The turret contained twin Dahlgren guns, each weighing 42,000 pounds and firing shot that weighed nearly a quarter of a ton. Steam-driven ironclads with revolving turrets came to play an effective part in the Civil War.*

*Emancipation
as a political expedient*

LINCOLN'S own party was badly split over the question of slavery. While Lincoln himself belonged to that group which placed the preservation of the Union above all other considerations, another segment of the Republican Party was fervently abolitionist and took every opportunity to criticize the president scathingly for not concentrating upon emancipation. Lincoln was also in favor of emancipation, but he subordinated it to the larger issue of preserving the Union and refused to proclaim emancipation before it appeared politically feasible to do so. Only after the apparent victory at Antietam did Lincoln take the decisive step. He issued his famous Proclamation of Emancipation, to become effective on January 1, 1863. In it Lincoln declared all slaves free in those parts of the United States then at war against the Union and not occupied by Union troops, but permitted slaves to be retained in those loyal to the Union. Although the proclamation did nothing to change the military situation, its announcement earned the North great moral support among liberty-loving peoples throughout the world, convincing the laboring classes in England and France especially that they were justified in supporting the North despite the preferences, which we shall shortly examine, of their governments for the South.

*The end
of the Confederacy*

AFTER Antietam, the Confederates continued to hold their own in the East. By the following May they twice defeated renewed invasions of Virginia. Then, in an effort to offset Confederate defeats in the West and to conserve the dwindling resources of   249 the South, Lee marshaled his forces and invaded the North. For three days (July 1-3, 1863) battle raged at Gettysburg, Pennsylvania, before the Confederates withdrew.

In the western campaigns the Union cause had progressed well from the outset. By the end of 1862, a northern army under General Ulysses S. Grant controlled the Mississippi as far south as Vicksburg and a naval force had captured New Orleans. These successes greatly heartened the North, whose morale had been shaken by threats of intervention from Europe and by defeats on the eastern front, and caused the governments of England and France to be cautious in their expectations of an ultimate southern victory. On July 4, 1863, right after Lee's setback at Gettysburg, Vicksburg fell to Grant. A few days later, northern forces won complete control of the Mississippi, severing Arkansas, Louisiana, and Texas from the rest of the Confederacy. Grant now went to the aid of the federal forces fighting around Chattanooga, and before the following winter he had temporarily forced the Confederates out of Tennessee. Atlanta, Georgia, a vital railroad and manufacturing center in the Confederacy, was occupied in September 1864 by a Union army under General William T. Sherman, and then some 60,000 men, virtually unopposed and systematically wrecking and looting, marched through Georgia to Savannah.

Thus the war moved into its final stages. Lincoln had given Grant command of all the northern armies early in 1864 and brought him east to hammer at Lee. The succeeding months witnessed a series of costly battles in which Grant wore down the forces of Lee through sheer attrition. A defeated Confederacy, its strength sapped by the long years of naval and military exertion, could no longer hope for aid from Europe. Lee was now caught in a vise, with Grant closing in on the north and Sherman from the south. Forced to abandon Richmond, he retreated to Appomattox Court House, where he surrendered to Grant on April 9, 1865. Meanwhile, Sherman was driving relentlessly northward and the remaining Confederate forces in the East surrendered to him on April 26. The Confederacy was no more.

European opinion and the American Civil War

THE NORTH'S victory had been due in considerable part to the handling of the campaign waged on the diplomatic front. Both sides had appreciated from the outset the importance of gaining European support. The North wanted, while cutting off the exchange of southern raw cotton for European manufactured goods, to avoid provoking Britain and other countries into intervening by diplomacy or arms on the side of the South. The Confederacy expected that the strength of economic factors would secure European recognition and intervention. Its president, Jefferson Davis, had even acceded to a futile plan calling for the emancipation of slaves in exchange for the recognition of the Confederacy by

250   Great Britain and France.

The North's blockade worked great hardships on the British and French textile industries. British imports of cotton from America declined from 2,580,000 bales in 1860 to 72,000 bales in 1862. Half a million mill-workers in Lancashire and elsewhere were thrown out of work, and cotton manufacturers and commercial interests began to apply pressure upon their government to recognize the Confederacy and break the blockade. Yet despite the tremendous hardships inflicted upon mill-workers by the shortage of cotton and the closing of the mills, the American minister in London, Charles Francis Adams, with the assistance of Canadian public opinion, of John Bright, Cobden, and other liberals, and of some able propagandist agents expressly sent over for that purpose, kept the British public amicably disposed toward the North and convinced of its ultimate success.

Government circles in Britain and on the Continent were inclined to be favorable to the Confederacy. The privileged classes in Europe were sympathetic to the aristocratic planters in the South and looked upon the Confederacy as a legitimate expression of self-determination. They were all the more averse to the American experiment in republican government because the working classes—even the suffering mill-workers—hoped for a northern victory and were prepared to think of such an outcome as a triumph of popular principles. Furthermore, European governments hoped that the splitting of the Union would reverse the Monroe Doctrine and open the way for the acquisition of territory or for diplomatic advantage in the New World. Napo-

In this sketch made by a special artist of the Illustrated London News, *the Garibaldi Guard, made up of Europeans who enlisted to fight for the North in the Civil War, passes in review before President Lincoln on July 4, 1861.*

251

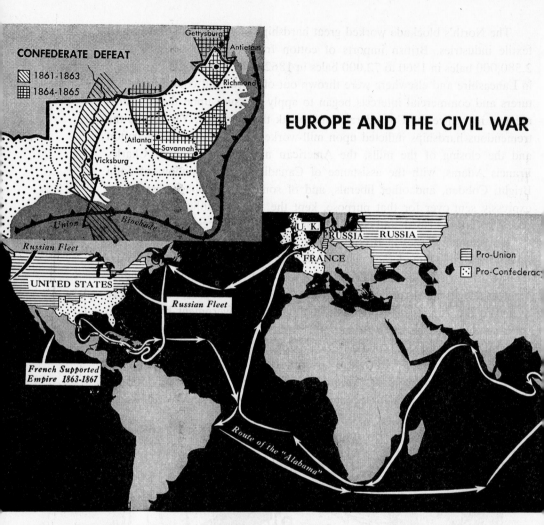

EUROPE AND THE CIVIL WAR

CONFEDERATE DEFEAT

- ▨ 1861-1863
- ▦ 1864-1865

Gettysburg
Antietam
Richmond
Atlanta
Savannah
Vicksburg
Union *Blockade*

Russian Fleet
UNITED STATES
Russian Fleet
French Supported
Empire 1863-1867

U. K.
PRUSSIA
RUSSIA
FRANCE

▤ Pro-Union
⬚ Pro-Confederacy

Route of the "Alabama"

The conflict of official European sympathies in the American war of secession (indicated by corresponding hatching on the larger map) was intensified in 1863 by a Polish war of secession (page 254). In this case also Great Britain and France favored the dissidents, while Russia tried to prevent rebellion. Fearing a blockade by the British, Russia sent her fleets to northern ports for haven. The two western European powers from the first had maintained only an imperfect neutrality. Fast Confederate raiders like the Alabama were built in British shipyards, and in a divided America Napoleon III saw an opportunity to establish a French-supported empire in Mexico. However, as southern military fortunes declined (inset map), the governments of Great Britain and France readjusted their policies.

leon III proposed more than once that France and Britain intercede for the South, but the British government was restrained from joining in such a plan by the strong pro-Union sentiment of English antislavery groups and the working classes. British antislavery sentiment was buoyed by the Emancipation Proclamation. Other factors favoring the Union were Britain's growing dependence on northern wheat, Lee's failure to win a decisive battle, the South's deteriorating military position after Gettysburg, and the friendly attitude of Russia, Prussia, and the Scandinavian countries toward the North.

252

**The Trent Affair
and the Alabama Affair**

BEFORE the war ended, diplomatic rupture between the North and Great Britain was only narrowly averted on at least two occasions. One was the crisis that arose when a northern warship stopped the British steamship *Trent* on the high seas and removed the Confederate commissioners en route to Britain and France. The British government viewed this act as a violation of neutral rights on the high seas and demanded the release of the commissioners and an apology. Lincoln saw that the American act had violated the nation's traditional policy regarding the freedom of the seas. He wisely yielded to the British position, and the storm blew over. The other incident was a violation of neutrality by Britain in its turn. Its prosouthern government permitted Confederate cruisers, such as the *Alabama* and *Florida,* to be constructed in British shipyards, and also allowed British ports to be used as bases of operation against northern commerce, which suffered millions of dollars worth of damage. After repeatedly ignoring the North's protests, the British government was compelled in 1863 to heed Adams' warning that the "escape" of any more Confederate commerce-destroyers would be an act of war, and became more concerned with enforcing its neutrality obligations. The damage caused by these Confederate cruisers with the connivance of groups in the British government later resulted in the United States' successfully pressing the *Alabama* claims against Great Britain (page 320).

**France
and the Mexican Empire**

NAPOLEON III envisaged in the split of the American republic a golden opportunity to reëstablish a French empire in the New World. In Mexico the disillusionment and financial distress following the war with the United States had led first to the exile and then to the dictatorship of the greedy and ambitious Santa Anna. But the dictatorship proved short-lived, and in two years gave way before a revolt of the Liberals under the Indian leader Benito Juárez. The Liberals in turn found their government resisted by the Conservatives, who resented especially the laws separating church and state. In the course of the ensuing civil wars, the Mexican government suspended payment of interest on its foreign debt; and Napoleon III, thinking that his chance had come, assumed the responsibility of protecting the investment of a European banking house whose head had but recently become a naturalized French citizen so as to give the French government a better right to interfere.

For a while the Monroe Doctrine was openly disregarded. French troops occupied Mexico City in 1863, and Archduke Maximilian of Austria was made emperor in 1864. The United States, especially when already engaged in a life-and-death civil struggle, did not want to get into war with France. Secretary of State Seward therefore refrained from mentioning the Monroe Doctrine when he informed Napoleon that the American people were not favorably disposed to the French venture in Mexico. After the close of the Civil War, Seward took a stronger tone in demanding the withdrawal of French troops. As we have already seen (page 193), Napoleon reluctantly complied. Unsupported, Maximilian fell into the hands of Juárez and was shot by a firing squad in June 1867. Juárez restored the republic and became its president.

The international crisis of 1863 in America and Europe

AT ONE point the American Civil War got somewhat mixed up with the bitterness engendered in France and England by Russia's pitiless repression of Poland (page 185). Russia looked upon Lincoln in a friendly spirit because, like the czar of Russia, he was dealing with the problems of emancipation and revolt. This friendliness was shared by Prussia, which wished not only to suppress the Poles but also to effect a union with the countries to its own south. The French and English governments, on the other hand, were sympathetic with Poland and hostile to the North. Fearing that, if a war should break out between Russia and England, the Russian fleets would be bottled up, the Russian naval minister ordered the Pacific fleet to San Francisco and the Baltic fleet to New York as if on friendly visits. The presence of Russian fleets in both American ports was long regarded in the United States as a bold act of support in a time of need, though its explanation actually was somewhat different. Yet if a war had come in Europe over Poland, the sympathies of the North would probably have been on the side of Russia and Prussia, and those of the South on the side of England and France.

Financing the American Civil War

THE MAGNITUDE of the American Civil War forced both sides to take drastic financial measures to raise revenue. Funds came chiefly from taxation, loans, and the issue of legal tender notes. For a few years before the war, the United States had had almost a free-trade economy. But during the struggle, Union tariff duties were introduced and increased until, by the Act of 1864, the average rate of duties on imports had advanced to 47 per cent. This new tariff policy was to remain for decades after the war the basis of a high protective system designed to profit American manufacturing. Another form of war taxation was that placed on incomes. In 1861, for the first time in American history, a graduated income tax was levied, and it rose steadily during the war. But most of the Union's revenue came from heavy borrowing through bond issues. Loans differed widely in duration, interest payments, and methods of redemption. They were floated by agents, the most outstanding of whom was the Philadelphia banker Jay Cooke. United States bonds found buyers abroad, particularly in Germany. The northern government resorted also to the issuance of fiat or paper money. In June 1864 some $431,000,000 of these "greenbacks" were still in circulation. They were legal tender for all debts, yet had no metallic backing. Since they failed to inspire popular confidence, they declined in value and contributed to inflation. In keeping with well-known economic laws, these greenbacks resulted in the disappearance of precious metals, and Congress was reduced to printing fractional paper money, called "shinplasters," in denominations as low as three cents.

A financial measure of the first importance resulted from the passage in 1863 of the National Bank Act. Its main purpose was to regulate both the banking business of the country and the issue of bank notes. Before its passage 1600 banks established under the laws of twenty-nine states were issuing several thousand different kinds of bank notes of widely varying soundness. The new act provided for the creation of national banks, and, to stimulate the sale of federal bonds, each national bank had to buy federal bonds to the extent of one third of its capital. The banks were then allowed to issue bank notes up to 90 per cent of the market value of bonds owned. In a relatively short time, the country had a new banking system, with a soundly backed currency replacing the old state bank notes (which were subjected to a 10 per cent tax in 1865 to hasten their demise).

The Confederacy also had to resort to stringent financial measures. Among them were property taxes, a graduated income tax, a profits tax, and a 10 per cent tax on farm produce. Staples such as cotton and tobacco were used as security in floating bond issues in Europe, while weak credit resources forced the South to print about a billion dollars' worth of fiat paper money. During the last days of the war, this paper money became practically worthless. The financial bankruptcy of the defeated states was made complete by Section IV of the Fourteenth Amendment to the American Constitution, adopted in 1868. By that measure the war debts of the late Confederate government and of the separate states were held illegal and void, so that bondholders, domestic and foreign, received nothing for them. The same amendment forbade compensation for the loss or emancipation of any slaves.

Boom in the North and depression in North and South AFTER a few months of business slackness at the start of the war, the North experienced unprecedented expansion and prosperity. The production of raw materials increased, with the output of coal, for example, jumping from 14,600,000 tons in 1860 to 23,600,000 tons in 1864. The discovery of oil in northwestern Pennsylvania resulted in the petroleum yield's rising from almost nothing in 1859 to 128,000,000 gallons in 1862. Oil was used chiefly for domestic purposes, particularly for lamps, and the rise of the petroleum industry brought the decline of the whale oil industry. Wheat and hog production also made great gains despite the drawing of thousands of farmers into the armed services, and these gains were in no small measure due to the growing use of new farm machinery, such as the mechanical reaper invented by Cyrus McCormick in

1831 and the scouring steel plow invented by John Deere in 1837. Military and civilian needs stimulated northern manufacturers to unprecedented endeavor; the consumption of wool, for example, increased from 85,000,000 to over 200,000,000 pounds. The improvement of facilities in water and land transportation kept pace with the expansion of the North's agriculture and industry, and the famous Union Pacific Railroad was chartered, though not constructed, during the war. Large-scale industrial techniques and the foundations of "big business" came to the United States largely as a result of the demands made upon industry during the Civil War. Northern prosperity was accompanied by a burst of social activity and even reckless extravagance. War profits created many new millionaires, and great numbers of people went in for heavy speculation and competitive ostentation.

Yet the laboring classes did not profit from this prosperity. The cost of living soared faster than wages, with the result that although the northern worker was earning more money at the close of the war than in 1863, he was actually worse off than in 1860. By 1863 hunger and industrial unrest were not uncommon in the larger cities, and the lot of the worker was made harder by the knowledge that if he quit his job, it would be immediately grabbed by one of the thousands of immigrants then swarming into the country. These immigrants had responded to the government's inducements to fill the ranks of the war workers. As the status of American labor declined, strikes became more common; and a number of national unions came into existence, including the American Miners' Association (1861), forerunner of the present United Mine Workers' organization, and the Brotherhood of Locomotive Engineers (1864). The trend toward unionism was accelerated still further during the late sixties.

In the defeated South, military destruction was so systematic that it paralyzed the economic system. Before the war, the South had enjoyed an agricultural economy based on the exporting of staple products and the importing of manufactured goods. The blockade had destroyed that exchange, had forced a costly conversion from staple products to foodstuffs, and had fostered new manufactures. The economy of the South was critically, if not fatally, weakened also by the destruction or deterioration of its transportation facilities, which had been inadequate even at the start of the war.

Lincoln's plan for southern reconstruction IN THE darkest hours of the war Lincoln, uncompromising but not unforgiving, had shown patience and restraint, tact and good humor. He never failed to make it clear that "our late friends, now adversaries" must one day be reunited as honorable, full-fledged citizens. The Republicans lost so many seats in Congress in the election of 1862 that it looked as if Lincoln might be defeated in 1864, but timely victories in the field helped him to win reëlection. His second inaugural

A large part of Richmond was left in flaming ruin when Lee evacuated the city after nine months of siege. The destruction was characteristic of that which befell many southern plantations and commercial centers.

address was a plea for the principles which he believed alone capable of rebuilding the nation upon a healthy foundation:

> With malice toward none, with charity for all, with firm-
> ness in the right, as God gives us to see the right, let us
> strive on to finish the work we are in, to bind up the
> nation's wounds, to care for him who shall have borne
> the battle, and for his widow, and his orphan—to do all
> which may achieve and cherish a just and lasting peace
> among ourselves and with all nations.

Two days after Lee's surrender at Appomattox, the president in a public address described his policy of reconstruction, upon which he had in fact embarked with the first reconquests in 1863. It was a policy founded not on vindictiveness but on magnanimity. Every southern state was to be read-mitted to its full privileges in the Union as quickly as feasible.

Lincoln was not suffered "to bind up the nation's wounds." On the night of April 14, while at the theater, he was struck down by an assassin's bullet. And when, in the early morning of the next day, the president died in the lodging house across the street from the theater, the nation lost the one figure of national stature who might have shielded the defeated South from malice and persuaded the victorious North to charity.

THE Civil War in America had been the most costly war in men and money that was ever fought up to that time—except perhaps for the Taiping Rebel- 257 lion in China (pages 273-279). The Concert of Europe had neither the authority to prevent war in America nor perhaps the inclination to do so, since several of the European rulers had no great desire to keep American republicanism from suicide. The war had demonstrated what the modern million-man military machine could do using steamboats, railroads, torpedoes, ironclads, long lines of trenches, Colt revolvers, submarines, breech-loading magazine rifles, and telegraph lines as military weapons. Casualties might have been greater if the revolving machine gun, capable of discharging 350 shots a minute, invented by Richard J. Gatling of Chicago in 1862, had been put into quantity production. French, German, and other correspondents and military observers on both sides reported these developments.

That the American republic survived and emerged, if anything, potentially stronger from the ordeal by fire helped the causes of nationalism and liberalism in several ways. It was a victory for strong federal government. It served as an inspiration to those Germans and Italians who hoped to complete the unifications of their countries. The emancipation of the last great body of slaves in the western world also justified the laboring classes of England and France in their confidence that the cause of the North was the cause of free labor. Lincoln was mourned in England and France only somewhat less sorrowfully than in the United States; and in France the victory of the North was, as we have seen, a defeat for Napoleon III from which he never recovered.

During the American Civil War, Canada had had to face its own problem of confederation. Confronted with a baffling puzzle in the unassimilable French Catholics in Quebec, the Canadian provinces thought of a limited provincial self-government and a union of the provinces into a single confederated dominion as the solution of their complications. In a convention at Quebec in 1864, four provinces drew up a set of resolutions to that effect and submitted them to London. If the American Civil War had resulted in a victory for the Confederacy, the British government might have felt greater hesitation in granting a system of provincial rights and centralized federation to Canada, for it might have been argued that the American precedent underlined the weaknesses of such a system. Shortly after the North's victory, however (as we shall soon discover), the London government created a federated Dominion of Canada.

It is also conceivable that if the United States had broken into two unfriendly nations, some at least of the Latin-American countries would have failed to maintain their republican institutions. The Mexican Empire probably would have continued under French domination. British interventions in Argentina, Honduras, and Uruguay (intermittently between 1838 and 1850) and the Spanish effort to recapture Peru (1865-1866) give reason to believe that other European countries might have taken advantage of American embarrassment to extend their systems to the Western Hemisphere. The victory of the North not only reinforced the Monroe Doctrine but meant also that Latin America was to become more clearly than ever before an area diplomatically swayed (though never fully controlled) by the United States.

On the other hand, the Civil War made upon American society some ugly scars that have remained visible ever since. The process of reconstruction, left to less merciful and tactful statesmen than Lincoln, was to put salt in old wounds, with the result that sectionalism was to remain a lasting feature of American politics. And the status of the Negro continues as "a great American dilemma," which time apparently has been solving only gradually.

Chapter five

EUROPEANIZATION AND

IMPERIALISM

IN ASIA

SINCE the sixteenth century Europeans had maintained fairly regular relations with the countries of the Far East. Until the nineteenth century, however, Westerners in Asia were forced to rely for safety upon the forbearance of the Orientals rather than upon their own strength. Distance, inadequate numbers, and insufficient armed might combined to keep the foreign intruders from exerting a decisive force upon the policies of Far Eastern governments. The foreigners handled their affairs preferably through trading companies; and the representatives of the trading companies, in order to keep their precarious footholds, had to depend upon the attractiveness of trade profits to the local authorities.

As time went on, these profits decreased. Hence, the political power of European governments had to be called upon more and more to protect the interests of their citizens. The regular, formally accredited emissary then made his appearance in China and other eastern areas, and a system of direct and official diplomatic negotiations gradually replaced the system of indirect and unofficial commercial negotiations. From the end of the eighteenth century on, the countries of Asia received an increasing number of formal demands to deal on a basis of equality with the representatives of western nations, whose strength and significance the relatively isolated states of the East appreciated little.

Until 1800, since neither side possessed overwhelming military preponderance, Europeans living and working in the Far East had been required to depend upon their own resources. Direct diplomacy, however, brought with it the support of naval armaments, in which the Westerners possessed marked superiority. Big guns quickly taught the Easterners to appreciate the merits of the European way of life, particularly its industrialism, for the 263 countries of the East had nothing to match the ever-expanding industrial strength of the West.

As the nineteenth century wore on, the technological gap widened, and the threat to the peace and security of the Far East became proportionately greater. In the West in earlier centuries, the Chinese, whose philosophy and art had won genuine admiration, had been symbolized by "the Chinese sage." Now, largely because of his technological backwardness, he was dubbed "the heathen Chinese" and looked upon as an inferior ready for conversion and exploitation. The increasing military, technological, and missionary pressure of the West, in turn, brought squarely home to the Asiatic peoples the question of how to preserve their own mores while equipping themselves to meet the threat of the West.

The pressure of the West was not constant even in the nineteenth century. At the beginning of the century, overseas expansion under government leadership was not generally regarded with favor. Colonies were thought by many to be too expensive, too much of a military risk to repay the effort required to build them up or too likely to interfere with missionary efforts among the natives. In France the memory of defeats in India and America was still fresh, and in England the successful revolt of the American colonies brought hesitation about new colonial ventures. The aggressive overseas imperialism that eventually characterized the nineteenth century did not become a potent force until after 1870, when the political and industrial developments of the earlier decades began to make profound and widespread changes in the economic and social fabric of western European life. Nevertheless, before 1870 certain western imperial projects, whether by economic domination or by colonization, had marked success.

THE DIVISION
OF OCEANIA

ENCOURAGED by the explorations and observations of Admiral George Anson and Captain James Cook in the eighteenth century, adventurers and fishermen from Europe and America sailed through the charted and uncharted South Seas in search of whales, trade, and loot. Missionaries also embarked for the Pacific islands in search of souls. Sometimes the flag followed fisherman, adventurer, or missionary.

Charles Darwin
and the voyage of the Beagle

THE PACIFIC world was not, however, to be explored only by naval officers, whalers, traders, adventurers, and missionaries. As in the eighteenth century, the scholars and scientists of Europe looked upon the opening of new lands as splendid opportunities for extending the frontiers of knowledge by the study of exotic plant and animal life, and of native customs, languages, and traditions. Alexander von Humboldt by his travels in Europe, South America, and the Russian Empire, and by his studies of the relations of geography and biology, had given an example to younger naturalist-travelers—Charles Darwin among them.

In the years 1831-1836 Darwin made a famous scientific voyage aboard the *Beagle,* a ten-gun brig of the Royal Navy. After a careful survey of the coastal area of South America and neighboring island groups, the *Beagle* carried Darwin across the Pacific to Tahiti, New Zealand and Australia. He was impressed by the multiplicity of coral formations, and they led him to publish a famous monograph (1842) on the origin of atolls and reefs. He was struck also by the relations between the plants and animals of the islands and those of the nearby continents, particularly by the fact that the island animals were clearly akin to but not the same as the continental species. This observation provided the initial impetus for his speculations about the modifications within genera, the starting point of his later theory of evolution (page 157).

The studies of Alfred Russel Wallace — IN 1854, the British zoologist Wallace (page 157) commenced his eight years of explorations and studies in Malaya and the East Indies. Like Darwin at an earlier date, Wallace observed and collected specimens of animal life in the insular and continental backlands of the South Pacific region. In the course of his observations he discovered what is still known as "Wallace's line," a narrow strip of sea in the East Indies waters on the two sides of which animal life is as widely divergent as in any two widely separated areas. Wallace, we have already seen, became a confirmed believer in evolution and a proponent of the theory of natural selection. After his return to England, he published his excellent account entitled *The Malay Archipelago* (1869). His later scientific writings also bear the imprint of his Pacific experiences.

Wakefield's scheme for systematic colonialism — WHILE DARWIN was engaged in his South Pacific researches, Gibbon Wakefield in England was sketching out his colonial ideas, particularly with reference to Australia and New Zealand (page 92). While imprisoned for attempting to trick an heiress into marriage, Wakefield produced his famous *Letter from Sydney* (1829). In this tract he maintained that the slow progress and heavy expense of colonizing efforts in Australia could be accounted for by the inefficiency of dispatching criminals to penal colonies and by the recklessness in donating lands to colonists there. He proposed the systematic sale at a reasonable price of small units of land, the proceeds from which should be set up as a fund for promoting voluntary emigration to Australia. Such emigration, he believed, would relieve the labor shortage in the colonies and simultaneously help to alleviate population pressures at home. After his release from prison, Wakefield became a leading figure in the organization of the National Colonization Society. The influence of this society (and of its individual members after its disbandment) was felt when the Colonial Office in 1831 placed New South Wales under regulations that embodied Wakefield's proposals. In 1833 he organized the South Australian Association; and the association's efforts were crowned with success when South Australia was created (1834) by an act of Parliament which borrowed considerably from Wakefield's theories. Contemporary settlements were made in Victoria and Western Australia.

Wakefield was also instrumental in organizing in 1837 the New Zealand Association, out of which developed the New Zealand Company. Determined to make of New Zealand a self-sustaining colony, he was bitterly opposed by those who looked upon the proposed colony as a useless expense or a potential interference with their missionary work. In this instance his enterprise forced the hand of the government, which in 1840 decided to annex the islands, just in time to prevent the French from gaining control over them.

The beginning of French interest in the East

SINCE THE Treaty of Vienna in 1815 had definitely established Britain as the winner in the old race for strategic overseas areas, the French had launched a new effort to regain their lost prestige. After 1830 they sought fresh laurels by explorations and annexations in Africa and the Pacific region. The story of the French imperial effort in Africa will be told in Chapter 7. Interest in France regarding the East, going back to the time of Louis XIV, rose after 1830, as diplomatic defeats in Europe and Africa whetted the appetite of King Louis Philippe for a more successful policy in Asia. Using the pretext of protecting Christian missionaries, the French became increasingly aggressive in Indochina and the islands of the Pacific.

The explorations of Dumont d'Urville

THE NAVIGATOR and hydrographic expert Jules Sébastien César Dumont d'Urville helped to stimulate French interest in the Pacific islands. In 1820 Dumont d'Urville had become famous for his discovery of what has since become perhaps the most venerated single piece of ancient Greek sculpture, the Venus de Milo. In 1826-1829 he made a voyage around the world, in the course of which he explored the South Seas. His account of these journeys deeply impressed the French people and government. Ten years later he undertook additional expeditions to the Antarctic and the South Pacific regions. These explorations enabled him to make a rough division of the Pacific island peoples into the Melanesian (Black Islanders), Micronesian (Tiny Islanders), and Polynesian (Many Islanders) groups—designations still in use, derived from striking characteristics either of the people or of the islands they inhabit. The

266   Melanesian and Micronesian Islands are located between the international

date line (the 180th degree of longitude) and the continent of Asia, the Melanesians in the southern sector and the Micronesians in the northern sector; the Polynesians are located east of the international date line.

The French policy of annexations in the Pacific

WHILE THEIR English rivals were engaged, as will be seen, in hostilities in Afghanistan and China, the French became particularly active in the Pacific. Suspicion of their aggressive intentions toward New Zealand, as already mentioned, was among the factors that induced England in 1840 to annex that archipelago. The French were not long, however, in getting compensation. Two years later they annexed the Marquesas Islands and established a protectorate over Tahiti and the Society Islands. The government of Napoleon III continued the imperialistic policy inaugurated by Louis Philippe. In 1853 the French annexed New Caledonia and in 1864 took over the Loyalty Islands. Although the French were neither the first nor the only ones in the scramble for Pacific possessions, it was they who pushed the policy of direct annexation the hardest. That policy was to lead to numerous diplomatic and naval embroilments during the nineteenth and twentieth centuries and to cause frequent wars between Europeans and the native groups that resisted them.

Americans in the Pacific islands

AMERICAN traders, fishermen, missionaries, and scientists also undertook to work in the Pacific islands. Moreover, the Washington government soon began to dispatch official expeditions for exploration and for protection of American interests. Although Westerners were sometimes welcomed by the natives, they were frequently attacked, particularly in areas that the white man had visited before. For example, in 1830 the *Friendship* of Salem, Massachusetts, was sacked by irate natives of Sumatra, in the Dutch East Indies (Indonesia today). Acting swiftly, the American government dispatched a naval expedition to investigate. As a consequence, the United States became one of the first western nations to support its traders and missionaries in the Pacific by naval action. In 1838, a scientific expedition under the command of Lieutenant Charles Wilkes, among other things, surveyed the great harbors of the Samoan group and confirmed the claim to Wake Island. The United States also began to display more than a passing interest in the future of the Hawaiian Islands, and on this issue came for a time into conflict with the older rivals in that area, Great Britain and France. Under pressure from the United States, the two European powers finally agreed in 1843 to recognize the independence of Hawaii and promised "never to take possession" of its territory. Several years later the United States concluded a treaty with the Hawaiian king establishing a temporary protectorate, and thereafter the question whether or not to annex the islands became an important issue in the United States' Pacific policy.

White supremacy among the Pacific islands — FOR ALL the western participants in the division of the Pacific islands, domination was accomplished with relative ease. Unable to resist the more powerfully armed white men and too widely dispersed to think of acting together, the island peoples were quickly obliged to submit. Their best hope lay in playing off the contesting powers against each other. In such cases, however, the islanders were generally the losers, no matter who won the decision. By the middle of the nineteenth century it was clear that the white man had come into the Pacific to stay.

CHINA'S WESTERN WARS

AND TAIPING REBELLION

THE CHINESE continued into the nineteenth century to patronize Westerners. At Canton, where alone the Westerners were permitted entry into the Celestial Empire, they were treated as inferiors who were graciously being granted the privilege of trade with China. Direct diplomacy with European governments was not looked on with favor by the "lord of ten thousand kingdoms" who ruled from the dragon throne in Peking. Nevertheless, western demands for equal treatment became more imperative and numerous.

The initiation of direct diplomacy in China — THE RELUCTANCE of the British to acquire additional colonies in Asia contrasted with their readiness to expand trade relations. This paradox was due in part to their unfortunate experience with chartered trading companies. British trading companies had sometimes acquired and administered vast empires as semisovereign rulers. Their decline in the eighteenth and early nineteenth centuries, however, had been rapid, marked by official investigations that had uncovered corruption and shocking scandal. Efforts followed to control the activities of the British East India Company through government regulations, such as William Pitt's India Act of 1784, and merchants outside the company felt encouraged to agitate for equality with company merchants. British public opinion was favorable to granting equal trading privileges, but it was opposed to new chartered companies that might build new empires. Hence the British government felt constrained to take over the British East India Company's responsibilities.

The traders of the British East India Company had dealt with the Chinese since 1684 at Canton. Until 1834 the company held a monopoly of the British trade with China, and its merchants were the only Britons permitted to conduct business at Canton. The Chinese had their own monopoly for handling trade at Canton. This monopoly was called the *Co-hong*. It was an organization of Chinese merchants with headquarters at Canton who were responsible to the imperial government at Peking for the conduct of trade with the Westerners. Thus a British monopoly dealt with a Chinese monopoly. When the British government attempted to deal directly with Peking, it began a new era in Anglo-Chinese relations.

Direct diplomacy with the Chinese government was first attempted by missions headed by Lord Macartney in 1793 and Lord Amherst in 1816 (page 62). It introduced into British commercial relations with China an element of official rigidity that had not existed before. So long as the British East India Company had acted alone, it had acted mainly for the interests of its stockholders, and it had been ready to make expedient compromises. Official diplomatic agents, on the other hand, could make no compromises with the Celestials without endangering the prestige of Great Britain. Thus, a widening source of conflict, hitherto unknown, developed between China and Great Britain in the early years of the nineteenth century, as Britain became more and more insistent that the Middle Kingdom grant to British traders and diplomats the recognition commonly accorded the representatives of countries having equal status.

The struggle for legal equality

THE STRAIN in Anglo-Chinese relations was almost brought to a breaking point when finally in 1834 the British government abolished the East India Company's monopoly of the China trade. To prepare for the admission of noncompany traders to Canton, the British in 1833 had dispatched to China an official known as the superintendent of trade. The first holder of this office was Lord Napier, who was firmly committed to the idea that China should recognize in word and deed the legal equality of all sovereign nations. His demands for equal treatment were, however, ignored or rebuffed by the Co-hong and the provincial officials at Canton.

China's weakness in controlling the opium trade

ALTHOUGH the Chinese imperial government continued to talk haughtily in the nineteenth century, the emperor was in no wise strong enough to keep the "barbarians" at arm's length. A startling example of the ineffectiveness of Chinese rule was to be found in the problems attending the importation of opium. The smoking of opium had developed into a widespread vice in China during the eighteenth century, and at the end of the century importation of the drug had been absolutely prohibited. During the first quarter of the nineteenth century, the Chinese made only a slight pretense of enforcing the law. Westerners remained eager to sell opium to the Chinese in order to balance their trade, which would otherwise favor the Chinese exporters, and Chinese merchants were no less eager to resell it at enormous profits to dope peddlers. Between 1828 and 1835 the annual average importation was over 18,000   269

These contemporary Chinese drawings, reproduced in Europe, show Chinese rural life in the early nineteenth century. Above, a threshing floor. Below, a farmer irrigates his fields with a primitive water wheel.

chests of opium, or more than four times what it had been in the previous decade. The breaking of the British East India Company's monopoly and the opening of the China trade to all British merchants after 1834 intensified the pressure to sell opium to the Chinese in return for silks and tea.

Within China two opposing camps sprang up. Some Chinese officials advocated enforcement of the anti-opium edicts; others, as they indicated in a memorial to the emperor, advocated legalizing a trade that they considered impossible to halt. Even while the imperial court sought a remedy for the opium problem, the trade at Canton increased in value to both the western and the Chinese merchants.

270

Captain Elliot
and the "opium crisis"

BY 1838 the imperial authorities had decided to proceed vigorously against the opium smugglers. Foreign merchants were ordered to turn their stores of the illicit drug over to the Chinese government and were placed personally under close surveillance. Meanwhile, Lord Napier had died and had been replaced as British superintendent of trade by Captain Charles Elliot. The Imperial Commissioner Lin Tsê-hsü and Captain Elliot carried on the negotiations that Napier had commenced but not on terms that Elliot was willing to consider equal. Although the British agent finally agreed to Lin's terms, he advised the British merchants to cease trading with China. Neither the British nor the Chinese officials, however, could halt the illicit coastwise traffic. The tense commercial and diplomatic situation that resulted came to be known as the "opium crisis."

To the Westerners this crisis was but a climax in a long series of grievances. The British officials were more concerned about receiving equal treatment commercially and diplomatically from the Chinese than they were in the trade itself. The Chinese, on the other hand, betrayed no consciousness that the British were angry over anything except the halting of the opium trade. For this reason the consequent hostilities (1839-1842) are sometimes inaccurately referred to as the "Opium War." In reality, the British resorted to arms primarily to force the Middle Kingdom to treat with them as nations of the West treated with each other. British persistence on this point was hard for the Chinese to understand.

The British attack
upon the Chinese coast

IN THE summer of 1839 Commissioner Lin, hoping to implement the embargo on opium, called on the Chinese people to arm themselves and to resist any attempts of the "English foreigners" to land. Bounties were offered for the capture of English ships and heads. In the fall British naval vessels arrived in Chinese waters to take protective and retaliatory measures. In the spring of 1840 they blockaded the port of Canton. By summer they were strong enough to attack and capture important points in the Chusan archipelago. Even the proud Chinese were forced to admit the superiority of British arms and equipment and the ineffectiveness of their own. Although some Chinese officials hoped to play the British off against other foreigners, the realization soon dawned, after the capture of Canton in 1841 and of the Yangtze city of Chinkiang in 1842, that China would have to make peace on Britain's terms. No longer could either the Chinese or the foreigners look upon the Middle Kingdom as invincible. The shell of China had been cracked, and the hollowness of China's military pride could be discerned.

The rapid successes of the British finally forced the emperor to sue for peace. Although the Manchu court was extremely reluctant to accept the

OPENING OF CHINA
1842-1844

Shanghai

Ningpo

Yangtze R

Foochow

Amoy

Canton

Hong Kong
(British Concession)

Shown here are the five Chinese ports opened to trade by the treaty between Great Britain and China following the Anglo-Chinese War of 1839-1842 and Hong Kong, which by the same treaty was ceded outright to Great Britain. France and the United States soon demanded and received the same right to trade at the five open ports, establishing a pattern that was to mark China's relations with the outside world throughout the nineteenth century.

British terms, only greater defeats could be expected from a prolongation of the war. Moreover, new defeats, it was feared, would probably intensify a serious internal situation. The unrest which was to burst forth in the Taiping Rebellion was already beginning to rumble as the weakness of the imperial government became obvious.

*The Treaty of Nanking
and extraterritorial authority*

AFTER ALMOST three years of intermittent hostilities, the Chinese government accepted the Treaty of Nanking. This treaty marks more than a mere cessation of hostilities between two belligerents. It formed the cornerstone of the diplomatic structure to be erected during the nineteenth century by foreigners with interests in China. Specifically, it provided for the cession of the island of Hong Kong to Great Britain, for opening Canton and several other ports to British trade, and for a war indemnity to Great Britain of $21,000,000. More important, however, than these specific provisions was the fact that the Chinese were forced for the first time to conduct diplomatic relations on a basis of equality. Yet the treaty was not itself an "equal" treaty, for it compelled China to accept the humiliating principle of extraterritoriality, or jurisdiction by British consuls over the persons and property of their fellow-citizens in China. Thus China began to lose her sovereign right to administer justice to foreigners within her own boundaries.

The principle
of the most-favored-nation

THE TREATY of Nanking and subsequent supplementary agreements between Great Britain and China in no way excluded other powers from entering upon similar relations with Peking. Indeed, implicit in the supplementary understandings was the possibility of equal treatment for all western powers. These understandings embodied a "most-favored-nation" clause—in other words, a clause stipulating that trade privileges extended to the nationals of any other power by China would automatically be extended also to British merchants. In the period 1842-1844 American and French diplomats, following the precedent set by their British associates, signed treaties with China by which they too were extended all the rights and privileges granted by China to any other power. Thus, whenever China made concessions to one foreign power she was bound to make equivalent concessions to every other power that had won or in the future might win most-favored-nation treatment. Although the most-favored-nation principle frequently worked in later years to the disadvantage of China, it also had the effect of protecting China somewhat against the claim of exclusive monopoly by any single power. In other words, it provided the legal background for what American diplomats came traditionally to refer to as the "open door," or the principle of equal opportunity, in China.

The "Great Peace"
and the "Heavenly Prince"

THE CHINESE reacted violently against the weakness of their government in dealing with the Westerners. Smoldering discontents were fanned into flames by the defeats of the war of 1839-1842, and by the unequal treaties which followed. Humiliation at the hands of foreigners was made even less tolerable to the Chinese by their own government's inefficiency and corruption. The Chinese were reminded more than ever that the reigning dynasty, the Manchus, although they had ruled China for three centuries, were themselves foreigners. The anti-Manchu sentiment was particularly vehement among the Chinese of the southern provinces, such as Kwangtung and Kwangsi, where the white foreigners were most active and where the power of the northern government had always been least secure.

In 1850 open warfare began in the south led by the Taiping rebels ("Taiping" means "Great Peace"). The Taiping Rebellion constituted a religio-political movement that gave lip service to certain Christian teachings but held more fervently the aim of overthrowing the Manchus and establishing a native dynasty. Under a leader who called himself the "Heavenly Prince," the Taiping rebels took advantage of the death of the emperor in 1850 to proclaim a new dynasty. Drawing their following from the peasants and other distressed elements of the population, of which China had many, the Taiping generals promised immediate betterment in the form of land and loot. The rebels looked for support from the foreigners who had so recently uncovered the weakness of the Peking government.

*The system
of "pin-pricking" the foreigners*

THE REBELS' hopes for foreign aid ran particularly high when tension mounted between Peking and the outlanders over the implementation of their recent treaties. Neither the government nor the people of China had accepted the principle of equality among nations for which the British "Opium War" had been fought. Insults to foreign representatives and to their national flags had never ceased, and numerous incidents took place as the foreigners began to trade and settle in the treaty ports. The residents of the five cities involved were not always willing to carry out orders from the capital in their dealings with the foreigners. Every right or concession granted under the treaties had to be fought out at the local level. At Canton particularly, the hostility of the native population proved difficult for the imperial government to handle. Charges of bad faith from both sides soon became common. The Taipings did their best to make the conflict between Peking and the Europeans hotter by encouraging animosity and recalcitrance among the natives of the treaty ports. Despite repeated incidents in the early 1850's, the British and the French, as long as they were engaged as allies in the war against Russia in the Crimea (pages 150-152), had to assume a conciliatory attitude in their dealings with Peking out of fear of forcing the Chinese into the arms of their enemy.

*The Anglo-French attack
upon the Manchu government*

AFTER THEIR decisive victory over Russia, the English and the French began again to demand concessions. In a sense, their joint pressure upon China was a continuation of the Anglo-French cooperation that had so recently won their brilliant success in Europe. It led in 1856 to an armed conflict, sometimes called the Second Western War against China. The Westerners were convinced that many of their troubles in China stemmed from not having legations in Peking and from being restricted to five port cities. Since China had not been fully opened by the first war, the aims of the new struggle were to chastise "John Chinaman" for his reluctance in observing his treaty obligations and to put the treaty structure on firmer and broader foundations. Thus the imperial government at Peking found itself fighting a civil war with the Taiping rebels and, at the same time, a foreign war with the Anglo-French alliance, though neither of the emperor's enemies felt a sincere friendliness for the other.

As in the earlier "Opium War," the utter inability of the Chinese to marshal their forces and to defend themselves against European attack astounded all observers. If anything, the Manchus acted less effectively than before. Still professing to be scornful of the "barbarians," the imperial court made but few direct efforts to halt the conquest of China's major cities.

Canton quickly fell to the British, who moved to the attack from their recently acquired base in neighboring Hong Kong. Then combined British and French forces advanced north toward Tientsin with the American minister, William B. Reed, in their entourage. Although both the United States and Russia were invited to participate in the hostilities directly, they declined. Each believed that, as had been true after 1842, it could achieve its objectives in China without sharing the danger or the expense. Moreover, the United States, as will be seen later, was simultaneously engaged in Japan, while Russia had another (and more ambitious) Asiatic program in mind.

*The series
of Tientsin treaties of 1858*

THE ANGLO-FRENCH forces moved fast. They arrived at the mouth of the Pei River in April 1858 and shortly afterwards took over the forts at Taku that guarded the river's entrance. They then occupied Tientsin. Thereupon the Peking government decided to reopen negotiations. A series of treaties was signed at Tientsin. The first ones were between China and the representatives of the nonbelligerent countries, Russia and the United States. Since their demands were not exorbitant, the Chinese quickly acceded to the American and Russian proposals for the opening of additional ports, the right to send diplomatic missions to Peking on special occasions, and freedom of travel for missionaries. Simultaneously, by negotiations at Aigun, Russia exacted important concessions in Manchuria, which will be detailed below (page 291).

"Gunpowder" is a name given to a kind of China tea widely used in England. Punch played on the word in this cartoon of Britain, France, and China discussing the Tientsin treaties around a tea table. Britannia: "A little more gunpowder, Mr. China?"

Allied troops storm the gates of Peking in October 1860.

The treaties with the belligerents, England and France, were much more comprehensive and much more deflating to Chinese pride. Particularly onerous were the requirements that French and British ministers be permitted to reside regularly at Peking and that traders as well as missionaries have freedom to travel and work in the interior of China. Nor was that all. The allied powers demanded and received the right to navigate the Yangtze River; on the initiative of both China and the powers, the opium trade was legalized; and the terms of extraterritoriality were spelled out in greater detail than before. The Manchu government agreed, in addition, to open five more treaty ports, to pay an indemnity, and (perhaps most humiliating of all) to cease referring to foreigners as "barbarians." Upon the imperial acceptance of these treaties, the allied forces were recalled in the expectation that China would now live up to her obligations without further military pressure.

*The sack of Peking
and the conventions of 1860*

THAT HOPE vanished quickly. Protesting that the treaties had been extorted under duress, the Chinese refused in 1860 to permit the English emissaries to proceed to Peking, fired upon the vessels in which they were passengers, and, despite a flag of truce, made captives of some other envoys. Thereupon the allies decided to make a condign reprisal by attacking the imperial city directly. After silencing the Taku forts, they advanced upon Peking, and the imperial court was forced to flee. As a punitive measure the British burned the emperor's beautiful summer palace at Yuen-ming-yuen. This drastic retaliation was intended to teach China the proper respect for western arms and international agreements.

At length, through the good offices of General Nicholai Pavlovich Ignatiev, the Russian envoy in Peking, new conventions were concluded in 1860. The emperor was forced to express his regret for the breach of peace and to agree again to permit resident ministers in Peking. Britain annexed the Kowloon Peninsula opposite Hong Kong. The Manchu government, which had been trying to prevent the nefarious practice of exporting Chinese laborers as indentured servants to other lands, was now required to legalize "emigration." Finally, China was obliged to pay an additional indemnity, which she could ill afford. For his "good offices," Ignatiev in a separate agreement acquired advantages for Russia in the north that easily matched the Anglo-French exactions (page 292).

*Shifting relations
of foreigners and Taiping rebels*

BY THE SERIES of treaties that since 1842 had been wrung from China by military force, the relations between East and West were now fixed. Particularly repugnant to China were the limitations upon her sovereignty, such as the removal of foreigners from Chinese jurisdiction by the principle of extraterritoriality. Ironic though it may seem, this bitter pill had been forced upon the Manchus, in part at least, as an indirect result of the activity of the antiforeign Taiping rebels. To be sure, the Taiping rebellion was a symptom as well as a cause of imperial weakness. Nevertheless, the feebleness of the Manchu regime's recent resistance to the West was easily attributable to the internal revolts with which it had simultaneously to contend. And the Taipings had made marked progress

OPENING OF CHINA 1856-1860

To Russia

Amur R.

Aigun

Ussuri R.

Pei R

Peking

Newchwang

Vladivostok

Tientsin

Taku

Têngchow

TAIPING
REBELLION

Yangtze R

Hankow

Nanking

Chinkiang

Kiukiang

Chaochow

FORMOSA

Kiungchow

Tainan

Taitung

HAINAN

KOWLOON PENINSULA
(To Britain)

France and Great Britain in 1858 occupied Taku and Tientsin on the Pei River and forced the formal opening of eleven more ports, which are underlined on the map. (In some instances the substitution of other ports or delay in the actual opening caused some subsequent modification of the original list of eleven.) Russia (page 291) profited by China's multiple troubles to exact simultaneously by the Treaty of Aigun (1858) the territory on the north bank of the Amur River, as well as joint control of the area between the Ussuri River and the sea. In 1860 the Kowloon Peninsula was ceded to Great Britain. Russia then demanded and received full title to the area between the Ussuri and the sea, where she had already pressed south and founded Vladivostok. The Taiping Rebellion had broken out in 1850 partly because of resentment of Peking's concessions to foreigners.

while Peking had been engaged with the foreign enemy. Though the rebels hated Peking partly because the Manchus had shown weakness in the face of the Westerner, they hoped for foreign support against the Manchus, the common enemy of the West and the Taiping rebels.

The victorious foreigners perhaps had good reason to feel indebted to and to encourage the rebels. They preferred, however, to look upon the conven-

278

tions of 1860 as the last in a chain of stipulations intended to place intercourse with China upon an enduring basis, which it would be good policy to preserve. Once the treaties of 1858 had been concluded, the foreign powers had begun to stop their ears to the siren songs of the Taiping leaders. Though Hangchow, Nanking, and other important cities had fallen to the rebels, the powers became adamant in their determination to maintain the Peking dynasty. This attitude met with severe criticism then and after. Many have argued that the Westerners should have supported the Taiping Rebellion because of the movement's formal adherence to Christianity. Others have contended that the rebels would have been more pliable than the stiff-necked regime at Peking. The western diplomats in authority believed, however, that little good and much evil might come out of the Taiping movement both for China and for those interested in preserving stability in China. Above all, the commercial powers of the West, once they had established satisfactory treaty relations with the Manchus, were determined to prevent chaos in a country where peace and order might be expected to bring limitless trading possibilities. Thus, in 1860, at the very moment that the allies were themselves fighting the Peking government in the north of China, they did nothing directly to support the Taipings in the south.

The defeat
of the Taiping Rebellion

THIS APPARENT inconsistency in western strategy was later accentuated by the policy of aiding the legal Peking government through both official neutrality and unofficial backing. The most significant help received by the imperial government came from an American military adventurer, Frederick Townsend Ward. In 1861 he began the formation of a force of adventurers under European officers, who received from the imperial government the title of "Ever-Victorious Army." Ward's enterprise was sponsored by Chinese bankers, and he was supported generously enough to be able to lure soldiers away from the regular English forces by promises of high pay. In 1862, Ward was killed in action and his place was taken by Major Charles George Gordon, an English veteran of the Crimean and Chinese wars, who soon won the nickname of "Chinese" Gordon.

With the help of Gordon's foreign troops the Manchu government gradually forced the Taiping rebels to retire southward. The efficiency of the imperial troops was remarkable on this occasion, mainly because of the great organizational and political abilities of Li Hung-chang and the military powers of Tsêng Kuo-fan. By 1864 the major cities of China had been recaptured and the Taiping forces dispersed. The rebellion had cost more lives than perhaps any previous conflict in history including the American Civil War. The damage to China in devastation and suffering continued to influence the course of events long after 1864.

Creation
of the Imperial Maritime Customs

INCIDENTAL to the main activities of this epoch a series of less spectacular but none the less significant events unfolded. As a result of the Taiping troubles and of the difficulties faced by foreigners trying to trade with turbulent China, the Imperial Maritime Customs was created in 1853. The Chinese welcomed the suggestion that until order could be restored the collection of duties should be supervised by a commission of foreigners. In 1863 the post of inspector-general was taken over by Robert Hart, a British subject. His administration met with favor from both sides, for he raised the collection of duties to the dignity of an extremely important official function until it became the mainstay of government revenue and credit. Through Hart's activities the Chinese postal service was also organized. Long after order had been restored, therefore, the system of foreign supervision of the customs prevailed in China, and Hart retained his post until 1908. Like numerous other infringements upon China's sovereignty, foreign administration of the customs had its beneficent as well as its imperialistic aspect.

The problem
of Chinese emigrant labor

ANOTHER significant outcome of the Chinese wars was the effect upon Chinese emigration. Since about 1845, Chinese laborers had been transported in large numbers to South American plantations and elsewhere by British and Portuguese shippers operating from Hong Kong and Macao respectively. Usually the laborers contracted to work for a period of years in return for their passage, keep, and wages; at the end of their periods of service, they might either re-contract or seek employment elsewhere. These "coolies" were thus theoretically indentured servants, though sometimes, because it was virtually impossible for a coolie to work off his debts in the course of a lifetime, he was practically a peon. The Chinese government tried to prohibit such labor contracts, and the British government looked upon them as a form of slavery in disguise; and in 1855 a British Chinese Passenger Act so stringently regulated coolie transportation that Chinese laborers who volunteered or were forced to become coolies were likely to fall afoul of their own law and Britain's. The traffic in coolies thereupon became largely a monopoly of the Portuguese. In 1859 the British undertook to legalize labor contracts by an agreement with Canton permitting emigration and limiting periods of service to five years.

As will be recalled, the Convention of Peking of 1860 included a provision granting Chinese the right to emigrate to other lands. Although the phrasing implied a concession on the part of the western governments, this provision in fact permitted the Westerners to exploit the overflowing Chinese labor market without serious government interference. At Macao and Hong

Kong the owners of plantations in South and Central America, the owners of mines in Australia and South Africa, and the railway and gold mine interests of the United States contracted for cheap coolie laborers. In many instances contract laborers were kidnaped by Chinese coolie collectors, who roamed the streets of southern China as agents for the Westerners. Although both the British and the Chinese governments strove to regulate these arrangements carefully, the evil practice nevertheless continued until in 1873 it was outlawed at Hong Kong by the British government and at Macao by the Portuguese.

THE REOPENING
OF JAPAN

ALTHOUGH the Japanese had legally closed their ports to Europeans since the seventeenth century, they had left a small opening at Nagasaki for the Dutch, who were permitted to trade there on a decidedly restricted basis. Through this opening the Japanese were able to keep somewhat abreast of major developments in the European world. From the Dutch they learned of the increasing interests of the occidental powers in the lands of the Far East. Japanese leaders soon became fully aware of the impossibility of rebuffing the unwanted attentions of the Westerners indefinitely.

Japanese reformers and "the Dutch learning"

DESPITE their isolation, some Japanese had acquired a vague knowledge of the outside world. In 1854 the Japanese reformer Sakuma Shōzan wrote:

When I was twenty I knew that men were linked together in one province.
When I was thirty I knew that they were linked together in one nation.
When I was forty I knew that they were linked together in one world of five continents.

Like many of his contemporaries, Sakuma had fallen under the influence of the "Dutch learning." The Japanese had been especially impressed by the medical and military skill of the Westerners, and some reformers sought, but unsuccessfully, to get state support and authorization to study the West.

The persistence of occidental interest in Japan

NUMEROUS attempts had been made by the Occidentals even before 1850 to persuade the sons of Nippon to reopen their ports, but they had failed ignominiously to achieve their purpose. For example, an American vessel, the *Morrison,* which sailed to Japan in 1837, was fired upon and moved off without landing any of the merchants or missionaries among its passengers. By the middle of the cen-

World events touched Japan but little in the first half of the nineteenth century. That occasional reverberations reached it is shown by this impression, from a mid-nineteenth-century Japanese book, of the British fleet assembling at London Bridge before sailing to attack China in the "Opium War."

tury, however, the Nipponese were forced to change their tactics. Internal difficulties were to combine with continued foreign pressure to bring doubts regarding the traditional Japanese policy of isolation.

Japan under the shoguns

IN THIS PERIOD, Japan was only theoretically ruled by its hereditary emperor. Although all Japanese avowedly were subjects of the emperor, the actual powers of the *tenno* (as the Japanese called him) at Kyoto had been strictly curtailed by traditional practices and political artifices. He was regarded as a sacred figure, too aloof to be concerned with practical matters. The real ruler was the "shogun," the hereditary military leader, who lived at Yedo. Since the seventeenth century the Tokugawa family had held the shogunal power and had ruled from behind the throne. The Tokugawa rulers had proved unable, however, to unite the country effectively, and disunion had helped to produce by the nineteenth century an explosive internal condition. Moreover, famines and peasant uprisings had become almost endemic by the 1850's, since the ruling classes in the Japanese feudal hierarchy had regularly failed to relieve the grinding poverty of the rural masses. Though the Tokugawa regime retained the unenthusiastic support of townsmen and merchants, all other classes in Japanese society had good reasons for desiring change.

A number of Japan's thinkers had advanced reform proposals, but reform was generally found to be unacceptable to the ruling classes. Gradually those who favored greater contact with the outside world grew in numbers, and they began to find fault with the shogun, who steadfastly continued to foster the traditional policy of isolation. The fate of China at the hands of the Westerners induced the anti-Tokugawa group in Japan to try to avoid an open challenge of the European powers and to advocate a policy of conciliation. At the same time, it frightened the shogun and his supporters into a desire for greater isolation.

The arrival of Perry's "black ships"

IN 1853, the American commodore Matthew Calbraith Perry appeared in Japanese waters with four "black ships" armed with big guns. His unheralded advent coincided with Japan's gathering conflict over its policy toward foreigners. Perry's fleet inspired less fear than might have arisen from the appearance of vessels belonging to greater powers. To Japan the nearby threats of the Russians and the British were more immediate and real than that of the United States, which was still a relatively unimportant, disunited, and harmless confederation on the other side of the vast Pacific. On the other hand, a contemporaneous movement of the Russians southward through Kamchatka and Sakhalin appeared seriously to endanger Japan's geographical isolation; and the successes of Great Britain in China appeared equally ominous to the culture of the sons of Nippon, who for centuries had respected the civilization and strength of the Middle Kingdom. Like the Chinese, but with much greater finesse, the Japanese hoped to gain time by playing the mighty western powers off against each other, and by collaborating with the one from which

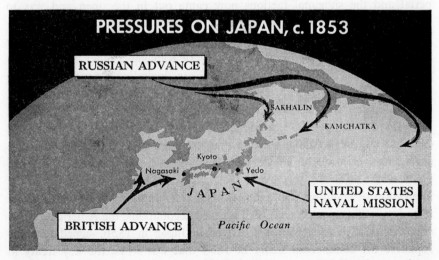

PRESSURES ON JAPAN, c. 1853

RUSSIAN ADVANCE

SAKHALIN

KAMCHATKA

Kyoto

Nagasaki · Yedo

J A P A N

UNITED STATES NAVAL MISSION

BRITISH ADVANCE

Pacific Ocean

At the time of Perry's arrival in Japan in 1853, the Russians had already moved into the Japanese horizon in the Amur area, Kamchatka, and Alaska, while England advanced up the neighboring Chinese coast.

283

they had least to fear. The Japanese hoped in this way for a time at least to halt western exactions.

Commodore Perry made a second trip in 1854 with nine ships. This time he was successful in obtaining an agreement. Japan consented to the Treaty of Kanagawa, which permitted the revival of Japan's foreign commerce. The treaty opened two Japanese ports to a limited trade and provided for better treatment of the shipwrecked. The United States also obtained a guarantee of most-favored-nation treatment as insurance against any preferential arrangement that any European power might later try to exact from Japan.

The decline of the Tokugawa shogunate

IT WAS not alone Perry's use of "guns as keys" (as the American poetess Amy Lowell was later to put it) but also the opportune situation upon his arrival that allowed him to succeed where so many others had failed. Afraid to assume entire responsibility for signing a treaty with foreigners, the Tokugawas had turned to the emperor for counsel and support. Their failure to expel the barbarians and to handle the negotiations independently provided their political critics with a golden opportunity to undermine the Tokugawas. Far from escaping responsibility for having signed the treaties, the Tokugawas were now saddled by their political enemies with the additional responsibility of having made the "divinely descended emperor" a party to their weakness. Since the emperor no longer could appear a remote, sacrosanct figure who did not deign to dabble in mundane affairs, the opponents of the shogun undertook a campaign to restore the *tenno* to his ancient powers as absolute secular ruler as well as spiritual head of the insular empire. The struggle between the imperial and the shogunal factions now came out in the open and was to constitute Japan's most difficult internal problem for over a decade.

Townsend Harris and the commercial treaty of 1858

WITHIN two years after the Treaty of Kanagawa other western powers, including Russia, also made "pacts of friendship" with Japan. None of these treaties was, however, detailed enough to establish normal commercial relations. Hence the several interested nations sought agreements that, as their Chinese experience indicated, should be broader in scope than the initial pacts. Japan's domestic crisis, however, brought delays. The shogun's government was caught in the predicament of having to appease the foreigners while creating at home the impression of standing firm against them. It temporized and evaded. Only after extraordinary persistence and lengthy negotiations, the American diplomat Townsend Harris, who had arrived in Japan in 1856, signed with the Japanese the commercial treaty of 1858 that was to be the key treaty in Japanese relations with the West in the nineteenth century. Besides opening more ports to commerce, the new treaty required Japan to accept a conventional tariff and the now familiar system of extraterritoriality. Thus Japan, like China, was forced to permit limitations upon her sovereignty. Again the other western nations followed suit, negotiating similar unilateral treaties with Japan.

*Reaction
in Japan against foreigners*

IF THE Tokugawa family, under pressure from its domestic critics and Perry's guns, finally consented to unbar Japan's doors, it did so only with great reluctance. Its reluctance soon seemed justified. After 1858, Japanese resentment of the foreigners and of the treaties that the foreigners had extracted multiplied alarmingly, and this attitude communicated itself to all parties. It was not long before the cry to "expel the barbarians" was heard throughout the land. Soon this demand was succeeded by acts of violence against foreigners who had entered Japan under the new treaties. The shogun's government at Yedo, however, was unable to muster enough military power either to act decisively against the foreigner or to maintain internal order, and its prestige was further undermined. As a substitute for military action, Yedo condoned attacks upon individual Westerners and upon their diplomatic and commercial establishments in Japan.

*Outbreak
of civil war in Japan*

THE TOKUGAWA rulers continued meanwhile to be plagued by demands for political and social reform. These demands, as we have noted, had preceded the demands for a firm policy against the foreigners. Both kinds of demands were now combined to weaken the long unshaken control that the Tokugawas had established over Japan. An accumulating sentiment demanded the overthrow of the shogunal government at Yedo and the reëstablishment of the imperial power at Kyoto. Although many pro-Westerners were to be found among the opponents of the Tokugawas, the now dismally obvious failure of the "barbarian-conquering" shogun to turn back the western intruders presented the opposition with a good chance to strike. In the decade following the signing of the Townsend Harris Treaty, civil war broke out. The enemies of the Tokugawas asserted that the shogun had usurped the imperial powers and that they were determined to effect the "restoration" of the emperor.

*The "restoration"
of the Meiji emperor*

THE TOKUGAWA armies fought several pitched battles with those of the clans supporting the emperor. The hated foreigners were shortly involved in Japan's civil war. Some clansmen murdered several Westerners and attacked western merchant vessels; and the naval forces of the West, American as well as European, made reprisals. In 1863, the bombardment of Kagoshima, a great center of clan strength, brought home to the antishogun feudal lords that their desire to "expel the barbarians" was impossible to realize. Consequently they devoted their efforts to the war against the shogun, and clustered more closely about the imperial standard. After surprisingly few military engagements the Tokugawas were turned out of power (1867). Important groups of Japanese had meanwhile reconciled themselves to the necessity of some degree of westernization.

The ruler at Kyoto at the time was the Meiji emperor. With the final resignation of the shogun in 1867, the reins of authority passed into his hands, and his court was transferred to Yedo (renamed Tokyo). Since the emperor was but a youth, the actual political control of Japan passed into the hands of the great clans of western Japan, which had provided the most active critics of the shogun. The leaders of these clans now assumed responsibility for "restoring" the emperor. They also launched Japan upon the road to modernization and inaugurated a carefully controlled program of political and social change. They applied a veneer of modernity to Japanese society, which remained, however, fundamentally feudal and backward in many important respects. The superficial Europeanization of Japan that resulted was thus not an enthusiastic imitation of Europe but rather a grudging reaction to European interference.

THE "CIVILIZING MISSION"
OF NAPOLEON III

INDOCHINA, in which France had been somewhat interested since Louis XIV's day, became the subject of serious French attention under the Second Empire. The Indochinese peninsula was strategically located and was rich in food and natural resources. Tu Duc, the emperor of Annam, ruled over most of this covetable land. Commercial relations inaugurated a policy of systematic penetration not unlike that being followed at the same time by Russia in northeastern Asia (page 292). The French set themselves up in eastern Asia, as they had done earlier in western Asia, as the protectors of Roman Catholic converts and missionaries. Such a policy made it possible to assign spiritual and cultural justifications for a program of economic and political penetration.

Armed intervention of France in Indochina

THE USE of gunboats to protect Christians and traders helped immeasurably by mid-century to intensify the bitterness of the Indochinese against the foreigners. To halt attacks upon Roman Catholics, King Louis Philippe's government in 1845 had dispatched an armed vessel to Cochin China, the southernmost possession of the emperor of Annam. The Annamites soon learned to fear French military proficiency. An Annamite edict of 1848 remarked of the Westerners: "In the art of making the cannon speak they are very clever." That year an official action by the emperor of Annam proscribed Christianity and prohibited commercial relations with the Westerners. France's preoccupation, first with the domestic problems that were the aftermath of the Revolution of 1848 and then with the Crimean War, kept the French government for a long time from taking steps against the defiant native regime. Not until 1855 did Emperor Napoleon III renew France's historic claims to protective interests in the Indochinese peninsula. The resumption of these claims was rebuffed, as he expected, and the rebuff provided him with an excuse to proceed vigorously against the natives in the name of religion and the dignity of the Second Empire.

After the Crimean War, Napoleon became more active in the Far East. As we have seen, his armies collaborated with the English in the Chinese War of 1856-1860. In 1858, the French emperor, seeking his own independent advantage in the East, declared in a brief statement:

> The ruthless persecutions of missionaries have brought our warships, on more than one occasion, to the coast of the Annamite kingdom, but their efforts to enter into relations with the government have been futile. The government of the emperor cannot allow its overtures to be spurned.

The Spanish had similar complaints to make against Indochina, and their nearby base in the Philippines furnished the French with an additional incentive for cooperation with them. A Franco-Spanish expedition against Annam was undertaken in 1858, just as France's war against China in cooperation with England seemed to have ended.

The conquest of Annam involved a long and difficult struggle for the Latin allies. Having superior weapons, the Europeans were able to capture the strategic cities of the peninsula with little difficulty. Tourane was quickly overwhelmed, and in 1859 Saigon fell to the French. But then the joint effort was brought to a standstill by the outbreak of war in Europe between France and Austria (pages 173-174) and by the renewal of hostilities in China. Fortunately for the French ambitions in Indochina, neither of these conflicts involved a protracted effort. Both were concluded by 1860, and Napoleon's government was free again to prosecute the war in Indochina, this time without Spanish assistance.

Treaty of Saigon between France and Annam

BY 1862, the emperor of Annam was ready to consider French terms. Tu Duc's capitulation came only after he had been regularly defeated on the battlefront and after riots sponsored by native Christians had begun to constitute an internal threat to the security of his dynasty. Lengthy negotiations at Saigon won for the French a set of concessions that made Annam virtually a French sphere of influence. The provisions of the Treaty of Saigon included religious freedom for Christians in Annam, a war indemnity, political control of three provinces of Cochin China, commercial freedom in three important ports, and the navigation of the Mekong River for trade purposes. In addition, Tu Duc yielded his rights in the neighboring state of Cambodia. The last stipulation was extended in 1863 by a secret treaty with Cambodia, which formally confirmed France as its "protector."

French conflicts with the king of Siam

THE DESIGNS of France upon Cambodia involved the Europeans in further complications. The king of Siam, Rama IV, like the emperor of Annam, possessed certain rights in Cambodia. Not yet having been exposed to occidental methods of persuasion, however, the Siamese ruler was not willing to give up his rights in favor of France, nor did he think it fair that France should unilaterally establish a protectorate over a territory of such vital importance to the security and prosperity of his country. From his court at Bangkok, Rama directed a set of schemes intended to play the British against the French. He realized that England had her own designs on his western neighbor, Burma, and so might support his efforts to prevent French annexation of the important states of Indochina to his east. Thus Siam might stand as a buffer between the expanding interests of France and of Britain in southeastern Asia. Moreover, Great Britain enjoyed an extraterritoriality arrangement and most-favored-nation relations with Siam by a treaty signed in 1855, which was modeled on the Anglo-Chinese Treaty of Nanking of 1842. And the United States and France had signed similar treaties with the Siamese court. King Rama dared to hope, therefore, that these nations would not permit the balance of power in southeastern Asia to be seriously altered, and for several years he dragged out negotiations skillfully enough to avert encroachment upon his rights in Cambodia. In the end, however, his expectations proved too sanguine, and in 1867 the Siamese relinquished their claims in return for some territorial gains at Cambodia's expense.

The annexation of Tonkin by France

CONTEMPORANEOUSLY with the diplomatic defeat of Siam, the French strengthened their hold upon Cochin China. They occupied another sizeable portion of the peninsula in their effort quickly to achieve control of its strategic possibilities and its wealth. A French expedition had meanwhile been exploring the Mekong River to decide whether or not it could be navigated into the Chinese province of Yunnan. When they discovered that ships could not reach so far north, the French began to explore the possibilities of the Red River in the Tonkin area. This new intrusion caused consternation once again in the Annamese court and led to further outbreaks, which were serious enough to keep Napoleon III's empire from establishing control of Tonkin. Before crumbling at Sedan, however, the Second Empire had obtained a firm grip upon the most vital parts of Cochin China, had set up a protectorate over Cambodia, and had won concessions from Annam similar to those which were being simultaneously exacted from China. Thus, the last French emperor bequeathed to France a Far Eastern empire that was well on its way.

RUSSIA'S

FAR EASTERN PROGRAM

WHILE FIGHTING the French, the English, and the Taipings, the ruling Manchus of China had been obliged also to protect their interests against the advances of Russia. Since the Treaty of Nerchinsk in 1689, Russia and China, separated by the longest common frontier in Asia, had lived at peace with each other. This peace had often been in danger in the eighteenth century, but the strength of China and the weakness of Russia in eastern Asia had served to deter the czars from inaugurating a more active policy of expansion. Their relative positions were reversed in the nineteenth century.

The objectives of the Russian push to the East AS THE western powers successfully challenged the might of the Celestial Empire, the Russian expansionists became more articulate. The report of Humboldt's expedition into central Asia excited great expectations of gold and diamond deposits in the east. Blocked in the desire to partition the Ottoman Empire, expansionists cast covetous eyes upon eastern Siberia, the north Pacific region, and the borders of China, and began to feel that Russia could not afford to fall behind in the scramble for concessions and influence in Asia and Oceania as she had done in the Balkans. With the reign of Czar Nicholas I, Russia became unmistakably aggressive in her designs upon the Far East. For the first time, the Russian government put into operation a policy that was to become traditional—of pushing simultaneously in the Near East and the Far East, hoping for success in the one area whenever forestalled in the other.

Because Russia had enjoyed since 1689 a virtual monopoly of the overland trade with China, the subjects of the czar had so far been expressly forbidden to engage in the lucrative trade at Canton; and the Chinese had stubbornly refused to deal commercially with the Russians at places other than the frontier trading towns, such as Kiakhta. Contacts by sea, however, were as easy as contacts by land between the trade centers of Russia and China, and now the Russians began to look for better seaports on the eastern seaboard of Asia. Furthermore, although the boundaries of China and Russia in northeastern Asia had been presumably settled in 1689, the Russians also began to press in the nineteenth century for a more precise settlement of frontier lines.

The advances
of Russia in eastern Asia

BEFORE the Crimean War, the spearhead of the Russian advance in eastern Asia was Nicholas Muraviev, the governor general of Eastern Siberia. Convinced that China was too weak and divided to halt his activities, Muraviev in 1850 sought to bring the Amur River under Russian control. The city of Nikolaevsk was founded at the mouth of the Amur along with several other frontier settlements. These outposts of Russian strength were manned by increasing numbers of settlers from western Russia. Meanwhile, Muraviev thrust Russia's Pacific naval base eastward into the north Pacific region by moving it from Okhotsk to Petropavlovsk on the peninsula of Kamchatka (see map, page 152). Other Russians were also active in eastern Asia. How little was known of this region was indicated when, around 1850, one of Russia's numerous scientific expeditions discovered for the first time that Sakhalin was an island rather than a part of the mainland, as had previously been supposed.

The advance
of the Russians toward Japan

THE RENEWAL of Russian activity aroused genuine concern, both friendly and unfriendly, in many quarters. Already under pressure from the West and the Taiping insurgents, the Chinese were forced to divide their attention still further. Nevertheless, the Russian move was not entirely unwelcome to them. The prospect of playing off the western powers against each other appealed to the court of Peking, particularly while the Manchus were confronted by domestic rebellion. The apprehension of the British over Russian activities in the Balkans, as well as farther east, was well known, and was shortly to lead to the Crimean War. And, as we have seen, the Japanese, watching with trepidation the southward advance of Russia through Kamchatka and Sakhalin, turned in their anxiety to the least menacing of the powers that were trying to break down their seclusion. The desire to offset the success of the American Perry in reopening Japan became a factor in the aggressive designs of Muraviev in eastern Asia.

Russian divisions
on Far Eastern policy

AT ST. PETERSBURG the accomplishments of Muraviev were not universally hailed as great triumphs. The Russian foreign minister, Count Nesselrode, deplored the excesses and the involvements of his compatriots in the Far East. Concerned about the dissipation of Russian energies at widely separated points, Nesselrode favored concentration upon western Asia and the Balkans as it became clearer that France and Great Britain were determined to thwart Russia's program in the West. Czar Nicholas, however, was credited with having stated categorically, "Where the Russian flag has once been hoisted it must not be lowered." At any rate, he committed himself to Muraviev's policy.

*Muraviev's actions
during the Crimean War*

HENCE, during the Crimean War, Muraviev was given a free hand in the Far East. He quickly embarked upon a program of expansion. The naval base at Petropavlovsk was strengthened, and in 1854, when Anglo-French naval units attacked it, they were firmly repulsed. This victory was one of the few bright spots in the generally depressing annals of the Russian forces in the Crimean War. Having strengthened his position in eastern Asia, Muraviev pushed boldly ahead in the Amur River region. Steamer service was opened on the river, and Muraviev began to write openly of the "Russian" Amur. Although these activities received the attention of the Peking government, China was not in a position to object or to take any advantage of Russia's embarrassments in the Crimean War. On the other hand, Muraviev, undeterred by Russian defeats in the Crimea, went full steam ahead. In fact, after the mortifying outcome of the war, the Russians sought even more eagerly for compensation in the East.

*Russia's program
during the Second Western War*

IN 1856, the outbreak of war between China and Russia's recent foes in the Crimean War presented Muraviev with another occasion to advance Russia's claims. He warned the Peking government of the strength of the western powers and insisted that Great Britain had territorial ambitions in northern China. Profiting by the traditional desire of the Chinese to balance "the near against the far," Muraviev in 1858 negotiated with the Chinese at Aigun while the other western diplomats were negotiating for their treaties at Tientsin. After intimidating the Chinese representatives, he finally induced them to agree to his terms. By the Treaty of Aigun the territory on the northern bank of the Amur was ceded to Russia along with joint control of the territory between the Ussuri River and the sea (see map, page 278). Moreover, it was stipulated that the main rivers of Manchuria might be navigated jointly by Russia and China, and that Russian goods were to be permitted legally to cross the frontier into Manchuria. These were the first concessions exacted from China by her northern neighbor, but others were to follow.

While Muraviev negotiated at Aigun, Count Putiatin pressed Russia's case at Tientsin in company with the other powers, and, as previously noted, the resulting Sino-Russian Treaty of Tientsin (1858) included the most-favored-nation clause. This stipulation permitted Russia to enjoy the same privileges as all other foreign powers with interests in China. Specifically, it meant that the old prohibition against Russo-Chinese maritime trade was removed, that the Russian government might establish consular agencies in the treaty ports, and that Russian subjects might live in China under extraterritorial jurisdiction.

The renewal of hostilities between China and the western powers in 1859-   291

1860 provided Muraviev with additional opportunities to advance the czar's standard. While the west Europeans planned and executed their attack upon Peking, Muraviev occupied the southern tip of the territory between the Ussuri River and the sea and planted the town of Vladivostok at the head of a magnificent harbor named (in honor of Peter the Great) the Petra Velikogo Bay. Meanwhile, as previously noted, General Ignatiev in Peking acted as mediator between the Westerners and China. For his trouble he demanded and received for Russia complete control over the Ussuri area, which then became the Maritime Territory of eastern Siberia. By this cession Russia received far more from the Second Western War against China than did the powers that actually had fought in it.

Russian pressure on China's western frontier

RUSSIAN activities in western China were contingent upon those in eastern China. Although no conspicuous advances were made for a time in the west, the Russians increased their pressure on the frontier trade centers. In 1851, they exacted the Treaty of Kuldja, which permitted Russian nationals to establish trading posts in two frontier towns and to live in them under consular jurisdiction. This concession was Russia's share of the first set of concessions made by China to the West after the "Opium War."

This Russian advantage on China's western frontier was succeeded by another resulting indirectly and somewhat belatedly from the general Chinese weakness reflected in the settlements of 1858-1860. After the suppression of the Taiping insurrection in 1864, the Manchu rulers of China confronted extensive revolts by Moslems in Sinkiang and several other provinces. The Moslem leader in Sinkiang was Yakub Beg, and he was courted intensely by both of the now inveterate rivals, the English and the Russians. Thus Sinkiang, on the northwestern boundary of China, became the scene of civil war and foreign intervention for more than a decade (1864-1878). When Yakub Beg made clear that he preferred the overtures of the British, the rejected Russians took matters into their own hands by dispatching military forces to the Kuldja area—as they declared, to maintain peace, order, and trade. Eventually the Chinese brought the rebels to heel, but too late to keep the Russians from establishing a virtual protectorate in northwestern China. Not until 1881 did Russia return the disputed border area to Chinese jurisdiction, and then only after receiving further commercial concessions.

The emergence of Russo-Japanese antagonism

RUSSIA'S vigorous maneuvers in Asia had meanwhile aroused the worst fears of Japan. This alarm was not without foundation. The southward advance of the Russian naval base from Petropavlovsk to Nikolaevsk in 1854 and from Nikolaevsk to the new town of Vladivostok in 1872 placed it on the Sea of Japan at a point where it seemed to be aimed at the very heart of Nippon. The conclusion of a

Russo-Japanese treaty in 1855 and supplementary arrangements two years later, in the wake of the Japanese treaty with Commodore Perry, did nothing to allay the qualms of Japan. Like the other western powers, Russia demanded and received most-favored-nation privileges and extraterritorial rights. For a period, however, the water barrier between the two empires, the preoccupation of Russia elsewhere, and the intentness of Japan upon westernization postponed a clash of arms. Yet astute observers already could perceive that a conflict was in the offing.

Russo-American relations in the Pacific and eastern Asia

AT THIS period Russo-American relations were remote from the center of the diplomatic whirlpool. Perry's treaties with Japan helped to establish the Americans firmly in Pacific affairs and served to rouse Russia and the other powers to the realization that any new Pacific balance would have to include America. Great Britain and Russia, though they disagreed violently regarding the partition of the Ottoman Empire, and though they were unfriendly in both the Far East and the Near East, had a common interest in the dismemberment of the Chinese Empire. But they had also become aware that the United States wanted to preserve the integrity of China. Throughout the negotiations with the Chinese, the representatives of the United States had sought to bolster China against the demands of the other Westerners. In effect, the United States had already begun to follow unofficially and almost unconsciously the policy of the "open door" in China that was destined to become a source of irritation to those who have been most vitally interested in dividing China. Meanwhile, Americans lent support to Japan also in its efforts to preserve independence and in its ambition to launch an extensive program of modernization.

Until the end of the American Civil War in 1865, the United States was handicapped in the Pacific region by domestic conflicts. In the postwar period Secretary of State Seward worked out for the new republic its first systematic Far Eastern policy. Aided by Anson Burlingame, the American envoy to China, Seward began to exert considerable influence over the foreign representatives at Peking and over the Chinese government. Burlingame usually receives the credit for inaugurating the cooperative policy of the United States in dealing with China.

While Burlingame increased America's prestige in Peking, Seward busied himself with the north Pacific area. The United States had agreed by treaty with Russia in 1824 not to colonize north of latitude 54°40', and the Russians in 1844 had abandoned their settlements in California. Alaska, the Russian colony in North America, seemed too remote and sparsely settled to offer a serious threat to the United States. Nevertheless, Seward began after the Civil War to negotiate for the purchase of Alaska. This northern land and its adjacent islands were held to be desirable in American strategical

293

calculations and in American plans for laying a cable across the northern Pacific. At the same time Russia was rapidly losing interest in Alaska as her interests in Asia expanded, and the cost of its defense and development began to appear extremely high as other areas became more attractive. America was thus able to purchase the peninsula from the Russian government in 1867 for the bargain price of $7,200,000. To have a strategic adjunct to Alaska, the United States navy in the same year occupied the Midway Islands. These acquisitions became bases for future American operations in the Pacific region. By retreating from the north Pacific, Russia, for her part, was better able in the years that followed to consolidate her holdings and to concentrate her energies upon the drive southward toward China and Japan.

BRITAIN'S

EASTERN EMPIRE (1833-1870)

Before 1870, British purposes in overseas possessions followed a wavering course. This hesitation was caused in part by strong "Little England" sentiment at home, and, in part, by Britain's preoccupation with domestic problems. By mid-century, nevertheless, for a variety of reasons the government felt impelled to give greater attention to counterbalancing the obvious growth of French and Russian interest in colonial possessions.

Abolition of Australia's transport system

SERIOUS attention was demanded by the Australian colonists, for instance, around the middle of the century. Some progress in solving land and social problems had been registered since the efforts of Wakefield in founding the colony of South Australia. In keeping with his admonitions not to use convict labor, the practice of penal transportation was discontinued except in Tasmania from 1840 to 1849, but then transportation of convicts was introduced into the sparsely populated and laborless colony of Western Australia. Protests against the system, however, were strong in "the continent down under." In Tasmania itself, where the first free settlement was made in 1816, the free settlers revolted in 1846 against the British governor, who advocated penal settlements, and the movement for abolition of the transport system was to meet with success in 1853. Western Australia continued to permit transportation until 1868.

Self-government in the Australian colonies

IN 1850 an important advance in the movement of the Australian colonies toward self-government was recorded. The people of New South Wales (which included Victoria at that time) led the fight for representative institutions. Prosperity had been characteristic of that colony since (about 1815) merino sheep, famous as

294

wool producers, had been introduced to graze in the vast areas beyond its eastern mountains. The "squatters" (the Australian equivalent of the American rancher) of New South Wales were the richest and most independent group on the continent. They were also the first to take steps toward the achievement of constitutional government and won a measure of self-government by 1842. In 1850 the Australian Colonies Government Act was passed by the British Parliament. It permitted the Australians to establish separate constitutional regimes and to create their own government within the British imperial sysem. In the movement toward constitutional government New South Wales again took the lead; and the leadership did not falter in either colony when Victoria became independent in 1851.

Discovery
of gold in Australia

THE GREAT turning point in Australia's development came with the discovery of gold in New South Wales and Victoria. Edward H. Hargraves, an English-born Australian who had learned some practical geology as a prospector in the California gold rush, after returning to New South Wales discovered gold near Bathurst in 1851. Shortly thereafter, rich deposits were also uncovered northwest of Melbourne in the recently created colony of Victoria. The discovery of gold in Australia, as in California, had far-reaching economic, social, and political effects. A rush toward the gold fields began immediately, and within five years the province of Victoria increased in population from 70,000 to 300,000. Its capital, Melbourne, as well as other cities in New South Wales and in Victoria, grew at a corresponding rate. Thousands left their diggings in California to seek their fortunes across the Pacific. The Australian population was hard put to retain its essentially British and pastoral character.

The constitutions
of the Australian colonies

AS THE Australians' numbers increased and their colonies prospered and expanded, the complexion of their political life changed radically. The spirit of earlier days was replaced by a new cosmopolitanism and a new feeling of independence. A written constitution, based upon the unwritten English model, went into effect for New South Wales in 1852. Three years later the colony of Victoria proclaimed a similar constitutional government. In the same year South Australia and Tasmania followed suit. Western Australia was not permitted self-government until it abolished penal transportation, and it received the right to govern itself only in 1890. Until 1900, all of the colonies continued to be separate political entities.

The Treaty of Waitangi
and the First Maori War

TO THE EAST of Australia, across the Tasman Sea, lie the islands of New Zealand, which had been annexed in 1840 by Great Britain. From the outset the grave problem of native resistance had been one of infinitely greater importance and complexity in New Zealand than the struggle against the backward aborigines in Australia. The Maoris of New Zealand had attained a high level of cultural development, approximately that of the Iroquois Indians of North America before the advent of the Europeans. In an effort to establish a basis for cooperation between white settlers and Maoris, the British in 1840 concluded with the natives the Treaty of Waitangi. In return for agreeing to British sovereignty the natives were granted the standing of British subjects and were guaranteed the ownership of their lands.

Almost at once conflicts arose over land titles. The New Zealand Company had felt obliged to make rapid purchases, sometimes in disregard of Maori customs and with resulting suspicions; and individual land-sharks unconnected with the company lost sight totally of the lofty objectives of Wakefield and his associates in their eager efforts to "purchase" lands for little or nothing. When a government land commission tried to set matters right after annexation, it was bedeviled by fraudulent native claims, vacillating governors, anticolonial missionaries, and political strife in Great Britain. The Maoris' resentment gathered strength until in 1843 they massacred some company settlers, and in 1845 open warfare broke out. It took three years for the British to bring the revolts under control.

The Second Maori War and limited self-government

CAPTAIN George Grey, who was sent to New Zealand in 1845 as lieutenant governor, crushed the Maori revolts, made a serious attempt to understand the Maoris, and won their confidence. He found himself in opposition to the company, which had outlived its usefulness. In 1850 it surrendered its charter. Under Wakefield's leadership it had done its work well, having selected good settlers and having begun the movement toward self-government. Governor Grey proved perhaps too zealous in his efforts to Europeanize the Maoris and under his less venerated successors, the preservation of Maori traditions became the major issue in a decade (1861-1871) of renewed Maori warfare. Meanwhile, with Grey's help, the six settlements in the islands—Auckland, Wellington, New Plymouth, Nelson, Otago, and Canterbury—had been united through the Constitution Act of 1852. Until 1875 New Zealand remained a loosely centralized series of settlements enjoying limited self-government within the British empire.

Extension of dominion in India

THE CONCERN of Britain's empire builders was not limited to Australasia (as Australia and the surrounding territories are often called). They worked diligently also in India to extend British dominion to the "natural frontiers" of the subcontinent. The responsibility for enacting British policy rested in the hands of the governor general. After the reform of the East India Company in 1833, this official, although still acting in behalf of the private interests of the company, was a governmental representative too. Moreover, the reform of 1833 stipulated that natives could no longer be kept from office by reason of "religion, place of birth, descent or color," and it opened India to colonization by Europeans. Hence the government of India ceased to be the monopoly of a company clique.

The reforms of Lord William Bentinck

UNTIL 1835, the governor general of India was the great social reformer Lord William Bentinck, whose work has already been mentioned (page 63). Not only did he overhaul the finances of the country and provide the native population with increased opportunities to take part in their own government but he was responsible also for setting up an educational system. Upon the advice of the historian and poet Macaulay, a member of his council, Bentinck decided that English should be the medium of instruction in government schools, for Macaulay persuaded the governor general to accept his oft-repeated assertion that "English is better worth knowing than Sanscrit or Arabic." Bentinck was also responsible for suppressing inhuman Hindu customs such as infanticide and suttee, or the custom of burning the widow on the funeral pyre of her husband, and for reducing the number of Thugs, a semireligious organization of assassins who strangled and robbed their victims according to a set ritual. His regime almost escaped bloodshed, except for a few minor clashes between British and native groups. On his statue in Calcutta are inscribed these words of Macaulay:

> He abolished cruel rites; he effaced humiliating distinctions; he gave liberty to the expression of public opinion; his constant study it was to elevate the intellectual and moral character of the nations committed to his charge.

The aggressive policy of Lord Auckland in India

WITH THE retirement of Bentinck in 1835, British emphasis upon social reform in India was temporarily replaced by military activity. The most immediate problem from the British viewpoint lay in the unstable and undefined character of India's northern boundaries. The Burma frontier on the east, however, was also a cause for concern and continued to provoke discussion and indecisive action. During his tenure of office (1835-1842) Lord Auckland, Bentinck's successor, inaugurated the above-mentioned policy of extending British power in India to its "natural frontiers." Auckland was primarily interested in the northwest of India. The fluid conditions and defenseless nature of the border regions in the Indus Valley left much room for improvement. The critical passes from central Asia into the subcontinent were in the hands of the Afghans and other untested peoples who might easily fall under the influence of an aggressive neighbor like Russia. Commercially also the failure of the British to control the Indus River was commonly looked upon as a definite liability. Trading missions between India and Afghanistan were subjected to levies by native groups such as the local rulers (known as "amirs") of the Sind area, who controlled the lower Indus, or the bellicose Sikhs of the Punjab, who controlled its upper reaches. In 1836, Lord Auckland could envisage no other course than a full-scale diplomatic and military effort to bring this strategic area under control either directly or indirectly.

Anglo-Russian rivalry and the First Afghan War

AUCKLAND'S first project was to win domination of Afghanistan through puppet rulers. Profiting by the friendship of the Sikhs, he moved swiftly to establish a prince of his own choosing over the turbulent Afghans. This step was designed in part to counter the activities of Russia in Afghanistan, for Czar Nicholas had a scheme of his own to establish a congenial ruler in Afghanistan. Lord Palmerston, the British minister of foreign affairs, and Auckland both believed that the aggressive Russian policy in the Balkans and Near East might now be carried over to the mountain fastnesses of central Asia. "Russia," according to Palmerston, "does not...wish to go to war with us, but is always trying to push on just to the extreme point of encroachment and aggression to which she may be allowed to go without war. She then halts to take breath and waits till people are looking another way to make another step or two forward." The British government felt that Russia was applying pressure to India's borders in an effort to force Britain to a more conciliatory attitude with respect to the Ottoman Empire.

When Auckland's diplomatic finesse in Afghanistan failed to fulfill his intention, he ordered military action in 1838 against the Afghans. Successful in his invasion, he proceeded to establish a puppet ruler, who, however, won almost no native support. To retain his appointee in power Auckland was forced to keep British troops in Afghanistan and to buy up adherents. The expense of such an occupation soon forced the adoption of a more limited policy, and garrisons and bribes were diminished. As the weakness of the British became obvious, the natives rebelled and forced a total evacuation. In the retreats of 1841 and 1842 thousands of British soldiers lost their lives, and Auckland was recalled as soon as news of the disaster reached Calcutta.

British annexations in the northwest of India

THE BRITISH defeat in the Afghan War encouraged other Asiatic groups to strengthen themselves for an eventual showdown with the British. Lord Ellenborough, successor to Auckland, struck out at once to reëstablish his country's prestige. A punitive expedition against Afghanistan and its capital city of Kabul accomplished its purpose in 1842. In the following year, he was pushed by the actions of his subordinates into annexing the Sind area in the lower Indus region. The story that Sir Charles Napier, who commanded the English troops in the capture of Sind, announced his victory in one word "Peccavi" (Latin for "I have sinned") is apocryphal—unfortunately, because it is one of the best puns in the annals of warfare. The story reveals rather the attitude of anti-imperialists. Two years later, the British under Lord Hardinge, a veteran of colonial wars, invaded the Punjab and, after overcoming severe resistance, forced the Sikhs to establish a government acceptable to Great Britain.

In 1848, Lord Dalhousie became governor general, and until 1856 he conducted the affairs of India with remarkable dispatch and efficiency. At first, however, he was confronted by many problems inherited from his predecessors. Dalhousie had not been in India more than six months before the Sikhs, abetted by the Afghans, rebelled again. After several bitter engagements, the Sikh armies were destroyed and their Afghan allies driven back into the mountains. Great Britain then annexed the Punjab and thereby finally secured her "natural frontier" on the northwest. The Afghans were left to their own devices, but their native hills have ever since remained a center of British and Russian intrigue in the complicated web of international politics in central Asia.

Annexations
of the British in lower Burma
A FEW years later, Burma, to the east of India, became a trouble center. In the First Burmese War (page 62) the British had extracted only limited concessions, and of those, the Burmese refused to live up to their obligations with regard to trade. Dalhousie resolved to take a "second bite of the cherry." He made careful preparations, and in a few months occupied the entire valley of the Irrawaddy River. Although severely defeated in several engagements, the king of Burma stubbornly refused to negotiate with the British. Dalhousie therefore issued a proclamation in 1852 by which Great Britain unilaterally annexed lower Burma. By this measure the remainder of Burma was isolated from the sea and the British East India Company gained control of the coast and ports of almost all south Asia. The Burmese government gradually learned in the years that followed to pay greater heed to Britain's terms.

Lord Dalhousie's
program of internal reform
AS BRITISH imperialists fondly recall, Dalhousie during his tenure of office extended by one third the area of India under British dominion. Like Bentinck, however, Dalhousie is more notable in the annals of Indian history for his constructive internal program than for his annexations of territory. He was the founder and planner of the Indian railway system, and was present in 1853 when the first stretch of track in that system was put into operation. He also helped to bring to completion the Ganges Canal. Through this British development program, the interior of India was opened to foreigner and native alike. By 1856 it had become possible to move native products readily to the port

cities and into the waiting holds of European vessels. Thus India's foreign trade expanded. Dalhousie facilitated its further expansion by introducing the telegraph and an efficient postal system. Finally, he carried to completion the social and educational reforms inaugurated by Bentinck. By the end of his term of office, India had made some sturdy strides along the road toward modernization, and India's millions had acquired for the first time an effective system of communication. Communication was eventually to accelerate the movement toward independence.

The mutiny
of the sepoys in 1857

ALTHOUGH Dalhousie is today looked upon as one of India's most enlightened governors, his domestic program aroused grave apprehension among the natives. Indian leaders became more and more fearful that the old traditions, the old economic structure, the old ruling elements in society, and especially the old religions would be seriously endangered by Dalhousie's radical program. When Lord Canning succeeded Dalhousie in 1856, he remarked with astonishing foresight:

> I wish for a peaceful term of office. But I cannot forget that in the sky of India, serene as it is, a small cloud may arise, no larger than a man's hand, but which, growing larger and larger, may at last threaten to burst and overwhelm us with ruin.

Anti-Christian feeling ran highest among the Bengal "sepoys" (a Persian word which had come to mean "natives who are employed by Europeans as soldiers"). The Hindus in the Bengal army constituted a homogeneous, high-caste group, and the army in which they served operated in the Ganges Valley well beyond the boundaries of Bengal. The belief grew among them that British strength in India was being maintained by them alone while British soldiers fought other Asiatics in the Crimea and in China. Thus the dissipation of British energies in other quarters provided the sepoys with both a justification and a chance to act. They received extraordinarily unanimous support from the landowners of Oudh, which Dalhousie had recently annexed and in which he had instituted some much-needed agrarian reforms.

The immediate cause of the mutiny was the indignation of orthodox Moslems and Hindus over an incident involving "greased cartridges." The Enfield rifle had recently been introduced into the British armies. It was loaded at the muzzle, and the powder was obtained by biting off the end of a paper cartridge first. The sepoys were outraged when they learned that the ends of their cartridges were said to have been greased with the fat of cows and pigs. The Hindus, who hold the cow to be sacred, were shocked by the possibility of sacrilege, and the Moslems, who believe the pig to be unclean, were revolted by the thought of tasting swine. Thus, the two religious

300

groups were able for once to agree on a common problem and to seek a common action.

Insubordination spread quickly. The first uncontrolled outbreak took place near Delhi. The mutineers marched upon that city, and there some Moslem sepoys declared British rule at an end and announced the restoration of the Mogul Empire. Thereupon, mutinous native troops set out on a campaign to exterminate the whites. Isolated garrisons of British soldiers, and in several places all British women and children, were butchered. Gory details of atrocities resembling the most legendary aspects of the Black Hole of Calcutta began to come out of India. More than a year passed before British relief forces, often including loyal Indian contingents, were able to restore order and to proclaim the country once more at peace.

*The end
of company rule in India*

THE SUPPRESSION of the revolt in India brought to an end only the military phase of the crisis. In London, the East India Company and its directors came under heavy fire. In spite of the able defense of the company by liberals like John Stuart Mill, its enemies won the political battle. Divided authority between crown and company agents in India seemed no longer justifiable. In 1858, therefore, the process of forcing the company out of India was brought to completion. New decrees made the governor general a viceroy and required that in London the affairs of India be handled through a special secretary of state for India. Subsequently India was deliberately prepared by a program of domestic rehabilitation and moderate rule to become the brightest jewel in the British crown. The control of the London government over all British Asiatic areas was rounded out in 1867 by the elimination of company rule in Malaya.

*The Victorian empire
in Asia and the Pacific Ocean*

BY 1870, the imperial structure of the Victorian age had been erected in the East, though new conquests lay ahead in Africa. Britain's possessions in eastern Asia stretched from India to Hong Kong, and in the eastern oceans from Ceylon to New Zealand. Australia had been transformed from a penal colony into a prosperous community rapidly moving toward self-government. And New Zealand was being colonized and coached for an important role in the British overseas family.

The end of company rule in India meant not only closer political control but also greater economic coordination in a governmental imperial system. The anticolonial attitude (later known as "little Englandism"), so prominent before 1870, was to be harder to find in subsequent decades. In the sharp political and economic competition with other industrial states, Britain was to be forced to pursue an increasingly aggressive policy if she meant to preserve her lead in the non-European world and to prevent its resources and markets from falling into the hands of her competitors.

IN THE age of the Romantic Movement the interest of Europe's writers and artists in the philosophy, arts, and crafts of China was largely replaced by a high regard for India. This regard was based upon Indian "mysteries" and especially the religious and philosophical ideals of the Hindus. In the middle of the century the attention of Westerners interested in oriental cultures shifted somewhat to Oceania and especially to Japan, which had hitherto been relatively unknown in the West.

*Scholarly interest
in China's geography and peoples*

THIS SHIFT did not mean that the attraction of the other parts of Asia ceased. The interest in China continued but was now in part diverted to a serious study by earnest scholars of its geography and languages. With the opening of China's interior to trade and missionary activity, it was possible to obtain a clearer conception of her size, diversity, and complexity. Moreover, explorations were undertaken into the mountain fastnesses separating India from China in an effort to establish more clearly the possibilities of intercourse by land routes. One of the most courageous enterprises was a purely scholarly effort. Sándor Körösi-Csoma, a Hungarian philologist, in an effort to discover the origin of the Magyars, crossed central Asia to Tibet in disguise in the 1820's, lived there for four years, and in 1834 published the first Tibetan-English dictionary and grammar. In 1844, over a decade before missionaries were legally permitted into the interior of China, the Abbé Évariste Huc undertook a similar journey. He traveled in disguise from Mongolia into Tibet with two companions. They reached Lhasa in 1846 and there they opened a chapel and studied the Tibetan language and customs until the Chinese ambassador obliged the Tibetan authorities to send the two European members of the party back to Canton. In 1850, Huc published *Souvenirs* of this memorable expedition and added substantially to the West's fund of geographical and linguistic knowledge of Tibet.

Studies of the Chinese language progressed rapidly during the middle years of the nineteenth century. Robert Morrison's *Chinese Dictionary* (six volumes) had appeared in 1815-1823. His place as the leading English Sinologist was taken by Sir John Davis, who wrote interpretative studies of China and translated Chinese tales, dramas, and romances into English. Davis' contemporary, the German Sinologist K. F. Neumann, collected one of the richest Chinese libraries in Europe, which eventually became the property of the University of Munich. Meanwhile, in China the German missionary Charles Gutzlaff was writing Chinese history from his own observations as well as from literary sources, and his American contemporary S.

Wells Williams was compiling data for his encyclopedic two-volume study, *The Middle Kingdom*. Williams' account remained standard in the field of Chinese history until the beginning of the twentieth century.

Sanskrit studies by European scholars

EUROPEAN scholars were endeavoring also to obtain accurate data from missionary and other sources to round out a realistic picture of India. Some carried on the tradition of Sanskrit studies inaugurated in the late eighteenth century by Sir William Jones. In this branch of scholarship the work of Max Müller was of outstanding significance. Born in Germany, Müller wrote and taught during most of his life in England, where the sources on India were more accessible. In 1850 he translated the *Rig-Veda* from Sanskrit into English. This work, one of the sacred books of the Hindus, is a primitive Aryan folk song of uncertain date, and is of primary value in reconstructing the history of ancient India. Müller and others devoted attention to the compilation of dictionaries and grammars. For example, between 1855 and 1875 a Sanskrit-German lexicon was published (in seven volumes) at St. Petersburg by Professor Otto von Böhtlingk and his collaborators. Almost all subsequent Sanskrit dictionaries are either abridgments or modifications of this standard work.

The missionary as a link between East and West

AS THE adventures of Abbé Huc and others show, the missionary spirit was a major force in the opening of the East. In the nineteenth century the Protestant missionaries of the great maritime nations became especially active in the Orient, although the Catholics continued to work there devotedly. The Protestant pastors and their families steadily grew in number and came to exercise an enormous effect upon the oriental policies of their native lands. The children of missionaries, who often obtained influence in other fields, as well as the missionaries themselves, acquired a knowledge of China, its language, its people, and its customs which often went far beyond that acquired by merchants and seafarers. They helped to mold public and official opinion in the West with regard to the non-Christian peoples of Asia. In scholarly associations such as the American Oriental Society, the views of missionaries regarding the Orient commanded respectful attention. Usually missionaries were anticolonial, but they sometimes became imperialistic when they met native opposition to their Christianizing efforts.

Russian interest in oriental studies

THROUGHOUT the period from 1830 to 1870, the advances made by Russia in oriental studies were particularly striking. We have already mentioned Böhtlingk's lexicon. The desire of the Russians to acquire special information about eastern Asia and the Pacific region was heightened by the policy of economic and military

303

Nineteenth-century Japanese prints depicting a funeral procession (above) and a primitive assembly line in a Japanese bakery (page 305). The delicate lines and coloring and the curious perspective of Japanese drawings enchanted nineteenth-century European artists and influenced the work of the French impressionists.

expansion toward the East. The German philologist Heinrich Julius Klaproth, a member of the St. Petersburg Academy, until his death in 1835 set the standards for Asiatic philology. Under his influence Russian scholars were primarily concerned with problems of comparative philology. A chair in the Mongol language was established as early as 1828 at the University of Kazan, and this university became the leading center of oriental studies in Russia. The first chair in Chinese studies in Russia was likewise established there, and also the first significant collection of oriental books to be found in Russia. I. J. Schmidt in 1831 published the earliest Mongol grammar in German at St. Petersburg. This was followed in 1844-1846 by O. M. Kovalevsky's Mongol-Russian-French dictionary. After the victories of Muraviev in the East, the chair of Mongol studies was transferred to the University of St. Petersburg, and greater official recognition was given to the entire field of oriental studies by the creation of a faculty of oriental languages at St. Petersburg.

Little work was done on Japanese studies in Russia until the late nineteenth century. With the opening of Siberia, however, the study of tribal customs and languages received marked attention. In 1842-1845, the Kiev professor A. T. Middendorf explored northern and eastern Siberia and published a monumental work shortly thereafter. From 1845 to 1849 the Finnish scholar Matthias Alexander Castren studied the Siberian tongues and gave support to the theory of Ural-Altaic family, in which he placed Finnish, Turkish, Mongol, and Tungusic (Manchu).

*The oriental vogue
in French art and literature*

IN FRANCE, a chair of oriental languages had been endowed in the Collège de France as far back as 1815, and an Asiatic Society had been founded in 1822. The French annexations among the Pacific islands and in Indochina awakened interest in the arts and crafts of those places, as well as in their linguistic histories. Soon it became stylish in Paris to affect curiosity about, or knowledge of, these still largely unknown regions. Things Japanese were especially in vogue during the Second Empire. The bold departure from conventional perspective, the delicate use of line, and the decorative charm of Japanese painting delighted Édouard Manet, Claude Monet, and Edgar Degas, all of whom sought to adopt the picturesque Japanese quality to their own work. At the Paris Universal Exhibition of 1867, Japanese prints, fans, and porcelains were shown and excitedly talked about.

In French literature, the influence of the Orient was likewise visible. The brothers Edmond and Jules de Goncourt, among their numerous works, produced the novel *Manette Salomon* (1867), which was the first of several of their writings to glorify the Japanese color print. The work of orientalist scholars stimulated the interest of Théophile Gautier (page 97) and his daughters. Among his verses and stories are a number that adapt Chinese and Japanese themes. He employed a Chinese to teach his daughters the language; he loved to talk about oriental civilization with literary friends such as Flaubert and the Goncourt brothers; and he followed with great attention the efforts of Victor Hugo to acquire a collection of oriental art objects. Charles Baudelaire (page 165), also through his friendship with Gautier, was inspired to collect Japanese art. A liking for Far Eastern art and oriental

themes appears to have been part and parcel of the French romantic poet's belief in "art for art's sake."

The Asiatic impact on American letters and farming

IN THE United States, the study of Sanskrit and other eastern languages had commenced about a score of years before the outbreak of the Civil War. At Yale University, Edward Salisbury set up a program of Sanskrit studies and began accumulating a respectable oriental library. With the organization of the American Oriental Society in 1843, scholars of the United States under Salisbury's leadership began to develop their own tradition in oriental scholarship. Emerson and other Transcendentalists, as we have seen (page 236), were earnestly interested in oriental literature, and Emerson was a member of the struggling but influential society. The oriental setting entered American fiction with Melville's *Typee* (1846) and *Omoo* (1847), which were autobiographical novels laid in a South Seas setting.

The impact of Asia upon preindustrial America, as was perhaps to have been expected, was more pronounced in the field of agriculture than of literature and art. Like Europeans of the previous century, Americans carried on ambitious efforts to adapt Asiatic plants and animals to the American soil. Serious projects were undertaken to compete with China in the raising of silk and tea, and oriental varieties of sugar cane, corn, and potatoes were tried out in various parts of the United States. The China pig, the Kashmir goat, and Brahmin cattle were bred with native American stock to improve and strengthen the strains. Several of these efforts proved successful and contributed significantly to American agricultural productivity.

Japanese adoptions of western techniques

WHILE Parisians adopted the *mode japonaise,* Japan was in process of adopting from the West the technological skills that had definitely established the superiority of the West in the struggle for power. Alone among the peoples of the Far East the Japanese realized that the salvation of their own ethos lay in cautiously accepting certain changes in their industrial and military techniques. Like the other peoples of Asia, however, the Japanese were determined to retain the essentials of a manner of life which they considered good. That determination won respect in the West, where the samurai, or warrior, though rarely seen in the flesh, became a symbol of Japan just as the familiar coolie was beginning to replace the sage as a symbol of China.

ALTHOUGH India, Japan, and China had been forced to adapt themselves in different ways to the onslaughts of the western powers, they continued to share a common hostility to foreign interference. Antiforeignism remained a significant factor in the countries of southeastern Asia also. In Oceania, however, the western countries made enduring progress, and in Australia, New Zealand, and numerous smaller areas the Westerners had gained a lasting victory by 1870. Significantly, these successes were won only where the natives were backward, where a systematic and solicitous program of colonization was carried out, and where the mother country quickly prepared the dependent area for self-government. On the other hand wherever a domineering attitude was retained, the white intruders were faced with difficulties that were sometimes the cause and sometimes the effect of that attitude. The Dutch in the Indies, the Spanish in the Philippines, and the French in Indochina continued throughout the nineteenth century to be troubled by unrest and revolt among the native populations. The British governments that in Australia and New Zealand allowed European immigrants to move toward self-government never had to cope with an effective resistance in Australasia, but they failed to grant autonomy to the native populations in India and so were obliged to deal directly with numerous knotty problems—many of which were not to be solved even by the proclamation of India's independence after the Second World War.

In the effort to withstand the West, the various eastern peoples were forced to westernize themselves at a greater or lesser tempo. Although native resistance to modernization continued emphatic outside of Japan, western scientists, missionaries, travelers, and educators everywhere pointed out effectively the value for increased health, wealth, and comfort of western hospitals, schools, engineering projects, agricultural and industrial methods, and transportation and communication systems; and these lessons were to remain vivid and to make their contribution to the nationalist movements, also frequently borrowed from European examples, that were eventually to drive out the Europeans. In some areas, particularly New Zealand and Australia, colonists and native peoples no less than the European investor prospered from the discovery of natural wealth by the Westerners. As the Asiatic world opened more widely to outside influences, natives came to realize the benefits as well as the handicaps of Europeanization, even as they came to resent the handicaps more.

The Asiatic paid for the lessons he learned from the Europeans and Americans. He paid not merely in the raw materials, art objects, and money surrendered in exchange for manufactured commodities but also in the labor of the Chinese coolie, the increased knowledge he provided for western students of oriental languages and culture, and the subtle ways by which he influenced western art and letters. The adoption of the *mode japonaise* in Paris, strikingly enough, was contemporary with the virtual completion of what Napoleon III conceived of as his civilizing mission in Indochina. Whether they realized it or not, the Napoleons (and the Muravievs, Perrys, and Wakefields as well) were helping to pave roads for a "two-way passage" in Asia and the South Pacific.

Part three

REALISM

AND POWER

1865-1890

RUSSIAN EMPIRE

UNITED KINGDOM

HOLLAND BELGIUM

GERMANY

FRANCE

ITALY

PORTUGAL SPAIN

Tunis

OTTOMAN EMPIRE

Mong.

MANCHU

Merv

Penjdeh

AFGHANISTAN

PERSIA

Tibet

Tripoli

CYPRUS

Suez Canal Cairo

MOROCCO ALGERIA

Cyrenaica

EGYPT (Occupied by British since 1882)

RIO DE ORO

Ferzan

INDIA

Nile R.

UPPER BURMA

Niger R.

Khartoum

L. Chad

ERITREA

SIAM

PORTUGUESE GUINEA

NIGERIA

SUDAN (Claimed by Egypt)

STRAITS SETTLEMENTS

SIERRA LEONE

LIBERIA

GOLD COAST TOGOLAND

White Nile

ABYSSINIA

SOMALILAND

FRENCH CONGO

Congo R.

CONGO FREE STATE (Belgian control)

Zanzibar (Br.)

GERMAN EAST AFRICA

ANGOLA

GERMAN SOUTHWEST AFRICA

MOZAMBIQUE

MADAGASCAR

ORANGE FREE STATE

Vaal R.

Orange R.

TRANSVAAL

NATAL Durban

CAPE COLONY

British   French   German   Spanish   Dutch   Portuguese   Italian

By 1890 most of the uncommitted areas of the earth had passed under European control. Germany, Italy and Belgium built huge empires in Africa, where France continued to encroach on the Ottoman Empire and appropriated large unclaimed areas. In the Near East, Russia, Austria-Hungary, and Great Britain profited from domestic unrest. China had been

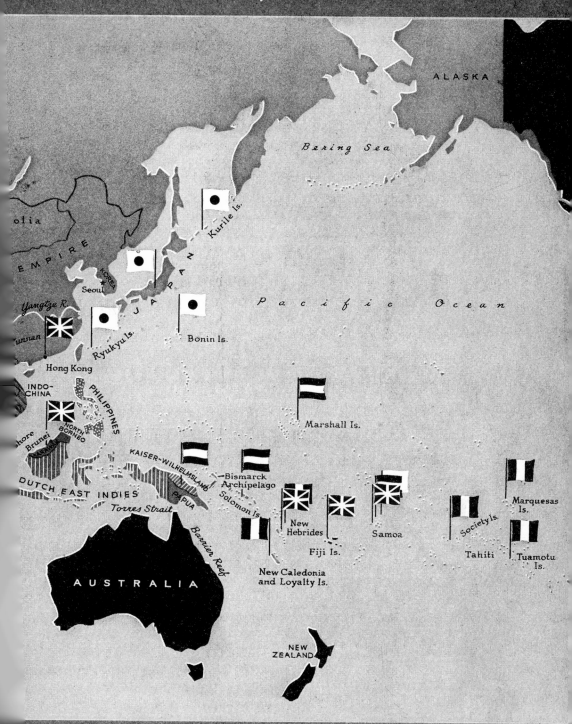

...rced to relinquish its suzerainty over Burma and Indochina to Britain and France respec-
...vely and was being challenged in Korea by Japan. Russia pushed her "peaceful penetra-
...on" of China, Mongolia, and Tibet. In the Pacific, Germany, France, and the United States
...dvanced their claims, and Great Britain countered to protect Australia and New Zealand.

Chapter six

NATIONAL RECONSTRUCTION AND INTERNATIONAL READJUSTMENT

c. 1870-1879

THE YEARS that may be roughly called the decade of the 1860's in a certain sense form a revolutionary period. They produced quick and conspicuous political changes in the United States, Canada, Japan, France, England, Germany, Italy, Austria, Spain, Russia, and elsewhere. Except in France in 1870-1871, however, those changes were not made from the bottom up but rather from the top down. They were not popular revolutions but were carried through by the established governments, sometimes by force and nearly always under the eyes of interested foreign powers. Hence, when the heat of debate and battle died down, the peoples in the countries affected had to take time to reconstruct their domestic patterns, and their governments had to readjust their foreign policies to new situations abroad. In a few instances, the governments sought compensation for loss of prestige at home or for late entry into the race for empire by extra efforts overseas, and showed a new spurt of imperialistic endeavor, which in turn brought on new international complications and readjustments.

These political developments went on alongside an intensification of industrial enterprise. Countries like England, France, and the United States that had already become familiar with big-scale manufacture increased their factory output and the numbers of their factory workers. Countries where political conservatism or disunion had previously interfered with economic innovation now were to find that their recent departure from the traditional ways or their new political unification helped to inspire a competitive business sense that soon made them rivals of the older commercial and industrial powers both for markets and for overseas sources of raw materials. In this struggle the United States and Japan, in the course of a relatively short time, had to be counted among the great imperialist powers of the world, along 315 with England and France. Italy and Germany, still held back by the problems that unification had just brought, were not to join the race for empire until the next decade.

Inevitably political and economic change was reflected in the literature and the art of the period. These years are the beginning of the "Gilded Age" in American culture and of the "Age of Naturalism" in Europe. The first term emphasizes the impact of the new wealth upon society, the second the impact of the new scientific attitude (or scientism) upon the products of the spirit and of the talents. Just as the straining for stern reality in politics spelled a new emphasis upon *Realpolitik* both in national and in international affairs, so the drive for a realistic portrayal of nature in writing and the fine arts, and a readier access to the things that man could make and money could buy, produced an emphasis upon the material at the expense, but not at the loss, of the spiritual. Political change, imperialism, industrialization, naturalism, scientism, *Realpolitik,* and materialism, and their concomitant problems were to continue—were often to grow more pronounced—in the decade of the 1880's. In fact the "Gilded Age" and the "Age of Naturalism," since they had only their beginnings in the years discussed in this chapter, will be left for consideration until the next.

The historian of Europe's role in world culture becomes increasingly less prone, when dealing with affairs after 1870, to concern himself with different parts of the world—Europe, Asia, the Western Hemisphere—in separate chapters, for the world after 1870 was growing more and more conspicuously interdependent. Though national and cultural differences persisted, the repercussions of major events—even in domestic affairs—were seldom limited by geographical boundaries, and the events themselves can usually be better understood even in their origins and development if seen in an international and intercontinental perspective. The workings of nationalism, industrialism, and imperialism were contemporaneous, whether in Japan, the European nations, or the United States, and they fused and meshed more and more after 1870 despite—sometimes, in fact, because of—cultural traditions, national rivalries, geographical barriers, and personal preferences. Even before 1870 the railroad, the cable, the steamboat, the international correspondent, the roving scientist, the immigrant, the curious writer and scholar, the investing capitalist, the merchant, the missionary, the explorer, the soldier adventurer, and a host of other technological changes or venturesome personalities had overcome intercontinental oceans and had disregarded, without destroying, national boundaries; and the process had been not merely accumulative but accelerating. After 1870 the separate consideration of Europe from the rest of the world (and vice versa) becomes less meaningful.

Accordingly, in the chapters that follow we shall widen our geographical perspective so as to include the whole world and proportionately narrow our chronological scope so as to get a better view of global interactions. In this chapter we shall examine a number of at least partly interdependent events that occurred on several continents during the years between the beginnings of Reconstruction in the United States and the realignments resulting from the great international Congress of Berlin.

AFTERMATH

OF THE AMERICAN CIVIL WAR

THE WAR between the Confederate States and the United States of America had been, in a fashion not always appreciated, a phase of the world-wide movement of the 1860's to achieve more complete national integrity. After the South's defeat Americans, like Europeans, were to find that technological developments seemed to favor the political unification of peoples of similar nationality. In the Americas, changes in technology came with amazing rapidity. Nevertheless, it remained to be seen whether certain patent cultural differences—between North and South in the United States, between French and English in Canada, between Europeans and Indians in Latin America—would permit unification or would lead to disintegration.

The problem of unification in Canada THE TRIUMPH of the North in the United States brought into focus another movement for unity on the American continent. The idea of a federal union of the provinces of British North America had long been under consideration. It grew out of three perplexing problems that seemed impossible of solution if the provinces were to act upon them separately. One was the inability of the French and English portions of United Canada to make their union, set up in 1840, work successfully. Another was the difficulty that the separate provinces were having in financing and executing the building of railroads. A third was the need for improved defenses against the United States. A decade earlier England had withdrawn British troops for use in the Crimean War, and the burden of defense had fallen upon the provincial governments.

Now that the United States had purged itself of its absorbing inner conflict, "manifest destiny" seemed again to threaten Canada. During the Civil War Northerners had voiced considerable sentiment for turning their armies upon Canada as soon as the war was over. Three disturbing events in the year 1866 heightened Canadian tension. One of these was a bill introduced in the United States Congress calling for the admission of Canada into the Union. Against the superior might of their southern neighbor the Canadian provinces would have been all but defenseless even if united. But another danger seemed far more immediate. The far Canadian west, many supposed, might fall to the United States through infiltration by settlers, as Texas and Oregon had done. Hence Canadian patriots urged a national effort to prepare their west for settlement and defense. The second disturbing event of 1866 related to the activities of the Irish-American Fenians (page 359). Anxious to strike a blow for freedom for the Irish homeland, the Fenians undertook to "twist the lion's tail" in Canada by instigating raids across the Canadian border. The third and most serious development was the abrogation of the Reciprocity Treaty of 1854 by the United States. With a tariff wall looming up between her and one of her best customers, Canada faced the necessity of reorienting her economic life.

The British North America Act of 1867

THE apprehension excited by these happenings led to an increased demand for unity among the provinces of British North America. The union of the maritime provinces of Canada had already been proposed by provincial leaders in 1864, and in 1867 the British North America Act was passed. Ontario and Quebec—i.e., the British and the French portions of United Canada—were happily separated again; with them were now associated the provinces of New Brunswick and Nova Scotia; and all four provinces were united in the Dominion of Canada. The Dominion's constitutional framework was a strong federal system that combined several features borrowed from both British and American institutions. The federal structure was somewhat like that of the United States—with a bicameral legislature in which the upper house, or Senate, represented the provinces (though the members were appointed for life by the Dominion government and the provinces were not equally represented). In drawing the line between federal and provincial powers, however, the founding fathers of the Canadian union considered the United States with its bloody sectional conflict a shining example of what *not* to do. Their constitution, neatly reversing the United States formula, specifically limited the powers granted to the provinces and retained all other powers for the federal government (though later judicial interpretation left both the Dominion and the provinces with only enumerated powers). The throne was represented by a governor general appointed by the London government. Ministerial responsibility, already well established in the provincial governments, was provided for the new Dominion as well. Criminal law, specifically enumerated as an area of Dominion legislation, did not come to vary from province to province as it did from state to state in the United States.

The growth of the Dominion of Canada

THE unification of the Canadian provinces was the work of patriotic leaders like John A. Macdonald. They had counted upon the power of the British, but unification prevailed despite some deeply rooted sectionalism because it was widely approved by the people of the provinces. It soon stimulated further national development. Within four years the Dominion of Canada expanded its territory to the Pacific coast. In 1869 it purchased the vast holdings of the Hud-

THE DOMINION OF CANADA 1873

Once Great Britain gave its support in 1867 to a strong Canadian federation, unification, as this map shows, was rapid. By 1873 the Dominion of Canada reached to the
Pacific and the Arctic, its biggest acquisition being the purchase of the Northwest
Territories in 1869 from the Hudson's Bay Company. The extension of federal organization met with occasional opposition like the Red River Rebellion of 1869-1870 (page
343) in what was soon to become the province of Manitoba. Dates on the map indicate
the year of entry into the federation. Newfoundland (including Labrador) was not to join
until 1949.

son's Bay Company, some of which was prairie suitable for settlement. This
area was reorganized as the Northwest Territories, and in 1870 the turbulent
Red River settlement was admitted to the Dominion as the Province of
Manitoba. In 1871 British Columbia was added to the Canadian federation
as its westernmost province. Two years later Prince Edward Island, in the
Gulf of St. Lawrence, joined the Dominion. After 1873 all that was needed
to complete the map of Canada was the admission of Saskatchewan and
Alberta, which came in 1905, and of Newfoundland, which did not enter the
Dominion until 1949. By that date ten provinces and the Northwest Terri-
tories stretched from sea to sea and filled in the continental area between the
United States and Alaska.

*The decline
of American expansionism*

IF THE "destiny" of the United
States was thus rendered less
"manifest," American expansion-
ism received an unexpected, though to a certain degree unwanted, impetus
when Secretary of State William Henry Seward, an ardent expansionist, acquired Alaska. At the time Seward found it hard to put the Alaska treaty
through the Senate. The attacks upon "Seward's folly" were symptomatic of
a decline in the expansionist spirit of the United States. After the Civil War, 319

the nation's energies and enthusiasms were absorbed in repairing the devastations of war, filling out the territories already acquired, and developing a new industrial civilization. Seward undertook negotiations also for acquiring naval bases in the West Indies but could not muster support from the rest of the government to carry his plans through. His interest and that of the United States navy in Pacific island bases resulted only in the taking of the Midway Islands by an American naval officer in 1867.

Improved relations
of the United States and Britain

HAMILTON FISH, Seward's successor, inherited a number of difficulties to iron out by direct negotiation with Britain. Skillful diplomacy on both sides led to the Treaty of Washington in 1871. This treaty provided for arbitration of three outstanding disputes—the United States-Canadian boundary in Puget Sound, the United States-Canadian fisheries dispute, and compensation for the damage inflicted by the Confederate commerce raider *Alabama* and two other raiders that had all been built in England during the Civil War. The boundary dispute was submitted to the German Kaiser William I, and his decision, favorable to the United States, was gracefully accepted by both sides in 1872. The fisheries question was left to a three-man commission of arbitrators, of whom the Austrian minister at London chose the neutral umpire; and that commission in 1877 awarded $5,500,000 to Great Britain for American fishing privileges in Canadian waters. When, however, the Canadian fish for some unaccountable reason began to show a preference for United States waters, the United States abrogated further payments (1883). The subsequent settlement of the *Alabama* claims was an especially great victory for arbitration as a means of resolving international disputes. Never before had two such great powers submitted such thorny, explosive, and expensive questions to an international commission for settlement. The commission in this case consisted of five arbitrators selected one each by the American president, the British queen, the Italian king, the Swiss president, and the Brazilian emperor. This method of selection betokened a patent effort to neutralize possible regional and political preferences. The commission met at Geneva and in 1872 awarded the United States $15,500,000 compensation for the damage done by the raiders.

The continuation
of industrialization in the North

VICE-PRESIDENT Andrew Johnson in 1865 became president upon the assassination of Abraham Lincoln. The Civil War, with its heightened demand for transportation, guns, uniforms, shoes, iron, oil, and the like had given enormous impetus to industrialization in the North. At the war's end the rising trend continued. The protective tariffs instituted as war measures were retained, and, thus secured from European competition, output zoomed. Railroad lines shot across the prairies toward the Far West, opening up new regions for settlement and providing transport back east for the commodities that energetic settlers produced. Industrial organizations, east and west, swelled in size and multiplied in number. The corporation, enabling many investors to pool their resources without incurring more than a limited liability, became the dominant form of business organization. Fabulous personal fortunes mushroomed.

Economic problems of the seceded states

IN CONTRAST to this rapid development of the North and West, the South emerged from the Civil War an economic cripple. The war had been fought on its soil. Its roads, bridges, and railroads were ruined. Great stretches of its farmland reverted to wilderness. Several of its cities were devastated. Its currency was worthless. Some of its outstanding leaders had fled abroad. And it had lost what many considered the very foundation of its economic system, its slave labor. The Thirteenth Amendment (ratified December 1865) made abolition a part of the American Constitution. The collapse of the Confederate and state governments meant the breakdown of law and order, and the South became the happy hunting ground for vandals from both armies, rootless and bewildered ex-slaves, and all sorts of economic adventurers. For a year or two after the war many Southerners resigned themselves to a mere struggle for physical existence. As the southern poet Sidney Lanier put it, "Pretty much the whole of life has been merely not dying."

What to do with the vanquished South and its newly freed Negroes was the most pressing postwar problem of the federal government. A Bureau of Refugees, Freedmen, and Abandoned Lands was set up in 1865 for the relief of Negroes and white refugees in war-torn areas. The South became the victim of transients called "carpetbaggers," typified by the carpetbag in which they carried their entire worldly goods. They were men who came from the North to make personal or political capital out of the chaotic conditions in the South. Most of them were adherents of the Republican Party. Some were starry-eyed agents of the Freedmen's Bureau promising the freedman "forty acres and a mule." Some were human vultures ready to prey upon a wounded South. A few were real reformers who wished to help the former slaves. Economic life revived, however, principally through the efforts of the Southerners themselves, sharecropping and crop-lien systems largely replacing the old plantation system. These systems were eventually to create economic complications of their own, but temporarily they made it possible to secure freedmen as farm laborers without ready money for wages.

Johnson's plan of reconstruction

POLITICAL "Reconstruction," on the other hand, was dictated by the victorious North. Unfortunately, Reconstruction became a political football in a conflict between Congress and President Johnson. Himself an antisecession Southerner, Johnson favored a plan for Reconstruction resembling in broad outline the conciliatory   321 policy that Lincoln had put into partial effect before the end of the war. It was based on the theory that the southern states could not, under the Constitution, secede from the Union, that they had simply been, as Lincoln had said, "out of their proper practical relation with the Union," and that the aim of Reconstruction was simply to restore the proper relationship. Under this conciliatory plan Johnson amnestied all but high officers and officials and wealthy citizens who had taken part in the rebellion if they swore allegiance anew and recognized the state governments formed by men who took such an oath of allegiance. This policy was based upon the extraordinary war powers of the president. By 1866 all the seceded states but Texas had thus been "reconstructed." The new governments assumed control of state affairs, drew up "black codes" regulating the relations of Negroes and Whites, generally disfranchising the Negroes, and elected representatives to the national Congress in 1866.

Reconstruction policies of the radical Republicans

MEANWHILE the advocates of a more radical form of Reconstruction, outspoken opponents of Johnson, had begun to win the upper hand. Their policy was based on the theory that the southern states had actually seceded from the Union and could now be treated as conquered provinces. This vindictive attitude was held both by idealists, who were morally indignant at the southern defense of slavery and disfranchisement of the freedman, and by a dominant faction of the Republican Party called the "radical Republicans." Johnson, a less able and popular man than Lincoln, and a Democrat, could not hold these vindictive groups in check. The basic element in the radicals' plan—and the one most resented by the Whites of the South—was Negro suffrage. Over Johnson's veto they prolonged the life of the Freedmen's Bureau and passed a Civil Rights Bill making all persons, black or white, born in the United States full and equal citizens.

The Fourteenth and Fifteenth Amendments

DESPITE Johnson's opposition Congress also submitted to the states for ratification a fourteenth amendment to the Federal Constitution. The proposed amendment gave federal and state citizenship to "all persons born or naturalized in the United States," forbade states to "deprive any person of life, liberty, or property, without due process of law," and reduced proportionally the membership in Congress of any state denying the vote to adult male citizens.

In the Congressional elections of 1866 the radical Republicans won a comfortable majority, and they proceeded more vigorously to apply their policy of "Thorough." Both houses of Congress refused to seat the congressional delegates elected by the new southern governments. It became clear, when in 1867 Tennessee was readmitted to representation in Congress, that

ratification of the Fourteenth Amendment was a condition of re-entry into the Union. A set of Reconstruction Acts in 1867 and 1868 put the South (except readmitted Tennessee) once again under military rule, dividing it into five military districts, and required the occupied states to draw up new constitutions giving the Negro the right to vote, and to accept the Fourteenth Amendment. In the ensuing conflict between the president and Congress, Johnson won the dubious honor of being the only president of the United States ever to be impeached by the House of Representatives. The Senate acquitted him, however, by a single vote short of the two-thirds necessary for dismissal.

Meanwhile the southern states were being "reconstructed." Johnson's own denial of the vote to a large proportion of leading ex-Confederates meant that the voice of the plantation owner was all but silenced, and the new governments elected in 1867 in the occupied states were formed of southern Republicans (generally poor Whites called "scalawags"), freed slaves, and carpetbaggers. It was the intention of the radical Republicans to form a loyal following out of these potentially subservient, politically inexperienced, or coolly exploiting elements and thus to emasculate the power of the plantation class. These Republican groups drew up new constitutions for the secession states and ran the state legislatures for varying numbers of years.

In 1869 the Fifteenth Amendment was submitted to the states by Congress. In order to circumvent future legislation once more disfranchising the Negro, it provided that no citizen should be denied the right to vote because of "race, color, or previous condition of servitude." The last four states to be readmitted to the Union had to ratify this amendment, too. By 1870 the entire process of "reconstruction" according to Congressional dictates had been completed in all the secession states.

The outcome of the policy of "Thorough" THE vindictive Congressional policy of Reconstruction and the radical and often corrupt government of the carpetbag regimes were more than many conservative Whites in the South would pacifically bear. Sometimes legally, but more often by terrorism through secret societies such as the Ku Klux Klan, the Negroes were forced or frightened out of politics. In one state after another the carpetbag-scalawag-Negro regimes were ousted and white control of the government was restored. By 1877 "white supremacy" was complete throughout the "reconstructed" South, and in that year the last federal troops of occupation were withdrawn. The plan of the radical Republicans for a subservient, pro-Negro, Republican South boomeranged. White supremacy became synonymous with the Democratic Party, and the "solid South," a South that could be counted upon to vote regularly and overwhelmingly for the Democratic candidates, was born.

Many decades of sectional dispute and four years of bloody war would doubtless have left their scars upon the states even if a policy of moderate 323 reconstruction had prevailed and even if the enfranchisement of the Negro had been left to local option. The policy of "Thorough" heightened the bitterness of race relations, increased Southern resistance to social reform, and reinforced the persistent sectionalism—all problems that still cast a shadow over the American scene. In addition, the Negro was given a bad start in the race for life, liberty, and happiness. Usually only half comprehending the freedom suddenly thrust upon him, he at first made a sorry showing when given political responsibilities under the self-seeking guidance of machine politicians. His brief moment of triumph in local politics served only to galvanize the forces against him and to harden the convictions of his ill-wishers that he was politically incapable, at best, and guilty of overbearance, at worst. The specter that has haunted the white Southerner—at least until recently—was "black domination" rather than "red revolution"—domination fostered or, in any event, approved by misguided or selfish Yankees; and so he built his future around a policy of keeping the Negro "in his place" at home and the Yankee at a safe distance.

MAJOR POLITICAL
ADJUSTMENTS IN EUROPE

THE PROCESS of unifying Germany, completed in 1871, had involved several continental countries. It had brought major changes to Austria, Italy, and France as well as to Germany. Each of these states now had to readjust to new constitutional arrangements and to make new diplomatic alignments, and each found itself with special problems to solve because of internal opposition to its new governmental policies. Spain, which had been only indirectly concerned in the unification of Germany, continued to struggle with its ancient problem of church and state, with royal pretenders, and with provincial privilege. Russia, which had not been directly involved in the wars of German unification either, faced its own difficulties in the disillusionment of liberals with Czar Alexander II, who until recently had appeared to be intent upon making Russia a modern state.

The beginning of the
V Narod movement in Russia

THE REFORMS of Alexander seemed by the 1870's to have been too few and to have come too late. Among other things, the land allotted to the peasants recently emancipated from serfdom consisted of plots too small for them to make a living, and many peasants found it necessary to rent additional land. Rent payments were high. Crop failures occurred during the 1870's, and the general price level went up. The peasants became restless.

The mood of nihilism, compounded of philosophical pessimism and
324 political do-nothingism, persisted among the Russian intelligentsia but proved

A contemporary sketch of a Russian peasant of the 1870's from the French periodical L'Illustration.

so unattractive that other more active movements developed along with it and in part out of it. One set of Russian intellectuals made the peasants' cause their own. The less serious among them merely affected to dress like peasants and to imitate rural habits. The novelist Leo Tolstoy set the pattern, though it did not keep him at this stage from living a comfortable life at his own manor. Others, however, identified themselves with the peasants seriously. They accepted positions as teachers, physicians, and workers in the villages. This group was called the *Narodniki* (men of the people) and their movement was called the *V Narod* (to the people). Unfortunately they met with distrust on the part of the very ones they wanted to help.

Thus rebuffed, many of these populists moved to the big cities to stir up unrest among the poor. They formed "revolutionary circles," particularly the society known as Land and Liberty (1876) in St. Petersburg. Its members still put their faith in reform through education rather than violence, but they soon found themselves engaged in a constant underground warfare 325

A group of cartoons from an 1876 issue of L'Illustration *satirizes the various attitudes of members of France's new Chamber of Deputies.*

with the police, and they moved more and more in the direction of economic and political revolution. The government suppressed as many revolutionary circles as it could reach. Since it was often impossible to utter grievances in the press, the revolutionary circles printed and distributed their views clandestinely.

A period
of political crises in France

MIDDLE-CLASS liberals were more successful in France. Defeat in the war with Prussia and the overthrow of Napoleon III had brought Adolphe Thiers, historian and statesman, to the fore. He had taken a lead in quashing the uprising of the radical Paris Commune against the new monarchist National Assembly in 1871. It seemed now only a matter of time until the National Assembly would reëstablish the monarchy. The Monarchists could not agree on a king, however. Some wanted the Bourbon heir, the Count of Chambord; others wanted the Orléanist heir, the Count of Paris; and a few wanted Napoleon III's son. As they bickered and bargained, Thiers, himself an Orléanist, who had hitherto been given the noncommittal title of "chief of the executive power," was vested with the title of "president of the Republic," which was obviously a commitment. Thiers finally espoused the republican form of government openly, on the ground that it divided Frenchmen least. But the Monarchists were strong enough to force his resignation in 1873 and to choose one of their own number, Marshal MacMahon, as president. To make sure that their victory would be a lasting one, they voted the Septennate Law giving the president a seven-year term. If Chambord had been a more realistic and less stubborn man and had insisted less upon the white flag of the Bourbons, he would have accepted the tricolor, and he might have regained his ancestors' throne. But since he did not think Paris was worth a flag, he kept the National Assembly in suspense until 1875, when it finally decided to set up not a definitive constitution but a series of laws "organizing" the state authorities. The first of these laws—the Wallon amendment, adopted by a bare majority of one vote—repeated the phrase "president of the Republic." This and other "organic laws" subsequently passed in 1875 became the only constitution France was to have until 1940.

This so-called Constitution of 1875 set up a legislative system based upon two elective chambers, the Chamber of Deputies and the Senate. Laws were to be enacted by concurrent majority votes of the two. The chambers were to meet in a joint session known as the National Assembly whenever the constitution was to be amended or a new president elected. The Chamber of Deputies was to be chosen by the direct universal suffrage of all adult male citizens, the Senate by an indirect method. The ministers, though selected by the president, were declared "jointly and severally responsible to the Chambers." It remained to be seen what would happen if the president and the chambers disagreed.

Republicanism versus clericalism CONVINCED French republicans believed that they had a serious grievance against the Catholics. Church leaders had consistently given their support to the restoration of the Bourbon monarchy. They were perhaps justified in believing that but for the stubbornness of the Bourbon pretender the Monarchists would have succeeded with the aid of the church in reëstablishing the domination of the altar and the throne. When the church in 1875 dedicated France to the Sacred Heart and began to build the Church of the Sacred Heart on the hill of Montmartre dominating the city of Paris, the Republicans became alarmed. As long as the promonarchical Marshal MacMahon was president, the clerical influence in French politics was marked. The Republican leader Léon Gambetta declared that clericalism was "the enemy."

The establishment of legislative superiority WHEN the new legislature met for the first time in 1876, the Republicans had a majority in the lower house. MacMahon tried to establish the president's control of the executive authority by censuring the Republican premier Jules Simon so severely that he felt called upon to resign. This bold step came to be known as "the coup

of the *Seize Mai"* (i.e., of May 16, 1877). It failed to achieve the presidential prerogative that MacMahon had hoped for. The new Monarchist ministry he appointed was in its turn censured by a vote of no confidence from the Republican Chamber of Deputies; and when MacMahon called for new elections, he was disappointed in the results. No French president subsequently has ever tried to dissolve a Chamber of Deputies once elected. In 1879, when the Republicans also established control of the Senate, MacMahon resigned, and with him went the last good chance of the Monarchists to regain control of the government of France. France has remained ever since (except for an interlude between 1940 and 1946) a country ruled by its legislature almost without check or balance.

Austria-Hungary under the Ausgleich *of 1867*

IN Austria-Hungary on the other hand, the legislatures proved ineffective. The new governmental structure set up in the Compromise of 1867, known as the *Ausgleich,* proved clumsy. It made necessary three defense ministers and three finance ministers —one of each for Austria, for Hungary, and for Austria-Hungary. There was only one minister of foreign affairs, but discretion dictated that the successive ministers be taken alternately from Austria and from Hungary. Each of the two parts of the empire had its own parliament, but there was also a common parliament called the Delegations, a sort of committee of 120 men for common affairs. Although the government machinery creaked under this burdensome system, it muddled through until the 1890's.

Readjustment in the kingdom of Italy

ITALY's major domestic problems after 1870 centered around the Vatican and the backwardness of Naples and Sicily. The Vatican, having lost its temporal possessions to the newly united Kingdom of Italy, proved unwilling to accept the olive branch offered in the shape of a generous Law of Guaranties. The law was enacted in 1871 to maintain the income, dignity, freedom, comfort, and special rights of the pope as head of a world religion, permitting him to consider the Vatican as a state over which he ruled as an inviolable and independent sovereign, and granting him 3,500,000 lire a year from the Italian treasury. Pius IX spurned this bid for friendliness to Italian unification and insisted upon considering himself an involuntary prisoner of the Italian government that had usurped his lands. He confined himself to the Vatican grounds, thus setting a precedent that his successors followed until 1929.

No special effort was made to improve the status of the benighted lands of the former Neapolitan monarchy. But they did profit somewhat from the general attempt made on a national scale to improve the country's economy. Railroads were built at a rate which increased the mileage by 1876 to about four times what it had been (1200 miles or so) in 1860. By 1877 Italy's merchant marine had developed to a point where it was second only to that of England and France in tonnage. A compulsory school law for children of six to nine was passed in 1877. The peasant's best solution, however, to the problems of poverty and illiteracy was to emigrate, and Italian immigrants to America, North and South, rose to flood levels by the turn of the century. They did not all come from southern Italy, for the workers of the industrial north also sought new opportunities in newer lands.

From republic to monarchy in Spain THE devotion of many Spaniards to their church, their provincial traditions and privileges, and their strict interpretation of the ancient laws of inheritance kept them interested in the cause of the pretender, the conservative Catholic Don Carlos. When Queen Isabella was forced to flee to France by a revolution in 1868, a provisional government was set up under General Juan Prim. It found itself caught between Carlists on the right and republicans on the left; and Prim resolved that the best way to steer a middle course and avoid both reaction and revolution was to seek a new occupant for the throne who would rule in accordance with a moderate constitution. The honor was first offered to Prince Leopold of Hohenzollern-Sigmaringen. The offer created the international crisis that precipitated the Franco-Prussian War, but by that time Leopold had declined it, and it went to a younger son of the king of Italy, the Duke of Aosta, who became King Amadeus I. After two years (1871-1873) Amadeus decided he could not win the loyalty of the Spanish and abdicated. Despite Carlist opposition, the Cortes declared Spain a republic, hoping to satisfy provincial loyalties by some system of federalization.

Both Carlists and federalists continued their hostility, however; and the military finally decided that the Bourbon family divided Spain least. They offered the throne to Isabella's son, who in 1875 became King Alfonso XII. The Carlists kept up armed opposition for about another year. In 1876, the Carlist wars came to an end, and the Cortes accepted a new constitution that steered closer to the old Bourbon absolutism than to republicanism. It left great power in the hands of the king, but created a bicameral legislature in which the lower house was elected by a restricted suffrage. The pope was appeased when the new government provided greater financial support of the church and a tighter control over schools and the family by legislation that barred Protestantism and civil marriages. The new king established order, kept Carlism in check, and introduced a certain amount of industrialization, railroad transportation, and material prosperity. Though universal suffrage was permitted in 1890, Spain remained until after the First World War essentially an outmoded monarchy—clerical, feudal, dynastic, agrarian—despite the persistence of republicanism and despite the introduction of radical movements like syndicalism, anarchism, and socialism.

*The beginning
of the Kulturkampf*

AFTER the Franco-Prussian War and creation of the German Empire in 1871, Chancellor Bismarck's domestic policy centered upon an effort, while promoting German nationalism, to defend his country against those he considered its enemies. For that reason he engaged in the Kulturkampf (or, the struggle for the national culture) with the Catholics. The struggle arose out of the proclamation of the dogma of papal infallibility in 1870. That proclamation, stating that the pope's *ex cathedra* decisions on morals and faith are immutable, had put several German state governments in an awkward position, and especially Prussia. A number of Catholics refused to embrace the new dogma and separated from the Catholic Church, setting up a sect of their own, called Old Catholic. The Old Catholics wanted to be spiritually ruled by bishops of their own choosing who would not be subject to papal authority. They sought the same protection and financial support as other Christian denominations were entitled to have under the different state constitutions. If the state were to grant these demands, however, it could count upon the opposition of the Center (i.e., Catholic) Party both in the state diets and in the German Reichstag. Furthermore, a conflict between the German government and the Vatican would be certain to result. Bismarck at first tried delaying tactics, but after a year or so he decided to take the offensive. The resulting strain between the German Empire and the Catholic Church brought on the Kulturkampf, a name that Rudolph Virchow, the discoverer of cellular pathology and a member of the Prussian Diet, claimed to have coined.

Bismarck himself gave the Polish question as the reason for the beginning of the Kulturkampf. Prussia was a Protestant country that had united Germany by defeating Catholic Austria and Catholic France. Catholics seemed un-Prussian, and Catholic Poles doubly so. The Catholic Department was a part of the Prussian ministry of education and religious affairs. It regularly favored the Catholic Poles over the German Protestants in the eastern provinces of Prussia. Bismarck feared that special treatment for German citizens of non-German nationality might weaken their links with German national culture, and he persuaded Emperor William I, in his capacity of king of Prussia, to abolish the Catholic Department by royal decree. The German bishops, for their part, saw in this measure an attack upon the legal rights of Catholics. When they protested, Bismarck added fuel to the fire by granting the demands of the Old Catholics.

The next step was an attack upon the religious orders. They were forbidden to teach in the schools, and the Jesuits were expelled from Germany. Bismarck's reason for special animosity against the Jesuits was that he suspected them of being the instigators of Pope Pius IX's "Syllabus of Errors," issued in 1864, which had listed nationalism among the errors of modern times and had reaffirmed the independence of the church from the state. A

330

Prussian Law on Secular Inspection of the Schools was enacted, and diplomatic relations with the Vatican were severed. All this occurred in 1872.

Bismarck's alliance with Liberals and Progressives

IN THESE measures Bismarck was enthusiastically supported by the powerful National Liberals and the Progressives (customarily in the opposition), because they regarded Catholicism as "backward" and believed in separation of church and state. The Socialists were neutral at first because they rightly guessed that, if special laws were enacted against Catholics, they might be the next target. To Bismarck's surprise his own class, the Conservatives, the Junkers, and finally the high aristocracy represented in the Prussian House of Lords (with the backing of the Empress Augusta) turned against him. They feared that the weapons now aimed at the Catholic Church might one day be turned upon the Protestant denominations if Bismarck became dependent upon the anticlerical parties' support. Bismarck thus found about half of Germany against him.

The peak of the Kulturkampf

AS THE atmosphere became more envenomed, the "May Laws" were enacted—so called because they chanced to come in May of 1873, 1874, and 1875. They prescribed that no one be appointed to a clerical office in Germany unless he was a German, had studied at a German high school and a German university, and had passed a German state board examination. They made all seminaries for priests state-controlled, and all clerical appointments subject to state approval. They declared marriages performed by a priest null and void unless previously registered with the civil authorities. Whoever violated any of these provisions was to be deprived of his position (whether or not he was a cleric). If he was a cleric, his state-guaranteed salary was to be withheld, and he was to be jailed. In extreme cases he was to be deprived of his German citizenship and expelled from the country. In a short time, several Catholic bishops were in prison, and hundreds of parishes were without a priest. The Kulturkampf took on the aspect of a veritable anticlerical revolution that might put the Catholic Church under the control of the German state.

Catholic response to the Kulturkampf

POPE PIUS IX denounced the May Laws as godless and enjoined every German Catholic, whether cleric or layman, to disobey them. He threatened to excommunicate any Catholic who dared to observe them. In this heated atmosphere a Catholic fanatic made an unsuccessful attempt on Bismarck's life (1874). The chancellor publicly intimated that the Center Party approved, perhaps had even instigated, the crime. He went so far as to make the pope's attacks upon him a matter of diplomatic negotiations with Italy, in the erroneous belief that Italy, at odds with the pope ever since the conquest of Rome, would readily side with Germany. But the suggestion was coldly rejected.

331

The situation at the end of 1875 presented an impasse. German clericalism had become militant; and it has remained a militant factor in German politics ever since. Nearly all German Catholics stood by the Center Party, which, until 1914, was to be the strongest party in the German Reichstag. Until the end of the Kulturkampf, the Center made common cause with its ideological enemies, the materialistic, revolutionary German Socialists, because they had a common enemy in the chancellor. The clerical party joined with the Socialists in demanding a program of social legislation. Bismarck soon had reason to regret his anticlerical policy, since it made him dependent upon the Liberals, whom he disliked only slightly less than he did the Socialists.

The end
of the Kulturkampf
AFTER 1875, though he did not discontinue it, Bismarck let the Kulturkampf fade away. He now trained his sights upon the Socialists; and when Leo XIII became pope in 1878, a new orientation toward the papacy became possible. Leo was not a firebrand like his predecessor. Realizing that the church had won the Kulturkampf, he saw no danger in being conciliatory. A gradual rapprochement between the Vatican and Bismarck took place. The church yielded in matters of small importance, e.g., civil registration of marriages, and by 1886 most of the May Laws were abolished. The law against the Jesuits remained in force until much later, when it was abolished by two acts (1904 and 1917).

German labor
and the Socialist parties
THE Socialists replaced the Jesuits as Bismarck's *bête noire*. As a nationalist he had good reason to doubt their "Germanness." When war between Prussia and France had broken out in 1870, the two Socialist members of the then North German Reichstag had voted against war appropriations. In the international crises of the early 1870's, the German Socialists proclaimed that the defense of the "fatherland" was not their business, because, as they put it, Germany was but the fatherland of the rich. Instead, they urged their fellow proletarians all over Europe to join them in striving for international revolution.

The destruction in 1871 of the Paris Commune by a new National Assembly, however, had taught the workers of Germany as well as France and elsewhere to expect no mercy from even a revolutionary government. Workers, it appeared, would have to protect themselves. The trade-union movement already had made a start in Germany. Printers had formed a union in 1864, and tobacco workers in 1865. But the way to trade unionism was blocked or hampered by legal barriers, and though workers sought defense in strikes and in slowing down production, they resorted above all to politics.

Socialist parties became more than ever the favorite weapons of the workers in the struggle against capital. Before the 1870's two rival factions had developed among the German Socialists. One group was made up of the followers of the late Ferdinand Lassalle and the other of those of Karl Marx. At a Socialist congress at Gotha (1875) they merged into one, the Social Democratic Workingman's Party, the SPD. The Gotha Congress adopted the so-called Gotha Program, which despite Marx's criticism on the one hand and Bismarck's on the other, was a program of nonrevolutionary political action for the betterment of the worker.

Bismarck's campaign against the German Socialists

THE government and the non-Socialists became alarmed at the Socialists' energy. Bismarck at first thought he could dispel the danger by repressing the SPD. A pretext for severe measures soon was found. In the spring of 1878 two attempts were made on the life of Emperor William I. Although neither of the would-be murderers was a Socialist, Bismarck used the events as the grounds for outlawing the SPD. The Reichstag enacted a law "against Socialist activities dangerous to the public welfare." It forbade Socialists to engage in any political activity except at election time; it prohibited the printing, selling, or distribution of Socialist books or other printed matter; it gave the police the right to seize Socialist printing presses, to dissolve Socialist meetings, and to arrest and imprison Socialists or persons suspected of Socialism. Socialists and suspects were liable to imprisonment or exile by court-martial. Finally, the law created a special federal committee for the purpose of supervising its execution. It was re-enacted several times and expired only in 1890 with Bismarck's departure from the chancellery.

The effect of the law was not all that Bismarck intended. The provisions on the press were easily circumvented by smuggling Socialist literature from foreign countries, particularly from Switzerland. Snooping, spying, and counterspying transformed many Germans into informers and led to indignation even among non-Socialists. Furthermore, the law intensified the resentment of the SPD, solidified the German workers behind it, and made a divisive movement within the party impossible for a long time. Socialist groups met as singing clubs or bowling clubs, and they held party conventions in Switzerland. With every new election the number of Socialist representatives in the Reichstag increased. In 1878 they numbered only 9; by 1884 they were 24; and by 1890 they were 35. Thus Bismarck's campaign against the Socialists was no more successful ultimately than his Kulturkampf.

The reform program of the second Disraeli ministry

IN THE 1870's two great reformers were prime ministers of England. William Ewart Gladstone's ministry (1868-1874), among other celebrated measures, disestablished the Anglican Church in Ireland, eased somewhat the land-hunger of the Irish farmer, increased the government support of schools, and reorganized the law courts and the army. In 1874 the Conservative Benjamin Disraeli became prime minister for a second time. He embarked immediately upon a program of domestic reform that caused historians to speak of the year 1875 as the *annus mirabilis* of social reform. The Public Health Act provided the basis for Britain's future system of sanitation, giving the whole country the benefit of the best previous local legislation. *"Sanitas sanitatum,"* said Disraeli, parodying a well-known Biblical phrase, *"omnia sanitas."* The first full-scale slum clearances in Britain were plotted, and the Artisans' Dwelling Act provided for new housing. The Sale of Food and Drugs Act pioneered in its field. A trades-union act expressly legalized peaceful picketing and laid a legal foundation for collective bargaining. The Agricultural Holdings Act required landlords to compensate tenants for improvements made at the tenants' expense when a holding changed hands. Nor was that all. In the year before the *annus mirabilis* had come the Factory Act, and in the year after it came the Merchant Shipping Act. The former established a ten-hour day as the maximum for workingmen; the latter attempted to protect sailors from the dangers of overloaded or unseaworthy vessels. Subsequent measures confirmed and supplemented some of these acts before Disraeli was again replaced by Gladstone in 1880. Thus Disraeli's program of direct social legislation anticipated and in some ways outdid the perhaps more famous program of Bismarck (pages 377-378).

BIG BUSINESS,
LABOR, AND SOCIALISM

THE UNITED German nation had the largest population in Europe next to Russia's, with an obviously great industrial potential. Bismarck's need to win the support of the National Liberals and the Progressives against the Center and the Socialists gave him a set of middle-class allies who pushed him in a direction where his own Junker prepossessions might not otherwise have let him go. In the 1870's he took the initial steps that put Germany in a position eventually to rival the older industrial nations—the United States, Britain, France, and Belgium. Industrialization brought on labor problems and the development of Socialist parties. In this period, the strongest Socialist parties, though also the most persecuted because the strongest, were to be found in Germany and France.

Nationalization of the railroads in Europe

THE PRUSSIANS largely ascribed their victories in their recent wars with the Austrians and the French to the railroads, which had enabled the Prussian general staff to move large bodies of troops from place to place within a short time. The obvious strategic importance of the railroads raised the question in several countries of whether they should be nationalized. Bismarck was the first European statesman actually to do so. The railroads of Alsace-Lorraine, since that area was a federal territory, became federal property. Bismarck would have preferred to see the others also pass directly under the ownership of the German Empire, but the separate German states were reluctant to let such a huge industrial enterprise slip through their fingers, and the Reichstag opposed imperial annexation. So Bismarck bought for the Prussian state the railroads located on Prussian territory and nationalized them, setting up the Royal Prussian Railroad System (1879). The other German states followed suit. By 1885 private railroad lines in Germany had practically disappeared, and seven different German railroad systems had come into existence, together constituting perhaps the biggest industrial enterprise in Europe. Not until after the First World War were they taken over by the federal government.

In the course of time state ownership of railways became common in Europe. Austria-Hungary, Italy, Russia, and Switzerland followed the Prussian example. France at first nationalized only one railroad system. The other French railways were not nationalized until the 1930's, and the British railways were not nationalized until after the Second World War. The railroads by their very nature as a public utility were frequently the first industry of national scope to become the property of the respective states.

A contemporary engraving shows the passage of the first locomotive through the newly completed tunnel under the Mont Cenis pass in the Alps in September 1871.

Banking,
big business, and cartels

IN THE 1870's it became obvious that financial and industrial enterprise had become so complicated that the one-man or the single-family bank was diminishing in relative importance. Leaders of finance found it expedient for administrative reasons, and profitable in addition, in some cases to combine the efforts of two or more enterprises. The small private banker gradually became exceptional in the larger cities. In every European country, highly bureaucratized big banks established branches all over the land. Founded in 1875, the Reichsbank, the imperial note-issuing bank of Germany, became a sort of bankers' bank for the whole country, as was already true of older banks like the Bank of England and the Bank of France. Big banks were needed to finance the giant industrial enterprises that were growing up everywhere.

In commerce, department stores came into being. Paris' Bon Marché (founded 1852) was probably the first one. Small shopkeepers were sometimes ruined by them. In Germany and Austria, where some of the leading department stores were owned by Jews, the coming of the department store had as a by-product an increasing anti-Semitism. This brand of anti-Semitism had hitherto been directed against Jewish family banks, like that of the Rothschilds, which were now receding before the large corporate banks. In the United States, department stores appeared in the 1860's, but mail-order retailing was at first more common, and retail chain stores also grew in numbers.

In industry especially, large combines developed. In large part their development was due to a depression that hit Europe after the international financial panic of 1873. This panic, we shall find (page 342), essentially originated in a bankruptcy in the United States. The structure of industrial combines was different in different countries. In Germany they took the form of "cartels." Cartels are not "trusts" in the American sense. In a trust the constituent parts give up their independence to a joint administrative superstructure; in a cartel they do not. Hence, a trust is more likely to be a combination established in order to achieve administrative efficiency, while a cartel is more likely to be an agreement arranged in order to avoid competition, though they may each tend toward both objectives. Cartels were organized to alleviate or eliminate the cutthroat competition that characterized the depression after 1873.

Some of the cartels became known as "syndicates," which meant that they fixed the selling prices and sold their output through a single sales organization set up for that purpose. In many cases, they restricted either production or sales in order to create an artificial scarcity and to keep prices high. Germany's Corporation Law of 1884 gave legal sanction to such organizations.

Bismarck's
protective policy

THE PANIC of 1873 was particularly hard on Germany. The money that had come in as indemnity from France until that year and had helped business to boom was no longer forthcoming, France having paid it off. The industrialists, often important members of the National Liberal Party, whose support the chancellor had needed in his campaigns for *Kultur* and still needed against the Socialists, demanded protection against English, French, and American competition; and the Conservatives, largely the big landlords, wanted to keep out the flood of cheap agricultural products from Russia and the New World. Some Liberals were unwilling to desert free-trade principles. They joined the Progressives, who now became the chief opposition in the Reichstag. In 1879 Germany deserted the free-trade policy which it had so far followed and adopted a high protective tariff law. With the support of the Conservatives, the Center, and the National Liberals, Bismarck was able to continue his war against foreign competition and domestic Socialists. Big industry benefited enormously in the ensuing years.

Working conditions
and the laboring classes

THE 1870's were years of growing social awareness for the European worker. To be sure, wage levels registered some gains between 1853 and 1873, and apparently did not fall as rapidly as price levels after the Panic of 1873. Nevertheless wages were low, and legal wage regulations did not exist. The nightmare of possible unemployment without compensation was constant. Working hours were long, usually twelve or more per day. When, exhausted and worried, the workingman came home from the factory, he would enter his noisy, dirty, and run-down tenement, which he frequently had to share with disreputable characters. Tuberculosis and other diseases were rampant. Despite the advancements in contemporary medicine (pages 383-384), because of unsanitary conditions the mortality rate remained high.

The poor could turn to few places for education. If a worker could read, he could go through his Socialist daily. Often it was of a highly inflammatory kind intended to fan his dissatisfaction with working conditions and to prepare him for the revolution that his leaders were sure or pretended to be sure would come some day. But such papers had at least the merit that they gave the worker a limited opportunity to learn what was going on in the world of science, literature, and art. Otherwise the worker had little opportunity to learn. He would often avoid church because he felt betrayed by the clergy. He was, as a rule, excluded from higher education, and until he took things into his own hands by setting up workers' academies, he had few opportunities beyond an elementary education. In rare instances the son of a worker might receive a secondary school scholarship if he were an un-

337

usually gifted boy, but then he ran the risk that his classmates would ridicule and ostracize him. The intelligent worker, frustrated in his desire for higher learning, would easily turn to envy and hatred of those who could afford to study at the high schools and universities and would take a resentful or belittling attitude toward matters of the spirit. This attitude, in turn, confirmed the middle and upper classes in the belief that the worker was an incurable ignoramus good only for menial work. The gap between upper and lower classes was rarely bridged.

If the worker wanted amusement, he had some choice. Public sport events were relatively uncommon, except horse races, and admission tickets even to the races were generally beyond his means. Tickets came high also at theaters, concerts, and variety shows. Once in a while he might take his family to a circus performance. He might go to a public dance hall on a Sunday, but in Great Britain that outlet was denied him because of the strict enforcement of the Sabbath laws. To escape from boredom and to find companionship, workingmen might join a vast variety of voluntary organizations —unions, cooperatives, friendly societies, sport clubs, debating clubs, etc.—if they preferred to stay away from church activities. The saloon, however, was nearly always open to them. In many instances, workers, in order to escape from the drabness of their surroundings, turned to the pub or beerhall. Alcohol was a social scourge in Europe, where, with the exception of Italy and some parts of France outside of Paris, the number of alcoholics among the working class was high. Émile Zola in his novel *L'Assommoir* (1877) described in unforgettable scenes the unholy alliance of alcohol, poverty, and crime.

*The worker
and the Socialist parties*

PARTICIPATION in the political activities of the Socialist Party of his region presented the workingman with another outlet for his energies. He could go to Socialist mass meetings, listen to the speeches of his leaders, and once a week participate in the discussions of the local group of his party. Often these groups were supervised by the police and sometimes they were dissolved at the order of the government. They were infiltrated by informers, who were likely to report any irreverent remark made about those in authority. If his remark were taken amiss, the worker might lose his job or be sent to jail. In Russia any part in such discussions exposed the worker to the danger of being exiled to Siberia, and under Bismarck's Anti-Socialist Law, he was permitted if a Socialist to engage in German politics only during election time.

*The growth
of socialism in France*

IN FRANCE orthodox Marxism was not as widespread as in Germany or, later on, in Russia. The crushing of the Paris Commune in 1871 had left the French working class stunned. Many of their leaders had been shot, jailed, or exiled. They now looked for some other doctrine that might give the workers strength. During the period of the Monarchist government of France, they turned in surprising numbers to anarchistic doctrines, fearing the policies of a regime they regarded as reactionary. The spirit of the French workers reached its lowest ebb when in 1872 a law was passed making it a crime to belong to the International Workingmen's Association.

With the eclipse of the Monarchists, the French workers regained some hope of achieving greater justice through government. Meetings of the workers were permitted now without interference by the police, and in 1880, a Republican legislature pardoned the exiled Communards. Quarrels between different schools of socialism, however, continued to keep the workers politically weak. They were divided between moderate "Possibilists," who were prepared to cooperate with existing governments to get whatever was possible for the workingman, and stricter Marxians. Gradually Jules Guesde, a thoroughgoing Marxist, became the most prominent leader of the French workers. In 1879 a single French workers' party was organized, but by 1882 it broke into two again.

EUROPE
AND AMERICAN INDUSTRIALIZATION

AFTER THE Civil War America experienced the same kind of rapid industrialization that was going on in Europe. The physical environment and the psychological outlook were quite different, but the results were much the same. Machine production and the factory system became the characteristic form of industry; output increased enormously; new industries, especially "heavy" industries, became dominant; business was concentrated in the corporation, and further concentrated in pools and trusts; and the line between capital and labor became more sharply defined.

The role of the railroad — EVEN MORE than in Europe, for tracks did not have to cross frequent national boundaries, a dominant feature of this rapid industrialization was the railroad. In western Europe the great age of railroad building had been the fifties and sixties; in the United States it stretched from the Civil War to about 1900. In 1865 the United States had about 35,000 miles of track; in 1900 it had almost 200,000, more than the total mileage of Europe. The railroads were largely financed by private enterprise, like those in Europe in the early stages, and much of the capital, the technical skill, the materials, and the labor were European. As was generally true of Europe, the railroads were considered national blessings and were aided and encouraged by the government. Federal aid took the form of subsidies and fabulously generous land grants. State and local governments that hoped to benefit from the new railroads helped them in the same fashion. The giants of the railroad age were the transcontinental lines. Between 1865 and 1884 four great railroad lines were pushed through to the Pacific coast. Whereas in Europe the railroads linked together established communities, the transcontinental locomotives of the United States puffed through largely virgin territory, which now lay open to settlement.

Importation of European workers

IN ORDER to settle the territory, as well as to provide a labor force, the railroad builders systematically encouraged immigration from Europe. They would advertise glowingly in European countries, sometimes find recruits at the embarkation or debarkation dock or hire them as section hands at the railhead, and then sell them land for $1 to $10 an acre. These immigrants could raise crops to be transported back east, thus making the railroads pay. As soon as they became farmers, their railroad jobs would be taken by the next immigrant contingent. In this way a tremendous exodus from Europe was stimulated, its numbers rising with each decade.

Between 1861 and 1890 over ten million immigrants entered the United States, many of them enticed by high-pressure railroad and steamship salesmanship. The majority were from northern and western Europe—Ireland, Scandinavia, and Germany in particular. They usually became farmers in the Middle West, where, together with native Americans who had trekked westward, they raised wheat that by the 1880's was flooding and undercutting the markets of the countries from which they came. A small but increasing number came from southeast Europe, Italy, and Austria-Hungary. They usually settled in the industrial cities, where they worked for low wages as unskilled laborers. A small percentage came from the Orient. As we have earlier remarked, emigration from Europe to the United States had noteworthy effects in the emigrants' homelands. While it relieved overpopulation in these countries, the loss of manpower and of restless individuals was not an unmixed blessing. It also gave to imperialists the appealing argument that colonies to which to send an overflow of population were the alternative to the loss of overflow population forever to another country.

The growth of new industries

UNDER THE stimulus of railroad building in America new industries burgeoned and old ones grew to full size. Mountains were leveled and robbed of their iron ore. The Bessemer and open-hearth processes of steelmaking were widely adopted, and Pittsburgh became the steel capital of the country. Cleveland, Toledo, and Milwaukee tried to keep pace. By 1890 the United States outstripped every European country in the production of both steel and pig iron. Mining of coal, copper, and other metals was stimulated. The petroleum industry mushroomed.

340

The railroad gave the meat producer a wider area of operations. The slaughterhouse's raw material was shipped alive on cattle cars from the "Wild West" grazing industry that flourished for several decades on the prairies between Texas and the Dakotas. The refrigerator car, borrowed from Europe around 1875, stimulated the meat packing industry, making Chicago (with due allowance for poetic overstatement) "Hog Butcher for the World." The invention of barbed wire brought to the United States an "enclosure movement" that contrasted with the earlier English movement. Barbed wire fences limited the movement of cattle and enabled the farmer to convert the fenced-in area to farmland or grazing lots.

The railroads helped to turn farming also into an industry. The pioneer farm devoted to the complete needs of one family was replaced by the farm that sold one crop—in most areas wheat or corn—for profit. New machines such as the reaper and the threshing machine aided this transformation. The same thing was happening in Europe.

Exchange of resources between Europe and America

SOME scientific discoveries and inventions were borrowed from Europe and put to use on a large scale in the post-Civil War period. The dynamo, developed by Sir Charles Whetstone, Z. T. Gramme, and others, and Sir Charles A. Parsons' steam turbine were especially important. Still, native inventiveness and technological skill contributed most to the advance of industry at home. The telegraph followed the railroads across the country, and in 1866 the first successful transatlantic cable was laid after the English scientist William Thomson answered a large part of the preliminary engineering problems. Physical chemistry and mathematical physics, to the understanding of which the European-trained American scientist Josiah Willard Gibbs made notable contributions in the 1870's, was applied to such American industries as petroleum, aluminum, and photography. Europeans later seized on Gibbs' principles to develop commercially such synthetics as nitrates, fertilizers, and explosives. In 1876 Alexander Graham Bell invented the telephone; in 1880 Thomas A. Edison produced the electric light, and in succeeding years he developed the central power station for distributing electricity over a large area. Inventions like these, favored and encouraged by friendly patent laws, not only made other industry more efficient but became major industries themselves, both at home and abroad.

The Americans generally improved on what they borrowed. They found ways of producing things faster, better, and sometimes more cheaply. They were the first to develop standardization and interchangeability of parts, making minute specialization of labor and eventually belt-line mass production possible. Americans became famous for their mechanical ingenuity, and European visitors were struck by the innumerable "gadgets" they found in America. At the international exhibitions of London in 1851 and of Paris in

1867 and 1878 Europeans became aware as never before of American mechanical ingenuity displayed in reapers, mowers, revolvers, the cable, and numerous other "contraptions." If in the early stages America borrowed its industrial revolution from Europe, by 1890 Europe was beginning to be the more frequent borrower.

European financing of American industry

IN THE financing of American enterprise European capital played a fundamental role. European capitalists subscribed to American stocks, and sometimes Europeans set up firms of their own in America. Wealthy Britishers, for example, made heavy investments in cattle and mining, and, as has already been said, Europeans invested heavily in American railroads. When the firm of Jay Cooke and Co., which financed the building of the Northern Pacific Railroad, overspeculated and closed its doors in New York, it helped to precipitate the world-wide panic of 1873. Before the First World War Great Britain was the world's largest exporter of capital, and the United States was one of the largest importers, owing about $6,000,000,000 abroad. European capital was similarly ventured in Canada and in South America, where the more advanced countries like Brazil, Argentina, and Chile were also building railroads and experiencing small-scale industrial revolutions. The Latin-American countries depended on American capital, too, but leaned more heavily upon Europe than upon the United States.

Difficulties of federal development in Canada

UNDER the premiership of Macdonald, the engineer of confederation, the new Dominion of Canada did its best to emulate the success of its neighbor to the south. With capital derived largely from English and American investors, a coast-to-coast railroad uniting far-off British Columbia with the rest of the nation and known as the Canadian Pacific Railway, was begun. Systematic recruiting of immigrants from Europe had thitherto failed to produce the desired numbers because life was easier and the land more fertile in the United States. The Homestead Act of 1872, offering 160 acres after three years of residence (that of the United States, passed in 1862, required five), would, it was hoped, help to populate the prairie west. But things at first did not go well. The world-wide depression of 1873 hit the Canadian economy particularly hard. The foreign market for Canada's goods had been severely depleted with the end of United States reciprocity (page 318), and the depression of the seventies took most of what remained. In fact, throughout this period a steady stream of Canadians, especially French Canadians, left for the United States. In an effort to build up home markets Canada in 1878 instituted a high protective-tariff policy that with modifications has been retained ever since. But home markets developed very slowly, and prices fell almost steadily for twenty-five years. The completion of the Canadian Pacific Railway in 1885 tended to divert some immigrants to the Canadian west. The Canadian Pacific also entered the transatlantic and transpacific steamship commerce with marked success. When Macdonald died in 1891, Canada was a self-supporting area of great promise as a nation.

A persistent and sometimes bitter sectionalism harried the new nation, in spite of its carefully centralized government. Louis Riel, as a leader of the métis, or French-Indian half-breeds, twice led armed rebellion against the Dominion. The first uprising, in 1869-1870, was in defense of the Catholic populations around Winnipeg against the English encroachments. This was known as the Red River Rebellion (see map, page 319). The rebellion was never a serious threat, and when Manitoba became a member of the Dominion, Riel for a while was a loyal and useful subject. He was to become obviously insane, however, and in 1885 to lead a bloody and impassioned revolt in the Northwest Territories at the fork of the Saskatchewan River. This Northwest Rebellion was to end only with the capture and execution of Riel.

Prevalence of laissez-faire attitudes

IN AMERICA industrialization brought the same social problems —discontent of workers, slums, extremes of wealth and poverty—as in Europe. It generally brought the same responses to these problems, such as labor unions and agrarian movements, but in the United States a different setting gave a different turn to these responses. So strong was the American laissez-faire psychology that people who prospered under the system, frequently unaware of the horrible conditions of the poverty-stricken, believed social blights could be cured by private philanthropy. To many of them any modification of laissez faire seemed a curb upon the liberty and opportunity that were the essence of America. The poorest immigrant was free to become another John Jacob Astor, who started as a small shopkeeper and died as a fur and real-estate magnate and the wealthiest man in the United States, or another Andrew Carnegie, who started as a bobbin boy in a cotton factory and rose to the headship of an industrial empire that sold for $250,000,000. If he remained poor, he was unfit—incapable, lazy, or immoral. It was the same view of poverty held by the mid-Victorian English businessman, but in the United States it seemed even more plausible because there was no incubus of hard and fast class distinctions carried down from a medieval past. No strong socialist party was ever to arise in the United States.

Attack by the farmers on laissez faire

NEVERTHELESS, the depression of 1873-1878 brought attacks upon the American economic system from two different quarters—the farmers and organized labor. The farmers were particularly hard hit by the decline in the prices of their produce during the depression years. A growing but rather amorphous resentment focused upon the high rates and arbitrary practices of the railroads on which 343 the farmers were almost completely dependent for transport of their goods to market. Sentiment gathered volume and momentum at meetings of the National Grange of the Patrons of Husbandry, a farmers' social and educational organization founded in 1867. Though its program was at first non-political, the "Grangers" fostered discussion of problems and exchange of ideas, and the meetings of their local Granges became forums of protest. The Grangers also established cooperative grain elevators, mills, and stores. This ferment led in a number of Midwest states to the creation of farmers' parties, which in the years 1870-1875 secured state legislation—sometimes called "Granger laws"—establishing state commissions to regulate the railroads. In 1876 the United States Supreme Court upheld this regulatory legislation, thereby driving an entering wedge of government regulation into the prevailing system of privately owned public utilities.

Attacks by labor: unorganized   DEPRESSION led to severe wage cuts, unemployment and corporation campaigns against trade unions. In 1877 wage cuts on the part of four railroad lines set off a series of unorganized but violent strikes that quickly spread to Baltimore, Pittsburgh, Chicago, and other large railroad centers. Pennsylvania coal miners organized the "Molly Maguires," a gang that deliberately resorted to violence in the coal fields. This was the "Great Strike" of 1877. Violence was of such dimensions that President Rutherford B. Hayes ordered federal troops to quell the disorders. Hardened capitalists and even some of the liberal

An incident revealing the violence of the "Great Strike" of 1877 was the burning of Cincinnati's Union Station, shown here in a contemporary engraving from Harper's Weekly.

344

press attributed the riots to recent immigrants "to whom," in the words of the New York *Nation,* "American political and social ideals appeal but faintly, if at all." But immigration was perhaps less to blame than the faulty labor conditions that, whether in America or Europe, accompanied rapid industrialization.

Attacks by labor:
the Knights of Labor

THE FAILURE of the strike and the reprisals of employers sent workers flocking to the one substantial labor organization already on the scene. That was the Noble Order of the Knights of Labor, organized as a secret fraternal society in 1869. In 1878 it held its first general assembly. The Knights of Labor, dropping their fraternal character, now became an all-embracing union, open to everyone, regardless of race, creed, or craft, who worked and sympathized with labor —excluding only liquor dealers, professional gamblers, lawyers, and bankers. Its leaders were somewhat visionary, with a dream of political action, producer's cooperatives, and a world organization with branches in Europe and the antipodes. Uriah S. Stephens, its founder, had been to Europe, and traces of Marxism and of the Paris Commune were discernible in his philosophy. His idealism did not permeate the ranks, however, and the chief attraction of the union to the workers lay, ironically, in its ability to win strikes. Though the union grew and reached the height of its power in the 1880's with 702,000 members, it was not to prove a lasting organization, and soon gave way to something more effective (pages 408-409).

IMPERIALISM

AND ORIENTALISM

EXPANDING capitalism and industrialization gave a new twist to imperialism. The concept *imperialism* before the nineteenth century emphasized the meaning of *empire* in the root word *imperium.* That phase of imperialism was most concerned with acquiring territories as colonies and expanding the size of one's country's immediate holdings. With the economic changes of the eighteenth and nineteenth centuries, though the pride of sheer territorial expansion did not disappear, the idea of *control* implied in the root word *imperium* received greater emphasis. Control no longer needed to be exerted by eliminating or enslaving the natives and establishing direct colonial government. It might instead be a product of indirect political, economic, or cultural influences within developing or even largely industrialized areas. It might arise as an accidental by-product of capital investments intended to build local industries, to monopolize local markets, or to extract raw materials. Such investments were, as a general rule, made on the assumption that the home governments would protect investors against default or fraud by diplomatic or, if need be, by military measures. The European or American managers of such enterprises generally used native labor but maintained an attitude of social and economic superiority to the natives. The new imperialism thus had a pronounced element of racism in it.

*The better side
of the imperialist urge*

SIR CHARLES DILKE in his book *Greater Britain* (1868) and Disraeli in a well-known speech at the Crystal Palace in London (1872) were among the first to give expression to the new imperialism. Professor John Robert Seeley in his Cambridge lectures on *The Expansion of England* (1883) became its historian. To millions among the white race it appeared only natural that the European should carry his culture to the "colored" races. The obvious technological superiority of the Europeans and Americans encouraged them to look upon ancient civilizations like those of India and China as inferior. Hence, if the natural resources of such countries were to be exploited for the general service of mankind, Europeans would have to do it; and many sincere men, ready to make genuine personal sacrifices, considered it their duty to spread the blessings of what appeared to them to be the white man's superior moral, political, and religious institutions.

*The exploration
of the "Dark Continent"*

THE NEW imperialism was staged largely against a new backdrop. Asia remained prominent as a scene of rival imperial urges, but the Western Hemisphere had been practically closed off by Seward's recent insistence upon the Monroe Doctrine. In the proscenium arose the "Dark Continent" of Africa, whose interior vastnesses had recently begun to be explored. The Scottish missionary David Livingstone was merely the most prominent among a number of African explorers. In a series of expeditions (1849-1866), he crossed the Kalahari Desert, discovered the Victoria Falls of the Zambezi River and Lake Nyasa, and became the first white man to traverse the southern part of Africa. Lake Tanganyika was discovered by two Englishmen, Richard Burton and John Speke, and the latter discovered also the Victoria Nyanza. Then, together with Sir Samuel and Lady Baker, Burton and Speke found the sources of the Nile. Livingstone later came upon the Laulaba River. On that expedition he became ill and was believed lost, but in 1871 the English-born Henry Stanley, then in the service of the New York *Herald,* found him dying on the shore of Lake Tanganyika. The meeting of the two men has provided a folk-saying: "Dr. Livingstone, I presume." From 1874 to 1877 Stanley accomplished some important feats of his own, including the descent of the Congo River. After Stanley's exploits the Franco-Italian Savorgnan de Brazza explored all the Congo basin. The course of the Niger had been traced early in the century by Mungo Park and others. Hence all Africa's great river systems—the Niger, the Zambezi, the Nile, and the Congo—were now known.

After the creation of the Empire, the Germans entered the competition for spoils in Africa. The Baltic German Georg Schweinfurth explored Abyssinia and first proved the existence of Pygmies. Gustav Nachtigal traversed Africa from Tripoli south to Lake Chad and then, turning east, visited Borku and Darfur and reached Egypt via Khartoum in 1874.

The exploration of Africa, it goes without saying, went on after the chronological limit of this chapter. Hermann von Wissmann explored the remote recesses of central Africa in the 1880's. Brazza founded the town of Brazzaville (1880), now the flourishing capital of French Equatorial Africa. The German explorer Eduard Schnitzer became an Egyptian official and took the name Emin Pasha. In the late 1880's Emin Pasha and his men were besieged by some Mohammedan fanatics known as Mahdists (page 424), and Stanley went with an expedition to his rescue. On the way Stanley discovered the legendary "Mountains of the Moon," now known as the Ruwenzori Mountains, of which the highest is called Mount Stanley, and observed the Pygmies in their native habitat. All these discoveries were greeted with an enthusiasm such as had not occurred since the great explorations of the fifteenth and sixteenth centuries. Once again greed and power politics came into full play along with the scientific and the missionary spirit.

Opposition to British annexations

IN THE push for African territory the British had a head start. Britain's naval superiority, the daring of British explorers, and her traditional policy of staying out of continental entanglements while concentrating on her overseas empire gave her big advantages. The accumulating British control of the African hinterland, however, encountered opposition from the inhabitants of Africa. The Kaffirs and the Zulus, aggressively engaged in building empires of their own, made war against British expansion in south Africa, but they were both crushed in the late 1870's. In the Zulu War, Prince Louis Napoleon, the only son of Napoleon III, was killed while serving as a lieutenant with the British forces.

Meanwhile Britain had become involved in continual disputes with the Boers. As proud descendants of Dutch pioneers, many of the Boers, since the annexation of Cape Colony in the Napoleonic wars, had looked upon the British as foreign conquerors. When slavery was abolished in the British empire in the 1830's, large numbers of Boer ranchers and farmers, resenting what they considered inadequate compensation for their slaves, and cynical about the British missionaries' sympathy for the natives, moved into the wilderness of the Orange and the Vaal valleys and of the eastern coast in a wholesale emigration that has come to be known as "the Great Trek" (1835-1837). They hoped thereby to pass from under the jurisdiction of English law, to keep their slaves, and to avoid interference with their exploitation of the natives. The English did not, however, relinquish their claims to the new territories or their feeling of responsibility for the natives, and in 1843, despite the Boers' armed resistance, the hinterland around the harbor of Durban (already English) was annexed as the colony of Natal. But in 1852, by the Sand River Convention, the British recognized the Boer area across the Vaal River as the independent South African Republic (now Transvaal) and did not interfere when the Boers in the area between the Vaal and the Orange rivers organized the Orange Free State (1854).

The discovery of diamonds in the Orange River valley was followed by the rapid development of the diamond industry around Kimberley. Land disputes led to complications which the inefficient Boer governments did not handle satisfactorily, nor were they capable of guaranteeing safety from continuing Zulu depredations. The British government under Disraeli (now earl of Beaconsfield) tried to settle these difficulties by creating a confederation of the several South African colonies and states. In 1877 the governor of Cape Colony annexed the South African Republic despite some Boer protest, and the British then proceeded to crush the common enemy in the Zulu War mentioned above. When the Liberals returned to office in 1880, Gladstone, though he had roundly denounced annexation, did not grant the Boers the self-government that had been promised, and the Boers of the Transvaal revolted. The British met defeat at Majuba Hill in 1881, and Gladstone saw fit to discontinue the war. In 1884 a convention was concluded at London. It fixed the boundaries of the "Transvaal State," and it stipulated that, though self-governing, the republic was not to conclude any treaties with foreign powers except with the approval of Great Britain.

Victoria proclaimed the empress of India

DESPITE the constant irritation with the Boers, the sentiment favoring imperial growth spread in Great Britain. Disraeli had a poet's attachment to faraway places. He combined the daydreams of an excellent novelist with the schemings of a cool-headed statesman. These personal traits enabled him to grasp, portray, and exploit the splendor of imperialism. When he was prime minister he bought the Suez Canal Company shares of the bankrupt khedive of Egypt for £4,000,000 (1875). As its guardian Great Britain took a special interest in the Suez Canal, now the principal avenue of communication with India.

The need for trained personnel in opening India meanwhile expanded the Indian civil service and provided new opportunities for soldiers and adventurers as well. At this juncture, as had happened several times before, the British and the Russians came into conflict in their efforts to control the rulers of Afghanistan. The impatient Russians threatened in 1876 to invade India and dislodge the British. Partly to convince the world of the strength of Britain's hold in India, Disraeli decided to confer upon Victoria the title of empress of India. In 1877 he stirred the imagination of the world by having the queen proclaimed empress of India at a magnificent spectacle set on the historic 348 ridge overlooking the Mogul capital of Delhi. The revivification of India's ancient imperial glamour lifted the pride of Indians no less than of Englishmen. Yet even as the potentates of India were assembling at Delhi to honor the absent queen, dark clouds began to gather ominously. Drought and crop failures in two successive years brought famine to India; and although the British imported grain and other foodstuffs, thousands died of hunger.

European studies
of Asiatic cultural origins

INDIA's place in the western imagination was steadily becoming something more than that of a mere appanage of the British Empire. Scholars were now establishing that India was the birthplace of the Indo-European languages and of some modern religious concepts. In 1870 Theodor Benfey, German philologist, published a history of oriental philology which remained the standard work on that subject until very recently. Benfey's study brought out clearly the predominance of German scholarship in the various branches of oriental studies. Among those who had studied Sanskrit at Berlin was the Yale philologist William Dwight Whitney. He received the first Franz Bopp Prize in 1870 from the Berlin Academy of Sciences for contributions to Sanskrit scholarship. The most notable of his works was his *Sanskrit Grammar* (1879). Eight years later, Karl Brugmann published a *Comparative Grammar of Indo-German Languages*. Meanwhile, at Oxford, Bopp's former student Max Müller was turning away from Sanskrit philology to the study of comparative linguistics and mythology. These researches led him naturally into the study

The Prince of Wales, later Edward VII, represented the British crown in a tour of India in 1876. Here, depicted by an English artist, is his welcome at the city of Agra. 349

of comparative religions. In 1875 the invaluable series called *The Sacred Books of the East* began to appear under his editorship. Completed in fifty-one volumes, the collection included the fundamental non-Christian scriptures translated by the best scholars of the day.

The oriental vogue
in French art and letters

ADMIRATION for the Orient was not limited to India. In France, *japonisme* continued to be a vogue. It was also a vogue in England. Collections of Japanese color prints and literary works became numerous in Paris after the Franco-Prussian War. That of Edmond de Goncourt became particularly celebrated as he acquired more Japanese prints and wrote more extensively about Japanese life and art. French painters shared the interest in the Orient. In 1874 the first exhibition of the school known as "impressionists" revealed that they were intrigued by Japanese paintings. On this occasion, along with Monet and Degas, Auguste Renoir exhibited his work, which showed him to be influenced, among others, by Boucher and Watteau, eighteenth-century rococo painters who had been noticeably interested in *chinoiseries*. Like his French colleagues, the American painter J. A. M. Whistler borrowed some of his simplified tone and subordinated detail from the Japanese. Japanese influence, however, was greater in decoration than in painting.

The influence of China was especially clear in the work of Judith Gautier, the daughter of Théophile Gautier. She never traveled in the Orient, but she learned the Chinese language well. Eventually she loosely translated a num-

An early member of the impressionist school, which began to flourish in the 1860's, was Camille Pissarro. Above is a Pissarro sketch, "Rue St. Vincent at Montmartre" (1860).

"Grey and Silver: Battersea Beach," by James McNeill Whistler (1863).

ber of Chinese poems into French verse. Her intention was to transmit literary quality rather than linguistic accuracy. The resulting *Livre de jade* (1867) was admired as the best work of its kind by outstanding men of letters and Sinologues in France and England. She also wrote several novels about China and eventually, in collaboration with Pierre Loti, a Chinese play entitled *La fille du ciel*. As travel between East and West became more common, orientalists of her type—men and women who had never actually seen the Orient—were replaced in western letters and scholarship by travelers, missionaries, and others who had been to the Orient to see and learn for themselves.

NATIONAL
ASPIRATIONS IN ASIA

In the last half of the nineteenth century, the Occidental's mechanical knowledge reduced the distances between East and West at a rate that would have been incredible to the voyagers of earlier days. After ten years of heartbreaking labor, the Suez Canal had been opened to traffic in 1869. It cut short the long voyage to the East, eliminating the tedious trip around Africa en route. In America, meanwhile, the completion of the Union Pacific Rail-

The tenno pays a visit to an arsenal and foundry in 1872. In this European engraving he is shown, with his entourage of western and Japanese dignitaries, witnessing a demonstration by European workers of western foundry methods.

way, the first transcontinental line, had brought the Atlantic and Pacific oceans within a week of each other, and by 1885 five great lines stretched across the North American continent. As quicker means of transportation reduced distances, the flow of trade in both directions continually swelled in volume. More vessels tied up at better docks, which were connected by more dependable links to the hinterlands. Through the opening of new and more efficient arteries of communication the industrial areas on both sides of the Atlantic came much closer to Asia and from opposite directions were better able to penetrate, and influence the course of life in, the countries of the East. The eastern land that borrowed the most readily and sacrificed least was Japan.

The Charter Oath of the Meiji emperor — THE MIKADO known to his people as the Meiji tenno had in 1868 been restored from traditional inactivity as a sacred figure to political control. "Meiji" means "enlightened government." Having learned quickly that western strength was founded in great part upon technological superiority, the Japanese of the Restoration era launched a comprehensive program of industrial enlightenment. The Meiji planners were aware of the marked reactions to be expected from prescribing such strong medicine. In the light of European experience, they were able to anticipate the social and economic problems of adjustment that almost inevitably accompany industrialization. Since theirs was to be largely a planned

352

industrialization, it would be possible, they believed, to control the predicted changes to a degree. They were right. The transformation that swept Japan in the late nineteenth century was never to get out of hand.

To accompany their controlled economic revolution, the Meiji planners inaugurated a movement designed gradually to bring about corresponding political changes. In a Charter Oath of 1869, the Meiji emperor promised that "learning shall be sought for throughout the world," that "all measures shall be decided by impartial discussion," and that he would permit "limitations upon the imperial prerogative." The last concession was taken to mean that the emperor would agree to the establishment of a constitutional government in which the people would exercise a measure of political power. For the next two decades, therefore, popular agitation for parliamentary institutions and political parties was forestalled by reference to changes being prepared by the royal planners.

The growing power of the clansmen

IN THE meantime the feudal and decentralized political organization of Japan was replaced by a more highly centralized government, as feudal chieftains *(daimyos)* more or less voluntarily surrendered their fiefs and their autocratic local powers. The western clansmen, who had brought about the "restoration" of the emperor and the downfall of the once supreme Tokugawa shogunate, now dominated the imperial ministry and the new civil bureaucracy. They also acquired the most important posts in the national army and navy. By weakening the monopoly of the old clans, the western clans automatically rose to prominence among the new nobility and the new councils that were being contrived in the name of the Meiji emperor. The economy of the country was in fact reoriented toward greater industrialization, but the clansmen assumed more and more influential posts in the developing industrial structure. The social transformation of Japan was thus in large part merely the replacement of clan by clan and therefore more apparent than real. Nevertheless, some fundamental changes did occur in Japanese society. Names were changed, customs altered, and reforms inaugurated. But the reins of power remained in the hands of the clansmen, who ruled in the name of a "divinely descended" emperor.

The spirit of revolt in the Philippines

IF THE Japanese were repressed, it was at least by people of their own kind. Other Asiatics were less fortunate. Among these were the Filipinos. Held in thrall by the Spaniards since the sixteenth century, the Filipinos at last began to organize in the nineteenth century for revolt. The Spanish revolution of 1868 and the events attending it in Europe provided the angry natives with an opportunity to lash out against the local authorities. As in Spain itself, the Catholic fathers exercised firm control in the Philippines over hospitals, education, and

353

charity. When the Filipinos revolted in 1872, they betrayed their deep resentment against their religious as well as their secular overlords. The leaders of these first revolts called for the expulsion of the friars no less loudly than for economic reforms. The Filipino insurrection was crushed quickly, but the agitation for reform persisted throughout the years that followed (page 497), and secret societies conspiring for independence became increasingly common.

The quest for Indonesian independence

THE DUTCH in Sumatra were also forced to defend themselves from native defiance. Revolts in the island had been frequent since the middle of the nineteenth century as the Dutch thinned out their forces in striving to consolidate their hold upon the peripheral areas. By 1873 the intensity of feeling among the native Mohammedan rebels had been converted into a resistance movement by the sultan of Achin. The Dutch troops sent to pacify the islanders at first suffered summary defeat, and reinforcements in substantial numbers had to be ordered to Sumatra. Finally thousands of soldiers brought the rebellious natives under control, and the sultan was quickly deposed. The civil administration of Achin was then entrusted to a Dutch governor, but the military forces of Holland had to be retained to hunt out guerrillas and bandits. Not until the end of the nineteenth century was Dutch control over the entire island firmly secured.

Annexations in the Pacific islands

THE NATIVES of Oceania did not always resent the encroachments of the white man. The Fiji Islands provide an instance of annexation with native approval. While the Dutch were fighting off attack in Sumatra, the British extended their Pacific possessions by annexation of the Fiji Islands. Financial ruin and general chaos had threatened the islands, and Australian commercial interests, feeling Australia's security threatened if other powers were to take advantage of the situation to extend their Pacific holdings, had long pressed for British action—particularly to forestall the efforts of France. In 1874 a British governor of Fiji was appointed by amicable treaty arrangements and entrusted with control over all British subjects in the western Pacific.

During the remaining years of the nineteenth century the few Pacific islands not already annexed by one of the great powers were quickly brought under their protection. The United States in 1878 began the development of the beautiful harbor of Pagopago in Samoa. Two years later the French formally annexed Tahiti. And at about the same time Japan, after some ten years of dispute with Peking, asserted de facto control over the Liukiu (or Ryukyu) Islands off the coast of China. Thereafter treaty arrangements were made among the powers in an effort to fix their Pacific spheres of influence peaceably (pages 413 and 417).

*The recognition
of the emperor of Annam*

THE LEADERS of the Third French Republic carried Napoleon III's program of conquest in Indochina ahead and finally brought it to completion. In 1873, just as the last German occupation garrison was leaving France, news was received in Paris of the defeat and death of the explorer Francis Garnier at Hanoi. By having ambushed and destroyed Garnier's forces, the Annamites temporarily constrained the French to put a stop to their annexations in the delta of the Red River, especially since it was known that Tu Duc, the emperor of Annam, was acting with the support of the Manchu government of China. Nevertheless, in the following year a new French expedition forced the Annamese emperor to capitulate. By the Treaty of Saigon France divided Annam from its traditional overlord, China, by recognizing its sovereignty and independence. In his turn Tu Duc confirmed the French ownership of Cochin China, agreed to conduct his foreign policy in line with the policy of Paris, and opened the Red River cities to French tradesmen and missionaries. The ancient technique of "divide-and-rule," which the French so profitably employed in these negotiations, was to be imitated repeatedly by other powers.

The Chinese government protested as strongly as possible against the French project of releasing Annam from its vassalage. Tu Duc himself encouraged the Chinese reaction by continuing after 1874 to negotiate with his Chinese overlord. This utter disregard of the French-Annamese treaty aroused unconcealed anger in Paris, but the French had not yet recovered sufficiently from the war of 1870-1871 to risk any direct action that might bring about a conflict with China as well as Annam. The Third Republic had first to win out over its domestic foes, before it dared to take definite steps to resolve the situation in Indochina (pages 414-415).

*The associations
of Korea with foreign nations*

ALTHOUGH known for centuries as the "Hermit Kingdom," Korea attracted the attention of Westerners and Asiatics alike in the nineteenth century as fair ground for expansion. After the reopening of Japan, the strategic location of Korea became increasingly apparent. Lying directly between Japan and the continent, the Korean peninsula seemed bound to play a pivotal role in the affairs of the Far East.

The problems attending the opening of Korea, "the Land of the Morning Calm," were in some ways similar to and in other ways different from the problems that had attended the reopening of Japan. Like the Japanese, the Koreans were inhospitable to mariners who chanced to be wrecked upon their shores and to merchants who came seeking trade. Like the Japanese, the Koreans were also highly suspicious of foreign diplomats who sought to engage them in negotiations. Unlike the Japanese, the Koreans had not had 355 centuries of preparation for contacts with the West. In Korea's case also no strong native groups urged the opening of the country to foreign contacts. Korea's vassalage to China, however, was very clear, and her vassalage to Japan, though less clear, was distinct enough.

The decline of China and the ascent of Japan

IN THE race to open Korea Japan became an important contender from the outset. Russia's movement southward and eastward also put her seriously in the race. Vulnerable because of concessions to the western powers by the set of treaties of 1858-1860 and exhausted by the calamitous Taiping Rebellion of 1850-1864, China had good reason to fear that her weak suzerainty over Korea might at any time be broken by Russia or some other western power. Japan, however, seemed less menacing. Although in 1871 China signed a commercial treaty with the island kingdom, the Japanese before the last decade of the century did not loom large in the political reckonings of China. Perhaps for that very fact the Japanese were to be the most successful in bringing Korea out of her traditional hermitage into the full glare of modern imperialism.

Shortly after the Meiji restoration in 1868, Japan set out deliberately to build an empire. While Europe anxiously watched the Franco-Prussian War, the Japanese, we have already seen, boldly began to incorporate the Liukiu Islands. Three years later they advanced claims to Formosa, thereby presaging a conflict that has lasted to our own day. In 1876, two years after France had forced the Annamese emperor to sign the Treaty of Saigon, the Japanese signed a commercial treaty with Korea in which China's suzerainty was also studiously disregarded and the complete sovereignty and independence of Korea were recognized. The Manchu rulers in Peking denounced the diplomatic chicanery of the French and the Japanese with equal bitterness. It made small difference that among the imperialistic powers which China now sought to play off against each other one was Asiatic.

COMPETITION

AMONG THE GREAT POWERS

SEVERAL centuries of political development had conspired to make Europe largely a congeries of nation-states before 1870 and, since the French Revolution especially, to render the terms "people," "nation," and "country" nearly synonymous. The nationalist aspirations of several dependent peoples remained a source of international complications during the 1870's (and beyond). At the same time there developed among the older nations a highly exaggerated sense of national pride that came to be called "jingoism." Nationalism and jingoism now combined with other factors to produce a local war that led to a European-wide congress of peace.

356

**The rise
of popular nationalism**

PRESENT-DAY nationalism is in one important regard a product of the French Revolution. Before that epoch popular sovereignty was no more than a theory. The recognition of all men as citizens and of the totality of citizens as the sovereign found formal expression in the patriotic documents of the Revolutionary assemblies and led to the close identification of the individual with his nation that characterizes modern popular or, as it is sometimes called, "integral" nationalism. A man today belongs to his nation body and soul—in body more than he ever belonged to his king, in soul more than he ever belonged to his church; and few men care and fewer dare to repudiate their dependence. On the contrary, nearly all take pride in it.

Modern nationalism requires a sense of nationality, i.e., a sense of belonging to the same people. This feeling is a product of several bonds that may be found in different combinations among different peoples. The primary bond may be religion, but not necessarily so, as for example in Germany, where the people are both Protestant and Catholic. Or it may be language, but not necessarily so, as in Belgium or Switzerland, where more languages than one are officially spoken. Or it may be loyalty to the same state, although at times it is better expressed by hostility to the state to which one belongs, as among the Czechs of Austria or the Bulgars of Turkey in the 1870's. Or it may express itself in a local patriotism, although Poles, Irish, and Jews scattered throughout the world have had a sense of national solidarity that centered in each case around a locus they may never have seen. It may, as Enlightenment "fraternity," be rationalized on the principle of legal equality of citizenship emphasizing the rights of man or, as romanticist "folkdom," be glorified into a biological bond of blood and language emphasizing the concept of statehood. Whichever of these bonds a people might lack, however, one thing it had to have to develop a dynamic national feeling, and that was a sense of belonging together because of sharing the same historical and cultural tradition. Industrialization, permitting the building of "national" economic systems with "national" communications lines and "national" markets, reinforced the national tradition and the sense of national interdependence.

**The rise
of aggressive nationalism**

A MODERN nation, strictly speaking, is one whose cultural tradition has a geographical setting that is under the control of a state that represents in some fashion or other the people who share that tradition. A country may have a state without being a nation because its people do not have a sense of nationality, as was true of Austria-Hungary during this period. A people may have a nationality without being a nation because they own no country, as was true of Czechs, Poles, Irish, Jews, and others during this period. Nationalism often expresses itself in the desire of nationalities to become nation-states and hence in hostility to foreign states that control them. In English the word *nationalism* may but does not necessarily convey the undertones of national aggressiveness and false pride that it has acquired in some other languages.

By 1870 the Germans and the Italians had experienced a decisive degree of success in their national efforts. The success of the Prussian and Sardinian kings in achieving their national revolutions from on high brought a significant change in international politics. It meant not only that two new or, at least, different powers had appeared in Europe, requiring readjustments of traditional policies and alignments; it meant also that aggressive nationalism by virtue of its very aggressiveness, by its policy of blood and iron, had won huge awards where the old Mazzinian or humanitarian nationalism, preaching self-determination for each cultural group but cooperation among them toward a united Europe and even a united world, had failed.

Some characteristics of aggressive nationalism

NATIONALISM must be distinguished from mere patriotism. Patriotism binds an individual to his country by a sense of loyalty independent of other considerations or the behavior of others. Gilbert and Sullivan, in their own hilarious way, poked mild fun at the English patriot in their chaffing operetta about the British navy, *HMS Pinafore* (1878):

> And in spite of all temptations
> To belong to other nations
> He remains an Englishman.

In its more aggressive forms patriotism becomes "chauvinism," a word derived from the name of a soldier, Nicolas Chauvin, whose demonstrations of loyalty to the first Napoleon became notorious. Nationalism has patriotism as one of its ingredients, but it is a social rather than an individual phenomenon. It needs to be shared by a people. The word *nationalism* in strict usage does not necessarily carry a connotation of chauvinism, but writers have often given it that connotation. And, in fact, to a large extent nationalism became chauvinistic, though not everywhere, after 1870. It led to policies such as forcing peoples to accept a culture that was not theirs (e.g., Russification or Magyarization), excluding peoples from equal consideration because of alien qualities they were supposed to have (e.g., anti-Semitism), getting even as a people for some wrong done by another people (i.e., *revanche*), and "redeeming" a piece of territory controlled by a foreign government in which lived people of one's own culture (i.e., irredentism).

Revival of national languages

LANGUAGE naturally became a powerful vehicle of national unity. The revival of half-forgotten languages as a means of propagating nationalism became a passion of nationalists. In the course of the nineteenth century the Irish rediscovered Gaelic and proposed to make it their official language; the Czechs turned away from German to Czech; the Norwegians adopted Landsmaal, their peasant dialect, as their official language; the Flemish discarded French for Flemish; the Zionists decided to adopt ancient Hebrew, until then largely ritualistic, as the language of their future state; the Catalans and the Basques preferred to avoid using Castilian Spanish; and even in centralized France ancient Provençal underwent a revival through the essentially unpolitical poetry of Frédéric Mistral. In France, the exhumation of a half-dead language had no disruptive political consequences. In other instances, however, a language might be linked either with the separatism of a people that wished to become independent or with the irredentism of a government that wished to claim nearby territory. Italy thus claimed the Southern Tyrol and Dalmatia, Greece claimed Epirus, and, in the course of time, Germany claimed Austria and the Sudetenland.

The quest for an independent Ireland NATIONALISM brought to Ireland a strikingly complex concatenation of intrigue and rebellion. The rebellion centered around the Fenians, patriotic Irishmen in the United States who sent money and help back home to achieve an independent Irish republic and harried Britain by attacking Canada from United States territory (page 318). When Gladstone was prime minister of Great Britain the first time, the Fenian movement and his own liberal principles convinced him that something had to be done to alleviate the plight of Ireland. The Disestablishment Act of 1869, which went into effect in 1871, and the Irish Land Act of 1870, both of which we have already mentioned, were bold strides toward that objective. Fenian agitation and agrarian revolt in Ireland did not cease, however, with these "half measures," as the Irish nationalists considered them. When the Conservative Party was victorious in the election of 1874, Disraeli, the new prime minister, inherited the Irish problem.

The Irish cause found a devoted leader in Charles Stewart Parnell, an Irish Protestant landowner of English descent and education. Parnell was elected to the House of Commons to sit for County Meath, Ireland, in 1875. In 1878 he was made the leader of the Irish party in Parliament. Parnell's program proposed to solve the land question by making it easier for the peasant to acquire his land outright and to solve the nationalist question by setting up home rule for Ireland. In order to reach both goals, the Irish party turned to filibustering against laws intended to promote the welfare of England, hoping thereby to gain concessions for Ireland.

The Irish Land League, organized in 1879, now became the rallying point of Irish nationalists. Parnell was its president. It advocated the by now familiar program of "the three F's"—fair rent, fixed tenure, and free sale—for Irish farmers, and resorted to collusion and violence to prevent or punish violations of "the three F's." One form of collusion was an agreement not to 359 communicate or cooperate with officials who had incurred dislike. Among such officials in 1880 was Captain Charles C. Boycott, a land agent in County Mayo. The secular excommunication of Captain Boycott led to a new practice in farmer and labor disputes and gave his name to the practice. The "boycott" was especially effective because, so long as no violence accompanied it, it was hard for the police or courts to handle. Parnell's obstructive tactics in Parliament and the activity of the Land League became especially noticeable with the bad harvests and depression of 1879, and violence plagued the country. In the years that followed, the British government was constrained to make concessions (page 437).

The situation
of international affairs in 1870

WHILE THE national aspirations of the Irish remained essentially a domestic problem of Britain, the delicate international situation in the 1870's made of Balkan nationalism a dangerous diplomatic issue. Bismarck was perhaps the focus of international politics of that decade. After the Treaty of Frankfurt had ended the Franco-Prussian War, Bismarck's foreign policy centered around his desire for peace in order to build up the new German Empire. He could feel quite certain, however, that the French would seek *revanche* at the first good opportunity. The shame of defeat, the resentment over the loss of Alsace-Lorraine, the indignation over the huge indemnity, the humiliation of occupation, and the still inadequate readjustment to the new constellation in central Europe made extremely unlikely France's peaceful acceptance of a secondary role in continental affairs. Bismarck recognized, however, that France, torn between Republicans and Monarchists, would not take the offensive without allies. Hence an important aim of his foreign policy centered upon cowing and isolating France. England could be expected to persist in her policy of "splendid isolation." Italy, having found cooperation with Germany against France profitable, might be counted upon to maintain it. The Russian czar had taken advantage of the war between a friendly Prussian king and an unfriendly French emperor to deneutralize the Black Sea, and Bismarck hoped that the czar would see neither appropriateness nor advantage in cooperating with a French republic. Only Austria, still resentful of her collapse in the Seven Weeks' War with Prussia in 1866, might consider alignment with an equally resentful France. Bismarck therefore continued the effort initiated immediately after that war with the easy terms of the Treaty of Prague to win the Austrian Emperor Francis Joseph to his side.

The League
of the Three Emperors

SEVERAL meetings of the German Emperor William and his Austrian confrere in 1871 led to the expectation that Bismarck's policy would succeed. The Austrian foreign office had no intention of upsetting the new German Empire. On the other hand, it was fearful that its own readjustment to the unification of Italy and Germany by means of the Dual Monarchy of Austria and Hungary, might be upset by continued agitation of minority nationalities. Russification, Pan-Slavism, and Russian ambitions in the Balkans were among the sources of agitation that kept Austria-Hungary's Poles, Czechs, Serbs, Croats, and other Slavic elements in turmoil. If only Russia would accept the status quo, then the traditional cooperation of old Prussia, the old Austrian Empire, and Russia might be renewed. Bismarck found the Russians entirely amenable. In 1872 he was able to arrange a meeting of the three emperors, and the next year to establish the Three Emperors' League. A series of loose agreements among the three governments looked toward the preservation of the status quo in the Balkans, reciprocal aid in the event of revolution, and mutual support under specified conditions in case of war. The Three Emperors' League was more of an informal entente than a binding alliance, but it did mean the more effective isolation of France. The French in a great show of patriotism paid off their indemnity and obliged the withdrawal of the German army of occupation (1873) faster than had generally been thought possible, but continued peace seemed assured because France could hardly consider going to war alone.

Bismarck
and the crisis of 1875

IN FACT, Bismarck's diplomatic success almost backfired. The rapidity with which France paid its indemnity led, as we have seen (page 337), to an artificial boom in German industry and made the depression that followed in 1873 seem all the deeper. French prosperity, accompanied by the stabilization of the French government by the organic laws of 1875 and the reorganization of the French army, presented a fearsome contrast. In the spring of 1875 a German paper published an article under the headline: *Is War in Sight?* Most Frenchmen and a large part of Europe were under the impression that Bismarck had inspired the article and was about to launch a new attack on France, again putting the blame on her, as he had so successfully done in 1870. Possibly Bismarck meant only to use intimidation both as a warning to France and as a means of rallying the Germans, then divided by the Kulturkampf and the revolutionary attitude of the Socialists. Fortunately this time the French did not desire war, as they did in 1870. The Russian and English governments indicated openly and the Austrian government indicated secretly that they would not be indifferent to an attack upon France; and after a visit of Czar Alexander II to Berlin, his minister Prince Gorchakov publicly declared: "Peace has now been assured." Bismarck denied that peace had ever been in danger, but he had to recognize that at the first serious test the Three Emperors' League had failed in its purpose. Instead of being isolated, France had come close to isolating Germany.

*Insurrection and war
in the Balkans (1875-1878)*

HARDLY had the crisis of 1875 passed when another danger spot developed. The Near East, relatively somnolent since Rumania's unification in 1862, once more flared up. The English, through Disraeli's daring speculation in Suez Canal Company shares, had acquired a controlling interest in the company and an increased stake in the status quo in the Near East. In the summer of 1875 several communities in Bosnia and Hercegovina, two of Turkey's Balkan provinces, struck a new blow for independence. In 1876 sedition spread to the Serbians and Bulgarians, and the Russian protégé, the prince of Montenegro, helped fan the flames of rebellion. The Bulgarian rebellion was crushed by the Turks with great cruelty, whereupon Serbia declared war on Turkey.

Gladstone, then the leader of the Liberal opposition in the British Parliament, denounced "the Bulgarian atrocities," but, undaunted, Prime Minister Disraeli adhered to the traditional British policy of preserving the Ottoman Empire. He entered upon a series of negotiations intended to bolster Turkish morale and to deter the Russians from military intervention on behalf of the Balkan Slavs and Christians. The Austrian government approved of the British policy. Without Russian help the Serbians were crushed by the Turkish army and were compelled to ask the great powers for help.

The Russians, moved by the distress of their coreligionists, lent a willing ear to Serbia's plea. Czar Alexander II, always ready to pursue the traditional Russian policy in the Near East, saw in the new crisis a chance also to deflect internal unrest, whose seriousness was evidenced by the success of the *V Narod* movement. He decided to heed the outraged cry of the Russians: "Help our Serbian brothers!" In the fall of 1876, he secretly sounded out Bismarck as to whether Germany would remain neutral in case war broke out between Russia and Austria-Hungary over the Balkan situation. Bismarck answered that Germany could not afford to have either of them injured to such a degree as to impair its status as a European power. Nevertheless, in 1877, risking the certain displeasure of England and Austria and despite the uncertainty of Germany's position, Russia made war on Turkey in order to save the Serbs. The Russians at first bungled the war, and a Russian victory was won only when the Rumanians, whose aid at first had been spurned, joined them. The allies stopped outside of Constantinople because the British let them know that a Russian conquest of the Turkish capital would not be tolerated. A British fleet had in fact started out for the Straits, and English chauvinism acquired the new name, "jingoism," from a popular verse:

> We don't want to fight,
> Yet, by Jingo! if we do,
> We've got the ships,

> We've got the men,
> And got the money too.

THE RUSSIAN people had expected a short campaign culminating in the conquest of Constantinople and the expulsion of the Infidel Turk from Europe. Instead, the war lasted nearly a year and the Russian losses were unnecessarily heavy. Constantinople was never taken, out of deference to British wishes. On March 3, 1878, in the preliminary Treaty of San Stefano, Turkey and Russia formally confirmed the independence of Serbia, Rumania, and Montenegro, and cut a huge fresh chunk out of Turkey for the purpose of setting up an autonomous Bulgarian state. Despite its military and diplomatic gaucherie, Russia seemed to have won a great victory in the struggle for control of the Balkans by establishing a system of satellite principalities. In addition, the treaty provided certain boundary "rectifications" in favor of Russia.

Peace and the calling of a congress

The British were dissatisfied. So were the Austrians. They wanted to reduce the size of Bulgaria because so large a state under Russian control would doubtless mean Russian domination of the Straits. The armistice terms that had preceded the Treaty of San Stefano had stipulated: "His Majesty the Sultan agrees to come to an understanding with His Majesty the Emperor of Russia in order to maintain the rights and interests of Russia in the Straits of the Bosporus and the Dardanelles." That stipulation was ambiguous, and it was disquieting to the British. Russia's "rights" as fixed by several international agreements were far from coinciding with her "interests."

Disraeli wished, however, to avoid publicly humiliating Russia and so embarked upon a series of secret negotiations with Russian, Austrian, Turkish, and German diplomats. Bismarck had special reasons for wishing to keep British and Austrian dissatisfaction from leading to war. Chief among them was that a general European war might impede his efforts to isolate France and would certainly end either Austria's or Russia's cooperation in a Three Emperors' League. In a speech to the German Reichstag he declared that he wanted nothing more than to play "the role of an honest broker." All the countries involved were more or less ready to accede when Austria-Hungary suggested a European conference, on the grounds that any territorial changes in the Balkans ought to have the approval of all the signatories of the Treaty of Paris of 1856. Actually, a fairly comprehensive understanding was brought about between Britain and Russia before the congress met; and from the sultan the British received the right to administer the island of Cyprus in return for having saved Turkey from worse destruction and as a base for speedier intervention against future aggression on the part of Russia in the Near East.

*The Congress
and Treaty of Berlin*

THE Congress of Berlin, attended by all the powers that had signed the Treaty of Paris—Britain, France, Russia, Turkey, Austria, and Italy (in lieu of Sardinia)—and Germany, met for a month (June 13-July 13, 1878). The Russians had hoped that Bismarck would insist upon a softening of the Anglo-Russian terms. But Bismarck, though playing his part carefully, did not oppose the British and the Austrians. The resulting Treaty of Berlin recognized the independence of Rumania, Serbia, and Montenegro, and enlarged each of them, though on a smaller scale than had the Treaty of San Stefano. Rumania received the Dobruja as a compensation for ceding Southern Bessarabia to Russia. Russia also received a few Caucasus cities. But a striking Russian defeat was registered in the rearrangement of Bulgaria. The northern part alone of that area became an autonomous principality; the southern part (called Eastern Rumelia) was returned to Turkey, to be governed by a Turkish-appointed Christian governor; and Macedonia, to the southwest, was given back to Turkey on no conditions other than a promise to institute some reforms. Bosnia, Hercegovina, and the district of Novi Bazar were to be policed or garrisoned by Austria-Hungary, although, on the protest of the Turkish delegation, they were allowed to remain Turkish territories in name, the Austrians calling their occupation "provisional." England's occupation of Cyprus was approved. France's share of the spoils was a secret understanding that she might occupy the territory of Turkish Tunisia at any time. Italy received nothing but even vaguer promises regarding Albania. Germany claimed to seek, and received, nothing but prestige. Without going to war, Great Britain and Austria-Hungary had gained all that they wanted. Disraeli had achieved "peace with honor." Russia had cut a poor figure. And the Balkan nations felt frustrated.

*The Dual Alliance
and the three emperors*

THE WRATH of the Russian nationalists was aimed most directly at Germany. Russia had with rare exceptions been on Prussia's side for more than a century. Without Russia's benevolent neutrality Prussia might easily have been less successful in the wars of 1866 and 1870-1871. Thus, the Russians saw in Bismarck's attitude during the Congress a glaring manifestation of ingratitude. Despite his protestations that he had continued his customary pro-Russian policy and had acted "like a third Russian delegate" the fact remained that the Russians felt cheated and held Bismarck to blame. The Russian press openly attacked the Germans, and the Russian government's communications ceased to be couched in conciliatory language.

Ever since his diplomatic defeat in 1875 the German chancellor had been haunted by what a Russian official called "the nightmare of coalitions."

THE NEAR EASTERN QUESTION 1878

When Russia went to war with Turkey in 1877-1878, the other European powers united to curb her. As the large map shows, in addition to Russia and Turkey all the other signatories of the treaty of 1856, as well as Germany, combined to write the Treaty of Berlin in 1878. Several furthered their own interests at the expense of the faltering Ottoman Empire. France getting a free hand in Tunisia, and Italy receiving similar promises regarding Albania. Great Britain had already obtained Cyprus from the sultan for blocking Russia from Constantinople and the Straits. The inset map shows the treaty arrangements for the Balkan areas. (Russia also got a few Caucasus cities.)

Bismarck knew that, with Russia estranged and France getting stronger, Germany, instead of isolating France, might itself be isolated, and ought to look for an ally on the Continent. Since Austria feared Russia as much as Germany feared France, Austria was chosen as that ally. A secret treaty (1879) provided: (1) that the two parties assist each other with full military aid in case either should be attacked by Russia; and (2) that if any other power should attack either of them (which could mean only an attack by France upon Germany), the other party would observe a friendly neutrality—unless 365

Russia aided the attacker, in which case full military aid would be called for. The treaty was to be communicated to Russia in case of an international crisis, but the pact was not made public until 1888.

The Dual Alliance thus formed was binding for only five years, but it was regularly renewed and lasted until the collapse of Austria in 1918. Russo-German estrangement was patched up later on (page 427), but the German government had meanwhile learned to dread the possibility of an attack by Russia, and the Russians for their part never overcame their apprehension that Germany might gang up with Austria-Hungary or some other power against them. That mutual fear, though temporarily allayed, has remained a decisive factor in Russo-German relations ever since. Bismarck is often quoted as having said that the whole Near East was not worth the bones of a single Pomeranian grenadier; yet his involving Germany through the Congress of Berlin in the Near Eastern Question has perhaps cost Germany much, much more.

THE Congress of Berlin was the last important congress in which European powers alone (if indeed Turkey could be considered a European power) were represented. The world of international might was no longer an elongation of the European shadow, as subsequent congresses were to show and as, indeed, Japanese and American imperialism had already begun to show in the Pacific and elsewhere. Nevertheless Europe was still the great economic center, the leading source of capital investments, of scientific discovery, of practical inventions, of business and industrial ideas. If the United States and Japan were catching up, they were still a good distance behind.

Before the 1870's five great powers had long dominated the world. They were England, France, Austria, Prussia, and Russia. Austria was now only the shadow of a once great empire, though it was to take several decades to make its lack of substance manifest. France, an empire turned republic, was internationally isolated and domestically unstable but was soon to emerge again as a great colonial power and a force in European politics. Prussia had become the German Empire (or, more accurately, the dominant fraction of it) and as such was to act a more self-conscious role in European affairs than it had ever before presumed to act and, in the course of time, was to become bolder still. The British crown had passed from empire to Empire— that is to say, from a policy of ruling by thumb over scattered areas to a more systematic colonial organization whose ruler was formally recognized as an empress in one of her realms—but she had in Canada taken the first important steps that were to convert the British Empire into a British Commonwealth of Nations. Russia, a big bumbling giant, looked too large and strong to be seriously restrained even though still checked both in the Near East and the Far East by more efficient and skillful adversaries.

Three new world powers now were bidding to join these five—a United States no longer torn by the threat of nullification and secession, a unified Italy, and a Japan that was rapidly leaving feudalism behind in its urge for centralization and industrialization. As yet, however, these three were not first rankers. The United States still had the problem of its South, and Italy had a similar problem, while Japan looked like an impudent pygmy beside China, which no first rank power any longer feared. So three continents, instead of one, now provided real or potential world powers. And one other continent had become more of an arena than ever for the world powers to exercise their imperialistic drives. To Asia, Australasia, and Oceania as theaters of colonial operations (the fiasco in 1867 of Napoleon iii's dream to build a Mexican Empire having demonstrated once more that the Western Hemisphere was closed) was rapidly being added the once "dark" Africa.

Each of the great powers had its domestic problems. To mention only one for each, England had its Ireland, France its royalists, Austria its minorities, Germany its Socialists, Russia its land-hungry peasants, the United States its Negroes, Italy its papal question, and Japan its clansmen. Of course, the little nations had their problems, too, both international and internal; and, of course, the little nations made their contributions to world culture (as we shall soon see). But the domestic problems of little nations, when they are independent, rarely become the world's problems; and their international problems are unlikely to disturb world peace unless the big powers take sides.

1849-1871	Livingstone's explorations in Africa
1850-1864	Taiping Rebellion in China
1859-1870	Unification of Italy
1861-1865	American Civil War
1862-1871	Bismarck engaged in the unification of Germany
1867-1868	Reconstruction in the United States
1867	*Ausgleich* establishes Dual Monarchy of Austria-Hungary
1867	British North America Act
1868-1876	Revolution in Spain
1869	Suez Canal opened to traffic
1870-1871	Franco-Prussian War
c. 1870	Beginning of *V Narod* movement in Russia
1870	The dogma of papal infallibility announced
1871	The rise and defeat of the Paris Commune
1871	Thiers given title of "president of the Republic"
1871	Pius ix refuses to accept Law of Guaranties
1871	Treaty of Washington provides for arbitration of outstanding Anglo-American disputes
1872	Filipinos revolt against Spain
1873-1875	Peak of the Kulturkampf
1873	Three Emperors' League
1873	Marshal MacMahon becomes French president
1873	World-wide financial panic
1875-1878	Balkan crises and Russo-Turkish War
1875	French National Assembly sets up "organic laws"
1875	Reichsbank founded
1876	Alexander Graham Bell invents telephone
1876	Japanese-Korean commercial treaty
1877	The coup of the *Seize Mai*
1877	Italian compulsory school law
1877	The "Great Strike" in the United States
1877	Victoria proclaimed empress of India
1878	Bismarck's Anti-Socialist Law
1878	The Congress and Treaty of Berlin
1879	Germany deserts free-trade policy
1879	MacMahon's resignation ends monarchist threat in France
1879	Parnell organizes Irish Land League
1879	Royal Prussian Railroad System established
1879	Dual Alliance of Germany and Austria
1879	Thomas A. Edison produces electric light
1880-1881	Revolt of the Boers

Chapter seven

REALISM

AND REALPOLITIK

1879-c. 1890

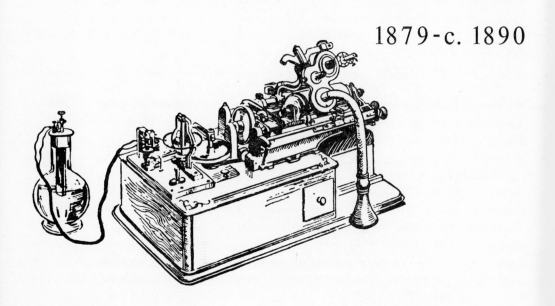

UNTIL THE 1890's confidence in continuous progress seemed to be the dominant credo of the western world. Europeans and Americans seldom doubted their ultimate ability to master whatever difficulties might arise. On the surface at least the United States and the countries of western Europe became more and more prosperous and more and more alike, with their parliamentary institutions, their engineering triumphs, their successes in preventing epidemics and curing disease, their programs of social reform, their devotion to realism in the arts and materialism in philosophy and the world of practical affairs. The names of great healers like Joseph Lister, Louis Pasteur, and Robert Koch were widely known; Lord Tennyson, Émile Zola, and Henry James belonged to the world; and Alfred Nobel and Thomas A. Edison were hailed as technological geniuses in Europe as well as America. Accumulating inter-European agreements were regarded as promises of either closer harmony or a better balance of power among the nations. A moderate program of social legislation made its appearance as a solemn obligation of governments. To the superficial observer, it seemed that permanent peace among white men would ultimately be assured and that all the world's mysteries would be cleared up.

Nevertheless, a countermovement had already set in. What came to be known as "the social question" continued to cast a dark shadow over Europe during the 1880's. Anarchism and anti-Semitism became more prominent. The encroachments of big business, class warfare, racial hatred, militant clericalism, and (in several countries) the plight of the peasants caused anxiety. *Raison d'état* (the overriding interest of the state) became increasingly the guiding light of statesmen. Patriotism assumed more and more the 371 features of that particularly aggressive form of nationalism and militarism which in a later era was to be the curse of Europe.

The prevailing cheerfulness and the counteracting apprehension will be dealt with in this chapter. One of the results of this conflict was a continent-wide disillusionment, which we shall find clearly reflected by a number of men of letters, who probed the intellectual, social, and religious shortcomings of their day, attacked its smugness and overconfidence, and stirred up uneasy consciences. As critics of evil attitudes and institutions some of these men found appreciative audiences, but they could not stay the current of their times.

THE "SECOND INDUSTRIAL REVOLUTION" IN EUROPE (TO 1890)

N EW INDUSTRIES were discovered at so fast a pace in the decades preceding the First World War that the development is sometimes called the "Second Industrial Revolution." In Germany after its unification, Bismarck adopted a policy of deliberate encouragement of German industry. He yielded to demands for high protective tariffs intended to allow German factories to compete with those abroad. The heavy industries of Germany soon compared favorably with those of Belgium as the best on the Continent. The industries of France and Sweden were not far behind, but none of them as yet could overtake the advanced factory system of England.

Heavy industry: coal and metallurgy

COAL MINING and the metallurgic industries became the economic backbone of continental Europe. Nature had favored France with important iron ore deposits and with vast and abundant coal fields; Germany and Belgium also had rich coal fields; and the three countries met with keen competition from British coal. The abundance of coal speeded the development of the metallurgic industries, particularly after the 1870's, when two Englishmen, Sidney G. Thomas and Percy C. Gilchrist, perfected a process by which iron ore with a high phosphorous content could be used in making steel.

In mining, the Germans had an advantage over their western neighbors. No other country produced as much lignite as Germany. As a fuel for household purposes it is almost equal to coal, and although it cannot be used in the production of steel, it has other industrial uses. It is dug from open pits and therefore does not call for workers as sturdy as those engaged in mining coal. Hence it is cheaper than coal. In Germany lignite was so extensively employed that large quantities of it were imported from Bohemia, Moravia, and Austrian Silesia.

Thus Germany could export coal to countries without significant deposits

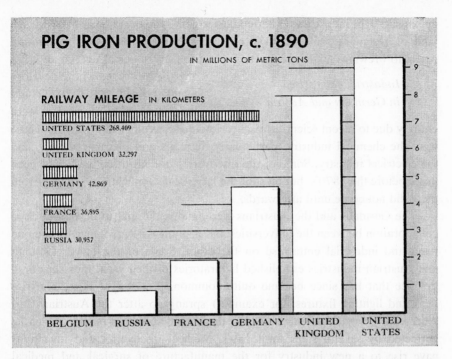

PIG IRON PRODUCTION, c. 1890

IN MILLIONS OF METRIC TONS

RAILWAY MILEAGE IN KILOMETERS

UNITED STATES 268,409

UNITED KINGDOM 32,297

GERMANY 42,869

FRANCE 36,895

RUSSIA 30,957

BELGIUM RUSSIA FRANCE GERMANY UNITED UNITED
KINGDOM STATES

In the face of the rapid development of the United States, the United Kingdom by 1890 had lost its early lead in the production of pig iron. A new contender, Germany, had already overtaken France, and Russia ran a poor fifth. The correspondence between industrial and railroad development is illustrated by the relative length of track, although, in part because of its size and in part because of its greater use of water transportation, the United Kingdom fell somewhat behind in railway mileage. Though as late as 1911 Belgium had only 2907 miles of track, it had a greater railway mileage in proportion to its area than any other country.

of their own like Italy, Switzerland, and Denmark. Until the loss of Lorraine in 1919, Germany also had a large though insufficient supply of iron ore. The eastern part of that disputed province gave its iron ore to the German steel industry. But France has always been richer in iron ore than Germany, and German heavy industry could not do without French iron. The Schumann Plan of our own times is a belated recognition of the interdependence of French iron and German coal. Likewise Sweden with its abundant iron ore and copper deposits played an ever increasing role in the development of Germany's heavy industry. The Eiffel Tower, which dominated the Paris Exposition of 1889, was a sort of monument to the steel industry of its day and a forerunner of the giant steel structures to come.

Light industry: textiles, instruments, etc.

THE LIGHT industries were more evenly distributed. In these too Germany played a prominent role. Her textile manufacture was highly developed, and her optical instruments became world-famous. The French were especially interested in textiles, silk, perfumery, wines, and liqueurs. Italy, because she is poor in coal, had to   373 emphasize light industries. Other countries with little or no coal, like Switzerland or Denmark, but with a strong agricultural or dairying background resort to brewing, textiles, cigarettes, precision instruments, and candy.

Industrial enterprise
in Germany and Austria

TWO INDUSTRIES whose developments few in the 1870's could have been able to predict were entirely due to recent scientific discoveries and technological advances. These were the chemical industry, particularly dyestuffs and pharmaceuticals, and the electrical industry. Some of the discoveries in both those fields had been made before the 1870's, but most of the large-scale applications growing from them did not come until afterwards.

The Germans and the Austrians were among the first to develop a close collaboration between the universities and institutes of technology on the one hand and industrial enterprise on the other. Some of the bigger German and Austrian industries established laboratories of their own, thus starting a practice that has since become quite common. A series of new industries (gas and lighting fixtures, for example) sprang up after the Austrian Carl Auer von Welsbach patented (1885) the incandescent gas mantle, which he perfected by several steps until 1893. Medical discoveries and inventions gave rise to a new industry for the manufacture of surgical and medical instruments such as Helmholtz's ophthalmoscope.

American contributions
to European industrialism

IN THE 1880's Europe began to feel the impact of several important American inventions. In addition to agricultural machinery (page 342), they were the telephone invented by Alexander Graham Bell in 1876, the incandescent electric bulb invented by Thomas Edison in 1879, and the roll film and the kodak, or portable camera, invented by George Eastman in 1888. In 1880 the German engineer and industrialist Emil Rathenau visited the United States. What he learned from Edison impressed him so much that after his return to Berlin he founded the AEG (Allgemeine Elektrizitäts-Gesellschaft), the German equivalent of the General Electric Company. The AEG in the course of time developed into one of the greatest industrial empires on earth. Concrete reinforced with iron, though first patented by a French inventor, F. J. Monier, was more fully exploited for building purposes in the United States. In the 1880's it began to become common in the building of houses and roads in Europe as well.

New printing devices
and popular journalism

IN THE 1870's Ottmar Mergenthaler, a German-American immigrant, perfected the linotype (patented 1885), which did by machine the process of composing type that had hitherto been done by hand. Together with the rotary press, which was invented in 1846 by Richard M. Hoe and perfected in 1865 by William Bullock, both Americans, this process made the printing of books and newspapers faster and cheaper. When Robert Miehle of Chicago in 1883 perfected the printing machine which prints an entire sheet in two revolutions, the modern big-scale printing industry became an actuality. The first successful two-revolution printing machine was set up in America in 1888.

The combination of these engineering feats hit Europe in full force during the 1880's and 1890's. Until that time there had been four kinds of European newspapers: (1) papers merely acting as mouthpieces of the various governments; (2) newspapers read almost exclusively by workers and usually strongly socialist; (3) papers serving professional, ecclesiastical, hobby, and sports interests; and (4) dailies that, in addition to the news, published "highbrow" articles and appealed only to small groups. The American inventions gave enterprising men the opportunity to create quite another kind of press organ. By the turn of the century the linotype, the rotary press, and, later on, the rotogravure were to make it possible to reach the mass of humanity; and, willingly or unwillingly, publishers, whether of papers or magazines or books, found that, if they wanted to make money despite the huge costs of these new installations, they had to cater to the taste of the average man. Literature, once dependent on aristocratic patrons, now became largely dependent upon mass appeal, in Europe and in America. A kind of press developed which in the English-speaking countries became known as the "yellow press." It played up crime, scandal, sports, accidents, and other sensational events, and became the favorite reading matter of millions of people (many newly enfranchised) all over the world.

The spread of industrialism to Russia

RUSSIA did not begin to industrialize effectively until the 1880's, in the ministry of the financial wizard I. A. Vishnegradsky, and in the 1890's, in that of his pupil, Count Sergei Witte (page 434). Then developments came rapidly. The vastness of the country explains why Russia was often considered a country without industry. Factories were thinly spread, but they grew in the bigger cities. Russian Poland had an important place in textile manufacture. By the 1870's Russia, along with the rest of Europe except the Iberian Peninsula, had a considerable system of railroads. As head of the railways department of the ministry of finance, and later as minister of communications, Witte helped to develop the Russian railroad system, and he was in a sense the father of the Trans-Siberian Railroad. When finally he succeeded Vishnegradsky as minister to finance (1893), he introduced the gold standard and, by securing a series of huge loans from France, was able to create a strong gold reserve.

Widening of the gulf between capital and labor

"BIG BUSINESS" now came to mean business on a national scale. In 1886 the British Nobel Dynamite Trust, for example, was founded and, because of its patent on dynamite, quickly became a monopoly on a national scale. In the next decade these 375

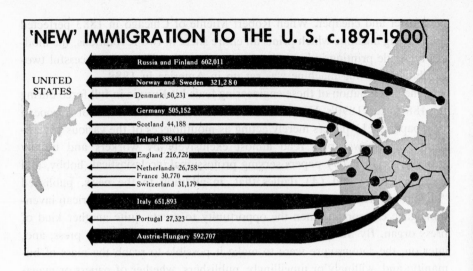

'NEW' IMMIGRATION TO THE U. S. c.1891-1900

UNITED STATES

Russia and Finland 602,011

Norway and Sweden 321,280

Denmark 50,231

Germany 505,152

Scotland 44,188

Ireland 388,416

England 216,726

Netherlands 26,758

France 30,770

Switzerland 31,179

Italy 651,893

Portugal 27,323

Austria-Hungary 592,707

national trusts began to acquire international scope (pages 452-453). The worker on the Continent formed part of these new industrial empires though he rarely had a sense of belonging to them. In some favorable cases where an old-fashioned paternalism lingered on, he could still hope to improve his position by a man-to-man talk. When industrial enterprises assumed gigantic proportions, the worker rarely, if ever, saw his employer. The managers who stood between the worker and the employer were interested in the worker, as a general rule, only as a cog in the efficient operation of the company. They were dependent themselves upon their superiors, who, in turn, were dependent upon a board of directors, who might themselves be guided by highly specialized corporation lawyers or engineers. The bureaucracy of big business was sometimes no less cumbersome than that of government.

America invaded by the poor of Europe

THE LONGING for a better status drove many of Europe's workers to the Americas. Between 1880 and 1900 a torrent of poor immigrants gushed forth from Europe into the United States—over 5,000,000 in the 1880's and over 3,500,000 in the 1890's. They came from Italy, the United Kingdom, Russia, Austria-Hungary, Germany, and Sweden. They were not consciously in search of liberty, about which they knew little. But they were ready to undergo the hardships of immigrant life because they held four things as certain: (1) that people would not spurn them merely because they were workers; (2) that they would earn a better living in America; (3) that they, or at least their children, would have a chance to acquire an education; and (4) that they and their children would avoid military conscription. Many European workers (mostly Germans and Italians) went also to Argentina, Brazil, and Chile. But their numbers were small in comparison with those who migrated to the United States. Some European governments felt misgivings about losing

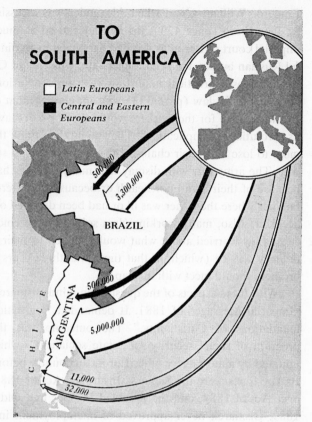

TO SOUTH AMERICA

☐ Latin Europeans

■ Central and Eastern Europeans

BRAZIL

500,000

3,300,000

CHILE

ARGENTINA

500,000

5,000,000

11,000

32,000

By 1890 a marked change in the European sources of migration to the United States was evident. As the figures (for the years 1891-1900) in the map at the left show, great numbers now came from the southern and eastern areas. A large current also flowed in from Canada and, to a lesser extent, from China, the West Indies, and Mexico. The map at the right indicates the main currents of the European migration that set in toward Latin America in the last half of the nineteenth and the first quarter of the twentieth centuries. This "new" immigration in both Americas was offset in part by a high proportion of returns to the country of origin, reaching, in Brazil, as much as 50 per cent.

so many workers and potential soldiers and tried either to discourage emigration by stigmatizing it as unpatriotic or to establish colonies that might absorb their surplus populations. But such measures did not effectively stop the exodus to America.

Bismarck's program of social security legislation

BISMARCK was, if not the first, at least the foremost continental statesman to grasp the desirability of legislation to increase social security. Yet, like most of his contemporaries, he opposed the regulation of working hours by law. His argument was that of his era: "The regulation of working hours," he declared before the Reichstag, "necessarily entails regulation of wages because, otherwise, there will arise the danger that when we reduce the working hours by twenty per cent, wages also will, slowly or rapidly, drop by twenty per cent. The government will be unable to prevent that from happening. Who is supposed to bear that loss? Who will make good for it? Do you want the government to compensate the worker for what he suffers from the loss in wages?" In 1885, this argument was widely considered unanswerable.

But Bismarck had a good political logic for providing other benefits for the workingman. Czar Alexander II of Russia was a nephew of the German

377

Emperor William I, and when Alexander was assassinated on the streets of St. Petersburg (page 433), his murder caused as much consternation at the imperial court of Berlin as if it had happened in Berlin itself. If the all-powerful Russian autocrat was no longer safe, what might German princes expect? Bismarck as a practical man drew realistic conclusions. He recognized that his antisocialist law (page 333) was not enough, that only if something positive were done for the workers would they be lured away from Marxism and its revolutionary implications. They might then think that they had something more to lose than their chains. The Prussian general staff felt much the same way. The army saw with dismay that many draftees had to be rejected either because of their own poor health or because they were the only providers in families where the father was ill or had been disabled or killed in an industrial accident. Also, many working-class soldiers were emotionally unreliable because they worried about what would happen to their families if during their military service (which, at that time, was three years) their fathers or elder brothers should meet with mishap.

With these aspects of the question in mind Bismarck inspired the so-called "Imperial Message" of 1881. It demanded "legislation based on the moral foundations of Christianity." The outcome was the German legislative program of social security—of "state socialism"—which was destined to be imitated by almost every other European country before the First World War. Its keystones were the Sickness Insurance Act of 1883, the Accident Act of ance Act of 1884, and the Disabled Persons and Old Age Insurance Act of 1889. Bismarck never approved of unemployment insurance, which he believed to encourage laziness. Except for accident insurance, which the employer paid for entirely, the costs were divided between employers and employees; and the state made contributions toward old-age pensions. The Socialist members of the Reichstag voted against each of those bills, partly at least because their leaders did not wish to see themselves deprived of their most telling article of propaganda—the alleged indifference of the capitalist state to the proletariat. And in fact Bismarck's state socialism had the effect of making many Socialists all over the world wonder whether better results might not be achieved by cooperation with rather than opposition to the capitalist state.

Nevertheless, the laws did not have the effect Bismarck had hoped for. As the workers saw it, state socialism was costly to them because they had themselves to pay a good share of the insurance premiums. Fundamentally, they remained hostile to capitalism, and the vote of the Social Democratic Party continued to rise. Early in 1890 Bismarck became aware that neither the antisocialist law nor the insurance legislation had shaken the workers' belief in Marxism. He contemplated a new electoral law that should curtail even more stringently the workers' right to vote. But at this juncture the new emperor, William II, balked. The difference over the treatment of Socialists became one of the reasons for Bismarck's subsequent dismissal (page 440).

**The French Socialists
and the Second International**

IN THE 1880's the French Socialists were divided and hence did not play an important role in French politics. The workers made one important gain, however. In 1884 the French Trade Union Act legalized unions (though they had been tolerated by the government since 1868). Since the suppression of the Commune, the International Workingmen's Association, founded in 1864, had lost much of its vigor. Transfer of its headquarters to New York moved it even farther from the centers of Socialist activity, and it broke up in 1874. At the world's fair in 1889 which marked the centenary of the French Revolution, the leaders of many Socialist parties of the Continent and Great Britain met in Paris and created a Second International Workingmen's Association.

Like its predecessor, the Second International proved ineffective as an arm of international revolution. In fact, many of its members were "revisionists," or "possibilists," or "opportunists," prepared to "revise" strict Marxism in favor of a program of cooperation with bourgeois governments like Bismarck's in order to achieve whatever was "opportune" or "possible" in the way of social legislation. The Second International did, however, give a certain semblance of solidarity to world socialism. In a series of international socialist meetings it reaffirmed workingmen's solidarity. But when war came in 1914 the boasted solidarity turned out to be an illusion.

**The origin
of Fabianism in Great Britain**

THE BRITISH labor movement developed along different lines. Orthodox Marxism never took firm root in Great Britain. Well-meaning British intellectuals were deeply impressed, however, by Henry George's *Progress and Poverty* (page 407), first published in America in 1879. They realized, however, that they could not take over George's theories as a whole, conditions in Great Britain being different from those in the United States. They eventually organized the Fabian Society, so called from Fabius, the Roman general whose strategy consisted of delaying actions. As early as November 1883 they adopted a resolution which stated "that the competitive system assures the happiness and comfort of the few at the expense of the many and that society must be reconstituted in such a manner as to secure the general welfare and happiness." The guiding principle of the Fabian Society was "the subordination of material things to spiritual." For this purpose the society demanded the supplanting of the competitive spirit through the best possible education of the young, which should endeavor to teach simplicity of living, the dignity of manual labor, and religious communion. The word *socialism* was first introduced into their program in June 1884.

With rare exceptions the Fabians were not workingmen but middle-class intellectuals. Among them were some whose names became famous in later years, like Annie Besant, Sidney and Beatrice Webb, and George Bernard

Taking on laborers at the East India docks, London, in 1889.

Shaw. They decided not to engage in party politics and to refrain from being candidates in parliamentary elections, but rather to fight their fight mainly with the printed word. The "Fabian Tracts" (1889) written by outstanding writers like Shaw and the Webbs became known the world over and in the course of time deeply influenced British legislation.

Rural conditions at the close of the century — ON THE Continent much more than half the population was still rural in the 1880's. In general, the peasant on the Continent west of the Elbe River and north of the Alps and the Pyrenees was able to gain a livelihood. East or south of that line he was usually poor. He had a few chickens or geese, a horse or a pair of oxen for ploughing. If he was lucky, he owned a sheep or a cow. West of the Elbe he lived in a fairly substantial house that had come down to him from his forefathers. East of the dividing line his dwelling was more often a ramshackle affair. In Hungary or the Balkans it consisted of a hut. Rarely was there any plumbing or other modern sanitation anywhere. If the peasant were bold enough to wash himself, he had to use the pump in his back yard, the village pump, or the public or semipublic village bathhouse. Rural telephone service began to appear only shortly before the First World War. Farm technology and American farming machinery did not reach the countryside to any significant measure until after the war. The only exceptions were the use of water turbines (a great improvement over water wheels) and of threshing machines in central and northern Europe. Shortly before the war the beginnings of rural electrification came to parts of Germany, Sweden, and Switzerland.

The backwardness of industry in Austria-Hungary

IN AUSTRIA and especially Hungary, which formed a single customs union, the landholding system was obsolete. The peasant was worked hard on large estates, whose aristocratic owners were called "magnates." They were, if anything, even more conservative and haughty than the Prussian Junkers. Except for Vienna, Bohemia, and Moravia, industrialization and the ensuing urbanization came later and were less intense in Austria-Hungary than in Germany. For that reason the agricultural surplus population of Austria and Hungary did not migrate into the cities to a large extent, as the German rural population was able to do. On the other hand, hundreds of thousands of Austrian and Hungarian peasants of all nationalities emigrated to America. A veritable stream of Croats, Slovenes, Germans, Italians, Slovaks, Czechs, Hungarians, Rumanians, Poles, and Ruthenians flowed from the Austro-Hungarian Empire to the American shores. They took with them the resentment of their homelands against the domination of Vienna and Budapest, and nurtured from abroad the nationalist aspirations of their native lands.

The farmers of Italy, Spain, England, etc.

THE PEASANTS of northern Italy often became landowners, but southern Italy and Sicily still lived under an almost medieval feudalism. In the south particularly, the system of *mezzadria* (sharecropping) persisted. There the absentee landlord, owner of tremendous latifundia, either leased to tenants who subleased to others who subleased again or left the tilling of his land to a superintending leaseholder who put the farmers to work on individual small holdings on a sharecropping basis (usually half and half). Seasonal laborers went about the south in fairly well-organized gangs with recognized leaders. Peasant revolts of an anarchistic character were frequent, and millions of Italians emigrated. Many of them went to France, others to the United States or South America.

Much the same situation prevailed elsewhere in Europe. In Spain the unrest among the peasants exploded in anarchistic revolts. Many peasants emigrated to France. In Rumania the agricultural situation was similar to that of Hungary. Bulgaria and Serbia had expelled feudalism with the Turkish overlords, but the peasants often were very poor and could afford no modern agricultural equipment. In Ireland the agrarian question was linked with the struggle for home rule (page 437), and in post-emancipation Russia with the struggle for constitutional government (pages 463-466). In prosperous England, many young people left the farms. Only 10 per cent of the population tilled the land by the end of the nineteenth century. In the 1880's about 45 per cent of all grains and in the 1890's about 80 per cent of the wheat were imported.

*The preponderance
of the Junkers in east Germany*

IN EASTERN Germany (i.e., in the so-called "old provinces" of Prussia and in the two grand duchies of Mecklenburg) large estates were the rule. The soil was poor, fit only for rye, potatoes, and in some places, sugar beets. Because the peasants could seldom afford to buy farm machinery, they could not compete with the aristocratic landlords and preferred to be farm laborers rather than tenants. Thus, eastern Germany was the land of the "Junkers" (meaning literally "young lords"), as the frequently reactionary and overbearing aristocracy were reproachfully called. East Prussian estates were inherited by primogeniture—i.e., the property all went to the first-born son. Younger sons frequently received the choicest positions in the army and the civil service.

The serfs had been legally liberated in eastern Germany during the Prussian reform era of 1807-1813. But in fact little else had changed in the traditional relations between the Junkers and the peasants. In the province of East Prussia, for example, the Junkers had the legal right to whip the servants of their manor as late as 1918. They also appointed the village school teachers and had a veto over the appointment of the Lutheran Church ministers of their parishes. No teacher or minister was likely to receive a position unless they were sure that his views were sound.

*The German retreat
from the policy of free trade*

DESPITE their privileged position, the Junkers had been hit hard by the economic crisis of the mid-1870's. They had put much capital into improving their soil, but the investment looked like a bad one. Sharecroppers or farm hands became hard to find, because many of the younger peasants, disgusted with the hard labor on unyielding farms, moved to the large cities and joined the industrial proletariat or emigrated to America. Shortage of labor increased the Junkers' inability to compete with the cheap food imported from the more fertile areas of the United States, Russia, Rumania, and Hungary, and roused their opposition to proposals to push the industrialization of Germany. The army, in which the Junkers generally were officers, was likewise averse to greater industrialization and was bent on saving agriculture because, in the era before mechanized warfare, the soldier of peasant stock was considered superior to the urbanized soldier, and because it wanted to make Germany agriculturally self-sufficient in case of war.

Bismarck proposed that the state should go to the rescue of the Junkers. He had by this time broken his alliance with the National Liberals (page 331), who believed in free trade, and was seeking the support of the industrialists, landowners, and clericals in the Conservative and Center parties. The industrialists, concentrated in western Germany for the most part, not only wanted protection from foreign competition but also preferred that eastern Germany remain agricultural so as to provide Germany with food

382

and stay out of the race for the domestic market in manufactured articles. The combined pressure of Junkers, army, civil service, and industrialists induced Bismarck to introduce a tariff law placing high duties on imported foodstuffs and manufactures. The new policy was adopted by the Reichstag in 1879, reversing among the great commercial powers the trend toward free trade that had begun with the repeal of the English Corn Laws in 1846.

Protection proved advantageous to industry but could not offset falling agricultural prices on the world market. About 1890 the Junkers were again in the same predicament as in the 1870's. Mortgage foreclosures became frequent. Mass migration from the countryside to the industrialized urban centers went on as before. The Junkers, despite Bismarck's qualms about increasing the Polish minority, brought in Polish workers from Russia because they lacked farm hands and the Poles worked hard for low wages. Bismarck put a stop to Polish labor immigration in 1885, but his successor was to restore it. On the other hand, his successors continued the protective tariff policy, and other nations eventually followed suit.

REALISM IN SCIENCE
AND THE ARTS

REALISM as understood during the last decades of the nineteenth century tended to differ from earlier forms of realism in its emphasis upon empiricism, the doctrine that experience and experiment are the best means of ascertaining truth. It allowed room for rationalism, the doctrine that human reason is also a source of knowledge, but only if reason is based upon empirically ascertainable facts. It therefore became more closely affiliated than before with materialism, the doctrine that the only basis of the world is perceptible matter, and that everything, including spirit and psyche, is but a function of matter. The historical materialism (or economic determinism) of Karl Marx was a special application of philosophical materialism. In America during these decades there emerged an ethical philosophy known as pragmatism, which held that good and evil are not absolutes but are relative to the outcome of thoughts and actions. The astounding advance of the sciences in the 1880's helped to promote this empirical, materialistic, and pragmatic realism.

The germ theory
and other advances in medicine

SCIENTIFIC advance was particularly notable in the field of medicine. Perhaps the greatest discoveries made in the nineteenth century were in connection with the study of the microbe. On the basis of work done on bacteria since the seventeenth century, the German physician Robert Koch isolated the anthrax bacillus (1876), the tuberculosis bacillus (1882), and the cholera germ (1883). His   383 work made the germ theory of medicine inescapable, and the French chemist Louis Pasteur was able to apply the growing knowledge of germs to the treatment of several diseases of humans and plants. Pasteur, a pious Catholic, spent a long time in prayer before he first applied an antirabies vaccine (1885), for vaccination had hitherto been used only for smallpox, and he saved his patient's life. Modern methods of treating disease by immunization and of purifying foods by heating to high temperatures (pasteurization), although indebted to earlier theory and practice, really date from Pasteur's experiments.

Some great psychologists and psychiatrists of this period dared to step across the boundary between medicine and psychology. Jean Martin Charcot in France studied the diseases of the nervous system and promoted the science of neurology. Cesare Lombroso in Italy, though his theory on the congenital criminal has been proved wrong, provided a scientific foundation for the study of criminology.

*Some discoveries
in physics and technology*

THE AGE of realism was especially proud of its accomplishments in physics and chemistry. Helmholtz, Maxwell, and Mendelejeff are among the scientists already well-known whose work continued in this decade. Marcelin Berthelot systematized the science of organic chemistry, showing, among other things, that organic chemical phenomena need no "vital force" to operate but are subject to the laws valid throughout the physical universe. In addition, he did valiant work in thermodynamics and explosives at the same time that he served France as

Louis Pasteur is pictured by L'Illustration *in his laboratory.*

a senator and then as a minister. Heinrich Hertz, working with the electromagnetic theory of light developed by Faraday, Maxwell, and others, produced (c. 1888) the invisible waves that have since become known as "Hertzian radiation" and studied their optical properties. Hertzian waves were in turn to furnish the theoretical basis for wireless communication (page 452).

*Science
and scientism in history*

THE REALISTIC spirit, sometimes sneered at as mere "scientism," also crept into the writing of history. Historical objectivity, it was now generally felt, must not be warped by any system of philosophy or any set of values. The "scientific" historian Theodor Mommsen, the only historian ever to win a Nobel Prize (1902), nevertheless betrayed in his works on Roman history his enthusiasm for liberalism. Hippolyte Taine was another representative of the school of historians who deliberately sought to make history an empirical science. In keeping with the theory of literature which he had propounded, Taine gave a prominent place in his historical method to the *faculté maîtresse* (the predominant characteristic) in the man, movement, or age with which he was dealing. Once he became convinced he had found it, he went into minute detail to characterize his subject within this selected pattern. When he wrote his monumental work on *The Origins of Contemporary France* (1876-1894), he was still pained and distressed by the indignities he had witnessed during the Commune. He attributed the history of France since the eighteenth century largely to the French *esprit philosophique* (speculative nature). As a result, the work leaves the reader with the feeling that the French Revolution, to which he devotes most of his space, was all an avoidable error.

With the historian Heinrich von Treitschke, German historiography, though still striving for scientific objectivity, became notoriously nationalistic. Treitschke was the son of a Saxon officer. As a young man, under the impact of Bismarck's empire-building, he became the herald of Prussianism. Treitschke did not consider himself any less a realist because of his preference for German nationalism. In his search for data he was conscientious and careful. But the result was somewhat less than detached. His major work, *The History of Germany in the Nineteenth Century,* began to appear in 1879, after the Reich was safely founded, though at the time of his death his account was to reach only the year 1847. To him and his generation (outside the Socialist parties) an outstanding reality of political life was the nation, and to him the German nation, as embodied in the German Reich and ruled by the military power of Prussia, was the fulfillment of the history of mankind. He saw in Great Britain the enemy *par excellence* of Germany—which was something relatively novel in German thinking. The popularity of Treitschke among Germans was enormous.

The idealist historians of the late nineteenth century

THREE historians of this period stand out as contributors in the field of cultural history. One of these was Lord Acton, who wrote no books but produced so many essays, reviews, and lectures that they have been posthumously published in several volumes with enough left over for several more. In the 1890's he planned the *Cambridge Modern History,* a systematic symposium of the world's outstanding specialists. He thought of history not as class struggle or as the inexorable and amoral outcome of either a dialectical process or of political conflict but as man's conscious striving for liberty. His German contemporary Wilhelm Dilthey reacted to the scientistic trend in historical research by insisting upon the difference between the natural sciences and the social sciences. He propounded the concept of the human personality as a product of historical development and contemporary conditions. In several biographies of German philosophers and literary figures he tried to *understand* rather than to *describe* them—to place them in their setting, both historical and contemporary, in order to grasp more fully the interplay between the individual mind and its historical and social setting. The unique values of a given era or individual rather than the establishment of general historical laws were the object of Dilthey's scholarship.

Perhaps most aloof from the trends of his time was the Swiss historian Jakob Christoph Burckhardt. During his lifetime he was known as the foremost expert on the civilization of the Italian Renaissance, although he is today also well known for his lectures on the place of force and freedom in history. His central thesis was that the struggle for power in itself is evil, that the core of history is the development of the human spirit. But he had little faith in the future. He was skeptical of Americans, Jews, democrats and socialists, and he saw in force a stark reality that might ultimately prevail. His pessimism led him to fear the emergence of totalitarian states in the twentieth century.

The European intellectuals' criticism of American culture

AN APPRECIABLE shift in the attitude of European intellectuals toward America now began to be discernible. While the New World continued for some to be the land of promise, for others it was only a land of a new barbarism. Burckhardt and others said disparaging things about America. A fast-settling conviction in certain European circles held that America was but a new Rome borrowing heavily from a better culture and with very little intellectual depth of its own.

At least four reasons can be assigned for this impression. In the first place, from the early 1880's on, America had become the great melting pot of the white race, whereas in the same period the European intelligentsia had become prone to think of their respective countries as inhabited by homogeneous nationalities that had lived there for centuries. Secondly, few towns of America were over a century old, and so they generally could boast no cultural accumulation, no medieval churches or universities, no Renaissance theaters or baroque opera houses, no eighteenth-century palaces or nineteenth-century museums, and they had to be content with a modest school or library, crude houses, or mansions and university buildings that were often patent copies of European models. Thirdly, a blatant materialism and corruption had characterized the two administrations of President Grant and had shocked Europe's intellectuals, who preferred discretion at least in such matters. Fourthly, the fact that in America money could be more quickly acquired than culture led to the appearance in Europe of a large number of American tourists who were perhaps not entirely representative of their countrymen but who were judged as Americans rather than as tourists. More friendly views of America appeared with Lord Bryce's *The American Commonwealth* (1888) and the novels of Henry James, the American expatriate, whose frequently rich American characters were not always lovable but did not suffer in comparison with their frequently effete European confreres.

*Naturalism
in French literature*

THE TREND of the realistic novel toward naturalism was particularly marked in France during the 1880's. "Naturalism," in this usage, describes the literary tendency to observe natural and particularly psychological phenomena with scientific thoroughness and to describe them with painstaking detail and conscientious truthfulness. The novelist Gustave Flaubert and the historian-critic Taine had prepared the ground for this thorough literary realism. But the first avowed French naturalists were the Goncourt brothers. Beginning as historians of art and of manners, they developed an interest in the strange and exceptional that soon found vent in fiction based upon extraordinary characters of their own acquaintance.

Émile Zola soon rivaled the claim of the Goncourts to have founded the naturalist "school" of French novelists. Zola was aware that realistic emotions could hardly be expressed without the intrusion of the author's feelings. On the other hand, he aspired to make his novels "experimental." He never quite succeeded in reconciling the two tendencies. But that very fact gave his writings an attractiveness they might not have had otherwise, for he dealt with lowly, coarse, and sometimes repellent subjects in the effort to achieve the detachment of the chemist in his laboratory or of the surgeon in his operating room. Although his novels became best sellers, his contemporaries sometimes found it hard to feel any sympathy with his characters. He had drawn them from life, and he took careful notes in preparation for the description of some of them, studiously avoiding the sentimental and the hypocritical. In the twenty volumes of his Rougon-Macquart novels (1870-1893), he traced the story of a family descended from insane and stupid ancestors. Several generations of drunkards, seducers, and murderers, redeemed by an occasional honest peasant, beautiful actress, or brave soldier were accounted for before their creator deserted the genealogical novel to turn to novels of reform. Zola's friend and protégé, Guy de Maupassant, particularly in his sometimes brutal short stories, was a thorough realist. He had an eagle eye for the pettiness of men and things, and in conciseness and precision of writing he had few equals. Paul Bourget became the foremost realist in the field of the psychological novel.

Literary naturalism in some other countries — IN THE late 1880's naturalism invaded German literature. The foremost German naturalistic writer was Gerhart Hauptmann. His play *Before Dawn,* first performed in 1889, opened up what in German literary history became known as "the literary revolution of 1889." Theatergoers were not accustomed to seeing man's misery rawly portrayed on the stage. Hauptmann's most famous play, *The Weavers* (1892), dealt with an episode during the Silesian weavers' strike of 1844. Contemporaries found it harsh that the only person of unblemished character in the play was the one who was killed at the end. The prevalent Victorian sentimentality preferred a happier ending.

Even if the outstanding English poets of this day were still the great moral idealists Browning and Tennyson, several British novelists were realists. Robert Louis Stevenson, despite the fantastic symbolic elements in *The Strange Case of Dr. Jekyll and Mr. Hyde* (1886), may well belong among them because of the painstaking realism of some of his other works. Although Thomas Hardy also wrote some tales of fantasy, perhaps his best novels are realistic accounts of man's frustration, and they have sometimes been interpreted—perhaps wrongly—as indictments of certain social institutions—for example, of marriage, in *Jude the Obscure* (1896).

Realism was nothing new in Russian literature. In the 1860's and 1870's Ivan Sergeevich Turgenev had written realistic novels for which he became famous. Russian realism, blended with lofty idealism and religious contrition, reached its summit in the works of Tolstoy and Feodor Mikhailovich Dostoyevsky. Tolstoy's *Anna Karenina* (1873-1876) was perhaps his greatest triumph after *War and Peace.* In it he described the dull aristocratic society of St. Petersburg as the background for an unhappy marriage that ends in adultery and suicide. He wrote several less famous novels during the 1880's. But by that time Tolstoy had begun to be a mystic, firmly convinced of an inner communion between God and man that needed no civilized institutions or cultural paraphernalia to be realized. Dostoyevsky's greatest masterpiece,

388

The Brothers Karamazov (1879-1880), tells the story of the psychological crises through which four temperamentally different brothers pass when one of them murders their father. Some critics have seen in the four brothers an effort to symbolize four national types prominent in Dostoyevsky's Russia—the mystic, the soldier, the intellectual, and the maladjusted.

The influence of impressionism in painting

NATURALISM found expression in the fine arts chiefly through the works of the impressionists. Monet, Pissarro, and others painted scenes of everyday life with a vision and technique that had developed out of the tenets of the older Barbizon school yet made use of advances in the knowledge of color and optics. They sought to portray the full character of light in its fleeting aspects by dabs of pure color, to paint on canvas what the eye sees unencumbered by memory or intellect. Monet painted several pictures of the same subject (e.g., the Cathedral of Rouen) under different light conditions in order to emphasize this aspect of change in nature. Degas and Pierre Auguste Renoir used impressionist color to construct designs from nature.

In the course of time, impressionism was to move abroad from France. The Dutchman Jozef Israëls and the German Max Liebermann were outstanding among those who were influenced by the work of the impressionists.

"The Café de la Nouvelle-Athènes," a meeting place of the impressionists, was sketched by Edgar Degas in 1878.

389

Rodin: A study in bronze for "Burghers of Calais," 1884.

In fact, the impact of the movement was so great that it soon became the basis of instruction in most of the art academies; and so in a sense impressionism became academic and other painters were to revolt against its strictures.

*Realism
in the art of sculpture*

REALISTS were also to be found among the sculptors. Two great men dominated the sculpture of the 1880's—Constantin Meunier, a Belgian, and Auguste Rodin, a Frenchman. Meunier robustly rendered subjects barred by academic conventions—

farmers, miners, and laborers. Rodin tried to convey the underlying spirit of a subject. He did not hesitate to let a work emerge only partly from a block of stone or to leave sections roughly finished if by so doing he might more strongly express his meaning. Émile Antoine Bourdelle, a pupil of Rodin, continued the tradition of his teacher but developed the free-moving quality of Rodin into a strict simplicity. Paris in 1900 created a Rodin Museum, one of the few museums ever devoted exclusively to a single artist.

Verdi, Brahms, Wagner, and other composers

IN MUSIC romanticism, classicism, and realism existed side by side during this period. An already marked nationalistic trend continued and induced some composers to rely for their material on folklore and history. Outstanding among them was Modest Petrovich Moussorgsky. Romanticism found gifted exponents in the Russian Tchaikovsky and the Czech Anton Dvořák. Classicism in the Italian tradition was represented by the last great works of Verdi. In *Otello* (1887), and *Falstaff* (1893), completed when he was eighty years old, he continued his reputation as one of the greatest composers of opera. Classic forms persisted also in the works of the Belgian-French César Franck and the Austrian Anton Bruckner. The German composer Johannes Brahms stands out as an individualist in this century of musical individualists because while his contemporaries were writing program music, he confined himself to the classical style of Beethoven's day, emphasizing purity of form and clarity of development rather than impressionistic tone-color. Brahms' symphonies, sonatas, string quartets, and choral works are rich and warm, but their emotional qualities are expressed within the framework of the composition—the reverse of Wagner's work, where dramatic requirements dictate form.

In the 1870's and 1880's Wagner at last gained world-wide attention. Verdi's *Aïda* (1871), written at the request of the extravagant Egyptian khedive Ismail Pasha, reveals a Wagnerian influence. In Bayreuth in 1876 all four parts of Wagner's tetralogy *Der Ring des Nibelungen* were performed for the first time, and each part was repeated twice. The German emperor and princes graced the occasion. In 1882 an opera house built solely for the presentation of Wagner's works was inaugurated in Bayreuth with the first performance of his *Parsifal*.

Realism in musical composition

DRAMATIC realism flourished notably in opera, where it became known by the Italian word *verismo*. Georges Bizet, who is said to have done for spoken rhythm in opera what Verdi did for melody and Wagner for instrumental music, was among the first to introduce *verismo,* in the form of local color, realistic characters, and contemporary settings, into his operas. This was particularly true of his last and best opera, *Carmen* (1875), based on the well-known novel of Prosper Mérimée. *Verismo* was thereafter to be found chiefly in Italian opera. Among the best-known veristic operas were eventually to be found *Cavalleria Rusti-cana* (1890) by Pietro Mascagni, *I Pagliacci* (1892) by Ruggiero Leon-cavallo, and *La Tosca* (1900) and *The Girl of the Golden West* (1910) by Giacomo Puccini. In these operas peasants, actors, prisoners, and gold-rushers sing their hearts out in melodramatic situations that do not seem totally implausible.

Realism in orchestral music started with the so-called "program music" introduced in earlier decades by Berlioz and Liszt. Music was no longer con-sidered self-sufficient or "absolute"—mere music and nothing more—but was expected to convey also an underlying meaning or mood. Depicting natural sounds was not new in music. Beethoven, for instance, had used that device in his "Pastoral Symphony." But the realistic rendering of such sounds by means of orchestration did not come to full fruition until Richard Strauss and Claude Debussy. Both of these composers were young in the 1880's, however, and their greatest work lay in the future.

THE REVOLT

AGAINST REALISM

NOT ALL the people at a given period of history can be correctly said to have subscribed to the prevailing "climate of opinion." In the midst of the realism of the 1880's, large numbers, obviously, were utopian, Christian, idealist, nonobjective—repelled by realism and by materialism in both the economic and the philosophical sense of that word. Obviously also, many people—we have already cited Tolstoy as an outstanding example—vacillated and would switch from one attitude to another. Hence, the prevalent realism and materialism had to contend with other isms for control of the hearts and minds of men.

The significance of Nietzsche's philosophy BECAUSE of some rash words quoted out of context Friedrich Nietzsche has sometimes been re-garded as an exponent of German imperialism and Teutonic lust for war. Notwithstanding, Bismarck's Germany did not have Nietzsche's approval, and he thoroughly despised the Germans, as he did most nationalities. Early in his life Nietzsche was under the influence of Richard Wagner, but he later became one of Wagner's bitter critics.

Nietzsche's first important book was *The Birth of Tragedy from the Spirit of Music* (1872). It contained an exposition of the antagonistic forces in the human character. One of them was the artistic impulse that looks for harmony in the universe; to this Nietzsche gave the name of "Apollonian." The other was the artistic impulse that seeks to express the dynamic will to live and to acquire power; to this Nietzsche gave the name of "Dionysian."

This book and subsequent writings made clear that the Dionysian attitude, according to Nietzsche, is "the most extreme limit of a yea-saying attitude to life." Since he put great store by a proud, affirmative view of life, he rejected the humble, submissive Apollonian philosophies of Socrates, Judaism, Buddhism, and Christianity as "life-undermining" forces. He called their ethics "a slave morality" detrimental to achieving man's destiny. Man's destiny, according to Nietzsche, was a society that would be ruled by a new aristocracy. He was convinced, however, that the new aristocracy, the "supermen," would not come unless mankind were set free from old and (according to Nietzsche) bad ethical standards. Therefore, he demanded "a transvaluation of all values" for the stalwart few who would be ready to bear the burden of ruling the world.

The highest virtue for Nietzsche was the kind of courage that he called the "will to power." It was to be used for the better development of already well-developed individuals. Convinced that truth was not for hoi polloi but for the few, he candidly set forth his shocking credo in his greatest work, *Thus Spake Zarathustra* (1883-1885), which urged man not to let traditional concepts of morality stand in the way of human perfectability. It was couched in a symbolic, dithyrambic style that had been used by some of the Hebrew prophets and pre-Socratic Greek philosophers and is sometimes said to be the summit of German prose. He was to return to the subject again in his last work *Ecce Homo* (1900), which was written a few weeks before his mental collapse. Nietzsche thus brought up the end of the procession of nineteenth-century philosophers of progress.

The impact of Nietzsche on continental civilization

THE REACTION to Nietzsche's startling philosophy was perhaps just what his contempt of his contemporaries had led him to expect. The Socialists, whom he had attacked as preachers of the ancient Judaeo-Christian ethics in materialistic guise, immediately labeled him an enemy of the proletariat. Convinced democrats rejected him because he scorned the democratic state. The organized religions were against him because he considered Christianity a religion of the weak. At first, the intellectuals of Scandinavia, Russia, Italy, and, above all, France understood him better than did the Germans. It was Georg Brandes, the Danish literary critic, who in the late 1880's first made him famous.

Petty nationalists and racialists eventually were to adopt Nietzsche as their prophet. Mussolini as a young man became acquainted with his philosophy and apparently applied it to himself. Some German businessmen and officers of the general staff, already intoxicated by Wagner's and Treitschke's nationalism, thought of themselves as Nietzsche's supermen. But a few men understood him, and through them many learned that a German philosopher had dared to scorn the whole conventional moral code for what he audaciously considered a higher morality.

The Danish cartoonist Olaf Gulbransson caricatures the Norwegian dramatic titan, Henrik Ibsen.

*Henrik Ibsen
and Björnstjerne Björnson*

A SECOND titan among writers who—in a different way—went beyond realism was Henrik Ibsen of Norway. He, too, had started as a romantic. In his middle years he became famous as the foremost realist playwright and, next to Zola perhaps, the greatest continental critic of the stuffiness that flourished—alongside Promethean radicalism and divine discontents—in the long and varied Victorian era. Realistic plays, like *A Doll's House* (1879), *Ghosts* (1881), and *An Enemy of the People* (1882), came as an irritant to many of his contemporaries. In these plays he laid bare the dependent position of wives, the falseness of married life without love, and the corruptibility of some of the pillars of society. He won a following as a playwright and a reformer, and Norwegian society was split in two over the question of puritan morality versus the new freedom.

In the mid-1880's, however, Ibsen grew less concerned with revealing the raw truth about social problems and more concerned with the inner workings of the human personality. His lyrical play *Peer Gynt* (1867) had already shown that a man may mistake the true sources of contentment. Perhaps he came to believe that under certain circumstances what men call

394

truth might do more harm than good. That is the message of his play *The Wild Duck* (1884), whose heroine commits suicide upon learning from a well-intentioned fact-finder the secret of her illegitimate birth. He turned to writing psychological plays, of which *The Wild Duck* itself was the first one in which the stream of consciousness or the conflict of character is the principal theme. Naturalism as portrayed in the analysis of specific social problems had been superseded by a kind of symbolism—the examination of a single character as representative of an enduring moral conflict.

Björnstjerne Björnson, Norway's greatest novelist and poet, and, next to Ibsen, her greatest dramatist, had an intellectual career that to a lesser degree reflects a similar literary development. Though he began as a romantic, his work belongs usually to the realist school, consisting largely of social plays and novels of peasant life rich in local color. In the first part of his play *Beyond Our Power* (1883; the second part did not come until 1895) he turned to mysticism, and portrayed the intensity of the religious experience. For him, too, realism was not always enough.

The rise of the symbolist school

ABOUT the time of Ibsen's espousal of what has loosely been called symbolism, a school of symbolists appeared, with men like Stéphane Mallarmé in France, Maurice Maeterlinck in Belgium, and William Butler Yeats in Ireland. How far these younger men were influenced by the example of Ibsen is a matter of controversy, but they too felt that realism was not enough, that the true artist must probe deep into man's abiding inner conflicts, into the clash within human minds rather than between natural forces.

A group of poets associated with Mallarmé and including Arthur Rimbaud and Paul Verlaine made up a loosely organized school sometimes called the "French symbolists." They used image, analogy, archaisms, and obscure figures to express symbolically rather than directly the thought which they sought to convey. They adopted free verse, the prose poem, and metrical innovations in protest against dead forms. But philosophically they had the same motivation as that which had induced Ibsen and Nietzsche to revolt against positivism and materialism: Nature was not enough; science was inadequate to explain the deeper mysteries of the universe; introspection, mysticism, a higher speculative morality might help to fill the gap.

Esthetics and estheticism

THE EFFECTS of industrialization, social unrest, nationalism, and the teachings of Nietzsche and Ibsen bewildered many intellectuals. Some of them tried to find an escape in a purely esthetic outlook. To them beauty in itself became the only goal worth living for. That attitude found its foremost advocate in Walter Pater in whose novel *Marius the Epicurean* (1885) the hero gropes through paganism toward high principles of action. Pater promoted among English

"The Bedroom at Arles," by Vincent van Gogh.

intellectuals the movement favoring "art for art's sake." In two short books on art criticism the Anglo-American painter James McNeill Whistler taught that the artist should be selfishly occupied in seeking artistic perfection. Estheticism eventually took a turn toward deliberate intellectual snobbishness. That attitude was particularly characteristic of Oscar Wilde, whose unconcealed defiance of convention (combined with his bad judgment) led to his spending two years in jail, from which was to come his melancholy "Ballad of Reading Gaol" (1898). One of the most popular of the rollicking English operettas for which Sir Arthur S. Sullivan provided the music and W. S. Gilbert the libretto, *Patience* (1881), burlesqued this "very singularly deep young man," who is portrayed as privately admitting:

> In short, my mediaevalism's affectation,
> Born of a morbid love of admiration!

Still, Wilde was to produce some of the most brilliant epigrams in English stage comedy, a great tragedy (*Salomé*, 1894), a fine symbolist novel (*The Picture of Dorian Gray*, 1891), and some beautiful tales.

Antirealism in the fine arts

IN THE fine arts the term "post-impressionism" is loosely applied to a number of painters who, although differing in aim and technique, broke away from the impressionists and set out in new directions far removed from the exact copying of nature.

Georges Seurat exploited more fully the new findings in optics and color. His works are formal, almost stylized arrangements painted with little dots of color (pointillism). Paul Cézanne recognized the essential structural and geometric quality of natural forms and portrayed their relationships in space by means of color. Paul Gauguin used brilliant hues and radical simplification of line to awaken imagination. His subjects are not lifelike or true to nature but serve to construct his imagery. The Dutch-born Vincent van Gogh used the impressionists' colors and his own spontaneous sense of form to express his personal emotions. The link that united these men was their belief that the artist may amplify or distort the visual impression in order to give it his own interpretation. The French sculptor Aristide Maillol, like the post-impressionists, revolted against merely representational art. His work emphasized the massive quality—strength and repose.

A liberal pope and the Catholic tradition

THE CHURCHES of all creeds steadfastly refused to believe with the Socialists and others that the traditional morality was a historically determined class morality or with Nietzsche that it was outworn. To them it was the result of divine inspiration, Christian teaching, and age-old interpretation. The hierarchical organization of the Catholic Church made it possible for the pope to speak authoritatively for Catholics in such matters—especially after the proclamation in 1870 of the dogma of papal infallibility.

Leo XIII became pope in 1878. One of his first acts was to restore Catholic learning to a higher level than it had occupied for a long time. By his encyclical *Aeterni Patris* (1879) he made the study of Thomism (the rational, common-sense philosophy of St. Thomas Aquinas) the central subject of Catholic philosophy. Leo XIII held also that there was no necessary antagonism between religion and science, and the recent careers of devout men of science like Mendel and Pasteur seemed to prove him right.

The decree of papal infallibility had created a crisis in church affairs and had led to the threat of a serious schism of the "Old Catholics." To counteract this hostility, the loyal clergy helped to create Catholic political parties in countries where they did not exist, and strengthened such parties in countries where they already existed. Where there were no clerical parties, as for instance in Great Britain and the United States, Leo XIII now encouraged nonpolitical Catholic organizations, in order to make the church's voice heard in an indirect way. In England, a Catholic revival had been in progress for several decades, with John Henry Newman, turned Catholic in 1845, as one of its leading figures. Newman had gained great prominence by his lectures on university education in the 1850's (published in 1873 as *The Idea of a University Defined*), in which he pleaded for a broad philosophical and moral rather than a factual education. In his *Apologia pro Vita Sua* (1864), he explained why he had espoused Catholicism. Leo XIII made him a cardinal 397 in 1879, and even non-Catholics were pleased. In America, to counter the anti-Catholic politics of the American Protective Association, the pope gave his support to the founding of the Catholic University at Washington (1887) and made James Gibbon, archbishop of Baltimore, the first American cardinal.

Although Leo negotiated with Bismarck to bring the German anti-Catholic campaign to a close (page 332), he refused to make any compromise with the Italian government. He continued Pius IX's policy of refusing to recognize Rome as the capital of the Kingdom of Italy. He spurned the Italian Law of Papal Guaranties and, upon failing to win satisfactory concessions, like Pius IX confined himself to the Vatican grounds.

The Ferry Laws and anticlericalism

ONE OF Leo's greatest successes was the partial peace that he effected between the French Republic and the clericals. When Grévy became president of France, Jules Ferry was named minister of education and immediately undertook to diminish the political influence of the French clergy. This policy he continued as prime minister, and when he was forced to resign (page 429), his successors carried it on. Ferry was convinced that the Republic was endangered so long as the clergy retained the powerful role in the educational system that had been assigned to them when Louis Napoleon was president of the Second Republic. One of Ferry's most famous anticlerical bills (1880) was intended to reform education. It forbade anyone "to teach in state or private schools or to direct a teaching establishment of any kind if he belongs to an unauthorized religious order." Since the Jesuits, having been expelled in the eighteenth century, had returned to France without official sanction in the nineteenth, they were not "authorized." The bill was defeated in the Senate, but Jesuit teachers were now again expelled from France by ministerial decree; and another such decree obliged other unauthorized orders to become authorized within three months or face dissolution. Another important step was the opening of *lycées* (government secondary schools) for girls. Until then the education of girls had been almost exclusively in the hands of the nuns. A law of 1882 made primary education obligatory, gratuitous, and secular.

Social and economic anti-Semitism

MEANWHILE another religious issue had begun to assume significant political proportions. The Jews had been granted emancipation by a series of laws in the late eighteenth and early nineteenth century in several countries of western and central Europe, but they were often driven by social pressure into a few circumscribed professions—business, art, literature, the press, the theater, medicine, and the bar—where they were regarded as conspicuous intruders and where whatever success they won made them all the more conspicuous. In the backward parts of Austria-Hungary, in eastern Europe, and occasionally even in France and Germany, religious anti-Semitism was strong. Several times in the 1880's and after, it found expression in an accusation of "ritual murder" —that the Jews had killed a Christian child to use his blood in some religious ceremony. Such accusations were made in Hungary (Tisza-Eszlar, 1882), in Greece (Corfu, 1891), in Bohemia (Polna, 1899) and in Germany (Xanten, 1892, and Konitz, 1900). In Russia, pogroms (organized massacres of Jews) became especially notorious, and the government, if it did not instigate them, did little to prevent them.

The pseudo-science of races and anti-Semitism

UNTIL the 1850's anti-Semitism could be accounted for on religious and economic grounds. It was explained by the religious separateness of the Jews, resentment of the Jews as an allegedly unassimilable element in society, fear or jealousy of their power in business and the professions, danger of pollution by intermarriage with Jews, or other considerations, valid or invalid. Anti-Semitism did not become a systematic political ideology, however, until Count Arthur de Gobineau published his *Essay on the Inequality of the Human Races* (1853-1855). In it he developed a pseudo-scientific racial theory to the effect that the Aryans were the superior race, to which all other races were inferior. The Semites, originally close to the Aryans, had adulterated their blood by intermarriage with inferior races, and from that adulteration had come the Jews. This pollution had in modern times reached France—in fact, the whole of Europe. The hereditary Aryan aristocrats, whom Gobineau identified with the blond peoples, in modern times had become a hapless minority, while the teeming dark-haired—i.e., inferior—masses held political power. Thus Gobineau made anti-Semitism a weapon for hard-pressed conservatives in the war against the rise of democracy.

Gobineau's book remained practically unnoticed for many years, and might have remained innocuous but for Richard Wagner. Wagner had long been a notorious anti-Semite. He and Gobineau collaborated on an anti-Semitic essay entitled "Heroism and Christianity" which was published in the Wagner Society's bimonthly *Bayreuther Blätter* in 1881. Political anti-Semitism made more rapid progress among central European nationalists thereafter. Totally unscientific though Gobineau's anthropology was, it found ready listeners among those whose ire had been roused by other anti-Semitic considerations.

THE GILDED AGE

IN AMERICA (c. 1865-1890)

MATERIAL progress and a maturing industrial economy were bringing to America the same sort of economic and social problems as those western Europe was concurrently experiencing—urbanization, slums, labor-employer antagonisms, and unsettled relationships between agriculture and industry. At the same time the United States was being pulled into the arena of European politics, now spread over the greater part of the globe. In the New World, as in the Old, industrialization was accompanied by the rise of the corporation as the dominant form of business organization and by the corollary combination of industries in pools and trusts. The generation that followed the Civil War saw perhaps more new millionaires than any other period of history. American art and letters benefited from their wealth and suffered from their lack of cultural background.

Combinations and trusts in American business

THE PANIC of 1873, followed by depression and the rapid decline of prices, had led in the United States to industrial pools for controlling prices and dividing markets. In the eighties, pools were superseded by trusts, of which John D. Rockefeller's Standard Oil Company was among the first (1879) and largest. As in Europe, these organizations squeezed little businesses out, separated the worker from the owner by the vast impersonal wall of stocks and bonds, and concentrated tremendous wealth and power in the hands of a very few. In the United States economic power was used, through pressure and manipulation both legal and illegal, to gain political power; political power in turn was used to enhance the position of big business. Hence the post-Civil War era was generally one of high protective tariffs and (until discontinued in 1871) of land grants for railroads (with a hands-off-business policy otherwise). It was an era of Republican predominance in federal politics. Between 1868 and 1912 only one Democrat, Grover Cleveland, was able to win the presidency though he did so twice (1885-1889; 1893-1897).

Despite the Democratic president's inclination to frown upon "Big Business," the Supreme Court's interpretation in 1886 of the Fourteenth Amendment gave the corporation a peculiar immunity from the control of local government. The prohibition upon each state of any action that would "deprive any person of life, liberty, and property without due process of law," intended to protect the freed slaves, was interpreted to apply also to the legal "person" of a corporation. This interpretation, when applied also to the Fifth as well as the Fourteenth Amendment, made any kind of regulation, whether federal or local, liable to disapproval by the courts as a deprivation of the corporation's liberty and property rights "without due process of law." Social legislation, already well under way in several European countries before the First World War, was thereby delayed in the United States.

American competition in the markets of the world

THE RAPID industrialization of the United States and the high protective tariff enabled American business gradually to dominate the home market. Furthermore, American iron, wheat, meat, shoes, and other products competed directly with Euro-

A contemporary drawing from a French magazine pictures an American barber shop of the 1870's. In such "tonsorial parlors," the American businessman discussed the issues of the day and, if a regular customer, could have his personal shaving mug placed in the rack.

pean products abroad and often undersold them. Thus American industrial expansion was indirectly a cause of the Europeans' search for new markets and new sources of raw materials in the late nineteenth century. It also contributed to the high-tariff movement of the eighties. The German and the French governments put high tariffs on American pork, for example, to protect domestic production. These protective measures led to a kind of tariff war in the 1880's. In the French instance it became known as the "Great American Pork Question" because the French government claimed American meat was contaminated and the American government retaliated with a tariff on French works of art (including wines). The "Great American Pork Question" did not prevent good feeling, however, between the citizens of the sister republics. A Franco-American Union presented F. A. Bartholdi's "Statue of Liberty" to the people of the United States, and several American Francophiles presented a smaller copy of it to the people of France. From islands in New York harbor and the Seine River, the two statues have ever since gazed in each other's direction across the ocean.

*Optimism
of American industry*

THE AMERICAN'S ability to compete successfully with European industrialists was in some part due to his having a new country to exploit. That newness meant not only vast and unused resources; it also meant being able to start new factories unencum-

401

bered by tradition and equipped with the latest mechanical processes and commercial techniques. American business knew little of the "cake of custom" and cared less for it. A psychology of "unlimited horizons," perhaps more convincing than the doubtful fact, developed. At any rate, almost every young, white American believed that he had only to apply himself to rise to fame. That conviction was popularized by the numerous novels of Horatio Alger, Jr., nearly all of which had the same plot of the country boy who by honesty, courage, and good fortune becomes the rich and honored man. Americans never wearied of that story, and enough striking successes happened in real life to make the stories seem plausible. In their exuberance the Americans peopled the vast reaches of the habitable West, drove the Indians from their lands and cooped them up on reservations, knit the American East and West together with a web of railroads and an interdependent economy, founded churches and universities, dug up fabulous riches in gold, silver, copper, coal, iron, and oil, cut down fabulous riches in virgin timber, and created within their own boundaries one of the world's greatest industrial empires, protected from without by a tariff wall and from within by free trade among the states. Mark Twain, writing in the seventies, called his times a Gilded Age. Often gaudy, crude, vulgar, and acquisitive, the generation of the Gilded Age was also vigorous, assertive, self-confident, and promising.

National color
in American literature

THE CHANGE in cultural standards was epitomized in the waning influence of the New England literary great (though most of them were still writing) and the rise of the western individualist and humorist Mark Twain (Samuel Langhorne Clemens) as the dominant literary figure. Despite his sentimentalism and his tall tales, Mark Twain was a realist. As chronicler of the Middle West and Far West in a series of stories that made the heroes of *Tom Sawyer* (1876) and *Huckleberry Finn* (1884) boon companions of many a boy in the western world, he brought the fresh air of the frontier to the East, where his earthy good humor found ready audiences. In collaboration with Charles Dudley Warner he depicted his own era, not altogether unsympathetically, in *The Gilded Age* (1873); and in *Innocents Abroad* (1869) and *A Connecticut Yankee at King Arthur's Court* (1889) he poked fun at archaic European manners and customs. Other western local-color novelists flourished in the seventies and eighties, although none of them achieved Mark Twain's stature.

At least two eastern novelists penetrated beyond local color to the spirit of the society in which they lived. William Dean Howells' earlier works were genteel chronicles of the middle-class East. A less sympathetic and more incisive dissecter of society was Henry James. His novels were subtle and penetrating psychological masterpieces. Both Howells and James were concerned from time to time with the contrast between European and American culture. James, whose brother William espoused the most American of philosophies (page 406), found the "rambunctious" American culture so little to his taste that he emigrated to England in 1876, eventually becoming a British citizen.

American poetry could boast several figures of lasting reputation. Longfellow, Whittier, Lowell, and Holmes all continued their work until the late 1880's or early 1890's. In addition, the younger generation produced at least two poets of genuine talent. The poetry of Sidney Lanier was rooted in the South. He had served as a Confederate soldier, and he lived a sick and broken man in the shadows of southern reconstruction and industrialization. But he was concerned not so much with the local scene as with poetry as art, particularly with its musical qualities and imagery. Another contemporary poet, Emily Dickinson, lived a retired, maidenly life in Amherst, Massachusetts, and wrote highly introspective and often mystical and cryptic lyrics for herself and her friends. With few exceptions, they remained unpublished in the Gilded Age and were unknown until 1924, when they were found to have a delicacy of thought, an epigrammatic quality, and a flair for the right word that put her in high critical esteem. On the whole, the first quarter-century after the Civil War was for American literature an interlude between the ebb of high romanticism and the flood of full-bodied realism that was to come with big-scale industrialization and the impact of European naturalism.

Dependence upon European fashions

VICTORIAN fashions, like Victorian architecture, did not emphasize simplicity. Both men and women of good society wore a large amount of clothing and exposed as little of the body as possible, even in bathing and cycling costumes. Whalebone corsets, high collars, high shoes, long gloves, large hats, large pieces of jewelry, ruchings, flounces, pleats, laces, satin, bustles, long trains, and somber colors marked women's attire. The gentleman's clothing rarely changed—stiffly starched collars and cuffs, dark cloth (or checked cloth for "sports"), stiff straw hats or derbies, black cravats. London and, more often, Paris dictated what the American woman of fashion would wear. Men's fashions were usually set by England and, more particularly, by England's aristocracy.

American artists under European influence

MORE THAN one American artist or writer, like Henry James, deserted the American milieu for the more mature cultural climate of Europe. Of the painters, Whistler and John Singer Sargent were the most noteworthy. Whistler, settling in England, executed notable portraits, including the familiar "Arrangements in Gray and Black" of Whistler's mother and of Carlyle, and a number of "Symphonies" and "Nocturnes." Sargent, painting first in France and later in London, became celebrated for his portraits in the tradition of Gainsborough and Reynolds.

Most young American artists of the period went abroad to study, usually to the École des Beaux-Arts in Paris, where they imbibed the pseudo- 403 classicism of the Second Empire or the landscape techniques of the Barbizon school. The Barbizon influence was apparent in the poetic landscapes of the painter George Inness; and William Morris Hunt, as painter and teacher of art, introduced the Barbizon school to Boston. John La Farge, after studying in Paris and in Hunt's atelier, became famous for his murals and particularly for his revival of medieval stained-glass-window decoration. La Farge's monumental approach in mural decoration was paralleled in the portrait sculpture of Saint-Gaudens, who was also trained at the Beaux-Arts and was schooled particularly in Renaissance art. Saint-Gaudens' figures of Farragut, Lincoln, and other national heroes express a dignity not seen before in American sculpture. His statue of a draped figure in Rock Creek Cemetery in Washington is poetic, almost mystical. He was the greatest single influence on later American sculpture. In painting, Thomas Eakins, also educated at the École in Paris, shows little European influence in his work, which is notable for its vigor and realism.

Eclecticism and American architecture

ARCHITECTURE in America reflected the esthetic confusion of Europe's architecture. The simple classical style gave way around the Civil War to an avalanche of period styles. Architects felt free to use and to combine the various styles of the past; and churches, public buildings, and houses of the rich boasted the "French" or the "Italian" or the Gothic style. A few of them reflected dignity, restraint, and good planning. Richard Morris Hunt, brother of the painter mentioned above, was one of the first American graduates of the École des Beaux-Arts. The houses he built for the rich were more than mere ostentatious imitations of the styles of earlier periods, but lesser architects and jerry-builders were guilty of extravagances in cheaper homes and buildings, which were often overloaded with wooden or iron ornament. Many architects of America as well as in Europe were aware of the architectural ills of their day. Henry Hobson Richardson, who also had attended the École, was one of them. He introduced the Romanesque style in the United States, hoping that its simplicity would mould a new architectural medium. Others thought that through a combination of the features of several past styles (eclecticism) a new idiom might arise.

The elevator and the American skyscraper

THEIR HOPES were premature. Period revival continued far into the twentieth century. But in the 1880's a new commercial architecture was born out of the ashes of the Chicago fire (1871). The opportunity to build anew; the development of the elevator from steam to hydraulic and eventually to electric power; the clay soil of Chicago (which made necessary some innovation if it was to be made to support the weight of high structures); the tremendous cost of land in the

404

city's central district—all combined to suggest skeletal iron or steel construction of tall buildings. Weight could thus be distributed throughout the metal frame and not borne entirely by the outside walls. Although most of the "skyscrapers" were decorated with classic or Gothic trim, those of Louis Sullivan proudly announced their commercial function and were unadorned by period dress. Sullivan's concept, "form follows function," was to have immense influence on future architecture.

Evolutionary theory and progress in America

IF EUROPEAN building styles were frequently imitated in the United States, the translation of European philosophy into the American vernacular was far more happily achieved. The impact of Darwinism and its broader implications was as great in America as it was in Europe. Darwin himself suggested that America might be the proof of his pudding: "The wonderful progress of the United States," he wrote (1871) in his *Descent of Man and Selection in Relation to Sex,* "as well as the character of the people, are the results of natural selection; for the more energetic, restless and courageous men from all parts of Europe have emigrated during the last ten or twelve generations to that great country and have there succeeded best."

Translated into Herbert Spencer's philosophy of inevitable social progress through evolution, Darwin's formula of change was particularly harmonious with the spirit of the Gilded Age. Its great American proselyte was John Fiske, exuberant social philosopher, historian, writer and lecturer, adept in reconciling religion with scientific evolution. Fiske's view was that evolution, far from denying God and the human soul, enhanced their glory. God is the infinite and rational power behind the evolutionary process. "In the deadly struggle for existence which has raged through aeons of time, the whole creation has been groaning and travailing together in order to bring forth that last consummate specimen of God's handiwork, the Human Soul." If this philosophy renewed faith in God, man, and enduring moral values, it was also a convenient justification of the status quo, whether good or bad.

Peirce, James, and the philosophy of pragmatism

THE PHILOSOPHY of pragmatism was in a way an adaptation of Darwinian theory to the realm of morals and thought. Rooted in the Darwinian concepts of change and chance in nature, pragmatism also reflected the utilitarianism of the Benthamites, the positivism of Comte, and the development of experimental psychology. Questioning the transcendental entities, major premises, categorical imperatives, and absolutes of "genteel" philosophy so popular in the mid-century, pragmatism asserted that truth is not an absolute in and of itself; the truth of any concept is to be tested by its logical or empirical consequences. The new thought, intended by its founders as a philosophical   405 inquiry into the nature of God and truth, became in the popular mind a justification of the active life. In any set of alternative choices, whatever worked, whatever was successful, was truest. Hence, truth, good, beauty are both variable and relative. What is true at one time and in one environment may be false somewhere else or at some other time.

The name "pragmatism" and the germ of this philosophy were first put forth by Charles S. Peirce, an American scientist, about 1875. Similar ideas were occasionally uttered among European men of science, but in America, where change was an accepted feature of everyday life, where a man's achievement was likely to be more important than his status, a philosophy that seemed to equate truth with success found ready listeners. William James, already famous for his exposition of experimental psychology in *Principles of Psychology* (1890), was later to popularize the pragmatic view in his *Will to Believe* (1897) and *Pragmatism: a New Name for Some Old Ways of Thinking* (1907). James found in pragmatism a means for restoring free will to philosophy. The deterministic meliorism of the Spencerians he replaced with the will to believe in free will derived from the necessity for positive action.

Suspect to most European philosophers as a piece of unredeemed American materialism or as a brazen denial of philosophy, pragmatism has nevertheless had a profound influence in American life. Its influence has even penetrated into Europe, in spite of its general rejection there. As a formal philosophy it has had few followers even in America, but as an attitude of mind and an approach to ethical problems it has borne fruit in many fields.

Evolutionary thought upon law and social theory

IDEAS OF evolutionary change of continuity through struggle, and of survival of the fittest—all of which tally with Darwin's teachings though they have older and broader foundations—permeated late nineteenth-century political concepts. In *The Common Law* (1881), Oliver Wendell Holmes, son of the physician and author, explained law as organic, as evolving according to "the felt needs of the times," instead of the static and changeless "law of nature and of nature's God." The application of an evolutionary view to social institutions created two opposing schools of the science of society. William Graham Sumner, Yale economist and sociologist, saw in Darwinism a good argument for laissez faire: "Liberty, inequality, survival of the fittest; non-liberty, equality, survival of the unfittest. The former carries society forward and favors all of its best members; the latter carries society downwards and favors all its worst members." On the other hand, Lester Frank Ward, professor of sociology at Brown University and the first president of the American Sociology Society, took an approach that departed from both laissez faire and Marxism. Social progress, he contended, evolved through conflicts of group needs and desires. Human intellect ought to be able to raise this struggle above the blind forces of evolutionary nature and to give it rational means and purposes. Arguing that only through the conscious direction of the evolution of social traditions and institutions could individual liberty be maintained, he was the precursor of the movement for "the scientific control of the social forces by the collective mind of society" that has received concrete expression in America only in recent years. Sumner was vastly influential; Ward went largely unheeded. Laissez faire remained the popular social philosophy for the America of their generation.

Social protest and realism in literature

LIKE WARD, Henry George, a poor San Francisco journalist, challenged the free-enterprise system. But, unlike Ward, he did not attack any basic American shibboleths, and he attracted an enormous following. In *Progress and Poverty* (1879), George argued that poverty resulted from progress because land, which was a natural gift belonging to society, tended as progress advanced to be appropriated by a few, who received in increasing rents the benefit of values created by and rightfully belonging to society. Of the agents of production— land, labor, and capital—only labor and capital were truly productive. Yet the increasing demand for land as societies developed created for the landlord an "unearned increment" that reduced the share rightfully belonging to labor and capital. George's solution was the "single tax"—to "appropriate all rent by taxation" and to "abolish all taxation save that upon land values." In this way the unearned increment would be returned to society without expropriation or violence. *Progress and Poverty* had an enormous sale, several millions in fact, not only in America but all over the world. Though his single-tax program was never adopted in its entirety, the idea of heavy taxes on increases in land values was fitted into existing tax systems in several European countries, Australia, Canada, and parts of the United States.

The popularity of Henry George was an indication that many looked upon expansion and industrialization as somewhat less than unmitigated progress. In the eighties this attitude was further expressed in several realistic novels and novels of social protest. Easily the most successful was Edward Bellamy's utopian novel *Looking Backward, 2000-1887* (1888), which sold over a million copies. It criticized the new industrial society by advocating communistic life within local communities. For a time Bellamy had a popular following in America comparable to that of Henry George. In Europe his book was also widely read, and its picture of a communistic Boston in 2000 A.D. contributed to the ground swell of socialism in the 1880's. In 1890 Howells, profoundly influenced by the pre-mystical Tolstoy, turned to literary realism with *A Hazard of New Fortunes*, in which he introduced poverty and injustice into his hitherto complacent writing.

*The last years
of the Knights of Labor*

THE LEADING labor organization at the beginning of the decade was the Knights of Labor. When the completion of the Union Pacific Railroad threw many Chinese laborers out of work, the Knights threw their weight behind the passage of a law intended to benefit the white American worker at the expense of the coolie. The outcome was the Chinese Exclusion Act, which suspended for ten years the immigration of Chinese, on the grounds that their low standard of living depressed wages in California. In 1885 the Knights helped to push through a law forbidding the importation of contract labor from any source. The Chinese Exclusion Act was to be renewed in 1902 and given a lasting effect that was modified only during the Second World War.

In 1886 many union groups, including the Knights of Labor, participated in a general movement for an eight-hour day. A series of strike disorders roused passions on both sides. In Chicago a strike of McCormick Harvester Company workers led to police violence culminating in a counter-demonstration in Haymarket Square. There someone threw a bomb that killed several policemen and injured over sixty other persons. Though the prosecution never established the identity of the real culprit, the court sentenced seven anarchists to death and one to life imprisonment for murder; and despite protest at home and abroad, and despite the suicide of one anarchist and the commutation of sentence for two others, four of them were actually hanged. The Knights of Labor were not directly implicated in the Haymarket affair. Its officers in fact denounced the accused anarchists. But outraged public opinion coupled them with the anarchists, while their failure to encourage solidarity and to display vigorous leadership in a labor crisis alienated the more radical members. Membership declined rapidly.

*The new union movement:
the American Federation of Labor*

WORKERS now turned to a new federation of unions which had been forming since the early 1880's and had emerged in 1886 under the name of the American Federation of Labor. It was headed by a group of hard-headed, realistic, opportunistic labor organizers. The most famous was the London-born Jewish cigar-maker Samuel Gompers, who was to be its president for almost forty years. Having deliberately borrowed its construction from European labor institutions, particularly the British Trades Union Congress, the American Federation of Labor differed from the Knights of Labor in several respects. (1) The new organization was a federation of craft or trade unions—that is, of workers organized locally and nationally by their specialized type of work. Its members were not individuals but national unions, represented by their officers in the Federation. (2) It limited itself strictly to workers' problems such as wages, hours, and conditions of work, and to the direct methods of

408

the strike and the boycott, deliberately eschewing political action except to lobby and exert pressure upon parties and officials. (3) It accepted the capitalist framework and set itself to improve labor's bargaining position within that framework. Though taking a frank stand on the opposing interests of capital and labor, it carefully avoided the militant class struggle and the political radicalism of Marxism. (4) It included labor unions in Canada as well as in the United States. For fifty years after its inception, unimpeded by any rival organization, it was the spearhead of the labor movement in America and determined the character of that movement.

Regulation
of interstate commerce

THE Granger movement (page 344) and a series of railroad strikes in the eighties underlined the demand for government regulation of the railroads, whose practices were obviously exasperating both their customers and their employees. So obvious was the need for some form of regulation that Congress, after several times balking at similar action, in 1887, in a Democratic regime, passed the Interstate Commerce Act. The Act dealt primarily with the question of rates, prohibiting pooling (or agreements to avoid genuine price competition), special rates for long hauls, rebates, and other exorbitant or discriminatory price practices of railroads engaging in interstate commerce, and set up the Interstate Commerce Commission to police the Act and hale offenders before the courts. This feature for a long time negated the Act, since the courts, generally strongholds of laissez faire, hamstrung the Commission; but in the course of time the Commission was to receive greater authority to prevent the major potential abuses of private ownership. Hence, unlike the experience of most European countries, nationalization of the railroads of the United States has not taken place.

Farmers' Alliances
and the agrarian movement

THE 1880's were a decade of mounting distress and protest among the farmers. They turned to a more aggressive type of farm organization than the Grange, known as the Farmers' Alliance. A severe drought in 1887 and a general deflation of land values ushered in a prolonged period of unusually hard times for the farmer. By the late eighties most local and regional Alliances had amalgamated into the Farmers' and Laborers' Union of America with around 2,000,000 members. Some Alliances that stayed outside the Union nevertheless in 1890 federated with it in a National Farmers' Alliance and Industrial Union. Active in social, educational, and cooperative endeavors to a greater degree than the Grange, the Alliances also had an even more positive political program. In 1892 the Alliances were to disappear almost suddenly in favor of a full-blown political organization known as the Populist Party (page 477).

*The Sherman Anti-Trust
and the McKinley Tariff Acts*

CAUGHT between pressure by populists, laborers, and farmer organizations on the one hand and laissez-faire industrialists, merchants, and bankers on the other, a generally Republican Congress found it hard to steer a middle course between national regulation of enterprise and a hands-off policy. Meanwhile, many large business combinations, frequently amounting to monopolies in their fields, had been created, sometimes by buying or forcing out weaker competitors. Such "trusts" were, in the eyes of some, as much a menace to truly free enterprise as nationalized industries might have been. Among the most hated monopolies was the Standard Oil Company, reorganized in 1882, whose monopolistic practices made the name "trust" synonymous with monopoly or near-monopoly. In the Standard Oil Trust many associated firms surrendered their stock to one board of trustees, receiving in return trust certificates entitling them to a pro rata share of the total income of the combination.

In the year 1890 the protests of farmers, laborers, reformers, and plain people finally bore fruit in the Sherman Anti-Trust Act. This act declared: "Every contract, combination in the form of trust or otherwise, or conspiracy in restraint of trade or commerce among the several states or with foreign nations is...illegal." It also made any attempt to establish a monopoly a misdemeanor and fixed heavy penalties for violations. The Sherman Anti-Trust Act had the effect of slowing, in the United States, the growth of monopolies and cartels such as flourished in Europe (page 336) and of making the United States government responsible for preserving free enterprise against those who would create vast trade empires that might eliminate competition. Subsequent court decisions were to extend its scope to railroads and labor unions.

In the same year Congress enacted the McKinley Tariff. This bill, except for providing reciprocity with Latin America (page 413), was openly protectionist. In it tariffs were pushed to new highs by various business lobbies anxious to prevent competition from foreign manufacturers. Thus Congress regulated business with one hand in order to preserve the competitive principle at home and erected a high tariff wall with the other in order to discourage competition from abroad. Competition for the abundant resources of the United States was to be kept open for Americans but restricted for foreigners.

*Intensification
of world rivalries*

IN THE PERIOD after the Civil War a few signs indicated that Americans were becoming more aware of the need for playing a part in international affairs. The United States joined in 1866 with other interested powers in inflicting a tariff treaty on Japan. The International Postal Union won the adherence of the United

States from its very start (1875). In 1880 the United States, together with some European powers, entered into an agreement for the protection of foreigners in Morocco. In 1884 the United States sent a representative to the Berlin Conference on the Congo (page 426). Twice during the eighties the United States took steps looking toward the building of a United States-controlled canal in Central America, but both times the project was dropped because of a treaty with England in which a canal under the control of the United States was specifically outlawed. In the late 1880's the country began to build a new navy of armored battleships. Public opinion had been won to favor a big navy partly by the naval historian Captain A. T. Mahan, who argued with telling examples from the past that world power was synonymous with sea power.

Major developments in some Latin-American countries

ALTHOUGH, under the protection of the Monroe Doctrine, the Latin-American countries seldom became involved in world affairs, they had some aggravating domestic problems. One such problem was the depressed condition of the natives. The first country confronted with this Indian question was Mexico. Benito Juárez, the hero of the war against the Napoleonic empire in Mexico, had died in 1872. After his death Porfirio Díaz came to the fore and became virtual dictator from 1876 to 1911 with one interruption (1880-1884). Díaz disregarded the welfare of the Indian, and he was only slightly more interested in the white man. He was a Mestizo, and his political strength came from the Mestizos. He spared the feelings of the white native-born Spanish (Creoles) but let them have little political power. They were, however, the holders of the big estates, and to offset their influence, Díaz created a new class by giving to Mestizos small estates (*ranchos*). The land generally came from expropriation of the Indian communal holdings. Since no law prevented the new Mestizo landlord from selling his land, the old Creole landlords eventually got hold of many of the *ranchos* by purchase. Nevertheless, by the end of Díaz' rule, more than 47,000 *ranchos* still existed. Fewer than a thousand men owned the far greater part of Mexican soil, however; and around 10,000,000 Indians had no land at all and were peons (little better than serfs).

Argentina experienced a prosperity analogous to that of the United States after the Civil War. It solved the Indian problem partly by exterminating the Pampas Indians in a series of Indian wars in the 1870's and 1880's. British-sponsored railroads opened up the vast country and huge cattle kingdoms then originated. In 1881 Argentina and Chile divided the Tierra del Fuego between them.

In 1889 Brazil became a republic, and the last independent monarchy of the Western Hemisphere disappeared. Ironically enough, that development resulted from the last emperor's liberal attitude on the question of slavery. Pedro II had been well liked, and under his benign leadership, emancipation without compensation to slaveholders came peaceably in 1888. Thousands of former slaves left the plantations, flocked to the cities, and became republicans. On the other hand, many landowners, the strongest supporters of the monarchy, became impoverished. When the army also became disaffected, the monarchy was overthrown by a bloodless revolution. Brazil adopted a federal constitution as the United States of Brazil but was under a military dictatorship from 1889 to 1894. In the twentieth century, Brazil became one of the great meccas of immigration. Around 3,000,000 workers emigrated from Italy, Spain, and Portugal between 1889 and 1914 to find employment mostly in the coffee and rubber industries of Brazil.

A large part of Chile's history after independence was a chronicle of conflict with her neighbors. In 1879 Chile became involved in a war with Peru and Bolivia known as the War of the Pacific. The war was caused by a dispute over control of certain guano and nitrate deposits. Peace was concluded in 1883. Peru ceded the province of Tarapaca to Chile, and Bolivia conceded to Chile control of the provinces of Tacna and Arica for ten years. Thus Bolivia was excluded from access to the Pacific. Chile solved its Indian question by carrying on drastic war against the native Araucanians. Eventually the Indians were isolated in reservations. Meanwhile domestic politics centered around the question of the authority of the president. Most of the time he was a dictator holding highly centralized authority by military power, but parliamentary practices slowly evolved. A civil war in 1891 brought to an end the era of autocratic government.

Pan-American movement of the 1880's

DURING the eighties a movement for a Pan-American conference developed under the persuasion of the Republican leader James G. Blaine. Blaine was particularly interested in diverting the flow of South American trade to the United States. South American countries exported large shipments of raw material to the United States but generally bought their manufactured goods from Europe. Blaine was eager to shift this trade to America and, if possible, to draw Latin America into a customs union with the United States after the manner of the German *Zollverein*. In 1889, the first Pan-American Conference convened in Washington with seventeen Latin-American states attending and Blaine, as United States secretary of state, presiding. The delegates, however, could not agree on most matters. The Latin-American countries were afraid of domination by the more powerful United States, and several European countries, fearful of losing their South American trade to the United States, stirred up opposition wherever they could. One signal outcome nevertheless did emerge—the establishment of the organization that eventually became the Pan American Union, a clearing house for information on Western Hemisphere affairs (excluding those of Canada and the European colonies).

412 The Conference also set a precedent for other such gatherings, and proved

to be a lever for tariff reciprocity between the United States and South America. The reciprocity was first provided in the McKinley Tariff of 1890.

American involvement in the Samoan Islands

IN THE YEAR of the Pan-American Conference the United States became involved in a struggle with two European powers for control of the South Pacific archipelago of Samoa. This archipelago lies athwart the trade routes connecting Panama, California, Hawaii, New Zealand, and Australia. As early as 1850 German, British, and American commercial agents were active in the Samoas. Having acquired the Aleutian Islands in the northern Pacific with the purchase of Alaska, the United States was particularly eager in the years after the Civil War to annex the Samoas as a parallel line of influence in the south. By 1878, as we have seen, the United States had established a coaling and naval station at Pagopago, and had volunteered to mediate any difficulties Samoa might have with the nations of Europe. Great Britain and Germany in turn in 1879 established their own naval and coaling stations in the Samoas. Trade rivalries, domestic intrigues, civil war, and international struggle marked the next twenty years of Samoa's history, and Robert Louis Stevenson tried in vain to present the natives' side of the story. Naval units of the three European powers lay in the islands as silent threats to one another, but the tense atmosphere was broken by a hurricane that beached some of the German and American ships and forced all three rivals to go to one another's aid. Bismarck had meanwhile proposed a meeting of the three powers for peaceful resolution of the Samoan question. In the spring of 1889 the representatives of Germany, England, and the United States met at Berlin. The United States thus, for a second time (page 411), took part in an international conference in Bismarck's capital on imperialist problems. The conferees agreed to restore the native dynasties, to neutralize the archipelago, to recognize its political independence, and to establish a joint board of control to protect the interests of foreigners. This three-power condominium preserved peace in the southern Pacific until the Spanish-American War of 1898 (page 497) once more disturbed the balance of power in the Pacific area.

IMPERIALISM

IN ASIA AND AFRICA

IN 1879 Li Hung-chang, the Chinese minister of foreign affairs, warned the Korean emperor at Seoul:

> As matters stand,...is not our best course to neutralize
> one poison by another, to set one energy against another?   413

> You should seize every opportunity to establish treaty
> relations with western nations, of which you would make
> use to check Japan.

The ensuing tug of war, not only in Korea but in other non-European
areas, was thus forecast. As the bigger nations jockeyed for advantage, the
weak countries that were the stakes in their race for power seldom had a
better choice than to delay the final but all too clear outcome by playing
one of the stronger nations against another.

*The rivalry
of China and Japan in Korea*

KOREA and Indochina were among
the larger stakes of the power
game. While China fought in In-
dochina against France, the advice of the Chinese statesman Li Hung-chang
guided the policy of Korea with regard to Japan. Between 1882 and 1886
Korea signed treaties with the interested foreign states similar to her treaty of
1876 with Japan. These agreements were concluded with the approval and
sometimes the military and diplomatic aid of Peking. In 1884 the Japanese
diplomat Prince Ito Hirobumi journeyed to Peking to make a request in no
uncertain terms: that neither power should dispatch troops to Korea without
first forwarding to the other a written notice of its intention. Being obliged
contemporaneously to defend her suzerainty over Indochina and Burma,
China reluctantly agreed to this demand in 1885, and in so doing practically
surrendered her traditional suzerainty over Korea without saving it in the
other threatened areas. Both countries thereupon withdrew their troops
from the coveted peninsula. In the course of the ensuing decade, Korea was
to become a focal area of international contention, especially bitter between
Japan and China. Supported by the West, the Chinese continued for a decade
longer to exert some influence, which the Japanese tried to offset, over the
court at Seoul.

*The conquest
of Indochina by France*

MEANWHILE China lost its claim
of suzerainty over Indochina. Under the imperialistic program of
Jules Ferry (page 398), in 1882 the French again began to push ahead
in Indochina in spite of repeated warnings from Peking. The war party at
Peking refused to accept the French annexation of Indochina passively.
Numerous local conflicts in Indochina led finally to a full-scale Franco-
Chinese war in 1884. But China proved unable to put up a protracted resistance. The court of Peking experienced in quick succession the destruction
of its fleet, the blockading of the Yangtze River, and the bombardment of
several port cities.

Though Ferry was forced to resign in the course of the war (page 429),
his aim was secured. Peace was concluded by the Franco-Chinese treaty of
414 1885: China gave up her claims in Tonkin and Annam, agreed to conclude

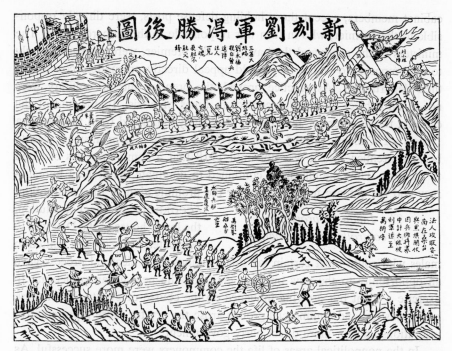

A contemporary French engraving of a Chinese drawing depicting the Franco-Chinese War of 1884. The artist, glorifying Chinese prowess, pictures the French (foreground) in retreat from Chinese forces.

a new commercial treaty with France, and expressed a preference for French engineers in the building program going on in Yünnan. Thus, France not only obtained control of Indochina but also carved out an important sphere of interest in southern China across the border. Isolated groups in Indochina continued to resist after 1885, but by the end of the century the entire peninsula had come under French control.

Clan authority confirmed by Japan's constitution of 1889

JAPAN'S ability to play the role of a great power was in part attributable to the efficient, stabilized, centralized, and militarist regime that she had recently established. A constitution finally was promulgated in 1889. It conformed largely to Japan's past feudal system and distribution of authority. The central government was carefully safeguarded from interference by the representatives of the people. On paper the powers of the Imperial Diet, as the bicameral representative assembly was called, were numerous and included approval of the annual budget. The new document was modeled in part upon the Prussian constitution of 1850. Hence, any failure of the Diet to approve a new budget would mean simply that the government was thereby empowered to carry on with a budget similar to that of the preceding year. The cabinet was not directly responsible to either house of the Diet but was so organized as to give it perhaps even greater freedom from parliamentary control than that of Prussia. The 415 cabinet members, except those holding defense posts, were directly responsible to the premier, who in turn was responsible to the emperor alone. The ministers of the army and the navy, like the premier, were responsible only to the emperor, to whom they could appeal directly on matters concerning their departments. As practice proved, the premier and the military were not at all subject to popular control in times of crisis. To the end of the century, the premiers of Japan were alternately appointed from the Satsuma (navy) or Choshu (army) clans. In 1898 the first nonclansman was to become premier, and it was not until 1918 that a commoner was elevated to the post. Thus the clansmen continued to dominate the civilian bureaucracy and the defense forces even after the promulgation of the constitution.

The Japanese program of controlled social change

ACCORDING to the constitution, the lower house of the Diet was to be elected by a suffrage limited to males who could meet certain tax qualifications. The electoral process gave an opportunity to the new business elite and the new urban proletariat to exercise a slight but growing influence on the course of events. From these new industrial and commercial groups arose the cry for more representative institutions and for more direct party government.

In the nonpolitical areas of life the commoners were more successful. As Japan expanded her industrial and commercial operations, various skills were required and gave greater importance to a greater number of people. No longer was it enough for the Japanese farmer to produce rice merely for domestic consumption. Agriculture, through more intensive production, had to produce large quantities for export in order to pay for the purchases of machinery and industrial equipment in foreign countries. A laboring force had to be trained for mining, industry, and commerce. The cities began to grow rapidly as rural youth sought employment in the new enterprises. Better measures of sanitation and higher standards of living brought a rapidly expanding population. Thus, although the advisers of the Meiji emperor sought with some success to control the rate of change, the new social forces nevertheless brought a few innovations that could not be forestalled. And ultimately those few were to hasten others.

The success of the controlled change within Japan was a concomitant of the success of the Meiji foreign policy. Under the guidance of Great Britain and the United States, Japan by the end of the century was to win her struggle for equal treatment in the family of nations. Moreover, her international position became secure enough for her to venture upon an aggressive policy toward her weaker Asiatic neighbors. In her negotiations with China and Korea after 1870 Japan regularly demanded concessions similar to those enjoyed by other "civilized" powers. The success of this program won a respect and loyalty at home that helped the domestic program to succeed.

416

*The partition
of eastern New Guinea*

WHILE hostilities between Japan, China, and France were building up on the continent of Asia, the great powers of the world were carrying their conflicts to the islands of the Pacific. The first of several international incidents in Oceania developed around 1884 over the question whether England or Germany should control the eastern half of the large island of New Guinea. The island's western coast had been held by the Dutch since the end of the eighteenth century. As the Pacific was being partitioned during the nineteenth century, the Australian colonies became increasingly concerned lest annexation by a foreign power of the undeveloped eastern parts of New Guinea endanger their freedom to use the Torres Strait and the splendid waterway of the Barrier Reef in time of war. The Germans were a special source of uneasiness, since they had but recently entered the race for colonies and appeared to have designs upon every uncommitted portion of the colonial world. Under considerable pressure from Australia, Great Britain in 1884 proclaimed a protectorate over the region. At the same time, a German trading company raised its flag on the northeastern coast of the island. The following year the two European governments divided the wild portion of the island east of the 141st meridian into the British territory of Papua on the south facing Australia and the German territory of Kaiser-Wilhelmsland and the Bismarck Archipelago on the north. Not until the twentieth century did the German and British regions of New Guinea begin to be developed commercially. German influence was further extended in 1885 by annexation of the Solomon and the Marshall islands. Great Britain, however, was to have no further trouble with Germany in the islands, since the two countries agreed tacitly in 1885 to limit further acquisitions in the western Pacific.

*The agreements
on the New Hebrides and Borneo*

THE BRITISH continued to have complications with the French and the Dutch. In the New Hebrides chain, for example, French and British nationals who were engaged in trading and missionary activities had long been urging annexation upon their respective governments. Since the New Hebrides were closely adjacent to the French colony of New Caledonia, the influence of France was particularly strong; and, as in New Guinea, Australian interests in the New Hebrides were significant in determining Britain's position. In 1878 Britain and France agreed to declare the islands neutral and to go no further in their efforts to acquire them. The proclamation of neutrality, however, did not prevent the natives from rioting against the intruders from Europe. A serious demonstration by the natives in 1886 brought French forces from New Caledonia, and the following year an Anglo-French convention placed the islands under joint jurisdiction, excluding other European nations. Although the condominium over the New Hebrides was bitterly criticized in Australia, 417 it was extended by further treaty arrangements, and the system of joint rule is still preserved.

Criticism of this policy in Australia was somewhat mitigated by British victories elsewhere. In 1888 British protectorates were established over North Borneo, Brunei, and Sarawak, thus splitting Borneo, the largest island next to New Guinea in the Pacific, with the Dutch. In 1889, it will be recalled (page 413), probably the most complicated of the Pacific disputes of the late nineteenth century was amicably settled by the establishment of a condominium of Britain, Germany, and the United States in the Samoan Islands.

The rivalry of England and Russia in Afghanistan

THE *bête noire* of the British imperialists was Russia. As in the Crimean War, Anglo-Russian hostility in the Near East in the 1870's was carried over into central Asia. It was partly in response to Russia's aggressive attitude in central Asia that Disraeli had threatened Russia with war before the Congress of Berlin in 1878 and then acquired Cyprus as a defense of the Suez route to the East. In India, Governor-General Lord Lytton put into operation his own plans for protecting the empire against Russian maneuvers in Afghanistan. He sent British troops over the mountain passes into Afghanistan a few months after negotiations were completed in Berlin. For two years Great Britain continued the war against the Afghans to make sure that an unfriendly ruler would not control the Khyber Pass. When the Gladstone government replaced the Disraeli government in 1880, it put Lord Ripon in charge of India. British military skill succeeded in bringing an end to the hostilities against Afghanistan, permitting the British choice, Abdu-r-Rahman, to act as emir at Kabul. Though Lytton had instituted an enduring policy of taking measures in advance to counteract recurrent famine in India (his so-called "famine insurance"), Ripon proved to be a much more popular viceroy because of his personal sympathy for the people.

Peace in central Asia was reared on shaky foundations. Smarting from the defeat handed her at Berlin in 1878, Russia continued to regard central Asia as one of her legitimate areas of expansion. Tension developed again when the Russians, in 1884, annexed the principality of Merv in the border area north of Persia and Afghanistan. When they followed this open aggression in 1885 by the occupation of Penjdeh, a territory claimed by Abdu-r-Rahman, even the anti-imperialist Gladstone conceded that Britain might have to go to war with Russia. Fear of a full-scale resort to arms spread to every European capital in 1885 (page 429), until Gladstone won Russia's agreement to a proposal for arbitration. Subsequently, numerous joint Anglo-Russian commissions were organized to define the frontiers of northern India, Afghanistan, and Russia. Although the area remains to this day a point of international friction, the political boundaries of the countries involved were delimited by the end of the nineteenth century.

The military activities of the British materially affected the course of India's development in the years following Queen Victoria's acceptance of the imperial title. Native troops had given a good account of themselves in the campaigns in Afghanistan. At the time of the Penjdeh war scare in 1885, a feeling arose that the Indian defense should be strengthened. As a result, in 1889 the Imperial Service troops came into being as permanent military units. They were drawn from the native population and paid for by the Indian princes but trained and organized along British lines.

The rise
of Indian nationalism
THE British *raj* (government of India) justified its regime in India, in part at least, by its con-tributions to the modernization of the country, to the mitigation of plague and famine, to a new system of justice, to education in the British tradition of freedom, and to projects of irrigation and forestry. The towns now had more factories than ever before; better roads and a few railroad lines con-nected the bigger cities; ports had been improved; a small native capitalist class had developed; and some of the worse customs had been abandoned under the guidance of the *raj*. On the other hand, generally without intend-ing to do so, the British rulers enhanced the Indian national sentiment. Indian nationalist critics of the *raj* became ever more articulate. In the course of time they were to charge (though the truth was not always as they painted it) that the British sometimes sacrificed the trade interests of India to those of Britain, that the government was unnecessarily autocratic, ex-pensive, and wasteful, and that the British were studiously reserved in their relations to the Indians. The affairs of India were conducted directly from the Indian Office in London, it was further charged, and Indians were excluded from the top offices in the central administration of their own country. Although Indians had been granted the right to work in the Indian civil service, the obstacles placed in their way were many, and as a general rule Indians received appointments only to provincial posts. Indignation was not keen, however, among the English-educated Indians who, advised by Englishmen and adopting English precedents, organized in 1885 an Indian National Congress as a pressure group. This Congress was the first political organization along western lines in any of the eastern lands. At first, the Congress advocated a program of gradualism and was pro-British, but it was eventually to become less patient and more demanding.

British advances
in Upper Burma and Tibet
WHILE the British were occupied in gaining a toehold on the north-western frontiers of India and in becoming more firmly established in India itself, the question of Burma again came to the fore. At this period the British were concerned about the expansion of French power in southeastern Asia and sought therefore to complete their conquest of Burma. Of particular concern to London were 419

the close relations developing between the French and King Thebaw of Upper Burma. The immediate cause of hostilities was the king's restriction of British trade. Exasperated by what they considered Thebaw's tortuous and devious policies, the British attacked Upper Burma in 1885, and in the following year formally annexed it to the British crown. During the remaining years of the century the British had to shoulder the formidable burden of pacifying the country and bringing order out of chaos.

The annexation of Upper Burma provided Britain with a counterweight to France's control of Indochina. In dealings with China, however, the British fared much better than had the French. China did not advance her tenuous claims to suzerainty in Burma with the same vigor as she had employed in the case of Indochina. Her involvement in Korea and the failure of her belligerent policy in Indochina rendered her now a more pliable opponent. In a convention of 1886, she formally recognized Britain's control over Burma in return for a guarantee that Britain would not advance rapidly toward Tibet and would not interfere with the dispatch of Burmese tribute missions to Peking.

The reference to Tibet in the negotiations started a new lap in the international race in the Far East. In the mountainous reaches of Tibet an ancient theocracy held sway under the nominal suzerainty of the Chinese Empire. There China, Russia, and Great Britain were shortly to present new threats to international peace as they maneuvered for advantage.

British advances in the Malay Peninsula   TO THE southeast of Burma, Britain also forged ahead. In 1867 the British had organized the major cities of the Malay Peninsula, despite the distances between them, into a single crown colony called the Straits Settlements. These included Penang, Malacca, Singapore, Province Wellesley, and the Dindings. The rest of the Malay Peninsula consisted of native sultanates acknowledging the loosely exercised suzerainty of Siam. In 1885, while British armies were active in Upper Burma, and Europe was talking about the possibility of an Anglo-Russian war over the Penjdeh affair, the sultan of Johore, a state at the southern tip of the Malay Peninsula, accepted British protection.

The sultan of Johore thus commenced a process by which Britain not only came to control the sea route from India to China but also got a start ahead of the other European powers in southeastern Asia. By the end of the century (1895) another group of Malayan sultans was to organize the Federated Malay States, which came into being as a British protectorate. Still later, several of the other sultanates were to disavow the shadowy Siamese overlordship and to pass singly under British protection. In that way the British acquired in Malaya one of the areas of the Far East richest in natural resources. The tin of Malaya helped the British immeasurably in retaining economic predominance in the prewar world.

*Pressures
toward Australian cooperation*

IN THE same period came a steady growth of self-government in the "white" parts of Britain's Pacific holdings. In Australia particularly, the British attitude had been most enlightened since the days of Wakefield. The Australian colonies earned a world-wide reputation as pioneers in new fields of social legislation, such as women's suffrage, old age pensions, minimum wage laws, and proportional representation. The sixth and last colony, Western Australia, received responsible government in 1890. For reasons of history and geography each colony on the island continent developed its own set of democratic institutions, its own policies, railroads, tariffs, land laws, etc. Rivalry was especially keen between Victoria, which was pursuing a protectionist policy, and New South Wales, which retained free trade. The smaller states feared that New South Wales, the richest and most populous of the colonies, would dominate a confederated government.

In the second half of the nineteenth century, however, the movement toward political unification of the continent advanced rapidly for reasons that for the most part recalled the United States and the Canadian precedents. Other pressures finally overcame the smaller colonies' deep-seated fear of the dominant colony. Economically, the continent suffered increasingly from attempting to operate as six independent entities, since both overseas trade and intercolonial trade were badly hampered by the tariff barriers of the various colonies. Moreover, the encroachments of rival powers in the neighboring regions aroused fear that a divided country would be unable to protect itself against foreign depredation.

One important inducement toward confederation had no American precedent, however. The Australian colonies, like other areas south of China, ran grave danger of being flooded by immigrants that they did not want. As their standard of living advanced they faced the prospect of thousands of immigrants not only from totally foreign countries like China and Japan but also from India and other parts of Asia under British rule. Asiatic immigration, the Australians feared, would threaten white supremacy and the institutions cherished by peoples of European extraction. These pressing problems quickly overcame the Australians' antipathy to centralization.

The advocates of Australian federation drew strength from the example of New Zealand. In 1875 the islands had abolished their provinces and established a centralized government. Five years later a conference was held at Melbourne to discuss Australian federation. It was not until 1890, however, that the movement began to take final shape. In the convention of that year New South Wales proposed a federation to include New Zealand as well as the six Australian colonies. The leadership in this major step was taken by Sir Henry Parkes, "the father of the Commonwealth of Australia." In the convention of 1891 at Sydney, Parkes was mainly responsible for

421

drawing up the rough draft of a federal constitution. Thereafter, leagues and associations were organized to urge the colonial legislatures to accept that constitution (pages 519-520).

The specter of the "Yellow Peril"

BY THE 1880's the potential wealth of the natural resources of China had become fairly well understood in the West. Between 1877 and 1885 Baron Ferdinand von Richthofen had published three large volumes and an atlas under the title *China*. Richthofen's work was far more detailed and precise than the travel accounts of earlier writers. Here for the first time was a geographer's systematic estimate of China's economic resources. In his account of his explorations of Shantung province, for example, Richthofen drew attention to its coal fields and ports, and thereby prepared the way for Germany's later interest in the province. The works of the Swedish explorer Sven Hedin on Tibet and central Asia also made known the natural wealth of those areas, and so did the explorations and writings of the American W. W. Rockhill.

Even while the western powers were planning to divide China, the growing knowledge of Asia stimulated the fear of the "Yellow Peril." Richthofen was at least partly responsible for inspiring this fear. In calling attention to the huge population of China, he further excited the already keen dread in Australia, New Zealand, Canada, and the United States of oriental emigration as an endless supply of cheap labor threatening the living standard of white workers.

Russia's "peaceful penetration" of China

MEANWHILE Russian scholars had been preparing systematic studies that were to prove useful in their country's later military expansion along the Asiatic frontier. Russia's activity in Afghanistan since mid-century led to some interesting contributions to the philological and geographical knowledge of central Asia. Extensive exploration and research had also preceded and now accompanied Russia's new burst of energy in the penetration of China. Long interested in Mongolia, the Russian authorities realized that the accumulation of data on China and Mongolia was a desirable and apparently innocuous way of promoting Russia's ambition to become paramount in northeastern Asia. "Peaceful penetration" would thus, on the surface at least, replace more belligerent methods without in fact changing her traditional policy. The Russian Geographical Society organized several expeditions to explore Mongolia, China, and Tibet. The University of St. Petersburg acquired a large collection of Mongol manuscripts. This scholarly accumulation on eastern Asia was further enriched by the reports of several noted Russian explorers. As a by-product of Russian explorations, the key to the ancient Turkish language was discovered. Moreover, the explorers, for their own edification, translated into Russian most of the available Chinese works on geography.

THE EXPANDING store of knowledge of Asia and the insular world of the Pacific, as one might expect, stimulated the imagination of European writers and artists. Among them was Julien Viaud, better known as Pierre Loti, a name given him by the daughters of the last queen of independent Tahiti while he was visiting the island as an officer with a French naval squadron in 1872. The "loti," according to its namesake, is a rare East Indian flower. On this memorable voyage Loti went to Easter Island, where he was intrigued by its prehistoric megalithic monuments. In 1880 he published his South Seas idyl, originally entitled *Rarahu* and later *Le mariage de Loti*. It helped to establish his reputation as a writer of exotic novels of remarkable charm and originality.

Loti's subsequent novels (about forty) are mostly about other lands he visited in the East, although the most famous one *The Iceland Fisherman* (1886) is about Brittany. The first European of genuine literary talent to visit the Far East, Loti arrived in Japan in 1885 for the first time. He was fascinated by it. Two years later he published *Madame Chrysanthème*, a semireminiscent account of Japanese life and manners. In this and his other tracts on Japan, he sometimes wrote disparagingly of the Nipponese and held their way of life to be decidedly inferior. In his later works Loti was less contemptuous of the Oriental, but throughout his writings there runs a constant strain of criticism. The widespread influence of his writings led many Europeans to look upon Japan as a land of fantasy and curiosity. Not until the Russo-Japanese War of 1904-1905 were Europeans generally to realize that the exotic picture of Japan was far from complete.

Robert Louis Stevenson also became interested in the East. Having long coped with his tuberculosis in England and the United States, in 1888 he went out to wander among the romantic islands and to write reports of his travels for American journals. In Samoa he settled down for the last few years of his life. One of his most famous writings of this period is in defense of Father Damien, whose mission among the lepers on the Hawaiian Islands had been misrepresented in Europe. Damien himself died of leprosy on Molokai in 1889. Some of Stevenson's last works were about the Pacific, notably his *Footnote to History,* pleading the Samoan case with the people of England. He ended his career in the South Seas (1894).

The oriental collection of the Goncourts, which continued to grow until the death of Edmond de Goncourt (1896), proved but the first of several. Another collection of Far Eastern antiquities was assembled by Émile Étienne Guimet, an industrialist of Lyons, and became the nucleus around which the Musée Guimet, a national museum of Far Eastern art and archaeology, was built at Paris in 1885. Henri Cernuschi, an Italian-born politician and economist, at this time also assembled a fine collection of Japanese art objects. It formed the core of the Cernuschi municipal museum of Paris.

*The British
and the French in Egypt*

MEANWHILE, Europeans had steadily been learning more about the Dark Continent. The British had become painfully involved in northern Africa. When in 1875 the extravagant and bankrupt khedive of Egypt, Ismail Pasha, had sold his Suez Canal Company stock to the British, he had invited British interference with the finances of his realm. Since his fiscal institutions were not such as Europeans would approve, in 1876 a joint French-English control of his receipts and payments was set up. Ismail, suspected by all parties, was dismissed by his overlord, the Turkish sultan, in 1879.

Egyptian nationalism grew under the new khedive, Tewfik Pasha, especially in the army. In 1882 the French and the English issued a joint note in support of the khedive and made a show of naval power in the port of Alexandria, but, as soon as the fleets withdrew, riots broke out that brought death to dozens of Europeans. The French proved unwilling at this point to use force, but, impelled by their fear for the Suez Canal, the English retaliated alone. They bombarded Alexandria, occupied Cairo, suppressed the nationalist movement, and by 1883 had laid the foundation of British control of Egypt.

*Gordon
and the Mahdi*

DURING these very years Egypt had got bogged down in the Sudan. Egypt had long claimed that area, but in 1881 the Sudanese tribes rebelled under the leadership of Mohammed Ahmed. His followers regarded him as "the Mahdi," which meant that they considered him the reformer of Islam predicted for their year 1300 (i.e., 1882) by a Mohammedan legend. The Mahdi now declared war on Christians, pagans, and Mohammedans alike, considering himself the savior of the world. He had a strong and well-disciplined army, whose nucleus was the so-called "mad dervishes," religious fanatics who followed him blindly. An Egyptian army under the command of the English general William Hicks was trounced near El Obeid in 1883, and Hicks and his staff were killed. The Mahdi then threatened to invade Egypt itself.

In 1884, the Mahdists actually began to descend the Nile Valley. The Egyptian government, advised by Sir Evelyn Baring (later Lord Cromer), the British agent and consul general, then decided to give up the Sudan, and the khedive sent General "Chinese" Gordon, who had helped suppress the Taiping Rebellion, to Egypt to take charge of the evacuation. He reached Khartoum early in 1884 and tried to negotiate with the Mahdi, who would not accept his terms. In January 1885 the Mahdists occupied Khartoum, killing Gordon and his force of 34,000 half-starved Egyptians and ransacking the city. That year the Mahdi died, but his successor continued his semimessianic, seminationalist regime, and not until 1896 were the Egyptians able to renew the war against the whirling dervishes (page 509).

*African acquisitions
of Germany, Italy, and Belgium*

THE BOMBING of Alexandria by the British in 1882 caused in Germany an outbreak of anti-British feeling dictated by a mixture of envy and moral indignation. Implacable nationalists quickly came to think that the Germans should have a few slices of Africa, too. A Bremen businessman named F. A. E. Lüderitz founded the first German settlements in southwest Africa in 1883. In 1884 a Society for German Colonization was founded by the enterprising explorer Karl Peters. That year Bismarck proclaimed German Southwest Africa, the Cameroons, and Togoland to be German protectorates. In 1885 Peters and some other private subjects of the Reich, as members of the German Colonization Society, acquired a big chunk of east Africa, which formally became a Reich protectorate in 1891.

Meanwhile, Italy and even tiny Belgium had entered the contest in Africa. Belgium was brought in through the personal efforts of King Leopold II, who put his private fortune into so-called "International Associations" for the development of the Congo basin. The Italians, once unified, had hastened to join the scramble, and had acquired a foothold in Eritrea in 1870, which was to lead to their claiming the whole in 1885; and Somaliland, as far as it was not already occupied by the British or French, passed under Italian control in 1889.

A battalion of the South Staffordshire Regiment moves up the Nile in an attempt to relieve General Gordon trapped at Khartoum.

425

THE Anglo-French rivalry in Egypt and the Anglo-German rivalry in southwest Africa almost coincided in time with disputes over control of the Congo basin and brought about several conferences in London and Paris in 1884. The conferences were intended to adjust these disputes amicably. At these meetings the world beheld the unusual spectacle of friendliness between German and French representatives, cooperating to embarrass the British. Finally Bismarck and the French minister Ferry collaborated to bring about in Berlin in 1884 the first international congress exclusively concerned with colonial affairs. Fourteen nations, including the United States, sent representatives to the conference, over which Bismarck presided. The domain of Leopold II was set up as a neutralized Congo Free State. All the colonial powers and Leopold, as sovereign of the Congo Free State, promised to end the slave trade.

By this time, usually by tacit rather than explicit agreements, most of Africa had been divided up into what were euphemistically called spheres of influence. "Influence," of course, sometimes meant proprietary rights based on an illiterate native chief's "X" to a document he did not understand. West Africa, except for a few Spanish possessions of old title, was distributed among France, Great Britain, and Germany; central Africa between the International Association's Congo Free State and the French; southwest Africa among Portugal, Great Britain, and Germany. South Africa, outside the British Cape Colony, still had the two Boer republics of Transvaal and the Orange Free State. Southeast Africa was Portuguese and British, and east central Africa British and German. Morocco was independent under an international agreement reached in 1880. The rest of north Africa was still under Turkish suzerainty, except that France now held Algeria and Tunis. Abyssinia (Ethiopia), which proved able to beat off successive Egyptian and Italian efforts at conquest, was not as yet a European sphere of influence. The Nile Valley (i.e., Egypt and the Sudan) was regarded as a British zone. Somaliland was divided among the British, the French, and the Italians. Finally, the republic of Liberia, founded in 1847 by "repatriated" American slaves, remained an independent Negro state. By 1890 little was left of Africa that was not already apportioned among the imperial powers, but that little was enough to create some major disputes.

TRIPLE ALLIANCE

AND REINSURANCE (1879-1890)

THE DOMINANT figure in international politics in the 1880's was Bismarck. His primary purpose in diplomacy remained the desire to keep Germany so strong and France so isolated that *revanche* by a resort to arms would appear obviously foolhardy even to the most nationalistic French and would not be attempted. England's policy of "splendid isolation" from continental affairs and Czar Alexander III's dislike of republicans played into his hands. Until Bismarck's removal from office in 1890, his policy met with astounding success.

The renewal
of the Three Emperors' League

THE SUSPICION on the part of Russian diplomats that Bismarck had betrayed them at the Congress of Berlin (page 364) was not long the major determinant of Russo-German relations. The desire of Germany to be safe from a Russian attack upon Austria or from Russian flirting with France, and the desire of Russia to prevent too close cooperation of Germany with Austria in the Balkans, forced each of the two powers to reconsider its attitude toward the other. Upon Bismarck's insistence the Russians consented to admit Austria into their negotiations. In 1881 the emperors of Germany, Russia, and Austria made a more formal alliance than their earlier understanding had been. This time all three secretly pledged to one another for a period of three years a friendly neutrality in the event that any of them was involved in a war with a fourth power; and no change was to be made in Turkey except by previous agreement among them. The treaty, though negotiated by Alexander II, was signed by Alexander III. It was renewed in 1884.

The Triple Alliance
of Germany, Austria, and Italy

THE Dual Alliance of Germany and Austria-Hungary signed in 1879 was regarded as still valid by the two signatories. Within a few years Italy joined the alliance, thus making it a Triple Alliance. Italy's readiness to combine with Germany, despite her traditional hostility to Austria, was a tribute to Bismarck's astuteness. Bismarck at Berlin had encouraged the French to seek compensation for the gains the other powers were making at Ottoman expense by occupying Tunisia. In that way he hoped to keep the French occupied outside of Europe and embroiled with the Italians, who were known to have their own aspirations in north Africa. In 1881 Ferry declared Tunisia a French protectorate, and the Italians regarded that French success as a direct and terrible blow. Their resentment led them (1882) into a pact with the Central European powers. Italy agreed to support Germany if it were attacked by France or any combination of powers, and to support Austria if it were attacked by a combination of powers (meaning, of course, primarily Russia aided by France). In return Italy received the promise of aid from both her allies if she was herself attacked by France or by a combination of powers. In the event of being obliged to take the initiative in making war, each signator was promised the benevolent neutrality of the other two.

Such an agreement with Italy fitted exactly into Bismarck's purposes. He thus killed two birds with one stone. (1) The pact with Italy further isolated   427

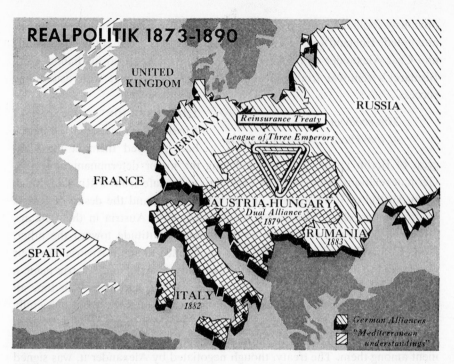

REALPOLITIK 1873-1890

This map shows the network of alliances by which Bismarck maintained peace in Europe from the end of the Franco-Prussian War until his dismissal in 1890. The crux of his plan was a weak and friendless France, and he counted on Britain's "splendid isolation." The League of the Three Emperors (1873-1879 and 1881-1887) linked Russia and Austria-Hungary to Germany. The firmer Dual Alliance of Germany with Austria (1879) expanded to include Italy (1882) and Rumania (1883), and a ring of "understandings" between England, Spain, Italy, and Austria was encouraged by Bismarck in 1887 (page 431) to maintain the status quo in the Mediterranean, north Africa, and the Near East, thwarting French and Russian ambitions in those regions. The Russo-German "Reinsurance Treaty" of the same year (page 432) capped Bismarck's delicate diplomatic structure, but it was to crumble after his removal from power.

France, since, in case of war, the French would have to fight not only the Germans and Austrians but the Italians as well. (2) It strengthened Germany's alliance system, since the pact diminished the ill will between his two allies, making it impossible for Italy (or so it seemed) to clamor for the "unredeemed" Italian-inhabited Austrian districts of Southern Tyrol and Trieste, while at the same time impeding the Austrian government's interest in restoring the secular power of the pope. Thus, the mutually resented ambitions of both Italy and Austria-Hungary were checked, and a double danger to the peace of Europe was neutralized.

The Triple Alliance was renewable in five years, and in fact it was renewed in 1887 and regularly thereafter until 1915. Several features were added in 1887. One stipulated that any territorial advantages in the Near East for either Austria-Hungary or Italy should be arranged only after an agreement providing proper compensation for the other. That provision was

428

largely to determine Italy's attitude in the First World War. By another set of new clauses Germany pledged military aid in case Italy took the offensive to prevent France from occupying Morocco or Tripoli. In this way the Triple Alliance, at first merely defensive, acquired an aggressive quality. The Triple Alliance became a sort of quadruple alliance when in 1883 Rumania, at last a sovereign state, made a secret alliance with Austria.

Bismarck's growing difficulties with Russia

DESPITE the secrecy that regularly surrounded these understandings, the espionage, diplomatic, and journalistic agencies of the various foreign ministries enabled them to suspect much more than was permitted to become public. Hence the Russian foreign office became uneasy upon learning of negotiations of Berlin not only with Vienna but also with Rome and Bucharest. Despite Bismarck's skill in avoiding conflicting engagements in his complex undertakings, he became involved in some highly delicate combinations. An alliance with Russia, Austria, Italy, and Rumania, all with varying interests in the Balkans, was bound to raise some justifiable doubt regarding Germany's bedrock loyalty in case of conflict.

The Three Emperors' alliance was renewable every three years. Since it pledged Germany only to friendly neutrality in the event Russia or Austria was involved in war with a fourth power, it did not literally contravene Germany's obligations to go to the aid of Austria if attacked by Russia. No insurmountable difficulty had prevented renewal in 1884. But when the treaty again came up in 1887, renewal was to prove impossible (page 431).

Crises in Europe because of imperialism overseas

IN THE meantime European imperialism had penetrated widely in Asia. It caused one war scare and one major cabinet crisis in Europe during the eighties. The war scare arose as the Russians in the 1870's and 1880's increased their interest in central Asia, particularly Afghanistan (page 418) and the British became uneasy. For a moment it seemed as if war might break out between the two European powers. But following the Russian and Afghan clash at Penjdeh in 1885, Anglo-Russian tension diminished in that area.

Imperialism in Asia was the cause of the overthrow of perhaps the strongest cabinet the Third Republic had so far been able to boast. For the very reason that Bismarck encouraged France to become engaged in colonial ventures, the French statesman Georges Clemenceau insisted that France should refrain from expanding her colonial possessions. Clemenceau in the 1880's was a powerful figure in the Chamber of Deputies. His opportunity to overthrow the colonial-minded Prime Minister Jules Ferry came with a temporary French reversal in Annam (page 414). Early in 1885, the Chamber voted a resolution of nonconfidence, and Ferry was out.

*The rise of Boulanger
as a figure in world affairs*

THE REPUDIATION of Ferry came at a tense moment. The English and the Russians were snarling at each other across the Afghanistan border. The rivalry of the English and the Germans in southwest Africa had become keen (page 425). The Russians and the Austrians were taking opposite sides in a brief, contemporaneous Serbo-Bulgarian crisis. If France were now to turn her attention from colonial enterprise to *revanche* in Europe, Bismarck had good reason to fear that the ill will among the imperialist powers would enable her to find assistance in one camp or another despite his skillful juggling of alliances. The situation was particularly dangerous because of a burst of nationalist fervor that followed in France close upon the fall of Ferry. The French glared again with angry and envious eyes at "the hole in the Vosges Mountains," the lost provinces of Alsace and Lorraine. General Georges Ernest Boulanger, the ambitious and eloquent minister of war, took advantage of the situation and quickly became a political power to be reckoned with. He was first backed by ardent republicans like Clemenceau who were also nationalists. Soon he turned to "the people," as both Napoleons had done. But toward the end he also came to a secret understanding with the house of Orléans, which counted upon him to use his power only to turn the government of France over to the grandson of King Louis Philippe. The voters did not learn about the subterranean connections of Boulanger. All they knew was that he was a respected general who seemed interested in the welfare of the people and who seemed to loathe politicians. He was elected deputy by several electoral districts at the same time with huge majorities.

A dramatic event soon gave Boulanger the opportunity to pose as the first Frenchman since the 1870's to stand up to Bismarck. In 1887, the Germans arrested a French frontier agent named Guillaume Schnaebelé on the ground that he was a spy. In France the League of Patriots, organized by the poet-politician Paul Déroulède in 1882, and Boulanger himself began to talk loudly of *revanche* and honor. The moment seemed well chosen, for the contemporaneous crisis in the Balkans made it appear likely that France might find ready support from Russia.

*Tensions
over Bulgarian politics*

RUSSIA and Austria had nearly come to blows over autonomous Bulgaria. The Russians had never stopped their agitation for the "Big Bulgaria" of the San Stefano Treaty and had roused thereby the enmity of the Serbs, who had their own ambitions regarding Macedonia. In 1885 a bloodless revolution brought about the temporary union of Eastern Rumelia with Bulgaria. Up to that time Russian influence had been unquestioned in Bulgaria. That Bulgaria's puppet ruler, Prince Alexander of Battenberg, now acted without Russian advice enraged

Czar Alexander III, the more so since the British, reversing their policy of 1878, quickly recognized the new Bulgaria. Serbia was outraged and declared war on Bulgaria but had to give up after two weeks of defeat and retreat. The outcome of the Serbo-Bulgarian War prompted the Turkish sultan to appoint Prince Alexander governor general of Eastern Rumelia, keeping it nominally separated from Bulgaria so as to preserve the Berlin Treaty in outward appearance. But then Prince Alexander was kidnaped by Russian-inspired conspirators, and when he returned, he was forced by pressure from Moscow to abdicate. Bulgaria came practically under Russian administration for more than a year. Eventually, the Bulgarians chose Prince Ferdinand of Saxe-Coburg, an officer in the Austrian army, as their prince (1887); and it took nine years for Russia, which saw Bulgaria slip thereby from her grasp, to recognize him.

War crisis
and peace efforts of 1887

ALTHOUGH many lives had been lost, the whole episode had the air of an operetta, and as a matter of fact eventually became the basis of *The Chocolate Soldier,* a comic opera by Oscar Straus, based on Bernard Shaw's *Arms and the Man* (1894). But it had its serious side. In the Serbo-Bulgarian War of 1885, Russia had given moral support to the Bulgars, and Austria and England to the Serbs. Though nothing much came of this war, it made the breach between Russia and Austria too wide for Bismarck to bridge, and that at the very moment when nationalists in both France and Russia were anti-German. Neither Austria nor Russia wanted to renew the Three Emperors' League. Yet in 1887 war threatened in two areas—between Germany and France, as French nationalism took the menacing form of Boulangism and resentment over Schnaebelé, and between Austria-Hungary and Russia, as Russia forced the abdication of the Bulgarian ruler and tried to make Bulgaria a satellite.

Bismarck realized that Germany did not want war. She had a ninety-year-old emperor, a cancer-stricken heir to the crown, and an eighty-seven-year-old chief of staff (the elder Moltke). Bismarck also believed that France would refrain from war, if she had no allies. Thus he urged a set of understandings among the several Mediterranean powers (England, Spain, Italy, and Austria) in favor of maintaining the status quo in the Mediterranean (at this time chiefly threatened by Russia's Black Sea and France's African ambitions). He also renewed the Triple Alliance, making it more of an offensive alliance than before (page 428). By the spring of 1887 it was clear that neither the French ministers, except Boulanger, nor Bismarck wanted war. The German chancellor even made a friendly gesture toward France by releasing Schnaebelé. That Schnaebelé had been arrested by German agents only after he had been lured to a conference with them provided a convenient pretext for this generous treatment of an alleged spy.

Reinsurance Treaty
of Russia and Germany

AT THIS juncture Bismarck succeeded in bringing about what
some historians consider to have
been his diplomatic masterpiece. He concluded a secret treaty with Russia.
When after his dismissal, he caused the treaty to be published (1896), it
became known as the "Reinsurance Treaty." It was to last for a period of
three years from its signature in 1887. It provided that if France took the
offensive against Germany, Russia would remain neutral, and if Austria-
Hungary took the offensive against Russia, Germany would remain neutral,
leaving each signatory free to act as it saw fit if the other were the aggressor.
In all other wars, each promised the other a friendly neutrality. So far, though
Bismarck had made commitments to the two great antagonists in the Balkans,
they had not been contradictory commitments. The same cannot be said of
the clauses in the Reinsurance Treaty by which Germany promised to raise
no objections if Russia occupied the outlet of the Black Sea (which meant
the Straits or Constantinople) and to recognize Russia's special interest in
Bulgaria. That provision was not contrary to the letter but it did violence to
the spirit of the German-Austrian treaty of 1879. For the Dual Alliance
could not but have induced Austria to believe that if Russia took the offensive in the Balkans in order to upset the status quo there and Austria resisted,
the least Austria could expect from Germany would be a friendly neutrality,
and (if Russia were joined by some other power) military aid also. The
Reinsurance Treaty, however, led Russia to believe that under such circumstances she would have Germany's moral support. Therefore, the Reinsurance Treaty was concealed from the Austrians. It also ran counter to the
spirit though not the letter of the Mediterranean understandings that Bismarck had just sponsored, since those understandings, though they contemplated the possibility of change of the status quo in the Mediterranean, had
centered, as far as Russia was concerned, around the Anglo-Austrian desire
to erect a barrier against a Russian conquest of Constantinople.

After the conclusion of the Reinsurance Treaty, Bismarck felt less endangered by the threats of Boulanger. But he took care to let the world know
as much about his treaties with Austria and Italy as he thought necessary to
dampen anti-German feelings in France and Russia.

Bismarck's success
in preserving peace

UNTIL his dismissal in 1890,
Bismarck succeeded in isolating
France, setting Austria-Hungary
and Italy off against each other, and neutralizing Russia in the affairs of
Europe. What would have happened if Russia had occupied Constantinople
under the secret clause of the Reinsurance Treaty is easy to conjecture. For
before the year (1887) was out, England, Austria, and Italy entered what has
come to be known as the "Second Mediterranean Agreement," pledging
themselves to occupy Turkey jointly if necessary to protect Bulgaria and the

Straits. Bismarck did not lend his moral support to this agreement as he had to the earlier understanding of that year among the Mediterranean powers. The fragility of Bismarck's alliance system was not so apparent to contemporaries as it has since become. Yet it countered threat with threat, and it kept the peace. Crisis had succeeded crisis without a war breaking out between any two major European nations since 1878.

AGITATION

AND REFORM IN EUROPE

THE YEARS between the Congress of Berlin and the dismissal of Bismarck not only were years of international peace, they also were relatively calm years in the domestic affairs of the nations of Europe. No movement that can accurately be called a political revolution occurred in Europe during that interval or was to occur until the Russian Revolution of 1905. Nevertheless, in some areas—Ireland, Russia, the Christian provinces of Turkey—tensions were high and disorders were not infrequent.

*The murder
of Alexander II*

THE RUSSIAN people looked upon the Berlin Treaty as a national humiliation. It disgusted the more radical element among the Nihilists and led to the formation of a new society in Russia called the "Will of The People." This society was ready to accept the views of Bakunin that the state was evil and that terror was a justifiable weapon against the "mere camarilla," the "usurping gang," known as the Russian government. They undertook a series of political murders. In February 1880, the Terrorists made two unsuccessful attempts on the life of Alexander himself. After a year of terror, he decided to re-embark on his program of reform. On March 13, 1881, he approved a proposal to call the Russians together in a representative assembly to consider some new laws. The proclamation was countersigned by his son Alexander and his brother Constantine. It is one of history's most ironic tragedies that on that very day, before the proclamation could be published, Alexander II was badly mangled by a Terrorist's bomb and died within a few hours. The "Executive Committee" of the Terrorists sent the new czar, Alexander III, a letter dated three days before the assassination of his father, demanding a National Assembly: "And now, your Majesty, decide! Before you are two courses, and you are to make your choice between them." Alexander III did not publish the proclamation which he had countersigned. After a lapse of ten days he issued another: "The Voice of God orders us to stand firm at the helm of government...with faith in the strength and truth of the autocratic power, which we are called to strengthen and preserve, for the good of the people, from every kind of encroachment."

*Alexander III
and Pobyedonostzev*

THE NEW czar had a giant's body and a strong will, and he allowed himself to be directed by his former tutor, a man with probably a stronger will and certainly a superior intelligence. That man was Konstantin Petrovich Pobyedonostzev. As the procurator of the Holy Synod, Pobyedonostzev, though a layman, controlled the Orthodox Church and was the most powerful man in Russia from 1880 to 1905. Though at first no reactionary, he now hated the West and all it stood for. He wanted no constitution for Russia, no freedom of the press, no freedom of conscience, no social reforms for the workers or the peasants. He wanted the minorities within the Russian Empire to be curbed, and non-Orthodox Christians and non-Christians to be second-class citizens until they embraced the Orthodox Church.

A policy that became known as "Russification" thus began. Immediately after the accession of the new czar, persecution of the Germans in the Baltic provinces started, and the Poles also were harassed. The Jews were victimized both because they were not Christians and because they were not considered Russians no matter how long their families had lived in Russia. A wave of murderous pogroms swept Russia in 1881, and an exodus of millions of Russian Jews to America began. The army, the police, and the civil service were given extraordinary powers for the protection of the autocratic system.

*Industrialization
and radical activities*

POBYEDONOSTZEV was powerless, however, to prevent the industrialization of Russia. As we have indicated, Russian industrialization went on under the efforts of Vishnegradsky and Witte (page 375). The industrialization of Russia led to a mass immigration of peasants to the big cities, where they hoped to find work in the factories. Witte wanted industrialization badly, but he had envisaged no program of social legislation. Hence the worst evils of the industrial era were duplicated in Russia. Night work for children was permitted in the factories. Many employers compelled their workers to buy their commodities from the factory shops and kept them steadily in debt. Workers sometimes had to toil for more than eleven hours a day. The government was to prove unable to prevent or to alleviate a great famine in 1891-1893, or to combat effectively a cholera epidemic in 1892. These dismal developments spurred workers, peasants, and intelligentsia to join new radical societies.

The inefficient bureaucracy responded with harsh police methods, and repression combined with the evils of industrialization to increase Terrorist activities. A series of murderous attempts was made on high government officials and members of the imperial family. Terror seemed so effective a weapon that in 1882 Marx thought that Russia would be "the vanguard of the European revolutionary movement." Police repression under Alexander III at length proved more than a match for the Terrorists. Georgi V. Plekhanov had in the meantime seceded from the Terrorist movement and formed the first Russian Marxist group (1883). The leaders of this group lived a good part of the time in exile. Being a Socialist was only slightly less dangerous than being a Terrorist. It might entail the loss of a job, a period in jail, or banishment to Siberia. Plekhanov was nevertheless willing that the Socialists cooperate with any group that was against the autocratic government. The exiles, however, were not only unable to find effective cooperation inside Russia, they also broke up into factions abroad. Terrorists and Socialists seemed to serve no other purpose than to goad the police to more repressive measures.

The Wilson Scandal and the Boulanger Affair

WHEREAS the Russian autocracy had to fear violence from radical groupings, the major threat to the French Republic came from the intrigues of the Right. In 1887 the Republic lost the popular confidence because the son-in-law of President Jules Grévy was caught using his influence to secure membership in the Legion of Honor for those who were dishonorable enough to pay him in cash. Because Grévy's son-in-law was named Daniel Wilson, this unsavory episode became known as the Wilson Scandal. Grévy, though innocent himself, was forced to resign.

General Boulanger made good use of the Wilson Scandal to win votes. The return of Schnaebelé, which looked like a victory for Boulangism, likewise played into his hands. When he was sent by an exasperated prime minister to serve in the provinces, crowds lay down on the railroad tracks in the vain hope of keeping him in Paris. Despite his "exile" at Clermont-Ferrand his popularity grew. Returning to Paris without official leave, he was dismissed. But then he won more elections. On January 27, 1889, he carried a particularly important one in Paris itself—important because the Republicans had chosen especially to contest it. He might perhaps have become the dictator of France by a coup d'état that night. Nearly everybody expected that he would. But he did nothing, and the opportunity was lost forever. He soon fled to Belgium and faded practically out of sight until he committed suicide on the grave of his mistress in Brussels in 1891. *Opéra bouffe* though the "Boulanger Affair" was, it had the effect of persuading many royalists and clericals that the Republic was not so unstable as it appeared to be, and it played a not insignificant role in persuading some of the French clergy to rally to the Republic. Moreover, the Third Republic had survived the first serious effort of the military to dominate the civil government, and international peace seemed more secure therefore.

A crowd gathers in front of the offices of La Cocarde, *a pro-Boulanger newspaper, on the announcement of Boulanger's dismissal.*

The Panama Scandal and the rise of anti-Semitism

A FEW years after the Wilson Scandal, another scandal fouled the French political atmosphere. The Panama Company, created to build a canal across the Panama Isthmus, went bankrupt in 1889 as a result of incompetence and graft in high places that became more and more manifest in the ensuing investigations. The antirepublican forces took full advantage of the Republic's embarrassment. Baron Jacques de Reinach, who had helped to finance the company, committed suicide; as president of the company, Ferdinand de Lesseps, the engineer who had built the Suez Canal, was fined and sentenced to prison, though the penalties were remitted on appeal; several others were tried but only three (including a cabinet minister) were found guilty. The public was outraged that so many had been accused and so few found guilty. The episode increased the hostility against Jewish financiers like Reinach and prepared the way for bitter political anti-Semitism in France.

Leo XIII and the French Ralliement

IN THE midst of the Panama Scandal the French clergy rallied to the support of the French Republic. As might have been expected, the church had not taken kindly to Ferry's challenge of its power over the young people of France, and many

French Catholics had given support to General Boulanger's tragicomic effort to overthrow the Third Republic. Pope Leo XIII, however, with the lesson of the Kulturkampf behind him, shared the opinion of several leading French clergymen that the Republic had come to stay and that the church would be well advised to cooperate with the more friendly parties in French politics. When in 1890 the French cardinal Lavigerie indicated by his public declarations that he thought French Catholics might and should rally to the Republic, Leo XIII sided with him rather than with his critics. "The civil power," said the pope, in an encyclical dated 1892, "upon every theory, comes from God," and he advocated the so-called *Ralliement*. He recommended to French Catholics that they forget their royalism and give support to the moderate element in the Third Republic, and many of them were ready and glad to make their peace with the Republic.

The Third Reform in Great Britain under Gladstone

THE BRITISH tradition of reform by parliamentary action permitted a major change to be made without terrorism or attempted coups d'état. Gladstone inaugurated his second ministry in 1880. Among the measures he undertook was an effort to make Parliament more representative, since the Reform Bills of 1832 and of 1867 had left many still disfranchised. By the Franchise Bill of 1884 the right to vote was extended to all but small, especially designated groups of the male population. About 2,000,000 new voters were thus created. Moreover, by the Redistribution Bill of 1885 votes were made practically equal by the redistribution of seats in Parliament among single-member constituencies of fairly equal size (with some exceptions). The Franchise and Redistribution Bills together are known as the Third Reform Bill.

Gladstone, Parnell, and the check of Irish Home Rule

GLADSTONE'S party also made a conscientious effort to solve the Irish question. He had Parliament enact the Land Act of 1881, which attempted to embody the three F's (fixed tenure, fair rent, and free sale), and which organized a system of courts to adjust disputes arising under its provisions. The Irish found the new law insufficient because it did not make outright ownership of the soil easy enough, and the landlords disliked it because it put curbs upon their disposal of their property.

Boycotts and terror continued. Parnell was arrested as a leader of the Irish terrorists but consistently denied responsibility for acts of terrorism, and in fact was released from prison on the understanding that as "uncrowned king of Ireland" he would use his influence with Irishmen at home and in America to check violence. Nevertheless, on May 6, 1882, two high British officials in Ireland were assassinated by a group of Irish extremists in Dublin. Although the jails already contained about 900 Irishmen, in July an outraged Parliament passed the Prevention of Crimes Act, giving the police 437 extraordinary powers to make arrests of suspects who could not give satisfactory explanations of their behavior, and due court processes were suspended in such cases. The Irish retaliated by scores of actual or attempted political murders and by throwing bombs at the Houses of Parliament, the Tower of London, and other public buildings.

By this time Parnell controlled a large block of votes in Parliament. He generally threw the weight of the Irish Party on the side of the Conservatives. The tragedy of Gordon at Khartoum was laid at home to Gladstone's mismanagement, and for that and other reasons he lost his grip on his party. Defeated on a budget matter, he resigned in 1885, and Lord Salisbury became prime minister. The Conservatives did not renew the Crimes Prevention Act, which expired that year, and they passed the Ashbourne Act making £5,000,000 available for easy loans to Irish land purchasers.

In the elections of 1885, Parnell's party won enough votes to give the Irish-Conservative combination a tie with the Liberals. Only with Liberal support, however, could he hope for a majority to pass a home rule bill, so Parnell threw his weight to the Liberals' side, and in 1886 Gladstone came to power again. Without the Irish, the new government could command no majority in Parliament. Therefore Gladstone went farther than he had been willing to go before and introduced a Home Rule Bill. But this bill met fierce opposition from the Protestants of Ireland's northernmost province, Ulster, centering around the city of Belfast. Many of these people were descended from immigrants who had come to Ireland from Scotland and

The eviction, in the early 1880's, of a tenant family from their cottage in the west of Ireland.

England since the seventeenth century, and their industrial, English, Protestant outlook made them unsympathetic with the nationalist aspirations of the Irishmen to the south of them. Some of the Liberals, who came to be called "Liberal Unionists" and broke away from Gladstone's party, championed their views. The Home Rule Bill was defeated in the House of Commons. New elections brought back the Conservatives and Lord Salisbury, who succeeded in passing the Perpetual Coercion Act (1887), which gave almost dictatorial powers to the viceroy of Ireland. With theatrical abruptness, Parnell's political life was ruined when he became involved as corespondent in a divorce scandal. He died in 1891. But Irish Home Rule remained a live and heated issue.

Defensive measures of the Salisbury government

ELSEWHERE in the empire Britain was more successful. The war scare of 1886-1887 led England, we have seen, temporarily to forsake her policy of isolation and to join two international combinations designed to preserve the status quo in the Mediterranean against a Russian threat. The year 1887 was the Golden Jubilee of Queen Victoria's reign, and was the occasion for calling the first Colonial Conference of the British Empire. It was attended by representatives from the Dominion of Canada and from the other colonies, and dealt chiefly with the problems of defense. Two years later Parliament passed the Naval Defense Act, which stipulated that the British Navy must preserve a "two-power standard"—that is, be as strong as any two potential enemies combined (Russia and France particularly, since Germany and Italy had no naval significance). These measures were an indication of England's determination to rely on her own resources, to build up her empire, and to stay out of European entanglements. It was to prove a vain hope.

Tension between the Kaiser and Bismarck

ONE OF THE reasons for the ultimate failure of England's policy of isolation was the personality of the new ruler of Germany. William I of Germany died in March 1888. His son, Frederick III, victim of cancer of the throat, reigned for only a few months. In June, Frederick was followed on the throne by his eldest son, William II, who became known at home and abroad as "the Kaiser." He was twenty-nine years old at the time of his accession to the throne. Frederick had always been a liberal, who had not approved of Bismarck's methods. But Bismarck expected to guide the young William II as he had guided the grandfather. For a while the chancellor seemed right in that assumption, but the characters of the two men proved incompatible. The Kaiser, an intelligent but vain man, sensitive about his withered left hand, was jealous of his prerogatives. "Regarding myself as an instrument of Heaven," he was to announce in a speech at Königsberg in 1910, "I receive my inspirations only from God, and I do not owe any account to anybody." In the words of Bismarck, William II wanted to be "his own chancellor." A final break was not long postponed. We have mentioned (page 378) their disagreement over domestic policy, particularly Bismarck's desire to crush the Socialists, which William did not share. An additional but less pressing reason for the final break developed in the field of foreign affairs.

Bismarck's dispute with the Kaiser over "reinsurance"

WILLIAM did not fully appreciate Bismarck's policy of "reinsurance" with Russia. The new chief of the Prussian General Staff, Count von Waldersee, who perhaps hoped to become chancellor himself, encouraged the Kaiser's doubts. In this connection they found a curious ally in the self-styled "Baron" Friedrich von Holstein. Holstein had started his career as Bismarck's secretary, when the latter was Prussian ambassador to Russia. Bismarck rewarded his personal loyalty and his good service at the Congress of Berlin by making him a councilor in the Foreign Office in Berlin. That was the highest office Holstein ever held, but it was by no means a measure of the influence he was to acquire. Holstein seems slowly to have developed a secret, deep-seated resentment of Bismarck. In the winter of 1889-1890, as the gulf between the Kaiser and Bismarck was widening, Holstein apparently let various persons close to the Kaiser learn that the Reinsurance Treaty was contrary to the spirit of the Austro-German alliance, and the Kaiser, whose preferences lay with the English and the Austrians, found another reason for disagreement with the "Iron Chancellor."

The immediate cause of Bismarck's dismissal was, however, his insistence that the separate ministers should report to the Kaiser only in his presence. When the Kaiser asked him to rescind that order, he refused, and the Kaiser then asked for his resignation. It was offered in March 1890 and accepted immediately. Thus, the man who had dominated Europe for more than a generation was chased from his position—like "an unfaithful servant," as he put it himself. He was in the end a victim of his own political philosophy that neither parliament nor ministry but the monarch was the ultimate source of authority. He retired to Friedrichsruhe, one of his estates, where he died in 1898.

Five days after Bismarck's dismissal, the German government decided not to renew the Reinsurance Treaty, and it was allowed to lapse. With it lapsed the complicated pattern of German alliances, English isolation, and French diversion which for a long time had meant relative peace in Europe.

WITH A certain justification the years between 1871 and 1890 have sometimes been called the Age of Bismarck. Those who call it so have politics foremost in mind. For the age that could boast Wagner, Brahms, and Verdi in music, Nietzsche in philosophy, Ibsen in drama, Hardy, Zola, Tolstoy, and Dostoyevsky in fiction, Verlaine, Tennyson, and Browning in poetry, Helmholtz in physics, Pasteur in biology, Manet and Van Gogh in painting, Rodin in sculpture, Edison in technology, and Nobel and Rockefeller in business cannot well be described as dominated by any one illustrious man. Even in politics, other statesmen's names claim attention—Disraeli and Gladstone perhaps foremost among them. Yet the name of Bismarck represented a long entrenched and a largely self-directed power, unbroken by the hazards of elections and only partly shaped by party pressures.

Bismarck knew his power. "Without me," he once admitted, "three great wars might not have been, 80,000 men might not have died, and parents, brothers, sisters, widows would not be in mourning. Nevertheless, I have made my peace with God." The three wars of which he spoke came before 1871. Since that time the greatness of Prussia which he had sought by forcibly unifying Germany had been a reality, and he had devoted himself to the preservation of peace—by alliances and by a show of strength, not hesitating to make seemingly contradictory promises to Germany's friends or to encourage the colonial ambitions of Germany's potential enemies in the hope of diverting them from Europe's quarrels to ventures and perhaps to disputes in distant places. If eventually he permitted Germany to become involved in tariff and colonial rivalries, it was not only because he was yielding to pressure but also because he sought in industry and empire new avenues to German greatness. Thus Berlin became not merely the seat of great international conferences but also the capital of an empire that now stretched overseas, an industrial and commercial center attempting to rival London, and a cultural mecca striving to outstrip Paris and Vienna.

In the hands of so skillful a player as Bismarck the game of *Realpolitik* could be so played as to make war or to avoid war. Since 1871 Bismarck had avoided war and, aided by the *Pax Britannica,* Italy's and Austria's dependence, France's preoccupation with domestic crises and colonies, and Russia's cumbersomeness, he had even helped to preserve peace. But his skill had helped to destroy the cushioning that a loose confederation in central Europe had once provided between Prussia and Austria and between eastern and western Europe. Instead of buffers, central Europe now constituted a hard, strong force, pressing upon and resisting pressure from all sides. Some of Bismarck's successors, less skillful than he in the game of *Realpolitik,* thought of the German Empire not as something gained that must be preserved but as something strong that must be made stronger still, and they were to form alliances rather to be victorious in case of war than to avoid war by a show of strength in times of peace. By their miscalculations Bismarck's Germany was to be undone—no one can yet say with certainty how profoundly or how irretrievably.

Part four

Part four

THE WORLD ON THE

FROM CRISES
TO CATACLYSM
1890-1914

THE WORLD ON THE

Arctic Ocean

RUSSI

CANADA

NEWFOUNDLAND
(Labrador)

UNITED
KINGDOM

St. Petersburg

BELGIUM

GERMANY

AUSTRIA-HUNGARY

FRANCE

BULGARIA

UNITED STATES

Atlantic Ocean

ITALY

OTTOMAN
EMPIRE

Bagdad

Gibraltar

Dardanelles

Persian Gulf

British West Indies
French West Indies
BRITISH GUIANA
DUTCH GUIANA
FRENCH GUIANA

MOROCCO ALGERIA

LIBYA

EGYPT

Panama Canal

FRENCH WEST AFRICA

ERITREA

SUDAN

SOUTH
AMERICA

NIGERIA

TOGOLAND

CAMEROONS

FRENCH
EQUATORIAL AFRICA

BELGIAN
CONGO

GERMAN
EAST
AFRICA

GERMAN
SOUTHWEST
AFRICA

UNION
OF
SOUTH
AFRICA

MADAGASCAR

Capetown

Delagoa Bay

German   U.S.   British   French   Japanese   Russian   Italian   Belgian

By 1914 large parts of the earth had been partitioned among the European powers either as colonies and protectorates or as "spheres of influence." When assassination in the Balkans set in motion the delicate alliance mechanisms that had been built up in Europe during the preceding decades, they necessarily went into operation at unprecedented distances. Naval supremacy was expected to enable the Allies to attack Germany's colonies, to call on the colonials of the Allied powers for aid, and to cut off raw materials and foodstuffs coming to Germany from overseas. The contiguity of the Central Powers seemed to make mutual military support easy for them, but it also increased their fear of attack on two fronts. Hence Germany's need for a speedy decision on the Atlantic front.

Chapter eight

IMPERIALISM AND
PROSPERITY
c. 1890-1905

ALTHOUGH no special magic attaches to the opening year of a new century, like 1900, popular imagination is stirred by the conspicuousness given to the passage of time as people stop assigning themselves to the earlier century and begin to associate themselves with the next. Some looked upon the *fin de siècle* (the century's close) with awe, some with hope, some with depression. Nevertheless, the pace of change in the 1900's was probably no faster than in the 1890's. In all the fifteen years between 1890 and 1905 great technological advances and impressive scientific discoveries were being prepared or actually announced, important constitutional changes and imperialistic enterprises were undertaken, the arts and letters continued to flourish, and the fiscal year 1900-1901 was probably much like any other year to most businessmen.

Several great changes, however, were taking place that future decades were going to be better able to appreciate than contemporaries. In science the principles of Newtonian physics were to be challenged by the Einstein theory. In technology electricity was beginning to vie with steam as an important source of energy. In international affairs the two great non-European powers, Japan and the United States, emerging as victors from wars with European nations, were to command greater respect as forces in the world. In the domestic affairs of the nations the concession of a constitutional regime for the Russian people was to mark the beginning of the collapse of Russian autocracy rather than, as many contemporaries thought, its consolidation.

One set of events was probably more shocking to contemporaries than it might seem to the generations that were to follow and to live through two world wars. After a decade of almost unbroken peace save for some imperialist skirmishes in Afghanistan, the Sudan, and other outlying areas, four wars (not counting the Italo-Ethiopian War of 1896 and the Greco-Turkish War of 1897) followed close upon one another, each involving at least one of the eight great powers of the time, and the last three involving a European nation on one side. These were the Sino-Japanese War of 1894-1895, the Spanish-American War of 1898, the Boer War of 1899-1902, and the Russo-Japanese War of 1904-1905. These wars enmeshed other countries indirectly through diplomatic channels, breaking the "splendid isolation" of England, bringing Japan and the United States into the quarrels of Europe, and forecasting the split of Europe into two armed camps (the German and the Anglo-French systems of alliances). Yet they were wars with limited objectives, and one might still hope, when they were settled, that the growing efforts for international peace might yet outweigh the growing tensions in international diplomacy.

EUROPEAN CULTURE

AT THE START OF THE ELECTRIC AGE

SINCE THE day in 1831 when Faraday had demonstrated that electricity could be induced from the magnetic field, the commercial production of electricity had made important advances. Steam was still the chief source of power when the nineteenth century ended, but the age of electricity was just around the corner. The Chicago Exposition of 1893 was brilliant with electric lights. In 1895 three 5000-kilowatt electric generators were installed at Niagara Falls. At the Paris World's Fair of 1900 electricity came into its own, and many who visited the exhibition went home with the feeling that the world would enter a new phase with the dawn of the new century.

Electric power and national economies

FOR COUNTRIES short of coal but rich in lakes and streams, electricity was to help solve the problem of industrial power. France and Italy took a prominent part in pioneering hydroelectric plants. Sweden and Switzerland soon proceeded to develop huge hydroelectric programs. Hitherto poor countries were able to increase their industrial wealth, to raise their standards of living, and, despite their small populations, to play an increasingly important role in the world economy. The Swiss, famous for the high professional standards of their engineers, began to electrify their whole railroad system, though the process was not to be completed until the 1930's. Electric railroads made the most beautiful mountain scenery easily accessible to tourists, and tourism in turn grew as an industry by leaps and bounds after 1900. Russia and Ireland also made use of water power for generating electricity, though only on a small scale until after the First World War. Outside Europe, Canada, the United States, New

The coming of the age of electricity revolutionized not only the industrial world but the entertainment world as well. This elaborate system of dynamos and controls was installed in 1887 for the electric stage lighting of the Paris Opéra.

Zealand, and Tasmania also developed hydroelectric projects. Areas that lacked water power as well as coal went in for thermoelectricity (steam-generated) particularly after 1920, when costs were reduced by more efficient methods of using coal.

Electricity, the theater, and advertising

ELECTRICITY had interesting incidental effects on the theater and advertising. For the first time great dramas and operas could be staged with lighting effects and other theatricalities that had existed hitherto only in the imagination of their authors. Good stage managers like Sir Herbert Beerbohm Tree in England and his young contemporary Max Reinhardt in Germany used the new possibilities to full advantage. The response of the public justified their efforts. The great classics in drama and opera became popular because they appeared literally "in a new light." Max Reinhardt, shortly before the First World War, staged the mystery play *The Miracle* in London, and then, after the war, in New York. His stage setting fascinated not only Londoners and New Yorkers but the whole theatrical world, and lifted the art of stage setting from an incidental to a major place among the dramatic arts. With the improvement of the electric light bulb, electric signs made their appearance, and after 1910 signs in the shape of moving lights on roof tops and house walls were to become a favorite method of advertising.   451

*The infancy
of some major industries*

THE TOTAL number of different kinds of employment grew as new industries sprang up. Some indus-
tries that were to develop only after the First World War had already laid their foundations around 1900. Karl Benz showed his first (three-wheeled) motorcar in 1885 at Mannheim, and the European automotive industry be-gan. Guglielmo Marconi in the 1890's perfected the inventions that laid the foundation for wireless telegraphy. Edison's gramophone, or phonograph, invented in 1877, began to be manufactured for sale shortly after but made a poor showing until the tinfoil record was replaced by wax cylinders and the cylinders by hard-rubber discs. The first moving picture was exhibited to the public by the Edison Company in 1896, but film production long remained an infant industry, despite the mechanical genius of Edison and the French Lumière brothers, because of the confused and ruthless competition among those engaged in it. The German Count von Zeppelin produced a practical airship in 1900, and the American Wright brothers a practical airplane in 1903, but the aircraft industry did not come into its own before the war of 1914. Petroleum was used chiefly as a fuel for lighting and heating, and rub-ber chiefly for erasers, boots, waterproofing, and bicycle tires before the pro-duction of a cheap automobile; and the Diesel engine (first patented in 1892) experienced no wide application until its adaptation to ships just before the First World War.

*Cartels
and cooperatives in Europe*

UNLIKE the American govern-ment the European governments did not make "combinations in restraint of trade" illegal. In 1886, as pointed out above (page 375), the British Nobel Dynamite Trust was founded. The Rheinisch-Westfälisches Kohlensyndikat, the German coal combine, was established in 1893. In some instances national cartels assumed the character of monopolies with the ap-proval of their governments. In 1910, for instance, the German Reichstag was to enact a law setting up a federally controlled potash syndicate, which had a total monopoly. Some businessmen reasoned that what seemed good on a national scale might be even more effective on an international scale. By agreements among them the first international combines came into being.

In some forms of enterprise large combines were checked or restricted by various means. Cooperative organizations, formed by persons willing to com-bine to own the stores in which they shopped and to distribute the profits among themselves, were especially strong in the English-speaking countries. Inaugurated in 1844 with the Rochdale Society, the cooperative movement extended to other kinds of cooperation—producers' cooperatives, bank coop-eratives, agricultural marketing cooperatives, and credit unions—and is now to be found in some form or other all over the world. Around 1900 there

452   were 1400 cooperative stores in the United Kingdom alone, and about 30,000

credit unions in the world, and it was estimated that the total world membership of cooperatives was around 6,000,000. In 1895 an International Cooperative Alliance was formed. Yet the cooperative movement has never been a
serious threat to "big business." In some countries, like France and Switzerland, the small businessman has held his own and is still rather strong. But
even in those countries, basic materials like iron, steel, dyestuffs, cement, and
electric appliances are controlled by combines. At the close of the nineteenth
century, the new stratum of rulers, the lords of industry, were growing in
numbers and in strength. Like the potentates of yore, they tended to found
dynasties. Some of these lords of industry were descendants of fairly old
families—like the Krupps in Germany, the Vickerses in England, and the
Schneiders in France; others were of humble origin, particularly in the United
States.

*Leo XIII
and the encyclical* Rerum novarum
THE SOCIALISTS taught that the
church was, consciously or unconsciously, merely the tool of the
capitalists. In part to win the workers away from their anticlerical leaders,
Leo in 1891 promulgated his famous encyclical *Rerum novarum*. In it he
castigated the evils of both socialism and capitalism. He warned the governments and the ruling classes that "some remedy must be found, and quickly
found, for the misery and wretchedness which press so heavily at this moment on the large majority of the very poor." While he defended the institution of private property, he also advocated labor unions (which were still
outlawed by some governments), collective bargaining, and social legislation. "Every one must put his hand to work which falls to his share, and that
at once and immediately, lest the evil which is already so great may by delay
become absolutely beyond remedy. Those who rule the state must use the
law and the constitutions of the country; masters and rich men must remember their duty; the poor, whose interests are at stake, must make every lawful
and proper effort; since Religion alone...can destroy the evil at its root, all
men must be persuaded that the primary thing needful is to return to real
Christianity." Leo's encyclical has been the yardstick of the Roman Catholic
Church in measuring social and economic proposals ever since. It was reaffirmed and enlarged by Pope Pius XI in 1931.

The Socialists dismissed the encyclical as the wry idea of a priest secluded
from the world. It nevertheless had an effect that was more fully understood
half a century after the event. It threw the church on the side of social reform.
Millions of Catholic workers refused to become Socialists, with resulting loss
to the Social Democratic movement. On the other hand, in many countries,
Catholic labor unions, springing up in the path of the encyclical, became so
strong that governments had to adopt programs of social legislation because
it was no longer possible to resist the combined pressure of Socialists and
Catholics. Nevertheless, the church had not gone radical. Leo himself re-

buked the "Americanism Movement" of some clergy who wished openly to espouse social reform. When workers threatened the social order, as, for example, in a series of strikes in Italy between 1903 and 1905, the pope (now Pius X, Leo having died in 1903) removed the injunction (*Non expedit*) against Catholic participation in Italian politics in order that Catholics might throw their support to the constituted authorities.

French syndicalism and the founding of the CGT

SOCIALISM in most European countries had a distinctly Marxian character. Under the leadership of Jules Guesde, French workers were increasingly attracted by the idea of the general strike (the cessation of all work), which many of them were sure would usher in the revolution and the seizing of power by the proletariat. Advocates of the general strike differed only on whether the revolution was to be brought about by the cessation of work alone or, in addition, by an armed conflict between the workers and the capitalists' army and police. Direct action by means of workers' unions to accomplish a revolution is known as "Syndicalism" (from the French word for trade union—*syndicat*). In the 1890's some bloody strikes and strike-breakings took place. The leaders of the French workers soon became insistent upon one point—namely, that a central organization of the workers of all France had to be established. In 1895 the General Confederation of Labor (Confédération Générale de Travail, or CGT) came into being. The most important provision of its charter required that it should "remain outside of all political schools," thereby announcing its intention to resort to direct action to attain its ends. On several occasions the syndicates started strikes affecting whole industries, and only after the dismal failure of the great railroad strike of 1910 were they to become more cautious. Meanwhile, however, Guesde in 1903 succeeded in bringing the various wings of the French Socialists together to form a single United Socialist Party, strictly Marxian and revolutionary in character. The Dreyfus Affair (page 466) had persuaded the Socialists of the necessity of union.

British labor and the Independent Labour Party

IN THE United Kingdom socialism developed independently of the continental movement. The British worker naturally desired to have representatives in Parliament. In 1892, though the Fabian Society (page 379) took no direct part in politics and no formal workers' party existed, fourteen trade-unionists were elected. In response to this demand Keir Hardie, in 1893, founded the Independent Labour Party. It was frankly a political party drawing its support from the trade unions and having a distinct political program of its own. To coordinate the work of their members in Parliament, in 1900, the Labour Representation Committee was organized, and by 1906 this organization led to the for-

454

mation of the British Labour Party. The Fabians were associated with it, but some of them now sat also as liberals in Parliament. In the general elections of 1906 the Labour Party was to gain twenty-nine seats.

The warfare of religion and science

SOCIALISM was not the only target of the church. The idea that science does not necessarily contradict religion had been advanced by some of the greatest scientists—for example, Mendel and Pasteur—of the age of realism. Nevertheless, as was perhaps to have been expected, many scientists, studying a universe that they thought they could explain by physical laws alone, were indifferent or even hostile toward religion, which they regarded as obscurantism. In 1899 the German biologist Ernst Haeckel, an outstanding Darwinian, published a book called *The Riddle of the Universe.* It became a best seller. In it Haeckel expounded a monistic materialistic theory—that the world is of one substance throughout. Everybody was able to understand his theory and to recognize that if it was right, the world was ultimately entirely intelligible in materialistic terms. The movement spread into religion in the form of "modernism"—an effort to bring religion into conformity with recent scientific developments. That movement met with disgust or outright hostility on the part of the Roman hierarchy. In 1907 Pope Pius X issued the decree *Lamentabili,* in which he listed over sixty modernistic errors, and an encyclical *Pascendi gregis,* in which he tried to check the growing scientific naturalism in church schools and seminaries. Nevertheless, the Catholic Church, having long permitted an allegorical interpretation of the Bible, found it easier than some of the fundamentalist Protestant sects to adjust its teachings to recent discoveries in the natural sciences.

The trends of the time in contemporaneous literature

CONTINUING the realistic vogue of earlier decades, the literature of the day reflected the controversies over industrialization and materialism that were being aired from pulpit and party platforms. Among the younger Russian realists of the day was the playwright and short-story writer Anton Chekhov. Chekhov was perhaps Russia's greatest short-story teller, not because of his plots, which his stories frequently lacked, but because of his straightforward descriptions of man's inability to understand his fellow men. His *Cherry Orchard* (1904) is a play illustrating the unpreparedness of a Russian noble family to readjust to the new urbanization going on around them.

Several great writers of the age were remarkable for their blending of science, particularly technological data, with fantasy. The pace in science fiction had already been set by the Frenchman Jules Verne, whose best scientific novels were behind him in the 1890's but who still exerted a marked influence on the others. The Englishman H. G. Wells was perhaps the leading writer of science fiction of the 1890's, although, an early Fabian, he also wrote novels of a Utopian nature and occasionally merged the two themes. Sir Arthur Conan Doyle brought to life, in a series of stories beginning in 1887, the scientific detective Sherlock Holmes, perhaps the greatest of the type in all fiction.

Anatole France
as the outstanding French author

ANATOLE FRANCE (pseudonym of Jacques Anatole Thibault) is often referred to as a realist because of the way he dealt in his series of four novels, *Contemporary History* (1897-1901), with the problems of his time. But in a sense he was rather the spiritual descendant of Montaigne and Voltaire. He was a skeptic, a rationalist, a satirist, an agnostic, and an Epicurean devoted to the beautiful, particularly women. But his sensuality was counterbalanced by a strong love for justice and a smiling compassion for the follies and miseries of his fellow men. His outraged sense of justice made him plunge into the turmoil of the Dreyfus Affair. All these personal qualities are blended in a fascinating way in his novels, most of which appeared before 1905, though two of the best, the satire *Penguin Island* and *The Gods Are Athirst* (1912), dealing with a well-intentioned but fanatical judge of the French Revolution who is himself finally guillotined, appeared in the next decade.

Conrad and Shaw
as figures in English letters

JOSEPH CONRAD provides a rare example of the novelist who gained fame from works written in a language not his mother tongue. He was born a Pole, served as a sea captain in the British merchant marine, and eventually settled in England, where he became one of the greatest prose writers English literature has ever had. He, too, dealt with his topics realistically and had a profound understanding of human tribulations. His real hero, however, was not man but the sea. *Lord Jim* (1900) and other stories are narrated by Conrad's favorite character, Marlow, who seeks to understand not facts so much as the meaning hidden beneath them.

George Bernard Shaw, whom we have already encountered as a Fabian (page 380), was a realist only in a limited sense of the word. He was a man motivated by an ethical fervor, softened by a sparkling humor, against convention and snobbery. Most of his plays are political pamphlets in dramatic form, the prefaces to which read like Fabian tracts written by a secularized, witty clergyman. His early plays, *Candida* (1897) and *Arms and the Man* (1898), are among the few nondidactic plays that he wrote, and even in these he lampoons two kinds of political figures—"the strong man" among the reformers and the romanticized soldier. Shaw's plays were to receive acclaim on the stages of the whole civilized world for more than half a

century.

**D'Annunzio's place
in Italian literature**

AS A professed esthete Oscar Wilde was matched in the 1890's by the poet-novelist-adventurer Gabriele d'Annunzio. The topics of D'Annunzio's plays and novels were realistic; his ideal was esthetic, and he had a magic power with the Italian language. His proclivity for writing about the morbid and the erotic exceeded that of perhaps any other author of his time. As a lover, D'Annunzio was a tattletale; as an aristocrat, he was haughty. His ties, his goatee, and his flamboyance set a fashion. And yet he had a genuine and abiding faith that Italy was destined for unlimited greatness. He was to volunteer in the First World War, when he was in his fifties, and to lose an eye in air combat. The novels and plays of D'Annunzio held a sway over the intellectuals of the Continent comparable to the music dramas of Wagner, the operas of Verdi, and the plays of Ibsen. The rude awakening was to come when D'Annunzio, as we shall see, became one of the fathers of Fascism.

**The beginning
of the fear of "Americanization"**

AMERICAN influences upon European culture were becoming more noticeable in the 1890's. The years of industrial expansion had seen European capital poured into the United States; now the trend was beginning to reverse itself. United States investment abroad began as a mere trickle in the 1890's, mostly in Canada and Latin America. In 1901 a British government loan was floated in the United States—the first such move by a European government. In addition, the early years of the twentieth century saw the establishment of branch factories of American concerns in Europe, a trend not wholly pleasing to European businessmen. Europeans felt obliged to emulate American techniques, advertising, and salesmanship in order to compete successfully. With the adoption of American methods and the invasion of such American products as electric bulbs, sewing machines, farm machinery, and phonographs, Europeans, fearful of "machine culture," began to speak disgustedly of "Americanization."

The apprehension about American "barbarism" was often voiced in literary circles. The French novelist Paul Bourget engaged in a controversy with Mark Twain about marital life in America. Most European intellectuals appeared to believe that Bourget was right in attacking the common American view of marriage as a private contract between a man and a woman rather than as a family, church, and state affair. Paul Claudel, then a young consul in the United States, joined the controversy with his tragedy *The Exchange* (1893), in which he charged that American marital arrangements were basically immoral because the religious and social purpose of marriage was misunderstood. In 1895, Bourget published *Overseas,* a two-volume journal of his observations in the United States, which was essentially friendly   457 but did not increase the number of Americanophiles in Europe, because it spoke also of America's "incoherence and haste...the crudity of its streets and big cities...its lack of equilibrium, measure, and taste...the too artificial tension of its culture...the ferocity [of] competition between businessmen, the corruption of its police, its magistrates, and its politicians."

Naturalism in musical composition

THE importation of realism into music made rapid strides with some young composers of the 1890's. Richard Strauss was one of the greatest programmatic music writers of the period. In his so-called orchestral "tone poems," particularly in parts of *Till Eulenspiegel's Merry Pranks* (1894), he went into a minute musical reproduction, a sort of orchestral onomatopoeia, of everything that was narrated in the underlying story. Concertgoers did not easily take to that kind of music, and Strauss was derided at first as a composer. In his later operas, *Salome* (1905), *Elektra* (1909), and *Der Rosenkavalier* (1910), Strauss gradually became more conventional.

The tone poem entered French music with the compositions of Debussy, especially his "Afternoon of a Faun" and *La Mer* (1903-1905). In his opera *Pelléas et Mélisande* (1902) he deliberately moved away from melody to a *parlando* (speaking style) supported by orchestra for the better expression of feelings and moods—in this regard falling into the tradition of French opera of the late baroque period and counteracting the Wagnerian influence. In his piano and orchestral compositions he endeavored to make his instruments convey the effect of water, light, rain, clouds, moods, and abstractions which few had previously attempted to portray by means of the musical scale. One of his preludes (1910), entitled "Footprints on the Snow," carries the instruction: "The rhythm of this piece ought to have the tone value of a lonely, frozen landscape." His intention to paint background by musical effects explains why he is sometimes said to have introduced impressionism into music.

Anthropology and oriental studies

UNTIL the 1890's the preponderant influence among students of the Orient had belonged to the philologists like Max Müller (page 349). Müller's work was strongly attacked in 1897, however, by the Scottish scholar Andrew Lang, himself a student of folklore, mythology, and religion, for its emphasis upon language and literary sources for the understanding of early Asiatic religions. Other attacks upon the philological domination of Oriental studies came from the newly developing sciences of archaeology and anthropology. After the establishment of European political control over important segments of the Asiatic world, expeditions to investigate the origins of its peoples were more frequently sent out by European and American museums and universities. In 1891-1892 one of the most startling discoveries in the history of evolution

458

"Head of a Tahitian." A drawing by the French post-impressionist, Paul Gauguin.

was uncovered in Java by the Dutch physician Dr. Eugene Dubois. He unearthed the fossilized bones of a creature that apparently came somewhere on the evolutionary scale between man and the higher apes of the Pleistocene age. To the being whose remains these bones were, the name *Pithecanthropus erectus* has been assigned by the scientific world. This being constitutes a valuable link in the chain of man's ascent from the lower animals.

Continuation of Oriental influences in Europe THE SCIENTIFIC and scholarly concern with the Far East was accompanied by a continued sentimental interest. Loti and Lafcadio Hearn (page 490) won vast audiences. The painter Gauguin (page 397), enamored of the beauty and romance of Tahiti, made the South Seas familiar through his numerous canvases. Intending to follow his vocation freely and cheaply, Gauguin in 1891 went to live there. The remaining years of his life he spent in the South Seas except for a short visit to Paris in 1895. In his autobiographical novel *Noa Noa* he described his life on Tahiti and revealed his admiration for the island people. He painted the bronzed natives among their exotic plants and crude dwellings and depicted the luminous and natural charm of the tropical landscape, which lent itself rewardingly to his theory of vivid color and expression even at the expense of the exact copying of nature. Moreover, he was influenced by the primitive wood carvings and terra cottas found on the islands. In the last 459 years of his life Gauguin sided with the natives in their political quarrels with the French.

Russia provided a striking example of cultural interchange with the East. Like several contemporaries in western Europe, Leo Tolstoy evinced a deep appreciation of Chinese thought and religion. In the twenty-five years before his death (1910), he turned to the Asiatic peoples for help in his quest for religious and moral understanding and showed interest particularly in the concepts of Confucianism and Taoism. He read many of the best contemporary appraisals of China and of its religions in western languages as well as translations of the Chinese classics. In his own writings on China, numbering ten separate titles, Tolstoy urged the Chinese not to follow the course of Japan in imitating the West. China and Russia, as the great independent, agricultural countries of Asia, should, he felt, be spiritually allied against the West. Tolstoy was also impressed by the Taoist doctrine of nonresistance, and he corresponded with Mahatma Gandhi (Chapter 11) on the effectiveness of passive resistance in political crises.

Japanese contributions to the sciences and the arts

AS JAPAN underwent political readjustment, Japanese scientists, scholars, and artists made important contributions in their respective spheres. The germ of the dreaded bubonic plague, so fatal to Occidental and Oriental alike in the past, was discovered in the 1890's by Kitasato Shibasaburo, a student of Koch and one of the world's foremost bacteriologists, about the same time that the Swiss bacteriologist Alexander Yersin and Koch himself were likewise shedding light upon the causes of the plague. Kitasato also discovered the bacilli of tetanus and diphtheria and made other bacteriological contributions. Takamine Jokichi isolated adrenalin in 1901. In art and letters Japanese and other Orientals continued to interest Europeans and to exert some influence upon them. In return the Japanese accepted western clothes, sports, and art forms to a limited extent. Several Japanese artists began to use oils and other techniques of western painting, and a few even went west to study. The big-scale importation of gramophones after 1896 made occidental music widely acceptable to the Japanese. But in all fields of artistic expression the traditional forms continued to predominate.

New departures in the physical sciences (to 1916)

AT THE TURN of the century the physical sciences underwent a veritable revolution. For one thing, the science of physical chemistry emerged, largely through the application of the laws of thermodynamics to chemical processes. In addition, a number of great physicists succeeded in providing, on the basis of the now familiar kinetic-molecular theory, a mechanical explanation of the thermal properties of matter and in making a quantitative inference about its ultimate building blocks (molecules). The study of the constitution of matter was greatly advanced by the discovery in 1895 by Konrad Röntgen of X-rays, most familiar today by their use in medicine and surgery. With their aid the presence and arrangement of atoms in crystals was demonstrated. By studying the scattering of X-rays, J. J. Thomson, the discoverer of a particle now called the "electron," was able to explore the inside of atoms, establishing the number of electrons per atom. He conceived a historically important (though incorrect) model of an atom, which guided Ernest Rutherford in some of his subsequent investigations. In 1911 Rutherford improved Thomson's model by conceiving of a tiny positive "nucleus" surrounded by a cloud of electrons. He thus laid the foundation for the still better model proposed in 1913 by Niels Bohr. Rutherford thus was the principal founder of another new science, nuclear physics. Among the pioneers in this science were Henri Becquerel, who discovered (1896) the phenomenon of radioactivity (the spontaneous decomposition of nuclei accompanied by radiations) in uranium, and Marie and Pierre Curie, who discovered radium (1898) and some other radioactive elements. This discovery overthrew the belief in the immutability of the elements of modern chemistry.

Another revolutionary discovery was made in connection with the nature of energy. Max Planck, attempting to interpret theoretically his law of black body radiation, found he could do so only if he assumed that the emission of energy from a vibrating electron proceeds not in a continuous wave but discontinuously in the form of definite "energy packages." He called such a package of energy a "quantum." Whereas previously only matter had been believed to come in discontinuous parcels (atoms), now Planck's quantum theory (1900) required the assumption that energy also must come in discontinuous parcels (quanta).

The greatest innovations in physical science came with the work of Albert Einstein. One of his contributions was to interpret Planck's quantum theory to mean that light is not emitted in spherical pulse waves but rather in the form of particles, which he called "photons." This photon theory alone does not explain all the phenomena in optics but is indispensable along with the wave theory, providing explanations where the latter fails. Einstein's most significant contribution during this period was his theory of relativity, first set forth as a special theory in 1905 and then generalized in 1914-1916. The theory of relativity assumes that the only constant mechanical norm is the speed of light, which had been measured and shown to be independent of the motion of the observer by A. A. Michelson and E. W. Morley in a series of experiments begun in 1881. Other quantities, such as length, duration, and mass, as well as the judgment of simultaneity, Einstein contends, vary according to the motion of the observer relative to the observed system. The Einstein theory modified the basis of mechanics (the study of forces and motion) and hence the basis of all physics. Moreover, it gave the physicist a stimulating precedent for further bold speculation.

Frazer, Lévy-Bruhl, and Freud

THREE well-known students of the irrational laid the foundations of their work in this period, though they continued and broadened their influence until the Second World War. Sir James George Frazer in *The Golden Bough* (1890-1915) advanced the understanding of myth and folklore and, in part to correct his errors, hastened the development of a scientific anthropology. Lucien Lévy-Bruhl, though formally a philosopher, also studied primitive man and exerted a significant influence upon the study of primitive religion in anthropology. The first of Sigmund Freud's many writings appeared in the 1890's.

Freud's major contribution was his development of psychoanalysis as a method of treating certain emotional disturbances. Several of his theories had been intuitively anticipated by the great dramatists, novelists, and poets, whose genius had led them to an understanding of the depths of the human personality, but he lifted their intuitive insights to the level of scientific verification—or, at least, testing. For example, he conceived the idea of the psychopathology of everyday life (Freudian slips) and the interpretation of dream material on a scientific basis. He contended that children have a sexual life quite their own, a contention which at first aroused shocked hostility. He laid stress upon the role of totem and taboo, holding that in certain mental disturbances patients revert to these and other beliefs and practices of primitive man, and in so doing resort to either mental and psychic repression or "sublimation" (i.e., deflection toward creative work). He expounded the Oedipus complex (the repressed sex relationship of child to parent) and other psychological complexes and their role in the formation of personality. He postulated the theory of the "Ego" and the "Id" (or the conscious and the subconscious) and he began the scientific investigation of compulsion neuroses. By the eve of the First World War students of psychiatry from all over the world were flocking to Vienna to study under him.

The literature of anti-Semitism

DESPITE (and possibly because of) the reputation of Jews like Einstein and Freud, anti-Semitism mounted at the turn of the century. Intellectual anti-Semitism became still more inflammatory with the publication in 1899 of a book by Richard Wagner's son-in-law, Houston Stewart Chamberlain, the son of a British admiral. The book was *The Foundations of the Nineteenth Century*. To the Gobineau-Wagner theories (page 399), Chamberlain added one important thought of his own. This was that modern culture was a component of five strains—the Greek, the Roman, the Christian, the Teutonic, and the Jewish—of which the Jewish alone was alien and destructive. But the world was not yet lost, he said, because Germany was destined to rule it and to save it from the sinister plots of the Jews. The Germans (or Nordics, Teutons, or Germanics, as he sometimes called them, and among them he included the Slavs and the Celts) had done everything great since the sixth century; most great men had been Teutonic, including Jesus, Dante, and Leonardo da Vinci. His book had an amazing influence upon large sections of German society, especially university students.

CONSTITUTIONALISM

AND NATIONALISM IN EUROPE

THE END of one century and the dawn of another led to many remarks about social and political anachronisms. The phrase "The Twentieth Century" somehow seemed synonymous with attainment and progress. Trains, clubs, restaurants adopted it as their name, as if to boast of being modern and progressive. Yet all over the world, as many observers pointed out, some peoples lived without constitutional rights that others had earned in the seventeenth and eighteenth centuries, and minorities were still deprived of national self-determination. More than the 1880's, the ensuing decades produced popular agitation, and more often now such agitation led not to reform measures alone but also to the grave instability of governments. In Russia it produced a revolution of significant proportions.

The accession — DESPITE the Terrorists, Alex-
of Czar Nicholas II — ander III died a natural death in
1894 and was succeeded by his son Nicholas. Nicholas II was not so strong of will or purpose as his father, though well intentioned and attractive. He was dominated by Pobyedonostzev (page 434) and the czarina, a strong-willed German princess inclined to religious mysticism.

A new wave of terrorism engulfed Russia after 1902. Two of the czar's ministers and his governor of Finland were assassinated within two years. New pogroms broke out. Witte, perhaps the only man able to forestall a revolution, was "promoted" to the honorific but uninfluential post of president of the committee of ministers, while more politic men took over. He nevertheless continued to lead the demand for administrative reform.

Mounting protests — THE VARIOUS parties which were
from the people of Russia — more moderate in character than
the Terrorists also grew in vigor as well as in numbers. Among the Socialists, Nikolai Lenin had come to the fore since 1900. His family name was Ulyanov, but revolutionaries now hid their identity by pseudonyms in order to protect their families against police retaliation. Lenin looked for no mass movement to establish the dictatorship of the proletariat but rather a dictatorship of a selected group of Marxists—a dictatorship *for* the proletariat. In 1903, at a congress held in London, the Russian Socialists split into two groups: the Bolsheviks (or the majority, as   463

"Bloody Sunday." Russian troops charge the crowd assembled before the Winter Palace in St. Petersburg. A contemporary drawing from L'Illustration.

they happened to be at that congress), who followed Lenin, and the Mensheviks (or minority), who followed Plekhanov (page 435). A peasant party, descended from the old populist, or *V Narod* movement (page 325), also arose about the same time in the so-called Social Revolutionaries. So great was the accumulated discontent in Russia that, as events were to show, only the police strength of the government kept the seething grievances from explosion. The goverment's repressive forces soon were to be weakened, however, by war and defeat. Shortly after the Socialist congress at London, Russia became involved in war with Japan (pages 521-524). The war was for Russia a continuous series of bunglings and military disasters.

The Zemstvo Congress and the "Bloody Sunday" massacre

THE accumulating discontents burst their bonds long before the final defeat at the hands of the Japanese. In November 1904, less than a year after the outbreak of war, a conference of *zemstvos* met informally and made a series of demands. They asked for a bill of rights, specifying such rights as freedom of conscience, speech, and assembly. They decried official discrimination because of creed, race, or class. They advocated elective local governments and a program of legislation to alleviate the plight of peasants and workers. Finally, they asked for a national assembly. Since the conduct of the war was not yet a public scandal, the czar was not ready to grant them full satisfaction. His reply was simultaneously to reprimand the Zemstvo Congress and, in a vague way, to promise reform. But he rejected the demand for a national assembly.

464

Various groups of lawyers, physicians, and other professional men now took up the demands of the Zemstvo Congress. The workers meantime organized strikes. Many of them put their faith in a priest, Father George Gapon, who proposed a direct personal appeal to the czar, the "little father." One Sunday in January 1905 he led a parade of several thousand workers with their women and children, carrying ikons and singing "God Save the Czar" and other hymns, to the Winter Palace in St. Petersburg. As they approached the square outside the palace, they were fired on by soldiers of the regular army. Several hundred were killed and several hundred others wounded. The massacre became known as "Bloody Sunday," and that Sunday the Russian workers began to lose their faith in czarism. Later on, it turned out that Gapon was connected with the secret police. In that day of rudimentary underground revolutionary activity, it must sometimes have been hard even for an agent himself to tell whether he was a policeman spying upon the revolutionaries or a revolutionary spying upon the police. At any rate, a few genuine revolutionary leaders tracked Gapon to Finland, where they killed him for his treachery.

Revolts, strikes, and the "October Manifesto"

TERRORISM revived. In February, an uncle of the czar was killed by a Terrorist's bomb in Moscow. Thereupon the czar, though reaffirming his faith in autocracy, granted that "the worthiest persons" should take part in preparing the country's law in a Duma, or elective assembly. In August the czar, though still speaking in nebulous terms, promised to call such a Duma.

But the patience of the people had run out. The sailors on board the battleship *Potemkin* mutinied. The railroad workers struck, and the printers and the electricity workers joined them. Schools and universities closed. The peasants, who for decades had dreamed of a partition of the land, invaded the estates and undertook to divide them up themselves. In October the first soviet—that is to say, a council of delegates from all the unions of the capital—was formed at St. Petersburg. Its vice-president was a still obscure moderate socialist, or Menshevik, who went under the name of Leon Trotsky. By this time the strike was general, the first example of a general strike as a revolutionary weapon. In addition the many different minorities of Russia had begun to demand that their national interests be respected. The government machinery had practically collapsed.

When Witte returned from the humiliating peace negotiations at Portsmouth (page 524), the czar, counting on Witte's popularity, dismissed Pobyedonostzev and his hated colleagues and made Witte chief minister. The new minister told the hesitant czar that only the granting of a constitution could save the dynasty. Even some of the haughty grand dukes entreated the czar to grant a constitution before it was too late. Nicholas finally issued the famous "October Manifesto." It granted most of the demands that the Zemstvo   465

Congress had made a year before. It also promised a national Duma based on a bicameral, representative system. At long last constitutional democracy appeared to have come to Russia. Immense joy filled the crowds gathered in the streets of the capital, but it was to be short-lived.

The aftermath of the Revolution of 1905

RIOTS occurred still during November and December, but revolutionary solidarity vanished. The Octobrists accepted the czar's manifesto as the basis of a constitution. The Constitutional Democrats wanted a popular assembly to draw up a new constitution. The Socialists and the Social Revolutionaries clamored for wider economic reform. Witte, now backed by loyal troops returning from the war, arrested many Socialists. By the end of the year 1905 the revolution was over. A reaction had in fact already set in. The landlords, the officer corps, the clergy, and the high bureaucracy set up a Union of the Russian People whose purpose was to organize and equip terror gangs known as the "Black Hundreds." They took the land away from the peasants who had expropriated the estate owners, and turned the fury of the disappointed people against the Jews, who became the victims of a series of more terrible pogroms than ever before. It was clear that, if any reform took place at all, it would be in keeping with the imperial will as expressed in the October Manifesto. Something that might be called civil order was restored by the spring of 1906.

The origin of the Dreyfus Affair

FRANCE, so frequently the nucleus of revolutionary fervor in the past, managed to escape revolution during this period, though not without crises. French nationalism in the 1890's found profound expression in a semireligious, semipolitical guise. The investigations of the Panama Scandal (page 436) continued until 1893, and the association of some Jewish bankers with the malodorous affair encouraged French anti-Semitism to come more clearly into the open. Many officers of the army (who were sometimes aristocrats, Bonapartists, royalists, or clericals whose loyalty to the Third Republic was not beyond question) were inclined to attribute at least some of their country's ills to Jews and Protestants. Their suspicions and fears were nurtured by the *Libre Parole* (*Free Speech*), a widely read anti-Semitic newspaper.

In its issue of November 1, 1894, the *Libre Parole* revealed that the rich, reticent Captain Alfred Dreyfus, the first Jew to secure a post in the French General Staff, had about two weeks earlier been arrested for giving secret intelligence to a foreign power. Thus began an intricate affair of justice that lasted for nearly twelve years. The counterespionage department of the French General Staff had known for some time that somehow Colonel L. C. von Schwartzkoppen, the military attaché of the German embassy in Paris, was learning French military secrets. The preceding September, Major Hubert Henry of the French counterespionage department had come into possession of scraps of paper picked up from the German attaché's wastepaper basket by a French scrubwoman. Henry pasted the scraps together, and the resulting document (which thereafter became known as the *bordereau* or "memorandum") showed that some French officer was betraying staff information.

*The trial
and condemnation of Dreyfus*

DESPITE the hesitation of the minister of foreign affairs, the historian Gabriel Hanotaux, Captain Dreyfus was arrested because his handwriting resembled that found on the *bordereau* and because the General Staff officers assumed (erroneously, it ultimately proved) that the traitor was on the staff. Dreyfus insisted upon his innocence but was put in solitary confinement after several graphologists, who did not agree among themselves, had been consulted. When he came up for trial before a military court, the public was not admitted. The judges found the *bordereau* to be insufficient evidence, but the General Staff introduced secret documents shown only to the judges and about which neither Dreyfus nor his lawyer was informed. The judges were so much impressed that they sentenced Dreyfus to degradation (public expulsion from the army) and life imprisonment. He was transferred to Devil's Island off the coast of French Guiana, and the affair seemed closed.

*The defenders
of Dreyfus' innocence*

DREYFUS' family and friends did not believe he was guilty. But they could make no progress until Colonel Georges Picquart was put in charge of counterespionage. Picquart found that, despite the elimination of Dreyfus, Schwartzkoppen continued to receive French military intelligence. Then Schwartzkoppen's wastepaper basket yielded a draft of a letter written but not sent to a French major, Count Marie Charles Walsin-Esterhazy, and Picquart convinced himself that Esterhazy's handwriting was identical with that of the *bordereau*. Picquart tried in vain to convince his superiors that Esterhazy should be arrested and the Dreyfus case reviewed. Persuaded more than ever of Dreyfus' guilt by new documents "discovered" by Henry, the General Staff stubbornly refused and transferred Picquart to Tunisia. Henry (now Colonel) took his place at the head of the counterespionage department. Esterhazy had meanwhile become so suspect that he had to stand trial, but he was acquitted, and Picquart was arrested for having communicated army secrets.

*The reopening
of the Dreyfus case*

BY THIS time the Dreyfus family had won many prominent supporters. Two days after Esterhazy's acquittal Émile Zola published a fiery open letter to President Félix Faure under the title "J'Accuse." The letter was an all-out attack by name on

The Dreyfus Affair. A thoughtful Émile Zola on trial for slandering the French army in his open letter, "J'Accuse," to the president of France.

everyone guilty of errors of omission or commission in the affair. Zola had to stand trial twice. He was convicted of slandering the army and fled to England to avoid sentence of a year in jail.

The affair now was splitting families asunder, and riots broke out in the streets between "Dreyfusards" and "anti-Dreyfusards." Leading literary lights took sides. Anatole France and the poet Charles Péguy gave their pens to the Dreyfusards; the journalist Charles Maurras and the novelist and essayist Maurice Barrès gave theirs to the anti-Dreyfusards. To check public disorder, the minister of war read to the Chamber of Deputies Henry's latest "discovery" of documents, which were immediately suspected of being forgeries. Thereupon Henry was arrested, and he committed suicide.

President Faure, who leaned toward the anti-Dreyfusards, died suddenly and was succeeded by Émile Loubet, who was more friendly to the Dreyfusards. In 1899 Loubet authorized a reëxamination of the case by the Court of Cassation, the highest civil court of the land. Esterhazy meanwhile had fled to England and there admitted in the newspapers that he had written the *bordereau*. The Court of Cassation ordered a new court-martial. Political passions were still so strong that the second court-martial (September 1899) found Dreyfus guilty, though "with extenuating circumstances," and sentenced him to ten years' imprisonment. President Loubet pardoned him, however, and amnestied all like Zola who had been indicted in connection with the affair and the resulting riots. In 1906 Dreyfus was cleared by the Court of Cassation and reinstated in the army with the rank of major.

The Socialist-Republican bloc and the Associations Law of 1901

THE ISSUE in the Dreyfus Affair had early ceased to be that of justice for a single man and had become that of the honor of the French army, still largely dominated by antirepublican, aristocratic officers. Hence, the longer it lasted, the more it became a struggle for control of a nation, with royalists, conservatives, and nationalists on the one side, and republicans and socialists on the other. Leo XIII did not permit the Catholic Church as such to take a formal stand in the case, and some Catholics, both lay and clerical, had been Dreyfusards. Nevertheless, most clericals had been in the anti-Dreyfusard camp. To counteract this imposing alliance, the Socialists not only serried their own disunited ranks but also looked with favor upon uniting with the Republicans. The Republicans had been strong enough in the Chamber of Deputies in 1899 to make René Waldeck-Rousseau prime minister with Émile Combes minister of public instruction. It was this ministry that advised President Loubet to pardon Dreyfus. Shortly afterwards (1900) the Socialists and Republicans united to form a parliamentary "bloc," and Combes pushed through the Chamber an Associations Law (1901) intended to weaken the clerical forces. It forbade religious "congregations" (meaning particularly monastic orders) to organize without the legal sanction of the Chamber. The unauthorized religious "associations" or "congregations," however, refused to dissolve voluntarily, and Waldeck-Rousseau preferred to resign (1902) rather than to adopt a policy of force. Combes, a country physician who had once studied for the priesthood, had no such scruples. As Waldeck-Rousseau's successor he induced the Chamber to turn down application after application for authorization and closed about 3000 "congregational" schools.

President Loubet's visit with King Victor Emmanuel III

LEO XIII with great astuteness avoided a break with France, "the eldest daughter of the Church." But under Pope Pius X, who succeeded him in 1903, the Vatican became the adversary of a now thoroughly anticlerical French government. Relations snapped over an incident in power politics. Since 1870 the Vatican had demanded that the heads of Catholic countries should not visit the king of Italy in Rome, because the church still regarded Rome as the capital of the Papal States and the presence of the king of Italy as a usurpation. Since 1902 Italy and France had been negotiating an entente pledging each other neutrality in the event of unprovoked attack (page 522). To demonstrate the new Franco-Italian friendship to the world, the president of France made a formal visit to the king of Italy in 1904. Thereupon the papal secretary of state sent a note to all Catholic governments, including the French, decrying the very idea of Loubet's visit. Anticlericals in France now argued that the Vatican was aiming to overthrow the Combes cabinet and became indignant at what they termed an unwarranted meddling with French domestic affairs.

*The separation
of church and state*

COMBES is sometimes believed to have deliberately intended to provoke the Vatican by sending President Loubet to Rome. He now recalled the French ambassador to the Vatican. Then he introduced a new series of bills in parliament. In July 1904, he called for the suppression of all congregations within ten years, and in November demanded complete separation of church and state. That demand meant abolishing Napoleon's Concordat of 1801, which for over a century, though with modifications from time to time, had regulated the relations of church and state in France. Without the Concordat, the clergy would receive no salaries or other support from the state. The Combes cabinet was overthrown, for other reasons, before the law was enacted, but an able young Socialist leader, Aristide Briand, steered it through both houses, and in December 1905, it received the signature of President Loubet. Thus, the Concordat of 1801 came to an end after a century of controversy, and, legally at least, the church and the state were separated in France.

Under the terms of the new law, voluntary religious associations (*associations cultuelles*), Catholic or other, were to be established that would be entitled to full property rights over their existing churches and other ecclesiastical properties, provided the local communities did not choose to acquire them. These associations would pay the salaries of such priests, ministers, or rabbis as they chose to have. The clergy would be permitted to use the churches for religious services, which were put on the same legal footing as other public meetings. Where no such voluntary associations were formed, the communities became the owners of ecclesiastical properties. They were not obligated to take care of the buildings, and some communities let them fall into ruins. It remained to be seen how the church would respond to the Act of Separation (page 540).

*Chancellor von Caprivi
and Germany's tariff problems*

GERMANY experienced no disorderly controversies in domestic affairs in the period now under examination. Bismarck's successor as chancellor of the German Empire was General Georg Leo von Caprivi. He did not persist in Bismarck's program of persecution of the Socialist Party, and it grew rapidly in the next two decades. In 1891 a party congress at Erfurt adopted the Erfurt Program, repudiating "revisionism" and redeclaring its confidence that the historical process led inevitably toward class revolution and the dictatorship of the proletariat.

Caprivi's major domestic problem arose from the new tariff policy that his predecessor had handed on to him. German industry's tariff program was opposed to that of the agrarian Junkers. Industry needed raw products from foreign countries. To get them cheaply, German industrialists demanded that the tariff walls for foreign agricultural products be lowered. Caprivi acceded to their demand in 1892, when renewing some old trade treaties; import duties on cattle, wood, and grain were abolished altogether. The new trade agreements provided the factories with cheap raw materials, and workers with cheap food, but the Junkers were outraged. In 1893 they sponsored a mass movement among the German peasants, founding the German Agrarian League, which they dominated. Once more Germany had to choose between becoming mainly an industrial state or mainly an agricultural state. Fearing that the Junkers were right in their claim that their ruin would also mean the ruin of the army and the civil service, and sympathizing with those who opposed Caprivi's moderate foreign policy, the Kaiser ousted him (1894); and for the time being Germany tried to be both industrial and agricultural. When Caprivi's treaties expired in 1902, a new tariff intended to protect German agriculture from foreign competition was enacted. The new tariff lulled people into a misplaced confidence that Germany could provide for herself in time of war.

Industrialization and Austria's minorities

BY THE TURN of the century a profound social cleavage had become apparent in the Dual Monarchy. Great changes had been wrought in the Austrian portion by industrialization. Previously the Germans, though numerically a minority, had been predominant in the economic life of Austria. But with industrialization had come a large increase in population. The majority of the factory workers were Slavs, and the Slav population grew much faster than the German population. Just before the outbreak of the First World War, Austria-Hungary was to number over 50,000,000 inhabitants, of whom less than one quarter were Germans; the rest were mostly Slav or Magyar. The Slavs, whether urban workers or peasants, were restive with the ancient complaint—they wanted to be dominated by Germans no longer. The most outspoken in this respect were the Czechs, but all Slavic elements still sought, as they had for decades, a greater degree of autonomy, recognition of their own language as official in the areas in which they lived, and universal suffrage throughout Austria, which they expected would automatically give them a Slav majority in the Diet.

Emperor Francis Joseph, however, insisted upon German at least as the only language for the military. He feared that if different languages were introduced, the army would cease to be a compact body. To compensate for his stubbornness in that regard, however, he was willing to accede to other linguistic demands. In 1895 he made Count Kasimir Badeni, who was a Pole, his prime minister. Badeni issued a set of ordinances in 1897 giving the local language in Bohemia official status, and royal decrees prescribed in which districts and under what circumstances German or Czech might be used; all Bohemian officials were to use both languages. German objections to such concessions transformed the lower chamber of the Austrian parliament into a prize ring, where, however, noise more often than fists was the major

471

weapon. Mark Twain in his reports from Vienna in 1897 gave a sardonic picture of what went on at one meeting of the Austrian Reichsrat: "Yells from the Left, counter-yells from the Right, explosions of yells from all sides at once, and all the air sawed and pawed and clawed and cloven by a writhing confusion of gesturing arms and hands." Finally parliamentary activity came to a total standstill. In 1898 the government could prevent pitched battles between Czechs and Germans only by declaring martial law in Prague. In the absence of parliamentary decisions, the government of Austria was obliged to rule mostly by imperial decrees, as the constitution permitted in emergencies. Austria remained, in fact, until its dissolution in 1917 a constitutional monarchy in name alone, since the Reichsrat had abdicated its functions and the emperor ruled by emergency measures.

Irish agrarian and British educational reform

IN BRITAIN Conservative and Liberal governments alike moved toward reform. Gladstone, who became the British prime minister for a fourth and last time in 1892, tried to have a new home rule bill enacted in 1893. Although it passed the House of Commons, it was rejected in the House of Lords, and Gladstone resigned early in 1894. Parliament did, however, approve of a more lenient land policy in Ireland. In 1891 and 1896, under the Conservative governments of Lord Salisbury that preceded and followed Gladstone's last ministry, it increased the sums available for easy land purchases. With the land act of 1903, the so-called Wyndham Act, passed at a time when Arthur Balfour was Conservative prime minister, the ownership of the Irish soil fell practically into the hands of the tenants. This act provided a sum that might eventually reach £100,000,000 for the purchase of Irish farms by Irish peasants and induced reluctant British landlords to sell by providing bonuses of 12 per cent.

Balfour's ministry also put through the Education Act of 1902. It increased the efficiency of the government's control of the publicly supported schools and subsidized formerly independent schools (mostly Anglican)

The English black and white artist Phil May made this sketch of Gladstone in the House of Commons in 1893, shortly before the prime minister's resignation.

out of local taxes, requiring them to accept in return a certain number of appointed members of their managing bodies. Nonconformist opposition dwindled when it was found that the public appointees acquired greater authority than had been expected. This episode marked the last battle between Anglicans and Nonconformists in British politics. The outcome was a marked increase in the number of schools and of pupils and the admission of many more working-class and middle-class children to the universities. The Conservatives could well claim that by moving more slowly they had advanced farther than the Liberals.

Political reform in some of the smaller countries

THE QUEST for more liberal constitutions or for national independence of minorities created complications among the small nations no less than among the larger ones. The Treaty of Berlin of 1878 had made Serbia and Rumania independent states and had created the semi-independent principality of Bulgaria. In those countries, formal constitutions and parliamentary institutions existed but produced little truly democratic spirit. In Rumania alternating cliques of the landed gentry held the power. In Bulgaria a tyrannical ruler played hide-and-seek with the constitution. In Serbia, a pro-Russian clique murdered the hated king and the despised queen and placed an anti-Austrian constitutionalist, Peter Karageorgevich, on the throne (1903). Switzerland, the oldest democracy of the Continent, revised its constitution in 1874. When the Swiss in 1891 celebrated the seven hundredth anniversary of their independence, they introduced into their constitution the "referendum," whereby the people voted on important laws passed by both houses of parliament, and the "initiative," whereby, if fifty thousand Swiss citizens demanded legislative action on any subject, the proposal had to be submitted to a referendum. In Belgium a system of proportional representation was adopted in 1899, assuring to minority groups some representation in government. The Norwegians had long found Swedish rule, imposed upon them since 1814, an unwelcome burden, and the grant of universal manhood suffrage in Norway in 1898 strengthened the movement for separation from the less democratic Sweden. In 1905 the Norwegian diet passed an Act of Dissolution, which was submitted to the voters and ratified by plebiscite. A treaty of separation followed with Sweden's full accord.

Theodor Herzl and the rise of Zionism

ZIONISM was a peculiar nationalist movement, since it developed among a scattered people of an ancient tradition who had to go in search of a country. The founder of Zionism, Theodor Herzl, was born a Jew but at first thought of himself rather as an Austrian. During the Dreyfus Affair he lived in Paris as a reporter for a Vienna newspaper. What he saw in France convinced him that nowhere in Europe were the Jews certain of a permanent welcome. He conceived the idea that the Jews should have "a home secured by international law, a home for those Jews who cannot or will not become assimilated." At first his followers vacillated about where this home should be established. Eventually, for reasons of history and religious sentiment, they decided it should be in Palestine, then a Turkish province. Herzl's writings found an eager response among the Jews of eastern and central Europe, where other leaders had already set forth similar ideas. In 1897 the first Zionist Congress met at Basel, Switzerland. The Jews were not all united behind Zionism, but it gradually acquired an increased following among them before the First World War. The Jews of the United States provided a large part of the money, influence, and energy that was ultimately to achieve this nationalist goal.

POPULISM AND PROTEST

IN THE AMERICAS

By THE TURN of the century the United States exhibited several of the same disturbing paradoxes that were discernible in European culture. The country had become industrialized, but agrarian interests had not yet bowed to industrial dominance. Its businessmen had acquired enormous political power, but the worker and the reformer were not accepting their dominance without protest. Faith in social evolution was still strong, but that faith had not yet produced the best of all possible worlds.

In addition, the United States had to cope with two paradoxes that were peculiarly its own. (1) It had long been a land of opportunity and a haven for the oppressed, but the "new" immigrants from south and east Europe were not so welcome as those who had preceded them. (2) American public opinion would brook no foreign interference in the affairs of the Western Hemisphere, but circumstances had given the United States a voice in the affairs of Europe and Asia. These and other paradoxes became political issues, debated with much the same arguments and with much the same methods as were familiar in the more democratic countries of Europe, though with some striking differences.

The Panic of 1893 in the United States
THE interdependence of American affairs with the affairs of the world was once more clearly demonstrated in the early 1890's. Because the old English banking house of Baring Brothers made some bad investments in South Africa and South America and had to undergo reorganization, English investors became uneasy in 1890 and began to sell their American stocks and bonds. This sale led to a panicky flurry in Wall Street, but good harvests prevented widespread distress. Congress, however, attempted at about the same time to bolster the price of silver (the Sherman Silver Purchase Act) by requiring the Treasury

474

to buy and coin a vast quantity of the white metal. The consequence was a steady stream of gold from the United States and a persistent anxiety in American financial circles. Months of apprehension led finally to panic in 1893, with a run on the United States Treasury for gold payments. The Treasury found these payments hard to meet because its income had been reduced by prohibitive tariff rates and its outgo had been increased by its purchases of enormous quantities of silver. President Cleveland's successful insistence upon repeal of the silver purchase act did not prevent the panic from spreading ruin widely among American business and banking houses.

Labor conditions in the industrial areas

HARD TIMES underlined the conflict between capital and labor, which, as industrialism advanced, had become more bitter. The year 1890 saw the largest number of strikes in any single year of the nineteenth century. Discontent arose generally from long hours and low wages, though real wages tended to be higher than they had been in the 1880's. Even in 1900 workers in the steel industry typically worked a twelve-hour day seven days a week, while 70 per cent of all industrial workers put in a day of ten hours or more. Between 1880 and 1910 the average industrial worker's income was not more than $600 a year, and if a reasonable allowance is made for the depreciation of money in the interval, that sum would be worth somewhere between $1800 and $2400 in purchasing power today. The American laborer nevertheless was well off compared to the European laborer of that day.

Immigration and Chinese exclusion

AN IMPORTANT factor in the American labor market was the constant flow of immigration from Europe. In the 1900's, as many immigrants entered American harbors as did in the two preceding decades together—over 8,500,000. Most of them came from Italy, Austria-Hungary, Poland, and Russia. These immigrants came to better their economic lot, or to escape persecution as Jews or other minorities, or to bring up their families in the "land of the free." They were enticed by the advertisements of railroad and steamship companies or by patriotic outbursts such as the lines of Emma Lazarus inscribed on the pedestal of the Statue of Liberty:

> Give me your tired, your poor,
> Your huddled masses yearning to breathe free,
> The wretched refuse of your teeming shore.
> Send these, the homeless, the tempest-tost to me,
> I lift my lamp beside the golden door.

The wage earners of these immigrant families were not usually farmers as early immigrants had been. They were often unskilled laborers, and they usually settled in the industrial cities of the Northeast and Middle West. 475

Tenement houses occupied by immigrant families largely of one nationality in neighborhoods largely of one nationality became characteristic of the larger industrial centers. The wretched refuse from Europe's "teeming shore" often remained huddled *inside* "the golden door," their breadwinners taking whatever jobs they could find.

In the western states racial prejudice aggravated the economic complexities of immigration. By the last quarter of the century, opposition in the Pacific states to the influx of Chinese began to constitute a serious problem. As a result of continuous agitation and numerous riots, the United States, as we have seen (page 408) began to pass laws limiting Chinese immigration. In 1894, Chinese laborers were by treaty "absolutely prohibited" entrance to the United States for ten years, a decision which led immediately to strained relations and ticklish negotiations between the two countries. In 1902 Congress made this exclusion perpetual; and after 1904 the United States refused to negotiate further, regarding the problem as a purely domestic issue until 1943.

Discontents of factory and farm

THE CLIMATE of opinion was still generally unfavorable to labor combinations. In the depression of the early 1890's this hostility became apparent in two great labor conflicts —the strike in the Homestead (Pennsylvania) plant of the Carnegie Steel Company in 1892 and the Pullman (Illinois) strike of 1894. The Homestead strike brought on an open and bloody war between strikers and detectives from the Pinkerton Detective Agency (a common source of "strikebreakers") hired by the Carnegie Corporation, and was finally broken by state militia. The Pullman strike, which spread far beyond its origins, stalled railroad traffic throughout the North, and, by preventing the delivery of mail, became a matter of concern to the federal government. It was put down by use of federal troops and a federal injunction against the recently organized American Railway Union, which, under the leadership of Eugene V. Debs, was conducting the strike. The federal courts decided that the Sherman Anti-Trust Act applied to the labor union as engaged in a "conspiracy to hinder and obstruct interstate commerce." Debs went to jail, and the antitrust act, so far rarely invoked against trusts, became an effective weapon to use against trade unions.

With the drought of 1887 (page 409) and with the years of depression in the 1890's the lot of the farmer grew worse. Foreclosures multiplied and farm tenancy increased. The farmers felt that they were the victims of rising costs and falling prices, high interest rates, and high freight and storage charges, and they directed their discontent against the railroads, the industrialists, the eastern banks that held their mortgages and determined their interest rates, and the financial and business lobbies that often persuaded government to act against their interest.

*The brief career
of the Populist Party*

THE SWELLING discontent among farmers and factory workers turned them away from the old Democratic and Republican parties. The Farmers' Alliances began to think in terms of political power and to demand at their conventions the formation of a people's party. A new party arose to channel protest into action. It took the name of the "Populist Party." Drawing its strength and its leadership mainly from the Farmers' Alliances, it also embraced the factory workers, the followers of Henry George and Edward Bellamy, and the discontented everywhere. Its first national convention in 1892 drew up a sorry indictment of American society.

The Populists rapidly became a factor to be reckoned with in both local and national politics from 1892 to 1896. The Panic of 1893, followed by hundreds of business failures, cascading prices, labor unrest, and widespread unemployment, swelled the Populist membership. This crystallization of fundamental discontents forced a radical reorientation of political issues and political parties. In the presidential election of 1896 the Democratic Party, under the flamboyant leadership of William Jennings Bryan, embraced the Populist viewpoint, particularly their "easy money" proposal of "free silver" (i.e., a silver standard for money), and brought the new party into the Democratic fold. More than ever the Democratic Party platforms thereafter were to be expressly designed to appeal to the worker, the farmer, and the immigrant.

*Election of 1896
and the return of good times*

THE presidential contest between Bryan and the Republican candidate William McKinley, with Bryan the eloquent voice of protest and McKinley the heavily financed candidate of resistance, was one of the most bitterly fought political battles since

An American family of the 1890's on holiday at Rockaway Beach, New York, is shown in this contemporary drawing from Harper's Weekly.

477

the Civil War. The dominant issue was whether the country was to have a single gold standard for its currency or a gold and silver standard with free and unlimited coinage of silver. The defenders of the gold standard won, and with the discovery of gold in the Klondike Region of Canada and in Alaska, adoption of the gold standard was assured. The policies of government continued to be guided mainly by the theory that what was good for business was good for the whole people. A new high tariff, the Dingley Tariff Act, was passed in 1897. Bigger and better trusts were formed in the last years of the decade, care being taken to by-pass the Sherman Anti-Trust Act. But good times returned with the increase of the world's gold supply, and the protest movement temporarily lost ground.

Reform, philanthropy, and the progressive movement

TO BE SURE, the protest remained —a continually growing factor in politics. Yet, to the bafflement of many a European observer, no important labor or socialist party developed, even after Debs, released from prison, took over the leadership of the small Socialist Party. Government ownership of business enterprises had small attraction for the American worker, who frequently thought of himself as a potential businessman, and the American Federation of Labor persisted in working with existing parties rather than forming a party of its own. Protest rather took the form of an active "progressive movement" aimed at improving government administration, regulating railroads, utilities, and finance, and making the government more sensitive to popular opinion through the direct election of senators, women's suffrage, initiative, referendum, and the like.

Paralleling the movement for political reform was a humanitarian movement aimed at alleviating the distress of the more miserable victims of industrialization. To help the poor in the cities, their numbers swollen by the new immigration, settlement houses modeled on the famous Toynbee Hall in London were established, some hundred of them by 1900. Many new charity organizations were founded, and an attempt was made to improve housing conditions in the slums. Private philanthropy flourished. Men of means, frequently "self-made men," founded universities and gave huge fortunes to charity in order to help the unfortunate—some of them victims of the very system that had made the huge fortunes possible.

Protest and disillusionment in the literature of the 1890's

PROTEST found expression not only in party platforms but also in the literature of the nineties. Jacob August Riis, himself an immigrant from Denmark, described, in several excellent works of reportage, the shocking conditions that prevailed in the slums. H. D. Lloyd's *Wealth vs. Commonwealth* (1894) was an attack on monopoly based on a case study of the Standard Oil Company. As in England several decades earlier, industrialization put the social prob-

478

lem into creative literature. Stephen Crane's *Maggie: A Girl of the Streets* (1893), written under the naturalistic influence of Zola, revealed a facet of life in the slums that shocked Victorian prudery rather more than the Victorian social conscience. Young Theodore Dreiser's novel entitled *Sister Carrie* (1900) was banned for its realistic portrayal of a debased actress' life. Howells' new interest in social themes led to *A Traveler from Altruria* (1894), which, by picturing a more sympathetic community, indicted the contemporary politico-economic system that showed the individual no mercy. The poet Edwin Markham pled for "humanity betrayed, plundered, profaned, and disinherited" in "The Man with the Hoe" (1899); and William Vaughn Moody in *Gloucester Moors* (1900) denounced the "haggard ruthless few."

Protest took the form of an economic theory in the writings of Thorstein Veblen. *The Theory of the Leisure Class,* the first of a dozen or more of his books, appeared in 1899. Rejecting classical economics as an apology for things as they were and Marxian economics as oversimplified, Veblen emphasized the role of the consumer rather than the producer. Distinguishing between industrials, whose objective is production of goods, and nonindustrials, whose objective is "emulation" or "invidious comparison" (i.e., rivalry in prestige), he asserted that the modern economy was controlled by the latter. The modern "leisure class" is distinguished from primitive predatory marauders by modern efficiency and modern moral concepts; the "leisure class" indulge at different levels in "conspicuous leisure," "conspicuous consumption," and "conspicuous waste," and thus, by their competitive ostentation, dominate the price system. Veblen was not indignant, and he advocated no system of reform, but he seemed to think that the contemporary price system would sooner or later give way to a planned economy.

The dependence of American music and art

AMERICAN musicians revealed less originality than American writers. Since the death of Gottschalk (1869), only two American composers had achieved more than local reputation. They were Edward A. MacDowell and Victor Herbert, both of whom studied in Germany (MacDowell also in France). Both composed in the classical vein, but Herbert later achieved his greatest popularity with operettas. MacDowell, as professor of music at Columbia University, and Herbert, as conductor of the Pittsburgh Symphony Orchestra, helped to make music a respected part of American society's education, but nearly all the music and most of the musicians continued to come from Germany, Italy, and France, and most of the Americans who seriously studied music continued to go to Europe for their training. By the end of the century all the big cities—New York, Brooklyn, Boston, Philadelphia, Chicago, Cincinnati—could boast at least one symphony orchestra, and some of them had opera companies; New York even had rival opera houses. Nearly always the conductors were foreigners or foreign born (outstanding among them being German-born Theodore Thomas of Chicago, and Leopold and Walter Damrosch, also German born, of New York). Most of the outstanding performers were immigrants or specially imported virtuosi. Only with the military band, largely because of the excellence of American-born John Philip Sousa as a composer of military marches and as a band leader, did native musical talent excel.

In art the European influence was also dominant. Still, American painters like Whistler, La Farge, Sargent, and Mary Cassatt commanded respect abroad; the skyscraper, appearing now more often in New York than Chicago, excited curiosity and some admiration outside the United States.

Roosevelt
as a political reformer

UPON THE assassination of McKinley (1901), Theodore Roosevelt became president and enthusiastically set out to cure the domestic ills from which the nation was suffering. With a moral fervor that was contagious, Roosevelt launched a crusade embracing some of the Populist program. He set out to "bust the bad trusts," to regulate the railroads, to give labor a "square deal," to write new immigration legislation, to conserve the nation's natural and human resources, and to do a dozen other gallant deeds. If the "Old Guard" in his Republican Party was plunged into the deepest gloom, the country at large was delighted with both his program and his enthusiasm.

Muckrakers
in American literature

THE POPULARITY of the causes Roosevelt espoused was greatly stimulated by a literary phenomenon known as "muckraking." Muckraking, or exposing evil and corruption in business and political life, was a pastime Roosevelt deplored, in spite of the fact that it played into his hands. It was he who coined the epithet "muckraker," after the man in *Pilgrim's Progress* who was so busy raking muck that he would not even look at the celestial crown that was offered him.

The muckrakers of the Roosevelt era were in some ways the American equivalent of the Dostoyevskys and the Ibsens—spokesmen of the world's troubled social conscience. They exposed the malpractices of the trusts, the unholy alliance of business and politics, corruption in municipal government, corruption in the Senate, the dubious origins of great fortunes, the deplorable conditions in the slums, the exploitation of the Negro, the white-slave traffic, and child labor. A group of popular magazines—*McClure's, Everybody's, Collier's, Cosmopolitan,* and *American*—were their major vehicles, but most of their writings were so topical as to be ephemeral as literature.

Some muckraking books roused a resounding indignation among the class that had to learn about poverty, corruption, and injustice at second hand. Ida M. Tarbell's devastating *History of the Standard Oil Company* (1904) and Lincoln Steffens' *The Shame of the Cities* (1904), an exposé of big-city political corruption, were factual reportage. Muckraking crossed with Zola-inspired naturalism to produce some popular novels as well. Frank Norris' books dealt with the wheat farmer: *The Octopus* (1901) described how the choking tentacles of the railroad wound themselves around the life of the country that nourished it, and *The Pit* (1903) portrayed the Chicago grain speculator who ruined himself in the process of exploiting farmer and consumer. Jack London, an uncompromising portrayer of violence and brutality, inveighed against entrenched injustice and preached class war in his stories of adventure about California, the sea, and Alaska.

Finley Peter Dunne's lovable character Mr. Dooley appeared first in newspaper articles and then between 1898 and 1919 in a series of books whose humor and dialogue-form did not permit the righteous indignation characteristic of the muckrakers. Nevertheless, Mr. Dooley's penetrating pronouncements on the foibles of contemporary politicians, delivered in Irish accent from behind the bar of his Chicago saloon, won a response from an audience that could not be reached by aroused journalists and novelists. To counteract the shock to public opinion dealt by these literary blows, big business in the course of time not only undertook voluntary reforms but also increased its philanthropies and engaged professional publicity agents to present its better nature.

Labor and the "Square Deal"

EARLY in the Roosevelt tenure the president began to wield his eloquence, energy, and toothful smile in favor of a "square deal" for labor. A bitter strike had begun in 1902 in the Pennsylvania coal mines, where the United Mine Workers (organized in 1890) struck for higher wages, a nine-hour day, and union recognition. The mine operators bluntly refused, expecting the government to follow the usual precedent and break the strike for them. But Roosevelt and public opinion were on the miners' side this time. As winter drew near, Mr. Dooley summed up the national concern about fuel:

> Th' rich can burn with indignation, thinkin' iv th' wrongs
> inflicted on capital...an' th' poor can fight among thim-
> silves an' burn th' babies....At wan stroke ye can keep
> th' baby warrum an' th' rest iv th' fam'ly comfortable.

After four months of stalemate Roosevelt threatened to take over the mines and run them with federal troops if the operators did not negotiate with the miners. J. P. Morgan thereupon induced the operators to arbitrate, and labor won an important victory.

Roosevelt's trust-busting campaign

AS A REFORMER and a good politician, the president undertook to fight the "bad" trusts. In spite of the Sherman Anti-Trust Act the movement toward combination had accelerated rather than diminished, impelled in part by a wave of prosperity after 481

"And He Asks for More." All the nation is required to pay tribute to King Monopoly in this antitrust cartoon which appeared in the American magazine Puck *in 1890.*

the Spanish-American War (page 497). In 1901, the world's first billion-dollar corporation was listed on the stock market under the name of the United States Steel Corporation. An investigator writing in 1904 found that economic power had become so concentrated and interlocked that the huge Rockefeller and Morgan groups together made up the core of the nation's business and commercial life. With few exceptions the great corporations were run by small groups of men, who often wielded their tremendous power almost solely for the benefit of the stockholders. That condition was especially true of the railroads.

Roosevelt seemed to take his trust-busting seriously. To permit more effective supervision of the national economy, he induced Congress to create a new cabinet department, the Department of Commerce and Labor, and a Bureau of Corporations to investigate interstate trusts. He ordered his attorney general to begin active prosecution of certain trusts under the Sherman law. The railroads were a favorite target. The Elkins Act outlawing rebates was passed in 1903, and in 1906 the Hepburn Act was to give the Interstate Commerce Commission the power to regulate railroad rates. But Roosevelt was unable to get through Congress a comprehensive law regulating trust activities. A few trusts dissolved after prosecution, but some of them reappeared in more legal guise.

Domestic growth of the Dominion of Canada

WHILE the United States was growing to its full stature, its neighbor to the north was, in a belated spurt, also reaching maturity. The revival of world trade after the Panic of 1893 imparted new vigor to the Canadian economy. With the growing importation of foodstuffs by the industrialized countries of western Europe, Canadian wheat found a ready and expanding market. Now that the more fertile and accessible United States lands were largely staked out, Canadian prairie lands at last became attractive. Many Canadian emigrants to the United States returned home, and many immigrants came from the British Isles and central Europe in response to the Canadian government's search for labor and citizens. Between 1891 and 1916 Canada's population jumped from 4,800,000 to 8,000,000; in the same years her wheat exports climbed from 2,000,000 bushels to over 150,000,000 bushels. Beginning in the nineties Canada's resources of lumber, gold, lead, zinc, and especially copper and nickel began to be exploited in response to the growing world demand. Iron, steel, paper, and textile mills flourished, and two more transcontinental railroad lines were built to accommodate the increased traffic.

Capital and labor developed along the same general lines as in Europe and the United States. The giant corporation became the characteristic business unit, though it was subject to somewhat more government scrutiny than was usual elsewhere. A trade-union movement arose as the natural accompaniment of industrial expansion. While borrowing some inspiration from British sources, many unions were influenced by American models and some were affiliated with the Knights of Labor in its heyday or, later, with the American Federation of Labor. As in Europe and the United States, unions had sometimes to cope with the indifference if not actual hostility of the general public.

The Dominion in international affairs   LIKE THE United States, Canada in the nineties evinced a growing interest in her role as one of the world's nations. While without any desire to sever the British tie, Canadians nevertheless sought to preserve their autonomy within the Empire—at a time when Britain, finding her European leadership challenged both economically and politically by rising continental powers, was trying to draw her empire closer. These efforts of the mother country were gently but firmly resisted by Canada and the other self-governing colonies. In 1897, on the occasion of Queen Victoria's Diamond Jubilee, a third Colonial Conference was held, broadening the precedent that affairs concerning the mature members of the Empire be discussed and decided in concert. Joseph Chamberlain, British colonial secretary, had hoped for an imperial customs union but got no favorable response at the conference and gave up the idea. Canada of her own accord, however, had given Britain preferential tariff reductions before the conference had opened and increased them afterwards. This was the first step in the system of imperial preference later extended to the whole Empire (page 517). In the nineties Canada also assumed the prerogative of negotiating her own trade treaties. Although Britain insisted upon retaining the right to make other kinds of diplomatic arrangements involving Canada, the time was not far off when Canada would, without fuss, take its place as a full-fledged member of the family of nations.

Some major developments in the Latin-American countries "GRINGO," or "Yankee," exploitation of Latin-American fruits, mines, oil, and other resources has been a frequent cause of irritation and suspicion on the part of the Latin Americans. Nowhere during this period was the exploitation by American capital greater than in Mexico. In 1901 Díaz opened Mexico to the American oil industry, exempting from taxes the importation of oil machinery and the exportation of oil. Investments also were tax-exempt for ten years. Most foreign capital (increasingly derived from the United States) went into gold, silver, and copper mining. Roads, railroads, and telegraph lines had been built, mostly with American capital and technical skill. The federal budget of Mexico began to show a surplus, and Díaz was admired all over the world. Nevertheless, the country's prosperity did not seep down to the agrarian proletariat. It came from oil, a young industry, fed by foreign investments and enriching a few absentee landlords. Mexican dissatisfaction was not totally concealed and was soon to break its bonds (page 550).

A war between two major Latin-American countries (Argentina and Chile) threatened during the 1890's over a boundary dispute in Tierra del Fuego. In 1899 and 1902 the disputes became critical, but a final agreement was reached by arbitration. To perpetuate the memory of this peaceful settlement, the famous statue of the Christ of the Andes was erected near the Uspallata Pass, marking the boundary between the two countries.

The most dramatic episodes of this period in the development of the Latin-American nations were the Venezuelan controversies of 1895 and 1902, the vanishing of the last vestiges of the once gigantic Spanish empire in America, and the Panama Revolution. They will be discussed below. The desire in the United States for closer relations with the Latin-American countries led in 1889-1890 to the First Pan-American Conference and the establishment of a Pan-American bureau (later called the Pan American Union), which has since flourished and expanded as a sort of clearing house for affairs of mutual interest. A second Pan-American Conference met in Mexico City in 1901-1902, and there have been similar conferences at irregular intervals up to our own day.

DUAL CONVENTION

AND CHINA QUESTION (1894-1899)

W HEN "the pilot" Bismarck was dropped, the German ship of state seemed to be sailing steadily in safe waters. Austria and Italy were allies; Russia's friendliness was "reinsured"; England was voluntarily, and France involun-

484

tarily, isolated; and the United States was well disposed. Within a few years little remained of the Bismarckian alignment save the loyalty of Austria. To a considerable extent this "diplomatic revolution" was due to the skill of French statesmen, particularly Théophile Delcassé, but it was also attributable to the blunders of Kaiser William II and the German Foreign Office. Until 1905, however, the errors in their maneuverings were not apparent, largely because of the weakness of Russia, and they could congratulate themselves and be regarded by others as successful. One of the most serious war scares that post-Bismarckian Germany had to deal with came in the Far East.

William II's
early friendliness to England

BISMARCK'S successor, Chancellor von Caprivi, was unfamiliar with foreign policy and this shortcoming worked in favor of a pro-English orientation. It meant an increase in the mysterious influence of Friedrich von Holstein, who had never been a friend of Russia and was inclined at first toward friendship with England. So was William II. The Kaiser was the son of an English mother, Queen Victoria's daughter, and had been brought up to admire everything British. He introduced British sports like soccer, regattas, and golf into Germany, and the Germans eagerly accepted them. Despite the German insistence upon the purity of their language, the English word *sport* became common usage.

Within two weeks after the Russo-German Reinsurance Treaty expired in 1890, Germany's new orientation in foreign affairs became still more visible. In July, Germany and Great Britain concluded a treaty by which the Germans ceded the protectorate over Zanzibar, off the coast of German East Africa, to the British. In return the Germans received the tiny island of Helgoland in the North Sea. Since it was nothing but a small area of crumbling sandstone while Zanzibar was a vast island producing cloves and ivory, the Germans received the treaty with a storm of indignation. The treaty, nevertheless, had its justification. The Kaiser wanted to assure good relations with England by giving up disputed claims in east Africa; at the same time, he proposed to transform Helgoland into a German Gibraltar, defending the German coast against England and all comers.

The diplomatic crisis
of the Empress Frederick episode

AS WAS to be expected, the demise of the Reinsurance Treaty caused some diplomatic maneuvering. The Kaiser began to feel concerned lest, as Bismarck had feared, a rapprochement between France and an apprehensive Russia should come to pass. In order to forestall that possibility, he decided to court the French by personal amiability. As part of this program, he sent his mother to Paris in February 1891 to visit an art exhibition. Unfortunately, Victoria, or Empress Frederick as she called herself, not only failed to buy any pictures but she also committed the blunder of visiting the ruins of the palace at St. Cloud, which had been destroyed during the Franco-Prussian War. Boos greeted her

485

in the streets of Paris, and she felt it wise to leave the city in a hurry. The scrupulously correct behavior of both governments smoothed out the incident, but it turned the Kaiser in a violently anti-French direction. Since the Empress Frederick was Queen Victoria's daughter, English public opinion in this crisis sided with Germany. The next May the German Foreign Office rushed through the renewal of the Triple Alliance with Austria and Italy; and taking advantage of Germany's desire for haste, Italy was able to insert a provision that gave her a free hand in North Africa. In July the Kaiser visited his grandmother in London, and a great show was made of the occasion.

The Dual Convention
between France and Russia

COMMON distrust and fear of Great Britain and Germany now brought France and Russia closer together, even though each was contemptuous of the other's political institutions. Their navies exchanged visits (though the Russians waited until 1893 to make theirs), and the French government encouraged loans to help build Russia's new railways as a manifestation of friendliness. In 1891 Alexander III provided an ironic touch when he stood bareheaded to hear the French naval band play the *Marseillaise* at Kronstadt although Russians were forbidden to sing it as a revolutionary song. That year an entente between the two countries was reached. The Russians were reluctant to move as fast as the French wished. Nevertheless, the entente was superseded by a military convention in 1894. Since it remained secret until 1897, and never was submitted to the French Chamber of Deputies for ratification, as the French constitution required of formal treaties, it was considered merely a military understanding binding the two armies. It was frankly intended to counteract the Triple Alliance. It provided (1) that Russia and France would immediately mobilize their forces as soon as any power in the Triple Alliance mobilized; (2) that if France were attacked by Germany alone or with the aid of Italy, Russia with all her military power should assist France; and (3) that if Russia were attacked by Germany alone or with the aid of Austria-Hungary, France would similarly assist Russia. The complicated but effective alliance system by which Bismarck had intended to isolate France thus was undone while he watched powerless but not silent from retirement.

The pressure
toward imperialism in Germany

A STATE of great unrest now came to Europe. Two rival alliance systems faced each other and clashed everywhere. After 1894 hardly a year passed without a threat of war. Under the pressure of the increasing international alarm, a group of Germans banded together in what became known as the Pan-German League (reorganized in 1894). It demanded a strong colonial policy, the union of all Germans wherever they lived, and a German *Weltpolitik* reaching beyond the seas. The League criticized even the Kaiser because he did not go far enough in imperialism. It was strongly inspired by Treitschke's nationalistic interpretation of German history, particularly by his anti-British bias. Together with the German Colonial Society (founded in 1887) and the German Navy League (organized in 1898) it exerted a pressure on German public opinion far greater than might have been expected of its 20,000 members. In the decades that followed, numerous youth groups were organized, and they responded to this imperialistic propaganda with enthusiasm.

Increasing tension between China and Japan IN THE Far East a situation was developing that gave the imperial impulse of Germans and others new opportunities. Li Hung-chang's policy of balancing off the nearer menace against the farther one had conspicuously failed. The success of the French in Indochina and of the British in Burma and Malaya brought home to the Peking government the danger of submitting to western methods of penetration in the hope that eventually the exploiters might fall out. That hope had been based on the illusion that all the exploiters would seek to penetrate the same areas at the same time. It had failed to take into account the possibility that the imperial powers might pursue a policy of cooperation in certain areas of exploitation or that one exploiter might advance in one quarter while China's attention was occupied with another exploiter in another quarter. Moreover, it flew in the face of the fact that, no matter which of the imperialist powers won, China was bound to lose unless she were willing and able to protect her own interests. Thus the Chinese government now had to answer an old question in diplomacy: If direct action against aggression must eventually be taken anyway, why not immediately, as a preventive of long drawn out hostilities? China was to answer that question in the affirmative and to regret her answer.

Located at one of the major crossroads of Asia, Korea occupied a position similar to that of Belgium in Europe. It lay, like Belgium between England and France or Germany, across the path leading from China to Japan, constituting a dagger pointed at the heart of Japan or a bridge leading into China and Siberia. The mutual distrust of Japan, China, and Russia in Korea provoked the most crucial international conflict of the late nineteenth and the early twentieth century. Peking's earlier policy of encouraging the western powers in Korea served not only, as intended, to put obstacles in the way of Japan's effort to obtain exclusive control but also to encourage the interested powers to interfere openly in the domestic affairs of that unfortunate peninsula. Plots and counterplots at court and in the embassies became common events in the life of Seoul. Riots also disturbed the generally quiet tenor of Korean life as the conspiring groups more frequently came into open conflict. Foreigners and Koreans alike were killed in the streets of Seoul, and the nations readied themselves for war in Korea.

Japan recognized
as an equal among the nations

ALTHOUGH vitally interested in Korea, the "Land of the Morning Calm," Russia for the time being pursued a policy of watchful waiting. The new Japan was an unknown quantity in world diplomacy and military affairs. Though China had suffered repeated defeats at the hands of better armed western forces, the vast military potential of an aroused China was not thought of lightly in 1894. The odds were generally felt to be against the courageous and progressive Japanese in their struggle with the powerful, if stumbling, giant of the East, but the war might not be a short one. Russia preferred to move cautiously. Only if either eastern power were to win a decisive victory over the other did she propose to take some definite step.

The war crisis of 1894 was the first one to find Russia and France united in their Dual Convention (also commonly called Dual Alliance) for joint action in European affairs. The awareness of that alliance materially influenced the power balance in the Far East by increasing British and Chinese suspicion of French and Russian designs. Great Britain now drew nearer to Japan and revealed an unwonted tolerance of Japanese advances in areas where Russia had contrary interests. In July 1894 the British signed an unprecedented treaty with Japan—the first of the so-called "equal treaties." By its terms Great Britain was gradually to relinquish her extraordinary rights—extraterritoriality and tariff control in Japan. Thus the British took the lead in putting Japan on an equal basis with other members of the family of nations. The treaty was both an effort to offset the Russian entente with France and a tribute to Japan's great progress in modernizing her industries and political institutions.

The humiliation
of China by Japan

THE SONS of Nippon were to prove still more unmistakably how well they had learned some lessons from the West. Without notice to China that a state of war existed, the Japanese in the summer of 1894 seized the royal palace at Seoul, placed their puppet on the Korean throne, and through him ordered the Chinese out of Korea. When China resisted, war ensued. It was waged in Korea, Manchuria, China proper, and the surrounding seas. From the outset China betrayed a woeful lack of military preparation and organization, and the superior training and preparation of her insular foes took a heavy tribute. China suffered a series of military and naval defeats and, to prevent Peking from falling into the hands of Japan, finally agreed to the terms prescribed by the "dwarfs from beyond the Eastern Sea," as the Chinese called the Japanese.

In the Treaty of Shimonoseki (1895), China was stripped of her last shreds of international prestige. As the price of peace, the ancient Middle Kingdom was required to agree to the complete independence and autonomy of Korea—a provision recalling earlier treaty arrangements between China

彤海監 (along with vertical Chinese text columns in the upper right of the image)

A Chinese artist's impression of a naval battle of the Sino-Japanese War. The Japanese have just crippled the Chinese vessel Kow Shing, *and Japanese sailors are firing on Chinese struggling in the water near the sinking ship.*

and France regarding Indochina. China was also to cede to Japan Formosa and the Pescadores Islands as well as the strategically valuable Liaotung peninsula in southern Manchuria. Like the western powers in their dealings with China, Japan demanded also a monetary indemnity and the opening of new treaty ports with the waterways leading to them. Finally, China had to concede a new treaty of commerce granting Japan the privilege of extraterritoriality, treatment as a most favored nation, and the right to establish industries and businesses in the treaty ports. Japan's demands not only made explicit her equality with the West in dealing with China, but even, by the workings of the most-favored-nation clause, put her in the position to pass on to the western powers a right never before conceded by China—the right to establish industries and business houses in the treaty ports.

The humiliation of Japan by Russia, Germany, and France

THE WESTERNERS, however, showed something less than gratitude for the success of the Nipponese. Even the incidental benefits accruing to them from the Treaty of Shimonoseki were not enough to allay their fears of Japanese expansion on the mainland. For the first time, the Chinese were to benefit, but at much too late a date, from the rivalries of the imperialist powers. At the initiative of Russia in 1895, the representatives of Russia, Germany, and France in Tokyo "advised" Japan to retrocede the Liaotung peninsula to China. Al-   489 though smarting under this indignity, the Japanese yielded, receiving only an additional monetary indemnity in return. The unwillingness of the three western powers to recognize the equality of the new Japan fully was to constitute for the next decade a sore point in Japanese relations with the continental powers of Europe, and to push her more firmly into Britannia's embrace.

The specter of the "Yellow Peril"

JAPAN had by this time ceased to be the picturesque fairyland of Pierre Loti and had become for the West a menacing, unknown quantity. Lafcadio Hearn (page 459) was perhaps the only western literary figure who had a realistic if sympathetic understanding of Japan. Unlike his contemporaries, Hearn fell completely under the fascination of Japanese institutions and ideas. He went to Japan in 1890 to work as a newspaper correspondent and teacher of English. There he married a Japanese and became a convert to Buddhism and a naturalized citizen. Unlike Pierre Loti, Hearn combined an intimate knowledge with literary skill to produce a series of books that revealed the genuine life of Japan for the first time to the western world. His works gave clear and intimate glimpses into what he referred to as "unfamiliar Japan." Those who read Hearn carefully must have been better prepared for the events of the decade following the Treaty of Shimonoseki.

The victory of Japan over China in 1895 posed the potential danger to Europe and America of a teeming Asia under enterprising Asiatics. Fear of industrial competition also pervaded the thought of the Europeans, for Von Richthofen had warned that "the slumbering factors of an immense industrial production all exist in China." Although of questionable accuracy in the light of later developments, the prophecies of Von Richthofen and others set off a train of thinking that had widespread repercussions. Czar Nicholas II of Russia was obsessed by the Yellow Peril to eastern Siberia and to the Christian world, and his fears were enhanced by the letters of his German cousin William II. The growth of sentiment against Asiatic immigration to the United States and Australia resulted in discriminatory actions and legislation against Asiatics (pages 408 and 520). The subsequent decision of the United States to retain the Philippines and to embark upon an imperial course in the Pacific (page 498) must be laid in part to the growing concern over the Yellow Peril. In America that part of the press which for unrelated reasons was called "yellow," in Britain the jingoists and imperialists, and in Germany the Kaiser himself were all persuaded that the oriental tide would have to be stemmed before it should overrun the Christian West.

France in the exploitation of China

THE dismemberment of the prostrate oriental giant thus found a moral justification in the eyes of many who might otherwise have felt some qualms. France was the first of the European powers to claim its share of China. In 1895 China granted

490

France options on mines in its southern provinces, permitted the extension of railways from French Indochina northward, and reduced tariffs on goods shipped across its southern frontier. Meanwhile, in contradiction of the Socialist claim that capitalists dictated governmental policy, French and Belgian capitalists were prodded by the Paris government into advancing loans to Russia. In turn, Russia was eager to advance loans to China on the valid assumption that the banker holds a whiphand over his debtor, especially if little likelihood exists that the loan can be repaid in a reasonable length of time. While helping to support Russia's financial imperialism, France continued to round out her holdings in the south of China. In 1898, as Russia advanced against the northern gates of China, France obtained a ninety-nine-year lease to the Bay of Kwangchow, a natural adjunct to the port and river systems of Indochina.

Russia
in the exploitation of China

ADVANCING her frontiers overland, Russia had begun pushing east and south before the middle of the century. In 1891, Russia started the Trans-Siberian Railway, to link Vladivostok and eastern Siberia to St. Petersburg and the west. The first section of the railway was opened in 1895, and shortly afterward St. Petersburg announced the formation of a Russo-Chinese bank, supported by French funds, which had for its aim the financing of railways in Manchuria. In the following year Li Hung-chang concluded a defensive alliance with Russia, giving the Russians permission to build a railway across northern Manchuria that would considerably shorten the Trans-Siberian line.

In disputed Korea, meanwhile, Russia continued after 1895 to promote her own interests. Having initiated the tripartite intervention, Russia stood as the most formidable obstacle to Japan's control of the "Land of the Morning Calm." But both sides were for the moment unwilling to resort to blows. Hence, in 1896, they made an agreement fully recognizing the predominance of Russia in the north and of Japan in the south of Korea. The two powers were also to share the police and advisory posts in the Korean government. Although the British looked askance at these arrangements, Japan and Russia seemed committed to a policy of mutual respect and cooperation in northeastern Asia.

The powers, including Russia, remained too deeply involved in the scramble for concessions in China to be diverted by disputes in peripheral areas like Korea. Although counsels were divided in St. Petersburg about the methods of expansion, the Russians were united in their determination to move into the vital Manchurian and north China areas, while containing the Japanese advance in Korea. As a logical result of this policy, the czar in 1898 concluded two conventions with China by which Russia obtained a twenty-five-year lease, with mining and commercial concessions, of the southern tip of the Liaotung peninsula, including the cities of Port Arthur and Talienwan (now Dairen), and permission to extend the projected railway line in Manchuria by building a branch south from Harbin to Port Arthur.

By virtue of these arrangements Russia occupied the very area from which Japan had been excluded three years before by the tripartite intervention. Moreover, Russia's new position strengthened her hold upon northern Korea and gave her greater weight in the councils at Peking. The rapid ad-

DIVIDING THE SPOILS

Concessions

Spheres of influence

Independent

MANCHURIA
(Russian)
R.R. Concession

Trans-Siberian R.R.

Harbin

Vladivostok

KOREA

LIAOTUNG PEN.
Talienwan
Port Arthur

Seoul

Peking

Weihaiwei

Kiaochow
(German)

C H I N A

Shanghai

Nanking

(British)

Yangtze R.

(Japanese)

FORMOSA

Pescadores Is.

(British)

KOWLOON
PENINSULA

(French)

BAY OF KWANGCHOW

HAINAN

492

Following the Sino-Japanese War of 1894-1895, Japan exacted from China not only the independence of Korea but land and unprecedented trading privileges as well. Subsequently (1896) Japan and Russia agreed upon the predominance of the one in south Korea and the other in north Korea respectively. The other powers were quick to secure their share of strategic areas by long-term leases. A series of nonalienation agreements with China created large "spheres of influence" wherein the favored power enjoyed exceptional rights of economic exploitation. Concessions and (in the case of Japan) outright cessions are marked by the flags of the various powers.

vance of Russia southward brought her into direct conflict with a furious Japan, and at the same time aroused suspicions among the western powers about the monopolistic character of Russia's ambitions in China. But would it be possible to trap and hold "the bear that walks like a man"?

Germany in the exploitation of China

THE ADVANCES of France in southeastern Asia and of Russia in northeastern Asia were particularly disturbing to Germany. Successful collaboration of France and Russia in eastern Asia strengthened their Dual Convention in other parts of the world. Moreover, the demands within Germany for "a place in the sun" had been mounting steadily, much to the satisfaction of William II. While urging the czar to move eastward—that is, away from the Balkans, where Germany now had her own ambitions (page 509)—the Kaiser was careful to enter the lists also in China in a general effort to check the Russian drive. Russia's plan to move upon Port Arthur was offset by the German occupation of Kiaochow on the Shantung peninsula in 1898. In addition to a ninety-year lease of Kiaochow, Germany obtained from China a preferential commercial position in Shantung as well as definite mining and railway concessions. Germany also became one of China's creditors by extending a sizeable loan to the Peking government.

Great Britain in the exploitation of China

GREAT BRITAIN, too, claimed a place in the partition of northern China. British commercial and financial interests in China, already stabilized and respected, might normally have led her to prefer the status quo, but she was forced to take measures similar to those taken by the others in order to maintain her dominant position in China. After Germany and Russia staked out their claims in northern China, the London government signed a convention with Peking for the lease of a naval base at Weihaiwei across the Gulf of Po-Hai from the Liaotung peninsula "for so long a period as Port Arthur shall remain in the occupation of Russia." Shortly afterwards, Britain also took a ninety-year lease on the remainder of the Kowloon peninsula opposite Hong Kong. Meanwhile, London had protected its interests in the Yangtze Valley by requesting from Peking a declaration of nonalienation—that is, a promise to the effect that China would not lease or cede "any territory in the provinces adjoining the Yangtze to any other power." Under the most-favored-nation clause France soon received a similar nonalienation agreement regarding southern China, and Japan regarding Fukien. By such agreements the powers helped China to protect her soil against the depredations of their fellows, much like the legendary Jurgen, who defended his lady's honor against others by violating it himself. The realization that one of her "protectors" was Asiatic could have given China small consolation.

Anglo-American reaction against the partition of China

THESE concessions exacted from a defenseless China were but the most important of the list. By the end of the century it looked as if a complete partition of China would be hard to forestall. Imperialism by loans, the acquisition of leaseholds and naval bases, the extraordinary business privileges of foreigners in the treaty ports, and the continuing weakness of the Peking government frightened the British and the Americans particularly. The English-speaking nations' fear was not attributable to their greater virtue (England had never before hesitated to exploit China) but rather to their financial interests, which were closely tied to the maintenance of an independent China. Equality of opportunity for all in the whole of China rather than exclusive control for each in a limited district became the objective of the English-speaking powers, and it was to be formalized in 1899 by the action of the United States in proclaiming the policy of the "open door" (page 504).

THE RISE OF THE UNITED STATES
AS A WORLD POWER

MEANWHILE, what some Europeans had feared as a consequence of the decisive victory of the Federal forces in the American Civil War had come to pass. The United States had become a leading contestant for world empire, but with certain differences. While late European entries like Germany and Italy had been content to carry on their contests in outlying areas without claim or under contestable claim by other European nations, sentiment and the strategic and economic interests of the United States directed American interests not alone to such areas but also to those already held by a once great colonial power—Spain. Moreover, some of American sentiment for imperialistic enterprise was based on the desire to liberate as well as to dominate, and so in certain instances an element of trusteeship rather than overlordship was to enter into American concepts of colonial rule.

American concern with the Hawaiian Islands

UNTIL THE 1890's Americans had not seriously entered the race for empire. Nevertheless, as already indicated, the United States had become involved in the Pacific islands, particularly the Samoans and the Hawaiians. In the seventies and eighties a group of thriving American sugar planters, some of them sons of missionaries, managed to secure two thirds of the land in Hawaii and a corresponding degree of political power. In the early nineties these planters, who exported most of their product to the United States, found the high McKinley Tariff harmful to their market and began a movement for annexation to the United States. American missionaries and consular agents gave them support.

494

In 1891 the Hawaiian throne passed to Queen Liliuokalani, a vigorous character who attempted to shake the monarchy free of American influence and restore "Hawaii to the Hawaiians." The American planters thereupon engineered a revolution, with the probable connivance of the American minister, who supplied American troops at crucial points. After the revolution the minister, acting on his own responsibility, declared Hawaii an American protectorate.

In the United States, American destiny again became manifest. "Liliuokalani, give us your little brown hannie!" became a popular jingle. Expansionists argued that if the United States did not annex Hawaii, the islands would fall to Britain or Japan, which were both covetous of these rich and strategic way stations. But before the Senate could ratify the annexation treaty, President Cleveland was inaugurated for his second term and as an anti-imperialist withdrew it from the Senate. A sober investigation revealing the high-handed American methods and the wrongs perpetrated against the natives somewhat dampened expansionist ardor. For the remainder of the Cleveland administration the question of Hawaiian annexation lay in abeyance.

Cleveland's extension of the Monroe Doctrine

CLEVELAND'S anti-imperialist sentiments were so convincingly demonstrated in the Hawaiian affair that when in 1895 he vigorously revived the Monroe Doctrine, his vehemence burst on the world like a bombshell. The occasion was a dispute of long standing between Venezuela and the British in Guiana over their mutual boundary. Venezuela, to whom the boundary was most important, early enlisted the aid of the United States. But Britain, in whose immense empire the boundary dispute was insignificant, several times refused the mediation of the United States. Clever propaganda on the part of Venezuela persuaded American opinion that the British were aggressors in Venezuela and that they were thus violating the Monroe Doctrine. Thus prompted, Cleveland's secretary of state, Richard Olney, sent a stiff note to Britain demanding arbitration and stating: "Today the United States is practically sovereign on this continent, and its fiat is law upon the subjects to which it confines its interposition."

Olney's tone, coupled with bellicose statements by the government and the press, astonished the European world. It was a kind of proclamation of the entry of the United States into world affairs on her own terms. The defiant position taken by the United States made a bad impression throughout Europe and aroused much ill will, particularly in Germany. In England sentiments were mixed. At first arbitration was rejected in unqualified terms. But war with the United States seemed, as Chamberlain called it, "fratricidal"; and both countries, deciding that friendship was worth losing a bit of face over, agreed to submit the dispute to arbitration.

American prestige was greatly enhanced by the entire episode. Despite English doubt that the Monroe Doctrine was applicable, it had received a pragmatic reaffirmation. And European powers looked with respect if not with friendliness upon the brash young titan who had suddenly shouted from the housetops that his fiat was law over half the world. In South America weak nations were pleased and strong ones resentful. Venezuela was so disappointed at the outcome of the arbitration that, ironically enough, pressure from the United States was required to bring her to sign the final treaty.

The rise of sentiment favoring American imperialism

DURING Cleveland's four years in office American imperialism had been fairly successfully pent up. When it came, it came full flood. In 1890 the superintendent of the census had formally stated that "there can hardly be said to be a frontier line" within the United States. The *Overland Monthly* in 1898 put its own interpretation on the closed frontier: "The subjugation of a continent was sufficient to keep the American people busy at home for a century. ... But now that the continent is subdued, we are looking for fresh worlds to conquer." Captain A. T. Mahan was of the opinion that "whether they will or not, Americans must now begin to look outward." The new navy was augmented with several first-class battleships and other armored war vessels, and a determined group of naval expansionists pushed for an even stronger navy to defend American coasts, protect American commerce, and back American diplomacy. A jingoistic press fanned the flames.

American intervention in the rebellion in Cuba

A MAJOR danger point was Cuba. In 1895 this island had rebelled against Spanish misrule, and the subsequent war between Spaniards and natives was ferocious, unscrupulous, and exceptionally careless of human life. American investments of some $50,000,000, the recent reassertion of the Monroe Doctrine, a ready sympathy for any rebel against tyranny, and the frank imperialism of some younger politicians like Theodore Roosevelt made Americans pro-Cuban from the start. Meanwhile the new yellow journalism went to work to whip public sentiment to fury against the Spanish. The New York papers of William Randolph Hearst and Joseph Pulitzer, each of whom sought to outdo the other in building up his circulation, competed in scare headlines and sensational news. Their sheets were filled with stories of Spanish atrocities, outraged virtue, and bloody debauchery.

In spite of the outcry in the press and Congress and among the public at large, Cleveland had refused to accede to the demands for war. The situation was still critical when McKinley came to office, and early in 1898 the battleship *Maine* was sent to Havana harbor to protect American life and property and to impress the Spanish. When in February a mysterious explosion (whose origins have never been determined) sank the *Maine* with a large loss of life, the American clamor grew irresistible. Throughout the land the cry went up: "Remember the Maine! To hell with Spain!" McKinley, who wanted peace no less than Cleveland had, was accused by Theodore Roosevelt of having "no more backbone than a chocolate éclair." Finally, in April 1898 McKinley acceded, and the United States went to war to free Cuba from Spanish misrule. It was the United States' first war with a European country since 1814 and the first war in which a European country was involved with a major power anywhere since 1878.

International implications of the Spanish-American War THE Spanish-American War was to be a brief affair. Its Cuban phase was notable chiefly for easy victories that increased the Americans' self-confidence and chauvinism—the battles of Santiago and San Juan Hill. Since, like Germany, Italy, and Japan, the United States was a late entry in the race for colonies and concessions in the Pacific, and since the best colonial areas were already occupied by the older participants, its best chance of success lay in replacing one of them. And so the Spanish-American War at once became a Pacific struggle. The United States had had no naval base in the far Pacific in 1898, and the American Far Eastern squadron under Commodore George Dewey was based at Hong Kong. Upon the declaration of war, Dewey sailed to the Philippines, attacked and destroyed the Spanish fleet at Manila, and then blockaded the harbor. At this juncture the German navy entered the scene. Having themselves looked for a long time with covetous eyes upon Spain's Pacific possessions, the Germans refused to stand idly by while the United States took over the remnants of the oldest surviving Pacific empire.

The future of the Philippines, however, was not to be settled entirely by distant powers. A native movement to oust the Spanish and to establish an independent regime was already under way (page 354). The Americans encouraged Aguinaldo and the *insurrectos* to throw off the rule of Spain. Meanwhile the Spanish, encouraged by the German Pacific fleet, sought to overcome the rebellion and fight the Americans at the same time. The American fleet in turn received moral and material support from units of the Japanese and British fleets. Thus the problem of the ultimate disposition of the Philippine Islands was from the beginning a delicate international issue.

Actual warfare between Spain and the United States ended within four months, and through the friendly offices of France, peace was signed in December. The Peace of Paris required Spain to relinquish the Philippines, Guam, and Puerto Rico to the United States and to free Cuba, which was placed under American protection. The decision of the United States to annex the Philippines prompted new native outbreaks, and it was not until 1902 that the rebellions were crushed. Meanwhile, Germany had somewhat reconciled herself to the new state of affairs in the Pacific through the purchase of the Carolines, Marianas, and Pelew Islands from Spain, which considered them less desirable without the Philippines. Thus ended over three centuries of Spanish empire in the West Indies and the Pacific.

The United States was now drawn fully out of isolation. No matter how many Americans might regret this development, they were headed toward both the Atlantic and the Pacific arenas, where other world powers were jockeying for resources, markets, and prestige. The impending change was carefully noted in Europe—with annoyance on the Continent, with pleasure in England. In their no longer splendid isolation the British were pleased to see in the United States a potential friend, whose new status might help to counterbalance the weight of their European rivals.

Causes and consequences
of annexing the Philippines

WHEN THE United States decided to annex the Philippine Islands, the decision marked an important departure in the Pacific policy of the United States. The Yellow Peril, the strategic and commercial advantages of the Philippines, and the active competition of the Germans for them helped to overcome idealism in Washington. In part, the switch to imperialism can be accounted for by the rapid transition from agriculture to industry that was then taking place in the United States with a consequently greater interest in foreign trade and empire. Besides, Protestant missionaries were eager for opportunities to penetrate untried areas. Finally, President McKinley believed that the Filipinos were not yet ready for independence, and that to grant it would merely be to invite the Japanese or some European power to move in. The scramble for concessions in China, he believed, furnished an object lesson as to what the future held in store for an oriental nation unable to protect itself from outside pressures.

English experience with empire-building ought to have made clear what would now happen. In order to hold what had been conquered, the United States would have to acquire still more—or so it seemed to some. In anticipating the annexation of the Philippines, American expansionists, naval and civil, warned that the United States would be unable to provide the islands adequate protection without possessing other coaling stations and naval bases in the Pacific. The decision to embark upon an imperial program in the Pacific led to the decision to annex Hawaii even before the Philippines were conquered. Hawaii in 1897 signed a treaty of annexation which, in the midst of the Spanish-American War, was formally carried out. Territorial status for Hawaii received authorization from Congress in 1900. In January 1899 the United States also occupied Wake Island in the Pacific.

Germans and Americans
in the Samoan archipelago

NEITHER Japan nor Great Britain, each of whom had turned covetous eyes upon the islands, was happy about the American decision to annex Hawaii, but they did not interfere. In regard to Samoa, on the other hand, Great Britain actively cooperated with the United States in an effort to limit the ambitions of Germany. Since 1889 (page 413) the Samoan archipelago had been under the joint rule of Great Britain, Germany, and the United States. As Germany drew apart from the English-speaking powers, the effectiveness of their threefold condominium diminished. During the Spanish-American War, Samoan difficulties, reflecting external influences, burst into civil war. The British cooperated with the Americans in bombarding Apia in Samoa when the Germans established a puppet ruler there. While intertribal hostilities went on in Samoa, the commissioners of the three white powers met and decided to partition the islands. Arrangements agreed upon in 1899 allowed the United States to annex those islands, including Pagopago, that lay east of the 171st meridian. The other Samoan islands went to Germany; and Great Britain was compensated by being permitted to annex the Tonga (Friendly) Islands and Savage Island to the south of Samoa.

Status of Cuba: conditional independence

THE STATUS of Cuba was hard to determine. In declaring war against Spain the United States had publicly disclaimed "any disposition or intention to exercise sovereignty, jurisdiction or control" over the island. Still, in addition to the reluctance to surrender so profitable an area, a genuine apprehension arose that Cuba's unsteady political condition might become an invitation to some foreign power—such as Kaiser William's colony-hungry Germany—to establish its own control. So in 1901 Congress adopted the Platt Amendment, which established a virtual protectorate. The Platt Amendment, which the Cubans were required to write into their constitution, provided that Cuba would permit no third power to establish colonies or coal bases, would limit her indebtedness (in order to forestall any episode like the Napoleonic affair in Mexico), would permit United States intervention if necessary to restore order or to maintain Cuban independence, and would provide the United States with sites for naval and coaling stations. In 1902 the United States withdrew its troops from Cuba.

The new American role in the affairs of the world

AFTER the Spanish-American War the United States candidly assumed a role as a world power. In 1899 United States delegates attended the First International Peace Conference at The Hague, where they helped to sponsor the establishment of the Permanent Court of International Arbitration. In the same year the United States proclaimed the "open door" policy with respect to China and in the following year played a leading part in the relief of Peking during the Boxer Rebellion (pages 504 and 514).

In the election of 1900, Bryan, again the Democrats' candidate, ran against President McKinley on a platform opposing imperialism as well as advocating free silver. McKinley won, and Theodore Roosevelt was elected to the vice-presidency. In 1901, McKinley fell victim to an assassin's bullet, and Roosevelt became president. In 1904 he was elected to succeed himself. Thus, during most of the first decade of the twentieth century, the highest office in the United States was occupied by a man eminently fitted by temperament, conviction, and physique to play the role of leader of the United States as a world power. Roosevelt had made a dramatic debut on the international stage first when, as assistant secretary of the navy, he had helped build the new fleets that had performed so brilliantly against Spain. He increased his popularity as the moving spirit of the Rough Riders, a regiment of cowboys, Indians, and adventurous elite from the East whom he had recruited to fight in Cuba. During his almost eight years as president his conduct reflected an attitude he had announced in 1900: "I have always been fond of the West African proverb: 'Speak softly and carry a big stick, you will go far.' " As a willing orator in the days before public-address systems, he had to strain his high-pitched voice and did not often speak softly, but, at any rate, he tried to carry a big stick.

The issue of an isthmian canal

ONE OF the most important questions agitating the United States after the Spanish-American War was that of a canal across the isthmus connecting the two American continents. During the Spanish-American War the battleship *Oregon* had had to go clear around Cape Horn to get from Pacific waters to the Caribbean, and its long voyage had dramatized the importance of an isthmian canal to United States defense.

Several obstacles stood in the way of a United States-controlled canal. One was a treaty with Great Britain by which both countries were bound not to fortify or exercise exclusive control over any isthmian canal. Several attempts had been made to get Britain to modify the treaty, but Britain had been unyielding. Now the British proved more amenable. They were seriously involved in the Boer War (pages 511-512), which not only occupied their armed forces but made them many enemies on the Continent. To counterbalance their European rivals, they openly courted American friendship. In the Hay-Pauncefote Agreement of 1901 they consented to an American-controlled canal.

Acquiring a canal route (1903)

PRESIDENT Roosevelt was anxious to "make the dirt fly." A private French company had already acquired rights and spent many years and $260,000,000 in trying to dig a canal through Panama. The United States therefore proposed to cut its canal through Nicaragua. The Panama route was finally chosen, however, after an agent of the French company pointed out to United States senators that an active volcano made the Nicaraguan route hazardous. The way through Panama was not all clear, however. The French company, having become mired in jungle and scandal (page 436), had been reorganized and now was eager to sell its rights to the United States, but Colombia, of which Panama was a province, proved unwilling to grant the United States the strip of land across the isthmus where the canal was to be dug.

Panama long had been known as a reluctant province of Colombia, having staged an average of about one revolt a year for the preceding fifty-five years. When negotiations bogged down, three American warships were ordered to join another already anchored at the Panama coast, and on the day they arrived, a new revolt broke out in Panama. It was engineered by a small group of Panamanians and members of the French canal company, with funds borrowed from the New York financier J. P. Morgan. The next day they declared Panama a republic independent of Colombia, and the American warships prevented Colombian troops from landing to suppress the rebels. Three days after the rebellion began, the United States recognized the new republic and twelve days later it secured a perpetual lease of a ten-mile strip of land across the isthmus. The "soft voice" and the "big stick" were suspected by everyone. Europeans frowned, and Latin Americans took careful and sometimes fearful note of their northern neighbor's tactics. Not even all Americans were pleased, and in 1921 the United States was voluntarily to pay $25,000,000 to Colombia by way of apology and reparation.

The Venezuela affair and the Drago Doctrine

THE YEAR before Roosevelt's "cowboy diplomacy" in Panama, a crisis arose in Venezuela. The occasion was a repetition of the familiar story—political chaos threatening ruin to foreign investments. In a series of uprisings that made Cipriano Castro dictator of Venezuela, financial and property losses were inflicted upon both Americans and Europeans. In 1902 Germany, Italy, and Great Britain sent some warships to Venezuela in order to collect their debts. The European powers, out of deference to the Monroe Doctrine, had made sure of the official American attitude before taking such a step and Roosevelt had given them his blessing despite the clamor of certain sections of the American press. What was originally intended to be only a naval demonstration degenerated into a blockade, the sinking of ships, and the shelling of Venezuelan ports. Thereupon Roosevelt intervened on the grounds of maintaining the Monroe Doctrine. Facing the muzzles of European cannon, the Venezuelan dictator accepted arbitration. The European blockaders were also glad to arbitrate, and the dispute was settled by a commission appointed by the Hague Tribunal. The settlement gave all the big powers, including the United States, reasonable satisfaction, though it scaled their payments down to about one-fifth of what they had claimed. Roosevelt commended both England and Germany for their "honorable good faith which merits full acknowledgement on our part."

In the course of the blockade, the Argentine government had proposed 501 to the United States government an extension of the Monroe Doctrine. It wished the world to recognize the principle "that public debts should never bring about any armed intervention, much less the material occupation of the soil of American nations by European Powers." This so-called Drago Doctrine (Luis Drago was the Argentinian minister of foreign affairs) was subsequently discussed at the Pan-American Conference of 1906 and in 1907 embodied, with modifications, in a resolution presented at The Hague and known, after the American representative Horace Porter, as the Porter Proposition. The Porter Proposition permitted the forceful collection of public debts only after arbitration had been attempted and failed.

*Disputes
over the Alaskan boundary*

WHILE the Panama and the Venezuela affairs were being worked out under Roosevelt's coaching, in the northwest corner of North America the big stick came into play against Canada. The discovery of gold in the Klondike region in 1896 had brought forth a dispute over the boundary between Alaska and Canada. In 1903 a commission of six jurists, two Canadian, one British, and three American, was appointed to settle the dispute. Roosevelt let it be known that if the decision were not to his liking, he would occupy the disputed area with United States troops and establish the line himself. Fortunately, the British jurist sided with the three Americans, and the boundary agreed upon favored the American claims—to the great discomfiture of Canada.

*The Roosevelt Corollary
applied to the Dominican Republic*

IN 1904 the big stick was brandished against the Dominican Republic. Here again civil war and bankruptcy threatened to bring European warships to the Western Hemisphere to collect European debts. Roosevelt decided to forestall such action. He admitted that the Europeans had a reasonable case, yet as he interpreted the Monroe Doctrine it barred European powers from intervention to secure redress. Hence, he concluded, it was up to the United States to make the smaller American countries behave. Roosevelt enunciated this principle in the Roosevelt Corollary to the Monroe Doctrine: "Chronic wrongdoing . . . may in America, as elsewhere, ultimately require intervention by some civilized nation, and in the Western Hemisphere the adherence of the United States to the Monroe Doctrine may force the United States, however reluc-

Between 1895 and 1905, the United States rapidly acquired colonies: Puerto Rico, Guam, and the Philippines by the Spanish-American War; the Hawaiian Islands by annexation; and eastern Samoa by agreement with Germany and Great Britain. After the Spanish-American War, the United States also "protected" Cuba for a time and formally occupied Wake Island. In 1903 the American "big stick" ensured the establishment of the Republic of Panama and a perpetual lease across the isthmus. United States interests in the Western Hemisphere were affirmed in the Venezuelan disputes of 1895 and 1902, the Alaskan boundary dispute with Canada, and the Dominican Republic's financial crisis. The United States in 1899 took its place among the nations at The Hague and in 1900 took part in the relief of Peking. It proclaimed the "open door" in China, mediated the Russo-Japanese War, and participated in the Algeciras Conference on Morocco following the Tangier episode (page 562).

THE U. S. AS A WORLD POWER

PHILIPPINE ISLANDS
Acquired from Spain 1898

Manila

U. S. defines "open door" policy in China with British support

U. S. delegates at First Hague International Peace Conference 1899

U. S. troops in relief of Peking 1900

U. S. participates in Algeciras Conference on Morocco 1906

GUAM
Acquired from Spain 1898

WAKE ISLAND
Occupied by U. S. 1899

ALASKA

'Big stick' in boundary dispute 1903

U. S. mediates Russo-Japanese Peace Treaty 1905

DOMINION OF CANADA

Apia

Pearl Harbor

Portsmouth

DOMINICAN REPUBLIC
"Roosevelt Corollary" means U. S. policing 1904

UNITED STATES

HAWAIIAN ISLANDS
Annexed by U. S. 1898

PUERTO RICO
Acquired from Spain 1898

SAMOA
Divided with Germany 1899

Havana

VENEZUELA

Monroe Doctrine invoked against Great Britain in 1895 and against Great Britain, Germany and Italy in 1902

PANAMA

CUBA
U. S. protectorate 1898-1902

'Big stick' policy aids independence and acquires perpetual lease for canal 1903

tantly, in flagrant cases of such wrongdoing or impotence, to the exercise of an international police power." Following this pronouncement, Roosevelt set up a customs collector to take charge of the collection of duties in the Dominican Republic, alloting 45 per cent of the income for home expenses and 55 per cent for repayment of foreign debts. It made the Dominican Republic a kind of financial protectorate of the United States for many years.

The "open door"
as Anglo-American policy

ALTHOUGH in the Western Hemisphere the United States usually succeeded in being a benign if self-interested neighbor to the smaller states, in the East this policy proved somewhat harder to apply. But the attempt was made. If the United States preferred to hunt with the hounds among the Pacific islands, it nevertheless felt sympathetic with the hares in China. Fearing the imminent partition of China, the United States, with the support and urging of Great Britain and without the knowledge of China, enunciated the "open door" policy. McKinley's secretary of state, John Hay, defined the "open door." It was nothing more than a formal reiteration with specific application to China of the most-favored-nation policy, which had in fact been followed since 1844. In a series of notes exchanged in 1899, Hay sought and obtained formal assurances that England, Germany, Russia, France, Italy, and Japan would respect the territorial integrity of China and would permit equality of economic opportunity within their respective spheres of interest or influence. Although the exchange of notes on the "open door" did not prevent the further development of spheres of influence, it probably helped to check the partitioning of China. The motivation of England and the United States was not pure altruism, however. Those powers (and England was among them) that had already made annexations geographically inside or close to China stood to gain most by further annexations, but the greatest commercial powers in China were England and the United States, and they stood to gain most by keeping China's doors open, with or without her permission. Fortunately for China her national interests at this period coincided with the national interests of the English-speaking powers. Temporarily at least, the good feeling of the United States, England, and Japan toward each other seemed to guarantee the status quo in the Far East.

THE BOER WAR

AND THE END OF "SPLENDID ISOLATION"

BRITAIN was governed by frankly imperialist cabinets from 1894 to 1905. In international affairs they adopted the policy of containing Russia in the Near East and the Far East and hence befriending Turkey and Japan. In

Africa they more or less openly supported the British empire-builders and thus came into conflict with the empire-builders of France and Germany. At first the British avoided seeking allies, but the complications in Africa and the Far East were to convince them of the worth of complacent friends in times of need.

International tensions over Armenia and Crete

THAT THESE were times of need soon became apparent. In 1895 temperatures climbed once more to fever heights in the Near East (among other places). The major irritant there was the policy of the Turkish sultan ("the great assassin," in Gladstone's phrase) toward the minorities within his empire. The Turks had begun to massacre Christians again, this time in Armenia, after the Armenians had made a new armed bid for autonomy. Everywhere in western Europe, hearts bled for the Armenians. Fearful of a renewal of the Balkan free-for-all, in 1895 Prime Minister Lord Salisbury attempted to coax the German emperor, on a second visit to England to attend the Cowes regatta, into a closer association with Great Britain. In an audience with the Kaiser, he took up the idea that had once shocked Palmerston and suggested the partition of Turkey among the great powers of Europe. But the attempt was unsuccessful and left bitter feelings on both sides.

Christian-Moslem feuds continued in the Near East, however, and now became additionally acute in Crete. In 1896 that island, inhabited almost entirely by Greeks, rose in insurrection (not for the first time), hoping to be permitted to join the Kingdom of Greece. Meanwhile, more Armenians kept acting in a fashion that the Turks continued to punish by massacre, and organized bands of Greek patriots attacked the Turkish forces in Crete and Macedonia. To keep the Balkan question from bringing Russia, Austria, and England to blows, the diplomats of Europe negotiated and proposed bargains. They agreed on a joint expedition to Crete, largely to prevent its formal annexation by Greece. That maneuver did not prevent the Turks, however, from going to war with Greece. Greece expected aid from Serbia and Bulgaria, but the Austrians and Russians used their power to keep the war from spreading. Left alone, Greece found the Turkish army more than a match and had to beg for the intervention of the big powers. An armistice was arranged within a month of the outbreak of war, and protracted negotiations led in 1898 to the recognition of Crete as an autonomous state within the Ottoman Empire but under a prince of the Greek royal house as governor general. Crete was not to become part of Greece until the Balkan War of 1913 (page 568). The Cretan crisis had created consternation among the powers at several points, but it had not raised a general war scare, largely because, no matter what governments thought regarding their interests at stake, public opinion was everywhere in Europe on the side of Greece and of the bleeding Armenians. Nothing was done, however, for the Armenians   505 and they finally submitted, to await future opportunities for rebellion against Turkish control.

The defeat
of the Italians in Ethiopia

IN THE midst of the Cretan controversy another limited war took place, but without gravely endangering the general peace of Europe. The future of Ethiopia became of interest to three European empires—Italy, which hoped to make it a sphere of influence; France, which hoped to be able to unite its holdings on the eastern African coast with those on the western coast; and England, which was anxious to keep the French away from the Nile. By placing a puppet, Emperor Menelik II, on the Ethiopian throne and making a treaty of alliance with him in 1889, the Italians had seemed about to gain their purpose. But the puppet proved less tractable than they had bargained for and gave railway concessions to the French. With the blessing of England the Italians moved troops into Ethiopia in 1895, but Menelik defeated and annihilated a force of over 6000 Italians at Aduwa the next year. Thereupon Italy, aggrieved and humiliated, overthrew the government of Prime Minister Francesco Crispi, recognized Menelik as unconditional sovereign of Ethiopia, and paid an indemnity of $2,000,000 into the Ethiopian treasury. It was the first lasting victory of a non-European people over a European army, and it was to rankle in Italian hearts for years to come, but it led immediately to no crisis outside of Italy.

Rivalry of the Germans
and the British in South Africa

AS AN ALLY of Austria and of Italy, Germany had been only indirectly involved in the Cretan and Ethiopian episodes. A notorious German outburst against England had meanwhile occurred in connection with England's African ambitions, which the Germans considered of more direct concern to them. Cecil Rhodes, already famous as one of the greatest and most daring British empire-builders, enjoyed a virtual monopoly of the African diamond industry and, was prime minister after 1890 of the Cape Colony. His ideal had long been to have the whole of South Africa, as far as it was not German, under joint Boer-British rule and to construct a railroad "from the Cape to Cairo."

The situation had become more complicated when gold was discovered in the Transvaal area in 1886 and large numbers of foreign prospectors and businessmen flocked into the area. The Boer government exploited these *Uitlanders* (foreigners), most of whom were English, and although they now formed the overwhelming majority of the population, put obstacles in their way to naturalization and hence to equality of treatment. Trade and investment rivalries made the situation still more tense. The Boer South African Republic had constructed with German and Dutch capital a railroad line connecting the Transvaal with Portuguese Delagoa Bay. The Cape Colony legis-

506

lature had helped financially to complete it, for both the new line and the older Cape Colony line were expected to run profitably. The Boer government gave the new line a monopoly, however, going so far at one time as to block the fords on the wagon routes that fed the Cape Colony line. In addition, Rhodes learned that Germans were making huge investments in Transvaal business, and he feared that these were but the first steps in establishing a virtual German protectorate over the two Boer republics.

The Jameson Raid and its repercussions

LORD SALISBURY was reluctant to do anything about the situation, but his colonial secretary, Joseph Chamberlain, was less cautious as a statesman and much franker as an imperialist. Chamberlain had put a businesslike efficiency in the Colonial Office, and in the crown colonies he had promoted reforms such as the building of hospitals, scientific research, medical schools, and the study of tropical agriculture. Everyone knew that the *Uitlanders'* patience had been exhausted and they were ready for revolt. How much Chamberlain knew of an actual conspiracy to overthrow the Boer Republic is still debated. It is beyond question that Rhodes encouraged Dr. Leander Starr Jameson to make a "raid" into the Transvaal. "I did not want to know too much," Chamberlain is reported to have said afterwards. Late in 1895 Jameson started his raid with about 500 mounted police of Rhodes' company, but he and his men were quickly captured by the Boers, and the raid was over.

Chamberlain disavowed the raid as soon as he heard of it and while it was still in progress. Thus it might have passed as a discredited coup in an overreaching empire-building program if it had not become an affair of international "honor." Germany was in an unfriendly mood and did not hesitate to add to international complications at a moment when President Cleveland was addressing bellicose messages to the British because of the Venezuela question (page 495). On January 3, 1896, the day after Jameson's capture, the Kaiser sent a telegram of congratulation to President Paul Kruger of the South African Republic. It was immediately published, and the British were thunderstruck. The telegram read:

> I express to you my sincere congratulations that without appealing to the help of friendly Powers, you and your people have succeeded in repelling with your own forces the armed bands which had broken into your country and in maintaining the independence of your country against foreign aggression.

The British never forgave the Kaiser for the all too evident satisfaction in his telegram, and German public opinion became more clearly anti-British than before.

The beginnings
of the armament race

MOUNTING military expenditures added to the international tension. The German constitution of 1871 had made military service obligatory for all able-bodied men. Since then, the tensions in European diplomacy had led to growing concern about military preparedness. Because of the Boulangist turmoil in France (page 431), Bismarck had wanted to increase the size and the equipment of the German army in 1887. He had won his point only after a hard struggle with the Reichstag, and a new army bill increasing appropriations was adopted. In 1893 Bismarck's successor, Caprivi, carried another army bill—again only after a hard battle in parliament. It lowered the service in the infantry from three to two years, but it also did away with most exemptions from conscription, so that actually the size of the army was increased. As a consequence, France and Russia increased their armies too. By 1890 the cost per capita for military expenditures was higher in all three countries than it had been in 1870 but was lower in Germany than in France.

After the episode of the telegram to Kruger, the Kaiser decided also to increase the strength of the German navy. Germany's overseas trade, her investments in undeveloped countries, and her empire had grown by leaps and bounds. Naval affairs were within federal jurisdiction under the German constitution, and the Kaiser was not handicapped in his supreme command of the navy by the obligation, as in the case of the army, to treat with the other rulers in the federation.

Admiral von Tirpitz
and the rise of the German navy

THE NAVAL program made rapid progress under Admiral Alfred von Tirpitz, the foremost German naval expert, whom the Kaiser appointed to the position of secretary of state for naval affairs. Tirpitz immediately inspired the founding of the German Navy League (page 487), an organization that made propaganda for a large German fleet. His naval ambitions, as we have seen, collided with American ambitions and brought Germany and the United States very close to a shooting war in Manila harbor in 1898. Actually, however, Tirpitz was more concerned about the British than the American navy, and this naval rivalry was ultimately to weigh most heavily in turning English preferences away from alliance with Germany. As England's isolation became clearer in the midst of the continental scramble for allies, she had developed the program of maintaining a fleet big enough to match any two potential enemies (page 439). Tirpitz devised the "risk theory" to counteract that program: If Germany should build a fleet big enough to destroy a large part of the British fleet, then England would altogether have to avoid risking her navy against Germany's out of fear that even a victory would involve so great a loss as to render the surviving British fleet inferior to the next two naval powers'. On this theory Tirpitz pushed through big navy bills in 1898 and 1900.

The Bagdad Railway and the Turko-German entente

THE KAISER also cultivated German glory in other fields. Germany's part in the partition of China in 1897-1898 has been narrated elsewhere (page 493). Germany also became deeply involved in the Near East. Since 1888 the Germans had been working on the construction of a railroad crossing Anatolia (or Asia Minor). In the 1890's, after several years of negotiations, a new phase of German economic penetration opened up in Turkey. The Kaiser used his influence to win investment opportunities for German capitalists. In 1898 he made a trip to the Near East, and at Damascus, in November, he delivered another of his flamboyant declarations. He wanted the 300,000,000 Moslems to know, he announced, that the German emperor would be their friend at all times. Since there were 250,000,000 Moslems living within either British-controlled or Russian-controlled territories, the British and the Russians were not so favorably impressed with William's oratory as the Germans were, but the Turks were especially pleased. The next year a German-financed Bagdad Railway Company obtained a concession for constructing what was called the Bagdad Railway, thousands of miles of track linking the shores of the Bosporus opposite Constantinople with the Persian Gulf. It was a dazzling project, which might bring the industrialization and rejuvenation, with German capital, of the Turkish lands.

The Sudan War and the Fashoda Incident

IN ONE connection Bismarck's successors remained loyal to his foreign policy. They were glad to promote French colonialism in areas where it might conflict with the colonial ambitions of others. In 1894 the French, with the acquiescence of Germany, undertook to conquer the central Sudan. A French expeditionary force under Major Jean Baptiste Marchand marched from the French Congo eastward to the Upper Nile Valley. In July 1898 Marchand established himself at Fashoda (now Kodok) on the White Nile and claimed the surrounding area for France. The British regarded that claim as an intrusion into their sphere of influence. In 1896, in order to counteract French and Italian maneuvers around the Nile, the British had resumed their war against the "mad dervishes," who had overrun the Sudan since their destruction of "Chinese" Gordon (page 424). General Herbert Kitchener, serving under Egypt but assisted by British forces, crushed them in a series of battles ending in 1898 with the Battle of Omdurman. Kitchener then quickly marched to Fashoda, where the French under Marchand had entrenched themselves. Kitchener politely insisted upon the withdrawal of Marchand's forces, and Marchand replied with equal politeness that he could not until the French government ordered him to do so.

As the two forces faced each other on the Nile, London and Paris became the scenes of astonishing diplomatic fencing. Despite the bitterness of the French people, the French foreign minister, Théophile Delcassé, held that Germany was the more inveterate enemy of France and therefore France must avoid any conflict with Great Britain. The French government accordingly ordered Marchand to evacuate Fashoda, and in the course of a year the French formally gave up their claims to the Nile. Since the feud between England and France over Egyptian interests was a hoary one, the French public looked upon this retreat as a confession of weakness resulting from the Dreyfus debacle. Actually it was the first bit of coquetry in Marianne's wooing of John Bull, who still had fresh in mind the tongue-lashings of the Kaiser (pages 507 and 509).

Nobel prizes, Olympic games, and the first Hague Conference

AS WAR scares followed one upon another, the race for military preparedness grew more desperate. The perfecting of nitroglycerine after 1862 by the Swedish chemist Alfred B. Nobel made the prospects of future wars appear ghastly. On his death in 1896 Nobel lent a particularly paradoxical touch to the quest for a good world, since he left the money he had made by the sale of explosives to endow the world's most famous prizes for science, literature, and peace efforts. As early as 1889, the Austrian baroness Bertha von Suttner in *Lay Down Your Arms* had tried to show what an armament race would mean. The book became a best seller and in 1905 she won the Nobel Peace Prize. Sir Norman Angell, later also a Nobel Peace Prize winner, in *The Great Illusion* (1910) argued that neither side could profit from a war. The problem, however, was not one that yielded to exhortation or argument. Nor did it yield to the good intentions of Baron Pierre de Coubertin, who succeeded in 1896 in reviving the ancient Olympic games. Although every four years since then (except when war prevented) many nations have sent their best amateur athletes to compete for honors in different cities of the world, friendly athletic rivalry did not displace unfriendly rivalry for armaments.

In 1898 Czar Nicholas II, distressed by the cost of his growing army and navy, issued a proclamation inviting the powers to a disarmament conference. He suggested that the armies and navies of all powers be frozen at the status of January 1899. The idea was enthusiastically received in the English-speaking countries, which had no compulsory military training, and among the small nations. Some Germans saw in it a Russian trap intended to dissuade the German government from developing the naval program upon which it had just embarked. Nevertheless, twenty-six nations from all parts of the world met and conferred at The Hague for several months in 1899.

A limitation of armaments in fact proved unfeasible, though accepted in principle. The conference did, however, constitute perhaps the most important step so far taken toward collective action for the preservation of international peace. A Permanent Court of Arbitration was established at The Hague. Between 1900 and 1914 forty-five nations adhered to this Hague Tri-

510

burial and it arbitrated fifteen international disputes involving sixteen nations from four continents. The conference also adopted a set of conventions for humanizing warfare but was unable to provide machinery for enforcing these rules.

The Boer (or South African) War

HARDLY had the Hague Conference ended when the question of the status of British residents in the Transvaal precipitated the outbreak of war in South Africa. Ill feeling had not diminished since the Jameson Raid. In fact Kruger had consistently followed a policy of greater discrimination against the *Uitlanders* and of resistance to English pressure. Conferences of Kruger with Sir Alfred Milner, governor of Cape Colony and high commissioner for South Africa, led only to mutual distrust. As troops began to arrive from England to reinforce the fewer than 15,000 British regulars in South Africa, Kruger sent an ultimatum on October 9, 1899, which the British rejected, and war began three days later. The Orange Free State joined the South African Republic in the fighting.

Great Britain was not prepared for war and suffered heavy defeats for a brief time. When Lord Roberts, hero of the Afghan wars, took over the command, with Baron Kitchener of Khartoum as his second, the tide turned. After the British captured Pretoria, the capital of the Transvaal, the Boers confined themselves to a skillful guerrilla warfare. Kitchener, now in com-

Boer volunteers, with rifles and cartridge belts, entrain from Johannesburg for Natal. A drawing from the Illustrated London News.

511

mand, counteracted the guerrillas by erecting a system of block houses and concentration camps for Boer women and children, in which about 20,000 died. Eventually the Boers capitulated. Peace was concluded at Vereeniging in 1902. The two Boer republics, having been annexed by the British in the course of the war, received the promise of self-government under British rule; the Boer language was granted official status; and the Boers were given compensation for their war-devastated farms.

The British
in search of an ally

THE PEOPLES of Europe and America had been shocked by Kitchener's ruthlessness during the war. The French, remembering the humiliation at Fashoda, were vociferous in their denunciations. In Germany the outspoken hatred of Britain sometimes embarrassed the government. When the defeated Boer generals went on a visit to Germany, though they were not formally received by the authorities, the people greeted them with ovations. In the United States a large part of the public had persuaded themselves that the Boers were an unfortunate small people who had failed to make good in their war of independence against a big bully.

Rarely had England been more isolated or seemed less splendid. At the beginning of the war, shortly after a visit of William II to England, Chamberlain had gone so far as to suggest in a famous speech at Leicester the creation of a British-German-American alliance. But the ill will arising out of the Samoan controversy (page 499) and the German naval program doomed the proposal. In fact, incensed by British interference with German ships engaged in trade with the Boers, the Germans in 1900 increased the size of their navy again; and in February 1901, when King Edward VII went to Germany to visit his cancer-stricken sister, the Empress Frederick, he encountered patent unfriendliness. Alliance talks nevertheless continued until early in 1902, when it became certain that an alliance with Germany was not feasible.

Reform in China
thwarted by Tz'u Hsi

IN THE MIDST of the Boer War things had been happening in the Far East that made Japan look like a good second choice as an ally for Britain. The proclamation of the "open door" without consulting the Peking government had done little to diminish the bitter resentment of the Chinese people over the dismemberment of China. It had been clear for a long time that the Manchu government was unable to prevent the dissolution of the empire. China's role as "the sick man of the Far East" stimulated ideas of reform among the educated and official classes. The Kwang Hsü emperor in the last decade of the century came under the influence of those who believed that reform along western lines would save the empire from disintegration. Societies were organized to work for reform legislation. One of the most influential tracts urging reform was written by Chang Chih-tung, the viceroy of Wuchang. It was entitled *Learn.* Unlike many of his contemporaries, Chang asserted that "the present condition of things is not due to outside nations, but to China herself."

Another of the great reforming spirits was K'ang Yu-wei. His influence was paramount in inaugurating the "Hundred Days" (June 11-September 22, 1898) of reform under the Kwang Hsü emperor. In slightly over three months decrees were issued which, if followed up, would have overturned the customs and institutions venerated for centuries. The reform movement was thwarted, however, by a struggle for power inside Peking. Tz'u Hsi was empress-dowager and the power behind the throne. Learning that the emperor and K'ang Yu-wei were plotting to imprison her, Tz'u Hsi, acting through Yüan Shih-kai, captured and imprisoned the emperor instead. As a result of this coup, reform was checked as abruptly as it had begun, and most of the radical decrees of the "Hundred Days" were quickly rescinded.

China's effort to lock the "open door"

A SUCCESSFUL reform movement might have taken support away from those who advocated extreme measures. Among the Left extremists was Dr. Sun Yat-sen, who, operating from exile abroad, advocated outright revolt against the dynasty. At this period his following in China, however, was relatively small and unorganized. No force now was strong enough to oppose the empress-dowager, who stood forth as an extremist of an opposite persuasion. She sought to achieve salvation for China by stirring up the antiforeign feelings of her subjects and by revitalizing the military prowess of the empire. She encouraged the rebirth of secret societies to help in the revival of the empire's military glory. From the gymnastic exercises practiced by one of these secret societies, the Righteous Harmony Fists, the Westerners coined the term "Boxers" and applied it to all the antiforeign elements. Rallying around the banner of the empress-dowager, these societies became popular and militant. They unfurled defiant slogans like "Protect the Ch'ing [dynasty] and destroy the foreigners." Hostility toward foreigners was further aggravated after 1898 by famine in the northern provinces. Violence broke out, especially in Shantung, where foreign missions were firmly entrenched and where the foreign concessions had been made but recently. In 1899 attacks upon foreigners and native Christians occurred with alarming regularity.

The suppression of the Boxer Rebellion

UNDER THE protection of their soldiers and gunboats the foreigners were for a time safer than native Christians, but the situation inland steadily grew more serious. In 1900 the powers that maintained legations in China became anxious over the safety of their emissaries. An international force was quickly assembled at Tientsin. When this force attempted to go to the aid of the emissaries at Peking, its march was interpreted by China as an act of war. Thereupon the Boxers laid siege to the legations at Peking, even though the imperial court understood quite well the status and immunities of emissaries under international law. Many of the empress' advisers warned her of the probable consequences of this folly, but she urged the attack forward. The international force from Tientsin managed to crack the Boxer resistance and to lift the siege of the legations only after it had lasted nearly two fearful summer months. Upon the defeat of the Boxer forces, the imperial court fled from Peking, leaving the ancient capital to the international expeditionary force, which plundered it thoroughly. The failure of the Boxer movement marked the nadir of China's international prestige.

Since the German minister to China had been the most prominent victim of the Boxer assassins, Germany had taken a leading part in suggesting the international crusade to crush the Boxer Rebellion. William II succeeded in getting Count von Waldersee named leader of the expedition (although the "world marshal" did not reach his post until the fighting was over). Other governments, however, felt misgivings when the Kaiser, addressing the German sailors embarking for China, admonished them to avenge the crimes once committed by Attila the Hun: "No quarter will be given. No prisoners will be made." The speech caused consternation even among the German people. Often referred to as "the speech of the Hun," it had a different effect from that which the Kaiser intended, for in future years, the Germans were to be labeled "the Huns" in enemy propaganda.

The aftermath of the Boxer Rebellion HOW LOW China had sunk was to become clear when a settlement was extracted by the aggrieved powers. While the negotiations were still in progress, the empress, in an effort to anticipate the powers' demands for reform, issued an edict proposing a long-term program of reconstruction (1901). The powers, meanwhile, disagreed among themselves as to the best way of handling what was virtually an unprecedented problem of international relations. Germany was the most vindictive and launched on her own initiative a punitive expedition into areas most seriously hit by the antiforeign movement.

After considerable diplomatic by-play, the crusading powers (eleven in number by this time) signed with China the settlement known as the Boxer Protocols (1901). Twelve long articles obliged China, among other things, to make a formal and general apology, pay indemnities to each of the powers, offer special regrets to Germany and a special indemnity to Japan, punish the Boxer leaders, suspend for five years the official examinations for administrative officials in Boxer towns, forbid the importation of arms and ammunition, permit the establishment of permanent legation guards in Peking, raze the fort at the mouth of the Taku River, revise commercial treaties, organize a ministry of foreign affairs along western lines, and accept military occupation of strategic points between the capital and the sea. Li Hung-chang signed this treaty—the last of the Chinese treaties in the humiliating nineteenth-century tradition. Two days later the aged statesman died.

The Boxers' xenophobia helped to bring understanding in one regard. The "sack of Peking" brought historical treasures to the West that made the libraries and museums of Europe and America extremely rich in Chinese literature and history at a time when western scholars were fairly well prepared to profit from their good fortune. For Far Eastern studies had made great strides in the last quarter of the nineteenth century under prominent scholars like James Legge in England, and Edouard Chavannes and Henri Cordier in France.

The powers agreed in 1901 to withdraw their occupation forces from China. But Russia, which had sent an army into Manchuria at the beginning of the Boxer outbreak, exhibited no serious intention of withdrawing her forces. And in the Korean peninsula Japan had in fact strengthened hers. Thus, at the beginning of the twentieth century China lay helpless between two powers whose ambitions in eastern Asia were but thinly disguised, and was beset at the same time by a host of long-range domestic problems.

The alliance of England and Japan

TO LONDON the Russian advance into Manchuria was but another example of Russia's determination to rule over the borderlands of Asia. Anxiety led Britain to request Japanese cooperation in the protection of India. Although the Japanese refused at first to become involved there, the British, feeling an intense need for breaking through their isolation, nevertheless went ahead with negotiations and in January 1902 signed an alliance with Japan. The Anglo-Japanese Alliance was restricted to the Far East. In its preamble it stressed the concern of both parties for the independence and integrity of China and Korea, and their common determination to preserve the status quo in eastern Asia. The signatories then recognized their common "special interests" in China and the "peculiar degree" of Japan's interests in Korea and promised to aid each other in preserving their respective positions. It was further agreed that if either party should become involved in war with a third power in defense of its Far Eastern interests, the other would remain strictly neutral; in case the third power were aided by a fourth, the allies committed themselves to go to each other's aid. Concluded for a five-year period, the alliance was actually to be renewed twice and to remain in force until 1922.

Though the Americans feared the consequences of giving Japan a free hand in Korea, the possibility of Russo-Japanese cooperation in eastern Asia appeared an even greater danger. Secretary Hay was primarily concerned "that, no matter what happens eventually in northern China and Manchuria, the United States shall not be placed in any worse position than while the country was under the unquestioned dominion of China." And President Roosevelt expressed the opinion: "We cannot possibly interfere for the Koreans against Japan. They could not strike one blow in their own defense." Thus the United States government, agreeing with Great Britain that the realities required the courting of Tokyo, was prepared to refrain from interference with Japan's obvious designs upon Korea.

Repercussions upon European diplomacy THE END of England's diplomatic isolation and the conclusion of the Anglo-Japanese Alliance helped to crystallize the alliance systems of Europe. Great Britain's hostility to the Asiatic ambitions of Russia was viewed hopefully in Berlin as presaging a conflict involving two of Germany's potential enemies. The Germans were also hopeful that the Anglo-Japanese Alliance might add to the hard feelings between France and England because of France's commitments to Russia under the terms of their Dual Convention. The British, however, had guarded against such an eventuality by providing for their neutrality in case of hostilities in the Far East limited to Russia and Japan alone. Under the terms of her alliance France was similarly protected from involvement on the side of Russia in an outbreak in eastern Asia. Neither the Anglo-Japanese nor the Franco-Russian treaty, therefore, put obstacles in the way of an entente of France and England regarding their common interests in Europe and Africa; and an Anglo-French entente was soon to become a reality.

THE BRITISH EMPIRE

AND THE RUSSO-JAPANESE WAR

THE Anglo-Japanese Alliance of 1902 brought a fourth diplomatic constellation into world politics. The oldest was the Anglo-American entente, never formally written down, almost unrecognized, and sometimes stretched to the breaking point, but resulting nevertheless in their usual cooperation to prevent any threat to the domination of the Atlantic Ocean by any third power. Much more formal was the Triple Alliance of Germany, Austria, and Italy. Less formal but no less binding was the military convention of the Russians and French. Thus, with the Anglo-Japanese Alliance to complete the list of commitments, each of the eight world powers had assumed toward at least one of the others some kind of obligation, written or understood, that in some fashion or other was likely to color its attitude toward the rest in the event of a crisis; and since the eight powers were located on three continents and had interests all over the world, the whole world was willy-nilly involved in their attitudes and disputes.

High tariffs
and economic competition

EACH OF the big powers except Great Britain by now had taken refuge behind a high protective tariff wall. As we have seen (page 383), Germany introduced a protective tariff in 1879. In 1891 she lowered it, but it was still high enough to involve her in a customs "war" with Russia, after the Russians turned to protectionism in 1891. France adopted protectionism in 1887, and soon became involved in a tariff war with Italy (1888-1899). Italy herself became protectionist in 1891. The United States, too, committed to a high protective policy under the Republican predominance since the Civil War, adopted in the 1890's the exceptionally high McKinley and Dingley tariffs.

Only Great Britain, of all the big countries, persisted in a policy of free trade. Nevertheless, it seemed obvious to some British statesmen that some answer would have to be found to the gradual exclusion of British products from the markets of other countries. When Chamberlain, moved by sentimental as well as trade considerations, brought up the idea of a regular imperial council at the Colonial Conference of 1897 and met with decided opposition from the assembled colonial statesmen (page 483), he was not daunted. He persisted in his protectionist attitude and in 1903 organized the Tariff Reform League to agitate for a reversion of the traditional free-trade policy. The outcome of the gradual return to protection by the countries of the world was a series of tariff conflicts and bargainings. Nevertheless, trade showed a general tendency to rise from 1896 to 1914.

The British
in India and Egypt

TWO great colonial administrators brought luster to the British imperial throne during this period. The most influential British statesman in Asia at the beginning of the century was Lord Curzon, viceroy of India. A farseeing imperialist, Curzon believed in the benevolent administration of India as a means of promoting both Britain's interests and the welfare of India. He overhauled the administrative, educational, and irrigation systems and insisted upon economy in all branches of government. Like many of his predecessors, Lord Curzon was also plagued by the problem of pacifying and policing the northern frontiers of India, but unlike many of his predecessors he acted with vigor. Through a mixture of administrative reorganization, bribery, and threats, Curzon won the tribesmen of the frontier to the support of Great Britain. Beyond the frontier passes of the north and the west he kept a set of active agents working on imperial business.

Contemporaneously Baring (page 424) was modernizing Egypt. Virtual ruler of Egypt for a quarter of a century from 1883, Lord Cromer (as he became in 1892) reformed its system of finances and its army. He made some much needed changes in the laws, courts, and prisons. He promoted education and public sanitation. When he resigned in 1907, Egypt was materially far ahead of where it probably would have been without his ministrations and at the same time probably better prepared for self-government.

The Persian Gulf area
a disputed sphere of influence

THE AMBITIONS of the French, Germans, and Russians to obtain control of actual or potential land routes between Europe and India constituted for the British Empire one of its most delicate international problems. Persia was not only on the route to India; it was also an area into which British capital had been poured since the 1860's and where recently a British company had received the right to prospect for oil. The efforts of the French to obtain footholds on the Persian Gulf were resented only slightly less than those of the Germans and the Russians. The proposed Berlin-to-Bagdad Railway (page 509) roused British fear that the Germans might entrench themselves in the same general area with the cooperation of the Turks. Furthermore, the traditional hostility between England and Russia had become particularly acute in Persia during the Boer War, when the Russians had attempted to replace British capital and had sent Russian ships into Persian waters. Shortly after the Anglo-Japanese Alliance alleviated Great Britain's apprehension of the Russians in eastern Asia, the British through Lord Curzon made known their intention to protect, by arms if necessary, the integrity of southern Persia. Thus a new crisis area was added to the growing list.

Tibet
in the affairs of the big powers

AS ON India's western frontiers, Curzon's handling of the problem on the eastern frontier was also in the best imperial tradition. Technically under the suzerainty of China but actually ruled by the Dalai Lama (grand priest) at Lhasa, the mountain state of Tibet has been a point at which Indian, Chinese, and Russian interests have periodically clashed. Shortly before the outbreak of the Russo-Japanese War (page 521), the relations between St. Petersburg and Lhasa became so friendly as to arouse suspicion in London. Meanwhile, trade between Tibet and India was interrupted by a Tibetan boycott. Thereupon Lord Curzon sent an expeditionary force to Lhasa, and the Dalai Lama was forced to accept a treaty forbidding the establishment of foreign agencies at Lhasa without British approval. With war facing them in Manchuria, the Russians were in no position to counter Curzon's high-handed methods. Nor was China strong or independent enough to assert its rights of suzerainty. Thus, after 1904 England retained a paramount interest in Tibet.

Kipling, Curzon,
and Indian nationalism

UP TO Queen Victoria's Diamond Jubilee in 1897, the contributions of India to the world and to the wealth and strength of the British Empire far outweighed the costs of holding the great peninsula as a colony. By the turn of the century, however, doubt was beginning to arise whether the balance sheet would always show a profit. The British were having ever greater trouble with the Indian nationalists, and the material returns to Britain from the colony fell off proportionately. The Diamond Jubilee had brought forth great pride over "the Empire on which the sun never sets." But the novelist and poet Rudyard Kipling, who was born in India and was a lifelong champion of what he called "the white man's burden," enlightened colonization, shortly after the Diamond Jubilee reminded his countrymen of their serious responsibilities:

> Lord of our far-flung battle-line,
> Beneath whose awful Hand we hold
> Dominion over palm and pine—
>
> . . . .
>
> For frantic boast and foolish word—
> Thy mercy on Thy people, Lord![1]

As viceroy of India, Lord Curzon had to cope with the new Indian nationalism. Determined not to recognize the growing national sentiment, Curzon repeatedly outraged both the nationalistic and the particularistic sensibilities of important native elements. In an effort to divide the old Bengal state into two separate provinces in order to make its administration easier, he ran headlong into fierce native resistance. Although Bengal had never been an independent nation, the Bengalis boasted of their race and language unity. Curzon paid no attention to these claims. The sentiment for his removal mounted both in England and in India, until in 1905 he was recalled. Indian national resistance thus won its first significant victory.

The constitution of the Commonwealth of Australia

THE REORGANIZATION of Australia advanced rapidly in the 1890's. For six years the separate colonies discussed the proposed federal constitution (pages 421-422). Finally a formal constitutional convention was called at Adelaide in 1897. All colonies except New Zealand and Queensland sent representatives. The delegates borrowed from the cabinet system of the British, making the prime minister responsible to the parliament, and from the Canadian constitution, making the king of Great Britain and Ireland also their king, represented by a governor general. Aware, however, that the Australian problem of 1897 was reminiscent of the American problem of 1787, they borrowed most from the Constitution of the United States. In both cases the strength of the small states had to be buttressed without encroaching upon the rights of the large states. As a result, a bicameral legislature with a strong lower House of Representatives was proposed, and in the upper house, the Senate, all states were to have equal representation. In deference to the continuing particularism, the constitution permitted the states to retain all powers not expressly accorded by the constitution to the central authority, and the constitution was to be interpreted by a Supreme Court—in these regards, too, borrowing from the American precedent. In 1900 the constitution of the new Commonwealth of Australia received the approval of the British government, and the continent "down under" was able, on the first day of the twentieth century (January 1, 1901), to make its bow as one of the most important units in the British family of nations. Since then Australia has consisted of five continental states (Victoria, New South Wales, Queensland, South Australia, and Western Australia) and the island state of Tasmania, administering dependent territories of its own.

Major political developments in Australia and New Zealand

UNTIL serious naval rivalry with Germany began, the royal navy accepted the responsibility of guarding the colonies. It was supported by voluntary colonial money contributions, but it neither expected nor received much aid from practically nonexistent colonial fleets. In return, the colonies, also voluntarily, assumed a responsibility for aiding the mother country in her difficulties. Canadian and Australasian contingents fought in the Boer War; and in the years before the First World War, Australia and New Zealand, as well as Canada, began to build their own navies.

Australia is not a highly industrialized country. Its major occupation is sheep raising, and it has long been the world's greatest exporter of wool. Its political history is remarkable for the fact that trade unions came before industrialization; hence, among the three major parties, the Labour Party became predominant in the 1890's, even before the Commonwealth was created. It is as little Marxist as the present British Labour Party. It succeeded in creating a complicated system of labor arbitration, which at that time was unprecedented, and later also in getting approval of old-age pensions (1909), invalid pensions (1910), and maternity allowances (1912). Australia has frankly limited immigration to Whites. By acts of 1902 and 1905, immigration of colored people was made practically impossible.

New Zealand has continued independent of Australia. Like Australia, it is remarkable for its social legislation. As early as 1894 it accepted an Industrial Conciliation and Arbitration Act, and shortly thereafter an eight-hour-day law and old-age pensions. Like Australia, New Zealand became a great exporter of wool. A restrictive immigration policy came even earlier (1899) than in Australia. On the other hand, after the Maori wars ended (1871), the Maoris were given representation in Parliament, and they usually have a representative in the cabinet.

520

Russo-Japanese War
and international diplomacy

DESPITE British commitments to her colonies and to Japan, the Anglo-Japanese Alliance did not involve her as a belligerent in the war that commenced in the East in 1904. Having failed to iron out the difficulties in Korea and Manchuria (page 515), Japan launched a surprise attack upon Russia in February. In the ensuing hostilities Great Britain remained neutral while the United States acted practically as a moral ally of Japan. President Roosevelt warned Germany and France not to intervene, and strongly intimated that intervention would bring the United States to the side of Japan. The president believed that the two "annexationist" powers of the Far East should be permitted to battle it out. Realizing that Japan might cause trouble in America's Pacific possessions, Roosevelt in 1905 extracted from them an "agreed memorandum" (often referred to as the Taft-Katsura agreement): Japan reassured the United States that "Japan does not harbor any aggressive designs whatever on the Philippines"; in return the president virtually became a silent partner to the Anglo-Japanese Alliance, committing his administration to a policy of which but few persons in the United States had any specific knowledge.

The significance
of Japanese successes

THE Russo-Japanese War was the first war in which an Asiatic nation challenged a European power and came off the victor. In many parts of the world the triumph of pygmy Japan over gigantic Russia aroused admiration. Among the peoples of the Orient the picture of a small and but recently "reopened" Asiatic nation trouncing the armies and the battle fleets of the czar revived the flagging spirit of resistance to the white man. In the United States, too, the traditional sympathy for the "underdog" worked in favor of Roosevelt's pro-Japanese policy. Finally, the Russian government's autocratic mismanagement of the Revolution of 1905 (page 465) alienated the western world and aided the Japanese cause correspondingly. The weakness of Russia was laid bare for all to see, as that of China had been laid bare a decade before. At the same time the world came to realize that a new power of first rank importance in oriental affairs had taken its place beside the other great nations of the world.

The beginning
of an Italo-French rapprochement

MEANWHILE events had played into the hands of Delcassé, enabling him further to strengthen the French system of alliances. Shortly after England's isolation had come to an end with the Anglo-Japanese Alliance, a rift had developed in the Triple Alliance. Italy had never been happy as an ally of Austria, and France had already (1900) made a friendly gesture by recognizing Italy's predominant interest in Tripoli in return for Italy's recognition of France's predominant interest in Morocco. Having become convinced at the renewal of the Triple Alliance in 1902 that no further concessions would be forthcoming from Germany, Italy now began to flirt with France. A secret Franco-Italian agreement was reached later that year. It provided that Italy would remain neutral if France were attacked or provoked into a declaration of war. This was Italy's own policy of reinsurance, no more and no less a violation of her obligations than Bismarck's Reinsurance Treaty with Russia had been. The Italian foreign office took the occasion to inform the French foreign office that Italy had no obligations that would force her to take part in a war in which France was on the defensive; and since the Triple Alliance was itself ostensibly a defensive one (except in so far as Italy had insisted on aid even if she took the offensive), this information was not literally false. It had the effect of reassuring the French, as the visit of President Loubet and Delcassé to Rome in 1904 (page 469) testified.

The formation of the Entente Cordiale

NEVERTHELESS, when Japan started her war on Russia, the French had good reason to be disturbed. They feared that, with their only ally entangled in the Far East, they might be weakened in counterbalancing Germany in Europe, especially if England felt constrained to support her ally Japan. For that reason they were more than willing to come to an agreement with Great Britain. The British also saw the desirability of making sure of a clear field in Europe in the event that the Russo-Japanese War spread to include Britain. The war in fact almost did involve Britain when the Russian Baltic fleet, on its way to the Far East, fired at some innocent English fishing vessels at the Dogger Bank in the North Sea, apparently mistaking them for Japanese warships.

Even before the Russo-Japanese War, Edward VII had visited Paris, and Loubet had visited London—so that people understood something was going on. The British sought no alliance. They wanted only to smooth out old grievances, and thus create an atmosphere of friendliness. A series of negotiations led to an understanding that came to be called by the old name "Entente Cordiale" and was contained in a treaty concluded in April 1904. A series of minor issues was ironed out, and by the main convention France gave up her pre-Napoleonic claim to Egypt and recognized British control there. In return Britain recognized France's special interest in Morocco, provided that in any partition of Morocco, France would give a share to the Spanish and that the port town of Tangier (opposite Gibraltar) would not be fortified. The parts of the treaty that dealt with the partition of Morocco were, of course, secret.

The Moroccan issue and the Tangier episode

WHEN THE open provisions of the Entente Cordiale were published, the German government was in a quandary. At first the Germans counted on a Russo-British war, especially after the Russian attack upon the English fishing vessels at the Dogger Bank. Such a war would have put the French in an awkward position,

FRANCE FINDS ALLIES

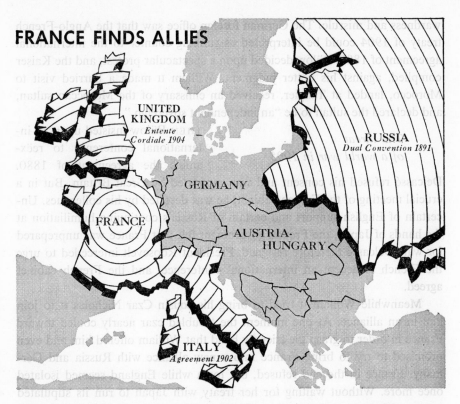

Bismarck's system of alliances aimed at keeping the peace largely by isolating France. It began to disintegrate in 1890, the year of his dismissal. Germany's Reinsurance Treaty with Russia lapsed in 1890, and Russia entered into a Dual Convention with France in 1891. A series of events around the turn of the century had made plain to Britain her need of allies. England's "splendid isolation" was dropped for an alliance with Japan (1902) followed by the Entente Cordiale with France in 1904. Italy, the third member of the Triple Alliance, negotiated its own "reinsurance" treaty with France in 1902.

obliged to choose between their Russian allies and their British friends. The Dogger Bank incident was turned over to the Hague Tribunal, however, and the prospect of war between Russia and Great Britain vanished. Meanwhile, Russia, suffering one defeat after another at the hands of Japan, demonstrated an augmenting incapacity to aid France if war should break out between France and Germany. Also, Holstein reckoned that Great Britain would not stand by France if war came. He and Chancellor von Bülow determined to take a strong stand against the Entente Cordiale.

An occasion was not hard to find. Since 1880, by international agreement, the leading European powers and the United States had recognized Morocco as an independent state open for commercial purposes equally to all. Actually, Morocco was not a state in the modern sense of the word. It was ruled by a tribal bureaucracy that, in its turn, was controlled by the Moroccan sultan. The government was corrupt and inclined to take bribes from foreign countries. The country offered an excellent example of back-

523

wardness and misrule. The German foreign office saw that the Anglo-French treaty of 1904 could be interpreted as running counter to the international agreement of 1880. Bülow decided upon a spectacular protest, and the Kaiser complied, against his better judgment. William II made a hurried visit to Morocco, landed at Tangier, received an emissary of the Moroccan sultan, and declared the sultan to be "an independent sovereign."

The threat
of a world war in 1905

THEN Bülow insisted upon an international conference to reëxamine the agreement of 1880. Delcassé refused his consent and was supported by Great Britain. But in a crucial meeting of the French cabinet, he was deserted by his colleagues. Uncertain of English support and certain of Russia's continuing humiliation at the hands of Japan, the French government felt that France was unprepared for war. Delcassé therefore resigned. President Roosevelt interceded to urge the French to accept an international conference, and the French cabinet agreed.

Meanwhile William II tried to bring his cousin Czar Nicholas II to join him in an alliance. At one moment the troubled czar nearly cooled toward France in order to grasp the friendly hand that William offered him and even promised to try to bring France into a new alliance with Russia and Germany. France in the end refused, but for a while England seemed isolated once more. Without waiting for her treaty with Japan to run its stipulated course of five years, she renewed the alliance for ten years more, recognizing Japan's "paramount...interests" in Korea again in return for Japan's extending the alliance to cover India, where Curzon's policies were creating the complications already considered (pages 518-519). Fortunately, Russia's inability to continue the war in the face of her military defeats and domestic revolution made her ready to end hostilities before any other European powers became further involved. When Roosevelt offered to mediate between the two belligerents, his offer was accepted.

The Treaty of Portsmouth
and the new balance of power

DIRECT peace negotiations between Japan and Russia began in the summer of 1905. The meetings were held at Portsmouth, New Hampshire. During the course of the negotiations, the president of the United States effectively exerted his influence to bring about a settlement. The Treaty of Portsmouth provided Japan with the materials needed for founding an empire in Asia. Russia, like the United States and Great Britain earlier, recognized in 1905 the "paramount interests" of Japan in Korea. Manchuria was to be evacuated and returned to China, but the strategic Liaotung peninsula was to be leased to Japan, and the railway from Port Arthur to Changchun was also to be controlled by Japan. Furthermore, Russia ceded the southern half of the island of Sakhalin (see map, page 553) to Japan and undertook to pay a substantial indemnity.

Thus Japan became the dominant power in northeastern Asia. China was not consulted in the changes brought about in her affairs by the Portsmouth arrangements.

Japan's victory altered the world balance of power significantly and rendered possible many agreements of the succeeding decade. England felt inclined thereafter to leave Far Eastern affairs to Japan, permitting the Entente Cordiale countries to turn their attention to European and African affairs— with results that were to be fairly satisfactory to them. The victory of Japan was soon followed by secret negotiations between Russia and Japan, resulting in their gradual rapprochement on all aspects of Asiatic affairs. The worst fears of President Roosevelt seemed about to be realized, however, as Japan and Russia moved closer together in the handling of their relations with Manchuria and China. Despite repeated American protests, it appeared after 1905 as if the "annexationist" powers might successfully close the open door and settle Far Eastern problems to suit themselves.

The beginnings of Japanese-American hostility

WITH THE military defeat of the "Colossus of the North," and the domestic effort of 1905 to overthrow the czarist government, Japan was left for a time to pursue her own ends in eastern Asia. The diplomatic and military entanglements of the European powers and their growing fear of world war forced them to deal circumspectly with Japan. After 1905 the United States was the only power free enough of entanglements to stand in the way of Japanese expansion. Although the United States had supported the island empire against Russia, the Washington government quickly realized that a powerful Japan could constitute a serious threat to the stability of the Far East, to the maintenance of the open door in Manchuria and China, and to the security of American Pacific possessions. The year 1905 marks the beginning of the serious tension between Japan and the United States that ultimately helped to bring about the Second World War. Some Americans wondered at the time whether it had been wise for Americans to side with Asiatics against Europeans, but only after another generation was the world to understand that the political supremacy of Europe was beginning to collapse and that world hegemony was passing into the hands of non-Europeans.

THE END OF "splendid isolation" marked the end of a phase of the Pax Britannica. Despite the efforts of British diplomats to retain a free hand, their country, they were to find, was in fact bound to throw its weight on one side against the other. Hence they could no longer hold in check the side that most endangered peace by the threat to throw their country's weight on the other. The best they now could do was to restrain their own friends by warning that Britain might have to remain neutral and to overawe potential 525 enemies by warning that it might not remain neutral. Britain's action in future crises was therefore not certain, and both sides had to take that uncertainty into account. French diplomacy would therefore be pointed to making sure that Britain would give real support, and German policy would aim at keeping Britain neutral, in forthcoming clashes.

The British Empire was still strong enough in 1905 to make it appear rash for any power to commit itself to war with a combination which included Britain's navy, her capital, her hundreds of millions of people, and her far-flung dominions. The Pax Britannica therefore seemed not yet to have come to a close as the reign of Victoria ended and that of Edward VII began. Despite recurrent war scares and diplomatic crises, uninterrupted prosperity and progress were generally expected, and if uninterrupted peace seemed too much to hope for, at least the likelihood of any long and general war seemed too desperate to assume.

1840-1917	Auguste Rodin
1856-1939	Sigmund Freud
1856-1950	George Bernard Shaw
1862-1918	Claude Debussy
1877	Edison invents phonograph
1885	Karl Benz exhibits his first motorcar
1891-1892	Dubois unearths bones of *Pithecanthropus erectus*
1891	The Dual Convention between France and Russia
1891	Pope Leo XIII's encyclical *Rerum novarum*
1892-1894	Gladstone's fourth (and last) ministry
1892	Diesel engine patented
1893	Financial panic in America
1894-1906	The Dreyfus Affair
1894-1895	The Sino-Japanese War
1895	Guglielmo Marconi invents wireless telegraphy
1895	French General Confederation of Labor established
1896	Italo-Ethiopian War; an African nation defeats a European power
1896	Edison Company exhibits first moving picture
1897	Greco-Turkish War
1897	First Zionist Congress
1898	Spanish-American War ends the Spanish empire in America and the Philippines
1898	Marie and Pierre Curie discover radium
1899-1902	The Boer War
1899	First International Peace Conference at The Hague
1899	The Boxer Rebellion
1899	"Open door" policy formally reiterated
1900	Zeppelin produces practical airship
1900	Max Planck's "quantum theory"
1901	First billion-dollar corporation (United States Steel) formed
1902	Anglo-Japanese Alliance
1903	Russian Socialists split into Bolsheviks and Mensheviks
1903	The Wright brothers' first successful flight
1904-1905	An Asiatic power defeats a European power in Russo-Japanese War
1904	The Act of Separation of French state and church
1904	"Entente Cordiale" formed by France and Britain
c. 1905	Establishment of the Sinn Fein
1905	Albert Einstein develops his special theory of relativity
1905	Revolution in Russia
1905	Norway separated from Sweden
1906	British Labour Party formed

Chapter nine

ALLIANCE vs. ENTENTE

1905-1914

In the decade before 1914, the earth for many, perhaps most, peoples of European culture did not seem to be merely a vale of tears, and life seemed more than an idle interval between nothingness and nothingness. For those who were religious—and their number was legion—the old faiths still carried their message of comfort and a divine plan, and the new scientific knowledge supplemented or modified but did not obliterate faith. For those whose religion was the new science, determinism or naturalism or evolution had taken the place of Providence. Yet both camps were prepared to believe that the human race was destined to progress—to move ever onward and upward toward worthier institutions and a finer humanity. The skeptics who doubted both Salvation and Progress were few. Marx's classless society, Nietzsche's superman, Leo XIII's idea of a Christian state, American philosophical pragmatism, were, each in its own way, expressions of the general optimism. Henri Bergson's *Creative Evolution* was to formulate that feeling most clearly in the course of the decade now to be examined.

Confidence was based on more than the politician's, philosopher's, or priest's pious hopes. Despite the misery and the backwardness, the poverty and the colonialism, the abuses of power and the arrogance of office that prevailed in much of Europe and of Europe's overseas empires, never had so many enjoyed so much. Commodities were more abundant, carried by every steamboat and train to and from all corners of the earth, processed by bigger machines in bigger factories, and sold by methods more strange than any pre-twentieth-century Sinbad or Münchhausen could have imagined—by words that traveled almost instantaneously thousands of miles through space and by men who were learning to ride horseless carriages and to fly in machine-propelled kites. Populations were increasing steadily, not only because the food supply was growing but also because the world's scientists had learned enough about the health and diseases of man to increase his life expectancy. Life was not always an unmixed blessing and wealth was not always an unmixed good, but general prosperity led many to believe that they might so become.

Even the abuses of power seemed less incorrigible than at many times in the past—at least in domestic politics. The programs of social security for workmen, the increasing strength of trade unions, the extension of the franchise to the unpropertied had made the state less the servant of the aristocrat and the propertied and more the agent of the common man, and few voices as yet were raised in warning of the tyranny of the majority. Moreover, constitutional limitations upon the power of governments had come or were to come to even the most unlikely places in Europe—to Russia and to Turkey. If the existing constitutions did not always establish in fact the rights and the separation of powers that they mentioned in theory, nevertheless hope persisted that constitutionalism was still a youthful and flourishing precept with a bright future.

In one sense, this prewar Europe, where progress seemed constant, prosperity sure, and freedom possible, was also a peaceful Europe. At least, since 1871 it had done its fighting abroad—in America, in Africa, in Asia—or, as was to be true in this decade, on the periphery of Europe—the Mediterranean Sea and the Balkans. Yet peace had always seemed to be in jeopardy, so much so that often statesmanship appeared to be better marked by planning how to preserve peace or to prepare for war than by planning how to spread the blessings of prosperity. Some dared to hope for an enduring world peace. They could point to the fact that the rulers of England, Germany, and Russia were by blood or marriage related to Queen Victoria and thus to each other. They could point to The Hague Tribunal.

But the prophets of peace were to prove false prophets. Queen Victoria was hardly in her grave when the things that her name had come to symbolize began conspicuously to vanish. Despite the miserable lot and submerged conditions of much of humanity even in the most advanced areas of the world, despite corruption and hypocrisy in high places, the word *Victorian* has often been used to designate serenity, gentility, and complacence, a high level of middle-class culture, and a puritan standard of public and private behavior no less than an express assurance of peace, prosperity, and continuous progress. For a few years under Edward VII the prevailing spirit of Europe continued to carry all the connotations of the word *Victorian*. But by the time that George V ascended the throne of Great Britain and became ruler of the British Empire, the dominant note had changed to a shrill cry of dispute and anxiety. A few years more and that cry would become part of the fury and anguish of a world war.

530

CONFLICTS OF DEMOCRACY
AND NATIONALISM IN EUROPE

BEFORE 1914 most of the countries of the world were still monarchies. The notable exceptions were to be found largely in the Western Hemisphere rather than Europe. Yet France after the Dreyfus affair seemed more steadily republican than ever, and the Swiss Confederation remained loyal to a republican tradition that went much farther back than the American. In Asia, China joined the republican fold in 1911. Nevertheless, outside of the Americas, monarchy was generally taken for granted; and even in Europe, except for the more advanced western states, ruling castes were prone to speculate how best to limit the participation of the governed in their government.

The first Russian Duma and the Manifesto of Viborg

IN RUSSIA that issue was settled temporarily in a relatively undemocratic fashion. With the imperial armies returning from the Manchurian front, and with the Black Hundreds (page 466) repressing malcontents throughout his realm, Czar Nicholas once more was complete master in his home. As soon as Witte was no longer needed, the czar dismissed him, since Witte personified the program of concession, and replaced him with a routine bureaucrat. The election of the Duma had meanwhile taken place. On the eve of its initial meeting the czar's government undertook to supplement the October Manifesto with an exposition of the "Fundamental Laws" of the empire. These Fundamental Laws reconfirmed the autocratic powers of the czar in the executive branch of the government and, while granting the Duma a certain share of legislative authority, restricted it greatly.

Hence the Duma never fulfilled its promise. When it met for the first time in May 1906, it was dominated by a liberal party known as the Constitutional Democrats, or, from the party's initials, as the Cadets. The Cadets immediately demanded a more democratic constitutional program than the Fundamental Laws, and the czar replied by dissolving the Duma. Some of the Constitutional Democrats, insisting that the Duma could not be dismissed, adjourned to Viborg in Finland and there issued a manifesto calling upon the people of Russia not to pay taxes that were not constitutionally levied by the Duma. But the tired people of Russia paid them no heed. The second Duma met in 1907 and soon underwent the same fate as the first.

Stolypin and the new kulak class

THE CZAR'S prime minister, Piotr Arkadevich Stolypin, then proposed to combine reform with repression. By a new electoral law the peasants and workers lost and the propertied classes gained representation in the Duma. The third Duma met with official approval and was suffered to live out its term of five years. Nevertheless, it enacted a series of reforms, including a great rural reorganization. This act had been earlier decreed by Stolypin, and the third Duma gave it formal approval. It provided that either the entire communal property of the village (or *mir*) might, by majority vote of the peasants, be divided into lots among the individual peasants or any individual peasant might take out his own share. On the whole, the richer peasants preferred to take out their shares and the poorer ones preferred to sell out and migrate. Stolypin hoped eventually to build a class of independent landowners who should be conservative and loyal to the czar. Stolypin was assassinated in 1911 by a Jewish lawyer, but whether the assassin was an agent of the reactionary secret police or of the revolutionaries remains uncertain. That Stolypin's agrarian policy would ultimately have destroyed the *mir* and created a small-farmer agriculture is impossible to say. The fourth Duma kept up his program of building a loyal kulak class, or landowning peasantry, at the expense of the poorer peasants, or *muzhiks*. But the czar and his wife came under the influence of a religious charlatan named Grigori Rasputin, and war and revolution soon swept away the Stolypin reform.

The check in Germany
of representative government

WHILE reaction was the order of the day in Russia, developments of a democratic character made small headway in Germany. Without the cooperation of the Center (Catholic) Party, no working majority had been possible in the Reichstag since the end of the Kulturkampf. In 1906 the Center refused to vote credits for the crushing of a native Negro revolt in the German colony of Southwest Africa. Chancellor von Bülow thereupon had William II dissolve the Reichstag. The subsequent elections gave Bülow the opportunity of forming a majority bloc composed of the two conservative parties (Conservatives and National Liberals) and the liberals (the Progressives), while the Center, the Social Democrats, and the Poles formed the opposition.

Bülow's new majority was precarious from the beginning. The Conservatives, dominated by the Lutheran Junkers, and the National Liberals, dominated by freethinking industrialists, felt uneasy in alliance with each other and with their former opponents, the Progressives. Besides, Bülow was never quite sure what the volatile Kaiser would do next. Perhaps worst of all, the chancellor had no fixed political policy of his own, being an amiable cynic in personal life and an opportunist in politics. His major objective was to retain the good will of his erratic imperial master. Bülow realized that the undemocratic Prussian electoral law gave the Junkers a dangerous hold over all of Germany. By the three-class system of voting, the Junkers, together with their propertied allies, controlled the lower house of the Prussian Diet; they also dominated the upper house by hereditary right. Their power in the Prussian Diet gave them a powerful voice in the Prussian government. The

Prussian government, in turn, virtually controlled the Bundesrat, the imperial council of the representatives of the German states; and without concurrent majorities in both the Bundesrat and the Reichstag, no federal law could be enacted. In this way the Junkers retained a disproportionate influence in German legislation in addition to dominating the army and the civil service, at a time when membership in the German Social Democratic Party was increasing and its representation in the Reichstag was growing.

Out of apprehension of Junker influence Bülow was more sympathetic with the Progressives in his bloc than with the Conservatives. But he dared not split from the Conservatives. He had been able to retain office despite a series of international complications (pages 524, 562, and 564) only with their support, and, as time went on, his position became increasingly delicate. In 1908 William II made his chancellor's political life still more difficult by an indiscreet interview with a representative of the London *Daily Telegraph,* in which, in order to play up his own Anglophile sympathies, the Kaiser declared that the German people as a whole did not like the English. The Reichstag was furious. Shortly afterwards when Bülow's advocacy of a democratization of the Prussian electoral law became known, the Junkers united to forestall him. He then proposed in the tax bill of 1909 to include an inheritance tax, which, by reducing their estates, might have had the same effect in the course of time. Thereupon the Conservatives were able to bring about his downfall by deserting the "Bülow bloc." In this way, the democratizing of Germany was frustrated, and the power of the landowning aristoc-

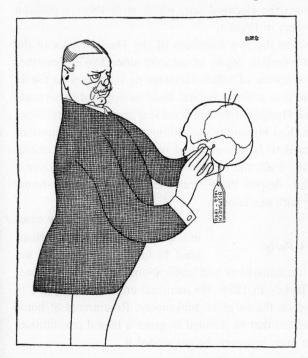

Chancellor von Bülow contemplates the skull of Bismarck. A caricature by the Danish black-and-white artist Olaf Gulbransson.

racy remained unbroken. Even though the parties of the Left won a great victory in the Reichstag elections of 1912, the Junkers retained their great influence over the Bundesrat.

In several parliamentary crises after 1912, the Reichstag tried to establish the principle of ministerial responsibility (i.e., that the minister must resign if he cannot control a majority). Bülow's resignation had looked like a victory for that principle; and in 1913 the Leftist majority even went so far as twice to pass unprecedented votes of "no confidence" in the government. But Bülow's successor, Dr. Theobald von Bethmann-Hollweg, on taking office in 1909, had expressed his attitude plainly: "Put me in a minority if it pleases you. I shall remain at my post just the same, as long as I retain the confidence of my sovereign." Before 1914 ministerial responsibility did not seem close to attainment in Germany.

Monarchical power in Austria and Hungary

IN THE Dual Monarchy, political confusion tended to increase the reliance on monarchical authority. Austria took an apparent step toward democracy in 1907 when it introduced an electoral system based upon universal suffrage and the secret ballot. But there democratic progress ended. Because of the struggle of the many nationalities a workable majority in an obstreperous parliament was often impossible to obtain; and the government, as we have seen (page 472), would prorogue parliament and enact laws by imperial decree. In Hungary the situation was similar to that in Prussia. The Magnates succeeded in blocking any attempts to change the electoral law, which gave them a position similar to that of the Junkers in Prussia.

In the relations between the two members of the Dual Monarchy the *Ausgleich* had preserved a certain degree of amenity since 1867. Nevertheless, the tariff issue, the question of which language or languages to use in the army, and the dispute over a single federal bank as opposed to separate banks for Austria and for Hungary frequently created crises in the relations of the two partners in the Dual Monarchy. In addition, the national minorities in both countries continued to be discontented with the dual arrangement, which excluded them. All in all, the Emperor Francis Joseph ruled over a congeries of peoples who, despite their economic interdependence, found difficulty in getting along with one another.

The founding of the Young Turk Party

A NOTABLE popular victory came in a quarter where it was perhaps least to have been expected before 1914. A series of assassinations and abdications had made Abdu-l-Hamid II the sultan of Turkey in 1876. He acquired an empire engaged in civil war (page 362) and on the verge of bankruptcy. Resentment at home and abroad seemed so heated that he decided to grant a liberal constitution. The moment danger was over, however, he suspended it.

Abdu-l-Hamid was the embodiment of what is often meant by the term "oriental despot." To stay in power by any means, fair or foul, was his guiding principle, and he surrounded himself with sycophants and spies. He tolerated only mediocre ministers because he believed that any other kind might be dangerous. Meanwhile, as already indicated, the Turkish empire was crumbling at the edges. In the Balkans, Tunis, Egypt, Crete and elsewhere, Ottoman suzerainty was displaced. Abdu-l-Hamid instigated the Armenian Massacres, at least in part to divert the attention of the Turks from his own misrule and to make the Christians of Armenia the scapegoats of his shortcomings. Thus Abdu-l-Hamid became *par excellence* "the unspeakable Turk" (another of Gladstone's phrases), averting Christian vengeance by playing one European power against another.

By the beginning of the century, the Turks had become thoroughly dissatisfied with their sultan. Secret revolutionary societies had been organized in Turkey and in Paris, of which the most effective was the Committee of Union and Progress, with several Turkish officers stationed at Salonika as its leaders. These societies called themselves the "Young Turks." Their members belonged to a new generation, many of whom had studied in foreign countries. From what they had learned abroad they had come to believe that unless Turkey became westernized, their country was doomed.

The revolution of the Young Turks in 1908

IN 1908 the Christian population of Turkish Macedonia again rose in revolt against the Turks, and the Turkish army took the field to suppress it. While the fighting was going on, the Young Turk officers sent an ultimatum to the sultan informing him that unless he reinstated the Constitution of 1876, they would no longer obey him. The sultan gave in, and a burst of joy swept the Ottoman Empire. It was quickly dampened, however, when the Bulgarians and the Austrians decided that Turkey's preoccupation with her revolution provided a fitting opportunity to promote their own territorial advantage at Turkey's expense (page 564). Meanwhile the danger of an army revolt had passed, and Abdu-l-Hamid attempted a counterrevolution. But the Young Turks proved strong enough to depose him (1909), to intern him at Salonika, and to place one of his brothers upon the Turkish throne as Mohammed v. They so modified the constitution as to take power from the sultan and give it to parliament.

The Young Turks failed to understand, however, that the mere introduction of democratic trimmings like parliamentary responsibility would not in itself create the spirit upon which such institutions must depend. The longer they stayed in power the more they had to contend with the inadequate preparation of the Turkish people for democracy. Furthermore they soon felt called upon to suppress the nationalism of minorities like the Armenians and Arabs, who would not willingly accept the idea of union under Young Turk   535 hegemony. To gain more prestige in international affairs, the Young Turks put their military reorganization under German officers and their naval reorganization under English officers. This nationalist-military policy only helped to hasten a series of international crises that proved disastrous for Turkey (pages 564-568).

Liberal reforms
in Great Britain and Ireland

IN ENGLAND significant constitutional changes took place, as had become the national habit, without domestic violence. These changes came about largely as a result of a Liberal victory at the polls in 1906. The greatest progress in a democratic direction was made by curbing the legislative power of the aristocracy. A Parliament Act of 1911 provided: (1) that if a money bill passed the House of Commons, it became law one month after being sent to the House of Lords, regardless of whether the Lords voted it or not; and (2) that if the Commons passed any other kind of law and the Lords rejected it, it became the law of the land nonetheless, provided that the Commons adopted it in three successive sessions and that the last vote was separated from the first by at least two years. These provisions had the effect of destroying the ancient veto power of the House of Lords over legislation passed by the House of Commons. The most the Lords thereafter could do was to delay general legislation for two or more years, but they could not delay money bills for more than a month. In addition, the Parliament Act of 1911 reduced the life of any single Parliament from a possible seven years' duration to no more than five years.

Another significant set of reforms of the Liberals was the adoption of a program of social legislation. A workmen's compensation act had already been passed (1897) through Chamberlain's efforts, and it was now extended. Between 1906 and 1912, the Liberals passed laws providing old age pensions, sickness insurance, unemployment insurance, and minimum wages in certain industries. In general, the English had every reason to be proud of their ability (at least outside of Ireland) to achieve domestic liberty by orderly processes. Nevertheless, in Britain as almost everywhere else in Europe, women did not yet participate in the election of legislators. Only Finland (in 1906), Norway (in 1913), and Denmark (in 1915) allowed women the right of suffrage before the end of the First World War.

Ulster
and the Irish question

BY THE turn of the century, Irish nationalism had become a popular cult in all of south Ireland. It expressed itself through a genuine revival of Irish literature, though ironically the great figures of Irish literature wrote in English. Poets like Yeats and A. E. (pseudonym of George W. Russell) won admiration all over the world. The Abbey Theatre in Dublin became famous not merely for the plays of Irish life by Yeats, John M. Synge, and Lady Gregory but also

An episode of the campaign for women's suffrage in England. A suffragette invades the sacred precincts of the House of Commons. She gets in a last word before being led away.

for the excellence of its players. Yet as national sentiment grew in south Ireland, opposition to home rule for Ireland grew apace in Ulster. Private armies—the Ulster Volunteers and the Irish Volunteers—threatened to jump at each other's throats.

Hence, the British Parliament balked on Irish home rule. Twice in 1913 a home rule bill was passed by the Commons but defeated by the Lords. The Parliament Act of 1911, as will be recalled, had taken from the House of Lords the power of vetoing a bill if three successive Houses of Commons had passed it in the course of not less than two years. Unwilling to assure the passage of the bill by this untried course, in May 1914 the Liberal government of Prime Minister Herbert Asquith introduced in the House of Lords a new home rule bill which differed from the original one by permitting each county of Ulster, if it so voted, to have a six-year leeway in joining an independent Ireland. The Lords had the right to modify the new bill—and modify they did, proposing instead to exclude all of Ulster permanently from home rule. The Commons were still considering the two home rule bills when world war burst upon them.

Ulster in the spring and summer of 1914 had armed itself to the teeth against Irish home rule. Under the leadership of Sir Edward Carson, 85,000 Ulster Volunteers declared they would resort to civil war rather than tolerate the application of home rule to Ulster. German observers meanwhile had been induced to conclude that Great Britain, threatened with civil war, would have to avoid involvement, should war break out on the Continent. That appraisal proved false, however. The British government did enter the war, but, as a consequence, the Home Rule Bill of 1914 was doomed to remain a dead   537 letter. The original bill was passed for the third time in September, but accompanied by a suspending act providing that it was not to be put into force until a year after the end of the war.

*Self-government
among the British dominions*

IN DEALING with her larger overseas colonies, Great Britain had continued success. As quickly as seemed feasible, the British redeemed the promises made to the Boers by the terms of the Peace of Vereeniging of 1902. The Transvaal in 1906 and the Orange River Colony in 1907 were given self-government. In 1910 the Union of South Africa came into being by the federation of Cape Colony, the Transvaal, Natal, and the Orange Free State. It was an unusually strong federation, the separate provinces of the Union retaining less self-government than is generally true in federal governments. Both English and Dutch were recognized as official languages. The racial problem remains, however, and has caused frequent complications, since discrimination against black natives and brown and yellow immigrant laborers has been incorporated into the laws as well as into the social customs of the white population.

The idea of British imperial loyalty moved steadily forward in the period before the First World War. A fifth conference of the self-governing colonies was held in London in 1907 and it hastened the day that was fast approaching, though not yet fully arrived, of frank recognition of the sovereign equality of the self-governing colonies with the mother country. The phrase "Colonial Conference" was replaced by the phrase "Imperial Conference," and the phrase "self-governing colonies" by "self-governing dominions." At the next Imperial Conference (1911), the list of self-governing dominions included Australia, Canada, Newfoundland, New Zealand, and the Union of South Africa.

*British labor unions
and the British Labour Party*

ONE OF THE prewar Liberal measures, intended to diminish the inequality of the workers in their bargaining with employers, was the Trade Disputes Bill of 1906. Among other things, that bill freed trade unions from the obligation to pay for damages caused by otherwise legal action during strikes or other trade disputes. It thus liberated the unions from the threat of civil suits as a result of strikes alone. They now used their funds more often for political purposes. Those who raised doubts regarding the legality of such expenditures were silenced by the Trade Union Act of 1913, which gave unions the right to use their funds freely upon a majority vote of their members.

These measures were ultimately to weaken the Liberal Party, for the trade unions threw their support to a new workers' party. The Independent Labour Party had been organized in 1893, but its representation in Parliament had been numerically negligible. Then the Trades Union Congress in

538

1899 turned its attention to that end, and in 1900 it created a Labour Representation Committee, which was made up of representatives from both the Independent Labour Party and the Trades Union Congress, and which that year elected two of its candidates to Parliament. In the election of 1906 the committee took the official title of the Labour Party and succeeded in electing twenty-nine members of Parliament. In 1910 it returned forty-two. In 1911, when a law providing pay for members of the House of Commons was passed, the Labour Party looked upon that law as a victory, since poor men could now afford to serve.

Georges Sorel's philosophy of revolution   SOME continental intellectuals, contemplating the programs of labor legislation inaugurated in several western states, began to fear that the workers, having made great strides since the days when Bismarck had first made the capitalist state an ally of the workingman, might themselves become stodgy and bourgeois-minded. Most outstanding among them was Georges Sorel, who in several treatises, particularly in *Reflections on Violence* (1908), took a bold step beyond Marxism. First of all, Sorel was a moralist rather than a socialist. He saw in the proletariat, history's instrument for bringing on a more moral society than the bourgeoisie had been able to accomplish. Secondly, Sorel, though an engineer by training, considered reason (science) merely a negative force; on the other hand, the imagination (myth) acted, he contended, in a positive way by kindling the will to constructive behavior. He denied that economic processes determine historical developments, as Marx had maintained. Hence Marx's conclusion that the end of capitalism would inevitably be brought about by a series of class struggles and a final revolution of the workers seemed to Sorel to be a faulty "myth." He advocated instead the "myth" of the general strike, which would enable the workers to do away with a morally corrupt and economically inadequate bourgeois parliamentary society and at the same time increase production, which, in his opinion, is the all-important goal of economic life.

Sorel's philosophy had relatively little influence upon practical affairs. On several occasions, but not because of his urging, the French syndicates called strikes affecting whole industries. But the great railroad strike of 1910 was a dismal failure, principally because Aristide Briand as prime minister, though a Socialist and once an advocate of the general strike, drafted the railroad men who were army reservists to keep the railroads running. After that, the syndicates were more cautious about resorting to direct action, and Sorel associated himself with royalists and nationalists. Sorel is perhaps most important as a representative, like Nietzsche, of an element in prewar society that had ceased to believe in either the way of God or the processes of history and yet hoped for a moral regeneration.

IN PREWAR France the major domestic issue of the Republican-dominated state was the bitter opposition of the clericals and the church. The papacy adamantly refused to accept the Act of Separation of 1905 (page 470). It contended, first of all, that the Concordat was an international agreement which the government of Paris could not unilaterally abrogate. Furthermore, the associations of worship, as voluntary organizations of laymen, were, in its view, a violation of the hierarchical principle upon which the church was organized; the priest could not be chosen and controlled by his parish. Professing Catholics refused to form the voluntary associations envisaged by the act, and when municipal authorities tried to take over their churches, civil disorder resulted. Sometimes blood was shed.

Heated conflict raged until 1907. Then Briand as minister of public instruction proposed a compromise whereby Catholics were permitted to use ecclesiastical properties without forming associations of worship. Nevertheless, when the First World War broke out, separation was still a bitter issue. The congregations, legally doomed to disappear in 1914, were being steadily driven from the schools, and no one could tell when Briand's policy of opportunism regarding the use by Catholics of the churches would change again to one of strict application of the original law of separation.

Religious controversy threatened to destroy the unity of the French people on the eve of war. It was carefully nurtured by royalists and nationalists on ideological rather than theological grounds. Foremost among the nationalist groups was the society known as the Action Française (French Action). Founded as a "committee" during the Dreyfus affair with money provided by the widow of Marshal MacMahon, it was the elongated shadow of Charles Maurras, an intense nationalist who had come to the conclusion that France could be an integrated state only under a hereditary monarchy. Though himself an avowed atheist, Maurras believed that a unitary French nation had to be Catholic. Reorganized as a league in 1905, the Action Française put out a newspaper called *L'Action Française,* founded in 1899, which in 1907 became a daily and for which Maurras, Barrès, Léon Daudet, and other nationalists wrote regularly and vigorously. Maurras himself distinguished between French Catholicism and what he called "Hebrew Christianity," which he considered foreign to France. He gathered around him a gang of tough young men who styled themselves the *Camelots du Roi* (King's Hawkers), forerunners of the paramilitary nationalist organizations of the future.

IN CONTRAST with Maurras' nationalist philosophy an outright humanitarian doctrine came to the foreground with Henri Bergson, who was born in England of Polish-Jewish parentage and naturalized and educated as a Frenchman. Bergson, faced with the query: "What is God (or Reality)?" answered, in his *Creative Evolution* (1907): "He is unceasing life, action, freedom." This answer was a repudiation not only of the materialists, who would answer that the ultimate reality was matter, but also of the idealists, who would answer that the ultimate reality is idea or consciousness. Bergson's answer was somewhere between the two: reality is the life force pervading the universe in time and space (or what he preferred to call "duration") with its generations of all kinds of living things and its droplets of individuals. "As the smallest grain of dust is bound up with our entire solar system, drawn along with it in that undivided movement of descent which is materiality itself, so all organized beings, from the humblest to the highest, from the first origins of life to the time in which we are, and in all places as in all times, do but evidence a single impulse...All the living hold together, and all yield to the same tremendous push." This push (what he called the *élan vital*) almost took the place that cause-and-effect had held in materialistic thought. To Bergson plant, animal, and the whole of humanity become "one immense army galloping beside and before and behind each of us in an overwhelming charge able to beat down every resistance and clear the most formidable obstacles, perhaps even death." Man is able to grasp this process of "creative evolution" by "intuition," or conscious instinct. Bergson thus seemed to repudiate the Darwinian theory of evolution by natural selection without man's cooperation and to substitute for it a nonrational or perhaps superrational participation by all mankind in the life process.

Old and new figures in the arts and sciences

MANY OF the great literary, artistic, musical, and scientific figures we have already considered were still active during the decade before the First World War—Chekhov, D'Annunzio, France, Hauptmann, Shaw, Maillol, Thomson, Debussy, Freud, and Einstein (to mention only a few). The young Russian naturalist, Maxim Gorki having already won a reputation with his gruesome play *The Lower Depths* (1902), was to enhance his reputation in this decade with his novels, which stirred the conscience of the world over its neglect and ignorance of the poor and wretched. The novelist-dramatist John Galsworthy began in 1906 the two series of novels entitled *The Forsyte Saga* that, completed only in 1935, gave an illuminating picture of a middle-class English family through several generations. The Austrian dramatist and poet Hugo von Hofmannsthal reached his greatest success during this period, with several plays put to music by Richard Strauss and staged by Max Reinhardt.

In science the Germans made some especially notable contributions. Fritz Haber in 1913 perfected the process for synthesizing ammonia from nitrogen and hydrogen, thus obtaining nitrogen from the air and enabling the German explosives industry to survive during the First World War despite blockade. The physician Paul Ehrlich in 1910 gave great impetus to the study of chemical therapy when he discovered the arsenic compound arsphenamine or salvarsan, which has helped to reduce the ravages of syphilis. Because it was the result of his 606th experiment it was also called "606."

In painting, the radical development known as "expressionism" now became prominent. The expressionists sought to paint what they saw subjectively in an object rather than the object itself. They became more and more interested in pattern and geometric construction, sometimes abstracting and distorting physical appearances to achieve a more striking effect. Henri Matisse, who relied on simplicity of color and rhythmic draftsmanship, was outstanding among these *fauves* (untamed), as their critics called them. Matisse himself derided Pablo Picasso and his school for their "cubist" form of expression (Chapter 13).

In music a similar revolt against classicism brought several new names into prominence or gave new prominence to familiar ones. The Austrian Gustav Mahler and the Finn Jean Sibelius in their later works avoided the academic development of themes. The Hungarian Béla Bartók and the Russian Igor Stravinsky, whose early works aroused scandal wherever they were performed, rebelled against the conventional rules of tonality. The Austrian Arnold Schönberg disregarded the rules entirely. Thus in music as in painting shortly before the First World War a group arose who refused to be bound by what the more conservative called objectivity but which appeared to them to be academicism, and insisted upon experimenting with the abstract. This revolt against classicism and academicism in the arts mirrored the widespread dissatisfaction with traditional norms all over the prewar world.

THE AMERICAS

BEFORE THE FIRST WORLD WAR

IN SPITE of doubts, dislocations, and innumerable problems the United States still seemed on the eve of the First World War to be a land of promise. Inventions continued to pour forth, the most conspicuous bringing improvements in the automobile and the airplane. Europe, accustomed to look at America as an unsaturated field of opportunity, now found other things there too. As a formidable industrial competitor, a world power, and a purveyor of machine culture and mammon-worship, the United States was regarded somewhat warily by Europeans. In Latin America it was feared as a possible conqueror and an actual exploiter.

Henry Adams and American pessimism SOME AMERICANS were themselves wary. One of the most gloomy of them was the historian Henry Adams. Upon visiting the World's Columbian Exposition at Chicago in 1893, where he had admired the work of Hunt, La Farge, Saint-Gaudens, and other American artists in the classical and medieval tradition (and gave no attention to Louis Sullivan's Transportation Building, which stood out in bold defiance of the classical tradition), Adams had seen the exhibition of the latest mechanical and electrical devices and had mused about them. He continued his musings at the Paris Exhibition of 1900 and the St. Louis Exposition of 1904. He wondered how a civilization that could be symbolized by the electric dynamo could feel the united power and the serene faith that had once long ago been the western world's when its symbol was the Virgin: "Chicago asked in 1893 for the first time the question whether the American people knew where they were driving." Adams admitted that he for one did not know. That did not keep him, however, from privately printing in 1904 a book entitled *Mont-Saint-Michel and Chartres* (published 1913), in which he propounded his idea that the Virgin had been a symbol of medieval unity, and following it with a private printing in 1907 of *The Education of Henry Adams* (published 1918), in which he portrayed himself as a victim of modern confusion.

European distrust of American "barbarism"

EUROPEAN intellectuals were perhaps more inclined to agree with Adams than was the average American. The conviction in Europe of American "barbarism" was still rife. It was exemplified in the writings of the Italian historian, Guglielmo Ferrero. After a visit to the United States just before the First World War, Ferrero wrote two books (*Between the Old World and the New* and *Ancient Rome and Modern America*) intended to show that America was intellectually inferior to Europe and was tending to replace "Quality" with "Quantity." The 1909 edition of the famous German guidebook on America known as "The Baedeker" had to assure its readers that throughout the United States travel was "as safe as in the most civilized parts of Europe and the carrying of arms unnecessary."

American philosophy, literature, and architecture

DESPITE Adams' and Ferrero's warnings, the popular trends in the arts that were already familiar in the United States continued during the decade that preceded the First World War. In philosophy the pragmatists were still led by William James, though John Dewey was rapidly coming to the fore as their spokesman, as we shall see. The muckrakers still were prominent in literature. Upton Sinclair's *The Jungle* (1906) was a searing indictment of the unscrupulous quest for profit in the meat-packing industry by the exploitation of the immigrant laborer and the consumer. Theodore Dreiser joined forces with the latter-day muckrakers with *The Financier* (1912) and *The Titan* (1914). The leading character in both novels was the same, and the resemblance between him and the Philadelphia and Chicago street-railway magnate, Charles T. Yerkes, who also helped build the London Underground, was not entirely coincidental. It was typical of the American "tycoon" of the day that Yerkes was also the founder of the Yerkes Observatory (1892) of the University of Chicago (itself founded by John D. Rockefeller in 1891).

In architecture "functionalism" (the wedding of form to utility) was gaining ground. New skyscrapers made their appearance all over the country, the most notable being perhaps the Woolworth Building in New York (1912). Frank Lloyd Wright, a pupil of Louis Sullivan, was rapidly becoming one of the foremost of American architects. He began to find followers in Holland and Scandinavia of his "organic view" of architecture (i.e., of buildings designed to blend with the surrounding landscape and made of local materials) and he introduced western building design and engineering into the earthquake-ridden islands of Japan. His Imperial Hotel (Tokyo) was completed in 1916. In Japan he found native examples of the organic view of architecture.

Imperialism in the Western Hemisphere

IN THE Western Hemisphere a twofold international development took place before 1914. On the one hand, Pan-Americanism—that is, the spirit of cooperation among the American nations—was growing. A third Pan-American Conference took place at Rio de Janeiro in 1906, and a fourth at Buenos Aires in 1910. At the same time, business interests in the United States, generally with the backing of their government, increased their commercial exploitation of Latin America. This exploitation brought on suspicions and tensions such as existed in the Eastern Hemisphere, and for somewhat similar reasons. In many parts of Latin America, the creole ruling society was only a thin layer superimposed upon a dense but silent stratum of Indians. The question was how long the Indians would remain silent. Rival generals and dictators engaged in intrigue and civil war, often involving the great powers in their conflicts. There was, however, a striking difference between Western and Eastern Hemisphere imperialism: with the exception of the Panama Canal Zone, the smaller states of Latin America did not have to give away their political sovereignty, as did so many of the states of Africa and Asia.

Nevertheless, Latin America was economically dependent on European and United States capital, at least in part because of its turbulent political life. As we have seen, coups d'état, civil wars, and dictatorships formed a familiar cycle in nearly every Latin-American country, depleting treasuries and hindering social advance. Hence capital for expansion, and often for the expenses of government itself, had to be sought abroad. Before the First World War this capital came chiefly from England. By 1914 the British had about $10,000,000,000 invested outside of the British Empire; the French and the Germans were not far behind in investments abroad. Much of this money went into stocks and bonds of United States corporations and municipalities, but a good deal of it found its way into Latin America. United States bankers were also investing greater and greater sums in Latin-American enterprises. Like the United States and Canada, the Latin-American countries encouraged immigration from Europe and thereby procured the labor necessary to man their economic development, but for technical skill they remained dependent largely on European and North-American engineers. Railroads were built, mineral resources exploited, and ranches and plantations developed with foreign capital and skill. Seldom did the natives rise above peonage. To be sure, an occasional victory for democracy was registered in the statute books, as when Argentina introduced the secret ballot and universal suffrage (1912). But where a third of the potential voters were illiterate, such a law had little practical meaning.

The application of the Roosevelt Corollary

AMONG THE reasons for the growth of United States investments in Latin America was the readiness of President Theodore Roosevelt to protect American interests abroad. As has already been indicated, Roosevelt announced by means of his so-called "Corollary" to the Monroe Doctrine that it was the obligation of the United States to preserve order in the Western Hemisphere, and for that reason he had intervened in the domestic affairs of the Dominican Republic (page 502). In still another United States protectorate in the Caribbean, Roosevelt also felt obliged to apply the "Corollary" and exercise police power. In 1906 disorders in Cuba became serious enough to lead the president to send United States troops there to restore order, as he was permitted to do under the Platt Amendment. Somewhat to the surprise of the rest of the world, they were withdrawn three years later when the American government considered their mission accomplished. After a few years of the Big Stick, the actuality of the Monroe Doctrine was established beyond all doubt in the eyes of the world. But Roosevelt's vigorous diplomacy did not confine itself to making America strong at home. In pursuance of American prestige and the establishment of an international balance of power, he took the United States to the forefront of world politics by assuming a prominent part in controversies far from home (pages 524 and 562).

Theodore Roosevelt and government regulation

WE HAVE previously mentioned Roosevelt's trust-busting activity (page 481). Under the Roosevelt aegis government regulation was extended in other ways. A meat inspection law was passed in 1906 (the year Sinclair's *The Jungle* was published), and in the same year Congress passed the first Pure Food and Drugs Act, intended to prevent at least the more easily detected frauds in patent medicines. At the end of the Roosevelt era the federal government had greatly broadened its control over business enterprise. In 1910 (when Taft was president) government regulation of rates was extended to telephone and telegraph lines.

Roosevelt applied his energies also to the reduction of the waste of the country's natural resources. Americans were still carrying on mining, lumbering, fishing, and even farming as if they thought that these resources were inexhaustible. Roosevelt thought otherwise, and laid out a systematic conservation campaign. He appointed a National Conservation Commission (1908). He withdrew millions of acres of timber land from public sale, stopped the looting of public lands by railroads, ranchers, and timber companies, inaugurated a federal reclamation and irrigation project, made the American public conscious of the need for conservation, and secured the cooperation of the state governors and of other North-American countries in a continental approach to the conservation problem. The conservation policy provided the American people with national parks and forest preserves and increased their penchant for touring the country in their new automobiles. If it also closed the frontier more tightly by removing millions of undesirable acres of public domain from the possibility of legal settlement, nevertheless homesteading (page 496) went on at an accelerated rate, and particularly between 1913 and 1923.

A "Gentlemen's Agreement" regarding Japanese immigration SINCE THE 1880's immigration had become a hotly debated issue in the United States. Around 20,000,000 immigrants entered the country between 1880 and 1914. The number might have been greater had not certain European governments adopted measures to discourage emigration. The German government in 1913 totally forbade the emigration of young men who had not yet performed their required military service. The flood from southeast Europe made those Americans who had originated earlier elsewhere especially apprehensive. Indignant groups, the labor unions not the least among them, denounced unrestricted immigration as threatening labor standards and bringing in foreign agitators and radical ideas. But the only immigrants that were newly restricted during Roosevelt's administration were the Japanese, and that restriction was effected only by indirection. After the Russo-Japanese War, Japanese came by the thousands to America, settling mostly in California, where they encountered segregation and open hostility. Discrimination by Californians threatened to become an international incident when the Japanese homeland took offense. In order to avoid an open rupture Roosevelt pressed the Californians to be more politic and at the same time concluded with Japan a "Gentlemen's Agreement" whereby Japan voluntarily agreed to issue no more passports to coolies bound directly for the United States.

Recent tensions led Roosevelt to feel the necessity of impressing the Japanese and the rest of the world with the power and glory of the United States. So in 1907 he ordered the country's battle fleet, now second only to Britain's and Germany's, on a cruise around the world. It returned in 1909. It constituted an impressive demonstration of power and greatly enhanced American prestige both in the Orient and in Europe. It also caused the Japanese to wonder apprehensively whether they were secure in their eastern strongholds (page 559).

Domestic changes
under President Taft

WITH THE departure of Roosevelt from the White House the tumult and the shouting died down. His successor, the fat and jovial William Howard Taft, sought no imperial trophies, and the "Old Guard" dominated his Senate. Little occurred to change the conservative tenor of the American polity during Taft's administration, and yet that little was significant. Congress submitted to the states the Sixteenth and Seventeenth Amendments to the Constitution. The first legalized a federal income tax, making possible for future, less conservative legislatures to lay a large share of the cost of government upon those of highest income. The second provided for popular election of senators (who previously had been selected by state legislatures), thereby holding out the promise that future Senates might be less conservative. More important immediately was the new attitude of the Supreme Court on the Sherman Anti-Trust Act. In obliging the Standard Oil Company and the American Tobacco Company to reorganize, the court drew a distinction between "reasonable" and "unreasonable" restraint of trade, thus encouraging the Department of Justice to concentrate its efforts on the worst offenders.

Increasing
American investment abroad

UNLIKE Roosevelt, Taft did not thrust the United States into the councils of Europe. His interest lay rather in opening opportunities for American investment abroad and enhancing American influence in the areas of investment. The growing availability of American capital abroad was gradually changing the United States from a debtor to a creditor nation.

Taft's policy of enhancing American influence through investment became known as "dollar diplomacy." It was carried out principally in China and Latin America. In China the main purpose was to prevent Russia and Japan from establishing economic control over Manchuria and other strategic areas. The details of this story are recounted elsewhere (page 554). Its main effect was to irritate the European powers which were involved in China and to draw Russia and Japan together against the capital-exporting nations.

Dollar diplomacy in Latin America was motivated in considerable part by the desire to protect the Panama Canal. Taft's strategy was to force European capital out of the canal neighborhood and to replace it with American capital. This replacement, it was hoped, would eliminate the danger of European intervention to collect debts, would give United States investors a good profit, and would preserve peace in Latin America. Unfortunately it also produced a growing ill will on the part of Latin-American states.

Taft and his secretary of state Philander C. Knox succeeded in guiding considerable American capital into Nicaragua and the Republic of Haiti. The Nicaraguan venture brought on big-stick methods reminiscent of Roosevelt. A Nicaraguan revolution in 1909 produced the usual fear of European intervention to protect investments, a possibility that the United States could not good-humoredly countenance because the alternate canal route might thus fall into European hands. Diplomatic pressure, backed by a quite unsubtle warship, persuaded the Nicaraguan government to accept an American loan for refunding the debt owed to British investors. In 1911 an American was made customs collector in Nicaragua, and in subsequent years the United States Marines landed several times to protect American interests. While both Europe and Latin America frowned, Taft's dollar diplomacy not only kept Europe out of Latin America but let American influence in.

The Progressive Party and the election of Wilson

ROOSEVELT soon made it obvious that he intended to run for president again. The Old Guard preferred Taft, however, and so the more liberal Republicans in 1912 split off and formed their own Progressive Party (the "Bull Moose" party) under Roosevelt. In a program he labeled the "New Nationalism," Roosevelt advocated not only government regulation of big business but the establishment of equal opportunity for all by removing government from control by the "vested interests."

"The Latest Arrival at the Political Zoo," a cartoon on the 1912 presidential campaign in the United States. Theodore Roosevelt (the Bull Moose) joins the donkey and the elephant. The reference to the "Harvester Trust" had to do with charges that Roosevelt's candidacy, despite his campaign against the "vested interests," was supported by certain representatives of big business.

SUFFERING SNAKES! HOW THEODORE HAS CHANGE[D]

WATER FOR STOCK PURPOSES

Compliments of the HARVESTER TRUST

The situation resembled that created by the Populist Party in 1896. But in this instance the reform group did not unite with the Democrats as the Populists had then done. Instead the Democrats put forth a progressive candidate of their own, Woodrow Wilson, whose "New Freedom" rivaled Roosevelt's "New Nationalism." The ensuing election was a rare event in American history—a three-cornered fight in which the newly created party was a serious contender. The Democrats, profiting by the Republican split, placed their man in the White House, the only Democrat except for Cleveland to be elected president in over half a century. Perhaps the most significant feature of the election was that progressivism, represented by Roosevelt, Wilson, and Debs, the Socialist candidate, polled three fourths of the vote.

Domestic reform aimed at the "plutocracy"

THE NEW president, a staid scholar who had only recently entered politics, lost no time in translating progressivism into law. The Underwood Tariff (1913), designed to restore effective competition, lowered the average duties by 10 per cent, reversing the upward trend of half a century. A bank panic in 1907 had led again to a demand for easy money, which the Republicans had essentially ignored. The Federal Reserve Act of 1913 now established a new national banking and currency system designed to avoid control of money and banking by a few powerful New York financiers and to provide more elastic credit. It was to be supplemented in 1916 by a Federal Farm Loan Act providing easier credit and lower interest rates for farmers.

Monopolies were a special target of Democratic attack. A five-member Federal Trade Commission was established in 1914 and given special powers of investigation and regulation of corporations engaged in unfair competition and other malpractices. The Clayton Anti-Trust Act, also passed in 1914, outlawed particular practices of mammoth enterprises, such as price discrimination and interlocking directorates, and made corporation officers personally responsible for violations. Labor unions were specifically exempted from the provisions of the act, and the use of the injunction in labor disputes was outlawed except in extreme cases.

During the first years of the Wilson administration the paradox of an economic plutocracy in a political democracy received special attention. The reaction to industrialization that in Europe had brought comprehensive programs of social legislation on the one hand and an increase in government-run business enterprises on the other was beginning to take place in the United States, now among the greatest industrial nations of the world. The federal government still avoided programs of social security, but several states had assumed responsibility in one regard or another for the economic welfare of their citizens, and workmen's compensation laws, child labor laws, and minimum wage laws had found their way into the statutes of individual states.

*Dollar diplomacy
replaced by watchful waiting*

WILSON and his secretary of state William Jennings Bryan openly repudiated the dollar diplomacy of Taft and sought the friendship of Latin America. But in spite of a high idealism that was to be Wilson's—and America's—chief contribution to wartime world affairs, he found himself tricked by events into using the methods of his two predecessors. He brought to conclusion a treaty initiated by Taft leasing islands off the Nicaraguan coast and a naval base on the coast itself. He bought the Virgin Islands from Denmark to forestall their acquisition by a European power. He sent American marines first to Haiti and then to the Dominican Republic to restore order after chaotic revolutions. He was obliged to deal with a particularly delicate situation in Mexico.

Revolution and counterrevolution followed in quick succession when the Mexican dictator Porfirio Díaz was forced to resign and flee for his life (1911). A murderous agrarian insurrection then swept over Mexico, and the Mestizo "Pancho" Villa became a popular hero, although regarded as a bandit in the United States. The arrest of some American sailors forced President Wilson to intervene, despite his personal preference for a policy of "watchful waiting." A war between the United States and Mexico was avoided only by the mediation of Argentina, Brazil, and Chile (the so-called ABC powers of Latin America).

In all of this Wilson's guiding policy was protection of the Panama Canal. The canal was formally opened only in 1914. Building it had taken nearly ten years, not merely because of the difficulty of the terrain but also because of the constant war against yellow fever. The Cuban physician Carlos Juan Finlay and the American army surgeon Walter Reed had already proved that a certain kind of mosquito carried the yellow fever germ. The American sanitation expert, Major William C. Gorgas, having earlier controlled the fever in Havana, was able to apply this lesson also in the Canal Zone. The canal immediately became the strategic link in American naval planning. The gathering war clouds in Europe, and the war itself, made more imperative than ever that Europe be kept out of the neighborhood of the "American lifeline."

*The moral tone
of American foreign policy*

SIGNIFICANTLY enough, Wilson's frequent use of American forces in the Caribbean was less alarming to the Latin-American countries than the activities of his predecessors. Here, as elsewhere, his frequent expressions of idealism carried conviction. In a speech in 1913 he declared that "the United States will never again seek one additional foot of territory by conquest." And of his Mexican policy, whereby he refused recognition of a dictator whose rule he believed would mean peonage for the Mexican masses, he stated: "Morality and not expediency is the thing that must guide us....It is a very perilous thing to determine the foreign policy of a nation in the terms of material interest." Here

550

was a foretaste of that penchant for moral pronouncements that was to baffle old-fashioned diplomats at the conference table after the First World War.

Probably most Americans in 1914 admired Wilson's moral fervor. But they were to find that material interests could not be disregarded. The United States was no longer isolated. It had vested interests and sentimental claims all over the world. It was a world power and a "melting pot" of all the world's peoples. Ostensibly neutral in Europe's quarrels, America seethed with the conflicting sympathies of immigrants and descendants of immigrants whose homelands were pitted against one another in the most devastating conflict the world had yet experienced. Americans were soon to find that the day of the wilderness frontier and of the impassable ocean was over. American frontiers lay on the Atlantic and the Pacific and beyond.

THE FAR EAST

AND THE PACIFIC ON THE EVE OF WAR

THE VICTORY of Japan over Russia in 1905 had a great influence upon subsequent developments throughout eastern Asia. The victory of an oriental nation over one of the great occidental powers released in Asia forces of nationalism and antiforeignism which had long been seething beneath the surface. To oriental idealists, however, Japan's rise in Asia was a source of mixed feelings. Proud though they might feel that a Mongolian people had matched its strength against a Caucasian people and had come off victorious, the Japanese disregard of Korean national aspirations brought out clearly that a strong Asiatic neighbor might be as great a menace to the independence of smaller Asiatic countries as were the colonial powers of the West. Moreover, the colonial ambitions of the West showed no signs of abatement.

Southeastern Asia on the eve of the First World War

IN SOUTHEASTERN Asia the patterns laid out during the nineteenth century underwent but few changes. The French continued to pursue their civilizing mission in Indochina, and the British proceeded to consolidate their hold upon India, Malaya, and Burma. Only Siam, "the Land of the White Elephant," seemed to have some future as an independent state. Great Britain and France had agreed in 1896 to guarantee its sovereignty. But then had come the Entente Cordiale. In 1904 the two western countries defined their respective spheres more explicitly, and by 1909 Siam had to make some minor frontier concessions to Indochina and Malaya respectively. Siam's tin, rubber, and wood could be expected to keep on attracting the western industrial powers and endangering Siamese integrity. Still, on the eve of the First World War, Siam seemed assured of an independent future because it served as a buffer between British and French interests.

*The origin
of the Manchurian question*

WITH THE looming of Japan's imperial might, the pattern of colonial rivalry in northeast Asia underwent an obvious change. Manchuria became one of the hottest subjects of diplomatic conversations after 1905. Upon the signing of the Treaty of Portsmouth, China was called upon to give formal recognition to the arrangements concluded between Japan and Russia regarding Manchuria. This recognition she gave before the end of the year in the Komura Treaty: Manchuria once more was formally turned over to China to administer, and China acknowledged Japan's new lease on the Liaotung peninsula. But thereafter the Chinese were obliged to watch silently and impotently as the Nipponese, acting from their bases in Korea and Liaotung and moving along the Manchurian railway line, rapidly consolidated their hold upon southern Manchuria. To protect their movement into Manchuria, the Japanese were prepared to establish a friendly understanding with their recent foe Russia, as the only nearby power still in a position to challenge Japan's advance on the Asiatic mainland. This ironic twist coincided with the equally ironic negotiations that were to mesh Russia in a Triple Entente with France and England (page 563). Thus, as a result of her poor showing in the Russo-Japanese War, Russia, no longer regarded as so serious a menace as Germany, was associated with the Anglo-Japanese Alliance, which had originated out of fear of Russia.

Through a subsequent series of treaties, both secret and open, with Russia and France, Japan established herself as an associate of the Triple Entente. These treaties divided Manchuria, which was nominally under Chinese sovereignty, into Russian and Japanese spheres of influence. Furthermore, Russia freely recognized "the relations of political solidarity" between Japan and Korea; in return Japan recognized the "special interests" of Russia in Outer Mongolia. Meanwhile, the three powers tacitly agreed that the Chinese southern provinces bordering on Indochina should be looked upon as a French area of influence. Thus Japan tied her program of expansion into the framework of European alliances and counteralliances.

*Roosevelt's restraint
of American resentment of Japan*

THIS TREND of events, as might have been anticipated, roused the anxiety of the other powers interested in the Far East—China, Germany, and the United States. Despite reiterated lip service to the principle of the open door, Japan, France, and Russia, without interference from Great Britain, seemed determined to complete their dominance over the major continental areas of the Far East. The immigration problem provided a further irritating factor in American-Japanese relations. Proud of their new glory in world affairs, the Japanese were unmistakably sensitive to the implied slander in the popular agitation in the

United States against Oriental immigrants. Counting upon the increasing tension between Japan and the United States, Kaiser William II proposed a German-Chinese-American alliance to counterbalance Japan and her allies and to prevent the further partition of China. But nothing ever came of his proposal. The American-Japanese strain was somewhat lessened in 1907, as previously indicated (page 546), by the so-called "Gentlemen's Agreement." Relations were further eased in 1908 by an exchange of messages (the Root-Takahira notes) regarding the two countries' common Pacific and Far Eastern interests. The notes soothed the fears of President Roosevelt particularly about the security of the Philippines; and in Japan they were taken to mean that the United States would not resist Japanese annexation of Korea so long as the open door was respected in Manchuria and China.

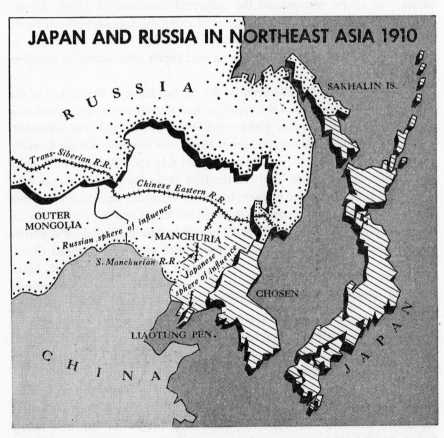

The Russo-Japanese War had created a new imperialist pattern in northeast Asia. Japan now controlled the strategic Liaotung peninsula, formerly leased by Russia from China, as well as the southern half of Sakhalin Island (page 524). The two former enemies also divided the rest of northeast Asia into "spheres of influence," Russia dominating Outer Mongolia and northern Manchuria, Japan dominating southern Manchuria and "independent" Korea. In 1910 Japan annexed Korea outright, renaming it Chosen (page 554). The raised areas indicate the actual borders of the respective countries, flat surfaces, similarly hatched, their spheres of influence.

Japanese successes
in Manchuria and Korea

NEVERTHELESS, the United States had reason to apprehend that the open door principle was being repeatedly violated in Manchuria. Unaware of the precise treaty arrangements between Japan and Russia, American diplomats and financiers found themselves blocked time after time in their Manchurian enterprises. With the beginning of the Taft administration in 1909, the United States began more actively to try to check the advance of Japan in Manchuria and of the other powers in China by extending to the Far East the policy of dollar diplomacy. By encouraging railway loans to the Chinese government, the American government made its policy partly effective. When, however, the United States proposed in 1909 "the complete commercial neutralization of Manchuria," its efforts encountered the concerted resistance of Japan, Russia, and France and brought on a new series of secret agreements between Japan and Russia guaranteeing the status quo. The failure of the Taft policy in Manchuria left small doubt that Russia and Japan were acting in collusion in northeastern Asia.

The stage had meanwhile been set for the last scene in the history of the Korean Empire. Since 1904 the Japanese had treated that tragic nation as a vassal state, and the Koreans' pleas to the world for help had gone unheeded. Yet despite the complete helplessness of Korea, the Japanese did not formally annex the country until they could confidently rely upon American inactivity and Russian acquiescence. In 1910 the final steps toward annexation were taken, and Korea, renamed Chosen, became a Japanese dependency, the first of Japan's outright continental acquisitions. No longer was Nippon merely an insular empire. The "dagger of Korea," which had been pointed for centuries at the heart of Japan, was thereafter turned with great effect against China.

The effort
to stave off revolution in China

THE GROWING threat of Japan was but one of the problems of China's rulers in the declining years of the Manchu dynasty. For the Peking regime's obvious weakness led to numerous domestic plots and rebellions. Since the Boxer outbreak in 1900 the Ch'ing (or Manchu dynasty) had had to wrestle with the problem of assuring national security and internal peace. Little was accomplished in the way of reform before 1905, even though persistent demands poured in from all parts of the country. The indignities suffered by China, such as having the major battles of the Russo-Japanese War fought on her soil, finally forced the Tz'u Hsi empress to issue a series of sporadic decrees that she hoped would rehabilitate her country. Pursuit of knowledge abroad was mildly encouraged, the better assimilation of the Manchus with China was advocated, the old system of civil service examinations was abolished, and special missions were sent to Europe, Japan, and the United States to study modern political systems. As in contemporary Russia (page 466), for a time the imperial regime of China appeared ready to accommodate itself to the progressive demands made upon it. The strength of the dynasty was most seriously shaken, however, by the death of the empress-dowager in 1908. The throne fell to a three-year-old child, Pu Yi. To hold in check the advocates of radical and immediate reform, the regency in Peking issued statements of their intention to permit the gradual development of a limited and constitutional monarchy.

Sun Yat-sen and the Chinese Revolution

BUT DEVELOPMENTS soon made clear that China would not be allowed to complete her transformation from an obsolete to a modern system by a policy of gradualism. Transformation was obviously inescapable, but rebellions, chaos, and civil war were destined to accompany it. In the contest for control the figure of Dr. Sun Yat-sen took on heroic proportions. He had organized a Kuomintang (National People's Party) at the beginning of the century. He had carried on agitation against the dynasty from within China and from his various homes in exile. Educated along western lines, Dr. Sun would not hear of the gradual development of a limited monarchy in China. Monarchy seemed to him particularly objectionable because Tokyo was exerting pressure upon China to model her government upon Japan's. He and his party, strong in central and southern China, called for the immediate overthrow of the dynasty and the establishment of a constitutional republic.

Sun's major rival for political power was Yüan Shih-kai, the former confidant of the empress-dowager and the outstanding military leader of northern China. Although Yüan held office under the Ch'ing as senior guardian of the heir apparent, his loyalty to his ward was open to question, and his enemies repeatedly accused him of being a pawn of the Japanese. For a time Yüan worked to prevent the overthrow of the child-emperor, but in the end he sought a compromise with the radical forces of central and southern China. The union of Sun Yat-sen's party with Yüan Shih-kai's military spelled the collapse of the ancient but defenseless Chinese Empire. In return for his cooperation in the revolution, Yüan was elected first president of the Chinese Republic and was permitted to preside over the dissolution of the Manchu dynasty (1912).

No sooner was the dynasty overthrown than hostilities developed between Yüan and the cohorts of Sun. In part, the early conflicts stemmed from lack of political experience with the republican form of government. More deep-rooted, however, was the conflict which developed as Yüan's ambition to use the republic as a stepping stone toward a new dynasty became increasingly clear. He received from foreign sources huge loans that gave him great financial power and won him the support of the countries to which he was most heavily indebted. The loans had been sought ostensibly for a governmental reorganization, but he used the borrowed funds to bribe politicians 555 and to build up his personal military strength. The rapid increase in his personal power did not diminish the distrust of his motives, and in 1913 he was confronted with a rebellion of the Kuomintang. He took advantage of his financial and military superiority to dissolve the parliament and began openly to work for a constitutional monarchy of his own. Despite the support of Japan, he was not strong enough to beat down the rebellion of the republican forces at home. In 1916 he had to acknowledge his defeat by reëstablishing the republic. Shortly afterwards he died.

The Morley-Minto reforms and rising nationalism in India

A NOTABLE advance in the direction of more democratic government was registered in India on the eve of the First World War. In 1905 Lord Minto succeeded Curzon as viceroy of India, and upon the accession of the Liberals later that year John Morley, the celebrated biographer, was named chief of the India Office. In response to the increasingly violent agitation in India for a greater degree of participation in government the Indian Councils Act was promulgated in 1909. It increased the number of members of the provincial legislative councils and required that indirectly elected nonofficial members (those not representative of the *raj)* be in the majority; it increased the number of elective members of the central legislature; and it added Indians to the Executive Councils of the governors and the viceroy in India. Although an important step toward self-rule, the reforms failed to satisfy the most active nationalists in India, and they emphasized an old element of discord by providing special representation for Moslems. Unrest continued, particularly in response to a partition of Bengal. Lord Minto in an effort to end the rising terrorism resorted to deporting the native leaders of opposition to his program. In 1911 the partition of Bengal was rescinded. On the eve of the First World War, even though India was calm upon the surface, the British realized that the Indian nationalists would continue to increase in numbers and that their loyalty in a crisis, though of paramount importance to the whole empire, was doubtful. Fortunately for Great Britain, the Morley-Minto reforms, despite their shortcomings, constituted for many Indian nationalists a warrant of Britain's good intentions and gave Indians an incentive to cooperate with the empire.

Japan and the Japanese on the eve of the world wars

AMONG THE nations of eastern Asia, Japan alone before the First World War had earned a respected position in the society of nations. Effected as rapidly as it was, the transformation of Japan from a semifeudal and isolated east Asiatic state to a largely modern state was far from complete. While technological readjustment and political reform lent her the appearance of complete modernity, life beneath the surface continued to follow a traditional and well-worn rou-

A European drawing of Japanese cadets leaving for the front during the Russo-Japanese War. The twentieth-century military dress of the cadet, center, bidding farewell to his family, is in strong contrast to the almost medieval garb of his parents. Such a contrast is representative of the simultaneously traditional and modern aspects of pre-First World War Japan, which came about as a result of that country's rapid leap from semi-feudal isolation to the position of the only eastern Asiatic country of respected status among the world powers.

tine. At the local levels social and economic relationships of individuals and of classes remained largely feudal. In religion and other patterns of thought the people of Japan in all classes generally held tenaciously to the beliefs of the past. It was only after Japan had catapulted herself into a position of international power that the faults in her transformation began to show up. The external shell of modernity was found to be thin indeed, and it soon began to show cracks under pressures from within and without. What remained was a nation wholly prepared physically but rather reluctant spiritually to face life in the modern world.

That reluctance did not mean that the individual Japanese was less intelligent or less effective socially than the individual Westerner. On the contrary, the contributions of Japan to modern intellectual life were amazingly forward-looking in many respects. In diplomatic, military, and naval strategy the Japanese had learned their lessons well. In the building of industrial and commercial empires they exhibited extraordinary skill and adaptability. Their achievements in the arts and sciences were often significant. They failed, however, to understand fully or to realize effectively the ways of living together that had so far enabled the nations of the West to maintain a high degree of internal peace and security along with a modicum of international peace and order. They failed to readjust their institutions to the requirements for such cooperative religion, democracy, and world order as were to be found at more or less advanced stages in the West. They turned away from the great international religions like Buddhism, Christianity, and Mohammedanism for the native Shinto cult. Emperor-worship and clan rule discouraged popular interest and participation in government. Open disregard of international law in such things as sudden attack without declaration of war made for a brooding suspicion in all international dealings with Japan. To be sure, many western nations at the same period failed equally to live up to the ethical, social, and religious values basic to the western way of life. The Japanese, however, not only had not tried them but were often not aware of or had deliberately refused to recognize the place of these virtues in the fabric of modern life in the West. They had not even paid to these western virtues the homage of hypocrisy.

Japanese success in foreign affairs helped to perpetuate the domination of the government by clansmen, militarists, and bureaucrats. Nevertheless, the newer political forces (page 416) carefully nurtured their own influence. With the continuing development of commerce and industry, the strength of the financial interests grew. Furthermore, political parties made their appearance in the Diet and at the local levels of government. Taking advantage of the continuous struggle for power between the civilian and the military groups, the advocates of responsible party government won important successes before 1914, and they were now more frequently permitted to designate party leaders to hold cabinet portfolios. No *commoner* was to be able, however, to win the post of premier until the dislocations of the First World War brought party politicians to power.

*Mutual suspicion
of the United States and Japan*

JAPAN'S glorious Meiji era came to an end with the death of the emperor in 1912. Just before his demise the empire had added to its prestige by the renewal of the Anglo-Japanese Alliance (1911) for another ten-year period. In the same year Japan concluded a commercial treaty with the United States on a basis of equality, and this treaty remained in effect until it was abrogated by the United States in 1939. Thus the Japanese cemented their ties with the West more securely.

Across the Pacific the new Japan won an admiration mixed with suspicion and hostility. American concern was stimulated by the monopolistic tendency in Japan's exploitation of continental Asia and by her independent action. The possibility of Japan's expanding southward toward the Philippines also created a latent fear among American admirals and diplomats. Recurrent international crises in Europe forced them to recognize that the United States was the only power in a position to oppose Japanese aggression in the event of war. The strategists in Washington hoped by combining strength with gentleness to ward off difficulties with Japan. In the years before 1914 the policy of the "mailed fist in the gloved hand" took form. The glove did not well conceal the iron, however, especially when after the Russo-Japanese War the American fleet was dispatched to the Pacific on its famous round-the-world voyage (page 546), and fortifications in the Philippines and Samoa were expanded and strengthened.

Still more disturbing to the Japanese was the open secret of the Panama Canal. The canal was ready for traffic just in time for the outbreak of the First World War. It cut a hemisphere in two in order to shorten the sea route between New York and San Francisco by at least half, and the route from New York to Yokohama by over three thousand miles. The United States was therefore able to count upon readier cooperation between its Atlantic and Pacific fleets. Moreover, through its possession of a good naval base in Hawaii, it was able to dominate without question the sea lanes of the eastern Pacific and to menace the western Pacific. No matter how loudly or sincerely Americans might proclaim that these arrangements were exclusively for defensive purposes, to Japan the increased naval strength of the United States implied a threat. As the course of empire took its way westward, along with it went the problem of maritime control, and a generation raised on Mahan's interpretation of history could be expected, on either side of the Pacific, to be worried about the outcome.

Japan and the United States as opponents in the Pacific region THE UNITED STATES was particularly anxious to preserve the other independent states of continental Asia from the fate of Korea. Revolution in China rendered the American assignment still more difficult. In 1914 China appeared tied to the chariot of Japan's ambitions, and the United States appeared to be the only power free to challenge Japan's triumphal parade through eastern Asia. Had it not been for the intervention of Washington, Tokyo might have steered the Chinese Revolution of 1911 even more openly than it did. From that date Japan began to look upon the American policy of the open door as a program especially designed to thwart her, and the conflict thus begun was to increase in intensity. Two non-European powers, quarreling over non-European lands and oceans but employing techniques and concepts developed largely in Europe, thus engaged in a struggle that was part of Europe's destiny as well as of their own.

559

Many EXPLANATIONS have been offered as to why the Victorian Age failed to fulfill its promise of continuous peace, prosperity, and progress. One that will perhaps appear more patent than the rest is the growing tension between two rival European systems of alliance that divided the forces or sympathies of practically the whole world between them. As has been true of neatly balanced power systems through the centuries, it is possible to argue that war might have been averted had the two sides been less evenly matched. For in an uneven controversy the weaker alliance is likely to yield (especially if the issue is not one of survival) to the stronger. In fact, in the recurrent crises from 1905 to 1913, as we are now to see, that was exactly what did happen. Another explanation frequently advanced for the failure to preserve peace in 1914 was the lack of an effective world organization to enforce peace. That lack brought international anarchy.

*The feeble success
of the Hague Conferences*

IN THE LIGHT of what we now know about the collapse of peace efforts in 1914, the Hague Conferences and Tribunal seem significant chiefly as a pioneer attempt at world government. To contemporaries, however, they carried a great hope of ultimate success. A second conference took place at The Hague in 1907 on the initiative of President Theodore Roosevelt and on the invitation of the czar. Forty-seven nations this time were invited to send representatives. This conference revised the conventions already reached at the earlier one (page 510) and took steps for calling a third. It looked as if a world organization of permanent conferences with a permanent tribunal had come into being, but the First World War was to shatter that illusion. The third conference never met.

*Growing armaments
and mounting militarism*

ONE SIGN of the weakness of the Hague organization was its inability to meet the problem of growing armaments. It did not even get a genuine discussion of the issue. From 1908 to 1914, expenditures expressly earmarked for armaments went up for the six European powers at the rate of a half billion dollars a year. A vicious circle resulted. Because nations trusted only to their own power to defend themselves and distrusted the intentions and promises of others, they dared not consider disarmament unless the others disarmed first. None of the great powers dared to be the first to disarm or the last to arm. By 1914 the per capita cost of armaments, already high (page 508), reached an unprecedented height and now was greatest in Germany. Nowhere was military discipline or respect for the uniform more conspicuous than in Germany (unless it was Japan). The spirit of unquestioning obedience entered the home, the school, and the civil service. To the charge of foreigners that Germany had developed an unhealthy degree of militarism, Germans replied that they were being encircled by France, Russia, and other potential enemies, and encirclement *(Einkreisung)* must be offset by military efficiency, as it had been in the past.

The unreliability
of Austria-Hungary as an ally

AS THEY watched the alleged *Einkreisung,* the Germans became more and more disturbed by the weaknesses in their own system of alliances. The introduction of universal suffrage in Austria in 1907 solved no problems, and in fact it aggravated the minorities issue. The Slavs now were in the majority, and the Austrian Germans' resentment of the Slavs became more bitter. Meanwhile Hungary was having similar problems with its minority groups. In Transylvania the Rumanian population sought union with independent Rumania. In Croatia, the Yugoslavs (or South Slavs, consisting chiefly of Croats and Serbs), although Catholic Croats did not always get on with Orthodox Serbs, found a common bond in their dislike of Magyar rule. The Yugoslav problem was rendered still more complex by the fact that in Bosnia-Hercegovina, which Austria garrisoned by virtue of the agreement at Berlin in 1878, the population was largely Serb. The heir to the Habsburg throne, Archduke Francis Ferdinand, was prominent among those who favored the conversion of the Dual Monarchy into a Trial (threefold) Monarchy, with the Yugoslavs as the third member. The Trialists hoped to deflate the irredentism of Yugoslav nationalists at home in Croatia and abroad in Serbia. Liberal elements also advocated the transformation of Austria into a federation of states. But Emperor Francis Joseph stubbornly opposed any such changes. To make matters worse, the relations between Italy and Austria-Hungary were impaired because the Italian irredentists claimed autonomy for the Italian minority living in Austrian Tyrol, Trieste, and Dalmatia. The threatened disintegration of Austria-Hungary became a factor that all European cabinets had to consider in their calculations. It weakened the Triple Alliance, and Germany was handicapped in her international bargaining because of Austria's lack of domestic cohesion.

For its part, the Austro-Hungarian government was distressed by the growing estrangement between Great Britain and Germany. Good terms with Great Britain were a practical necessity for Austria's Balkan policy so long as Russia had designs on the Straits. The possibility of a war between Great Britain and Germany was an alarming prospect to the Vienna government, but it was helpless to prevent Anglo-German tension. It had to support Germany, which was its only dependable ally in case of armed conflict with

561

Russia; and the danger of that conflict increased from the very condition—the Slav nationalisms—that caused the Dual Monarchy's domestic dangers.

Austria's difficulties with Serbian nationalism

INSIDE OF Serbia, shortly after the murderous coup d'état of 1903 (page 473), the anti-Austrian party grew strong enough to make its leader, Nikola Pashitch, prime minister. Through secret societies and outspoken declarations, Serbian nationalists multiplied their efforts in favor of annexing the Yugoslav areas of Austria-Hungary. Austria soon became involved in a tariff war with Serbia intended to stop the importation of hogs from that country. Since the trade in hogs was a life-and-death question for the Serbian farmer, the ensuing "Pig War," despite its humorous possibilities, was no laughing matter. It greatly intensified the political estrangement between Serbia and the Austro-Hungarian Empire, increasing both Serbian irredentism and Austrian impatience with Serbian "insolence." After two years (1905-1907) the Pig War ended with the total defeat and exasperation of the Serbian pork farmer, who thereafter was prepared to look only with an unfriendly eye on Austria's behavior. Secret societies aimed at promoting a Yugoslav national spirit among Austria's South Slav subjects prospered in Serbia more than ever.

Germany's defeat at the Algeciras Conference

AUSTRIA'S weakness in a pinch was made manifest at the international congress called, upon Chancellor von Bülow's insistence, to consider the Moroccan dispute that had arisen between France and Germany in 1905 (page 524). The conference opened at Algeciras, in southern Spain, in January 1906. As soon became clear, Bülow's scheme to isolate France once more had boomeranged. Instead, Germany, with only a distraught Austria-Hungary to support her, was isolated. Even Germany's supposed ally Italy, cultivating the newly discovered friendliness between Rome and Paris (page 522), stood with France. So did the United States. When the conference closed in April, Germany had suffered a spectacular diplomatic setback. Holstein was made the scapegoat and dismissed. The German defeat was even greater than appeared on the surface, for the English and the French military and naval staffs had held secret conversations on how to arrange their forces in case of war, and hypothetical plans for strategic cooperation resulted from these conversations. Though the parliament of neither nation learned about these hypothetical commitments, they became the basis of future strategy and had a certain moral force that would have been close to betrayal to repudiate.

The conference drew up the Act of Algeciras, which was an ambiguous document. It guaranteed the sovereignty of the sultan of Morocco, but it provided loopholes like a police force and a state bank through which the French were permitted to preserve a dominating surveillance. Thereby France was able to accomplish what became known as the *pénétration pacifique* of

Morocco. Germany was allowed to save face by the public confirmation of Moroccan sovereignty but otherwise gained little for all her efforts.

The completion of the Triple Entente

THE FRENCH government now exerted itself to bring about rapprochement between Russia and Great Britain. Russia was chastened by war and revolution. Furthermore, having been defeated in the Far East, she wished to recoup her prestige in the Near East and recognized that she could do so only if Great Britain did not object. Great Britain, for her part, wanted a friendly Russia, if for no other reason than that Germany was revealing herself as a potentially more dangerous opponent.

By this time the British government had ample proof that the German navy was being constructed for the express purpose of challenging the maritime supremacy of England. In 1906 H.M.S. *Dreadnought* was launched. It not only was more heavily armored than any other warship; it also had guns that could outshoot both in number of shots and in distance anything else afloat. It made every other type of battleship obsolete. Immediately, however, the *Dreadnought* was recognized as meaning an ultimate advantage to Germany rather than England, since England would have no more than a one-ship start in the competition for superiority in the dreadnought class at the same time that her greater strength in other classes was automatically diminished by the fire superiority of the new type.

The Germans immediately laid down a program of naval building to profit fully from this windfall. In 1906 Germany enacted a new naval bill; in 1908 another one followed. In reply, the British practically scrapped their old fleet because they found it outmoded. They created a new one, which was to be dominated by the new type of battleship. Also, the British laid down two warships for each one the Germans constructed. No one knew yet that the submarine would ultimately reduce the significance of the surface ship.

As we have seen (page 552), Russia and England's ally Japan were meantime reaching an understanding. Under pressure of the Anglo-German naval race a parallel British-Russian entente was concluded in 1907. It delimited the Russian and the British spheres of influence in Persia and recognized the predominance of England in the conduct of Afghanistan's foreign affairs and of China in all the affairs of Tibet. This settlement of the major differences of the two countries was intended to enable the Russians and the British to work more easily with each other and with France in forthcoming international disputes. The arrangement completed the triangular understanding that was commonly called the Triple Entente. Subsequently England withdrew its objections to a modification of the treaties concerning the Straits in favor of Russia and Russia accepted Britain's domination of the Persian Gulf.

*The crisis
over Bosnia-Hercegovina*

THE NEW Triple Entente was quickly put to the test. The Young Turk Revolution (page 535) raised a difficult question for Austria-Hungary and Bulgaria. By the Treaty of Berlin of 1878, Bosnia, Hercegovina, and the district of Novi Bazar, though all of them were Austrian-occupied, were still nominally Turkish territory. The same was true of Bulgarian Eastern Rumelia. The new illness of "the sick man of Europe" looked to his European neighbors like a good opportunity to claim his various properties. Moreover, the ambitious Austrian minister of foreign affairs, Count von Aehrenthal, felt that Austria had to do something spectacular to dazzle the multinational population of the tottering Dual Monarchy. In a face-to-face conversation in 1908 he told the Russian foreign minister, A. P. Izvolsky, that if Russia would not object to Austria's annexation of Bosnia and Hercegovina, Austria would not object to Russia's opening of the Straits to Russian warships. Izvolsky claimed afterwards that he thought the Austrian minister had in mind merely a hypothetical situation and so raised no immediate objection. Nevertheless, the Russian minister shortly undertook a tour of the European capitals to win general consent to the hypothetical proposal (if such it was). But without waiting for a sign from Izvolsky, Austria-Hungary formally annexed Bosnia and Hercegovina, returning the district of Novi Bazar to Turkey. Meanwhile Bulgaria had already annexed Eastern Rumelia, and Prince Ferdinand had proclaimed himself the independent czar of Bulgaria. In reply to these inroads, the recently triumphant Young Turks started a boycott of all Austro-Hungarian goods.

The situation immediately became explosive. The Serbs, who thought that they had a better right to the annexed provinces than Austria and who felt that they were entitled to compensation to counterbalance Bulgaria's new prestige, mobilized their army, confident that Russia would support them in case of war. Russia thereupon raised strong objections to the Austrian violation of the Treaty of Berlin. The Triple Entente suggested an international congress, but before the congress could meet, Austria got Turkey to surrender her claims to the disputed area by paying a cash sum for them. The Serbs still wanted to fight it out, but Germany supported Austria, and Russia, still weak from the Japanese war and the Revolution of 1905, yielded. Serbia consented reluctantly to the annexation (March 1909), and no international congress took place. This time it was the Dual Alliance that, having hung together, carried off the diplomatic victory—to the discomfiture of Russia, which had not received its allies' whole-hearted support.

*Diplomatic crises
at Casablanca and Agadir*

IN THE MIDST of the hullabaloo about Bosnia-Hercegovina, the smouldering Moroccan issue blazed anew. In 1908 French soldiers invaded the German consulate at Casablanca looking for deserters from the French Foreign Legion. Their intrusion was clearly a breach of international law, not totally justified by the fact that the German consul had likewise disregarded international law in giving shelter to a deserter who was not a German. The air, already tense with the Bosnian crisis, nevertheless cleared when the Casablanca affair was turned over to the Hague Tribunal. In fact, in February 1909, France amicably agreed that Germany might have certain commercial concessions in Morocco in return for Germany's conceding political control to the French.

For about two years the German nationals in Morocco grumbled, feeling that they were getting the worst of the bargain as the French tightened their political hold. In July 1911, a German gunboat, the *Panther,* anchored in the harbor of Agadir, Morocco. The gunboat was sent there, the Germans vaguely explained, to "protect German interests." It looked as if Germany had decided to challenge the French in their "peaceful penetration" of Morocco. What Germany actually wanted was compensation for France's accumulation of power in Morocco. The German minister suggested the French Congo as good compensation. The French refused, and Great Britain supported them. Lloyd George, the British chancellor of the exchequer, generally regarded as a pacifist, declared in a belligerent speech at the Mansion House in London that England could not be ignored "when her interests were vitally affected." The speech was readily understood in Germany and elsewhere. It meant that England considered the Entente Cordiale a vital interest. Secretly the British and French made plans for military and naval cooperation, to supplement their earlier agreements. This time the Germans accepted diplomatic defeat. In November, an agreement was concluded between Germany and France that left Morocco entirely to France. As compensation Germany received a few slices of French territory in and around the French Congo—which were considerably less than the Germans had originally suggested. In 1912 France formally declared Morocco a French protectorate.

The growing ambiguity of Italy's foreign commitments

THE VICTORIES of France and the setbacks of Germany in the Algeciras and the Agadir controversies were due in no small part to their allies. The moral support that the British government had extended to France in both instances was unmistakable. On the other hand, Austria's domestic complications had diminished the effectiveness of her support of Germany. And Italy's position was growing increasingly ambiguous. In 1909, between the two crises, Italy had secretly reached an understanding with Russia somewhat similar to her earlier secret understanding with France (page 522). The two powers agreed to support each other's imperial ambitions—Italy, Russia's in the Straits and Russia, Italy's in Tripoli. Though neither the German people nor their government realized it, the Triple Alliance was crumbling.

Russia was only one of the several European governments that since the 565 crushing defeat at the hands of the Abyssinians at Adua in 1896, had encouraged the Italian government to consider Tripoli as its field of expansion. When it became clear that France would take over Morocco, the Italians felt that it was time for them to act. One day in September 1911 they sent an ultimatum to Turkey demanding consent to their occupation of Tripoli and the next day declared war. Thus began the Italo-Turkish War; six years separated it from the Russo-Japanese War—the longest stretch of peace since Bismarck had ceased to be Germany's chancellor.

The war put the Germans in a most awkward position. Officially they were still allies of Italy. On the other hand, Germany now considered herself also the friend and protector of Turkey. Furthermore, Austria, anxious to preserve the status quo in the Balkans (in so far as she did not upset it herself), made clear to the Italians that she would disapprove of any attack on Turkey's Balkan areas. The Triple Alliance thus was visibly strained. But it did not break, because the crisis passed quickly. Turkey, fearing attack from her Balkan neighbors, was ready to buy Italy off after a year of undistinguished desert warfare, and by the Treaty of Lausanne in 1912, the hard-pressed Turks surrendered both Tripoli and Cyrenaica, which thereupon became the Italian colony of Libya. Italian troops also continued to occupy the Dodecanese Islands.

International tensions during the First Balkan War
THE BALKAN states saw in the multiplying difficulties of Turkey a golden opportunity. Under Russian sponsorship Serbia, Bulgaria, and Greece concluded a series of alliances providing for the distribution among them of Albania, Macedonia, and other Turkish areas in the Balkans. Montenegro acceded verbally. In October 1912,

THE NEAR EASTERN QUESTION, 1912-1913

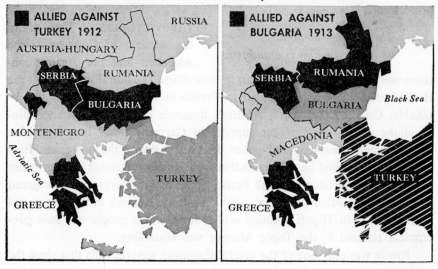

just before the Turks' war with Italy ended, Montenegro struck. The others joined in shortly.

Turkey's armies had had several highly reputed German instructors for years. Hence, when the Balkan War broke out, the Turks were expected to win. Except for the Germans, however, no one wanted them to gain the fruits of victory. Russia in fact openly supported the Serb irredentist aspirations, and the other great European powers favored the status quo.

Much to the general surprise, the Balkan allies won sweeping victories. In November, Serbs and Montenegrins stood on the Albanian shores of the Adriatic and the Bulgarians at the gates of Constantinople. The Albanians, hoping thereby to avoid being divided among the victorious Balkan nations, declared their independence of Turkey. Italy and Austria supported Albania, both making clear that they would not welcome Serbia as a third contestant in their dispute for control of the Adriatic. Russia at first backed Serbia and Montenegro, and France backed Russia. Great Britain, however, did not share Russia's enthusiasm for a Greater Serbia at Turkish and Albanian expense. Hence Sir Edward Grey, the British secretary of state for foreign affairs, invited the powers to a conference at London to decide what to do about the new situation in the Balkans.

At London two complexities made a settlement difficult. First, Serbia supported by Russia demanded an outlet to the Adriatic and for that purpose proposed to annex Albania. The Austro-Hungarians would allow no such annexation, letting it be known that any Serbian or Montenegrin attempt to occupy Albania would be met by a declaration of war. The Austrians were encouraged in this attitude by the Italians, who coveted Albania for themselves. In the second place, Turkey was not so badly beaten that she would

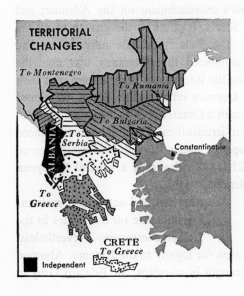

TERRITORIAL CHANGES

To Montenegro

To Rumania

To Bulgaria

To Serbia

ALBANIA

Constantinople

To Greece

CRETE
To Greece

Independent

In 1912 the Near Eastern question threatened to involve most of Europe, as the Balkan Alliance (first map) made a successful grab for Turkey's Balkan holdings. (The disputed Balkan area and Crete are indicated by light shading.) The Albanians declared their independence of Turkey with the support of Italy and Austria-Hungary, which wished to keep Serbia sealed off from the Adriatic. Russia (and France) backed Serbia. General dissatisfaction brought a second Balkan conflict in 1913 (second map), in which Bulgaria attacked and was beaten by her former allies, Serbia and Greece, who were joined by Rumania. Turkey fought Bulgaria on her own. The peace treaties of Bucharest and Constantinople gave most of the spoils to Bulgaria's neighbors, as the third map shows. Greece's share included the hitherto autonomous Crete; and Albania's independence was recognized.

567

meekly give up all that the Balkan nations demanded, especially as a series of cabinet changes gave Young Turk nationalists increasing control at Constantinople. The London Conference broke down within a few weeks, and war was resumed by the Balkan nations. In May 1913 Grey again brought the powers together in London, and this time they were able to force a peace upon the reluctant Balkan states, distributing slices of Turkish territory among them.

Continued tension during the Second Balkan War

PEACE LASTED about a month. Serbia, deprived of Albania by Austrian disfavor, coveted compensation out of the big conquest the Bulgarians had made in Macedonia. Austria wished to check Serbia, and Russia backed Serbia. Again the danger of war lurked in the councils of the great powers. In June, Bulgaria attacked her former allies. The Turks found this an excellent occasion to renew the war against Bulgaria; and Rumania too, though she had remained neutral during the First Balkan War, decided to improve the shining hour by joining the attack upon Bulgaria. Bulgaria gave in after a short struggle. By the Peace of Bucharest in August, Rumania received a slice of Bulgarian territory, and Serbia, Greece, and Montenegro divided the Turkish spoils among themselves, consoling hapless Bulgaria with three bits of Turkish territory. Greece got the biggest share, including the island of Crete. Some weeks later, in September, the Turks made peace at Constantinople, taking back a slice of Bulgaria's earlier spoils. The powers recognized Albania as an independent principality. The elated Serbians and the Greeks again dared to invade Albania. But threats of war by Austria and Italy made them pull out again.

Assessment of the profits and losses of the Balkan wars among the great powers is difficult. What Austria lost by the growth of Serbia, it offset by successfully resisting Serbia's encroachment on the Adriatic; and what Russia lost by the restraint of Serbia, it offset by the growth of all the Balkan states at Turkey's expense. The Balkan muddle nevertheless had critical consequences. The Turks, convinced that Germany was now the power most concerned with preserving the integrity of their empire, put their army more fully and openly under German officers. The Serbs, convinced that Austria would never willingly permit a Greater Serbia, became more than ever committed to secret anti-Austrian irredentism. The Russians, convinced that the Balkan states would not cooperate under Russian leadership, agreed in secret crown council (February 21, 1914) that only a general European war would give them control of the Straits.

The failure of the Haldane mission

BRITAIN had acted as a restraining influence on both sides in the Balkan controversy. Nevertheless, by this time she had an additional reason for loyalty to the Entente. Alarmed by the steady increase of German strength in warships, Sir Edward Grey in

1908 suggested to the Germans that the two countries stop their naval race. Tirpitz, however, thought the Germans were winning the race and so turned a deaf ear to the proposal. In consequence, the British passed a new naval bill in 1909, but they did so only with undisguised reluctance.

Naval limitation appeared increasingly desirable to the British since Chancellor of the Exchequer Lloyd George and others felt uneasy about extending social legislation as long as enormous sums were being swallowed up by naval armaments. Early in 1912, shortly after the Italians began to nibble at the Turkish empire, the British government sent Lord Haldane, the war minister, to Berlin to have some informal talks with the German author-ities. Lord Haldane when a young man had studied at a German university and was now a philosopher of recognized stature as well as a government minister. He was a genuine friend of Germany, and he sincerely wanted to bring about an understanding between the two countries. The idea of war between Great Britain and Germany was utterly abhorrent to him. Bethmann-Hollweg, the German chancellor, was in favor of a naval agreement if Great Britain would promise to remain neutral in case of a continental war, but Tirpitz was against it, and the Kaiser supported Tirpitz. Since Germany was a semi-absolute monarchy in which the chancellor took orders from the emperor, the Haldane mission came to naught.

New armaments in Europe in 1912-1914

HALDANE'S failure was the signal, in fact, for a new burst of speed in the armaments race. A new German naval bill was almost immediately passed by the Reichstag. In reply the British concentrated their fleet in the North Sea, leaving the protection of the Mediterranean to the French, thus making the Entente Cordiale morally more binding than it ever had been before. The French and the Russians about the same time came to an understanding about the coopera-tion of their fleets.

Then under the impact of the Balkan crises, the French and the German governments almost simultaneously introduced new army bills. The French proposed extending the two-year compulsory service to three years. The German proposal increased the army over 50 per cent in size and called for a special one-time levy of about 1,000,000,000 marks, dubbed the Imperial Emergency Defense Sacrifice. Both bills encountered opposition, especially from the Socialists, but the French opposition was more heated than the German, and the German proposal passed first. By the summer of 1913 both France and Germany were armed more extensively and expensively than ever before in peacetime. The British navy, with plans for patrol of the seas already based upon moral commitments to France, in 1914 began conversa-tions to provide for the cooperation of the Russian navy. That year, we already know (page 560), armaments budgets reached an unprecedented height among all six European powers.

*Efforts
to prevent conflict*

THE CHAIN of crises in Morocco and the Balkans since 1906 had demonstrated that diplomatic victory lay with the side that appeared to have the greater cohesion, domestic stability, and unimpeded military strength. Hence, expecting new diplomatic crises at any moment, each side exerted itself to be recognized by the other as united and strong. At the same time efforts were made to avoid conflict over issues that did not appear vital. At the end of 1913 the Germans chose not to make a major issue of the place of German generals in the Turkish army and agreed, upon Russian protests, that General Liman von Sanders should be merely an inspector-general without an actual command. And as late as June 1914 English and German negotiators reached an understanding about the Bagdad Railway, settling a dispute of nearly two decades as to how far the tracks were to run and what were the limits of the commercial spheres of each country. Had this understanding ever gone into operation, one of the big stumbling blocks in Anglo-German relations would have been removed. The understanding was supposed to be formally signed on August 4, 1914. That day Great Britain declared war on Germany.

By 1914, the eight nations generally regarded as great powers were scrambling not only for colonies or spheres of influence, and not only for commercial, military, and naval advantages, but also for alliances. They sought not only the good will of lesser countries like Mexico, Serbia, Turkey, and China but also agreements with each other. These agreements sometimes took the form of open alliances, sometimes of secret conventions, sometimes of promises of neutrality, and sometimes of tacit understandings. Occasionally the same nation would make commitments that, in spirit at least, appeared like a betrayal, or at least a misleading, of its presumed allies. Now and then the commitments were only conditional and hypothetical propositions of cabinet officials or of generals and admirals, and hence not binding upon parliaments and parties.

By 1914 this complicated system of alliances had reached a stage of extremely delicate equilibrium. The two major systems—the Triple Alliance and the Triple Entente—faced each other, each fearful both of its own potential lack of cohesion and of its opponent's potential diplomatic and military advantages. Each member of the two alliances was more or less committed to move, even if to move reluctantly, in a dangerous direction if some new diplomatic crisis were either to betray weakness in its own alliance or to give new strength to the other.

In such a situation a higher power or a stronger spiritual force than national sovereignty might have preserved peace. But no agency existed strong enough to bring order into the anarchy in which the nations lived in relation to each other. The Hague Conferences and Tribunal had only such strength as the separate nations voluntarily chose to give them. International law was only a growing compendium of conventions, agreements, and precedents that had no more binding force than custom, good will, and world opinion could give it. The Concert of Europe, which had prevented a worldwide war since 1815, had not yet broken down, as several international congresses (such as Algeciras and London) amply demonstrated. Yet the Pax Britannica (the ability of England to preserve the peace by threatening to throw her sword into the scales) had vanished. For England had allowed the expectation to arise that though she might remain neutral, she would probably be friendly to one side, thus obliging the other side to make its preparations on that presumption. No single strong detached nation of Europe could now admonish both alignments, calling upon them to halt their threats and mobilizations lest it too feel obliged to move and thus upset all previous calculations.

Every foreign office, every general staff among the great powers of Europe had made its guesses as to what to do as circumstances might require. The diplomatic chess game had been played so often by the same opponents that each knew, or thought he knew, the other's moves and how to counteract them. And yet the balance of power and skill was so delicate that no one could be sure that it would remain balanced from day to day. And so each opponent watched jealously that no slight accident should upset it to his disadvantage. The accident came when a chauffeur took a turn down the wrong street of Sarajevo on June 28, 1914.

1842-1910	William James
1859-1952	John Dewey
1860-1911	Gustav Mahler
1881-1945	Béla Bartók
1881-	Pablo Picasso
1905	The *Action Française* organized as a league
1906-1912	The Liberals' program of social legislation in Britain
1906	The Algeciras Conference
1906	First Russian Duma
1906	The Pure Food and Drug Act in the United States
1907-1909	The United States' battle fleet's cruise around the world
1907	Henri Bergson's *Creative Evolution*
1907	The Triple Entente
1907	The "Gentlemen's Agreement" between the United States and Japan
1908-1909	Revolution of the "Young Turks"
1908	Bosnia-Hercegovina crisis
1908	Georges Sorel's *Reflections on Violence*
1908	Roosevelt appoints National Conservation Commission
1909	Morley-Minto reforms promulgated in India
1910	Union of South Africa created
1910	Korea becomes Japanese dependency
1910	Paul Ehrlich discovers arsphenamine ("606")
1911-1912	The Italo-Turkish War
1911	The Chinese Revolution
1911	Anglo-Japanese alliance renewed
1911	Parliament Act weakens veto power of House of Lords
1911	Revolution and counterrevolution in Mexico
1911	Partition of Bengal rescinded
1912-1913	The Balkan wars
1912	The Haldane mission fails to slow up European armaments race
1912	Leftist victory in *Reichstag* elections
1912	Roosevelt supporters form Progressive Party
1912	Woolworth Building erected
1913-1914	Irish Home Rule controversy
1913	The Sixteenth Amendment permits taxing of American incomes
1913	Kuomintang rebels against Yüan Shih-kai
1913	Huber perfects process for obtaining nitrogen from the air
1914	Clayton Anti-Trust Act
1914	Panama Canal opened
1916	Chinese Republic reëstablished
1916	Frank Lloyd Wright's Imperial Hotel (Tokyo) completed

Chapter ten

THE "WAR
TO END WAR"

1914-1918

WAR COULD probably have been averted in 1914 if peace had been the major consideration on both sides. But the major desire on one or both sides in prewar controversies usually is not to preserve peace but to preserve "vital interests" or to win political advantages and ends even at the cost of peace. Unfortunately each side in 1914 was thoroughly convinced that the other side would either back down first or be handily defeated in a short, localized fight, and so was prepared to run the risk of war.

Who was responsible? Historians still argue that question, and we shall attempt an answer in the following pages. But it will bear repetition that almost no one wanted war for its own sake. Diplomats, soldiers, and peoples wanted only to win advantages or at least to avoid incurring disadvantages. Unfortunately, miscalculations regarding diplomatic and military potentialities were made on both sides, and so all the originally participating nations "staggered and stumbled" (to use Lloyd George's phrase) into a catastrophe that probably each would have tried to avoid if its governmental authorities could have guessed how wrong their calculations would soon prove to be. Indeed, efforts to avoid war were made on both sides, but earlier commitments abroad, or divided councils at home, or mutual suspicion regarding ulterior motives made those efforts too limited or too late.

And so because Bismarck's scheme of isolating France and winning Russia had been abandoned since 1890, and because two fairly equal camps had divided Europe and a great deal of the rest of the world between them since that date, and because each side felt that this time it could not afford to yield and would be victorious if it persisted, the first of the World Wars burst upon a horrified world. The outcome was not only the disruption of the settlement in central Europe that Bismarck had done so much to create, and not only an enfeeblement of that Europe which had dominated the world's politics till that time, but also an end to that peaceful and prosperous Victorian society which since the Congress of Vienna had had reason to believe that progress was an inevitable outcome of the passage of time. When the war was over, a world order was to be attempted, the specter that Marx had announced in 1848 really began to haunt Europe in earnest, the "Yellow Peril" had assumed more menacing proportions, and the Western Hemisphere had come to take a decisive part in European affairs.

A TRAGEDY OF ERRORS

THE PRECIPITATING cause of the war of 1914 was an assassination. Since the victim of the assassination was the Austrian heir apparent and the assassin was a Serbian nationalist, the event called for an initial step by Austria, and that initial step tripped off a concatenation of events that were to place the diplomats of Austria, supported by Germany, in a more and more militant and uncompromising position. They hoped at first to win a diplomatic victory by a show of force. When it became clear that a mere show of force would not be enough, the fitting moment to compromise had passed; diplomatic engagements and military plans that had been prepared for decades had to be put in operation if the risks of betraying one's allies were not to be run. The military made the final decisions.

*The assassination
of the Archduke Francis Ferdinand*

ON SUNDAY, June 28, 1914, the Archduke Francis Ferdinand of Austria and his morganatic wife, who were visiting Sarajevo, the capital of recently annexed Bosnia, were shot and killed by a member of a Serbian irredentist society called "Union or Death." It is conceivable that if the chauffeur of the archduke's car, having taken the wrong road on the way back from the official reception at the town hall, had not backed up in order to correct his error, the assassin would not have been successful. On the other hand, another assassin might have been, because the plot to kill the archduke had been carefully laid under the direction of the colonel in charge of the intelligence division of the Serbian general staff, and more than one assassin was lying in wait that day. A bomb, in fact, had earlier been tossed at the royal pair, only to bounce off their car and kill several other persons.

*The Austrian reaction
to the Sarajevo assassination*

THE WORLD was stunned at first by the assassination of the Austrian heir apparent. It was obvious that another of Europe's recurring crises would follow. Yet few believed that the assassination of a none too popular Austrian prince would bring about a general war. Nor did the eighty-four-year-old Emperor Francis

Joseph think so. In fact, the death of his nephew, with whom he was on bad terms because of his morganatic marriage, did not deeply grieve the old man.

A certain uneasiness, however, spread throughout Europe. The assassin and his accomplices, though Austrian subjects, were of Serbian extraction. Moreover, the complicity of at least some Serbian government officials was assumed. The emperor was put under heavy pressure by some of his advisers, who felt that a golden opportunity for punishing Serbia had arrived, since world opinion would doubtless be on Austria's side and Serbia's defenders would find it hard to adopt an air of righteousness. The chief of the Austro-Hungarian general staff, Count Conrad von Hötzendorf, was an unabashed militarist. Contrary to other generals and high officials who did their utmost to vindicate themselves after the war was lost, Conrad honestly admitted that he had not been averse to war, preferably a limited war for the cowing of Serbia, because he believed that a war was the only means of keeping the Austro-Hungarian empire from tottering to its ruin. Other Austrian officials, and particularly Count Leopold von Berchtold, the minister of foreign affairs, agreed with him (and in so doing hastened the end they sought to avert).

The reaction of the German government

YIELDING to this pressure, Francis Joseph appealed to Kaiser William II. In a letter delivered on July 5, the old emperor expressed the opinion that the assassination at Sarajevo was "not the bloody deed of an individual, but the result of a well-organized conspiracy, the threads of which reach to Belgrade." Even though the complicity of the Serbian government could probably not be proved, "the efforts of my government," he said, "must in the future be directed toward the isolation and diminution of Serbia." The Austrians, Francis Joseph announced, would demand full satisfaction, and if that was not forthcoming, would march into Serbia.

Francis Joseph's letter practically put it up to Germany to decide what should be done about Serbia, for, without German backing, Austria would scarcely have embarked upon the grandiose scheme of Conrad and Berchtold. The German government did not see any danger that a limited war between Austria and Serbia might spread. On the other hand, the danger seemed real that if Serbia did not undergo fit punishment, she would become an ever greater menace to Austria and hence to the Dual Alliance. "Our own vital interests," wrote Chancellor von Bethmann-Hollweg, paraphrasing the Kaiser's words to him, "demanded the unimpaired maintenance of Austria." Hence the Kaiser told the chancellor that, while it was "not our business" to guide Austria in this case, Emperor Francis Joseph should nevertheless be informed "that we could not desert Austria-Hungary in time of need." The chancellor agreed with the Kaiser, and so sent to Vienna the telegram that has since become notorious as the "blank check": "His Majesty will faithfully stand by Austria-Hungary, as is required by the obligations of his alliance and of his ancient friendship." The Austrian ministers took Germany's reply as *carte blanche* to proceed as they liked.

*Preparation
of the Austrian ultimatum*

ON JULY 7, 1914, the joint ministers of Austria and Hungary, the prime minister of Austria, the prime minister of Hungary, Count Conrad as chief of the General Staff, and a representative of the navy met to decide what steps to take against Serbia. Count Berchtold announced that Kaiser William as well as the German chancellor had "assured us with every emphasis the unconditional support of Germany in case of complications leading to war with Serbia." He then conceded the possibility of Serbian resistance to Austrian attack and of Russian support of Serbia. The Hungarian prime minister, Count Stephen Tisza, was against a surprise attack on Serbia, arguing that Austria-Hungary would thereby alienate the rest of Europe and would earn the hostility of all the Balkan countries except Bulgaria. Tisza's argument persuaded Berchtold not to make unannounced war on Serbia but to present her with an ultimatum so severe that Serbia could be counted upon to reject it. An ultimatum was soon made ready, but the Austrian government deliberately delayed its delivery at Belgrade a few days because President Raymond Poincaré and Premier René Viviani of France happened then to be visiting St. Petersburg, and it was thought wiser to wait until they should leave Russia, thus making communications between Russia and her ally less simple and direct.

*The Austrian ultimatum
and its rejection by Serbia*

ON JULY 23, the Austro-Hungarian envoy to Serbia delivered the ultimatum. It accused Serbian officials of being willing accomplices of the assassins of Francis Ferdinand (although the proof of this accusation was incomplete). The ultimatum required the Serbian government to issue through official journal and army orders a proclamation prepared by the Austrian government expressing Serbia's regret at the assassination and threatening rigorous punishment for any who thereafter made propaganda against Austria-Hungary. Also, the popular nationalist association Narodna Odbrana, believed to have had connections with the assassins, was to be dissolved, and similar societies were to be prohibited in the future. Civil functionaries and army officers whom Austria might designate as having agitated against the Dual Monarchy were to be dismissed. School teachers and teaching were to be purged of all anti-Austrian tendencies. Other demands of a similar nature were included. But the demand most calculated to rouse Serbian resentment was that in the suppression of future anti-Austrian propaganda delegates of the Austrian government should take part. The ultimatum gave the Serbian government forty-eight hours to answer.

Never in modern times had the world witnessed such an ultimatum. When

Sir Edward Grey learned of it, he called it "the most formidable document I had ever seen addressed by one State to another that was independent." And indeed it was taken for granted, in Austria-Hungary and Germany as elsewhere, that no self-respecting government would accept it. Russia, supported by the other Entente powers, asked for an extension of the forty-eight hour limit, but Austria-Hungary bluntly refused.

The Serbian government mobilized its army, thus becoming the first country to take military precautions. Then at almost the last possible moment on July 25, it informed the Austrian envoy that Serbia was ready to accept the ultimatum in part. Upon this the Dual Monarchy broke off diplomatic relations. The Kaiser himself was deeply disturbed. When he had received a copy of Serbia's answer to the Austrian ultimatum, he wrote in the margin, "A great moral victory for Vienna; but with it every reason for war disappears." Only little by little did it dawn upon him that the encouragement he had given the Austrians on July 5 had stiffened their determination for the "diminution" of Serbia.

*Russia's
and Austria's belligerency*

NEITHER Serbia nor Austria had a strong moral position in the eyes of the world. Though proof was lacking, the complicity of Serbian officials in the Sarajevo outrage was generally suspected. Austria, on the other hand, seemed extraordinarily anxious to pick a quarrel with Serbia. Even if other European governments had wished to stand aside, the balance of power was endangered, and inactivity, they felt, was impossible. Russia, the least pacific of the Entente powers and the one that would be most disadvantaged by an Austrian victory over Serbia, had already decided upon "the period preparatory to war"—that is, the taking of preliminary steps toward mobilization, although her military realized that mobilization, once begun, would be hard to stop. Russia thus made the first military decision that was based upon the assumption of the possibility of a war involving big powers on both sides. The French government assured Russia of its support.

Peace now depended upon what Austria would do. On July 26 the British foreign secretary, Sir Edward Grey, without knowing how far Austria and Russia had gone, suggested to Germany that the great European powers should hold a conference and in concert should try to induce Serbia to give Austria every reasonable satisfaction. But the German government hesitated and made conditions. On July 27, the old Emperor Francis Joseph, reluctant to end his unhappy career in war, was tricked by a forged telegram into the belief that Serbian troops had already invaded and occupied portions of his country. Upon this pretext the Dual Monarchy declared war upon Serbia on July 28, and Belgrade was bombarded the next day. By actually resorting to arms the Vienna government converted what might have remained a diplomatic quarrel into a probable cause of war among the big powers. The

German government now realized that it had miscalculated—that the Austro-Serbian war, if not stopped at once, might bring in Russia, and it became clearer and clearer from actions and statements in Paris and London that Russia's allies might support her. War would thus mean no cheap localized victory for the Triple Alliance.

Beginning
of Russian mobilization

IN RUSSIA the military situation by this time was confused. The military wanted a full mobilization, convinced that Germany would support Austria and that partial mobilization would mean an irreparable loss of time. Czar Nicholas, engaged in personal correspondence with Kaiser William (the famous "Willy-Nicky" correspondence, in English) and hopeful that it might still preserve peace, wished to take no irrevocable step. The well-informed knew that Germany's military plans required her in case of war with both France and Russia to overwhelm France first and then turn on Russia. Hence Germany had to count on Russia's being slow and elephantine in mobilizing; she could not allow the Russians a big head start, and would have to consider Russian general mobilization a *casus belli* (occasion for war). Yielding momentarily to the urgings of his advisers, the czar ordered general mobilization on July 29, but on William's promise to continue efforts for peace in Vienna, Nicholas revoked general mobilization in favor of the resumption of partial mobilization against Austria alone.

Failure
of England's peace effort

THE GERMANS, on the urging of London, now asked Austria to occupy Belgrade and then stop hostilities while general negotiations were resumed. But the Austrians paid no heed, partly, it seems, because the German military authorities secretly encouraged the Austrian military to go ahead. Bethmann-Hollweg, thoroughly distressed by this time, in the predawn hours of July 30 telegraphed to Vienna: "If Austria refuses all negotiations, we are face to face with a conflagration in which England will be against us, Rumania and Italy according to all indications will not be for us, and we shall stand two against four Powers....Under these circumstances we must urgently and emphatically urge upon the consideration of the Vienna Cabinet the adoption of mediation in accordance with the [proposed] honorable conditions. The responsibility for the consequences which would otherwise follow would be for Austria and for us an uncommonly heavy one." Berchtold made no satisfactory reply.

Germany's
declaration of war on Russia

DIRECT though limited negotiations were in fact resumed by Vienna with St. Petersburg on July 30; and perhaps, with Germany and England urging moderation, a peaceful arrangement might have come from them. But the decisions by that time were out of the diplomats' hands. The Russian military authorities either could not or would not call off general mobilization; the machinery was simply too cumbersome to halt effectively once it was put in motion. And so on July 30 the czar once more ordered general mobilization. This step made it practically impossible to avoid war with Germany. On July 31 the Germans sent Russia a twelve-hour ultimatum to call off military activity on the German frontier, which Russia did not do, and on August 1 Germany declared war on Russia.

Thus another miscalculation was added to the growing list. In both Germany and Russia the civil and diplomatic arms of the state had thought that they could control the military. But the military felt that they had to act and, as a matter of fact, acted in certain contingencies in accordance with plans and pledges made long before. At the same time that William was trying to get Francis Joseph to talk peace and Bethmann was lecturing Berchtold, Helmuth von Moltke, the German chief of staff and nephew of the great Moltke, was secretly urging Conrad to "mobilize against Russia at once." Count Berchtold is reported to have remarked, "That is odd. Who is boss? Moltke or Bethmann?"

Outbreak of war between Germany and France

THE FRENCH had consistently encouraged the Russians to back Serbia, but they had been willing to accept the British proposals for negotiation. Meanwhile they had taken preliminary war measures should mobilization prove necessary. Full German mobilization could be assumed to be the signal for full French mobilization. Hoping that perhaps the French would not move, the Germans tried to get the French first and then the English to guarantee French neutrality. But the French mobilized their army at almost the same moment as the Germans (August 1), even though French mobilization could be expected to result in a German declaration of war upon France.

In the fatal game now to be played every opening move had been more or less envisaged. The German strategy for a two-front war was charted in the famous "Schlieffen Plan" (named for the late chief of the German General Staff). It called for a short and successful invasion of France through neutral Luxemburg and Belgium, while at the same time a defensive force from Germany and Austria-Hungary warded off the Russians; then after a quick French defeat, which the German General Staff regarded as a foregone conclusion, Germany would turn and overwhelm slow-moving Russia. The war would thus be short, cheap, and victorious. Moltke was to prove utterly mistaken in every one of these assumptions.

Before beginning the invasion of France, Germany asked France about her intentions. Obviously, if the French wavered in their support of Russia, another strategy might be considered. The French answered they would do what their honor and their interests commanded them to do. Any surviving hope of preserving peace now disappeared completely, for both the German and the French blueprints of war called for speedy action. Thus, to use Beth-mann-Hollweg's words of warning to Berchtold (July 28), Germany was "drawn by Vienna into a world conflagration frivolously and in disregard of our [German] advice." A declaration of war against France was postponed for a few days, for reasons that will soon become apparent, but the attack on France began forthwith.

British hesitation to declare war on Germany

FORMALLY, until August, the war was one of Austria against Serbia and of Germany against Russia. In each case Germany and Austria had been the ones to declare war, although the enemy had mobilized first. Meanwhile, the situation of France presented Britain with a dilemma. According to an earlier Franco-British agreement (page 569), the French had concentrated their fleet in the Mediterranean, while the British had concentrated their fleet in the North Sea. If Great Britain remained neutral, the northern and western shores of France were without protection. Winston Churchill, first lord of the admiralty in 1914, had (with the knowledge of Prime Minister Asquith only) kept the fleet together after the regular summer maneuvers and had sent it to the naval base at Scapa Flow to be ready for any emergency. But need the emergency be war if Germany carefully avoided provoking the English? The ambiguously worded agreements between military, naval, and civil officials of Great Britain and France had never been submitted for approval to the British Parliament, nor was the public informed about their existence. Actually, the agreements had questionable constitutional standing in both countries. The German government also promised to make no attack on the French coast if Great Britain remained neutral. What was the British government to do? Should it of its own will rush into a possible conflagration that it might be wiser to watch from a safe distance? Could it look on idly while France defended itself against the Germans in a struggle that, no matter what the outcome, could not fail to influence Britain's future?

The British cabinet split on that issue. German strategy, however, played into the hands of the pro-French group. The Belgian Neutrality Pact drawn up in 1839 was still binding upon its signatories, including Great Britain, France, and Germany, the last as the legal successor of Prussia. On July 31, 1914 Great Britain had asked both France and Germany to respect the neutrality of Belgium, which the British regarded as an essential to their own security. France's blueprints for war did not necessitate a move through Belgium if Germany did not move there first, and she replied that she would. Germany refused a definite answer. In fact, without declaring war on France, the Germans put the Schlieffen Plan into operation. They invaded Luxemburg and sent an ultimatum to Belgium (August 2) demanding access to France across Belgian territory in return for an indemnity. The king of the Belgians appealed to both France and Great Britain as guarantors of the Belgian Neutrality Pact, and at the same time he replied to Germany that he would resist German aggression with all his resources.

Declaration of war by Britain upon Germany

ENGLAND, faced with civil war in Ulster (page 537), was anxious to avoid international conflict. Two anti-war British ministers had already resigned because they were opposed to Foreign Minister Grey's policy favoring support of France, and public opinion in England was divided. But the threatened violation of Belgian neutrality convinced the undecided. Great Britain dispatched an ultimatum to Germany requesting "assurance that the demand made upon Belgium will not be proceeded with and that Germany will respect the neutrality of Belgium." But, as Bethmann-Hollweg later stated, "necessity knows no law." On August 3 Germany declared war on France on the pretext (among others) that French airplanes had bombed Nuremberg; on August 4 it began the invasion of Belgium; and that day England declared war on Germany. That afternoon the German chancellor admitted in the Reichstag that Germany had violated the neutrality of both Belgium and Luxemburg. He admitted that Germany's conduct was contrary to the precepts of international law and asserted that "the wrong we thereby commit we will try to make good as soon as military aims have been attained." And when the British ambassador took leave, the German chancellor remarked that Great Britain had gone to war "just for a scrap of paper." One after another the British dominions declared their support of the mother country.

Rounding out the respective alliances

WITHIN a few days of the outbreak of war, the other powers with commitments to one side or the other indicated where they stood. Italy long had made clear that she would fight no war against the British navy. Besides, she had a secret understanding with France (page 522) not to join in an aggressive war against her. Hence it should have surprised no one that Italy formally declared her neutrality on August 3. On August 5, Montenegro, which had fairly consistently followed the lead of Serbia, declared war on Austria and, three days later, on Germany. Austria declared war on Russia on August 6. By August 12, when France and England declared war on Austria also, all the belligerents on one side were officially at war with all the belligerents on the other. Germany and Austria, generally called the "Central Powers," stood alone against a coalition, generally called the "Allies," of Serbia, Russia, Belgium, France, Britain and her dominions, and Montenegro. The assassination of an Austrian prince had produced a world war, not so much because the prince was of world importance as because each of the great powers expected victory and at least an avoidance of strategic loss if not a chance to profit.

The question
of responsibility for the war

ALL THROUGH the war, each side accused the other of starting it. After the war was over, when the Austrian Empire was broken up into bits and the Russian Empire was rent asunder by revolutions, interventions, and civil wars, a helpless and defeated Germany was obliged by the much-debated Article 231 of the peace treaty to accept "responsibility...for causing all the loss and damage to which the allied and associated governments and their nationals have been subjected as a consequence of the war imposed upon them by the aggression of Germany and her allies." That "war-guilt" clause only intensified the debate among politicians, journalists, and historians as to whether Germany was alone or primarily responsible for "causing all the loss" and for having "imposed" the war upon the others. The question was to play a significant part among the causes of the Second World War.

The degree
of Serbian responsibility

SERBIA as the country that took the first step in bringing about a state of belligerency can not avoid a certain share of the war guilt. That Serbian officials were accessories to the assassination of the Archduke Francis Ferdinand is now known (though the Austrians acted at the time without sufficient proof of their complicity). That the Serbian government had not discouraged the nationalist and irredentist Serbian societies—had in fact encouraged them—may even be taken for granted. It is not yet clear, and may never become clear, that the Serbian government as such knew of or participated in the Sarajevo plot. Its apparent guilt consists of sympathy with Pan-Serbism to the extent that it did not adequately suppress movements and actions that were potentially dangerous

"You see how I manage to keep the enemy out of my country." The Belgian cartoonist Louis Raemaekers pictures the Kaiser shielding himself behind the aged Francis Joseph of Austria-Hungary.

to international peace. When, however, the crime was committed and Austria demanded punishment and repression of future subversive activity, Serbia (apparently, however, only because of uncertainty of how far Russia would support her) was willing to make honorable amends. What she did not prove willing to accept were dishonorable conditions that would have meant the loss of her national sovereignty. All the European governments, including Germany's, thought that Austria ought to have been content with Serbia's reply. War could have been avoided if Austria had been content. Serbians (and, to some extent at least, the Serbian government) were guilty of providing the *casus belli*. They were not guilty of having made the preservation of peace impossible. Serbia was also the first country to begin mobilization, but her mobilization was apparently only for defensive purposes.

The degree of Austrian responsibility

IN THE extenuation of Austria's aggressive attitude toward an apologetic Serbia, Austria's exasperation with Serbian Austrophobia and Serbian irredentism, and Austria's own internal dissensions and weaknesses take a significant place. Austria, as the events were to prove, was fighting for existence as a multinationalist anachronism in a nationalistic age. Federalism might have saved her, but her statesmen did not care to try that remedy. The opportunity to settle, perhaps once and for all, with the Serbian tormenters must have been extremely tempting. A brief local war seemed all that was required if Germany would hold off Russia. That reasoning was responsible for the decision to resort to arms and to tempt Russia to resort to arms in reply. Austria cannot be exculpated from the readiness, even eagerness, to make war on a small neighbor and to risk war with a large one because she believed her advantage would be promoted thereby. To be sure, she did consent to direct negotiations with Russia after hostilities with Serbia had begun and it was Russian mobilization rather than Austria's military maneuvers that rendered those resumed negotiations futile, but it was Austrian action that had impelled Russia to mobilize. The Austrian government was guilty of aggression against Serbia and of provocation of Russia, and it was soon to pay a dire penalty.

The degree of Russian responsibility

THE FIRST big power to decide to mobilize any of her forces against another big power was Russia. The world knows now, having experienced two world wars (and the better informed must have realized then), that mobilization of one power necessitates countermeasures by its potential adversaries unless they are willing to concede an enormous advantage. In being the earliest to mobilize, first with partial mobilization against Austria and then with general mobilization against Germany and Austria, the Russian foreign minister and military were willing to accept the risk of countermeasures by Austria and Germany. The provocation of Russia, it must be admitted, was great. Not only had Austria taken a bullying attitude toward one of Russia's Slavic protégés, but it was also possible that Germany might not support Austria and that therefore Austria could be administered a sound diplomatic or military beating. Russia's guilt is extenuated somewhat also by the facts (1) that everyone knew how lumbering her mobilization processes would be even though she had stationed large numbers of troops near the Austrian and German borders since the previous spring) and that therefore in spite of a good head start upon her potential enemies she might not win the race, and (2) that at every moment up to the German declaration of war Russia was willing to negotiate directly with Austria. Nevertheless, the Russians also knew that once they mobilized, the Germans would have to take into their calculations not only the Russian mobilization but also the probable French mobilization and therefore would have to be extremely forbearing if they were to remain inactive once they learned of Russian mobilization. Hence the Russians must be held guilty of taking the first steps that moved the issue from the realm of big-power diplomacy into the realm of big-power military strategy, thus withdrawing the major decisions from statesmen and giving them to soldiers. If Russia had not mobilized, conceivably the controversy might have been settled by a *quid pro quo* arrangement short of war.

The degree of German responsibility   MORE farsighted and less aggressive statesmen than William II and Bethmann-Hollweg would have avoided at least three of the miscalculations of which they were guilty. (1) Their anxiety for Austria to profit from Serbia's criminality led them to give to Austria an unconditional promise of support (the *carte blanche*) that they were to rue only after it was too late. (2) The willingness of a semiautocratic ruler to give great authority to the military permitted a none too competent chief of staff to act in a fashion that counterbalanced the civil government's peaceful efforts when at last the ruler and his chancellor became fearful that a general war might result. (3) The German government, without making sure of how Italy or England would react, was ready to gamble all, including honor, on a plan of war which to succeed required (a) that the French forces should be divided between the Belgian-German frontier and the Italian frontier, and (b) that the Belgians and British should go to the aid of the French, if at all, too late and with too little. German statesmen thus were indirectly responsible for Austria's provocation of Russia, and German generals for Austrian hesitation to accept the mediation of the big powers. And since German military strategy called for an "offensive defensive," Germany did in fact begin the general war. In extenuation her apologists can point to the danger she ran of vital losses if she did not go to the support of Austria and did not mobilize in answer to Russian and probable French mobilization. It nevertheless seems possible that if Germany had not begun the shooting among the big powers, Russian mobilization might not have led to war with Austria because Austro-Russian negotiations had in fact begun and Russia's allies were ready, England in fact anxious, to submit the whole controversy to pacific international consideration.

Germany's war guilt was great, but she was not the only culprit, and it was certainly not true, as was commonly believed among her enemies during the war, and for a while after, that she had foully engineered the war so as to entrap an unsuspecting and unprepared Belgium and France. On the contrary, just before the situation passed out of the hands of the civil government into those of the military, the German emperor and his chancellor were earnestly engaged in trying to prevent Austria and Russia from taking irrevocable steps. Their conversion to pacific measures, alas, came too late.

The degree of French and English guilt

APOLOGISTS for Germany have insisted that France and England were guilty of egging on Russia and of hiding their true intentions so as to lead Germany into a trap. They point to the ancient enmity of France and Germany, to the French passion for *revanche,* to the colonial rivalries in Africa and the East, to the commercial competition that Germany was giving England, to the Anglo-German naval race, to the bitterness engendered by the Bagdad Railway dispute (arrangement of which was to have been signed on that fateful August 4), to the encirclement of Germany by the Entente powers, and to a host of other motives for hostile behavior on the part of France and England. The fact remains, however, that England tried, until the shooting actually began, to limit the war as much as possible and to induce the Austrians and Russians to consent either to direct negotiations with each other or to the mediation of other powers. It is also true that France, though more definitely committed to Russia than England was to either France or Russia and therefore more concerned with Russian susceptibilities, was ready to go along with England in this step. France also urged Russia to be cautious in its military preparations. Both powers, however, indicated their moral diplomatic support of Russia, and France promised all along that she would abide by her obligations as a military ally. With their previous commitments, neither could well have done less, and the Germans apparently did not expect that they would do less. The French were careful not to mobilize until Germany had proclaimed a "state of danger of war" and had issued an ultimatum to Russia. Their mobilization orders anticipated the Germans' by only five minutes.

The French slate is not entirely clean, however, and neither is the English. The French might have been less ready to support Russia, might perhaps even have done more to dampen Russian military ardor. The English might have done the same; and in addition, it is sometimes argued, they might have made clearer that they would ultimately support France and Russia in a showdown. In extenuation of France, the previous defeats of Russia in the Balkans (pages 564 and 568) must be taken into account. If France had not now loyally carried out her alliance obligations, she might have found herself deserted by a disillusioned Russia and once more isolated by a triumphant Germany. And England's unwillingness to pledge her ultimate participation openly either to Germany or to her allies was not a deliberate effort to mislead. Perhaps the Russian foreign minister, S. D. Sazonov, was right when he urged that if England would declare her solidarity with Russia and France, Germany would back down, but Sir Edward Grey could constitutionally make no such commitment. He not only did not have the full support of his cabinet but, until the invasion of Belgium, it was doubtful whether Parliament would have supported even a united cabinet that proposed a declaration of war. The facts indicate that Grey did all he constitutionally could do, including giving broad hints to the German ambassador at London, which unfortunately received attention too late in Berlin, to prevent a general war.

International anarchy:
the fundamental cause of the war

THE REAL culprit in 1914 was not a man or a government or a people. It was an international system, or lack of system, that had developed since the Concert of Europe had begun to split apart in the 1820's. That lack of system had induced governments to seek security for what they considered their vital interests in a set of international alliances backed by vast armaments and secret pledges. Those alliances were delicately balanced one against the other. They had nearly the same amount of military and naval power and diplomatic prestige. They were nearly equal in economic and human resources. They had prepared secret plans of military operations that, attempting to foresee every possible move of the enemy, called for countermoves in a predetermined fashion. A wholesome fear of each alliance for the other had preserved European peace for a long time. Yet the danger was constant that at one time or another the vast military machines that each had built up in its quest for security would go into action, and once one was known to have made a move, the others could be expected to make their countermoves. It was almost like an expert game of chess, but between opponents who were prepared to break the rules if it should prove to their advantage, since they were playing with vast armies for what they believed to be the safety and welfare of their native lands. Only a stronger force than either of the two alliance systems could have kept international order; and where was that force?

THE INDECISIVE WAR

(TO AUGUST 1918)

As STATED above, the Austro-German strategic plan called for a quick defeat of the French by the Germans, while the Austro-Hungarians and a small part of the German army held off the Russians. Then the Germans were to turn east with all their might and defeat the Russians, who were expected to plod along only slowly in the early stages of the war. That plan miscarried, as we shall soon explain, and the war that was to have been as clean and as speedy as lightning bogged down into a four-year test of endurance.

The failure of the Schlieffen Plan

THE GERMANS moved rapidly, making effective use of the railroads and giving the automobile its baptism as an instrument of war by sending armored motor trucks along with their cavalry. Nevertheless, the Schlieffen Plan was botched from the very start, and for several reasons. Among them four are notable: (1) Because of Italy's neutrality, the French were able to move more troops against the Germans than had been expected. (2) Belgian resistance was unexpectedly strong, holding up the Germans for eighteen days. (3) Because of Japanese cooperativeness, the Russians had been able to leave eastern Siberia unprotected and to amass troops near the German and Austrian borders as early as the spring of 1914. (4) The French plan of campaign—named the "Joffre Plan" after the French Chief of Staff Joseph Joffre—called for a quick attack on Germany in the Alsace-Lorraine area, and Moltke had to weaken the German armies in Belgium in order to make a counteroffensive in that area. The French invasion quickly met with decisive defeat, but it helped to throw the German advance off schedule. In short, the Belgians, the French, and the Russians were stronger than the Germans had calculated. It was not until August 20 that Brussels surrendered to the Germans. Only at the end of August did the Germans invade France where, according to their plans, they should have been more than two weeks earlier. At this point Moltke, thinking the French situation was well in hand, further weakened his forces in order to send a large contingent to the hard-pressed Russian front.

The Belgians, British, and French kept retreating until September 5. On that day the Germans were so close to Paris that they could see the Eiffel Tower. But they were in a dangerous strategic position. Their lines were overextended, entire army commands had lost touch with each other, and intelligence service was inadequate. Joffre took full advantage of the German difficulties. He rapidly moved all the troops and supplies he could spare against the Germans, mobilizing Paris taxis to transport troops. From September 5 to 12, the invaders were thrown back in the Battle of the Marne.

The race to the sea and the start of trench warfare

THE GERMANS to the northwest retreated to the Aisne River, and those to the east therefore had to retreat likewise. The western flanks of both armies were now exposed, and a race to the sea began, each contestant striving to outflank the other. The highlight was the First Battle of Ypres (October 30-November 24), in which for over three weeks Europe's manhood was slaughtered in the longest and

THE FAILURE OF THE SCHLIEFFEN PLAN

UNITED
KINGDOM

Masurian Lakes

RUSSIA

Tannenberg

BELGIUM

Ypres

GERMANY

Paris

GALICIA

Marne R.

AUSTRIA-
HUNGARY

FRANCE

MONTENEGRO

SERBIA

BULGARIA

TURKEY

▨ *Allies 1914*
■ *Central Powers 1914*
•••• *Farthest German advances
on western front*

German strategy and diplomacy in 1914 was predicated on a quick paralyzing swing through Belgium and northeastern France, while a holding army contained the Russians until the full German force could be transferred against them. When the Schlieffen Plan stalled—partly because Italy, the third member of the Triple Alliance, remained neutral, and Belgium and France put up surprisingly strong resistance—the war on the Western Front became a four-year stalemate. On the Eastern Front the Central Powers were more successful, defeating the Russians at Tannenberg and the Masurian Lakes.

bloodiest battle to that time. Neither army succeeded in outflanking the other. The lines became frozen, figuratively at first and soon literally as winter set in. Two lines of trenches extending from the Channel to the Swiss border were to face each other for nearly four years without either being able to make a good-sized dent in the other until March 1918. The Germans had, however, won the coal fields of Belgium and northern France, the iron deposits of French Lorraine, and the food supplies and harvests of the conquered peoples. Without these essential resources they might not have been able to hold out as long as they did.

*The war
on the Eastern Front in 1914*

MEANWHILE, the Russian armies had marched against Austria-Hungary. Austrian troops already dispatched to the Serbian border had suddenly to be diverted to meet the threat. Railroad lines became clogged, with resulting dislocation of army units. The Russians quickly conquered almost all of the province of Galicia. The Austrians never fully recovered from that setback. Their defeats, amounting to a military catastrophe, made it impossible to "punish" Serbia. Two weak invasions by Austria in 1914 were beaten back.

In their invasion of East Prussia, the Russians did not fare so well as in Galicia and suffered two heavy defeats. The first took place in the Battle of Tannenberg (August 26-30), where they were defeated by Generals Paul von Hindenburg and Erich von Ludendorff, who from that time on became popular German heroes. As the Russians retreated, they suffered a second great defeat in the Battle of the Masurian Lakes (September 6-15). In both battles the Germans took nearly a quarter of a million prisoners all together. In November and early December they succeeded in carrying the war deep into Poland. The eastern frontiers of Germany were never again seriously menaced.

The war
on the seas and in the colonies

THE BRITISH conducted the naval war with fairly traditional strategy. Before the year was over, the German cruiser squadrons were forced off the high seas by the Battle of the Falkland Islands (December 8), and only the German home fleet remained, stationed in the North and Baltic seas. The British also attacked the enemy's colonies. The German Pacific islands, Asiatic stations, and African colonies were picked off one by one by nearby dominions or allies. At the same time the British subjected the Central Powers to blockade, cutting them off from foodstuffs and raw materials. As early as January 1915, the food situation became so serious in Germany that bread rationing was introduced. Little by little practically everything edible and everything essential for the conduct of war, like metals, textiles, and raw materials, were rationed by the Central Powers. The added responsibility, particularly in Austria, made the bureaucracy creak under the strain.

The Germans' naval tactics were far from traditional. They made raids upon the British coast with battle cruisers; they employed the submarine for the first time as an effective instrument of war; and they rendered large stretches of ocean dangerous to the "Mistress of the Seas" by improved mine fields. One day in September a German submarine torpedoed three British cruisers in the North Sea in quick succession. Thus an entirely new offensive weapon made a spectacular entry into the history of warfare.

The winning
of new allies on both sides

THE SOUND of the opening guns in Europe had reverberated throughout the Orient. The war at first seemed a strictly European quarrel; yet the nations of Asia were concerned about possible armed conflicts between Europeans in the East and the effect that European war might have upon the balance of power in Asia and the Pacific region. Shortly after the outbreak of the war, Japan proposed to participate on the side of her British ally. Seldom was the aid of an ally less welcome, since there was good reason to fear that Japan meant to take advantage of Europe's difficulties to increase her holdings in eastern Asia. Unable to convince the Nipponese of their ability to fight without aid, the British vainly sought an agreement that Japan should limit her activities to naval actions against German shipping and war vessels. While reassuring London of its peaceful intentions with regard to China, Tokyo prepared to move against the German installations on the Shantung peninsula.

Upon the outbreak of war, President Yüan had proclaimed China's neutrality and requested the European belligerents not to extend their battles to China's waters or territory. Although Germany had a lease on Kiaochow, technical sovereignty in the peninsula remained in the hands of China. Tokyo in an ultimatum to Berlin required that Germany "deliver...to the Imperial Japanese authorities without condition or compensation the entire leased territory of Kiaochow, with a view to eventual restoration of the same to China." This ultimatum, however, was dispatched to Berlin without consulting China, and the Chinese were suspicious of Japan's motives. Peking tried to gain American support in restraining the Japanese but met with a coldly polite refusal. Acting Secretary of State Robert Lansing observed that "it would be quixotic in the extreme to allow the question of China's territorial integrity to entangle the United States in international difficulties." No satisfactory answer having been received by the date set, Japan declared war on Germany on August 23 and on Austria two days later. In the ensuing campaign against Germany's forces in Shantung, the Japanese ruthlessly violated China's neutrality, but the powers were not prepared to intervene on questions so far removed from their own war area and basic interests. By the end of the year the Japanese were in complete control of the territory in China formerly leased by the Germans. The German base at Kiaochow was besieged with British aid without regard to the fact that such an operation meant a violation of Chinese neutrality, and was taken after a two-month's siege.

The Turks were the next non-European power to enter the war. Fearful of a Russian victory, Turkey had made a secret treaty on August 1 pledging to join the Central Powers as soon as their military preparations were completed. Meanwhile they showed obvious favor to the Germans, allowing German battleships to escape pursuit by entering the Dardanelles. Without warning, Turkish warships fired upon the Russian coast (October 29), and Russia declared war a few days later (November 2). England and France followed suit on November 5.

The military and diplomatic fronts in 1915

OFFENSIVES by both sides on the Western Front in 1915 netted nothing substantial for either except unprecedented numbers of casualties. Many casualties were due to poison gas, which was used for the first time that spring by the Germans. In the hope of breaking the stalemate, offensives were undertaken on other fronts. (1) In May, the Germans and Austro-Hungarians started an attack in Galicia. It met with marked success and did not come to a stop until September, when the Central Powers held a line stretching from the Bukovina to the

Gulf of Riga. (2) From March to December, in an effort to unite forces with the Russians, an Anglo-French armada attempted to force the opening of the Dardanelles, defended by a new line of fortifications and a rejuvenated army under Liman von Sanders. After sustaining very heavy losses in men and ships, the Allied forces finally withdrew to Greece, still formally neutral, and elsewhere; and the Russians were left effectively isolated.

Meanwhile, on the diplomatic front, the Allies had won a great victory. If Italy had gone into the war on the German side, France might have been overwhelmed in 1914 as she was to be in 1940. Sympathy for the Allied cause grew steadily in Italy after the war began. Moreover, the government, anxious to win as much unredeemed territory as possible, and having some reason to believe that Italy's intervention would be decisive, negotiated secretly with both sides. Since most of the territory that Italy wanted was Austrian and Turkish, Italy signed a secret treaty at London in April and entered the war on the side of the western powers on May 23, 1915. The new front did not, however, prove decisive. Fighting between the Italians and the Austro-Hungarians, mostly along the Isonzo River, remained inconclusive all during 1915.

Bulgaria, inveterate enemy of Serbia, offset the Allied diplomatic success somewhat when she entered the war on the side of the Central Powers in October, since in this instance the situation was reversed and the Germans were prepared to offer Bulgaria more territory that Serbia also coveted than were the Allies. The Bulgarian intervention was fairly decisive in the Balkans. Despite the removal from the Dardanelles campaign of an Anglo-French force to nominally neutral Greece, the Bulgarians crushed Serbia and forced the Serbian army to take refuge on the island of Corfu, thereby opening a direct line of conquered territory from Berlin to Constantinople. Montenegro, overrun by the Austrians, was the first belligerent to quit.

The new character of maritime warfare

AMONG THE German admirals a conflict raged over whether the battle fleet should be sent against the British or kept in the German ports to serve as a bargaining asset in case the war should prove indecisive. Except for limited engagements, no naval battle was to take place until 1916, since the Kaiser and Admiral von Tirpitz had concluded that the risk was too great. Although they had insisted previously upon constructing huge battleships, they now decided in favor of submarine warfare. In February 1915, Germany declared a blockade of Great Britain, intending to enforce the blockade by means of submarines. Great Britain's reprisal was to declare that it would no longer recognize the time-honored distinctions between contraband of war and other kinds of goods and would seize any goods, neutral or otherwise, intended for the enemy. The United States as the largest and most vulnerable neutral was again, as in previous wars, badly hurt by blockade and counterblockade. Since the beginning of the war, it had sternly protested British restrictions upon American goods intended for Germany and the British practice of blacklisting American firms believed to be trading with the Central Powers. Nevertheless, the British were given to understand that President Wilson's government did not intend to make war on these issues.

Growth of anti-German sentiment in the United States

GERMANY'S use of the submarine, whose international standing as a war weapon was in considerable doubt, seemed a greater menace to American shipping. It added to the ill-feeling against the Central Powers already created in America by the "rape of Belgium," the Turkish massacre of the Armenians in 1915, and the generally superior British propaganda. When the United States complained about German restriction of the freedom of the seas, Germany proclaimed her willingness to abandon submarine warfare provided Great Britain would grant free access to foodstuffs and raw materials intended for the Central Powers. Great Britain declared that she was ready to make concessions only so far as food was concerned. That, the Germans contended, was not enough, and they went ahead with their submarine war. Americans were outraged when they learned that passenger ships (including one American vessel) were being sunk without warning. But worse was yet to come.

Early in May the British luxury liner *Lusitania* was scheduled to leave the port of New York for England. The German ambassador at Washington publicly warned American citizens through a newspaper advertisement adjacent to one for the *Lusitania* not to embark on her because she was liable to destruction by German submarines. The ship actually was carrying American-made ammunition for Great Britain, but that fact was not known to the American public, and the warning, coming on the day of departure, was too late anyway. The *Lusitania* was unarmed, but as an enemy vessel carrying war material she was subject at least to capture according to international law. A submarine, however, cannot take prizes easily. When the *Lusitania* was south of the Irish coast, she was torpedoed without warning. About 1200 people went down with her, among them more than 100 Americans.

International law regarding submarine warfare was relatively untried. Judicially, the Germans were perhaps within their rights, though it was certainly controversial whether an unresisting passenger ship might be sunk without warning. Politically, the Germans had committed another blunder. What made things worse was that all over Germany the sinking of the *Lusitania* was celebrated as a great victory, with flags and parades of war-intoxicated citizens. And indeed, if public opinion in the largest remaining neutral country had not been at stake, the Germans might well have believed they had won a major victory, for the sinking of the *Lusitania* demonstrated that the submarine was an effective instrument of blockade.

AT THE TIME, the United States was involved in confused, warlike relations with Mexico (page 550). Moreover, despite the rising public disgust, a strong anti-Allied sentiment survived in the United States among citizens of German descent, among American Poles and Jews who resented Russian mistreatment of their peoples, among inhabitants of the West Coast who were apprehensive about Japanese aggrandizement, and among the Irish-Americans and large numbers of other Americans who had learned in school to look upon England as the traditional enemy. In general, the people of the United States preferred to remain at peace, regardless of which side had their sympathies. Hence President Wilson, who hoped to keep the country out of the war, restricted himself to a stern demand for an apology, reparations, and a promise not to torpedo any other passenger vessels without warning. Bryan resigned as secretary of state because he thought the president's attitude too belligerent. The German government, lest America enter the war against her, ordered her submarine commanders not to attack passenger ships. In August, nevertheless, two Americans went down with another unwarned British liner. Finally in September the German ambassador let the United States government know that passenger vessels thereafter would be sunk only if they had been warned beforehand and if they then either tried to escape or offered resistance. All together more than four hundred Allied and neutral vessels were sunk in British home waters by German submarines (in addition to the vessels sunk by mines) before the end of 1915, and England was hard put to it to keep her sea lanes open. The Germans, however, were probably worse off. Early in 1916 they began to feel the brunt of the British blockade.

The Western Front: Verdun and the Somme (1916)

MOLTKE having suffered a breakdown, his successor as chief of staff, Erich von Falkenhayn, decided to destroy enemy resistance on the Western Front, which by common consent was the crucial theater. In February 1916, a formidable German force attacked the fortress of Verdun. Despite the attackers' initial successes, the French were able to prolong the titanic Battle of Verdun for nearly five months. Around 300,000 German and 350,000 French casualties filled the cemeteries and the hospitals. The French had determined that "they shall not pass," and they did not. French losses were so high that France's manpower was seriously crippled. Nevertheless, strategically Verdun was a German defeat, and the Allied front stood firm though shaken.

To reduce the pressure on Verdun, the Allies started a counteroffensive on the Somme. During the last week of June two thousand heavy guns kept the German lines continuously under fire. This barrage was followed by a drive that also lasted almost five months, until it was stopped by rain and mud. The Battle of the Somme proved as much of a disappointment to the Allies as the Battle of Verdun had been to the Germans. Again the losses were terrific on both sides. The first day the British alone lost 60,000 men. A new weapon, the tank, was thrown into battle by the British, but in numbers too small to be effective. The losses on each side were almost twice those at Verdun. In the two battles together the Germans lost around 850,000 and the Allies 950,000. The Germans could afford such losses less than could the Allies.

The struggle for control of the seas (1916)

MEANWHILE, blockade clashed with counterblockade. The Germans announced a new submarine campaign in February 1916, and the American president soon had to protest against new sinkings without warning that took the lives of several American citizens. A threat to break off diplomatic relations brought a new promise not to sink merchant vessels without warning, but the submarine took an enormous toll of Allied ships and cargoes even so. The only great naval battle of the war took place off the coast of Jutland on May 31 and June 1, 1916. The Germans won a tactical victory, the British losses in men and tonnage far exceeding those of the Germans. Strategically the battle was a British victory, however, for the Germans lost the same number of vessels and the British more than ever controlled the seas—or, at least, the surface of the seas. The German battle fleet, having had a narrow escape from annihilation, remained bottled up in the German ports for the remainder of the war.

The Eastern Front and the diplomatic front (1916)

THAT JUNE the Russians made a comeback. They conquered the Bukovina again, and the Austrians suffered such heavy losses and such a blow to their morale that from then on it was necessary to amalgamate Austrian and German forces in the east, with a consequent weakening of German forces in the west. The Russian advance was brought to a standstill in August. Meanwhile Russian success and the promise of pieces of territory at the expense of Hungary (especially Transylvania) induced Rumania to enter the war on the side of the Allies. This seeming diplomatic victory proved an almost fatal error. Rumania was crushed by a combined Austro-German army and lost most of her territory to the Central Powers, and her wheat fields and oil fields replenished the disappearing German supplies. Offsetting their victory over Rumania somewhat, the Germans had had to declare war on Portugal, which they could not reach. From the very outbreak of the war Portugal had remained loyal to her ancient alliance with Britain. She had taken part in the raids on German African colonies and had interned German ships. In 1916, therefore, the

Central Powers declared war upon her. The balance sheet at the close of 1916 showed that the Central Powers had won some tactical victories, but the Allies seemed still to hold marked strategical advantages.

Ireland and the Easter Rebellion

SO FAR Britain was the only belligerent power to have a serious civil conflict on her hands. A small Irish radical organization known as Sinn Fein ("We Ourselves") which had come into being around 1900, now resorted to open rebellion. The romantic Irish leader Sir Roger Casement proved willing to act with the Germans on behalf of Irish independence. A German submarine landed him on Good Friday, 1916, on the west coast of Ireland, with plans for an insurrection and promises of support. Accordingly, on Easter Monday (April 24) between 700 and 1000 Irish Volunteers rose in rebellion in Dublin under the leadership of an idealistic schoolteacher named Patrick Pearse. They seized several public buildings and hoisted the white, green, and orange flag of the Irish Republic on their roof tops. A big railroad station was occupied by the rebels under the command of Eamon De Valera. For a whole week fighting raged in Dublin between the Irish "Citizen Army" and the British, with heavy casualties on both sides and the main street of the city ablaze. Finally the revolt was crushed. Pearse and several other Sinn Fein leaders were shot. Casement was hanged for high treason in the Tower of London. De Valera got away with a prison term because he was a native American and the British were reluctant to put a national of a prospective ally to death. He was released from prison a year later. Although the Easter Rebellion was ill-advised and ill-timed, it ultimately proved helpful to the Sinn Fein cause, for the severe punishment meted out to the rebels created much resentment among the Irish.

The effect of the war upon the neutral countries

THE WAR brought serious predicaments to some of the neutral countries. Because of the blockade by both sides, neutrals as well as belligerents had sometimes to endure the rationing of essential commodities. Most of the neutral countries, even previously half-bankrupt Spain, became prosperous because the belligerents were ready to pay huge prices for their products, but politically they were often under a heavy strain. The neutrality of Luxemburg, Belgium, Greece, and China had been violated by one side or the other. An invasion of the Netherlands, proposed by Ludendorff, was prevented only by the veto of the Kaiser. Every neutral country had a pro-German and pro-Allied party. Switzerland set an example of immaculate neutrality, not even allowing its press to color its articles in favor of either party. In the United States, on the other hand, the heated debate between the pro-Germans and the pro-Allies became a major issue in the presidential election of 1916. By only a narrow margin, Wilson was reëlected to the presidency, appealing to the peace vote under the slogan: "He kept us out of war." Wilson, believing that the war had now reached a stalemate, thought the moment ripe for mediating peace. Lest the United States also be dragged into the war, he now tried to get both sides to agree to "peace without victory."

The peace probe
of Emperor Charles I

FEW KNEW it, except in a hazy way, but Austria had also begun to probe for peace. The assassination of the Austrian prime minister by a prominent Socialist in October 1916 revealed how thin the patience of the starving population had worn. Emperor Francis Joseph died the next November. His successor Charles I (or Charles IV as king of Hungary) wanted peace badly. He publicly declared that he had had no part in starting the war, thus dissociating himself from the warmongers. He realized also that the loyalty of the Slav nations of his empire was uncertain, and he rightly feared that if war were not brought to an end soon, the empire would fall apart. His wife's brother, having been rejected by the French army because of his family, was serving with the Belgians, and Charles approached the Allies through him. But this peace feeler ran into headlong collision with the war aims of Italy. The king of Italy felt that he could not accept peace on any terms that the Austrian emperor dared to offer. In the midst of these secret negotiations, the United States entered the war, and the Allies, sure of ultimate victory now, turned their backs upon this opportunity.

The renewal
of unrestricted submarine warfare

WITHOUT Wilson's knowledge, his peace efforts coincided with the urgent demands of Hindenburg, now chief of staff, and Ludendorff, Hindenburg's principal adviser, for a resumption of unrestricted submarine warfare. They believed that even if a German decision to that effect should bring about America's armed intervention, the submarines would have starved Great Britain into submission before any American army could be sent to Europe, and the submarines would also be able to prevent its landing.

During the whole of January 1917, President Wilson negotiated with both sides. Neither showed any inclination, however, to be the first to make concessions, though he was left with the belief that his general peace effort was approved by the German government. Meanwhile, Bethmann-Hollweg, who had hesitated to renew unrestricted submarine war, gave in to the generals, and a crown council decided that unrestricted submarine warfare should begin again on February 1. The day before that, Germany publicly declared that certain sea areas surrounding Great Britain, France, and Italy were zones in which all traffic was prohibited and would be "prevented by all weapons."

598

The World at War 1914-1918 labels on map:
JUTLAND

German submarine blockade

Dardanelles

Kiaochow

TOGOLAND

CAMEROONS

GERMAN EAST AFRICA

GERMAN SOUTHWEST AFRICA

MARIANAS IS.
MARSHALL IS.
CAROLINE IS.
SAMOA
GERMAN NEW GUINEA

THE WORLD AT WAR 1914-1918

FALKLAND IS.

⇨ *Allied and Associated Powers*

▢ *Central Powers*

The war, which at first seemed a strictly European affair, soon became worldwide. New allies joined both sides, until by 1918 only the areas shown in light shading remained neutral. The land war spread from the Western and Eastern fronts envisaged by Schlieffen to northern Italy, the Near East, and the Middle East where, as on the Eastern and Western fronts, land offensives are indicated by arrows. Naval warfare raged on all the oceans, particularly from the North Sea to the South Atlantic. Germany's holdings in China and Oceania north of the equator were seized by Japan early in the war, German New Guinea and Samoa by Australia and New Zealand. In Africa, German Togoland and Cameroons fell to French and British forces, South African forces took German Southwest Africa, and German East Africa eventually was conquered by British, Indian, and Portuguese efforts. The short-lived German empire overseas thus ceased to exist.

The entrance of the Americas into the war

THIS ANNOUNCEMENT put an end to Wilson's position, proclaimed shortly after the *Lusitania* episode, that the United States was "too proud to fight." As he had threatened on an earlier occasion if unrestricted submarine warfare were renewed, he immediately broke off diplomatic relations with Germany. In the expectation of that contingency, the Germans had taken another miscalculated risk. The German foreign office had proffered Mexico an alliance. Mexico, it was proposed, should mediate peace between Germany and Japan, and in return for siding with Germany the Mexicans were to get back some of the territory acquired by the United States in the Mexican War of 1846-1848. That fantastic suggestion became known as the "Zimmermann note," after the German minister of foreign affairs who had dispatched it. The text of the note came to the knowledge of the British secret service, who informed the United States government of it.

Meanwhile Wilson had asked Congress for permission to arm American merchant vessels, but a filibuster by four antiwar senators made it necessary for him to do so on his own authority, as a law going back to the "Undeclared War" with France permitted. Despite this armed neutrality, German subma-

599

rines torpedoed five American vessels without warning, and American lives were lost. At the same time, the Zimmermann note became known, shocking a large part of the American public into an anti-German furor. Then the welcome news of a democratic revolution in Russia (page 603) arrived, removing the scruples of those who had hesitated to fight on the side of czardom. On April 6, 1917, the United States declared war upon Germany. Although she did not join the Allies formally, she immediately began naval, economic, and military cooperation as an "associated power." Before the war ended, a number of Latin-American countries—Panama, Cuba, Brazil, Guatemala, Nicaragua, Costa Rica, Haiti, and Honduras—followed the United States into the war.

The "Twenty-one Demands" upon China by the Japanese — IN AUGUST 1917, China entered the war on the side of the Allies, including Japan. Strange as this step may seem, it was a result of accumulating tension between Tokyo and Peking regarding Shantung (page 592). As a climax to their growing hostility toward China, the Japanese in 1915 had presented the Chinese government with "Twenty-one Demands." These "Demands" provided conspicuous symptoms of Nippon's increasing aggressiveness. Highly complex and detailed, they virtually required China to become a Japanese protectorate. Arranged in five groups with numerous subheadings, the demands called upon China to permit the Japanese in the name of peace in eastern Asia to assume virtual control over its wealthiest and most strategically located provinces, to grant the Japanese a dominant role in the railway systems of China, to accept Japanese political and military advisers, and to agree to a system of joint police administration. With the example of Korea's gradual annexation in mind, China and the powers viewed Japan's "Demands" as the first step in a studied Nipponese effort to shear the locks of the Samson of the Far East.

Upon learning of the compromising character of Japan's proposal to China, the United States sought to restrain the islanders. Washington was joined by London in making overtures calculated to let the Japanese appreciate how suspect their "Demands" appeared to the West. The Japanese nevertheless delivered an ultimatum to China requiring the acceptance of most of their "Demands." At this juncture Bryan, who was American secretary of state at the time, let it be known that no matter what agreements Japan should impose upon China, the United States would not recognize any that violated American treaty rights in China, the political or territorial integrity of China, or the policy of the open door. Thus, Bryan laid the foundations of an American policy of nonrecognition, which was to play an important part in later efforts to halt aggression. In spite of Bryan's pronouncement the Japanese forced China to accept an amended but still highly objectionable version of the "Demands." The result was a Sino-Japanese treaty (1915) that became a serious complicating factor in later international relations, since many doubted whether the treaty was legal.

Declaration of war by the Chinese Republic

IN CHINA, little resistance arose against Japan's "Demands," and that little was forced into the background in 1916 by the death of President Yüan. Despite his machinations to revive the monarchy, Yüan had been able to serve as a symbol, however feeble, of the ancient unity of China. Upon his death China's military leaders (war lords) began to fight among themselves, and civil war again swept China. The powers continued to recognize the Peking governors as the legal rulers of China, but Peking's area of jurisdiction was sharply cut down as the civil war went on. In the south the Kuomintang (National People's Party) proceeded after 1916 to organize an independent government.

The Japanese, meanwhile, put the domestic confusion of China to their own advantage. By 1916 the European powers had come to realize that the war would be long and desperate, and Japan's allies were anxious to preserve her good will. The beleaguered czarist government of Russia readily signed a treaty with Japan providing that Russia would support Japanese claims in the Far East at the forthcoming peace conference. Russia consented to the Sino-Japanese arrangements in return for Japanese recognition of Russia's special interest in another province of China, Outer Mongolia. When the Japanese in 1917 extended their control into Inner Mongolia, some Chinese troops put up an ineffective resistance. The result was only new demands by Japan, which China had to allow. Great Britain, France, and Italy likewise made agreements with Japan, supporting her claims in the Far East.

In 1917, however, the American declaration of war against the Central Powers considerably reduced the need of the European powers for Japanese cooperation. Thereafter, they began to pursue a more independent course and to become more wary of promises for the future. At the same time, the prospect of American participation in the peace negotiations led the Chinese to feel hopeful. Hostility to Japanese aggression was almost the only thing on which the diverse groups in China could reach even temporary agreement. To rid China of foreign control, all Chinese factions were prepared to concede that China too must participate in the postwar negotiations. Defying Japan's objections, therefore, the Peking government in 1917 declared war upon the Central Powers, expecting thereby to assure itself of at least a seat at the peace conference. The Allied governments had cajoled China into that step by releasing her altogether from her German and Austrian obligations and surrendering their own Boxer indemnities for five years.

If the American declaration of war encouraged Japan's rivals in the Far

East, it also tied the hands of the United States somewhat. As a logical step in preparing for peace, Japan now sought an agreement that would assure American support in the peace arrangements. Being in no position to offend Japan, the United States consented to an exchange of notes between the two foreign offices. The resulting Lansing-Ishii notes recognized that "territorial propinquity creates special relations between countries, and, consequently, the government of the United States recognizes that Japan has special interests in China." In return for this concession Washington received Tokyo's consent to respect the policy of the open door in China. It was soon to become clear, however, that Washington and Tokyo differed widely in their understanding of what "special interests" Japan could rightfully claim to have in China.

The beginning of total warfare (1916-1917)

BY NOVEMBER 1916, Germany had become the first power since France in the days of the Terror to undertake total war. Every German unable to take up arms was rendered liable to serve his country in some other capacity. Thus the whole nation was mobilized. Manpower, whether military or noncombatant, economic resources, and public opinion were put under the control of the state. Everything essential or scarce was rationed, and the state became the provider as well as the provided. The German people did not take kindly to these innovations. To make matters worse, the winter of 1916-1917 was one of the longest and harshest winters in European history. It became known as the "turnip winter," because turnips in every conceivable form constituted the major food of a large part of the population. Rumblings of popular protest were plainly audible, but the generals, intent upon ending the war with a brilliant victory that spring, failed to understand the mood of the people. Similar mobilization measures were applied in Austria. Although they were less efficiently administered there, the same rumblings could be heard.

The Allies solved the shortage of factory and farm hands in a different way. British control of the seas enabled the French to import thousands of African Negroes and Indochinese coolies from their colonies either to work on the farms and in the factories or to serve in the army. The stresses in England, France, and Italy were, however, also severe. All three countries had resorted to rationing essential products through "munitions dictators" and "food dictators," although they were not so close to the "bottom of the barrel" as was Germany at the end of 1916. All of them too, including Great Britain (1916), had resorted to conscription to raise armies of millions. Hard pressed though the Allies were, by 1917 they were buoyed up by the conviction that American armies and supplies would arrive in time. The Germans could harbor no such consolation. The list of their possible allies was exhausted. But an unexpected event might have saved them, had they used it wisely.

*Two revolutions
in St. Petersburg in 1917*

IN MARCH 1917, czardom in Russia broke down. The backwardness of her industry, the inefficiency and corruption of her bureaucrats, the mismanagement of her military, and the strange conduct of an imperial court given to pseudoreligious mysticism made Russia unfit to wage a long war. The victory of Turkey in the Dardanelles campaign had left Russia without direct naval or commercial contact with her allies or the ability to rearm, particularly after heavy defeats had deprived her of most of her artillery and ammunition. Dismissals, concessions, even the assassination of the empress' holy man, Grigori Rasputin, did not assuage the Duma or the people. Then to top off their troubles, the Russians had to face the hard winter of 1916-1917 without sufficient food supplies to stave off famine. Strikes began in St. Petersburg, and finally the whole people revolted. Within a few days czarist rule collapsed. A provisional government including the Constitutional Democrat historian Paul Milyukov and the Social Revolutionary Alexander Kerensky took over. A cry went up in Russia for "peace without annexations and without indemnities." Nevertheless, the new Russian government, anxious to play its international role well and to restore domestic confidence, started a new offensive in the summer of 1917. The offensive was stopped by the Germans, who now added some new conquests to the vast Russian territories they had already occupied.

Internal dissensions tore Russia asunder. The Bolsheviks (who have since become known as the Communists) were bent on ending the war and beginning the long-prognosticated international socialist revolution in Russia. To instigate further dissension in Russia, the Germans allowed Nikolai Lenin and a few of his exiled friends to pass from Switzerland through Germany in a sealed railroad car. The German authorities hoped that Lenin would pull Russia out of the international war in order to concentrate upon a civil war inside Russia. In the ensuing anarchy Lenin skillfully organized a military corps of revolutionary soldiers and workers. In November, with the support of these "Red Guards," the Bolsheviks seized power in Russia, and they soon announced to the world that they were inviting all the warring peoples to conclude "an immediate armistice on all fronts, with the purpose of immediately opening *pourparlers* for the conclusion of a democratic peace."

*Bethmann's resignation
and the ascendency of Ludendorff*

A GOODLY portion of the people of the belligerent countries sympathized with the Russian demand for a negotiated peace without annexations. When czardom first broke down, the German people had expected their government to take advantage of the enemy's willingness to negotiate. But as the months wore on and the German government did nothing, they became restive. The Bolshevik peace proposal brought about a political crisis. Bethmann-Hollweg had lost the support of the conservative parties because, to win greater popular support for the war effort, he had granted reform of the Prussian franchise, at long last abolishing the three-class system of voting. With his approval, the Center Party now placed before the Reichstag a so-called "Peace Resolution." Hindenburg and Ludendorff, believing that Russian collapse was imminent, hastened to Berlin and obliged the Kaiser to require Bethmann's resignation. A combination of Center and Left deputies nevertheless adopted the Peace Resolution on July 19. But its effect was vitiated from the start because the new chancellor, Dr. Georg Michaelis, a puppet of Ludendorff, publicly declared that his policy could not be carried out within the framework of the resolution.

An attempted mediation by Pope Benedict XV in the interests of peace met with a similar fate, and for much the same reason. Ludendorff had become the virtual dictator of Germany, with the Kaiser and the chancellor as figureheads. Despite his great gifts as a military leader, the general lacked political understanding. He failed especially to take account of the situation of Germany's allies, Austria-Hungary, Bulgaria, and Turkey, all of which were fast approaching the end of their endurance. The Greek statesman Eleutherios Venizelos had made a better guess as to the probable outcome. Only the pro-German sympathies of the Greek king, Constantine, kept his country nominally neutral, but in June 1917, Constantine abdicated, and Greece declared war on the Central Powers.

The near-success of the Central Powers in 1917

MEANWHILE the fighting went on uninterruptedly. The Germans, to save man power, retired in certain areas on the Western Front to prepared trenches known as the Hindenburg Line. This operation was completed just in time to receive the great Anglo-French offensive of April 1917. The Allied attack was repelled with very heavy losses, and as a consequence mutinies broke out in several French divisions. Later that year (October), Italy suffered a disastrous defeat at the hands of an enlarged German-Austrian army in the Battle of Caporetto, which almost entailed the collapse of the Italian army, already exhausted by two years of effort on the unfavorable Isonzo front. Russia gave up late in November. Encouraged by these favorable turns, Ludendorff persisted in the thought that he would still be able to win the war and to dictate the peace. But before the peace negotiations with Russia started, two events occurred that were ominous for Germany's ultimate success. One was a series of victories of the Arab countries (page 612), which heralded the end of the Ottoman Empire. The other was the appearance of the tank in decisive quantities.

New weapons in a technological war

THE FIRST WORLD WAR was a contest in technological skill. Just as naval warfare had undergone great modification by the use of dreadnoughts, submarines, and improved mines, so land warfare had been revolutionized by the use of the automobile,

604

the land mine, the hand grenade, the flame thrower, poison gas, the tank, and improved artillery and machine guns. The dirigible was used for reconnaissance and occasional bombings; airplanes were useful for these purposes as well and also to fight dirigibles and each other. The Diesel engine burning oil as a fuel was used for the first time to drive war vessels. The Germans had a gun called the "Big Bertha" (named for Bertha Krupp) that for a period of nearly five months bombarded Paris about every three days from a distance of over seventy-five miles.

The weapon that perhaps more than any other was responsible for the ultimate victory of the Allies was the tank. It was first used in large numbers by the British during the two weeks' Battle of Cambrai in November 1917. Nearly four hundred of these iron monsters caused terrible havoc among the Germans. The Germans were saved from disaster only because the British themselves, not realizing the potentialities of their new weapon, had not provided enough infantry to follow the tanks, and the exhausted foot soldier could not, against the inevitable German counterattacks, keep the ground that the tanks had captured.

The Conference and Treaty of Brest-Litovsk NONE OF THE belligerents accepted the invitation of the Bolshevik government to make peace without annexations or indemnities. So the Bolsheviks, considering the war a capitalist error anyway and unwilling to divert attention from their domestic revolution any longer, decided to make peace themselves. In December Russia signed an armistice with her enemies, and peace negotiations were opened at Brest-Litovsk.

From the very beginning it was obvious that to the Russians the peace conference was, among other things, a sounding board for revolutionary propaganda. Therefore they strove to delay the negotiations as long as possible. To the Germans the conference was just a means of dictating a peace that a defeated Russia was to sign on the dotted line. The Germans wanted a peace treaty quickly so that they could devote their full attention to their enemies in the west before the Americans arrived; since the Bolshevik Revolution (November 7), they had been shifting the bulk of their eastern armies westward. The Russians, however, refused to consider any annexations. The Germans agreed to ask for none if Russia's allies would accept the principle of no annexations and no indemnities. The Allied powers, uncertain of what attitude to take toward the Bolshevik government and fairly certain of ultimate victory, declined to answer directly (page 608) when Leon Trotsky, the people's commissar for foreign affairs, asked them. Thereupon the Germans made some stiff demands. In February 1918, Trotsky broke off negotiations, claiming that the war was over even though no peace had been signed. Thereupon German and Austrian units marched into Russia practically unopposed. The Russians finally capitulated and in March signed a peace.

The terms of the Treaty of Brest-Litovsk were so severe that they have frequently been considered justification for the severity that the Germans themselves were later to encounter. The Russians gave up Poland, Courland, and Lithuania. They evacuated Livonia, Estonia, Finland, and the Aland Islands. They not only evacuated the Ukraine but had also to recognize the treaty of alliance that the Central Powers had concluded with the puppet government of the newly created Ukrainian People's Republic. They restored the Transcaucasian districts to Turkey. Finally, they promised to demobilize and to refrain from "any agitation or propaganda" in the lands of the Central Powers as well as "all interference in the internal relations" of the ceded territories. Most of these provisions were merely recognition of *faits accomplis,* since the Russian Empire had begun to disintegrate the moment the czar was overthrown. The German intention was obviously to assure and to hasten the process.

Civil war and Allied intervention in Russia

THE ANTI-BOLSHEVIKS in Russia were numerous, but they were split into many factions. Some of them, however, joined forces temporarily for the purpose of driving the Bolsheviks from power. The Bolsheviks, having adopted the red flag as their symbol, became known as the "Reds." The anti-Bolsheviks became known as the "Whites." Even before the conclusion of the Treaty of Brest-Litovsk the Allied powers had openly planned to intervene in Russia. Among the Allied countries France became most insistent upon backing the Whites. Ever since the rapprochement of France and czarist Russia in the 1880's, Frenchmen had invested heavily in the numerous loans made by French banking houses to Russia. Since such an investment blended patriotism with good business, France had put about 16,000,000,000 francs into Russia between 1887 and 1917. Now the Communists repudiated the czarist debt (January 1918), and the French Government was foremost among those who hoped, by ousting the Bolsheviks, to bring back a government that would honor old debts and resume interest payments. But, if the French were to lose the Russian alliance along with their investments, they hoped to build up a new Poland as a substitute to help them counterbalance Germany. Hence they supported the Polish claims on former Russian territories. Furthermore, the Allies had set up huge ammunition and matériel dumps in Murmansk, Archangel, Vladivostok, and other ports, and, looking upon the Bolsheviks as Germany's henchmen, they feared that the Germans would step in and seize these war supplies. Finally, the Russians annoyed the capitalistic countries with Communist propaganda and the threat of the spread of Communism.

Confusion of motives led to confused military situations. The Germans tried to retain control of the Ukraine; the French and the British seized Murmansk and Archangel; a Czech legion made up of Austrian army men who had escaped from Russian prisons held the Trans-Siberian Railroad. Simultaneously, the Whites moved in from east, west, and south. The situation became so dangerous in the summer of 1918 that the Bolshevik government found it expedient to have the czar, his wife, and their children murdered in a little town where they were held captive, and thus do away with one rallying-point of reaction.

Japan's designs upon eastern Siberia

A NEW STRAIN in the relations of Washington and Tokyo arose from the temporary collapse of Russia as a factor in the Far Eastern balance of power. Although Russia's withdrawal as a contestant left Japan in a weightier position, Japan evinced profound concern over the unilateral action of the Bolshevik government in stepping aside. Japan had little to gain from a German victory. Moreover, the Japanese too, like the French and the English, suffered financial losses when the Bolsheviks repudiated the debts of the czarist regime. Moreover, Japan, like the other Allies, distrusted the Bolsheviks as henchmen of the Germans, shared the fear of the spread of revolution, and sought to preserve the stockpiles of Allied war materials in Russia. Rumors spread that German and Austrian prisoners of war in Siberia might be given arms and supplies stored at Vladivostok and elsewhere to use against the Allied powers and the heroic pro-Ally Czechoslovak force.

England, France, and Japan exerted pressure on President Wilson to cooperate in military action against the Bolshevik regime. But the memory of joint intervention in the Chinese Boxer Rebellion and of the subsequent international complications prompted the United States to view a multipower intervention in Russia with foreboding. The ultimate decision of Wilson's administration to acquiesce was perhaps influenced more by fear of Japan's stated determination to "act alone" in eastern Siberia than by the pleas of the European powers for aid. Agreeing in the summer of 1918 to participate in the intervention, Washington sought to limit the number of troops engaged.

In Siberia leadership in the intervention fell by force of circumstances to Japan. Taking advantage of the capture of Vladivostok by the self-directed, rampaging Czechoslovak forces, the Allied powers placed the city under Allied protection. Thereupon, the Japanese, without waiting for their allies except for some Chinese contingents, poured streams of troops into eastern Siberia through Manchuria, Korea, Vladivostok, and Nikolaevsk. It soon began to look as if Japan's intentions were not merely defensive. Upon arriving on Russian soil, the Japanese forces pushed swiftly westward along the Trans-Siberian Railroad and through the Maritime Territory of eastern Siberia. On Sakhalin a Japanese force began to invade Russia's northern half of the island. In their determination to control Siberia east of Lake Baikal the Japanese combined forces with all anti-Bolshevik elements in Russia. The slight deference paid by Japan to the wishes of her allies aroused bitter feeling and dark suspicions about her ultimate aims.

*The Treaty
of Bucharest (1918)*

THE APPARENT doom of Russia had meanwhile brought on the surrender of Rumania. In December 1917 the Rumanians signed an armistice, and peace was concluded at Bucharest the next May. Its terms were in some ways as harsh as those imposed upon Russia. By putting the Carpathian passes under the control of Austria-Hungary it practically transformed Rumania into an Austrian military outpost, and by giving the Germans a ninety-year lease on Rumania's oil it converted Rumania into a German sphere of economic influence. The treaties of Brest-Litovsk and Bucharest shocked Allied public opinion and helped to strengthen Allied determination, because the man in the street, no matter how defeatist he had become, thought he knew what to expect if the Allies lost the war.

*The "Fourteen Points"
of Wilson's peace proposal*

WHEN THE ALLIES refrained from expressing their adherence to the Bolshevik principle of "no annexations and no indemnities," they had to decide what terms they would consider as a satisfactory basis for peace, and two statements were soon forthcoming from Allied statesmen. In a speech to the British labor unions on January 5, 1918, Lloyd George laid down a set of war aims that corresponded with President Wilson's famous "Fourteen Points" enunciated three days later in an address to Congress. But the correspondence was far from perfect. The first of Wilson's Fourteen Points—his famous demand for "open covenants of peace openly arrived at"—was hardly welcome to Lloyd George and others who felt bound by the secret treaties among the Allies. Nor could a spokesman for Britain feel unreserved enthusiasm for some of the points that followed—"absolute freedom of navigation upon the seas" (point 2) and "absolutely impartial adjustment of all colonial claims" (point 5). And France, ever fearful of renewed German strength, might be expected to have some reservations regarding "the establishment of an equality of trade conditions among all the nations" (point 3) and the reduction of national armaments "to the lowest point consistent with domestic safety" (point 4). Nor, in view of their vested interests in Russia, could either France or England agree unconditionally to "the evacuation of all Russian territory and.... obtaining for her an unhampered and unembarrassed opportunity for the independent determination of her own political development" (point 6). For that matter, large sections of American opinion, in and out of Congress, had their own doubts about the wisdom of the first six points.

But the next eight overlapped Lloyd George's earlier proposals to a considerable degree. The first seven of these dealt with the areas that had come directly or indirectly under German domination during the war: the evacuation and restoration of Belgium "without any attempt to limit the sovereignty which she enjoys" (point 7); the evacuation and restoration of all French territory, and the righting of the "wrong done to France by Prussia in 1871 in the matter of Alsace-Lorraine" (point 8); the readjustment of Italian frontiers "along clearly recognizable lines of nationality" (point 9); "the freest opportunity of autonomous development" for the peoples of Austria-Hungary (point 10); the economic independence and territorial integrity of the several Balkan States (point 11); "absolutely unmolested opportunity of autonomous development" for the various nationalities within the Otto-man Empire (point 12); and an independent Polish state including "the terri-tories inhabited by indisputably Polish populations" and having "a free and secure access to the sea" (point 13). Finally, Wilson proposed the establish-ing of "a general association of nations....for the purpose of affording mutual guarantees of political independence and territorial integrity to great and small states alike."

Reactions to the Fourteen Points were mixed. The Allied governments publicly did not qualify them, but they regarded them with mental reserva-tions, well aware that some of the points were contrary to secret agreements concluded among the Allies. The Germans scorned the proposals because in January 1918 they still expected to win the war before American troops could arrive in significant numbers in Europe.

The German offensives in France (March-July 1918)

AT THE beginning of 1918 the Germans at last had practically a one-front war to fight, since Aus-tria was doing well against the Italians, and since the Arab revolts (page 612) seemed as yet indecisive for the Ottoman Empire. In the spring of 1918, Ludendorff with 600,000 men (many of them boys who should not have been called before 1920) attacked the British front in France on a fifty-mile sector from Arras to La Fère with more poison gas and more guns than had ever been used in one action before. This line was at the juncture of the Brit-ish and French forces. The British, outnumbered more than 3 to 1, gave up 90,000 as prisoners and 1300 guns the first day. They had to retreat and soon lost contact with the French. But the Allied lines did not break. In April, Ludendorff once more attacked the British, this time between Ypres and La Bassée. Here again he opened a wide gap in the British lines but could not break through. In neither offensive did he reach the coveted Channel ports.

After the first shock was over, the Allies appointed General Ferdinand Foch as supreme commander, unifying French, British, and Americans into a single army for the first time. The British sent 350,000 fresh troops across the Channel. The United States had adopted selective conscription in May 1917 and within a month had begun to send troops to France. The Americans in 1918 promised to send more than 600,000 men to France between March and July. That promise, despite German submarines, was

An American airfield in France. A study by J. Andre Smith, an official artist of the American Expeditionary Forces.

more than kept; by July over 1,000,000 and by November over 2,000,000 American soldiers had poured into France.

At the end of May, Ludendorff had started another offensive against the French. He gained so much territory that he again reached the Marne, but the gains did not give him the decision he sought. The American troops in France had finally acquired training in large enough numbers to be thrown decisively into battle. Shortly after the Ludendorff offensive began, the American First Division started a counteroffensive at Cantigny. Early in June, the Second and Third Divisions joined the French in first checking and then stopping Ludendorff's advance at Belleau Wood and Château-Thierry.

The last German thrusts and the defeat of Ludendorff

A NEW GERMAN thrust started on July 15, 1918. This time the Germans actually crossed the Marne, but that apparent success led to their undoing. For on July 18 Foch attacked their exposed right flank on a twenty-eight-mile front from around Soissons to Château-Thierry. No artillery barrage had given previous warning as hordes of tanks, covered by a creeping barrage, and all the air squadrons moved ahead of a huge Franco-American force of which the American contingent alone was nine divisions. Thereafter the initiative lay with Foch. This Second Battle of the Marne developed into a battle engulfing all of northeastern France.

The Germans never again gained the upper hand. August 8, 1918, was what Ludendorff later called his "black day." That day a combined Australian and Canadian tank army broke through the German lines. The Australian general John Monash, an engineer by profession, urged unremitting tank attacks. Foch, not grasping the magnitude of the German defeat on August 8, was more cautious, and the Germans rallied again. But, outnumbered and exhausted, they were steadily pushed back. In the ensuing Meuse-Argonne

610

offensive (which was only one of several Allied attacks on German trenches and railway lines) the American forces in less than two months fired more ammunition (by weight) than had been fired by the North during all four years of the American Civil War.

THE COLLAPSE
OF THE CENTRAL POWERS

THE EVENTUAL collapse of Bulgaria, Turkey, Austria-Hungary, and Germany is closely connected with the development of President Wilson's program of peace. In contemplating armistices, the Central Powers hoped that the Allies would feel bound by the idealism that had pervaded his public utterances. They were doomed to disappointment. Wilson may have been sincere when he described the conflict as "the culminating and final war for human liberty." But a more cynical sentiment, sometimes ascribed to Lloyd George, ultimately proved to be truer: "This war, like the next war, is a war to end war."

The collapse
of Germany's allies
THE GERMANS had been fighting practically without aid from their allies since June. Between June 15 and June 24 the Austrians had suffered a heavy defeat at the Piave at the hands of the reorganized Italians. The Italians then went on the offensive, and Austria's power of resistance broke completely at Vittorio Veneto (October 30). Meanwhile the subject peoples of the Dual Monarchy had declared their independence. Bulgaria and Turkey were at the same time nearing collapse. Nevertheless, it took the Allies until November to bring the war to a victorious conclusion. Victory was determined not so much by the defeat of Germany in France as by the total collapse of Germany's allies.

Bulgaria was the first to fold up. By June 1918 the Allies had an army of over 700,000 Italians, Serbs, French, English, and Greeks encamped north of Salonika. Finally, in September the Allied army drove through the Bulgarian lines. On September 30 Bulgaria signed an armistice that in effect meant surrender to the Allies. The first consequence of this surrender was that Rumania re-entered the war and the Allies mopped up all over the Balkans.

Turkey's position, already bad, thereby became worse. The Allies by the secret Sykes-Picot Agreement in 1916 had agreed on how they would split the Turkish empire among them. But this agreement did not take account either of Arab national aspirations or of promises made to Arab chiefs to induce them to revolt. Later that year Colonel T. E. Lawrence, thereafter known as "Lawrence of Arabia," by a combination of diplomatic skill and soldierly daring, induced the Arabs to revolt against Turkey. He afterwards described his venture in *The Seven Pillars of Wisdom,* one of the great war books of all time. While the Arabs were successfully pursuing their guerrilla warfare under Lawrence, the Turks were more occupied with their war against Russia, especially when the recovery of Transcaucasia became possible (page 606). The British under Sir Stanley Maude drove the Turks from Mesopotamia, taking Bagdad in March 1917. Toward the close of 1917, a British army under Field Marshal E. H. H. Allenby invaded Palestine from Egypt, and in a masterful campaign took Jerusalem. The need for his soldiers in France in the spring of 1918 obliged Allenby to go on the defensive. But in the early autumn he routed the Turks in Palestine, and with the aid of an Arab army, took Damascus. The way to Asia Minor lay open. On October 30, 1918, Turkey concluded an armistice with the Allies.

Meanwhile the Dual Monarchy had fallen asunder. On October 7, a Polish assembly at Warsaw had proclaimed an independent and united Polish nation. The Czechs declared their independence at Prague on October 28. The Serbs proclaimed a new Yugoslav (i.e., South Slav) union on October 29; they were rapidly recapturing their homeland, and they re-entered Belgrade on November 1. On the same day, Hungary declared its independence. Two days later the Italians captured Trieste, and that day (November 3, 1918) Austria-Hungary signed an armistice that was practically a surrender. Thus Germany was threatened by an invasion from the south at the same time that her generals were ready to admit defeat in France.

Wilson's commitment to the dissolution of Austria

WHEN COLLAPSE was close at hand, the Turks, the Austrians, and the Germans, in turn, remembering Wilson's plea for a world "fit and safe....for every peace-loving nation" turned to him for an armistice based on the Fourteen Points. But by that time the situation had changed. The Fourteen Points were perhaps valid in terms of American national interests, but they had already run into the harsh and uncompromising realities of European national interests. As a war measure, Wilson had recognized the Czechoslovak National Council as a *de facto* (and not merely "autonomous") government (September 2). When Austria-Hungary later asked "all belligerents to send delegates to a confidential and nonbinding discussion of basic principles," the president rejected the appeal on the grounds that he had already stated the basic principles. Furthermore, when the ruler of Austria-Hungary belatedly offered to federalize his empire, thus giving his subjects "the freest opportunity of autonomous development," the president rejected the offer, declaring that the United States could no longer accept "mere autonomy." Thus an Austrian Confederation, which some experts then and since have considered the best solution of the problem of economic interdependence and national incompatibility of the various countries in the Danubian area, was ruled out.

The German request
for a cessation of hostilities

EVEN BEFORE any of Germany's allies had surrendered, Ludendorff, with Hindenburg's approval, had urged upon the Kaiser (September 29, 1918) that an armistice be requested at once. The Kaiser immediately appointed a new chancellor who might appeal to the Allies as a relatively liberal statesman. He was Prince Max von Baden, heir to the grand-ducal crown of Baden. The prince felt that in order to obtain an armistice based on the Fourteen Points, two conditions would have to be met: (1) the generals must have no say in shaping Germany's foreign policy; and (2) the German constitution must be so remodeled as to transform Germany into a constitutional monarchy.

The sudden collapse of Germany caught the Allies unprepared. They had set up no machinery for peace negotiations. The first appeal for an armistice was made jointly by Austria and Germany on October 4. President Wilson lost several weeks making sure that the Germans were no longer ruled "by the arbitrary power which has hitherto controlled the German nation." The lapse of time meant more German setbacks on the battlefields and hence less pressure upon the European Allies to abide by Wilson's principles. It also gave Ludendorff, who had insisted on an armistice in September, a chance to begin insisting again on continuing the war, and it gave color to the subsequent legend in Germany that an army still able to resist was "stabbed in the back." But Ludendorff was dismissed from office on October 25; and on October 28 the German constitution was amended as Prince Max had suggested. Finally, on November 5, President Wilson informed the German government that it might apply for an armistice to Marshal Foch. The basic questions had been negotiated between London, Paris, Rome, and Washington; a large margin of freedom was left to Foch.

The overthrow
of the Second German Reich

DISRUPTION in Germany had advanced so far that the German government had to submit to anything Foch might impose. By the end of October the German sailors had reason to believe that the German admiralty had decided upon sacrificing the German fleet in a last-chance battle. Had that plan been carried out, it would perhaps have meant the pointless death of tens of thousands of sailors. The sailors at Kiel mutinied. Soldiers stationed in Germany and the workers sided with them. Within a week the revolutionary movement spread all over Germany, and all the ruling princes of Germany abdicated.

The Kaiser, who was at his general headquarters in Spa, Belgium, now made few heroic gestures. On the morning of November 9 he offered to abdicate as German emperor but not as king of Prussia. Prince Max was exasperated. In order to avoid a civil war, he declared on his own authority that the Kaiser had abdicated as emperor and king and that the Hohenzollern crown prince had renounced his rights in favor of his twelve-year-old son,   613 for whom a regency would be set up. Prince Max himself resigned from office, turning over the chancellorship to Friedrich Ebert, the leader of the Social Democrats. The Kaiser and the crown prince fled to Holland.

Ebert would have preferred to preserve the monarchy, but that course proved impossible. The leftist Independent Socialists and the newly organized Communists demanded a republic, and the Social Democrats stole their thunder lest the country be overtaken by a Communist revolution. They proclaimed the German Republic that afternoon. They did it without enthusiasm. A German government consisting of six commissars of the people and headed by Ebert was set up. It declared that it would stay in power only until, after a general election, a national constituent assembly determined the form of government.

The arrangement
of the terms of an armistice

BEFORE HIS resignation Prince Max, as directed by President Wilson, had sent an armistice commission to wait on Marshal Foch at Compiègne. Except for some military advisers, the German armistice delegation was composed of civilians—in part because the government hoped to counteract the deep-rooted distrust the Allies felt for the German militarists and in part because the military preferred to side-step the onus of surrender. Few could have foreseen that shortly Ludendorff would maintain that Germany had not lost the war, that the army was "stabbed in the back" by Social Democrats and Jews, and that if the generals had conducted the armistice negotiations the armistice would not have been so harsh. Still fewer could have foreseen that he would be believed by a large section of the German people.

The armistice terms indeed were not lenient. Germany was required to evacuate Belgium, Luxemburg, France, and Alsace-Lorraine within two weeks. All German territory west of the Rhine had to be evacuated within a month. The Allies were to occupy that territory and, in addition, a zone of thirty kilometers in width on the east bank of the Rhine. Russia, Rumania, and Turkey were to be evacuated. The Germans were obliged either to surrender or disarm their warships, submarines, and naval aircraft. These and some less significant provisions of the armistice conditions were no more than the Germans had expected. They had not expected, however, to be called upon to surrender such huge amounts of railroad stock and so many motor trucks that their whole transportation system would be disorganized. Nor had they expected that the blockade of Germany would be continued, with consequent malnutrition and economic stringency inside Germany. The intention behind these severe terms was to make Germany unable to renew hostilities. If they seemed harsh to the Germans, some among the Allies, especially among the French, who felt it was unwise to make any terms at all with the Germans before Berlin was captured, thought them too lenient. The armistice

614   was signed in a railroad car in the Forest of Compiègne on November 11,

1918. It became effective at 11 A.M. the same day. The new German Republic had made peace, but the Germans were never to be allowed by some of their countrymen to forget that it was a peace without honor.

THE IMPACT OF THE WAR

AND THE REVOLUTION

THE WAR of 1914-1918 had not been the first war fought all over the world. The wars of the so-called "Second Hundred Years' War" (1689-1815) had involved the world-wide empires of England, France, Holland, Spain, and Portugal, and hence had been fought on all the continents and high seas. But those wars had nevertheless been struggles of Europeans with only occasional and secondary participation by non-European peoples. The war of 1914-1918 was essentially a European war but one nevertheless in which non-European nations and peoples took prominent part both in Europe and at home. It was, in more than the geographical sense, the first global war, and its implications were global.

The United States
the principal victor of the war

A STRIKING result of the war was the shift of the center of gravity, political, military, and economic (but not yet cultural), from Europe to America. Before the war six great powers had maneuvered for advantage in Europe. When the war was over, Austria-Hungary had ceased to exist; Russia was in the turmoils of civil war, intervention, and revolution; Germany was in a state of chaos; only Great Britain, France, and Italy were left as Europe's great powers, all three in a state of exhaustion. The might of two non-European powers, the United States and Japan, had correspondingly increased. The United States had provided the Allies with guns, ammunition, and other military equipment long before it had entered the war. The Allies became heavily indebted to the United States largely because of loans made by the Washington government. A transfer of capital from Europe to America had taken place as European corporations and investors liquidated their holdings to meet the demands for money arising from increased taxes and the expansion of war industries at home. For the first time American loans and investments abroad were greater than foreign loans and investments in the United States. The United States was transformed from a debtor country into a creditor country. The stock exchange of New York became the world's foremost stock market, replacing London in that role. Europe was weary, damaged, and impoverished, and the United States was still fresh. Europeans felt that Americans had suffered little and profited much from the war. Americans believed that without their timely aid Europe might have been crushed by the heel of Prussian militarism.

615

THE WORLD WAR had provided Japanese, Chinese, Indians, and Indochinese with an opportunity to play a part in the Allied defeat of Germany and to advance their own aspirations. Like the United States, the countries of Asia sent troops and supplies to Europe. What had once been Europe's back yard, peculiarly fitted for colonial exploitation, had started to become a non-European community of independent nations. Colonialism in all of its ramifications was dealt a body blow by the events of 1914-1918. The slogan of "self-determination of nations," meant by those who shouted it loudest and most often to apply to European minorities, sounded remarkably appropriate to Asiatics, who had long found that their destinies were determined for them by others. And the Bolsheviks' cry of "capitalist imperialism" found them ready to respond with pent-up resentment.

The principle of the self-determination of nations was in fact eventually to become a telling factor in the disintegration of the British Empire. No good reason dictated that self-determination should stop with the disintegration of Austria-Hungary and Turkey. After 1918 the subject peoples of the British Empire were to continue, with fervor enhanced, their prewar struggle for independence. In many cases they explicitly referred to Wilson among the sages whose pronouncements justified their action. We have already noted that the liberation movements received a new impetus in Ireland during the war. The same was true in India, Malaya, Ceylon, and Burma; and the movement spread to the Dutch and the French empires.

Japan's primary motive in entering the war had been aggrandizement. She intended to capture German territories and concessions in the Far East and the Pacific, and to elevate Japan to an imperialist status in Asia similar to that of the powers of the West. Japan's war arrangements with her allies, if allowed to stand, not only would make Japan heir to all Germany's concessions in China but would also give her concessions elsewhere, especially in Manchuria and Inner Mongolia, and would widen Japan's influence in Chinese domestic affairs. China had little therefore to hope for from the victory of the Allies. The Chinese had taken little part in the war except to send labor battalions to several fronts and some troops under Japanese direction to intervene in Bolshevik Siberia. Torn by internal faction, China had but one source of hope for preserving her independence of Japan—the growing tension between Tokyo and Washington.

As for the British dominions, impelled by their own patriotism and fear of German domination, they had voluntarily gone to the aid of their mother country. Their self-reliance made itself felt during the war, and by the end of the war they had earned world-wide recognition and respect as essentially **616** independent and sovereign countries.

Political developments in India during the World War THE DEVELOPMENT of a national spirit in India called for special attention during the war. Almost a million Indian soldiers and almost half a million noncombatants (all volunteers, for India had no conscription) were sent to the colonial, western, and Turkish fronts, and they gave a good account of themselves on the battlefields and in the workshops. The war stimulated heavy industry in India, but it also necessitated huge Indian expenditures, not only in supporting India's war machine but also in gifts to the British (one alone of £100,000,000). When the war at last came to a close, India's currency system was near collapse. India had meanwhile found a loyal political leader in a frail, gentle, ascetic, London-educated patriot named Mohandas K. Gandhi.

The fear that the Indian nationalists might take advantage of Britain's preoccupation in Europe to revolt against the British *raj* proved unfounded. Nor did the Moslems of India endeavor to aid their Turkish coreligionists in their war against the western powers. The British felt secure enough indeed during the war years to remove all but a handful of their British military units from India to Europe. Even after the outbreak of the Russian Revolution, India remained relatively quiet. The British government appeared willing to bow gracefully and gratefully to India. The secretary of state for India promised in the summer of 1917 "increasing association of Indians in every branch of the administration and the gradual development of self-governing institutions with a view to the progressive realisation of responsible government in India as an integral part of the British Empire."

The promise of "progressive realisation of responsible government" involved a radical departure from past policy. The British government instructed Lord Chelmsford, the viceroy of India, and E. Samuel Montagu, the secretary of state for India, to investigate thoroughly the problems which might stand in the way of introducing fundamental changes in India's government. The proposed investigation called forth varying responses from interested groups. Imperialists warned that it was unreasonable to expect the vast subcontinent with its huge and varied population to be prepared for the responsibilities of independent government in any acceptable length of time. Among hopeful nationalists, the British promise appeared to herald a new day. In 1918, the celebrated Montagu-Chelmsford Report was submitted to the British Parliament. It observed that enough educated Indians were available to staff important sections of government and recommended reforms intended to give such Indians significant opportunities.

Some of India's leaders, however, were opposed to what they considered halfway measures. Among them were B. G. Tilak and Mrs. Annie Besant. Long conspicuous among the Indian extremists, Tilak advocated violence in achieving self-government. In 1907 Mrs. Besant, an Englishwoman, had become the president of the Theosophical Society, a religious group which believed that the true religion should combine the teachings of the Hindu Vedas and the Christian gospels. She was also a strong believer in Indian nationalism. In 1916 she created the Indian Home Rule League, and in 1917 she was elected president of the Indian National Congress. (In 1926-1927 she was to undertake a tour of England and America in order to announce to the world her discovery of the new Indian Messiah.)

The views of these leaders were rendered more explosive by current complications. High taxes, high prices, severe crop failures, and influenza epidemics swept the country at the end of the war. Indian extremists charged the British rulers with the major responsibility for the starvation stalking the country. Discontent rose to ominous levels. "I wish," complained Montagu, "I could get the damned Bureaucracy to realize that we are sitting on an earthquake." The eruptions in Russia made India seem all the more volcanic.

The first phase of Russia's Marxist revolution IT WAS ironical that the proletarian revolution should have begun in Russia, industrially a backward country where the proletariat was sparse. In order to modernize their country, the Bolsheviks planned to industrialize it. But this they could do only if they could avoid antagonizing the peasants, who otherwise might turn against the revolution and starve the cities. The classes that were regarded as incorrigibly hostile to the revolution might well receive less considerate treatment. Almost the first step of the Bolsheviks on taking power was to confiscate large estates and distribute them among the peasantry. In rapid succession, banks were nationalized, foreign debts repudiated, factories confiscated and turned over to the workers, church properties nationalized. In February 1918, to be sure, the Bolshevik state nationalized all the land of Russia, but actively working peasants were for the time being left undisturbed in their enjoyment of the usufruct of their farms.

The pattern of counterrevolution and foreign intervention of the French Revolution now was repeated. Those at home who were against the new government joined with its enemies abroad, and devastating civil wars, aided and abetted by foreign interventions and revolts of subject nationalities, followed. This triple danger in turn caused the revolutionary government to heighten the pitilessness of its terrorism at home and the fervor of its missionary propaganda abroad, partly in order to stay in power and partly out of genuine conviction of the righteousness of its cause. Several essential differences have in the course of time become distinguishable between the French and the Russian Revolution. In the numbers involved, the terroristic thoroughness applied, and the doctrinaire devotion exhibited on both sides, the later upheaval probably exceeded the earlier one. It has also lasted longer, and presumably therefore has made a more indelible impression than the earlier one.

618 But little of this lasting quality was suspected in 1917-1918, when every

day was expected to be the Communists' last. In August 1918, an attempt on the life of Lenin was made, and he was severely wounded. This plot unleashed a wave of terrorism over Russia. The government had at its disposal only two forces upon which it could count for survival. They were the Cheka, its secret police, and the small Red Army created by Trotsky, now the commissar of war. Together they numbered only about 100,000 men. Wherever the Whites were victorious, however, they attempted to take the newly acquired land away from the peasants. Moreover, the White soldiers were badly led and were given more to killing and looting than to fighting. Though, as the result of the November 1917 elections had shown, most of the peasants did not prefer the new rulers of Russia, the Whites' counterrevolutionary policies induced the peasants to side with the Bolshevik government.

It was still gravely doubtful at the time of the armistice whether the Bolsheviks could last. World war, civil war, and nationalist revolts had caused dislocations in transportation and in the distribution of food and industrial products, and the Bolsheviks had added to the dislocations by precipitate and punitive nationalizations, often carried out by inexperienced men and in a wasteful, bureaucratic way. Shortages could not be overcome by foreign commerce, for foreign countries hesitated to trade with a country where trade was a state monopoly, whose debts had been repudiated, and whose collapse was regarded as imminent. But meanwhile Communism had also begun to spread abroad (Chapter 11).

The growth of nationalism and democracy aided by the war — AT THE END of 1918, nevertheless, it looked as if the World War had made the world safer for democracy (and self-determination was theoretically the application of the democratic principle to national sovereignty). The democracies of France, England, Italy, and the United States had won the war. Only Japan on the Allied side was still a relatively despotic empire, but it too had of late been moving in a constitutional direction (page 558). Semi-absolute empires had toppled in Germany, Austria, Turkey, and Russia, and several minority nationalities had in each case achieved a long-sought national dignity. Most of the succession states (i.e., states created from the defeated empires) had accepted or were about to accept republican constitutions. The British Empire was making or was expected to make concessions in the direction of greater self-government to its colonies and dominions. The Communists were still feared and hated but were so exhausted that they no longer seemed to present a serious threat. Democracy and nationalism seemed safer than ever.

Economic and social dislocations — IN THE SENSE in which Sir Norman Angell and others had predicted (page 510), no nation in Europe profited from the war. All countries only suffered different degrees of loss. The entire economic life of belligerents and neutrals alike had been geared to war production. In an unprecedented fashion the home fronts had been marshaled to meet the demands of the armed forces in belligerent countries, and in neutral countries high prices for war materials had concentrated labor and money on supplying them. The attention of scientists and writers had also been largely mobilized to meet the uninterrupted and importunate demands of the war. In the belligerent countries at least, all forms of activity had been more or less regulated by the governments. The sudden end of production after the armistice caused intellectual, social, and economic dislocations, which in some countries were to assume a semi-revolutionary character.

In industry the effect was ruinous. Machines for peacetime production had not been in operation for years; machines used during the war had worn out. Production for an assured government-paid war market gave way once more to competition, and owners of once artificially stimulated enterprises closed their factories or resumed work on only a small scale. Many workers lost their jobs, and returning soldiers could not find jobs. Unemployment figures mounted. In many cases war had severed European relations with overseas customers, and they were never to be renewed, because, as was the case with some Latin-American countries, the customers found that they could buy from the United States and Japan as well as from Europe. The great Russian market was gone because of the revolution.

New states like Poland and Czechoslovakia had yet to build commercial ties with each other and with western markets, since their old roads, railways, communication lines, and business methods had centered on the major cities of the empires of which they had once formed part. Making new ties was likely, however, to prove complicated by their natural desire

"The New Rich," a French cartoon. The war profiteer surveys his hoard of scarce food-stuffs—dried vegetables, pâtés, butter, fruits, rice, sugar, and eggs.

to defend their national industries and markets and to raise revenue by high tariffs. As business and government finance were dislocated, the expenses of rebuilding new governments and fiscal systems mounted. War and revolution, shortages and war debts had unsettled finances and tax collections, and the credit of new governments was too feeble to enable them to float satisfactory loans. They resorted to inflation of the currency and in several instances inflation was to prove disastrous. As we shall see (Chapter 11), economic conditions were worst, of course, in the countries of the vanquished, where they were further complicated by waves of revolutionary disorder.

Scientific and technological advances

IT IS PROBABLY true, as has been contended, that wars of themselves do not produce intellectual giants, except perhaps among strategists, and it certainly is true that they destroy men, women, and products of talent and genius. Nevertheless, total wars mobilize a people's talents along with their other resources, and, by giving purpose and unity to the national effort, may call forth intellectual energies, resources, and abilities that might otherwise remain unused, uncoordinated, or aimlessly dissipated. The First World War at least lifted the speed and shifted the channels of performance by men of talent who might otherwise have been content with less urgency and other aims, and put at their disposal money, labor, laboratories, and opportunities that the more leisurely demands and the normal indifferences of peacetime would hardly have made available.

Technology and science were mobilized on both sides to fight for victory. The First World War was a "chemist's war," with results, such as poison gas, that we have already had occasion to note. Few nondestructive scientific advances resulted directly from the war, and they were chiefly in medicine. One of them was the work of the Austrian neurologist Julius Wagner-Jauregg. During the war he was the head of a military hospital for the insane. There he made an observation that baffled him at first; he noticed that patients in the early stages of general paresis (syphilitic softening of the brain) recovered if by chance they contracted malaria on the battlefields. He therefore artificially induced malaria in patients showing the early symptoms of general paresis, and they were cured. From those experiments he concluded that the malaria parasite was a good antidote in the early stages of general paresis. Increased knowledge of immunization and prophylaxis greatly reduced the damage that might have been expected from the old "military" plagues like typhus. The large number of wounds, amputations, and operations resulting from the war led to marked improvements in surgery. Alexis Carrel and Henry D. Dakin developed a method of treating open wounds, called "the Carrel-Dakin treatment," with a solution of sodium hypochlorite and sodium bicarbonate as a germicide. Blood transfusions saved many from bleeding to death and also increased the time available to the surgeon for successful operation on a bleeding patient. Anesthesia and asepsis (freedom from germs, etc.) became better understood and better applied. Encouraged by the discovery of vitamin A in 1913, the science of dietetics made big strides during and after the war, in large part because of food shortages and the necessity of feeding adequately the huge numbers that poured into camps, factories, and hospitals. The great medical defeat of the war was the inability to cope adequately with the pandemic of Spanish influenza of 1918.

Big industry
and mass production

THE WAR also gave a tremendous impetus to industry. Concrete was used extensively in building. Rubber was developed for use in tires for automobiles, trucks, and airplanes. The automobile became common. The airplane demonstrated its practicality to the point where it was frequently conceived of as a profitable commercial vehicle and as a decisive weapon of the next war. The electric bulb was brightened by the use of tungsten for filaments that had been invented just before the war. Artificial silk (later called rayon), invented around 1900, was improved. The moving picture industry moved rapidly ahead in the United States, having developed the feature picture and having become a good medium of propaganda.

Mass production, a phenomenon rarely found anywhere outside the United States before 1914, was a determining factor in the outcome of the war. By "mass production" is meant the manufacture of great quantities of standardized goods, which usually consist of parts made by special-purpose automatic machines and assembled by a series of workers alongside a moving conveyor belt. The Ford Company was one of the first industrial enterprises to use this new production method before the war, and the Model-T came off its assembly lines by the hundreds of thousands. The war accelerated the application of mass production methods to industry everywhere. Mass production had obvious socioeconomic effects, of which one calls for special mention: it stressed the importance in industry of the managerial staffs—the efficiency expert, the engineer, the salesman, and the business executive—and proportionately cut into the prestige of the mere financier.

The war promoted the trend toward trusts, cartels, monopolies, and industrial combinations in Europe as well as in America. In 1919 a Committee on Trusts was to find ninety-three monopolistic organizations in Britain and to express the fear that they "might within no distant period exercise a paramount control over all important branches of trade." In the United States, the need for industrial concentration in the war effort led to official connivance to promote combinations and trade associations through agencies such as the War Industries Board, and the Webb-Pomerene Act of 1918 authorized trusts for foreign trade. In Germany, where monopolies were not illegal, several kinds of combinations in industry were officially encouraged not to compete, to fix prices, and to divide markets among themselves.

THE IMPACT of four years of waste and slaughter on society was such as might easily have been anticipated. On the one hand, it caused spasms of artificial and superficial pleasure-seeking, as wars, rendering the future more than ever uncertain, generally have done. With the armistice the sobering effects of war sacrifice vanished, and peace was to bring in its wake disillusionment to a generation of young people whose faith in the traditional values had been severely shaken, and who were to become known in American literature as "the lost generation." Large parts of the same generation were lost in a more literal sense likewise. The war had cost about 10,000,000 dead and 20,000,000 wounded on all sides (not to mention an estimated money cost of over $330,000,000,000). Germany and Russia had suffered well over 1,500,000 deaths each, France and Austria-Hungary well over 1,000,000 each, Great Britain just under 1,000,000, and Italy, Turkey, and the United States almost another 1,000,000 all together. The rest of the killed were distributed among the Canadians, Australians, the other British dominions, and other belligerents. These men included the flower of the world's youth. It was frequently remarked in the next generation that old men continued to control politics in Europe. How many writers, scientists, and artists were lost the statistics do not reveal. Rupert Brooke and Charles Péguy were among them.

LITERATURE during the war sometimes sank to low levels. Historical writing often descended to propaganda in all countries; moving picture scenarios and the theater rarely rose above it; and journalists were sometimes paid propaganda agents. The popular songs were the usual barrack and sentimental ballads that soldiers sing. Occasional poems by a poet-soldier like Rupert Brooke's sad war sonnets entitled *1914* or Siegfried Sassoon's indignant *Counter-Attack* or Wilfred Owen's bitter *Dulce et Decorum Est* earned a well-deserved immortality. The war gave birth also to few outstanding works in other branches of literature. Lawrence's *The Seven Pillars of Wisdom* has already been mentioned (page 612). Several novels of the soldier's life at the front thrilled and saddened contemporaries, particularly *Under Fire* (1916) by the Frenchman Henri Barbusse. A series of short nightmarish sketches about war called *Man Is Good* (1917) by a self-imposed exile, the German pacifist novelist Leonhard Frank, perhaps contributed to the weakening of the German war spirit. The French novelist Georges Duhamel, a surgeon by profession, produced *The Life of the Martyr* (1917), a poignant account of his experiences in the military field hospitals behind the trenches.

Old masters also contributed to the war literature. H. G. Wells' *Mr. Britling Sees It Through* (1916) was a story of a writer's adjustment to the cruelties and incongruities of war. Shaw's *Heartbreak House* (1917) was a philosophical discussion in dramatic form of the causes of the war. Romain Rolland wrote a pacifist essay entitled *Above the Battle* (1915). Maurice Barrès wrote daily columns in the *Écho de Paris,* which were reissued in book form under the titles of *The French Soul and the War* (1915-1919), and *Chronicle of the Great War* (1920-1924). To him the war was the justification of his life's work. In general, the literature that came from the war, when it departed from propaganda and patriotism, was a literature either of resignation or of indignation. The price of glory seemed too high.

The phrase "the end of an era" occurs frequently and with greater or less justification in books of history. The war of 1914-1918 is described by that phrase perhaps more accurately than most historical episodes. Before the war, progress was taken for granted by most, peace was regarded as the normal state of international relations, and prosperity was more or less assured in the course of time for those who were energetic. After the war, progress began to appear to some at least as a huge fraud that led only to bigger and better wars, rendering peace always precarious and prosperity a monopoly of those who made profits while others fought.

Most still hoped, however, that the ideological slogans of the war had more than a propaganda value. Perhaps this war had indeed ended war. Was it not at last sufficiently clear to all that war did not pay, that imperialism cost more than it could possibly produce, that armaments and alliances were insufficient guarantees of international security? Would not nations at last be willing to surrender some of their sovereignty to establish an international order that would enforce peace among them? Perhaps an organization of nations might be created that would become the instrument not only of collective security but of peaceful change in the direction of international justice. Hopeful people all over the world, sometimes well organized in pressure groups, shared Wilson's belief that even an imperfect international union might become a channel toward a better world order, ironing out injustices that centuries of selfish power and mistaken principles had inflicted on the less powerful or better principled.

Twenty-one years after the Armistice of 1918 the Second World War was to break out. The First World War had been the end of an era perhaps, but it was destined neither to end war nor to make the world safe for democracy. It was to appear that some things were more weighty with some peoples than the preservation of peace or democracy—racial superiority, national independence, unification or aggrandizement, glory, *revanche,* employment, and many other things that peace apparently did not bring and that war might. To those people the First World War was primarily a source of lessons to apply if one hoped to win the next war.

624

June 28, 1914	Assassination of Archduke Francis Ferdinand
July 5, 1914	German chancellor's "blank check" to Austria
July 23, 1914	Austrian ultimatum to Serbia
July 28, 1914	Dual Monarchy declares war upon Serbia
July 31, 1914	Britain asks France and Germany to respect Belgium's neutrality
August 1, 1914	Germany declares war upon Russia
August 3, 1914	Germany declares war upon France
August 4, 1914	Germany invades Belgium
August 4, 1914	Britain declares war upon Germany
August 5-8, 1914	Montenegro joins the "Allies"
August 6, 1914	Austria declares war upon Russia
August 12, 1914	France and England declare war upon Austria
August 23-24, 1914	Japan enters war on the Allied side
October 29-November 2, 1914	Turks join the "Central Powers"
January-May 1915	Sino-Japanese negotiations on the Twenty-one Demands
March-December 1915	Allied failure to force the Dardanelles
May 7, 1915	Sinking of the *Lusitania*
May 23, 1915	Italy enters the war on the side of the Allies
October 1915	Bulgaria joins the Central Powers
April 24, 1916	Easter Rebellion in Dublin
August 27, 1916	Rumania joins the Allies
1916	Central Powers declare war upon Portugal
1916	Wilson reëlected to the presidency
1916-1917	Wilson's peace negotiations with both sides
1916-1917	Beginning of total warfare
January 19, 1917	"Zimmermann note" offers Mexico alliance with Germany
February 1, 1917	Germans renew unrestricted submarine warfare
March 1917	Overthrow of czarist regime in Russia
April 6, 1917	The United States declares war upon Germany
June 1917	Greece declares war upon the Central Powers
August 1917	China enters the war on the side of the Allies
November 7, 1917	The Bolshevik Revolution
January 8, 1918	Wilson's "Fourteen Points" speech
February 9, 1918	Treaty of Brest-Litovsk
September 30, 1918	Bulgaria signs armistice
October 30, 1918	Turkey concludes armistice with the Allies
November 1918	Overthrow of the Second German Reich
November 11, 1918	New German Republic signs armistice

Part five

Chapter eleven: Postwar settlements and unsettlements 1919-1925

Chapter twelve: From hopefulness through depression to anxiety

Chapter thirteen: The eve of the Second World War

THE WORLD

BETWEEN TWO WARS

1918-1939

ICELAND

NORWAY

SWEDEN

FINLAND

U S

Leningrad
ESTONIA
LATVIA
LITHUANIA
EAST PRUSSIA

UNITED
KINGDOM

BELGIUM
NETHERLANDS
DENMARK

Baltic Sea

EIRE

*Berlin
GERMANY

POLAND

CZECHOSLOVAKIA
AUSTRIA HUNGARY

FRANCE

ITALY

Rome*

RUMANIA

YUGOSLAVIA

BULGARIA

Istanbul
TURKEY

PORTUGAL SPAIN

ALBANIA

GREECE

SYRIA

IRAQ

IRAN

AFGHANISTAN

TIBET

MOROCCO

TUNISIA

Suez Canal

ALGERIA

LIBYA

EGYPT

TRANS-
JORDAN

INDIA

SAUDI
ARABIA

FRENCH WEST AFRICA

FRENCH
EQUATORIAL AFRICA

ANGLO-
EGYPTIAN
SUDAN

ITALIAN
EAST
AFRICA

| ■ Axis-controlled areas | ▨ British possessions | ▨ French possessions |

By September 1939 the face of Europe, Africa, and Asia had already been changed by the Fascist powers. Albania, Austria, and Czechoslovakia had disappeared as sovereign states, and the Rome-Berlin Axis dominated central Europe from the Baltic to the Mediterranean. In Africa, Italy had incorporated Ethiopia into the new Italian East Africa bloc; Egypt, though sovereign and independent, was bound by military arrangements to Britain. Japan had since 1931 been building a "New Order" in Asia at the expense of China. The French and the British empires had undergone no major territorial changes since the 1920's.

Chapter eleven

POSTWAR SETTLEMENTS

AND UNSETTLEMENTS

1919-1925

In europe the period following the First World War was to be an era of extraordinary uncertainty. Some of the prewar problems had remained unsolved, new problems had been produced by the war, and fresh problems arose during the postwar period. All together they seemed to presage a new catastrophe.

Above all the uncertainties loomed the shadow of Communist Russia. Little was done in Europe after 1917 economically, politically, socially, and militarily that was not done with an eye to Russia. In countries that had no democratic tradition or had acquired one only recently, large landowners, big business, the middle class impoverished by inflation, and the unemployed white-collar workers soon found that dictatorship need not be a proletarian monopoly. They fell in readily with movements for a great national plan to be implemented by a leader whom they would follow with unquestioning loyalty. The ideas of national planning and of unquestioned leadership were not new in the 1920's. Examples had been furnished as recently as the Terror and Napoleon I. But the Bolsheviks improved upon the older models, and Lenin in turn was to become the prototype for a Mustafa Kemal Ataturk and a Mussolini during the period now under consideration, and they in their turn for a Hitler later.

The First World War, as might have been expected, had hammered out a new pattern of international affairs. Until 1914 the other continents had been Europe's satellites, as European influences, despite occasional retreats, had advanced steadily over the rest of the globe. By 1918 the centripetal force of these influences had drawn the greater part of the world into a total war that had begun as a seemingly local difference in the Balkans. When the war was over, the leadership of Europe had sadly diminished, and nations outside of Europe—particularly the United States—had taken leading, if not commanding, positions in world affairs. For a time at least, Europeans who hoped for a better world looked to the American president, Woodrow Wilson, as their leader in a crusade for democracy, self-determination, and collective security. The war seemed thus to have brought to a fitting maturity the period of conspicuous participation of the United States in world politics, a participation that had begun in the 1890's.

Americans, however, were reluctant to accept their place in the new world pattern. With the coming of peace, the United States, for reasons that will soon appear, turned its back on Europe, and for over a decade attempted to follow a policy of isolation. It was to prove a vain attempt. American blood, American money, American ideals, and American careers were too deeply invested in European affairs to permit either complete withdrawal or complete exclusion.

Perhaps no set of events reflects so clearly the new pattern of international affairs as the changes in the parts played by Far Eastern peoples in European diplomacy and warfare. Until the eighteenth century the colonial peoples of Asia had generally been permitted to act only passive roles whenever the powers of Europe fought with each other. With the passage of time Asiatics were frequently recruited to fight in the local battles of their foreign overlords, as was generally true in the imperial wars of the nineteenth century. In the twentieth century, and particularly since the rise of Japan to a power position, the countries of Asia have figured prominently in diplomatic entanglements and, when war has come, have fought for their own interests. The interwar epoch of 1918-1939, of which we are now to examine the first years, was to witness long steps in a kind of anticolonial revolution in Asia.

The political, social, and economic history of the period 1918-1925 makes a logical unit—from the armistice at Compiègne to the Treaties of Locarno. To consider the year 1925, however, as a breaking point in the cultural development of the postwar years is less logical. Culturally, the generation that came between the two world wars for good reasons seems to require consideration as a whole. Hence the discussion of artists, writers, and scientists of the years from 1918 to 1939 has been left for Chapter 13.

PEACE CONFERENCES
AND TREATIES (1919-1923)

OVER TWO MONTHS elapsed between the signing of an armistice at Compiègne and the opening of the Congress of Paris that was to make the peace. In the interval several events occurred that augured ill for the new German republic. Allied troops occupied various strategic areas in Germany; the blockade of Germany continued to work hardships on the German population; Allied statesmen made promises to their electorates that German "war criminals" would be condignly punished and that the Central Powers would be required to pay the costs of the war; a Spartacist (i.e., Communist) uprising broke out in Berlin and was suppressed only after ten days of hard fighting. All these events seemed to emphasize that the forthcoming peace negotiations would be between resentful victors and their vanquished foes incapable of further resistance. Germany was not invited to send a delegation to the opening of the conference.

The clash of principles among the peacemakers at Paris

WILSON HAD decided to attend the peace conference himself as head of the American delegation. When he came to Europe at the end of 1918, the people in the Allied countries received him as the herald of peace everlasting. His triumphal procession through England, France, and Italy confirmed him in the expectation that he could still be the mediator he had been before the armistice, when the Allied governments still had Germany to fear and had looked to America for salvation. Moreover, he was convinced that if governments proved recalcitrant, he could successfully appeal over their heads to their peoples. Of the deep-rooted nationalism and inveterate distrusts of the European nations, of their concepts of vital interests that could not be compromised and of nonvital interests that could be bartered away in a manner that seemed to him unjust, he had only a second-hand knowledge. He was soon to find that though the peoples of Europe cheered his ringing pronunciamentos, they also wanted guarantees of their future safety and compensations for their past sufferings at the hands of a hated enemy and were prepared to support their statesmen, who believed that safety and compensation could best be derived from annexations and indemnities. Before long the American delegation and the delegations of the European allies were at odds, suspecting each other of bad faith. In the end Wilson, still believing that peace would be secured if he could tie the plan for a league of nations into the peace treaty, proved willing to consent to arrangements of which he did not approve in principle.

The Fiume question as a test of the Fourteen Points

THE ITALIANS, the very ones who had feted Wilson the most, were the first to abandon him. They insisted on getting Fiume, Hungary's only good seaport, which the new Greater Serbia (or Yugoslavia) also wanted. The Hungarians and the Yugoslavians claimed it because they needed it as an outlet to the Adriatic. The Italians claimed it because most of the people there spoke Italian and because it was among the prizes promised Italy by a secret provision of the Treaty of London (page 593) when she had entered the war. Lloyd George for one understood the Italian delegation's predicament. Wilson regarded the Italian demand as a flagrant violation of the Fourteen Points, which had included statements to the effect that Italy's boundaries would be fixed on

633

"clearly recognizable lines of nationality" and that Serbia would be "accorded free and secure access to the sea." Wilson believed that the opposition to his views came only from the Italian peace delegation, and he made an appeal direct to the Italian people. He was amazed when they supported their premier, Victor Emanuele Orlando. An outcry arose all over Italy: Why then had Italy suffered her nearly two million casualties? Hadn't the war been fought to preserve the sacredness of "scraps of paper"?

Disputes and compromises among the Allied "Big Four" THUS WILSON found that the Allied diplomats were in no mood to abandon the secret agreements they had concluded before America entered the war. He also found the European governments hampered by the demands for vengeance made by their peoples in the heat of war. That lack of freedom was especially true of Lloyd George, who had been prime minister in a coalition government since 1916 and had just made statements to the British in the first postwar general elections (December 1918) that some of them interpreted as a promise to "hang the Kaiser"; and it was true also of the French premier, Georges Clemenceau, who had made statements to the French that seemed to mean that "the Boche will pay for everything."

Clemenceau, who had created France's "victory cabinet" in 1917, wanted a peace with victory. He was prepared to make the proper obeisance to Wilson's aspirations for international justice and order, but he also had a proper respect for harsh political realities. He sought French security through German weakness rather than through a lenient peace. The French meant to separate all the territory west of the Rhine from Germany and make it into an independent Rhineland. Wilson and Lloyd George were adamant in opposing that intention because they did not want "to create a new Alsace-Lorraine," as Lloyd George put it. But in order to assuage the justifiable French feeling of insecurity, both Lloyd George and Wilson consented to separate treaties binding Britain and the United States respectively to go to the assistance of France in case of an unprovoked German attack upon her. Counting upon such a triple alliance to protect France against future attack, Clemenceau gave up his insistence upon a separate Rhineland and even became friendly toward the idea of a league of nations.

Wilson, Orlando, Lloyd George, and Clemenceau were the "Big Four" of the Paris Conference. They had led their peoples through a costly war to a great victory, and they seemed at the time to enjoy the confidence of their constituents. They often exchanged heated words and enacted dramatic scenes at Versailles, but in the end they did not come to blows, for even the American president, champion of "peace without victory," was realist enough to yield to pressure when he had to, especially since he counted on the proposed league of nations ultimately to right all temporary wrongs. Furthermore, all four represented democracies, and they would eventually

A caricature of Clemenceau by the French artist Charles Leandre.

have to answer to their electorates; and so they could not be blind to political considerations and the vote-appeal of their decisions.

The guiding principles of the Conference of Paris

COMPARED to the statesmen who were prominent at the Congress of Vienna of 1814-1815, the men of 1919 cut but a drab figure. The Paris Conference did not dance as had the Congress of Vienna; rather it advanced over much ground very rapidly. But the problems of an industrial society communicating by telephone and telegraph and traveling by train, steamer, automobile, and airplane were more complex than those of the society the earlier statesmen had had to handle. By and large, the provisions set up in 1815 enabled the European peoples to enjoy a century rarely disturbed by great wars, but the work of the men of 1919 was to collapse within a few years and to engender a new world war within a single generation.

Essentially the principles that guided the diplomats at Paris were the old ones. Punitive annexations were demanded and many pieces of territory changed hands, but frequently the spirit of nationalism and democracy, so often disregarded at Vienna, received tribute in the form of "self-determination" by means of plebiscites among the traded peoples. Punitive indemnities also were required, although they were given the more euphemistic name of "reparations" and justified by Article 232 of the final treaty as "compensation for all damages done to the civilian population of the Allied and Associated Powers." The concept of legitimacy or status quo was somewhat more difficult to retain, because victors and vanquished were all committed to further change: either a redistribution of the lands of the crumbling empires or a reorganization of Europe on the principles of justice and world organization. Moreover, about half of the European system was in revolution—Germany, the former Austrian states, the one-time czarist empire, the Turkish and Arab areas—and out of Russia particularly stalked a revolutionary spirit that was no longer a specter but a stark reality.

To erect new states on strictly national foundations proved impossible, since many countries, old and new, contained mixed nationalities. The peacemakers at Versailles realized that unless something were done for the protection of the minorities within the several national states, a new explosion was likely to burst over Europe as in 1914. The peacemakers hoped at least to mitigate this problem by including in the different treaties provisions for the protection of the racial, linguistic, and religious security of the minorities. In addition, Poland, Czechoslovakia, Rumania, Yugoslavia, and Greece—states to which the war settlements had assigned or would assign areas containing well defined minority groups—undertook special obligations for the protection of minorities within their respective territories.

President Wilson had a hard time getting the minority guarantees accepted, for each of the states concerned attempted to evade the issue. They pointed out that such obligations were an infringement upon their sovereignty. Nevertheless, Wilson remained adamant, and eventually they all had to submit. After pressure was removed, however, they were to fail to live up to their obligations in several instances.

The signature of the Treaty of Versailles THE GERMANS were invited to the conference only at its close in order that they might sign the treaty drawn up in their absence. They were given three weeks to make up their minds, and they had to present their observations in writing without previous discussion with any of the Allied delegates. This process led to some minor changes, but the incumbent German government resigned rather than accept the treaty even as modified. In fact, however, Germany had no choice. A large part of its people were already on the point of starvation. So a new government agreed to sign the somewhat modified document. By a studied gesture of humiliation, the ceremony of signing the treaty was scheduled for the fifth anniversary of the assassination at Sarajevo (June 28, 1919) in the very hall at the Palace of Versailles where William I had been crowned German emperor. The German delegates in accepting the treaty announced their conviction "that these conditions of peace represent injustice without example." And Germans everywhere soon learned to call the treaty a *Diktat* (an arbitrary dictation).

Since the Covenant of the League of Nations (page 692) was Part I of the Treaty of Versailles, the Germans, along with Wilson, had reason to believe that eventually, as an international government, the League might rectify the grosser injustices of the peace settlement. Nevertheless, Germany was not permitted as yet to become a member of the League. From the very start the treaty encountered noncooperation and eventually forceful resistance from most of the German people.

Territorial provisions of the Treaty of Versailles

OF THE MANY difficult territorial questions provided for in the treaty, probably the most complex concerned the parts of Poland that had formerly belonged to Germany. A new Poland had come into existence during the war, as each side intrigued to win Polish support against the other. Its nucleus was the former Russian Poland. The Prussian province of Posen, overwhelmingly inhabited by Poles, was now given outright to the restored Poland. Difficulties arose over what to do about Upper Silesia and West Prussia, both of which contained large numbers of German-speaking people, and over how to assure the Poles free access to the sea. Three compromises were made. (1) In Upper Silesia a plebiscite was scheduled to determine the allegiance of the majority. (2) The greater part of West Prussia was given to Poland. In that way East Prussia was separated, as it had been before the first partition of Poland in 1772, from the rest of Germany. The intervening area became known as "the Polish Corridor." (3) The essentially German city of Danzig and its surrounding territory became a free city under the administration of a high commissioner to be appointed by the League of Nations. Such compromises share the character of an epigram, which has been defined as a half-truth bound to irritate those who believe the other half; both Germans and Poles were to find each of these three compromises a source of future irritation.

Other territorial changes were arranged with little or no compromise. The treaty deprived Germany of all her colonies, which were to become "mandates" of other nations under the supervision of the League of Nations (page 695). Germany returned Alsace-Lorraine to France. The Saar Basin was put under a special regime responsible to the League of Nations: its coal output was given to France; and after fifteen years the people were to decide by plebiscite whether to retain the League of Nations regime, go back to Germany, or be annexed by France. Schleswig was divided into two zones, each of which was to decide by separate plebiscites whether it wished to go under Danish or to remain under German rule. Germany was enjoined never to annex Austria, which was now a small German area around the city of Vienna (page 640), except with the consent of the League. The dis-   637

Six new nations were created by the diplomatic arrangements of 1917-1919—Czechoslovakia, Yugoslavia (which included Serbia and Montenegro), Lithuania, Latvia, Estonia, and Finland. Poland was re-created, and Hungary was separated from Austria. Italy, Greece, Belgium, and Rumania were enlarged at the expense of Germany, the former Dual Monarchy, Turkey, Bulgaria, and Russia. France regained Alsace and Lorraine. Compromise agreements made Danzig, Memel, and Fiume free entities under the supervision of the League and provided for eventual plebiscites to determine the disposition of disputed areas such as the Saar Basin and Schleswig. The Rhineland was demilitarized and occupied by Allied troops. The Greco-Turk boundary was in dispute.

trict of Memel was set up as a territory under the supervision of the League of Nations. Small pieces of German territory were allotted to Belgium and Czechoslovakia.

The disarmament and occupation of Germany

THE Fourteen Points had envisaged general disarmament, but the Allies were not willing to wait to disarm Germany until a general agreement could be reached. The disarmament of Germany had already begun under the terms of the armistice. The Treaty of Versailles now required Germany to surrender what remained of its navy. When, accordingly, the German fleet the next June sailed into Scapa Flow, the crews scuttled their ships rather than leave them in the possession of the Allies. The treaty allowed Germany to have no more than six warships, in addition to a limited number of small craft, and forbade submarines altogether. The Kiel Canal and Germany's rivers were opened to all nations. Germany was permitted only an army of 100,000 without airplanes or big guns. The left bank of the Rhine and a fifty-kilometer zone on the right bank were to be permanently demilitarized (i.e., free from any kind of German military fortification or activity). In addition, the Rhineland and the bridgeheads along the right bank of the river were to be occupied by Allied troops in various stages of five, ten, and fifteen years, or longer if Germany failed to meet her obligations; and Germany was to pay the costs of the armies of occupation. From the very beginning the Germans did what they could to circumvent these provisions.

War guilt and the reparations question

THE PROVISION of the treaty dealing with the "aggression of Germany and her allies" (page 584) was a partly correct statement of historical fact. It was intended only to justify the payment of reparations by the vanquished, but it implied a moral condemnation and was accepted by the German nation in the last analysis only under duress. The "war-guilt question" became an obsession with the German people and a wedge that split open public opinion in Allied countries. Another provision demanded the surrender of "war criminals." The Germans never did conform to this demand, and it is possible that the Allies would have been embarrassed if they had conformed.

The treaty did not fix the total amount of the reparations that the Germans were to pay, leaving the sum for an Allied Reparations Commission

638

MAJOR TERRITORIAL CHANGES
IN EUROPE 1917-1919

FINLAND

ALAND
IS.

ESTONIA

DENMARK

Schleswig

Memel

LATVIA

RUSSIA

LITHUANIA

Polish Corridor

Danzig

EAST
PRUSSIA

GERMANY

POLAND

BELGIUM

Rhineland

UPPER
SILESIA

Saar Basin

CZECHOSLOVAKIA

Alsace
Lorraine

FRANCE

AUSTRIA

HUNGARY

RUMANIA

ITALY

Fiume

German losses

Bulgarian losses

Austro-Hungarian losses

Russian losses

YUGOSLAVIA

Serbia

BULGARIA

*To
Greece
from
Turkey
1923*

Montenegro

ALBANIA

GREECE

TURKEY

to decide later. Germany had meanwhile to surrender most of her merchant marine, large parts of her fishing fleet, and huge quantities of her coal. While the Reparations Commission was trying to determine the full claims of the victors, Germany was also required to pay 20,000,000,000 gold marks (equivalent to about $5,000,000,000), installments on which were to begin   639 as soon as the Commission demanded. The size of the provisional sum made the Germans feel victimized and increased their anxiety about the future. These feelings were fully exploited by both the Communists and the Nationalists of Germany, and they met with sympathy abroad.

Keynes' evaluation of the Treaty of Versailles

OUTSTANDING British and American economists warned that Europe's problems were not being squarely faced at the Conference of Paris. John Maynard Keynes, in *The Economic Consequences of the Peace* (1920), probably the most eloquent and incisive and certainly the most popular criticism of the conference, was to write: "The Treaty includes no provisions for the economic rehabilitation of Europe,—nothing to make the defeated Central Empires into good neighbors, nothing to stabilize the new States of Europe, nothing to reclaim Russia; nor does it promote in any way a compact of economic solidarity amongst the Allies themselves." Herbert Hoover, then director-general of the International Relief Organization, warned that Europe's productive capacity had been largely destroyed by war, disorder, political uncertainty, unemployment, soil exhaustion, human fatigue, undernourishment, and other factors. But said Keynes: "It is an extraordinary fact that the fundamental economic problems of a Europe starving and disintegrating before their eyes, was the one question in which it was impossible to arouse the interest of the Four. Reparation was their main excursion into the economic field, and they settled it as a problem of theology, of politics, of electoral chicane, from every point of view except that of the economic future of the States whose destiny they were handling."

The Treaties of Saint-Germain and Rapallo

PEACE WITH Austria was signed at Saint-Germain-en-Laye the next September. This treaty confirmed the fate that Austria had deliberately gone to war to avoid. Austria had fallen apart as an empire. All the Allies could do was to recognize that fact by reconstituting a little Austria from the compact German-speaking central provinces of the former Austrian Empire. The new Austria was obliged to recognize the independence of Czechoslovakia, Hungary, Poland, and Yugoslavia. To Czechoslovakia went a tiny part of Lower Austria, most of Austrian Silesia, and all of Moravia and Bohemia. Galicia went to Poland, and Bukovina to Rumania. The duchy of Teschen was divided between Poland and Czechoslovakia. Bosnia, Hercegovina, and most of Dalmatia were given to Yugoslavia. Austria was permitted an army of no more than 30,000 men. She was obliged to pay reparations and was forbidden to join Germany except with the consent of the League.

Under the secret provisions of the Treaty of London, Italy had been promised large pieces of Austria, and the Treaty of Saint-Germain awarded her South Tyrol, the Trentino, Istria, Trieste, and two Adriatic islands. Now that Austria had fallen apart, the Italians wanted still more, hoping to establish their complete control of the Adriatic. The conflict mentioned above regarding Fiume could not be settled at Paris because the Italian delegates temporarily walked out of the conference, and it was left to Italy and Yugoslavia to settle between them. In the midst of the negotiations, the flamboyant Gabriele D'Annunzio seized Fiume and set up an Italian government (page 674), although he was disavowed by Rome. Only in November 1920 did Italy and Yugoslavia agree to a peaceful distribution of the disputed territory, and then by the Treaty of Rapallo Fiume became a free city.

The Treaties of Neuilly and Trianon

SETTLEMENT with Bulgaria was delayed because of a series of revolutionary crises that it underwent upon its defeat. Finally, in November 1919, a treaty was concluded in the Paris suburb of Neuilly. Bulgaria had to cede Western Thrace to the Allies, who gave it to Greece. She had to surrender her navy, limit the number of her soldiers, and agree to pay some reparations.

Peace with Hungary was delayed not only by a series of revolutions but also by wars in which her neighbors took from her what they could. Finally Admiral Nicholas Horthy, leader of the monarchist party, set himself up as regent and virtual dictator (page 684). His government signed a peace treaty in the Grand Trianon Palace, located on the palace grounds of Versailles, in June 1920. Austria received the German-speaking Burgenland from Hungary. To Yugoslavia went Croatia-Slavonia and about half of the Banat of Temesvar. Rumania got the other half of the Banat and all of Transylvania. Czechoslovakia's share was Slovakia and Carpathian Ruthenia. Hungary also agreed to assume some of the burden of reparations and to limit her army.

The Turkish refusal to accept the Treaty of Sèvres

TURKEY had likewise been undergoing a series of revolutions and, in addition, had to endure invasions by Greek and Italian armies seeking pieces of Turkish territory. A strong man emerged in the person of the Nationalist general Mustafa Kemal Pasha, who had covered himself with glory in the victorious Dardanelles campaign of 1915 (page 593). When it began to appear that the peace negotiations might leave the old Ottoman Empire badly dismembered, the Turkish Nationalists led by Mustafa Kemal demanded that Turkey keep all territory where a clearly Turkish majority of Islamic faith existed. That demand was rejected, under the influence of the Allies, by Sultan Mohammed VI. Kemal then called together a national assembly at Angora in April 1920. The assembly elected him head of the government, disregarding the powerless sultan. A separate peace conference at San Remo led the

641

Allies to the decision to make peace with the sultan's government at Constantinople rather than with Kemal's republican government at Angora.

In August 1920, the sultan's representatives signed a treaty at the Parisian suburb of Sèvres. They ceded all Turkey's territories inhabited by non-Turkish populations, and those territories were set up either as independent states or as mandates of the League or were assigned to Italy or Greece. The treaty, though it was doomed to only a brief validity, was a milestone on the road to limbo for the Ottoman Empire, which had been no less an anachronism in a nationalist world than the old Dual Monarchy, for the non-Turkish peoples remained separated from Turkey thereafter.

The British stood behind the sultan's government in Constantinople, largely because they wished to keep the Straits open and feared that a Nationalist government, disavowing former international agreements, might try to close them. Lloyd George wanted to curb Kemal, but was aware that his war-weary country could not and would not undertake an extensive military campaign for that purpose. It appeared, however, that British exertions would be unnecessary, since the Greek prime minister offered to undertake such a campaign in the hope of obtaining not only the large Greek city of Smyrna, as promised by the Treaty of Sèvres, but other lands as well. But after two years of bitter fighting in Anatolia, Kemal defeated the Greek armies completely. In September 1922 the Turkish army recaptured the badly battered Smyrna. British intervention kept the Turks from other probable victories. Kemal proclaimed the sultan deposed, and the friendless monarch fled, as several friendless monarchs had before him, to asylum in England.

The Treaty of Lausanne with the Republic of Turkey

IN JULY 1923, peace between the Republic of Turkey on the one hand and the Allies and Greece on the other was concluded at Lausanne, Switzerland. The Treaty of Sèvres was scrapped. Turkey retained Asia Minor and the Aegean Sea islands of Imbros and Tenedos in Asia. In Europe she retained Constantinople and Eastern Thrace with Adrianople and the Gallipoli Peninsula, thus keeping control of both sides of the Straits, which she agreed to demilitarize. Capitulations, which were special privileges for the nationals of foreign Christian powers and consequently were a mark of Turkish inequality in the family of nations, were abolished.

A cruel innovation in the settlement of minorities problems was devised at Lausanne. Regardless of the wishes of the individuals involved, the Greeks and the Turks agreed to exchange Turks living on Greek territory for Greeks living on Turkish territory. Not many Turks had to be expatriated, but more than a million Greeks had to leave Asia Minor, where they and their ancestors had lived since Homeric times. Greeks who had resided in Constantinople before the end of the war, however, were allowed to stay there. Although Turkey had lost the whole Arabic-speaking part of her possessions, Kemal had saved a large and now cohesively Turkish portion of the former Ottoman Empire.

Japan's
new international position

THE DELIBERATELY aggressive role of Japan in the postwar world was one of the most intricate problems that the powers were called upon to face. During the war years the conservative political and social groups had continued to dominate the government of Japan, and had profited considerably from the rapid expansion of the nation's foreign trade and industrial plants. The western powers had hired Japanese commercial vessels and placed large orders with Japanese industry at a time when their own industrial and commercial enterprises were overtaxed by military demands. The Japanese had also been able during the war years to penetrate the Asian, African, and South American markets formerly controlled by Westerners. The rapid increase in exports provided Japan with a favorable balance of payments and elevated the insular empire, like the United States, from debtor to creditor status.

The Japanese
at the Paris Conference

WHILE international tension mounted over Japan's aggressive tactics in the Siberian intervention, Japanese diplomats at the Conference of Paris sought to obtain new international recognition of their nation's status as a great power. They at once encountered the unwillingness of the Big Four to take an oriental diplomat into their confidence. That embarrassment induced the Japanese to press all the more vigorously for the inclusion of the principle of racial equality in the Covenant of the League of Nations. In this ambition they were thwarted by the growing antagonism in the United States, Canada, Australia, New Zealand, and the countries of Latin America toward Asiatic immigration. It was particularly difficult for the Japanese to understand that major resistance to their equality should come from the United States, whose president had talked in high-flown phrases of justice and right. They failed to understand how embarrassing it was for a Democratic president to seem to advocate racial equality.

In their other objectives at the peace conference the Japanese were more successful. They won the right to hold under mandate to the League of Nations the formerly German islands in the Pacific north of the equator. Australia and New Zealand were granted mandates in the islands south of the equator. The Japanese, depending on the guarantees accorded them during the war by all the powers except the United States, also laid before the conference their claims upon the former German holdings in Shantung. The Chinese delegation, supported by President Wilson, meanwhile sought the 643 abrogation of all spheres of influence in China. After lengthy and generally discomfiting discussion, it was finally agreed that Japan should be permitted to take over Germany's former rights in Shantung with the proviso that certain concessions should in due course be returned to China. In China, all groups looked upon the Shantung decision as a betrayal of the national interest, and the government at Peking refused to sign the Treaty of Versailles. Once more they learned that little power resided in high-sounding phrases. Technically, China did not make peace with Germany until they concluded a bilateral treaty in 1920.

Embarrassments
of the western powers in Siberia

JAPAN'S designs on Siberia seemed for a time also to prosper. Her vigorous espousal of the anti-Bolshevik cause there continued to cause grave doubts regarding her motives. Could not Japanese zeal be due chiefly to the desire to upset the balance of power in the East? Besides, counsels were divided as to what the ultimate objectives of the intervening powers ought to be, and some of the western statesmen were beginning to doubt the merits of intervention in Russia altogether. In Siberia the establishment of a White Russian government under Admiral Alexander V. Kolchak shortly after the armistice brought out these differences clearly. Supported mainly by the European Allies, who wished to put an anti-Communist in power, the Kolchak regime was undermined by the Japanese military, who saw no advantage in stabilization under any Russian authority, and by their Cossack supporters, who sought power for themselves. Kolchak failed and was executed by the Bolsheviks in 1920. His failure discouraged the western powers and China, and in the spring of 1920 they began gradually to withdraw their forces from Siberia.

In eastern Siberia, meanwhile, the Bolsheviks had begun to make headway through guerrilla activity and the establishment of local governments. By the time the western powers and China had withdrawn their intervention forces, the Bolshevik guerrillas (or "partisans," as they were called) were descending in armed raids upon the Japanese and their Cossack supporters and slaughtering them in great numbers. Provoked to reprisals, the Japanese military engaged in massacres of Reds who resisted their authority, and burned down the cities and villages that opposed them. Since the Japanese continued to act in the name of the Allies, the western powers felt called upon to repudiate these dismaying actions and requested the withdrawal of Japanese troops as soon as possible.

The rise and fall
of the "Far Eastern Republic"

UPON THE withdrawal of their allies, the Japanese concentrated their activities in the Maritime Territory and on the island of Sakhalin. In the remainder of eastern Siberia, the Communists, as they recovered the once-occupied territory, organized an "independent-democratic" state known as the "Far Eastern Republic." Denouncing Japanese ruthlessness to the world, the Far Eastern Republic sought to win aid in its effort to force the withdrawal of the Japanese. Sympathy came from the United States. In 1921 the American government, as it had done six years before, declared that it would recognize no changes brought about by force if they violated existing treaty rights. At the same time the United States and the other powers prepared plans for a conference to meet at Washington to deal with eastern problems.

Consequently the Japanese government decided to proceed more cautiously in eastern Siberia and agreed to negotiate at Dairen with representatives of the Far Eastern Republic. Here discussions went on for over eight months. Meanwhile the Washington Conference had begun, and Japan became more and more involved in complications in simultaneous meetings at Dairen and at Washington. Taking advantage of Japanese embarrassments, the Communists increased their demands at Dairen. The issues of Siberia and Sakhalin were, however, aired but not acted upon at the Washington Conference, and few conclusions were reached at Dairen.

Subsequent efforts of the Russians and Japanese to negotiate their differences also met with failure. Because of domestic pressure (page 663) and the changing pattern of world affairs, the Japanese finally decided to evacuate Vladivostok in October 1922. The next month, the thinly disguised fiction that the Far Eastern Republic was independent of Russia was given up when its government voluntarily dissolved itself and turned control over to Moscow. The question of Northern Sakhalin was not resolved until the resumption of official Soviet-Japanese relations in 1925 (page 662), when the Japanese acquired oil and coal concessions there in return for the evacuation of their troops.

The continuation
of tensions in the Far East

PEACE elsewhere in the Far East was far from a reality at the conclusion of the Versailles Treaty. A contest for control of China was going on unabated between the Kuomintang (National People's Party) in Canton and the government in Peking (page 660), and hostility to Japan was about the only point on which the Chinese could now cooperate. The general irritation was increased by the support Japan accorded certain of the Chinese aspirants for political power. At length, the Chinese undertook a nation-wide boycott of Japanese goods. The fears of the western powers about Japanese intentions mounted further because of the threat of Japan as a commercial and naval rival. The naval race constituted a particularly heavy burden upon the capacities of all the maritime nations and rapidly became a problem of first importance to their war-stricken economies. To Japan inflation, the Chinese boycott, and the expenses of naval armaments and of an unsuccessful Siberian intervention were a bitter yield for her toil and expense during the great war, and the people began to groan under the onerous responsibilities that their government had shouldered.

The major question of Far Eastern international relations left over from the prewar period was the future of the Anglo-Japanese Alliance. Twice renewed since 1902, the alliance was scheduled to expire in 1921. The United States and Canada were particularly opposed to the continuation of the alliance, for it became increasingly clear that Great Britain was thereby obliged to close her eyes to Japan's growing aggressiveness. At a meeting in London of the prime ministers of the Commonwealth in 1921, the prime minister of Canada argued vehemently against renewal of the alliance and in favor of a congress on Pacific affairs to include all powers having Far Eastern interests with the exception of Soviet Russia. In the meantime the people of the United States began to clamor for an end to the race in naval armaments and expressed the expectation that the British and the Japanese would also welcome some agreement that might reduce the burden of expanding naval competition. Hoping for such a coordination of interests and aspirations, President Warren G. Harding in 1921 issued invitations to a Pacific conference. Nine powers—Great Britain, France, Italy, the United States, Japan, Portugal, the Netherlands, Belgium, and China—accepted.

Pacific and naval problems at the Washington Conference IT WAS THE Washington Conference (from November 12, 1921 to February 6, 1922) rather than the earlier Conference of Paris that erected the postwar structure of the Far East. The results of the Washington meetings were embodied in six treaties and thirteen resolutions, and in addition two separate treaties were simultaneously negotiated outside the formal sessions. The Anglo-Japanese Alliance was terminated, and the hopes of China for removal of the limitations upon her sovereignty were encouraged by definite promises regarding tariff autonomy and extraterritoriality. Few failed to note that these decisions promoting amity among the nations were taken outside the League of Nations because the United States was not a member of the League. The League thereby had to forego a rare opportunity to win prestige.

Two of the Washington treaties were concluded with the intention of bringing the naval race to an end and establishing a naval balance of power in the Pacific. The Four-Power Pacific Treaty signed by the United States, the British Empire, France, and Japan specified the rights of the powers "in relation to their insular possessions and insular dominions in the region of the Pacific Ocean." In case of a threat to their rights, it provided that they should consult with each other "to meet the exigencies of the particular situation." Concluded for a ten-year period, this treaty replaced the Anglo-Japanese Alliance as the stabilizing factor in Far Eastern diplomacy.

Directly thereafter, the powers concluded the Five-Power Naval Pact.

Great Britain, the United States, France, Italy, and Japan agreed to limit the capital ships (battleships and cruisers) of Great Britain, the United States, and Japan by a formula of 5:5:3 (i.e., five ton units each for England and the United States to three for Japan) for a period of ten years. Because the United States was in a position to outbuild England, the English consented to parity with the American naval program. France and Italy were allowed to have each a strength of somewhat more than half that of Japan, with a ratio number of 1.7. To maintain the status quo with regard to naval fortifications and bases in the Pacific region, certain islands were not to be fortified. But no limitations could be agreed upon for minor seacraft like light cruisers, submarines, torpedo boats (and a new world war was soon to prove how important these lighter craft can be). In keeping with the terms of the agreement, about 40 per cent of the heavy naval craft, mostly outmoded, was scrapped. Although the Japanese smarted under the "inferior ratio" on new capital-ship tonnage accorded them, the naval arrangements concluded at Washington were officially in force until 1936.

The Chinese problem at the Washington Conference

THE GREATEST achievement of the Washington Conference was the Nine-Power Pact and related agreements pertaining to China. Determined ultimately to rid China of its inferior status, the Chinese delegates adopted as their immediate objectives the winning of tariff autonomy, the elimination of the treaties and notes based upon the Twenty-one Demands of 1915, and the regaining of control over Shantung. At the conference it again became clear that Japanese policy was the major obstacle to the realization of China's hopes. Referring repeatedly to the chaotic condition of China as a danger to the peace of the Far East, the Japanese delegates protested Japan's peaceful objectives and retreated only gradually from the special position won during the war. Their protestations were belied somewhat by the military activities still going on in eastern Siberia.

In many regards the Washington agreement was a victory for China. To be sure, belligerent Chinese nationalists resented the fact that the conference assumed jurisdiction over numerous problems relating to the internal affairs of China. Yet it was noted by the world at large that at Washington, China was permitted for the first time in the twentieth century to have a voice in determining her own future. Moreover, even though divided by internal faction and defenseless against foreign enemies, China had no new impositions placed upon her. On the contrary, she received the support (no less real though qualified) of the United States and Great Britain in her struggle to loosen Japan's grip and to win assurances of eventual control over her own destiny. The Nine-Power Pact constituted the only serious effort so far to frame approved principles for the conduct of international affairs relating to China. All the powers with definite stakes in China (except the Soviet Union) agreed therein "to respect the sovereignty, the independence and the territorial and administrative integrity of China," to aid China "to develop and maintain an effective and stable government," to help advance "the principle of equal opportunity," and "to refrain from taking advantage of conditions in China to seek special rights or privileges" (the open door). In her turn, China, also a signatory of the pact, agreed to support and work within the existing treaty structure.

China's efforts to achieve full sovereignty THE NINE-POWER PACT promised but did not actually include provisions for the major demands of China, which were arranged rather through a series of accompanying treaties and resolutions. Particularly pressing was China's need for tariff autonomy. The establishment of the "effective and stable government" called for in the pact hinged upon the ability of some Chinese ruling group to tap a continuous and adequate source of revenue such as would be provided by the customs, but several of the powers, and especially Japan, insisted that "effective and stable government" was a necessary prerequisite to tariff autonomy. Lengthy discussions at Washington led finally to a compromise providing for revision of the tariff system and for the convocation of a special tariff conference. Accordingly, a few years later, a plenary conference convened at Peking (1925), and the powers agreed to the gradual removal of restrictions upon China's tariff autonomy. Although the political situation was to continue chaotic in China, the powers nevertheless kept their promises. In the spring of 1930 Japan was at length to sign the last of the treaties on customs, thereby according full tariff autonomy to China.

China's effort to revoke extraterritoriality was not fated to reach an equally quick and favorable conclusion. Although the Chinese delegation at Washington referred to extraterritoriality as a "national humiliation," the other representatives pointed out that the administration of law in China was disordered, inefficient, and often corrupt, and that aliens still required consular jurisdiction to protect their lives and holdings. The powers were willing, however, to make a minor concession. They relinquished their control over China's postal services, which had hitherto been a part of the extraterritorial system. The Chinese assumed control over their postal system only in 1923. A score of years had still to elapse before the principle of extraterritoriality in China would be fully abandoned, and then only after it had virtually ceased to function in fact.

Direct negotiations of China and Japan at Washington THE MAJOR points at issue between China and Japan were not included in the formal agenda of the Washington Conference. It was agreed beforehand that these were matters that might best be settled by direct negotiation between the two Asiatic powers. China's hesitation, however, to deal with Japan except in the presence of less interested parties, stimulated the western powers to urge that such direct negotiations take place at Washington. Though reluctant, Japan submitted to this international pressure. Accordingly, at Washington the treaties of 1915 that had emerged from the Twenty-one Demands and the question of Shantung were reëxamined by Japanese and Chinese delegations. The Chinese argued that the treaties of 1915 "vitally affected the very existence, independence, and integrity of China" and should be revoked in the common interests of China and the western powers. On their side, the Japanese contended that China as "a free, sovereign nation" had entered into the treaties of 1915, and that revocation would constitute an "exceedingly dangerous precedent" for the whole treaty structure relating to China. The Japanese proved successful in warding off the Chinese onslaught against the treaties of 1915. Nevertheless, they agreed in 1922 (as earlier) to relinquish the civil control of Kiaochow to China, to transfer the port of Tsingtao to China, and, most important, to withdraw their troops from Shantung. Certain railway holdings and other capital investments of Japan were, in turn, to be purchased by China. Thus China won another major diplomatic victory. In the former German-leased territory she could point to the first major piece of land ever to be returned to China. As an aftermath of discussions at Washington, the British also restored territory to China—the port of Weihaiwei, which was once again placed under Chinese jurisdiction in 1930. The French base at Kwangchowan was not returned until 1945.

Evaluation
of the Washington Conference

THE WASHINGTON treaties occupy a unique place in the history of international agreements. They appeared to many Westerners a longer step toward international order than Versailles. They had resulted in an apparently important victory for disarmament, seeming to put a halt to the Anglo-American-Japanese naval race. The cancellation of the Anglo-Japanese Alliance helped to remove uncertainty about British policy in the Far East and released Britain from an unwilling partnership in Japan's aggressions in China. The accompanying arrangements for the Pacific region were designed to discourage aggression and to support the integrity and independence of a non-European country even at a time when it was in no position to defend itself. The general feeling arose in the West that perhaps a new system of international justice had been born at Washington. The world was to realize only later that the limits placed upon naval building and fortifications in the Far East were to induce Japan to believe that she could command Asiatic waters without fear of a successful challenge from the western powers. And the Japanese, having failed to win recognition of racial equality at Versailles and having lost their alliance with Britain at Washington, were not sanguine about international justice.

649

THE BURDENS of war had forced upon the United States unwelcome responsibilities. Its armed might and wealth, just beginning to be tapped as Europe's resources were reaching exhaustion, had turned stalemate into victory. Wilson's faith and eloquence had called forth a vision of a world order guaranteeing peace with justice. But the people of the United States hesitated to accept the new mission. With the defeat of the Germans, revulsion against war and power politics brought new life to the tradition of deliberate isolation, which had always vied with the tradition of deliberate involvement in European affairs.

The return
to isolationism in America

MOST AMERICANS were generally under the impression that, no matter how the war had come to America, they had engaged in an essentially ideological crusade and not a bout for political advantage. When, therefore, President Wilson came home with a peace treaty that contained patent compromises, many felt that he had been outwitted. The Bolsheviks had published the secret agreements that they had found in the Russian archives, and Americans were shocked to see to what an extent the treaty they were now asked to ratify confirmed those secret covenants secretly arrived at.

The war had not destroyed the spirit of isolation in America. As Americans watched the wrangling and bargaining and spoiling that went on in postwar Europe, they felt that perhaps it had been a mistake to become too closely involved in Europe's imbroglios. Hence the opposition crystallized around Articles 10 and 11 of the Covenant of the League of Nations. Article 10 read in part: "The Members of the League undertake to respect and preserve as against external aggression the territorial integrity and existing political independence of all Members of the League"; and Article 11: "Any war or threat of war, whether immediately affecting any of the Members of the League or not, is hereby declared a matter of concern to the whole League, and the League shall take any action that may be deemed wise and effectual to safeguard the peace of nations." These provisions, it was feared, would bind Americans to go to war without the consent of Congress as provided by the Constitution of the United States.

American repudiation
of the Treaty of Versailles

THE Republican Party made itself the channel of expression for the revived isolationism. Even before Wilson returned, Republican senators had voiced their fear of the surrender of American sovereignty to an international organization. They won support not only from isolationists but also from liberals, pro-Germans, anti-British,

An American cartoonist's view of the futility of the economic and political isolation of the United States. It appeared in the Louisville Courier Journal in 1923.

and others who felt that the treaty was a betrayal of the fine principles of the Fourteen Points. Since the Covenant was an integral part of the peace treaty, rejection of the Covenant meant rejection of the treaty.

President Wilson tried to explain that the United States by signing the Covenant would undertake only a moral, not a legal obligation to enter a war against an aggressor. If he had been willing to permit entrance into the League with reservations, he might have won a majority, but he insisted upon ratification without reservations. While he was campaigning for his views, he became sick, never fully to recover. The electoral campaign of 1920 was fought in part on the issue of membership in the League, and Warren G. Harding, a relatively obscure Republican senator, running on a platform that was ambiguous regarding the League (though he promised League membership during the campaign), defeated a still more obscure Democratic candidate. Harding's victory meant that the Covenant was never ratified by the Senate. Instead, in July 1921, Congress adopted a joint resolution declaring the war at an end without a peace treaty. The next August, almost three years after the armistice, a peace treaty was concluded at Berlin by which the signers accepted many provisions of the Treaty of Versailles. Reparations and disarmament were among them; the League was the chief feature repudiated. Subsequently parallel treaties were made with Austria, Hungary, Bulgaria, and Turkey.

An immediate consequence of the rejection of the Versailles Treaty was that the United States also rejected Wilson's proposed treaty of alliance with France. Britain thereupon repudiated hers. That left the French in a dangerous position if Germany should ever recover from its defeat, and they felt that they had been betrayed. This attitude was ill understood in America. The harshness that the French applied toward Germany was generally misinterpreted as sheer vengeance. On the other hand, the French regarded the outbursts of moral indignation in America as the height of Anglo-Saxon hypocrisy. On both sides of the Atlantic a sense of distrust grew, even though personal and international contacts grew at the same time.

American attitudes toward the League of Nations THE NET effect of the United States' refusal to join the League of Nations was to reduce the prestige and to narrow the objectives of that body from the very start. Some have argued that, even with United States membership, the League would not have succeeded in keeping the peace, since the problems and hatreds which the war had bequeathed were too numerous and too knotty for pacific solution. But others have believed that the possibilities for its success would have been much greater. Their argument ran: The United States was the one country that the small nations of Europe trusted as more or less disinterested in Europe's quarrels; with its withdrawal the confidence of the little nations and the hopes of millions of little people sank, and France, unable to count upon an Anglo-American-French alliance to shield her against a German *revanche,* had to resort to a balance-of-power policy against Germany. Americans were to become more and more saddened or revolted as Europe's politicians pursued their old objectives outside the League or turned that body into an arena of old-fashioned international diplomacy, and to regret or rejoice accordingly that the United States was not involved.

The official dissociation of the United States from the League was at first so complete that even its communications were ignored. After months of silence, the entire accumulation was answered at once in September 1921. Public opinion was, nevertheless, widely favorable to the League; the United States began to send unofficial observers to some nonpolitical League meetings, and after 1925 took an increasing part in the League's social and cultural activities. American citizens served on the World Court from its inception, though the United States did not formally join that body.

The United States did not carry the other American nations with it in its relapse into isolation. Most Latin-American countries joined the League promptly, and during the years of its existence referred to it several disputes for settlement. Canada early joined the League, insisting, despite Wilson's objections, on membership as a full-fledged sovereign rather than as an adjunct of Britain. Because of the important part played by Canadian troops during the war, Canada was able to secure unconditional membership. This was a significant victory for Canada's diplomatic independence. It was followed by another in 1920, when she was also given the right to name a resident minister to the United States, although the post was not filled until 1927. In subsequent years Canada appointed ministers to some other countries. Thus Canada reached a mature international status, and the concept of a dominion in the British Commonwealth underwent a radical though peaceful modification.

Though the United States had repudiated the idea of collective security through League action, it was all in favor of maintaining peace through other means. How far even a Republican administration was committed to international cooperation was demonstrated in 1921 when it initiated the conference of nine naval and Pacific powers (excluding Russia) at Washington. The Washington Conference was the first world-wide diplomatic congress to meet in the United States and did much to spread international good will abroad and provide a counterbalance to the isolationist atmosphere at home.

Economic changes brought to the Americas by the war FOR THE Americas economic readjustment to peace was not, as in Europe, a matter of rebuilding devastated areas, reviving peacetime industry and trade, and coping with catastrophic financial difficulties. It was rather a matter of readjusting expanded wartime industries to peacetime conditions. The war and the collapse of Russian trade had forced the rest of the world into an economic interdependence favorable to the Americas. While the European powers were battling it out on Europe's soil, the Americas had supplemented Europe's reduced production and had provided huge quantities of war materials. Argentina had supplied meat and wheat to the Allies. Chile had provided nitrates, Venezuela, oil. Canada had sent wheat, meat, minerals, wood products, and munitions abroad. The United States had provided all kinds of war materials, food, money, and credit. In the absence of European competition new industries had developed for home markets.

This stimulation had wrought vast changes in the economic systems of the American nations and in their economic relationships with the rest of the world. Industry assumed a big role in Canada, which became a leading industrial nation, trailing behind only three or four of the big powers. Though wheat production remained a basic element in her economy, manufacturing, mining, and lumbering also came to be of first importance. An index of the extent of Canadian industrialization was the increase of urban population to the point where in 1921 it almost equaled the rural population. Latin America experienced a similar rapid industrialization in some areas, although others remained industrially backward. To some extent the war accentuated the tendency to one-product rather than diversified economies and brought a greater dependence on the world market. For example, the great wartime demand for nitrates and the postwar falling-off of that demand left Chile with a grave problem of readjustment. By and large, however, the war-stimulated prosperity continued in Latin America until 1929.

The war made the United States, already one of the leading industrial nations of the world, a mature economic giant. Not only did the industrial production of the United States outstrip that of its rivals; it had taken over many European and Latin-American markets and had become one of the greatest creditor nations in the world. Private investments and both public and private loans gave the United States economic stakes everywhere and in turn made the economies of other nations highly sensitive to American economic policies. For a year or so following the armistice, while peacetime commodities were still scarce, the Americas enjoyed an unprecedented prosperity. Then, as in Europe, a sharp depression followed (1920-1922), brought on partly by postwar deflation and partly by the resumption of normal production and shipping in other parts of the world.

*American business
and the Fordney-McCumber tariff*
THE CONSEQUENT economic readjustment of the United States was, like its political readjustment, fraught with complications for other countries. In 1922 Congress passed the Fordney-McCumber Tariff Act, a protective measure that walled out certain commodities by means of the highest duties in American experience. The act was intended to emphasize agricultural protection and to promote the self-sufficiency of the United States by encouraging the manufacture of such products as chemicals and dyestuffs ("war babies") that had formerly been imported mainly from Germany and now had been developed to a high point in the United States largely through the use of German patents confiscated as war booty. Also given higher protection from foreign competition were some older and better entrenched industries, such as sugar, woolen textiles, and luxury goods, which would have suffered severely from the renewal of foreign competition.

This protective policy undoubtedly gave certain American enterprises a fillip, but it also hampered European recovery by cutting off United States markets, and made it more difficult for nations indebted to the United States to pay their obligations. The initial American insistence on carrying out wartime debt arrangements, coupled with the American tariff policy, exasperated European merchants and governments. "Uncle Sam" became "Uncle Shylock" to Europeans, who quickly lost their vision of Americans as Wilsonian idealists and thought of them instead as crass materialists and mammon-worshipers.

Harding's campaign promise of "return to normalcy" as actually practiced meant favor to business, especially big business. Not only was a prohibitive tariff law enacted, but wartime excess-profits taxes were repealed, and corporation taxes and heavy taxes on high incomes were reduced. The Federal Trade Commission and the Supreme Court were staffed by "safe" men, who did not feel it their special mission to "bust" trusts or to recognize and regulate abuses by big business. A series of strikes in the early postwar years alarmed conservatives, and an open-shop drive conducted by employers against labor unions received government backing, notably in 1922 when a strike by 400,000 railroad shopmen brought forth a sweeping federal court injunction against the strikers. Herbert Hoover as secretary of commerce until 1929 and later as president encouraged the formation of associations of manufacturers to promote efficiency and to standardize industrial conditions; he also fostered business combinations which by price-fixing and voluntary regulations moved business enterprise farther and farther away from the self-regulating competitive market that the classical economist held up as ideal.

Concomitant with the development of big business went the spread of the practice of sharing the profits of production. Henry Ford was one of the leading exponents of profit sharing. Ford did this by means of higher wages and bonuses. Other huge industries preferred the distribution of stock shares among workers on easy terms. Ford and other industrialists reasoned that prosperous workers make potential consumers who can buy more of industry's commodities than underpaid workers. They expected also that prosperous workers would not be good subjects for Communist propaganda or for union organizers.

Nationalism and immigration quotas

A STRIKING tendency of the postwar American mood was its xenophobia (antiforeign impulse). Americans also became, more conspicuously than before, anti-Negro, anti-Catholic, and anti-Semitic, and more insistent than ever upon "100 per cent Americanism." This heightened nationalism sprang not only from the pride engendered by American feats during the recent war but also from the fear of German sympathizers ("pro-Germans") at home during the war and from the revolution in Russia afterwards. Americans were alarmed by the appearance of a small but active group of revolutionary Communists in the United States, avowedly attached to the Third International, which was controlled by Moscow and dedicated to the overthrow of democracy and capitalism. In 1919 several public officials received in their mail packages containing bombs, and other bombings were directed at prominent officials and wealthy businessmen. This violence, whether the work of cranks or of radicals, was easily associated in the public mind with foreigners, union leaders, and Negroes. The great migration of Negro workers from southern farms to northern war industries led to the segregation of large Negro populations in the

North and fear in certain quarters in both North and South that the Negro might not remain as amenable as he had hitherto been. Returning Negro war veterans felt entitled to equal treatment with white veterans. Xenophobia, as in the days when Federalists and anti-Federalists fought over the merits of the French Revolution, became a political issue.

One expression of the new Americanism was the passage of laws restricting immigration. "Emergency" laws passed in 1921 and 1922 were superseded by a law of 1924, which limited the number of immigrants per year from each country to 2 per cent of the number that the census of 1890 showed as having come from that country and being then in the United States. Orientals including Japanese were to be excluded entirely, despite the "Gentlemen's Agreement" of the Roosevelt administration (page 546). The effect of this legislation was to permit relatively easy immigration for north Europeans, who predominated before 1890, and to discriminate against the would-be "new" immigrants from southern and eastern Europe. North Europeans were considered better bred, better educated, more easily assimilable, and less radical. The United States was no longer willing to serve without restriction and discrimination as a haven for "the wretched refuse" of Europe's "teeming shore." The middle-class, white, Protestant, native-born American did not relish the prospect of becoming a member of a minority group.

Intolerance, persecutions, and alarm INTENSE "nativism" immediately after the war found expression in the phenomenal rebirth of the Ku Klux Klan. Taking the name and the nativist spirit of the Klan of Reconstruction days (page 323), the new Klan, founded in 1916, grew, sometimes at the rate of 100,000 a week, to a claimed membership of 5,000,000 in 1925. Anti-Negro, anti-Catholic, and anti-Jew, it operated outside of the law, through threats and terror and midnight parades of white hoods and fiery crosses. For a brief time the Klan became so powerful that in some places it controlled local politics, and even the national political parties avoided taking an open stand against it. Some men who afterwards were to regret their action found it good politics to become affiliated.

"Red" scares and "witch" hunts became a familiar part of the postwar reaction. The Industrial Workers of the World, frankly revolutionary, was the target of a concerted, violent, and generally effective attack. Five representatives were expelled from the New York State legislature because they were Socialists. Personal ambition and public indignation caused by the bomb incidents of 1919 prompted Attorney General A. Mitchell Palmer to seek out and deport suspect aliens in a manner that has made "the Palmer raids" proverbial as a violation of the American tradition of civil liberty.

The extremes of reaction represented by the Ku Klux Klan and the Palmer raids were largely confined to the early 1920's. Even when suspicion was at its highest, many editors, lawyers, judges, and laymen insisted upon fair play and the traditional liberties. Nevertheless, the fear of an alien radicalism remained to inflame the political atmosphere. It deepened the capitalist's distrust of labor, stiffened resistance to change, reinforced the nativist's determination to seal his country off from left-wing importations from Europe, and even led to extensive approval of strong-arm methods at home and abroad that stamped out radicalism and kept the Communists in check.

The new era in American business

IN THE Americas business recovered quickly from the postwar depression of 1920-1922, and except in agriculture prosperity was general again until almost the end of the decade. Laymen and some reputed economists spoke of "a new era" of continuous prosperity. The famous Teapot Dome scandal, involving two cabinet secretaries and some oil magnates in conspiracy to defraud the government, only slightly ruffled the smooth surface of "normalcy." Harding died in office in 1923. His successor, Calvin Coolidge, added to American lore the dictum: "The business of America is business." Secretary of Commerce Hoover and others lauded "rugged individualism."

A trend toward monopoly and combination in business fostered by the war was now further nourished by the benign attitude of the government. In manufacturing, mining, transportation, trade, banking, utilities, newspaper publishing, the new field of radio, and many other industries, small businesses were frequently replaced by a few mammoth concerns. Nationally owned chain systems of grocery stores and five-and-ten-cent stores invaded even the smallest country towns and often forced the local grocer or variety store out of business. Holding companies and investment trusts (corporations whose property was not an industry but stock certificates in other corporations) gave a relatively few financiers inordinate power over the management and policies of large corporations. Frequently a single man might be a director of several or many related companies, thus bringing about a kind of chain system of corporations (or, as it was generally called, an interlocking directorate). A carefree public, blessed with accumulated war bonds to convert into something more profitable, provided a horde of stock brokers with a steady flow of ready cash for a few trusted financial wizards to invest for them in what appeared to be a solid capital structure.

The condition of the farmer and of labor

AMERICAN prosperity of the golden twenties was not universal. The farmers had lost their wartime markets and farm prices had come down, but farm costs remained high. Since they still depended a great deal on sales abroad, the high United States tariff did them little or no good. The reduction in the total of international trade cut down their overseas markets and encouraged competitive production abroad. Canada, Australia, and Argentina became successful competitors with the United States in grain and meat export, and several European countries tried actively to promote a greater degree of self-sufficiency in agriculture. At the same time, farmers were forced to pay for farm machinery and manufactured goods at prices pegged by a protective tariff and by "gentlemen's agreements" among manufacturers at home.

Labor shared more than the farmer in the prosperity of the twenties. Yet even in the peak years at least a million and a half were unemployed. The average working week remained fixed at about fifty hours and average wages rose only slightly during the decade. Union membership and union activity had been abnormally high during the war, but it now declined. This decline was due largely to the concerted campaign against the closed shop begun in 1919 (page 655). The American Federation of Labor, strongest of the unions, retained a conservative, skilled-craft organization, but the great mass of unskilled laborers remained unorganized. Much of the American Federation of Labor's energy was absorbed in a harassing battle with a small but militant group of revolutionary Communists who were attempting to bore from within. Thus American labor found itself under attack from both Right and Left.

Economic interests and intervention abroad

CONSERVATIVE, unsentimental, and isolationist, the government of the United States remained throughout the 1920's a businesslike but flexible creditor to European debtors. Calculated arrangements were made with various debtor countries to scale down interest rates, but in its refusal to cancel the principal the United States was adamant. While the Europeans wanted the United States to write off its loans as America's free contribution to the winning of the war, the United States regarded them as genuine business obligations. "They hired the money, didn't they?" Coolidge asked. When Charles G. Dawes helped to ease tension within Europe by negotiating the scaling down of German reparations (page 707), his contribution to the solution of what was officially considered a purely European problem had little formal backing from the United States government.

Yet, though sternly isolationist, the United States did not hesitate to support its investors abroad, and its government actively aided its businessmen to get raw materials from all over the world. In particular, it fostered control of overseas oil supplies. In Mexico and elsewhere in Latin America, Americans began to outstrip competitors from other countries, but had to spar with the British and Dutch to secure oil concessions in the Near East and the Dutch East Indies. Oil interests in Mexico indeed threatened for a time to embroil the United States in the civil wars of her neighbor south of the Rio Grande, until General Álvaro Obregón was elected president (1920) and made peace at home and arrangements that were satisfactory abroad. Investments in other Latin-American countries, added to the concern over the Panama lifeline, brought the United States Marines to more than one of the little republics. The United States evacuated Santo Domingo in 1924 amidst general approval, and a less aggressive attitude presaged a new era in inter-American relations (Chapter 12).

Disillusionment and revolt against "Victorianism" AMID THE GENERAL conservatism and complacency of a fabulously prosperous era some querulous voices were heard. While slick-paper magazines and tabloid newspapers sang the praises of business efficiency and success, a new generation of novelists and social critics (Chapter 13) pointed out the shortcomings and dilemmas of a civilization rooted in mammon, materialism, and the machine. Cynicism, disillusion, and the revolt against puritanism were in part a product of the war, but they also expressed tendencies beginning to be apparent before the war. The identification of mind with matter in Freudianism and behaviorist psychology, along with the baiting of traditional morality in the writings of Oscar Wilde and the French primitivists, had already wrought havoc with prewar conventions. Then in 1920 the Volstead Act so inclusively defined "intoxicating" beverages as to encourage its violation as a law intended to enforce the Eighteenth (the Prohibition) Amendment to the Constitution (1920). The emancipated youth of the "Jazz Age," the "flapper" in loose-fitting and graceless clothing and her "boy friend"—and their elders, too—drank highballs and cocktails made with bootleg whiskey or gin and home-brewed beer, perhaps in greater quantities than they might ever have consumed of the legal stuff, and it became fashionable to cultivate intemperance and to circumvent the law. This curious phenomenon of official self-denial and private self-indulgence favored the highly organized bootleg industry, which in turn fostered other forms of organized vice, from gambling to blackmail and murder. And the Nineteenth Amendment (1920) at last gave women the right to vote. The flagrant and wholesale disrespect for the law of the land and the new emphasis on freedom and equality for women combined with the older intellectual trends to produce a scornful attitude toward what were called "Victorian conventions," the genteel tradition, and the custom banning sex from polite letters and conversation.

THE GROWTH

OF NATIONALISM IN THE EAST

TWO GREAT slogans came out of the West during the war to hearten the patriots of China, India, and other countries of the East. One of them was Wilson's "self-determination of nations," the other the Communists' "capitalist imperialism." The Japanese, who were well on the way toward imperialism themselves and who reacted to these slogans somewhat differently than did the peoples struggling toward national dignity, could nevertheless unite with them in the desire for equality of Asiatics with Europeans.

China's problems and the Kuomintang

THE GREAT need of the Chinese people and their leaders was to reconcile their internal differences and to undertake seriously the construction of an efficient and honest republic. At both the Versailles and the Washington conferences, foreign statesmen had repeatedly called upon China to do so. Such admonitions usually came from persons who had but a slight acquaintance with China's problems. Ravaged for over a century by an inefficient and corrupt dynasty, and exploited without payment by the great powers of the West, China was in a state of moral and economic confusion that rendered the achievement of order and central authority difficult indeed. This task was made still more complex by the determination of foreign powers to have a voice in the development of the republic. Resentful of outside interference, many of the Chinese leaders steadily became more antiforeign, and their determination grew to repudiate any government whose hands had been soiled by foreign money. In this regard the record of the Kuomintang was fairly clear in its earlier years.

At the end of the war the Kuomintang, though its strength was limited to the Canton area, began actively to plan the overthrow of the northern Chinese government at Peking, internationally recognized and supported by the war lords. Repeated efforts in the postwar years to heal the internal wounds of north and south and to compromise the differences between Canton and Peking were fruitless. Compromise was rendered difficult by divisions within each major group. Complications arose also from the fact that a number of military leaders had established control of armies that obeyed only them and that acted independently of each other. The individualistic aims of the northern war lords and the splintered character of the Kuomintang forces postponed decisive action from either the north or the south. After the Washington Conference, however, the Kuomintang was able to muster sufficient force to begin extending its control outside of the Canton area.

The leadership of Dr. Sun Yat-sen

THE NEW STRENGTH of the Kuomintang was due largely to Dr. Sun Yat-sen. Sun's father was a Christian, and so was Sun throughout his life. He had acquired a medical education in a missionary school in British Hong Kong and began to practice in Portuguese Macao. There he had become interested in the movement for political reform that swept China in the last years of the imperial regime. He engaged in ill-calculated plots to overturn the Manchu empire, founded the Kuomintang, and was ultimately forced to flee the country. Working among overseas Chinese, Sun wandered through Japan, southeastern Asia, America, and Europe. In public speeches, debates, and writings he gradually began to formulate a guiding political philosophy for the Kuomintang.

Like most western-educated Chinese, Sun was concerned with removing the limitations upon China's independence and with organizing a strong central government. This revolution he proposed to accomplish through the promotion of "The Three Principles of the People (*San Min Chu I*), which have formed the starting point of Chinese political thought in the twentieth century. The first of these three principles was to be the achievement of *nationalism,* or unity. After a period of further preparation, China would be ready for democratic self-government of the western type; this was Sun's second principle, *sovereignty*. Unlike many of his western-educated contemporaries, being concerned with the welfare of the poor, he believed that a third principle, a degree of economic security and equality for the masses, would have to be provided to insure the success of the other elements in his program. Around this third principle of *people's livelihood* the most bitter debates of recent Chinese history have raged.

Sun's principles were soon to be put to the tests of experience. The deep resentment felt in China over Japan's Twenty-one Demands and the disappointment with the decisions of the Paris Conference brought out clearly the overwhelming desire of the people for political independence and integrity. The enthusiasm for Sun's positive program among the Chinese students, a powerful political group in a country where the scholar has traditionally been venerated, helped him considerably in the postwar years to fix his position of leadership in the party. In his search for support, Sun also approached the United States, the western European powers, and Japan. Following their avowed policy of refusing to interfere directly in the affairs of China, these powers rejected Sun's overtures.

Sun's relations with the Communists

WHEN Sun approached the Soviet Union, however, he had greater success. Praising him for marching "at the head of Chinese democracy" and for struggling against "the foreign imperialistic powers of oppression," Moscow promised aid and quickly dispatched diplomatic and military missions to Canton. Sun and his Soviet supporters agreed in 1923 that "the Communistic order or even the Soviet system cannot actually be introduced into China, because there do not exist here [in China] the conditions for the successful establishment of either Communism or Sovietism." Nevertheless, the Russians immediately began to exert a considerable influence upon the reorganization of the Kuomintang and the development of an effective Nationalist fighting force. From the beginning, collaboration with the Soviets threatened to break the Kuomintang into Communist and anti-Communist groups. Until his death in 1925, however, Dr. Sun was able by skillfully balancing opposing forces to prevent an irreparable break. After his death, the party leaders, as well as their Soviet cohorts, began to maneuver for control of the party and for the position vacated by Dr. Sun.

Soviet policy in the Asiatic countries

THE Union of Soviet Socialist Republics (as Russia was now officially called), smarting from the indignity of the Allied intervention, the unwillingness of the major western countries to recognize her, and the refusal of the nations to invite her to the peace conferences, made a special effort to cultivate her Asiatic neighbors. Although she was initially rebuffed, the affable proposals of Moscow soon began to sound attractive to Asiatic governments accustomed to peremptory demands. The Russians associated themselves in their public statements with the victims of western imperialism and blamed the ills of Asia upon the misdeeds of Europeans and Americans. Imperialist capitalists, they repeated, were pumping dry the reservoirs of Asia's wealth, forcing the natives to starve. Their claims, persistently broadcast by every instrument of propaganda, appeared convincing, since Russia's defeat of the combined forces of intervention made the Soviet Union appear to be the only continental Asiatic nation to resist successfully the depredations of the technologically superior powers. Since the czarist regime had succumbed on occasion to oriental and European nations alike, the simplest explanation for Russia's new successes seemed to be the effectiveness of the Soviet system and the Bolshevik regime. The political policy of Russia in Asia was as a rule skillfully promoted by the activities of the Communist International (page 668).

In line with their policy of making friends in Asia, the Bolsheviks dissociated themselves as much as possible from the system of unequal treaties. While the western powers did little more than talk of self-determination for the Asiatics, Russia offered new treaties on an equal and reciprocal basis. Such treaties were signed with Turkey, Iran, Afghanistan, China, and Japan between 1921 and 1925. In the Chinese treaty (1925) Russia relinquished the czarist titles to extraterritoriality and returned to China her concessions at Hankow and Tientsin. The treaty with Japan, already mentioned in connection with Northern Sakhalin (page 645), reëstablished consular and trade relations between the two countries at a time when many of the western nations were still boycotting the USSR.

Party rule inaugurated in Japan

WHILE CIVIL WAR and differing political and social philosophies divided China, Japan in the interwar epoch struggled with problems arising in part from her new position as a world power. The swift expansion of Japan from the annexation of Korea in 1910 to the withdrawal from Siberia in 1922 (page 645) redounded to the glory and power of the armed forces. Nevertheless, the period of the twenties was not to be one of marked militarism. Business and other groups with international connections held the center of the stage for a time, and in the years immediately after the World War, Japan passed through an era of comparative liberalism. Although the parties were far from democratic, the islands were to experience their longest stretch of party rule.

During the war years Japan in some regards had had the appearance of prosperity. The growth of foreign trade and the demands of the military produced high profits for industrial, commercial, and certain farming groups. Unfortunately rapid economic expansion also produced inflation and grave dislocations. Wages, as they often do, lagged behind prices, no matter how high the inflationary spiral mounted. Although working full time, workers in factories and those on fixed incomes found it increasingly difficult to fill their rice bowls. By the end of the war the concentration of industry upon war manufacture combined with the uncontrolled inflation to produce acute shortages in most vital consumers' goods, and hunger finally brought about a series of rice riots.

The inability of the war government of bureaucrats and militarists to deal with the economic situation led to the first government by a parliamentary party in Japan's history. Hara Takashi, the first commoner to hold the post of premier, came to power in 1918, and brought with him a political machine almost completely under his personal control. In 1919 a limited franchise reform extended the vote to all men over twenty-five who paid a small tax (formerly 10 yen, now 3 yen). The tax, though sufficient to deprive propertyless laborers of the right to vote, doubled the number of voters from around 1,500,000 to over 3,000,000. Although giving lip service to the principle of responsible government, Hara's party was held together mainly by its interest in the spoils system and in lucrative government contracts. In the three years of his regime, the new businessmen of Japan became prominent in government by taking over posts formerly held by clan leaders. In 1921, a few days before the opening of the Washington Conference, Hara was assassinated by a young "patriot," who thought thereby to take a shortcut to honest government. There followed a quick succession of noble premiers as the demand grew for a wider franchise. Finally, in 1925, a Universal Manhood Suffrage Bill altogether eliminated the property qualification for voting, and the number of voters was more than quadrupled (14,000,000). It remained to be seen whether the broader franchise would really mean a greater popular voice in the government of Japan (Chapter 12).

The Amritsar Massacre and the Government of India Act
IN INDIA postwar unrest was more violent than in Japan. Famine and the influenza epidemic of 1918-1919 that killed millions all over the world caused enormous distress in India, and Nationalist extremists resorted with growing brazenness to acts of terror. Since 1906, hundreds of bombings, murders, and gang robberies had taken place in Bengal alone, with but few convictions of the offenders. To meet the rising discontent, the Rowlatt Act of 1919 permitted the government in 663

emergencies to intern agitators without trial. Though the law was never actually put into force, it was deeply resented as a token of repression.

The bad judgment of a British officer soon brought on an outrage condemned by nearly all the world. In Amritsar General R. E. H. Dyer, meaning "to strike terror into the whole of the Punjab," ordered his men, without warning, to fire upon an illegal but unarmed assemblage. Around 1400 people were killed or wounded. "The Amritsar Massacre" caused a storm of indignation in Great Britain and India alike. Dyer was censured by the House of Commons, and he was obliged to resign. The Indian National Congress bought the site of the massacre and set it up as a "martyrs' memorial." The amir of Afghanistan, believing that India was ready to drop into his lap like a ripe plum, began an attack upon the subcontinent, but he was rapidly shown the error of his calculations.

As became increasingly clear, quiet in India depended on good judgment. The Montagu-Chelmsford Report had been under consideration since 1918 (page 617) and finally became the basis of a new constitution in the Government of India Act of 1919. The act called for the decentralization, democratization, and reorganization of the government. Increased powers were granted to eight Indian provinces, and the central and provincial legislatures, in all of which now the majority were to be preponderantly elective, were permitted to have jurisdiction over specified affairs. The most striking feature of the new constitution was its provision for double government, or what came to be called the "dyarchy." This unique system of administration divided provincial-governmental functions into *reserved* and *transferred* categories. Administration of justice and control of the police (i.e., the instruments of peace and order) were *reserved* to the British governor and the professional civil service. In matters of education and sanitation, the responsibility was *transferred* to the elected legislatures. From this arrangement developed a provincial administrative hierarchy, some of whose members answered to the appointed governor and others to the elected legislatures.

The reaction of India against the dyarchy

ALTHOUGH the authors of the constitution of 1919 looked upon the new provincial system as temporary and transitional, the reaction against it and the central authority in India was immediate and profound. The Indian National Congress denounced the dyarchy as wholly inadequate, and paid slight heed to the British statement that it would be but the first step toward genuine self-government. As the critics pointed out, the new system applied to only eight of the British provinces; the provincial legislatures would be elected by one-tenth of the male population, who alone could meet the high property tax and educational qualifications; and the powers of the legislatures would be more important in theory than in practice, for the new India Act reserved to the governor complete powers under extraordinary circumstances. The Indian

National Congress split in two over the question of whether to accept the new government. The seceding faction became known as the Moderates or Liberals.

Mahatma Gandhi and civil disobedience IN THIS charged situation a new Indian personality rose to world prominence. Educated for the bar in London and having practiced law for twenty years in South Africa, Mahatma ("the holy man") Gandhi had until 1918 been friendly to England and had only recently become one of India's most daring opponents of Britain's rule. Unlike most modern political leaders, Gandhi viewed his mission as both religious and political. In the struggle against discrimination in South Africa he had learned to believe in a policy of exerting political pressure through noncooperation and passive resistance. Zealous and influential among the common people, Gandhi put his crusade on both a spiritual and a material plane. In his campaigns of civil disobedience he pleaded with his followers not to resist, but also not to obey. As might have been expected, many Indians resorted to violence in the name of nonobedience, but Gandhi

An Indian, Sjt. Kanu Desai, made this drawing of Mahatma Gandhi in 1925.

665

promptly repudiated their actions. On the other hand, he sought to put teeth into his measures by encouraging a boycott of British goods and the patronizing of home industry. His fight to break the hold of the British textile industry in India, reflective of his personal hostility to the machine as well as to the British, took the seemingly impractical form of encouraging home spinning. The spinning wheel became for his more fervent disciples a kind of religious symbol.

Gandhi's devotion to a simple and ascetic life endeared him to the millions of India. Like the peasants he dressed simply, lived frugally, respected the ancient traditions, and shared their trials. He rounded out his program of nonviolent resistance and social reform by calling for an end to drunkenness, for unity between Hindus and Moslems, for the restoration of human dignity to untouchable groups, and for the elevation of women to a dignified position in society. His nonviolent doctrine of *Satyagraha* ("defense of truth") spelled out his deep conviction that human beings are unable to rid the world of evil by force and that evil will succumb only to good will, sacrifice, patience, and love. He was willing to base his fight for India's freedom upon the hopeful premise that the better nature of man will eventually triumph over all problems if only violence be not employed.

Hindu nationalism and nonviolent resistance

SINCE THE Government of India Act of 1919 provided that the constitutional experiment should be reviewed within ten years, the Indian Nationalists planned to use the intervening decade to agitate against the limitations on home rule still in force and to call loudly for a new national struggle against imperial control. In the meantime, the system of dyarchy prepared a trained group of native administrators. All was not peaceful in those years within the National Congress party itself. Trouble began in 1920 when Gandhi was elected leader of the Congress. Gandhi's civil disobedience campaigns of 1921-1922 failed to win their objectives and thus estranged important segments of the Nationalist Party. Nevertheless, his campaigns served to stir the political consciousness of the lower classes and to enlist their active support in the struggle against British rule. It was only by imprisoning the Mahatma and other nationalist leaders in 1922 that the British managed to halt the civil disobedience campaign, which had been growing in seriousness for over a year. Gandhi was not released until 1924. Thus, in India, as in other parts of Asia, the postwar era was one of bitterness and agitation.

Nationalist aims in colonial Asia and Oceania

LIKE THE people of India and other contemporaries, the peoples of colonial Asia and Oceania began to expect a greater degree of independence and equal treatment from their European masters. The French in Indochina, the British in Burma and Malaya (as well as in India), the Dutch in the Indies, and the Americans in the Philippines were challenged vigorously and repeatedly by dissident native groups demanding a stronger voice in government and administration and a larger share of the wealth produced in their lands. Many groups in Europe and America were sympathetic with the nativist movements, and both economic and political advances were recorded, but the western governments rarely went beyond discussing measures preparatory to independence. Though of recognized merit, the arguments used by the western governments were often thought to be only foils in an endless duel between those who wanted freedom for Asia and those who opposed it.

The several nationalist movements of colonial Asia proclaimed similar objectives because they had grown out of similar circumstances. To the rice-producing natives, autonomy had little meaning except in terms of what it might contribute toward easing the hardships of daily life. Their western-trained leaders, however, even in the prewar decades had implored the western governments to introduce changes leading not only to greater economic and political security but also to full independence. Demands for reform had increased as the rapid development of communication and transportation between the colonies and their "mother" countries made the natives ever more aware of the great gulf between eastern and western ways of life. This growing consciousness of inferior status had led to compromises of native differences and to a consequent development of oriental unity and a concomitant spread of revulsion against white exploitation and control.

The failure of "self-determination"   DURING THE war slogans of democracy and self-determination reached into remote corners where perhaps western orators had not intended to be heard. Colonial soldiers and workers who had been shipped to European fronts in 1914-1918 often returned with brilliant phrases still ringing eloquently in their ears. Hope ran particularly high because Wilson had proposed as Point 5 of the Fourteen Points "a free, open-minded, and absolutely impartial adjustment of all colonial claims based upon a strict observance of the principle that in determining all such questions of sovereignty the interests of the populations concerned must have equal weight with the equitable claims of the government." With the acceptance of Wilson's terms as a basis for armistice negotiations, many Asian groups believed that a new day was dawning. Their expectations were bitterly dashed, however, when it became clear at Versailles that the powers of the West were determined to make the basic decisions of the peace without permitting Japan, the leading nation of the East, to have a voice in the deliberations of the "Big Four." The fatal blow to their hopes came when the Japanese failed to get a racial equality clause accepted as part of the Covenant of the League of Nations. The mandate system, in which Wilsonians found some basis for hope, appeared from the oriental viewpoint to be simply a new device for the extension of imperial exploitation and control, in which the 667

Japanese now would also take part. As in China, the peace arrangements of 1919 and afterwards were looked upon in colonial Asia and Oceania as a "white peace" from which Orientals could expect but little.

The Soviet program of opposition to colonialism

IN THEIR disillusionment the nationalist groups turned to the suave voices calling from the Soviet Union. Marxism taught that capitalism thrived on imperialism and would die when the colonies were lost or squeezed dry. By opposing imperialism the Bolsheviks hoped to win allies among the Asiatic peoples who were ripe for revolutionary efforts, and at the same time to deal a death blow to capitalism. By repudiating the extraordinary privileges claimed by the former Russian government, the Bolsheviks persuaded people throughout Asia and in certain circles in Europe of their sincerity. Unlike other white powers, the new Russia, once it had professedly repudiated its colonial claims, felt free to encourage the anticolonialism of the natives of Asia. The Comintern's agents aided the ill-coordinated native societies and parties to work out their organizational problems and to choose wisely the time and the targets to strike. Through Communist leadership the inarticulate unrest of colonial Asia was gradually transformed into an organized political and military resistance. The effectiveness of Communist methods increased the Russians' prestige among Asiatics, made numerous converts to Communism, and enabled Communists to exercise an increasingly important degree of influence upon native movements. In the eyes of many in the Asiatic world *capitalism* became synonymous with *status quo* and *exploitation,* and *communism* with *change* and *freedom.*

Eastern Asia and the Communist International

CONSISTENT with their doctrine of world revolution, the Communists began in 1919 to organize the workers of Asia. At Shanghai, Peking, and Canton they "bored" within the labor unions and among the students, while the Soviet government won confidence by offering up all "special privileges" acquired at China's expense by the Russian imperial government (page 492). In Japan, the Communist experiment in Russia seemed an attractive model for some of the working classes; a Japanese branch of the party was organized in 1921, and the next year the Japanese radical Katayama Tetsu was asked to preside over a congress of the Communist International at Moscow. In French Indochina the Communists, working with radical student groups, supported and encouraged their attacks upon white imperialism. In India and elsewhere in the Asiatic tropics the agents of Communism also propagated hatred of the "capitalist exploiters" from the West. Thus from its earliest years the Communist movement sought to take advantage of the nationalistic spirit of the Orientals to extend Russian influence in Asia. This alliance between nationalism and Communism was to become one of the most dynamic forces in the development of the Far East.

EUROPE SAFE

FOR DEMOCRACY?

THE END of the war brought profound relief to the nations of Europe, to be sure, but also new maladjustments. The entire economic life of all countries, belligerents and neutrals alike, had been geared to war production. The sudden cessation of war orders after the armistice caused social and economic dislocations, which in some countries assumed a semirevolutionary character. As business and government finance became more and more dislocated, the expenses of rebuilding new governments and fiscal systems mounted. War and revolution, reparation and war debts unsettled finances and tax collections; and the credit of new governments was too feeble to enable them to obtain satisfactory loans. They resorted to inflation of the currency, and in several instances inflation was to prove disastrous. New nations like Poland, the Baltic States, and Czechoslovakia had yet to rebuild commercial ties with each other and with western markets, since their old roads, railways, communication lines, and business methods had centered on the major cities of the empires of which they had once formed part. Making new ties was, however, complicated by the desire to defend national industries and markets and to raise revenue by high tariffs.

National planning and international order

WHEN EUROPE emerged from four years of bloodshed and destruction, many of its old institutions were thoroughly discredited. They had not been able to prevent, and in some instances they had helped to provoke, the outbreak of the most catastrophic war in history. The world had suffered so horribly that many felt a change was needed. In the beginning, not even the drastic Russian experiment looked so forbidding to large numbers in the West as it was to look later. Europeans generally thought that only a greater degree of democratization of government and a more just economic and social setup could prevent a recurrence of what had happened in 1914. They were prone to believe that governments rather than peoples made wars. Hence, if peoples could be made content by a just social order and if they could control their governments by more democratic institutions, war would become an archaic memory. Social planning and international organization, as well as democratic constitutions, won adherents everywhere. But they also had their opponents.

About the hardest prewar questions carrying over into the postwar world were the cleavages between capital and labor inside countries and between nationalism and international order among countries. This double cleavage complicated developments in most of Europe. The postwar growth of Communism and the hobbled career of the League of Nations made both problems more complex. Communism caused Socialists to wonder whether the state, in order to plan its economic and social program, needed to be authoritarian, and the challenge of the Comintern raised the question whether planning was better done on a national or an international basis. Hence parties arose that were nationalist first and socialist afterwards (Fascists), to compete with those that were socialist first and nationalist afterwards (Social Democrats) and those that were international socialists (Communists).

The problem
of capital and labor in Britain

VICTORY did not bring prosperity to the United Kingdom. It had suffered around 3,000,000 casualties on the battlefields and the seas. It had poured out billions of pounds sterling to finance its own forces and those of its allies. During the war, the United States and Japan had entered many markets previously monopolized by Great Britain. And cheap labor as well as efficient techniques now permitted Japanese industry to undercut British prices. The high value of almost any kind of foreign money in terms of the inflated postwar German mark made German merchants also anxious to sell abroad at undercutting prices. Furthermore, the war and the collapse of Germany in 1918 deprived the British of one of their best customers; and subsequent German reparations to Italy and France in kind, particularly of coal, deprived Britain of other customers. For these and similar reasons British industry did not do well after the war. British shipping stagnated, unprecedented numbers of workers were unemployed (about 1,000,000 in 1921; about 2,000,000 in 1924), and the government had to pay "doles," or employment insurance benefits, which in 1920 were extended to cover nearly all unemployed industrial workers. Discontent led to several strikes.

In 1918 Great Britain enlarged the franchise to all males over 21 and all females over 30. The major domestic issue now was the retention of a free trade policy. On that issue Lloyd George's coalition government broke up in 1922, and the Conservative government that succeeded it put the question up to the people in December 1923. The Conservatives' protective policy won a plurality, but Labour and the Liberals combined controlled Parliament. In January 1924 the Labour Party went into power for the first time. It was headed by Ramsay MacDonald, who had opposed the war and had only recently regained the leadership of his party. The Labour government lasted a little over eight months and, having no majority, could accomplish little of significance. Its major act in the field of foreign policy was to grant formal recognition to Soviet Russia. It proved unable to remedy the widespread unemployment and hardship.

England
and the "Irish Republic"

IN IRELAND, when the war was over and the election of December 1918 took place, the anti-British mood swept Sinn Fein into a great victory at the polls. The seventy-three victorious Sinn Fein candidates decided not to attend the sessions of the British Parliament. Instead they constituted themselves the Constituent Assembly of the Irish Republic and convened in Dublin. On January 21, 1919, they declared Ireland's independence and named Eamon De Valera president. They sent a delegation to the peace conference at Paris, but it was unable to win formal recognition.

The six northern counties (Ulster) still refused, however, to be included in an autonomous Ireland, and the south Irish refused not only to relinquish Ulster but also to accept allegiance to the British crown. De Valera (page 597), who had recently been rearrested and had escaped from prison, was in the United States in 1920. He declared that any home rule arrangement envisaged by the British would be inconsistent with the independent Irish Republic proclaimed in 1919. A desultory "Anglo-Irish War," consisting mostly of assassinations on both sides, had been going on since 1919. When Ulstermen expelled several thousand Roman Catholic workers from the shipyards of Belfast in 1920, the civil war between the two parts of Ireland was intensified. The British sent to Ireland the Royal British Constabulary, popularly known from the colors of their uniforms as "the Black and Tans." These men were a military police composed chiefly of tough noncommissioned officers who had served in the World War. World opinion swung in favor of the south Irish when the Black and Tans shot the lord mayor of Cork, fired into a Sunday football crowd, and burned down part of the city of Cork. Irish stubbornness was revealed when the new mayor of Cork, Terence J. MacSwiney, and his companions starved themselves to death on a hunger strike that lasted, in MacSwiney's case, seventy-five days.

The creation of the Irish Free State THE WAR IN Ireland went on through 1920 and 1921. Eventually Lloyd George, then prime minister, offered to compromise. Despite the opposition of De Valera, five delegates of the Dáil Éireann (the Republican parliament of Ireland) went to England to confer with the prime minister. In December 1921, a treaty was signed granting to the "Irish Free State" recognition as a dominion, with its own parliament and an executive responsible to that parliament. Together with the other "autonomous communities" within the British Empire it was "united in a common allegiance to the Crown," and an oath of faithfulness to the king was required of members of the Dáil Éireann. The agreement gave the six northern counties the right to choose for themselves whether or not to adhere to the new Ireland, and no great insight was required to anticipate that they would prefer to remain in the framework of the United Kingdom.

The Irish divided heatedly over the treaty with Great Britain. Those who believed with De Valera that Ireland was already a sovereign republic spurned the proffered dominion status. The Dáil Éireann accepted it, however, and De Valera in disgust resigned as president of "the Republic." A civil war now broke out between those, on the one side, who favored the treaty with Great Britain and, on the other, the Irish Republican Army, which stood for a totally independent Ireland. Meanwhile, members of the Irish Republican Army also made raids into the territory of Ulster. Field Marshal Sir Henry Wilson, formerly head of the Imperial General Staff, appointed by Ulster to defend the country, was assassinated in London by two Irishmen in June 1922. Michael Collins, one of the signers of the treaty and prime minister of the Irish Free State, was assassinated in August. Nevertheless, the De Valera forces were ultimately crushed.

The Dáil had meanwhile adopted a democratic constitution. In December 1922 the Irish Free State was proclaimed, and a few days later the last British troops left southern Ireland. The Irish Free State became a member of the League of Nations in 1923. But Ireland had to wait until 1925 for long overdue economic and social reform.

Complications
in the British control of Egypt

THE British Empire underwent change also in other areas. We have already considered the new status of Canada (page 653) and India (page 664). When war broke out between Great Britain and Turkey in 1914, the British by a unilateral act had declared a protectorate over Egypt, nominally a vassalage of the Turkish sultan, and had deposed the khedive. The Egyptians resented British rule, partly for religious reasons, partly because of British war measures, partly because the European conception of nationalism had gained a foothold in Egypt. The Wafd, a steadily growing popular nationalist party, was at the bottom of a large-scale insurrection in 1919, to which the British replied by additional acts of repression and by a commission of investigation under Lord Milner. The commission issued reports proposing conditional independence. On February 28, 1922, the British declared that their protectorate had come to an end and that Egypt was a sovereign state. At the same time, however, they proclaimed that the defense of Egypt and the Suez Canal, the protection of foreigners, and the administration of the Sudan were British obligations, though subject to discussion with Egypt. Sultan Fuad took the title of King Fuad I and in 1923 granted a constitution creating a liberal regime with universal suffrage and a responsible ministry. The Wafd soon gained the upper hand in the new Egyptian parliament. Riotous demonstrations not only against the British but also against the king were frequent.

French dependence
upon German reparations

THE WORLD WAR had been fought longest and had left its ugliest scars in France. France had suffered nearly 5,000,000 casualties. About 13,000 square miles of her territory were in ruins. In many areas the horses and the livestock had been abducted or slaughtered by the German occupation forces. The fields had been destroyed, the fruit trees deliberately cut down, the mines systematically flooded, the railways thoroughly ransacked. The French peasants and workers, still under the influence of war propaganda, which had taught that scheming Prussian militarists had without cause attacked an unsuspecting France, believed that if ever a war had been caused by one side alone, this one was it, and that therefore the Germans were solely responsible. To them it was self-evident that "the Boche," having made France pay through the nose in 1871, ought now to pay for everything. To make matters worse, France was deeply indebted financially to Britain and the United States, and the Bolsheviks had repudiated the French loans made to the czarist government. If the Germans and the Russians did not pay them, how could they pay Britain and the United States? France's economic problems thus had both domestic and international repercussions.

*Inflation
and instability in France*

VICTORY brought prosperity to France even less than to Great Britain. France's major domestic complication after the war was monetary inflation, which reached a threatening level in 1924. The parties on the Left hoped to stop it by emergency measures including a high tax on capital itself (the so-called "capital levy") and a high income tax as well. The parties on the Right wanted to increase indirect taxes, which, being transferable to the prices paid by the ultimate consumer, would hit the poor harder than the rich. Poincaré's ill-starred invasion of the Ruhr (pages 702-707) only increased the financial instability of France without collecting reparations. In the elections of 1924 a coalition of parties on the Left (Cartel des Gauches) won a majority. The Cartel des Gauches, however, proved incapable of solving the monetary problem. The open and conscious cleavage between capital and labor in France made almost any solution unacceptable to one side or the other. The coalition broke into fragments over this question, and inflation continued to mount.

*The French
in Morocco and Algeria*

THE FRENCH empire also encountered its difficulties. After the French had established their protectorate over Morocco in 1912, they succeeded in a surprisingly short time in pacifying the country. This pacification was mostly the work of Marshal Louis H. G. Lyautey. Although he was sometimes sharply criticized for his arbitrary methods, he combined in his person the administrative ability of the Roman proconsul with the boldness of the British empire-builder. He had founded cities with modern sanitation, streets, and lighting. He had partly industrialized Morocco. He had made it so secure for the French that during the World War they were able to pull most of their troops out of Morocco without encountering subsequent difficulties from the natives.

The French situation in Morocco became dangerous only after the war, when Spanish Morocco was rocked by a rebellion under the Riff chieftain Abd-el-Krim (page 687). The Riff Berbers were overwhelmed only after the French went to the assistance of the Spanish. But Morocco was no longer the safe place for the French that it had been. As nationalism crept into Morocco, however, it tended to diminish (but without disappearing) in Algeria, which formed an integral part of metropolitan France, largely because in 1919 the French granted French citizenship to great numbers of Algerians who either had served the French well during the war or had reached a certain stage of culture as demonstrated by their literacy or property.

Italy's problems after the First World War ANOTHER of the victors, Italy, by the end of the war was suffering from many ills. It was an overpopulated country. Its industry, concentrated in the north, had to import coal and all but a few raw materials. Its agriculture, concentrated in the south, was outdated. Economically and physically it was exhausted by sacrifices (including nearly 2,000,000 casualties) that had been much greater than all but a few Italians had anticipated in 1915. Its currency was inflated, and the lira retained only one third of its prewar value. The people were confronted with a severe food shortage. Many veterans found themselves unemployed. It did not improve their morale to learn that the Conference of Paris hesitated to give Italy all the *Italia irredenta* which they had conquered or any of Germany's former colonies or control of the Adriatic, which the Italians called *mare nostrum* ("our sea"). Unrest was the inevitable consequence of these economic and political discontents. Many of the discontented were dazzled by the picture of the "glorious revolution" in Russia, and some even refused to cheer for their own king. A revolutionary mood seized the country. Scribblings on house walls commonly read: "Long live Pope Lenin!"

D'Annunzio's adventure in Fiume D'ANNUNZIO, prince of literary snobs and master of the Italian language, had long made a cult of the wedding of poetry with action. Though already in his fifties, he had volunteered as an aviator during the war and had lost the sight of one eye in battle. Bored with peace, he now sought new heroic experiences. His opportunity came when President Wilson refused to let the Italians have Fiume, and the Fiume question was left unsettled by the peace conference. Until such a settlement should be made, the town and its surroundings were to be occupied by the regular Italian army. When an officer of that army suggested to D'Annunzio that he seize Fiume, the histrionic poet-adventurer jumped at the chance. He pictured himself in a role combining the Renaissance condottiere, Lord Byron in Greece, and Garibaldi in Sicily. At the head of a Falstaffian band of disgruntled ex-officers and adventurers, among whom were a few genuine "liberators," he seized Fiume in September 1919 without encountering resistance and made himself dictator of the disputed seaport.

D'Annunzio's role now changed and he became a benevolent despot ruling with the assent of his community, which was held in trance by his

oratory. *Opéra bouffe* though this may have been, D'Annunzio's Fiume venture gave play to all the heroics without which the future movement of Fascism could not have captivated the crowds. The balcony harangues, the so-called "Roman salute" (with the raised right arm, which was in fact a salute more often given by Roman slaves than by their masters), the Fascist yell *A noi* ("For us"), the black shirts, and other things that were later thought to be typical of Fascism were D'Annunzio's inventions. After fifteen months of D'Annunzio as "Duce" ("leader"), the Fiume question was peacefully settled between Italy and Yugoslavia (page 641), and the Italian government decided to oust him. D'Annunzio, confronted by the booming guns of Italian battleships, preferred to call his adventure off and retired to his estate on the shores of Lake Garda. Many of D'Annunzio's band now joined a new Duce.

The early career of Benito Mussolini

THE NEW Duce was the heavy-jawed, heavy-shouldered, and heavy-strutting Benito Mussolini, son of a revolutionary-minded blacksmith of Romagna and of a school teacher. He had been named Benito after Benito Juárez, the Mexican revolutionary leader. As a young man he had been a revolutionary himself. He had joined the Italian Socialist Party, had done some teaching, and had worked for a time as a mason in Austria and Switzerland. In both countries he had fallen out with the police because of his revolutionary activities. At one time or another he appears to have been exposed, whether directly or indirectly, to   675 the ideas of Machiavelli, from whom he thought he derived the maxim that the end justifies the means; of Nietzsche, from whom he thought he derived the conviction that nineteenth-century ideals were not fit for the men of the future; and of Georges Sorel, from whom he thought he derived the expectation that decadent democracy would yield to direct violence.

Consistency was no hobgoblin of Mussolini's mind. At one time he had been strongly antimilitarist, attacking in his editorials the Italian war against Turkey. In 1912 he became the editor-in-chief of *Avanti,* the leading newspaper of the Italian Socialists. When Italy's entry into the World War was in the offing, he changed his mind, advocated joining the Allies, was obliged to resign his editorship, and withdrew from the Socialist Party. He now became a passionate nationalist. Some people ascribed his change of mind to a genuine conversion. Others believed, however, that he simply saw from which direction the wind was blowing and decided to set his sails so as to take the greatest advantage of it. With money secretly given to him by the French government, he founded an interventionist newspaper, the *Popolo d'Italia (Italy's People),* which carried as its mottos: "Who has steel has bread" (said to be from the socialist Blanqui) and "Revolution is an idea which has found bayonets" (said to be from Napoleon). After war was declared he became a soldier, was wounded accidentally by an Italian weapon, and was discharged from the army.

As has been indicated in the analysis of earlier revolutionary movements, a revolution to succeed not only needs widespread dissatisfaction on the part of people who are ready to support each other in a struggle for betterment under recognized leaders, but must come at a time when the conservative forces are unable or unwilling to put up effective resistance. The so-called "Fascist Revolution" came at just such a juncture. Mussolini founded the Fasci di Combattimento (Combat Bands) in March 1919 and gave them a program that seemed somewhat paradoxical. The *Fascisti* were to be at the same time nationalistic, revolutionary, republican, anticlerical, and authoritarian. At first this contradictory program did not attract a great many advocates.

The elections of 1919 and 1921 in Italy IN THE elections of November 1919, hard times were the major issue. They were the first elections held under a recently adopted law granting universal manhood suffrage and proportional representation. In consequence, they produced a large anti-monarchist Socialist vote. Hoping to offset the growing radicalism, politically conscious Catholics had recently formed the Partito Popolare (Popular Party), and subsequently Pope Benedict xv had given Italian Catholics permission to take an active part in politics; but the new Catholic Partito Popolare trailed the Socialists. Mussolini's Fascists gained not a single seat in the Chamber of Deputies; Mussolini himself, running in Milan, received fewer than 5000 out of a possible 346,000 votes.

Continued social unrest led to strikes and lockouts, and union leaders induced the workers in many places to seize their factories by "sit-down" strikes, because they felt that the slow-working parliamentary machinery was not apt to cure their economic ills. Street fighting broke out in several cities and agrarian uprisings in several provinces. Mussolini now had taken over D'Annunzio's myrmidons and trimmings, and appealed to the millions of the unorganized middle class who were fearful of the workers' trade unions and the Socialist Party, to disgruntled army officers, and even to Socialists bored with a drab and unsuccessful Marxism. Factory invasions by the workers and unrest among the peasants were met by Fascist head-breaking expeditions.

The elections of May 1921 were carried on amidst mounting disorder. The result was a clear plurality for the Liberal and Democrat parties, which supported the government. Only thirty-five Fascists (including Mussolini) had succeeded in getting elected, and still fewer Communists. The revolutionary movements seemed over. In July, Mussolini himself conceded in his newspaper: "To say that there still exists a Bolshevist peril in Italy is to substitute certain insincere fears for the reality. Bolshevism is vanquished."

The tactics of Mussolini's "Black Shirts"

NEVERTHELESS, the anxiety that the Communists had caused among businessmen, landowners, and the middle class remained. Their confidence that the government could keep the workers from again seizing the factories had been thoroughly undermined, and they were prepared to look with favor upon unconstitutional measures. The propertied classes doubted that the Catholic Partito Popolare, though it was opposed to the existing government, would suit their purposes, since it stood for a program of social, especially agrarian, reform. The propertied wanted a party that opposed both the government and social reform. They found what they sought in the Fascisti.

Businessmen and landowners had by this time begun to show open appreciation of Mussolini and what was more, they provided him with money to feed, clothe, and equip his *squadre d'azione* (action squads) and to transport their black-shirted *squadristi* on their "expeditions." It now was a common event for *squadristi* to converge in great strength upon a given objective—a trade-union center, a factory whose workers were on strike, a Socialist meeting, or a Communist city council—and, outnumbering their adversaries, to beat them up. Communist "Red Guards" at first retaliated in kind whenever they could, but the initiative quickly passed to the "Black Shirts." They learned to practice their strong-arm tactics when they knew the police would not be present or could be expected to be indifferent or to show favor to the Fascist side. The police became more and more favorable as the Fascists infiltrated little by little into the administrative system, as they seized control of city after city, and as weak ministers, with the frightening example of the Russian Communists in mind, consented to private warfare against the "Reds." Sometimes judges would acquit Fascists who had to stand trial for acts of violence.

As the movement grew, the instability of cabinets (five between June 1919 and February 1922) and impatience with the parliamentary system led many people to condone the ways of Fascism. Ambitious intellectuals joined the Fascist ranks, giving the movement an air of respectability. Leading businessmen, high-ranking army officers, and celebrated clergy became interested, though such "élite" seldom joined the movement directly. Gradually, workingmen, too, moved over into the Fascist ranks.

The surrender to the "March on Rome" IT STOOD Mussolini in good stead that Italy had in the cabinet of Prime Minister Luigi Facta a weak and inept Liberal and Democrat government, and in the Socialist and Popular parties weak and internally divided opposition. Finally the labor unions woke to the realization that they were fighting an ambitious man rather than a program. Mussolini by this time had revealed his hand: "Our program is simple: we wish to govern Italy....It is not programs that are wanting for the salvation of Italy, but men and will power." The labor unions called a general strike in August 1922, but by this time the Fascists had hundreds of thousands in their ranks. They succeeded in breaking the strike. On October 24, at a Fascist rally in Naples, 40,000 *squadristi* passed in review, shouting "On to Rome!" Mussolini sent an ultimatum to Facta: "Either the government will be given to us or we shall seize it by marching on Rome." Within a few days the demonstration of strength known in Fascist annals as the "March on Rome" began. By this time the king and the church recognized that Mussolini's republicanism and anticlericalism had vanished. When the prime minister weakly urged the king to declare martial law (weakly, for it was not certain that the army would obey) and to make an end to Mussolini's "Black Shirts," the king refused. Instead he called Mussolini to Rome (from Milan, where Mussolini had safely retired during the "March") to form a new government.

The Fascists in power in Italy AS PRIME minister Mussolini's first concern was to have the legislature enact an enabling law giving him dictatorial powers. Fascism, supposedly a revolutionary movement, thus came to power by a "legal" coup d'état. Once in power it proceeded to set up a dictatorship by studied parliamentary acts. Hitler was to copy this method eleven years later. Within a year Mussolini brought all the provincial governments, the army, and the legislature to heel by a series of decrees and laws and won official recognition of his "Black Shirts." He himself became responsible to the king alone, and the king was a weak man.

Mussolini was no longer mere "prime minister" but the "head of the government," and to the Fascists he was "il Duce."

It took several years, however, for the Fascists' Duce to become the undisputed master of Italy, and a large part of the population remained in more or less discreet opposition to him throughout his dictatorship. In that respect his situation was different from that of Hitler's (Chapter 12). Like other dictators Mussolini did not feel safe if he permitted civil liberties to prevail. He organized an efficient secret police. Censorship of newspapers, books, and teaching was attempted, though it was much less thorough than in Nazi Germany or in Soviet Russia. Those who dared to speak out against Fascism were often subjected to the infamous "castor oil" treatment. People considered dangerous to the government were exiled to remote villages or the Lipari Islands and occasionally done away with. In the elections of April 1924, the Fascists, wielding cudgels and castor oil and counting the votes themselves, received (so they announced) 4,700,000 votes—about twice the number of all the other parties combined.

The Matteotti Affair
and the Aventine Secession

AT THIS juncture a Fascist assassination almost brought about Mussolini's collapse. A young Socialist deputy, Giacomo Matteotti, had published anonymously a book that in English translation was entitled *The Fascisti Exposed: A Year of Fascist Domination* (1924). In it he disclosed the violence and corruption of the Fascist government in the year 1922-1923. He repeated these charges in a speech to the Chamber of Deputies, despite the angry protests of the Fascist members, and otherwise indicated that he meant to bring his chronicle of violence and corruption up to date. Matteotti's charges scared Mussolini, whose popularity among the workers was endangered by such disclosures. It is possible that Mussolini himself instigated the assassination of Matteotti. In any case, some outstanding Fascisti kidnaped and killed him.

The murder upset the whole country. Had the anti-Mussolini forces acted energetically, his downfall might have resulted. But, weak in numbers and in leadership, they merely bolted the Chamber of Deputies in what they called, in reminiscence of a famous protest in ancient Roman history, "the secession to the Aventine" (one of Rome's seven hills). Thus of their own volition they did for Mussolini what other dictators had to risk doing themselves. They purged the parliament of the opposition.

Mussolini for a moment was shaken and began to make concessions. But the anti-Fascists fumbled the situation, relying chiefly upon verbal attacks. Mussolini soon regained his self-assurance. He arrested opponents, bought up or repressed the opposition newspapers, and proceeded to pass laws with a rump parliament. Thus the Aventine Secession presented him with a well-exploited opportunity to tighten his hold upon parliament and the press. By 1925 it was clear that Fascism was not going to be easily deposed. **679**

*President Ebert
and constitutionalism in Germany*

IF IT COULD be questioned whether the war had brought more grief than glory to the victors, for the vanquished it was beyond question both grievous and inglorious. The Germans had fondly hoped that their new republic would not be held to answer for the sins of the German Empire. Blockade and *Diktat,* however, got the new republic off to a bad start. The revolutionary government of 1918 was dominated by the Majority (i.e., the more moderate) Socialists, under the leadership of Friedrich Ebert and Philip Scheidemann. In order to give a permanent constitution to the new Germany, this government called for a national assembly to meet at Weimar, famous as the residence of Goethe. The Weimar Assembly elected Ebert the first president of the German Republic, suppressed some Communist uprisings in the spring of 1919 (page 688), and accepted the Treaty of Versailles.

The so-called "Weimar Constitution" was adopted in July 1919. It provided a seven-year term for a president who was to be chosen by universal suffrage. He was to name a cabinet, which was to be responsible to the majority of the lower house (Reichstag) of the legislature. The upper house (Reichsrat) was to consist, like the old Bundesrat, of representatives of the German states (now reduced to 18). It could no longer veto legislation, but, being permitted a consultative voice, still could delay legislation. The Reichstag was to be chosen by a system of proportional representation, designed to give each party a number of representatives proportional to its size. This feature of the Weimar Constitution was generally greeted as a highly commendable democratic innovation, for it promised to give a proper voice to all shades of opinion. In practice, it proved a means of strengthening the party organizations (since all but the smallest could hope for some offices and since candidates were selected by the party central committee and not by the voters). It encouraged small parties to avoid absorption by stronger ones and obliged a chancellor to compromise and combine with several parties in order to be sure of a majority. In the end many Germans came to prefer the one-party system, but, for the nonce they thought, and the world agreed, that the Weimar Constitution was perhaps the most liberal in the world.

*Weaknesses
in Germany's democracy*

THE Weimar Constitution looked democratic indeed on paper, but it was counteracted in practice by the civil service, the military, the aristocracy, and the big businessmen, many of whom looked either back to the monarchy or forward to an authoritarian republic. Two flaws in the constitution helped these antidemocratic elements. One was proportional representation, which produced more than a dozen parties and eventually paralyzed the legislature. The other was the ill-advised Article 48. It gave the president the right in times of threatening disorder to set aside certain constitutional requirements and promulgate emergency decrees. If, therefore, a government were to prove unable to carry its measures in the Reichstag because the splintering of parties made majorities uncertain, it might take advantage of Article 48 to enact the same measures by presidential decree. The Reichstag had the right to revoke a presidential decree, but in that case the president might dissolve the Reichstag and appeal to the electorate. By the use of Article 48 the legislative process was eventually to be undermined.

The conflict of capital and labor in Germany

IN THE EARLY years of the Weimar Republic the Social Democrats, the moderate workers' party, predominated. They participated in several state cabinets, and in Prussia they were almost permanently at the helm from 1919 to 1932. Although after 1920 Ebert's cabinet was usually dominated by the Center, he remained president until his death in 1925. German labor in that interval won several goals for which it had long been striving. Trade unions became powerful political and economic organizations. On the other hand, big business, backed by former aristocrats and the impoverished middle class, became afraid of the growing power of the workers. In addition, the traditional pacifism of the Socialists was suspect to the army. Thus for military as well as for economic reasons, big business and the army backed the several nationalist groups that opposed the Socialists. In this way the issue of capital vs. labor became confused with that of nationalism, and nationalism, it turned out, was of greater importance than any other consideration to most Germans.

Financial and economic complications

AS WAS to be expected, defeat and revolution had induced many Germans who had money to send it abroad. The extraordinary flight of German capital into foreign countries, particularly the Netherlands, Sweden, and Switzerland, magnified the financial hardships already visible from the war's destruction (Germany's casualties numbered over 6,500,000) and the postwar blockade—the dislocation of business, the decline of national income, the meagerness of foreign trade and customs revenue, and the difficulty of collecting taxes. A tremendous national deficit and consequently the beginnings of a German inflation appeared as early as 1920.

To these factors of economic instability were added the international disputes over reparations payments. The fact that inflation had already set in before the reparations total was fixed (page 701) and before any payments had been made in significant amounts indicates that reparations were not the only cause of the subsequent disaster. The exorbitant cost of the war, the collapse of the German fiscal system, the unwillingness of the men of big fortunes to submit to the taxes that would have been necessary for good government finance, and their preference to pass on the costs to others by the "hidden taxation" of inflation must also be counted among the factors leading to the ultimate collapse of the German mark. But the general fear of the mark's shakiness was emphasized by the reparations negotiations, and the political insecurity that reparations negotiations engendered further accelerated the flight of German capital, weakened the government's credit, and lowered the paper mark's value in foreign exchange.

Business magnates and the "vertical" trusts   A NEW FORM of industrial enterprise rose to prominence in Germany in the wake of the war and the blockade, which made raw materials scarce, and of the inflation, which made big purchases easy for those who had money. The 1920's were the years when the "vertical" trusts came into their own in Europe. A vertical trust is a gigantic industrial combination encompassing every stage of production from the raw material to the finished product. It differs from a "horizontal" trust in that it attempts to combine many plants engaged in working the same materials at *all stages* instead of combining *all competitors* on the same market. Huge trusts may easily acquire characteristics of both vertical and horizontal types where the law does not intervene. Since neither horizontal nor vertical trusts were restricted by German law, enormous combinations were able to encompass all stages of manufacture from raw material to finished product and numerous competitors, and to extend their control to the newspapers in order to expound their economic and political philosophies, to the films in order to direct the public sympathies toward their views, and, in the last stages of the inflation, to the growing paramilitary organizations in order to use an extralegal force in protecting their interests and intimidating their opponents.

Frequently a vertical trust was under the control of a single magnate. The most notorious of the German trust magnates was Hugo Stinnes, whose political and economic influence was paramount between 1920 and 1924. He had started his trust before 1919, becoming interested in coal and inland navigation. He built wharves and had his own ships constructed there. He bought coal mines for the fueling of his ships. He acquired entire forests, sawmills, ironworks, newspapers, cinema companies, hotels.

If the big German industrialists did not already know from economic theory, they would soon have found out in practice that the farther the German inflation advanced, the more easily they could expand their power. As prices went up and the purchasing power of money went down, they got more and more money for the things they produced although their old debts stayed at the same number of marks. They hastened to pay their old debts in depreciated currency, and thus achieved their independence of the banks. They bought up small enterprises that were forced to the wall by hard times. They sent their excess profits abroad for saving or investment, and thus, while promoting the inflationary trend, they could hedge against their own losses by inflation. Every time the German government made a token reparations payment the national deficit increased, and that meant that the government printed more paper money; and more paper money meant more inflation and more power to the big industrialists. To Stinnes, Fritz Thyssen, the steel baron, Alfred Hugenberg, newspaper and cinema magnate, and other rulers of trusts, the inflation was a windfall.

An attempt
at counterrevolution in Germany

ECONOMIC conditions were further aggravated by waves of revolutionary disorder. We have already mentioned (page 680) and shall soon mention again (pages 688 and 705) the Communist efforts to win control of Germany. In order to defend itself the German Republic called upon volunteer veteran units. After peace was signed, the blockade lifted, and the Weimar Constitution adopted, the government decided to dissolve the volunteer units. Thereupon they mutinied (March 1920) and under their monarchist officers, started the so-called "Kapp *Putsch.*" (*Putsch* is German for coup d'état.) The rebels occupied Potsdam and Berlin, demanding the abolition of the republic and a military dictatorship for the purpose of restoring the monarchy. The rebellion was commonly recognized to have been planned by Ludendorff.

The conspirators failed, however, to win the support of the civil service, though it was still very conservative, or of the regular army. The republican government retreated from Berlin to Stuttgart, and the workers and the civil service went on general strike, swiftly bringing about "Chancellor" Kapp's collapse and flight. It was ominous, however, that almost no one was punished for armed sedition, though hundreds of cases were examined by the courts. Ludendorff was called only as a witness. The enemies of the German Republic were emboldened and its adherents discomfited by the weakness it had shown. The Weimar Republic somehow weathered Communist and monarchist storms, but its problems continued acute, intimately tied up with the international negotiations concerning reparations (pages 699-707).

Socialism
and nationalism in Austria

WHAT REMAINED of Austria after the collapse of the Dual Monarchy in 1918 became, like Germany, a federal republic. Austria's first chancellor was the Socialist Karl Renner, the same man who was to become its president after the Second World War. The new Austria had one advantage over many other European countries: it had no ethnic minorities. It was inhabited by people of German stock speaking a dialect of the German language. But it suffered from one notable difficulty: nowhere in Europe was the antagonism between town and country so pronounced as it was in Austria. For that reason the city of Vienna (with 1,600,000 inhabitants out of the total of 6,700,000) was organized as a special federal state. The countryside resented what it considered

683

Vienna's undue strength. To make the issue more pronounced, Vienna was largely socialist in its economic outlook and liberal in its social and cultural outlook, while the small towns and the farms were strongly Catholic, conservative, and nationalistic. Many of the peasants felt profound distrust for the Viennese, whom they regarded as godless and unpatriotic. The Vienna state government's enterprise, for example, in the field of public housing (the Karl Marx Hof) became an object of admiration among other Europeans, but the Austrian peasants and small-town dwellers regarded it as socialist squandering of the taxpayers' money.

In Austria no more than in Germany did a democratic spirit grow deep roots. The two leading parties, the Social Democrats and the Christian (i.e., Catholic) Socials, were of almost equal strength in the Austrian parliament. The Nationalists did not play a big role until the 1930's. At first Social Democrat and Christian Social governments alternated or formed coalitions, but the latter gained ascendancy during the 1920's. Each party created its own armed force, and democracy in Austria was undermined little by little by two extraparliamentary paramilitary organizations, the Christian Social Heimwehr (home guard) and the Socialist Schutzbund (security league).

Revolution and dictatorship in Hungary

AMONG THE vanquished nations Hungary perhaps was the hardest hit. The country was proclaimed a republic a few days after the armistice. Prisoners of war from Russia, who had been exposed to Communist doctrines, streamed back home; and when they could not find jobs, they attributed their ills to the newly established bourgeois republic. The revolutionary mood came to a head in March 1919, when a Hungarian Soviet Republic was established under the leadership of an ex-prisoner of war in Russia, Bela Kun. The new government was short-lived. The Rumanians occupied Budapest, and the members of the Soviet government fled to Russia.

Meanwhile an antirevolutionary government had been established under the leadership of Admiral Nicholas Horthy at Szegedin. His army, consisting of fanatical nationalists and counterrevolutionaries, marched into Budapest in November, and the Rumanians withdrew. The counterrevolutionary terror was no more tender than the revolution had been. Admiral Horthy was proclaimed regent of the kingdom of Hungary. The country became one of Europe's anomalies—a kingdom without a king ruled by an admiral without a navy. Hungary became under Horthy the first dictatorship of postwar Europe outside Russia. Horthy took control on the pretext of saving the country from Communism, but only after the major danger was in fact already past, and he was able to hold on to power because the fear of Communism continued to be strong. His was a pattern that was, as we have already indicated, soon to be followed in Italy.

684

*An experiment
in democracy in Czechoslovakia*

AMONG THE new nations set up in postwar Europe, Czechoslovakia became a model democracy. She owed that success to two outstanding men, Thomas Masaryk, who was president from 1918 to 1935, and his foreign minister, Eduard Beneš, who succeeded him as president. Masaryk, well known as a sociologist before the war, had long been a student of the liberal tradition of England and the United States. He applied his democratic convictions to his own state when he and his followers set up the Republic of Czechoslovakia. He also took a leading part in creating the Little Entente of Czechoslovakia, Yugoslavia, and Rumania (1920-1921), aimed not only at defending its members against a recrudescence of Hungarian aggression but also at making up somewhat for the economic and political inconveniences incurred from the splintering of the old Dual Monarchy.

Next to its democratic constitution the most important domestic accomplishment of the new Czechoslovakian republic was its land reform. Like many other parts of Europe, Czechoslovakia, under the old Austrian regime, had had a powerful class of landowners, who together owned more than one-fourth of the land. What was particularly galling to the Czechs was that these lands were owned either by the Habsburg family or by a German-speaking aristocracy that had acquired them by confiscation from Czech patriots after the failure of the Czech war of independence in the seventeenth century. In 1919 an expropriation law was enacted, and the expropriated land was divided among the peasants. Although the former owners, with the exception of the Habsburgs, were compensated for their losses, the payments were made in depreciated currency.

Czechoslovakia's chief domestic difficulty was her minorities problem. In the first place, the relations between Czechs and Slovaks had never been completely harmonious. The Czechs were generally urban and literate; in Slovakia a large percentage of the population was rural and illiterate. In the second place, the Germans in the Sudetic Mountains, later known as the Sudeten Germans, were of doubtful loyalty to the new republic. The other minorities—Magyars, Poles, and Ukrainians (here called Ruthenians)—caused relatively little trouble, though the autonomy promised the Ruthenians was never granted. Schools were made available to the Germans as well as to the other minority groups, and their rights as citizens were protected by the constitution. Yet the Germans were dissatisfied. They had been accustomed to dominate Bohemia, and they could not reconcile themselves to their new status as just one of several minorities in Czechoslovakia. Once they had been masters because Vienna was strong. Now they cast hopeful glances northward across the border to Berlin. But Germany was to give them no encouragement until Hitler came to power.

Conditions
in other Danube succession states

THE OTHER states that had arisen in whole or in part from the ashes of the Habsburg empire—Poland, Rumania, and Yugoslavia—were considerably less democratic than Austria or Czechoslovakia. In two of these countries the antidemocratic tendency was linked to the land question. The example of Czechoslovakia had clearly shown the big landowners that only so long as they could control the government could they hope to keep their large estates. In order to control the government, they had to have an antidemocratic rule. During the final stages of the war, Poland had been torn among several factions, one of which was under the leadership of the pianist and composer Ignace Jan Paderewski, who had the support of the Allies. Another was led by General Joseph Pilsudski, who at first had had the support of the Central Powers. After the war Pilsudski acquired greater and greater power, and Poland gradually fell under his dictatorship. Rumania, bloated by annexations at the expense of Hungary, Russia, and Bulgaria, was torn between the two leading parties, the urban Liberal Party and the National Peasants' Party, and the king frequently exerted extraordinary powers. In Yugoslavia the complications were ethnic rather than agrarian. Croats, Slovenes, Macedonians, and Montenegrins resented the domination of the Serbs, and King Alexander ruled with an iron hand, ruthlessly suppressing minority rights.

The reorganization
of the Turkish Republic

FOR SEVERAL years after the Armistice of 1918 Turkey was engaged in international war as well as domestic revolution (page 641). On October 29, 1923, Turkey was formally declared a republic, and Mustafa Kemal became its first president. Although the new republic had a constitution that provided an elective parliament, actually Kemal's influence was so great that he became the dictator of Turkey. If he was no Turkish George Washington, neither was he the usual kind of dictator. He had little in common with either the Fascist or the Communist dictators or with the military dictators of some Latin-American countries. He became for Turkey a gentler version of what Peter the Great had been for Russia, the man who modernized and westernized his country.

Kemal's first problem was to counteract the conservative influence of the Moslem clergy. He abolished the caliphate in 1924; the next year religious orders were suppressed. The disestablishment of Islam brought a change in customs. The man's fez was replaced by the European hat; the woman's veil began to disappear. The Moslem clergy were no longer allowed to wear clerical garb in public. Every Turk had to assume a family name. Polygamy was abolished; the divorce laws were modernized. Turkish words and names replaced foreignisms in Turkish language and geography. Constantinople, for example, became Istanbul and Angora, now the country's capital, became Ankara. By 1925 a social revolution seemed well under way in Turkey.

Spancesilon...

Spain
under the dictatorship of Rivera

POSTWAR unsettlement reached into the countries that had been neutral. Spain was one of the most backward countries of Europe. The percentage of illiteracy was high. The educational system was mostly in the hands of an inflexible clergy. The preponderance of large estates belonging to absentee landlords was as great as in Hungary or czarist Russia. The peasants were among the poorest in Europe. The workers had practically no rights and voted, whenever they did vote, under the direction of employers, priests, or *caciques* (local bosses). The army regularly played a high-handed role in politics.

Like other neutrals, Spain had made large profits selling to both sides during the World War. But her prosperity died with the end of the war, and unrest seethed among dissatisfied elements throughout the country—Catalans and Basques who wished autonomy, workers who were socialists or anarchists or syndicalists, and intellectuals who were liberals and republicans.

The flower of the Spanish army was in Spanish Morocco. In 1920, as we have seen (page 673), the natives of the mountainous Riff, headed by a Berber chief named Abd-el-Krim, rebelled. Twenty thousand Spaniards suffered a terrible military defeat in 1921; twelve thousand of them were killed and the rest captured, and their general committed suicide. The report of a committee appointed to fix responsibility for the disaster was not at first made public, possibly because the king was among those guilty of bungling. The attempted conspiracy of silence only increased the public outrage and endangered the monarchy. King Alfonso XIII, much impressed by the Mussolini regime, thought that what had apparently served the monarchy well in Italy might also profit Spain. In September 1923, while Alfonso was conveniently visiting France, General Miguel Primo de Rivera suspended the constitution, proclaimed military law, and began to rule as a dictator. During the next two years Rivera strengthened his position by fairly arbitrary means.

The Russian Revolution
and international Communism

WHEN THE Bolsheviks came to power in Russia, they had been so busy with political and military maneuvers that they had prepared no economic blueprint along Marxist lines to put into effect. We have already described how haphazardly and incoherently the new society arose out of the ruins of the old (pages 618-619). International intervention, civil war, famine, the resistance of the peasants to attempted grain levies, and the dissatisfaction of the urban population brought every aspect of Russian activity nearly to a standstill by the end of 1920. Such a complete economic and political collapse had not occurred in a European nation for nearly three centuries.

The Bolsheviks, for their part, believed that the world revolution was on its way. One of the great hopes of the Soviet government in 1918, when the German Revolution occurred, was that Germany would have a Marxian upheaval on the Russian pattern. Communist Germany might then pass under Russian auspices, and that prospect seemed to the Russian leaders to hold out the possibility of economic survival of their own country. Germany suffered two waves of Communist revolt. The first one took place from Christmas 1918 to January 1919 in Berlin; the second and more serious one (April and May 1919) resulted in a short-lived Communist republic in Bavaria. The repression was more thorough than the revolutionary attempts themselves and certainly much more thorough than was the subsequent procedure against rebels on the Right (page 706). Russian hopes flared again when Communist uprisings occurred in Austria and Hungary, both of which were trying to readjust themselves to the collapse of the Dual Monarchy. The Austrian Communist movement, however, produced only agitation without victory. In Hungary a Soviet dictatorship was actually set up, as we have seen, but it was driven out within a few months. Russia determined thereupon to concentrate upon Asia (page 662), but remained the mecca for Communists and Communist-minded people ("fellow travelers") everywhere. It took the Communists a long time to realize that they had overrated their strength in countries outside Russia and that the world was not yet ready to conform to the Marxian prognostication of an international revolution. Temporarily they were forced to postpone the world revolution until Communist parties and movements everywhere could be backed by a more powerful Russia.

By 1920 the Russian civil war was effectively ended. A few Allied soldiers mutinied. The White Russian soldiers were badly led and were more given to killing peasants and looting than to fighting. Thus, despite some pitched battles, the counterrevolutionary and interventionist campaigns collapsed inside Russia. Nevertheless, the Japanese continued to hold Vladivostok until 1922; and Soviet Russia became involved in a war with Poland, largely over the question of control of the Ukraine. The Russians advanced as far as the outskirts of Warsaw, and but for the strategic plan which the French General Maxime Weygand worked out for the Poles, the Russians would have won the war. In March 1921 the Poles and the Bolsheviks made peace at Riga on a compromise basis, but most of the Ukraine remained within the new Russian-dominated federation (known after December 1922 as the Union of Soviet Socialist Republics).

Lenin's
New Economic Policy
AFTER several years of civil war following upon several years of disaster in the World War, Russia was in a chaotic condition. Originally the Soviet leaders had planned to nationalize banks and industry only gradually. But because of the resistance of businessmen, the government started to nationalize here and there, in order to punish particular firms rather than to carry out a plan. Thus, to the dislocations caused by years of world war and civil war were now added the

Lenin. A sketch from life made by Nathan Altman in May 1920.

dislocations caused by precipitate nationalizations, often carried out by inexperienced men and in a wasteful, bureaucratic way. Shortages could not be overcome by foreign commerce, for many foreign merchants refused to deal with a country where trade was a state monopoly and payment uncertain. When in 1920 a crop failure occurred and millions starved while a million or more idle peasants roamed the roads, the breakup of Russia was daily anticipated abroad.

That a Bolshevik party of merely 2,500,000 men and women would be able to control a federation that, despite its various losses, still numbered around 160,000,000 people seemed highly improbable. Lenin himself was forced to recognize that for the time being he would have to put a stop to the installation of pure communism and beat a strategic retreat. Most of all, he realized, he would have to appease the peasants, if he were to save the revolution. Therefore, in 1921-1922, they were freed from the previous wholesale levies of grain and were allowed to sell in the open market as much of their products as exceeded a fixed grain tax that had to be paid to the government. They might rent their land. They might even hire some farm hands. Many peasants took advantage of the new regulations.

A certain degree of freedom was also extended to commerce and industry. Employers of fewer than twenty workers were to be left more or less alone by the state. Thus, free enterprise and private trade inside Russia were tolerated to a limited extent, though the state retained supervision of commerce, industry, and agriculture and continued to monopolize transportation, utilities, foreign trade, banking, and large industries. The new setup became known as the NEP (New Economic Policy). It was meant as a temporary expedient only, although people in foreign countries misinterpreted it as recognition of the impossibility of a communist economy. This compromise between the capitalist and the communist system was in force when Lenin died in January 1924.

The struggle within the Communist Party

LENIN's death removed the main check upon the fairly open factional jealousies among his lieutenants. As has often happened upon the demise of a dictator, personal rivalries among the would-be successors now came to the surface. Four men had most prominently shared the limelight with Lenin. Like him, these men were known by the pseudonyms they had taken as revolutionaries to avoid implicating their families with the czarist police. Frequently regarded as first among them was Leon Trotsky, the creator and commander of the Red Army, to whom the successful conduct of the civil war and the victorious resistance to foreign intervention were generally attributed. Another was Grigori Zinoviev, the creator of the Third International, who was considered both cruel and weak by friend and foe alike. A third was Lev B. Kamenev, who was vice-president of the Council of People's Commissars and thus a sort of vice-prime minister. Finally there was Joseph Stalin, general secretary of the Russian Communist Party, who was to prove to have a keener sense of political realities than the others (Chapter 12).

The Third International and Russian foreign policy

FROM ITS beginnings Soviet politics had been a double-pointed shaft. One point was aimed at Russia, which was to become the model Soviet state; the other was aimed at the rest of the world. Trotsky contended that the revolution could not succeed in Russia alone, and Stalin insisted that "socialism in one country" was feasible. They were not to split openly on this question, however, until 1926. To foster Communism everywhere, the Third International had been founded in 1919. Officially, the Third International and the Russian government were strictly separate bodies. But actually, the foreign Communist parties became,

690

via the Third International, willing tools in the hands of the Soviet government.

Russia's foreign policy had two main aims. The first was to obtain *de jure* recognition from as many countries as possible, and the second to nip in the bud any recurrence of a foreign anti-Soviet *cordon sanitaire* such as had existed immediately after the Revolution of 1917. On the whole, the Russians were successful in these aims. The Treaty of Rapallo with Germany (page 703) broke Russia's isolation from the rest of the world in 1922. Mac-Donald's Labour government made a commercial treaty with Russia in 1924; Italy and France followed suit; in 1925 a commercial treaty was made with Germany; and Turkey, Iran, Afghanistan, China, and Japan extended the hand of friendship between 1921 and 1925 (page 662). Other countries then also gave Russia recognition. The United States was to be the last of the great powers to recognize her (1933).

The instability **THE** Russian Revolution of 1917
of the Russian succession states had been a signal for several of
the non-Russian peoples within the former czarist empire to seek their independence. The Finns, the Estonians, the Letts, the Lithuanians, the Poles, the White Russians, the Ukrainians, the Bessarabians (Rumanians), the Georgians, and the Armenians, with greater or less alacrity, and frequently with the aid of the Germans, sought to establish their independence. The Treaty of Brest-Litovsk had recognized several of these states. As we have seen, the Allies, including the United States, also believed it to their interest and at the same time in keeping with the Wilsonian principle of self-determination, to support the national aspirations of the seceding states. So Bessarabia was assigned to Rumania; the Russian Poles were added to the Austrian and German Poles to make the new Poland; and the new states of Finland, Latvia, Estonia, Lithuania, White Russia, Ukrainia, Georgia, and Armenia emerged. The last four were soon incorporated in the Union of Soviet Socialist Republics. The others continued to live in fear of reannexation. In 1925, however, they looked relatively safe, since Russia had her hands full with her domestic problems and since Germany, Poland, England, France, and the Little Entente (page 685) had good reason to favor their independence.

COLLECTIVE SECURITY,

MANDATES, AND REPARATIONS

FOR OVER A decade after the armistice few in power thought of a general recourse to arms as a means of resolving conflicts, no matter how frequently nations might resort to limited warfare in order to attain local objectives. The major diplomatic efforts of governments all over the world were directed until 691 the 1930's toward disarmament and the pacific solution of international disputes. At first it seemed as though the League of Nations, despite American defection, might reach full height as an instrument for the rectification of international injustice by means of peaceful change; and important decisions also took place outside the League.

Organization
of the League of Nations

THE COVENANT of the League of Nations made up the first twenty-six articles of the Treaty of Versailles. At the start the League had only twenty-four member nations. In the course of time their total number was to increase to sixty, but some of them were again to withdraw before the League ceased to exist. The League was actually not a league of *nations* but a league of *governments*. The permanent site of the League was at Geneva, Switzerland.

The League consisted of a Council, an Assembly, and a Permanent Secretariat. The Council included both permanent and nonpermanent members. The permanent members were designated by the Covenant as "the Principal Allied and Associated Powers," but, in the absence of the United States, they were only Great Britain, France, Italy, and Japan. The United States, Russia, and Germany were not members of the League when it opened its sessions; but the Covenant permitted naming additional members with permanent membership in the Council. Until 1922 there were only four nonpermanent members, but six thereafter. The nonpermanent members were elected by the Assembly.

The Assembly, composed of representatives of all the member countries, might deliberate and vote on any subject of interest to the League. Every member exercised but one vote and might have no more than three delegates. Though the Assembly controlled the budget and had other specific duties, in the course of events its major task became to advise the Council. Because the Council met three or four times a year, and the Assembly only once, the members of the Council came to know each other better than did those of the Assembly. Difficult questions and controversies, it was believed, could be settled more easily in the club-like atmosphere of the Council than amid the forensic agitation of the Assembly.

The Permanent Secretariat consisted of the secretary general and his staff. The first secretary general was Sir Eric Drummond (later Lord Perth). The Permanent Secretariat's task was to prepare the agenda of the sessions of the Assembly and the Council, to register all treaties any member concluded, and to keep the League going in the intervals between meetings.

International bodies
affiliated with the League

NOT DIRECTLY connected with the League, but authorized by the Covenant, was a Permanent Court of International Justice. It had the right to "hear and determine any dispute of an international character which the parties thereto submit to it." It also

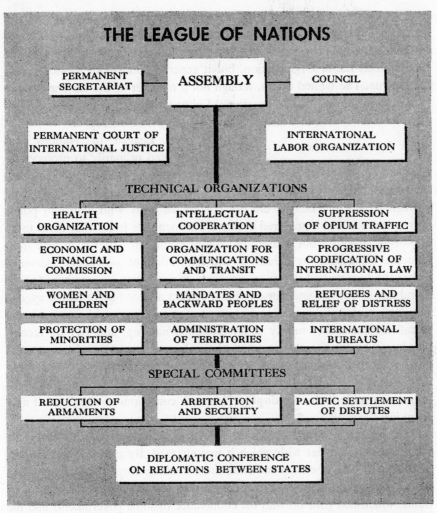

THE LEAGUE OF NATIONS

| PERMANENT SECRETARIAT | ASSEMBLY | COUNCIL |

| PERMANENT COURT OF INTERNATIONAL JUSTICE | INTERNATIONAL LABOR ORGANIZATION |

TECHNICAL ORGANIZATIONS

HEALTH ORGANIZATION	INTELLECTUAL COOPERATION	SUPPRESSION OF OPIUM TRAFFIC
ECONOMIC AND FINANCIAL COMMISSION	ORGANIZATION FOR COMMUNICATIONS AND TRANSIT	PROGRESSIVE CODIFICATION OF INTERNATIONAL LAW
WOMEN AND CHILDREN	MANDATES AND BACKWARD PEOPLES	REFUGEES AND RELIEF OF DISTRESS
PROTECTION OF MINORITIES	ADMINISTRATION OF TERRITORIES	INTERNATIONAL BUREAUS

SPECIAL COMMITTEES

| REDUCTION OF ARMAMENTS | ARBITRATION AND SECURITY | PACIFIC SETTLEMENT OF DISPUTES |

| DIPLOMATIC CONFERENCE ON RELATIONS BETWEEN STATES |

At the point of its greatest membership (sixty members in 1935, before the announced withdrawal of Japan, Germany, and Paraguay became effective) the League of Nations included all of the leading states of the world with the exception of the United States. Counting Costa Rica (which withdrew in 1924), Brazil (which withdrew in 1928), and Egypt (which entered only in 1937), sixty-three nations belonged to the League at one time or another. (The USSR belonged from 1934 to 1939.) Comparison of the League organization with that of the United Nations (page 915) will reveal certain similarities (large Assembly, smaller executive Council, Permanent Secretariat, and numerous specialized commissions).

could give its "advisory opinion upon any dispute or question referred to it by the Council or by the Assembly." It was located at The Hague, where it held its first session in 1922. This court went a step farther in the direction of international order than the Hague Permanent Court of Arbitration (page 510); the court envisaged by the Covenant of the League of Nations was to be a court of law and not merely one of voluntary arbitration.

Set up independently of the League by the Treaty of Versailles, the International Labor Organization was established in 1919. It had its offices also

693

in Geneva and worked closely with the League. Its purpose was to devise international agreements for protecting the lives, health, and welfare of workers. The members of the League were automatically members of the International Labor Organization, but it generally had more members than the League. The United States, though not a member of the League, was to become a member of the International Labor Organization in 1934. Several other international bodies also became affiliated with the League.

Some purposes and achievements of the League THE League of Nations was planned primarily to preserve international peace. To do so effectively, it should have had the power to protect its members from external aggression. But the League did not possess an army with which to police aggressors, nor was it prepared to protect its members from what came to be known as "boring from within" or "the fifth column"—that is to say, from domestic weakening by means of the infiltration of subversive elements. Hence the League had to put its emphasis on protecting its members (a) by moral means (mobilizing world opinion against a would-be or actual aggressor), (b) by judicial means (arbitration), (c) by coercion short of war (in so-called "sanctions," mostly of an economic nature), and (d) by recommendation by the Council to some of the League members of a concerted military effort against any member of the League engaged in or contemplating aggression. Nonmembers were to be invited to accept similar obligations in order to settle their own disputes "on such conditions as the Council may deem just."

The League's most lasting achievements perhaps were to result from the humanitarian activities with which it was charged. By partly suppressing or restricting the sale of opium and other habit-forming drugs, the League was to reduce somewhat the appalling conditions arising from the international drug traffic, which had gone on with the connivance of some governments and the indifference of some others. The League also assigned the great Norwegian explorer, Fridtjof Nansen, to the task of returning war prisoners to their home countries and of providing aid and assistance to the refugees from the Russian Revolution. With the aid of the International Red Cross and other existing agencies and by new methods of his own devising, Nansen solved those problems in a truly humanitarian spirit. Among other things, he provided the "paperless" victims of the Russian Revolution with a special and internationally recognized passport which became known as the "Nansen passport" or the "League of Nations passport." Many international measures for the regulation of slavery, armaments trade, and quarantine and other hygienic purposes were taken by the League. It also supervised the exchange of Greek and Turkish nationals (page 642) and the plebiscites required by the Treaty of Versailles and subsequent treaties. Until 1935 the League ruled the Saar Territory and until 1939 helped to rule the Free City of Danzig.

694

*Minorities problems
before the League of Nations*

THE League of Nations was entrusted by the various peace treaties with watching over the treaty rights of minorities. Time and again it had to intervene on their behalf. That it did not have better success was sometimes attributable to overzealous nationalism. Nor did the minorities make it easy for the majorities. For instance, in Czechoslovakia, which adopted a minority policy that, for all its shortcomings, was fairly liberal, the German minority persisted in a sullen attitude that led to complications both within and without. Some member countries, particularly Poland, used every available device to circumvent whatever the League of Nations undertook to provide for the minorities. In case of showdown, the League was hampered in this respect as in many others by the fact that it lacked the physical or moral force to impose its decisions upon recalcitrant members. After Mussolini came to power in Italy, it proved impotent, for instance, to protect the German-speaking South Tyrolians from the Italianization that Mussolini imposed upon them. Mussolini was prepared to defy the League because he was well aware that other members of the League, for reasons of their own, would not care to antagonize him. If they did not have guilty consciences regarding their own treatment of minorities, they had bargains to make and interests to serve that seemed to them more important than that justice should be done in South Tyrol. Despite its shortcomings, the League did nevertheless manage to do some good work in protecting minorities.

*Types of mandates
under the League's supervision*

THE LEAGUE'S supervision over colonial administration was likewise to prove more theoretical than real and yet far from futile. This experiment with international responsibility for colonial administration formed one of the more enduring phases of the League's influence, and continues today in the Trusteeship Council of the United Nations. When Germany had to give up her colonies and Turkey had to accede to the surrender of her non-Turkish possessions, Wilson saw to it at Paris that they were assigned only as "mandates" to their new rulers. In other words, the new ruling powers were to act only as "mandatories," or trustees, for the League and were required to make annual reports to the League on their respective trusteeships.

Mandates were divided into three classes. Class A mandates consisted of the former Turkish territories of Palestine, Trans-Jordan, Iraq, Syria, and Lebanon. They were regarded as so far advanced toward national sovereignty that some of them at least might be recognized as states "subject to the rendering of administrative advice and assistance by a Mandatory until such time as they are able to stand alone." The mandatory for Palestine, Trans-Jordan, and Iraq was Great Britain; that for Syria and Lebanon was France. Class B mandates comprised the six located in Central Africa. Parts of the

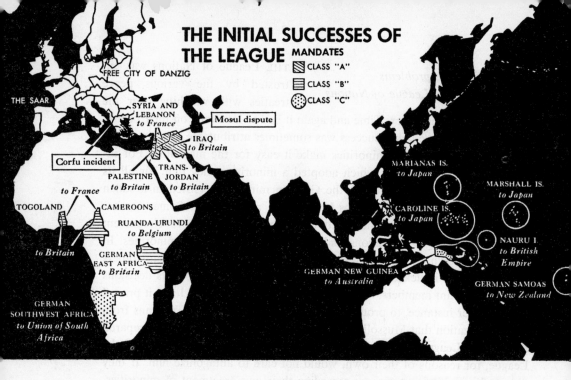

MANDATES
- ▨ CLASS "A"
- ☰ CLASS "B"
- ⦿ CLASS "C"

FREE CITY OF DANZIG

THE SAAR

SYRIA AND LEBANON
to France

Mosul dispute

IRAQ
to Britain

Corfu incident

TRANS-JORDAN
to Britain

PALESTINE
to Britain

to France

TOGOLAND

CAMEROONS

RUANDA-URUNDI
to Belgium

to Britain

GERMAN EAST AFRICA
to Britain

GERMAN SOUTHWEST AFRICA
to Union of South Africa

MARIANAS IS.
to Japan

MARSHALL IS.
to Japan

CAROLINE IS.
to Japan

NAURU I.
to British Empire

GERMAN NEW GUINEA
to Australia

GERMAN SAMOAS
to New Zealand

The first years of the League were marked by several successes. The former colonies of Germany and Arabic Turkey were divided among the victors under mandate to the League. The Saar Basin and the Free City of Danzig were governed without major crises. Austrian and Hungarian finances were put on a sound footing. League prestige rose with the successful settlement of several international disputes, of which the Italian-Greek "Corfu Incident" in 1923 (page 708) and the Iraqi-Turkish dispute over Mosul in 1925 (page 699) were perhaps the most noteworthy.

Cameroons and Togoland, and the whole of German East Africa, now called Tanganyika, went to Great Britain. The rest of the Cameroons and Togoland became French mandates. Belgium received the mandate of Ruanda-Urundi. Class C mandates were those which, owing to the sparseness of their population, their small size, their remoteness from the centers of civilization, their geographical contiguity to the territory of the mandatory, or other circumstances, "can best be administered under the laws of the Mandatory as integral portions of its territory." But the League of Nations retained the right of supervision "in the interests of the indigenous population." Numbered among the Class C mandates were the former German colony of South-West Africa, which was allotted to the Union of South Africa, and certain islands in the Pacific Ocean, which were allotted to Japan, Australia, and New Zealand.

Arabs, Zionists, and British in Palestine

PALESTINE became the most embarrassing mandate. Britain found her administration hampered there by overlapping pledges made during the war. One of these was the Balfour Declaration. It was made in 1917 to win the support of the Jews throughout the world and especially to reward the brilliant war work of Chaim Weiz-

696

mann, a Russian-born, Zionist professor of chemistry at the University of Manchester. Weizmann, among other things, had developed a process of making acetone, an essential ingredient of the high explosive called cordite, out of horse chestnuts and other cheap materials. The declaration took the form of a letter from the minister of foreign affairs, Arthur Balfour, to Lord Rothschild. It stated that the British government looked favorably upon the proposal to establish in Palestine a national home for the Jews, provided that nothing should be done to infringe the civil and religious rights of non-Jewish communities there.

Immediately the Zionist cause, hitherto a valiant but apparently unrealistic hope nurtured chiefly by a faction of Jewish intellectuals, became a practical matter. Difficulties could easily have been foreseen, however. More than nine-tenths of Palestine's population (about 750,000 at the time) were Arabs, mostly Mohammedan and partly Christian, and less than one-tenth Jews. Moreover, the Jews of the world were themselves divided. Some were anti-Zionists, and those who were Zionist disagreed over the kind of national home they wanted: Was Palestine to be merely a Jewish cultural center and refuge or a sovereign political entity?

From the beginning the Balfour Declaration ran into cross fire. The Jews saw in it a promise of unrestricted Jewish immigration. The Arabs, on the other hand, had been told by Colonel Lawrence that they would gain domination of all Arab-inhabited countries formerly under Turkish domination, and until 1920 they persisted in believing that the age-old city of Damascus in Syria would become the center of a refurbished Arab world in a kingdom ruled by Emir Feisal of the Hashemite dynasty. For that reason they had not objected to the Balfour Declaration, believing that once they ruled over Palestine they could regulate Jewish immigration. The British had also come to a secret agreement with the French (the Sykes-Picot Treaty of 1916), which, while leaving room for an Arab confederation and a special regime for Palestine, promised the French domination over Syria and Lebanon. The Bolshevik revelation of the secret treaties damped Arab hopes, and Colonel Lawrence, after unsuccessfully trying, as an Arab representative at the Paris Conference, to implement his promises, gave up in disgust, enlisting as a mechanic in the British air force. French, Jews, and Arabs saw in the apparent contradictions a new example of the alleged British habit of divide-and-rule, while British critics considered them another case of muddling by trial and error. When the first British high commissioner of Palestine, Sir Herbert Samuel, in 1922 proclaimed a constitution setting up a legislative council, the Arabs refused to have anything to do with it. They did not even go to the polls.

The hostility between Arabs and Zionists was only in part religious, symbolized by the frequent outbreaks over the rites at the Wailing Wall in Jerusalem. What aroused the Arabs most was that the Zionists bought up   697 large tracts of land to settle immigrants. Arab landlords were willing to sell the land, since they wanted the money, but, afraid of becoming eventually outnumbered, they did not want the Jewish immigrants, who acquired land and employment while Arabs were landless and unemployed. Nor did Arab landlords, still flourishing in a semifeudal, seminomadic society, look with favor upon the business, industrial, and agricultural methods or the social ideas that the Jewish immigrants brought with them from the West. In 1921 bloody anti-Jewish riots broke out, and it seemed doubtful that a safe Jewish refuge would ever be created in Palestine. The creation of the Hebrew University at Jerusalem in 1925, although it admitted the few qualified Arabs who applied, did not diminish Arab hostility. The Jewish population mounted, nevertheless, from around 10 per cent to around 20 per cent of the whole even before the great flight from Nazi persecution took place in the years following 1933. The League of Nations left the Palestine question to the British to solve.

British mandates
in Trans-Jordan and Iraq

THE MANDATE question was an easier one in the totally Arab countries. In Trans-Jordan, Emir Abdullah of the Hashemite dynasty became king in a British-mandated country. Abdullah's brother, Feisal, became king of Iraq. Originally Feisal was thought of as the probable ruler of the united Arab kingdom with its capital at Damascus. But, when that idea collided with the Franco-British agreements on Syria and Lebanon, Feisal was made king of Syria. That dignity, however, lasted only from March to July 1920. A resolution of the special Conference of San Remo in April 1920 (pages 641-642) made Syria and Lebanon French mandates, and King Feisal gave up, temporarily as much disgusted as Colonel Lawrence had been.

Shortly thereafter Feisal became king of Iraq. When the war was ended, the Iraqis had been in no mood to become the subjects of a mandated territory. They wanted independence. But for the remarkable efforts of Gertrude M. L. Bell, Iraq might have been lost altogether to the British. That extraordinary woman before the war had traveled through the Arabic-speaking countries, visiting areas where European women had rarely been seen before. During the war she had done intelligence work for the British government. After the war she became the oracle of the British government in oriental affairs. When anti-British riots broke out in Iraq in 1920, she recommended to her government that the British mandate, without being formally abolished, should be transformed into an Anglo-Iraq alliance. She felt that otherwise the British might lose all their influence in the Near and Middle East. Sir Percy Cox, with whom she had previously worked harmoniously, was named high commissioner, and he provided for a plebiscite, which by 96 per cent of the vote asked for a kingdom under Feisal.

A treaty of alliance with the new king was concluded in 1922. But such was the animosity of the Arabs that the pact could not be ratified until 1924. To all outward appearance Iraq remained a mandate, but actually it became a semi-independent state under British supervision, giving to the British behind the scenes perhaps more influence than they might have had if they had retained mandatory power. The area around Mosul remained in dispute with Turkey until 1925, when the dispute was settled by the League mostly in favor of Iraq.

French mandates in Syria and Lebanon

THE FRENCH divided the former Turkish territories allotted to them into three parts—Alexandretta, Syria, and Lebanon. Alexandretta, in which the Turkish population was dominant, became autonomous in 1923 and was finally ceded to the Turks in 1939. In the rest of Syria religious complications were particularly troublesome. Most of the people (around 2,500,000 for Syria and 800,000 for Lebanon) were Mohammedan, but they did not all subscribe to the same sect, and the people known as the Druses, inhabiting the area in the south known as Jebel Druse, were so different as to be regarded as enemies by the other Mohammedans. A minority of the population was Christian, mostly Greek Orthodox or of a sect affiliated with Roman Catholicism known as the Maronites, found chiefly in Lebanon. The French divided the whole mandate into five parts, one of which was the Christian-dominated Lebanon, hoping to be able to rule the remaining four parts more easily. The Mohammedan Syrians were upset not only because they felt cheated in their political aspirations when their preferred ruler, King Feisal, was forced to flee Damascus but also because they suspected the French of favoring the Christian Syrians. The French decision to put the country under military police because of the constant threat of disorder only added to their resentment. The League of Nations interfered little with the French mandates.

The origin of the problem of reparations

THE Treaty of Versailles, ratified (without the participation of the United States and China) on January 10, 1920, brought, instead of the longed-for "normalcy," a rude awakening. The hydra of reparations made its appearance. As we have seen (page 638), the final settlement of the total sum that Germany must pay was left to a Reparations Commission. The commission was to consist of one member each from the United States, Great Britain, France, Italy, and a fifth country (usually Belgium) to be selected, but since the United States Senate did not ratify the treaty, no American member took part. The French representative, for a time Poincaré, who was most insistent upon full reparations from the Germans, generally won majority support in the commission. Poincaré probably was interested in creating economic hardship for Germany as well as in compensation for France. Either would add to France's future security, which was his major objective.

*German unwillingness
to pay reparations in full*

A FEW Germans were ready to concede that elementary justice required them to replace in kind the livestock which they had destroyed and the rolling stock which they had taken away, and that the coal output of the Saar mines should go to France because the retreating Germans in 1918 had deliberately destroyed the mines of northern France (even if they were inclined to excuse German destruction as acts of war). But what about "all damages done to civilians"? This was a principle that Wilson in the pre-Armistice negotiations had reluctantly admitted, principally upon the insistence of the French, as an amendment to the requirement in his Point 8: that invaded portions of France must be restored. The French now argued that it included pensions to soldiers or their heirs.

Negotiations among the European Allies and between them on one side and the Germans on the other dragged on throughout the year 1920. The Germans were recalcitrant from the beginning. They naturally wanted to pay as little as they could get away with paying. It is also probable that they could not pay as much as the Allied governments wished to collect. Germany now had practically no international credit and few raw materials except coal. In addition, as we have noted (page 682), the reparations negotiations themselves further weakened the government's domestic credit and hence the already declining purchasing power of the paper mark. Whether cause or symptom or outcome of Germany's economic weakness, reparations payments were eventually to be considered by both sides as based on Germany's ability to pay.

But, as might have been expected, in the course of time more and more Germans came to oppose payment. They contended that reparations were based upon Germany's "war guilt," which most Germans flatly denied. They regarded "reparations for war damages" as a hypocritical metaphor to hide their true nature as old-fashioned indemnities extracted from the conquered; and they were determined to sabotage them.

*German resistance
to reparations payments*

UNTIL THE spring of 1921 the German representatives tried to diminish the demands upon Germany in all negotiations dealing with reparations, and they met with great success. Yet they considered the total now demanded still too high. In March, the Allies occupied three leading cities in the great industrial area of the Ruhr district. This act was ominous. It indicated that the Allies had become convinced of Germany's bad faith and were prepared to "apply sanctions" (diplomatic euphemism for "use force") to collect what they claimed as their just dues. The Allies set up a customs border on a line running east of the occupied cities from the Dutch to the Swiss border. In that way western Germany was separated from the rest of the country. The Allies kept the customs receipts collected on the new border line.

Only then did the German government give way to the Allies. Negotiations were renewed, and finally Germany was confronted with an ultimatum at a conference in London (May 1921): she was to pay $33,000,000,000 (132,000,000,000 gold marks) in annual installments of $500,000,000 (2,000,000,000 gold marks); in addition, she would make annual payments amounting to a tax of 26 per cent on German exports. The latter provision was particularly resented by the Germans because they saw in it a means of restricting German competition in the world's markets. The German government submitted, however, believing that a policy of fulfillment and compliance *(Erfüllungspolitik)* would prove within a short time that Germany was unable to pay such huge sums, and that the Allies would then see for themselves that a new settlement would have to be made.

This policy of compliance was reasonable but impracticable. A large part of the populace regarded the cabinet members as traitors, and every day the average German was confirmed in this view by the newspapers, many of which were directly or indirectly controlled by big business. (Radio was not yet an effective propaganda medium.) Two German statesmen, one a Catholic and the other a Jew, were assassinated as supposed traitors to their country (1921 and 1922 respectively). The assassins were members of secret organizations knowns as the Feme (from the Vehme, secret and irregular tribunals of medieval Germany). Also, the reparations payments made in accordance with the "fulfillment policy" helped to lift German inflation to a flood level. And the big industrialists openly resisted the efforts of the government to levy high taxes on a gold basis, which might have permitted "fulfillment" without resorting to further inflation. The mark, worth twenty-five cents in 1914, fell to one third of a cent in June 1922. In July, the German government asked the Allies for a moratorium (i.e., a postponement of the payments due) until 1925 lest revolution break out in Germany.

The default in reparations payments

THE GERMANS hoped for some understanding abroad. Although Great Britain was having to weather her own economic crises, the British government proved willing to renounce her claims if a general debts settlement could be reached. But the United States would cancel none of the war debts owed by the former Allies (page 654). On the contrary, Congress, on the theory that the American economy could be shielded against European complications, adopted the Fordney-McCumber Tariff Act, thereby making it difficult for European countries to bolster their faltering economies or reduce their indebtedness by trading in the United States.

The French did not regret Germany's embarrassment. They not only had less of a stake in Germany's future recovery than the British but they also were more suspicious that German complaints were made in bad faith. At a new reparations conference in London in August 1922, Poincaré was prepared to accept a moratorium only if German business were made more fully responsible for guaranteeing ultimate payment. Franco-British relations became strained, but the Germans got no moratorium.

Meanwhile the "fulfillment policy" led to more payments of reparations and thus to acceleration of the downward slide of the mark. Inability to cope with the panic of all elements of the German population brought about the fall of the moderate Center government. The big industrialists and the leaders of the small but highly professional German army saw to it that it was replaced by a nationalistic cabinet headed by an amenable chancellor, Wilhelm Cuno. He was the manager of the Hamburg-American Steamship Company and had close contacts with the Ruhr industrialists. Cuno changed the government's reparations policy, deliberately choosing to stop reparations payments in kind.

At the end of 1922 the representatives of Great Britain, France, Belgium, and Italy met again in London. Bonar Law, the British representative, proposed that Germany be granted a moratorium, and was willing in return to cancel the debts the other countries owed England. Poincaré still declined, regarding the exchange as both financially and politically unwise for France. Subsequently the Reparations Commission declared Germany in default on reparations in timber. France, Italy, and Belgium voted against Great Britain.

The Ruhr invasion   ON JANUARY 10, 1923, the French
and the collapse of the mark   government published a brief declaration stating that because of Germany's default, a control mission would be sent into the Ruhr district. The next day French and Belgian troops began to occupy the whole Ruhr area. The Italians participated in the occupation only through a few technicians. The English made public their doubts regarding the legality of the invasion but did nothing. Supported by the big industrialists, and particularly by Hugo Stinnes, who now was perhaps the most influential person in Germany, the German cabinet embarked upon a policy of passive resistance.

But highly industrialized Germany was not Gandhi's India. Passive resistance was doomed from the very beginning. About 10 per cent of the German population lived in the Ruhr area. It was the most important industrial district on the Continent. Poincaré believed that by occupying the area he could either compel the Ruhr workers to work for the benefit of France or force the German government into paying reparations. The German government believed that if the Ruhr workers refused to work, the occupation costs would ruin France financially. The striking workers, however, had to be helped financially lest they starve, and in order to help them, the currency had to be increased by printing fantastic sums. That increase meant a runaway inflation. In June 1923, the mark stood at 100,000 to the dollar. In early August, the dollar fetched over 5,000,000 marks, and worse was yet to come.

*The paradox
of German-Russian relations*

IN THE OFFING lurked the fear
of Communism. The German government and big business believed
or pretended that unless Germany was saved from the French, a Communist
revolution might break out in Germany, and they intimated to British and
Americans that in order to save their skins, they might be compelled to come
to terms with Russia. Germany had in fact been negotiating with Soviet
Russia during all this time. By the Treaty of Rapallo (April 1922) the two
countries, both outside the League of Nations and outcasts from the international family, had drawn together, promising each other neutrality in case of
attack by a third power and renouncing all reparations claims on each other.
Since then Germany had kept in close economic touch with Russia.

These two were strange bedfellows indeed. While the Moscow-guided
Communists of Germany started demonstrations amounting almost to civil
war in unoccupied Germany, the Communists in the Ruhr area supported the
Berlin government by passive resistance against "French capitalism." While
German police battled Communists in the streets of German cities, German
experts secretly tested new German weapons inside Russia, German volunteers trained Russian troops, German industrialists joined in close economic,
and often political, collaboration with the Kremlin, and revived German
manufactures found a good market in Russia.

*The effects
of invasion and inflation*

PASSIVE resistance in the Ruhr
soon proved irksome to the French
and Belgians. In order to break
it, they declared a state of siege over the Ruhr area, sealing it off from the
rest of the country. Manufactured goods were not to be exported to other
parts of Germany. Food was let into the Ruhr only in amounts sufficient to
keep the population from starvation. Railwaymen, postal clerks, white-collar
workers, and industrial workers were dismissed whenever they showed signs
of resistance. More than 100,000 Germans were expelled, were sent to jail,
or voluntarily fled. A few were killed in anti-French demonstrations.

Meanwhile, in unoccupied Germany inflation advanced like a galloping
fever, making paupers out of some and profiteers out of others. It consumed
investments, savings, and salaries. Everything was available in the stores, but
few Germans were able to buy anything. Popular irony pointed out that
whereas once the shopper had brought her money in a purse and taken
home her purchases in a basket, now the reverse was true. On the other hand,
European and American tourists and profiteers descended upon the big
German cities, living the life of *nouveaux riches*. They could exchange a
few lire and francs or fewer dollars and pounds for millions (later billions) of
marks, and they were able to buy nearly everything. Every new quotation
of the mark on foreign exchange wiped out some Germans and made the

Inflation in postwar Germany. A billion mark bill.

foreign visitors richer and more jubilant. An intense xenophobia developed among the Germans.

The German middle class, the people who had put their savings into mortgages, bonds, annuities, insurance policies, and bank deposits, were ruined. The nest eggs that they had carefully fostered for a rainy day or old age were insufficient now to buy food. As in most inflationary periods, the farmer prospered. The industrial workers were better off than the middle class because in many cases they were organized and could force their employers to raise wages, though wages always lagged behind rising commodity prices. Not only the Federal Printing Press but practically all the printing presses of unoccupied Germany were at work twenty-four hours a day seven days a week. In August 1923, the government had to admit that the printing presses were no longer able to keep up with the demand for currency. The banks, the factories, the offices, and most of the stores closed. In Berlin the department stores barricaded their windows. Everybody believed that Germany was on the brink of a revolution. The Cuno cabinet resigned, bankrupt in every respect. The ruined German middle class longed for a leader.

Stresemann's ministry and galloping inflation

PRESIDENT EBERT now appointed Gustav Stresemann chancellor. Stresemann at first seemed to be the leader the German middle class sought. Although unattractive in appearance and voice, he became one of the most popular orators Germany ever had. By inclination he was a monarchist, an imperialist, and a believer in capitalism. In 1918 he had founded the Volkspartei (People's Party), which had opposed the policies of the successive postwar governments. He now organized a coalition cabinet including Socialists and Centrists.

Stresemann's task was to put an end to the Ruhr conflict, as the only way to restore some semblance of order and stop the disastrous inflation. This undertaking proved most difficult, for the few months of the Stresemann ministry were the very ones when the inflation went through its worst stages. Employees had to be paid day by day, since wages varied mightily from day to day. Money was no longer counted but weighed. Workers would carry their pay in suitcases and, as soon as they received it, would rush to spend it because it would buy much less the next day. In August the peasants began to repudiate the official currency and would part with nothing except in return for something else of at least equal value. Those who had nothing to barter or who were not among the happy few illegally possessing foreign currency were in a tragic position. Families would sell all their valuables in order to subsist. Sometimes, when the last valuable object had been bartered away, a whole family would commit suicide. The possibility of despair driving the people to revolution grew ever greater, but it was not clear whether the revolution would be by international Communists or national monarchists.

Growing unrest and the National Socialists   AMONG THE several nationalist groups one, led by an Austrian-born ex-corporal named Adolph Hitler, was especially active. It called itself the National Socialist German Workers' Party. Its program was a composite of superpatriotism (including a growing anti-Semitism), socialist promises, and paramilitary, fascist discipline. Its opponents derisively abbreviated "National Socialists" to "Nazis," and the name stuck.

Stresemann felt that passive resistance had to be stopped in order to stop the inflation. Various nationalist groups in Germany, nevertheless, favored passive resistance as a patriotic measure. Political passions were inflammable in the late summer of 1923, but Stresemann did not lack courage. In September he called off passive resistance, and in October he informed the Reparations Commission that Germany was ready to resume payments provided her financial and economic status was reëxamined by the Allies. The Reparations Commission thereupon appointed two committees to look into the matter. Weeks went by, however, without any sign that the French would relax their grip on the Ruhr. The Germans became convinced that Poincaré's real aim was not the securing of reparations payments but rather the disorganization of Germany.

The atmosphere of uncertainty led to several abortive revolutions. In October the Communists attempted a revolution in Hamburg, meant to be the signal for a Communist revolution all over Germany against a government that had sold out to French capitalism. At about the same time the people of the Rhineland declared an independent republic, probably at the instigation and certainly with the approval of the French and the Belgians. And in November, Hitler's Nazis attempted in Munich a tragicomic coup d'état since known as the Beer Hall *Putsch*. It was crushed next morning and Hitler was put in jail for about a year, although Ludendorff, who had aided and abetted the Nazis, got off scot-free after a brief arrest. The other revolts were also suppressed and with greater severity.

The new currency and deflation in Germany

ON NOVEMBER 15, 1923, the dollar at Cologne was worth around four trillion marks. It cost hundreds of billions of marks to mail a letter. The paper on which currency was printed had long been worth much more than the currency itself, and the government had been obliged to print new denominations across the faces of old bills and postage stamps in order to save paper. Before anything could be done with regard to the reparations question, it was obvious to everyone concerned that German currency would have to be put on a sound basis. In October the Stresemann government had appointed the banker Hjalmar Schacht as special currency commissioner. He put into circulation a new currency called the Rentenmark. A special bank, the Rentenbank, was set up to issue it. The currency was nothing more than this bank's printed promises to pay one new Rentenmark for every trillion of the old, but since the new bank had important agricultural holdings and business investments, the people had faith in it. It worked. After a transitional period, and after Schacht had been made president of the Reichsbank, a new permanent currency called the Reichsmark was established.

Meanwhile, the government began a stringent deflation policy. The new mark enabled the government to keep its budget balanced. Business returned to normal; the feverish activity of inflationary markets came to a halt. The government dismissed hundreds of thousands of its employees. Unemployment rose rapidly, and Germany experienced the horrors of deflation right after she had undergone the horrors of inflation. But harsh measures were deemed necessary in order to prove to the Allies that Germany was determined to put her economic house in order.

International repercussions of the German inflationary trends

INFLATIONARY tendencies in other countries were stimulated by the German inflation. In Austria inflation was almost as bad as in Germany. In Czechoslovakia it was less virulent. In both Czechoslovakia and Austria a harsh deflationary policy ended the inflation. The new measures were resented so much in Czechoslovakia that the minister of finance, Alois Rasin, one of the founders of the republic, was assassinated in 1923. Austrian finances required the intervention of other European governments. Great Britain, France, Italy, and Czechoslovakia granted Austria a loan of $135,000,000, upon which a new Austrian currency was based. Austria lost still more of her sovereignty as a result, being obliged to promise that she would renounce the issuing of paper money and the floating of loans unless she were authorized by her creditors

706

to do so. The French also caught the contagion. The enormous government expenditures for rehabilitation of the ruined areas, the failure to collect reparations, and the cost of keeping an army of occupation in the Ruhr all helped to push the value of the franc down on the international market (page 673), but French inflation was not to reach disastrous proportions until 1926.

The Dawes Plan
for reorganizing German economy
THE COMMITTEES appointed by the Reparations Committee for the purpose of studying Germany's economic status had meanwhile begun their work. The American government raised no objections to the participation of two Americans in the discussions of the first committee. They were General Charles G. Dawes, a Chicago politician and banker, who presided over the committee, and Owen D. Young, chairman of the board of directors of the General Electric Company. The other committee was headed by Sir Reginald McKenna, a London banker. The Dawes committee, hoping to take reparations out of politics and put it entirely into the realm of finance, recommended the following steps: evacuation of the Ruhr district; the incorporation of the German federal railroads into a special nonfederal company to be assigned as security for whatever loans Germany should receive; payment by Germany for four years of a graduated annual sum for reparations (fixed at a sum insufficient to pay even the interest on the total reparations the Allies had once intended to collect), subsequent payments to be determined according to a prosperity index; a loan to Germany of $200,000,000; and the creation of a supervised German central bank, with a long-term monopoly on the issue of paper money. The McKenna committee concurred with these recommendations. Germany accepted the reports. They were adopted (with some minor changes) at a conference in London in 1924, in which the Allies and Germany participated. The Dawes Plan became operative on September 1, 1924. The French and the Belgians began to evacuate the Ruhr at once.

International insecurity
and the question of disarmament
ALTHOUGH the entire question of reparations had been handled by a diplomatic machinery unconnected with the League of Nations, the League had not meantime been idle. Among the questions it tried to deal with was that of disarmament. Not only governments but large numbers everywhere believed in 1919 that the prewar armament race had been one of the reasons, if not the main reason, for the war. The view was common that if a recurrence of catastrophe was to be avoided, armaments had to be restricted. The only question was how to attain this desirable goal; and, in the arguments about the method of disarmament, the ways parted. Each nation sought security for itself and feared aggression from others. Hence none wished to throw away its weapons until it felt safe, and each feared the armaments of the others. Armaments, it appeared, were both a cause and a result of insecurity.

The first conspicuous step by international action in the direction of disarmament had been taken when Germany had been obliged to accept a severe reduction of arms by the Treaty of Versailles. The Germans, however, proceeded surreptitiously to circumvent most of the restrictions imposed upon them. Millions of Germans received secret military training in the ranks of the Steel Helmet, a paramilitary, nationalist organization, and the Nazi Brown Shirts. Secret cooperation between former officers of the German army and the Russian government enabled the two outcast nations to build supplies of poison gas, tanks, heavy artillery, and airplanes in Russia. Military aviation, also forbidden under the terms of the Treaty of Versailles, was likewise resurrected. Some Allied officials closed their eyes to the Steel Helmet and the Brown Shirts because they felt that such training was necessary to combat the influence of the Communists and the old army officers inside Germany. The arms restrictions imposed upon the Germans proved a bonanza to them. It obliged them to get rid of antiquated material, to invent novel methods of combat, and to eliminate waste, while the French and British remained satisfied with the outmoded methods of the last war.

The League
and the Corfu incident

DISARMAMENT and mutual security were placed high on the agenda of the first meeting of the League in 1920 and remained continually under consideration thereafter. The League was first put to a serious test as a body for the prevention of war after Mussolini came to power in Italy. The occasion was an attack in August 1923 upon an international commission designated to draw a boundary between Greece and Albania. The attack, allegedly by bandits, occurred on Greek territory. Several Italian members of the commission were killed. Mussolini was pleased with this opportunity to "live dangerously"; some even suggested that he had himself instigated the murders. He dispatched an ultimatum to Greece, demanding among other things an investigation at which the Italian attaché should be present and an indemnity of 50,000,000 lire. Greece rejected these demands. Thereupon, Mussolini ordered the Italian fleet to shell the Greek island of Corfu and then to occupy it. In the shelling fifteen unarmed occupants of the ancient citadel were killed.

The world was stunned by this abrupt violence, which bore an ominous resemblance to Austria's treatment of Serbia in 1914. The Greeks asked the League of Nations to intervene. Mussolini's representatives at Geneva contended that the affair was none of the League's business and that it could all be settled between Italy and Greece. But in 1923 the war was still fresh in everybody's memory, and world opinion was so decidedly against Mussolini that he had to give in. The Council of the League ordered an investigation of the affair. The investigating commission reported that it could not find who the murderers were and recommended that Greece pay the 50,000,000 lire demanded by Mussolini. The Greeks submitted, and thereupon the

Italians evacuated Corfu. The Corfu incident thus appeared as an obvious victory for the League and raised the hope of those who prayed for its success.

The proposal and defeat of a protocol against aggression

AFTER the Corfu incident, the prestige of the League mounted. Édouard Herriot, premier of France, and Ramsay MacDonald, prime minister of Great Britain, came to the conclusion that the moment was ripe for a clear-cut program of collective security. They introduced in the League a "Protocol for the Pacific Settlement of International Disputes," which came to be known as the Geneva Protocol. It proposed disarmament and the compulsory adjudication of international quarrels either by the Permanent Court of International Justice or by arbitration. A country that went to war in violation of the Covenant or the Protocol was automatically to be considered an aggressor, and the other members of the League were to apply economic and military sanctions against it. Sixteen nations ratified the Protocol. In the interval, however, MacDonald's Labour government was soundly defeated at the polls, and the new Conservative government under Stanley Baldwin, preferring to assure peace on the Continent by direct negotiations between France and Germany, repudiated the project that the preceding British government had sponsored. And so the Geneva Protocol came to naught.

Security for France or equality for Germany?

THE MISCARRIAGE of the Geneva Protocol encouraged an already visible trend to by-pass the League of Nations in international negotiations and to resort to old-fashioned diplomatic methods. French insecurity presented itself to the French government as a stark reality, particularly after the League's proposal for joint action against aggression came to nothing. As long as Germany was disarmed or nearly disarmed, the French had not felt endangered. But in the mid-twenties the French government and General Staff could no longer remain blind to the fact that Germany was more or less secretly rearming.

Security for France was now a burning question because the time had come when the Cologne zone, if the Allies consented, was by the terms of the Treaty of Versailles to be evacuated. The French held, however, that unless some substitute for the still-born Geneva Protocol could be found before evacuation took place, their security and the security of the whole Continent would be in jeopardy. They therefore declared in general terms that, since German disarmament was incomplete, the Cologne zone must not be evacuated unless a special pact was first accepted.

The French attitude put the British in a quandary. Though ready to cooperate with the French, the British wished also to avoid incurring German displeasure. They hoped to steer clear of a continental crisis in view of their own domestic economic difficulties and the unwillingness of the dominions to become involved in European affairs. But if the Cologne zone 709 were not evacuated, a new outburst of German nationalism was to be expected and, with it, a recurrence of militarism. On the other hand, if both the French desire for security and the German longing for "equality for Germany" could somehow be satisfied, a period of stability might result. They hoped also that if Germany could be brought into the orbit of the West, she would serve as a barrier and balance against Soviet Russia.

German balancing between Russia and the West

THE GERMAN government was likewise in an awkward position. Stresemann, now minister of foreign affairs, wanted the Cologne zone to be evacuated on the stipulated date, because he, too, feared that otherwise German nationalism might again explode. He recognized, however, that the French would probably not consent without other guarantees; yet if he were to make even reasonable concessions, that very gesture might also cause a nationalistic outburst in Germany. On the horns of that dilemma he hinted to the British ambassador, Lord D'Abernon, that Germany would like to reach an understanding with France provided the British took part in the negotiations.

Anglo-German friendliness in opposition to Bolshevism had a determined advocate in the person of Lord D'Abernon; and the British foreign minister, Austen Chamberlain, eagerly fell in with D'Abernon's spirit. He felt, however, that it would be good diplomacy to keep in the background and advised Stresemann to approach the French directly. The same advice was given by the American ambassador. Just as the scene seemed well set for a western entente, President Ebert died (February 28, 1925). His successor, Field Marshal von Hindenburg, was not impressed by what he learned of the negotiations, and Stresemann now adopted a less pliable manner. Briand, recently appointed French minister of foreign affairs, and Chamberlain were both lovers of peace but capable of driving a diplomatic bargain. They had reason to wonder whether Hindenburg might not be calculating that Germany was better off with close military collaboration with Soviet Russia than with a loose understanding with France; and they made a special effort to win over the Germans. Ultimately the German government, recognizing that for a long time to come Germany would need financial assistance from Great Britain and the United States, and not wishing to antagonize either of the two English-speaking powers, leaned toward the West. The completion of the French and Belgian evacuation of the Ruhr in July encouraged Stresemann further.

German cooperation with England and France

THE FINAL negotiations took place in the idyllic Swiss town of Locarno, on beautiful Lake Maggiore. The chief participants of the conference were Chamberlain, Briand, and Stresemann. Italy, Belgium, Czechoslovakia, and Poland were also represented, and the United States, which had had a hand in the secret negotiations preceding the conference, was kept posted upon what was going on

710

behind the closed doors of the conference. After twelve days of friendly meetings and negotiations, a series of seven agreements and an explanatory note were signed on October 16, 1925, and together became known as the Locarno Pact.

The main instrument consisted of a treaty of mutual guarantee between Germany, Great Britain, Belgium, France, and Italy. They guaranteed, collectively and individually, the inviolability of the frontiers between Germany and Belgium and between Germany and France, and the permanent demilitarization of Germany west of the Rhine and of a zone fifty kilometers in depth east of the Rhine. Germany, France, and Belgium undertook never to make war upon or attack each other or invade each other's territory except to uphold the Locarno Pact or the League. On the other hand, in case of flagrant violation of any of the pact's provisions the signatories agreed to go to the assistance of the victim of the violation. The pact was to come into force when Germany became a member of the League of Nations.

The significance of the Locarno agreements THE REAL importance of Locarno lay in the fact that Germany voluntarily reaffirmed a large part of what she had signed under compulsion at Versailles. The pact recognized that Alsace-Lorraine was French, that the districts of Eupen and Malmédy (which Belgium had annexed after the war) had definitely become Belgian, and that the Rhine Valley should be demilitarized. Although Germany had acted voluntarily at Locarno, protests were voiced in both the nationalist and the Communist press of Germany. The nationalists objected to the concessions made on Germany's western frontiers; the Communists feared Germany's rapprochement with the capitalist countries. Among some Germans the Locarno Pact became known as "the Locarno *Diktat.*"

Another set of agreements was also signed at the same meeting in Locarno by Germany, France, Belgium, Czechoslovakia, and Poland. They provided that all difficulties between them should be adjusted by peaceful means. But Stresemann in his own mind put "the readjustment of our Eastern frontiers" among the great tasks of German foreign policy. He recognized, also, that German public opinion would back the nationalists and Communists in opposing concessions on Germany's eastern frontier. Hence he refused to guarantee the boundaries of Czechoslovakia and Poland. In consequence France, in separate treaties with those countries, pledged that she would immediately go to their defense if Germany violated their territories.

The signing of the pact caused jubilation in the western world, including America. The joy was justified in that tension on the Continent was temporarily diminished and the way seemed open to the readmission of Germany to full status in the world's affairs.

THE WAR and its aftermath had wrought so much material and moral havoc that it took until 1924 for even a temporary economic stabilization to come to Central Europe, and in France it was to take until 1926. In Great Britain fiscal administration was never so speculative, the taxpayer so irresponsible, or diplomacy so tied to the exchequer as on the Continent, and as a result the economic atmosphere never was cleared (if *cleared* is the appropriate word) by an uncontrolled inflationary storm. The Russian Communist appeared to have some reason to believe that international capitalism was dying—as he would put it, under the impact of its own contradictions.

But capitalism refused to die. In the United States a "new era" of widespread and unparalleled prosperity was confidently expected. In 1925 Britain returned to the gold standard. And world industry seemed to have recovered its prewar healthiness. The international revolution that the Communists had expected was defeated in Germany, Austria, Italy, Hungary, and elsewhere; and in several countries of continental Europe fascist dictatorships were set up that, instead of working for the downfall of capitalism, sought rather to mold it to the dictators' purposes. In 1925 the Communist Party in Russia was itself divided between those who believed in "revolution in one country" and those who believed that revolution was "for export." Communism seemed to be on the retreat, having accepted a limited degree of free enterprise.

In 1925 the world on the whole looked no less "safe for democracy" than it had in 1918. Democracy flourished in Czechoslovakia as nowhere else among the newly created states. Germany and Austria, though beleaguered by dissident elements, still managed to cling to their republican constitutions. Canada, Australia, New Zealand, South Africa, Ireland, Egypt, and India had won new status in the British Empire, and Algeria in the French empire. Equal and universal manhood suffrage and the secret ballot had been introduced in most European countries after the war, as well as in Japan. Only a few western countries, and France was conspicuous among them, continued to exclude women from the polls and from holding elective office. After the war more and more women were employed in offices and in business. The political and economic emancipation of women produced neither the millenium some had expected nor the dire consequences predicted by others.

Peace also seemed assured. The Dawes Plan gave promise of stopping inflation in Germany and bringing reason into the reparations controversy, and held out the prospect of a return to Europe's "normal" prosperity. Locarno, if not by the League of Nations, seemed to guarantee collective security. Austen Chamberlain was knighted and shared with Dawes the Nobel Peace Prize for 1925. And yet the promise of prosperity was shortly to prove a sham and the assurance of peace a delusion. Depression and the spread of Fascism were only around the corner.

1917-1924	Lenin as head of the Council of People's Commissars
November 2, 1917	The Balfour Declaration
1918-1935	Thomas Masaryk as president of Czechoslovakia
1918-1919	Communist movements in Germany and Hungary fail
April 22, 1918	Montagu-Chelmsford Report on India
September 29, 1918	Hara becomes Japan's first commoner premier
1919-1922	British coalition government under Lloyd George
January 18, 1919	Peace Conference opens at Paris
March 2, 1919	Founding of the Third International
March 23, 1919	Mussolini founds the Fasci di Combattimento
April 13, 1919	The "Amritsar Massacre"
June 1919-August 1920	The Treaties of Versailles, Saint Germain, etc.
July 31, 1919	Adoption of the Weimar Constitution
September 12, 1919	D'Annunzio's regime in Fiume begins
December 23, 1919	The Government of India Act
March 13-17, 1920	The "Kapp *Putsch*"
November 2, 1920	Harding elected president of the United States
November 15, 1920	First meeting of the League of Nations
1921-1925	Sun Yat-sen heads national government of China
1921-1924	The United States limits immigration
1921-1922	Washington Conference on naval and Eastern affairs
1921-1922	Gandhi's first civil disobedience campaigns
1921-1922	Irish Free State created
1921	United States makes separate peace with Germany, etc.
February 15, 1922	Permanent Court of International Justice opens
February 28, 1922	Termination of the British protectorate in Egypt
September 19, 1922	Fordney-McCumber Tariff Act
November 22, 1922	Mussolini given dictatorial power
1923-1938	Mustafa Kemal as president of Turkey
January 1923	French and Belgian troops occupy the Ruhr district
May 1923-January 1924	First Baldwin ministry
July 24, 1923	Treaty of Lausanne
August-September 1923	The Corfu incident
September 13, 1923	Primo de Rivera assumes dictatorial power in Spain
November 8-11, 1923	Hitler's "Beer Hall *Putsch*" in Munich
1924	Beginning of Stalin-Trotsky feud in Russia
1924	Britain's first Labour cabinet under MacDonald
1924-1929	Second Baldwin ministry
1924	The Dawes Plan
1925	The Locarno Conference and Pacts
1925	Japan's Universal Manhood Suffrage Bill

Chapter twelve

FROM HOPEFULNESS THROUGH

DEPRESSION TO ANXIETY

THE WORLD at the mid-twenties had some reason for hopefulness. The Dawes Plan held out for Europe the promise of economic stability, and the Locarno treaties seemed to assure political stability. The Washington treaties, it was confidently expected, would guarantee peace in the Pacific region and the Far East, as Pan-Americanism would in the Western Hemisphere. The League of Nations bade fair to grow in prestige and influence. Perhaps warfare on a global scale was obsolete after all, and even obsolescent on a limited scale.

To be sure, the western concept of democracy did not seem altogether safe in Russia under the Communists or in Hungary, Turkey, Italy, and Spain under dictatorships. Still no country with a lengthy democratic tradition had yet succumbed to either Communism or Fascism, and on the other hand several states (Germany, Czechoslovakia, Finland, and Austria were outstanding examples) now had regimes that were considerably more democratic than their prewar regimes had been. Even the dictators did not yet appear a serious menace to liberty; with a little indulgence one might easily persuade oneself that they were more in the Roman republican tradition of dictatorship (vested with emergency powers that at the first good moment they might lay down) than after the Roman imperial model. In 1925, to hope for a united, free, peaceful, and prosperous world did not seem sheer madness.

A world-wide depression was to set in with the Wall Street crash of 1929. Whatever semblance of prosperity Europe had previously displayed quickly began to vanish. One country after another fell into an economic and political quagmire. National attempts to bring about recovery were to prove for the most part too late, too feeble, or too dangerous. Nor had international economic cooperation, despite the valiant efforts of the brand-new Bank of

International Settlements, reached the stage where the calamity of overproduction in one area could be neatly adjusted by extending international credits to forestall the tragedy of scarcity in another. Though the Russian Communist had troubles of his own, he looked to a state-planned economy for more rational results and thought he had better reason than ever to believe that international capitalism was on its last legs. National self-interest led to desperate attempts on the part of the separate nations to insulate themselves— in the economic sphere against external fluctuations by fostering self-sufficiency, in the political sphere against disunion by the creation of authoritarian states, and in the diplomatic sphere against external dangers by making bargains at the expense of other nations. The trend toward national economic autonomy became global. World trade shrank, with each nation a tight economic unit, deflation-ridden, fear-ridden, and struggling desperately to lift itself by its own boot straps from the international economic debacle.

The depression brought with it a new threat to the control of the western nations over India, eastern Asia, and Oceania. The determination of the native peoples to remove colonial bonds was seriously complicated by the rising appeal of Communism and by the imperialism of Japan. Although the movements for independence and the development of Communism were to be relatively unsuccessful until the outbreak of war in Europe in 1939, the western powers, pressed by their own economic complications and hampered by the spread of hard times in the farthest recesses of the East, were continuously forced to retreat from their former positions in deference to either native resistance or Japanese aggression.

The various economic expedients to which governments resorted did not bring the desired relief to the depression's victims, and downhearted peoples became ready listeners to repeated urgings toward agitation and rebellion. In almost any country a political crackpot with a panacea could raise a following. A hungry man might listen to Communists who promised that his class would someday rule the world or to Fascists who promised that he would have work, bread, and glory under a national leader; or he might simply express his desperation in uninstigated and aimless rioting. Economic unrest fed political unrest, only to be fed by it in turn, until everywhere men began to wonder whether the old institutions could be saved even if they were worth saving.

BOOM AND BUST

(1925-1929)

FOR THE AMERICAN businessman (though not for farmers and certain kinds of workers) the first postwar decade appeared to be one of great prosperity, and he was prone to identify prosperity with progress. The era was characterized by the assembly line producing automobiles and electric appliances. To the European businessman prosperity was still elusive. The assembly line was, as already indicated, largely unknown except as an American innovation, and mechanized land vehicles still played a less significant role than in the United States, though much was being done with aircraft. Nevertheless all parts of the world were under the influence of a new phase of the "Industrial Revolution."

New industries and their effects on daily life

SOME NEW industries radically changed the American social pattern. The automobile became an indispensable possession of great numbers of American families. The radio began to occupy an intimate place in the American home. The movie industry grew with phenomenal rapidity to the status of a major industry. Nonferrous metals (aluminum, copper, chromium, lead, etc.) began to replace or supplement steel in electrical appliances, building construction, airplanes, machinery, furniture, plumbing, cutlery, and other uses. Steam-generated electricity (page 451) and the Diesel engine (page 452) were becoming more and more common. Plastics appeared in everyday objects in the factory and the household.

Americans isolated before the war on farms or in remote areas were brought by the automobile, the radio, and the movies into the main stream of American life. Taste, recreation, dress, and manners were further standardized. There ceased to be a great deal of difference between the urban housewife and her country cousin. Electrical gadgets, such as vacuum cleaners, refrigerators, washing machines, and victrolas, synthetic textiles and plastics, sanitary plumbing, and processed foods ballyhooed with fancy names in fancy packages by the mushrooming advertising industry all contributed to the standardization as well as the simplification of American daily life. Standardization often meant lifting the level of those who without the newer media of transportation and communication might have lived isolated and untutored lives, but it also meant that frequently printing, the films, and the air channels were devoted to mass appeal rather than to high standards.

"Victorian" prudishness, as stated above, was on the wane in the America of the "Jazz Age," and in many European countries the rising interest in sports, fun, automobile travel, and outdoor living resulted in simpler and less, though not less colorful, clothing, particularly in women's styles. Large-scale manufacture and chain clothing stores led to greater uniformity of dress. The influence of Freud and of "progressive education" (pages 462 and 836), led to a widespread feeling that the repression of natural impulses and the obligation to conform to conventional types were not good for healthy mental development. Privacy, easily available in dark moving-picture theaters or secluded automobile roads, made the time-honored institution of chaperonage ineffective if not obsolescent.

717

*The revolution
in communications*

THE RADIO was soon to change the lives of men everywhere. When in 1920 a station in England and another in the United States had begun to broadcast programs of speech and music, a wholly new industry came into being that was one day to give employment to hundreds of thousands of people. It would enable the old, the sick, and the remote to hear about happenings in the great centers of activity as if they were present. It could reach the Negroes of central Africa and the Eskimos of the Arctic, and bring them into closer contact with the world of the white man. For the first time people living outside the big cities were able to enjoy the best musicians, actors, lecturers, and news analysts, if they chose to do so; and many people might come to an understanding of music and the theater to whom the works of Beethoven or Verdi, of Shakespeare or Ibsen, might have otherwise remained unknown. Radio also provided a means—unfortunately not free of abuse—of teaching the young. It offered a most profitable (and frequently annoying) means of commercial advertising, though less so in Europe, where the communications systems were more strictly state-supervised than in the United States. On the other hand, in Europe it was more easily to become a medium of political propaganda, with dictators and would-be dictators dinning their slogans into the ears of ubiquitous listeners. The year 1926 saw the first wireless telephone between New York and London; and in the following year transatlantic phone service was put into operation, bringing the two hemispheres still more closely together.

*The impact
of the automobile on modern life*

IN THE MOTOR vehicle industry the postwar period saw the small manufacturer driven to the wall by the assembly line and automatic machinery to make parts. Before 1914 the automobile was still being greeted on the streets of the smaller American cities by children crying "Get a horse!" During the 1920's the horse as a draft animal was rapidly disappearing in the United States. Even on the farm he was giving way to the truck and the tractor. Along with him went the livery stable and the blacksmith. In their place the filling station, the taxi stand, the parking lot, and the garage sprang up. By 1929, at six people per car, enough automobiles existed in the United States to transport its entire population simultaneously. Less dependent on streetcars, subways, and suburban trains, businessmen and workers were enabled to live farther from their places of employment, with the result that new city areas and suburbs (and rush-hour traffic jams) rapidly developed. Although the automobile has speeded up transportation and communication, it is also a dangerous menace that has killed and maimed many hundreds of thousands.

The leadership in automobile manufacture definitely passed from Europe to the United States after the war although the vocabulary (garage, chauffeur, chassis) remained French. The automotive vehicle, particularly the truck, forced both Americans and Europeans to rebuild their streets and road systems, the Europeans on a much smaller scale and at a much slower pace. To compete with the automobile and motor truck, railroads all over the world were eventually forced to improve their rolling stock, accommodations, and speeds. Automobiles and roads created a tremendous demand for petroleum products, steel, rubber, concrete, and asphalt, and thus made "the automobile age" a distinguishable stage of the "Industrial Revolution."

Modern mechanization has caused considerable change in the habits of some Africans and Asiatics. The "auto" helped to conquer the deserts and in the late 1920's had begun to replace the camel, although the conquest is still incomplete because driving has proved to be an enormous strain on drivers in these desolate areas. Factories have caused cities to grow and social disruptions to appear, as in Europe a century or more earlier. So have oil wells and refineries. Indians and Africans have learned to use the technological devices of the white man, although their use has not yet produced a notable degree of technological inventiveness. The Russian factory commissar and the Japanese industrialist were able to teach assembly-line methods with ease to their countrymen, even those who had had almost no previous acquaintance with mechanical devices. Despite the universal adaptability of modern technology, however, many areas of the world remain relatively untouched in their native beliefs, superstitions, and customs.

The development
of the talking picture
MOTION-PICTURE photography advanced with great strides in the 1920's as film and cameras improved. The sound film made its appearance in 1926 and the first "all-talking" picture in 1928, greatly adding to the common enjoyment of the "movies" and, for a while, even threatening to drive the "legitimate" theater out of business. The impact of the "talkies" was almost as far-reaching as that of the radio, allowing people in remote provinces and rural areas to see news events photographed on the spot and the finest of plays (along with a plethora of bad ones) produced in many countries in several different languages. They educated people who had few other means of education in diction, manners, taste, and moral standards (all too often miseducating them, too). The educational "short" also became a regular tool of the schools as well as a fill-in for the feature pictures. The movies, like the radio, became an obvious avenue for advertising and propaganda, and, like the automobile, were an industry in which the United States produced the most but not always the best.

Export of American movies to Europe brought a strong American vogue in such externals as dances and slang but gave Europeans a rather distorted view of American culture. Even Europeans who had visited American universities, museums, concerts, and theaters sometimes spoke of American

719

culture as if it were made up exclusively of sex, romance, glamour, money, bootleg whiskey, jazz, and crime. Europeans frequently made better movies at less cost, but the American films nevertheless were popular, especially animated cartoons and the comedies of Charlie Chaplin, the English-born clown and master of comic pathos. The late 1920's witnessed a general revulsion in Europe against the domination of the moving-picture field by low-standard American films, and since that time an effort, only partly successful, has been made to lift the level of American productions.

The development
of air strategy and travel

DURING THE war the airplane had passed from the trial stage to the status of a dependable means of conveyance. In the postwar decades General Giulio Douhet of Italy and General "Billy" Mitchell of the United States advocated the centering of military strategy thenceforth on the air force. First used in warfare in the Tripolitan War, the airplane had been adopted by armies on both sides in 1914, although the Germans preferred the Zeppelin for bombing purposes and the English preferred the balloon for submarine detection. The Germans introduced a machine gun that could fire between propeller blades. For better defense the Allies then adopted formation flying, which pointed to the feasibility of tactical air operations on a fairly large scale, and to new theories of warfare. The aircraft carrier had also appeared during the First World War. Douhet and Mitchell, however, were regarded as air enthusiasts and encountered the hostility of traditional military thinkers in their countries.

After the war, air traffic was no longer a curiosity. Flights were so common that an international code became necessary to police the air. In 1919 an International Flying Convention was ratified by all the Allies except the United States, which, however, followed the convention in its own legislation. Longer and longer nonstop flights were made. The first nonstop transatlantic flight in an airplane, from Newfoundland to Ireland, was completed by John Alcock and Arthur Brown, English air officers, in 1919. Commercial flights by dirigible across the ocean at first seemed more practical than plane flights and soon became regular events, pioneered mostly by the Germans. The dirigible, however, in addition to being unable to compete with improvements in heavier-than-air transportation, proved dangerous in storms and highly inflammable because of its hydrogen-filled envelope. Charles Lindbergh made the first nonstop solo flight across the Atlantic from continent to continent and proved that the airplane could fly directly from New York to Paris (1927). By 1929 French pilots in planes or dirigibles had flown to various parts of Africa, Portuguese pilots to Brazil, Roald Amundsen and Umberto Nobile to the North Pole, Admiral Richard E. Byrd to both poles, and British pilots to various parts of the Empire.

In 1919 the first commercial airline was established, a British company that flew the Channel. The next year an American airline opened for business. In 1924 around 500,000 miles of air routes were in commercial operation. Commercial air travel necessitated more planes, new airports, and higher grade gasoline, and in other ways increased the demand for commodities and labor. The British first used air mail in 1919.

*The development
of the plastic industry*

THE RAPID development of synthetic or specially treated natural substitutes (plastics) for wood, leather, metal, glass, rubber, ivory, wool, silk, cotton, and paper was another postwar phenomenon. Begun in the 1860's from efforts to find a substitute for ivory in the billiard ball, celluloid was commonly used for billiard balls, gentlemen's collars, and photographic film before the war. The demand for ersatz (substitutes) in blockaded Germany during the war stimulated research in synthetic materials. An improvement in cellulose plastics came with the development of cellulose acetate, which answered the need in the automobile and airplane for such things as handles and panels, and in the telephone for mouthpieces. Synthetic resin had been developed before the war by L. H. Baekeland, and his product, Bakelite, had found use in phonograph records, pipe stems, etc. His product was more fully developed when his patent ran out in 1926, and synthetic resin products were adapted to the radio, the electric switch, automobile battery boxes, etc. After the war, casein came to be used largely for buttons and novelties; and cellophane, lucite, and a number of other plastics were marketed as substitutes for glass, cloth, wrappings, and metals. Rayon and other synthetic or treated fibers were substituted for natural silk and cotton. These synthetic industries sometimes provided entirely new commodities, but they also provided substitutes for old ones, and hence though they employed many hands and apparently increased man's total productive capacity, they displaced old industries. The silk industry in China and Japan was hard hit by the development of rayon, but worse was yet to come (page 806).

*The creed
of "bigger and better"*

IN THE United States, after the brief depression of 1921-1922, business boomed once more and the creed of "bigger and better" won new successes. The longest underground conveyor in the world hauled coal after 1924 near Pittsburgh. The Americans' pride in their long and majestic bridges, going back to the extraordinary engineering feat of the Roebling family in erecting the Brooklyn Bridge in 1883, was heightened when the longest swing-span bridge in the world went up at Fort Madison, Iowa, in 1926 and the next year the longest suspension bridge appeared at Philadelphia. United States Steel built the widest continuous hot strip mill in the world in 1927, and in 1928 the largest electric furnace. The tallest building in the world, the Chrysler, went up in New York in 1929 (only to be outstripped by the Empire State Building in 1930). In 1929, too, the world's largest airship hangar was constructed in 721

Akron, Ohio. Though some doubted whether these things, though bigger, were necessarily better, the nation's glory in them was nevertheless enormous. That Europeans were not all innocent of the worship of mammon and the mammoth was indicated by the founding of huge trusts during this period—e.g., the German Interessengemeinschaft Farbenindustrie (I. G. Farben) in 1925 and the British Imperial Chemical Industries in 1926.

Conservatism
in American law and politics

THE WIDESPREAD nativism relaxed somewhat as the fear of Communism diminished. Nevertheless, it was demonstrated in two conspicuous instances. In 1921 two Italian-born anarchists, Nicola Sacco and Bartolomeo Vanzetti, had been tried in Massachusetts for the murder of a paymaster in an alleged robbery attempt and found guilty. Many held that their guilt had not been proved beyond a reasonable doubt, and their case was bitterly debated all over the world for several years. Their defenders maintained that they would not have been found guilty if they had not entertained unpopular political opinions. The higher courts, however, did not reverse the decisions of the trial court. When Sacco and Vanzetti were finally executed, the public protest in the United States and abroad was considerable and the applause only scattered. The Sacco-Vanzetti case became the subject of poems, plays, and novels by leading American writers, nearly always sympathetic with the executed men. But this literature may not have reflected the opinion of the public at large as well as did the new law on immigration of 1929. This law limited the total number of immigrants who might enter the United States from Europe to 150,000 annually, and apportioned them among the countries of origin in accordance with the numbers from those countries in the census of 1920. This quota basis favored the northern Europeans and especially the English. "The myth of the melting pot" was not popular enough to counterbalance the antipathy to the "hyphenated American" (to use phrases current at the time).

General hopefulness
in America and Europe

THE GENERAL satisfaction of the American people with their government was demonstrated by the overwhelming electoral victory of Herbert Hoover, the Republican candidate, over Alfred E. Smith, his Democratic opponent, in 1928. The "solid South" did not vote as a bloc in favor of the Democrats, although that failure to follow precedent must be attributed largely to Smith's being a Catholic and an opponent of prohibition. Rarely was the country more cheerful. The stock market went into a steady and unprecedented upward swing. Only the farmers exhibited any notable departure from the general cheerfulness, since the price of agricultural commodities was disastrously low; and the Hoover administration made an effort to afford them relief. Of several legislative efforts toward this end, the most significant was the creation in 1929 of a Federal Farm Board with a fund of $500,000,000 to make easy loans and to encourage cooperation among the farmers. The "new era" looked as if it would reach into all sections of the country and all levels of the population.

American money seeking investment was eagerly accepted abroad, and wherever it went, the appearance of prosperity was apt to go with it. The American boom was thus indeed mirrored in certain European areas. Furthermore, although inflation continued in France, hard times in England, and revolutionary sacrifice in Russia, the Locarno Pact and the Dawes Plan had nevertheless helped to promote a feeling of international friendliness and to stimulate commerce. The more cheerful in Europe could find reason to believe that the worst was behind them, and the years 1925-1929 were on the whole years of hopefulness in Europe as well as in America.

Germany, Hindenburg, and the Dawes Plan
PRESIDENT EBERT of Germany was succeeded by the seventy-seven-year-old Field Marshal von Hindenburg in April 1925. Hindenburg was the first president to be elected by the people (Ebert had been chosen by the Weimar Assembly). As a war hero and a trusted patriot, he was expected to be a stalwart leader in a time of crisis. He regarded himself, however, as the vicar of the Kaiser, and he hoped that after his death the Kaiser or some other Hohenzollern would return to the throne. Hindenburg observed the terms of the Weimar Constitution whenever they were unequivocal, but wherever a loophole permitted, he was to show himself favorable to an authoritarian solution.

The Dawes Plan had already gone a great way toward restoring German confidence. But many Germans had accepted the Dawes Plan with tongue in cheek. They were still determined to pay nothing at all in reparations, if they could help it. The plan had been adopted by the Reichstag only with great reluctance and against marked opposition, and immediately a fight against it was launched by both the Nationalists and the Communists. The Dawes Plan, nevertheless, continued to produce the desired effects during its first years, and business picked up notably. Concurrent with its obligations under the Dawes Plan, the German government contracted several loans from private banks. German cities, towns, counties, and industrial enterprises likewise borrowed from foreign banks (mostly American). On this borrowed capital Germany recovered by rapid strides from the ravages of war, blockade, occupation, inflation, and deflation, and began to look prosperous once more. But it was only a borrowed prosperity and could last only as long as prosperity at the source lasted.

Regrowth of German military power
WHILE THE bankers of the former enemy countries were lending Germany money for short terms and trying to restore its economic usefulness, the military of those countries were worried. According to the British general J. H. Morgan, "the development of interior lines of communication, the reduction of railway rates, the

promotion of state factories and aluminum manufacture, the contribution to vast electrical power stations" were "but a few of the undertakings upon which public moneys have been lavishly expended, and all of them, be it remarked, have a military usefulness." In other words, the very process of building up Germany's economic self-reliance meant also building up her military potential. While ostensibly maintaining an army limited to the 100,000 men permitted by the Treaty of Versailles, the Germans had more than that number organized in a police system and large numbers "unorganized" in "free corps" and paramilitary groups. In 1926, Philip Scheidemann, still leader of the Social Democrats, revealed in the Reichstag that during the preceding three years Germany had spent almost $17,000,000 for secret rearmament. This money came indirectly from foreign bankers, some of whom probably did not mind German rearmament because they were convinced that it was intended to ward off Soviet Russia if need be. But the secretive German General Staff, under the command of the able General Hans von Seeckt, was at the time cooperating with the Russians (page 703). German technicians had built war factories in several Russian cities, and German industries were extending credit to Russia to buy German equipment.

Hard times in the United Kingdom

IN 1925-1929, while defeated Germany looked prosperous, victorious Britain seemed to have deteriorated economically. At the end of 1925, a million and a half wage-earners in textiles, coal, steel, and other old staple exports were out of work. The restoration of the gold standard at the old parity put the British coal industry into competition with increased coal output from European countries with cheapened currency. Bad working conditions in the mines and outmoded coal-mining methods became notoriously worse, and government subsidies helped the mines only temporarily. The British workers more than any other stratum of society resented this state of affairs. When the coal mine owners demanded that workers accept either lower wages or increased hours, the miners refused both. The operators then declared a lockout and the miners retaliated by a strike on May 1, 1926.

The General Council of the Trades Union Congress thereupon ordered a general strike. About 2,500,000 workers responded with work stoppages in printing plants, iron and steel mills, building trades, and other industries, and in all transportation services. The Conservative prime minister, Stanley Baldwin, called the strike illegal, and this castigation, upheld by the courts, made a deep impression upon many workers. The general strike lasted only nine days and ended in defeat for the workers because thousands of volunteers rushed to man the depleted transportation lines and factories. Some of the labor leaders felt relieved when the strike was over, because they had begun to fear that it might degenerate into a revolution. Both sides had conducted themselves with extraordinary restraint.

The miners kept up their strike until November, but finally surrendered. When it was over, the plight of the coal mines and the miners was worse than before. Some of the mines had to be closed as unprofitable. Unemployment increased, sometimes with a subsequent lowering of wages or lengthening of the working day. The Conservative majority in Parliament passed the Trades Disputes and Trades Union Act (1927) outlawing sympathetic strikes or any strike or lockout intended to influence the government either directly or by imposing discomfort upon the public and permitting trade unions to use a member's dues for political purposes only on his written authorization.

The coal-mining situation and this Trades Union Act remained thorny issues, rallying the workers behind the Labour Party. The Liberal Party, split between Asquith Liberals and Lloyd George Liberals since 1916 (pages 634 and 670), had closed its ranks in 1923 to defend free trade, but now it broke up again over Lloyd George's control of political funds and over the issue of the coal mines, Lloyd George advocating a government subsidy to the mines and Lord Asquith opposing it. This split strengthened the relative position of the Labour Party in the political arena. Another advantage perhaps fell to Labour in 1928, when Parliament by a new Representation of the People Act at last gave women exactly the same political rights as men, increasing the numbers of voters by about 5,000,000, most of whom probably shared the general dissatisfaction with Baldwin's labor policy. The result was that in the national election of May 1929 the Labour Party ran ahead of the other two parties, though again unable to win a majority, and MacDonald became prime minister again in a second Labour cabinet.

Inflation and stabilization in France

NO DAWES PLAN had been extended to France to help solve her spiraling inflation, since France was not under international tutelage. In July 1926, the French inflation assumed disastrous proportions. The franc, worth 20 cents in 1914, dropped to 2 cents in 1926; the cost of living had gone up altogether about 700 per cent since 1914. In order to forestall complete disaster, President Gaston Doumergue asked Poincaré to take the premiership again. Few liked the black-bearded, stubby Poincaré, but he was universally respected. When he rose to deliver his first speech as the new prime minister in the Chamber of Deputies, the Communists taunted him with the cry, "We see you only in bad times!" and rose singing the Communist anthem, "The International." Nevertheless, the French counted upon his undoubted ability and personal integrity to save the situation. He named five other former prime ministers to sit with him in a "National Union" cabinet. He restored confidence, balanced the budget, and was able to stabilize the franc at about 4 cents. He did it mostly by establishing a sinking fund and by administrative economies, but he also enacted a few hated taxes, including new indirect taxes and an inheritance tax. Confidence reappeared in France and

Premier Poincaré proudly escorts a Madame Republic enriched by the stabilized franc. A cartoon by Werner Hahmann.

was to stay for a while after it had vanished in other countries in the early 1930's.

The continuation of Turkey's westernization

UNDER Mustafa Kemal's benevolent dictatorship, Turkey continued its program of westernization. Islam remained the creed of nearly all its people, but Islam now lost its exclusive status as the state religion. Marriage was made a civil matter in 1926. Since Islam was based on the Koran, which was written in the Arab language, Kemal was enabled to use the devotion to the Koran itself to increase western influence among his people. In 1928, he replaced the Arab alphabet by the Latin alphabet, and all Turks under forty had to go back to school to learn the new lettering. Few of the rising generation, educated in the Latin alphabet, were able to read the Koran in the original. Thus at one stroke Kemal brought Turkey closer to Europe without necessarily diminishing its affiliation with Arab culture. Perhaps Kemal's most astonishing innovation was the adoption in 1926 of the Swiss code of civil law as the basis of the new law of Turkey. When the new social revolution seemed well under way, Kemal commenced the industrialization of Turkey. By 1929 it seemed that Kemal had done what no other Asiatic ruler outside Japan had ever succeeded in doing; he had modernized his country without sacrificing its independence.

The victory of Stalin in Russia

UNTIL 1925 it seemed possible that Trotsky would become the recognized successor of Lenin as the leading figure in the Communist Party of Russia. At first, his rivals, Zinoviev, Kamenev, and Stalin, banded together in the expectation that their alliance presented the only way to outweigh Trotsky's enormous prestige. The issue, it may be repeated, was not merely one of personalities. Stalin,

726

finding the party greatly discouraged by the defeats of the Communists in Hungary, Germany, China, and elsewhere, proposed to devote attention to the stabilization of Soviet Russia at home and, leaning upon the Russian peasantry, advocated "socialism in one country." Trotsky on the other hand believed that stabilization within Russia was not possible so long as capitalist states outside Russia were free to oppose it. Therefore, he favored the promotion of "permanent" world revolution, and in domestic policy leaned on the urban population, particularly the factory workers, as the truly revolutionary class. Trotsky denounced Stalin for reviving capitalism by pampering the wealthier peasants (kulaks) and the NEP capitalists. Kamenev and Zinoviev shared Trotsky's philosophy but at first feared Trotsky more than Stalin.

Stalin proceeded cautiously at first, even attempting at one point to form an alliance with Trotsky. His position as general secretary permitted him gradually to acquire control of the Communist Party. When he felt strong enough, he saw to it that Trotsky resigned as commissar of war (1925). After that, the pro-Stalin triumvirate broke up, and Trotsky was able to make an alliance with Zinoviev and Kamenev, but it was already too late. In 1927, all three of them were expelled from the Communist Party. Zinoviev and Kamenev recanted their "deviation" from what was now the approved party line, but in 1929 Trotsky was exiled from the Soviet Union.

Stalin became, so far as any outsider could tell, the uncontested ruler of Soviet Russia. A "Fourth International," which the discredited Trotsky organized among his followers, served chiefly as a means of giving Stalin the opportunity to accuse his opponents in Russia of being "Trotskyites." For the time being, the victory of the principle of "socialism in one country" was complete over the principle of "permanent revolution." So long as it prevailed it meant that the Russian Revolution was to be primarily a national and not an international phenomenon, even though the Third International was permitted to survive. The business of the Bolsheviks became to stabilize their control of their own sixth of the globe's surface.

Shortly after Stalin's triumph, when the government found itself unable to purchase enough grain from a reluctant peasantry to feed the cities, Stalin reversed his attitude. Announcing that the "kulak was disrupting the Soviet economic policy," he turned his favor toward the urban proletariat. Convinced that neither the haphazard methods of 1917-1920 nor the NEP would suffice to solve the economic inadequacies of Russia, he proclaimed a "Five-Year Plan" in October 1928. Its purpose was to transform Russia into a large-scale industrial country and to "collectivize" agriculture. In order to do that, extraordinary emphasis was to be put on state-owned heavy industry and the merging of small, privately owned farms into large mechanized, state-owned or state-supervised farms. Heavy industry (i.e., the production of machinery for factories) was to be built up by an extraordinary concentration 727 of effort within five years even if the Russian people would have to forego consumers' goods in the meantime.

The creation of a giant heavy industry could be accomplished only by a huge labor supply, which in an agricultural country like Russia would have to come mostly from the peasants. This shortage of factory labor was one of the reasons why industrialization had to be accompanied by the collectivization of agriculture. Collectivized and mechanized farms could be managed by fewer farmers than would have been possible with small, individually owned farms. The surplus farm hands, whether they liked it or not, would be forced into the cities, where they would become factory workers, as the government wished. But in order to improve the factories, to feed the increasing urban population, and to keep rural collectivization going, factory and agricultural machines, particularly tractors, would be needed. They would obviously have to be imported, at least during the first few years of the Five-Year Plan. What was perhaps not fully foreseen by those responsible for Russia's planned economy was the extent to which, in order to pay for imported machinery, grain would have to be exported. A vicious circle was soon to develop: the harder the Russian workers worked, the more machinery they had to use; the more machinery used, the more machinery had to be imported; the more machinery imported, the more grain had to be exported to pay for it; and the more grain exported, the less food remained inside Russia. Hence, the harder the Russian workers worked, the less food they had. Despite incredible difficulties, the Soviet government was nevertheless to succeed in carrying out its program to industrialize Russia, but at a tremendous cost in human lives and human happiness.

The tightening of Mussolini's hold on Italy

PROGRESS in Russia toward a Soviet dictatorship was matched by progress in Italy toward a Fascist dictatorship. The Aventine Secession (page 679), far from weakening Mussolini's hold on the Italian legislature, made it a more docile tool in his hands. Between 1924 and 1926 an obedient Chamber of Deputies passed a series of laws suppressing all opposition newspapers and parties, thus making the Fascist Party the only legal one in the country. As if to make certain that the meaning of this change would be clear, the Chamber also gave the head of the state the dictatorial power to issue decrees. The lenient treatment meted out to Matteoti's murderers, when they were finally tried in 1926, indicated that extermination of the Duce's enemies was not to be considered a serious offense.

Mussolini's next step was to make sure of the loyalty of the working class. In 1927 a "labor charter" put questions of capital and labor under government control. It set up thirteen (eventually reduced to nine) "confederations" of syndicates (unions), six for employers, six for employees, and one for intellectual workers (mostly self-employed). They confederated all the existing syndicates in agriculture, banking, industry, insurance, commerce, the professions, and the arts. They had the authority to regulate hours of labor, wages, and working conditions. Their decisions were binding, and strikes and lockouts were outlawed. Shortly (1928) these confederations were given the power, in place of the proscribed parties, of suggesting to the Fascist executive committee, the Fascist Grand Council, most of the candidates for election to the Chamber of Deputies. In 1929 the corporative organization of Italian industry was capped by the creation of a Council of Corporations, made up of deputies from the syndicates and the government. This Council was vested with authority to settle labor disputes of national scope.

The new labor organization of Italy was hailed in many countries as a solution of the labor-capital conflict. Actually, it proved a cumbersome way of regulating the politico-economic life of the country. It did not end, and may even have increased, the dissatisfaction of employers and employees alike. Conflicts were now more likely to arise, however, between employers' and employees' syndicates. The number of unemployed remained high. In 1928, to make still more certain that no labor opposition would arise, only members of syndicates, high taxpayers, government pensioners, and clergy were permitted to vote (the number of voters thus being greatly reduced), and they were permitted to vote only for nominees submitted to them by the Fascist Grand Council.

Pius XI
and the Lateran agreements

THE "Roman Question" (page 328) now seemed ready for solution. The old animosities between the popes and the house of Savoy had lost their momentum in the course of the nearly sixty years since their origin. Continued stubbornness by the Vatican seemed less likely than ever to bring any advantage to the papacy, and in the face of rising Communism it might even prove disastrous. At first, when Mussolini, in creating a one-party state, had suppressed the Popolare, friendliness between the old church and the new state looked impossible. Nevertheless, after protracted negotiations, the Duce and the Vatican succeeded in coming to an understanding, and in 1929, they signed a treaty, a concordat, and a financial convention in the Lateran Palace.

By the treaty, Italy recognized the pope as the sovereign of Vatican City. It comprised, among other buildings on the right bank of the Tiber, the Vatican Palace and Saint Peter's Church. In addition, some churches and ecclesiastical buildings on the left bank came under papal sovereignty. The person of the pope was declared "sacred and inviolable." He received the right to send and receive ambassadors and to make treaties. Thus Vatican City became a sovereign state, much like any other state in outward appearance, with an army, subjects, a postal system, coinage, and a radio station.

By the concordat, Italy recognized the Roman Catholic religion as the only state religion of Italy. Marriages performed in accordance with canon law were recognized as legal by the state. Religious instruction from church-approved books and by church-approved teachers became compulsory in the elementary and secondary schools. No apostate or censured priest was to be allowed to teach in Italy. Clerics were to receive special consideration with regard to military service and court procedure. In return for these concessions, the Holy See promised to appoint no bishops or archbishops within Italy who were not acceptable to the government, and to keep Italian ecclesiastics out of politics. By the financial agreement, the pope received a cash payment of about 750,000,000 lire (when the lira was about 19 to the dollar) and 1,000,000,000 lire in 5 per cent government bonds as final settlement for all his claims.

Pope Pius XI now made clear that the Roman Question was settled once and for all and that he recognized the Italian kingdom with Rome as its capital and the house of Savoy as its dynasty. He brought to a close the voluntary imprisonment in which he and his predecessors had lived since 1870 and stepped on Italian soil. Disputes were to arise over the training of children, since the pope wished to make good Catholics and Mussolini good Fascists of them, but these disputes were settled without an open break. In fact, the Lateran agreements were to be among the few made by Mussolini that would outlast their author. The final arrangement of Italy's old quarrel with the church made Italian Fascism look to observers at home and abroad like a huge success.

*Mussolini
and the "monolithic" state*

FASCISM, rationalized if not actually caused by the wish to combat Bolshevism, had used several tenets from the Bolsheviks' creed. A "monolithic" (single stone) state was one of the big ideas in both camps. The monolithic state requires a subservient church, but in enforcing that subservience the two new cults differed somewhat. Bolshevism was frankly atheistic, permitting only a grudging tolerance to those addicted to the "opiate" of religion. Fascism allied itself with the church, but it too was essentially non-Christian. Mussolini had been a frank atheist in his younger days. In 1904 he had written a little book entitled *God Does Not Exist,* in which he maintained that the universe is nothing but "the manifestation of matter, which is one, eternal, indestructible, never had a beginning, will never have an end." Instead of the brotherhood of man, Mussolini taught the brotherhood of Italians and the "otherhood" of non-Italians. Instead of turning the other cheek, he sought vengeance for real or imaginary face-slappings of Italy. Instead of the Golden Rule, he implied that it was permissible to do anything unto others: "Today among the things for which there is no room, must be included the opposition." Instead of only the things that were Caesar's, he demanded that everything be rendered unto Caesar: "The Fascist State...includes all the form of the moral and intellectual life of man. ...It...disciplines the whole person...the very soul of the soul." Instead of peace on earth, he believed "neither in the possibility nor the utility of perpetual peace." If he made a settlement with the Vatican, he did so because, in the manner of Napoleon before him, he thought that the Catholic Church was a good police force for a regime that had substituted for "Liberty" the slogan of "Order, Hierarchy, Discipline."

Meantime, to some opponents of democracy Mussolini appeared a paragon. His Fascist modification of the old idea of syndicalism seemed a better answer to the old problem of the relation of the state to business than the Communist answer. His bargain with the church looked more respectable than the Bolsheviks' atheism. His one-party state was less ruthless than the Russian Communist state. Even outstanding advocates of democracy hailed Mussolini as a great man who was clearing Italy of beggars, making its trains run on time, and cleaning up Rome.

Armaments, cartels, and speculative holding companies — IF THE YEARS 1925-1929 were on the whole years of well-being, there were also indications that Europe's prosperity was only illusory. One of the serious omens of the disaster ahead was the purposes for which governments were spending their revenue. Some share of the loans the Germans were receiving was beyond doubt being used for rearmament in secret defiance of their international obligations. France, too, was engaged in huge expenditures for war purposes —the Maginot Line (page 788) and big loans to the members of the Little Entente for their arms programs. Thus a large part of Europe's goods was being sidetracked from the production of consumers' goods.

Another unhealthy sign was the increasing activities of international cartels and holding companies. Cartels originating in different countries sometimes cooperated despite national rivalries. For instance, the French armament company of Schneider-Creusot owned a considerable interest in the Czech Skoda works and had an agreement with the German Krupp works. The Krupps in 1928 made an agreement also with the American General Electric Company regarding patents on tungsten carbide. The British Imperial Chemical Industries had understandings with the German I. G. Farben, and both of them entered certain arrangements with the American DuPont interests and Standard Oil Company. New companies were formed, sometimes by old ones, sometimes independently, that carried on as subsidiaries of the old ones or as collaborators with each other in several countries at once. Such international arrangements were formed by big concerns with a view to fixing supply, controlling patents, distributing market areas, or in other ways causing artificial shortages and ruling out competition in order to maintain stable prices for their products. This practice was especially true of several metals monopolies and of the match cartel, headed by Ivar Kreuger of the Swedish Match Company, who, when finally unmasked as a swindler, committed suicide (1932). Holding companies—i.e., companies whose assets 731 consist primarily of securities in other companies—were known since the nineteenth century, but they now engaged more than formerly in stock deals for speculative reasons. Mergers of companies also became more frequent on a speculative basis.

Monopolistic and speculative practices like these were not necessarily illegal (except perhaps in the United States where they might run contrary to the antitrust acts), but they encouraged questionable business practices. Kreuger had his counterpart in Clarence Hatry of England, Alexander Stavisky of France, and Samuel Insull of the United States. Businessmen and laymen who knew of and deprecated speculation and shady dealings were legion, and they, no less than the unsuspecting, were to be among those who, when crash and panic came, would lose faith—at least momentarily—in the banks, governments, stock markets, and credit system that had permitted or encouraged such practices.

The United States and European economy

SINCE THE center of economic as well as political gravity had shifted to the United States, a healthy international commerce depended largely on American policies. If Americans wanted full repayment for what they had loaned to the Europeans, the Europeans should have been given a chance to work off their debts or to pay off old debts out of new loans. In consequence of a high American protective tariff, however, Europe could profitably export few goods to the United States. The fundamental inability of Europe to meet its debts was visible to some Americans who lamented it and to others who were indifferent to it because they believed in an American economic isolation. For most Europeans as well as Americans, it was not visible so long as the United States pumped loans into Europe, but in 1928-1929 American sources began to dry up. From 1920 to 1931 Americans bought $11,600,000,000 of foreign capital issues, about 40 per cent of them European. If depression were to come to America, the train was laid for an economic and social explosion in Europe.

The Wall Street crash and the coming of the depression

FEW SAW the full extent of the danger. Long ago the American farmer, shipyard worker, mass textile worker, and soft-coal miner had ceased to share in the "new era" prosperity, much of which was a false prosperity based upon market speculation and the assumption that American business could prosper regardless of how the rest of the world might fare. In 1923-1929 several thousand American banks, mostly in the corn and wheat belt, had closed their doors. About 1927 economic activity began to slow down in such basic areas as the building trades, the automobile industry, and foreign investment. By 1927 the number of unemployed was estimated at around 1,500,000 and was mounting. The trend was scarcely noticed, however. It was obscured by a stock market boom that began about the same time and sent stock prices rapidly to dizzy heights.

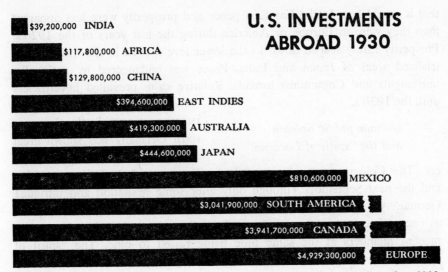

$39,200,000 INDIA

$117,800,000 AFRICA

$129,800,000 CHINA

$394,600,000 EAST INDIES

$419,300,000 AUSTRALIA

$444,600,000 JAPAN

$810,600,000 MEXICO

$3,041,900,000 SOUTH AMERICA

$3,941,700,000 CANADA

$4,929,300,000 EUROPE

This chart indicates the extent of the major United States investments abroad in 1930. The largest sums are invested in the Western Hemisphere (almost $8,000,000,000) and in Europe ($4,929,300,000). The other investments here indicated total $1,545,300,000.

Stock speculation spread like a virus. As the popular song "The Twentieth-Century Rag" put it, "Millionaires all worry/how to get another/million dollars in a hurry." For a while all one needed to do to get rich quick, it seemed, was to buy certain stocks, hold them until they went up to the desired amount, and then sell them again, pocketing the profit. A fairly large number of Wall Street stocks seemed capable of achieving this magic effect rapidly.

Once more, alas, a hard lesson was in store. Modern businesses are so intertwined internationally that prosperity is international, and a crash in one place may cause the ground to shake in another. By mid-1929 the world prices of metals, wool, cotton, and wheat were dropping. Banks in Japan, Italy, Austria, and Belgium were in trouble because they had been financing risky ventures, and creditor countries like the United States and Great Britain were exporting less and less capital. Then in London Hatry's speculative companies failed (September 1929), and he was sent to jail. His English victims, needing cash, dumped their American securities. Immediately stock quotations fell sickeningly; the bottom dropped out of Wall Street in October; and a depression (probably the worst in history) soon engulfed the world.

AN INTERLUDE

OF COMPARATIVE PEACE (1925-1930)

As A RESULT of the conferences of Washington and Locarno, a sweet reasonableness seemed to reign in international relations. Contemporaries spoke sanguinely of the "spirit of Locarno in Europe," and dared to hope that it would last. In the Far East peace and prosperity were less apparent than they were in Europe or America during the last years of the 1920's. Prosperity rarely seeped down to the lower levels, even in the more industrialized areas of Japan and India. Peace was endangered by nationalist movements and Communist inroads. Relative calm prevailed nevertheless until the 1930's.

German public opinion and the "spirit of Locarno"
IN KEEPING with the Locarno spirit Germany was shown great consideration by the western powers. The Cologne zone of occupation was evacuated in February 1926, and the next September (though only after some hesitation and intrigue) Germany was admitted to the League of Nations. She was granted a place as one of five permanent members of the Council, the number of nonpermanent members at the same time being raised to nine. The "spirit of Locarno" was so much talked about that it began to assume the aspect of a reality. For their work at Locarno not only Austen Chamberlain (in 1925) but also Briand and Stresemann (in 1926) were awarded the Nobel Peace Prize. For several years it looked as if Locarno marked, in Chamberlain's words, "the real dividing line between the years of war and the years of peace."

Unfortunately, Chamberlain was to prove mistaken in believing that pacts and promises would preserve peace. From the very start, a large part of the German people were opposed to the pact. Stresemann found it hard to get the Reichstag to accept it. Plots against his life were discovered by the police. Nationalists and Communists, though they could agree on little else, as if by a concerted effort tore him to bits in their press, accusing him of having sold pieces of Germany like Alsace-Lorraine for the almighty dollar. The irony of the situation was that Stresemann himself regarded the pact merely as a matter of expediency, albeit a necessary one—a finesse in a tight diplomatic match.

Stresemann's "reinsurance" policy with Russia
GERMANY was literally caught between two forces. Stresemann had gained by the Locarno Pact what he wanted from the West—namely, the easing of French pressure and the confidence of Great Britain and the United States. But Soviet Russia, always suspicious, became restive; and Germany, for several reasons, was not willing to sacrifice her understanding with Russia. Only with Russian aid could the Germans regain the provinces they had lost to Poland. Furthermore, the Germans had good ground for believing that they could not prosper economically without Russian trade. An unfriendly Russia, besides, could block Germany's rearmament and leave Germany isolated without support against France. Especially during the months that the League was hesitating about admitting Germany, an eastward orientation appeared desirable.

Therefore, Stresemann concluded in April 1926 a mutual neutrality pact with Russia that became known as the Berlin Pact. Its main provision was to the effect that neither signatory would take part in any economic or financial boycott against the other. This pact dashed the high hopes that the British had built upon the Locarno Pact. From the British Conservative's point of view, Locarno should have been only the beginning of a close cooperation between Germany and the West, a cooperation whose chief purpose was to create an anti-Russian coalition. The Berlin Pact on the contrary harked back to Bismarck's Reinsurance Treaty.

The partial success of the Briand-Stresemann efforts
THE LOCARNO PACT nevertheless seemed to indicate that the Germans were genuinely determined to end the age-old European boundary quarrels once and for all. The high point of good feeling between Germany and France came in the fall of 1926 when Briand and Stresemann had a several hours' talk in Thoiry, a little French town near Geneva. Stresemann, climaxing an eight years' struggle for German equality in the family of nations, had just made a triumphal entrance into the League of Nations, and Briand, representing a tired people anxious to return to a stable, pacific world, thought the time had come for a full accord. Alone, except for an interpreter, the two men sought an understanding. The results of their meeting were that French troops evacuated the Saar region and that Germany recognized the Permanent Court of International Justice as the proper place where all potential international disputes should be settled.

But further efforts to draw Germany into closer cooperation with the West were defeated by the colleagues of Briand on the one hand and by Stresemann on the other. Stresemann was not ready to agree that Germany be used exclusively as a tool of the West in its dealings with Russia. As one of Germany's leading historians afterwards discerned, in the rapidly developing three-cornered struggle "old Prussian and Russian sympathies were revived, and the common antagonism to western culture became more pronounced." Still, official Franco-German relations did not deteriorate as long as Stresemann lived, and the French government, fondly believing that defensive measures would now be enough to ensure France from invasion, proceeded to build the "Maginot Line" (page 789), which gave her a false sense of security. After Stresemann's untimely death in 1929, Franco-German relations were to deteriorate rapidly.

The appeasement of Mussolini in Tangier
BRIAND'S policy of conciliating France's potential enemies induced him to yield to the belligerent Mussolini. If the Corfu incident of 1923 had been a victory for the League of Nations, it had not been a humiliation for the Duce. Once the incident was settled, however, he bided his time until he might win a more

clear-cut triumph. He glorified war by every means—in speeches, textbooks, the daily press, and pamphlets. He held up the Rome of the Caesars as a shining example for modern Italy, and he publicly ridiculed the League as an obstacle to the vitality of nations.

In October 1927, the Duce felt strong enough for another coup. In a gesture recalling Kaiser William II's tactless performance in 1905, he sent three Italian warships to Tangier at a moment when France and Spain were engaged in negotiating a renewal of the Statute of Tangier of 1923, while at Rome he made plain that he expected to be included in any Mediterranean deal. Instead of rebuffing Mussolini or appealing to the League of Nations, France and Spain gave in, and Italy received a voice in the international administration of Tangier. Mussolini was now enabled to pose as the man of action who had brought glory at the sword's point to Italy. Although the Tangier affair was of minor importance in itself, it was ominous, because none of the other governments of Europe showed any inclination to resist the Italian show of force, and the League of Nations did nothing about it. The Tangier incident thus improved upon the Corfu pattern of threat and appeasement. With less provocation Mussolini had taken bolder action against a bigger opponent and had come off with a more impressive victory.

An American attempt
to extend naval disarmament

WHILE WILLING to send observers to Geneva and to cooperate with some of the League's agencies, the government of President Coolidge had to act independently of it in major undertakings. Interested in economy as well as in staying out of European imbroglios, Coolidge was disturbed by the League's failure to achieve any kind of disarmament. In 1927 he called another conference to discuss ways and means of preventing a race in naval vessels of smaller size, which had not been restricted by the Washington arrangements. He hoped that the capital-ship ratio of 1922 could be extended to such vessels, putting an end to a race already well under way and into which the United States had no desire to enter. The conference met at Geneva. Of the great naval powers France and Italy, suspicious of each other, declined to take part, and only Great Britain and Japan joined the United States at the conference. But the British and the Americans were unable to agree. The United States wanted a few big cruisers capable of carrying large forces on lengthy voyages between distant naval bases, while Britain, already having a distinct advantage in cruisers, wanted a number of smaller vessels for nearer, defensive expeditions. The conference failed.

The Kellogg-Briand Pact
regarding the outlawry of war

IN THE FOLLOWING year the American secretary of state, Frank B. Kellogg, became an understudy of Briand in the quest for peace. The failure of a sufficient number of members of the League to ratify the Geneva Protocol led to efforts outside the

League to achieve a substitute for it. In 1928 the Pact of Paris was adopted in its stead. It became known as the Kellogg-Briand Pact, after its sponsors. It declared wars "outlawed" as an instrument of national policy, and it expressed the intention of its signers that all international disputes should be settled by no other than peaceful means. But it had no teeth in it, and it was signed by fifty-three nations largely because it committed them to nothing but pious wishes. Nevertheless, the Pact of Paris was hailed at first as a real victory for international peace, and nowhere more than in the United States, where people and government, having less at stake than Europeans had, were less distrustful and more ready to take a mere declaration of intentions for a realistic political fact. It gave hope to those who believed in the efficacy of moral purposes backed by public opinion in preventing war, but others spoke cynically of an "international kiss." The Kellogg-Briand Pact was in a sense another blow to the prestige of the League of Nations. Now more than ever it appeared good international practice, while paying lip service to the League, to conduct important diplomatic negotiations outside its framework.

The mandates of England and France THE LEAGUE made a somewhat more impressive record in connection with the administration of the mandated territories. King Feisal's government in Iraq, having its hands full with the Kurdish tribesmen, who had risen in rebellion in 1924 and threatened to do so again, looked to the British forces in his kingdom for defense. England also championed the Iraqis against the Turks in the dispute over the Mosul oil area. The boundary dispute was settled in the League in favor of Iraq; and thereupon Iraq granted to the British the right to exploit the immensely productive Mosul oil fields (1926). Iraq also leased three airports to the British and agreed to have her army trained by British instructors.

Britain was not equally fortunate in her dealings with the Palestine mandate. There the immigration of Jews still was a fighting issue for Arab nationalists, and in 1929 a particularly widespread and bloody anti-Jewish riot spread havoc in Palestine's cities and ports and led the British to contemplate putting an end to Jewish immigration (page 756). In Palestine's affairs the part of the League of Nations was no more than formal.

The French meanwhile had their hands full in Syria. Not least among the complicating factors there were the Druses. As a particularly proud minority, they had been the leaders of defiance in the Near East on many occasions in the past. Now protesting French favoritism to the Christians, they started a rebellion that developed into a great Syrian upheaval (1925-1927). The French bombarded the Druse villages, and when revolt spread, they systematically burned down the rebels' villages. Damascus was the target of heavy artillery and planes in 1925, and again in 1926. Since Damascus was one of the oldest cities on earth, dearly beloved by the Arabs, an outcry went up throughout the Islamic world. The situation became so tense that 737 the Mandates Commission of the League of Nations intervened and its subcommission, after investigation, condemned the French for their faulty administration.

In 1928 the French felt that order was sufficiently restored to permit elections of a constituent assembly. But, as might have been expected, the majority of the representatives elected were Mohammedan nationalists, who aimed at an independent Syria. The French thereupon suspended the constituent assembly and proceeded to draw up a constitution of their own devising. It was to be promulgated in 1930 and was to provide for a republic under French mandate with French control of Syria's foreign policy. The Syrians temporarily submitted, though obviously discontented.

Pan-Americanism
in the Western Hemisphere

THE GOOD WILL of Latin America toward the United States grew during these years as American interference diminished. Only in Panama, which was maneuvered in 1926 into accepting a treaty giving the United States a large control over its foreign affairs, and in Nicaragua, where United States Marines supported the government against Liberal insurgents (1926-1928), did the big neighbor exercise open pressure. Good will was magnified in 1928 by the official repudiation of the Roosevelt Corollary (page 502), whereby the United States had arrogated the right to regulate the finances of "backward" Latin-American countries. At the fifth and the sixth Pan-American Conferences at Santiago (1923) and Havana (1928), the Pan American Union reached maturity, receiving a permanent governing board made up of the American secretary of state and the Washington emissaries of the other member states and providing a forum for the pacific discussion and the possible arrangement of disputes. In most Latin-American areas the influence of the United States through commercial investment was now so great that military investment seemed no longer necessary.

The Young Plan
and inter-Allied war debts

ONE OF THE problems that continued to cause fiscal uncertainty in Europe was the relationship of German reparations payments to the Allies' war loans. The United States government persistently denied any such relationship. The mood of the American people, disillusioned by the outcome of the war, dictated an unwillingness to pay for any part of it but their own. All during the 1920's the question of inter-Allied war debts envenomed the relations between the United States and its former allies. Nevertheless, as long as Germany honored her annual reparations payments according to the Dawes Plan, the European Allies regularly paid installments on their war debts to the United States. In 1928 the four years of annual reparations stipulated by the Dawes Plan expired and a new schedule of payments was called for. A still more

738

lenient plan was worked out in 1929 by an international committee under the chairmanship of Owen D. Young.

The Young Plan revealed the changes that had come about in official thinking regarding international indebtedness. In the first place, the close kinship of reparations with war debts was acknowledged (since the United States was not formally a party to the plan) by turning the banking problems of reparations payments over to a Bank for International Settlements and by providing that any cancellation of war debts would immediately be reflected in a proportionate reduction of reparations. The new plan further acknowledged the desirability of making reparations payments reasonable and definite both in size and in number, requiring Germany to pay annual installments that were smaller than those of the Dawes Plan and were to end entirely in 1988. If they had all been paid, they would have totaled $9,000,000,000 (which was only a little over a fourth of the sum which the Reparations Commission had originally designated). In addition, Germany was to have a more dignified role in the transactions connected with the proposed payments. The Bank for International Settlements would be managed through representatives of the central banks of the interested countries, Germany having equal status with the others. The Young Plan, though subsequent developments were to cut short its operations, stands nevertheless as testimony of the new spirit in Europe's international relations. It was an effort to treat reparations as a dignified business matter rather than as a football of bargaining diplomats dependent in last analysis upon the power of their armed forces. Actually the last occupation troops began to move out of the Rhineland while the Young Plan was still under discussion, and occupation was over by June 1930. Haggling over the Young Plan continued from June 1929 to January 1930, when finally the representatives of the countries involved affixed their signatures. But no sooner did it go into operation than it proved impracticable, for a world-wide depression was by that time under way, and Germany was to be one of its worst victims (page 747).

The trend toward party rule in Japan

HIROHITO became emperor of Japan in 1926, shortly after the Universal Manhood Suffrage Act (page 663). Domestic changes began in his country that soon became of major concern to the entire world. The military still occupied a sheltered spot under the Constitution of 1889, and their reluctance to take orders from a civilian government increased, but it was not until the 1930's that aggressiveness was to become the outstanding characteristic of Japanese foreign policy.

In the general election of 1928 several new labor parties came into existence. The tendency of the working classes to form parties of their own, however, proved easy to check and control by the major political parties, the "liberal" Minseito and its leading opponent, the Seiyukai. Drawing for support upon the *zaibatsu* (the great financial families), the old parties had little difficulty in holding their voting strength. Where pressure and bribery failed, the government of the old parties and big business ruthlessly suppressed opposition by police action. Many Japanese came to look upon party government as the puppet of the great financial families or as synonymous with inefficiency and corruption. This readiness to cooperate against labor parties did not mean that either the old parties or the great financial families were in agreement on the objectives of government. The Seiyukai was allied with the Mitsui family of bankers and industrialists, and was ordinarily more conservative than the Minseito, with its backing from the Mitsubishi family of shippers and industrialists. In the last years of the twenties, the Minseito advocated a moderate program: domestic retrenchment, expansion of foreign trade, and a policy of conciliation in dealing with foreign countries. To business interests in Japan and abroad this seemed to make sense, but to the landed groups domestic retrenchment appeared ruinous. The Seiyukai proposed a "positive" program in which were included an energetic diplomatic and military policy, particularly with regard to China, the expansion of foreign trade by superior vigor rather than by conciliation, and the acceleration of both agricultural and industrial production at home. The "positive" program appealed from the beginning to the farmers and the armed forces; after its successes had brought profit, commercial and industrial interests were also to rally behind it.

In the field of foreign relations the Minseito was criticized roundly for its weakness. Particularly disturbing to its critics were the growing strength of the Kuomintang in China and China's growing hostility toward Japan. The success of the Soviet Union in the Far Eastern Republic (in 1926 renamed the Far Eastern Area) and Russia's increasing interest in Manchuria also held prominent places on its list of potential sources of international challenge. The weakness of the Minseito policy in Asia appeared to the proponents of a "positive" policy to have an insidious counterpart in Europe. Japan's cooperation in the Kellogg-Briand Peace Pact and her association with western disarmament programs seemed to them to be dangerous pacifism. Throughout the later 1920's, however, the moderate program of the Minseito prevailed.

The Simon Commission and its failure in India

BY THE mid-twenties five policies were obviously competing for support among India's nationalists. Nonviolent noncooperation with a view toward ultimately achieving swaraj (self-government) won prestige as the policy of Gandhi, who in 1925 was chosen president of the Indian National Congress. In the Congress two other groups, despite their loyalty to Gandhi, raised doubts about the correctness of his program. One was led, among others, by Motilal Nehru (father of Jawaharlal Nehru); it advocated cooperation with the *raj* to the extent at least of electing members of the legislatures who should engage in obstruction and nuisance tactics. They became known as the Swaraj Party and were approved by the Congress. The younger Nehru, educated in Britain and advocating the modernization of India, was developing a more revolutionary program, one that was ready to use direct action and violence as its means and included in its ends both complete independence and a program of economic reform. Even more definitely opposed to the Congress' policies was Mohammed Ali Jinnah, the leader of Mohammedan nationalists, organized (since 1906) in the All-India Moslem League. Appealing for a return to traditional Moslem institutions, Jinnah resented particularly the efforts of Gandhi to unite Hindus and Moslems. The Moslem minority, he feared, would suffer in an independent India, and he advocated the establishment of separate Moslem and Hindu states. Although Jinnah too was western-trained and unorthodox, his program for Moslem India attracted millions of followers among orthodox Moslems. Still another party operating outside the Congress was the Liberal (or Moderate) Party, which advocated loyal cooperation with the dyarchy. All these parties had one thing in common—some form of self-government for India.

The Baldwin government gave heed to the Indian clamor. It appointed in 1927 a commission of six members of Parliament under the leadership of Sir John Simon to gather the data needed for determining its future policy for India. Since no Indians were included on the Simon Commission, and since its objectives were but vaguely stated, the native groups once more resorted to civil disobedience, disorder, strikes, and terrorism to impress the commission and the world with their determination to bring British control to an end in India. The most important native leaders refused to appear at the hearings of the commission. The Swaraj Party accepted the elder Nehru's report proposing dominion status, but the younger Nehru now organized an All-India Independence League outside the Congress. The British government at the end of 1929 decided to call a series of round-table conferences in London to examine the desirability of dominion status for India. But would dominion status now be enough?

The one-party state of Chiang Kai-shek in China

THE NATIONALIST movement in China had contemporaneously exhibited greater unity than in India. The death of Sun Yat-sen in 1925 precipitated a free-for-all among his disciples for leadership in the Kuomintang, but after a period of appalling chaos, Chiang Kai-shek, a young officer who had visited Soviet Russia, emerged as the recognized leader of the party. Trained in military science in Japan and Russia, Chiang early displayed also a diplomatic aptitude for playing one side against the other. Not committed to either extreme in the Kuomintang, he managed by adroit political manipulations to gain and hold the ascendancy in the party against all comers. Moreover, his military training and his hold upon the Nationalist armed forces gave him a distinct   741 advantage over his civilian competitors, and were to stand him in good stead throughout his long and variegated political career.

Chiang Kai-shek did not break at once with the Communists. After becoming leader of the Kuomintang he gave his attention first to organizing his military forces and to preparing an expedition against the northern government at Peking. For this purpose he found his Soviet advisers of great help in providing financial aid and military advice. Chiang conducted the campaigns of 1926 and 1927 so successfully that by the spring of 1927 the rich Yangtze Valley with the wealthy cities of Nanking and Shanghai had fallen to the southern forces.

Having captured the great emporiums of China, Chiang listened with rapt attention to the Yangtze capitalists. In response to their suggestions, he put an end to the marriage of convenience between the Kuomintang and Communism. The next summer the Communist elements in the party were purged at Hankow, and a reconciliation followed between Chiang and the strongly anti-Communist groups in the party. Chiang's ties with the wealthy elements of Chinese society were strengthened at the end of 1927 by his wedding to Soong Mei-ling, a member of the respected and influential "Soong dynasty." Madame Sun, the widow of Dr. Sun Yat-sen, was a sister of the new Madame Chiang.

The year after the break with the Communists was devoted to the completion of the northward expedition and the establishment of a "constitutional" regime at Nanking. Peking was taken by the Kuomintang forces in June 1928, and to symbolize the trend toward modernity and unity the name of the old city was changed to Peiping (meaning "northern peace," whereas Peking means "northern capital"). At Nanking (meaning "southern capital"), meanwhile, preparations went ahead for the proclamation of the National government of the Republic of China, which took place in October. Operating under an organic law, the new republic was set up frankly as a one-party government. It professed to have realized Dr. Sun's first principle of *nationalism* and advertised that it was about to embark upon a period of preparation for *sovereignty* or *democracy*. The economic principle of *people's livelihood* was presumably to be realized only after the achievement of the party's political objectives.

Communism among the Asiatic peoples

TO ASIATIC peoples who wanted to rid themselves of the white man's rule or of their native landlords' privilege, Russian Communism, fighting for advantage against foreign hostility and seeking to promote the international class war, seemed a natural ally or at least an admirable example. And in Japan, India, southeastern Asia, and especially China, the Communists had been active in the organization of labor and student movements. After the suppression of Communism in China, the movement went underground and several of its unsuccessful leaders were purged. The focal point of Communist activity was then shifted for a time to the minor states of eastern Asia. In French Indochina, for example, the Communists became particularly active after 1927 in the anti-French movement. In Java, too, they were successful in stimulating riots and attacks upon the Dutch rulers of the East Indies. The Japanese viewed Communist activity with the utmost distrust and placed elections and labor movements at this period under careful police surveillance. The Chinese Nationalists assumed that Soviet agents were continuing to operate as Communist propagandists in China even though Communists had been purged from the Kuomintang. Non-Communists have difficulty in distinguishing between Russian and Comintern policies, and the Chinese government suspected that the differences were only nominal. After 1927 diplomatic relations between China and the USSR were strictly limited and curtailed.

The Russo-Chinese conflict over the Chinese Eastern Railway

A SIGNIFICANT Russo-Chinese diplomatic and military conflict nevertheless arose over the question of Manchuria and the control of the Chinese Eastern Railway. So long as the Chinese had been at war with one another, Japan and Russia had been left free to push their economic and political advantages in Manchuria. The establishment of a central authority at Nanking, however, was followed by a concerted effort on its part to resume China's control over Manchuria in fact as well as in name. This reassertion of Chinese dignity ran counter to the plans being laid in 1928-1929 by the USSR to reinforce its own hold upon the Chinese Eastern Railway and to make that line the main instrument of Soviet economic expansion in Manchuria.

The balance of power in Manchuria had by that time become a key point in Far Eastern diplomacy, and the Chinese Eastern Railway was a prominent factor in that balance. Completed in 1904 as a joint enterprise of Russia and China, the Chinese Eastern Railway had been a source of friction between the two countries ever since. During the course of the Far Eastern intervention in Russia (page 644), the railway had been for a time (1919-1922) under a control board of the various interested powers. It was later restored to the joint supervision of Russia and China, but Russia had of late been trying to augment her share in the railway's management. Upon Japan's military withdrawal from Siberia, the Nipponese sought to offset the Soviet program by sponsoring and financing new Chinese railway lines in Manchuria. They hoped thereby to divert traffic toward the South Manchurian Railway and the port of Dairen, both under their domination. Although they were themselves disturbed by the reassertion in Nanking of authority over Manchuria, the Japanese watched with quiet interest the brewing of the more imminent storm between China and Russia.

Nanking's show of vigor in Manchuria was encouraged by the major powers of the West. They recognized the National Chinese government 743

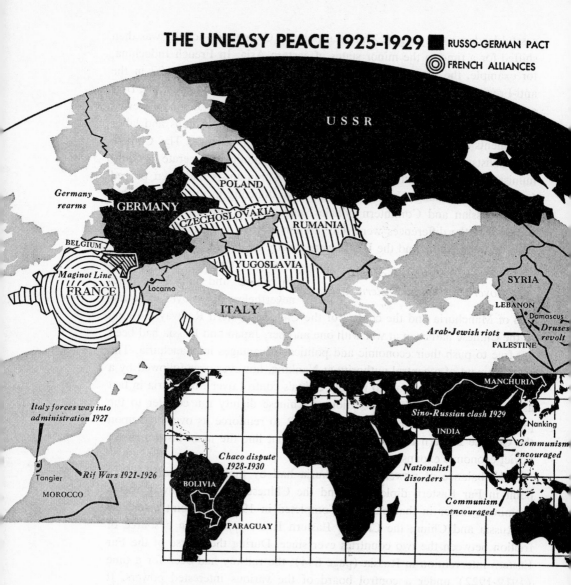

THE UNEASY PEACE 1925-1929 ■ RUSSO-GERMAN PACT
◎ FRENCH ALLIANCES

Though the world still talked peace in the years between Locarno and the Wall Street panic of 1929, various steps were taken in fear or expectation of war, international or civil. Czechoslovakia, Rumania, and Yugoslavia had already aligned themselves in the Little Entente (1920-1921) to preserve the status quo in central Europe (page 685). France signed defensive agreements with the Little Entente, Poland, and Belgium (page 711). Germany negotiated a "reinsurance pact" with Russia (page 734). Large funds went in Germany toward secret rearmament and in France toward the Maginot Line (page 735). Russia openly clashed with China in Manchuria and encouraged Communism in China, French Indochina, and the Dutch East Indies. In Morocco, the Riffs defied Franco-Spanish forces until 1926 (page 687), and Italy won a place in the Tangier government (page 736). In Palestine Arabs rioted against an increase in Jewish immigration. In French-governed Syria, the Druses touched off a nationalist uprising (page 737). The Chaco area dispute between Bolivia and Paraguay flared up in 1928, and was temporarily arranged in 1930. Indian nationalist agitation against British rule led to strikes and disorders throughout the decade.

744

officially and concluded with it a series of new commercial treaties. In addition, the Nanking government was among those to sign the Kellogg-Briand Peace Pact, the only recent international agreement to which both China and Russia were equal parties. This new dignity for their country led the impatient Nationalists toward a more aggressive policy. They were not above the desire to profit from the general international ill will toward Russia. They appear to have felt that since a Russo-Chinese contest would cut the only railway between Europe and the Far East, the resulting obstruction would bring the powers to their side against a nation already feared and suspected.

China's defeat by direct negotiations
THE RUSSO-CHINESE quarrel quickly became a matter of international concern. China in 1929 completely severed the only tenuous diplomatic ties that she had preserved with Russia after 1927 and showed a manifest determination, regardless of the consequences, to regain her share of control in the Chinese Eastern Railway. The League of Nations could not feasibly attempt to stem the impending clash, since Russia was not a member. For the same reason only futility could be expected from invoking the Nine-Power Pact signed with such great *éclat* at Washington in 1922. The threat of war in Manchuria, however, could be acted upon internationally under the terms of the new and loosely constructed Kellogg-Briand Pact. Early in the dispute the western powers, on the initiative of the American secretary of state, Henry L. Stimson, reminded both China and Russia that the Kellogg-Briand Pact obliged them to renounce war as a means of resolving their differences. This was the first test of the renunciation-of-war agreement, and it was quickly to be found wanting.

The summer of 1929 passed in continuous crisis and sporadic military activity. Worsted in the field, the Chinese continued to hope that either the Japanese or the western powers would support them with more than diplomatic measures. The powers, however, were reluctant to become involved actively in a clash of arms in a remote, although vital, corner of eastern Asia. The United States undertook, however, to initiate an appeal to the reason of both parties on behalf of the major powers with Far Eastern interests. Other signers of the Kellogg-Briand Pact made individual appeals. Although the Chinese welcomed even such feeble activity, the Soviet government replied bitterly to these representations, protesting that it could not "forbear expressing amazement that the Government of the United States, which by its own will has no official relations with the Soviet, deems it possible to apply to it with advice and counsel."

Throughout the international negotiations the Soviet Union insisted upon resolving the dispute by direct agreements with China and the war lords of Manchuria. In the end that method was followed. As a result of arrangements accepted in December, the situation was restored to what it had been 745 before hostilities began in Manchuria, thus giving the victory to Russia. Nor was the lesson of the Soviet success lost upon Japan. If the Russian Communists could set aside Nanking's legitimate claims without exciting a world-wide reaction, what was to prevent Japan, a respectable, capitalistic nation, from similarly advancing her ambitions in northeastern Asia?

THE QUEST

FOR LEADERSHIP IN EUROPE

THE IMPACT of the financial maelstrom of 1929 was all the greater because the sailing had been so smooth. The Washington treaties, Kellogg-Briand Pact, Dawes and Young plans, League of Nations, Pan American Union, Geneva conferences, and other international understandings and agencies had been effects as much as causes. They had represented, stage by stage, the recognition of global interdependence, and at the same time they had helped to promote that interdependence. The "Great Depression" undermined the foundations of peace laid by the conferences of Paris and Locarno. It not only affected Germany's ability to pay reparations and made difficult any payments by the Allies of their war debts to the United States, but it also almost put an end to any sense of moral obligation to repay international loans. Moreover, it intensified the groping for strong men to guide the bewildered peoples out of their confusion and fright.

Financial instability and Anschluss in central Europe

BECAUSE OF the depression the flow of American capital to Germany was checked. Money shortages in turn caused German factories to close down or to work only on a restricted scale. Unemployment resulted, with all its pathetic social consequences. Countries with raw materials to sell were hard hit because they could not sell to countries like Germany, whose industrial apparatus had become paralyzed. The industrialized countries could not sell their finished products, because their customers could no longer afford to buy them. The vicious circle assumed the proportions of a catastrophe in central Europe when to the price, production, and trade crises a financial crisis was added.

This phase of the general financial crisis had its origin in Austria. Under the terms of the treaties of Versailles and Saint-Germain, Germany and Austria were not to unite in any way. On receiving an international loan in 1922 (page 706) Austria had once more confirmed her obligation "not to alienate her independence...and [to] abstain from any negotiation or from any economic or financial engagement calculated directly or indirectly to compromise this independence." Still, a large percentage of the population of both countries favored just such a compromise, hoping to bring about an *Anschluss* (a "linking") of the two German countries. During the twenties the issue had had mostly sentimental overtones.

But when Austria was hit by the world depression, the Austrian chancellor, Johann Schober, renewed the proposal on economic grounds. Could not a customs union be established which would do away with Austria's helplessness once and for all? By joining the far greater Germany, Austria might eliminate the economic difficulties that had been her lot since the destruction of the Austrian Empire. The German chancellor, Heinrich Brüning, and his foreign minister, Dr. Julius Curtius, Stresemann's pedestrian successor, readily fell in with Schober's proposal. But when the treaty creating an Austro-German customs union was made public in April 1931, France, Poland, Czechoslovakia, and Italy, all of which had reason to fear a stronger Germany, protested to the League of Nations. The League asked the Permanent Court of International Justice for its advice. The court decided in September that Austria had violated her pledge of 1922, and that decision put an end to the customs union project.

The tottering
of the German banking system
EVEN BEFORE the court rendered its decision, financial palsy had struck both German-speaking countries. Once more politics determined economic developments. France felt the impact of the world depression much later than the other countries, and its economic system was not yet as close to a knockout as were others. Not until 1934 did France too begin to reel under the blows of international hard times. In 1931 the French, strong in international finance since Poincaré had stabilized the franc, sought to discourage Austria's ardor for *Anschluss* by promising a badly needed loan if Austria would give up the idea. Although this demand came at a moment when Austria's largest private bank, the Vienna Kreditanstalt, could no longer meet its debts, the Austrian government hesitated, and the resources of the Rothschilds, the Austrian National Bank, the Bank for International Settlements, and the Bank of England were pooled to meet the emergency. The Kreditanstalt was reorganized without going completely into bankruptcy. The loss of confidence in the Kreditanstalt brought on the total collapse, nevertheless, of one of the largest German banks, the Danatbank. Badly shaken, the whole German banking system started to totter as American, Dutch, and Swiss bankers, facing depression themselves, called their short-term loans back from Germany.

Moratorium
and "standstill" agreement
EVEN BEFORE the failure of the Danatbank central Europe had seemed again to be on the verge of a catastrophe as bad as the inflation of 1923. To avoid that horror President Hoover had suggested that all reparations payments on the part of Germany and all other intergovernmental debts be suspended for one year. In

July 1931 Congress ratified the "Hoover moratorium," but it came too late. No soothing words or mere suspension of payments could reassure panicky bankers, who wanted their money back from their tottering German debtors before they crashed themselves. The closing of the Danatbank and the impending insolvency of the whole German banking system forced the government to close all banks and the stock exchange for three weeks. When that period was over, the government embarked on a policy of rigorous economy, which proved as terrible to the average citizen as the inflation had been. Eventually about 25 per cent of the labor force was thrown out of work. Many of the unemployed rushed into the Nazi Party. When Charles G. Dawes' Chicago banking house underwent financial stress, Dawes became a favorite subject for Hitler's derision. In language made familiar by the Communists, he attacked "America's dollar diplomacy and economic imperialism" that could not help itself but wanted to play financial preceptor to Germany.

Dr. Hans Luther, president of the German Federal Bank, in dismay sought aid abroad. He went to London and Paris, but the British could not help him, and the French, still outraged because of the customs union affair, would not. An American committee, called in by the Bank for International Settlements, suggested a "standstill" on all payments on private short-term loans, and the proposal met with general approval. The standstill period was at first intended to last only through February 1932, but it was extended every year until the Second World War. By that time Germany still owed to American banks alone about $400,000,000.

England
off the gold standard

WHEN THE standstill agreement came into force, the bankers in Belgium, the Netherlands, Sweden, and Switzerland had a new access of panic. The agreement meant that British bankers, among others, might no longer call their short-term loans back from Germany. That state of affairs in turn alarmed the bankers of the small countries, who, fearing that the British banks might close, hastened to make heavy gold withdrawals from London. Therefore, in September 1931, Great Britain again "went off the gold standard" (i.e., refused to pay its foreign obligations in gold).

The financial uncertainty of England was felt around the world. The British dominions had been drawn more tightly together by Imperial Conferences in 1926 and 1930. By the Statute of Westminster (1931) they were explicitly declared to be, as indeed they had long been, "equal in status, in no way subordinate one to another...freely associated as members of the British Commonwealth of Nations." They had been applying a policy of "imperial preference"—i.e., trade concessions to each other and England; and in 1932, partly in reply to American protective policies (page 776), Britain adopted a moderate tariff after almost a century of free trade, and drew her empire still closer about her by her system of imperial preference. And the United

States went off a full gold standard in 1933 (page 779). France, Italy, and the countries that tied their economy to the French franc were almost the only ones left on the gold standard. The franc now was "the strongest currency in the world," and it was the turn of the American tourist in France to discover what it was like to have one's money depreciate on foreign exchange.

The end
of reparations and war debts

IN JUNE 1932 an international finance conference opened in Lausanne, Switzerland, for the purpose of deciding the future of the Young Plan. The plan in effect was canceled, and Germany was requested to pay in place of reparations the sum of $750,000,000 (3,000,000,000 marks) for European reconstruction. At the same time Great Britain, France, Italy, and Belgium entered a "gentlemen's agreement" to the effect that they would not ratify the proposed substitute for the Young Plan unless the United States met their concessions on reparations with "satisfactory" proposals regarding Allied war debts.

The United States officially turned a deaf ear to the suggestion. Drawn-out negotiations with the European debtors began, but only Great Britain, Italy, and Finland made any payments on their war debts after 1932, and after 1934 Finland was the only country to do so. Germany never resumed payments on reparations either, and so the Lausanne Conference marked the virtual end of a period in which reparations had been a major, if not the major, international issue. During that period Germany had paid in reparations an estimated $8,500,000,000 (of which about $6,000,000,000 worth was in kind). This total was even less than the $10,000,000,000 that Keynes in 1919 had estimated Germany could pay. During that time Germans had borrowed $5,000,000,000 from abroad. But only one sixth of that sum had been loaned to the German government; the rest had gone to private borrowers and helped to modernize German industrial plants and equipment.

Deflation,
autarky, and autarchy

THROWN INTO the depths of depression, the countries of the world tried to adjust themselves to their trying situation as best they could. They all turned to a greater or lesser degree to a policy of planned deflation, self-sufficiency, and economic isolation ("Buy American!" "Buy English!" "Buy French!"). This policy is sometimes called "autarky."

The word *autarky* describes an economic system and is to be distinguished from the word *autarchy,* which describes a political system. *Autarky* means "national economic self-sufficiency." For modern industrialized nations it is difficult to prosper without regard to the economies of other countries. Raw materials and commodities not produced at home have to be imported, and in order to pay for them, home products or money or promises to pay have to be exported. But after 1931 the international transfer of money was increasingly cut down by governments anxious to protect their already depreciated na- 749 tional currencies from greater depreciation through competition and comparison with the currencies of the less hard-hit countries. As a result, in the years 1931-1939 international trade returned to a marked degree to a barter rather than a money and credit basis. Since barter was frequently based upon limited bilateral agreements, world trade was further restricted.

The Germans, particularly after Hitler became dictator (page 755), proved past masters in concluding such barter agreements to their own advantage. For instance, in order to obtain certain minerals from Yugoslavia, which the Yugoslavs had to sell for their economic survival, the Germans offered them in part payment such things as cosmetics, alarm clocks, pianos, and other German products for which the Yugoslavs had no vital need. But the Yugoslavs had no choice, if they wanted to sell their minerals. Similarly, some American exporters found themselves paid in harmonicas. Sometimes inspired by the socialist ideal of "planned economy" and sometimes by the Stalinist concept of "socialism in one country" and nearly always by a desire for national self-sufficiency, German economists developed an erudite theory that autarky was superior to other forms of economy. It was in some respects reminiscent of the old mercantilist philosophy. Together with the historians who were prognosticating the decline of the West (page 797), this school of economists built up a profound and widespread doubt as to whether Europe could survive without reversing some of its older traditions.

Some dictators and kinds of dictatorship

ONE OF EUROPE'S most ancient traditions is the aspiration for liberty, which is deeply rooted even though it is counterbalanced and often braked by a complex of sometimes counteracting traditions, among which are the quest for order and the readiness to trust the great leader. The potential antagonism between liberty and order, though they are not necessarily hostile forces, has been a factor in a string of revolutions followed by reaction, sometimes led by a man on horseback. The career of Adolph Hitler presents many striking parallels with other men on horseback like Napoleon Bonaparte and Benito Mussolini. Hitler too found a people who were for the most part united by fear of a revolution from the Left more than of one from the Right, though the danger from the Right proved to be the greater. Unlike Napoleon but like Mussolini, Hitler was able to use media of mass communication like the public-address system, the radio, the movies, and the cheap press to feed popular fear and prejudice. He too had a program of reform which, like Napoleon's and Mussolini's, was a curious mixture of philosophy, practical experience, and personal ambition. In Hitler's case it was compounded in part from Wagner's anti-Semitism, Chamberlain's Aryan myth, Nietzsche's anti-Christian superman, Ludendorff's apologetics for German defeat, Mussolini's Fascist state, and Stalin's socialism-in-one-country. Some of the compound was learned second-hand from the intellectuals among his followers; but mostly it was derived from his own frustrations, aspirations, and ambitions. He too found conspirators in high places ready to overthrow the government and seeking an alliance with a leader who had an armed force behind him. He too was ready to challenge the status quo at the very juncture when those whose interest should have placed them on the side of the status quo were too weak or too unwilling to defend it against a would-be dictator.

Even when distinguished from tyranny, dictatorship is an ancient institution. In the course of Europe's history new dynasties had arisen—Caesars, Carolingians, Bonapartes—because in unsettled times, some commanding figure had been assigned extraordinary powers by general consent or had usurped them by force or ruse and then had somehow passed them on to his successors. By the nineteenth century the idea of constitutionally unlimited authority in the hands of one man who had recently acquired it was familiar—historically, at least. More recently Europe had developed two new versions of the idea. One was the concept of dictatorship as a stage in the development of the classless society (as in Russian Communism). The other was the concept of dictatorship as the culmination of national unity (as in Italian Fascism). Class and nation could easily be merged when it suited the advocates of either philosophy to do so. It remained for German Nazism to add a third to the modern versions of dictatorship—that the dictator spoke for a superior "race" and exercised authority on its behalf.

The rise of the Nazi Party

WHEN HITLER went to jail in November 1923 after the Beer Hall Putsch blew up in his face, the Nazi movement seemed ready to die of ridicule. Months in a prison fortress gave him a chance to write his masterpiece, *Mein Kampf,* a mixture of autobiography, personal philosophy, and blatant prejudices, which after his rise to power sold by the millions of copies in Germany and perhaps has had greater influence than any other German work outside of Luther's translation of the Bible. Here he betrayed how frustration in his early career and bitterness over German surrender in the World War had led him to lay his own and Germany's sufferings to the Communists, the international capitalists, the Jews, and the "November criminals" who had "stabbed the German army in the back" by making an armistice on uneven terms although, according to him, Germany had not been defeated. Somehow they all became identified in his mind with Jews, and he used the terms interchangeably, only half believing their identity himself but hoping to concentrate hatred upon a single symbol by taking advantage of the new gust of anti-Semitism that blew over Germany in the wake of the inflation of 1922-1924. For, he stated: "The great masses of a people...will more easily fall victims to a great lie than to a small one, since they themselves perhaps also lie sometimes in little things, but would certainly still be too much ashamed of too great lies." He also frankly set forth his ambition to become Germany's Führer (leader) and to

steer the united German "race" to the mastery of Europe, conquering "Black-Jew France" and the inferior Jewish-Slav Russia in the process. The ambitious but vague socialist schemes of the National Socialist Party receded more and more into the background as nationalism and racism advanced.

The apparent prosperity of Germany from 1925 to 1929 had meant hard times for Hitler. Most Germans refused to take seriously this pasty-faced Austrian with the comic moustache, high-pitched voice, and guttural accents, who seemed destined to no greater glory than to be satirized (as he eventually was) by the comedian Charlie Chaplin. But with distress and unemployment in 1929 his party grew and his brown-shirted "Storm Troops" became more numerous and more violent. In the elections of 1930 the National Socialists won over a hundred seats in the Reichstag—about thirty more than the Communists and about thirty fewer than the Socialists—and the party continued to grow and to become more violent in the ensuing months.

The short ministry of Chancellor von Papen UNTIL APRIL 1932 German democracy still seemed capable of survival. The eighty-four-year-old Hindenburg was renamed president of Germany, this time as the candidate of the democratic parties, in an election in which he received over 19,000,000 votes, Hitler over 13,700,000, and Ernst Thälmann, the Com-

752

munist candidate, around 4,000,000. Chancellor Brüning, a leader of the Center Party, embarked on a program of social reform and put a ban upon the Nazi paramilitary forces. But he aroused the displeasure of the Junkers, especially because he wanted to put an end to unprofitable estates, many of which could stay out of bankruptcy only by means of constant subsidies, the so-called *Osthilfe* ("help for the east"), paid by the federal treasury at the taxpayers' expense. The money had been intended to keep agricultural enterprises going and thus to supply food and employment. It was sometimes manipulated, however, so as to provide fine houses and expensive equipment for the landlords. Hindenburg, maintaining that Brüning's policy was Bolshevism, dismissed him curtly in May.

The relatively obscure Franz von Papen now became chancellor. Papen was not a Junker but the scion of an aristocratic family of the ancient Holy Roman Empire. Papen was a rich man, a regular churchgoer, and an excellent raconteur. And Hindenburg and his son took a fancy to him. He became chancellor just in time to receive the credit that should have gone to Brüning for putting an end to reparations. He courted Nazi favor by removing the ban upon the "Brown Shirts," and he offered to make Hitler vice-chancellor but with restrictions that Hitler, convinced of ultimate victory, refused to consider. Papen thought of himself as a sort of Bismarck, governing by authority of the head of the state and despite the opposition of the Reichstag. In July, claiming that the legal government of Prussia, which was Socialist, was too friendly to the Communists, he deposed it by a military coup d'état, though he used the emergency powers conferred by Article 48 of the Weimar Constitution (page 680) as a pretext. The Prussian ministers put up no resistance. Papen now took charge in Prussia. Thus the Socialists lost their last chance to use force to maintain the Weimar Republic.

Still Papen encountered growing dissatisfaction except among the Junkers and the big industrialists. He was forced to dissolve the Reichstag twice within three months. Both elections returned overwhelming but disunited majorities in opposition to the government. The Nazis were now the largest faction, but the second election (November 1932), coming at a juncture when economic conditions seemed to be getting better, indicated that for the first time in two years the Nazi tide was also receding; and the impression was general at home and abroad that the movement would now disintegrate. Papen had to give up finally when the Nazis made common cause with the Communists in a streetcar, bus, and subway strike that paralyzed Berlin.

The ministry of General von Schleicher

HITLER, still insisting upon "all or nothing," refused the deliberately restricted offer of Hindenburg to make him chancellor; and so the president turned to General Kurt von Schleicher. Schleicher had been a driving force behind Germany's secret rearmament program and collaboration with the Russians. He now thought, with a field marshal as president and a general as chancellor, that the moment was not far off when Germany could tear up the Treaty of Versailles, openly rearm, and extract compensation for her losses at the end of the World War. In order to carry out this ambitious program, he sought first to gain the confidence of union leaders and the workers. Schleicher was also convinced that the *Osthilfe* scandal had to come to an end, if for no other reason than to convince the workers that the government was not reactionary. The Junkers were outraged. They dubbed Schleicher "the Red Chancellor."

As Schleicher knew, Hindenburg would never willingly accept his program. But he knew also that Hindenburg's son was engaged in an effort to avoid paying inheritance taxes on his father's estate. By using this knowledge he hoped to coerce the president into submission. The president, however, proved hard to coerce, and in January 1933, he obliged Schleicher to resign. Though Schleicher played with the idea of a military revolt, he apparently could not bring himself to defy a field marshal. This hesitation proved his undoing.

The advent of Adolph Hitler to power

SINCE THE elections of November 1932, Hitler's party had actually begun to show the expected signs of disintegration, and Hitler, who had refused hitherto to take office either as chancellor or as vice-chancellor unless he could do so without conditions or restraint, now was chastened. His party was financially bankrupt after two election campaigns, and top Nazis were in defection. He himself had even contemplated suicide. In January 1933 he was ready to accept conditions that two months earlier he might have spurned. He and Papen met at the home of a rich banker, the Baron Kurt von Schroeder, in Cologne. These men represented the opposition to "the Red Chancellor"—Nazis, aristocrats, the industrialists. Hitler was apparently told that if he could win the forthcoming state elections in the tiny state of Lippe-Detmold, thereby placing his party again in the forefront, the debts of the party would be paid and Papen would arrange that he be made chancellor, provided that Papen was himself made vice-chancellor and that the majority of the cabinet posts were entrusted to non-Nazis. That, at any rate, was the order in which things actually did happen. Hitler seems to have accepted these conditions. Papen then used his influence to stiffen Hindenburg against Schleicher and to name Hitler instead. Forty-eight hours after Schleicher's resignation Hitler was appointed chancellor and Papen vice-chancellor.

In the hope of getting a clear majority in the Reichstag, Hitler immediately called for new federal elections. Throughout the month of February, street fights, kidnapings, and political murders took place all over Germany. Many people became disgusted with the violent methods of the Nazis. Moreover, economic conditions showed some signs of improving and the cessation of reparations had gone far to weaken German resentment of the Versailles *Diktat*. The Nazis, haunted by the fear that they had lost their hold and might not win the elections, felt they had to do something spectacular to convince the Germans that Hitler was the only man capable of saving them from Bolshevism. A few days before the election, henchmen of Hermann Goering (Hitler's lieutenant, who had been appointed Prussian prime minister) set the Reichstag building afire. The blame was put on a feeble-minded Dutch youth believed to be a Communist and on the Communist Party of Germany. Millions of Germans saw in the fire the flaming hatred of the Communists for Germany. At the polls on March 5 the Nazis combined with the Nationalists, the party of big business and the aristocracy, to gain a small majority.

The Gleichschaltung
under "the Third Reich"

MEANWHILE Hitler, declaring that Germany was on the eve of a Communist revolution, had received semi-dictatorial powers by an emergency decree of President von Hindenburg. The Communist Party was outlawed, and its representatives in the Reichstag were not admitted. The rump parliament, despite Socialist opposition, then voted an Enabling Act that gave Hitler for four years more power than Mussolini had ever had and in effect destroyed the Weimar Constitution.

Then followed an era of arbitrary arrests, concentration camps, censorship, spying by the police, and all the other odious methods and institutions of dictatorship. Hitler astonished the world by officially sanctioning a one-day boycott of all Jewish stores and Jewish doctors and lawyers' offices. The next steps were the prohibition by government decree of all political parties except the Nazi Party, the dissolution of the labor unions, and the confiscation of union funds. The state governments were brought under the chancellor's control by an appointive, centralized system of administrators, and the unification of Germany was completed by the abolition of the federation. All this was accomplished in the name of the *Gleichschaltung* ("shifting everything into even gear"), or the "coordination," of the new Germany—"the Third Reich."

Jewish persecution
and the Palestine question

JEWS WERE treated worse than other victims of the Nazis. They were excluded from office, whether as teachers or as deputies. By the Nuremberg Laws of 1935 they were deprived entirely of citizenship, and marriage or other sex relations between Jews and Germans (or related peoples) were prohibited. Those who protested were humiliated, bullied, arrested, and sometimes murdered, and their property was "coordinated." Many committed suicide. A mass emigration, usually without proper authorization, took place such as had not been witnessed in modern times for religious reasons since the Huguenots fled from

Louis XIV's France. Hitler, possibly with the Greek-Turk exchange of population in mind, thought to replace fleeing Jews by "Aryans" immigrating from other lands.

Even before the great flight from Nazi persecution after 1933, the few Jews who had sought refuge in Palestine had encountered bloody anti-Jewish riots, occasioned by Arab fears of being dispossessed by a Jewish state. For that reason the British had restricted Jewish immigration to Palestine in 1930. This restriction was considered among the Zionists a violation of the Balfour Declaration. Whatever the British did, they were bound to displease either the Arabs or the Jews of Palestine, and sometimes both. It was obvious, however, that from 1930 on, the British were more inclined to support the Arab majority than the Jewish minority. In 1930, the Mandates Commission of the League criticized the British for providing inadequate police protection in Palestine, and in 1932 a restricted Jewish immigration was again allowed. As a consequence, new anti-Jewish protests came from the Arabs, followed by a boycott of the British. In 1933, as the need of a refuge for Jewish victims of Nazism became pitifully clear, the Jews began riots of their own in protest against the restrictions that still remained. The British, on the assumption that limited action meant limited commitment, acted as little as possible, but they appointed a series of commissions to study the Palestine

The apelike figure has the face of Joseph Goebbels the Nazi minister of propaganda. He says: "You see, there is no place for the Jew in our cultural life." An English cartoon.

question. By 1936, Jews and Arabs were beginning to arm for eventual conflict.

The liquidation of the opposition to Hitler

ADHERENTS of the Christian religion in Germany did not escape unscathed. In the effort to "coordinate" religion, the Protestant sects were early united in a single Evangelical Church, and those who refused to accept the union soon found themselves in prison or concentration camps. The Catholic Church was obliged, by a new concordat with the Nazi government (1933), to withdraw from politics; no bishops were to be appointed without Hitler's consent. Yet Catholic clergymen likewise found themselves in prison or concentration camps. Nazis who had begun to have their doubts for one reason or another about the Führer's program were summarily executed in a "blood purge," which included also non-Nazis like Schleicher and failed, only by accident apparently, to include Papen (June 1934). When Hindenburg died (August 2, 1934), Hitler arbitrarily took the powers of the president but, spurning the title, submitted to the German people a plebiscite on the question whether he should be the nation's Führer. The German people saw in Hitler the strong man who was going to lead them to prosperity and to glory once more. Extensive rearmament and open contempt for the hated *"Diktat"* (page 787) seemed to justify both expectations. They approved the plebiscite by about 9 to 1. Though the voting was so manipulated as to make a negative vote an act of great courage, the returns probably represented the wishes of the overwhelming majority of the German people at the time. And so by popular consent the Third Reich accepted Hitler's monolithic state—"One people, one Reich, one Führer!"

The structure of the monolithic state in Italy

THE DEPRESSION found Italy farther advanced than Germany on a nationalistic program of economic endeavor. Like other rulers, Mussolini tried to meet the global crash by tightening the autarkic structure of his country. He instituted a "Buy Italian" campaign, engaged in a "battle for wheat" (draining the Pontine Marshes to increase Italy's farmland), promoted a set of public works (including archaeological excavations intended to borrow for modern Italy the glory of ancient Rome), and subsidized industry (particularly ship and airplane building). In 1934 Italy's economic life was divided into twenty-two kinds of enterprise (wines, textiles, theater, etc.), and twenty-two "corporations" were created representing the syndicates and other designated individuals or groups, including capital and labor, concerned with each of the twenty-two kinds of enterprise. A National Council of Corporations was their national coordinating body. Economic life soon was controlled by the National Council of Corporations rather than the Chamber of Deputies, just as political life was controlled by the Fascist Party through its Grand Council; and Mussolini was automatically chosen the head of all corporations and councils. The Chamber of Deputies was now no more than an obsolete survival, but it was not to be abolished altogether until 1938, when a National Council of Fasces and Corporations was created to take its place. The monolithic structure of Italy had no more visible cracks than that of Germany. The Fascist slogan, "All in the State, nothing outside the State, nothing against the State," appeared to have become a reality.

Fascism
in southeastern Europe

FASCISTS in several smaller nations of Europe likewise saw in the inspired intuitions of a leader their main chance for salvation. But they were not rewarded with performances that matched Mussolini's and Hitler's. Austria was among these smaller nations. The world depression had hit truncated Austria in 1931, increasing the antagonism between its two armed groups, the Christian Social *Heimwehr* and the Socialist *Schutzbund*. Tensions finally became so taut that they led to a short civil war in Vienna (February 1934), the first armed conflict between Fascists and anti-Fascists. The Socialists were crushed, the Karl Marx Hof was largely destroyed, and the Christian Social chancellor, the diminutive, vigorous Engelbert Dollfuss, was able as a result to establish a one-party dictatorship.

In Rumania the Iron Guard, a nationalist, anti-Semitic, paramilitary organization, had been steadily growing in following and prominence as palace intrigues and fiscal ineptitude increased dissatisfaction. The Iron Guard attracted a number of followers because King Carol's publicly acknowledged mistress, Magda Lupescu, for whom he had once renounced his claim to the throne, was a Jewess, and it was simple to attribute Rumania's ills to her. In 1933 a premier was assassinated; a plot to kill the king was foiled. Until 1938 it remained unclear, however, whether the fascists or the king would triumph. But in that year the king seemed to win a decisive victory. He was to receive approval by plebiscite, suppress the Iron Guard, and rule as a royal dictator, authoritarian though not anti-Semitic.

Other states of southeastern Europe tended also in an authoritarian direction. In 1932 Julius Gömbös became the real ruler of Hungary, and immediately pushed fascist policies to a point where Horthy's earlier premiers had not cared to advance. Before his death in 1935, "Marshal" Gömbös had made Hungary all but a satellite of Mussolini's Italy. In Yugoslavia King Alexander continued to be royal dictator until his assassination at Marseilles in 1934. He had tried to unite Croats, Slovenes, and Serbs into a strong nation and to keep Yugoslavia tied to France in foreign policy. His assassin was a Croat nationalist operating from Hungary and apparently with the connivance of Hungarian officials. In Greece, where an unstable republic had been created in 1924, the royalists had remained loyal to their cause, and in

758   1935 the monarchy was restored; the next year General John Metaxas was

to become Greece's "leader." In Bulgaria, intrigues by Communists, army officers, and Macedonian nationalists led finally to King Boris' emerging as virtual dictator (1935-1936).

The advent
of Salazar as Portuguese dictator

THE REPUBLIC of Portugal, opposed by monarchists and would-be military dictators, had managed to survive until 1926, when the army seized power. General Oscar de Fragoso Carmona then set up a military dictatorship but was no more able to cope with his country's problems than the kings and presidents before him. In 1928 Carmona appointed a professor of economics, Antonio de Oliveira Salazar, minister of finance, and in 1932 made him prime minister. Salazar declared that one of the great errors of the nineteenth century had been to "consider the English parliamentary system capable of adoption by all European peoples," and set up a dictatorship of his own, though Carmona remained president. Salazar succeeded in stabilizing Portugal's currency and in bringing moderate prosperity to Portugal. Approved by the church and by the people in several plebiscites, he is still at the helm. Portugal remains a police state, very harsh toward intellectuals, particularly university professors. But it seems to have attained a greater stability than has been true of other police states in the West.

A brief dictatorship
followed by a republic in Spain

THE ONE important defeat of the fascist ideology during this period took place in Spain. King Alfonso XIII, in attempting to imitate the fascist model (page 687), had committed two blunders. He had entrusted the national power to a general, and he had openly violated the constitution, whereas in Italy and Germany the coup d'état had been engineered by a man ostensibly of the people conforming outwardly to legal procedure. Primo de Rivera never had any popular following, despite a grandiose program of public works intended to restore prosperity, and dissatisfaction soon threatened the monarchy again. The army mutinied; writers were imprisoned; the universities were shut down; workers rioted. The collapse of the *peseta* after the crash of 1929 caught the general unawares. Plagued by revolts and ill health, he resigned in 1930, dying shortly afterwards.

The king, now seriously alarmed, promised to restore the constitution of 1876 but did nothing to keep that promise. Meanwhile, the demand for a new constitution grew. Municipal elections in April 1931 resulted in huge republican majorities almost everywhere. The king gave up in disgust. Without a formal abdication, he left for France with his family. A republic was immediately proclaimed, with Niceto Alcalá Zamora as provisional president. The elections of June 1931 resulted in a distinct victory for Left Republicans and Socialists, and the next December, a new republican constitution proclaimed "a republic of the workers of all classes." It gave the franchise to men and women over the age of twenty-three. Legislative power was vested in a one-chamber Cortes. The president of the republic was to be chosen for a six-year term by an electoral college consisting of the Cortes and electors chosen by the voters. Executive power was entrusted to a cabinet responsible to the Cortes. To cope with recurrent separatist demands, autonomy for the provinces was made possible under certain conditions. The church was explicitly separated from the state, thus repudiating the Concordat of 1851, which had recognized the Roman Catholic religion to the exclusion of all other cults.

Reform and opposition in the new Republic of Spain

THE Spanish Republic was confronted with formidable tasks. Little could be accomplished unless the opposition of the clergy was broken. Since the Middle Ages the church had always been a state within the Spanish state, and the church was the biggest landowner. In 1929 over 80,000 men and women were members of the clergy. In January 1932, the Jesuit order was dissolved, and a large fraction of its property was ordered confiscated. This was an economic as well as a religious reform, for the Jesuit order in Spain owned or co-owned banks, maritime companies, and other kinds of business, and its property was valued at $30,000,000. Marriage was made a civil matter, and divorce was permitted. The next year an Associations Law stipulated that no member of a religious order should engage in business or teach anything except religion, that church property should be taken over by the state, and that priests should cease to receive support from the government.

This situation was not unfamiliar to the Catholic Church. Exactly as in France after 1905, the clergy of Spain tried to counteract the separation of church and state. The leading men of the new republic were well aware that in the disestablished and impoverished clergy they had implacable enemies ready to join any who were against the republic. Building of schools, diminution of the army, confiscation of large estates, redistribution of royal lands, reduction of hours of labor, granting of special privileges to Catalonia, and other reforms were intended to win popular support for the new government.

At the same time these reforms could be expected to incur opposition from those who paid or thought they paid for them. Before long a Catholic Popular Action Party was formed. In November 1933, the elections resulted in a defeat for the moderate Left and a victory for the Catholics and Royalists. Several Rightist governments followed each other between 1933 and 1936 and, despite a general strike in Madrid and Barcelona and an insurrection in Asturias and Catalonia as protests, undid by administrative means much that had been done by legislative reforms. Thus in the one postwar monarchy of Europe which in the Great Depression had turned to republicanism rather than fascism for deliverance, it was uncertain whether republicanism would meet the test.

THE HARDSHIPS of the Russian people were due not directly to an unpremeditated and unexpected drop in the business curve but were the by-product of a planned economy. While Russian grain was being dumped on the world market to pay for the machinery systematically imported in order to make Russia an industrial nation, Russia's agricultural population went hungry, and large numbers of its urban population literally starved in a famine of 1932-1933. The kulaks resisted collectivization, slaughtering their livestock and attacking the collective farms. Thousands of them were deported to Siberia or to the territories near the Arctic Circle for sabotaging the government's program. They roamed the land and died of hunger and disease, and before long the kulaks ceased to exist as a class.

Despite (and, in a sense, because of) the great famine, most of the Five-Year Plan was carried out by 1934. Forty-five million acres of land were transformed into state or collectivized grain factories, sometimes hundreds of thousands of acres in extent. A huge electric power plant at Dnepropetrovsk was completed. The Turkistan-Siberia Railroad (1100 miles) was completed ahead of schedule. Thousands of new office buildings, paved streets, factories, and power plants had been conjured into existence. The production of oil and machinery exceeded the goal set in the Five-Year Plan.

But the planning was not equally successful everywhere. Production lagged behind in the coal and the steel industries. And the production of consumers' goods fell so far short of the people's needs that the government felt something drastic had to be done. Therefore, a Second Five-Year Plan (1933-1937) was announced. It called for more housing, textiles, foodstuffs, footwear, and other consumers' goods. Some of the harshest measures of farm collectivization were mitigated, allowing the peasants to keep or sell some of their produce.

By 1937 the Soviet government was to be able to boast several achievements of the two five-year plans. More than half of Russia's people lived in towns and were a true urban proletariat, even some peasants had become class-conscious proletarians; Russia had taken a place among the industrial nations; and the standard of living had risen for her poor since czarist days. The Russian achievement seemed all the more impressive when contrasted with the contemporary crash and depression in the rest of the world. Yet outside of Russia some voices were heard asking whether these achievements had been worth what they had cost in human effort, terror, and sacrifice.

RUSSIA had not paid for its economic progress merely in deprivation, hunger, and starvation. The quarrels within the ruling clique had continued. But now they went on underground in the conspiratorial fashion that had long been familiar to the

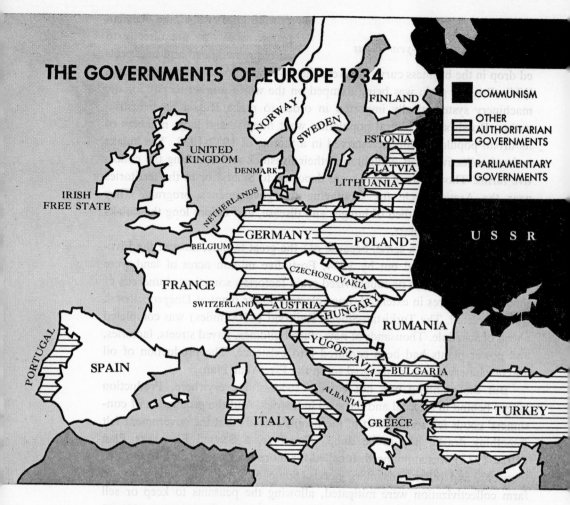

THE GOVERNMENTS OF EUROPE 1934

COMMUNISM

OTHER AUTHORITARIAN GOVERNMENTS

PARLIAMENTARY GOVERNMENTS

NORWAY

FINLAND

SWEDEN

ESTONIA

UNITED KINGDOM

DENMARK

LATVIA

LITHUANIA

IRISH FREE STATE

NETHERLANDS

BELGIUM

GERMANY

POLAND

USSR

FRANCE

CZECHOSLOVAKIA

SWITZERLAND

AUSTRIA

HUNGARY

RUMANIA

PORTUGAL

SPAIN

YUGOSLAVIA

BULGARIA

ALBANIA

TURKEY

ITALY

GREECE

By 1934 a distinctly threefold pattern had developed in the governments of Europe. Most of the northwestern states retained some form of representative government, and a republican experiment in Spain survived precariously. The experiment had failed in the postwar Baltic states of Estonia, Latvia, and Lithuania where the republican constitutions had been suspended. In the Balkans, Rumania and Greece were for the time being still resisting fascist attempts. Otherwise some brand of authoritarian rule prevailed in the central and southwestern states of Europe, except in Czechoslovakia. Meanwhile Communism gathered strength in the USSR.

Russians. In 1933 about one million members were expelled from the Communist Party. On December 1, 1934, Sergei Kirov, the Bolshevik official generally conceded to have the best chance to become Stalin's successor, was assassinated. Whether it was a political assassination or a murder for private reasons has never been clearly established. Stalin used the death of his friend, however, as the grounds for a far-reaching reign of terror. Trotsky, then living in France, was accused of having instigated a conspiracy to overthrow Stalin in connivance with the Nazi government of Germany. All the leaders of the opposition, mostly old-party intelligentsia, were wiped out. Zinoviev and Kamenev were tried twice; the first trial ended in imprisonment, the second in execution. Their "accomplices" were haled into court with them, and other groups of "conspirators," including several prominent generals, were likewise indicted. If they did not commit suicide, the accused were found guilty and executed. Their trials usually astonished the outside world by the apparent readiness of the defendants to admit their guilt.

These purges were to last from 1935 to 1938. Meanwhile, the secret police held Russia in an iron grip. The Orthodox Church and all other religions were persecuted as "opiate of the people." Churchgoing was discouraged, though not actually forbidden except for members of the Communist Party. Religious services were discountenanced though not outlawed, and many churches were either destroyed or transformed into clubs or antireligious museums. By 1935 the Communist Party speaking through Stalin had established an unquestioned control over a thoroughly planned society and, feeling secure at home, contemplated amending the Russian constitution so as to grant a greater degree of political freedom to the Russian people (page 807).

IMPERIALISM, NATIONALISM,

AND COMMUNISM IN THE FAR EAST

BOTH RUSSIA and Japan looked upon the growing strength and unity of China under Chiang Kai-shek as a threat to their interests. Nevertheless, the defeat of China in her dispute with Russia in 1929 had brought out for all to behold the reluctance of the powers of the West to help China maintain her territorial integrity and international position by strong measures. While China's enemies anticipated that the fiasco of 1929 would constitute a precedent, the Chinese hoped that future crises would meet with prompter and sterner measures. They attributed western clumsiness in Asia primarily to the inefficacy of the only legal machinery that had been available to apply to Sino-Soviet difficulties. If they thought, however, that that deficiency would in the future be remedied, they were for the most part doomed to disappointment.

Dislocations in Japan and popularity of the military

DURING THE time that Mussolini was making himself master in Italy and Hitler in Germany, the proponents of authoritarian control were also winning successes in Japan. Japan's discontented were to be found mostly in the urban proletariat, the farmers, and the army, and not among the politicians and the middle and upper classes as in Europe. To meet the depression the moderate Minseito government proposed financial retrenchment, but that program was not welcomed by the poor already facing imminent disaster from unemployment, low land values, low farm prices, and rapidly rising population figures (at the rate of about 1,000,000 per year). Emigration provided little relief, since several countries restricted Japanese immigration. The urban and rural masses of Japan wanted a more immediate solution of their economic problems, and the military with their policy of expansion abroad and at home seemed to offer such a solution. The growing popularity of the military was fought by the political parties and their financial backers, but the parties failed, as previously, to win the confidence of the rank and file. Party government was derided as corrupt, inefficient, and western, and new slogans called for a return to Japan's traditions of simplicity, sincerity, and forthright action.

*Naval problems
at the London Conference*

FORTHRIGHT action in foreign affairs was nearly ruled out by a naval conference called at London in 1930. The conference seemed an excellent opportunity for the Minseito government to work out a system for handling Far Eastern and Pacific problems within the framework of the cooperative principles established at the Conference of Washington. But other things by that time took precedence over the creation of a regular system for preserving Far Eastern peace. In 1930, as in 1922, the maritime powers proved anxious above all to reduce naval armaments so as to relieve their peoples, already under stress from the Great Depression, of the heavy financial burden required for naval programs. In Japan, as in the United States, the government was intent upon economy and retrenchment. Even though European nations were at loggerheads because of the increasing aggressiveness of Mussolini's government in the Mediterranean, the need for immediate economy prevailed.

As a result, the conference made no proposals for the general peace of the East. It did agree, however, to extend the holiday on building capital ships to 1936. In heavy and light cruisers the ratio between the United States and Japan (5:3) fixed at Washington in 1922 was practically preserved, but in destroyers Japan was allowed over 70 per cent of the United States' strength, and in submarines was granted parity. The possibility that Italy might launch a naval building program regardless of her treaty obligations was met by the introduction of an "escalator" clause, which provided that interested powers might legally scale their navy programs proportionally upward if any other power should do so first. In so far as the Pacific was concerned, the Washington arrangements remained virtually unchanged.

*The opportunity
of the Japanese in Manchuria*

AT HOME the Japanese reacted strongly against the London treaty and the policy of retrenchment as inappropriate to the national dignity and the need for jobs. The compliant program of the Minseito was blamed by chauvinists and military hotbloods for Japan's economic difficulties. Many of the soldiers were recruited from the farm population, which had been particularly hurt by the depression. Highly articulate organizations of old soldiers and raw recruits attacked the civilian government for not providing a positive economic program and for being weak in its dealings with China and the West. When the Minseito also sanctioned tariff autonomy for China, the opposition decided to take matters into their own hands. The military planners in Tokyo worked out the details of a plan for action without reference to the civilian government.

Many Japanese had again begun to cast covetous glances toward Manchuria. Not only was the mineral wealth of Manchuria a desirable possession but, as was often openly admitted, there was danger in letting it remain in the hands of a united and aggressive China or in leaving it for a predatory Soviet state to gobble up. From Korea to Manchuria the step seemed easy and inevitable. In the eyes of the Japanese the control of Manchuria's markets and resources rapidly became the most vital of Far Eastern problems. They spoke even more fondly of their "special position" in Manchuria and of their determination to preserve and extend it. Moreover, the Japanese repeatedly asserted, and some of them undoubtedly believed, that their country stood as a barrier against the aggressive designs of China and Russia in Manchuria.

Until 1931 the unmistakable belligerency of China's Nationalists toward foreign interests and the omnipresent suspicion of Russia had won for Japan a degree of support from the western powers. The adoption of a "positive policy" by Japan, however, was quickly to cool the sympathies of the non-Asiatic nations for her Asiatic program. From Japan's viewpoint the autumn of 1931, for the very reasons that excited the misgivings of the West, appeared the auspicious moment to move ahead swiftly in Manchuria. According to some suspicious observers in the West, depression-stricken Japan deliberately bided its time to launch its poorly disguised aggression until a moment when the powers of Europe and America were seriously preoccupied with depression problems of their own, Russia was involved in grave internal troubles such as the collectivization of her farms, and China was suffering from famine, floods, and serious civil war.

The invasion of Manchuria and the victory of the Seiyukai

THE MOMENT chosen was in any event an opportune one. It was provided by an explosion in September 1931 on the tracks of the South Manchurian Railroad. The Japanese military immediately moved armed units into Manchuria's most important cities, although they were technically under the jurisdiction of Nanking, and other strategic centers were also quickly occupied. Meanwhile the civilian government in Tokyo reassured China and the world that Japan had no aggressive intentions and was engaged only in a police action designed to punish those who had violated treaty rights.

In truth, however, the Japanese foreign office was not apprised either before the incident or in the ensuing months of the true intentions of the military. As events moved ahead, it became increasingly clear that the civilian and the military authorities of Japan were often divided upon the correct 765 policy to follow in Manchuria. Despite the fact that both groups were equally responsible to the emperor, their disagreement appeared to give a dual character to all authority in Japan. At first many western statesmen were inclined to believe that the Japanese army had gone out of control and that the nations of the world, in order to aid the civilian authorities of Japan to reëstablish themselves, ought to refrain strictly from interfering in the Manchurian affair.

Unfortunately Japanese politics soon passed entirely out of the hands of the more pacifically inclined elements. In combination with the Seiyukai, the military and agrarian groups had been working feverishly to overturn the Minseito government. In December 1931 their efforts prevailed, and Inukai Takishi, a civilian proponent of a "positive" foreign policy, was asked to form a new government. Although the militarists thereby succeeded in establishing the Seiyukai in power, they continued to rail against even the new civilian authority, since it failed to suppress altogether the protesting elements in Japanese society.

China's appeal to the League of Nations

THE CHINESE were not disposed to accept the hesitations and assurances of civilian Tokyo at face value. Nanking shortly presented a letter to the Council of the League of Nations asking for international action on the Manchurian incident. Although both Asiatic powers were League members, the Japanese maintained from the beginning that it was a local incident and could best be handled by direct negotiations between Tokyo and Nanking. On the other hand, the Chinese persisted in viewing the affair as a threat to world peace and worked feverishly to get action from the powers with interests in eastern Asia. Only slowly did the western powers become convinced of the seriousness of the situation, more because of the continuing military operations of Japan than because of the sound arguments of the Chinese.

The reaction of the United States

ALTHOUGH not a member of the League of Nations, the United States became particularly disturbed at the end of 1931 over the failure of the League to take positive action with regard to Manchuria. While cooperating with the League, Secretary of State Henry L. Stimson became impatient with its failure to move and undertook to strike out for himself under the terms of the Nine-Power Treaty and the Kellogg-Briand Pact. Having relatively limited economic interests on the Asiatic mainland, the United States ran small risk and hence was in a particularly strong position to act with vigor in Far Eastern crises. Thus, as in the case of the Sino-Russian imbroglio of 1929, the United States took the lead, demanding that nothing should occur in eastern Asia to disturb the existing treaty structure fundamentally. Although Stimson sought League support for the American action, it was not immediately forthcoming. In

January 1932 he took the initiative completely away from the League of Nations by bluntly stating that the United States "cannot admit the legality of any situation *de facto*....which may impair the treaty rights of the United States or its citizens in China." This policy became known as the Stimson Doctrine of nonrecognition.

The "Shanghai War" and western intervention

THE POLICY of nonrecognition seemed to the European governments merely a set of bold words. The British in the midst of the financial crisis that caused the desertion of the gold standard and free trade (page 748) were particularly reluctant to second nonrecognition. Moreover, like the Japanese they had recently suffered from the Chinese Nationalists' antiforeign trade policies and were ill disposed to act against Japan on Nanking's behalf. London wanted most of all to work out a peaceful compromise of the Sino-Japanese difficulties, for if war were to come from opposition to Japan's ambitions, the British fleet and British investments would bear the brunt of hostile action. In France and other countries of western Europe, no greater enthusiasm could be evoked for Stimson's proclamation.

The episode known as the "Shanghai War" (January–March 1932) was finally to arouse Britain's active concern over the aggressions of Japan. The Chinese had renewed boycott and terror in the Yangtze Valley, and had inflicted great losses upon the Japanese. Hoping to restore peace and quiet to the vital Yangtze commercial region and at the same time to shift attention away from their "independence" program in Manchuria, the Japanese landed a huge contingent of troops in the great metropolis of central China. The protest of the United States against this patent act of aggression was immediate and was shortly followed by strong British representations at Tokyo. Again the Chinese government appealed to the League of Nations, and on this occasion their appeal received a more sympathetic hearing. Meanwhile the Chinese military forces at Shanghai gave a good account of themselves in their battles with the Japanese bluejackets, and the Chinese boycott was greatly intensified.

On this occasion the European powers and the United States acted with unusual dispatch. A special on-the-spot commission of investigation quickly went to work at Shanghai, and American naval vessels were dispatched to the scene of hostilities. Early in February the powers proposed terms for an armistice, but they were speedily rejected by the Japanese. The American government used the opportunity to tempt the British to a course of action in line with the doctrine of nonrecognition. The British were, however, not easily tempted. Although visibly troubled by the "Shanghai War," they preferred to wait for a League report on events in the Far East. Impatient with the British and the cautious procedure of the League, Stimson issued an open letter in which he candidly accused Japan of violating the treaties with and

767

pertaining to China. On March 3, the Assembly of the League convened in special session and the next day called upon both China and Japan to cease fire in and around Shanghai. One week later the same body virtually adopted by a unanimous vote Stimson's policy of nonrecognition.

By devious routes the interested powers had finally come to act jointly in the effort to focus upon Japan the full force of world opinion. Although the Japanese retorted indignantly to this universal moral condemnation, hostilities ceased, armistice arrangements were concluded, and the Japanese military forces were withdrawn. It was not altogether clear whether Japan's change of heart came as a result of this international condemnation or of an independent military decision in Japan, but in any event the halting of the "Shanghai War" cost the Nipponese heavily in prestige both at home and abroad. It seemed a great victory for world opinion, but it also led to the Japanese determination to seek redress.

"Independent" Manchukuo and the end of party government — WHILE JAPAN was engaging the Chinese at Shanghai, a movement for Manchurian independence sponsored by the Kwantung army of Japan (i.e., the army operating from Port Arthur and vicinity) was making rapid headway. On February 18, 1932, the birth of the "state of the Manchus," or Manchukuo, was announced to the world from Mukden. The new regime in what had once been Manchuria was headed by Henry Pu Yi, the last of the Manchu emperors of China. The western powers were stiffly reticent in their attitude toward the puppet state.

Although the Japanese government insisted that the new country had come into being as a result of spontaneous native drive, the rest of the world was persuaded that the policies and plans of Manchukuo emanated in final analysis from Tokyo. Even at home some voices were raised in protest. The weakness of the Seiyukai in failing to stifle domestic criticism of the military's activities in Manchuria and at Shanghai was violently attacked in the popular press. In the summer of 1932, after their disappointment at Shanghai, the military groups began to take matters even more fully into their own hands, not stopping at assassination of those who dared to oppose their program. One of their victims was Inukai, the third premier of Japan to be assassinated since 1921. With his successor, Admiral Makoto Saito, party government ceased to exist.

The Lytton Report and the failure of the League — THE BIRTH of Manchukuo had been broadcast to the world just as a League commission headed by the Earl of Lytton arrived in the Far East. After six months' study of the Manchurian problem, the commission completed its report. Thus, just one year after the Mukden explosion, the League was informed (September 1932) that Japan's actions in Manchuria could not "be regarded as measures of

DISARMAMENT

MANCHURIAN PROBLEM

A Soviet cartoon satirizing the League of Nations' avoidance of the pressing issues of Manchuria and world disarmament.

legitimate self-defense." The commission, moreover, reported that the Manchukuo government "is regarded by the local Chinese [the large majority of Manchukuo's population] as an instrument of the Japanese." Although the Japanese denounced the lengthy report as inadequate and biased, a special assembly of the League, after long and heated discussions, in February 1933 adopted the Lytton Report in its essentials and formally decided to follow Washington's lead in extending the doctrine of nonrecognition to the recent Manchukuoan developments. Nonrecognition now applied to both Shanghai and Manchukuo. Angered by this decision, Japan, no longer impeded by a civilian government, withdrew from the League in March. The next year she also repudiated all obligations and limitations under the naval agreements of 1922 and 1930 (page 764).

In its first major trial the League of Nations thus exhibited over a period of almost two years its inability to halt a large power threatening the peace of the world. Japan had acted when the big western powers were in the midst of an economic crisis and a popular wave of pacifism. Lacking the support of the USSR, and able to count upon only the moral force of the United States, the League delayed action when action might have produced a quick decision. Nevertheless, in the course of the long debates over Shanghai and Manchuria the League also managed to appear the guardian of the world conscience. World opinion gradually crystallized to the point where, by the spring of 1933, Japan was almost universally branded as an aggressor. Unfortunately moral condemnation and nonrecognition of Japan's position in Manchuria were not sufficient to halt the Japanese march toward empire, and the League's feebleness in the face of its first defiance by a big power set a precedent that was to be fatal both to the League and to peace.

Creation of the Chinese Soviet Republic   CHINESE warlords of unpacified areas and Chinese politicians interested in personal advancement had responded in different ways to the threats of Japanese attack. Some were willing to bury the hatchet and cooperate with the Nanking regime in a common front against the "dwarfs" from across the eastern sea. Others attempted to use the opportunity offered by Japanese military success to undermine and, if possible, overthrow the Kuomintang. In the general confusion, the Chinese Communists reappeared as an active political and military force. Although the Kuomintang at first repeatedly asserted that Dr. Sun's first principle of *national unity* had already been realized in its essentials, foreign observers and less partisan Chinese remained unconvinced that the Nanking government had achieved internal strength and security.

Among the domestic enemies of the Kuomintang the Communists were the most obdurate. Operating underground after the purge of 1927, under the leadership of Mao Tse-tung, the Communists developed close relations with the hard-pressed and restive peasants of southern and central China. In isolated backward areas Soviet units of government had begun to appear since 1930, and the peasants of these areas had regularly been recruited and trained for a Chinese Red Army.

The steady growth of Communism within China contributed to the reluctance of important elements in the Kuomintang to become too deeply involved in war with Japan. Chiang Kai-shek, now the Kuomintang's generalissimo, and Wang Ching-wei, Dr. Sun's successor as head of the party's executive body, were particularly concerned about the expansion of Communist activity. Measures of strict surveillance were inaugurated and enforced through the Kuomintang's secret police. In December 1930, the generalissimo dispatched an expeditionary force to the Red areas to wipe out the Soviets. By skillful retreat the Communists baffled Nanking's efforts. Employing greater numbers of troops, the generalissimo sought again in the summer of 1931 to exterminate the Red forces, but again his endeavor was in vain. The Manchurian and Shanghai affairs then forced him to suspend hostilities against the Communists for a time.

While Nanking was confronting the growing Japanese menace in Manchuria, the First All-China Congress of Soviets convened in the province of

Kiangsi in November 1931. On that occasion the Chinese Soviet Republic was proclaimed with the objective of releasing the peasantry from economic and political oppression and placing sovereignty in the hands of the toilers. Denouncing the Japanese as aggressive imperialists, the struggling Soviet movement sought to attract further attention to its program by boldly declaring war upon Japan in April 1932, shortly after the declaration of Manchukuo's independence.

The T'ang-ku Truce as a national humiliation

WITHIN THE Nationalist government itself agreement on a positive program of action seemed virtually impossible. Bargains and counterbargains were arranged to appease or checkmate individuals and groups that were too recalcitrant to cooperate and too powerful for the government to liquidate. Student groups meanwhile called upon the government to take up the task of leadership, to conciliate aggrieved party and nonparty groups, and to unite the nation for action against the Japanese threat. They pleaded that "Chinese stop fighting Chinese." The government long was split over whether to pursue a conciliatory or a belligerent policy toward Japan. The unforgivable Japanese attack upon Shanghai in 1932 temporarily won the day for the proponents of vigorous action, and the resulting vigor accounted in part for China's ability to hold the Japanese in check and to bring upon them the moral condemnation of the rest of the world (page 767).

In Manchuria, however, the threat from Japan was considered in many quarters to be neither so immediate nor so serious as that from the Communists at home. Hence a policy of vacillation and withdrawal—perhaps unavoidable anyhow in view of Nanking's weaknesses—won out and resulted in the abandonment of Manchuria to the Japanese. In May 1933—after Japan's indignant withdrawal from the League of Nations—the two contending powers concluded a truce at T'ang-ku. The armistice left the Japanese in control of Manchuria and established a buffer zone between the two armies. This arrangement was viewed in China as a surrender and a crowning national humiliation, and to Nanking's irreconcilable critics it appeared as an admission that China had neither the military power nor the spiritual unity required to halt the Japanese advance.

Revolt at Foochow and the war with the Communists

THE DEEP divisions within China now quickly came to the surface. In November 1933 a group of opponents of the Kuomintang merged their interests, made an alliance with the Nineteenth Route Army, heroes of the "Shanghai War," and sought to establish a new regime for China at the port city of Foochow. The Foochow rebels not only looked for support from the notoriously individualistic warlords of the southern provinces in the vicinity of Canton but they also sought to establish relations with the Soviet regime in neighboring Kiangsi. They failed, however, in their effort to obtain Communist support and succumbed quickly to the military forces dispatched against them by Nanking.

The Communists remained a serious menace, however. In the spring of 1933, Chiang, determined once and for all to finish them off, launched an "annihilation drive." Proceeding cautiously and methodically, the Nanking forces spent a year surrounding and closing in upon the entire Red area. Shortly before the expected final assault upon their positions, the Reds attacked and broke through the weak southwestern sector of the encircling enemy. Though harried by the Kuomintang troops, units of the Red army skillfully managed to flee westward into the provinces of Kweichow, Yünnan, and Szechwan. At this point their "Long March" was directed northward to the isolated border region of Shensi province. There the weary and sorely tried Communists reunited their forces and began to build anew. The "Long March" ranks with the classic exploit of Xenophon's Ten Thousand as a military epic—and the Chinese were numbered in the hundreds of thousands. Thwarted in his effort to eliminate the Red Army, Chiang was never again able to reckon without the Communists and would one day have to retreat before them. In the barren hills of Shensi, the Chinese Soviet Republic was reëstablished; by 1936 the Communists had taken the city of Yenan and made it their capital.

Japan's program
of expansion and collaboration

THE T'ANG-KU Truce put no end to the demands by the Japanese upon Nanking. Using Manchukuo and Korea as bases, Japan sought to extend its control by economic and military maneuvers in northern China. Through bribes, threats, and political pressure the Japanese, particularly in the provinces of Chahar and Hopeh, instigated autonomy movements of the kind that had been successful in the founding of Manchukuo. They endeavored also to break the Chinese boycott of Japanese goods and at the same time to deprive Nanking of badly needed customs revenue by using their military to protect the smuggling of their traders.

The western nations, of course, protested repeatedly against the depredations of the Japanese. Seriously in need of foreign markets, the depression-stricken countries of the West sought by economic and diplomatic pressure to halt Japan's effort to close the open door in China. In this effort the United States and Great Britain took the lead, although Italy and Germany also sought to bolster China's defiance of Japan by advancing financial assistance and military advice. At no time, however, did the United States or the European powers show an inclination to use enough force to stop Japan's "quiet expansion."

But if the deeds of the western world were too slight to save China, they were bold enough to provoke Japan. When the British tried to aid China to stabilize its inflated currency, they collided with charges from Tokyo that the

Westerners were merely endeavoring to promote their financial imperialism in China. Japan's resentment of western "interference" in eastern Asia was proclaimed openly in 1934 by a "Japanese Monroe Doctrine." The Tokyo Bureau of Information announced: "We oppose...any attempt on the part of China to avail herself of the influence of any other country in order to resist Japan. We also oppose any action taken by China calculated to play one power against another." In response to this declaration the European powers objected only mildly. The United States, through Secretary of State Cordell Hull, was, however, more outspoken, reminding Japan that a unilateral declaration from Tokyo could not legally modify the international treaties and agreements relating to China. In general, the western powers continued, in spite of Japan's admonitions, to lend money, send military advisers, and promote trade with China.

While engaged in threats and hostile acts, Tokyo was paradoxically formulating a policy designed to bring Nanking into collaboration with Japan. The objectives of this policy were embodied in a program announced in 1935 by Foreign Minister Koki Hirota. The so-called "Hirota Principles" required that the Chinese recognize the autonomy of Manchukuo and North China, cease appealing for help from the western powers, and join Japan in a crusade to rid eastern Asia and the Pacific region of Communism. Although the Kuomintang leaders might not have been averse to a joint crusade against Communism, they realized that recognition of Japan's puppets and the severance of relations with the West would be tantamount to political suicide for China. Chiang neither accepted nor rejected Hirota's three principles, leaving the next move to Japan (page 830).

Reform and propaganda within the Chinese Republic

IN THE 1930's in addition to incessant civil war and constant Japanese pressure, the Kuomintang faced economic depression as well as China's perennial floods and famines. Although thwarted by practically insoluble domestic and international problems, the Nanking government endeavored in certain areas to reform along western lines the political, legal, and educational institutions of the country. This endeavor was part of its announced program of preparing China for the eventual introduction of democracy. In 1931, a provisional constitution was promulgated designed to carry the nation through a period of political tutelage preparatory to a permanent constitutional regime. Simultaneously, a new civil code was instituted in an effort to modernize social and economic practices and to outlaw undesirable practices such as child labor. School reforms attempted to meet the need at all levels for greater emphasis upon practical and scientific subjects. A program of mass education called the "New Life Movement" was planned under the patronage of Generalissimo and Madame Chiang Kai-shek to inculcate among the Chinese people a respect for such "western virtues" as order, efficiency, punctuality, sanitation,

"The New Generation" by a Chinese artist, Ku Yuan.

and simplicity of organization. Other virtues not specifically western, such as frugality, were also included.

Although highly impressive on paper, the reforms of Nanking did not in actuality produce significant changes in the traditional ways or relieve the grinding poverty of the Chinese masses. Constitutions, law codes, educational reforms, and imported concepts of virtue meant little to people who were primarily concerned with subsistence. Nanking's failure to inaugurate Dr. Sun's third principle, *people's livelihood,* undermined its other reform programs. The Communists were quick to recognize and to preach that promises of political privileges at some future date, laws in favor of humane and modern social practices, and admonitions to sanitation and punctuality could not substitute for food. They focused their program and propaganda upon rural reform and quick economic relief for the peasants, the very area in which the Kuomintang most seriously fell short of providing the basic needs of China. The Kuomintang, having failed to annihilate the Communist army, failed also to undermine its potential popular appeal by a program of genuine agrarian reform.

Revolution and "new order" in Siam

IN SIAM, the only independent state of the Asiatic tropics, the western capitalist, the Russian Marxist, and the Japanese capitalist contended for ascendancy in much the same way as they did in China. As in the nineteenth century, the economy of Siam was still dominated by Great Britain, with some competition from France and the United States. Tin, rubber, and wood were exported to the West in return for manufactured goods, while rice was exported to China,

774

India, and Japan. One of the most prosperous of the peoples in the tropics, the Siamese have been among the most difficult for the Communists to attract. Siam's relatively strong position in international affairs was demonstrated by the fact that she won full freedom from extraterritoriality by the end of the twenties, more than a decade before China.

Like the major capitalist countries, Siam suffered seriously from the depression of the 1930's. Particularly discontented were the civil servants and army personnel, who were forced to take large salary cuts. As in Japan, these groups rebelled against the government's program of retrenchment. In 1932-1933 they staged a revolt against King Prajadhipok and forced the establishment of a constitutional monarchy. Their success led others to resort to direct action. After a period of hectic turmoil, Prajadhipok abdicated (1935) and left the country. Since then a series of strong men have dominated the monarchy. The "new order" in Siam chose to collaborate with the "new order" of Japan, and became strongly anti-western in its feelings and actions. The Communists nevertheless continued their work among the lowly elements of the population.

Civil disobedience and the Government of India Act

THE DEPRESSION hit India hard, and misery spread among her poor, who had little or no margin of safety against starvation. Civil disobedience, which had led to refusal to cooperate with the Simon Commission (page 741), easily passed into rioting and destruction. Civil disobedience became still more drastic when the Indian National Congress refused entirely to participate in the first round-table conference, called for 1930 in London to examine India's perplexities, and officially went on record against "dominion status" and in favor of complete independence. Gandhi and other leaders of the Nationalists were put in jail. Only when his objectives were clearly formulated and understood did Gandhi, temporarily released from prison, agree to a suspension of civil disobedience and consent to attend a second round-table conference. Although he contributed but little to the discussions in London in 1931, the report of the Simon Commission and the recommendations of the round tables led to the publication in 1933 of a "white paper" (i.e., a printed report to Parliament) which eventually became the basis for the Government of India Act of 1935.

Though avoiding dyarchy as an unworkable administrative device, the new constitution was intended to introduce self-government at the provincial level, going beyond the pattern worked out in 1919. A complicated system of separate electorates for members of specified geographical groupings, professions, workers, women, creeds, and castes guaranteed representation for various minorities as well as for the general population, and increased India's voters to around 30,000,000. The provinces were freed of control from the central authority in certain specified areas, although the British governors retained wide powers. The constitution also proposed the creation of a Federation of India, including those of the 562 native states (ruled by native princes) that might choose to join as well as the provinces of British India, but it left the governor general in charge of foreign affairs, defense, and several other areas of federal scope.

Gandhi was not satisfied with this compromise, but he was willing to use the India Act of 1935 as a basis for further negotiations. His refusal to use more than oral persuasion in the Congress in its favor (although he was ready more than once to "fast unto death" in order to win support for some of his own points) permitted the widest differences to reign among the nationalists of India. Jawaharlal Nehru and his supporters called for vigorous opposition to the new constitution because it contained too many safeguards of Britain's interests. Since the India Act was not to go into force until 1937, agitation pro and con continued among the several Indian parties.

THE NEW DEAL

IN AMERICA

For THREE and a half years the downward spiral of deflation continued in the United States. The once most prosperous nation in the world watched helplessly as its prosperity vanished. Americans who had sought to isolate the United States from foreign entanglements or who had so far refused to see the effects of American policies on world economy had now to face in aggravated form the economic problems from which they had sought to shield themselves ever since the World War.

Moratorium, defaults, and protective tariffs

THE AMERICAN stock market crash brought to a stop the curious circle in which war debts and reparations payments had been moving. Realizing that both the United States government and United States private investors would lose by a complete collapse of the European economy, President Hoover called for a moratorium, which, as we have seen (page 747), was welcomed by the European countries concerned. The United States government coupled this generous action, however, with a refusal to cancel or further reduce any of the war debts, a stand which in the end negated the favorable effects of the moratorium, and soon the defaults that Hoover had hoped to avert had become general.

Meanwhile the United States, in trying to bolster its internal economy, had taken a further step toward the walling up of world trade. The Hawley-Smoot Tariff Act of 1930, initiated before the crash in an ostensible effort to help the farmer, had brought among the most vocal pressure groups a free-for-all that raised tariff walls to unprecedented heights. Over the protests of the American Bankers Association, exporters, and more than a thousand economists, the bill became law and further lessened the ability of European countries to pay their war debts. Retaliation by other countries was immediate and seriously harmful to world trade. Tariffs, quota systems, and exchange controls were directed against the United States by a score and more of America's best customers.

The early expectations
of recovery in the United States

FROM 1929 TO 1933 depression dug deeper into the pockets and the spirit of the people of the United States. Millions of dollars worth of savings were wiped out, leaving many families on the verge of destitution. The number of unemployed rose in 1933 to over 13,000,000. Breadlines, war veterans selling apples on street corners, and outright beggary became familiar scenes in American cities. Farmers could no longer sell their produce because hungry people had no money to buy it, and many farmers lost their farms. Prices fell steadily, and thousands of firms, no longer able to produce at a profit, went into bankruptcy, as ruined businessmen jumped out of hotel and office windows. The entire economy seemed to be grinding slowly to a snail's pace.

Experts differed on what should be done to give the wheels new speed. Until the end of the Hoover administration the business-centered philosophy of the twenties motivated the government to stimulate recovery by propping up sagging businesses with government funds. The administration hoped to maintain or increase employment as the benefits of government aid trickled down through business budgets to the worker. A Reconstruction Finance Corporation (RFC) was established in 1932. It loaned money to banks, railroads, industries, farm organizations, and local governments. A limited public-works program was also undertaken, in keeping with Hoover's policy of restricting the government's competition with private enterprise. But these measures went as far as Hoover was willing to go in a "socialist" direction, and he deliberately avoided direct relief by the federal government on the grounds that it would discourage "the spirit of charity and mutual self help through voluntary giving and the responsibility of local government."

Private charity and local relief proved thoroughly inadequate to cope with the widespread and acute distress. But radical agitation, Share-the-Wealth Clubs, and a veterans' march on Washington in July 1932 brought no change in government attitude. Congress did, however, in 1932 try to assuage the farmer and the laborer. It distributed Farm Board surpluses of wheat and cotton, and passed an act outlawing "yellow-dog" contracts (contracts which obliged workers not to join unions) and certain uses of the injunction in labor disputes.

Despite the depression and unemployment of the 1930's, the trend toward the "bigger and better" continued, and the feeling persisted that American prosperity had not permanently ended but was to be found "just 777 around the corner." Rockefeller Center in New York City was built in 1931—the world's largest building project. So was the longest arch-span bridge, at Bayonne, N.J., and United States Steel broke its former records with a 96-inch rolling process strip-sheet mill to meet the still substantial demand for sheet steel for automobiles and other steel products.

*Defeat of Hoover
and the election of Roosevelt*

THOUGH THE operations of the RFC in 1932 did save some shaky businesses, the downward spiral continued. It hit bottom in the autumn and winter of 1932-1933 as the banking system of the United States, already tottering in the rural districts, began to collapse in some of the large cities. In the midst of this downward trend the presidential election of 1932 took place. The Democrats profited from the general dissatisfaction with the Hoover policy of "recovery without reform," and the presidency passed from Hoover to Franklin Delano Roosevelt.

President Roosevelt was cheerful and confident despite having to drag around ten pounds of iron on his legs because of an attack of infantile paralysis in his late thirties. He combined to a rare degree the qualities of shrewd politician, calculating opportunist, and speculative reformer. Friend and foe were both kept guessing, throughout the longest presidential career in United States history, which set of qualities would be foremost at any given time. With an unmistakable popular mandate and the aid of a cooperative Congress, he attacked the depression boldly along a broad front.

*The "brain trust"
and "the new liberalism"*

ROOSEVELT surrounded himself with a group of young lawyers and professors, who came to be called the "brain trust." Several of these "brain-trusters" subscribed to the economic theories of Keynes, the brilliant English critic of the Treaty of Versailles. Keynes in several recent writings, most striking of which was *The End of Laissez Faire* (1926), had presented the doctrine that came to be known as "Keynesianism." While accepting as a historical tendency the ups and downs of prosperity known as the "business cycle," Keynes believed that they were subject to rational control by governments. Accordingly, if the tax power were used to reduce private spending in boom times, demand, and hence prices, could be kept down, and if government revenues were used for public-works programs in times of depression, demand, and hence prices, could be kept up. Thus, if Keynes was right, the fluctuations of the business cycle could be more or less ironed out by government action without resort to government ownership and socialistic planning. The "Keynesian" no longer assumed that an unregulated, competitive market was the best thing for the country at large. That system, which had placed most of the nation's wealth in the hands of a small percentage of its population, seemed discredited by the near economic collapse. The "new liberalism," without totally abandoning

778

"free enterprise," laid major stress upon "controlled capitalism" and the government's responsibility for the welfare of the individual.

The new president confidently announced at his inaugural address that "we have nothing to fear but fear itself," closed the banks of the nation to prevent runs, and immediately undertook a vigorous program of reform. Within a year measures had been passed affecting almost every kind of economic activity. Much of it was short-lived emergency legislation; some of it endured. Nearly all of it was inspired by the new attitude toward the interrelations of government, business, and the individual. After more than a decade of "hands off business," the "new liberalism" revived and extended the governmental paternalism of the early Wilsonian era.

Banking, currency, and relief legislation

THE ATTACK on the depression began with emergency banking legislation bolstering solvent banks with government credit. Subsequent monetary legislation broadened government control over currency and credit, and under this legislation the United States, following European countries in abandoning the gold standard, prohibited the export of gold, called in gold coins and certificates, and increased the gold value of other currency by offering to buy gold at much higher than the old price. These measures were intended to raise prices by reducing the official gold content of the dollar about 40 per cent and thus encourage production and business enterprise.

Roosevelt further revised the Hoover policy of limited governmental action with a bold program of federal relief, giving aid directly to the needy in the hope of stimulating business with increased purchasing power. Half a billion dollars of federal funds were made available for state and local relief. Numerous federal work relief agencies were set up. A Civilian Conservation Corps provided youth with jobs in tending the forests, the soil, and the plant and animal resources of the country. The Tennessee Valley Authority (TVA) became the model for several government organizations created to construct and operate dams for flood control, power production, and "the economic and social well-being of the people." They not only provided employment to thousands in a bold public-works program but inaugurated a far-reaching experiment in regional planning and government operation of public utilities. A general public-works program employed millions; manual workers were kept off the relief rolls by building schools, hospitals, and bridges, improving parks and roads, and clearing slums, while intellectuals had a chance to maintain a modicum of their dignity by making sociological studies, library catalogs, and indexes to historical materials, painting murals in public buildings, and giving community concerts and plays. The longest hingeless arch bridge was completed over the Hudson in New York (1935), and the longest bridge of any kind over San Francisco Bay (1936). Home owners were helped to build new homes or to save their old ones from foreclosure, and farm owners to save their farms by federal mortgage loans on liberal terms. The Twenty-first Amendment, which repealed the Eighteenth Amendment to the Constitution, was prompted not only by the obvious failure of prohibition but also by a sober desire to revive the once profitable alcoholic beverages industry.

The Roosevelt program of farm relief and conservation

THE LONG-RANGE problem of farm relief was attacked with equal boldness by an attempt through government action to tilt economic operations in the farmer's favor. The essence of the plan was to raise the farmer's income by reducing surpluses, thus creating a relative scarcity of supply and raising the market prices of farm products. Farmers received benefit payments for acreage withdrawn from cultivation, for planting crops other than soil-exhausting staples, and even for products not placed on the market. The objectives behind this extraordinary program, which by government subsidies induced farmers not to raise or sometimes even to destroy food when city-dwellers were receiving relief from the same treasury, was to preserve the soil and to vary the crops, as well as to readjust supply and demand. The Supreme Court almost put an end to the experiment in 1936 by declaring the principal act in the agricultural reform program (the Agricultural Adjustment Act of 1933) an encroachment on states' rights and hence unconstitutional. But some of its features survived in the Soil Conservation Act of 1936 until a new agricultural act could be passed (page 841).

A voluntary program for the regulation of industry

RELIEF FOR business was continued through an expanded RFC. In addition an attempt was made to permit the entire industrial community of the nation, with governmental good will, to regulate itself through a National Recovery Administration (NRA). The act that created this agency permitted voluntary organizations of manufacturers (provided no monopolies resulted and governmental officials were able to supervise the arrangements) to draw up voluntary codes of fair practice. It was hoped in this way to revive business confidence, eliminate unfair competition, and produce a price level profitable to industry. Under these NRA codes industry was to govern itself under the watchful eye of the government and the public at large. The purpose was reform as much as recovery. The government provided a blanket code as a model and a working code until specific codes for each industry could be worked out. The model fixed minimum hours and wages, prohibited child labor, and guaranteed to laborers the right to organize freely and to bargain collectively. To implement the section on labor a National Labor Board (later superseded by a National Labor Relations Board) was created to help settle labor disputes.

In its two years of operation the NRA was not a great success. The tendency toward monopoly quickly betrayed itself, and big business inevitably

"Sweatshop" by William Gropper, an American artist.

outshouted small business in drawing up the codes. Businessmen disagreed with government administrators, revealed a vast impatience with governmental red tape, and loudly resented government's attempts at regulation. In 1935 the Supreme Court declared this measure, too, unconstitutional on the grounds, among others, that the act gave the president "an unfettered discretion."

Renascence of the labor movement

THE EARLY depression years marked a low ebb for labor. Unemployment, wage cuts, and desperate insecurity had been the worker's lot. Strikes had practically disappeared, for no one dared risk his job when millions were unemployed. Profiting from Roosevelt's courtship of the labor vote, the dormant labor movement reawoke. The establishment of NRA wrought something of a labor revolution. Within a few months membership in the American Federation of Labor swelled to 4,500,000.

The suddenly revitalized labor movement clashed head-on with indignant businessmen, and labor strife became widespread. Encouraged by NRA's protection of labor rights and by the beginnings of economic recovery, labor unions began a chain of strikes. In 1934 striking workers numbered over a million. A great textile strike spread clear across the country. A big strike tied up the automobile industry. San Francisco witnessed a general strike, which frightened many as a tactic borrowed from Europe and associated with political radicalism. All the strikes were broken, some of them by professional strikebreakers and special police, with great violence and bloodshed.

With the demise of NRA, the most important features of its labor provisions were re-enacted in the Wagner Act (July 1935), and a permanent National Labor Relations Board was established. The Wagner Act confirmed, with modifications, the provisions protecting free organization, collective bargaining, and negotiation through representatives of labor's own choosing. The National Labor Relations Board was given power to conduct union elections, investigate complaints, and issue "cease and desist" orders against unfair labor practices.

In 1935 the growth of the union movement was both intensified and complicated by a split within the American Federation of Labor. The "horizontal" or skilled-craft organization embodied in the American Federation of Labor was challenged by a movement to organize all workers in a given industry, whether skilled or unskilled, in a single industrial union, which, it was hoped, would have a stronger strategic position in collective bargaining. The "vertical" industrial-union principle met with stubborn resistance from A. F. of L. officials, but the leaders of the new movement, notably John L. Lewis, were equally stubborn. Forming a Committee for Industrial Organization, they began an intensive campaign to organize industrial unions, particularly in mass-production industries employing large numbers of unskilled workers, to whom union membership had hitherto been neither open nor attractive. Expelled from the A. F. of L., they reorganized as the Congress of Industrial Organizations (CIO) and soon were to rival the parent organization, reaching a membership of four million by 1937.

The New Deal and increased federal power

THE URGE TO reform was applied well beyond the spheres of relief, the farm, and labor. Legislation was passed regulating banking practices, insuring bank deposits against certain losses, and attempting to limit speculation and to eliminate misrepresentation in securities, investment businesses, and stock exchanges. The power of the old Interstate Commerce Commission was modified, and new commissions or coordinators were set up to supervise radio, federal water-power projects, and other public utilities engaged in interstate or international activities. One of the most significant reforms was the Social Security Act of 1935, providing for cooperation with the separate states in the creation of a system of old age and unemployment insurance for workers and of other benefits for the needy. Through this legislation the United States, having long resisted social insurance as an undesirable interference by government in private affairs, caught up with the European governments that since the time of Disraeli had accepted responsibility for the social security of their peoples.

782

The measures of the Roosevelt administration came to be known collectively as the New Deal.

Depression and discontent in Latin America

SIMILAR changes were under way in other American countries. In Latin America the expansion of trade and industry brought by the war, the prosperity of the twenties, and the vast amount of foreign investment, had greatly strengthened the middle and proletarian classes, and thus the simple, traditional class pattern of landlords and agrarian workers had changed into something more complex. The depression sharpened class controversies and increased the demand for social legislation. The familiar Latin-American pattern of coup d'état and dictatorship was now apt to be cast in terms of socialist or fascist ideologies; and social legislation, whether sponsored by liberals or conservatives, socialists or fascists, became a dominant issue.

Much was achieved, sometimes by progressive governments, sometimes by fascistic leaders. But in several countries the economic situation remained unstable and the general direction of affairs obscure. For instance, when Europeans could no longer afford with their inflated currencies to buy the coffee crops upon whose export the stability of Brazil's economic life depended, Brazilians were reduced to solving their problem of oversupply by dumping their coffee into the sea or using it as locomotive fuel. Depression produced extensive reform measures in Argentina, Brazil, Chile, Mexico, Cuba, and some other countries, sometimes by means of displays of violence by Communist or Fascist groups, resulting, as in Brazil and Cuba, in or from the establishment of a dictatorship. Foreign investors generally looked with favor upon the less revolutionary dictators.

Social reform in the Dominion of Canada

IN CANADA the depression, aggravated some years by drought and grasshoppers, meant declining prices and vanishing markets for her primary products. Between 1930 and 1932 Canada, while adhering to "imperial preference," raised her tariff duties to prohibitive levels, partly to favor the depressed home market and partly to have a bargaining weapon against the protective policies of other countries like the United States. At the same time the Canadian government moved in the direction of friendlier relations with the United States by advocating joint United States-Canadian development of a seaway to the Great Lakes via the St. Lawrence River. In spite of President Roosevelt's backing, the treaty drawn up in 1932 to provide such a seaway was defeated in the United States Senate. As deflation and unemployment continued, reform sentiment grew among Canada's farmers, wage-earners, and intellectuals. This trend drew a response from the Conservative Party, in which some leaders were moved by a genuine desire for social reform and others by the hope of holding their parliamentary majority. In 1935 the Conservative government enacted a sweeping program of social legislation. It included amendments to the criminal code dealing with questionable business practices, acts setting minimum wages and maximum hours, unemployment and social insurance, extension of farm credit, government aid in marketing of natural products, and strengthening of antimonopoly legislation. Its purpose, the prime minister frankly declared, was to reform capitalism by government intervention and control. Some of Canada's legislation was inspired by the Roosevelt New Deal and, like the New Deal, it did not escape censure. In the following year much of it was declared invalid by the Canadian Supreme Court, and shortly afterwards the judicial committee of the Privy Council in London declared most of it unconstitutional. Reform sentiment remained strong, however. In the elections of 1935, in which new parties polled over a quarter of the vote, the Liberals won by a landslide.

*Isolationism
in American economic policies*

IN THE EARLY depression years naked fascist aggression had appeared, tearing the already threadbare fabric of international peace and cooperation. "Moral sanctions" quickly proved (page 769) not of the substance to deter aggressors. The "great debate," as old as the Republic, over the foreign policy of the United States now split public opinion into two schools. Isolationism was even more pronounced in the early thirties than it had been in the previous decade. Europe's problems, it was said, were none of America's business. America had better put her own house in order, had better concentrate on her own national recovery and social problems, come what might abroad. This was in part the philosophy behind the Hawley-Smoot Tariff—the securing of the home market to home producers. It was also behind the American refusal to cancel the war debts and the subsequent Johnson Act (1934) barring debt-defaulting nations from making loans in the United States. Roosevelt himself was not at first free from this isolationist outlook. At the World Economic Conference in London in 1933 the new president did not cooperate in stabilizing the major world currencies, at least in part because he wanted freedom to manipulate the exchange value of the dollar or of an ounce of gold. Economic self-sufficiency was implicit in the AAA, which tacitly assumed the loss of the world market for American farm products and was geared to a policy of balancing supply and demand within the domestic market.

*The United States
as the "Good Neighbor"*

ISOLATIONISM was at first a factor in Roosevelt's foreign policy. It entered to a certain extent into the motivation behind the Tydings-McDuffie Act, passed in 1934, providing for Philippine independence after a ten-year probationary period. The United States hoped thereby to diminish its obligations abroad. Isolationism also figured in the changing attitude toward Latin America. Americans, turning

784

their backs at the same time on Europe and imperialism, substituted either good will where economic interests might dictate or indifference where they might not.

President Roosevelt's inaugural address in 1933 dedicated the nation to "the policy of the good neighbor." At the Seventh Pan-American Conference meeting at Montevideo later in the same year, the United States subscribed to a nonintervention pact adopted unanimously by the conference. The American government soon proved that its change of policy was sincere. It refrained from intervention to quell disorders that arose in Cuba and in 1934 abrogated the Platt Amendment authorizing intervention there (page 545); in the same year it withdrew its marines, sent during some disorders in 1929, from Haiti; and in 1936 it ratified a treaty restoring to Panama its sovereign powers.

Attempts to improve United States contacts

ECONOMIC isolation was repudiated by Roosevelt's secretary of state, Cordell Hull. Hull attempted to secure economic cooperation at least in the Western Hemisphere, if not with transoceanic countries. He initiated a strenuous campaign to expand United States exports and loosen the barriers to world trade. His principal weapon was the Reciprocal Trade Agreements Act of 1934, by which the president was given the authority for a period of three years to raise or lower tariff duties up to 50 per cent in order to apply pressure upon other countries to make tariff bargains with the United States. Under this act Hull in five years negotiated twenty-one treaties, and their tariff concessions were extended also to other countries having most-favored-nation treaties with the United States. One of the new treaties was with Canada, lowering duties and thus removing the recently erected bars to cordiality between the two countries. By this piecemeal bartering the channels of world trade began slowly to be widened. In a further effort to improve foreign relations, the United States in 1933, after sixteen years of diplomatic estrangement, recognized the government of Russia. The United States also joined the International Labor Organization in 1934, and participated in international silver, wheat, and sugar pacts designed to avoid overproduction and to control prices.

Fascism, Communism, and the "Roosevelt revolution"

AMERICANS became worried as democratic governments in Europe faded out and quarrels between Left and Right arose over their wraiths. Similar agitations muddied the always turbulent stream of politics in Latin America. They occasionally disturbed the usually more serene course of affairs above the Rio Grande. In Louisiana Governor Huey Long became virtual dictator of the state and threatened to sweep the country with his share-the-wealth program. Several new nativist movements sprang up. Among them the most popular was that of the demagogic priest Father Charles Edward Coughlin, who, by clever use

785

of radio and press, amassed a tremendous following for his fascistic and anti-Semitic program of "Social Justice." The German Bund (Union), under emissaries working directly with the Nazis of Germany, organized in the United States a paramilitary group that received its support mostly from German-Americans. Sinclair Lewis' novel *It Can't Happen Here* (1935) was a product of the fear that a fascist dictatorship *could* happen even in the democratic United States.

In the end Lewis' fears proved unjustified. Huey Long died in 1935 by a bullet from the revolver of a young man who had had enough of the Louisiana dictator. And Father Coughlin was discouraged by the disapproval of his superiors. But Fascism abroad continued both figuratively and literally on the march. A fair number of young American intellectuals who joined the Communist Party or became "fellow travelers" did so in apprehension of the spread of Fascism throughout the world. The same apprehension induced others to listen more attentively to the nativist and Bund leaders who warned against the dangers of Communism in the United States. Sometimes out of genuine fear and sometimes for political purposes, Roosevelt's opponents accused him of revising the traditional American policy of laissez faire and private initiative and starting his country down the road to a socialist serfdom. Only the wise conservatism of the Supreme Court, they claimed, had prevented catastrophe. His advocates replied that no New Deal measure had basically modified the system of free enterprise or had struck at the sacred institution of private property, but that the New Deal had in fact preserved these institutions by inaugurating the timely reforms necessary to forestall violent revolution from Right or Left. It had thus, they insisted, given American capitalism a "new lease on life." Despite nativist movements and "old-fashioned liberal" doubts regarding the wisdom or the constitutionality of the New Deal, Roosevelt was reëlected in 1936 (with only 7 electoral votes for his opponent).

ARMS AND THE MAN

THE BASIC ideas of Hitler's foreign policy were fixed. They had become visible years before he came to power when he had published *Mein Kampf*. One of his unshaken tenets was that France must be destroyed as a major power, though it might be allowed to survive as a German satellite. Russia was to be destroyed altogether; its rich grain lands were to come under German domination and be resettled with German peasants. Great Britain might be spared, provided she returned the former German colonies to Germany. Despite a ready flexibility in adjusting means to circumstances, Hitler never lost sight of these fundamental objectives, and he was to meet with amazing success in playing off the western democracies against Soviet

Russia.

*The place of Russia
in Hitler's calculations*

GETTING ALONG with Russia had consistently been a calculated Prussian (and later, German) policy. Perhaps without realizing it, Hitler reversed this policy and followed the old Austro-Hungarian anti-Russian strategy. Mixed with his desire to restore the prestige of Germany were the ideas that he retained from his grammar-school days in Austria about the romantic aura of the Holy Roman Empire with its *Drang nach Osten*—its impulse to push toward the east and the southeast. To that impulse he had added another derived from the recent teachings of Professor Karl Haushofer about a new class war—the "have not" nations against the "have" nations for more Lebensraum (room to live). The new *Drang nach Osten,* imperialistic though it was, was not a simple quest for territory and resources. It sought also to destroy Communism. But to what extent the war on Communism was pretext and to what extent genuine motivation is hard to say. The hypothesis is at least tenable that Hitler would have undertaken an attack upon Russia no matter what kind of regime she happened to have. Before an assault upon Russia could be seriously planned, however, Hitler, in addition to making Germany a "coordinated" unit, had also to create a strong army and a system of satellite states. Only then could he hope to be economically and politically secure against surprise attacks or superior pressure from other countries while engaged upon his ultimate military objective.

*The failure
of disarmament efforts*

QUARRELS among the nations that had defeated Germany in the war of 1914-1918 induced Hitler to believe that they would not unite to circumvent his plans. They could not even agree on naval disarmament. To be sure, the naval conference in London in 1930 (page 764) had extended the naval holiday to 1936, but the naval holiday in fact ended before that date. The Japanese and the Italians evaded the London agreements; and the French did not dare to conform in the face of constant threats from Mussolini. The French indicated their willingness to comply fully provided that Great Britain would enter into a Mediterranean "Locarno" that might discourage Italy from threatening France. And the British were ready to enter into such a commitment provided that the United States would put teeth in the Kellogg-Briand Pact. But President Hoover, disappointed with the League in the Manchurian crises and following the now prevalent American trend to isolationism, refused to give any such assurance. In 1934 Japan formally denounced the naval pacts of Washington and London and started a new naval armament race.

The League of Nations had a special Preparatory Commission that had worked for years to bring about a general disarmament conference. Finally sixty nations, including Russia and the United States, met to discuss the limitation of armed forces. This meeting, the world's first disarmament conference, opened at Geneva in February 1932. From the beginning it was clear that the problem of disarmament could not be solved by merely wishing. Insoluble conflicts arose. Germany wanted equality of arms, but France insisted upon security first. An international police was proposed to deal with aggressors, but no agreement could be reached on how to recruit or organize it. Soviet Russia advocated proportional disarmament of all nations, but the French insisted that in an industrial age the paramount question was war potential rather than the actual number of men under arms in time of peace. Every new proposal met with deadlock in the form of criticism from one or several powers. In July 1932, the conference adjourned temporarily.

Germany's withdrawal from the League of Nations

THE GERMANS now declared that they would not return to the conference unless their claim for "equality" was recognized. In December 1932 the powers acceded to the German demand, and the conference reconvened in February 1933. By that time Hitler had come to power in Germany. Despite valiant efforts by the French, British, Russian, and American delegations, no further headway was made, largely because the Germans would not consent to count Hitler's paramilitary forces as soldiers and would not agree to an arms holiday unless it first got equality in those weapons which the conference should eventually label "defensive." In June the conference adjourned temporarily again. In the interval it became clear that France and the Little Entente were so frightened by Hitler and the Nazis that they would not consent to any rearmament of Germany. In October, two days before the delegates were scheduled to resume their meetings at Geneva, Hitler suddenly announced Germany's withdrawal from the Disarmament Conference and, a few days later, from the League of Nations on the grounds that the other nations had amply demonstrated that they had no intention either of disarming themselves or permitting Germany to rearm. The conference did not formally close until the summer of 1934, but its continuation was futile thereafter, for Germany had begun openly to rearm.

France's reactions to Germany's rearmament

HITLER took small pains to conceal Germany's preparations for war, and the French had good reason to remember Germany's war potential. But the French failed to act wholly upon their own apprehensions. On the very eve of the Second World War they would be able to count on but a small air force and a few inadequate armored units.

The principal explanation for France's unpreparedness was that she relied upon her allies and the Maginot Line. Since the "Eastern Locarno" of 1925 France had cemented her alliances with the Little Entente and Poland, lending them money for armaments and arranging for mutual defense. In 1933 the Little Entente was converted into a permanent "unified international organization." France gave this organization her support and blessing. Counting on the Little Entente to replace the prewar entente with Russia and on the Maginot Line to stop a German offensive, the French government and people developed a state of mind that afterwards was termed "Maginot psychology"—a confidence in the safety of France that in the age of the airplane was to prove misplaced. This strange sense of security was enhanced when in 1935 Russia and France, equally fearful of Hitler, formed an alliance for five years against unprovoked attack. The main Maginot Line, when completed (1933), stretched from the Swiss border to a point near Sedan.

No up-to-date fortifications shielded the frontier between Sedan and the North Sea. For this region France relied upon the protection Belgium might give her. But Belgium's new king, Leopold III, was isolationist; and in 1935 Belgium, displeased by the Franco-Soviet pact of that year and fearful of the "Rexists," a pro-Nazi group at home, announcing that she was once more neutral in international affairs, disentangled herself from her French alliance.

Domestic weakness of the French Republic — WHY DID France not attempt to prolong the Maginot Line along its northwestern frontier until it was too late? A part of the explanation is to be found in the rapidity with which cabinets came and went after the resignation of Poincaré in 1929 because of illness. Part was also to be found in the corruption in government that became particularly glaring when Alexander Stavisky either committed suicide or was murdered (1934) to avert his telling all he knew about skulduggery in high places in connection with his operation of a government pawnshop. Still another part was to be found in the alacrity with which French royalists, fascist groups, and Communists resorted to riot and bloodshed (1934) to express their indignation over the Stavisky scandal and their hatred of each other. The different French cabinets that were in office until 1936 (and beyond) were weakly supported by the makeshift blocs that gave them their majorities in the Chamber of Deputies and were bitterly attacked both inside and outside the Chamber. When the franc began to fall again in 1934 the government resorted to economy, which meant cutting the salaries of already underpaid government employees, and hence more riots. Between 1929 and 1935 France did not present an edifying example of how parliamentary government worked.

Russia as the chief opponent of Nazism — THE LEADERSHIP in the opposition to Hitler's rearmament came not from France or England but from Russia. The Russians knew that they were Hitler's major objective and that large sections of public opinion in the West were prepared to wish Hitler well if he turned against them. Nevertheless, Russia's progress toward the goal of a monolithic state had kept pace with Germany's. Moreover, she had won some striking victories in international affairs in recent years. The United

States, the last of the great powers to do so, recognized her in 1933. The next year she joined the League of Nations and was awarded one of the (now six) permanent seats in the Council. The main Russian setback came in China, where the Communists not only failed to dominate the Kuomintang but lost almost all influence for a time (page 771). Russia's foreign policy after 1933 pivoted on her relations with Germany. That was why Stalin reversed the policy of distrust of bourgeois states and formed an alliance with France in 1935. Out of this new policy was to emerge an effort to unite the world against Fascism.

In 1923 Edward P. Cheyney, president of the American Historical Association, had stated his conviction that among the laws of history, "there seems to be a law of democracy, a tendency for all government to come under the control of all the people." Few in the United States in the 1920's would have been disposed to disagree with him. By 1935 the "law of democracy" seemed of exceedingly dubious validity. The pre-Armistice revolutions in China and Russia had moved in the direction of totalitarianism. So had the postwar revolutions in Germany and Austria. Italy, Hungary, Poland, Portugal, Turkey, and Japan were already to a greater or less extent totalitarian in government, and in the Balkan countries (Yugoslavia, Albania, Greece, Bulgaria, and Rumania) a marked tendency toward totalitarianism was visible. In some of the countries that were still to be counted among the old democracies—France, Belgium, and the Latin-American republics—strong Fascist or Communist parties were preparing, at the first good opportunity, to create one-party systems. Some of the republics of recent origin, such as Spain, Austria, Czechoslovakia, Poland, Finland, Lithuania, Latvia, and Estonia, were in danger (as a few years would make clear) of being overrun by neighboring dictatorships. If the English-speaking countries (including Ireland), France, Belgium, the Netherlands, the Scandinavian countries, Switzerland, and Czechoslovakia remained overwhelmingly staunch in their devotion to representative government and were even holding out the hope of self-rule to areas under their control like India, the Philippines, and some of their mandates, nevertheless none of them had entirely escaped organized opposition against parliamentary bungling and laissez-faire economy. The opposition was expressed on the extreme Right by Fascist groups and on the extreme Left by the Communists.

In 1935, therefore, the world seemed much less safe for the old brand of democracy than it had in 1923. In fact in the three-cornered trial by combat that had begun to look imminent, it appeared possible that democracy might not even survive unless the democratic countries joined either the Fascist countries or Russia against the other. That democracies would have such a choice in the event of open conflict seemed a good risk in 1935, for few believed that Nazis and Communists would ever make common cause.

1923-1929	The "Great Boom" in the United States
1925-1929	Stalin's rise to power in the USSR
1925-1929	Hard times in Britain
1925	Hindenburg elected German president
1925	Gandhi chosen president of the Indian National Congress
1925	Chiang Kai-shek succeeds Dr. Sun as head of Kuomintang
1926	The British "General Strike"
1926	Berlin Pact of neutrality arranged by Russia and Germany
1926	Evacuation by the French of the occupation zone in Germany
1926	Germany admitted to the League of Nations
1926	First wireless telephone between New York and London
1927	Lindbergh's nonstop solo flight from New York to Paris
1927	Mussolini's Tangier coup
1927	Unsuccessful naval disarmament conference at Geneva
1927	Britain's Trades Disputes and Trades Union Act
1928	Stalin proclaims the first "Five-Year Plan"
1928	The Kellogg-Briand Pact
1929-1933	Construction of the Maginot Line
1929	Second Labour cabinet in Britain
1929	The Young Plan for the payment of reparations
1929	The Lateran agreements of Pope Pius XI and Mussolini
1929	The Wall Street crash
1930	Hawley-Smoot Tariff Act
1931	Spanish Republic created
1931	The "Hoover moratorium" on international payments
1931	Austro-German customs-union project made public and opposed
1931	Statute of Westminster confirms British Commonwealth of Nations
1932	Manchukuo set up as a Japanese puppet state
1932	International Conference cancels Young Plan
1933-1937	First years of Franklin D. Roosevelt's "New Deal"
1933-1937	Russia's Second Five-Year Plan
1933	Japan and Germany withdraw from the League of Nations
1933	World Economic Conference achieves little
1933	The United States recognizes the USSR
1934	Chancellor Hitler made Führer by a German plebiscite
1934	USSR joins the League of Nations
1935-1938	Russian purges wipe out opposition to Stalin
1935	The Nuremberg Laws to keep Germany "Aryan"
1935	The "Hirota Principles" in Sino-Japanese relations
1935	Government of India Act extends self-government
1935	Russian-French alliance formed

Chapter thirteen

THE EVE OF THE SECOND

WORLD WAR

THE WORLD had suffered a great shock in 1914-1918 and contemporaries often wondered whether it would ever recover. Philosophers inquired whether a society that had been so shaken and had wandered so far from its accustomed moorings would ever again achieve a sense of unity or even of direction toward unity. The growth of new anti-Christian cults in Nazism and Communism intensified the feeling of disunion, particularly since the countries that still believed in the representative system found difficulty in agreeing among themselves. For all Europe's technical accomplishment, was it on the verge of a disaster perhaps worse than war, the disaster of spiritual disintegration? Writers, artists, and scientists presumably asked this question more often than the statesmen and sometimes gave disturbing answers, but the statesmen had more power to act upon their conclusions, and their acts were to be still more disturbing. The answers that a groping generation gave to the quest for a new faith frequently took the form of sympathy with new dispensations—theosophy, Communism, Fascism, or world order, but most of the world continued to give at least lip service to the old faiths.

In the interwar period a self-assertive Asia added to the babel and disunity of spirit. The "white man's burden" was now less the advancement of the backward Asians than a losing fight to retain what had been won by earlier generations. In an effort to close the technological and political gaps between East and West, the peoples of Asia more and more modified their traditional principles and practices and adapted them to modern western patterns. The spiritual appeal of Asia's traditional ideas and historical personalities, however, was not diminished among western intellectuals by the rapidly changing character of Asian life under the impact of industrialization and nationalism. At the same time, three of the great revolutionary ideals of the   793

West were slowly being absorbed by the East, if only spottily and incompletely—the Judeo-Christian ideal that all men are brothers and none has been given domination over the others, the scientific ideal that all men may equally understand and benefit from nature, and the democratic ideal that all shall have an equal opportunity to improve their talents. In the twentieth century the East was to strive for these ideals all at once, although it had taken the West many centuries to understand them only imperfectly.

For the United States the period between the two world wars was one of contradictory movements. In the first postwar decade, a self-absorbed United States had tried to build a great business prosperity and had smugly reckoned itself independent of the rest of the world. Despite the large minority (by some estimates, even a majority) which favored membership in the League of Nations, the government had repudiated the philosophy of Woodrow Wilson, who had induced the country to embark upon a program of social legislation and to play a leading part in world affairs. Yet, as we have seen, those who had repudiated soon suffered repudiation. In the second postwar decade, the shock of world depression, having put an end to domestic conservatism, pushed the progressivism of Wilson onward under a second Roosevelt. The more jarring shock of totalitarian aggression was gradually to bring a reluctant United States again to consider favorably the internationalism of Wilson.

"SCHISM OF THE SOUL"

WHAT HITLER called "cultural Bolshevism" was in a sense an awareness on the part of writers and artists that the prewar era was dead and that other times required other mores. Intellectuals of this stripe rarely were Communists themselves, but they frequently were radicals in the sense that they found the accepted conventions of the prewar world no longer acceptable. This dissatisfaction with the conventions was felt by several outstanding writers as well as by the exponents of expressionism and the "new objectivity" in the arts. In general, the statesmen of the new totalitarianism disliked these intellectuals. Toward certain types of writers and artists Russia under Stalin was to take an unfriendly attitude which greatly resembled that of Germany under Nazism, and it did so for the same reason: such artists and their work did not fit well into the monolithic state under the unquestioned leader. Toward scientists the attitude was different. So long as scientists were not politically or "racially" unacceptable, they were encouraged, since their work was demonstrably useful and did not automatically involve a critical attitude toward society. Like Napoleon, the totalitarian rulers of the twentieth century encouraged science, which they respected and did not understand, and discouraged or prostituted the arts, which they thought they understood and did not equally respect.

Interwar developments in the physical sciences

BETWEEN the two world wars natural science made its greatest advances in the fields of physics and medicine. The work of several scientists like Pierre Curie and Albert Einstein (page 461) at the close of the nineteenth century and the beginning of the twentieth had led to speculation that mass, being equivalent to energy, might be transmutable into energy. At the same time scientists in several countries continued to study the structure of the atom. Rarely had scientific work been carried on with greater international cooperation. Niels Bohr in 1913-1915 described the hydrogen atom as consisting of a positively charged nucleus around which a negatively charged electron rotates. Rutherford (1919) was the first to "split" (i.e., cause to disintegrate) the atom and thus to give a new scientific turn to the alchemical idea of transmuting one element into another. The German physicists Walther Bothe and Otto Hahn, the Americans E. O. Lawrence and H. C. Urey, the Italian Enrico Fermi, the Frenchman Frédéric Joliot-Curie, and others further explored the inside of the atom. After 1930, when Lawrence constructed the first cyclotron, or atom-bombarding machine, at the University of California, atom-smashing became relatively simpler, and by 1939 scientists were freely discussing the possibility of deriving energy from the fission of the nucleus of the atom. Einstein, Fermi, and other physicists, driven to the United States by the unfriendly atmosphere of Germany and Italy were (fortunately for the United States) to continue their work in American laboratories.

Advances in surgery and medicine

MEDICINE made enormous strides between the two world wars. Brain operations became a common form of surgery, and it proved possible to cure certain mental disturbances by brain surgery. The American surgeon Harvey W. Cushing excelled especially in this field. Lung surgery and plastic surgery also became common.

The most famous and probably most glorious achievement of medicine in this period was the isolation, and in some instances the actual synthesis, of certain vitamins. A fuller understanding developed of the diseases caused by vitamin deficiencies, and the use of vitamins as prophylactics or remedies became general. Vitamin A was discovered in 1913; vitamins B to K were discovered between 1926 and 1939.

Hormones, chemical substances secreted internally by the ductless glands and each performing a specific function in stimulating the action of some other organ of the body, had been discovered by the English physiologists E. H. Starling and Sir William M. Bayliss as early as 1903. Now new hormones and their effect upon sex, personality, and disease were investigated more thoroughly. Insulin, for example, a hormone extracted in 1922 by the Canadian physiologists F. G. Banting, C. H. Best, and their collaborators, keeps diabetes under control.

New drugs and antibiotics were concocted. The sulfa and sulfonamide drugs were first produced in Germany by Gerhard Domagk but were developed in the United States. They proved invaluable in combating streptococcal and other bacterial infections. The antibacterial substance called penicillin was discovered in 1929 by the English bacteriologist Alexander Fleming but was not developed until 1939. Thereafter it proved to be potent in the treatment of pneumonia and venereal diseases and also helpful in the treatment of other diseases.

The social implications WITH HEALTH standards much
of the increase in the life span improved, many people lived to be older than had been thought possible a generation earlier. This new development confronted medical men and social scientists with new problems. A wholly new branch of medicine developed called geriatrics, dealing with the problems of old age. Social scientists are now seriously studying how best to adjust old people to society and society to old people. Insurance companies are confronted with new problems because of the ever-rising number of old people, which suggests the desirability of a constant upward revision of their actuarial tables. Because of the marked improvements in obstetrics (childbirth medicine), pediatrics (children's medicine), and dietetics (scientific regulation of diet) more children were born alive and stayed alive than ever before. The white child born about 1900 in the United States had a mean life expectancy of no more than 47 years; in 1949 its mean expectancy of life was to go as high as 67 years. Lengthening of life was not altogether an unmixed blessing. It increased the number of human beings without necessarily increasing food, wealth, or economic opportunities. Once more physiologists and sociologists began to debate the old Malthusian problem—whether the world's population might not eventually exceed all possibility of feeding it.

Physics FINDINGS IN the natural sciences
and the new metaphysics between the wars led to new speculations on the nature of the world. The investigations by the American physicists Robert A. Millikan and Arthur H. Compton of cosmic rays, or radiations apparently reaching the earth from outer space, have given a new impulse to the science of astrophysics. Supertelescopes afforded man a farther look into the outer spaces of the universe than he would once have dared to dream of. A new cosmology was in the making; scientists began to reëxamine the nebular hypothesis critically. The English astronomer James Jeans propounded a gaseous-tidal theory of the origin of the world. The German physicist Werner Heisenberg in 1927 set forth the "uncertainty principle" in quantum mechanics, which in oversimplified language means that both precise position and precise motion can not be attributed at the same time to such microcosmic things as atoms or electrons, and hence any prediction as to their future performance is subject to

error. Heisenberg's "uncertainty principle" induced some philosophers to hold the nature of the physical order to be indeterminate and perhaps immaterial and led even hard-headed physicists to think of cause as a set of probabilities rather than as a determined order. The English astronomer Arthur Eddington took a leading part in the effort to reintroduce into the study of physics a reconciliation of religion and science, and his compatriot, the philosopher A. N. Whitehead, attempted to create a scientific religion—a philosophy he called *organism*.

"Decline" and "Schism"
in the philosophy of history

TWO REPRESENTATIVE philosophies of history emerged in the period between the wars—one essentially materialistic, the other essentially Christian. Oswald Spengler published *The Decline of the West* (1918-1922), and Arnold J. Toynbee published the first six volumes of his monumental *Study of History* (1934-1939). Both works have one thing in common in that they deal with the histories of entire civilizations. But their basic concepts are totally different. Spengler's is a deterministic and pessimistic view of history. According to him, civilizations (or "cultures," as he calls them, after the German fashion) have an inexorable life cycle much like that of living animals. They are born, go through childhood, adolescence, middle age, and old age, and then they die. By drawing parallels between contemporary European society and societies that have already disappeared, he tried to show that western civilization had reached its state of maturity and would soon begin to decline and disappear. The Nazis were to regard him as one of their intellectual forerunners because he spoke of "Caesarism" as a forthcoming development in the West.

Toynbee was less deterministic. He proceeded from the belief that hardship rather than ease calls forth human creativity. He examined a series of problems and risks that civilizations have to face, trying to derive solutions from the experiences of twenty-six civilizations which are all now either dead or faced with the prospect of dying. He described their "geneses," "growth," "breakdowns," and "disintegrations." He found that they tend to break down and disintegrate because they no longer respond adequately to their complications ("challenge") and lose their social unity ("schism in the soul"). In these six volumes he did not come to a conclusion but seemed to imply that a civilization is on its way out when it can no longer, under the leadership of creative individuals or minorities, respond adequately to a challenge. In works written under the stress of the Second World War he was to make clear that he felt that western civilization can survive only if it develops unity centering around a set of values essentially Christian.

Not all the philosophers of historical bent were concerned with the morphology of cultures. H. G. Wells' *Outline of History* (1920) was hopeful of man's progress and ultimate unity. The Webbs returned from Russia to write *Soviet Communism: A New Civilization* (1935). The French anti-

Bergsonian philosopher Julien Benda caused a stir in the twenties with his book *The Treason of the Intellectuals* (1927). He accused European, especially French, writers of intellectual betrayal and moral cowardice. In departing from the realm of reason into the realm of emotion, he claimed, they were setting the pace for totalitarianism. In several subsequent writings he renewed his appeal for abstract intellectual daring against the emotionalism of the day.

Freud inevitably became a severe critic of present-day civilization. His book *Das Unbehagen in der Kultur* (translated as *Civilization and Its Discontents,* 1930) summed up his formidable indictment. Like Nietzsche he condemned contemporary standards of morality, but whereas Nietzsche assailed them because they seemed to him the morals of slaves and pygmies who barred the way to a potential future of supermen, Freud based his indictment on what he held to be their harmful psychological effects upon living generations. He saw no hope in socialism, because: "Suppose that personal rights to material goods are done away with, there still remain prerogatives in sexual relationships, which must arouse the strongest rancour and most violent enmity among men and women who are otherwise equal." Nevertheless, many of that interwar generation found it possible to be Marxian, Nietzschean, and Freudian at the same time, because they saw in all three philosophies a common denominator of disgust with bourgeois morality.

Irish literature in the period between two wars EUROPEAN literature between the two wars was perhaps not so prolific as it had been before 1914 but had its own significance. During these years Ireland had a galaxy of great writers. Yeats was still (page 536) the dean of this "Irish Renaissance," and among its younger writers were Liam O'Flaherty and Sean O'Casey. O'Flaherty in his novel *The Informer* (1925) gave an account of the mixed emotions among the poor in Ireland's war for independence. O'Casey's *The Plough and the Stars* (1926) was a drama, made famous by the Abbey Players, portraying the war of the Black and Tans. His *Within the Gates* (1933) reveals the conflicting attitudes of a number of persons encountered by a bishop in a London park. Both authors portrayed the confusion of purposes in strife-torn Ireland in the hope of leading their countrymen to some constructive purpose.

The Irishman generally regarded as the most outstanding of this generation preferred to live as an expatriate. He was James Joyce, universally acclaimed because his learned, allusive, word-conscious style and stream-of-consciousness method influenced a whole generation of writers and because his novel *Ulysses* (1922) is commonly described by critics as an artistic accomplishment of the highest order. He compressed the entire career of the average European into the ruminations by a simple Dublin advertising agent upon an ordinary twenty-four hours of his life, depicting hour by hour the loneliness, the frustrations, and the inanities of modern existence. Joyce used

A sketch of James Joyce by the British painter Augustus John.

here, and still more in *Finnegans Wake* (1939), in which by a similar method he made the whole history of the human race pass in review, an obscure language which, though easily parodied, has rarely been successfully imitated. Although *Ulysses* ends upon the word *yes* as a symbolic affirmation of life, it is a gloomy book—flashes of humor, sensuousness, and wit notwithstanding. The last chapter, written without punctuation, consists of a subconscious monologue which is among the best applications to novel-writing of the psychoanalytic findings of Freud.

Disillusionment among the younger writers

SEVERAL younger continental writers who had already gained reputations before 1914 now acquired still greater fame. Discontented and disillusioned even before the war, some of these writers felt constrained to immure themselves in a sort of dream world. Rainer Maria Rilke and Franz Kafka, both born in Prague, were among them. Rilke, one of the great German-speaking lyric poets, had been in his youth the secretary of the French sculptor Auguste Rodin. As a creator of beautiful phrases he had few equals. Rilke was a religious mystic, often despondent, glorifying poverty ("Blessed are those who stand in the rain and get wet"), speaking frequently of death, and preaching submission. Rilke wrote his *Duinese Elegies* and *Sonnets to Orpheus,* which are among his best poems, during and shortly after the war. Kafka's novels depicted a nightmarish despair that perhaps reflected his illness and disappointment in love. Though Kafka was a Jew and his God was a stern Jehovah, the same mysticism appears in his novels as in Rilke's lyrics along with the same kind of dream world and the same sense of frustration by realities. His posthumous, incomplete novel *The Trial* (1925; English translation, 1937), was symbolic of man's vain struggle against "the law" and other universal forces he could not understand. Kafka's works, for the most part published after the war, deal with the period just before it began and just after it ended.

The war itself became a setting for young men of letters who had endured its horrors. Robert Cedric Sherriff's play *Journey's End* (1929) told a story of futile heroism. Erich Maria Remarque's novel *All Quiet on the Western Front* dealt with the German soldier's anxiety to remain alive. Arnold Zweig's *The Case of Sergeant Grischa* was a novel that attacked the injustice of the Prussian military bureaucracy. The Austrian Jew Franz Werfel dealt in two novels with the problems of race and religion in wartime—*Barbara or Piety* (1929; translated as *The Pure in Heart*) and *The Forty Days of Musa Dagh* (1933).

Some novelists' critique of bourgeois, Communist, and Nazi THE OUTSTANDING contemporary figure in French literature was André Gide. Before 1914 Gide had written several novels that had won respect. His postwar works, like the autobiography *Si le grain ne meurt* (1924-1926, translated as *If It Die*) and the novel *The Counterfeiters* (1926) showed a greater maturity. The "counterfeiters" are those who teach the distressed hero of the novel a decadent middle-class morality. For a time Gide had pro-Communist leanings, originating in his first-hand contact with injustice while occupying several minor government posts. But after a visit to Russia he returned home thoroughly sobered and made a clean break with Communism in his *Retour de l'U.R.S.S.* (1936).

Gide's avowed "last work" was his little book *Theseus*. It was not published until after the Second World War (1946), but it may be assumed to summarize his whole message. The story of Theseus, king of ancient Athens, narrated as autobiography, is treated as symbolic of recent history. He develops from a turbulent youth into a responsible adult devoted to the well-being of his fellow men. The climax of the novel, if it can be called a novel, is in the encounter of Theseus with the blind king Oedipus. Through the words of Theseus, Gide rejects the heroic leader who sees only with an inner eye and

inflicts untold misery upon himself and his fellow men, though he rejects him with admiration, and ranges himself on the side of practical vision and accumulative progress.

The interwar novels of Thomas Mann reflect the schism in the society of his country. *The Magic Mountain* (1924) depicted German and, through representative characters, European society on the eve of the First World War. Its setting in a tuberculosis sanitarium permitted Mann to probe once more into his favorite topic of disease and the conflict between esthetic and practical values. In the four volumes of his "Joseph" series (1933-1944), he recounted the biblical story of Joseph and his brothers, again unfolding, this time against a scholarly panorama of ancient Egyptian civilization, the struggle of the artist with and for society. In *Lotte in Weimar* (1939; English translation, *The Beloved Returns,* 1940), Goethe's character Lotte, the heroine of *Young Werther,* visits old Goethe, and once more the conflict between bourgeois values and genius becomes the theme. Mann left Nazi Germany to live first in Switzerland, then in the United States, and then in Switzerland again. His *Dr. Faustus* (1948) was to depict Faust as a modern (and modernist) musician who sells his soul in exchange for some years of genius, which he is doomed to spend in tribulation in interwar Germany.

One expression of the revolt of the 1920's was a demand for social freedom. It ranged from the exploitation of sex themes by movies, magazines, and tabloid newspapers through D. H. Lawrence's cult of "the wise vices of the body" to the frank medical study of the place of sex in normal life. Lawrence caused a sensation with his antipuritan poems and novels. Few have doubted his genius, though many have condemned him for obscenity. Around him centered a coterie of English and American writers. Some of his many works, particularly the autobiographical *Sons and Lovers* (1913) and *Lady Chatterley's Lover* (1928), by general consent are among the good novels of the twentieth century. Lawrence's war with accepted bourgeois conventions led to regular banning of his books in English-speaking countries.

Europe's dramatists between two world wars

AMONG playwrights the same queries regarding human values and conflicts prevailed. Luigi Pirandello was the only one to enrich dramatic form by a new method. He was well over fifty and had written literally hundreds of short stories, novels, and plays before he became famous. Because of a case of insanity in his own family he was haunted by the question, "What is illusion? What is reality?" He wondered about the many-sidedness of human character, which nevertheless remains incomplete. These topics dominate his plays, of which *Six Characters in Search of an Author* (1921) became the best known. Six unfinished characters of the playwright appear upon the stage, each requiring that his story be completed.

Bernard Shaw wrote some of his best plays in his old age. *Back to Methuselah* (1921) was a humorous fantasy on one of Shaw's favorite 801 themes, the evolution of man. It depicted a time when men would be born at seventeen years of age and live to be hundreds of years old and become little more than thought vortexes. *Saint Joan* (1923) was an attack on historical man's stupidity and selfishness; it portrayed Joan of Arc as one who questioned the established order of her day and therefore appeared a dangerous "witch" to those who intended to maintain that order.

The continuing revolt against imitation in architecture

A STYLE of architecture that had developed before 1914 and had reflected a common determination to get rid of the imitative styles in which the nineteenth century had indulged, arose to new prominence in the interwar decades. This style was sometimes called "modern" or "international." Its practitioners, borrowing from the earlier work of Frank Lloyd Wright and inspired by the German architect Peter Behrens' philosophy of industrial art, laid emphasis on utility combined with beauty and simplicity and upon the use of modern and easily available materials. Their doctrine of "functionalism" was practiced and preached by the Swiss Le Corbusier (pseudonym of C. E. Jeanneret), who believed that dwellings should be built expressly for the efficient housing of people. They emphasized the use of corner windows, glass brick supported by steel and concrete, and steel furniture. The outstanding school of functional art was the Bauhaus, located first at Weimar, then Dessau, and then Berlin. Its leading teachers of architecture were Walter Gropius and Ludwig Miës van der Rohe. Among its instructors of painting were the Swiss Paul Klee, the Russian Vasily Kandinsky, and the Hungarian Laszlo Moholy-Nagy, all abstract artists. The Bauhaus architects avoided ornamentation and went in for straight lines and flat roofs. Their architecture incurred the hostility of the Nazis, who preferred the classic style and denounced modernism as "cultural Bolshevism" (while the Russians denounced it as "decadent capitalism"). The Bauhaus leaders sought refuge in America, France, and Switzerland.

New developments in painting and drawing

IN PAINTING the revolt against impressionism and realism turned in ever new directions. Before and during the First World War, Pablo Picasso (page 542) was for a time, along with Georges Braque, a leader of those who cultivated cubism. The striking characteristic of cubism is its analysis of natural forms into their basic geometric patterns and the projection of those patterns on canvas. Later Picasso developed a style of painting which is essentially individual and cannot be classified with other schools. The best known of his interwar pictures is "Guernica" (1937), an experiment in black and white, of which the leading figure is a horse driven wild in the destruction of the city of Guernica during the Spanish Civil War (page 813). Matisse (page 542) never joined the cubists; in this period he painted the interior scenes for which he is perhaps most famous.

Matisse: A line drawing made in 1936 by the French artist echoes the composition of his many paintings of odalisques (female harem slaves), who have been among his favorite subjects.

Several other artists, with or without having gone through a preliminary period of cubism, created new styles which, however, because of an inimitable technique did not give birth to new schools. Among them were Georges Rouault, the great religious painter of the era, whose angular figures, in bright colors outlined in black, frequently depict suffering, vice, or cruelty; Maurice Utrillo, who has become famous for the color and design of his paintings of streets; and Russian-born Marc Chagall, who sometimes (but not regularly) paints pictures that suggest fantasy. Two new movements of significance developed during and after the First World War. They were dadaism and surrealism. The most popular representative of surrealism was the Spaniard Salvador Dali. The school of dadaism was deliberately unruly, disrespectful, and iconoclastic in regard not only to the old forms but also to its own. It arose as a protest against the destruction of the First World War, and, as the horror of the war receded, it gave way to surrealism, which does not spurn technical exactness but protests against tradition through emphasis upon incongruities such as are to be found in dreams and the subconscious.

The art of the cartoon found great exponents during these decades. The German George Grosz became famous for his expressionist cartoons, in which he savagely derided militarism and bourgeois complacency. After his emigration to America he turned to landscape painting. The New Zealander David 803

Low time and again lampooned the dictators and those who appeased them. Low invented the unimaginative, conservative Colonel Blimp, and made Neville Chamberlain's umbrella the symbol of appeasement (page 820).

In sculpture, though unconventional forms also appeared (Chapter 15), two of the ablest artists—the Yugoslav Ivan Mestrovic and the English Eric Rowland Gill—employed the approved forms and subject matter.

Music in Europe between the two wars

NEW FORMS of music that had appeared shortly before the First World War developed more fully after the war. Maurice Ravel achieved popular acclaim with his orchestral work *Bolero* (1928). Igor Stravinsky, revolting against academic traditions, no longer constructed music on an easily recognizable theme, and Arnold Schönberg departed from the familiar seven-tone (diatonic) scale and the use of familiar thirds for musical chords, substituting the twelve-tone (chromatic) scale and unfamiliar fourths instead. The result was catcalls from his audiences, who did not understand what unfriendly critics called atonality or dissonance and what friendly critics called intellectualism, metatonality, or indifference to tonality. Bartók (page 542), Paul Hindemith, and Arthur Honegger also composed in the new musical idiom. Stravinsky and Bartók were among the exponents of "neo-classicism," which by 1926 was in full swing, with new forms of polyphony and rhythm and unusual instrumental effects. Sergei S. Prokofiev, Manuel de Falla, Ernest Bloch, and Darius Milhaud made frequent use of dissonances without always departing from conventionally melodic compositions and often indulging in tone poems and expressionism. Meanwhile, the works of Richard Strauss, Jan Sibelius, Ernst von Dohnanyi, Sergei Rachmaninov, Sir Edward Elgar, and Ralph Vaughan Williams continued the traditional techniques; and a few European composers like Ernst Krenek (in his opera *Jonny spielt auf*, 1926) gave support to the effort to lift jazz out of the realms of banality and improvisation to the level of symphony and opera. In England the fervent pursuit of happiness by the young through song and dance paralleled the American "Jazz Age" and gave to the first postwar decade the sobriquet "the roaring twenties."

Simplified jazz rhythm at the one extreme and nonobjective intellectualization of sound at the other perhaps typified in music the contemporary "schism in the soul." As nationalism made the atmosphere in central and eastern Europe unhealthy for nonconformist musicians, they (as well as nonconformists in science, literature, and art) took up their abode in western Europe and the United States, enriching the lands they adopted and impoverishing the lands of their birth, and demonstrating in still another way the interdependence of the globe. Rachmaninov gave up his residence in Russia in 1918; Schönberg, Bartók, Hindemith, Bloch, and other musicians of Central Europe fled their native countries to the United States in the 1930's.

*Changing standards
of the worth of the individual*

THE STANDARDS of decency and respect for the individual common to most of Europe before 1914 had been largely obliterated by the 1930's. For example, before 1914, a traveler wishing to go from Berlin to Paris could under ordinary conditions buy a railroad ticket without preliminary application, exchange some of his German marks for French francs without question, and expect to encounter no greater inconvenience than an examination of his baggage by a French customs official. No passports had been required for travel except to Turkey or Russia, and the very need for passports in those cases was generally regarded as an indication of the backwardness of those countries. But in the 1930's, especially after Hitler came to power, a German who wished to visit Paris had to apply for a passport at the local police station; he had to give a plausible reason for his intended travel; he had to indicate how much money he wanted to take with him, and how long he intended to stay in France. If he received a passport, he had to have a permit from the federal bank in order to exchange a prescribed amount of marks for French currency. Then he had to get a French tourist visa and a Belgian transit visa. At the frontier he would be examined by German officials checking whether he had exceeded the amount of money allotted to him for his travel. His passport would be examined at the Belgian and French frontiers by policemen of those countries. Upon his arrival at his stopping place in Paris he had to fill out for the police record a questionnaire about his travels, and, if he meant to stay for some time, to present himself at the police office of the district in order to obtain a sojourn permit. Upon going back to Germany he would have to repeat much of the same cumbersome process in the reverse order.

Personal insecurity became tragic after Hitler came to power and the mass flight of political refugees began. People who caused, or were likely to cause, displeasure to any dictatorial government were deprived of the official identification papers that they would need in foreign countries. When such people had to flee across the frontiers, they went without passports. Sometimes they were fortunate enough to acquire League of Nations passports, which some of the member states would honor. When apprehended by the police of countries that demanded national passports, they might be arrested, jailed, and finally deported back home or mercifully expelled to some other foreign country. In this way, thousands of people were hounded like criminals. Many others committed suicide. The quest for national security had led to insecurity for millions of individuals.

*Technology
in a shrinking world*

MEANWHILE, technological developments continued to make the world a smaller place. In 1933 twenty-four military planes under the Fascist general Italo Balbo flew from Rome to Chicago and back; and Wiley Post made the first around-the-world solo flight. By 1939, air line service for passengers had been established across both the Atlantic and the Pacific oceans. The silk industry of Japan and China suffered a body blow when nylon was commercially produced in the United States in 1939. In the year before the United States entered the Second World War it produced about 438,000,000 pounds of various plastics, about half of the total world supply for that year, bringing consternation if not ruin to laborers and craftsmen in leather, silk, ivory, and other natural materials in the old countries as well as the new. Technological improvements wrought in such new industries as radio, the automobile, and aviation emphasized an old lesson—that no matter how riven the world's peoples might be by their nationalistic differences, economically and intellectually they were being brought ever closer together.

POPULAR FRONT, PACIFISM,

AND ANTI-COMINTERN PACT

How far the dread of Communism was the real reason and how far it was used as an expedient pretext in the calculations of the Fascist dictators is debatable. Certainly some of the Communist scare was due to genuine apprehension, and certainly also some of it was studiously whipped up for purposes of anti-Communist propaganda designed to win fealty for the "leaders." The same kind of debate arises with regard to the Communists' dread of Fascism. How far it placed them genuinely on the defensive and how far it was but a convenient argument for persuading anti-Fascists to travel in company with the Communists is hard to say. But certainly anti-Fascism won fellow travelers for Communism in much the same way as anti-Communism won fellow travelers for Fascism. The two ideologies were excellent weapons in a struggle that nevertheless was largely if not fundamentally a power struggle. On the eve of the Second World War, the Fascist states took the offensive in that struggle.

Communist policy of collective security

PURGES AND five-year plans at home and Communist failures abroad had put Russia on the defensive by 1935. The desire for a respite partly explains why she had been ready to make an alliance with bourgeois France. That year Russia also agreed to a mutual assistance pact with Czechoslovakia. At meetings of the League of Nations the Russian delegation took a leading part in rhetorical displays on disarmament and collective security. Furthermore, the growing threat of Fascism induced the Third International as the representative body of the world's Communist parties to advocate a union anywhere in the world of all political forces opposed to Fascism. Hence arose a "Popular Front" of left-wing parties that in France and elsewhere from 1935 to 1939 gave some reason to believe that the Communist parties of the western countries and Russia might ultimately support the democracies against the Fascist states.

In keeping with this new departure the Russian constitutional commission under Stalin's chairmanship (page 763) in December 1936 gave the USSR (now a union of eleven federated socialist republics) an entirely new constitution. The Stalin constitution looked good on paper. In it a declaration of rights granted not only political liberties such as freedom of speech and press but also economic guarantees such as employment and social security. The franchise was granted to all normal persons over eighteen, and numerous elective assemblies were provided at all levels. Provision was made for the individual citizen to own a limited amount of private property. But the new spirit did not encompass a reduction of the power of the Communist Party in Russia or of its leader Stalin; it permitted only one party to exist. Whether the constitution was intended to be more than a gesture in the new bid for popular solidarity inside and outside of Russia is uncertain, for in any event a rapid sequence of international crises kept the Russian government from giving most of its more liberal provisions anything but nominal observance.

Léon Blum and the Popular Front in France   THE FIRST Popular Front was created in France, where two problems outweighed all the others. One was the obligation to counteract the growing menace of Nazism and Fascism both at home and abroad, and the other the hardships of the workingman as a result of the declining purchasing power of the franc after 1934. To meet these challenges the left-wing parties formed a bloc in 1935 consisting of Socialists, Republicans, and Radical Socialists, and the Communists now showed a readiness to cooperate with them. This Popular Front dominated the French government from 1936 until the diplomatic humiliation of Russia in 1938 (page 820). Léon Blum, who as a Socialist and a Jew was particularly obnoxious to the Action Française, the Croix de Feu (Fiery Cross), and other right-wing organizations, twice was prime minister during this period. A series of sit-down strikes in 1936 reinforced Blum's personal urge toward socialist reform. A forty-hour week and other labor privileges, nationalization of the Bank of France and of factories engaged in armaments production, suppression of paramilitary organizations, and laws to improve the lot of women, children, consumers, and the poor were decreed in quick succession. Blum's "New Deal" spread panic among the rich, and a flight of capital abroad to safer areas of investment reduced government revenue at the very time that growing international tension dictated additional expenditures for fortifications and armaments. The franc kept falling, and Blum was forced to resign after more than a year as premier. Until a reaction in 1938 (page 820), however, the Blum reforms were retained.

The Popular Front was considerably less successful in its foreign policy.   807

It faced defeats in Spain, Austria, and Czechoslovakia. Its cabinets were supported only by the makeshift bloc that gave them faltering majorities in the Chamber of Deputies and were bitterly attacked by the Right both inside and outside the Chamber. At one point a plot to overthrow the government by an armed royalist-Fascist organization known as the Cagoulards ("The Hooded Men") was discovered and nipped by police action. Yet, with unwonted unity, the Chamber voted funds for the fortifying of the Belgian front. The Superior War Council, dominated by the aging antiparliament "hero of Verdun," Marshal Henri Philippe Pétain, did not fully exploit the funds that were voted. A "small Maginot Line" was built on the Belgian front, neither as well constructed nor as well manned as the big line—a fact which the Germans apparently well knew.

The French also neglected their air force. Underneath the financial reason for this neglect lay two psychological reasons. (1) The French General Staff, resting on its First World War laurels and not having learned the lessons of tank and aerial warfare that the Italians and Germans were contemporaneously learning in Ethiopia and Spain (pages 812 and 813), expected any future war to be one of attrition with long drawn-out trench maneuvers. (2) France had suffered in blood so terribly from the last war and was so divided politically at home among pacifists, Communists, and Fascists that many, perhaps most, Frenchmen were defeatist.

A few Frenchmen and Englishmen realized how woefully unprepared morally and physically their countries were for modern war. Colonel (later General) Charles de Gaulle published (1934) a warning in his book *Toward a Professional Army* (translated in English in 1941 as *The Army of the Future)* in which he outlined what a modern streamlined army should be. The French paid as little attention to his warnings as did the British to Winston Churchill's. Churchill was regarded as too bellicose, and his proposals for building up England's war strength were thought more likely to goad an enemy into precipitate action than to provide a timely defense.

Complications
in Britain and Ireland

AS TROUBLES accumulated on the Continent, most of the British assumed that a solution short of war must be found. Young men, especially in the universities, took formal oaths not to fight in another war. Besides, the British government had its hands full with domestic and imperial problems. The year 1936 was a year of three kings. George V died; Edward VIII preferred to abdicate rather than give up a marriage of which his government disapproved; and his brother became George VI. The complications in India and other parts of Asia will shortly claim our attention (pages 827-833). Under De Valera's leadership the Irish Free State, though it no longer resorted to armed conflict, at first expressed its discontent with its status as a dominion by tariff discriminations. Then in 1936 it amended its constitution so as to cancel all association with the British crown in domestic affairs and to permit the king to act for Ireland in foreign affairs only as advised by its own Executive Council. Finally a new constitution, based on the assumption that Ireland was the sovereign republic of Eire, was adopted by plebiscite in 1937. England accepted Eire's new status when the royal government agreed in 1938 to turn over the Irish coast defense to the republic and made amicable tariff and other settlements.

The threat of civil war in Palestine

IN PALESTINE Jews and Arabs were clearly preparing for a fight. The British in 1936 sent Lord Peel and a new commission to investigate. The Peel Commission's report stated that the Jewish and the Arab populations were incompatible and suggested that the country, altogether no bigger than the state of Maryland, be divided into three parts, one controlled by Arabs, another by Jews, and a third by the British. But nothing came of the proposal. The World Zionist Congress accepted it conditionally, and a Pan-Arab Congress of self-appointed delegates repudiated it unconditionally. By 1937, the more extreme Arab nationalists resorted to systematic terror, and new riots broke out. Great Britain had to set up special military courts and send a large army to restore and maintain order. The Arabs boycotted the British officials; Zionist extremists organized their own system of terror. By 1938, Palestine was the scene of frequent bombings, terrorist "executions," pitched battles, and massacres. A new commission under Sir John Woodhead proposed a conference of Jews and Arabs in London, but when such a conference was called, it could agree to nothing.

Eventually, in May 1939, Great Britain by a narrow parliamentary majority approved a compromise plan. It permitted a total Jewish immigration of 75,000 in the course of the ensuing five years. After that, immigration was to cease entirely unless the Arabs consented; and after another five years, an independent Palestine was to be set up with guarantees for "the essential interests of each community." This so-called British Plan meant hopelessness for numbers of European Jews to whom Palestine might have been the only haven from the Hitler persecutions. Before the question of the Palestine mandate could be thoroughly aired in the League of Nations, the Second World War broke out.

Complications in other mandated areas

BRITAIN surrendered her mandate in Iraq, and in 1932 Iraq was admitted to the League of Nations, the first of the mandated areas to become a sovereign state. The Iraqis nevertheless remained largely dependent upon British forces for defense against the Kurds, who three times rose in rebellion. King Feisal died in 1933. Under his son, King Ghazi, the Iraqis showed greater dissatisfaction with the alliance, and when Ghazi was killed in an automobile accident (1939), the British consul at Bagdad was stoned to death by an excited mob 809 that accused him of arranging the accident. Iraq was infiltrated by Nazi agents, and the Iraqis were to cause the British much trouble during the Second World War.

The French continued to find the Syrians hard to manage. The constitution of 1930 won no great loyalty, as nationalism grew and with it a demand for Syria's admission to the League as a sovereign state. Unrest became epidemic and was accompanied by suspensions of parliament and frequent streetfighting. Finally, in the summer of 1939 the French high commissioner suspended the constitution altogether. In Lebanon, however, pro-French ministries consistently made the French government's problems much simpler.

The difficulties of Britain in Egypt

KING AHMED FUAD of Egypt was friendly to the British protectorate of his realm, but the growing nationalist party, the Wafd, was not. In 1930, King Fuad abolished the liberal constitution of 1923, hoping that he could get rid of the Wafd. In its place he promulgated a far less liberal instrument, and in 1934 he dispensed with a constitution altogether. But continued nationalist agitation obliged him in 1934 to reinstate the constitution of 1923. The Wafd wanted not only to get rid of the British but also to restrict the power of the king. The British, fearful of Italian ambitions in the Mediterranean and Africa (page 811), doubted whether the Suez Canal and other important interests in Egypt would be safe and whether a truly liberal regime was possible in a country where more than half of the population consisted of illiterate and miserably exploited lower classes.

The death of Fuad and the accession of his young son Farouk in 1936 proved an advantage to Egyptian nationalism. The looming European crisis dictated discretion to the British, and Farouk at first showed no inclination to continue his father's high-handed disregard of the Wafd. So Great Britain and Egypt concluded a new treaty. It provided for the withdrawal of British troops from Egypt, except for the Suez Canal area, and for a twenty-year defensive alliance. But Egypt had to grant several concessions in return. British troops were to be allowed free passage in case of war, the British navy was to be permitted to maintain bases at Alexandria and Port Said even in time of peace, and the British army was to instruct the Egyptian army. In 1937 the European powers agreed to cancel most of their Egyptian capitulations, and thereupon Egypt as a sovereign state became a member of the League of Nations. But unrest inside Egypt and suspicion between the British and the Egyptians continued.

Austrian sovereignty and the conference at Stresa

UNTIL 1938 Hitler carefully avoided making any conquests outside prewar Germany. In the first place he had his hands full coordinating the Third Reich and tearing up the Versailles and Locarno scraps of paper. In the second place, he was practically isolated diplomatically. Nevertheless, his henchmen were busy in Austria; they assassinated Dollfuss in 1934 in an unsuccessful attempt to seize power, and Dollfuss' successor, Kurt von Schuschnigg, was obliged to devote himself almost entirely to efforts to defend his little country against its native son now dominating the Third Reich. Austria's most probable defender seemed to be Mussolini's Italy. Not only Schuschnigg but the French and English thought so, and at a conference at Stresa in 1935 the three big powers issued statements that indicated a readiness to cooperate against Germany, partly in order to preserve the independence of Austria.

Austria counted also upon France. But France was patently unprepared for war. This state of affairs was one of the justifications that the several premiers used for a policy of appeasement that characterized French foreign policy from 1935 until it blew up in their faces in 1939. But it was not the only reason that they assigned for their lack of vigor. Pacifism, internal dissensions, ambivalence toward Russia and Communism, and doubts as to whether France's major efforts should not be directed toward internal reorganization along fascist lines also were factors. In addition, the hope persisted that Mussolini could be played off against Hitler and Hitler against Stalin.

Mussolini's conquest of Ethiopia

THIS GAME was tried when Mussolini decided in 1935 to invade Ethiopia. The Duce's intention was to take revenge for Italy's old humiliation (page 506) and win a big colony at low cost. Haile Selassie, the emperor of Ethiopia, had earlier in the

British cartoonist David Low cast a satirical eye on the Italian invasion of Ethiopia and his country's reluctance to take a decisive stand against the aggression.

year appealed to the League of Nations, which again had shown characteristic reluctance to act against a big power. But when the Fascist tanks actually began to mow down the Ethiopian infantry, the universal cry of outrage became loud enough to induce the League Assembly to declare Italy an aggressor and, for the first time in its career, to invoke economic sanctions against an aggressor. Premier Pierre Laval, supported by the British minister of foreign affairs Sir Samuel Hoare, in planning to get Mussolini to compromise, proposed to go far toward meeting his demands. The resulting burst of indignation in France and England obliged both perpetrators of the Hoare-Laval "gentlemen's agreement" to resign. For a while it looked as if England supported by other Mediterranean nations might go to war in the Mediterranean with Italy. But sanctions worked unequal hardship on League members; the League had little machinery for enforcing them; and they were almost ignored by nonmembers like Germany and the United States. On the other hand, Italy's people gathered around their Duce; the British fleet, out of respect for the Italian air force, stayed close to Alexandria; and Ethiopia's barefoot, ill-equipped army was no match for Italian air bombs and poison gas. In May 1936 Mussolini declared the king of Italy emperor of Ethiopia, and by 1938 England and France as well as other countries recognized his new status.

*Popular Front
and civil war in Spain*

ELECTIONS early in 1936 found the Spanish Communists endorsing the policy of Popular Front. Hence they joined with the Socialists, Republicans, and other left-wing parties and were able to win a clear-cut victory over the Conservatives and their right-wing supporters. By a series of decrees the new leftist government resumed its reform program, amnestied its supporters condemned by earlier regimes, and silenced army officers who had monarchistic leanings or were known to have been engaged in activities inimical to the Republic. Meanwhile strikes, assassinations, burning of monasteries, street fights, and peasant riots stained the whole of Spain with bloodlettings, in which the Fascist organization known as the Falange (or Phalanx) became notorious. These developments stirred the generals to armed resistance against the Republic. The assassination of a rightist member of the Cortes gave the pretext for a general revolt. It started in July.

*Hitler's victories
in the Saar and the Rhineland*

THE SPANISH Civil War seemed made to order to serve as a proving ground for the relative strength of the Fascist parties and the Popular Front. Hitler had by this time completed his coordination of Germany. Following the lead of the Japanese and Italians in their successful defiance of international treaties and the League of Nations in Manchuria and Ethiopia, the Führer had already begun his drive for aggrandizement. In 1935 he had scored his first diplomatic victory. It was altogether in keeping with the Treaty of Versailles that the Saarland should decide by plebiscite whether to rejoin Germany. Hitler had left nothing to chance, however. He had instituted, despite League supervision, a preliminary program of propaganda and intimidation in the Saar which, together with the obvious preference of the Saarlanders for Germany, caused the plebiscite to result in a 9-to-1 triumph for the Third Reich. Hitler was then emboldened to announce German rearmament, in blunt defiance of the Versailles Treaty. Pacifism in England and France prevailed over the desire to stop him, and nothing was done. In 1936, Hitler, declaring the Locarno accords no responsibility of his, marched German troops into the Rhineland, though its disarmament had been provided by the Treaty of Versailles and confirmed at Locarno; and a few months later he resumed control of Germany's rivers. France, England, and the other signers of those treaties, having their hands full already with the Italians in Ethiopia, let him do what they probably would have kept the Weimar Republic from doing.

The triumph
of Fascism in Spain

AT THAT JUNCTION civil war broke out in Spain between the Popular Front government and army insurgents. While pacifist England and Popular Front France kept hands off what they preferred to consider an internal affair, and the United States enforced its neutrality acts (page 842), Germany and Italy used arms and troops to insure final victory to the Fascists. Volunteers fought for both sides in Spain. On one side, anti-Fascist refugees from Germany and Italy, republicans and "fellow travelers" from France, England, and the United States, Communists from Russia, and others from elsewhere rallied to the aid of the Republic's "Loyalists." On the other side, Irish Catholics, German Nazis, Italian Fascists, and others went to the aid of General Francisco Franco's "Nationalists." The powers met in nonintervention congresses and drew up solemn nonintervention regulations. But as they could not agree on a strict supervision of their regulations, volunteering continued; arms were imported by both sides; a German cruiser was attacked by the Loyalists, and English shipping by the Nationalists; and the fight became considerably more than a renewal of the old Spanish feuds over Carlism, clericalism, and provincial autonomy. Mussolini's government took small pains to hide its intervention on the side of the Nationalists, and Italian Fascist units fought the Garibaldi Division of Italian anti-Fascists in more than one battle. After two and a half years of fighting, Franco's forces, better equipped by the Germans and Italians than the Republican forces were by the Russians, counting on large Moorish contingents from Spanish Morocco, and supported by scores of thousands of Italian Fascist troops and by German naval vessels and airplanes, pushed back the Republican forces to the provinces centering on 813

Barcelona and Madrid. When Barcelona fell and a Loyalist army of about 200,000 men fled to France and was disarmed, the Republic was decisively defeated (January 1939). The Madrid government, no longer recognized even by France or England, fled to France. The National Defense Council which it left behind soon had to fight Communists as well as Nationalists because the Communists wanted to continue the hopeless struggle. In the end (March 1939) Madrid surrendered to Franco, now "Chief of the Spanish State," without condition. Franco then instituted a reign of terror that wiped out the Loyalist leaders who had not fled. German and Italian troops paraded as such in a triumphal procession in Madrid, and then withdrew from Spain, leaving Franco behind as caudillo (chief) of a ruined state in which war and terror had claimed around a million lives, not counting the maimed, the starving, and those dying of disease in the prisons.

The spread of Fascism in the smaller European states NONE OF THE smaller states of the Continent escaped Communist and Nazi infiltration altogether. In a few—Holland, Switzerland, Denmark, Sweden, and Finland—the rival ideologies were kept under control. Belgium had its Rexists. Portugal's Prime Minister Salazar, despite the ancient alliance with England, gave aid and assistance to Franco all during the Spanish Civil War. Hungary adopted the Nazi "racist" laws in 1938, openly courted Hitler's favor, and was to join the Anti-Comintern Pact (page 818) in 1939. Yugoslavia made a nonaggression pact with Italy in 1936 and exchanged assurances of friendliness with Hitler. Czar Boris of Bulgaria and King Carol of Rumania were able to keep the Nazi sympathizers of their realms in temporary check only by assuming totalitarian authority themselves. Greece gave Metaxas the post of premier for life. In Turkey, Dictator Kemal continued until his death in 1938 to introduce enlightened western practices (women got the vote in 1934, at a time when they were being urged back into the kitchen in Germany); and Ismet Inonu, who was elected president in his place, followed in his footsteps. The Baltic countries (Latvia, Estonia, and Lithuania), located between the shadows of Russia on the east and Germany on the west, were unable to unite effectively for mutual defense, despite a Baltic Pact ratified in 1934, and they resorted to domestic dictatorships. Developments favorable to Fascism took place also in Austria, Czechoslovakia, Albania, Poland, and Norway, and are detailed elsewhere. Pope Pius XI was in a difficult position. In 1931 he issued the encyclical *Quadragesimo Anno* ("In the Fortieth Year" after Leo XIII's *Rerum Novarum*), calling for voluntary solutions of the capitalist-labor problem and denouncing Communism. In a similar spirit he showed sympathy with the Spanish Nationalists against the Republic. Nevertheless he supported the Catholic clergy of Germany and Austria against Hitler's "coordination" and disapproved of the racial laws of the totalitarian states. Pius XII, who succeeded him in 1939, continued his policies.

*The Nazi concept
of total war and mobilization*

THE NAZIS made no secret of their intention to fight a total war. In fact they exploited it as a frightening propaganda weapon. Total war connotes the full application of all industrial, economic, propaganda, and military devices to the pursuit of victory without distinction between combatants and noncombatants. Total war means regarding every man, woman, and child among a hostile people as an enemy, and every man, woman, and child at home as a war resource.

In any forthcoming war the Nazis intended that the upshot should be different from that of the First World War. All the obstacles of which the German General Staff had complained in 1914-1918 were to be removed. No longer could the Reichstag challenge the government, for the Nazi parliament had been reduced to a mere assembly affirming the Nazi creed. Labor unions dared not protest forced labor, and the humanitarian voices of the churches were muted if not silent. Whatever voluntary associations still were permitted to exist were thoroughly controlled by the Nazis. And worst of all, the press was a tool in the hands of the Nazi propaganda master mind, Dr. Paul Joseph Goebbels. Not only were news and editorials tainted with the idea that Germany was a peaceful country which a hostile world, particularly the Jews, would not allow to live in peace, but also sports news, book reviews, theater critiques, and serial novels were permeated with a militaristic spirit. When a half-crazed Jewish boy in Paris assassinated a German diplomatic agent (1938), Jews, synagogues, and Jewish homes were systematically attacked all over Germany by "Brown Shirts," and a fine of one billion marks (an average of about four hundred dollars for every Jewish man, woman, and child in Germany) was extracted from the Jewish community.

The German people were gradually put in a state of total mobilization long before the shooting started. Realizing that the blockade had been one of the main causes of Germany's defeat of 1914-1918, they planned to forestall a repetition of that horror. Borrowing another leaf from the Communist book, they started the so-called Goering Four-Year Plan in 1936. Not only was industrial production for war regulated by a Nazi bureaucracy but raw materials and foodstuffs were acquired from other countries by the barter system (page 750) and stockpiled. No worker could now change his job without a special permit. Industry was told what and how much it had to produce. Labor was conscripted long before the war started. Partial rationing was introduced. Goering's famous formula "Guns instead of butter" gave eloquent expression to the Nazi military spirit. The financial system of Germany and particularly the monetary policy of the Reichsbank had already been geared to total war. Autarky had no purpose more meaningful than to supply Germany with the raw materials and the food necessary for waging just such a war. The military training of both boys and girls from the sixth year on and their indoctrination inside and outside the classroom with an

815

unquestioning martial spirit—an educational system borrowed from the Communists and the Fascists but more systematically applied by the Germans—had among its avowed aims their preparation for a total-war emergency. Ruthlessness toward political prisoners had as one of its main purposes toughening the perpetrators for the cruelties that they would have to deal out to foreign enemies. No quarter was to be given by the German master race, and they must expect none. Psychologically, economically, and militarily, Germany had been in a state of constant alert long before 1939.

Fifth columns and German propaganda abroad

THE KINGPINS in Hitler's propaganda machines outside of Germany consisted of "fifth columns." The phrase came from a remark attributed to one of Franco's generals during the attack on Madrid (page 814). He is reputed to have said that he counted not only on the four armed columns he was deploying against the city but also on a "fifth column" of henchmen within it. The fifth column was a tactic as old as Ulysses' Trojan horse. The Communists referred to their adaptation of it as "boring from within" or "infiltration." Hitler gave to this hoary device a perfection that it had not known before. More than any of the conflicts since the French Revolution, the current one was a clash of conflicting ideologies, and exponents of the Nazi ideology (Order and Power at the expense of Freedom) were found to an amazing extent within the boundaries of Germany's potential enemies.

Hitler's tactics outside Germany after 1933 were surprisingly similar to those he had used inside Germany before he came to power. He "bored from within" the ranks of intended victims or unwilling associates. In this way armies, police, political parties, and the press were either paralyzed or became his more or less ready accomplices. Once in an advantageous position, he tried to win over apprehensive businessmen, ambitious politicians, disgruntled crackpots, and racial bigots. He presented "the Nazi philosophy" expounded by his approved philosopher, Alfred Rosenberg, as the bulwark against Communism, as the destroyer of the labor-union movement. The reports concerning unsavory aspects of his rule were explained away by Goebbels' propaganda machine as Communist and Jewish lies. He repeated over and over again that it was foolish and useless to resist the inevitable.

Not all the dupes of Hitler were fifth columnists. Many patriots came to anticipate the victorious course of fascism just as by similar methods others had been persuaded to expect the eventual triumph of Communism. Charles Lindbergh was impressed by the display of Nazi military power and became a leading exponent of isolation for America. Anne Morrow Lindbergh, his wife, set forth a philosophy of order in a book entitled *Wave of the Future* (1940). The distinguished Swedish explorer Sven Hedin and the Norwegian Nobel-laureate Knut Hamsun openly showed admiration for the Nazi cult.

Businessmen everywhere felt that you could "do business with" Hitler.

The "softening up"
of French public opinion

NOR WERE all fifth columnists dupes. Some French big businessmen, for instance, fully understood Hitler's anti-French feelings but wanted to believe that he was, nevertheless, their man, ready to protect them from the demands of their own workers. Their dislike for the Third Republic with its strong Socialist Party flourished side by side with their anti-German feelings, and no doubt they regarded both emotions as signs of true French patriotism. Circumstances were soon to reveal that, for some of them, anti-Germanism was the weaker feeling of the two. As practical men, they looked upon the efficiency of the streamlined Nazi organization and liked it. It seemed to promise relief from strikes, tiring negotiations with labor unions, red tape, and the annoying inefficiencies of party politics and parliamentary procedure.

Although some of Hitler's henchmen abroad were doubtless bought with Nazi money or honors, most, like Tacitus' Senators, voluntarily "rushed into slavery." Hitler had to spend little money for converting surprising numbers of foreign writers, artists, journalists, musicians, and actors. Lifelong anti-Germans like Charles Maurras, Léon Daudet, and their fellow-royalists of the Action Française were ripe for fascism. Always critical of the disunity that they considered the direct outcome of democratic freedom, they had even quarreled with the Roman Catholic Church in 1926, and their journal had been placed on the Index. Now they became well disposed toward Nazi Germany. So many other writers, scholars, and scientists, particularly in France, accepted the Nazis for one reason or another that Benda felt called upon to enter the lists once more in defense of democracy. His defense was entitled *The Great Test of the Democracies*. The manuscript, however, had to be smuggled out of France and published in New York (1942), because his country was by that time under the heel of the Nazis.

The real dupes among Hitler's fifth columnists were likely to be genuine pacifists. They honestly believed Hitler's contention that he meant nothing but peace and wanted only to be let alone to work out Germany's destiny. Ever since the holocaust of the First World War a very large fraction of Europe's population had been strongly pacifist. In France their leaders were often grammar-school and high-school teachers (who in Europe are generally male). Their pacifist propaganda fortified the French "Maginot psychology," leaving France unprepared spiritually or militarily to deal with a well-prepared enemy. The French *instituteur* (schoolmaster) was frequently a left-winger, sympathetic with the Popular Front, but he was frequently a pacifist as well. He was at this stage of the conflict likely to oppose expenditures for war purposes in favor of expenditures for domestic reform. Thus, whether he liked it or not, he shared the "Maginot psychology" of the anti-Semitic, anti-Socialist groups among his compatriots who openly stated a contrary preference: "Hitler rather than Léon Blum."

WHERE NECESSARY, Hitler did not hesitate to titillate the pocket nerve or the ambitions. Some trusted officials of foreign countries became fifth columnists of Hitler. Such people could not be "bribed," in the ordinary sense of the word, but they could be drawn into Hitler's orbit by the inducement of shares in the financial or industrial enterprises the Nazis might acquire or by the prospect of high office once the Nazis were triumphant. In this way, he won over the Norwegian official, Major Vidkun Quisling, whose name was to become a synonym for "traitor." Hitler rarely worked by common bribery except in cases where he founded pro-Nazi newspapers or magazines in foreign countries. Some of those publications were cleverly disguised as literary, art, fashion, or gossip sheets, all of them with a strong anti-Semitic bias.

A method of fifth columnism that worked well with the "small" man—the nonintellectual, nonofficial, nonsocialist artisan, farmer or worker—was "infiltration." It was borrowed from the Communist Third International but effectively modified. Hitler tried that method with varying success in Norway, the Balkans, the Americas, and elsewhere. Nazis would, like Communists, try to place sympathizers in key positions in government, unions, clubs, lodges, and other organizations. Infiltration proceeded also through the welding together of people of German "Aryan" descent, the setting-up of paramilitary organizations, huge parades, military exercises, pep talks, racial propaganda, whispering campaigns against the legitimate government, the disparagement of parliamentary processes, and little Führers like Sir Oswald Mosley in England, Léon Degrelle in Belgium, Fritz Kuhn in the United States, Colonel François de la Rocque in France, Arthur Seyss-Inquart in Austria, or Conrad Henlein in Czechoslovakia.

*The creation
of the Anti-Comintern Pact*

THE GERMAN Nazis had been studiously cultivating their Fascist colleagues by exchange of visits and friendly gestures. By 1935, when the League of Nations was being stultified in the Ethiopian debacle (page 812), three great powers had openly defied it: Japan and Germany had withdrawn, and Italy had refused to stop her aggression. Italy's loyalty to the Stresa front did not, however, vanish entirely during the Ethiopian fiasco. Despite the Duce's displeasure with France and England, he joined with them in protesting the German remilitarization of the Rhineland in 1936. But he was now an easy mark for Hitler's cajolery. When the Spanish Civil War broke out, the Anglo-French eagerness to prohibit intervention and the Italo-German intention to intervene came into direct conflict. A few months afterwards (October 1936), a formal entente of the Duce and the Führer was announced. From their subsequent support of each other this agreement came to be called the Rome-Berlin Axis. It was followed within a month by a Tokyo-Berlin Axis, which was obviously intended to serve as a counterweight to the Franco-Russian Alliance of 1935, although it was labeled an anti-Communist pact. By November of the next year Italy joined this anti-Communist pact to form a Berlin-Rome-Tokyo triangle known as the Anti-Comintern Pact. These pacts were in fact more than mere manifestos in a war of ideologies; they marked rather a conflict for Lebensraum of the self-pitying "have not" capitals against the "have" capitals— Moscow, Paris, London, and Washington.

The destruction of Austrian independence HITLER'S support of Italy in Ethiopia and Spain and of Japan in Manchuria and China was repaid by their loyalty as he now began to build his New Order in central Europe. His first aggressive step outside of Germany's old boundaries was directed against Austria. Schuschnigg and other European statesmen were still counting on Italy to keep Germany out of Austria and away from the Brenner Pass, the gateway to Italy. They were not prepared therefore for the browbeating which Schuschnigg received when he visited Hitler in February 1938; and when the Austrian chancellor complied with Hitler's demands by giving the Austrian Nazis full amnesty and leading posts in his government, they were not prepared for the wholesale disorders that followed, engineered by Nazis all over Austria. Schuschnigg's reply was to promise a plebiscite on whether Austria should remain independent, but, without waiting for the outcome, the German army in March moved into Austria. Schuschnigg resigned, and Seyss-Inquart became chancellor and proclaimed the union of Austria with Germany. A subsequent plebiscite approved the union by nearly 100 per cent. France and England, of course, protested. But Italy did nothing. The next August, Mussolini applied "racial" laws copied after Germany's to Italy's Jews and "non-Aryans."

The question of Czechoslovak independence HITLER'S next major blow was directed at Czechoslovakia. The Sudeten Germans had organized as a party under Henlein's leadership in 1934. The party grew rapidly when Czechoslovakia joined the Franco-Soviet pact of 1935 (page 806) and became the second largest of the nation's numerous parties despite the fact that it represented a minority nationality. By 1937 it had committed itself to a demand for autonomy for the Sudetenland. As Hitler's designs on Austria and Goebbels' denunciations of Czech pro-Communism and mistreatment of Sudeten Germans became more menacing, the Czech government (under Beneš as president since Masaryk's resignation in 1935) sought to defend itself by understandings with Austria, by building up its armaments, by police measures against Henlein's party, and by other measures. The government's measures led to further recriminations. To Henlein's demands for full equality of Germans with Czechs, autonomy for the Sudetenland, and a reversal of the country's foreign policy, the government made definite but unaccepted concessions; and to reports of German military maneuvers on its borders, it replied with mobilization.

So long as the Czechs felt that they could count on their allies, the Russians and the French, they were not afraid. But it soon became clear, from a special British emissary sent to Prague, that Britain was anxious to avoid war even if the Czech government had to make concessions it considered unworthy and unwise. Both sides took steps preparatory to war all during the summer of 1938, but in September Prime Minister Chamberlain, armed with his umbrella, went personally to see Hitler at the Führer's fortified mountain aerie in Berchtesgaden and came back convinced that a sacrifice by Czechoslovakia would save the cause of peace. Premier Édouard Daladier of France fell in with this decision, and both Daladier and Chamberlain put pressure on Beneš to accept. Although the Russian government did not join in this program of appeasement, Beneš reluctantly gave in. Thereupon Chamberlain went back to Germany and met Hitler at Godesberg. But Hitler's demands upon Czechoslovakia were now greater than Chamberlain had expected. They involved not only outright cession of Sudeten German lands but also plebiscites in other doubtful areas. Chamberlain returned home without accepting the new terms. War might have come immediately had not Mussolini, Roosevelt, and other interested statesmen joined Chamberlain in urging a conference to reëxamine the situation.

The conference at Munich and the collapse of Czechoslovakia

THE CONFERENCE met at Munich. Czechoslovakia was not invited to send a representative; Russia was not invited to send a representative; but Mussolini was present with a staff; and so were Hitler, Chamberlain, and Daladier. When their all-day meetings were done, Chamberlain and Daladier had been won over not only to granting Hitler's earlier demands but also to giving Poland and Hungary each a share of Czechoslovakia so as to leave a rump nation without any dissatisfied minorities. "Munich" has since come to mean in every language "peace without honor." Beneš resigned and sought refuge in the United States, as German, Polish, and Hungarian armies carried out the first partition of Czechoslovakia.

The delirious jubilation with which Chamberlain and Daladier were greeted upon returning from Munich proved that the French and the English were inclined to peace at almost any price. Nevertheless, the British were aroused. The government stepped up its airplane and war production, bought planes from the United States, and for the first time in a period of peace introduced military conscription. Daladier modified the forty-hour week and other workmen's benefits, despite a general strike in favor of them, and also speeded up armaments production. The Popular Front fell apart.

Rump Czechoslovakia quickly gave up the ghost. The Slovaks and the Ruthenians claimed and established their autonomy as Slovakia and Carpatho-Ruthenia respectively. Communists, Jews and other "non-Aryans," Freemasons, and other despised or suspect groups were made subject to various disabilities. The new president of autonomous Slovakia, Emil Hacha, quarreled with the new premier, Joseph Tiso. Tiso appealed to Hitler for support, and Hitler obliged by establishing a German protectorate over Bohemia and Moravia first and then by recognizing Slovakia as an "independent" republic and "ally" of Germany (March 1939). Hungary annexed Carpatho-Ruthenia. And so came about the apparent end of the only democratic state in eastern Europe. England and France, having solemnly guaranteed rump Czechoslovakia at Munich, stood revealed in all their helpless nakedness. But the occupation of Prague proved a turning point. Neither pacifists nor pro-Germans could easily persuade themselves any longer that Hitler's aggressions were intended only to unite Germans or to undo the wrongs of the Versailles *Diktat*.

The nonaggression pact between Germany and Russia

SINCE NOTHING worthy of respect seemed as yet to stand in the way, Hitler now reannexed Memel, and Italy annexed Albania. The Spanish Civil War having at the same time come to a close, the caudillo now joined the German Führer, the Italian Duce, and the Japanese mikado in the Anti-Comintern Pact, whose chief victims so far had not been the Comintern.

Although he had made a ten-year nonaggression pact with Poland in 1934, Hitler indicated that his next targets were the Free City of Danzig and the Polish Corridor. France already had a mutual assistance treaty with Poland. Great Britain now changed her do-nothing course and signed a similar agreement with Poland. The spring and summer of 1939 were spent in a scramble for allies, but few thought that a general war would actually ensue. Even Hitler, people supposed, would hesitate to attack Danzig and Poland against the combined wishes of England, France, and Russia. Stalin, however, with his exclusion from the Munich negotiations in mind and in apprehension that Russia might have to bear the brunt of Germany's attack, insisted on promises of armed support, on joint intervention, if necessary, in the Baltic and Balkan states that acted as buffers between Russia and Germany, and on the right to send troops into Poland. For all of these points his would-be allies showed some distaste. The Russian demands struck them as an attempt to tie their hands while Russia extended her sway over neighboring states the better to defend them against Germany. Obliged to choose between the probable aggrandizement of Nazi Germany and of Communist Russia, England and France hung undecided.

While his opponents hesitated, Hitler reversed his policy. He asked Russia for a pact of nonaggression. Stalin proved amenable. Promptly a treaty was signed providing neutrality if either signatory were attacked by a third party; and it also secretly provided that in the event of a Polish defeat in a 821

Rhineland
remilitarized
1936

Germany annexes
Memel, March 1939

GERMANY

Russo-German Pact, August 1939

POLAND

U S S R

Civil War in Spain
1936-1939

Saar plebiscite
1935

Czechoslovakia annexed
piecemeal 1938-1939

Austrian Anschluss
1938

SPAIN

Madrid   Barcelona

Italy annexes Albania
April 1939

ITALY

Rome-Berlin-Tokyo axis 1936

Italy takes
Ethiopia 1935

TOTALITARIANISM
ON THE MARCH 1931-1939

German-Polish war, Russia was to have a sphere of influence in the Baltic states, eastern Poland, and Bessarabia as compensation for German control in western Poland and Lithuania. In return for his sudden reversal of policy Stalin thus got some claims to territory in case of war between his potential enemies as well as a chance to remain neutral while they fought it out. Hitler's recompense was release from the dread of a two-front war.

*The final steps
toward the Second World War*

WHEN THE Russo-German non-aggression pact was signed (August 23, 1939), the rest of the world was astounded. The Anti-Comintern Pact became meaningless except as a pact against the democracies, and the Franco-Russian Alliance burst in thin air. Hitler immediately began to establish his control of Danzig and now

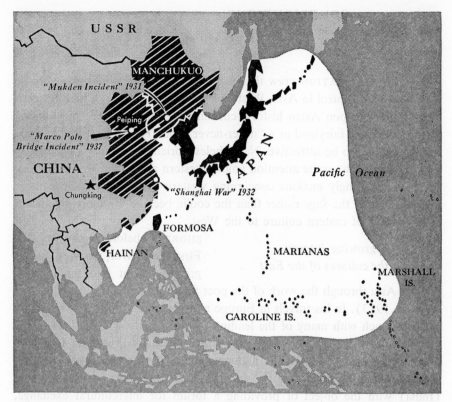

In the 1930's the Fascist governments of Japan, Italy, and Germany won some cheap victories in Asia, Africa, and Europe in the face of weak protest from the western powers and the League. (The solid black areas represent Fascist holdings as of 1931; hatched areas indicate later acquisitions or diplomatic triumphs.) In one of these, Spain became a testing ground for opposing Fascist and Communist maneuvers, as the western powers remained neutral; and the republic succumbed to the Fascists' attack. Hitler had meanwhile overrun Austria and been appeased in Czechoslovakia. Then, in 1939, Fascist Germany and Communist Russia signed a nonaggression pact. The German bogey of a two-front war was laid, and Germany put western indecision to still another test, the attack on Poland.

demanded special privileges in the Polish Corridor. Despite appeals and warnings from Chamberlain, Daladier, and Roosevelt, and in the midst of pacific negotiations, he launched a full-scale attack on Poland (September 1) without a formal declaration of war.

Hitler hoped that the appeasing governments of France and Great Britain, unprepared and deprived of Russia's support, would wring their hands and do nothing. But there Hitler made his first great miscalculation. France and Great Britain feared that their turn would come sooner or later, and perhaps sooner if Russia remained loyal to Hitler. His nonaggression pact with Russia for the purpose of destroying Poland also destroyed most of the support he had gained from anti-Communist sentiment in Great Britain and France. On September 3, the two western democracies declared war on Germany, and the Second World War was on.

CONTRIBUTIONS

AND CONFLICTS OF THE EAST

As THE REALIZATION grew that the western powers would probably be unable to keep control in Asia, Westerners ceased to look with merely sentimental interest upon Asian history, customs, literature, art or knickknacks. Far from being a fairyland or a "never-never" country, the East had become too threatening to be attractive. Nevertheless, oriental precepts for everyday living continued to excite attention among western artists and writers as they became increasingly anxious concerning western inadequacies. Once more the warrior and the sage rather than the coolie became the more significant embodiments of eastern culture to the West.

The growing interest in the cultures of the East

SHORTLY before and after the First World War, the West gained greater insight into the civilizations of Asia through the work of the poet Sir Rabindranath Tagore (Nobel laureate, 1913). In his travels in Europe and America in the 1920's, Tagore came in touch with many of the leading literary figures. His lectures in the metropolises of Europe and America decried nationalism, whether Indian or other, and spread a sympathetic understanding of Indian concepts of art and personality. He established an International University at Santiniketan (India) with the object of providing a forum for intercultural exchange. Though constantly critical of the materialism of the West and particularly of the class-struggle doctrine of the Russian Communists, Tagore stressed in his teachings the essential equality of all peoples under God. He sought to convince Oriental and Occidental of their need to work together. Perhaps Tagore's message to the peoples of the world can best be expressed by his oft-quoted aphorism: "Men are cruel, but Man is kind."

Tagore's message was all the more persuasive because of recent events. Sympathetic souls in the West saw in Gandhi an embodiment of the great leader who was trying by nonviolent means to achieve a national unity that in the West was being pursued with guns and whips. The carnage and pitiful waste attending the First World War had helped to upset the intellectual complacency of the West. Wells' popular *Outline of History* brought the Orient into the mainstream of human development in a way that no popular writer had previously made clear. Sanskrit studies had deep roots in Germany, and numerous translations of Hindu and Buddhist works appeared in the interwar years. In Hitler's Third Reich an affinity between the German "Aryans" and their Indian and Japanese counterparts was presumed. The Anti-Comintern Pact with Japan (page 819) acted as an incentive to serious study also of Japanese institutions and traditions.

824   A growing number of scholarly studies, popularizations, and works of

realistic fiction gave the English-speaking world a more detailed and accurate knowledge of oriental life and literature than it had previously possessed. The numerous descriptive works of Lin Yutang, especially *My Country and My People* (1935), provided intimate glimpses into the attitudes and beliefs of the Chinese. Excellent translations of Chinese poetry and prose by Arthur David Waley and Florence Ayscough helped introduce some elements of the Chinese literary tradition into the stream of English literature. The novels of Pearl Buck, especially *The Good Earth* (1931), put China on the best-seller lists and in the movies for over a decade. The fiction of Alice Tisdale Hobart, especially *Oil for the Lamps of China* (1933), brought out vividly for western readers and movie-goers the conflict in the Orient between the old and the new.

The influence of theosophy and Buddhism

SINCE THE beginning of the twentieth century, moralists had sought to find a sedative for western materialism in the mystical and exotic profundities of Tibetan Buddhism and Hinduism. Introduced to the West by Mme. H. P. Blavatsky, theosophy soon made converts, notably in Berlin literary circles. Profoundly affected by the "mysterious East," Yeats stressed in his poetry its occult and spiritual qualities. D. H. Lawrence, too, sought refuge in eastern lore in his effort to escape western rigidity of life and art. E. M. Forster's *A Passage to India* (1924) stressed the mystical character of personal relations. Suspicious of the modern world, Aldous Huxley sought to compound a panacea by refurbishing in his novels the teachings of Vedantism (an offshoot of Hinduism) and Buddhism; his conversion to metaphysical mysticism is recorded in *Eyeless in Gaza* (1936). Irving Babbitt, professor of French literature at Harvard, became an avid reader of Buddhist and Taoist texts; and convinced that neither the Enlightenment's rationalist nor the Rousseauan romanticist had grasped the enduring precepts of oriental thought, he stressed Buddhism's conviction that men possess both a "higher will" and the obligation to exercise it. Hence, in part at least, came his insistence upon a disciplined education (page 837).

Oriental models in occidental letters and music

WRITERS of the West sometimes imitated oriental literary models and adapted oriental literary themes. In France, experimentation with Japanese verse forms continued to attract the interest of poets, and the symbolists studied and commented seriously upon oriental esthetic theories. Even before 1914, French poets had begun to write lyrical epigrams consciously modeled upon the Japanese haikai (verses in three lines of five, seven, and five syllables each), and after the war they not only continued these poetical experiments but in addition wrote imaginative prose based on Far Eastern themes. Though also indebted to French *Japonisme,* the British and American poets of the imagist circle were particularly moved by the richness of Chinese literature and the humane   825 quality of Chinese manners. Recent English translations of Chinese master-pieces, new histories of Chinese literature, and especially Judith Gautier's classic *Livre de Jade* influenced these rebellious spirits of the twentieth century to experiment with themes and forms. Ezra Pound based his *Cathay* (1915) upon notes about Chinese poetry left to him by an orientalist scholar for whom he acted as literary executor. To John Gould Fletcher, another leading imagist, Chinese poems meant (in his own words) "an enormous revolution in English poetic technique." Amy Lowell also experimented with verses in the Chinese vein. Witter Bynner in his "Caravan" (1925) expressed the sentiments of many of his contemporaries:

> I went away a Western man
> But I'm coming back in a caravan.[1]

In music, too, the West occasionally borrowed from Asia. Since the world's fair of 1900 in Paris, oriental music and instruments had figured in western exhibitions and concerts. Debussy had been interested in the *salendro* scale employed in Javanese music and is said to have modeled his whole tone scale upon it. Mahler and Puccini employed oriental themes. Louis Laloy, French musical critic and teacher, visited the Orient and wrote an appreciative history of Chinese music as well as an account of his impressions in the *Mirror of China* (1933).

The importation of oriental products to the West
ONE OF THE most fruitful importations in the West from the Far East was the humble soybean.
Though first introduced in 1804, it was not widely grown in the United States until the end of the First World War. Particularly suitable for large-scale agri-culture, the soybean has become a crop of the first rank in the plains states. Since 1919, its production in the United States has multiplied sixteen times, largely because of the complications in Manchuria, which produced most of the world's soy crop, and in 1939 more than 8,000,000 American acres were given to it. In Europe, the soybean has usually been grown only in limited quantities, generally for fodder, and almost exclusively in the eastern coun-tries. In America, on the other hand, it has been used increasingly for a flour rich in proteins and in the manufacture of plastics, oil, ink, and other indus-trial products.

In drugs, too, the Far East has contributed significantly to Europe and America. Chaulmoogra oil (derived from the seed of a tree usually found in southeast Asia) has recently been applied in the treatment of leprosy and skin diseases. In 1887 a Japanese chemist prepared from a Chinese drug an alkaloid which since 1925 has been developed as ephedrine in the West and used with good results in the treatment of asthma. The possible efficacy of other drugs from the great Chinese herbarium is under regular study in the United States.

Even Chinese economic institutions have had their admirers in the West. Henry A. Wallace, before he became American secretary of agriculture (1933), had been impressed by the actual operations of the ancient Chinese system of "the ever normal granary," familiar in the West primarily as the system Joseph had inaugurated in Old Testament Egypt. In his writings, Wallace repeatedly credited the Chinese for the inspiration of his own plan. He proposed that the government purchase grain from the farmers in fat harvest years for storage in government granaries against the lean years, when it should be sold at a fixed and reasonable price, thus keeping a balance between supply and demand. Through the reforms instituted after 1933, the ever normal granary became an aim of New Deal policy.

Confusion in Asia's loyalties — THE ATTRACTIVENESS of oriental wisdom, however, did not diminish the reality of the peril to western control in the East. A great threat to both western imperialism and Communist activity in colonial Asia came in the interwar years from Japanese expansion. Having obtained the mandate over the Marshalls, the Marianas, the Palaus, and the Carolines, the Japanese entrenched themselves securely in the Pacific region. In their commercial program of the twenties, the Japanese undertook to produce the cheap consumers' goods required by the poverty-stricken natives of the region. By catering to such needs, the Japanese were able to obtain an increasingly larger share of the colonial market. Eventually, as they became bolder, they spearheaded their expansion program with an appeal to the less powerful peoples of Asia to cooperate with their great Asiatic neighbor in the development of a community which would be at the same time anti-Communist and independent of the West. For a time Japan's program of "Asia for the Asiatics" evoked a deep and sincere response among the Asiatics, matching the concern it created in the western capitals. As it gradually became clear, however, that the Japanese were also bent upon exploiting and controlling the nativist movements, some natives turned once again in the Communists' direction, but the Japanese program continued to attract a genuine following among the non-Communists in the fight for independence. Even sophisticated Europeans found it hard to evaluate the conflicting propaganda of Caucasian imperialists, Caucasian Communists, oriental imperialists, and native autonomists; the four-cornered ring made for great confusion in the minds of politically inexperienced Asiatics, particularly after 1936, as Comintern and Anti-Comintern maneuvered for advantage.

*The government of India
on the eve of a new world war*

IN INDIA still another factor added to the confusion—religious animosities among the natives. The first elections under the Government of India Act of 1935 took place early in 1937, when members of the various provincial legislatures were chosen. The Hindu independence party of Gandhi and Nehru was generally successful in these elections, and since it opposed the new constitution, the center of political attention shifted from the application of the constitution to the control of the All-India Congress. A tug of war ensued between the moderates under Gandhi and the radicals under Nehru. Meanwhile Jinnah's Moslem League (page 741) had grown and had become more persistent in its demands for Pakistan, an independent Moslem state; and a wing of the Congress developed to the left of Nehru which came out for more rapid socialism than Nehru thought he could advocate. Hence Nehru drew close again to Gandhi. In 1939 Gandhi appeared to have regained control of the Congress. The European war broke out, however, before a satisfactory solution of the problem of India could be found.

*Nationalist agitation
in southeast Asia and the islands*

IN BURMA AND Indochina, nationalistic groups had begun to call insistently for an end to colonial rule. In Indochina the French steadfastly refused to succumb to such demands, and unrest mounted swiftly. The British in Burma, as in India, were more inclined to satisfy the demand for reform and independence gradually. Until 1935 the British administered Burma as the largest province of India (page 420). In response to the increasing pressure for home rule and autonomy, they permitted Burma in 1937 to have its own constitution and government, and a position of qualified dominion status within the British Commonwealth of Nations. In Malaya, however, the British maintained the system of federated, unfederated, and crown states that had developed during the nineteenth century.

An anticolonial ferment seethed also in the insular areas of the southwestern Pacific. In the East Indies, and especially in Java, the Dutch were confronted by a swiftly growing nationalist movement in which the Communists were particularly active. Determined to hold their highly profitable islands securely, the Dutch pursued an uncompromising policy that was at the same time paternalistic. Demands for self-government were either stifled or ignored.

Unlike the Dutch in the Indies, the Americans in the Philippines yielded to Filipino demands by granting immediate reforms looking toward eventual independence. After the Jones Act of 1916 facilitated the transfer of Filipino offices to natives, native leaders had come to the fore, and the independence movement had won striking victories. The Republican administration in the United States of the 1920's temporarily checked the movement toward self-government with the argument that the islands were not yet ready to assume the full responsibility of independence. But the Tydings-McDuffie Act (page 784), accepted in 1934 by both the American Congress and the Philippine legislature, permitted the Philippine Islands eventually to become the first of the colonial states of Asia to win independence. In the intervening years, the Communists and the Japanese looked to the day when American political and military control would be removed from the islands.

The Popular Front in the politics of China

SINCE 1931 the Japanese had been using the puppet state of Manchukuo as a continental base for operations against the northern provinces of China. Japan's aggressive policy had the effect of switching the main interest of the Kuomintang from the effort to rebuild China toward the struggle to remain free of Japanese control. Nevertheless, the Chinese won a certain amount of success in both areas by 1937. They established a temporary solidarity at home, thanks in part to the Comintern's policy after 1935 of a Popular Front against Fascism (page 806) but more to a curious episode in the personal career of Chiang Kai-shek. In December 1936 he was kidnaped by a pro-Communist, anti-Japanese warlord, and not released until he had promised a greater degree of cooperation with the Communists. By the same token Chiang won an increased amount of financial and moral support in Russia. The outspoken bitterness in the West against Japanese aggressiveness also encouraged the Chinese. Unfortunately the same factors contributed in no small measure to Japan's determination to act quickly and forcefully in China.

Government by the military in Japan

ALTHOUGH the Japanese extremists after 1933 suffered occasional setbacks, the march toward totalitarianism moved ahead relentlessly along several avenues at the same time. Efforts of intellectuals, industrialists, and statesmen to halt the advance were quickly checked by assassination, terror, or military action. Terrorism in the name of patriotism became such a universal menace that in 1936 when a military group mutinied in Tokyo they openly refused even to obey an imperial command—almost unbelievable behavior in imperial Japan. The mutineers of 1936 also murdered several cabinet officers and occupied Tokyo's police headquarters, the Diet building, and the War Ministry. Although the mutiny was quelled after several days, it brought forcefully home to all Japanese that the militarists would stop at nothing to achieve their objectives. The government was now openly dominated by the military. Japan shortly joined with Nazi Germany in the Anti-Comintern Pact (page 819).

Successful in their military and political adventures, the Japanese militarists were at the same time reshaping their country's economy to fit the requirements of expansion. Control and regimentation of industry, trade, and agriculture became the watchwords of the economic planners. Regimentation involved reorganization of the nation's productive and distributive capacities for the purpose of providing the basic needs of a frank imperialism. Concentration upon these strategic requirements, however, helped to produce a shortage of consumers' goods and services. The ambitions of the military also forced the government to borrow, to print paper money, and thus to devalue the currency. These measures contributed to the forces already at work to encourage the rise of prices. Despite the efforts to regulate Japan's economy, wages and salaries lagged behind the sensational price increases of the 1930's. For the urban laborer and for professional and clerical workers on fixed incomes, inflation was a disaster. It served the temporary objectives of the military, however, by advancing the income of the agricultural groups and of certain business elements from which the government derived support.

Lest the critics of the "positive" program find an audience, education, religion, and mass media of communication were placed under strict control. The history taught in the schools became little more than "patriotic" propaganda: Japan always occupied the center of the stage, and all her acts were glorified. "Right thinking" along traditional lines was stressed in both schools and religious services, and "Japanese virtues" were universally extolled. The newspapers, periodicals, moving pictures, and radio were subjected to strict censorship. Discussion of topics that might have led to "dangerous thoughts" was not permitted in print or on the air. The Central News Agency (Domei) was the principal bureau of censorship, and it was charged with close scrutiny of all public information.

The "China incident"
and international repercussions
THE GREATEST failure of the "New Order" was its inability to wind up affairs in China. Advertised at home as a national crusade that would quickly bring stability to eastern Asia, the Chinese venture bogged Japan's army down and seriously drained her slender resources in arms and other materials of war. As the Chinese complications became more raveled, all groups combined efforts to bring the national mission to a successful end. An ever-widening circle of maneuvers, however, kept requiring larger and larger sacrifices at home, which were unswervingly exacted from all groups by the determined militarists in power.

Many Japanese had already begun to wonder whether the scales of fortune might not as readily tip away from their side as toward it when what the Japanese euphemistically called the "China incident" began. In July 1937 a Japanese force attacked some Chinese units stationed near the Marco Polo Bridge in Peiping. It was not long before the war spread to distant as well as nearby parts of China, while the capitals of the western world sought some diplomatic method for handling still another Sino-Japanese conflict. As on the occasion of the Manchurian incident, the Nanking government appealed immediately to the League of Nations. By 1937, however, the prestige of the white powers had suffered heavily in Asia, and the prestige of Japan was at its peak. Moreover, since Germany by this time had joined Japan in withdrawing from the League, it was a foregone conclusion that collective action short of sanctions or war would be even less effective than on the occasion of the Mukden outbreak.

In Geneva and Washington action was prompt but ineffective. Protests were drafted urging upon both parties to the "incident" the cessation of hostilities and the acceptance of mediation. Tokyo quickly rejected British and American offers to mediate and reiterated Japan's determination to deal with China directly and without the restraining influence of outsiders. In the League's deliberations it was decided, with special urging from the United States, to convene a meeting of the signatories of the Nine-Power Pact and others at Brussels. A special invitation to the Soviet Union was accepted, but Japan, supported by Germany, refused to be party to any international discussions of the "China incident."

The Brussels meetings lasted for three weeks in November, but almost nothing was accomplished. Russia called for positive action. Britain urged moderation. And Italy, since 1936 an open ally of Germany and a recent member of the Anti-Comintern Pact, withdrew in protest from the meetings. The American delegation pursued a wavering and uncertain course. The final conference report risked no positive recommendations, and the powers committed themselves only to the debatable generalization that "force can provide no just and lasting solution for disputes between nations."

Japan's "Co-Prosperity Sphere" and undeclared war against China — IN CHINA, meanwhile, the Japanese continued to carry out their program of a "New Order." Not yet committed wholly to conquest, the Japanese sought to force the Nanking regime to adopt a more conciliatory and cooperative attitude. After capturing many of China's major cities, they defined their "New Order" as "a tripartite relationship of mutual aid and co-ordination between Japan, Manchukuo, and China.... to secure international justice, to perfect the joint defense against Communism, and to create a new culture and realize a close economic cohesion throughout East Asia."

The coordination of China into Japan's "New Order" was to be accomplished through the medium of puppets. The Japanese moved very rapidly into China, even attacking the American gunboat *Panay* and other American shipping in the process. They established two separate provisional governments with headquarters at Peiping and Nanking, as the Kuomintang government painfully retreated west to Chungking in the mountainous province of Szechwan. Tokyo, meanwhile, through the good offices of the German ambassador in China, sought again to win Chiang Kai-shek over by offering to 831 make him ruler of a united China upon Japan's terms and as an integral part of the "New Order." To these blandishments Chiang remained aloof. After another period of dickering with various candidates, the Japanese struck a bargain in 1938 with Wang Ching-wei, old rival of Chiang, to head a Japanese-sponsored government of China. This new government was not actually proclaimed until 1940.

Nor was Wang the only Chinese to collaborate with the Japanese. After the withdrawal of Chiang's government into the hinterlands of western China in 1938, other malcontents and defeatists deserted the Kuomintang. Discouraged by continuous defeats, many Chinese believed that compromise with Japan was preferable to close association with the Communists or with the predatory powers of the West. The hopelessness of Chiang's position and the ineffectiveness of foreign aid seemed to others to call for a reassessment of China's aims and objectives. In other words, to a substantial number of influential Chinese the national welfare seemed to require some sort of compromise with the Japanese. In their estimation, little could be expected from a government located in remote Chungking whose authority was challenged by Communists and Japanese puppets alike.

The problems of the Chungking government

DESPITE the genuine efforts of the Nationalist government to maintain resistance and to plan simultaneously for the reconstruction of the country, defeatism was rampant in Chungking itself. Conservatives were afraid that growing dependence upon the West would lead Chiang to concede an increasingly greater role to liberals and Communists. In their determination to prevent the control of the government from slipping out of their hands, the right-wing members of the Kuomintang fought doggedly and successfully against reform. As the war settled into a stalemate, the old domestic hostilities, which had been temporarily erased, came back with renewed strength.

Uncontrolled inflation also played havoc with the economy of "Free China." Black markets were protected by corrupt officials who used them for their own private profiteering. Although the government called for sacrifice and patriotic service, open corruption flourished in the army and in civilian offices. Industrial cooperatives proved strikingly effective for a period in marshaling the limited and varied industrial resources of unoccupied China, but the government gradually withdrew its support from the movement, since it was looked upon with suspicion and disfavor by the seaport capitalists, merchants, and private industrialists. Reorganizations of local government and limitations upon provincial autonomy were among the most positive accomplishments to the credit of the Chungking regime. Even here, however, the government's failure to proceed democratically made it subject to criticism from domestic and foreign observers. Nevertheless, until the outbreak of the

832

European war in 1939, the Chungking regime managed—nominally, at least, in cooperation with the Chinese Communists—to maintain resistance against the Japanese and to hold together a coalition of disparate political groups.

AN AMERICAN GENERATION

LOST AND FOUND

THE AMERICAN youth of the 1920's was dubbed by the expatriate writer Gertrude Stein the "lost generation." It was "lost," not physically, as was the youth of Europe, which had died by the millions on the battlefield, but because it had lost touch with the traditional values of the prewar generation and was groping for other values to take their place. In a sense, this was also a "found" generation, one that was discovered by the rest of the world. Sinclair Lewis in 1930 was the first American man of letters to win a Nobel prize, and after him three other Americans of this generation (Eugene O'Neill, Pearl Buck, and William Faulkner) and the American-born T. S. Eliot were to win that recognition. Less exceptionally than in the earlier days, American literature was recognized as worthy of respect abroad. American men of science also won greater recognition abroad than had once been commonly meted out to them. By the 1930's the intellectuals had begun to find themselves again—usually in a set of political creeds ranging from Ezra Pound's pro-Fascism, through the "brain trust's" New Deal, to pro-Communism. The politics of the nation remained essentially isolationist, however, despite the tendencies nudging it in an anti-Fascist direction.

Literature during the "Jazz Age" THE ERA OF the "lost generation" became known also by novelist F. Scott Fitzgerald's term the "Jazz Age" because of its affinity for the blatant tones and elemental rhythm of the syncopated music that blossomed in the twenties. Fitzgerald's novels, notably *This Side of Paradise* (1920) and *The Great Gatsby* (1925), portrayed rather sympathetically the frenzied gaiety, the aimless carousing, the loveless sex life, and the intellectual futility to which prosperity and lack of faith condemned the "lost generation." Edna St. Vincent Millay put this bohemian spirit into numerous quotable and lilting stanzas. Though titled with words borrowed from literary classics, Hemingway's novels of the twenties were likewise in the new spirit. Probably the most memorable were *The Sun Also Rises* (1926), which dealt with the loves of the postwar generation, and *Farewell to Arms* (1929), which returned to the war for its setting and centered around the panic of the Italian retreat at Caporetto. Written in an unorthodox, uninhibited, stripped, colloquial style, they reflected the cynicism and embitterment brought by the war and the rootlessness of the generation 833 that had matured in its shadow. John Dos Passos' portrayal in *Three Soldiers* (1921) of character disintegration through military regimentation and boredom was followed in *Manhattan Transfer* (1925) by a study of the devastating effect of life in a materialistic and success-seeking metropolis.

Social criticism through fiction and drama

OTHER WRITERS less intimately associated with the "lost generation" also arraigned the American industrial culture for its shortcomings. H. L. Mencken in 1924 founded his monthly magazine *American Mercury,* in which he wielded a sophisticated and caustic pen "to combat, chiefly by ridicule, American piety, stupidity, tinpot morality, cheap chauvinism in all their forms," and became the arbiter of literary taste and the fount of wisdom for younger intellectuals who joined him in his attack on the "booboisie." Ring Lardner's and Damon Runyon's short stories chronicled with good-natured satire and in the slang of the semi-literate the struggles and frustrations of "lowbrow" and demimonde characters who tried to achieve the universal goal of wealth and success. Sinclair Lewis, in *Main Street* (1920), *Babbitt* (1922), *Arrowsmith* (1925), *Elmer Gantry* (1927), and other novels satirized the smugness, boredom, venality, and intolerance of the small towns of the Middle West, where, however, the local physician was likely to be an admirable character. Sherwood Anderson's short stories in *Winesburg, Ohio* (1919) and his novel *Poor White* (1920) were likewise indictments of small-town provincialism. Theodore Dreiser, still the brooding realist, produced his masterpiece, *An American Tragedy,* in 1925. It reversed the Alger story (page 402). It was based on the actual history of a youth who escaped the drabness of a poor Midwest background only to lose his moral standards completely when plunged into a wealthy urban environment, and who finally was executed for murder. William Faulkner told with brutal frankness stories of depravity in the Deep South, of which *The Sound and the Fury* (1929) was the most successful during this decade. With Eugene O'Neill's dramas of contemporary society the American stage reached maturity. His plays were usually about unhappy, uneducated people unable to understand the forces that drove them onward. The most memorable of American plays about the war was *What Price Glory?* by Maxwell Anderson and Laurence Stallings (1924). *Middletown: a Study in Contemporary American Culture* (1929), a sociological study of a middle-size Indiana town by Robert S. and Helen M. Lynd, provided a factual basis for comparison with the satire and debunking of the novelists.

The historical novel without direct social significance

SOME OF THE contemporary novelists had no immediate and burning message of protest to convey to Americans about America. Willa Cather continued to write, without condemnation or indignation and with warmth and grace, of pioneer families in the Middle West. Among her best works was her historical novel about missionaries in New Mexico—*Death Comes for the Archbishop* (1927). Thornton Wilder began his reputation with novels refreshingly unconcerned with contemporary social purpose, such as *The Bridge of San Luis Rey* (1927), a story of eighteenth-century Peru. Pearl Buck's novels of Chinese life (page 825) and Margaret Mitchell's best-selling romance about the South in Civil War times—*Gone with the Wind* (1936)—provided "escape" for those who wished to lose themselves in other lands or other times.

Poetry at home
and among the expatriates

IN CHICAGO Harriet Monroe's *Poetry: A Magazine of Verse* (founded in 1912) became the recognized organ of a striking number of gifted American poets. Here and in other media they found a more receptive audience than had usually been available to earlier American poets. E. E. Cummings, in poetry that carried the revolt against tradition to the point where he abandoned capitalization and ignored conventional punctuation, peopled his works with low-life characters and used "jazzy" language to disguise his none the less frequently

T. S. Eliot, a drawing
by Powys Evans.

835

familiar themes of romance and satire. Robinson Jeffers brought a dramatic cynicism into his poetic narratives and dramas. Edgar Lee Masters analyzed small-town life in *Spoon River Anthology* (1915) and in *The New Spoon River* (1924). Carl Sandburg's free verse sang of Chicago and the Middle West. Robert Frost wrote affectionate narrative poems of rural New England, and Edwin Arlington Robinson dealt in somber, ironic analysis of New England character. Edna St. Vincent Millay's prize-winning lyrics discussed love and social problems. Stephen Vincent Benét in *John Brown's Body* (1928) penned one of America's great epics.

A number of men and women of letters, finding or pretending to find the crassness of American life more than they could bear, fled to Europe, where life might be less materialist and certainly was cheaper. Even before the First World War, Ezra Pound had been well known as a leader of American literary expatriates and of the "imagist" poets (page 825). After the war he wrote the iconoclasm of the "lost generation" into his learned poems and looked to the East or to Mussolini to give meaning to his times. A resident of England since 1915, the American-born T. S. Eliot, who was gradually convincing the world that he was one of the great poets of English literature, proclaimed his protest against the spiritual diversity of the twentieth century in his best-known work of this period—the lengthy, symbolic and allusive poem *The Waste Land* (1922). Eliot moved quickly from disgust with contemporary mores to Anglo-Catholicism, conservatism, and classicism.

Instrumentalism and progressive education　THE REVOLT against traditional prepossessions found a champion in the outstanding American philosopher of the day. A student of Peirce and James (pages 405-406), the psychologist-philosopher-educator John Dewey gradually developed a version of pragmatism called instrumentalism. In two works published during the war —*The School and Society* (1915) and *Democracy and Education* (1916)—he applied pragmatic philosophy to education and civic behavior. In subsequent works—*Reconstruction in Philosophy* (1920), *Human Nature and Conduct* (1922), and *Experience and Nature* (1925)—he further developed his brand of pragmatism. Instrumentalism regards moral concepts as hypotheses to be tested by and adapted to their practical consequences—as instruments of correct action rather than as ends. Viewed pragmatically, education became for Dewey not the mastery of a body of crystallized knowledge but the development of the child "in cooperative and mutually helpful living." "The test of all institutions of adult life," he declared, "is their effect in furthering continued education." Dewey's ideas, complementing those of Rousseau, Pestalozzi, and Froebel, furnished the major rationale of the progressive-education movement that was to become widely adopted in the interwar period in

American schools and to find some vogue in Europe. The essence of progres-

sive education was that schooling was to be adapted to the developing interests of the pupil rather than that the child should be obliged to conform to a
curriculum determined by adult preferences. One of the major contemporary
American critics of this point of view was Irving Babbitt (page 825), who
championed a disciplined, humanist education based upon classical and
oriental learning and literature.

*Characteristics
of literature in the twenties*

IN GENERAL the socially conscious literature of the twenties
was apt to be querulous and de-
featist, in contrast to the crusading literature of the prewar muckraking era.
It was generally realistic or naturalistic, and often sensational. It exhibited
the interest in Freudian and behaviorist psychology and Marxian theory characteristic of the era. Much of it was experimental in style and form, showing
the influence of the symbolists and of James Joyce. The stream-of-consciousness technique was popular in prose writing and drama, while poetry featured
free verse, images—often learned and abstruse, with meticulous attention to
the sound and meaning of words. Words as sounds in prose as well as in
poetry became important to writers under the influence of Gertrude Stein,
who became the center of a devoted coterie of American expatriates and of
abstract painters living in Paris. She developed a prose style in which simple
words were used both for their sound and for their meaning; and through
repetition without regard to conventional grammar she sought to create moods
and evoke impressions rather than to tell a story.

*Literary impact
of the great depression*

THE DEPRESSION of the 1930's
called forth a new departure in
American letters. Whereas the
literature of the twenties had been satirical and nihilist in spirit, the major
works of the 1930's were indignant and purposeful. In his *U.S.A.* trilogy
(1930-1936) John Dos Passos portrayed savagely and with Marxian overtones the prewar, war, and boom years in the United States and the uniformly
devastating effect of an economic system he considered vicious, greedy, and
evil. A new writer, James T. Farrell, blasted his way to fame with his characters Studs Lonigan and Danny O'Neill, to each of whom he devoted a
trilogy of novels (1932-1935 and 1936-1940 respectively). They chronicled
with the detailed fidelity of sociological documents the sordid conditions and
spiritual poverty of the Chicago slums, and the destructive effect on promising
youth of a vicious environment and unamiable associates. It was (to use the
title of one of the Danny O'Neill trilogy) "a world I never made," in which
Danny fares better than Studs. In a more genteel vein Thomas Wolfe in his
novels *Look Homeward, Angel* (1929) and *Of Time and the River* (1935)
portrayed (in his own words) "man's inhumanity to his fellow man...suffer-
ing, violence, oppression, hunger, cold, and filth and poverty going on un-

heeded in a world in which the rich were still rotten with their wealth." His hero was a Southern small-town youth who became an intellectual. Ernest Hemingway's *To Have and Have Not* (1937) told the story of a man forced by hard times into lawlessness ending in tragedy. The widest read tract for the times was John Steinbeck's stark indictment of the system that sacrificed human beings to profit—*The Grapes of Wrath* (1939), the story of a migrant "Okie" (Oklahoma sharecropper) family in search of food and work in the California fruit ranches, where property rights fight an unequal battle with starving humanity. This was a decade when a new dispensation beckoned to young people who saw clearly the misery in the United States and who knew little about the misery in Russia, though only a few actually turned to Communism.

Music, architecture, and art in the Americas   IN MUSIC and in architecture post-bellum America developed native products. Jazz forced itself more stridently on the postwar world than before. Stereotyped sentimental ballads or comic verses set to simple melodic tunes, frequently stolen from the classics, became "hits" through the energetic and profitable media of "Tin-Pan Alley" and the Broadway musical review. American jazz bands traveled all over the world and played for dancers who joyously learned new American dances like the "Turkey Trot," the "Charleston," and the "Black Bottom," which required great vigor and none of the sedateness of the minuet or waltz. With John Alden Carpenter's *Krazy Kat* (1921) and *Sky-scrapers* (1926) and George Gershwin's *Rhapsody in Blue* (1923), jazz was raised to the level of serious ballet and concert music. In the next decade (1935) Gershwin was to put jazz elements into his opera *Porgy and Bess*. His contemporary, Aaron Copland, also used jazz idioms, along with the modern dissonant style. Roy Harris, Roger Sessions, Walter Piston, and others in their symphonies and chamber music gave a distinctly American accent to the current neo-classical idiom. The Brazilian Heitor Villa-Lobos and the Mexican Carlos Chávez composed in a style deliberately made imperfect in order to express some of the more primitive elements of their countries' lore.

Frank Lloyd Wright continued and taught his organic architecture. In 1923 his Imperial Hotel in Tokyo, designed seven years earlier to withstand earthquakes by being floated on the Japanese mud, was the only building in central Tokyo to remain unshattered by a great earthquake. Wright's reputation, together with the influence from abroad of Le Corbusier and the German Bauhaus group, made "modernism" a prominent feature of American architecture, furniture, and interior design. The relatively unadorned office buildings of Rockefeller Center in New York were more of a compromise with traditional styles than some of the newer apartment houses, office buildings, and industrial plants, which displayed straight lines, large windows, glass-steel-and-cement structure, unadorned walls, and chromium steel furniture.

Nevertheless the old styles still had their exponents. "Collegiate" Gothic and Georgian continued to flourish on American campuses. In Chicago the attempt was made (in the Tribune Tower) to adapt Gothic even to the sky-

The palatial movie theater, a monument of the "Jazz Age" in America. A drawing by Saul Steinberg.

scraper. The architects B. G. Goodhue and R. A. Cram were the leaders in a neo-Gothic movement that, beginning with the prewar plans of the Cathedral of St. John the Divine in New York, gradually spread to churches, schools, and chapels. A neo-classic vogue also flourished under the aegis of W. R. Mead, surviving partner of C. F. McKim and Stanford White, both disciples of Richardson (page 404). Until Mead's death in 1928, the firm of McKim, Mead, and White built university halls, museums, and public edifices with stately domes, arches, and columns, and their influence outlived them. John R. Pope was perhaps the greatest of the later classicists.

In painting a vigorous style with unorthodox subjects developed along-side of conventional work. A small group of painters as early as 1908 had rebelled against the representational and romantic subject. They became known as "the Eight" or "the ash-can school." Among them were Robert Henri and John Sloan, who brought verve, color, and realism to their can-vases. George W. Bellows' "Dempsey and Firpo" (1923), Grant Wood's, Thomas Hart Benton's, and John Steuart Curry's regional scenes, and Georgia O'Keeffe's still lifes were good examples of the unconventional subject or style. So are Rockwell Kent's lithographs and John Marin's watercolors. Despite a few abstractionists, sculpture, however, was still dominated by representational artists like Jo Davidson, Malvina Hoffman, and Lorado Taft.

*Science
in the United States*

IN SCIENCE most of the American achievements were immediately translated into technological improvements and have already been discussed as such—radio, plastics, the movies. Americans participated in the remarkable progress already outlined in the discussion of European scientific research. In 1926, Thomas H. Morgan published his *The Theory of the Gene,* expounding his findings that heredi-tary characteristics are determined by minute bodies in the chromosomes called "genes." With his findings and their further refinement, plant and ani-mal breeding have become more directly controllable. Americans, who before 1914 had won only one Nobel prize in the sciences (Michelson, laureate in 1907), won several after 1914 in physics, chemistry, and medicine (among them some who have been mentioned above—Compton, Lawrence, Millikan, Morgan, and Urey). When these men were joined by other Nobel laureates fleeing from Europe, like Einstein and Fermi, American science, no matter what the politics of the country might be, had broken whatever parochial or national bonds may once have held it. An extraordinary effort to provide "a better analysis through a more comprehensive synthesis" of the social sciences was provided through the collaboration of scholars all over the world in the *Encyclopaedia of the Social Sciences* (1930-1935) under the editorship of E. R. A. Seligman and Alvin Johnson.

840

Roosevelt's second term and continuation of the New Deal

IN POLITICS the major issue continued to be that of political and social reform. Considering his overwhelming victory in the election of 1936 as an endorsement of the New Deal, President Roosevelt undertook to challenge the opposition in one of its strongest citadels—the Supreme Court. He proposed (1937) to enlarge the court by adding younger men, whether or not the older judges retired. The proposal was immediately attacked even by some of Roosevelt's supporters as a scheme to subordinate the judiciary to the executive—"to pack the Supreme Court"—and was never carried through Congress. Nevertheless, having been publicly rebuked as "judges of retirement age who do not choose to retire or resign" several of the older federal judges now saw fit to retire, and their places were filled with men well known for their New Deal views. The Supreme Court, now dominated by Roosevelt appointees, reversed several previous decisions.

The country seemed to be climbing out of the depression by 1936. Nevertheless, in 1937-1938 occurred a recession. Over 16,000,000 people were estimated by the end of 1937 to be either partly or wholly unemployed. Laissez-faire advocates attributed the recession to the interference with the autonomy of the market, but Roosevelt and his supporters thought it due rather to a premature effort on the part of Congress to reduce government expenditures for relief and public works. With a now compliant Supreme Court, they reinvigorated the New Deal. A new AAA (1938) reëstablished acreage allotments and introduced "parity" payments (sliding subsidies to the farmers to encourage staple crops by making good the difference between market prices and "parity" prices). In addition it provided controls for the marketing of crop surpluses, offered crop insurance, and attempted to establish an "ever normal granary" by loans to farmers enabling them to carry over surpluses from good years to bad. The NRA was not revived but its features relating to labor standards were re-enacted in the Fair Labor Standards Act of 1938, which was aimed at achieving a reasonable minimum wage and maximum work week, and prohibited child labor in industries producing goods for interstate commerce.

Labor's battle for recognition

THE YEAR 1937 was notable for its labor turmoil. Almost five thousand strikes took about two million workers away from their shops. The C.I.O.'s attack was aggressive and militant. In the automotive industry it introduced the sit-down strike, borrowed on the spur of the moment from France, where it was currently proving successful (page 807). This kind of strike was widely regarded as seizure of private property and hence a violation of a sacred right, and it aroused the bitterest antagonism not only among employers but among large sections of the general public. Employers felt encouraged to resist the C.I.O.'s onslaught by their expectation that the Wagner Act, which they regarded as unfairly friendly to labor organizations, would be declared unconstitutional; they often ignored NLRB orders and sometimes resorted to shop spying, hiring of scab gangs, incitement to violence, and other shady means of strikebreaking. In April a ringing decision of the same Supreme Court that the president had recently rebuked declared the Wagner Act constitutional. Disappointed employers continued to resist, however. On Memorial Day ten people were killed and forty wounded when police at the Republic Steel Corporation in Chicago with little provocation fired on a workers' protest parade.

By and large the spoils of battle went to labor. By 1940 total labor-union membership in the United States was around eleven million. But the violence that had accompanied the resurgence of unionism created bad blood between labor and employers, while rivalry and antagonism between the C.I.O. and the A.F. of L. hampered the political influence of both and further complicated labor-employer relations by "jurisdictional" strikes (to determine which union would have the power to organize a particular shop).

Deepening isolationism and neutrality by legislation

AMERICANS could not be indifferent to the onrush of Fascism in Europe, with its ever increasing threat of general war. The presence of celebrated refugees was a constant reminder of impending catastrophe. Yet most Americans thought, in the mid-thirties, that the United States could remain a neutral bystander in the conflicts of alien ideologies. As Europe's crises deepened, determination mounted in the United States to "sit this one out." Many Americans regarded war as a foreign disease to which their country might remain immune. They thought the United States could make itself invulnerable to attack and scoffed at the fear that a Fascist triumph in Europe would be a threat to democracy and civilization the world over. Other Americans—but they were probably fewer—saw no reason to feel concern if the rival European nations bled each other white.

Accordingly all but a group of fearful Americans, whom the public opinion polls showed to be in a minority, sought to insulate themselves against war by a series of neutrality laws. Bills, hastily improvised in 1935 and 1936 as crises arose in Europe, forbade the sale or transport of munitions or the making of loans to belligerents wherever the president should declare that a state of war existed, and gave the president power to forbid Americans to travel on ships of belligerents except at their own risk. When civil war tore Spain asunder (page 813), an act of January 1937 forbade the sale of munitions to either side, a "neutrality" measure which meant that the Spanish Republican forces could not buy weapons to offset those the Germans and Italians were providing the rebel Fascists. Later in 1937 a "permanent" Neu-

842

trality Act reaffirmed the major features of the earlier bills, made travel on ships of belligerents unlawful, and added a "cash-and-carry" provision by which items listed by the president would have to be paid for before export and transported by the buyer. The act reflected the sentiment of the public, which was determined never again to be propelled into a European war by resentment over the destruction of American lives or property on the high seas. So intense was the sentiment to stay out of Europe's imbroglios that Americans by this legislation voluntarily abandoned the traditional defense of their rights as neutrals on the high seas, although several times in their history, the last only twenty years earlier, they had gone to war to defend them.

Positive efforts of the Roosevelt administration PRESIDENT Roosevelt and the State Department did not see eye to eye with the American public on the policy of withdrawal from world problems. In both Europe and the Orient they took as firm a stand against aggressor nations as it was possible to take in view of the ostrichlike state of public opinion. In October 1937 Roosevelt made a sensational speech in Chicago suggesting the quarantining of aggressor nations and asserting, "There must be positive endeavors to preserve peace." The following month the United States took part in the Brussels Conference intended to restore peace in China (page 831). In January 1938, shortly after the American gunboat *Panay* was attacked and sunk by Japanese bombers, Roosevelt asked for a billion dollars to bring the navy up to treaty strength, and a year later requested over a half billion more for national defense. The State Department, in keeping with the Stimson Doctrine of nonrecognition (page 767), repeatedly refused to accept any "New Order" in the Far East or to consent to any modification of United States interests, and in mid-1939 gave notice of its intention to abrogate the Japanese-American commercial treaty of 1911.

The aggressions of Germany and Italy were openly condemned by high American officials. President Roosevelt departed from United States precedent several times to appeal personally for pacific methods. During the Sudeten crisis (page 820) he cabled both Hitler and Mussolini urging a peaceful settlement. In the following spring he asked the two dictators to pledge not to attack any of thirty-one listed countries within the next ten years and suggested an international conference to discuss disarmament and trade. In August 1939, upon the signing of the nonaggression pact between Germany and Russia, which was regarded as a "green light" signal for war, he cabled the German Führer, the Italian king, and the Polish president in the hope of arranging a peaceful settlement of the Polish crisis (page 823). Although many isolationists in the United States felt that the administration was going too far in this verbal meddling with affairs across the seas, the president's words, however eloquent, had little or no effect. And Roosevelt's own preference to take a stand openly with England and France and to quarantine the aggressors was hamstrung by public opinion.

Strengthening
inter-American ties

ROOSEVELT'S inclinations fell in better with isolationist propensities in his effort to achieve a sense of collective responsibility in the nation's own hemisphere. The Good Neighbor policy and the Monroe Doctrine were now directed toward the formation of a hemispheric bloc to resist economic penetration and possible aggression from Fascist states abroad. In 1936 the president traveled in person to the Pan-American Conference at Buenos Aires and announced to an approving audience that potential aggressors from overseas "will find a Hemisphere wholly prepared to consult together for our mutual safety and our mutual good." Secretary of State Hull proposed also that the American nations act jointly to preserve American neutrality in the affairs of the other hemisphere. Latin-American states were not overhasty about accepting this virtual invitation to assume joint and co-equal responsibility with the United States for keeping out European aggressors, but the events of the next few years led in that direction. At Buenos Aires they agreed to confer on questions affecting hemispheric peace. Two years later, at the Pan-American Conference at Lima, the twenty-one countries that were represented unanimously adopted the Declaration of Lima, warning potential aggressors of their intention to consult together in case of threat to the "peace, security, or territorial integrity" of any of them and to defend themselves against all foreign intervention. The United States also sought to checkmate Fascist economic penetration in Latin America by strengthening economic ties, especially through loans and reciprocal trade agreements. The dispute with Mexico over oil and land sequestrations was allowed to die down with only a nominal payment for the sequestered land and with no agreement on oil until 1944, when Mexico agreed to pay $24,000,000 to the expropriated American oil companies. On a visit to Canada in 1938, Roosevelt in effect applied the Monroe Doctrine to Canada when he declared that "the people of the United States will not stand idly by if domination of Canadian soil is threatened by any other Empire."

The growth
of American interventionism

MEANWHILE some leading diplomats, novelists, newspaper correspondents, and other first-hand observers kept warning of the dangers to the United States in the pending cataclysm of Europe and the East. Hemingway was among the foremost of those who sensed that isolation—even hemispheric isolation—was a chimera. In a best-selling novel and movie about an American hero on the Republican side in the Spanish Civil War, *For Whom the Bell Tolls* (1940), he summed 844 up his attitude neatly in his frontispiece quotation from John Donne: "No man is an Iland, intire of it selfe; every man is a peece of the Continent, a part of the maine;...any mans death diminishes me, because I am involved in Mankinde; And therefore never send to know for whom the bell tolls; *It tolls for thee."*

IN DIPLOMATIC arrangements Germany in 1939 seemed far better prepared for war than in 1914. In 1914 the Central Powers had stood alone. In 1939 the Germans could count upon "the Rome-Berlin Axis of Steel" and probably also on the Tokyo-Berlin Axis. Mussolini's military forces would oblige the French to divide their forces even if he did no more than strike an attitude of friendly neutrality to Germany. The Japanese would be useful by threatening the British and the French empires in the East, thus obliging them to divide their naval forces, and keeping the attention of the United States, a potential ally of the western powers, fixed upon the Far East. And Russia, also an enemy in 1914, would now at least remain neutral. The French and the British, on the other hand, appeared unprepared physically or spiritually for the heroism needed in total war. The Führer appeared to have anticipated everything.

It remained to be seen whether an American conversion to collective security would come and, if it came, whether it would not be too late. Some American voices were heard to declare that the two halves of the world would not have to meet at Armageddon if the Germans were made to realize that, as in the First World War, they would have to deal with American industrial potential before they were done. Other American voices—pro-Communist, pro-German, and isolationist—were heard shouting, "The Yanks are not coming!" and "America first!" The studied neutrality of the United States encouraged aggressor nations to embark with confidence on their aggrandizement in the expectation that the United States would protest but would be too complacent and disunited to take effective action. In 1939 the chances looked better for continued American isolation than for collective action against aggression.

The German public did not rejoice in 1939 that war had come, as it had in 1914, but it was better marshaled behind its government. The opposition was dead, or was inside the barbed-wire fences of numerous concentration camps, or had fled abroad. The Poles, the British, and the French were still less elated than the Germans. Poland as an authoritarian state (under Marshal Edward Rydz-Smigly since the death of Pilsudski in 1935) was assumed to be better prepared for war than the western democracies, but even the Poles were far from ready for the heroic measures now demanded of them. And yet the Allies did not despair of ultimate victory. They counted upon 845 their superior navies, money power, and coal supply to win the war for them ultimately—the navies by blockading Germany, the money by buying armaments abroad faster than they could be made by slave-labor in Germany, and the coal by keeping British industry going while German industry struggled along on short fuel rations. But for these advantages to register their full weight a long war would be necessary, and no one knew how long the war could last. At the beginning of the Second World War, the situation certainly looked like a well-calculated risk from the German point of view.

1920	Sinclair Lewis' *Main Street*
1922	James Joyce's *Ulysses*
1922	T. S. Eliot's *The Waste Land*
1922	Insulin discovered by Banting and others
1926-1929	Discovery of vitamins B to K
1927	Heisenberg formulates the "uncertainty principle" of physics
1929-1939	Penicillin discovered and developed
1929-1937	The Great Depression
1930	Construction of first cyclotron
1933	Seventh Pan-American Conference at Montevideo
1933	Congress passes the Agricultural Adjustment Act
1933	Post flies solo around the world
1935-1939	"Popular Front" parties in Europe
1935	Stresa Conference seeks to protect Austria against Germany
1935	Italian invasion of Ethiopia
1935	Saarland adheres to Germany by plebiscite
1936-1939	The Spanish Civil War
1936-1939	Nazi mobilization of Germany by Goering's Four-Year Plan
1936-1938	Popular Front's domination of French government
1936	Pan-American Conference at Buenos Aires
1936	Franco proclaimed chief of the Spanish state by insurgents
1936	Ethiopia formally annexed to Italy
1936	Hitler remilitarizes the Rhineland
1936	Adoption of a new constitution by USSR
1936	Abdication of Edward VIII
1936	Mutiny and military domination in Japan
1936	The Rome-Berlin Axis and the Tokyo-Berlin Axis formed
1937-1941	Roosevelt's second term and extension of the New Deal
1937-1940	Chamberlain ministry in Britain
1937	Egypt becomes sovereign state and member of the League
1937	Congress passes the Neutrality Act
1937	Peak of labor turmoil in the United States
1937	The "China Incident" begins undeclared Sino-Japanese war
1937	The Anti-Comintern Pact of Germany, Japan, and Italy
1937	Gandhi-Nehru party dominates elections in India
1938	German invasion and annexation of Austria
1938	The Munich Conference appeases Hitler in Czechoslovakia
1938	The Declaration of Lima on Western Hemisphere defense
1939	German domination of Czechia and Slovakia
1939	Soviet-German nonaggression pact
1939	Beginning of the Second World War

Part six

Chapter fourteen: "Blood and toil and tears and sweat"

Chapter fifteen: Neither world war nor world peace

Chapter sixteen: Epilogue: Some persistent problems of the modern world

WAR

AND THE UNCERTAIN

PEACE

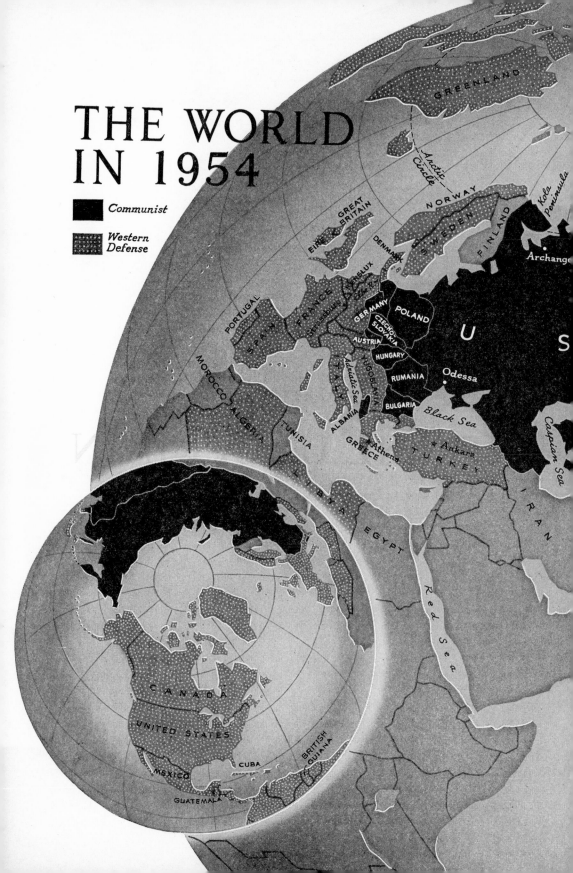

THE WORLD
IN 1954

■ Communist

▦ Western
Defense

In June 1954 tensions existed within both the Communist and non-Communist defense systems. In Indochina civil war raged, with Communists and West on opposing sides. In British Guiana and Guatemala the local governments at times were friendly to Communism. In certain satellites hostility to Communist control was widespread. Spain, Libya, and Pakistan were involved in western air-base or other military arrangements. (This map avoids showing the colonies of the western empires as part of their defense system.)

Chapter fourteen

"BLOOD AND
TOIL AND TEARS
AND SWEAT"

HISTORIANS do not dispute the question who was guilty of starting the Second World War, but they disagree on several issues that arose in the course of the war. For example, some maintain while others disagree, that the Soviet government did not intend merely to buy a respite from attack by the nonaggression pact of August 1939 but meant to encourage Germany to attack the "democratic" nations in order to profit from Russia's neutrality while the non-Communist powers bled each other white. Some assert and others deny that Belgium's and France's pitiful ineffectiveness and ultimate collapse on the western front were due to deliberate domestic sabotage as well as to a "Maginot psychology." Opinions differ as to why Hitler chose to attack Russia despite her apparent friendly neutrality to Germany. Arguments equally loud are made on both sides of the proposition that the United States should and could have shortened the war by going in earlier than it ultimately did. Different schools of thought exist regarding the degree of German instigation and American provocation of the Japanese attack upon United States territory. Certain features of President Roosevelt's policy after American entry into the war—such as his demand for the "unconditional surrender" of Germany and his readiness to make concessions to Russia—were to become heated postwar political issues.

A few tactical and strategic decisions of the war also have both their champions and their detractors. Should "saturation" bombing, involving destruction of noncombatant areas, have been employed? Should more attention have been given by the United Nations to the war against Japan? Should the French, Italian, Yugoslav, and Greek resistance movements have been allotted more support? Should the possibilities of a Balkan invasion have been exploited more vigorously? Should the western Allies have agreed to a line of demarcation between their front and the Russian front in a collapsed Germany? Should the atom bomb have been dropped on Japan? Questions like these remain controversial long after the epoch that gave them rise. We shall attempt below to answer them and other questions like them so far as our present knowledge and prepossessions permit.

A great aspiration was to color the postwar controversy. At no time in the history of mankind was more of the world's thought and material resources centered upon a single contest than in 1939-1945. Though divided into three camps—United Nations, Axis powers, and neutrals, each country with its own purposes—the countries of the world had reached a higher degree of interdependence than ever before. The war, and the uneasy peace to follow, were to show that no matter how hard it was for the sovereign nations of the world to live together, it was also hard for them to live isolated from and unanswerable to each other. Hence, in the midst of a death struggle the question how best to preserve a just peace arose more persistently than ever.

BLITZKRIEG
AND SITZKRIEG (1939-1940)

THE DIPLOMACY and strategy of the Second World War were complicated and confused largely because it was not one war, but, in a sense, at least four. (1) The western democracies had failed to embroil Russia with Germany and had themselves become embroiled with Germany. (2) Russia took advantage of the mutual destruction among her neighbors to pick up stray pieces of territory on her frontiers, until in 1941 she herself was confronted by a belligerent and confident Germany. (3) The Japanese, grasping the opportunity presented by the European powers' preoccupation with one another and by the American insistence upon neutrality until 1941, drove competitors out of their Asiatic sphere. (4) The Italians and Germans tried to expel the English and French from the Mediterranean and North Africa with remarkable success until 1941. In 1941 operations in all four theaters were to be more fully coordinated.

The Gestapo and the concept of total war   ONCE THE FATAL step had been taken, the Nazis applied outside Germany's borders the methods that they had practiced inside for a long time. They were efficient, well prepared, and merciless. Wherever the Germans invaded, the Gestapo (Secret State Police) followed immediately after the soldiers. Anyone in a conquered country capable of military or even spiritual resistance had to be rendered powerless. In the Slavic lands, particularly in Poland and eventually in Russia, a systematic extermination policy was carried out. The aim of the Nazis was to leave "inferior" nations without intellectual leadership, in order to make them more malleable to Nazi direction. All through the war, conflicts arose between the German military and the Gestapo. The generals, quite naturally, desired a quiet population in the rear of the German armies. The methods of the Gestapo, however, brought the conquered people to a white heat of anti-German hatred. Feeling that they had nothing to lose but their miserable lives, the citizens of the conquered countries took up arms as guerrillas against their conquerors.

Gestapo methods thus produced retaliation in a widespread underground movement. The Nazis had tried to figure out everything in advance, from lists of people to be arrested after conquest to the seizure of industrial and agricultural products. To one thing, however, they had not given sufficient weight—the spirit of the conquered people. Total war in the end proved to be a boomerang. The British cartoonist David Low bitterly caricatured the Nazi cross-purposes. One of his cartoons showed Hitler and Heinrich Himmler, chief of the Gestapo, standing in a conquered country against a background of corpses dangling from gallows; Hitler asks Himmler, "Why don't they love us, Heinrich?"

The war aims and methods of the Nazis　　AS BECAME clear as early as September 1939, the forthcoming war was to be first and foremost a war of self-preservation of all those who were endangered by the Nazis, the Fascists, and the Japanese war lords. In this respect it was to differ from the First World War, of which the aim had not been to obliterate nations or to reduce them to a permanent state of slavery. Atrocities had then been regarded as unfortunate extravagances of wartime passions and were not part of a fixed policy. In the Second World War, however, abduction or obliteration on an Assyrian scale was to become a set policy. After being attacked by Germany, the Russian government was to evacuate the Volga Germans, who had lived in southern Russia since the time of Catherine the Great. Hitler had around 6,000,000 Jews exterminated. Millions of people were to be shifted back and forth for purposes of slave labor. What later became known as genocide (the extermination of a whole people) was a political dogma with the Nazis. The vanquished faced subjugation or annihilation or both, like the vanquished in the wars of antiquity.

The ostensible German objective in the attack upon Poland was the reannexation of Danzig and the Polish Corridor. But the quick realization of this aim was not to end hostilities, for it had been in fact only a pretext for starting the war. The first real goal was the obliteration of the Polish state. Hitler's next goal was to reduce France to the position of a German satellite. And all this was only the overture to Hitler's higher objectives—the reorganization of Europe as a step in the direction of world conquest. Subsequent developments revealed that the temporary entente with Russia had not in fact changed the plans outlined in *Mein Kampf*. Soviet Russia was to be largely destroyed. When that was done, Germany would annex the territories of "the black earth" in southern Russia, settle German peasants there, establish a system of German-controlled satellite states in European Russia, and drive the Russians beyond the Ural Mountains. A sort of United States of Europe would then follow under German domination. The nucleus of that federation should be an industrialized Germany. It should be surrounded by the rest of Europe, which either should remain agricultural, where the economy had not yet emerged from an agricultural status, or (e.g., France) should be de-industrialized, reduced to an agricultural status, and rendered impotent to wage a modern industrialized war against Germany. Italy should be compensated by French territory and some European colonies in Africa, excepting the former German colonies, which must be returned to Germany. Japan should be paid off in eastern and southern Asia and, possibly, in some parts of Latin America. The rest of Latin America and the United States Hitler apparently hoped eventually to dominate by means of infiltration with the aid of German "fifth columns."

The defeat and partition of Poland

TO MEET THE mechanized onslaught of German planes, tanks, armored trucks, motorcycles, and infantry, the Poles, having neglected both their air force and their armored land vehicles, put their faith in their cavalry. Persuaded by their western allies, they delayed their mobilization until the day before war broke out. Germany had commenced her mobilization earlier, so that on September 1 she was fully ready for war, while the Poles had barely begun to get ready. On the first day of the war the Germans attacked Poland with their full air force and motorized units, leaving only a small force to protect their western front. The German General Staff correctly counted upon the French to stay within their Maginot Line and not to attack Germany while she was engaged against Poland. And so, while an uninformed public in all countries expected the French to strike with all their might against the weak German screen in the west, the French armies did next to nothing. They and the British General Staff still thought of war in the terms of the attrition of 1914-1918: they would wear Germany down by naval blockade and by holding the "impregnable" trenches of the Maginot Line. Thus they contemplated only a *Sitzkrieg* (a sitting war).

As a consequence, the Germans were able to win their great gamble against Poland easily. The German air force destroyed almost all of the Polish airfields, and German tank squadrons appeared in the rear of Polish armies. Despite two weeks of desperate and valiant fighting by the Poles, the Germans stood before Warsaw on September 15.

Two days later, notwithstanding the Russo-Polish nonaggression pact, the Russians invaded eastern Poland. Since Poland had ceased to exist as a state or government, they announced, Russia felt called upon to protect the White

POLAND REPARTITIONED 1939

Nazi aggression turned on Poland in 1939, and Russia quickly joined in to make sure of her share of the spoils. In the resulting partition, each took a large segment of Polish territory, granting small bits to subservient Slovakia and Lithuania. The rump Government General of Poland was occupied by German troops.

Russians and Ukrainians of Poland. "At the same time the Soviet government propose to take all measures to extricate the Polish people from the unfortunate war into which it was dragged by its unwise leaders." The German government publicly approved of the Russian move. The Russians occupied all of eastern Poland, and after twelve days of severe artillery and air bombardment Warsaw fell to the Germans. On September 29, Germany and Russia announced to a horrified world a new partition—sometimes called "the fifth partition"—of Poland. A western portion, including Posen and the neighboring areas, was annexed directly by Germany. The rest of German-occupied Poland, centering on Warsaw, became a German government-general to be administered under martial law (except for bits granted to Slovakia). Poland east of the partition line was annexed by Russia, which graciously granted a few thousand square miles around Vilna to Lithuania.

Thus, Poland once more became only a memory, a geographical expression, and a hope. The Polish government first fled to Rumania, then constituted itself a government in exile in France, and after the defeat of France finally transferred to London. The Germans undertook to Germanize the annexed provinces. They expelled the Polish population by mass deportations. About 1,500,000 so-called *Volksdeutsche* (people of German heritage without being either German citizens or living in Germany) were settled in 857

Poland. They came from Italian Tyrol, the Baltic states, Transylvania, and the Russian-occupied part of Poland. Against the nearly 3,000,000 Jews of Poland the Nazis began a program of systematic extermination in concentration camps and gas chambers.

*Russian domination
of the Baltic countries*

RUSSIA AND Germany were no longer separated by a buffer Poland. Their contiguity was an important step in Hitler's designs upon Russia, but until he could dispose of France, he did not feel free to divert his attention to Russia. Thus, when Soviet Russia, in September and October 1939, concluded "mutual assistance pacts" with Estonia, Latvia, and Lithuania, he acquiesced, much as he must have disliked the unilateral expansion policy of Russia. Each of those countries permitted Russia to establish military and naval bases on its territory.

The Russians' anxiety to control the Baltic and protect their flank against potential attack was not quieted by these concessions, however, and led them to demand the cession of certain Finnish territories and naval bases. The Finns procrastinated, and in November the Russians invaded Finland. The Finnish government complained to the League of Nations, but all the League could do was to expel the Russians and to condemn their behavior. The Russian government apparently believed that the Finnish army would be a "pushover," but "General Winter" for once fought on the side of Russia's enemies, and the Russians suffered a series of humiliating defeats. Only the next February did they begin to rally, and by March the Finns were forced to come to terms. By a peace treaty concluded at Moscow the Finns surrendered outright or leased several strategic pieces of territory, including the Karelian Isthmus, where their major fortification line was located. Startled by the collapse of France the next June and the danger from a ravenous Germany, the Russians, feeling that the "mutual assistance" of Estonia, Latvia, and Lithuania was not enough, encouraged Communist revolutions in those countries, and in August "admitted" them to the Soviet Union.

*The Sitzkrieg,
or "the Phony War"*

ON SEPTEMBER 3, 1939, Chamberlain and Daladier had to announce to their respective parliaments that their earlier promises of "peace in our day" had been premature. The war that ensued in the west until May 10, 1940, became known in the United States as "the Phony War." Warfare reverted to the maneuvering for position of the eighteenth century, when armies often confronted each other over long stretches of time without firing a shot. During this period the heavy guns spoke up once in a while and enemy aircraft would sometimes reconnoiter; but the Franco-British armies did little to disturb the Germans, and the Germans did little to disturb the Franco-British armies. Air warfare against civilians, so often predicted before the war, did not

materialize; the hastily issued gas masks were laid aside, and anxiety disappeared from the preparation of air-raid shelters. The western nations were soon lulled into the belief that warfare was not greatly different from what it had been in 1914-1918, and that in the end their superior resources would win for them.

Attention was focused upon the war at sea. The Germans immediately resumed the submarine tactics of the First World War. They sank without warning neutral as well as belligerent freighters and passenger liners. The day after the declaration of war by England they sank the British liner *Athenia* with about 1400 noncombatant men, women, and children, among whom were a number of American citizens. The United States did not react with the shocked indignation that had arisen when the *Lusitania* was sunk. The most spectacular event at sea in 1939 was a battle between a British naval squadron and the German battleship *Graf Spee* at the mouth of the Rio de la Plata. The German ship fled to the harbor of Montevideo. But, according to international law, a belligerent vessel might not remain longer than four days in a neutral port without being interned. On December 17, on the orders of Hitler, she was scuttled outside the harbor by her own crew.

On the diplomatic front, the Phony War permitted time to prepare for a "real" war. Great Britain and France concluded an alliance with Turkey, which, however, permitted Turkey to remain neutral throughout the war. More important to the eventual outcome was the partial repeal of the embargo on arms to belligerents that had been required by the American Neutrality Act of 1935. Under a new act passed in November 1939, belligerents were permitted to buy implements of war in America, but they could not buy on credit, nor could the matériel be delivered on American ships or airplanes. From these provisions the revised policy of neutrality came to be known as the "cash and carry" policy. The new act also provided that no American citizen or ship might enter combat areas and that no belligerent submarine might enter the ports and territorial waters of the United States. The American anxiety to avoid becoming involved in Europe's war was still patent, but since the Allies were in a better position to pay cash and to carry than the Germans, the new neutrality legislation was an ill-disguised act of friendliness to France and England.

BLITZ ON THE WESTERN FRONT
(APRIL-JULY 1940)

ALL THROUGH the Phony War, Hitler multiplied his infiltration and undermining activities. While his prospective victims rejoiced that they were protected by friendly agreements with the Nazis (as Denmark and Belgium) or derived a false sense of security from the feeling that war in 1940 was no different from that in 1918 (as France), Hitler's fifth columnists were busy as never before. In April 1940, his military preparations completed, he struck.

The invasion of Denmark and Norway

DURING THE Phony War, Hitler had used the Norwegian port of Narvik for transporting Swedish iron ore to Germany, and the British and the French determined to put a stop to that. Moreover, Hitler needed control of the airfields and sea lanes of Norway and Denmark to give his troops better coverage in the event of an invasion of the Low Countries and France. On April 7 the British discovered that huge Nazi convoys were moving in the direction of Norway. The next day Great Britain and France announced that they had mined the territorial waters of Norway at three points. The day after that, German troops invaded Denmark and Norway simultaneously. The Nazis informed both governments that they had come to protect Norway from an alleged British seizure of Norwegian ports, and they proposed to set up a German protectorate. The decision to attack Norway and Denmark was probably reached much earlier, however, because on the day of the actual attack fully armed Nazi soldiers emerged from apparently innocent German freighters in Norwegian harbors, as Greeks had emerged from the belly of Ulysses' "Trojan horse," and those freighters must have left Germany several days before.

After a short but futile struggle Denmark surrendered. Hitler treated Denmark as a "model" protectorate—at least until 1943. Norway proved a less easy victim. King Haakon VII and his government rejected the German demands. Fighting between the invaders and the Norwegians started at many points. The Norwegians were not unprepared like the Danes, and wherever they had a chance, they put up a valiant resistance. One single-gun Norwegian whaling vessel took on a whole German squadron. It was magnificent, but it was not war. From the start Norway was doomed because of the outright treason of Quisling and other officers. By their fifth column and "Trojan horse" tactics the Nazis gained easy access to the Oslo Fjord, otherwise difficult to enter, and to the port of Narvik. By noon of April 9, nine of Norway's most important towns were in German hands.

The Norwegian king refused to accept a new government under Quisling and continued to fight and retreat. The British and the French sent him some reinforcements. Although the Allies had a few initial successes, they and the Norwegians were eventually defeated. After two months' resistance, Norway surrendered. The king and the government fled to London, where they set up a government in exile.

Chamberlain's resignation and Churchill as prime minister

BRITISH RESENTMENT ran high against Chamberlain's government because of the defeat in Norway. It was held against him that at the beginning of the Norwegian campaign he had jubilantly said, "Hitler has missed the bus." Lloyd George, still leader of the Liberal Party, told Parliament, "It is the same old story of too little and too late." The leader of the Labour Party, Clement Attlee, cried out, "The Norwegian campaign is the culmination of other discontents." Severely criticized in the House of Commons, Chamberlain obtained a vote of confidence, but no less than thirty-eight members of his own Conservative Party voted against the prime minister. That was a moral defeat, and he resigned.

On May 10, Winston Churchill formed a new cabinet. As a young man Churchill had been a Conservative member of Parliament, as befitted a descendant of the great Duke of Marlborough. After a time he left the Conservative ranks to become a member of the Liberal Party. He had held several cabinet posts in the Asquith cabinet, and had been first lord of the admiralty at the time the First World War broke out (page 582). When, after the war, he went back into the Conservative fold, he was looked upon with suspicion by friend and foe alike. In the 1930's he made himself disliked by his repeated warnings of the bad intentions of Hitler and opposed the appeasement policy of Baldwin and Chamberlain. Regarded as too bellicose, he received no cabinet post despite his recognized abilities, until, upon the outbreak of war, he was again named first lord of the admiralty, and his was the only branch of the British armed forces that could point to any recent victories. He now formed a coalition cabinet, which included the outstanding figures of the Conservative, Labour, and Liberal parties.

When Churchill presented the new government to the House of Commons, he made a brief speech. It was a speech not of resignation but of defiance. "I have nothing to offer," he admitted, "but blood and toil and tears and sweat." Aware that Great Britain ran the risk of the treachery by which Norway had been handed over to the Nazi invader, Churchill immediately prepared and shortly carried in Parliament (May 23) a bill which in part suspended the liberties of the individual, though safeguards were incorporated into the law to prevent arbitrary decisions. The government rounded up all known and potential sympathizers of the Nazis, including the leaders of Sir Oswald Mosley's Fascist party (page 818) as well as some innocent German refugees.

*The invasion
of the Low Countries*

ALTHOUGH in 1937 Hitler had publicly declared that the German government was prepared to recognize Belgium and Holland as inviolable neutral territories, a few hours before Churchill's appointment the Nazis invaded Holland, Belgium, and Luxemburg. Luxemburg, though theoretically protected since 1867 by an international neutrality pact, was occupied within a few hours. The Dutch attempted to hamper the invader, as they had done in previous wars, by opening the dikes and flooding the countryside, but the Nazis were ready for such a contingency. They crossed the inundated areas in rubber boats. Among the

German soldiers were men who knew the language and were familiar with Dutch localities because as children they had been harbored by the Dutch to save them from the "hunger blockade" after the First World War.

The Dutch experienced a fuller application of the tactics of which the Poles had received but a foretaste. The Germans attacked with mechanized forces and bombers as in Poland. The city of Rotterdam was bombed in midday, its center was destroyed, and around 30,000 people were killed. The Germans deliberately dropped bombs on nonmilitary objects in order to kindle fires that might serve as beacons for other bombers at night. Flares in different colors lighted up the skies at night. The Germans made use also of dive bombers which they called Stukas. Planes machine-gunned the civilian population fleeing on the highways. This strafing of refugees was deliberate, so as to cause panic and clog the highways. Soon an avalanche of Dutch, Belgians, and Frenchmen was blocking the roads of France, making efficient military movement well-nigh impossible. By mid-June an estimated ten million refugees were roaming the highways of France. Also, the invaders literally dropped upon their objective by parachute, employing a device that the Germans had learned from the Russians. No fortress or Maginot Line could adequately protect the land behind it from attack by parachutists.

The collapse of the Low Countries

WITHIN FIVE days Dutch resistance came to an end, and an armistice was concluded. The royal family had a narrow escape but managed to flee to England. There they were met by the Dutch ministry, which set up as a government in exile. The Austrian "quisling," Arthur Seyss-Inquart, was made Reich commissioner of the Netherlands, and the Gestapo began its systematic work.

On the day of the invasion of Belgium and Holland, French and British mechanized forces had gone to the aid of the Belgians. The Allies hoped that the very strong Fort Eben-Emael dominating the Albert Canal Line would stop or at least delay the advance of the Nazis. But the hope crumbled before Nazi parachute detachments. In the ensuing confusion other Belgian forts fired at Fort Eben-Emael. On May 11 it fell to the Germans. After this initial success Nazi mechanized units rushed into Belgium. Once they overran the Ardennes area, they were in a position to outflank the Maginot Line on the north. The French now had to pay for having left the Line unfinished between Sedan and the North Sea.

The plight of France and Belgium

THE GERMANS invaded France near Sedan. A few of the most important bridges on the main highways had been left undestroyed by the retreating French. Whether they remained standing because of surprise, inefficiency, negligence, or treason has never been established. Certainly the morale of the French army had been sadly undermined by Fascist and Communist propaganda. The intact bridges

862

made the advance of the Nazi tanks easy. By May 19 the Nazis had opened a sixty-mile gap between the French armies and had reached Saint-Quentin. The French, British, and Belgian armies were in a desperate situation. The new French prime minister, Paul Reynaud, deposed the commander in chief, General M. G. Gamelin, replacing him with General Maxime Weygand, who had been Marshal Foch's chief of staff during the latter part of the First World War and had saved Warsaw for the Poles during the Russo-Polish War of 1920 (page 688). Despite Weygand's great reputation he could not stop the French rout. Whether his failure was due to his age (he was well over seventy), his inflexibility, and his defeatism, as his critics maintained, or whether the situation was already hopeless, as he later claimed, in the end the result was the same.

Even a general without any shortcomings might have proved unable to stem the Nazi tide, outmoded as the French army was. German tanks and motorcycle troops crisscrossed northern France almost at will. After desperate fighting the Belgian army was at the end of its resources. Forming the northern flank of the Allied armies, the Belgians were enduring the brunt of the German attack. King Leopold III was ready to surrender. The Belgian cabinet had already installed itself as a government in exile in London, and his ministers implored their king to follow them to London. But they pleaded in vain. Being a stubborn man of an autocratic disposition and having exalted ideas about the role of a king, he followed his inner promptings. On May 28, 1940, he capitulated with his army of 500,000 men.

His surrender left the British and French armies in the north dangling, without flank protection and exposed to possible destruction by the advancing Nazis. Neither the Allies nor a large segment of the Belgian population ever forgave the king his desperate action, particularly his refusal to go to England. The "royal question," as it was called, arose to bother the Belgians for more than ten years, particularly since, during the rest of the war, the king acted in a way that seemed to lend substance to the charge that he was a "collaborationist." Although he was eventually interned by the Nazis, more than half of the Belgian population came to regard him as their willing tool. After the war he was to be banished from Belgium, and eventually forced to abdicate in favor of his young son Baudouin.

The "Dunkirk"
of the British forces

EVEN BEFORE the Belgian capitulation the Allied army in northern France had been in an untenable position. It was cut off from the main French army and was strafed day and night by German planes without sufficient means of defending itself or of retaliating. On May 26 the British government, aware of what was about to happen to the Belgian army, ordered the British Expeditionary Force home. Over 650 volunteer reserve craft of every size, age, and description, some "manned" by women and children, and over 220 light naval vessels swarmed to the beach of Dunkirk. Evacuation took place upon mined seas under constant shelling by Nazi artillery and strafing by Nazi planes. The sea was choppy, but the wind was not so strong as to endanger the many small, rickety, and overloaded vessels. The evacuation beaches were crowded with soldiers waiting for embarkation, the city of Dunkirk burning in the background. The growing Royal Air Force risked its home defense strength to save the flower of the British army, and beat off the German air attacks. The main evacuation took place from May 26 to June 3; a few stragglers were still being picked up on June 4 and 5. The British Admiralty had hoped to save about 100,000 men at best. Actually, 330,000 British, French, Belgians, Dutch, and Poles were rescued, and only 30,000 men were lost. Their entire equipment, except for what the evacuees carried, was abandoned.

On June 4, Churchill gave an account of the evacuation to a sober Parliament. In a hushed House of Commons he concluded his speech with defiant and prophetic sentences that were broadcast to a tense and waiting world:

> ...we shall defend our Island whatever the cost may be, we shall fight on the beaches, we shall fight on the landing grounds, we shall fight in the fields, and in the streets, we shall fight in the hills; we shall never surrender, and even if, which I do not for a moment believe, this Island or a large part of it were subjugated and starving, then our Empire beyond the seas, armed and guarded by the British Fleet, would carry on the struggle, until, in God's good time, the New World with all its power and might steps forth to the rescue and liberation of the Old.[1]

The defeat
of the Third Republic

ON JUNE 10, 1940, Italy declared war upon France and Great Britain. Announcing this new diplomatic defeat, President Roosevelt said scornfully: "The hand that held the dagger has struck it into the back of its neighbor." Wishing to be in on the kill, Mussolini ordered a few Italian fighter squadrons to participate in the impending aerial onslaught on England. In the south of France, Italy occupied a few strips of land. French resistance collapsed everywhere. The French government, deciding not to risk the destruction of Paris, declared it an "open city" (i.e., undefended) and moved to Tours and later to Bordeaux. On June 14 the Germans entered Paris. French politicians began to waver, some of them out of genuine confusion. Churchill hurried to France, hoping to save the alliance. He offered a union of France and Great Britain with common citizenship for the French and the British. He urged that the French

[1]Speech delivered in the House of Commons, June 4, 1940, Winston Churchill, *Blood, Sweat, and Tears* (New York: G. P. Putnam's Sons, 1944), 297. Copyright, 1941, by Winston S. Churchill.

fleet, government, and army be transferred to French North Africa to carry on the war. The cabinet divided on that question, Reynaud trying to win consent to the continuation of the fighting. He was forced to resign.

Marshal Pétain, then eighty-four years old, became prime minister and named a cabinet in which the most influential figure was Laval, already notorious for his appeasement of Mussolini (page 812). Pétain immediately asked the Nazis for an armistice. In the forest of Compiègne, in the same railroad car in which Marshal Foch had handed the armistice terms to the German delegation in 1918, the German High Command, in the presence of Hitler and his top henchmen, made their terms known to the French delegates: More than half of France in the north and west (the parts closest to England) was to remain occupied by the Germans; all military installations in the area were to be handed over to them; the French were to pay for the costs of German occupation; the French fleet was to proceed to ports assigned by the Germans, and to remain there immobilized under German and Italian supervision; all military forces were to be disarmed and disbanded. An armistice with the Italians followed, permitting Italy to occupy some and demilitarize other areas on the Italian frontier of France or France's African colonies. The French accepted the terms of both armistices, and on June 25 France formally ceased hostilities.

The demise
of the Third Republic

ALL FRENCHMEN did not give in, however. General de Gaulle, for instance, as early as June 18, addressed the French people in a radio speech from London in which he said: "France has lost a battle; she has not lost the war." And he entreated "all Frenchmen" to "fight wherever they are." De Gaulle and the people who rallied around him formed the nucleus of what was to become the Free French movement.

France was now officially at peace with Germany. The possibility that the French fleet, most of it at anchor in the port of Oran, Algeria, might fall into the hands of the Germans or the Italians was a continuous nightmare to Churchill. The British proposed to the French admiral that his fleet should join them and continue to fight, or sail to England and be interned, or sail to the French West Indies and remain there for the duration of the war. If none of these suggestions was accepted, the French admiral was notified, the British would feel obliged to attack his ships. The French decided to risk attack, and the English, in the Battle of Oran, disabled the fleet that only a few days before had been fighting on their side. The Pétain government thereupon broke off diplomatic relations with Great Britain.

Vichy became the capital of unoccupied France. On July 9 the two houses of the French legislature, over the protests of their presidents, voted by big majorities to grant dictatorial powers to Pétain, enabling him to draft a new constitution. Two days later the French parliament adjourned for an indefinite term. Pétain abolished the national motto *Liberté, Egalité, Fraternité,* substituting for it *Honneur, Patrie, Famille.* Thus, Pétain put an end to the Third Republic. In July, Pétain made Laval prime minister. From then on, France, sometimes with Laval in the government, sometimes without Laval, moved more and more in a fascist direction.

BLITZ OVER BRITAIN

AND IN THE NEAR EAST

THE FATE OF the British Isles was the paramount question during the second half of 1940. The attack upon Britain could not be limited, however, to the fighting in the air over the British Isles. It had to be fought also on the sea lanes leading to and through the Mediterranean and the Suez Canal, by which indispensable aid went to Britain from India, the dominions, and the colonies. Until November the Russian government and the Communist parties everywhere seemed ready to hunt with the Fascist hounds. If Britain fell, it looked as if a truly isolated United States might then be confronted by a triumphant alliance of Germany, Italy, Japan, and Russia.

The lone stand *of the British Empire* THE FIRST round in the battle for Britain had been won by bringing the British Expeditionary Force safely home from Dunkirk, even if without its equipment. What saved the island from immediate attack was that Hitler preferred to concentrate his forces upon the subjugation of France in the belief that, once France collapsed, he could come to terms at leisure with a Britain which would then find itself in a hopeless position. The British expected an invasion at any moment, not knowing that Hitler was not yet contemplating an attack upon them. It is doubtful that he would have succeeded in such an attack if he had tried. His navy had sustained heavy losses in the battle for Norway, and the Germans did not possess sufficient landing craft for a large-scale amphibious operation.

All through the month of July, the German soldiers sang: "We shall sail against England," but they never did. Still, until far into 1941 Churchill and the British General Staff did not dare to discount the possibility of a German invasion. In a speech to the German Reichstag on July 19, Hitler tried the power of persuasion: "In this hour I feel I owe it to my conscience to make another appeal to reason in England. I believe I may do so because I do not speak up for reason as one who has been conquered and then pleads, but as a victor. I see no reason that makes the continuation of this struggle necessary." The offer was scornfully rejected by Great Britain three days later. Until the middle of 1941 the Germans often reiterated the appeal to "reason"—no longer in official declarations but through neutral countries and persons having contact with England.

*Air blitz
over Great Britain*

MEANWHILE, however, Hitler was finding Britain hard to crack in spite of the fact that German air superiority over the British was around three or four to one. The Germans had been carrying on daily air raids on England on a small scale since June, and regular mass air raids started in August, with more than a thousand German aircraft participating in some of them. They dropped both incendiary and explosive bombs. Most of the attacks were concentrated on London. Hitler declared publicly that the Germans would raze the British cities to the ground.

At that time the main German effort was aimed at terrorizing the civilian population of Great Britain rather than at destroying industrial and military installations—"in the silly idea that they will put pressure on the government to make peace," as Churchill put it. By that time, according to Churchill, 2000 civilians had been killed, and about 8000 wounded by the air blitz. Four fifths of the casualties were struck down in London.

The few aviators whom the Royal Air Force had been able to muster found only rare moments of rest as wave after wave of German attackers bombed the island. "Never in the field of human conflict," Churchill said in August, "was so much owed by so many to so few." The climax of the air blitz on London came on September 15. That day alone the RAF shot down a number of planes that the British believed to be 183 at the time (although it was found after the war actually to have been 56), a big enough toll to induce Goering to call off mass attacks on London for a while. Some British experts later admitted that if the air assault had lasted only a few days more, Britain's defense might have given way because of the physical exhaustion of the British aviators, the air-raid wardens, the firemen, and others whose task it was to protect the capital from destruction and to take care of the wounded and the homeless.

After their bad experience of September 15 the Nazis undertook a systematic air assault on the British Channel ports, shipping, and industrial areas. On November 14 German aircraft rained death upon the city of Coventry, and the heart of that city was utterly destroyed. The attack was intended as a "retaliatory raid" for a British bombing of Munich, where Hitler had recently given a pep talk to his cronies on the anniversary of his beer-cellar *Putsch* of 1923. Attacks upon Plymouth, Sheffield, and Manchester followed.

Meanwhile the bombardment of London continued, though on a smaller scale. Air raids upon large cities meant great loss of human life, the destruction of dwellings, factories, and office buildings, the bursting of gas, water,

The Bombing of London. This woodcut, which served as a cover illustration for the German periodical Illustrirte Zeitung *in October 1940, suggests that all of London is one vast industrial area. No monuments or church spires are shown.*

and drainage pipes with the consequent risk of epidemic, the burning of warehouses loaded with precious hoards of food and war materials, and strain upon the nerves and morale of the population. Although many private and public air-raid shelters had been constructed, a large section of the London population had to spend night after night on the platforms of the Underground (subway), which in London is very deep. Large groups of citizens were engaged every night in the tasks of air-raid wardens, helping firemen to extinguish conflagrations, warning people away from danger areas, or guiding victims from shattered homes. Firemen, police, physicians, and nurses stayed either on duty or on constant alert. Lack of sleep, inadequate food, unsanitary conditions in some of the mass shelters, and unceasing strain brought about a lowering of production in the war factories during the latter part of 1940.

The worst of all the blows on London fell on December 29. The Nazis seemed bent upon wiping London from the face of the earth on that day. An unprecedented number of incendiary bombs were dropped upon the British capital, starting a fire that made people think the day of judgment had come. St. Paul's Cathedral, though badly damaged, survived as if by a miracle, but it stood stark in the midst of a wide area of devastation. Other famous buildings in other parts of London, the Guildhall among them, were in ruins. The last large-scale air raid on London was that of May 10, 1941, when the chamber of the House of Commons and many other historic buildings were damaged or destroyed.

British defense and counterattack   THE BRITISH had developed ingenious tactics for dealing with air-raid emergencies. Lookouts climbed in regular shifts to roof tops and church steeples in order to give warning of approaching planes, not so much to save life as to avoid unnecessary strain and waste of time from false alarms. The inadequacy of the human eye for detecting objects through fog, in the dark, and at a distance was largely eliminated by science. Radar (an electronic finder that could locate distant objects) was given its first big-scale test during the Battle of Britain, and with amazing results. Chain radar stations were able to give advance warning of air raids, making it possible to reduce the number of planes engaged in patrolling the skies, to call out fighter planes only in cases of actual attack, and to reduce greatly the flying time and strain upon the hard-pressed defenders. Radar could even reveal the attackers' rate of speed. Anti-aircraft batteries and captive balloons forming a barrage around the city forced the enemy to fly high, making their marksmanship inaccurate. Demolition squads had the unenviable task of digging up unexploded bombs and rendering them harmless. But for such devices the carnage would have been more frightful than it was. The Nazi air assaults continued until June 1944, when the Germans began to use V-weapons (rocket bombs); but as the British gained experience, as their radar chain improved, and as their air force increased with increased production at home and imports from the United States and Canada, the Nazis ceased to be as successful as they had been in the beginning.

From the very start the British attempted to retaliate as well as they could. But it was harder for the Royal Air Force to reach Germany from bases in Britain than for the *Luftwaffe* (the German air force) to reach Britain from occupied France. During the latter part of 1940 the British kept the French Channel ports and the ports of the Low Countries under almost daily air attack, in order to destroy barges and other installations that might prove helpful in a Nazi attempt to invade England. Important German railroad and industrial centers were also subjected to British bombings. Limited resources obliged the British authorities not to retaliate by indiscriminate bombings but to concentrate on significant objectives one at a time. For that reason the British did not attack Berlin until August 1941. Berlin had never been the center of Germany in the sense that London was the center of England. The industrial center of Germany was the Ruhr district, which was, besides, closer to England. Thus, Ruhr cities like Hamm, Gelsenkirchen, and Duisburg, the greatest river port on the Continent, had to bear the brunt of British air bombardment.

*The obstruction
of Axis policy in western Europe*

WHEN HITLER realized that the conquest of England would be a long-drawn affair, he decided to change his political and strategic plans. The first step was the signing at Berlin of an alliance between Germany, Italy, and Japan (September 27, 1940), which became known as the Tripartite Pact. The three signatories promised "to assist one another with all political, economic, and military means" whenever one of the three contracting parties should be "attacked by a power at present not involved in the European war or the Sino-Japanese conflict." This seemed a clear reference to both Russia and the United States. In order to assuage Russia, a clause was inserted which stated that existing relations between Russia and the three contracting parties would not be affected by the pact. Nevertheless, Russia felt called upon to reconsider her foreign policy.

For the time being, Hitler in fact did not intend to break with the Soviet Union. He wanted first to bring Spain and France into the fight on the side of the Axis. Franco did everything short of war to please the Axis, but he could not be persuaded that it was yet to his advantage to make war openly, and Hitler could not bring him to attack Gibraltar or to declare war. Nor was Hitler more fortunate in winning France openly to his side. He promised the Vichy government a peace treaty with Germany, provided that it acquiesced in German troop movements through unoccupied France, the use of French ports both in metropolitan France and the colonies, and an open and official break with Great Britain. The Nazis also coveted all of the French fleet. And Laval seems in these matters to have been ready to collaborate with the Nazis. Whether Pétain was equally ready is a moot question. With their usual bluntness the Nazis destroyed any chance they might have had to win Pétain. While negotiations were still going on, they suddenly annexed Lorraine to Germany and expelled some of the people of Lorraine from their homeland. Thereupon Pétain's attitude toward Germany stiffened. American diplomacy at Vichy was directed toward encouraging Pétain to resist German demands. In December 1940, Pétain had Laval arrested for alleged conspiracy, but upon the insistence of the Germans Laval was released, although he was not immediately returned to office. Thus, the German plans for an alliance with the dictator of France met with no more success than with the dictator of Spain.

*The beginning
of war in the Balkans*

HITLER WAS more successful in the Balkans. In June 1940, immediately after the downfall of France, a Russian ultimatum obliged the Rumanians to return the frequently exchanged Bessarabia to Russia and to cede northern Bukovina along with it. Those cessions gave the signal for a general partition of Rumania. Both

Bulgaria and Hungary were eager to get back the provinces they had lost to the Rumanians at the end of the First World War. In order to avoid a Balkan war, which neither Hitler nor Mussolini wanted at that time, the Germans forced the Rumanians to cede the Dobruja to the Bulgarians and the northern half of Transylvania to Hungary.

The surrender of the Transylvanians to the hated Hungarians caused a political convulsion in Rumania. The Rumanian Nazis, the so-called Iron Guard, seized upon the popular resentment to get rid of the anti-German King Carol II, who once more had to flee, with Magda Lupescu, from the country. His son Michael became a puppet king under the rule of the Iron Guard Marshal Ion Antonescu, who styled himself "head of the state." With Antonescu's permission the Nazis occupied Rumania. Hitler had now secured one of his principal aims: Germany stood upon the shores of the Black Sea.

Mussolini so far had played the role of a very poor second to Hitler during the war. Germany's encroachments in the Balkans not only overshadowed the Italian dictator's aspirations but were positively dangerous to Italy's security. Therefore, he decided to act on his own without notifying Germany about what was to happen. In October 1940, the Italians invaded Greece.

Italian defeats
by the Greeks and the British

THE ITALIAN government had dreamed of a repetition of the Nazi blitzkrieg in Greece. Instead they were stalled by the Greeks. The Italian air force proved inefficient, the army ill equipped and badly led. Fantastic corruption in the Fascist hierarchy rendered the Italian forces inadequate for waging war even against so small a country as Greece. On November 7 the Italians suffered a heavy defeat at Janina. By the end of the year the Italians had been driven out of Greece, and the Greeks had invaded Italian-dominated Albania and inflicted one defeat after another upon the Italians.

In addition, the Italians suffered badly on the seas. A British air attack in November 1940 devastated their fleet gathered in the port of Taranto. The next March the British administered a heavy defeat to the Italian fleet off the coast of Greece near Cape Matapan. It was obvious that despite the excellence of the Italian army, air force, and navy on paper, Britannia still ruled the waves of the Mediterranean. By the end of 1940 Mussolini had to beg for German air support.

Meanwhile, the Italians had experienced successes and reversals in Africa. They had conquered British Somaliland in August 1940. In the fall they penetrated into Egypt as far as Sidi Barrani. But from December on, the Italian forces suffered a series of shattering defeats at the hands of the British. In February 1941, the British took Bengasi in the Italian colony of Libya. They also reconquered British Somaliland, occupied Italian Somaliland and Eritrea, and in May liberated Ethiopia, where Emperor Haile

Selassie, after five years of exile, resumed his rule. Mussolini lost face within Italy and without.

The Nazi conquest of the Balkan Peninsula

OUT OF CONSIDERATION for his own prestige as a dictator as well as to aid an ally, Hitler decided to go to the aid of the Italians. Before he did so, however, discretion required that he make sure that no complicating Balkan troubles should arise in his rear. He first endeavored, therefore, to bring the Balkans into the Tripartite orbit.

Here, for the first time, the Führer was to receive a setback. On March 1 the Nazis occupied Bulgaria with the acquiescence of King Boris III. The example of what had happened in Rumania and Bulgaria prompted Prince Regent Paul of Yugoslavia to submit to the German demands, and in March 1941, he acquiesced to a "nonaggression" pact with Germany. The prince regent realized that if he resisted Nazi pressure, an invasion by German, Bulgarian, and Hungarian forces was to be expected. But as soon as the Yugoslav people learned about the pact with Germany, they revolted. The prince regent and the government were ousted after a bloodless rebellion, and young King Peter was made head of the state.

Hitler's setback was not for long. He now forced the Hungarians to line up with him. The submission of Admiral Nicholas Horthy to the Nazi demands led to the suicide of his prime minister, Count Paul Teleki, who apparently preferred not to repudiate his recent treaty of friendship with Yugoslavia. On April 6, 1941, the Germans invaded both Yugoslavia and Greece. Belgrade was subjected to a terrific air attack, and the Nazis subdued Yugoslavia within a short time. The Germans then overran Greece despite desperate Greek resistance and soon came into the possession of such hallowed places as Mount Olympus, Thermopylae, and Athens. By the end of May continental Greece was in the hands of the Nazis.

The British, with what little troops and arms they could spare from their North African front, helped the Greeks as best they could. But by May 1941, the Greek and British armies were cornered on Crete. The Germans started the Battle of Crete with air tactics known only theoretically so far—mass invasion by glider-borne parachutists. Despite heavy losses, the Germans soon conquered the whole island. The discouraged remnants of the Greek and British forces were evacuated to Egypt.

A Nazi attempt to get a truce with England

A MOMENTARY but ultimately fruitless sensation was provided in May, when Rudolf Hess, the deputy Führer of Germany, landed in an airplane on the estate of the Scottish Duke of Hamilton and Brandon. Evidence brought out after the war during Hess' trial as a war criminal made clear that he had acted of his own accord. He was so imbued with Hitler's idea of neutralizing Britain in the prospective

872

war with Russia that he still pursued it, even though Hitler had by this time given it up. Like other Nazis, Hess failed to grasp either the mood of the British people or the political setup within Great Britain. He had flown a lone mission to Scotland believing that if only he could talk with representatives of a British appeasement group (which in 1941 hardly existed outside his imagination), he could easily arrange a compromise between Germany and Great Britain that would leave Germany free to handle Russia. He was arrested and held incommunicado for the rest of the war. The Nazis first declared Hess to be insane, and certainly he behaved at his subsequent trial in an abnormal fashion. But this explanation fitted too well into British anti-Nazi propaganda as a reflection upon the wisdom of Hitler's choice of deputies. The Nazi propaganda machine then changed its tune, saying that Hess was a misguided idealist. The Hess episode had no influence upon the course of the war. It did, however, mirror the intensity of anti-Russian feeling in certain high circles of Germany.

The impact
of the war upon the United States

WHEN WAR had broken out in September 1939, the American people had little doubt that Hitler had so willed it. Also, all but the Communists believed that he probably would not have undertaken the gamble without the acquiescence of Russia. Despite widespread disgust with Nazism and Communism, Americans generally hoped that the United States would stay out of the war, the more so as they saw no need to become involved, since the French army was still thought of as invincible.

But when between September 1939 and July 1940, Hitler conquered seven European countries including France, many Americans became disturbed about the security of their own country. The main question on everybody's lips was: Would Great Britain, too, fall a victim to Nazi aggression? Hope seemed forlorn. Yet Churchill's determination became an inspiration to Americans no less than to the British.

The fall of Paris was a personal loss to many of the American people. A nostalgic popular song, "The Last Time I Saw Paris," became a "hit" on radio and dance programs. A "great debate" raged between isolationists and nonisolationists, the former not necessarily appeasers, the latter not necessarily interventionists.

Arguments
for American isolationism

THE ISOLATIONISTS comprised four different groups. Some were "practical" men, who, dazzled either by sheer Nazi power or by what on the surface looked like Nazi efficiency, feared that intervention would end only in defeat. Others were idealists, who opposed any measures that might lead to war out of religious scruples or out of a feeling that the United States had too many shortcomings at home (illiteracy, slums, racial prejudice, inadequate medical care, corruption in city politics, etc.) to embark again on a crusade for democracy far beyond the seas. Then there were those who said that the affairs of Europe were no concern of the United States: Europeans had never been able to get along with each other, and it was not America's business to save those who obviously were beyond redemption; moreover, Europe was far away, and neither Hitler nor Mussolini could attack America even if he wanted to. The last group perhaps made up the plurality among the isolationists.

These three groups of isolationists acted out of relatively disinterested conviction. Other groups, however, considered America's future course a question of sheer politics. Since intellectuals who had joined the Communist Party to promote a proletarian revolution had dropped out, disgusted by the Kremlin's pro-Hitler policy, the "party line" was now anti-British ("The Yanks are not coming!"). And some conservatives, out of dislike for the domestic policy of President Roosevelt, hoped to replace him at the next election, and feared that if the United States became entangled directly in the European war, "that man" Roosevelt, despite the tradition that limited presidents to two terms, would attempt to be reëlected.

American precautions to defend the Western Hemisphere WITH EVERY new success of Hitler the United States felt compelled, for its own safety, to take another step in the direction of outright intervention. But it was a painful, mooted process. As early as May 1940, it became obvious that Hitler's victories would necessitate some strategic precautions for the Americas. Some of the European countries had possessions in the Western Hemisphere. What was to become of them? If Hitler laid claim to them, should he be allowed to control them directly or by proxy or not at all? What was to become of the French islands of Saint Pierre and Miquelon at the mouth of the St. Lawrence River? What about the French and the Dutch possessions in the West Indies? What about French and Dutch Guiana?

The French and Dutch possessions in other continents likewise presented complications. Those in Asia were coveted by the Japanese. Dakar, a sea and air port in French West Africa, in the hands of the Germans would be a serious threat to Brazil, since it is located at a point in Africa within only a few hours' flight from South America. President Roosevelt reminded Congress that "from the fjords of [Danish] Greenland it is...only six hours [by air] to New England." Denmark was already in German hands, and to keep the Danish outpost of Greenland out of Nazi hands, the Monroe Doctrine was extended to Greenland. In May 1941, after German aircraft were sighted in the neighborhood, the United States, though still at peace with Germany, put Greenland under its protection. It was found out then that the Nazis had installed a weather observation post on the pack ice of Greenland. The post was destroyed by American forces. The Faroe Islands and Iceland, both of them connected with the Danish crown, had been occupied by the British, but

874

only after an American vessel was sunk in the surrounding seas, in the summer before the United States entered the war, was Iceland garrisoned by Americans. None of these acts could be successfully counteracted by isolationist opinion.

The New World to the rescue of the Old

AFTER THE British Expeditionary Force fled the Continent with little more than the equipment its soldiers could carry, the idea of aiding Britain by "methods short of war" gained a firmer and firmer grasp upon the minds of Americans. From American arsenals and armament factories a steady stream of rifles, guns, tanks, planes, and ammunition flowed to England on a "cash and carry" basis. In September 1940, fifty allegedly overage destroyers were sent to the British, who needed them desperately in their struggle against German submarines and surface raiders. In exchange the United States received a ninety-nine year lease on naval and air bases to be constructed in the Western Hemisphere—in Newfoundland, Bermuda, the Bahamas, Saint Lucia, Antigua, Trinidad, Jamaica, and British Guiana. This was a two-pronged move in defense of the Atlantic.

Meanwhile, Roosevelt was also taking steps to build up hemispheric strength and solidarity. He promoted cooperation with Canada and Latin America. In October the first United States conscription act to be enforced in peacetime went into operation—the Selective Training and Service Act. Sixteen million men registered for the "draft." A few months later the National Guard was taken into the federal service. In December a board of four distinguished men—the Office of Production Management—was set up to eliminate the bottlenecks in the armament program. Its chairman was William S. Knudsen, a naturalized citizen who had become famous as an automobile executive; its other members were Sidney Hillman, a Jewish immigrant who was now an outstanding figure in the C.I.O., and two prominent Republicans whom Roosevelt had added to his cabinet, Henry L. Stimson, secretary of war, and Frank Knox, secretary of the navy.

The third election of Roosevelt as president

PRESIDENT ROOSEVELT, indeed, did bid for a third term. His Republican opponent was Wendell Willkie, a businessman who was a relative newcomer to politics and had been forced upon the Republican nominating convention by popular demand. Willkie refused to make foreign policy an election issue and spoke out against Hitler as much as Roosevelt did. Despite the fact that Willkie received more votes than any Republican candidate before him, Roosevelt received more than Willkie, and for the first, and presumably for the last time (because in 1951 the Twenty-second Amendment to the Constitution was to forbid more than two presidential terms) a United States president was inaugurated for a third term. The defeat of isolationism in both parties 875 did not end the great debate, which went on until the United States was itself attacked (page 883).

(page 883).

The abandonment of American neutrality

TOWARD THE end of 1940 it became increasingly clear that Great Britain was financially scraping the bottom of the barrel. The enormous orders that had been placed in America for foods, planes, tanks, and other implements of war had nearly exhausted the assets and security holdings of Great Britain. British gold flowed to India in a steady stream to pay for the welcome deliveries of products from the fast-developing Indian industries. The Indians thus were enabled to wield a most effective weapon—the power of the creditor—in their struggle for independence from the British.

The American government felt that something unorthodox had to be done to extricate Great Britain from a dangerous economic situation. Otherwise British bankruptcy and defeat would result. Roosevelt had never been satisfied with the cash and carry policy. Shortly after his third inauguration (January 1941), a bill was introduced in Congress for the purpose of authorizing the president to make available any implements of war, by loan or lease or any other way he might deem appropriate, to the British or any other nation taking part in the struggle against Germany or Italy. The Lend-Lease Act, as it was popularly called, was put on the statute books in March. Three days later Roosevelt declared, "Our country is going to be what our people have proclaimed it must be—the arsenal of democracy."

To the Nazis the Lend-Lease Act came as a hard blow. They had been confident that within a foreseeable time the British treasure chest would be exhausted and that then the United States, which they liked to picture as a country of 130,000,000 money-mad people, would refuse to help the British any longer. Their outcry against lend-lease testified to their profound chagrin. The Axis powers looked with dismay at the armament program America was undertaking. In answer to Mussolini's and Hitler's propaganda, Roosevelt shifted the anti-Nazi struggle to ideological grounds. In a broadcast on January 6, 1941, he enumerated for the first time what later became known as "the Four Freedoms"—freedom of speech, freedom of religion, freedom from want, and freedom from fear.

THE TRIPARTITE DIVISION

OF THE WORLD

HITLER WAS beyond doubt the victor so far. As yet, not even the historical tendency of the menaced to unite against the menace was operating against him. The United States was slowly awakening to the dangers of Hitlerism, to be sure, but in Russia the old anti-German feeling was slow to reassert itself. Nevertheless, Hitler now decided that England's doom would have to wait until he could make sure of Russia one way or another.

The strain between Russia and Germany

THE OFFICIAL Russian position at the outset of the war had been pro-German. "It was not Germany who attacked France and England," Stalin declared, "but France and England who attacked Germany, thus assuming responsibility for the present war." Although the German victory over France had to a certain extent been due to the friendly neutrality of Russia, the swift victory of the Germans produced Russian fear of a victorious and relatively unscathed Germany. For their part the Germans could not close their eyes to the aggrandizement of Russia at the expense of the buffer states on the Baltic and elsewhere; and they closed ranks with their other allies, Italy and Japan, and with their satellites through the Tripartite Pact (September and November 1940). As Ribbentrop put it in November: "Both partners of the German-Russian Pact had together done some good business." Now Hitler offered a division of the Eastern Hemisphere among Germany, Italy, Japan, and Russia. Russia, however, insisted upon certain assurances with regard to Finland, the Straits, the Caucasus, and Northern Sakhalin in addition to the proffered "territorial aspirations...south of the national territory of the Soviet Union in the direction of the Indian Ocean." Unwilling to make these additional concessions, Hitler began to toy with the idea of attacking Russia even before he settled with England.

The preliminaries of the Russo-German war

IN NOVEMBER 1940, the new turn of affairs dimly began to appear. Molotov visited Berlin but could accomplish practically nothing. The meeting left behind unmistakable signs of mutual distrust between Germans and Russians. Shortly afterwards Hitler ordered his generals to prepare for war on Russia. Yet the rulers of Russia refused to believe that a rupture was close at hand. Warnings from the British and the American governments were regarded by the Kremlin as suspect.

Nevertheless, the warnings were entirely justified. Early in 1941 Hitler amassed his armies at the borders of Russia. He was ready for an invasion by the spring. But the crowded events in Greece and Yugoslavia (page 872) forced him to delay his attack on Russia. The Russians, at last feeling uneasy, concluded a neutrality pact with Japan in April. Thereby the Japanese gained freedom from Russian threat in northeastern Asia, and the Russians, feeling secure in their rear, could concentrate upon their armies in the west. On May 6 Stalin assumed the premiership of Soviet Russia, thus symbolizing the union of the Russian Communist Party and the Russian state in the person of a single leader.

A Nazi view of the Soviet Union. The woodcut appeared in a German magazine in April 1943.

The invasion of Russia by the Nazi armies

THE NAZI INVASION of Russia started at dawn on June 22, 1941. The German armies were supported by the armies of Hungary and Rumania and (after June 25) Finland. Later Italian, Slovak, and Bulgarian units and French and Spanish "volunteers" were added to the German forces. The attack started on a front stretching from the Baltic to the Black Sea. The invading armies advanced slowly but relentlessly. Not fully mobilized and with an air force unequal to that of the Germans, the Russians could do no more than fight delaying actions. They exchanged space for time. They gave ground everywhere, but the Germans were unable to break through the Russian front.

As Hitler had expected, whole Russian units, especially among disaffected Ukrainians, surrendered without a fight. In several Russian towns and villages the German commanders were received with bread and salt, the traditional symbols of hospitality. In some areas the Germans were openly greeted as liberators. If Hitler had his prototype Napoleon Bonaparte in mind at all, he must have decided he could avoid the earlier invader's error. But he committed a worse one. His mind was set on enslaving the "inferior" Russians.

As a consequence, even the most disaffected groups within Russia began to side with their government. A savage guerrilla war started against the German invader. On July 3, Stalin announced a "scorched earth" policy: "In case of a forced retreat...all valuable property, including metals, grain, and fuel, that cannot be withdrawn, must be destroyed without fail...Blow up bridges and roads, damage telephone and telegraph lines, set fire to forests, stores, and transport." Whatever of Russian industry could be moved was somehow carried to the east, out of the way of the invaders.

England, Iran, and American lend-lease

THE DAY OF the German invasion Churchill announced that "any man or State who fights against Nazism will have our aid." On July 13 a Russo-British alliance was concluded. The United States soon extended its lend-lease aid to Russia. But before this aid could be carried to its destination a bottleneck had to be removed. Because of Germany's strength on the Baltic and the Black Sea, lend-lease goods had to take more indirect routes. One of them was via the Persian Gulf and Iran. But Iran was infested with German agents, and the shah, Reza Shah Pahlavi, did nothing to keep them under control. On the contrary, he resisted British pressure to do something about them. The shah had started his dazzling reputation as an anti-Russian officer in the First World War. Throughout his subsequent career he remained thoroughly pro-German and anti-Russian. After he placed himself upon the Peacock Throne, he retained his friendly attitude to the German cause. The British and Russians now sent troops into Iran and saw to it that he abdicated in favor of his son (September 1941). They arrested the shah and interned him on the island of Mauritius. Soon British and Russian troops occupied the most important railroad centers, ports, highways, and oil wells of Iran, and American supplies began going through to Russia.

The battle of the Atlantic

ANOTHER important line of delivery led to Murmansk, on the Arctic Ocean. The way to Murmansk became the most dangerous route on the seven seas. German submarines prowled the narrow channel between the coast of the Kola Peninsula and the drift ice of the northern seas. Ice, fog, snow, storms, and enemy submarines took a heavy toll of the Allied merchant marine. At the same time Great Britain and the United States were hard pressed by submarine warfare in the Atlantic. German submarines appeared as far west as the Atlantic coast of Long Island.

The U-boat menace was only slowly overcome by a defense system that employed both old and new devices. Depth charges and convoys (protected now by aircraft as well as warships) gave better protection than the same

879

tactics in the First World War. New devices like radar made detection of hostile craft easier and speedier. Yet defense of maritime shipments might have been impossible had not the British succeeded in driving German surface raiders from the seas. After a dramatic chase the British sank the German battleship *Bismarck,* the world's largest and swiftest, in May 1941.

The proclamation of the Atlantic Charter

BY THE SUMMER of 1941, the United States, despite the persistence of the isolationist attitude among large groups of the population, was in the war in all but name. Step by step the government, acting from sympathy with the Allies and fear of the Tripartite powers, had given all the "aid short of war" that it legally could (and, some maintained, more than it legally could). In June all German assets in America were frozen. During the same month all German and Italian consulates were closed by order of the United States government, and their officials expelled. The United States extended its naval patrol as far east as Iceland.

The American people did not feel, however, that they wanted to become involved in a new bloodletting merely to help the Allied nations. They felt that they were entitled to know what kind of postwar world an Allied victory might help to create. To enable him to meet the demand for a better world and also to discuss the many complex military, economic, and diplomatic questions arising from the war, Roosevelt agreed to a personal conference with Churchill. They met on a British warship off the coast of Newfoundland, and on August 14 they issued from shipboard the Atlantic Charter. It was cast in a framework of eight points. The American president and the British prime minister declared: "Their countries seek no aggrandizement, territorial or other" (Point 1); "they desire to see no territorial changes that do not accord with the freely expressed wishes of the peoples concerned" (Point 2). And they called for "a peace which will afford to all nations the means of dwelling in safety within their own boundaries, and which will afford assurance that all the men in all the lands may live out their lives in freedom from fear and want" (Point 6).

The declaration thrilled the Allied nations. But they probably read more into it than was intended. First of all, it was not a treaty; it bound England and the United States merely as a set of lofty principles, and it did not bind Russia at all. The response nevertheless weakened the isolationists of America and gave new enthusiasm to the movement for "aid short of war."

Undeclared war on the Atlantic Ocean

IN SEPTEMBER 1941, President Roosevelt, interpreting his position as commander in chief of the navy to give him the necessary authority, ordered that American sea forces strike at Nazi U-boat raiders in "any waters which America deems vital to its defense." The Germans struck back, attacking an American destroyer. Thereupon Roosevelt ordered the United States Navy to "shoot on sight." By October, the United States and Germany were actually though not formally at war on the Atlantic. Nazi U-boats heavily damaged one American destroyer and torpedoed another, which sank with about one hundred members of her crew.

The crest of Tripartite power

WHETHER EVEN an undeclared naval war would be sufficient to save the Allies now was doubtful. Russia seemed on the point of a collapse like that of France a year before. In September 1941, the Nazis occupied Kiev. On October 3 Hitler declared that Russia's power was broken "never to rise again." By mid-October the Nazis were at the gates of Moscow. The Russian capital was transferred deep inland to Kuibyshev (once Samara) on the bend of the Volga. The diplomatic corps and everyone not directly engaged in the defense of Moscow were forced to leave the city. In the south, Odessa, Kharkov, and Rostov fell in quick succession. On December 6 Goebbels alerted the Berlin journalists to stand by for an important announcement. He apparently meant to flash news of the fall of Moscow. But Moscow never fell.

A plan for conquest was unfolding on a scale that made the undertakings of Genghis Khan and Napoleon seem pale in comparison. Hitler was after the Caucasian oil wells, to be sure, but they were only part of a far more ambitious strategic plan. The German armies were supposed to make a two-pronged push eastward—via southern Russia into the northern Caucasus and via Turkey and Iran into the southern Caucasus to the shores of the Persian Gulf. The Italians were supposed to hold North Africa with the aid of the Nazis. The Japanese were supposed to hold down China and to conquer Oceania and Australia. Southeastern and southern Asia, once thought of as a possible award to a loyal Russia, might also now go to Japan—including India, if possible, by means of an Indian rebellion against the British. If feasible, the Japanese were also to attack Russia in eastern Siberia, and then the victorious German and Japanese armies would meet somewhere in the Middle East. This program of world conquest miscarried because (1) the Germans, for reasons still unknown, never attacked Turkey, and they did not succeed in making the Turks their allies; (2) the German advance was stalled in the northern Caucasus; (3) Stalingrad constituted an immense roadblock, where a huge Nazi army was annihilated during the winter of 1942-1943; (4) the Italo-German armies in North Africa were destroyed; (5) the Japanese carefully refrained from attacking Russia; (6) India did not revolt; and (7) from August 1942 the Japanese were to find themselves too much occupied with trying to save their own skins to carry out Hitler's grandiose scheme.

The failure
of American-Japanese negotiations

ALL THROUGH the year 1941 the relations between Japan and the United States had gone from bad to worse. By a treaty in the spring of that year between Japan and Vichy France, Indochina practically became part of the Japanese "Co-Prosperity Sphere." This action made the British hold in Malaya practically untenable, and the Americans agreed with Great Britain, Australia, and New Zealand to plan jointly for the protection of this strategic area. In the summer of 1941 the United States government froze Japanese assets and forbade the shipping of oil and scrap iron to Japan. Moreover, Roosevelt refused to engage in high-level direct negotiations with Prince Konoye, preferring the usual diplomatic channels. On September 6 an imperial conference, with the approval of the emperor, reached a decision which established, in the later words of Premier Prince Fumimaro Konoye, "a point...beyond which negotiations could not proceed." On October 16 the cabinet of the still hesitant Prince Konoye resigned, and the belligerent General Hideki Tojo became prime minister. The Japanese cabinet then decided upon war against America, provided a last effort for a compromise should fail. The price the United States would have had to pay was the abandonment of China and Indochina, but the Japanese probably did not expect the Americans to abandon these countries. Although many in Washington believed even at this early stage that the Chiang Kai-shek regime was undependable, no one considered it desirable to leave China and the vital resources of southeast Asia to the mercy of the Japanese. While negotiations were still going on in Washington, the Japanese sent their fleet out to attack Pearl Harbor.

Chinese women load ammunition for the war against Japan. A woodcut by Lu Tien.

The "day
that will live in infamy"

ON SUNDAY morning, December 7, 1941, the Japanese air force and some midget submarines attacked Pearl Harbor by surprise. The attackers destroyed 177 American planes on the ground, sank or badly crippled 8 battleships and a number of other vessels, did much damage to military installations, killed 2343 men of the American armed forces, and inflicted over 2000 other casualties. Never in all its history had the United States suffered a greater defeat. The success of the surprise attack was due to insufficient alertness on the part of the military authorities in Hawaii, which in turn was partly due to a lack of coordination between the army and navy commands in Hawaii, and between the state, war, and navy departments in Washington. The Japanese also succeeded in a similar attack, though one of lesser intensity, on Manila, although there Japanese success in destroying grounded planes and military installations was due both to American confusion and to inadequacy of air defense. British installations at Hong Kong and on Malaya were also attacked.

That day marked for the Japanese a bold and successful military maneuver and for Americans a day which "will live in infamy," as President Roosevelt put it. It forced a reluctant United States into the war. A few days before Pearl Harbor the *Chicago Daily Tribune,* a leading isolationist newspaper, and other newspapers had published a summary, with verbatim extracts, of certain government plans for war mobilization, and critics of the government in Congress had protested against these "secret war plans." But after Pearl Harbor isolationism practically disappeared. The next day war was declared upon Japan by the United States and England; and a few days later, Germany and Italy declared war on the United States.

The turning
of the Pacific tide

DURING THE first months of the new war, one catastrophe after another was inflicted upon English, American, and Dutch possessions in the Pacific. The Pacific became an almost uncontested Japanese ocean. The Japanese took from the United States Guam, Wake Island, the Philippines, and some of the Aleutian Islands; from Britain Hong Kong, Singapore, Malaya, and Burma; and from the Netherlands the Dutch East Indies. All these territories were conquered by the Japanese within a few days or, where heroic resistance was offered, a few months. Australia was in mortal danger. Anxiety on the American Pacific Coast reached the point where the military obliged all persons of Japanese descent, even if American-born citizens, unless otherwise authorized, to leave the coastal area, and established "relocation camps" in inland states for those who could not provide for themselves. By the next spring, an American fleet was reassembled in the Pacific, but the Japanese advance was not stopped until the Battle of the Coral Sea (May 7-8, 1942), which saved the supply lines of Australia from further cutting and the Battle of Midway (June 3-6),

AXIS POWER
AT ITS CREST 1942

By May 1942 the Axis powers controlled most of Europe, much of southeast Asia and the western Pacific, and a large part of Africa. German "blitzkrieg" had overrun Poland in 1939, then in 1940 Norway, Denmark, the Low Countries, and northern France. (The northern half and western coast of France were occupied outright, the remainder being held under Nazi domination through the Pétain government at Vichy.) Italy aided in the conquest of France, mostly by tying up a portion of the French forces in the south. In the North African theater, Italy enjoyed early

which kept the Japanese from Midway and the approaches to Hawaii. The United Nations took the offensive with the capture of Guadalcanal in the Solomon Islands by American landing forces in August. This was the first of a series of hops from one Japanese island stronghold to another, intended

884   ultimately to lead the Allies to the beaches of Japan.

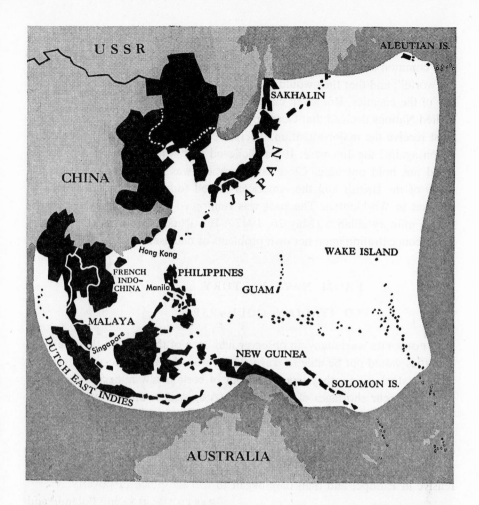

successes, but by 1941 Germany had to bolster her against British counterattacks. In the Balkans, Albania (now an Italian puppet state), Hungary, and Rumania joined the Axis in 1940, and Italy attacked Greece only to bog down at Janina. Bulgaria joined the Axis in 1941. A German drive through Yugoslavia and Greece followed. In Asia the third member of the Axis had by the end of 1941 gained great advantages at the expense of France and China. Japan waited, however, until her attack on Pearl Harbor to start her "blitzkrieg." By May 1942 Japan dominated French Indochina, British Burma, the Dutch East Indies, and several United States possessions—Wake, Guam, the Philippines, and several of the outer Aleutian Islands. The USSR had by 1940 extended her western outposts by annexing Estonia, Latvia, Lithuania, Bessarabia, eastern Poland, parts of Finland, etc., but these were overrun as well as much of southwestern Russia in the Nazi attack of 1941-1942. (The boundary lines here given for Europe are roughly those of 1939-1942 with some of the traditional names retained even where they had been officially changed.)

Establishment of the United Nations

ADVERSITY produced solidarity among the defeated. Toward the end of 1941 Churchill came to Washington. On New Year's Day, twenty-six governments, including those of the "Big Three" (England, Russia, and the United States), proclaimed in 885 a solemn declaration that they subscribed to the principles of the Atlantic Charter; that they would pool their "full resources, military or economic" in the "common struggle against savage and brutal forces seeking to subjugate the world"; and that they would not make a separate armistice or peace with any of the enemies. Roosevelt called the alliance "the United Nations." The United Nations decided that Germany, as the most dangerous of the enemies, must receive the major attention. Therefore, they must fight only a delaying action against the Japanese. It was believed that when Germany fell, Japan could not hold out long. Close collaboration was established between the heads of the British and the American armed forces. A permanent British staff sat in Washington. The pact was reinforced by a twenty-year Russo-British military alliance (May 26, 1942). But Russia remained more or less aloof, concentrating upon her own problems of defense.

FROM NAZI VICTORY
TO ITALIAN COLLAPSE

BEFORE THE war, many an observer had been of the opinion that the Axis countries would not be able to wage a long war. According to this view, for all their stock-piling, they would run out of certain raw materials and were bound to incur shortages of man power. Axis writers and military experts, however, had publicly declared time and again that supplies and man power would come from conquered countries. And such exploitation of the conquered was exactly what happened—as long as there were countries to conquer. By 1943, however, the Axis countries were forced to take the defensive in Europe, and then they began to feel the pinch of poverty.

Plunder, slave labor, and concentration camps

PARTICULARLY in Poland and Russia, the Nazis let the vanquished know by word and deed what it was like to be "inferior." Although no German soldier was allowed to loot anything for himself, the Nazi government systematically removed things from the subjugated nations. Whatever could contribute to the Nazi war effort was taken away—bedding, clothing, food, razor blades, machinery, and anything of metal like church bells and monuments.

The huge losses in German soldiers killed, wounded, or missing during the Russian campaign caused the Nazis to exploit the labor of the conquered peoples. Since every German or satellite national able to bear arms was drafted, a labor shortage resulted in the war industries and on the farms. For that reason the Nazis resorted to slave labor. Hundreds of thousands of inhabitants of the occupied countries, whether they wished to go or not, were shipped to Germany, Austria, and German-occupied Czechoslovakia to work in German factories and fields. Many Italians were "lent" to the Germans for the same purpose, the Fascist government selecting those Italians who were most likely to oppose the regime. The Germans treated these laborers no better than the nationals of a hostile power.

Recalcitrants among the men and women of the occupied countries as well as intellectuals suspected of despising the Nazis were likely to be sent to concentration camps. Huge numbers of people perished in these camps. Some of them were deliberately done away with; others were slowly starved or died from lack of medical care. Wherever the Nazis set foot, the Jews were arrested, shipped to segregated concentration camps, and exterminated in gas chambers. Literally millions of Jews disappeared thus. Before or after death the victims were stripped of everything valuable, even of the fillings in their teeth. With meticulous bookkeeping the Nazis kept track of all their confiscations and executions. The German population as a whole, however, knew little of these wholesale atrocities. Though the horrors of the concentration camps were suspected abroad during the war, only after the Americans and the British captured the camps in 1945 and liberated their inmates did the awful truth become generally known. The reports of United States Congressional and British Parliamentary committees, all of which made investigations on the spot, divulged unprecedented horrors. Names like "Buchenwald" and "Dachau" (the most notorious camps) became bywords for bestiality.

Underground and resistance movements

UNDER THE impact of Nazi treatment, underground movements sprang up in all the German-occupied countries. In Russia they were organized by the government. The underground waged a relentless war against the Germans, cutting supply lines, dynamiting the headquarters of German civilian and military authorities, sniping, burning supplies, and destroying ammunition dumps. The French underground became the best known of them. It was called the *maquis,* and its members were called *maquisards. Maquis* is derived from the Corsican word *macchia,* meaning the region of almost inaccessible and dense underbrush in Corsica. The name was given the French underground because its members often hid out in mountainous, forest-covered wastes hardly accessible to the enemy. Under elected or self-appointed leaders it developed a discipline and a cohesion. The *maquis* received weapons and secret instructions from General de Gaulle and from British military authorities, and were in constant radio touch with the British. The French underground was to prove its value at the time of the Allied invasion of France in 1944, when it harassed the rear of the German armies. It was to bring about the French rebellion in Paris on the eve of the liberation of that city, and thus was perhaps instrumental in saving Paris from the total destruction that Hitler is believed to have planned in case of a German retreat.

In the Axis countries, resistance movements met with varying success. The Italians had an underground that was eventually to be heard from (page

894). Something of the kind developed even in Germany. Through 1942, Gestapo repression and Nazi regulations worked smoothly. Dislocations in the distribution of raw materials and man power among the war industries started only in 1943, when the big German cities became the targets of English and American aerial bombings, but even then the Germans managed to construct and to run many camouflaged and subterranean factories at full or near capacity. Discontent reached notable proportions on the home front only as the war lengthened. As long as victory seemed assured, grumbling was at a minimum. But when the hope of victory began to fade, a people that did not dare to express its fears began to fall into apathy. A few idealistic clericals and university students risked their lives in a futile resistance. Some high-ranking officers and civil servants finally dared to make a nearly successful attempt on Hitler's life, but only after the evidence became convincing that he was leading Germany to destruction. The effectiveness of the Gestapo at home, the German readiness to submit to authority, and skepticism abroad about the real motives of the resistance movement in Germany kept it from acquiring the strength that the underground acquired elsewhere. In Japan, despite the average man's miserable lot during the war, no sign of organized resistance appeared.

Problems of the Allied home fronts

THE UNITED Nations also had home-front problems. Great Britain, having borne the brunt of Nazi attack almost alone for over two years, had by the end of 1941 mobilized all of her resources—man power, money, opinion, industry, housing, etc.— for victory. Total mobilization was accepted as a matter of course by the newcomers, Russia and the United States. The Russians relocated an important part of their industries in or near the Ural Mountains, in Siberia, and in central Asia, where they were not easily accessible to Nazi air attack. Strict regimentation and the low standards of living to which the Russians were accustomed facilitated the task of the Soviet government. They managed to produce an enormous amount of artillery and some of the world's best tanks.

The American home-front situation was quite different. Great reluctance was shown on all sides to interfere with private enterprise, and a business-as-usual attitude prevailed not only during the years of lend-lease but also after Pearl Harbor. The many million unemployed were easily absorbed into the war production program, and despite the draft no serious man power shortage occurred. Everyone realized after bombs started dropping on the soil of American territories that drastic changes would have to be made in the national economy, but in taking concrete measures, both capital and labor tried to shoulder as little of the burden as possible. Profits and wages, and hence prices, went up. The rate of taxation was raised, but not high enough to prevent an inflationary trend. Industry at first was only slowly converted to war production. When President Roosevelt announced as the American goal the production of 50,000 planes per year, he was derided in many quarters. Some of those who later boasted loudest of America's fantastic war production were, in the beginning, men of little faith. They were induced, however, by cost-plus-fixed-fee contracts (a guaranteed profit beyond the costs of manufacture) to run the risks of conversion. Eventually price and wage controls, rationing of consumers' goods, and allocation of basic materials were instituted. By the end of 1943 the American people had become reconciled to wartime restrictions, to doing without new automobiles and nylon stockings, and to putting up with rationed gasoline, tires, sugar, and aluminum ware.

Scientific and technological progress

WAR NEEDS required the government and research institutions to put more money and effort into scientific research than ever before. Some medical techniques worked out before the war were now applied on a vast scale. A remarkable feature of the war was that no epidemic struck British and American soldiers or civilians. Every person serving with the armed forces was immunized against a number of diseases, among them typhoid fever and cholera. Although the United States was cut off from its quinine supply by Japanese conquests, relatively few cases of malaria occurred because substitutes for quinine were found in time. Elephantiasis and a few other tropical diseases with which western medicine was not familiar did, however, occur in some instances. Penicillin and the sulfa drugs proved invaluable in the treatment of the wounded. And the general use of blood plasma may perhaps be the greatest achievement of wartime medicine. The people eagerly responded to the government's request for donations of blood.

In technology the necessities of war led to several outstanding achievements. These included the jeep, the bazooka, the improvement of infrared photography, the development of invasion craft, and the construction of artificial ports, for the purpose of facilitating invasion. Loran (long range navigation) enabled a navigator to plot his own position by means of signals from two or more known stations. Loran, the simplification of two-way radio communication, radar, and other electronic aids to navigation and to the landing of aircraft made possible "blind" flying and landing, and together with the speeding-up and perfection of plane construction largely accounted for the eventual establishment of Allied air superiority in every theater. The most dramatic scientific discovery was that of atomic fission, long known to be theoretically possible (page 795). It became a practical process only because the United States government was ready to put billions of dollars into an atomic-research program and because leading Italian, German, Hungarian, and other scientists, driven from their native countries and naturalized as Americans, could join forces with native American and other Allied scientists. The first self-sustaining atomic chain reaction was accomplished under the stands of an abandoned football stadium at the University of Chicago in December 1942. Its first use was as a war explosive (page 904). But it has also opened up new vistas for peacetime usages, the end of which, should mankind survive its explosive effects, no one can foretell.

Free France
and the Polish government in exile

WITH THE exception of Denmark, all the countries overrun by the Nazis established governments in exile in England. England became also the temporary home of the Fighting French, later called the Free French, under the leadership of General de Gaulle. These governments were important cogs in the "psychological warfare" machine that the Allies erected in the effort to win supporters in the enemy armies and vanquished lands by radio, pamphlets, and other forms of propaganda. The Big Three occasionally encountered friction with these governments. Difficulties arose from time to time with De Gaulle because of his inflexible spirit and the doubt in the American state department that he was the right Frenchman to deal with.

The greatest complications arose in connection with the Polish government in exile. As was customary in the long annals of Polish exile, the Polish refugees were divided against themselves. Their heroism glowed in the heat of the war, and few contingents in the uniformed forces or in the resistance movements gave a nobler account of themselves than the Polish volunteers on the west front or in the Polish home army. But the Polish government in exile presented a problem because the Russian government had its own Polish policy, which did not contemplate the restoration of Poland to the *status quo ante,* and in the Polish government in exile some were more ready than others to accept a *modus vivendi* with the Russians. Tact prevailed in the Polish government in exile as long as its first prime minister, General Wladyslaw Sikorski, was alive. But when he was killed in an airplane accident, the more conservative faction of the government became vociferous and exacting. It gave the Big Three a difficult time by its unwillingness to make concessions to the Russians, who responded by sponsoring their own Polish government in exile in Moscow. Before the war the Poles had failed to win the loyalty of the Ukrainians, who formed the bulk of the population of eastern Poland, discriminating against their religion and discouraging their separatist tendencies. Nevertheless, the Poles naturally wanted eastern Poland back. The Russians were equally determined that they should not get it and made the question a paramount issue (page 898).

The invasion
of North Africa

ALL THROUGH the first half of 1942 the situation of the United Nations remained bad. The Germans stood deep inside Russia. The Japanese overran the Pacific. In North Africa the British lost many of their gains to the Italians and Germans under the able General Erwin Rommel. In January, Rommel recaptured Bengasi. Tobruk fell the next June. In the summer he stood well inside Egypt.

Then the tide in the West began to turn. In October, the British general Bernard L. Montgomery started an offensive against the Italo-Germans in the Battle of El Alamein. In November, the British pierced through the left wing of Rommel's army, and the Axis troops started their long trek back to Tripoli. With them went the dream of an Italian empire in Africa.

Meanwhile the greatest convoy ever assembled had been gathering in the waters around Gibraltar. Its secret was not betrayed even by the Franco government. It was a huge expeditionary force of British and American troops, which, according to schedule, landed on November 8 on the coasts of Morocco and Algeria. The next day Algiers, Oran, and Casablanca were occupied. The French troops and especially the French ships stationed there put up a resistance that at some points was more than a token of their duty. They disregarded the urgent pleas of both General de Gaulle and General Henri Giraud, whom the Allies recognized as the head of the Free French in preference to General de Gaulle. The resistance from the Vichy forces might have lasted even longer but for the sheer accident that Pétain's right-hand man, Admiral Jean Darlan, happened to be in Algiers and was captured. Thereupon General Dwight D. Eisenhower, the commander of the Allied forces, recognized Darlan as head of the French administration in North Africa. This step was much criticized at the time because Darlan was deeply involved in collaboration with the Nazis and had been boastfully hostile to the British. But Darlan consented to issue a cease-fire order to all French armed forces in Africa, and that was what counted most at the moment. Another accident relieved Eisenhower of further complications, for the admiral was assassinated by an anti-Vichy Frenchman on Christmas Eve.

Three days after the Allied invasion of North Africa, the Germans took possession of all of "unoccupied" France. They attempted to get hold of the French fleet anchored at Toulon, but the crews scuttled the vessels before the Nazis could seize them. A savage battle broke out between the Germans and the motley population of the Old Port district of Marseilles. The Germans systematically destroyed the whole quarter, and 200,000 tons of scuttled shipping still blocked the harbor when the Americans arrived in 1944.

Allied objectives agreed upon at Casablanca

THE MAIN GOALS of the Anglo-American allies by this time had become obvious. They were (1) to strengthen their alliance with Soviet Russia and the other allies; (2) to induce nations still neutral to join the grand alliance or, in cases where that was not feasible, to keep them neutral; (3) to prepare a normally functioning government for France as soon as the country was liberated; (4) to agree upon terms that should be granted to defeated Germany and Japan; and (5) to lay the groundwork for a postwar peace organization. A series of conferences was held in the course of the war to consider these goals. The first important one took place when Roosevelt and Churchill met in January 1943 at Casablanca, Morocco. It had been hoped that Stalin would participate in that meeting. He did not appear, however, assigning as his reason that he had to concentrate his energies upon the offensive then unfolding against the Germans in Russia. Apparently, also, despite Roosevelt's desire to allay his fears, he was still distrustful of Anglo-American intentions. Roosevelt and Churchill at Casablanca found that they had other professional jealousies and political tangles to straighten out. De Gaulle and Giraud were outwardly reconciled, and a two-man rule of Free France was set up. But this arrangement did not last long. It was silently transformed into the one-man rule of De Gaulle, for Giraud, it developed, had no following among the French people, and De Gaulle eventually had to be recognized as the head of the liberated French state.

The most momentous outcome of the conference at Casablanca was the decision not to negotiate with the Germans until they were prepared to surrender unconditionally. This decision has been a matter of controversy ever since. According to some critics, the demand for unconditional surrender prolonged the war unnecessarily because it left the Germans no way out unless they were willing to accept complete defeat, and it discouraged in advance any thought of ousting the bitter-enders in favor of a government that might have been willing to compromise. Roosevelt and Churchill were motivated, however, by their apprehension that anything less than unconditional surrender would produce in Germany the same unfortunate results that the comparatively lenient terms of 1918 had produced. As they reasoned, if Germany were not definitely beaten by military force and its armies completely destroyed as military units, the Germans might again be beguiled into thinking that their army had not lost the war but had been "stabbed in the back," and Germany would then prepare for a new test of strength. Furthermore, in view of Russian fears that the "bourgeois democracies" might yet combine with the Germans to attack Russia, a categorical demand for German surrender seemed desirable at the moment that the Russians were making a decisive stand (page 894).

The first major Nazi defeat

MEANWHILE the first major setback of the Nazis was shaping. Montgomery's forces had pushed Rommel back toward Tripoli, which they occupied early in 1943. By ship and air the Nazis rushed an army into Tunisia, hoping to avert defeat and to retain a foothold in Africa. The Americans suffered some initial defeats and were stalled in Tunisia for several months. But by the spring of 1943 the Italo-Germans were crushed in a nutcracker formed by Montgomery's army moving from the east and the Anglo-American army moving from the west. The end of the Axis forces in Africa came in May, when about 250,000

Germans and Italians surrendered to the Allies in Tunisia. Rommel had been recalled by Hitler when defeat seemed inevitable, and he was not among the captives.

The dismissal and downfall of Mussolini

THE INVASION of Italy was now feasible, since Tunisia is only about a hundred miles from Sicily. The strategic island of Pantelleria fell to the Allies in June. In July, Sicily itself was invaded, and its complete conquest took only thirty-nine days. The Duce hastened to meet the Führer in the Tyrol in order to request more help, which Hitler apparently refused. Even while Mussolini was there, the Americans made their first air raid on Rome (July 19), carefully avoiding the Vatican City. This air raid shattered Italian morale. Upon his return Mussolini called the Fascist Grand Council together. In a night-long debate he was scorned and vituperated by those who had formerly basked in his favor, including his own son-in-law and foreign minister, Count Galeazzo Ciano. When the stormy session was over, the Grand Council, by 19 votes to 7, asked for his resignation. On July 25 he went to see the king, who told him that he was dismissed. Upon leaving, the fallen Duce was arrested.

Invasion and civil war in Italy

MARSHAL Pietro Badoglio, once Mussolini's chief of staff and conqueror of Ethiopia, became his successor. Badoglio declared at once that Italy would continue the war on Hitler's side, but at the same time he entered by intermediaries into secret negotiations with the Allies. Actually, both the king and Badoglio tried to steer between the Germans and the United Nations, hoping to escape both the fury of the one and unconditional surrender to the other.

Soon the United Nations became the greater menace. On September 3, the British landed on the "toe" of Italy. That day the Badoglio government signed an armistice with the Allies. Its main provisions stipulated the surrender of the Italian fleet, air force, ports, and airfields. The armistice terms were made public on September 8. The royal family and the Badoglio cabinet—half prisoners, half allies—fled into Allied-occupied territory in southern Italy. But they were not strong enough to guarantee that the rest of Italy would surrender with them.

The example of a fallen dictator brought as much chagrin to the Nazis as joy to their enemies. A few days later German parachutists kidnaped Mussolini from the hotel where he had been kept in custody and transported him to Germany. The Nazis tried to offset their loss of face by reëstablishing the "rescued" Mussolini. Under Nazi guidance he set up a National Fascist Italian Republic in northern Italy, while Nazi armies poured into Italy, overrunning the country as far south as Naples. Mussolini took his revenge on those who had been against him in July. Among others, his son-in-law was sentenced to death and was hanged. The greater share of the Axis effort in Italy now fell on the Nazis, because Mussolini's new regime, no less corrupt than the old one, encountered a widespread, heroic, and relatively well-coordinated "partisan" (i.e., underground) resistance.

The Allies were now committed to a war against what Churchill had once called "the soft underbelly of Europe." Contrary to his expectations, however, the campaign in Italy was one of the bloodiest and most difficult of the whole war. Allied losses in an outflanking attempt at Anzio Beach were heavy, and mountain warfare in the Apennines was tedious and costly. The campaign shocked public opinion when it caused the destruction of venerated classical and medieval monuments. Rome did not fall to the Allies until June 1944, and German resistance in northern Italy continued until the very end of the war in Europe.

FROM STALINGRAD

TO V-J DAY

IN 1943 AND 1944 Allied tactics worked like a huge grinder slowly pulverizing the military power of the Nazis. But Hitler still retained confidence in his "intuition." Though his generals were less confident, they had long ceased to contradict him because contradiction was too dangerous. By 1945 it was also to be too late.

The Russians
and the "second front"

THE SEEMINGLY irresistible onslaughts of the Germans were by the winter of 1943 converted into setbacks. Stopped by a Russian counteroffensive begun in November 1942, the entire German Sixth Army was destroyed bit by bit at Stalingrad with the loss of about 330,000 men. German morale at home began to crumble as defeat in Russia followed upon defeat in Africa. At the same time day and night attacks by British and American planes destroyed one important German industrial center after another. The damage now wreaked on Cologne, Hamburg, and other German cities repaid with good measure the damage done to Warsaw, Rotterdam, and London. As in the First World War, Churchill would have liked to widen the "soft underbelly" strategy by an Allied landing in the Balkans. But the American General Staff did not share his views, and he did not persist. Instead, at meetings with Roosevelt in Washington and Quebec (in May and August 1943 respectively), he agreed to an invasion across the English Channel in 1944.

The Russians had been clamoring since 1942 for a "second front" in the west to divert from them the brunt of the Nazi pressure. With their usual distrust of "capitalist" motives, they looked askance at the proposed Allied invasion of the Balkans as at least a pretext for avoiding a direct attack on
894 Germany if not as an effort to frustrate the Communist underground move-

ments in the Nazi-dominated Balkan countries. It looked to them like a Churchillian maneuver to keep them bleeding while the Anglo-American forces won easy victories. To reassure them, Churchill and Roosevelt traveled from their meeting with Chiang Kai-shek at Cairo in November 1943 (page 901) to meet Stalin at Teheran in Iran. Their conference dealt almost exclusively with the preparation of a "second front" and the coordination of Russian and Anglo-American war efforts. The western statesmen solemnly promised a cross-Channel invasion the next spring.

Communism in the liberated areas

THIS PROMISE did not end inter-Allied friction. Churchill found himself by prior commitments and by his monarchistic proclivities bound to try to save the thrones of the discredited kings of Italy, Greece, and Yugoslavia. The Communists suspected that his motives, if not really pro-Fascist, were certainly anti-Communist, and they made the most of appearances. Large sections of the populations of those countries—some with open eyes, others blindly—fell into the arms of the Communists. Thus, even while the three big nations were engaged as allies in a struggle to the death against the Axis, the English, usually supported by the Americans, were tugging against the Russians in the domestic reorganization of the countries they were all anxious to liberate from the Nazis.

Developments in Italy illustrate well the various cross-purposes at work. That the discredited king of Italy, Victor Emmanuel III, was not immediately dethroned was largely due to Churchill's readiness to forgive him. Badoglio also was protected by Churchill. Yet both king and minister were apparently distrusted by the Italian people, as subsequent events revealed, in part because they made no serious effort to weed out the now universally despised Fascism. The purging of Fascists from the civil service and other influential positions was vigorously undertaken only under Badoglio's successors. Meanwhile the Partisans wondered at the suspicious tolerance of the British and American governments, and many of them became easy marks for Communist propaganda to the effect that the "bourgeois democracies" were not anti-Fascist after all. The Anglo-American allies, for their part, wondered about Communist intentions in Italy. The Comintern had, to be sure, been abolished by the Soviet government as a mark of good faith early in 1943, but the national Communist parties still existed and had everywhere taken a leading part in the underground movements. In Italy the Communist party was now growing by leaps and bounds. Under American pressure, the king and Badoglio promised in March 1944 that they would retire as soon as Rome was taken by the Allies. Badoglio kept his promise, and Ivanoe Bonomi, a pre-Fascist prime minister, formed a new cabinet. But the king did not abdicate outright, as it was generally expected he would. In June, he announced that while retaining the title of king, he was transferring his powers to his son, Humbert, whom he appointed lieutenant general of the kingdom.

The attack
upon the Nazis in France

ANGLO-AMERICAN concern was concentrated most of all upon D-Day, the day of the long planned landing on the Continent. Hitler was well aware that the Allies were preparing for an invasion of France. He had built an Atlantic Wall, a system of fortifications stretching all along the western coast of France. He believed his system (unlike the Maginot Line) to be impregnable. But the Allies had devised a plan of attack simultaneously by naval, amphibious, air, parachute, and land forces that was to astonish him. On June 6, 1944, D-Day came. Under the supreme command of General Eisenhower, five divisions of Americans, British, and Canadians arrived at dawn in some 4000 ships covered by 11,000 planes. Under the protecting fire of their battleships they stormed the beaches of Normandy (a forty-mile stretch between the western tip of Cotentin Peninsula and the environs of the bathing resort of Trouville) which had already been "softened" by a terrific air bombardment. The Atlantic Wall was breached by nightfall. After heavy fighting through the months of June and July about a million Allied troops swarmed over Brittany and Normandy, and by mid-August they approached the lower Seine Valley from the west. Other American forces, supported by Free French troops, largely Negro contingents from Equatorial Africa, landed on the Mediterranean coast of France in August and began to move northward along the Rhône.

An attempt
on Hitler's life

FOR A LONG time some daring Prussian aristocrats, high civilian bureaucrats, and labor leaders had been engaged in a conspiracy to kill Hitler. They had won over quite a number of army officers, who now, realizing that Hitler would bring Germany to absolute destruction, took the lead. Among the conspirators were a few genuine idealists who wanted to liberate Germany from a regime which had become intolerable. When all was ready (July 20, 1944), an army officer who had access to Hitler left a bomb in a suitcase at Hitler's headquarters. The bomb exploded, but Hitler was only slightly injured.

Instead of killing Hitler the bomb made the Prussian Junkers an excellent target for him. If the plot had succeeded, the army officer class might have been able to stop the war or even form an alliance with the western powers against Russia—or so they seem to have believed—putting the blame for German excesses upon Hitler. Hitler immediately grasped the significance of the incident and had the Gestapo arrest thousands of people and eventually execute about 5000. The military aristocracy were made a special object of the Führer's wrath. Some of them preferred suicide to being shot or hanged. General Rommel, whose death was shortly announced, seems to have been one of these. Whole families were exterminated, since Hitler liquidated relatives

896

" 'Fresh, spirited American troops, flushed with victory, are bringing in thousands of hungry, ragged, battle-weary prisoners....' (News item)" The bedraggled American infantryman escorting equally bedraggled German prisoners was drawn by Bill Mauldin, cartoonist for the American service newspaper Stars and Stripes.

of relatives and friends of friends of the conspirators. It was a purge that lasted six months and resembled Stalin's purges of the 1930's. The Junkers as a class received a body blow, and control of the army passed completely into Hitler's hands.

Paris liberated and Germany invaded

THE OFFENSIVES from west and east meantime rolled on toward Germany. On August 25 the Allies liberated Paris. The same day Rumania declared war upon Germany. While the Russians marched on in Rumania, the western Allies drove the Nazis out of France by a two-pronged drive. In October the Russians invaded East Prussia, and the Americans entered Germany near Aachen, which fell on October 21.

The western Allies were stalled on German soil for quite a time by a last great effort of the Nazi armies. It was climaxed by a Nazi offensive in the Ardennes Forest against the most exposed lines in the Allied advance. From the shape of these lines the battle is commonly called the Battle of the Bulge (December 16, 1944–January 25, 1945). Only by great endurance and by a miracle of logistics were the American and British armies able to frustrate a Nazi attempt, characterized by both heroism and trickery, at a breakthrough in the direction of Antwerp; but the frustration of their efforts left the Nazis exhausted.

897

*The conference
of the Big Three at Yalta*

THE UNMISTAKABLE signs of collapse on all German fronts suggested the desirability of a conference of the Big Three to consider the full significance of "unconditional surrender." Since Stalin would not leave his country, Roosevelt and Churchill met with him in February 1945 at Yalta in the Crimea. There eastern Poland, among other territories, was promised to the Russians. The old Curzon Line was set up as the boundary between Russia and Poland. Poland was to receive compensation in Germany, and eventually this compensation was loosely fixed east of the Oder and Neisse rivers in certain Prussian provinces which the Poles had coveted for a long time. In their turn, the Russians, notwithstanding their recent neutrality pact (page 877), secretly promised to enter the war against Japan "two or three months after Germany has surrendered" and "to render assistance to China with its armed forces for the purpose of liberating China from the Japanese yoke." No other decision was contemporaneously so much criticized in America as the handing over of eastern Poland to Russia, although later Roosevelt was to be even more severely condemned for his promise to surrender to Russia certain territories and economic and political advantages then held by Japan in the Far East. The agreement on the Far East (Chapter 15) was not published until the first anniversary of the conference.

One paramount reason prompted Roosevelt to make these concessions to the Russians. The war looked far from finished. In Germany the Rhine had not yet been reached, and the West Wall reinforced the Rhine. The American military had no reason yet to believe in the feasibility of the atomic bomb, which was not to prove practicable until the next July (page 904), nor did they realize the extent of the damage already inflicted upon the Japanese, which only postwar investigations were to uncover. They expected to bring the war in Japan to a close only after the war in Germany ended and only by a direct invasion of the Japanese homeland; and they wanted to divide Japan's armies by a two-front attack if possible. For that purpose Russia's entry into the hostilities against Japan was highly desirable. Otherwise America might run the risk of bleeding itself white on the invasion beaches of Japan. With these considerations in mind President Roosevelt deemed it wise to accede to Russian wishes.

A communiqué on the Crimean Conference, issued on February 11, told only part of the story. It mentioned the agreement on Poland, but (since Russia was still at peace with Japan) nothing on the Far East. It further stipulated that Germany after unconditional surrender would be divided into three separate zones: "Coordinated administration and control has been provided for under the plan through a central Control Commission consisting of the Supreme Commanders of the Three Powers with headquarters in Berlin." The communiqué also indicated several other areas of agreement. The Proto-

898

col of the Proceedings of the Crimean Conference, when published after the war, revealed in greater detail what had been done: The three powers would "take such steps, including the complete disarmament, demilitarization and dismemberment of Germany as they deem requisite for future peace and security"; would assist the liberated peoples of Europe "to solve by democratic means their pressing political and economic problems," including "free elections of governments responsive to the will of the people"; would establish an Allied reparations commission in Moscow to work out a plan of reparations by Germany "for the losses caused by her to the Allied nations in the course of the war"; and would call a United Nations conference somewhere in the United States the next April. Both the communiqué and the protocol indicated that on the Balkan countries and some other problem areas further negotiation would have to be undertaken.

The plan for a division of all Germany into three coordinated parts could have worked only if Allied unity had been preserved after the war. Some think that, had Roosevelt lived longer, he might have preserved that unity. Others contend that even before he died Roosevelt had begun to doubt the willingness of the Russians to make it work. We shall never know. On April 12, 1945, he died suddenly of a brain hemorrhage.

The collapse of the Nazi regime

THE COLLAPSE of the Nazis came quickly after Yalta. Early in March the Allies stood on the left bank of the Rhine. On March 7 American troops crossed the Ludendorff Bridge (near Remagen), which the Nazis had failed to destroy. Once on the right bank of the Rhine, the Allies fanned out in many directions. The West Wall proved no more impregnable than the Atlantic Wall or the Maginot Line. Meanwhile, as the western forces moved eastward, the Russians were sweeping across Hungary and eastern Germany. On April 13 Vienna fell to them. On April 25 American and Russian units met near Torgau, on the banks of the Elbe River. Holland, Denmark, and Norway were also rapidly being liberated, and the Allies were overrunning Austria and Czechoslovakia. On April 29 some Italian partisans captured, "tried," and executed Mussolini.

In the last days of April the Russians started their attack on Berlin. The city had already been partly reduced to a rubble heap by American and British air attacks. The Russians finished the destruction by point-blank volleys of their heavy guns. On May 1 the German radio announced that Hitler had met "a hero's death" in Berlin. Actually, he had killed himself. Goebbels and his wife also killed themselves after having poisoned their children. The bodies of all these dead were then placed by faithful followers on gasoline fires and consumed, a "Twilight of the Gods" appropriate to the Nazi mentality. On May 2 all of Berlin was in the hands of the Russians. On May 7 representatives of the German High Command signed an unconditional surrender in a schoolhouse in Rheims, France. Next day the document

was confirmed by a ceremony held in the Berlin suburb of Karlshorst. On May 13 the last German resistance came to an end in Czechoslovakia.

Latin America and Canada in the war	ALL THE Latin-American countries had by that time entered the war on the side of the Allies. All

but Argentina and Chile broke with the Axis after an Inter-American Conference in Rio de Janeiro in January 1942. Nazi spies and fifth columnists were weeded out, with the exception of Nazis in Argentina. Mexico was the last country of Central America, and Brazil was the first one of South America, to declare war. Brazil actually sent to the Italian front the first Latin-American troops to fight on European soil. Only in 1945 did some of the other South American countries declare war. The last was Argentina (March 1945).

Canada loyally and ably played her role, along with the other British dominions, all through the war. By its share in the British Commonwealth Air Training Plan, Canada became, in Roosevelt's words, "The aerodrome of democracy." In 1940 by the Ogdenburg Agreement a program of joint defense was arranged with the United States, thus enabling Canada to divert larger forces from the home front to overseas duty. After the American Lend-Lease Act, Canadian-American cooperation in war production was planned and announced in the Hyde Park Declaration. In 1942 Canada gave a billion dollars to Britain and subsequently presented supplies to other Commonwealth countries and allies. The Canadian air force, navy, and army took a regular part in the war from start to finish.

"Island-hopping" toward the shores of Japan

WHEN V-E (Victory in Europe) Day came, V-J (Victory in Japan) Day was not far behind. The objectives of the war against Japan had been fixed by the conference of Churchill, Roosevelt, and Chiang Kai-shek at Cairo, Egypt, in November 1943 (page 895). (Stalin stayed away because Russia was still at peace with Japan.) Here the conferees reconfirmed that they were going to continue their fight until Japan was ready to surrender unconditionally. They spelled out the terms that would seem acceptable: "All the territories that Japan had stolen from the Chinese, such as Manchuria, Formosa, and the Pescadores, shall be restored to the Republic of China. Japan will also be expelled from all other territories which she has taken by violence and greed.... In due course Korea shall become free and independent." Postwar rivalries were to render at least one of these promises empty words (Chapter 15).

The fight against Japan was conducted according to strategic concepts quite different from those applied in the European theater. The first task in the East was to protect those countries which, though coveted by Japan, had not yet been attacked. They were Australia and some of the islands in the South Pacific. Several battles on New Guinea resulted in hard-won victories for the United Nations and assured the safety of Australia. Then, by "island-hopping in Oceania," the Allies gained stepping stones toward the main Japanese islands. On the mainland of Asia, Burma was liberated and the Ledo Road hacked from the jungle to join with the older Burma Road, establishing an overland supply line to China.

The difficulties of warfare in a tropical or semitropical climate—the ceaseless struggle against a merciless nature with torrential rains, jungle beasts, swarms of insects, malaria, and dysentery—presented one of the most trying challenges that ever an occidental army had had to face. The toll in American lives was a heavy one. The victory at Guadalcanal (page 903) was followed by the capture of Tarawa (1943) and Saipan (1944). Amphibious operations in the Aleutians (1943) and the Philippines (1944) brought them back under American occupation. The battles for the islands of Okinawa and Iwo Jima, now part of the American folk legend, then followed. Little by little the American forces, aided by Canadians, Australians, New Zealanders, and British, ground Japan's strength to pieces. Japan's uninterrupted loss of men and material that had started in China as far back as 1931 now began to tell. One of the most desperate devices of the Japanese consisted of the so-called

Kamikaze, aviators who would make a suicidal crash on the decks of American warships. It took a heavy toll of both lives and ships.

The Big Three
at the Potsdam Conference

BY THE SUMMER of 1945 the assault on Japan itself seemed imminent. The American General Staff told President Harry S. Truman, who had just succeeded to his office on the death of Roosevelt, that in case of an invasion of Japan, American losses would be tremendous. The president thought it desirable to warn Japan of the probable outcome before the supreme attack was made. To prepare the warning, a conference was held at Frederick the Great's palace at

THE UNITED NATIONS VICTORY 1942-1945

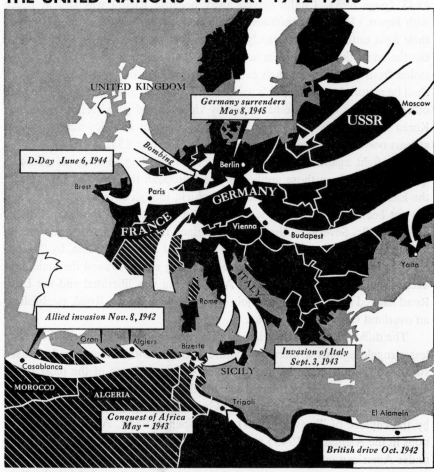

In the spring of 1942 the tide began to turn against the Axis powers though fierce submarine warfare harassed the west Atlantic coast up to the end of the war. The advance of the Japanese was stopped with the Battle of the Coral Sea in May and the Battle of Midway in June. The United Nations offensive began in the Pacific in August at Guadalcanal, in North Africa in October with Montgomery's drive from El Alamein, and in Europe with the beginning of the Russian offensive at Stalingrad, in November. The

Potsdam, Germany, in July and August 1945. It was attended by Truman, Stalin, and Churchill. In the midst of the conference a general election in England revealed that the British did not trust Churchill to lead them in peace as well as he had in war. The Labour Party was victorious, and the new prime minister, Clement Attlee, came to replace Churchill at Potsdam. Stalin alone of the original Big Three remained to make the peace. At Potsdam the principles were laid down for the Allied occupation, zoning, and administration of Germany, and the payment of reparations (page 899). A new Poland was set up, with remapped boundaries that a recently installed, Russian-oriented Polish government accepted but that were to be subject to

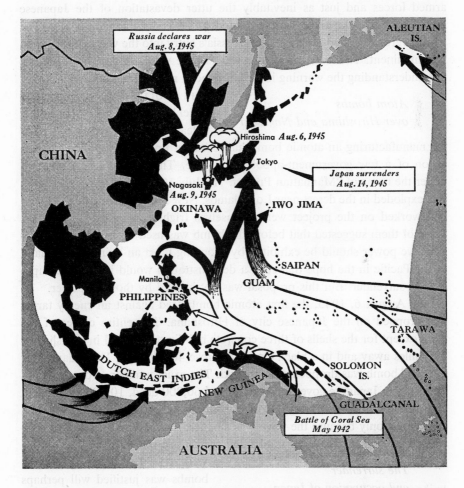

invasion of Italy began in 1943 and of France in 1944. Meanwhile the initiative in the air had passed to the Allies, and the submarine had been effectively counteracted. The objectives of United Nations strategy were planned and confirmed in diplomatic conferences at Casablanca, Washington, Quebec, Cairo, Teheran, and Yalta. By May 1945 both Italy and Germany had collapsed, and the atom bombs dropped on Hiroshima and Nagasaki in August hastened Japan's surrender.

final delimitation in the subsequent peace settlement. The Allies also created a Council of Foreign Ministers to deal with other defeated countries and with deadlocked questions. Obviously areas of deadlock were not going to be few—Poland, Czechoslovakia, Rumania, Bulgaria, Hungary, Finland, the Dardanelles, Korea, and other places where the preferences of Russia might run counter to the preferences of England and the United States. A large part of the next chapter will be devoted to them.

From Potsdam the Allies issued their solemn warning to the Japanese. In veiled language, the full significance of which was not immediately recognizable, the Allies informed Japan that "the full application of our military power will mean the inevitable and complete destruction of the Japanese armed forces and just as inevitably the utter devastation of the Japanese homeland." The Japanese were exhorted to surrender unconditionally. The words were understood to mean that Russia's entry into the war against Japan was imminent. That was true, but it was not the whole story. The Japanese, not understanding the warning in its full import, rejected it on July 29.

*Atom bombs
over Hiroshima and Nagasaki*

THE FULL IMPORT appeared quickly. Since the first controlled release of nuclear energy, a plant for manufacturing an atomic bomb had been set up under the secret supervision of a few government-appointed people. The project was concealed under the name of "Manhattan Project." In July 1945, the first atomic bomb was exploded in the desert near Los Alamos, New Mexico. The scientists who had worked on the project were themselves frightened by its possibilities. Some of them suggested that before the bomb was used against Japan its destructive power should be exhibited by dropping it on an uninhabited island of the Pacific in the hope that such a demonstration would induce the Japanese to surrender. But this proposal was not heeded by those in power.

On August 6, 1945, the first atomic bomb used against an enemy target was dropped on the Japanese city of Hiroshima. The entire center of the town except for the shells of three concrete buildings vanished in a flash seen 170 miles away and in a black cloud that rose 40,000 feet. Three days later a second bomb was dropped on Nagasaki. The exact number of deaths is not known. The Japanese government estimated 60,000 dead, 100,000 wounded, and 200,000 rendered homeless at Hiroshima. The casualties at Nagasaki were fewer only because the town was smaller, for the bomb itself was considered so far superior as to render the earlier one obsolete.

*The surrender
and occupation of Japan*

WHETHER THE dropping of these bombs was justified will perhaps always remain a matter of controversy. We now know that Japan would probably have surrendered anyway within a short time, worn out by long war, acute shortages, recent defeats, bombings, and blockade. The Russians declared war upon Japan on August

8, two days after the first atomic pyre at Hiroshima. Two days later, as the Allies were informed by the Swiss government, Japan was ready to surrender. On August 14 Tokyo indicated willingness to accept unconditional surrender provided the emperor might stay in office. That request was granted. On September 2 the Japanese signed the surrender document on the American battleship *Missouri*. With the single exception of the nominal recognition of the emperor's status, the Japanese surrender was as complete and unconditional as that of Germany. The country was occupied by foreign forces, mostly American, and was for all practical purposes ruled by General Douglas Mac-Arthur until his recall in 1951. The Japanese people accepted their defeat with philosophical submission.

Dumbarton Oaks and San Francisco

BEFORE HE DIED, Roosevelt had made plain that he thought the war would have been fought in vain if war as an instrument of policy were not abolished once and for all. For that reason he had advocated establishment of an international organization for the purpose of adjusting all international conflicts by peaceful methods. The new organization was to be something like the old League of Nations remodeled in the light of hard experience. Experience seemed to have taught that aggression, no matter how strong, might be frustrated if countered by still stronger resistance on the part of the peace-loving countries, and that to prevent delays in countermeasures, the United States ought to be among the participants from the start.

The groundwork for such a new organization was laid at two conferences at Dumbarton Oaks, an estate in Washington, D.C., in 1944. This organization was the one contemplated in the references to the "United Nations conference" in the Yalta protocol (page 899). A lengthy conference at San Francisco (April-June 1945) finally drew up a United Nations Charter (Chapter 15). Hope ran high in 1945 that the United Nations would actually bring about peaceful global cooperation.

IN TWO DECISIVE respects Hitler and his generals had repeated the mistake their predecessors had made in 1914. One of these was to underestimate the staying qualities of a people who think of themselves as responsible for their government. His plans had been based upon a quick, short war such as a well-organized dictatorship, counting upon the coordination, efficiency, and rapidity of movement of a highly disciplined people, can achieve. What he forgot was that the very parliamentary processes and differences of public opinion that render democracies slow to make war may render them slow also to make peace. It takes the imminence of defeat to make the citizens of a free country willing to surrender their liberties even temporarily, but the idea of an emergency dictatorship, acceptable in the democratic tradition since the

Plutarchian days of the Roman Republic, gives a democracy intent upon retaining its liberty a resource in defeat that an autocracy does not have. A democracy can make temporary dictators of its most able men; a dictatorship has no recourse in a crisis except to give more power to those who have brought the crisis about. Hitler had not understood this principle.

The second mistake of Hitler and the German General Staff had been to lose sight of one of the great lessons that the German military classic, General Karl von Clausewitz's *On War,* had drawn from the Napoleonic wars. The offensive, Clausewitz had taught (though generations of Prussian military cadets had apparently failed to grasp his lesson), sows the seeds of its own defeat, for the wider its success, the more effort it requires to maintain itself, while at the same time its opposition concentrates and accumulates. Hitler had repeated the error of the Kaiser. Unable to win in a blitzkrieg, he had been doomed to conquer more and more territory until he reached a point where his forces were spread thin while potential enemies became active enemies and threw fresh forces against his overextended and exhausted lines.

The Second World War ended with Germany dismembered, powerless, and at the mercy of those whom she had sought to destroy. This was the end of Hitler's Reich, supposed to last for a thousand years. And Germany's allies shared in its defeat. Japan was battered, humiliated, and occupied. Italy was not occupied, because it had been permitted to change sides in the course of the war, but it was also battered and humiliated—neither at war nor at peace with the victors. The various Nazi satellites were, like Austria, divided among four occupying powers or, like Hungary, Rumania, and Bulgaria, dominated by Russia. Some of the liberated countries, like Poland and Czechoslovakia, were trying to reach an understanding with Russia or, like China, Greece and Yugoslavia, were engaged in civil war between Communists and anti-Communists, the outcome of which might mean domination by Russia. And some, like France, Belgium, Holland, and Norway, were trying to capture the dignity that victory and recovered sovereignty should have brought.

Over all of Europe passed a sobering realization. No European nation had won the war! England had bled too freely to qualify as a victor. France, vividly aware of having been rescued by others' efforts after treason and inefficiencies at home, was obliged to leave to the Big Three the decision whether she would be allowed to run in their company. Only Eurasian Russia, sorely crippled but powerful still, and the United States of America seemed to have survived as truly great powers. At best Europe might be a third force balancing between them; at worst it might be an arena for their struggle for power, if they should fall out.

September 1, 1939	Germans attack Poland
September 3, 1939	England and France declare war upon Germany
September 29, 1939	"The fifth partition" of Poland
April 8-9, 1940	German invasion of Denmark and Norway
May 10, 1940	German invasion of the Low Countries
May 10, 1940	Churchill forms new British cabinet
May 11, 1940	German invasion of France
May 26-June 4, 1940	The evacuation of Dunkirk
June 10, 1940	Italy declares war upon France and Britain
June 22, 1940	France signs armistice with Germany
September 15, 1940	Climax of the air blitz on London
September 27, 1940	The Tripartite Pact
October 28, 1940	Italian invasion of Greece
November 1940	Roosevelt elected for third term
March 1941	The Lend-Lease Act
April 6, 1941	Germans invade Yugoslavia and Greece
June 22, 1941	Nazis invade Russia
July 13, 1941	Russo-British alliance concluded
August 14, 1941	The proclamation of the Atlantic Charter
December 7, 1941	Japanese attack Pearl Harbor
May-June 1942	Battles of the Coral Sea and Midway
October-November 1942	Allied offensive begun in North Africa
December 1942	First self-sustaining atomic chain reaction
January 1943	Roosevelt-Churchill meeting at Casablanca
February 2, 1943	Axis troops surrender at Stalingrad
May 7-12, 1943	Major Nazi defeat in North Africa
July-August 1943	Allied conquest of Sicily
July 25, 1943	Mussolini dismissed by Italian king
September 3, 1943	Badoglio government signs armistice
November 1943	Roosevelt, Churchill, and Chiang at Cairo
November 1943	Big Three meet at Teheran
June 6, 1944	Allied invasion of France (D-Day)
December 1944-January 1945	Battle of the Bulge
February 1945	Big Three confer at Yalta
April-June 1945	United Nations Charter drawn up
April 12, 1945	Death of Roosevelt
May 1, 1945	Hitler's death announced
May 7-8, 1945	Germans surrender
July-August 1945	The Potsdam Conference
August 6, 1945	Atom bomb dropped on Hiroshima
September 2, 1945	Formal Japanese surrender

CHRONOLOGY IN REVIEW

Chapter fifteen

NEITHER WORLD WAR

NOR WORLD PEACE

THE ESTABLISHMENT of the United Nations, the control of atomic energy, the settlements with the vanquished, the reëstablishment of the liberated countries, and the return of the belligerents to the practices of peace were among the more immediate and insistent problems inherited directly from the war. As rapidly became clear, reconversion to the *status quo ante* would be difficult and perhaps impossible, because of the underground practices of Russia, the spread of unrest across Asia and Africa, the political vacuum in defeated central Europe, the debilitating aftermath of liberation in western Europe, the physical and economic exhaustion of Britain, and the unpreparedness of the United States for international leadership.

Even before the war ended, many observers suspected that it had been in fact a three-sided struggle and that the defeat of one side would lead only to conflict among the two victorious ones. Hopeful of returning as quickly as possible to a new "normalcy," the United States was inclined to place the burden of making peace in Europe upon the newly constituted United Nations, in which the United States was predominant. The Soviet Union, on the other hand, pursued a strict policy of national interest (which by that time was hard to disentangle from the Communist cause) in both Europe and Asia. Weakened by war and overshadowed by Russia and the United States, the other major nations of the world retired into the background as the global arena was prepared for the struggle of the two titans. "Hot" war now was over, but in its place came, not peace, but something called "cold" war. In this eerie half light between general war and general peace, the struggle of the victors began. "East" and "West" took on new meaning—signifying, respectively, the Russian and the Anglo-American systems of alliance.

Once more, as after the First World War, Russia was able to benefit from the readiness of both radicals and conservatives to identify the Russian cause with the cause of revolution. Only this time the confusion was to be more widespread. Recognizing the possibility of gaining from disorder, the Communists moved rapidly in Asia and Europe at the end of the war. At first they met with little or no resistance in some areas, and with inadequate resistance everywhere. Not until after two years of reverses did the United States and the nations of western Europe strike back effectively anywhere. The struggle thereupon became an open one—essentially for power but between two camps generally professing different social and economic ideologies. Nearly all the rest of the world sympathized with one of the two. Each side was convinced of its right, and each determined to protect itself against what it labeled the arrogance, aggressiveness, and unrighteousness of the other. Had the most destructive war in history decided merely who would survive to fight a still more destructive one? Or was there room for hope that a third world catastrophe might yet be averted?

THE ORGANIZATION
OF THE UNITED NATIONS

LIKE SEVERAL outstanding earlier examples of concerted action among the powers, the United Nations had been conceived during the war years by the victors. They hoped by such an organization to preserve their wartime unity and to combine their forces for a united, peacetime assault upon common problems, such as international aggression, poverty, disease, ignorance, and discrimination. Though the uninspiring record of the League of Nations cast a shadow across the sunlit project, many felt that the League had charted the way to world organization and that the greater need now might lead to a better course.

National sovereignty and the United Nations Charter FROM THE very start, the new world organization, unlike the old, was associated with the United States. After two months of deliberation in San Francisco's neoclassic Civic Center from April 25 to June 26, 1945, an assemblage of diplomats and scholars had brought forth the basic instrument, or Charter, of the United Nations Organization. By that time Germany had surrendered, but the war with Japan was still going on. The Charter's preamble voiced the determination of the peoples fighting fascism "to save succeeding generations from the scourge of war,...to reaffirm faith in fundamental human rights,...to establish conditions under which justice and respect for the obligations arising from treaties and other sources of international law can be maintained, and to promote social progress and better standards of life in larger freedom, and for

910

these ends to practice tolerance and live together in peace with one another as good neighbors."

When the time came, however, to discuss methods of implementing these general principles, each nation continued to guard its individual sovereignty jealously. Hence the Charter, though dedicated to international cooperation and collective action, did not create a dynamic world government, as some had hoped it might; nor did it place ironclad restrictions upon the sovereignty of the member nations. The first chapter stated explicitly that "the Organization is based on the principle of the sovereign equality of all its Members" and that the United Nations possesses no authority "to intervene in matters which are essentially within the domestic jurisdiction of any state or...require the Members to submit such matters to settlement under the present Charter." Moreover, by Article 51, the separate states retained "the inherent right of individual or collective self-defense if an armed attack occurs" until the United Nations took measures to restore peace.

The architects of the United Nations sought, however, to make it a political, economic, and military machine of sufficient strength to provide world order and render unnecessary even wars of self-defense. They derived confidence from the fact that the United Nations at its beginning comprised fifty-one member nations, including the United States and the Soviet Union, neither of which had from the outset been a member of the League. Moreover, the changing concepts of distance and the soon-to-become universal nightmare of atomic warfare provided added inducements for nations to place their coveted freedom of action below their fear of a new holocaust. World unity did not look like an idle dream so much as a dire necessity. The only possible choice seemed to many to be between either "one world or no world."

General Assembly of the United Nations

THE UNITED NATIONS comprised six principal organs. These were the General Assembly, the Security Council, the Economic and Social Council, the Trusteeship Council, the International Court of Justice, and the Secretariat. The powers of these organs were specifically enumerated in the Charter.

Composed of representatives of all members of the United Nations, the General Assembly was intended to be its supreme body in all matters except international peace and security. In this body each member state received but a single vote. "The General Assembly may discuss any questions or any matters within the scope of the present Charter," says Article 10. The moral monitor of the world, the General Assembly became a platform for varied proposals and for bitter tirades, all too often merely for propaganda purposes. It is scheduled to meet each September, but special sessions may be convened if occasion requires. The General Assembly was destined to gain stature, for the Security Council was to fail as arbiter of international problems, and

911

Dean G. Acheson, who was American secretary of state from 1949 to 1953, was to adopt the policy of taking disputes to the Assembly for airing, at least, and for action wherever the Charter permitted.

Security Council of the United Nations

THE AUTHORITY of the Security Council was based upon a frank recognition of the predominant responsibility of the great powers for war and peace. No pretense of equality was preserved. The United States, Great Britain, Russia, France, and China were named permanent members, in the expectation that the problems which formerly had been handled through varying diplomatic channels might be considered, with better results for the general welfare, by a permanent committee of the great states. Six nonpermanent members of the Council were to be elected by the Assembly for two-year terms in order to give the smaller nations an opportunity to participate in decisions of high policy.

Each of the eleven members was permitted one vote. A distinction was drawn, however, between voting on procedural matters and on substantive matters, and it worked to the advantage of the permanent members. Roughly speaking, a procedural matter was one that dealt with the manner in which the council conducted its internal business; a substantive matter was one that concerned its decisions on international questions under consideration. A vote of any seven members would carry a procedural question. "On all other matters" decisions rested "on the affirmative vote of seven members including the concurring votes of the permanent members." Theoretically, this wording meant that each of the permanent members possessed the right of veto in all but procedural questions. Practically, the veto of the permanent members sometimes extended to procedural matters as well, for the question of what matters are procedural is apt to be considered a substantive one. Experience was soon to show that the Security Council did not really have the power to indict or punish one of the permanent members or its satellites, for the great power in question could exercise its veto if it chose.

The structure of the Economic and Social Council

COMPOSED OF eighteen members elected by the General Assembly, the Economic and Social Council concerns itself with "studies and reports with respect to international economic, social, cultural, educational, health, and related matters." Specially designated among these matters are "human rights and fundamental freedoms for all." This Council has also concerned itself with sanitation, the protection of minorities, the prevention of religious and racial discrimination, freedom of the press, the status of women, and the illegal trade in narcotics. From the outset, its Commission on Human Rights was required to propose a Universal Declaration of Human Rights, and the General Assembly approved the Commission's proposal in 1948. Several special commissions, such as the

Statistical Commission and the Population Commission, have also been organized by the Council. The Council can make recommendations for action to the General Assembly, individual member governments, or specialized UN agencies, but none of its recommendations is binding. It works through the voluntary cooperation of the nations and peoples of the world. It collaborates with and attempts to coordinate other specialized international agencies, such as the older International Labor Organization (page 693), the more recent World Health Organization, and the United Nations Educational, Scientific, and Cultural Organization. Such specialized agencies, however, are not under the jurisdiction of the Economic and Social Council except in a loose fashion. They report to it, and it in turn reports to the General Assembly.

The structure of the Trusteeship Council

THROUGH THE organization of the Trusteeship Council the San Francisco Conference sought to mitigate the problems of some of the dependent peoples of the world. The need for such a body was demonstrated by the fact that at the end of the war almost one third of the earth's inhabitants did not yet govern themselves. The first task of the Trusteeship Council was to provide for the former mandates of the League of Nations (page 695). A few of the former mandates—Iraq, Lebanon, and Syria—had become independent states and were now members of the United Nations in their own right. Since other formerly mandated areas were not yet ready to take their places as sovereign states, other arrangements had to be made for them. Britain, France, and Belgium shared in the rearrangement of the mandates in Africa; and the United States, Australia, and New Zealand in that of the western Pacific region. Certain territories detached from the vanquished states as a result of the Second World War were also placed in the new trusteeship system. The administering states, having accepted "as a sacred trust the obligation to promote to the utmost...the well-being of the inhabitants," were made responsible to the Trusteeship Council. Being permanent members of the Trusteeship Council, however, the administering states, unless they call one another to account for their stewardship, may be checked only by the nonpermanent representatives. The Council includes as many nonpermanent as permanent members, and because no nation has the power of veto, all decisions are made by a majority vote. But the effective control of the Trusteeship Council over administering powers is limited in practice to moral suasion.

The United Nations' International Court of Justice

TO REPLACE the Permanent Court of International Justice created in 1919, the Charter established the International Court of Justice as an organ of the United Nations. Like its predecessor, the new court is located in the Netherlands at The Hague. By its constitution all member states of the United Nations are members of the court; but nonmembers, such as Switzerland, have the right to request membership. Fifteen judges comprise its panel, and they represent a wide variety of nationalities and every major legal system of the world. Only states may bring cases to the International Court, but any state, whether a member or not, may do so. In addition, the Court acts in a consultative capacity on legal questions brought to it by agencies of the United Nations. Since most of the problems resulting from the war have been subjects of diplomatic negotiation, few international cases have so far been referred to it for decision.

The Secretariat THIS VAST network of UN organ-
of the United Nations izations is coordinated through the
Secretariat. The Norwegian statesman Trygve Lie was appointed in 1945 by the Security Council as secretary general, or chief administrative officer. Soviet hostility toward him developed after he lent his support to the UN decision to resist North Korean aggression (page 984), and in 1953 he resigned. He was replaced by a Swedish diplomat, Dag Hammarskjöld. Besides arranging for meetings of the various groups, and drawing up the annual report to the Assembly, the secretary general may, on his own initiative, bring to the attention of the Security Council those matters which he considers dangerous to international peace and security. A huge staff of experts has been drawn from all parts of the world and from almost every line of endeavor to assist the secretary general. With general headquarters in New York (but outside the legal jurisdiction of the United States), the United Nations today has its own territory, administrative offices, and flag. The visitor to New York City who looks upon the cluster of functional skyscrapers (largely a gift of John D. Rockefeller, Jr.) that constitute the headquarters of the United Nations may well wonder what has become of American isolationism and whether American commitment to the United Nations will render that organization more or less effective than the League of Nations.

THE MEANING OF
"UNCONDITIONAL SURRENDER"

THE "UNCONDITIONAL SURRENDER" of the vanquished enemies left the achievement of peace and security in the postwar years to the victors as their undivided responsibility. To crush the military forces of an aggressor (the world was again to learn) is less complex than to restore political and economic stability among the nations once they have undergone the horrors of total war.

As the facing diagram shows, the structure of the United Nations is much like that of the earlier League of Nations (page 693). In its membership the United Nations got off to a stronger start than the League, since it numbered at the outset fifty-one nations including the United States and the USSR.

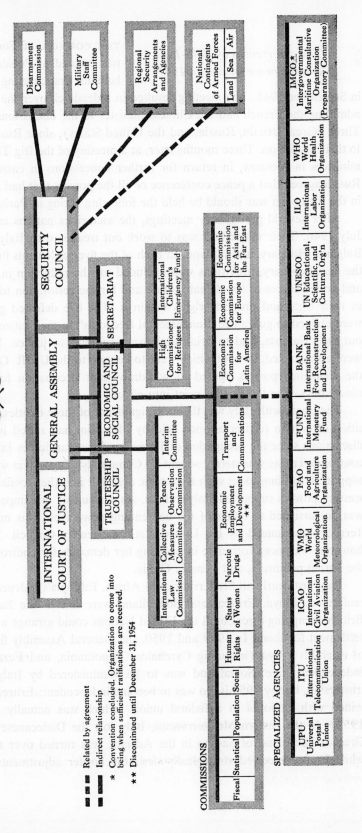

THE UNITED NATIONS

*The conferences of 1945-1946
and the peace treaties of 1947*

THE COUNCIL of Foreign Ministers created at Potsdam in 1945 held its first meeting in London in September 1945. The meeting resulted in a deadlock over the question of admitting the French and the Chinese minister to the discussions of the Big Three (Great Britain, Russia, and the United States), since Russia objected to their admission. Three months later, at a meeting of the Big Three foreign ministers in Moscow, in return for further concessions in eastern Europe, Russia agreed that a peace conference of all the powers that had participated in the European war should be held the following spring in Paris.

After several preliminary meetings, the victorious nations assembled in July 1946. Their major task was to work out treaties with Italy, Rumania, Bulgaria, Hungary, and Finland. In each of the five settlements finally signed the next February, provisions were included for the reduction in armaments and armed forces of the defeated state and for the restoration to the victors of their legal and property rights within it. The five defeated governments were obliged to guarantee "fundamental freedoms" to their citizens, to weed out their Fascists, and to bring their war criminals to justice. Reparations were also exacted, most of which were to be paid to the USSR. On their side the victorious powers agreed to withdraw their occupation forces within ninety days after the treaties went into effect.

The treaty with Italy was the most significant of these treaties. The disposition of certain territories once held by Mussolini had raised international discussions since the occupation of Rome by American forces in 1944. The control of Trieste was sternly sought by Communist Yugoslavia with Russian support. Unwilling to let such a strategic area fall into the Russian orbit, the western powers supported Italy's claim. As a result of this impasse, Trieste was not assigned to either of the contending powers but was made a Free Territory guaranteed by the United Nations Security Council. Yugoslavia, however, was more fortunate in realizing her demands for control of Fiume, the Istrian peninsula, and Venezia Giulia.

Italy lost nearly all her territories in Africa. Ethiopia's independence was reaffirmed. Libya, Eritrea, and Somaliland were left in the hands of the British occupying forces until the United Nations could arrange a permanent settlement for them. In 1949 and 1950, the General Assembly finally voted to establish Libya (including Cyrenaica, Tripolitania, and Fezzan) as an independent state; Somaliland was to be administered by Italy as a UN trusteeship, but by 1959 it too was to become independent; Eritrea was to be joined with Ethiopia in a federal union (which was actually realized in 1952). In the eastern Mediterranean, Italy lost the Dodecanese Islands to Greece. The island of Saseno in the Adriatic was turned over to Albania, while France received strategically desirable border adjustments at Italy's expense. With the exception of her temporary trusteeship in Somaliland, Italy was entirely deprived of her former colonies.

Politics and economics in Italy

THESE TERRITORIAL losses confounded the already confused domestic problems of postwar Italy. Until 1947 Italy was actually run by the Allied Military Government and its occupying forces. Nominally, however, Italy was still ruled by the house of Savoy. King Victor Emmanuel III yielded his crown to his son Humbert in May 1946 in an effort to save the monarchy, but the gesture came too late to restore the confidence of the Italian people. The question of Italy's form of government was submitted to a general referendum in June, and the monarchy was defeated. The dispossessed King Humbert II took refuge in Portugal, and Italy was officially proclaimed a republic.

Politics in postwar Italy centered around three of the numerous parties. Until 1953 the most successful political leader was Alcide de Gasperi, the founder and leader of the Christian Democrats. As the dominant anti-Communist party, the Christian Democrats have enjoyed the militant support of the papacy and the Catholic hierarchy as well as the encouragement of the western powers. The Communists have continuously been the second strongest party in Italian politics. The Left-Wing Socialists have pursued a policy which is pro-Communist.

Acute economic problems have helped the Italian Communists to maintain a strong grasp upon the working classes. Italy after the war was more than ever to be counted among the "have-not" nations of Europe. Land, raw materials, capital, and power were not available in sufficient quantities to accommodate her already teeming and constantly increasing population. Emigration had largely disappeared as a possible solution, particularly since Italy's colonies were gone and an increasing number of non-European nations, including the United States, had been gradually closing their doors. Agricultural reforms designed to modernize farming have helped the rural workers somewhat; and a set of laws passed in 1950 contemplated that farm land should be more evenly distributed; and a little has been done to break up the great estates. But the peasants of Italy are probably too numerous to be adequately supported by the potential amount of arable land. Though the Italian manufacturing districts of the north did not suffer heavily in the war, the number of jobs available were far too few for the many workers, and unemployment became chronic. The problem has been intensified by the continuous increase in prices. In the postwar period the Italian lira reached a new low. In the hope of relieving unemployment and inflation, Italy concentrated upon production for export. Increased trade, financial aid from America, and closer economic ties with France have alleviated the distress somewhat, but Italy's economic problems remain severe and essentially unsolved.

917

*The western orientation
of the new Italian government*

THE CONSTITUENT assembly charged with giving the new republic its instrument of government was dominated by De Gasperi and the Christian Democrats, and the document that it drew up returned to the western parliamentary tradition. A bicameral legislature consisting of a Senate and a Chamber of Deputies formed the nucleus of the new government. Except for a few honorary life-senators appointed by the president, representatives in the upper house are elected, on a regional basis, by citizens over twenty-five. The lower house is elected by citizens over twenty-one years of age. Executive powers are delegated to a ministry responsible to both legislative houses. At the head of the government is the president, chosen for seven years by an electoral body consisting mostly of the legislators. The constitution includes a bill of rights granting religious toleration but recognizing Catholicism as the official faith. Shortly after the withdrawal of the last occupation forces, the constitution was accepted (December 1947).

In the first elections under the republican constitution, a bitter struggle between Christian Democrats and Communists focused world attention upon Italy. The Communists received the support of Russia; the Christian Democrats were staunchly bolstered by the papacy and by American economic aid. The Christian Democrats emerged victorious from the elections; but the Communists showed up clearly as a strong second. As the rehabilitation of Italy proceeded, the Communist hold appeared to weaken, but this apparent weakness was debatable. In 1951 the Communists still claimed over 2,500,000 members. Their possible losses were attributable not only to the improvement of economic conditions and to American economic aid (page 977) but also to the political preferences deliberately accorded Italy by her former western enemies in order to offset Communist propaganda. Of the former Axis partners Italy, for example, was the first to be freed of occupying forces, permitted an independent government, and proposed for admission to the United Nations. Its admission was vetoed by the USSR. And Yugoslavia stood in the way of a pro-Italian settlement of Trieste's status.

The elections of 1953 revealed widespread discontent. The two left-wing parties polled over 35 per cent of the vote, and the Monarchist and Neo-Fascist parties almost 15 per cent. As a result the relative political stability that Italy had enjoyed under De Gasperi's ministry gave way to razor-edge maneuvering, although his successors were likewise anti-Communist.

*The German question
and the unsettled peace*

DEFEATED GERMANY was accorded much sterner treatment than Italy. As the major enemy and a second offender in the eyes of the victors, Germany was held more strictly accountable for the disruption of world peace than her European partners. Since she was economically and geographically the heart of Europe, her judges had to take into account, along with the desirability of reprisal, the economic health and military security of western and central Europe. In view of the mounting hostility between "the East" and "the West," the need for a buffer or a balance between them in central Europe was perhaps greater than ever. A dilemma troubled the western Allies: How could they punish the Germans and at the same time restore Germany as quickly as possible to its normal economic and diplomatic functions? The issue was further complicated by the pardonable fear that a revived Germany might again become an international menace. Those who were convinced of Teutonic perfidy (and their number both in the East and in the West was legion) were supported by those who argued that even angels in the position of the defeated Germans might feel called upon to play one side against the other.

The division
of Germany among the victors
"UNCONDITIONAL surrender" had made it necessary for the victors to rule Germany. It was divided into four zones of occupation (American, British, French, and Russian) and a joint administration was established for Greater Berlin by all four occupying powers. An Allied Control Council, which consisted of the four military chiefs, assumed supreme command over German affairs. Germany's eastern frontier was fixed along the Oder and Neisse rivers, the large agricultural area to the east being assigned to the revived Poland. East Prussia was also partitioned between Poland and the Soviet Union.

The internal reorganization of Germany proved hard. German refugees numbering around nine millions, whether they wished it or not, were transferred from east of the Oder-Neisse line to the remaining areas of Germany. Their transfer quickly created an aggravated refugee problem, which was made worse by an influx of dispossessed Germans from restored and vengeful Czechoslovakia and Hungary. Immediate arrangements for war crimes trials and for the punishment of Nazis or the "denazification" of the innocent were undertaken, and they added to the country's disorganization. The occupying powers found themselves at odds over Germany's economic rehabilitation and were obliged to rest satisfied with the general decision reached at the Potsdam Conference (page 903) that Germany should be "treated as a single economic unit" but that its "present excessive concentration of economic power as exemplified in particular by cartels, syndicates, trusts, and other monopolistic arrangements" should be decentralized.

Meetings of the victors in 1946 and 1947 resulted regularly in deadlocks on the various problems of German reorganization. The American proposal for the establishment of a unified German state whose demilitarization would be assured by a four-power agreement was rejected by Russia. The western states were equally adamant in their refusal to accept the Russian proposal for four-power control of the Ruhr industrial region. Conflicts over reparations, rehabilitation, and the German standard of living widened the rift. 919

The Soviet zone was sharply cut off economically, as well as politically, from the other zones; and among the zones of the western powers, the French blocked economic unification for a time in their determination to extract territorial and economic advantages. "Decartelization" was not carried out with equal zeal in all zones, and brought decisions that sometimes pleased those who were for severity and at other times pleased those who were for moderation, but usually displeased everybody.

Denazification and the Nuremberg trials

THE PROCESS of "denazification" also moved along zonal lines. In its zone the United States tried to carry out a comprehensive program, designed to clear away not only the Nazi leaders but the little Nazis as well. This program ran almost at once into the insurmountable problem of classifying and trying thousands of people. The American occupation authorities found (to take a striking example) that almost all teachers had been required to belong to Nazi organizations, whether they were actively in sympathy with Hitler or not. Had these teachers been removed from office, the educational system of Germany would have ceased to function. The Americans soon adopted a less stringent policy of purge. Neither the British nor the French attempted anything on so broad a scale as the original American plan, being content simply to punish those who had been well-known Nazis. The Russians tried only a few of the foremost Nazis in their zone.

On the matter of the major war criminals, such as Goering and Ribbentrop, the powers managed to reach agreement. They established an unprecedented International Military Tribunal to try certain Germans indicted as chiefly responsible for the outbreak of war. The Tribunal sat at Nuremberg, which the Nazis had made into a national shrine and where they had held their party congresses.

Within the western countries, serious disagreement arose as to the legality and desirability of the war trials. Some observers felt that trial by such a court would be little more than a justification of revenge upon the vanquished leaders by the victors, and would make a mockery of justice. Who would try the "war criminals" among the victors? Others believed that it was high time to set a precedent that would make political and military leaders realize that they were individually responsible for plotting aggressive war in violation of the Kellogg-Briand Pact.

While the debate continued, the highest ranking among the Nazi survivors were arraigned before the court on that count among others. After a trial which lasted for nearly a year and in which hitherto secret documents were read into the record, three of the defendants were freed, seven were given prison terms, and twelve were condemned to death. Goering cheated the hangman by suicide; the eleven others were hanged. One hundred and eighty-

The dilemma of West Germany. A British cartoon.

Ghilchik

five other leading Nazis were tried in a tribunal set up by the Americans in their zone, and over half of them were sentenced to death or prison.

Combatting inflation and chaos in the west zones

ALTHOUGH the barriers between Russia's eastern zone and western Germany constantly rose higher, the British and Americans worked toward the fusion of the western zones. At first, the prospects for German recovery and unification appeared dim. Economic revival and unification of the western zones were hampered by a confusion of currencies and by the mounting threat of inflation. Barter became a chief medium of trade. The American cigarette, neatly packaged and in great demand, became a common currency, and the American soldier, permitted to buy his cigarettes cheaply at his post exchange, was able to trade them for jewelry, household articles, and other valuables at tremendous bargains. The elimination of the old managerial groups, the physical removal of industrial plants, the dispersion of the labor force, the uncertainty surrounding the political future of the vital Saar and Ruhr areas, and the influx of refugees presented further economic complications. By 1947 the responsible officials in the three western zones began to attack these problems systematically without regard to the regular protests of the Soviet Union.

By 1948 they were able to announce a currency reform for the three western zones. The old reichsmark (worth nominally about thirty cents but bringing about one cent on the free market) was recalled and replaced by a new mark. The new mark proved more stable. Black-market operations diminished, barter became less common, and a large degree of confidence was restored to the currency of the western zones. Close supervision of the amount of money in circulation, including the requirement that the American occupation forces should not buy German produce or use German currency, was designed to check the inflation. The renewal of industry and trade promoted business relations and the economic unity of the western zones. The eastern zone meanwhile introduced its own measures of currency reform.

It was realized in most quarters that someday the occupation would have to end and that a responsible German government ought to be prepared gradually to take over the administration of the country. In the early days of the occupation new administrative units called *Länder* (singular, *Land*) had been created within all four zones. These *Länder* cut across traditional boundaries, such as those of the former state of Prussia, and were partly intended to destroy the ancient provincial (particularly Prussian) loyalties. With the breakdown in cooperation, territorial administrative questions were more and more frequently decided by the occupying power in each zone. Political collaboration in the western zones flourished with their joint attack upon economic problems. The British-American collaboration resulted early in the creation of "Bizonia," as the two fused zones were called. The economic revival of Germany frightened the French, however, and they showed an open reluctance to go along with the English and American policy without some compensatory concessions. Their desire for compensations was somewhat allayed by the economic union of the Saar Territory with France (1948), and that year the French agreed to convert "Bizonia" into a "Trizonia."

Soviet opposition and the blockade of Berlin

AT THIS JUNCTURE the Soviet Union, finding that verbal protests had no effect, sought by forceful action to bring a halt to the western unification. It chose Berlin as the scene of action, since that city, though administered and patrolled jointly by the four occupying powers, was located entirely within the Russian zone. The Russians inaugurated a blockade of Berlin. Explaining their actions as part of a hunt for illegal shipments and spies, they gradually closed off western supply lines, thus threatening the western-controlled portions of the city with starvation. The western powers retaliated as best they could. From June 1948 to May 1949, despite a terrible intervening winter, a gigantic "air lift" from England and the western zone of Germany supplied Berlin, through a "safe passage" air corridor, with commodities of all kinds. Had the Russians tried to cut off the air lift, the possibility of a new war would have been very great. That risk the Soviet leaders apparently did not care to run, and in the spring of 1949 the blockade of Berlin was relaxed. Its major outcome was that it had made plain the determination of both sides to act independently and in defiance of each other.

The development
of two separate German regimes

BY THIS TIME, within the separate *Länder,* German leaders had steadily resumed the initiative, preparing in all zones for the day when the occupation forces would retire. As self-government reappeared in the *Länder,* the hope had been born that Germany might gradually be reunited under a democratic and independent administration. The division between east and west Germany, however, required a reorientation in German thinking about independence. Neither side in the larger struggle, it was clear, would permit Germany to be unified under the auspices or influence of the other. The western occupation authorities encouraged moderate political parties in Trizonia; in the Soviet zone the various shades of political opinion were permitted to organize, but the official spokesman of Soviet policy was the Social Unity Party. Though all four powers were committed to the ultimate reunion of Germany, the western parties decided, while the Berlin blockade was in progress, to proceed with the organization of a separate west German state.

In the spring of 1949, the *Länder* sent representatives to Bonn to work out a "Basic Law for the Federal Republic of Germany." This document, like one being drawn up at the same time in the eastern zone, envisaged the eventual adherence of all the *Länder.* Drawing heavily upon former German constitutional documents, the Basic Law provided for a centralized state with certain administrative and political rights reserved to the *Länder.* The federal government was organized along parliamentary lines with the Federal Council (Bundesrat) representing the *Land* governments and the Federal Diet (Bundestag) representing the people. The lower house was to be elected by all persons over twenty-one. The executive power was lodged in a president, a chancellor, and a cabinet. The chancellor was made ultimately responsible to the Bundestag, but elaborate precautions were taken to avoid the cabinet instability of the Weimar Republic (page 680). Controversies over constitutional issues or clashes over jurisdiction between the *Länder* and the federal authorities were to be adjudicated by a special Constitutional Court.

As a result of the international cleavage two Germanies emerged. In the first West German elections (August 1949), the moderate and conservative parties won a decisive victory. The first chancellor was the Christian Democrat leader Konrad Adenauer, once a prisoner of the Gestapo, who included in his cabinet representatives from three non-Communist parties. The lower house chose Dr. Theodor Heuss, a liberal professor of history and constitutional law, as the republic's first president. In October the German Democratic Republic was created in the eastern zone under Soviet auspices, with its headquarters in the Russian zone of Berlin. The government of East Germany was organized along Soviet lines, and became an important part of Communist Europe (page 944).

While the organization of West Germany was in progress, the western 923 powers completed their trizonal fusion and began to replace their military directors with civilian representatives. An Allied High Commission was established to handle problems not yet placed within the jurisdiction of Bonn, such as reparations, foreign affairs and trade, displaced persons and refugees, and the protection of the Allied forces of occupation. The Bonn regime was accorded wide legal powers in domestic affairs, but final authority rested with the occupying powers and the Allied High Commission. Though a peace treaty between Germany and its former enemies was widely discussed, no progress was made, and central Europe continued to be an arena for the struggle between the Communist and the non-Communist powers.

The liberation and occupation of Austria AUSTRIA'S POSITION in the post-war world also remained anomalous. Though Austria had participated in the war as a part of Nazi Germany, the powers decided to treat her as a liberated rather than a defeated nation. Like Germany, Austria was divided into four separate zones of occupation, with Vienna under the joint administration of all four occupying powers. At the Potsdam Conference the powers had decided not to exact reparations from Austria, though Russia in her zone of eastern Austria was permitted to appropriate certain specified kinds of German assets in partial compensation for her war losses. Controversy over Russian expropriations in eastern Austria began almost immediately, and was further complicated by disputes over refugees. A deadlock resulted and, as in Germany, none of the powers governing Austria proved willing to be the first to withdraw its military forces. Hence the conclusion of a treaty and the transfer of full sovereign authority to the local officials were regularly postponed.

Nevertheless, a movement toward self-government in Austria got under way immediately after the defeat of Germany. Karl Renner, a Socialist leader of the earlier Austrian Republic (page 683), organized a provisional government in April 1945. As a coalition of Socialists, Communists, and People's (Catholic) Party groups, the provisional government undertook to denazify Austria. By the fall of 1945 Renner's government received the official recognition of the Allied Control Council.

With the sanction of the Austrian provinces the Renner government revived the constitution of 1920 as the fundamental law of the land. This decision meant the restoration of a parliamentary republic in which the source of power lay in a popularly elected lower house. The People's Party and the Socialists now gained control over the political life of the newly constituted republic, forcing the Communists into a weak opposition. In January 1946, the occupation authorities formally recognized the Austrian state and tentatively agreed that its frontiers should be the same as those of 1937. The Austrian government was permitted to conduct its own foreign relations, though always with the proviso that its decisions might be vetoed by the

Allied Control Council. In domestic political matters the Renner government managed to maintain authority in all zones. The zonal system ended in 1953.

The domestic economic enigma of Austria turned out to be harder to deal with. Like its predecessors, the Renner government was confronted with the problem of feeding and clothing the large urban population of Vienna from a small hinterland. Huge importations of food and machinery proved necessary, but Austria was unable to produce sufficient quantities of export goods to establish a well-balanced economy. The oil fields developed in eastern Austria might have helped to meet this need if Russia had not regularly refused to hand them over to the Renner government. The revival of industry was additionally hampered by Austria's severance from Germany and the other Danubian countries, her most accessible customers. Some experts doubted that Austria's economic problem could be solved even if good will existed among the occupational authorities.

Japan under the Allied occupation

WHEN THE Japanese government finally signed the Allied terms of unconditional surrender (page 905), the divinely descended emperor had to accept subordination to General MacArthur, the Supreme Commander of the Allied Powers (commonly abbreviated SCAP). Since Japan had been defeated mainly by the actions of the United States armed forces, the American government assumed primary responsibility for the occupation, disarmament, and reform of Japan. Though policy-making commissions, on which the other powers were represented, were set up in Washington and Tokyo, the final authority over Japanese affairs rested in the hands of SCAP. The functions of the Allied commissions were usually limited to a review of SCAP's proposals and programs.

As in Germany, the occupation authorities in Japan were faced with the dilemma of restoring the economy and society to health while at the same time making certain that a rehabilitated Japan should not again become a menace to world peace. The occupation of Japan by American forces proceeded smoothly, perhaps in part because of the decision to retain the emperor and the native government. Though key men of the former regime were quickly removed, SCAP worked through the bureaucracy and the traditional offices at almost every level. Demobilization of the armed services was achieved almost without incident. The precedent having been set in Germany, the top military and civilian leaders of Japan were placed on trial before an International Military Tribunal. Though public conflict raged in the Allied countries over whether the emperor himself should be tried, no one in authority apparently ever had any serious intention of arraigning him. Twenty-eight of Japan's other war leaders were, however, indicted on five different counts. The trials lasted for more than two years (1946-1948). Seven civil and military figures were given death sentences, including the wartime premier, General Hideki Tojo; sixteen were committed to life imprisonment; and the other 925 defendants received lighter sentences. No serious reverberations occurred among the Japanese public, who accepted the punishment of their erstwhile leaders more stolidly than had the Germans.

The occupation authorities sought initially to purge government, parties, business, labor, education, and religion of its authoritarian elements. At the same time SCAP sought to awaken the Japanese population to a sense of its political responsibility. The old devices of thought control were removed and free expression of opinion was encouraged. Though a number of the old political bosses were removed, the petty or corrupt neighborhood politician was much harder to discipline. The broadening of the franchise helped in some instances to displace the key men of the old order, but the electorate as a whole remained unorganized and uncertain. Despite all too obvious disappointments, the government of Japan nevertheless slowly and unevenly grew more democratic.

Reform
of Japan's economy

AS INHABITANTS of a country where agriculture is the most vital part of the economic system, the Japanese were most interested in the projected agricultural reforms. The Basic Land Reform Act of 1946 was greeted with especial concern. It undertook to redistribute the land by breaking up and putting on sale many of the larger estates. But the Japanese tenant-farmers usually found that they were too poor to purchase the lands thus made available. Moreover, inflation and shortages in agricultural commodities had helped to improve the farmer's lot in relation to that of other economic groups. Since he was doing better than before, many a farmer lost the impulse to advance from tenant to landowner. The land reform program therefore had only a limited success, aiding the smaller landowner rather than the tenant.

Industrial and commercial reform efforts met with even more limited success. Demilitarization of the economy was carefully graduated in an effort to prevent severe unemployment and economic hardship. SCAP at one and the same time had to deconcentrate and to rehabilitate industry and business—a double task that would have been hard enough to do without the additional burden of inflation, which bore particularly heavily upon the urban wage earner and salaried worker. The constantly mounting expense of supplying Japanese deficiencies during the period of occupation fell on the American taxpayer, with the result that considerable pressure came from the United States to make Japan as self-sufficient as possible in as short a time as possible. Consequently only the most notorious cartels, such as the great Mitsui and Mitsubishi trading companies, were dissolved, while other great houses were not "decartelized." In instances where the reputation of an organization was not widely known to be bad, deconcentration was sidestepped out of respect for the rights of private property. Socialization or nationalization of

926

the vaster economic interests was suggested by the more radical groups among the Allies but not seriously considered by SCAP; and since purchase of such holdings was usually beyond the financial capabilities of the smaller capitalists, they generally remained unmolested in the hands of their former owners.

A new constitution for the Japanese Empire

IN 1947, THE Constitution of 1889 was formally revoked and a new Japanese constitution, written in part by SCAP, became the basic law of the land. It contained a bill of rights modeled after the first ten amendments of the American constitution and declared, in elaboration of Lincoln's pithier statement, that "government is a sacred trust of the people, the authority for which is derived from the people, and the benefits of which are enjoyed by the people." It proclaimed Japan's eternal renunciation of war except in self-defense. The cabinet, to be composed exclusively of civilians, was, like England's, made responsible to the legislature, which was acknowledged to be "the highest organ of state power." The emperor, still a divinity to those who chose to regard him as such, became automatically a servant of a sovereign people. He took to appearing in public in frock coat and high hat, and an American teacher was sent to Tokyo to help educate his heir in the ways of democracy.

The re-recognition of Japanese sovereignty

WITH THE inauguration of a genuine parliamentary system, political parties assumed greater importance in Japan than they had had in the prewar period. For a time the Socialists and the Communists enjoyed a popular success, but SCAP stood firmly in favor of the more conservative parties. An effort to provoke a general strike in 1947 was halted by a ban issued by MacArthur. The Americans usually supported the political activities of Shigeru Yoshida, the leader of the Democratic Party and prime minister after 1948. He adopted a program of thorough rehabilitation, free enterprise, and close cooperation with the United States.

Fearful that reform without prosperity might lead to Communism, the occupation authorities began after 1948 to work for the rapid revival of Japan as "the workshop of Asia." Moreover, the resurgence of international conflict in the Far East aided Japan's comeback. The fall of the Nationalist government of China (page 947) was an undeniable defeat in the American effort to contain Russia and Communism. With the victory of Communism in China, Japan's former role as an implacable enemy was largely forgotten, and she became a vital link in America's chain of Pacific defenses against Russian expansion and a potential ally in the struggle against the spread of Communism. With these considerations in mind the United States began in 1949 to plan a peace treaty with Japan. The outbreak of an undeclared war in Korea (page 984) hastened the process.

TERRITORIAL
RE-ARRANGEMENTS
1945-1947

In November 1950 the United States government issued a statement of the principles upon which it was ready to base a Japanese peace treaty. This proposal, aimed to bring Japan closer to the West, met Soviet Russian and Soviet Chinese opposition. The western powers, though disagreeing on such matters as reparations, nevertheless went ahead with their plans. John Foster Dulles, the American in charge of preparing the treaty, managed by the summer of 1951 to arrange a settlement satisfactory to both Japan and the non-Communist powers with interests in the Pacific region. Japan renounced all claims and title to Korea, Formosa, the Pescadores, Sakhalin, the Kuriles, the former mandated islands, and outlying territories, and agreed to an American trusteeship over the southern Ryukyus. Japan was thus reduced to her four main islands. In consideration of the economic burden brought about by war and loss of territory Japan was not required to pay reparations. Moreover, Japan was permitted to apply for membership in the United Nations.

At a conference held in San Francisco in September 1951, forty-nine of the fifty-two United Nations signed the treaty with Japan despite outspoken

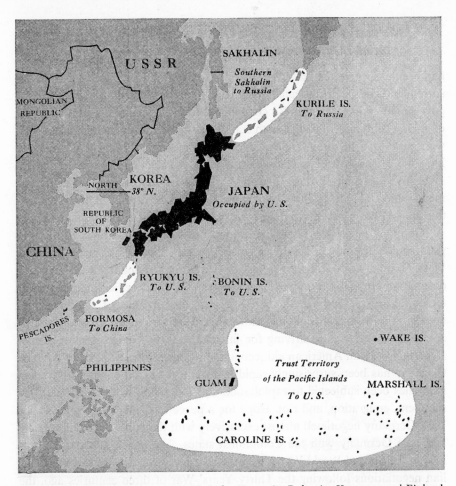

The treaties of 1947 made peace with Italy, Rumania, Bulgaria, Hungary, and Finland.
Italy lost Trieste, which became a Free Territory under UN supervision. Fiume, Istria,
and Venezia Giulia went to Yugoslavia, the Dodecanese to Greece, and pockets along
the French border to France. Italy's African empire was put under British occupation
pending UN disposition or, as in the case of Ethiopia, reverted to independence. Earlier
arrangements had stripped Germany of her gains of the 1930's and of other territory
as well. Germany lost East Prussia to the reconstructed Poland and the USSR, and a
large area upon her eastern frontier went to Poland as well. (Germany and Austria, as
indicated by the corresponding hatchings, and their capitals of Berlin and Vienna were
divided into British, French, Russian, and American zones of occupation.) Japan was
occupied meanwhile by American troops for the UN, and her Pacific mandates as well
as the southern Ryukyus were put under American trusteeship. Russia kept southern
Sakhalin, which she had occupied during the war. Southern Korea by 1947 had been
recognized by the United States and some other nations as a sovereign republic, but
Russia recognized a communist government in northern Korea.

Soviet objections. The Russians were particularly agitated by the simultaneous signing of a United States-Japanese military security pact providing for
the maintenance of American armed forces in Japan even after the end of
the formal occupation. These steps completed the relatively slow process by
which Japan definitely moved into the western camp as a sovereign nation.
American troops stayed behind—but as allies now, not as occupation forces.   929

The status in 1954
of Japan, Italy, and Germany

THUS, AFTER six years of occupation, reform and reëducation, Japan was readmitted, as Italy had been earlier, to the family of nations. To Japan and Italy, "unconditional surrender" had been mitigated somewhat by the continuation of a national government. American aid also contributed from the beginning to the revival of their economies. Though both nations lost their overseas empires, they were permitted to retain control over the homeland without division. Both have the support of the western powers and the antagonism of Soviet Russia (which vetoed their entrance into the United Nations) because their governments stand as yet against the expansion of Communism in their respective areas. Both must revive their foreign trade to achieve economic balance.

Germany's postwar rehabilitation was even more complicated. By its geographical location, it is sandwiched between the hostile camps of East and West. German unity still seems illusive. War, "unconditional surrender," and occupation brought not only inflation, disarmament, denazification, war trials, territorial losses, and reëducation but also the division of the truncated homeland into several economic and political units, and the creation of two antagonistic states each striving for jurisdiction over Germany as a whole. Nevertheless, with American aid, economic recovery in most parts of western Germany has been surprisingly rapid in recent years, although eastern Germany has been subjected to exploitation and repression, with consequent resentment, emigration, and riot. Hope for a peace settlement lingered on, but West Germany negotiated almost exclusively with the non-Communist states, and East Germany with the Communist states. The peace negotiations following the Second World War have exceeded in length of time the Westphalian negotiations following the Thirty Years' War of three centuries ago, the previous record. The western nations (except France) have shown great willingness to readmit West Germany into their international arrangements. Yet for the German patriot the future of Germany may well seem bleak, and a recrudescence of German nationalism in its worst forms remains a constant threat that all Germany's neighbors fear and have to take into account.

THE COST OF VICTORY

IN THE WEST

Six years of bombings, scorched-earth tactics, occupations, and liberations had brought ruin and hardship to the victors as well as the vanquished. In fact, it was hard to tell whether some of the victors would recover from the ill effects of war any more rapidly than the vanquished. The victors too had to fight off weariness, despair, and domestic unrest as again they sought the ways of peace.

*Material
and human losses of the war*

THE CONTINENTAL partners of Great Britain and the United States had all suffered from enemy occupation and the ravages of war by land and air. Belgium and Denmark were less damaged and disrupted than France; but Holland, particularly Rotterdam, was badly scarred by German aerial and ground actions. Paris suffered almost no military damage, but the towns on the Normandy invasion route, such as Rouen, had been hit heavily. War losses had been high in the Allied countries. Great Britain, with about one third of its total male population in the armed services, had suffered almost one million casualties, including the civilian victims of aerial bombardment. Large areas in the urban centers of Britain had been reduced to rubble by air raids or V-bombs. Numerous British battleships and merchant vessels also had fallen prey to Axis attacks. Though the continental United States had suffered only a few negligible direct blows, bombardment of the Hawaiian Islands and invasion of the Aleutians had brought the war uncomfortably close to the seaboard states and Canada. The battle casualties of the United States in Europe and the Pacific numbered close to 1,000,000, of whom 200,000 were killed. Out of Norway's total population of 3,000,000, over 10,000 lost their lives. In eastern Europe, the human and material losses were far greater still (page 941).

*The burdens
of occupation and reconversion*

HAVING COMMITTED themselves to "unconditional surrender," the victors were required to keep large numbers of men under arms in the states of the abjectly vanquished. The occupation program presented difficulties not only for the Allied armed services, called upon to assume the police authority of defunct or nearly defunct governments but also for the large civilian staffs required to coordinate the various activities of the victors among themselves and with the responsible officials of the occupied countries. Additional burdens grew out of denazification, reëducation, and war trials. The continual drain upon the depleted man power and financial resources of the occupying powers encouraged the feeling that the occupied countries should be rehabilitated and launched once again on an independent course at the earliest possible date.

That feeling was in a way only a mirroring of the demand for reconversion to peacetime practices within the victor countries. The urge to demobilize the armed forces and to rebuild the homeland was hard to resist. Outside of the United States and some of the neutral countries, living standards were steadily declining; and inflation was almost universal. Large numbers everywhere had to be relocated either by the change from war to peacetime economy or by migrations, both forced and voluntary. Occupation and rehabilitation took money, but to exact heavy taxes from populations still groggy from the blows of war became increasingly difficult. To the insistent clamor for disarmament and reconversion the victor governments could grant only partial satisfaction. No sooner had the Nazis been removed as a threat to world order than the non-Communist and the Communist governments began to look askance at each other. Security rather than reconversion therefore continued, after the defeat of the Axis, to be uppermost in some minds both East and West. As ill feeling mounted on both sides, each suspected the other more and more of evil designs and aggressive purposes, or at least made a public show of such suspicions.

*British economic problems
and the Labour Party's victory*

AMONG THE western powers the British in particular found recovery difficult. Damage to Britain's industrial and commercial centers had forced her former customers, if they had good credit or ready cash, to turn elsewhere. At the end of the war England's export trade was valued at only 30 per cent of its prewar figure, and England was a debtor rather than a creditor nation. Moreover, as after the First World War, Britain sorely missed her normal economic relationships with Germany. At the same time British trade suffered from the competition of American firms, whose reconversion to peacetime practices was achieved more swiftly than was possible for English firms. Meanwhile, the British empire in India was drawing to a close (page 951), and China was passing into the Communist orbit. The concomitant diminution of British investment opportunities in both areas dealt a hard blow to many a British fortune. At the war's end England had to try to nurse economic recovery while faced with the need to rearm and to readjust to changing positions in India, Egypt, and elsewhere. Churchill proposed to meet the crisis by a removal of wartime restrictions and by declining "to preside over the dissolution of His Majesty's empire."

To nearly everyone's surprise, in the general election held in the summer of 1945, the people of Britain put the Labour Party into power (page 903). Weary of war and stunned by sacrifice, they did so apparently in the hope that Labour might find a more radical solution to the country's needs than Churchill proposed. Under the leadership of Clement Attlee the Labourites offered a program of gradual socialization: broadening state ownership and control of key utilities and industries, and increasing the number and variety of social services. The British electorate was prepared to accept the Labour program, many believing that it offered a fundamental, if austere, approach to full employment, to an equitable distribution of goods and services, and to social security.

*Nationalization,
social services, and austerity*

THE LABOUR PARTY remained in power for over six years. In that time public ownership was considerably extended. The Bank of England, overseas cable and air services, coal mines, railroads, electric plants, gas works, and finally steel mills were nationalized. In keeping with the British aversion to revolutionary methods, the former owners were compensated, sometimes handsomely; and even after an extensive program of nationalization, about four fifths of British enterprise continued to be operated by private concerns. Government corporations were established to take over the management and operation of the nationalized industries. The Conservative Party in 1947 announced that it would retain most of these nationalization measures, when it should regain power, and so the danger of a thorough reaction largely disappeared.

The Labour government also put its social service program into practice. A National Insurance Act and supplementary measures broadened the existing health, accident, old age, and unemployment benefits and extended them to every Briton, the costs being distributed among employees, employers, and the state. A National Health Service Act granted every inhabitant of Britain free medical attention and supplies as well as hospital care and nursing. Physicians cooperating in this program were permitted to continue in private practice as well; patients taking advantage of it received the right to select their physician from a panel. The Labour medical program created great excitement both in England and abroad. According to its advocates it brought good medical care to many who previously had been obliged to do without, and according to its opponents it interfered with the proper relations of doctor and patient.

In providing Britain's consumer needs the Labour government undertook a stringent program of government control of trade, currency, agriculture, and industry. Rationing was not completely lifted, Britons being told that national austerity was required to save or to distribute fairly the country's limited economic resources. Heavily dependent upon imports, the British throughout the postwar years suffered from an adverse balance of trade and payments. To push exports the pound was devalued in terms of dollars. Loans from the dominions and Marshall Plan funds (page 977) from the United States were required to aid in the purchase of raw materials and other supplies indispensable for industrial rehabilitation and new housing. In the midst of this tremendous straining toward recovery the hard-pressed British felt obliged also to rearm in cooperation with the United States and the nations of western Europe. Rearmament efforts had to be intensified in 1950 as a result of the Korean crisis (page 984). Tired of the unceasing sacrifices and dissatisfied with the meager results produced by nationalization, the British electorate reduced Attlee's majority to an unsafe margin in 1950 and returned Churchill and the Conservatives to power in 1951.

France's recovery from occupation and liberation

FRANCE'S LIBERATION in 1944 had been perhaps more costly than defeat in 1940. It had wrecked whole cities and almost obliterated the transportation system of northern France. The activities of the French Resistance Forces against the Germans had inflicted heavy ruin also upon the French countryside. Shortages of food, fodder, and textiles added to the numerous exigencies that brought a flourishing black market into existence. Like Britain, France had lost many of her former markets and was experiencing difficulty in retaining some of her prize overseas possessions. At the war's end, but for British and Nationalist Chinese aid, the French might not have been able to reoccupy Indochina.

In Europe, however, metropolitan France was well on her way to national revival and a place in world councils by the close of the war. For about a year and a half after liberation De Gaulle ruled France mainly through executive decrees. He paid no heed to those who cried that France's days as a great power were over. Rehabilitation of the country, conversion of the Resistance Forces into a regular army, and reassertion of French prestige and influence in world affairs were the main lines of his policy. To facilitate economic recovery and somewhat to appease his political opponents of the Left, De Gaulle inaugurated a policy of nationalizing key industries and business not already under government control, such as the coal mines, the Renault automobile works, aircraft production, civil aviation, gas, electricity, and credit establishments. Less than a year after the liberation of France, a new army was outfitted and ready to take part in the German occupation. In December 1944, France, still more fearful of Germans than Russians and with a powerful Communist Party of her own, strengthened her international bargaining position by concluding a treaty of alliance and mutual assistance with Russia. Thus, while the war was still going on, France had moved into a position from which to reassume an important role in the councils of Europe and in the postwar race for foreign trade.

The leading political parties were now the Communists, the Socialists, the (Catholic) Popular Republican Movement (MRP), and the De Gaullists. For the time being, though not for the same reasons, they agreed on a number of vital issues, among them the arrest and trial of the Vichy collaborators. Pétain and Laval were the principal culprits. Both were condemned to death, and Laval was actually executed, but De Gaulle commuted the sentence of Pétain to life imprisonment. This severe treatment of celebrated men whose offense, in the eyes of many, had been bad judgment rather than evil intentions, stirred up doubts, particularly among the conservatives, and the De Gaulle government never carried through the wholesale punishment for wartime collaboration that had earlier been demanded in certain quarters.

The creation of the Fourth Republic ANOTHER ISSUE on which the Resistance parties agreed was that the constitution of the Third Republic should be discarded. A National Assembly was chosen in October 1945 to draw up a new constitution. In the ensuing debates, the Communists, whose strength stemmed from their gallant record in the Resistance as well as their ideology, advocated a government based upon a single-chamber legislature, which they hoped to dominate. Their De Gaullist opponents fought for a new document in which stability would be assured by a strong executive power, which they could easily picture in De Gaulle's hands. Standing between the two extreme parties, the Socialists and the MRP won the most votes by advocating something more like the traditional system of checks and balances. After a year of debates, plebiscites, and drafts, the nation approved a constitution that brought the Fourth Republic into being.

The Fourth Republic resembled the Third to a degree that made the relationship undeniable. The strongest unit in the state was to be a bicameral legislature composed of a National Assembly and a Council. Elected by universal secret suffrage, the National Assembly was planned to be the real seat of power, while the Council, chosen partly by the local governments, partly by the National Assembly, and partly by the overseas territories, was intended to act primarily in a consultative capacity. The cabinet, as formerly, was to be chosen from and responsible to the deputies of the people, who have retained a multiparty system and have been able to create majorities only by the formation of blocs. Hence, under the Fourth Republic as under the Third the tenure of premiers has regularly been short and their cabinets unstable. Stability is achieved by the fact that the other ministers do not change their portfolios as often as the premiers and that the bureaucracy stays on as premiers come and go. The president of France in the new republic was to be elected every seven years by the legislative bodies, and, as previously, honor and ceremony were attached to his post rather than power. He was given the significant power, however, of making the choice among the possible candidates on the occasions (eighteen between 1945 and 1954) when a new premier is to be designated. Vincent Auriol was elected the first president; Renée Coty succeeded him in 1954.

*Rehabilitation
in the French Republic*

WITH THE establishment of a new government, France once again addressed itself to its pressing economic problems. Unlike Britain, France removed most wartime restrictions and controls quickly. Though inflation mounted and the franc had regularly to be devalued in foreign exchange, the French modernized many of their factories, paying for imported raw materials and machinery with agricultural exports supplemented by the proceeds from the recaptured luxury market and the tourist trade. In addition France obtained substantial loans, especially from the United States. The industrial potential of the Rhône Valley was conspicuously raised by the construction of a series of huge dams. By 1948, French industrial production, partly replacing the deficiencies of German and British industry, exceeded its prewar figure. Farmers who could not make a fair living deserted their inadequate farms to go to the cities, often permitting the consolidation of the scattered holdings of former days and the greater use of farm machinery. Tax evasion and the constantly increasing number of low-paid civil servants continued to plague ministry after ministry.

Low wages caused strikes and ministerial crises, which successive governments tried to bridge by raising the legal wage minimum and increasing the social security benefits. Inflation too has been painful, especially to the middle class. It is attributable, at least in part, to the fact that France continues to import more than she exports, but unlike Britain, France imports almost exclusively machinery, industrial equipment, and armaments; in food, France is relatively self-sufficient, and its industrial potential is steadily increasing.

The French Union and French foreign policy

FRANCE'S RECOVERY has been slowed by a series of overseas complexities. The German occupation of France had stimulated nationalist activity in her African and Asiatic possessions. In an effort to appease the self-assertive colonials, the new constitution provided for the establishment of a French Union, a confederation composed of France, its overseas departments and territories, and "associated" territories and states. The overseas departments are the older colonies that are permitted direct representation in the National Assembly (Algeria, Martinique, Guadeloupe, etc.); the overseas territories are the older colonies not so honored (French Equatorial Africa, the India settlements, etc.); and the "associated" areas are the former protectorates (Tunisia, Morocco, and Indochina). Control in the new Union was intended to remain firmly centralized in Paris, while giving to the colonials a definite share in the decisions taken there. Though the Union represents a compromise of France's tradition of centralized colonial government, it does not altogether satisfy the colonies. French control in North Africa and in Indochina has been consistently challenged, and its maintenance has constituted a steady drain upon French man power, armaments, and financial resources at a time when they were badly needed at home. Indochina has been the scene of an especially costly war (page 956).

Despite the complexities of colonial resistance, unfavorable balance of trade (or "dollar gap"), and inflation, France's position in world affairs has constantly improved. A large and influential Communist party and the traditional fear of a rejuvenated Germany kept the new republic from moving fully into the western camp. By virtue of its alliance with Russia in 1944, France acted for a time as intermediary in the bickerings between Russia and the United States. This policy proved advantageous to France, even though it effected no international reconciliation. In the United Nations and in the occupation of Germany, France's voice was raised at first as a friend of both the eastern and the western camp. But after 1947 the unmistakable recovery of France, largely through American capital, and the unswerving devotion of the French Communists to the Soviet line had the effect of inducing most Frenchmen to apprehend the Russian alliance and favor closer association with the western powers. The foreign policy of the United States had been largely directed toward that end (page 977).

The prosperity of the United States

CONFRONTED FOR a third time in the twentieth century with reconversion as a result of either war or depression, many Americans feared, and the Communists hoped for, either widespread unemployment or a runaway inflation. Some observers warned of an engulfing crime wave unleashed by demobilized and demoralized veterans. The population was steadily growing so that early in 1954 it passed 161,000,000, because of a declining death rate and a sharp increase in the birth rate during and after the war. Urban centers continued to expand, and by mid-century accounted for 60 per cent of the total population. An outstanding feature of this urbanization was the migration of Puerto Ricans and Negroes northward and a sharp increase in the total Negro population. Racial tension was marked in almost every part of the country, and fear or hope caused many to prognosticate a widespread race war. None of these fears wholly materialized.

Unparalleled prosperity enabled American industry and agriculture to produce more than could be consumed at home. The demands of the rest of the world, however, continued to be great and, prompted by a combination of altruism and good business sense, the Americans made loans that enabled other countries to purchase needed goods in the United States. The expansion of home and foreign markets kept employment at the highest level in history, and personal income rose by July 1953 to a record annual rate of $288,000,000,000 for the whole country. In 1952 nearly 44,000,000 privately owned automobiles (not counting trucks and buses) were licensed in the United States; 6,490,000 individuals owned at least one share of publicly purchasable corporation stocks; and in 1954 over 50,000,000 telephones were in use. While those figures meant that many had no automobiles, shares, or telephones, and some had more than one, they seemed to indicate that in the United States at least the trend was not in the direction of a revolt in which the worker would have nothing to lose but his chains. High wages, high farm prices, and high taxes had in fact, for the time being at least, brought about a redistribution of the national wealth in favor of workers and farmers. The ones to suffer most heavily from the continuous price rise were unorganized consumers on fixed incomes, such as clerks, teachers, and pensioners.

American prosperity was derived largely from the domestic demand for consumers' goods pent up during the war, from the export of goods for relief and reconstruction, and from the continuation of heavy government spending. The unsatisfied demand permitted American commerce, industry, and agriculture to reabsorb without serious dislocations the more than 12,000,000 men and women quickly demobilized at the end of the war. Wartime restrictions, such as rationing and price controls, were likewise swiftly removed. Heavy pressure for lower excise and income taxes, however, had only slight success. The reduction of federal revenue was not feasible at a time when 937

American commitments for world-wide reconstruction and defense were constantly expanding. In fact, taxes rose, and in addition, paradox though it may seem, the richest government in the world resorted more and more to "deficit financing" (i.e., allowing its indebtedness to grow).

Labor disputes in the United States

INFLATION, THOUGH far from out of control in the United States, brought the usual reactions. For one thing, labor unrest became serious in almost all basic industries as the workers demanded higher wages to meet the rising cost of living. Though wage increases were frequently granted, strikes and walkouts continued. In strikes affecting the public welfare, such as in the coal industry and the railway lines, the federal government intervened to compel bargaining. Anti-labor sentiment increased sharply, and was codified by the Republican Congress of 1947 in the Taft-Hartley Labor Act. This lengthy act, among other provisions, outlawed the closed shop, banned jurisdictional strikes, authorized the injunction of strikes dangerous to national health or safety, permitted the president to call for a cooling-off period before strikes, made unions subject to suit for damages inflicted by union activities, and required "loyalty" (i.e., anti-Communist) oaths of union leaders. Though President Truman opposed the bill, Congress passed it over his veto.

Discrimination and social prejudices

WITH THE migration of Negroes to all parts of the country, segregation and discrimination became national rather than regional issues. A start was made in 1948 to eliminate "Jim Crowism" in the armed forces, with appreciable success. Discrimination in employment continued to be a common practice, and it was supported by large segments of management and labor. Several decisions by the Supreme Court, however, contributed to Negro welfare. In 1947 the Court declared that real estate covenants intended to keep certain racial or religious groups from so-called "restricted" areas were not enforceable by public authorities. The court also insisted upon equal educational opportunities for Negroes. And it nullified the "white primary" laws on the statute books of a number of southern states, though the poll tax continued in some of the same states to disfranchise the Negro. Local governments in the North frequently adopted laws calling for "fair employment practices," and church and philanthropic societies tried to counteract prejudice. The incidence of lynchings and other acts of violence diminished markedly. The number of Negroes in the schools showed an upward trend. The Negro problem began to seem ultimately solvable, though still acute. While not so conspicuous as the Negro question, prejudice against Orientals, Jews, and Catholics also produced internal discord and provided the enemies of the United States with an excellent propaganda weapon.

938

The controversy regarding civic loyalty

PREJUDICE AGAINST minority groups was in small part explained and in large part rationalized by the fear of subversive elements boring into the American structure. In the fight against the Axis, and later against the Soviet constellation, Americans gradually became alert to the danger of espionage and fifth-column activity. In 1938 the House of Representatives had first established a special committee to investigate "un-American activities." Subsequent acts of Congress, chief of which was the Alien Registration Act, sought to provide protection against subversive elements. The fear arose in liberal circles that these laws were based upon doctrines such as "guilt by intent" and "guilt by association," generally foreign to the American concepts of justice. In the hope of systematizing loyalty procedures and at the same time of heading off the accumulating attacks upon government officials for Communist sympathies, the executive branch of government established in 1947 a number of review boards of its own. Russia's success in spying out atomic secrets stimulated the creation by certain states, patriotic societies, municipalities, and educational institutions of special groups to investigate the loyalty of persons in government office, defense occupations, or education. Periodicals, politicians, and ex-Communists demanded investigations of governmental employees, professors, school teachers, writers, actors, and Communist leaders, and the attorney general made public a list of "subversive organizations." While liberals protested that this activity betrayed hysteria and either was or came dangerously close to being an infringement of civil rights, the Federal Bureau of Investigation and the Congressional Committees of Un-American Activities could point to a number of actual court convictions for espionage and for conspiracy to teach or advocate the overthrow of the government by violence. With each Russian success and with each conviction in the American courts the wave of "hysteria" and "counterhysteria" mounted until by mid-century it had become one of the most troublesome of America's domestic problems, reminiscent of the similar manifestations that had accompanied the French Revolution and the early stages of the Bolshevik Revolution.

Truman's victory in the elections of 1948

AMERICA'S DOMESTIC difficulties could be accounted for, in part, by the sudden termination of Roosevelt's strong leadership. President Truman did not win the popular approval that his predecessor had enjoyed, although he had the same opponents. Confident that this diffident and prosaic president could not rally the country behind him, the Republican Party in 1948 nominated Thomas E. Dewey, the young governor of New York who had been defeated by Roosevelt in 1944. But Truman, selected without much enthusiasm by his own party, showed an unsuspected campaigning ability. He went directly to the people, openly favoring a progressive policy at home and a stronger anti-Communist policy abroad. When the returns came in, the predictions of the political "experts" were completely upset. Truman's election demonstrated the continuing popularity of the New Deal (called the Fair Deal now).

The "great debate"
on American foreign policy

THE ELECTION of 1948 also brought with it the realization that foreign policy would play an ever larger part in American political decisions. Americans now assumed tardily and reluctantly the role in world affairs thrust upon them at the end of the war. Neither the government nor the people had seemed in the beginning to comprehend that a return to "normalcy" would be virtually impossible. They perceived only slowly that Britain and western Europe had lost (temporarily at least) their dominant position in global diplomacy, that violent nationalism and revolt were dooming colonialism in Asia, that the spread of Communism beyond Russia was not due merely to skillful propaganda but to fundamental dissatisfactions in eastern Europe and Asia. Because realization of the changed circumstances came only after widespread hesitation and obtuseness, the policies pursued by the United States were at first makeshift, uncertain, and confused.

Inclined both to parochialism and impatience, Americans differed widely on how to deal with Russia. Proposals ranged from the hopeful one of living peaceably with Communism in a single world government to the desperate one of attacking the Russians before they attacked. The more bellicose never numbered more than a few, and the persuasiveness of their argument evaporated when Russia exploded her own atomic bomb in 1949, sooner than the experts had thought possible. Acutely aware of the destructive possibilities of total war in the atomic age, Secretary of State Acheson embarked upon a policy of counterbalancing Russian and Communist strength by building up strong Atlantic, Pacific, and Mediterranean alliances (pages 976-983). American money had already been sent in large quantities into many European states, and American advisers and experts had usually accompanied it; Europe now in addition found its armies and navies largely advised, if not supervised, by American officers. The more dependent on America the older countries grew, the more their peoples divided into pro-American and anti-American groups, and the anti-Americans were often the more articulate (page 975). Hurt and bewildered by the failure of the rest of the world to appreciate their good intentions, the people of the United States developed a resentment that helped to breed disillusionment and confusion.

The election
of Eisenhower in 1952

NEVERTHELESS, as the presidential campaign of 1952 demonstrated, the country was not divided in its foreign policy. By that time only a minority wing of the Republican Party was isolationist. Both the Republicans (supporting General

Dwight D. Eisenhower) and the Democrats (supporting Governor Adlai E. Stevenson of Illinois) accepted the responsibility of maintaining the "positions of strength" that the Truman policies had provided, with disagreements primarily over which areas to emphasize. The major issues were concerned with domestic affairs. The Democrats stood for the Fair Deal and the Truman foreign policy. The Republicans hammered away upon the desirability of a change of parties, promising to diminish inflation, taxes, corruption, disloyalty, waste, diplomatic bungling, and costs and casualties in Korea (page 984). In the largest turnout of voters in American history, Eisenhower won a sweeping victory, and his party regained control of both houses of Congress, though by only narrow margins.

THE VICTORY

OF COMMUNISM IN THE EAST

THE WAR OF extermination waged by the Nazis in eastern Europe had brought devastation more horrible and extensive than anything western Europe had experienced. The Soviet Union, it is estimated, suffered around 7,000,000 deaths; Polish casualties numbered 5,000,000; Yugoslavia and Greece suffered comparably. Scorched earth tactics and widespread depredations caused unprecedented property damage. In Russia, almost 25,000,000 persons were left homeless, and millions in all countries were uprooted and scattered in various directions. Cities, industries, mines, bridges, dams, roads, and railways were demolished. Caught in the vortex, the despairing populations of eastern Europe hardly knew where to turn or what to do as the fury abated. Among these victims of demoralization, the Soviet Union, a pitiable fellow sufferer, moved quickly and deliberately, ready to provide leadership and claiming to have the only correct remedies for ancient grievances.

Rehabilitation
and readjustment in Soviet Russia

THOUGH THE Stalinist regime had narrowly escaped defeat in the war, it attacked the problems of reconstruction with vigor. The greatest losses of life and property, and the most severe dislocations, had occurred in the leading industrial and agricultural areas of western Russia. Following the patterns already set, the Russian government instituted a Fourth Five-Year Plan to be completed in 1950, with the general objective of raising industry to the prewar level of productivity and the particular objective of increasing the output of coal and electrical power beyond the levels of 1940. The emphasis on heavy industry (largely synonymous with war industry) meant a corresponding inattention to agriculture and consumers' goods.

The recovery program of Russia was helped considerably by reparations exacted from Germany and by confiscations at the expense of Austria and 941 the Balkan partners of the Axis. The development of Siberia was presumably made easier by the confiscation of former Japanese installations in Manchuria. Rehabilitation was further aided by the preferential position acquired by the Soviet Union in trade with eastern Europe and the Balkans, which together provided Russia in 1947 with about 75 per cent of her imports. Many German and Japanese prisoners were not released after the war and, along with native political prisoners, were used as what opponents of the Soviet regime labeled "slave labor." The free Soviet labor force was obliged to depend increasingly upon incentive wages to maintain what would be in American terms a subsistence livelihood, the higher rewards going to the intellectuals, the managers, and the officials.

By the end of 1950, despite the difficulties encountered, total Soviet production (at least according to the announced figures) was boosted by 73 per cent over the level of a decade before. In housing, the plan was somewhat overfulfilled. Particularly significant was the new geographic distribution of industry. In the Urals, pig iron production had jumped, while iron and steel figures for Siberia were impressive enough to be included in the published report for the first time. Not only was the Soviet Union beginning to develop backward regions, but it was also—through decentralization of its strategic industries—making the country less vulnerable to air attack. Farm output, however, did not come up to expectations; and in consumers' goods, production in some fields fell below the 1940 mark. And meanwhile the population had increased. Soviet economic reconstruction was made difficult also by the continued maintenance of large military forces.

The Soviet program of "normalcy" and "democracy" LIKE "democracy," "normalcy" was given a new meaning in the context of Soviet life. The most important aspects of Russian "normalcy" were a return to the tight control of the prewar years exercised by the central regime, the training of an enlarged Communist Party in Marxist thought, and the eradication of foreign influences, which had increased during the war. Several ethnic groups that had shown too much sympathy for the German invaders were deprived of whatever cultural and national autonomy they had previously enjoyed. The Soviet authorities insisted that these strenuous measures were necessary because of the historic inevitability of capitalist hostility and because of the atomic bomb, which some capitalists wished to "drop now." This new Russian belligerency ran counter to the hopes of the overwhelming majority in the West, who had seen in wartime collaboration the beginning of moderation and conciliation and the possibility of coexistence of the two incompatible ideologies.

"Democracy" in Soviet usage had become the "people's democracy," a tautologous phrase intended to emphasize the contrast with the so-called "bourgeois democracy" of the West. This "people's democracy" looked to the West little different from Nazi totalitarianism except in its proclaimed objective to achieve the classless society. The number of "people's democracies" grew as the Communists maintained and extended their hold over new territories. At the end of the war Soviet troops totally occupied Finland, Estonia, Latvia, Lithuania, Poland, Czechoslovakia, Hungary, Rumania, Bulgaria, and Albania, and were an influential force as well in Germany, Austria, northern Norway, and Yugoslavia. In Asia, the Soviet Union had annexed the small border state of Tannu-Tuva and had occupied Manchuria, northern Korea, southern Sakhalin, Sinkiang, and the Kurile Islands. Of these countries only Finland, Norway, and Yugoslavia were able to reëstablish full independence of Russian control before 1954.

The Soviet annexations had been confirmed by wartime agreements of the great powers. For Russia this meant the direct absorption of 185,000 square miles of new territory and a new population of around 25,000,000. The eight states that came directly under Soviet influence without being formally annexed had a population of almost 100,000,000, with annual national incomes roughly equivalent to about one half that of Russia. In wartime conferences the western powers had agreed to this Russian sphere of influence in return for Russian recognition of their preferred position in Greece and Italy. The western leaders had thought of this arrangement as merely a temporary expedient to prevent a huge administrative vacuum in the areas from which the Nazis and Fascists were retreating, and Stalin had agreed at Yalta "to form interim governmental authorities broadly representative of all democratic elements in the population and pledged to the earliest possible establishment through free elections of governments responsive to the will of the people." But phrases like "free elections" and "will of the people" did not mean to Communists what they meant in the western tradition. In the Soviet philosophy the "will of the people" was historically determined and needed only to be interpreted by the Communists; and elections were not "free" when "the enemies of the people" controlled them.

The descent of the "Iron Curtain"

EXCEPT FOR eastern Germany and Finland, the pattern by which "people's democracies" were created in eastern Europe did not vary in essentials. The victorious Russian forces, after weeding out "collaborators" from among the native leaders, turned the reins of government over to coalition governments made up of representatives from all parties that had participated in the fight against the Nazis. The Russian authorities insisted regularly upon the appointment of a Communist to the post of minister of the interior, the official in charge of the police in most eastern European countries. Meanwhile, under Soviet prodding, large enterprises not previously under government control were nationalized, and the means of transportation and communication were strictly supervised. On charges of treason or other serious offenses the Communists forced the representatives of the opposition parties from the government and replaced them with either Communists or crypto-Communists ("fellow travelers"). This gradual elimination of organized opposition was accompanied by the restriction or abolition of civil liberties; and political recalcitrants were imprisoned or executed unless they managed to go into voluntary exile. Education, art, literature, the radio, and the press were so manipulated as to augment the willingness to accept a Communist dictatorship.

"From Stettin in the Baltic to Trieste in the Adriatic," said ex-premier Winston Churchill in a speech in March 1946 at Fulton, Missouri, "an iron curtain has descended across the Continent," dividing the Communist from the non-Communist world. The final achievement of Communist domination east of the "Iron Curtain" came in different places at different times depending upon the strength of the non-Communist forces and of western influences. Total Communist regimes were not set up until 1947 in Albania, Bulgaria, Rumania, and Yugoslavia. Poland, Czechoslovakia, and Hungary succumbed to Communist pressure only in 1948. The key organization in the international Communist system, the Communist Information Bureau (Cominform), was established in September 1947, ostensibly in reply to the "Truman Doctrine" (page 976). Just as the abandoning of the Comintern had been a friendly gesture to Russia's allies during the war, the assembling of the Cominform was a mark of the renewed distrust. Its primary function was to assure the safety of the Soviet fatherland by tightening the Communist hold in eastern Europe and by making certain of the loyalty and cooperation of the Communist parties in the states that before the war had formed a "cordon sanitaire" against Soviet expansion.

In the Russian zone in eastern Germany, Communism was established only gradually. At first the Social Democrats and the Christian Socialists appeared to be worthy opponents of Communism, but gradually they were forced from all positions of prominence, and in 1947 they were outlawed. Thereafter, the number of refugees fleeing to the western zones of Germany increased. Many eastern Germans joined with western Germans in hoping for a clash between the occupying powers that would favor the reëstablishment of a unified German nation. But their hopes withered as the powers promoted instead the development of two republics, East Germany and West Germany, each of which claimed to be acting on behalf of the German people as a whole. Those who, counting on western appeasement, hoped for a reunited Communist Germany, saw their ambitions dashed by the failure of the Berlin blockade (page 922). Meanwhile the reality of Russian influence in East Germany became clear. The establishment of a single-party state under the leadership of Wilhelm Pieck placed East Germany in 1949 unquestionably within the Soviet orbit. Protest riots in 1953 were suppressed by Russian tanks.

*The split
of Yugoslavia from the Cominform*

THE SACRIFICE of the interests of the people's democracies to the rebuilding of the Soviet Union led to Yugoslavia's open break with the motherland of Communism. Marshal Tito had emerged from the war as the political leader of Yugoslavia most acceptable to the Soviet Union. A Moscow-trained Communist, Tito quickly established in his war-torn country an authoritarian regime cut after the traditional Communist pattern and at once began an extensive program of socialization and collectivization. Not having had to go through a stage of coalition with more moderate parties, and possessing a respectable armed force built up during the war, Tito was less troubled by opposition and "deviation" than most of the other rulers of people's democracies; and, being less dependent upon Russia, as well as farther away, he took no pains to hide his resentment of Soviet methods. In 1948 he declared his unwillingness to accept the decisions of the Cominform. Encouraged by the western powers, he maintained his defiance despite economic reprisals and open threats of war. Tito's "betrayal" stimulated the Cominform to redouble its precautions, and non-Russian Communists felt called upon to vow publicly that they placed their loyalty to the Communist motherland above their duty to their national homes. Despite the shock this preference for a foreign country gave to non-Communists and despite the alienation of some veteran Communists, such avowals were made by Communists all over the world.

Tito's action thus had greater significance than might have been expected. It was the first breach in the Russian satellite system. Yugoslavia continued to be a Communist state though not an ally of Russia, but pressure and aid from the West mitigated somewhat the totalitarian character of the Tito regime. Furthermore, Yugoslavia's revolt obliged Communists outside of Russia to speak like Russian fifth columnists as well as (and perhaps rather than) genuine revolutionaries. At the same time the support extended to Tito indicated that Communism was not regarded as the enemy in the West so much as was pro-Russianism.

*Russia's advance
upon China's Asiatic frontiers*

THE WEST'S victory in Yugoslavia was more than offset by the Communists' victory in China. The misfortunes of war had required the Chiang government for a time to pursue a conciliatory policy toward China's Communists; but after the western powers entered the fight and it became clear that Japan would be defeated, the rival parties prepared for an eventual test of strength. Armed clashes were frequent. Meetings between Mao Tse-tung and Chiang Kai-shek usually ended with manifestoes promising better cooperation, but they were promptly ignored by both sides. The Communists concentrated in the last years of the war upon establishing rural soviets north and south of the 945

Yangtze River, while the Nationalists concentrated upon regaining control of the important commercial cities and the railways. As the officially recognized government of China, the Nationalists, despite frequent accusations of corruption, received Allied aid to a much greater extent than the Communists.

When Russia joined the attack upon the Japanese, the struggle for power in China became still more complicated. The Russian annexation of Tannu-Tuva in 1944 (page 943) was a threat to China's border, and the Russian advance upon the Japanese in Manchuria put that vital area under Russian influence. Nevertheless, the Russians and the Nationalist Chinese with apparent amicability arranged their outstanding contentions in the Sino-Soviet Treaty of 1945.

The following year the tensions beneath the surface began to show, however. In keeping with the terms of the Sino-Soviet Treaty, Outer Mongolia voted its independence of China and continued to accept "advice" and leadership from Russia. Sinkiang, the key area of central Asia and traditionally a Chinese province, also began to move more directly under Soviet influence. Although Russia in keeping with the arrangements at Yalta actually, to the surprise of most Westerners, withdrew her forces from Manchuria, she did so only after removing every piece of machinery and material that could be moved and destroying the rest. The Soviet Union thus either established control of regions that had formerly acted as barriers to its expansion or made sure that potential enemies would secure only empty shells.

Failure
of the Marshall mission

AFTER THE WAR, the United States continued its wartime policy of supporting and aiding the Kuomintang, while at the same time urging internal reform and the cessation of civil war. At the end of 1945, President Truman appointed General George C. Marshall to undertake the role of mediator in China and announced that continuation of American aid to the Chiang regime would be dependent upon the willingness of the Nationalists to broaden the base of their government and to negotiate with the Communists. Though Marshall succeeded in bringing the hostile parties to a conference table, he found it impossible to get them to bargain. Convinced that the United States could not afford to let Communism prevail in China, the Nationalists at first refused to make any concessions. Their recent regaining of military control over China's most important strategic centers stiffened them in their uncompromising stand. The Communists, outraged by the continued American aid to the Nationalists, began to balk at participating in the conferences altogether. Although Marshall finally won a few temporary points, his mediation effort failed, as became clear in 1946 when the Nationalists proclaimed a new constitutional regime without previous agreement with the Communists. Marshall distributed the blame for failure evenly. "Sincere efforts to achieve settlement," he

946

asserted, "have been frustrated time and again by extremist elements of both sides."

The collapse of the Kuomintang

THOUGH THE liberals of China tried to act as mediators, they were too few and too uninfluential to effect a political balance. Moreover, both opposing sides possessed armed strength and foreign connections. Since each was essentially committed to a totalitarian solution of China's multitudinous problems and believed in its own ultimate victory, the prospects of compromise and workable coalitions probably never had been as bright as some hopeful Americans believed. Weary of bloodshed, famine, and brutal hardship, the Chinese peasantry welcomed any solution that promised freedom from war and hunger. Never having enjoyed liberty in the western sense, the Chinese in general sought primarily a modicum of physical comfort and security. After almost twenty years of Kuomintang rule, they looked for little from that quarter. The rural reform program of the Communists, which had been tried out in widely scattered parts of the country, appeared at least to have the merit of promising something positive.

The withdrawal of the Marshall mission and the subsequent curtailing of American aid diminished the Nationalists' prestige. Their armies over-extended, their means of communication and supply severely damaged, the Nationalists in 1947 were forced to take the defensive. In a country suffering from civil war, banditry, famine, and inflation, the faltering government was unable to command popular interest in its survival. On the other hand, the Communists captured the peasants' imagination and were able to wrest the leadership away from the Kuomintang. Concentrating their activities upon the cities and strongholds of the north, they cut off, surrounded, and reduced the Nationalist strongholds one by one.

The victory of the Chinese Communists

THE CHINESE Communists were frequently thought of abroad as essentially interested in agrarian reform. But in 1948, as their armies occupied the northern centers, the "line" of Communist thinking underwent a change. No longer were the rural areas and the peasantry to be the fulcrum of their nation-wide revolution; the movement turned increasingly toward the urban proletariat. The leaders of the Kuomintang were castigated as corrupt traitors and were charged with having brought China almost to ruin as the "running dogs of the American imperialists." Despite the dubious record of Russia in Manchuria and other peripheral areas, the Communists considered the Soviet Union China's true friend. As they piled victory upon victory, they refused all Kuomintang offers to negotiate. Once firmly entrenched in the north, they moved against the Nationalist strongholds south of the Yangtze. By the end of 1949 Nationalist resistance on the continent was broken, and Chiang Kai-shek and his supporters took refuge on the nearby island of Formosa, hoping someday to return and reconquer the empire they had lost.

International reaction
to the Chinese "Red" Revolution
THE CHINESE People's Republic had already been proclaimed (October 1, 1949), heralding the victory of Mao's forces. The powers now had to face squarely the question of recognizing the revolutionary government. The reality of the new regime's authority over China's resources, people, and markets could not seriously be questioned by the close of the year. The Soviet Union, the day after the proclamation of the new government, extended recognition to the Communists. A thirty-year Sino-Soviet alliance of friendship and mutual assistance came the next February.

In the United States, meanwhile, controversy raged. The Republican opposition charged the Truman administration with having failed the Nationalists and having thereby opened the whole of eastern Asia to Communist penetration. In response, the Department of State contended that no amount of money or material could have maintained the corrupt, inefficient, and tottering Chiang regime. The United States, nevertheless, refused to repudiate Chiang and withheld recognition from the Chinese People's Republic. Great Britain, on the other hand, granted recognition. The United Nations followed the leadership of the United States; it did not unseat the Nationalist Chinese and it did not invite the Chinese Communists to join.

With the victory of the Mao forces in China, Communist control extended across the Eurasiatic continent from Vienna in Austria to Canton in China. The rapid successes of Communism helped to increase Communist prestige, particularly in lands where the governments were new and relatively unstable. Even in western Europe, as French, Italian, Dutch, and other die-hard Communists vowed publicly never to take up arms against the motherland of Communism, the Communist parties presented a serious menace to the hard-won and still precarious stability. Were time and history in fact, as Communist philosophers said, on the side of Communism?

The "liberation"
of the Korean Peninsula
A GREATER URGENCY was lent to the struggle by the duel for Korea. At the Potsdam Conference (page 902), the military staffs of Russia and the United States had agreed that the Japanese forces in Korea north of the 38th parallel should surrender to Russian troops and those south of that line to American troops. Unable after the surrender to agree, the two countries permitted the military demarcation line gradually to become the frontier between a Communist and a non-Communist zone.

In both sectors, preparations went ahead, as in divided Germany, for the establishment of a permanent native regime that might have jurisdiction over the entire peninsula. Under American auspices an independent government of South Korea emerged in 1947 under the leadership of Syngman Rhee. In North Korea, a separate regime was organized under Russian auspices and with the collaboration of the wartime hero Kim Il Sung. In an effort to settle this dispute, the United Nations sought to hold supervised elections in Korea. Refused permission to proceed north of the dividing parallel, the UN Commission in the spring of 1948 supervised the elections of South Korea alone, where Rhee was confirmed in power. The United Nations recognized the Rhee regime as "a lawful Government...and...the only such Government in Korea."

Rejecting the decision of the United Nations, North Korea proclaimed its separate existence and proceeded to prepare for a showdown. Despite the approaching climax, the formal withdrawal of the Russian and the American "liberation" forces followed in 1949. The Rhee regime was left with the protection of some United Nations employees, a small staff of American advisers, and some American financial assistance, though North Korea was known to be engaged in active military preparations with the aid of Russian advisers and materials. It remained to be seen whether the United Nations could be any more effective in the Korean contest than the League of Nations had been in the Chinese and the Ethiopian crises of the 1930's.

THE COLLAPSE
OF COLONIALISM

THE SECOND World War had brought with it noble pronunciamentos on liberty by the Allies, a temporary defeat of the great colonial empires of England, France, Holland, and the United States, and the ultimate defeat of the lesser empires of Italy and Japan. The pronunciamentos and the defeats were not lost on those who sought liberty in Africa and Asia. The early successes of Japan had in some instances helped to stimulate latent native feelings into open hostility against the white overlords. The non-European subjects of the European empires had been required by the circumstances of the war to develop self-reliance, and the end of war did not end their determination to pursue their independent courses. Not having comprehensive colonial ambitions, and believing in the "self-determination of peoples," the United States assumed a neutral, though sometimes puzzling, role with regard to the new anticolonialism. Russia, having no colonies so called, took advantage of the strong national feelings in the colonial areas to win friends, and the Communists lined themselves up solidly with the insurgents to "bore from within" the national movements. While working for independence, the nascent states had to withstand or adjust to constant Soviet pressure from within and without. 949

*New developments
in the American empire*

SOME OF THE remnants of the vast Japanese Pacific empire went to Russia (page 943). The preponderant role of the United States in the occupation of Japan seemed to require American control of the more southerly approaches to Asia. To the string of naval and military stations in Hawaii, Alaska, Guam, and the Philippines, the United States now added authority over most of Japan's former Pacific possessions. Outright annexation, however, was not considered appropriate. The United States Navy occupied the strategic islands of Micronesia while American diplomats endeavored in the United Nations to arrange trusteeship over them; and in 1947 the United Nations, after bitter debate, approved the establishment of the Trust Territory of the Pacific Islands under American administration.

Though the United States thus became dominant throughout Oceania, it demonstrated its lack of imperialistic intent in other connections. The Philippines had been assured full independence upon the return of peace, and on July 4, 1946 (the first peacetime Independence Day) the American promise was made good. Since then, the Philippine Republic has maintained close economic and military ties with the United States. In addition to the problems created by the war's desolation and the new independence, the islands had to deal with the revolutionary activities of the Hukbalahap, a movement that had originated in resistance to the Japanese occupation but then had fallen under Communist control. Calling for peasant reform, land redistribution, and an end to American imperialism, the "Huks" engaged for eight years in guerrilla warfare against the "capitalists" controlling the new government of the Philippine Republic. Finally, in 1954, President Ramón Magsaysay induced the Huks to surrender. Meanwhile (1952) the American Congress had granted to the Commonwealth of Puerto Rico almost complete autonomy.

*Indian nationalism
during the Second World War*

NO LONGER ABLE or willing to maintain the colonial system, Britain granted self-government to all of its Asiatic colonies except Hong Kong and Malaya, which were strategically and economically vital to British interests and could be said to be less prepared for self-government. A number of concessions were made even to these surviving colonies, however.

Under Gandhi's pacifist influence, India had neither rallied officially to Britain's side nor risen in rebellion against the *raj,* though a few Indians were guilty of collaboration with the Japanese. The advance of Japan into southeastern Asia and the efforts of the Japanese to woo more Indians into collaboration brought the war close to India's doorstep. As the threat to India grew more ominous, the Congress Party and the Moslem League sternly attacked Gandhi's pacifism, and the Indian leaders demanded fewer concessions from

Great Britain. Even so, the Indian Congress in 1942 turned down as insufficient the famous Cripps proposals for dominion status after the war.

India nevertheless continued to play an important role in the war against the Axis. Indian soldiers were permitted to join the British as volunteers, and they gave a good account of themselves in Italy and Burma. At home India's industries made notable contributions to the war effort, meanwhile expanding at an unprecedented rate. Since these products were sold to Britain on credit and since the Indians made other loans to Britain, Britain soon went into debt to India. The war also brought new currents from the outside when India became a base for attack on Japan with a growing number of foreign soldiers and sailors, especially Americans, stationed on her soil.

Political deadlock permitted a new force to develop in India. The Moslem League under the leadership of Jinnah determined to bring an end to the Congress' domination of India's political life. Refusing to be classified any longer as a minority, the Moslems, particularly in the northwestern and northeastern corners of India, where they constituted majorities, insisted that the peninsula's Moslems were a separate nationality, and they called for the division of India into two independent nations, one of which should be the Moslem state of Pakistan in the north. Naturally, both Gandhi and Nehru fought against the Moslem separatist movement.

The independence and partition of India

AT THE CLOSE of the war the British put an end to the political stalemate in India. Hoping to find a peaceful and considered solution, the Attlee government negotiated assiduously with India's leaders. In India, however, impatience with conferences ran high, and repeated parades, strikes, and demonstrations called for the British to clear out of India immediately. Open hostility between Hindus and Moslems over the Pakistan issue, however, made the British hesitate to withdraw, for civil war was being but narrowly averted as the questions of independence and unity became enmeshed with rising famine, postwar dislocations, and unemployment. Finally, in 1946, a cabinet mission made proposals that caused Indians of all parties to realize that Britain really intended to grant independence. Thereupon civil hostilities became the order of the day as Moslems fought with Hindus for advantage. When the situation threatened to pass out of control, London prepared to act decisively. Lord Louis Mountbatten was made viceroy (March 1947), and in June announced that the British would withdraw immediately, transferring power to two separate states, India and Pakistan.

Because of the rapidity of Mountbatten's action, neither of the new states was prepared to take over at once. The viceroy, nevertheless, insisted that the British should get out and leave the native governments to their own devices as soon as possible. Both countries having expressed a preference for dominion status in the British Commonwealth of Nations, Parliament provided that it be conferred in August. The Union of India established its capital at New Delhi; Pakistan made Karachi its seat of government. This rapid transformation left the two states with many administrative, security, and personnel problems, but Hindus and Moslems rejoiced in their new freedom.

The difficulties
of the new state of Pakistan

THE NEW STATE of Pakistan was a striking anomaly. Separated into two areas about a thousand miles apart, Pakistan claimed a population of about 80,000,000, and 360,000 square miles of territory. Within Pakistan live about 20,000,000 Hindus, constituting a large and articulate minority. Western Pakistan is based on the valley of the Indus River and includes one of the most productive agricultural areas of the world. Though much smaller, eastern Pakistan is densely populated and also highly productive in rice and jute. Pakistan had never before existed as a single entity. Hence its founders were confronted with the problem of welding together a people who had little in common except religion and religious customs, and who had no linguistic, economic, political or administrative unity. Systems of communication, law, and administration had to be built up from scratch. Nevertheless, the state of Pakistan, with British and American help, has so far been able to maintain its independence.

The difficulties
of the new Union of India

PROBLEMS OF organization did not loom so high in the Union of India. Nehru and his followers inherited from the *raj* a capital, a civil service, and a relatively united nation. With a population of around 337,000,000, the Indian Union constituted one of the largest and most populous states in the world. Nevertheless, internal unity was only partial. The native states, such as Hyderabad and Kashmir, where British rule had not extended, were required to indicate after 1947 whether they would become affiliated with India or Pakistan. Most of the native princes whose territories lay in the center of the Indian subcontinent affiliated with India. Thus, though Pakistan remains a living reminder of India's traditional political and cultural disunity, a hitherto impossible political consolidation has been achieved in the rest of the peninsula. Rival claims upon Kashmir, however, soon provoked bitter disputes.

The territorial consolidation of the Indian Union has neither simplified the cultural heterogeneity nor filled the economic needs of its people. As in the past, the rulers of India were confronted with the task of integrating Sikhs, Mahrattas, Bengalis, Punjabis, and other peoples with differing languages, traditions, and customs. About 40,000,000 of these people were Moslems; about 85 per cent of the total population were illiterate. Moreover, India, left with twice the population and one third of the territory of the United States, had lost its richest agricultural areas to Pakistan and found difficulty in feeding its congested population despite the remarkable rapidity of industrial growth. The annual income is about $52.00 per capita.

In their planning for India's future, the leaders of the new state have concentrated upon the expansion and modernization of industry (especially textiles) and upon improving the peasant's agricultural methods. India, like Russia, has a five-year plan. However, native leaders, no less than the British, have encountered numerous obstacles in their efforts to reform rural practices and beliefs. Land holdings are normally small and scattered, making mechanization of agriculture unprofitable. The Hindu's reverence for the "sacred cow," proverbial all over the world, persists. India now has 60 cows for every 100 people, and no butcher will get them as long as Hindus continue to revere all life as sacred. Whatever the cows eat constitutes a drain upon the economy of a country where famine is a regular visitor. Custom also ordains frequent festivals, religious and social, which cut heavily into the farmer's working hours. Holy men and beggars roam the streets in large numbers and produce nothing. The death rate is high, but the population steadily increases and probably will increase faster as modern medicine and sanitation are introduced. Increased economic productivity has not accompanied population growth in India as it did in Japan. As in China, the unfavorable relation of arable land to population makes the importation of food a primary necessity. Some of India's leaders have favored birth control and planned families as an eventual solution of India's over-population.

Disputes over the native states

THE EMERGENCE of India and Pakistan as independent dominions in the British Commonwealth called for certain international readjustments. India was one of the original signers of the United Nations Charter, but Pakistan was not admitted to membership until 1947. Meanwhile, numerous conflicts had developed between the two states. In both dominions, minorities were persecuted, and millions of terrified migrants moved to and fro as minorities sought refuge with their own religious or communal groups. Some of the bloodiest riots in history claimed victims by the hundreds of thousands.

Relations between India and Pakistan were further aggravated over rival claims to native states. After considerable dispute, the Moslem state of Hyderabad was annexed to India by force in 1948. Kashmir's future was violently contested. Though the logic of geographical and economic ties suggested affiliation with the Moslem state, the ruling clique in Kashmir were Hindu and favored affiliation with India. Heavy fighting broke out in 1948, and the Indian government appealed the Kashmir question to the United Nations. The Security Council, after asking the rivals to cease fire, established a commission to study the problem, but although the fighting stopped, no solution had yet been found by June 1954. Hindu extremists murdered

Ghandhi in 1948 as he sought by his characteristic method of fasting to protest against the heated tempers on both sides. Pakistan extremists assassinated their prime minister, Liaquat Ali Khan, in 1951.

Nehru's leadership
in the affairs of Asia

OF THE men who had headed the Indian independence movement from its inception, only Nehru now survived. Shortly after the war, Nehru had taken the initiative in promoting regional cooperation among the new Asiatic nations. In 1947 New Delhi welcomed representatives of twenty-five governments to an Inter-Asian Relations Conference for exploratory discussions. The conference made clear that though the new nations had many problems in common, such as security against Communism, they were all too preoccupied with immediate domestic problems to move farther toward regional cooperation. Subsequent conferences of Asiatic countries served to rekindle interest in such cooperation but yielded few practical results. Though the governments agreed with Nehru that Asia should be relieved of western colonialism and shared his "neutralism" in the East-West conflict, some viewed with reserve his determination to "live with" the Chinese Communists.

In the United Nations, too, particularly on the question of recognition for China, India has endeavored to speak for Asia. On this issue, her voice has been heard with respect, if not with applause, since India is the only major non-Communist nation to maintain regular diplomatic ties with Communist China. Nehru's ardor in playing the mediator between the Communist and non-Communist camps was cooled somewhat in 1951 when the Chinese Communists marched forces into Tibet's mountains to assume control over that country's theocracy. Since Tibet lies on India's northeastern border, Communism thus became India's contiguous neighbor. Nevertheless, India was the only country considered genuinely neutral by both sides in the truce negotiations in Korea in 1953 (page 985).

Postwar settlements
in Burma, Ceylon, and Malaya

THE LOSS OF India as a colony diminished England's interest in retaining the neighboring areas, originally acquired, in some instances, as outposts in India's defenses. One of these was Burma. Until 1937, Burma had been managed as a part of India. Then Rangoon became its administrative center as the Burmese acquired a greater degree of self-government. The Japanese had occupied Burma during the war, but native resistance, both organized and unorganized, was strong and effective. After the war, in the midst of the complex problems of rehabilitation and pacification, public opinion in Burma moved decidedly in favor of immediate and complete sovereignty. Numerous conferences on the Burmese preferences led finally to the Union of Burma, which officially came into existence as a new and independent nation in January 1948. Tied closely to Great Britain by treaty, Burma was admitted to the United Nations the following

954

April. As an independent nation Burma has experienced numerous civil struggles which have been complicated by the rapid expansion of Communist influence in China and southeastern Asia. The government of Burma has, however, so far managed to steer an independent course.

Elsewhere in British Asia, native movements likewise advanced as Great Britain readjusted to postwar realities. After being ruled as a British colony for nearly a century and a half, Ceylon became a self-governing dominion in February 1948. In Malaya, no nationalist movement compelling respect had begun before 1940, and even after the war, the cry for independence was still small. On the other hand, the economic resources and strategic value of the peninsula were enormous, while the heterogeneous native population was obviously unprepared for self-defense and self-government in a competitive world. Bowing only slightly to the demand for change voiced by groups sometimes Communist-inspired, the British, likewise in February 1948, created a new Federation of Malaya. They retained control of defense, foreign affairs, and the courts by the new constitution, but accorded local self-government to the nine Malay states of the peninsula. The strategic island of Singapore, despite violent protests, remained a crown colony. Communist-led nationalism and terrorism continued in the Federation.

The readjustment of the Commonwealth of Nations THE VARIOUS CHANGES in British Asia dictated some readjustments in the British colonial structure. Burma was the only one of the new states to choose immediately not to become a member of the British Commonwealth of Nations. At the Imperial Conferences of 1948 and 1949 India, Pakistan, and Ceylon were represented along with the older dominions (with the conspicuous exception of Eire). The participating states decided that the word *British* should be removed from the official title of the Commonwealth. The relation of the British crown to India was further clarified. The preamble of the Statute of Westminster of 1931 had implied that the crown symbolized not only the "free association" but also the "common allegiance" of the Commonwealth nations. In a formula proposed by India, the crown now was described "as the symbol of the free association of its independent member nations, and, as such, the head of the Commonwealth." The other nations, however, continued to accept the obligation of "common allegiance" as well. In January 1950 India was able, in keeping with the new formula, to become a republic. While these discussions were in progress, Eire (April 1949) announced its withdrawal from the Commonwealth and took the title of the Republic of Ireland (thus reasserting its claim to the whole island). After George VI died (1952), his daughter was crowned "Elizabeth II, by the grace of God of the United Kingdom of Great Britain and Northern Ireland and of her other realms and territories Queen, head of the Commonwealth, defender of the faith."

A few other changes have taken place in the British Empire. Malta was made a self-governing colony in 1947. In 1948 Britain gave up her mandate in Palestine (page 959). Southern Rhodesia, a self-governing colony since 1923, was joined in 1953 with Northern Rhodesia and Nyasaland to form the Central African Federation. The numerous crown colonies—among them Gibraltar, Jamaica, and Hong Kong—and the protectorates have been otherwise retained. Britain's foreign policy has been determined largely by her loyalty to her Commonwealth and Empire—to a point that has inhibited any great ardor for participation in the projected European Defense Community.

*Rebellion
in French Indochina*
WHILE THE colonies of Great Britain were being gradually prepared for self-government, the French tried to continue the prewar colonial policy of "association." This policy was designed to make French political and cultural influence palatable by associating selected natives with the French government. It had had only limited success in Indochina. The anti-colonial feeling of Indochina for almost two generations before the outbreak of the Second World War had been unparalleled elsewhere in southeastern Asia. Moreover, the collaboration of Communists with Indochinese nationalists went back to about 1930. The French had contributed to the well-organized agitation by their unwillingness even to talk about complete independence. The French Constitution of 1946 made the three Indochinese states "associates" in the French Union.

The efforts of both the Communists and the Japanese to win Indochina during the war had pointed up its importance. It was well located strategically for the control of southeastern Asia and for a descent upon Singapore. Furthermore, its wealth in rice, rubber, tin, zinc, and manganese increased its attractiveness. The Japanese occupation of Indochina and the collaboration of the Vichy officials with the Axis served to further nationalist hopes in Indochina. Under the leadership of Ho Chi-minh, a Communist-trained nationalist, the Annamese in 1942 created the Viet Minh (League of Independence) and proclaimed the Viet Nam (or Annamese) Republic. At the conclusion of the war, French prestige suffered another blow inasmuch as the reoccupation of the peninsula had to be carried out by British in the south and Chinese in the north. In the north, meanwhile, the Viet Minh continued to strengthen its hold. French troops and administrators reappeared after the war, and the British and the Chinese withdrew in 1946.

The establishment of the postwar French Union proved easier on paper than in actuality. France's Atlantic and American colonies remained devoted, and she was also able to retain her hold upon her Pacific possessions, such as New Caledonia and the Society Islands. But the Union encountered open rebellion in Indochina. Though it permitted a great degree of colonial self-government, it did not provide for dominion status or independence. Fired by the brilliant successes of their neighbors of the British Empire, the Annamese nevertheless insisted upon recognition of their independence. Compromises, negotiations, and foreign pressures failed to bring a peaceful solution, for Ho Chi-minh, as leader of the Viet Minh, would accept none of the limited French proposals. With the victory of Communism in China in 1949, Ho refused still more emphatically to settle for less than complete sovereignty.

The "cold war" and the problem of Indochina

IN AN EFFORT to satisfy nationalist aspirations and at the same time undermine the hold of Ho Chi-minh, the French sought to establish a friendly native regime. Ignoring the Viet Minh pretensions, they sponsored a nominally independent Viet Nam under Bao Dai, the ex-emperor of Annam. After the proclamation of Bao Dai's government in 1949, both native regimes in Viet Nam claimed sovereignty over the entire country. Civil war raged—particularly in the north. Russia, China, and the Communist satellites in Europe extended recognition to the Ho regime; Great Britain and the United States lent their support to France by recognizing Bao Dai. When the war threatened to spread into Laos, and Cambodia, in the hope of winning more enthusiastic support from the natives the French in 1953 offered full independence except in the conduct of foreign affairs. The drain upon France's resources was one of the most serious aspects of this struggle. Frenchmen and Annamese have been killed, wounded, and captured by the tens of thousands, and in 1952 alone the French Assembly voted over $1,000,000,000 in military credits for Indochina. While economic and technical aid from the United States reinforced the French effort, Ho's forces were regularly supplied and augmented from Communist China. French defeats in 1954 raised the possibility that France would accept a face-saving truce unless she received direct military aid.

The "cold war" and the recovery of Thailand

THOUGH NOMINALLY a constitutional monarchy, Siam, now usually called Thailand, was run after the revolution of 1932-1933 by a clique dominated by Luang Pibul Songgram, the country's strong man, and the armed services. The growing struggle between Communists and non-Communists in southeastern Asia threatened the political stability and independence of Thailand. Never having lost its sovereignty to the colonial powers, it managed, before the war, to maintain its role as a buffer between French and British dependencies in southeastern Asia, and by skillful maneuvering, to work along with the Japanese during their brief period of ascendancy. With the decline of Japan, Thailand adroitly switched its allegiance to the western powers and organized an anti-Japanese underground. By returning border territories annexed during the war to British and French control, the Thailanders were able to win moderate treatment. Not having suffered serious damages or losses, Thailand was thus able, unlike its neighbors, to resume its former position in regional and world trade quickly. A moderate regime made its appearance at the end of the war, but before long Luang Pibul assumed power again. The greatest potential threat to Luang Pibul's strong-arm regime came from Communism, and he watched events in Indochina with growing apprehension.

The revolt against the Dutch in Indonesia

MORE THAN the British and the French colonies, the Dutch colonies were left to their own devices during the Nazi period of triumph. In the Dutch Indies the Javanese, farther advanced than the other natives, were particularly dissatisfied with the limitations upon their local autonomy. Even before the reappearance of the white armies, the nationalists proclaimed the Republic of Indonesia (August 1945) and established a capital at Jogjakarta. The Dutch were, however, unwilling to retire without a fight. Officially labeled a "police action," genuine war went on in Indonesia at intervals from 1945 to 1949. Though a settlement of the dispute had been arranged as early as 1946, both sides honored its provisions mainly in the breach. In 1947, the Security Council of the United Nations offered its good offices, designating Belgium, Australia, and the United States as arbitrators. The Dutch bitterly opposed the decisions of the Good Offices Committee but were finally brought by pressure from the United States to accept. In November 1949, at a round table conference in The Hague, an agreement for Indonesian independence within a Dutch-Indonesian union was concluded. The capital was moved to Jakarta (formerly Batavia).

The United States of Indonesia has found that independence has not solved its problems. Under the leadership of Sukarno (who, like many Indonesians, has no other name), the new state has continued to struggle with the Dutch. One of the major issues is territorial—for control over New Guinea. The gradual liquidation of Dutch interests and institutions in the islands has also created complications for Sukarno's regime. Lacking capital, personnel, and experience, the United States of Indonesia since independence has had to look to America and elsewhere for aid. Like other former colonial areas, Indonesia has also had its domestic problems. It is faced, especially in its more backward sections, with the problem of holding a strong native Communist movement in check. Indonesia has its own peculiar problem in the jealousy and fear of the other islands concerning the predominance of Java. Indonesia is strongly neutralist in the East-West conflict.

Pan-Arabism and anticolonialism

THE WAR BROUGHT with it the end of the mandates and the colonial system in the Near East. Syria and Lebanon received independence as early as 1941. Arabic-Moslem cooperation was stimulated by the formation in 1945 of an Arab League. It included the six independent states of Egypt, Iraq, Lebanon, Saudi Arabia, Syria, and Yemen, and the semi-independent Trans-Jordan also adhered to it. Together they controlled about 37,000,000 people and an oil-rich, strategic area of 1,000,000 square miles. The founders of this organization counted upon the sympathy of roughly 200,000,000 coreligionists in the Moslem

958

world. Frustrated for centuries by the control of foreigners (the Ottoman Turks, the French, and the British), Arab nationalists took advantage of the growing weakness of Europe to assert their freedom. In 1946 the British withdrew from Trans-Jordan, and the newly independent state became the Kingdom of Jordan. In Iraq and Egypt, the British continued to maintain troops, but the protests of native nationalists became increasingly vehement.

Rivalry in Iran of the English and the Russians THE EVENTS THAT took place in Iran immediately after the war were particularly alarming to the Arab nations, as well as to their former European overlords. Having jointly occupied the country (page 879), Russia and Britain nevertheless, at the Teheran Conference of 1943, guaranteed Iran's independence and integrity; and Iran became one of the original members of the United Nations. The shah immediately called for an end of the occupation, and a date was set for withdrawal (March 2, 1946). The British forces evacuated the south, but in the north trouble developed. There Communist political organizers with the protection of the Soviet forces had busied themselves with the formation of a Tudeh (Mass) party. Meanwhile, they had stimulated a secessionist movement in the Iranian border province of Azerbaijan and had organized a puppet government headed by Jaafar Pishevari, a native Communist. Iran protested against these activities to the United Nations, and Russia, evidently not prepared to make an issue of this case, withdrew its forces in May. Thereupon the Pishevari government collapsed; its leader took refuge in Russia; and Iran once again assumed control in Azerbaijan. As Iranian nationalism grew, it concentrated its fury upon the British domination of Iran's oil and soon led to the expulsion of the British (page 962).

The Palestine question and the independence of Israel AS IN OTHER parts of the Near East, the British Labour government insisted after the war upon relinquishing its control over Palestine. American Zionists meanwhile brought pressure upon the American government, urging that quick action alone could relieve the suffering of the more than one million displaced Jews in central and eastern Europe. The problem, however, was not one that could be answered by a quick fiat, since the population of Palestine was still less than half Jewish, and many of the Arabs objected more violently than ever to further Jewish immigration. An Anglo-American Committee was designated to find a solution, but its proposals looked too costly to the British, and the question was taken up in 1947 by the United Nations.

Meanwhile the ancient hostility between Moslems and Jews in Palestine reached a new peak as the Zionists made progress in their immigration program. When the UN in 1947 voted for a crazy-quilt partition of Palestine into disjointed Jewish and Arab states, organized warfare broke out. For the Arabs it was a war of extermination, for the Jews a last-ditch fight. The Arabs were badly organized, and the Jews held. Calling upon the Arab League for help, the Moslems of Palestine refused to negotiate with the Jews. Violence by extremists on both sides inflamed passions to the point where a rational solution appeared impossible. A climax in the reign of terror was reached when Count Folke Bernadotte of Sweden, the UN mediator, was assassinated by a Jewish terrorist. His post fell to Ralph Bunche, who was a living example of the fact that, though the Negro question in America was still far from solution, able Negroes were no longer totally deprived of the opportunity to rise high in the service of their country.

Meanwhile, the United Nations, having decided upon a threefold partition (a Jewish state, an Arab state, and an international city of Jerusalem), tried to settle the questions of frontiers, exchange of minorities, and control of Jerusalem. In May 1948, upon the unceremonious withdrawal of the British, the Zionists proclaimed in their share of Palestine the sovereign republic of Israel, with Chaim Weizmann as president. Though the Arab League threatened reprisal, internal divisions prevented the Moslems from taking effective action. War between the Arabs and the Israeli went on until an uneasy armistice was arranged in July 1949. In 1949 international recognition was accorded Israel, and its representatives were seated in the United Nations. The victory of Israel, greeted by Jews all over the world as the fulfillment of a two-thousand-year prayer, provoked outbursts of hostility throughout the Arab world—particularly against Great Britain and the United States, the two powers that had supported the Jewish cause most actively.

Israel, since its birth, has lived under arms, with hostilities breaking out spasmodically despite the armistice. In addition, the tiny republic has to solve a number of other problems. About 650,000 Arabs, induced by their own fears and Arab propaganda to flee the country, now live as pathetic starvelings on Israel's borders and are welcome neither in Israel nor in the Arab states to which they fled. Israel contains, besides, a large minority of Arabs who constitute a delicate problem within its boundaries. Weizmann's government also faced the task of establishing in a country of limited size and resources almost one million displaced Jews from Europe and the Moslem countries, more than the total Jewish population of Israel before their immigration. The new state, nevertheless, advanced steadily in stability and economic strength, many of its immediate needs being provided for by collections among Zionists and others all over the world. The American Jewish community in particular helped Israel to acquire necessary dollar reserves and war matériel; and in 1952 the Bonn government agreed to pay Israel $715,000,000 (in addition to $107,000,000 to other Jewish organizations) in partial compensation for the damage done by the Nazis to Jews. The growing strength of Israel by comparison with the neighboring Arab states further incensed and worried the Moslems. The future of Israel, however, remains precarious, surrounded as it is by more populous Arab states.

THE BREAKDOWN OF COLONIALISM

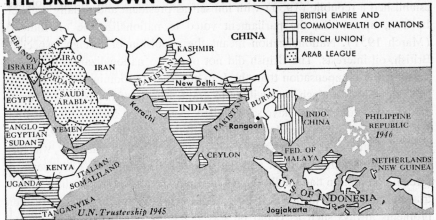

Subject peoples were loath to give up the independence they had had to develop during the Second World War, as this map of the more turbulent African-Asiatic areas shows. Of Italy's former colonial possessions only Somaliland was returned to her and then only under UN trusteeship. The British Commonwealth underwent new modifications, while Burma (and Ireland) left the Commonwealth entirely. Several of the former British and French mandates aligned themselves in the Arab League in 1945, and part of the British mandate of Palestine became the Republic of Israel in 1948. The Philippines were cut loose from the United States in 1946. The postwar French Union was unsatisfactory to nationalists in Indochina (as well as Morocco and Tunisia), while in the Dutch empire dissatisfaction resulted in the United States of Indonesia.

Other problems
of Arab nationalism

THOUGH HOSTILITY toward western interference served to unite the Arab peoples somewhat, the cooperative enterprises of the Arab League, whether economic, political, or military, repeatedly foundered in conflicting national interests. The struggle for control of the Arab League brought clashes between Ibn Saud of Saudi Arabia and King Farouk of Egypt. The small Moslem states, fearing for their own existence and integrity, rarely would extend whole-hearted cooperation to League projects. This lack of joint purpose and of coordination came out clearly in the ineffectual struggle against Israel.

In an effort to achieve greater cooperation and security, the Arab states of Egypt, Saudi Arabia, Syria, Lebanon, and Yemen initiated a collective security pact in Alexandria in 1950. Jordan and Iraq did not adhere to the pact because of League differences on Jordan's effort to annex Arab Palestine. Meanwhile a bitter feud developed throughout the Arab world over the attitude to take toward the western nations. Eager to obtain western arms, the rulers of the Arab League sought to repress demonstrations against British troops. Nevertheless, in Egypt particularly, the Arab nationalists continued to provoke riots and fights over the Suez Canal and other issues. In 1952 a military coup d'état engineered by General Mohammed Naguib drove out King Farouk. Naguib seemed consistently intent upon a genuine reform program. At first he proposed to establish a regency for Farouk's infant son

Fuad. When the exiled Farouk hesitated to return his son to Egypt, Naguib established a republic (1953) with himself as president and usually premier. In Iran, meanwhile, the parliament voted to nationalize the oil industry (March 1951). Nationalization meant the expulsion of foreign, especially British, oil interests. The British did not object to nationalization but asked for a greater compensation than the Iran government, dominated by Premier Mohammed Mossadegh, was willing to grant. Efforts of the United States to mediate that controversy have so far failed, even though Mossadegh was himself ousted and imprisoned for attempting to dethrone the shah in 1953.

The Arab world, as the western powers were forced to withdraw, was torn by social and political unrest and the threat of Communism. Long years of foreign domination had taught the natives some lessons of nationalism, industrialism, and social justice, but little about self-government. Nor were their problems always such as could be solved merely by good will. In several instances they were due to the lack of enough wealth to go around as well as to the concentration of what there was in the hands of a few. The Communists have not hesitated to cry aloud for drastic remedies. Whether a raging revolution can be avoided in these areas depends to a large extent upon whether reasonable reform can be made before it is too late.

THE ANXIETIES

OF THE ATOMIC AGE

THE BOMBS that fell upon Hiroshima and Nagasaki precipitated a great deal of apprehensive speculation all over the world. Would this new source of energy mean the improvement or the destruction of the world? Some thought that a chain reaction might be set off that would produce unending fission and destruction, and they predicted an atomic war after five years—when the Russians could be expected to learn how to make an atom bomb—in which both sides, and perhaps all of mankind, would be destroyed. Others, more sanguine, thought that the very horror of total atomic war might bring mankind at last to accept a supranational police authority to prevent future aggression. The atomic scientists themselves, startled by the havoc they had wrought, warned the world of the dire consequences of mishandling atomic energy. The American public read with foreboding John Hersey's *Hiroshima,* which told what the atomic bomb had done, and David Bradley's *No Place to Hide,* which told what the atomic bomb might do.

The problem of control of atomic energy

THE UNITED STATES Congress set to work immediately after the war to create a national committee to control research and development of atomic energy. Only after great public protest against military control did this committee become civilian. In

1946 the United Nations also established an Atomic Energy Commission to provide international control of research, management, and production. As a cooler evaluation of atomic power became possible, politicians and moralists began again to do business at the old stands, but no sober man ceased to be concerned that atomic energy should prove a blessing rather than a menace.

In the United Nations, disagreements soon developed over the control of atomic energy. Since the United States was the only nation with a stockpile of atomic bombs, and Russia (as we now know) was hopeful of solving the riddle of nuclear fission before the western experts thought she could, the crux of the dispute was whether the United States should retain its advantage in atomic weapons until a dependable international control could be created (as the United States wished) or whether all nations should start from scratch by outlawing the bomb at the very outset (as Russia wished). The United States proposed to the UN Atomic Energy Commission the creation of an international board with unrestricted and exclusive control of fissionable materials and of licensing and inspecting atomic plants, and promised successive disclosures of atomic information as successive stages of the control machinery were reached. The western nations supported the United States. The Russians rejected this step-by-step plan because they feared probably unfriendly inspection, because it left to the United States the head start of the bombs already made as well as the exclusive knowledge of how to make new ones, and perhaps too because they wished no solution until they could themselves learn how to make an atomic bomb. The Russians also wanted the atom bomb discussed along with disarmament in general, whereas the United States wished a separate and speedy agreement upon atomic weapons. Russia's steadfast refusal to compromise her position on the atomic bomb led her advocates to believe that she felt any other course would be suicidal and led her critics to insist that, after all, Russia did not act out of any sense of insecurity but out of a desire for specific advantages. Until 1949, the United States possessed the only atomic bombs, and as the "cold war" waxed hotter, a few Americans advocated a showdown with the Communists before the Russians had bombs of their own. When the Russians produced their own atomic explosions, it was hard to tell whether the outcome would be only a neutralization of the West's advantage (i.e., a stalemate resulting from each side's fear of reprisal from the other) or the greater possibility of a universal atomic war. The horror of mass-slaughter weapons became even greater in 1952, when American scientists conducted tests that appeared to signify their ability to produce a hydrogen bomb, a more powerful weapon than the atomic bomb. And in the course of the Korean "police action" (so called in the United States because it had not been declared as a war by Congress) United States ground forces began to receive training for the possible use in battle of new atomic weapons and the United States Navy began to build a submarine to be driven by atomic energy. "Modern weapons," said President Eisenhower, 963

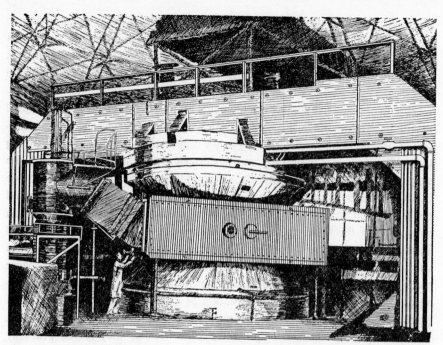

An atom-smashing cyclotron. This huge machine is a device for accelerating particles which will bombard and split the nuclei of target atoms, producing new nuclear species.

"can—in a single attack—visit upon an enemy as much explosive violence as was hurled at Germany by our entire air force throughout four years of World War II." Whether all this would produce or discourage general war was not clear.

Civilian uses of atomic energy and isotopes

WHILE HORRIBLE in its war potentialities, atomic physics helped to bring about notable advances in other sciences and techniques. Radioactive isotopes for use in physical, medical, agricultural, and industrial research were produced in nuclear reactors in quantities and varieties sufficient to make possible their distribution to widely separated research centers. Research groups in Europe and the United States experimented with radioactive isotopes as tracers whose behavior in animal bodies, soils, and plants could be followed by means of Geiger counters and other sensitive devices. This method was used in new treatments for cancer and thyroid diseases, experiments with enzyme systems, and studies of the effects of radiation upon heredity. Food-producing plants, animals, and fertilizers have also been traced in this way to improve the understanding of nutrition and photosynthesis. The biochemist W. F. Libby worked out a method of using carbon 14 to measure the degree of natural radioactivity remaining in organic products. This technique was increasingly applied after 1948 to problems of dating; through the measurement of the loss of radioactivity in their residual carbon, approximate dates for prehis-

964

toric wooden artifacts and other carbonaceous materials could be obtained. In the oil industry, radioactive antimony was introduced into long-distance pipe lines to separate products of different types. Of all the scientific accomplishments of the postwar decade perhaps future generations would celebrate most Einstein's "unified field theory" (published 1953), in which he embodied in a few mathematical formulae a set of laws that, despite Heisenberg's uncertainty principle, he believed would reduce the physical universe to a few simple, unified, and regular concepts, equally applicable to atoms and to galaxies. Except to the initiate, however, Einstein's formulae seemed less exciting than the palpable results of technology in electronics.

Other advances in the medical sciences

DRAMATIC ADVANCES were recorded in the medical sciences by other means as well, particularly in the manufacture of new drugs. Antibiotics, such as penicillin and streptomycin, were refined and increased in number, as were also the antihistamines (counteracting allergies) and anticoagulants (counteracting blood clots). New forms of the sulfonamide drugs appeared. In malaria treatment primaquine, used in conjunction with quinine, yielded excellent results. Understanding improved of the place of hormones, such as cortisone and ACTH, in the preservation of health. New drugs produced miraculous relief of asthma, of ulcers, and of arthritis and other rheumatic diseases. Surgery made progress, especially in the treatment of nervous disorders, such as certain types of ulcers and of psychoses, and in the correction of heart ailments. Virus infections did not generally yield to the new knowledge, but a form of immunization against poliomyelitis (infantile paralysis), believed also to be due to a virus, gave some hope in 1954 of taming that grave menace. Meanwhile the study of the mechanism of the living cell also advanced.

The development of electronics and radar

THE SECOND World War had also brought in its wake great advances in electronics and radar. In industry, electronic devices were used for sorting goods, detecting flaws in metal products, and selecting and matching textiles of various hues. In medical research, electronic devices detected metal imbedded in the flesh and produced fever artificially. The introduction of the radiotelephone in moving vehicles was also attributable to man's greater understanding of electrons. In sea and air travel radar gave warning of obstacles and made blind landings safer, and loran made navigation easier. Regular transoceanic flights now became commercially feasible. In 1952 the British Overseas Airways began regular jet airliner service. In 1946 a radar beam reached the moon, an achievement which probably will have future bearing upon stellar and planetary research and travel in space. Radar has also made possible "radio astronomy," the locating of stars invisible to the telescope by means of a great "dish" resembling a radar receiver. In 1952 the United States Air Force in Korea used electronically guided, pilotless planes to hit predetermined targets, and in 1953 NIKE, a guided-missile anti-aircraft defense, was announced.

In the prewar years television had become practicable, and a small number of home sets were in operation by 1945. At the end of the war commercial receivers appeared on the market in quantity. By 1950, the annual world production of television receivers had mounted to around 5,000,000. In September 1951, a transcontinental TV network was completed in the United States; this achievement tied together 108 local outlets into a nation-wide chain. The increasing use of television had a marked influence upon the American presidential campaign of 1952. The TV screen brought the candidates and the conventions and other activities directly into the home of the voter, who was no longer so dependent upon his local political machine or newspaper or upon his radio for his impressions. In the entertainment world, TV constituted a threat to radio and the motion picture industry. Practically all important political, entertainment, and sporting events and even many catastrophes were being televised by mid-century, and social-minded persons were seriously concerned how to use it for the promotion of, rather than interference with or commercialization of, the processes of education. Educators became more sensitive to the possibilities of audio-visual devices for supplementing the older processes of reading and oral instruction.

Science
in the Fourth Five-Year Plan

THE RUSSIAN state sought after 1945 to coordinate scientific research and to bring its conclusions into line with Marxist-Stalinist orthodoxy. In the Fourth Five-Year Plan (page 941), heavy emphasis was placed upon reconstruction of laboratories and libraries, the more effective utilization of natural resources, and research in the interests of defense. This trend was highlighted by the genetics controversy between Soviet and non-Soviet theoreticians. The Soviet agronomist T. D. Lysenko rejected the neo-Mendelian theories of heredity generally accepted by geneticists, and asserted that characteristics acquired through environmental influences are inherited. Since such a theory was congenial to Marxist social and political beliefs, Lysenko's assertions for a time became the official line in genetics. Soviet scientists seemed to accept this decision reluctantly and their western colleagues denounced it. In 1949 Julian Huxley, the British scientist, brought out the details of the conflict in his *Heredity East and West*. The Communist tendency to glorify Russian scientific achievements and to discredit the findings of non-Communist scientists became particularly acute in psychological research. The Soviet Academy in 1950 proclaimed the existence of "only two [psychologies], pre-Pavlovian and post-Pavlovian." The West dared underestimate Russian scientific and technological skill, however, only at great peril, as the development of the Russian atomic and hydrogen bombs and of the MIG jet plane amply showed.

966   The social sciences were also recruited for Russia's ideological warfare. Of

particular interest in this connection was the case of E. Varga, an outstanding economist. Instructed during the war to survey the impact of the war on the capitalist economies and to forecast their future development, Varga reached conclusions that apparently ran counter to official expectations. He held that a depression in the West was not likely before 1955, that the condition of western labor had improved, and that the capitalist states had been relatively successful in their economic programs. In 1947 Varga's "errors" were exposed by the Institute of Economics of the Academy of Sciences, and by 1949 he himself recanted. Soviet planning for the ultimate collapse of capitalism had, nevertheless, to recognize the continuing stability of the western economies, though the Soviets probably argued (as did many in the West also) that western stability was due to the emergency measures taken after 1947 rather than to inherent strength.

Soviet attacks upon bourgeois "intellectualism" SOVIET NATIONALISM also invaded the arts and letters. Writers of world-wide reputation were publicly accused of succumbing to the "foreign sickness." The editors of magazines, newspapers, and scientific periodicals were urged by Ilya Ehrenburg and Konstantin Simonov, Russia's approved novelists and literary arbiters, to stress the ideological and human superiority of the Soviet people brought up in the Soviet system. Russian history, theater, and fiction were mobilized to "show the Soviet man as he really is, and simultaneously as he ought to be." Mikhail Sholokhov, author of two novels well received in their English versions, was rarely heard of any longer in the West. Soviet musicians were accused of reflecting in their music "the decay of bourgeois civilization." The three leading Russian composers, Dimitri Shostakovich, Sergei Prokofiev, and Aram Khachaturian, were criticized for departing from the tastes of the Soviet people and indulging themselves in atonality and muddled combinations of sounds. At the same time a revival of the classical Russian composers was sponsored. Even the sports writers were reprimanded for encouraging "careerism and individualism" among Soviet athletes. Though the Russian teams covered themselves with glory in the Olympic games at Helsinki in 1952, they were criticized at home because they had not won firsts in certain events. Meanwhile, the Soviet radio and press sought to ascribe inventions such as the airplane, games such as baseball, and scientific advances such as atomic research to Russian origins. This nationalistic spirit was inculcated in part to counteract the foreign influences to which millions of Russians had been subjected during the war.

The new impact of the Orient on western thought EVEN AS THE Iron Curtain ever more sharply separated the new East from the new West, the desire to learn more of the old East developed in the West. It was engendered by a wholesome respect for the near-success of the Japanese attack, by   967 curiosity among the numerous occidental soldiers in the East during the war, and by the world-wide struggle for influence in Asia. One of the short stories of the Japanese writer Ryunosuke Akutagawa was shown in films in the West, and several were translated into English in 1952. Professor F. S. C. Northrop of Yale University published *The Meeting of East and West* in 1946, concluding that in personal and family relations, esthetic appreciation, and the acceptance of the transitory character of determinate things, the Orient had concepts which could contribute to emotional steadiness and peace of mind. In *Richer by Asia* (1947), Edmond Taylor, a former member of the American armed forces in India, was likewise impressed by the patience of India's people with their numerous problems and their adjustments to them. Both Northrop and Taylor deplored the cultural imperialism which appeared to accompany western plans for world unity, and advocated a modification of traditional values in East and West as a necessary prerequisite to mutual understanding and world order. In his survey of the Near and Middle East the American Supreme Court Justice William O. Douglas wrote in *Strange Lands and Friendly Peoples* (1951): "It is ideas that will win [in Asia] not dollars....We must go to the East with humility not condescension, mindful of our debt for the great cultures which the East has given us."

The quest for a new faith among Europe's intellectuals THE IMPENDING sense of doom in the West was not lessened, as in the Communist countries, by the persuasion that time was an ally. Conventional intellectual and artistic circles were jarred by the adherence of a number of leading intellectuals to Marxism as the wave of the future. Diego Rivera and Pablo Picasso, Louis Aragon and Paul Eluard, the leading surrealist poets of the French Resistance, Frédéric Joliot-Curie, a prominent French physicist, Howard Fast, a popular American novelist, and Hewlett Johnson, the "Red" dean of Canterbury, if not Communists, took small pains to hide their interest in Russia or Marxism. The revelation that several other scientists and intellectuals in France, England, and America were secret agents of the Soviet Union stimulated suspicions about the loyalty of persons in key scientific, administrative, and technical positions, though sensational investigations, special legislation, and extraordinary agencies to deal with the danger were rarely set up in Europe, as they often were in the United States.

Gloom pervaded what had been until recently the cheerful Bergsonian atmosphere of Paris intellectual circles. In the once carefree cafés around the old Church of Saint-Germain-des-Prés, the gloom was particularly thick. There Jean-Paul Sartre expounded the philosophy called existentialism to men who, like himself, had undergone the "total responsibility in total solitude" of the Resistance. Sartre's thought was based upon the Christian existentialism of the Dane Soren A. Kierkegaard, who had died in 1855, and of the German Karl Jaspers, still alive, and upon the atheistic existentialism of

968

the German Martin Heidegger, also still alive. These men were probably more learned and profound than Sartre. They had raised questions regarding the nature of reality, knowledge, essence, and being, in terms that the layman found hard to follow. Sartre gave them a following.

Sartre's writings, more through his plays and novels than through his philosophical work, made existentialism a vogue. Denying that God was essential to man's understanding of his place in the world, he posited man's existence as coming before man's essence (or, more simply stated, the individual as coming before the concept of mankind). The individual's responsibility for and helplessness in his existence were central to this doctrine. Yet, no matter how inadequate human reason might be for resolving the problems of life, no other force was regarded as more adequate. Man is alone and must determine his own destiny without regard for tradition or society. Nevertheless, Sartre saw a necessity for morality in action, in the unavoidable obligation to make decisions and choices: "Since by our very existence we influence our time, we must decide that this influence shall be deliberate."

The existentialist doctrine of a "dreadful freedom" for the individual has had a significant influence upon recent French literature and art. In the novels of Albert Camus a prevailing sense of the meaninglessness and utter futility of life was clearly reflected. In the rest of war-torn Europe, the lonely mood of the existentialists attracted followers among students and other young intellectuals. Sartre's own exposition of it in *Existentialism* (1947) pled for it as "optimistic, a doctrine of action": "There is no doctrine more optimistic, since man's destiny is within himself." Nevertheless, to those who believed in the primacy of either Matter or God, the primacy of Existence appeared the rankest heresy and despair, inflicting upon man the responsibility which the materialists denied without affording him the guidance in which the God-fearing trusted.

The Catholic response to Communism and modernism

THE SPREAD OF materialistic and atheistic philosophies such as Communism and existentialism provoked a quick response from Christian thinkers. The liberal French Catholic philosophers Étienne Gilson and Jacques Maritain expounded a doctrine of neo-Thomism. Maritain in *Existence and the Existent* (1949) claimed that the genuine existentialism is Thomism, the marriage of faith with reason that St. Thomas Aquinas had performed in the thirteenth century. He asserted that the individual's anguish over the absurdity of life and the nothingness of existence can best be relieved by recognition of the Fatherhood of God and the Brotherhood of Man. Not only is the traditional Christian faith for Maritain an answer to nihilism, it also provides the fundamental basis for the development of a democratic society.

The papacy itself felt called upon to take notice of the spread of modernism, atheism, and indifference. In an encyclical of 1947, *Optatissima pax,*

Pius XII called for an end to class hatred and urged class cooperation for the common welfare. Particularly disturbing to the Catholic world were the attacks upon Catholics living behind the Iron Curtain. Ancient strongholds of Roman Catholicism in eastern Europe were cut off by the Communists from communication with the papacy, and church holdings were nationalized. In Poland, Czechoslovakia, Hungary, and Yugoslavia, a number of the leading clergy were arrested and tried and sometimes signed "confessions" that puzzled western readers. Unable to help the persecuted Catholics directly, the papacy in 1949 excommunicated the Communists as enemies of religion, and the clergy, from the pulpits and through their publications, denounced the Godless teachings of the Marxists. In western Europe—for example, in the Italian elections—priests sometimes engaged openly in anti-Communist political activities.

The Catholic Church also proceeded vigorously against other dissenters within its ranks. Seeking to adjust their beliefs to contemporary scholarship, Catholic modernists in Europe had inclined after the war toward relativistic and evolutionary interpretations of the faith. Since 1950 was a Holy Year, when Catholics from all over the world made pilgrimages to Rome and religious fervor was at a high pitch, the papacy was in a particularly strong position to proceed against those intellectuals believed to be subverting the traditional faith. In the papal encyclical *Humani generis* (1950) this modernism was denounced and subsequently a number of offenders were removed from clerical posts. Meanwhile, Pope Pius XII sought to clarify Catholic doctrine in order to bring it into closer conformance with the teachings of science. In a series of encyclical letters and addresses of 1950-1951, he said that the account of creation in Genesis was not necessarily irreconcilable with evolutionary theory, that the material creation of the universe might have occurred from five to ten billion years ago, and that the church recognized the mutability of the inorganic world. These interpretations perhaps reconciled some of the fold who had wondered about the apparently growing chasm between dogma and science.

Proposals of reunion among Protestant denominations

THOUGH LIKEWISE concerned with the spiritual and moral problems of the atomic age, the Protestant churches concentrated rather upon church reunion in their efforts to strengthen Christianity. A milestone in this syncretistic movement was reached in 1948 with the convocation of the World Council of Churches at Amsterdam, where delegates from 150 Protestant, Eastern Orthodox, Anglican, and Old Catholic bodies discussed their common problems. Encouraged by the creation of a United Church of Canada in 1925 by all Methodists and Congregationalists and part of the Presbyterians, certain Methodist, Congregational, and Presbyterian groups in other English-speaking countries took

steps toward consolidation. In 1947, E. Stanley Jones, a famous missionary and theologian, was placed at the head of the Association for a United Church for America. The Roman Catholics, though willing to cooperate in interreligious and civil activities at the community level and in organizations like the Brotherhood Movement for toleration, continued to maintain that theirs is the universal church and that church union could best be achieved if the other Christian faiths would return to the jurisdiction of Rome.

New approaches in behavioral studies

ONE INDEX OF the general concern felt about humanity's future was the popularity of the one-volume abridgment (1946) of Arnold Toynbee's *A Study of History.* The new version centered attention once more (page 797) upon the disintegration of the great civilizations of the past. "We may and must pray," he concluded in a revised chapter, "that a reprieve which God has granted to our society once will not be refused if we ask for it again in a humble spirit and with a contrite heart." Toynbee thus stressed the spiritual factor in determining the adequacy of a civilization to meet its challenges.

The social scientists in general, however, continued to concentrate their attention upon environmental factors with great regard for psychological techniques and perceptions. When the Henry Ford family set up the Ford Foundation (the wealthiest philanthropic fund ever created), its directors decided in 1951 to give considerable emphasis to the promotion of behavioral studies. Psychiatry, psychoanalysis, and psychosomatic medicine expanded their range in the postwar epoch. Though Freudian techniques still held the field, a tendency grew to reëvaluate Freud's emphasis upon sexual motivation by reference to the importance of social and cultural factors in personal maladjustments. Startling results were achieved by the application of psychotherapy to diseases previously thought of as fundamentally physiological. Psychosomatic practitioners met with a significant degree of success in treating such disorders as stomach ulcer, heart disease, rheumatics, asthma, and endocrine disturbances. Nor were the advances in psychic research limited to the treatment of the sick. Research in human development, education, political science, and sociology was also influenced by psychoanalytic techniques, despite the numerous voices raised in fear of a possibly undue emphasis upon psychology.

Social behavior in an age of anxiety

A DECLINE IN morality appeared to accompany and to follow the war and inflation. Some observers wondered whether the appearance might not be due to improved methods of recording crime and communicating scandal as much as to the actuality. The problem attracted the serious attention of churchmen, educators, social workers, and psychologists, who, through the media of the theater, the movies, the press, the radio and television made valiant efforts to counteract the debilitating effect of the broken family, particularly in urban centers; at   971 the same time they attacked those media for spreading immorality. Juvenile delinquency and governmental corruption in Europe and America, if they did not actually increase, at least seemed to claim increased attention; and the statistics available to the American Federal Bureau of Investigation showed an absolute increase of criminal activity. Social taboos rapidly lost their power even in England, and the most brazen Victorian hussy might easily have paled at the conversation that was considered permissible in postwar society, novels, drama and commercial art. Professor Alfred C. Kinsey and his collaborators in *Sexual Behavior in the Human Male* (1948) and *Sexual Behavior in the Human Female* (1953), despite the criticisms of their statistical method, attempted to take discussion of the subject of promiscuity out of the realm of religion or morals, and put it on a factual scientific basis.

Literary developments during the postwar period

THE CLINICAL approach to the problems of human behavior was often adapted to literature, which also frequently reflected the social radicalism of the day. Among the most able or promising writers in the United States (in addition to Mann, O'Neill, Lewis, Hemingway, Steinbeck, Faulkner, and others already mentioned) were Erskine Caldwell, Lillian Hellman, Arthur Miller, and Tennessee Williams. Their plays and novels commonly dealt with social and moral degradation. Faulkner in 1949 was awarded the Nobel prize for literature. In France the novels of Sartre, Camus, Jean Cocteau, and François Mauriac (Nobel laureate, 1952) treated similar problems but with less emphasis upon degeneracy. Circulated widely in cheap editions, this type of reading matter ran second in popular demand only to the detective story and the "comic book." English novelists tended to be less morbid than the French. Aldous Huxley in his later writings moved toward the mystical; Somerset Maugham continued to write charming short stories with a punch, several of which were put into films; James Hilton and Graham Greene, among the younger writers, wrote dramatic stories also suitable for filming. Christopher Fry seemed to have taken Shaw's place as England's leading dramatist. No figures of like stature had yet appeared in Germany out of the literary confusion that prevailed after 1933. Among the English and American poets, Eliot, Frost, Sandburg, Jeffers, and Masefield continued to win laurels, though Eliot turned also to drama and essay, and Sandburg to history and fiction; and W. H. Auden received perhaps the greatest acclaim among the younger poets.

The acceptance of the abstract in art

IN PAINTING and sculpture, the abstract, experimental, and symbolical won widespread interest. Museums of modern art, established before the war in New York, Paris, and elsewhere, won greater popular appreciation. Rouault gained new admiration. Henri Matisse, perhaps the most famous of the surviving prewar painters next

to Picasso, designed a modern chapel at Vence in southern France, and a

retrospective showing of his works was held in various American cities from 1948 to 1952. Picasso, ever experimenting, maintained his leadership in the artistic realm. The Mexicans Rivera and José Orozco continued to excite comment by their frescoes and murals dealing with political subjects in a bold, characteristic style. At the Venice festival of painting in 1950, where four thousand recent works from twenty-five countries were assembled, the pictures of Rivera, the American water-colorist John Marin, and other Western Hemisphere artists elicited favorable comment. And European and oriental art have been exhibited to amazing numbers in American museums, evidencing an increasing art consciousness in a world of lessened distances.

In sculpture, classical concepts of mass continued to be opposed by "modern" concepts of space, achieved frequently by the use of metals and mechanical aids never before employed as media for modeling or chiseling. Mestrovic and the once-controversial American-born English sculptor Jacob Epstein were, without being imitative, among the older sculptors who for the most part put their influence on the side of the classical tradition, against the Rumanian-born French sculptor Constantin Brancusi, who was dean of the abstractionists. The British sculptor, Henry Moore, worked mainly in wood, stone, and cement; his works were characterized by their organic shape and the use of holes to achieve added three-dimensional effects. In the United States the Russian-born Aleksandr Archipenko carved abstractions that were sometimes only smooth, curved forms that suggested their subjects. In France, the home of artistic innovation, the American Alexander Calder became the leader of a school that created "mobiles," designs made of variant, flexible materials that have their full suggestive effect only when put in motion.

Crosscurrents in musical developments
IN MUSIC, a postwar neo-classical revival tended to counteract the trend toward abstract music, on the one hand, and simple popular tunes, on the other. In part the revival came from technological improvements in phonograph records and needles, increasing the demand for good music. As many as 20,000 sets of Wanda Landowska's harpsichord recordings of Bach's Goldberg Variations were sold within three months after they were issued. The bicentennial of Bach's death was the occasion in 1950 for commemorative festivals all over the world. The one at Strassburg also honored Albert Schweitzer, musician, physician, theologian, missionary, Bach scholar, and, subsequently, Nobel peace laureate. Throughout Germany and Italy, music lovers heard compositions previously forbidden, such as the works of Paul Hindemith.

Musical influences were now easily interchangeable in remote parts of the world. In Australia, orchestral development reached maturity in 1947 when Eugene Goossens accepted the directorship of the Sydney Symphony Orchestra. In Japan, the prewar interest in western music, and particularly jazz, was accentuated by the American occupation. In 1950, Gilbert and Sullivan's *Mikado* was for the first time played in Tokyo with Japanese characters. Perhaps still more surprising, in 1952 Gershwin's folk opera *Porgy and Bess,* parts of which were unmistakable jazz, was acclaimed in Berlin, Vienna, and London. In 1954 Japanese *kabuki* dancers were applauded in American cities.

At the same time, experimentalism in musical compositions continued to win adherents. The dissonant twelve-tone technique of Arnold Schönberg stimulated the founding in Europe of an international atonality society. Stravinsky was now dean of the musical composers. Milhaud and Honegger continued to produce compositions in the "modern" style. Milhaud, whose work had usually been *avant-garde,* with considerable influence from South American folk melodies, introduced his new opera, *Bolivar,* in 1950. English and American composers like Williams, Benjamin Britten, and Copland went in less for dissonance than did their continental contemporaries.

Americanization and anti-Americanism

IN SOME REGARDS, what was happening in music was typical of the "Americanization" of the older culture. Many of the best composers, writers, and artists were attracted to the United States by higher compensation and better living standards, while along with other American modes raging in Europe, "le jazz" swept the Continent. Jazz was perhaps the most strident testimony, and Marshall funds the most substantial, of what an indignant French deputy, decrying the importation of another American commodity, called the "coca-colonization" of culture. Anti-Americans looked upon such importations as signs of a new barbarian invasion. Pro-Americans insisted that America had a culture that might match any other in some regards, even though it was too young to compare favorably in some others, and that besides sharing in Europe's culture for the elite, it had a much more widely based, popular, nonintellectual culture of its own represented by American plumbing, household labor-saving devices, automobiles, telephones, movies, jazz, comic books, pulp magazines, and Coca-Cola. This argument usually failed to lull the fears of the anti-Americans; and aggravated by the communist-capitalist ideological controversy, by charges and countercharges of imperialism, by doubts for and against Congressional loyalty investigations, and by official propaganda on both sides, anti-Americanism became a large factor in the "cold war."

FROM "COLD WAR"
TO "HOT TRUCE"

EXCEPT FOR SOME extreme anti-Communists, sometimes deprecated as "redbaiters," the end of the war against the Axis had been welcomed in the West as a chance for peace and world cooperation. To the Communist leaders, however, the "redbaiters" did not seem negligible. Moreover, they looked upon the victory over the Axis as a mere episode in the permanent world revolution, in which a next logical step was encouragement of anticolonialism in Asia and Africa. To offset anti-Communist sentiments in the West and to promote Communist efforts wherever possible, the Russian government tried to provide leadership for the spreading revolutionary movements in the colonial or semidependent areas and stepped up their offensive against the "capitalistic-imperialistic" countries.

*The postwar success
of Communism and Russia*

AMERICANS, IN particular, after V-J Day had been lulled into a false sense of security. Possessing the secret of the atomic bomb, the United States easily assumed that it could protect its interests by push-button techniques. The overwhelming majority of Americans were eager to "bring the boys back home," and American withdrawal from Europe proceeded apace, even while the Russians were strengthening their garrisons in eastern Europe. In China, as noted, American efforts likewise were reduced, and the United States hoped, primarily through economic aid, to reinforce the Chiang government in its effort to win back control from the Communists. Pressures at home for lower taxes, more consumers' goods, and an end to rationing and government spending brought a sharp curtailment in the manufacture of armaments, planes, tanks, and other military equipment (pages 937-938).

In Russia, meanwhile, a new Five-Year Plan (page 941) emphasizing rehabilitation and heavy industries was launched without regard for the needs of the civilian populations. Russia also set to work to crack the secrets of nuclear fission and to manufacture atomic weapons. While the United States continued to send aid and relief to the stricken of Europe, the Communists took from their neighbors many of their raw materials and machines, much of their professional skill and labor, and other assets, often without pretense of compensation. But the Communists made bold promises of food to the starving and property to the dispossessed—and to the insecure, security may easily take precedence over liberty and democracy. Hence for a long time it seemed possible that the Communist program of forcible distribution of land and wealth might win more adherents in Europe and Asia than the democratic program of free and unfettered elections. Except in Iran (page 959) the Communists steadily advanced their cause until 1947.

*The enunciation
of the "Truman Doctrine"*

ALARMED FINALLY by the numerous Communist victories and warned by Winston Churchill and other anti-Communists, the western nations began to take countermeasures. Soviet efforts to lower the Iron Curtain around Greece and Turkey provided the incentive. The return to Greece of King George II after the war had set off civil strife between government and Communist forces. Since George II was suspected of collaboration during the war and was supported by well-known pro-Fascists, the issue was not a clear-cut one of Communists versus patriots, and sympathies even in democratic countries were divided. Receiving aid from neighboring Soviet satellites, Greek rebels carried out devastating guerrilla actions and slowed the badly needed reconstruction program.

Meanwhile Russia also put pressure of a nineteenth-century variety upon Turkey. Not having participated in the war against the Axis until the very last months, Turkey had successfully maintained her neutrality and integrity by balancing the Germans off against the Russians. The defeat of Germany left Turkey clearly at Russia's mercy. The Soviets made demands for territory and joint administration of the Straits, but they were boldly resisted by the Turkish government. As tension mounted, the hard-pressed Labour government of England prepared to withdraw its troops and financial aid from Greece. The American Department of State under General Marshall as secretary of state decided upon a bold move. President Truman, called home by plane from a holiday, in March 1947 announced to Congress and over a national radio hookup a policy that became known as the Truman Doctrine. The new doctrine was a far cry from the Monroe Doctrine: the United States would defend democratic countries wherever they were threatened by Communist aggression.

The program was immediately put into effect. Though Greece had regularly received short-term aid, the Truman program provided long-term economic and political aid. The strengthening of the monarchy internally and in international councils followed, aided perhaps by the death of King George and the accession of Paul in 1947. The threat of Soviet military action against Turkey was likewise checked by the shipment of American military supplies to Turkey. Since 1948, Turkey and Greece have undertaken large public works programs designed to stabilize their economy and to serve their needs in war or peace. Turkey's first free general election was held in 1950, and gave the Democratic Party a sweeping victory; the Democratic leader Jelal Bayar was elected president. Whether or not Greece and Turkey have been made safe for democracy, they have so far been saved from Communism.

*The operation
of the Marshall Plan*

IN WESTERN EUROPE, too, a number of shaky governments needed bolstering. Germany's collapse had had a debilitating effect upon the entire region, and the resulting disintegration, inflation, and consumer shortages contributed greatly to Communism's popularity. In 1947, Secretary Marshall in a speech at Harvard University invited Europe (including the Communist nations) to unite in a plan for recovery and promised American grants-in-aid for such a joint plan. The Communist countries, and Czechoslovakia under Communist pressure, refused to participate in this "Marshall Plan." Nevertheless, the United States in 1948 undertook a comprehensive program of long-term aid to sixteen (later, with the inclusion of West Germany, seventeen) European countries that united in an Organization for European Economic Cooperation (OEEC) in response to the Marshall Plan. By 1951, when it underwent modification, this so-called European Recovery Program had cost the United States over $11,000,000,000, mostly in equipment and materials. Repayments of these grants were placed in the "counterpart funds" of the debtor nation and were spent, with the approval of the American agency called the Economic Cooperation Administration (ECA), to promote European recovery.

When the four-year Marshall Plan ended in 1952, great strides had been made in the western countries. Though full European recovery had not yet been achieved, a less comprehensive program seemed permissible. It took the form of a Mutual Security Agency (MSA), American loans being earmarked more particularly for armament purposes. In 1953 Point Four (page 983) and Mutual Security programs were united under the Foreign Operations Administration. Despite American loans to Spain and growing pressures in Franco's favor, Spain had not yet been invited to become a member of the OEEC by 1954. Meanwhile the eastern European states steadfastly refused to cooperate with a program dominated by "American imperialists," and the absence of these states made it considerably easier to win the support of the American Congress for the program. Particularly large grants have been made to France, Great Britain, Italy, and West Germany. Switzerland was the only participating state prosperous enough to refrain from asking for aid.

The expansion
of European economic cooperation

THE ORGANIZATION for European Economic Cooperation, aside from representing Europe's needs to the American authorities, was charged with presenting a long-term plan for European recovery and cooperation. One of the conspicuous achieve-

Caricatures by Bernard Grambert of three leaders of postwar Europe: Winston Churchill of Britain, left; Robert Schuman of France, and Konrad Adenauer of Germany, page 979.

ments in economic integration of western Europe, planned since 1944, took place on January 1, 1948, with the creation of the customs union (called Benelux) of Belgium, the Netherlands and Luxemburg. Urged on by their neighbors, the three countries agreed to adopt common tariff rates in their trade with outside states and to work toward internal free trade and integration of their currency and economic systems. The Scandinavian states, including Iceland, set up a Committee on Economic Cooperation with a permanent secretariat, to work toward the same objectives. Such projects, still largely on paper only, received help and encouragement from Marshall Plan funds.

Meanwhile the French foreign minister, Robert Schuman, had been pushing a program of economic and political cooperation that might assuage the age-old bitterness between France and Germany. The Schuman Plan proposed a fifty-year treaty calling for a pool of both privately and publicly owned coal and iron industries in France, West Germany, Italy, and the Benelux countries. As eventually elaborated, the plan provided for a merger under the supervision of a supranational High Authority responsible to a Council of Ministers, representing the member governments, and a Common Assembly, representing the parliaments of the member states. In conjunction with the earlier French arrangement (page 922) of the Saar region (which, however, the West German government has consistently refused to regard as permanent), this plan may enable the French to prevent German domination of the economy of western Europe and may make more acceptable to France the inclusion of West Germany within the framework of the North Atlantic Treaty Organization. In 1951 the six countries accepted the plan in principle, and in 1952 they created the proposed Coal and Steel Community and took steps toward creating the supranational parliament that the Schuman Plan envisaged. No matter how far short of an ideal Federation of Europe the Coal and Steel Community might be, even the least sanguine had to admit that it marked greater progress in that direction than had seemed likely before the Truman Doctrine.

THE GROWING FRONT AGAINST COMMUNISM

*The expansion
of European defense cooperation*

AS THE Schuman Plan indicated, economic cooperation was paralleled by political cooperation. The first important step toward postwar unity among the non-Communist countries was taken by the Dunkirk Alliance (1947) of France and Great Britain. A year later, and within a month after a Communist coup in Czechoslovakia (page 983), a regional pact of France, Great Britain, and the Benelux countries created the "Western Union" to consult on common problems and on the establishment of a common defense organization. The Western Union received material and moral support from the United States. American links with Europe were fastened in April 1949 when the United States, Canada, and the Western Union powers announced the North Atlantic Defense Pact and invited the participation of other interested powers. Fourteen nations have signed this pact, which has for its major objective the consolidation and organization of the Atlantic and Mediterranean states against the threat of Communist expansion. Especially important to the European states was the guarantee that an attack upon one participating state would be considered

The growing Russian and Communist strength eventually forced some of the other nations of the world to combine, composing their differences as best they could. These maps show the major economic and military organizations that have been set up as defenses against the advance of the Communist bloc.

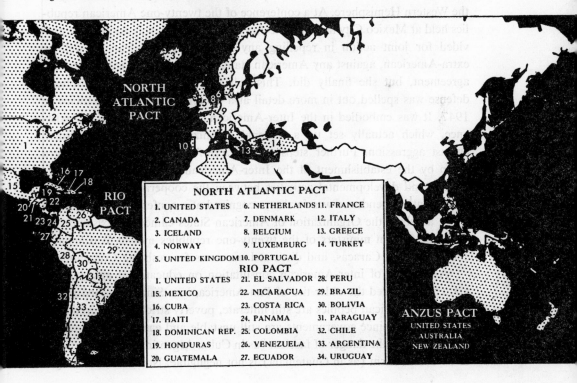

**NORTH
ATLANTIC
PACT**

**RIO
PACT**

NORTH ATLANTIC PACT		
1. UNITED STATES	6. NETHERLANDS	11. FRANCE
2. CANADA	7. DENMARK	12. ITALY
3. ICELAND	8. BELGIUM	13. GREECE
4. NORWAY	9. LUXEMBURG	14. TURKEY
5. UNITED KINGDOM	10. PORTUGAL	

RIO PACT		
1. UNITED STATES	21. EL SALVADOR	28. PERU
15. MEXICO	22. NICARAGUA	29. BRAZIL
16. CUBA	23. COSTA RICA	30. BOLIVIA
17. HAITI	24. PANAMA	31. PARAGUAY
18. DOMINICAN REP.	25. COLOMBIA	32. CHILE
19. HONDURAS	26. VENEZUELA	33. ARGENTINA
20. GUATEMALA	27. ECUADOR	34. URUGUAY

ANZUS PACT
UNITED STATES
AUSTRALIA
NEW ZEALAND

an attack upon all. A joint defense army and navy was created of which General Eisenhower was the organizer and first commander. For the United States, participation in the North Atlantic Treaty Organization (NATO) involved a definite commitment to the security of western Europe—a commitment far different from any undertaken before.

Further consolidation was achieved by the organization of a Council of Europe. A United States of Europe was advocated by such eminent statesmen as Churchill and Édouard Herriot. Some leading personalities formulated a statute for a Council of Europe, which they published in 1949. Ten western European states, including the Western Union powers, Norway, Sweden, Denmark, Ireland, and Italy, at once agreed to cooperate in this effort to achieve a federalized Europe, and five other states, including Greece and Turkey, joined later. The statute provides for a permanent parliamentary organization with headquarters in Strassburg, but the Council has so far been largely a forum of representatives from the legislatures of the separate members. A European Defense Community of the countries that formed the Coal and Steel Community was likewise seriously contemplated after 1952, first proposed and then delayed because of French fear of German recovery.

The Organization
of American States

WHILE BINDING herself closer to western Europe, the United States worked for greater solidarity in the Western Hemisphere. At a conference of the twenty-one American republics held at Mexico City in 1945, the Act of Chapultepec was adopted. It provided for joint action in repelling any aggression, American as well as extra-American, against any American state. Argentina hesitated to sign this agreement, but she finally did. This collective endeavor for hemispheric defense was spelled out in more detail at a conference at Rio de Janeiro in 1947. It was embodied in the Inter-American Treaty of Reciprocal Assistance, which actually set up a regional organization to initiate measures against aggression. Further steps toward Pan-American cooperation were taken by the establishment of the Inter-American Bank to facilitate commercial and developmental activities between the cooperating states. Hemispheric interdependence was further recognized at a conference at Bogotá in 1948, at which the Organization of American States came into existence. In 1951 the foreign ministers of the twenty-one republics met in Washington, and in 1954 at Caracas, and discussed measures for resisting Communism.

A program of inter-American consultation on educational and cultural matters reinforced the older ties of Pan-Americanism. Since large masses of the Latin-American peoples are still illiterate, poverty stricken, diseased, and exploited, and since governments are still unstable and easily overthrown by military coups, the danger of fascism (as in Cuba, Argentina, and Venezuela) or of Communism (as in Guatemala) is not negligible. Neither is the danger

982

of uncompensated nationalization of foreign capital (as in Bolivia). On the other hand, several Latin-American states (Mexico in particular) have developed socially progressive and politically stable regimes. Despite disorders and coups d'état in several countries, a solid base of hemisphere cooperation permits the United States to devote an increasing share of its resources and efforts to the more pressing problems outside of the Americas.

Point Four and the Colombo Program THE TRUMAN program, despite its successes, encountered two serious setbacks. In 1948 the Communist Party of Czechoslovakia seized control of the government by physical force, and in the course of time created a totalitarian regime, while the western nations helplessly fumed and did nothing. In 1949 the shortcomings of American policy in China became undeniable and provoked particularly vehement criticism of the State Department, calling for reconsideration of America's role in Asia. Fearful that Communist success in China would set off other revolutions throughout Asia, the United States prepared an Asiatic counterpart to the Marshall Plan. At his inauguration in January 1949, President Truman outlined as the fourth point of his foreign policy a "bold new program for making the benefits of our scientific advances and industrial progress available for the improvement and growth of underdeveloped areas." This program became popularly known as Point Four. It could not be, as was the recovery program for western Europe, a relatively short spurt of aid toward rehabilitation of normal standards. In "underdeveloped areas"—i.e., in countries where standards of living and production had never been adequate or even comparable to the West—aid had to take the form of building from the bottom. In June 1950 Congress passed an Act for International Development. By 1953 Point Four projects had been in operation in more than thirty countries, directed at improving water, power, and mineral resources, promoting social welfare, housing, and transportation, giving advice on public administration, farming methods, and industrial techniques, or combating famine, sickness, and illiteracy.

The Commonwealth of Nations also developed an assistance program for underdeveloped areas. In January 1950 at Colombo, Ceylon, a Commonwealth Plan was published by the participating countries, Britain, Australia, Canada, Ceylon, India, New Zealand, and Pakistan (but not South Africa, which had recently chosen a government that was committed to an anti-Negro, pro-White policy). The Colombo Plan called for the expenditure of over $5,000,000,000 in a six-year program of aid in the economic development of southern Asia. Unlike the American program, the Colombo Plan has the advantage of having Asiatic states as full-fledged participants. Point Four authorities work with the Colombo authorities, the United Nations, and the Organization of American States.

The first phase
of the "hot war" in Korea

IN JUNE 1950—in the midst of all this planning for Asia—the North Koreans, disregarding the known wishes of the United Nations, began a well-coordinated armed attack south of the 38th parallel, which divided them from South Korea. Within three days they had captured the South Korean capital at Seoul. Immediately, American forces from Japan were dispatched to Korea, and the United States government placed the matter before an emergency meeting of the Security Council of the United Nations. The Russians had been boycotting the Security Council because it would not seat the representative of Communist China, and in the temporary absence of the Russian delegate (who therefore could not exercise his customary veto), the Council held North Korea guilty of aggression and called for an immediate cease-fire. When this order failed to overawe the North Koreans, the Security Council called for more military aid, and appointed General MacArthur supreme commander of its forces in Korea. Seventeen nations shortly placed some contingent or other under the United Nations command in the "police action" in South Korea. Though the overwhelming majority of troops were South Koreans, the greatest number of other combat forces were American, and the burden of expense and equipment fell on the American taxpayer.

The military successes of the North Koreans were at first swift and devastating. Forced to retire to the southern tip of the peninsula, the United Nations fought a defensive action until reinforcements and supplies could be built up. Then came a quick breakout from this defense perimeter, and by the fall of 1950 United Nations forces, not stopping at the 38th parallel, gained control of almost the entire peninsula up to the Chinese border. MacArthur announced that the war would be over by Christmas.

The prolongation
of the Korean "police action"

THREE DAYS later the situation changed entirely. Alarmed by the presence of UN forces at their border, the new Communist regime of China in November 1950 entered the fight. The Chinese participation brought on an "entirely new war," in MacArthur's words. Once again, outnumbered United Nations forces were obliged to retreat. Not until the following March could MacArthur stabilize his lines in the neighborhood of the 38th parallel. Then the war in Korea settled down to a long stalemate.

Communist China sought to use the Korean war as a wedge permitting its entrance into the international councils so far closed to it. It wanted satisfaction on two issues especially, in both of which it was opposed by the United States: (1) the American decision to protect Formosa and to train the remnants of the Chiang army in refuge there, and (2) the refusal of the United Nations to unseat the representatives of Nationalist China and extend

984

recognition and a seat in the Security Council to Mao's government. While the Communists fought to have these questions linked with the war in Korea, the western powers refused to consider them until after the settlement of the Korean hostilities. In April 1951 MacArthur was recalled because the United States government disapproved of his apparent purpose to broaden the Korean war by carrying it to Communist China. The next June, truce talks were undertaken. They dragged on and on. Meanwhile, John Foster Dulles became United States secretary of state, Stalin died (March 1953), and the stalemate became more and more patent despite mounting costs. Finally in July 1953 a truce was signed creating a narrow neutral zone at the neck of the Korean peninsula, placing prisoners who preferred not to return home under the supervision of a neutral commission, and calling for a high-level conference to discuss the whole Korean problem.

Communism in check in Asia and Europe? THE FAILURE of the Communists to snatch a quick victory in Korea, and the promptness of the United States and the United Nations in defending the weak government of South Korea revived the hopes of the non-Communist nations all over the world. Though a number of Far Eastern leaders, like Nehru, had feared that the intervention of the hated "white powers" in Asia might strengthen the Communist cause, for the moment they seemed mistaken. The Japanese peace treaty had helped the western cause in Asia, and in 1954 a mutual defense treaty with the United States tied the new Japan more closely than ever to the western powers. The signing in 1951 of mutual defense pacts with the Philippines, Australia, and New Zealand, and conversations in 1952-1954 on a Pacific community to match NATO, also underlined the determination of the United States to resist Russian and Communist Chinese advance in Asia. Nevertheless, new aggressions, particularly in Indochina, continued. And the question was asked: In such aggressions could the United Nations be any more effective than in Korea? At least, Korea had not been left hopelessly undefended by the United Nations as China and Ethiopia had been by the League of Nations. But the United Nations had acted in Korea largely under the aegis of the United States. Did the future contain the promise only of a Pax Americana or a Pax Russica, or could a more genuine world order be achieved? The death of Stalin brought no immediate answer. Hidden tensions soon became visible inside Russia and the satellite countries as his successors (of whom Georgi M. Malenkov seemed the most dominant) struggled for his place. Yet it was anyone's guess how the outcome would affect international relations. A conference of the foreign ministers of the countries interested in Korea and Indochina took place at Geneva in the spring of 1954, but as this book goes to press it appears doubtful that the conference will take any decisive steps toward a general settlement.

985

BY THE MIDDLE of the twentieth century neither One World nor world destruction had come, and in fact it began to look as if at least three worlds might dominate the future: American, European, and Eurasian. The rivalry between the pro-Russian and anti-Russian worlds had accomplished what might not have been possible otherwise—the cooperation of Europe and America to rebuild Europe after what for a time had seemed to be an irremediable collapse.

Still there was little room for cheerfulness. Communication between the two halves of the world had almost broken down. Although the United Nations continued to represent the aspiration for world unity, the titanic battle between Russia (openly espousing communism) and the United States (openly espousing capitalism) overshadowed all other national, cultural, and economic rivalries or combinations, and endangered all efforts to unite the nations. The failure to agree on international control of atomic energy even for peaceful purposes, the indiscriminate use of the veto in the Security Council, and the deep distrust between the Russian and the American governments had frustrated nearly every important effort to reach a general settlement by peaceful negotiation. The "police action" had ended, but only to permit greater attention to the crisis in Indochina, and the nightmare of a possible total atomic war persisted.

International organization was, however, showing some likelihood of succeeding at the regional level. In the Communist sphere the Cominform had consolidated a large part of the Eurasiatic continent through a common ideology and discipline. Fear of Russia, foremost among many factors, had brought about the European Coal and Steel Community and the Council of Europe, and, if given enough time, might yet bring about a united western Europe. The North Atlantic Treaty Organization, though only slowly materializing, gave substance to the concept of the Atlantic Community, which had played a leading role in political and economic life since the seventeenth and eighteenth centuries. Regional pacts in America and in Asia (a fourth world?) consolidated other important economic and geographical groups. The Commonwealth of Nations (a fifth world?) was unique in that it stretched beyond regional boundaries to cement nations by sentiment. Dreams of an effective world government had not vanished by mid-century; and simultaneously the possibility of a world safely divided into three, four, five, or more regions peaceably balancing each other had perforce suggested itself. Yet the prevailing mood was one of anxiety.

1942	Viet Nam Republic proclaimed
1945-1953	Trygve Lie serves as the UN's first secretary-general
1945-1951	Labour Party in power in Britain
1945-1951	SCAP rule in Japan
March 22, 1945	Arab League stimulates cooperation among seven Arab states
August 14, 1945	Temporary Russo-Chinese agreements
August 17, 1945	Republic of Indonesia proclaimed
August 19, 1945	Russia's Fourth Five-Year Plan
January 1946	Austrian state recognized by occupation officials
June 1946	Italy proclaimed a republic
July 4, 1946	Independent Philippine Republic created
December 1946	Fourth French Republic adopts constitution
1947-1952	The Truman and Marshall Plans in operation
1947-1948	Communist regimes established in Albania, Bulgaria, Rumania, Yugoslavia, Poland, Czechoslovakia, and Hungary
June 1947	Allied Military Government rule ends in Italy
August 1947	British withdraw from India and Pakistan
October 5, 1947	Cominform established
January 1, 1948	Inauguration of Benelux customs union
February 1948	Federation of Malaya created
May 1948	Republic of Israel proclaimed
June 1948	Tito breaks with Soviet Russia
April 1949	North Atlantic Treaty Organization begins
April 1949	Republic of Ireland withdraws from Commonwealth
August 1949	Establishment of Bonn regime in West Germany
October 1, 1949	Chinese People's Republic (Communist) proclaimed
October 1949	German Democratic Republic created in east zone
November 1949	Indonesian independence agreement concluded
1950-1953	United Nations defend South Korea against aggression
March 1951	Iranian parliament nationalizes oil industry
September 1951	Japanese peace treaty
October 25, 1951	Conservative Party returned to power in Britain
February 1952	Elizabeth II ascends British throne
July 1952	King Farouk driven from Egypt
August 1952	The Schuman Plan inaugurated
1953	Eisenhower inaugurated president
1953	Death of Stalin; Malenkov apparent successor
1953	French offer independence to Indochina within French Union
1953	Publication of Einstein's "unified field theory"
1954	Conference at Geneva on Korea and Indochina

Chapter sixteen

EPILOGUE: SOME PERSISTENT PROBLEMS OF THE MODERN WORLD

IF WE COULD cut back to the Europe of the early nineteenth century, we would probably be astonished by a number of things that we would note or fail to note. Perhaps first of all we would be struck by the absence of numerous mechanical devices which now we take for granted. We might be relieved or distressed (depending on the nature of our problems and predilections) to find no television and radio programs, no phonographs, no telephones, no movies, no trains, automobiles, and airplanes, no asphalt pavements, no elevator buildings, no telegraph poles, no combines and tractors, no electric refrigerators and heaters, little sanitary plumbing and running hot water, no electric lights, no plastics, only experimental steamboats, almost no knowledge of germs, no antibiotics, no comptometers, no functional architecture, no abstract art, no photography, no ready-made clothing, no repeating pistols or guns, no atomic and hydrogen bombs—and (this would certainly be distressing) almost no knowledge of anesthetics. It might take us a while to realize that London was in many ways farther away from Paris than air lanes, cables, and radio had made Hong Kong from London by the middle of the twentieth century. Although the different parts of the world of the early 1800's had already developed close mutual ties, we would probably find in all of them appalling ignorance of many remote corners that are now within speedy and regular reach of one another, and we might miss a number of institutions and customs that were to develop from the increasing interaction between Europe and the rest of the world.

After a while we would probably be equally astonished by the relatively slight urbanization of the 1800's. In Europe and America, none of the cities would have approached their present mammoth size. New York, a city of around 8,000,000 in 1950, had only 60,000 inhabitants in 1800. Tokyo was

989

hardly known to the western world at the beginning of the nineteenth century. In western Europe, London, Paris, and Rome were, as they are now, densely populated commercial or industrial centers, and were (as now) challenged by the eastern cities of Berlin, Vienna, and Moscow; but Europe was essentially rural. A little reflection would enable us to recognize what the "Industrial Revolution" had meant to twentieth-century cities as centers of industry, art, education, and trade, and likewise what it had meant to the rural areas of the more advanced countries in bringing to them wider markets, improved transportation facilities, farm machinery, electricity, telephone, and radio.

In the midst of these palpable contrasts, a flashback to 1800 would perhaps astonish us by the similarities that we might discover in spiritual matters. We might observe that mankind, though today physically, economically, and intellectually interdependent as never before, is no less divided into national groups and hostile alliance systems than it was in 1800 and continues to think and operate on almost as varied national, economic, religious, and racial lines as in 1800. Moreover, we might find that the social structure within the separate nations of the two eras was similarly splintered into ideological camps; but whether it was over different ideologies, or over the same ones with different emphasis, would be hard to say. Solidarity within the several camps was constantly being in much the same way threatened from within as well as from without.

Machines, we might reflect, had obviously made simpler the labors of mankind, but had they made work more interesting or men freer and happier? At the middle of the twentieth century are anxiety, fear, frustration, and pessimism about the future more pronounced, or less, than they were at the end of the eighteenth century?

We do not propose to answer these questions in the remarks that follow. In fact, since we have no satisfactory method of weighing happiness, fear, and frustration (particularly of an age long departed), correct answers may be impossible. But a presentation of some of the data relevant to an answer might have some interest. Since we have tried in the above pages to look both forward and backward, some of the problems of which we shall speak have already been raised, and some repetition (for which we apologize) may occur.

NATIONALISM

AND IMPERIALISM

THE CENTURY and a half since the French Revolution has been constantly beset by the problem of nationalism. Though the old ghost of national sentiment has frequently been laid by international planners and theorists, it has continued to haunt those who seek for international peace through a supra-national order. International movements, tribunals, and organizations have appeared at various points throughout the interim, but the principle of national sovereignty has at no time been sacrificed completely to the interests of international order. Jealous of their national traditions, rights, and cultures, the peoples of the world, large and small, white and colored, have clung tenaciously to their political and cultural aspirations as nations. Indeed, loyalty to the national group has often transcended loyalty to race, faith, class, party, family, and self.

*The spread
of cultural nationalism in Europe*

ONE OF THE most lasting bequests of the French Revolution was its rallying of the French nation behind a set of attractive liberal principles. When Napoleon, emperor of the French, sought to enhance the glory of France by trampling roughshod upon his country's neighbors, revolutionary ideas spread as a by-product of his aggressions; the principles of liberalism and nationality found a hold throughout continental Europe. Upon his overthrow the conservative planners at the Congress of Vienna sought through a system of international agreements to create a system of international cooperation in the common fight against liberal revolt, but no statesman was ready to sacrifice his nation's interests in the common cause. Indeed, after the Congress of Vienna romanticist poets and scholars waxed lyrical over the sacred bonds uniting the nation, over the national language and culture, and over the glories of the nation's conquests, whether military or spiritual. The nation-state was for them the actual or potential embodiment of the national spirit, which was itself the sum total of the popular experience and the popular will.

*National destiny
and overseas exploitation*

AS NATIONAL sentiment won new converts in Europe, the doctrine of the nation as a mystical unit possessing a soul and a peculiar character also gained widespread acceptance. While the nation was usually considered to be first and foremost a geographical grouping, a unit made up of those who had been born or naturalized within a given area, the fashion of thinking about nationality as a subjective spiritual quality soon spread to those having little in common except their faith and their sentiment of solidarity, such as the Jews and various Moslem groups.

In Hegel's and Ranke's thought, the state, governed by a personal ruler and shaped by its own peculiar history, was conceived of as a transcendental entity. It was supreme even over every social structure; it was above any possible world state or confederation of nations; and the freedom of the individual was identical with voluntary submission to its will. In the view of Mazzini, liberalism and nationalism were twins; the freedom of a people and its national independence were identical, and each people had "a special mission to fulfill, a special work to be done in the cause of the advancement of humanity." But the Mazzinian concept of liberal, popular, humanitarian nationalism was one of the casualties of the abortive Revolution of 1848; the concept of the state as the creation of an upper-class government triumphed. Among the German historians, and particularly in the works of Treitschke, Mazzini's idea of the popular nation was modified into the idea of the disciplined nation, which was raised to the level of a creed; and the German Reich was looked upon as the nation with the supreme mission.

Contemporaneous intellectual developments were reflected in nationalist thought. To pseudo-Nietzscheans, nationalism became a belief in the moral obligation of the elite nation. For exponents of *Realpolitik,* morality, property, and life were mere tools in the achievement of the nation's destiny. The social Darwinists contributed to the spread of nationalist concepts by applying a biological concept, the survival of the fittest, to social and political phenomena to which it had dubious relevance.

Nationalistic pride helped to provide a rationale for imperialistic adventuring in the overseas world and for the complacent acceptance by the white man of the inferiority of Asiatic, African, and primitive peoples. In the very years when Englishmen and Frenchmen were painfully acquiring new political freedom at home, their fellow countrymen were systematically proselytizing or conquering, organizing or dominating, educating or exploiting the non-European peoples of the world. Houston Stewart Chamberlain voiced the creed of the extreme nationalists:

> Race lifts a man above himself: it endows him with extraordinary—I might almost say supernatural—powers....
> It is almost always the nation, as a political structure, that creates the conditions for the formation of a race or at least leads to the highest and most individual activities of race.

This racial nationalism found expression not only in overseas imperialism but also in various kinds of domestic xenophobias at the end of the nineteenth century: nativism in the United States, the Action Française, and anti-Semitism in central Europe.

Total nationalism in the twentieth century

IN THE TWENTIETH century nationalism in various seductive guises kept on beguiling Europeans and Americans, and rapidly began to make new converts in the colonial world. The race for national self-sufficiency led to accelerated programs of domestic development and to international protective measures like tariffs, preferential exchange relations, and barter agreements. International religious movements made little headway against the nationalistic currents, and international socialism barely survived the impact of the First World War. The advent of international communism in Russia seemed for a moment to threaten the uninterrupted progress of national sentiment, but the noncommunist nations, anticipating a threat to their traditional ways, boycotted the Soviet Union economically and politically until boycott became manifestly unprofitable; and in the meantime international communism had given way largely to Russian Communism, essentially a brand of Russian nationalism. Although a League of Nations arose out of the horror of the First World War to bring the nations together for peaceful settlement of their disputes, the national states, and the United States in particular, refused to surrender any appreciable degree of sovereignty to such an international organization. The international League proved helpless, or nearly so, to overcome the recalcitrance of the nations, and it collapsed. The colonial nationalities, having looked to the League to promote their hope for self-determination, realized (even before the League's demise) that freedom and independence would not always be forthcoming without a fight. Inspired by the prestige of a united Japan, the peoples of Asia swiftly became converted to a militant nationalism in their desire to overthrow colonial rule.

The Second World War presented the nations with another chance to bring a world order out of the anarchy that made world wars possible. The events leading to the war itself, however, attested to the strength and sometimes the irrational nature of national loyalties in all parts of the world. Italian Fascism was based on the premise of total devotion to the national glory. Whipped into a frenzy by Hitler's cries for German Lebensraum and for the unity of all Germanic peoples, the Nazis committed themselves to the achievement of a nation-race. They took up the sword against the Jews and other minorities accused of undermining the strength of the "Aryan race" and of conspiring against its historical destiny to lead the world. In Japan, nationalism took the form of aversion to the West and of glorification of Nippon's unique heritage. A hitherto relatively domesticated jingoism became a ferocious international imperialism as both Germany and Japan sought to realize their destinies and establish their superiority at the expense of their neighbors. Russian Communism, which had originated partly in protest against "capitalistic" nationalism and imperialism, became under Stalin an ideology directed toward mechanizing the Soviet state, inculcating the myth of the world leader, and compounding the traditional objectives of Russian foreign policy with the idealistic objectives of the Russian Revolution. And since the end of the Second World War, new nations, Communist and non-Communist alike, have declared their determination to weld themselves into national unities and to fight off zealously all forms of external control. Even as the United Nations was struggling to be born, new nations were issuing declarations of independence and vigorous pronouncements about their determination to stand free from their old ties, to unite against all aliens, and perhaps even to engage in imperialistic ventures of their own. Who could say that nationalism and imperialism were any less strong in the 1950's than in the

1800's? One thing seemed certain, however: Nationalism was less likely to be inevitably linked in men's minds as a twin with liberalism than once it had been.

FREEDOM,

ORDER, AND SECURITY

THE ASPIRATION to have order in freedom and freedom in order continues, in our day as it did at the beginning of the nineteenth century, to engage practical politicians and political theorists alike. The American and the French Revolutions, borrowing from many religious, philosophical, and historical sources, formulated and unleashed the doctrines of individual liberty and political equality that were to be among the most controversial issues of the succeeding 150 years. These doctrines had been set forth in a set of ringing declarations of independence and of rights, which, though they did not agree and though many people did not accept all of them, provided the philosophical and emotional basis for the liberal tradition of the generations that followed.

*Liberalism,
nationalism, and socialism*

THE LIBERAL tradition has conflicted, however, with other traditions. Liberalism, briefly defined, is the belief that the individual is entitled to certain liberties, even against the will of the government, even against the will of the majority. Whenever the people and the nation are regarded as one and indivisible, with a government that serves the people's will and does not dominate them, liberalism and nationalism appear to be twin forces. Challenged in the name of national order and tradition at the beginning of the nineteenth century by autocracy, aristocracy, and clergy, the liberals withstood these traditionalists with varying success, only to be confronted after the middle of the nineteenth century by an old but newly reformulated social doctrine, socialism, which placed economic guarantees both above national order and tradition and above individual rights.

The three-cornered struggle of our own day between national socialists, international communists, and old-fashioned liberals is partly a continuation of the ancient, though not irreconcilable, antagonism between the advocates of liberty and the advocates of order and security. The critics of the liberal creed see or pretend to see in democracy freedom for only the few at the expense of the security of the many, and liberty of action for only the few at the expense of a planned order and efficiency that would benefit the many. On the other hand, the critics of totalitarian doctrines like fascism and communism see in them political and economic preconceptions that call for the sacrifice of the individual and his liberties to the crushing needs of society

994

as determined by an elite party. Totalitarian states emphasize government *for* the people (at least in theory) and tend to identify the people with the state; the democracies emphasize government *by* the people and tend to identify the people with the majority party or bloc. Actual experience seems to indicate that the totalitarian planned society breaks down in certain regards and that the democratic free society can function only if certain restrictions are imposed. Actual experience seems also to indicate therefore that neither the totally planned nor the totally free society can provide an enduring solution of the socioeconomic problem. But the issue is one that may not be decided by the lessons drawn from experience alone, since the divorce of freedom from order (which are not necessarily incompatible) is rarely sought on economic or rational grounds alone but on grounds that are mixed up with national and power politics and so convey intense emotional overtones.

*The experience
of France with liberty*

A REVIEW of some highlights in the history of the struggle for liberty will underline this point. Tired of the disorders brought on by the quest for liberty and equality in the French Revolution, the solid citizens of France turned in 1799 to Bonaparte in the hope of achieving an orderly liberty. Bonaparte, while preserving the name of liberty, violated many of liberalism's fundamental tenets in his pursuit of personal glory and dynastic stability. The short-lived Napoleonic dream of wedding liberty with order was replaced by a constitutional Bourbon monarchy in which the old philosophy of "mixed government" was retouched. A shaky system of authority for a few (the court) and freedom for the many (the propertied) was attempted to the neglect of the authority and freedom of the people as a whole. When the balance swung too far in favor of royal authority, revolt followed in an effort to achieve once more the popular sovereignty and the individual rights of the revolutionary tradition. The balance between the tradition of order and the tradition of liberty has since been upset in France on a number of occasions, but France has preserved a high degree of individual freedom, sometimes at a very high price in destruction, blood, and treasure. In the process French business has developed a wider gap between workers and employers than is common in the West, and French government has had to forego whatever advantages are to be found in efficient, long-term ministries and has had to be administered by a bureaucracy whose roots go back to the Valois and Bourbon monarchs.

*National self-determination
as a force countering liberalism*

THE LIBERAL attack upon autocracy that had been sparked by the American and the French Revolution spread to other parts of Europe and America, and in more recent times to Asia. It frequently won tangible victories in the form of written constitutions that explicitly or implicitly recognized some of the "rights of man." In the nineteenth century, as the liberal doctrines spread into central and eastern

Europe, they collided with entrenched autocracies that at first refused to yield. By the middle of the nineteenth century, however, autocracy had permitted, or had been unable to forbid, a carefully guarded and limited liberalism to develop. In these areas, the liberals had themselves generally become ready to compromise the principle of national self-determination, particularly in countries where minority problems also existed. Whereas liberalism in western Europe had usually operated in alliance with nationalism, the events of the later nineteenth and of the twentieth century demonstrated that liberty and equality made their greatest gains in states, like England, France, and the United States, in which self-determination was not a major objective of minority groups. Where national unification of centrifugal ethnic or political groups was the immediate objective—as in Germany, Austria-Hungary, the Russian Empire, and Japan—the constitutional regimes were likely to center supreme power in a strong executive rather than in a representative legislature, to allot special privileges to the conservative upper classes and the military, and to emphasize centralization of government more than the consent of the governed. And where nations emerged or reëmerged by means of minority secession, as in Rumania and Poland, they sometimes were prepared to sacrifice the rights of the individual to the quest for national independence, power, and glory.

Economic security or political and social freedom? THE FRENCH Revolution came at a time when Europe was not conspicuously industrialized and when the major politico-economic questions were those of an agrarian society. Hardly had the political revolutions of the eighteenth century placed the middle class in a position to share political power with the landed aristocracy when Europe's major politico-economic questions began to be derived from the "Industrial Revolution." To the leaders of the French Revolution the effort to achieve greater economic security for the masses had been secondary and corollary to the effort to abolish absolutism and aristocratic privilege. After the middle of the nineteenth century the "economic rights of man"—the right to a living wage or its equivalent in social welfare programs—became of major concern as industry flourished and the working classes expanded. Although some historians now doubt that the lot of the city laborer was worsening, social and political theorists and humanitarian writers turned ever keener attention to the complaints of economic insecurity that grew ever louder as cities and factories mushroomed. Utopian and eventually Marxian socialists called for political and economic adjustments that would give the working classes a greater share of the national wealth and a greater voice in deliberations upon which their destinies depended. Individual profit, they asserted, could and ought to be limited in the interest of the common welfare, and individual initiative and enterprise restricted sufficiently to assure social justice.

*The development
of socialist and communist plans*
ALTHOUGH AT first only negligible minority groupings, the Socialist parties gained enough economic and political strength to become at the beginning of the twentieth century a force to be reckoned with in several western countries. To weaken their appeal to the working classes some governments began to adopt some of their program, giving the workers of the world something to lose other than their chains. In England, Germany, and France, the Socialists, while increasing their demands for security through government regulation of private enterprise and through government support of social services for the workingman, proved willing to achieve their ends through parliamentary action. In Russia, no such compromise emerged. The Bolsheviks simply overturned the moderate revolutionary regime established upon the overthrow of the czars in 1917 and put in its place another that became steadily more totalitarian, sacrificing freedom to the announced goals of common economic and military security.

The example of a Communist state in Russia was a source of fear to some and of inspiration to others no less concrete than had been the example of the United States as a democratic state since the eighteenth century. In Germany, Italy, and Japan, those who feared both democracy and Communism triumphed over those who admired either of them, and freedom declined in those countries. Their rulers formed the Axis—on the grounds, pretended as well as real, that they needed, on the one hand, to counter the Russian menace and, on the other, to obviate parliamentary inefficiencies; and they sought by programs of "National Socialism," internal repression, and external expansion to provide economic security at home and national prestige abroad. Meanwhile, in the United States, England, France, and other western areas, freedom survived the fears of both Communism and National Socialism. This outcome was achieved in part by means of government programs designed to provide at least a minimum security for all economic and social levels by supervision and regulation of private enterprise rather than by wholesale nationalization.

*"People's democracy"
versus "bourgeois democracy"*
AT THE END of the Second World War, statesmen throughout the non-Communist world had to address themselves even more earnestly to the question of reconciling freedom and order, and of providing enough economic security to prevent unrest and revolution; for the Russians claimed that a true "people's democracy" (as opposed to "bourgeois democracy") was possible only in alliance with the "Fatherland of Communism." One of the major issues of today is whether freedom of the individual can survive. Will it ultimately be sacrificed to social security and national planning or will some compromise be found compatible with both individual freedom and the ordered state? Meanwhile Communist

997

courts punish with execution some who are "guilty by association" in one form or another with advocates of western ideas, and in the United States lesser punishments such as dismissal are meted out by public and private employers to some who are "guilty by association" with Communists and other "subversive groups." In a conflict at least partly ideological, public tolerance of views considered dangerous was an early casualty. On neither side, however, is "association" alone—without treason, espionage, conspiracy, or perjury—yet deemed sufficient for punishment by due court process.

STANDARDIZATION
UNIFORMITY, AND ORGANIZATION

THE "INDUSTRIAL REVOLUTION" brought in a steadily intensified specialization of labor. The development of the factory system, the use of interchangeable parts, and the invention of the assembly-line technique placed a high premium upon standardized products. The individual artisan rapidly tended to disappear in the nineteenth century, and the commodities of everyday life, whether household wares, tools, ornaments, foods, or clothing, lost their individuality and were manufactured or processed by machines for mass consumption. Business firms were owned by numerous stockholders and managed by highly paid administrators under the supervision of often interlocking and more or less self-perpetuating directorates. Individual creativeness in industry rapidly became the prerogative of trained engineers, skilled mechanics, or research staffs. Ordinary industrial and farm laborers were not required or expected to experiment on their own. As a result, the world has been flooded with highly advertised and standardized products that the producers themselves may well hesitate to alter in blueprint design or ultimate packaging.

The rewards and penalties
of technical standardization

A CERTAIN amount of standardization was hardly avoidable in industry, agriculture, and communication. In the age of railway development it soon became obvious that tracks and rolling stock should be standard within nations, and also between nations if an international network of rails were to materialize conveniently. Telegraph and radio signals and equipment were also required to follow identical standards if the nations of the world could reasonably expect to be linked together in a comprehensive communications chain. The interests of the states and the monopolistic nature of such enterprises worked in the same direction. But more competitive enterprises followed the same pattern. Ready-made shoes and clothing, costume jewelry and cutlery, canned goods and packaged articles, prefabricated furniture and parts of houses led to a high degree of uniformity. Farm machines helped to systematize farming practices and to remove uncertainties from the farm. Even chickens were obliged to adopt standardized schedules for sleeping, molting, and laying.

Standardization has brought some rich rewards to the world. It has resulted in a high degree of specialization of industry, and specialization has helped to increase the volume of production many times, has made many easily learned jobs available, has brought down the price of most everyday commodities, and thereby has put more of them within the reach of more people. But it has also put men to work repeating the same simple and monotonous operation a stated number of times per minute for several hours a day and has taken from them interest in their work and pride in their workmanship. If it thereby has also tended to eliminate individual eccentricity from industrial design, it must also at times have discouraged inspiration.

"Rationalization"
of business and industry

INDUSTRIAL organization sometimes took the form of what some economists (usually German) have called "rationalization." Concerned about the defects, inefficiencies, overlappings, and duplications inherent in free, individualistic, and competitive enterprise, industrial engineers, economic planners, and efficiency experts advocated the adoption of overall programs (from raw materials to finished commodity) for particular fields such as the chemical or the optical industries, in the interest of standardizing their products, eliminating waste, minimizing effort, and reducing competition. At times, industries have been organized on such a "rational" basis without regard to national boundaries or national interests. The organization of pools, combines, trusts, and cartels enabled the organized firms to eliminate their small, unorganized competitors. Moreover, the rationalized enterprise could, through its greater financial power, exercise an increasing influence upon governmental policies.

Whether rational or not, the tendency of big business to acquire greater economic and political power is patent. Even laissez-faire economists sometimes look to governments to defend free enterprise from big business and monopolies. Others count upon new processes, inventions, and innovations to give advantages to some industries over others and thus keep real competition alive. Still others contend that the general urge toward bigness is not lamentable since the power of big industry can be counterbalanced by the power of big retailing establishments and each finds a "countervailing force" in the power of big labor unions. Meanwhile small business has shown a tenacious capacity for survival.

Labor
as an organized force

IN THE LABOR movement, widescale organization has been increasingly recognized as a means toward the economic welfare and political influence of the working classes. Though often illegal and generally weak and poorly organized in the nineteenth century, workers' unions have become huge labor cartels. They are sometimes confined to single industries or occupations but often cut across industrial and occupational lines to bring the full power of organized labor to bear upon a critical dispute. The great labor groups of the industrialized West have been no more hesitant than the industrial cartels to act in a politically conscious role; and in the western democracies, like France and England, they have brought tremendous political strength to the struggle for what they consider to be the interests of organized labor. So far they have had remarkable success on the whole, and not only in disputes with employers but also in competition with the unorganized elements of society, whether these are other workers or consumers and taxpayers.

The economic plight of the unorganized white-collar, professional, and artisan groups has deteriorated correspondingly in the twentieth century. The decline of their economic status has been abetted by a period of persistent inflation in which the rise of prices has often preceded that of wages, and in which the organized labor groups have usually managed to provide at least a short-term protection for themselves through direct or indirect action. Where unorganized workers are also unorganized voters, they have declined also in political influence, since organized political machines normally are inclined to pay little heed to the independent voter and generally rely upon organized pressure groups to provide election funds, to bring out the voters, and to deliver votes for a designated party or candidate.

Uniformity in the corporate state

THE INTEGRATION of political parties with labor unions and industrial cartels was but a step to organizers like Mussolini, who hoped through the "corporate state" to eliminate the weaknesses and inefficiencies of political democracy and free enterprise. Translated into political terms, standardization became political uniformity in countries like Italy, Germany, Japan, and Russia. Competitive political parties, like industrial competitors, were ruthlessly eliminated by the dominant political monopoly in the name of greater domestic order, economic efficiency, and national security. Elections were transformed from contests between opposing candidates and parties into national holidays for celebrating the achievements of the unitary party and for reaffirming the public's confidence in the national leadership. In these rationalized and standardized societies, individual differences were looked upon as potential threats to the integrated order and seemed to warrant drastic handling by the state.

The dangers of conformity for liberalism

EVEN IN nations where political uniformity had not triumphed, a premium was placed upon conformity of the individual to group and national preferences. The "rugged individualist" or old-fashioned liberal ran the danger of being looked upon as an eccentric or possibly as an obstructionist if he openly viewed with 1000 hostility, suspicion, doubt, or alarm the major aims and objectives of dominant industrial, labor, religious, racial, or national groups. The tendency to look askance upon nonconformist judgments helped to transfer ethics and esthetics from individual to group decisions, to make them subject to fashion rather than to conscience. Individual moral convictions were expected to give way before popular concepts or dictatorial precepts of the good of party or country even when these concepts or precepts were contrary to religious or ethical standards that the individual might hold as sacred or self-evident. Those liberals who retained confidence in eighteenth-century notions of rights and freedom were attacked as "bourgeois" and "capitalist" by both extreme Right and extreme Left in the democracies and fared badly indeed in one-party states.

The dictatorship of the majority was fraught with dangers to the individual personality perhaps no less than the dictatorship of a Führer or general-issimo. In the United States, where a Supreme Court had the right and obligation to declare even the wishes of the majority unconstitutional because they violated the fundamental rights guaranteed by the Constitution, the individual had an additional guarantee against the tyranny of the majority, but it was no stronger than the judges' readiness to live up to their obligations in doubtful cases. In countries whose institutions were not so deliberately based upon the principle of separation of powers and where, therefore, power rested largely with the legislative majority, the chief defense of the minority's or the individual's rights lay in what, as indicated above, came to be called in economic thought a system of "countervailing forces"—the possibility that strong competitive organizations would neutralize each other, leaving a safe margin for freedom. Historians have long been aware, for example, that the individual was more likely to find room for freedom where church and state were at odds than where they stood united. Political scientists assign to the concept of countervailing political forces the name "pluralism."

The diminution of regional differences

ONE NOTICEABLE result of the standardization of thought, commodities, and services in modern life is that differences between regions are less marked than they used to be. The small town has the same movies, radio and television programs, political organizations, fraternal lodges, school systems, syndicated newspaper features, patent medicines, canned goods, packaged foods, bottled beverages, and advertised brands as the big town, particularly in the United States, and even differences between nations in these regards are not so marked as they once were. The ready accessibility in the small towns and suburbs to labor supply, easy transportation, entertainment, good shops, superior schools, up-to-date housing, and other advantages once considered metropolitan have led to a tendency for city dwellers and factories to escape from crowded cities to the suburbs and rural areas. Backed by the desirability of decentralization of administration and industry in a time of potential atomic war, this tendency might conceivably reverse the prevailing trend toward urbanization.

If the diminution of regional differences has certain advantages, it is nevertheless no unmixed blessing; for a uniform set of cultural and economic values could conceivably deaden the urge for innovation and incapacitate individual creativity and initiative. What would happen in a free society growing accustomed to uniformity if its economic, social, and political life should fall under the control of ambitious and unscrupulous leaders? Have not the media of mass communication made the danger from such leaders greater than it once was? Even in societies where free majorities still rule, freedom may have to struggle hard to remain alive if diversity is to be regarded as disunity, if a new idea is too easily to be labeled subversive, and if the correctness of judgments is to be determined by majority vote. One of the hardest questions a monotone democracy may have to answer is: How is creative imagination to prosper if its criterion of success is to be the approval of the millions? Fortunately, creative and competitive spirits can thrive in many instances without wholesale approval, and majorities often respect individual genius and talent.

CREED AND COLOR

THE LINKING of the continents that began to take place in the fifteenth century (and even earlier) and was carried forward at a particularly amazing rate in the nineteenth and twentieth centuries brought pressing racial and religious problems. Peoples of still more varied beliefs and diverse ethnic backgrounds came into closer touch with each other, and their contact raised new issues. The colored peoples of the world, whether in Asia or Africa, were forced to open their gates to the dynamic white peoples of Europe and America, who brought with them their Christian faiths. As became clear by the middle of the twentieth century, the nonwhite and non-Christian peoples of the world were not going to accept passively the preferred position of European civilization and the Christian faith.

Continuing disunity among religions and sects

EVER SINCE its triumph in Europe, Christendom itself has been divided by heresies and schisms. The Reformation split western Christianity by internecine strife. The subsequent scientific and liberal revolutions increased both tolerance and indifference. The decline of religious fervor and the lack of interest in theological issues brought a reaction after 1800 from clerical and lay proponents of formal religion. It took the guise of hope for church reunion among the Christian peoples. The tendency of Protestant churches to divide into new denominations was matched by a decided effort to reunite groups of similar persuasion and to lay the groundwork for a possible reunion of all Christendom. The papacy meanwhile maintained its position of infallibility on questions of faith and morals, sought to clarify the Catholic Church's teachings in the light of the findings of modern science, politics, and economics without compromising the ancient faith, and worked for Christian unity by encouraging the return of Protestants and others to the jurisdiction of the bishop of Rome. Despite these efforts, Christendom remained divided in the 1950's and was increasingly plagued by the dangers of materialism, indifference, and atheism. The Greek Orthodox Church, in particular, faced the possibility of extinction after atheistic Communism took over in Russia. In the Balkans, Roman Catholicism also has been threatened with extinction since 1945.

The Jews
as an articulate minority

THE HISTORY of the Jews in the last century and a half has been filled with many troubles and not a few triumphs. In Russia, France, and Germany, discrimination against the Jews in the army and in public office was common. Led by articulate, educated, prominent, and wealthy spokesmen in western Europe, they fought arduously against prejudice and discrimination. Anti-Semitism, particularly as exhibited in the Dreyfus case in France, stimulated the growth of Jewish nationalism, or Zionism. After the First World War, anti-Semitism in central and eastern Europe raged with an astonishing fury. Within Judaism, meanwhile, splits continued to occur among the orthodox, the reformed, and the conservative branches of the ancient Hebrew faith. These religious splits were accompanied by splits along national lines, since Jews more frequently placed their current national affiliations above their allegiance to ancient Zion. Nevertheless, the Zionist movement grew as Jews sought relief from persecution by the reëstablishment of the dispersed nation in its original Palestine homeland. The new Israel became a political reality in 1947 and it has provided a refuge for many thousands of displaced Jews of Europe, Africa, and Asia. In some countries anti-Semitism never was a major issue, and in others, despite recent bursts of anti-Semitism in Communist countries, considerable progress has been made in the last decade in at least formally outlawing discrimination. Prejudice, however, is a social and psychological phenomenon not eradicated solely by fiat, and further solution of the problems must await the slower process of education, unless, as seems unlikely, the Jews should become unidentifiable as such outside of Israel.

The plight
of the Negroes in white countries

OF THE white-controlled nations of the world a few have had a genuine racial problem. The Negro minority in the United States, having been emancipated from slavery in 1865, constituted a trying social and political problem. In the South, where the majority of Negroes lived until very recent decades, discrimination along social, educational, and political lines has been a part of general practice and has been connived at and even sanctioned by the law. In northern urban areas, 1003 discrimination against Negroes, though less frequently practiced openly, has been aggravated in recent years with the immigration of large numbers of Negroes. Race riots in several urban centers and outraged public opinion stimulated the government to eliminate segregation in the army and to discourage government contractors from carrying "Jim-Crowism" into their hiring practices. Decisions of the Supreme Court discountenanced discrimination in the purchase of real estate and segregation in the schools. In South Africa, meanwhile, the white minority proceeded systematically to keep the overwhelming native Negro majority from enjoying equal rights with the white population. In Kenya a native secret society known as the Mau Mau obscured the issue by resorting to violence and primitive blood rites.

The Communists have played up racial inequities, especially in the United States, as typical of capitalism and imperialism, particularly stressing this point in their propaganda in Asiatic and African countries. They give little recognition to the facts that dark-skinned persons are by and large treated on a basis of equality in the capitalist countries of continental Europe and that Ethiopia, Liberia, the Gold Coast, French Equatorial Africa, and other African areas either retain sovereign independence or have made some progress toward autonomous administration and representative government with the white capitalist's assistance. Nor have the critics of the United States been willing to concede what all superficial indications at least point to as probable —that, no matter how great the distance still to go, great strides have been taken in the last generation toward economic and social justice for American Negroes.

The white policy of exclusion of Orientals

AS THE WORLD's melting pot, the United States has suffered other forms of racial animosity. Like the Negro question, the oriental problem has played a relatively minor role in the history of Europe; but the appearance of the Chinese on America's Pacific coast about a century ago inaugurated another critical problem in race relations for the United States. Unlike the American Negro of that day, the Oriental did not trace his roots back to an almost forgotten primitive culture, and he had not been exposed for centuries to the language, religion, and customs of the white majority. Proud of his own traditions and able to compete effectively against white labor, the oriental immigrant was not assimilated easily. Unlike the European immigrant, the Oriental, already easily distinguishable by his racial features, could find little in the New World with which to identify himself. As a result he joined with his fellow nationals in hard-knit communities.

Though second-generation Orientals quickly adapted themselves to the American scene, the dislikes and suspicions of their white neighbors brought about bitter disputes over social, educational, and religious questions. The doors of the United States, closed to Orientals in 1924 in response to pressure from the West Coast, have not to date been completely reopened. Physical relocation was forced, as a result of the panic created in the Pacific states by the disaster of Pearl Harbor, upon large numbers of persons of Asiatic descent, even when American-born citizens. Canada's oriental inhabitants underwent similar treatment. In South Africa, Australia, and New Zealand, the problem of oriental migration has likewise been regarded sometimes as a threat to the supremacy of the white majority, and strict laws governing immigration have been in force in those dominions during most of the twentieth century. The race problem is one that seems to bother English-speaking countries most. If a plausible explanation of their prejudice is that they are newer areas and thus attract oriental immigrants in large numbers, why are Latin-American countries so little subject to this particular form of prejudice?

The end of western superiority?

PREJUDICES toward individuals of other colors and creeds are in part a reflection of the Westerner's feeling of white and Christian superiority. Catholic and Protestant missionaries have preached to Asiatic, African, and insular peoples the omnipresence of the Christian God, the brotherhood of man, and the perfection of the Christian ideals. But in typical practice the white man has belied his missionaries in his dealings with persons and peoples not of European descent. Recently the supremacy of the white man has been threatened throughout the world, and the values of his Christian society have been openly called into question by European and non-European Marxists as well as other disbelievers. The "Yellow Peril" and the "Black Menace" have in certain areas appeared synonymous with the "Communist Revolution" and have become ominous to western Christian society. These threats to western supremacy have contributed in no small part to the anxieties of our age. Alongside of the old divisions between Christian and non-Christian, white and colored, capitalist and communist now runs a fresh dichotomy into pro-Russian and anti-Russian. Though the lines of separation are not always clear and the loyalty of citizens of color is generally taken for granted in all nations, the several sets of antagonisms reinforce each other.

DEMOCRACY:

EAST AND WEST

Since ARISTOTLE wrote about democracy in his *Politics*, controversy has raged over its definition. Political theorists until the seventeenth century feared rule by the mass of people as but a step removed from anarchy and disorder; but the term gained greater respectability and received stricter formulation in the eighteenth century. In the fervor of the revolutionary decades, democracy became a battle cry and an article of faith. The strait jacket placed upon French freedom by Napoleon provoked Jefferson in 1809 to name the Americas as the "sole depositories of the remains of human liberty." But within less than three decades Tocqueville was contending that rule by the people could not be avoided and urged his contemporaries to adjust themselves gracefully to it. The growth of labor movements, the spread of popular education, and the broadening of the franchise in the nineteenth century were among the factors that firmly established the majority party or bloc as the ruling force in western society. In the twentieth century two world wars have so far been fought, at least in theory and by avowed intention, to preserve this form of democracy.

Division over social and political democracy

SINCE 1945, the peoples of the world have had occasion to ask whether they have a common understanding when they use words like "democratic principles." The political democracy of nineteenth-century liberal thought could hardly satisfy the socialist thinker in his search for social and economic equality; for liberty and equality of opportunity necessarily lead to inequality of achievement. Nor could colonial peoples willingly conform to any interpretation of democracy that provided for free elections in Europe and America and arbitrary exploitation of the resources and lives of non-Europeans or non-Americans. Nor could Negroes or other minorities be counted upon loyally to cooperate in a system of democracy that granted them the right to vote but did not allow them to enjoy equal education, employment, and social privileges. Nor could the scientist and the scholar accept a definition of democracy that, even when it granted them employment and economic security, forced them in practice to yield to political dictation, whether of an elite party, an elected leader, or the majority. Rule by the majority of those who vote, even under a system of equal, universal suffrage, has seemed an inadequate basis for "democracy" to several groups, and conflicts over its definitions have never ceased.

"Cold war" has made the conflict between the concepts of "bourgeois democracy" and "people's democracy" the most fearful of our day. About a century ago, the cleavage between political and social democracy became a major issue. In 1848, Tocqueville denied the interconnection of democracy and socialism:

> Democracy extends the sphere of individual independence, socialism contracts it. Democracy gives to every man his full value, socialism makes of every man an agent, an instrument, a cipher. Democracy and socialism are linked only by the word "equality"; but note the difference: Democracy wants equality in freedom, socialism wants equality in constraint and enslavement.

Socialist and communist writers have argued, on the other hand, that political democracy without economic equality is a polite fiction agreed upon by the propertied minority to exploit and crush the unpropertied majority. In 1936, Stalin called capitalist democracy the "democracy of the strong." Anatole France had much the same idea in mind when he stated that "the law, in its majestic equality, forbids the rich as well as the poor to sleep under bridges." The theory of "bourgeois democracy" emphasizes liberty at the expense of economic equality, and the theory of "people's democracy" emphasizes economic equality at the expense of liberty.

The conflict over the liberated "democracies" THIS IDEOLOGICAL cleavage was given practical form in the treaties and agreements concluded during and after the Second World War. As already mentioned, the Yalta agreements of 1945 (page 899) provided for "free elections" in eastern Europe, and the Potsdam agreements promised to resolve Germany's future in line with "democratic principles." After 1945, it became clear that the same words possessed different meanings for the Communists and the non-Communists. The elections held in eastern Europe rarely met the western requirements for free elections; nor were the western powers impressed by the freedom of the new "democracies" which came into being on the borders of the Soviet Union. The violent elimination of opposition by the Communists was regarded in the nations of the West as a stultification of the elementary democratic principle of freedom for party, group, and individual expression.

Points of agreement on democratic objectives IN AN EFFORT to define "democracy" through international discussion, the United Nations Educational, Scientific, and Cultural Organization (UNESCO) conducted a mid-century symposium. As a result of this investigation, the committee in charge concluded: "The unanimity which appears in the statement of aims is an impressive fact." All parties could agree with Lincoln's assertion that democracy is "government of the people, by the people, and for the people." Moreover, they could also concur that each individual should be guaranteed by his government the greatest possible opportunity to realize his potentialities so long as his efforts did not jeopardize others' opportunities. The widest degree of popular participation in government was uniformly considered desirable, but all agreed that without education, leisure, and energy to study and understand the issues the masses could not participate fittingly. The unanimous opinion that all should be entitled to equal access to economic, cultural, and educational privileges was paralleled by an agreement that in democracy no room existed for discrimination on the basis of color, religion, birth, or "philosophical inclinations."

People in all camps seemed thus to realize that democracy is still an unrealized ideal rather than an accurate name for any existing social and political state. In the non-Communist West its complete fulfillment is balked by the fact that all too frequently it seems to operate through such things as pressure groups and party machines, and in societies characterized by social prejudices, governmental inefficiency, concentrations of wealth, and abuses of power. In the Communist East it is balked by the fact that governments employ such things as one-party systems, dictatorships, purges, censorships, state monopolies, regimentation, and restricted travel. Apparently nearly universal agreement that democracy is a good thing does not make clearer what it is or whether it is attainable in full.

SCIENCE,

THE ARTS, AND PHILOSOPHY

NOT ONLY CREED, color, and politics divide the world today. Science and art also remain, as they long have been, fields of hot dispute. In totalitarian states the answer to what is correct science and good art frequently depends upon the taste or preferences of the leader. Among peoples who reserve such judgments for the trained critics, the decisions are not always so easy.

The modification of the Newtonian world

THE RAPID and dramatic advances of invention and technology in the nineteenth century stimulated a firm confidence in the ability of man to understand and control his environment. Theoretical scientists forged ahead in the natural sciences with equal hopefulness; and in studying historical, psychological, literary, linguistic, and social problems, the nineteenth-century scholar, borrowing with almost unquestioning faith the scientists' methods and drawing analogies to their findings, came to similar conclusions. "Progress" seemed a sure thing. Darwin's evolutionary theories in biology and Marx's "scientific" socialism won friends in all layers of society. "Natural selection" and the "class struggle" swiftly became household words before the end of the century. By the dawn of the twentieth century, evolutionary theory and the idea of progress were often thought of as immutable laws of nature. The world of objective science was widely accepted as the real world, and each achievement of science was viewed as another step on the road to man's conquest of nature. In the twentieth century, however, this faith in the ability of science to solve man's problems, strong though it remained, was tinged with doubt as scientists themselves regularly exploded principles that had long been held irrevocable.

The decline of mechanistic physics at the turn of the last century profoundly shook the belief of many theoretical scientists that they would eventually be able to "explain" the universe in terms of the laws of mechanics.

Like the philosophers of the Newtonian age, some scientists, and many others who found consolation in the scientists' doubts about the all-satisfying nature of science, began to speculate with increasing freedom about nonmaterialistic factors in the natural world. This school saw new horizons open when Einstein expounded the general theory of relativity. The new school looked beyond the old materialistic limitations not so much because of any analogies to the metaphysical world drawn from the Einstein theory as because of the conclusion that the Newtonian principles which had hitherto ruled the world could no longer be regarded as final. From such a viewpoint physics was evidently no more permanent a guide of life than philosophy, and only God was good. Heisenberg's "uncertainty principle" led to analogies in the realm of human affairs.

In an effort to formulate a more satisfactory scientific outlook, a group of philosopher-scientists have founded the related schools of logical positivism and scientific empiricism. Renouncing philosophical speculation as a futile pursuit, the new positivists center their thinking around the relations of logic, mathematics, and science, and the assumption of a unity of science. Logical positivists have had a considerable following in Europe and America in their effort to formulate a new and independent Unity of Science Movement. Despite Einstein's warning that popularization of his unified field theory may "produce nothing but confusion in the minds of nonspecialists," his purely physical theory will probably not avoid the general fate of scientific theories— i.e., adaptation to a system of philosophy.

*Life
as a continuing mystery*

NEVERTHELESS, the neo-Platonists, neo-Thomists, and neo-Kantians continue to propound the dualistic nature of the universe. By mid-century, as atomic fission and fusion brought to mankind fear of annihilation, traditional science lost still more of its hold and had to face stiffer competition from the traditional religions and philosophies for the minds of men. Religious precepts have won great consolation also from a school of biologists and sociologists, sometimes known as ecologists, which has emphasized not struggle but cooperation (e.g., symbiosis and association) as a major determinant in the struggle for survival. Mechanistic explanations in the biological and social studies, furthermore, were viewed by some experts as inadequate. The biologist John Scott Haldane wrote in 1931:

> Though the physico-chemical, or mechanistic, conception of life is still very much alive in the minds of popular writers, I think it is now far from being so among serious students of biology. Such support as it still receives is, at least, nearly always very half-hearted, and depends

mainly on the absence of any clear conception of what can take the place of physico-chemical interpretation.

Even if correct for its own day, twenty years later this view would probably have been less representative of the prevalent feeling among biologists. Yet the questions whether life emerged from inorganic matter and if so, how, continued to baffle scientists looking for physical or evolutionary connections between the organic and the inorganic phases of nature.

The limitations of the science of human behavior THE STUDENTS of society had also to recognize that the progressivism of Comte and Spencer had probably been misplaced, or was at least premature. Instead of progressing in an orderly fashion from the heterogeneous to the homogeneous, the social organism continued to behave in a highly unpredictable manner. Though empirical and statistical methods in sociology, anthropology, and economics had brought new data and understanding to social scientists, irrational and unclassifiable factors in individual and social behavior imposed strict limitations upon the scholar's ability for the most part to predict social developments except within limits either too narrow to be widely applicable or too broad to be strictly applicable. Even when the anthropologist and the sociologist could establish to their own satisfaction that skin pigmentation has no necessary relationship to efficiency or morality, they could not easily apply their findings to the cure of the social ill of discrimination, and could still less easily apply them to the elimination of individual prejudices.

Like some of the natural scientists, students of society often wondered whether behind their data there lay something that was not explicable in scientific terms. Yet most of them insisted upon those terms. One growing school of social thought emphasized the role of society and culture as determinants of human behavior. In medicine, physiological explanations of illnesses had rapidly been making room for psychological diagnoses as well. As we already know, Freud was foremost among those who pointed out the limits in the physico-chemical diagnosis and treatment of human ailments. He and his followers, convinced of the existence of nonmaterial realities behind psychological symptoms, sought to examine the mental constitution of their patients. Though the psychoanalysts encountered sometimes amused, sometimes fierce resistance from almost every quarter, they appeared upon the scene at the point of crackup in the edifice of economic and material determinism. Though theirs was a determinism of a different sort—the determinism of biopsychological factors—they emphasized the role of the irrational and the immeasurable in social behavior. They contended, however, that the subjective could be objectively studied and that the irrational could be rationally understood. Psychology now no longer emphasizes so much as it once did the problem of abnormal behavior, important though that problem is, and concerns itself more with the study of man's normal behavior as a social animal. But even more than other social and biological sciences, it is still at an admittedly rudimentary stage.

The academic and the modern in art

ONE OF THE old conflicts of European culture is the quarrel between the "ancients" and the "moderns." This quarrel has its political reflection in the things that conservatives stand for as opposed to the things that radicals stand for, but it is generally thought of as a dispute in arts and letters between those who prefer academic standards elaborated from past practice and those who are friendly to innovations. The "ancients" and "academics" fear that low standards and bad taste may creep in without a proper set of criteria; the "moderns" are repelled by the danger of mere imitativeness and the discouragement of initiative if standards are regarded as fixed once and for all. How are new ideas to come to art, letters, or music if the artist must always aim to be like Michelangelo, Shakespeare, or Beethoven? To which the academics retort, "Look what happens when classic standards are forsaken!" And they use adjectives like *primitive, savage, abstract, nonobjective, atonal,* and *dissonant* as terms of derision and derogation. The artist particularly is in an awkward position, for if he paints what his eyes see, he is likely to be considered "unimaginative" or "photographic," and if he paints what his emotions dictate, he is likely to be labeled *"avant-garde"* or "hoaxer." In the latter case, he can find only small consolation in the reflection that in the course of time the moderns become ancient.

The role of science in the state

FOR THE SCIENTIST the question of what is right is likely to be answered by empirical tests. Hence that is right which "works" best until something better is found ("works" meaning either "produces the wanted results" or "explains the most"). But if the pragmatic question is relatively easy for scientists, the moral or ethical question is not, for science can be and is being used for destructive as well as constructive purposes, and the scientist is often troubled by the application of his knowledge. He sometimes takes refuge in a repudiation of responsibility, claiming that it is not his province to dictate how his knowledge will be applied, or he seeks through semiscientific, semipolitical pressure groups to urge constructive use of his knowledge.

A state at war or in fear of war will, however, mobilize its scientists as one of its major war resources, and it will require them (if indeed they do not volunteer) to find better weapons than the enemy's and to find them faster. It will also barely allow them free exchange of information or investigation in times of stress, and it will bring all kinds of pressure and persuasion to bear for the kind of research it wishes to have done. Is science then doomed to greater and greater deviation toward political, usually destructive, ends? The answer, of course, is only to a small extent within the scientists' power.

The special problem of growth in populations

THE MEDICAL scientist has a peculiar ethical problem to face. Certainly his scientific purposes and probably his government's pressure will suggest to him that his objective be the saving and prolonging of life. But the prolonging of life brings other problems. Some people, especially those suffering from painful and incurable disease, do not wish to live, and groups have been organized to permit "euthanasia" (gently bringing on death under certain circumstances), to which the clergy in general and some doctors are opposed. Similar divisions of opinion take place over proposals to provide systematic instruction in birth control. In addition, the decline of infant mortality, the prolonging of the life span, and the reduction of the killing power of diseases like pneumonia, mastoiditis, tuberculosis, appendicitis, typhoid, and peritonitis have created not only more old people, whom the young must support, but also bigger populations pressing ever more and more upon the available goods, particularly food. Will social science or empirical governmental enterprise be able to solve the economic and social problems that result from the physiologists' success in prolonging human life?

The place of the social sciences

THE NATURAL scientists have achieved an understanding of animals and things that far exceeds the social scientists' understanding of society. Man can make electronic machines that he cannot fully control or that by the new science of cybernetics will compute sums he cannot fully grasp; he can spread propaganda and suppress truth; he can travel at supersonic speeds and can convey thought faster than he can digest truth or learn standards of appreciation. Man's need to study man more and better is obvious; it is not equally obvious that he has the capacity to understand him sufficiently.

The lag between the natural and the social sciences is not altogether the social scientists' responsibility. For one thing, the natural scientists seem guaranteed at least a small margin of autonomy in that usually only fellow scientists feel capable of censoring their work in its preapplication stages. The social sciences are not so fortunate. Everybody, having lived all his life in some form of society, has at least a smattering of the social sciences, and only the rare citizen knows enough about them to realize his ignorance. Hence almost every legislator, school administrator, and prominent citizen feels competent to censor the social scientists. And since their conclusions are frequently hard to demonstrate, often are debated by other social scientists, and may sound dangerous to some element or other of society, the degree of censorship that they will encounter may be great.

1012 Moreover, the social scientists' problems do not readily yield to their answers, even when they agree—usually because application of the answers is politically hard to obtain. If physiologists agree that insulin may greatly diminish the danger of diabetes, insulin is quickly administered and the expected results follow. But freer trade does not follow when economists agree that free trade will diminish economic ills. The atom yields to bombardment of the cyclotron when once physicists have agreed that the atom is smashable. But a balance of world power or the creation of world order does not come from bombardment by the manifestoes of the political scientists.

Nevertheless the social scientists have scored some pragmatic victories. The tendency of governments, business houses, labor unions, and social service agencies to employ trained personnel spreads, with what may be presumed on the whole to be desirable results in policy planning, management, industrial relations, family relations, and the like. If, however, the bigger corporations are now trying to sell stock to their employees, if the number of stockholders is slowly growing in the more prosperous western countries, if in the course of time the ups and downs of the business cycle should ever be controlled, if business organizations should ever become the property of their employees and of the public at large, if countervailing political and economic forces should someday strike a nice balance, empirical and practical considerations rather than social science generalizations will probably have had the greater share in bringing that state to pass.

The place
of education in the state

IF MAN KNEW man better, the problems of education would presumably be easier. We might then know whether increased knowledge leads to increased skill or wisdom, and, if so, how. Would it be by direct correlation? Would it be by exhortation or precept or example? Would it be by free, progressive education or by non-elective study of the classics? Should the aim be better Christians, better materialists, better citizens, better scholars or better soldiers? Should everyone be educated to the extent of his educability or only to the extent of his utmost usefulness to the state as determined by educators and legislators? And who educates the educators? And what happens to the goal of the equality of man if there are to be permanent inequalities of education? At present an answer to these questions is more easily forthcoming in the states of the one-party governments, as most answers are, but not everyone is satisfied that the answers given are the right ones.

The plight
of the "beat generation"

THE RESTLESS minds in the West among the generation that followed the Second World War were bound to be more nihilistic than those among the "lost generation" after the First World War. The "lost generation," having been bereft of the Victorian tradition, had the cults of fascism and communism to fall back upon. But by the end of the Second World War those in the West without religious faith were bereft not only of "the God of their fathers" but also of "the wave of the future." Moreover, science, which had offered to the irreligious of earlier generations the hope of progress, presented this generation with the awesome spectacle of 100,000 dead at Hiroshima by means of atomic fission and the dread probability of greater destructive power by means of atomic fusion, particularly after the announcement by Malenkov in August 1953 that Russia too had developed a hydrogen bomb. This was, as some of its contemporaries called it, a "beat generation." Those who could not find consolation in a church or in a generalissimo tried to find what solace they could in the humanists' "great books" or the sociologists' "healthy society" or, as a last resort, in the proved fact that as a generation they "could take it." They might perhaps build, in the words of one of their mentors, Bertrand Russell, on a "firm foundation of unyielding despair." But to most of their contemporaries the reenthronement of God by some scientists and philosophers was a greater consolation, for how could God intend the destruction of humanity?

WAR AND PEACE

At the turn of the last century, the upper strata of western European and American society possessed a seldom troubled sense of security and well being. At the same time, the lands and peoples of Asia and Africa began to stir restlessly under colonial rule and incipient national upheaval. Hence, some Europeans had occasional premonitions of future disaster, but such forebodings were likely to be spread abroad by racial agitators who warned against the "Black Menace" and the "Yellow Peril" that would one day upset the equilibrium and engulf the white world with swarming masses of vengeful natives rather than by the fringe thinkers of radical and conservative camps, Marxist theorists or orthodox theologians who predicted a dire end to the Gilded Age. About the danger of future wars, however, only a few Cassandra voices were raised in warning; and rare indeed were those who would have foreseen that creed, class, color, and colonial status would all combine with power politics, nationalist aims, and economic competition as causes of global war in the near future.

*Limited war
as an extension of diplomacy*

GENERAL WARS involving most of the European nations and their colonies were thought at the beginning of our century to have ended with Waterloo. After Napoleon, war was considered an adjunct of statecraft, a pursuit of diplomatic ends by more forceful means. It had ceased to be regarded as a medium of ideological mission that must result in the total defeat or extermination of a heretical enemy. The wars of the nineteenth century were normally fought in limited areas, with limited resources, for limited objectives such as national unification, control of strategic territory or economic resources, or readjustment of the balance of power. Big-scale conquests in Europe and world control were not motives in the minds of even the most ambitious empire builders like Napoleon III, Cavour, Disraeli, Bismarck or William II. All of these men subscribed roughly to the same Christian, moral, capitalist, European principles, and their wars were fought mainly to achieve a national advantage, not to overturn any competing economic, intellectual, or social gospel. For them ideological warfare had passed with the Thirty Years' War and the wars of the French Revolution and Napoleon, except to the extent that nationalism was an ideology.

World war and world organization

FEW AUGURS could have predicted that a Balkan crisis in 1914 would set off a series of general wars complicated by ideological shibboleths. Nevertheless, the major wars of the twentieth century were fought all over the world; their numerous participants rallied in varying degrees to such ideals as "democracy," "racial superiority," and "freedoms"; and the wars did not end until they had brought about the modification of the European state system, the collapse of Europe's superiority in Asia and Africa, and the loss of world leadership to largely non-European areas like the USSR, the United States, the British Commonwealth, the French Union, China, and India. The League of Nations, the United Nations, and their cooperating agencies were symptoms of Europe's eclipse, visible signs of the aspiration of nations and peoples to chart their destinies on a world instead of a regional scale.

The disillusionment that followed in the wake of the First World War was accentuated by the inability of the new world association to assure collective action for peace. For diverse reasons the inhabitants of the smaller nations, American isolationists, Russian Communists, Orientals, and nationalists everywhere waxed suspicious of British and French predominance in the League of Nations. The failure of the League in the 1930's to check Japanese, German, and Italian imperialism lent substance to the far-reaching doubt that the League was well devised to preserve world peace. Thus, after the First World War, even though a world organization existed and operated effectively in limited areas, the choice between war and peace remained largely to the individual states.

Nevertheless, the concept of "One World" gained adherents. The very existence of the League, the growth of communist and fascist ideologies and of anticommunist and antifascist leagues, and the rapid development of commerce, industry, transportation, and communication tended toward transforming the European state system into an interdependent and interacting world system. Once certain statesmen of the interwar period began to think in world terms, a race began to determine which leader, which ideology, and which people should control the "One World" of the future. Private schemes for a federal organization of the world were also propounded in which various nations and peoples might enjoy the freedom of diversity under a unified though beneficent world government, but practical politics became a struggle for the power to decide the form, operation, and control of whatever world organization might win out.

The rise of irreconcilable ideologies

EVEN BEFORE the First World War the belief had been widespread in the West that eventually the entire world would move along a common path. Westerners generally expected the rest of the world to follow the example of the European nations and accept majority government, Christian morality, and free enterprise. The rise and spread of Communism after 1917 brought into the competition a militant ideology that, though a product of European culture, refused to accept the superiority of the western way of life and set out to extend its own doctrines of proletarian dictatorship, materialism, and economic collectivism by means of propaganda, infiltration, and local action. No less forthright in their convictions than the Communists, the fascists of Italy, Germany, and Japan intended to ride the wave of the future. Total war and a total peace after their own hearts became in the interwar years the objectives of leaders who looked upon compromise as a token of weakness, and upon weakness as a token of death. The western democracies were reluctantly forced to the realization that if the battle for world supremacy came, it would be limited neither in its objectives nor in its effects, and that it might not be a victory for democracy, even if the democracies should win.

Revolution and war regarded as desirable processes

UPON THE firm establishment of Communism in Russia, the world came face to face with the idea of permanent revolution not as a socialist theory but as the fixed policy of a mighty nation. Persuaded of the correctness of the Marxian tenet that bourgeois society must eventually give way to a dictatorship of the proletariat, the Bolsheviks after 1917 supported in any country of the world any group or movement that they thought might hasten the decline of capitalism. Confident, however, that history was fighting on its side, the Soviet Union seldom troubled either about the passage of time or the choice of means. Underground activity, popular fronts, non-aggression pacts, and the Comintern were emphasized or soft-pedaled as seemed expedient. When finally Russia herself became a target of Nazi aggression in the Second World War, the Comintern was disbanded entirely in order to demonstrate the solidarity of Russia with the "bourgeois democracies."

After 1945, the underground revolutionary war was resumed. This time the international agency of Communist activity was named the Cominform, and it now constituted a major instrument in the Communist program. The

Communists continue to speak of war as a capitalist instrument and of peace as their own aim. While preparing for war against the capitalists, and even resorting to limited warfare in certain instances, they have managed to transform limited warfare and peace propaganda into a kind of continuous revolutionary activity, pushing their capitalist opponents into the awkward position of seeming to favor war, colonialism, the status quo, and even reaction.

Like communism, the various brands of fascism developed their own anti-liberal philosophies of history. In the Italian Fascist doctrine, war, especially war for ideological ends, was frankly elevated to a positive virtue, bringing the nation to its highest peak of sacrifice, unity, and achievement. The racial teachings of the Nazis embraced a still larger concept than the nation-state. For Hitler, "race" meant conflict for superiority; politics was war; imperialism was inevitable and necessary; and world domination by the sword was the final objective of both foreign and domestic policy. To the Japanese, history appeared to teach the hard lesson that the meek would not inherit the earth but that the strong would rule and the weak would perish.

Victory without peace AS ELSEWHERE detailed, the three-cornered struggle of the western democracies, the fascist states, and Communist Russia led in the interwar period to several critical shiftings of sympathies among them. The twilight of the fascist gods descended only when the Soviet Union and the United States were forced by fascist miscalculations to combine with the Commonwealth and the exiled democracies. After the bloodiest and most nearly total war of history, a world organization of the victors, with the announced objective of eventually including all the world's nations, again raised the hopes of mankind for the permanent establishment of world peace and order.

The war, it soon appeared, had determined, so to speak, who had been defeated but not who had won. To begin with, the obliteration of the fascist powers as military threats was not followed by the complete elimination of fascist doctrine. Fascism survived openly in Spain and Argentina; fascists went underground more or less in other countries to reappear boldly in neo-fascist movements in Germany, Italy, and elsewhere within a few years. Nor did the defeat of the Axis powers signalize the beginning of a real world order. The old suspicions between the Communists and the western nations had not really died during the war, and each side deeply distrusted the other now that they had no common enemy to fear.

The world's worst war therefore did not put an end to the world's ideological struggle. The permanent revolution of the Communists threatened global equilibrium and security. Russian military power, propaganda, and infiltration were employed to subvert the independence of bordering states; and Communist parties and agents, aided by the genuine misery and desperation of war-ridden populations, carried on intrigue and subversion in the rest of the world. They sought, or so their apologists said, not merely social justice 1017 for the proletariat but also a system of buffers for their own security against capitalist imperialism. Eventually the western powers, in an effort to contain the spread of Communism, rebuilt their war machines and their alliances, undertook by programs of loans, grants, and technical assistance to help each other and the underdeveloped areas, and increased their counterintelligence efforts, sometimes to the point of exciting fears regarding civil liberties. To avoid the failure of the League of Nations to act against aggressors, they went to the aid of states like South Korea that they deemed to be the victims of aggression.

The world balanced between peace and war AT MID-CENTURY, mankind's problems in other areas of life were dwarfed by the threat of renewed global struggle and for the most part subordinated to it. Science, art, letters, education, industry, politics, finance, and social relations were wholly or largely shaped by the needs of the limited struggles in areas where the "cold war" had grown hot and by the fact that a general war might yet burst forth. Instead of rallying under the United Nations Organization, the world had rapidly divided into two hostile camps. Some less hopeful observers ventured to suggest that the concept of world organization was self-contradictory, for if the nations of the world could agree, no world organization was necessary, and if they could not agree, no world organization was possible.

The division of the world into East and West brought with it a bipolarity in international relations, politics, communications, scholarship, art, and thought that seemed to defy all efforts at bridging. The "Iron Curtain" separating the two ideological camps increased suspicion and fear as each accused the other of aggressive intentions and inhuman methods. The fear of eventual conflict was raised to an almost hysterical pitch by the universal feeling that a total war between two huge coalitions, each possessing cataclysmic weapons, would probably not result in a clean victory for either side and might bring about the destruction of civilization. To the prophets of doom the world appeared determined, just at the moment when an enduring peace and unity had seemed within humanity's grasp, to pull the pillars down in a final drastic effort to secure permanent release from constant strife and recurring wars. The utter irrationality of such a total war led the hopeful to prophesy an armistice or a recognition of stalemate and the gradual reëstablishment of normal relations. Few were those who dared to believe that an amicable settlement would rapidly be found, both sides agreeing to live and let live. Counting on the mutual fear of retaliation to deter both sides, most expected no more than a long and uneasy chain of bitter propaganda battles and of "local incidents," fought with conventional weapons. The peoples of the world were thus enabled to nourish the thought that general war and the surrender of the institutions they held most dear might in the end be averted.

*The persistence
of the European heritage*

IN THE PERIOD covered by this volume, the most notable change to record is the eclipse of western Europe's political primacy, accompanied by a loss of luster to its cultural heritage. As is the way of historical eclipses, Europe's has not been total. If the great powers of today are not located entirely in Europe, their culture— even Communist culture—stems from there. The European drama has been transferred onto a world stage. Even in the atomic age when man, driven by his inquisitive and acquisitive impulses and having tasted perhaps too freely of the tree of knowledge, may destroy himself before he can regain Eden, he remains an aspiring animal. His aspirations, whether in the East or in the West, derive some of their most striking features from the European heritage. Even Chinese Communists, while berating the Whites as imperialists, give full credit to Marx, Lenin, and Stalin for providing them with their doctrines; and, in an idiom that has acquired an orthodoxy of its own, these doctrines speak of a paradise lost by error and to be regained by sacrifice.

In the last century and a half Europe has indeed been transformed. Its power in world terms has declined. Its culture has spread to all parts of the globe and has been shaped by importations from all parts of the globe. Europe is no longer the proud creditor and unchallenged exploiter of the other continents. Its future is insecure—along with the future of the other continents. The Caucasian peoples, the Indo-European languages, and Christianity may not hereafter occupy the predominant places they once held. Nonetheless, the opposing ideas and forces that still flourish in one part or another of the modern world have many, if not all, of their roots in Europe's soil—Christianity and materialism, free enterprise and statism, capitalism and communism, nationalism and world organization, self-determination and federation, democracy and totalitarianism, science and several forms of creative art, the reason of state and the rights of man, materialism and historicism, realism and nonobjectivism, Sovietism and Americanism, the empires and anticolonialism. In the words of an old French proverb, the more Europe changes the more it remains the same, for, as we said in the beginning, history is a record of both change and continuity. It is still too early to believe that only the good things will change and the wrong things continue. And it is certainly not too late to hope that time for change will not run out, and that the day may yet come when, in the words of Dwight D. Eisenhower "men of the West and men of the East can fight and work and live together side by side in pursuit of a just and noble cause."

BIBLIOGRAPHY

To avoid repetition and to permit the fullest possible use of the space available for this bibliography, works which might profitably be consulted in connection with more than one chapter have been listed only once. Only works in English are given.

General

REFERENCE WORKS

Anderson, G. K., and Warnock, R. (eds.). *Our Hundred Years: The Literature of the Contemporary Period.* Chicago: Scott, Foresman and Company, 1951.

Cambridge Modern History. Planned by Lord Acton. Edited by A. W. Ward, G. W. Prothero, and S. Leathes. 13 vols. Cambridge: Cambridge University Press, 1934.

Cassell's Encyclopedia of Literature. Edited by S. H. Steinberg. London: Cassell & Co., Ltd., 1953.

The Catholic Encyclopedia. 18 vols. New York: The Encyclopedia Press, Inc., 1907-1952.

Columbia Dictionary of Modern European Literature. Edited by H. Smith. New York: Columbia University Press, 1947.

The Columbia Encyclopedia. Edited by W. Bridgwater and E. J. Sherwood. 2d ed. New York: Columbia University Press, 1950.

Concise Oxford Atlas. Edited by D. P. Bickmore and K. F. Cook. New York: Oxford University Press, 1953.

A Cyclopedia of Education. Edited by P. Monroe *et al.* 3 vols. New York: The Macmillan Co., 1925-1928.

A Dictionary of Music and Musicians. Edited by G. Grove. 6 vols. New York: The Macmillan Co., 1935.

The Dictionary of Philosophy. Edited by D. D. Runes. New York: Philosophical Library, 1942.

Encyclopaedia Britannica. 24 vols. 14th ed. Chicago: Encyclopaedia Britannica, Inc., 1954.

Encyclopedia of Religion and Ethics. Edited by J. Hastings. 13 vols. New York: Charles Scribner's Sons, 1911-1927.

Encyclopaedia of the Social Sciences. Edited by R. A. Seligman and A. Johnson. 15 vols. New York: The Macmillan Co., 1951.

The Jewish Encyclopedia. Edited by C. Adler and I. Singer. 12 vols. New York: Funk & Wagnalls Co., 1925.

Langer, W. L. (ed.). *An Encyclopedia of World History.* Rev. ed. Boston: Houghton Mifflin Co., 1950.

Lord, C. L., and Lord, E. H. (eds.). *Historical Atlas of the United States.* Rev. ed. New York: Henry Holt & Co., Inc., 1953.

Morris, R. B. (ed.). *Encyclopedia of American History.* New York: Harper & Bros., 1953.

Muir's Historical Atlas: Medieval and Modern. Edited by G. Goodall and R. F. Treharne. 8th ed. New York: Barnes & Noble, Inc., 1952.

The New Century Cyclopedia of Names. Edited by C. L. Barnhart. 3 vols. New York: Appleton-Century-Crofts, Inc., 1954.

The Reader's Encyclopedia. Edited by W. R. Benét. New York: Thomas Y. Crowell Co., 1948.

Shepherd, W. R. *Historical Atlas.* 7th ed. New York: Henry Holt & Co., Inc., 1929.

Van Nostrand's Scientific Encyclopedia. 2d ed. New York: D. Van Nostrand Co., Inc., 1947.

GENERAL HISTORIES

Ausubel, H. (ed.). *Waterloo to the Atomic Age.* (*The Making of Modern Europe*, Vol. II.) New York: The Dryden Press, Inc., 1951.

Barker, E., *et al.* (eds.). *The European Inheritance.* 3 vols. Oxford: The Clarendon Press, 1954.

Barnes, H. E. *A History of Historical Writing.* Norman: University of Oklahoma Press, 1937.

Baumer, F. Le Van (ed.). *Main Currents of Western Thought: Readings in Western European Intellectual History from the Middle Ages to the Present.* New York: Alfred A. Knopf, Inc., 1952.

Brandes, G. *Main Currents in 19th Century Literature.* 6 vols. New York: Boni & Liveright, 1923.

Brinton, C. *Ideas and Men: the Story of Western Thought.* New York: Prentice-Hall, Inc., 1950.

———. *The United States and Britain.* Cambridge: Harvard University Press, 1945.

Clough, S. B., and Cole, C. W. *Economic History of Europe.* 3d ed. Boston: D. C. Heath & Co., 1952.

Clyde, P. H. *The Far East.* 2d ed. New York: Prentice-Hall, Inc., 1952.

Cole, G. D. H. *A History of Socialist Thought.* 2 vols. (to 1890). New York: St. Martin's Press, Inc., 1954.

Collingwood, R. G. *The Idea of History*. Oxford: The Clarendon Press, 1946.

Corti, E. C. *The Reign of the House of Rothschild*. Translated by Bryan and Beatrix Lunn. London: Victor Gollancz, Ltd., 1928.

Croce, B. *History of Europe in the 19th Century*. Translated by Henry Furst. New York: Harcourt, Brace & Co., 1933.

Dampier, W. C. D. *A History of Science and its Relations with Philosophy and Religion*. Cambridge: Cambridge University Press, 1943.

Einstein, A. *Short History of Music*. 2d ed. New York: Alfred A. Knopf, Inc., 1938.

Fisher, H. A. L. *A History of Europe*. New ed. Boston: Houghton Mifflin Co., 1939.

Forbes, R. J. *Man the Maker: a History of Technology and Engineering*. New York: Henry Schuman, Inc., 1950.

Friedell, E. *A Cultural History of the Modern Age*. Translated by C. F. Atkinson. 3 vols. New York: Alfred A. Knopf, Inc., 1952.

Gardner, H. *Art Through the Ages*. 3d ed. New York: Harcourt, Brace & Co., 1948.

Gewehr, W. M. *The Rise of Nationalism in the Balkans, 1800-1930*. New York: Henry Holt & Co., Inc., 1931.

Gide, C., and Rist, C. *A History of Economic Doctrines from the Time of the Physiocrats to the Present Day*. R. Richards, trans., 2d ed. Boston: D. C. Heath & Co., 1948.

Grant, A. J., and Temperley, H. *Europe in the 19th and 20th Centuries (1789-1950)*. New York: Longmans, Green & Co., Inc., 1952.

Grousset, R. *The Civilization of the East*. 4 vols. Translated by K. A. Phillips. New York: Alfred A. Knopf, Inc., 1931-1934.

Halecki, O. *Borderlands of Western Civilization: a History of East Central Europe*. New York: The Ronald Press Co., 1952.

Hawkesworth, C. E. M. *The Last Century in Europe (1814-1910)*. New York: Longmans, Green & Co., Inc., 1912.

Hazen, C. D. *Europe since 1815*. Rev. ed. New York: Henry Holt & Co., Inc., 1928.

Heilbroner, R. L. *The Worldly Philosophers: the Lives, Times, and Ideas of Great Economic Thinkers*. New York: Simon & Schuster, 1953.

Hemleben, S. J. *Plans for World Peace through Six Centuries*. Chicago: The University of Chicago Press, 1943.

Hitti, P. K. *History of the Arabs from the Earliest Times to the Present*. 5th ed. New York: St. Martin's Press, Inc., 1952.

Höffding, H. *A History of Modern Philosophy*. Translated by B. E. Meyer. 2 vols. New York: The Macmillan Co., 1924.

Hogben, L. *Science for the Citizen*. London: George Allen & Unwin, Ltd., 1938.

Holborn, H. *The Political Collapse of Europe*. New York: Alfred A. Knopf, Inc., 1951.

Koht, H. *The American Spirit in Europe: a Survey of Transatlantic Influences*. Philadelphia: University of Pennsylvania Press, 1949.

Kuh, K. *Art Has Many Faces; the Nature of Art Presented Visually*. New York: Harper & Bros., 1951.

Latourette, K. S. *A History of the Expansion of Christianity*. 7 vols. New York: Harper & Bros., 1937-1945.

——. *A Short History of the Far East*. New York: The Macmillan Co., 1946.

McKay, D. *The United States and France*. Cambridge: Harvard University Press, 1951.

MacNair, H. F., and Lach, D. F. *Modern Far Eastern International Relations*. New York: D. Van Nostrand Co., Inc., 1950.

Makers of Modern Strategy. Edited by E. M. Earle, *et al*. Princeton: Princeton University Press, 1950.

Mangone, G. J. *A Short History of International Organization*. New York: The McGraw-Hill Book Co., 1954.

Mendenhall, T. C., *et al*. *The Quest for a Principle of Authority in Europe, 1715-Present*. New York: Henry Holt & Co., Inc., 1948.

Merz, T. *A History of European Thought in the 19th Century*. 4 vols. New York: The Humanities Press, Inc., 1897-1914.

Mettler, C. C. *History of Medicine*. Philadelphia: The Blakiston Co., 1947.

Miller, W. *The Balkans*. 3d ed. London: T. F. Unwin, Ltd., 1923.

Morse, H. B., and MacNair, H. F. *Far Eastern International Relations*. Boston: Houghton Mifflin Co., 1931.

Mowat, R. B. *The States of Europe, 1815-1870*. New York: Longmans, Green & Co., 1932.

Nef, J. U. *War and Human Progress*. Cambridge: Harvard University Press, 1950.

Randall, J. H. *The Making of the Modern Mind*. Boston: Houghton Mifflin Co., 1940.

Rippy, J. F. *Historical Evolution of Hispanic America*. 2d ed. New York: F. S. Crofts & Co., 1940.

Ruggiero, G. de. *History of European Liberalism*. Translated by R. G. Collingwood. New York: Oxford University Press, 1927.

Sabine, G. H. *A History of Political Theory*. New York: Henry Holt & Co., Inc., 1937.

Sansom, G. B. *The Western World and Japan*. New York: Alfred A. Knopf, Inc., 1950.

Schapiro, J. S. *Modern and Contemporary European History*. New ed. Boston: Houghton Mifflin Co., 1953.

Schevill, F. *The Balkan Peninsula and the Near East*. London: George Bell & Sons, Ltd., 1922.

Schumpeter, J. A. *History of Economic Analysis*. New York: Oxford University Press, 1954.

Scott, J. F., and Baltzly, A. *Readings in European History since 1814*. New York: F. S. Crofts & Co., 1931.

Seton-Watson, R. W. *The Balkans, Italy and the Adriatic*. London: Nisbet & Co., 1915.

Shryock, R. H. *The Development of Modern Medicine.* New York: Alfred A. Knopf, Inc., 1947.

Stearns, R. P. *Pageant of Europe.* New York: Harcourt, Brace & Co., 1947.

Sykes, P. *A History of Exploration: from the Earliest Times to the Present Day.* 3d ed. New York: The Macmillan Co., 1950.

Toynbee, A. J. *A Study of History.* 6 vols. London: Oxford University Press, 1948-1951.

Van Laue, M. *History of Physics.* New York: Academic Press Inc., 1950.

Vinacke, H. M. *A History of the Far East in Modern Times.* New York: Alfred A. Knopf, Inc., 1938.

Znaniecki, F. *Cultural Sciences: Their Origin and Development.* Urbana: University of Illinois Press, 1952.

NATIONAL HISTORIES

Albrecht-Carrié, R. *Italy: from Napoleon to Mussolini.* New York: Columbia University Press, 1950.

Allan, J., *et al. The Cambridge Shorter History of India.* New York: The Macmillan Co., 1934.

Altamira, R. *A History of Spain from the Beginnings to the Present Day.* Translated by M. Lee. New York: D. Van Nostrand Co., Inc., 1948.

Bailey, T. A. *A Diplomatic History of the American People.* 4th ed. New York: Appleton-Century-Crofts, Inc., 1950.

Baldwin, L. D. *The Stream of American History.* 2 vols. New York: Richard R. Smith Inc., 1952.

Baron, S. W. *A Social and Religious History of the Jews.* 3 vols. New York: Columbia University Press, 1937.

Beard, C. A., and Beard, M. *The Rise of American Civilization.* 2 vols. New York: The Macmillan Co., 1927.

Bemis, S. F. *A Diplomatic History of the United States.* New ed. New York: Henry Holt & Co., Inc., 1950.

Bertrand, L., and Petrie, C. *History of Spain.* New York: The Macmillan Co., 1952.

Billington, R. A., *et al. The United States: American Democracy in World Perspective.* New York: Rinehart & Co., Inc., 1947.

Blake, N. M. *A Short History of American Life.* New York: McGraw-Hill Book Co., 1952.

Brooks, V. *Makers and Finders: A History of the Writers in America 1800-1918.* 5 vols. New York: E. P. Dutton & Co., 1941-1953.

Cambridge History of British Foreign Policy, 1783-1919. Edited by A. W. Ward and G. P. Gooch. 3 vols. Cambridge: Cambridge University Press, 1922-1923.

Carman, H. J., and Syrett, H. C. *A History of the American People.* 2 vols. New York: Alfred A. Knopf, Inc., 1952.

Cheyney, E. P. *An Introduction to the Industrial and Social History of England.* Rev. ed. New York: The Macmillan Co., 1920.

Clapham, J. H. *Economic Development of France and Germany, 1815-1914.* 3d ed. London: Cambridge University Press, 1928.

Commager, H. S. *The American Mind.* New Haven: Yale University Press, 1950.

Craven, A., and Johnson, W. *The United States: Experiment in Democracy.* Boston: Ginn & Co., 1950.

Crawford, R. M. *Australia.* London: Hutchinson & Co., Ltd., 1952.

Creel, H. G. *Chinese Thought from Confucius to Mao Tse-tung.* Chicago: The University of Chicago Press, 1953.

Cross, A. L. *A Shorter History of England and Great Britain.* 3d ed. New York: The Macmillan Co., 1939.

Curti, M., *et al. An American History.* Vol. II. New York: Harper & Bros., 1950.

Curti, M. *The Growth of American Thought.* 2d ed. New York: Harper & Bros., 1951.

Dietz, F. C. *A Political and Social History of England.* 3d ed. New York: The Macmillan Co., 1947.

Faulkner, H. U. *American Economic History.* 6th ed. New York: Harper & Bros., 1949.

Fitzgerald, C. P. *China—a Short Cultural History.* New York: Frederick A. Praeger, Inc., 1950.

Florinsky, M. T. *Russia: a History and an Interpretation.* 2 vols. New York: The Macmillan Co., 1953.

Glazebrook, G. P. de T. *Canadian External Relations; an historical study.* London: Oxford University Press, 1942.

Goodrich, L. C. *A Short History of the Chinese People.* New York: Harper & Bros., 1943.

Grayzel, S. *A History of the Jews.* Philadelphia: Jewish Publication Society of America, 1947.

Guérard, A. L. *French Civilization in the Nineteenth Century.* New York: The Century Co., 1918.

Guignebert, C. *A Short History of the French People.* Vol. II. New York: The Macmillan Co., 1930.

Halecki, O. *The History of Poland.* Translated by M. M. Gardner and M. Corbridge-Patkaniowska. London: J. M. Dent & Sons, Ltd., 1942.

Hall, W. P., and Albion, R. G. *A History of England and the British Empire.* 3d ed. Boston: Ginn & Co., 1953.

Harcave, S. *Russia, a History.* Rev. ed. Philadelphia: J. B. Lippincott & Co., 1952.

Henderson, E. F. *A Short History of Germany.* Vol. II. New York: The Macmillan Co., 1931.

Hofstadter, R. *The American Political Tradi-*

tion: and the Men Who Made It. New York: Alfred A. Knopf, Inc., 1948.

Kerner, R. J. (ed.). *Czechoslovakia, Twenty Years of Independence.* Berkeley: University of California Press, 1940.

Kornilov, A. *Modern Russian History.* New York: Alfred A. Knopf, Inc., 1943.

Larkin, O. W. *Art and Life in America.* New York: Rinehart & Co., Inc., 1949.

Larsen, K. *A History of Norway.* Princeton: Princeton University Press, 1948.

Latourette, K. S. *The Chinese, Their History and Culture.* 3d ed. New York: The Macmillan Co., 1946.

——. *A History of Christian Missions in China.* New York: The Macmillan Co., 1929.

——. *The History of Japan.* New York: The Macmillan Co., 1947.

Lattimore, O. *Inner Asian Frontiers of China.* New York: Oxford University Press, 1940.

Linden, H. van der. *Belgium, the Making of a Nation.* Translated by S. Jane. Oxford: The Clarendon Press, 1920.

Lunt, W. E. *History of England.* 3d ed. New York: Harper & Bros., 1945.

Lützow, Count von. *Bohemia: an Historical Sketch.* Rev. and extended by H. A. Pilcher. London: Everyman's Library, 1939.

McGrane, R. C. *The Economic Development of the American Nation.* Rev. ed. Boston: Ginn & Co., 1942.

McInnis, E. *Canada, a Political and Social History.* New York: Rinehart & Co., Inc., 1947.

McLaughlin, A. C. *A Constitutional History of the United States.* New York: D. Appleton-Century Co., Inc., 1935.

MacNair, H. F. *Modern Chinese History.* Shanghai: Commercial Press, Ltd., 1927.

Marcham, R. G. *A History of England.* New ed. New York: The Macmillan Co., 1954.

Marriott, J. A. R., and Robertson, C. G. *The Evolution of Prussia; the Making of an Empire.* New ed. Oxford: The Clarendon Press, 1937.

Masaryk, T. G. *Spirit of Russia: Studies in History, Literature and Philosophy.* Translated by E. and C. Paul. 2 vols. London: George Allen & Unwin, Ltd., 1919.

Mavrogordato, J. *Modern Greece.* New York: The Macmillan Co., 1931.

Mazour, A. G. *Russia: Past and Present.* New York: D. Van Nostrand Co., Inc., 1951.

Miller, W. *A History of the Greek People (1821-1921).* London: Methuen & Co., Ltd., 1922.

Morison, S. E., and Commager, H. S. *The Growth of the American Republic.* 2 vols. New York: Oxford University Press, 1950.

Murdock, J. *A History of Japan.* 3 vols. New York: Greenberg Publishers, 1926.

Nowell, C. E. *A History of Portugal.* New York: D. Van Nostrand Co., Inc., 1952.

Oechsli, W. *History of Switzerland, 1499-1914.* Translated by E. and C. Paul. Cambridge: Cambridge University Press, 1922.

Pares, B. *A History of Russia.* Def. ed. New York: Alfred A. Knopf, Inc., 1953.

Parrington, V. L. *Main Currents in American Thought.* 3 vols. New York: Harcourt Brace & Co., 1927-1930.

Rawlinson, H. G. *India—a Short Cultural History.* New ed. New York: Frederick A. Praeger, Inc., 1953.

Reischauer, E. O. *Japan Past and Present.* New York: Alfred A. Knopf, Inc., 1952.

Robinson, H. *The Development of the British Empire.* Boston: Houghton Mifflin Co., 1922.

Sachar, A. L. *A History of the Jews.* Rev. ed. New York: Alfred A. Knopf, Inc., 1953.

Sansom, G. B. *Japan: a Short Cultural History.* New York: D. Appleton-Century Co., 1943.

Schmitt, B. E. (ed.). *Poland.* Berkeley: University of California Press, 1945.

Seignobos, M. J. C. *The Evolution of the French People.* Translated by C. A. Phillips. New York: Alfred A. Knopf, Inc., 1932.

Smith, G. *A History of England.* New York: Charles Scribner's Sons, 1949.

Smith, V. A. *The Oxford History of India.* Oxford: The Clarendon Press, 1920.

Snyder, L. L. *German Nationalism: the Tragedy of a People—Extremism contra Liberalism in Modern German History.* Harrisburg: The Stackpole Co., 1952.

Stomberg, A. A. *A History of Sweden.* New York: The Macmillan Co., 1931.

Strauss, E. *Irish Nationalism and British Democracy.* New York: Columbia University Press, 1951.

Taylor, A. J. P. *The Course of German History: a Survey of the Development of Germany since 1815.* New York: Coward-McCann, Inc., 1946.

——. *The Habsburg Monarchy, 1815-1918.* London: Macmillan & Co., Ltd., 1941.

Thomson, S. H. *Czechoslovakia in European History.* Rev. ed. Princeton: Princeton University Press, 1953.

Trevelyan, G. M. *British History in the 19th Century and After (1782-1919).* London: Longmans, Green & Co., 1937.

Valentin, V. *The German People, Their History and Civilization from the Holy Roman Empire to the Third Reich.* New York: Alfred A. Knopf, Inc., 1946.

Vernadsky, G. *A History of Russia.* New ed. New Haven: Yale University Press, 1954.

Wallbank, T. W. *India in the New Era.* Chicago: Scott, Foresman and Company, 1951.

Ward, A. W. *Germany, 1815-1890.* 3 vols. Cambridge: The University Press, 1916-1918.

Wilgus, A. C. *Development of Hispanic America.* New York: Farrar & Rinehart, Inc., 1941.

Williamson, J. A. *A Short History of British Expansion.* 2d ed. New York: The Macmillan Co., 1931.

Wolf, J. B. *France, 1815 to the Present.* New York: Prentice-Hall, Inc., 1940.

Woodward, W. H. *A Short History of the Expansion of the British Empire.* Cambridge: The University Press, 1921.

Wright, C. *Economic History of the United States.* New York: McGraw-Hill Book Co., 1941.

Chapter 1

Allison, J. M. S. *Monsieur Thiers.* New York: W. W. Norton & Co., Inc., 1932.

Artz, F. B. *France under the Bourbon Restoration, 1814-1830.* Cambridge: Harvard University Press, 1931.

——. *Reaction and Revolution (1814-1832).* Rev. ed. New York: Harper & Bros., 1953.

Beveridge, A. J. *The Life of John Marshall.* 4 vols. Boston: Houghton Mifflin Co., 1916-1919.

Brinton, C. *English Political Thought in the Nineteenth Century.* London: Ernest Benn, Ltd., 1933.

——. *The Lives of Talleyrand.* New York: W. W. Norton & Co., Inc., 1936.

Bruun, G. *Europe and the French Imperium: 1799-1814.* New York: Harper & Bros., 1936.

Cresson, W. P. *Diplomatic Portraits; Europe and the Monroe Doctrine One Hundred Years Ago.* Boston: Houghton Mifflin Co., 1923.

——. *The Holy Alliance; the European Background of the Monroe Doctrine.* New York: Oxford University Press, 1922.

Du Coudray, H. *Metternich.* London: Jonathan Cape, Ltd., 1935.

Ferrero, G. *The Reconstruction of Europe; Talleyrand and the Congress of Vienna, 1814-1850.* Translated by T. R. Jaeckel. New York: G. P. Putnam's Sons, 1941.

Gayer, A. D., et al. *The Growth and Fluctuation of the British Economy, 1790-1850.* 2 vols. New York: Oxford University Press, 1953.

Greenfield, K. R. *Economics and Liberalism in the Risorgimento, a Study of Nationalism in Lombardy, 1814-1848.* Baltimore: The Johns Hopkins Press, 1934.

Guedalla, P. *The Duke.* London: Hodder & Stoughton, Ltd., 1931.

Halévy, É. *The Growth of Philosophical Radicalism.* Translated by M. Morris. London: Faber & Gwyer, 1928.

——. *A History of the English People, 1815-1841.* Translated by E. I. Watkins. 3 vols. New York: Peter Smith, 1924-1928.

Hammond, J. L., and Hammond, B. *The Village Laborer, 1760-1832: a Study in the Government of England before the Reform Bill.* New ed. London: Longmans, Green & Co., 1920.

Hayes, C. J. H. *Modern Europe to 1870.* New York: The Macmillan Co., 1953.

James, M. *Andrew Jackson.* Indianapolis: The Bobbs-Merrill Co., 1933.

Knaplund, P. *James Stephen and the British Colonial System, 1813-1847.* Madison: University of Wisconsin Press, 1953.

Laidler, H. W. *A History of Socialist Thought.* New York: Thomas Y. Crowell Co., 1927.

Madariaga, S. de. *Bolivar.* New York: Farrar, Straus, & Young, Inc., 1952.

May, A. J. *The Age of Metternich, 1814-1848.* New York: Henry Holt & Co., Inc., 1933.

Mazour, A. *The First Russian Revolution, 1825; the Decembrist Movement, its Origins, Development and Significance.* Berkeley: University of California Press, 1937.

Nicolson, H. *The Congress of Vienna, a Study in Allied Unity, 1812-1822.* New York: Harcourt, Brace & Co., 1946.

Perkins, D. *Hands Off; a History of the Monroe Doctrine.* Boston: Little, Brown & Co., 1941.

Phillips, W. A. *The Confederation of Europe.* London: Longmans, Green & Co., 1914.

Schlesinger, A. M., Jr. *The Age of Jackson.* Boston: Little, Brown & Co., 1945.

Shine, H. *Carlyle and the Saint-Simonians; the Concept of Historical Periodicity.* Baltimore: The Johns Hopkins Press, 1941.

——. *Carlyle's Early Reading to 1834, with an Introductory Essay on his Intellectual Development.* Lexington: University of Kentucky Libraries, 1953.

Strakhovsky, L. I. *Alexander I of Russia, the Man Who Defeated Napoleon.* New York: W. W. Norton & Co., Inc., 1947.

Taussig, F. W. *The Tariff History of the United States.* 8th ed. New York: G. P. Putnam's Sons, 1931.

Temperley, H. *The Foreign Policy of Canning, 1822-1827.* London: George Bell & Sons, Ltd., 1925.

Thompson, J. M. *Napoleon Bonaparte.* New York: Oxford University Press, 1952.

Turner, F. J. *Rise of the New West, 1819-1829.* New York: Harper & Bros., 1906.

Viereck, P. *Conservatism Revisited; the Revolt Against Revolt, 1815-1949.* New York: Charles Scribner's Sons, 1949.

Webb, W. P. *The Great Plains.* Boston: Ginn & Co., 1931.

Webster, C. K. *The Congress of Vienna, 1814-1815.* London: Oxford University Press, 1919.

——. *The Foreign Policy of Castlereagh.* London: George Bell & Sons, Ltd., 1925.

Woodward, E. L. *The Age of Reform, 1815-1870* (*The Oxford History of England,* Vol. XIII.) Oxford: Oxford University Press, 1938.

Chapter 2

Ashton, T. S. *The Industrial Revolution, 1760-1830.* Oxford: Oxford University Press, 1948.

Barnes, D. G. *A History of the English Corn Laws, from 1660 to 1846.* London: London School of Economics, 1930.

Barr, S. *Mazzini, Portrait of an Exile.* New York: Henry Holt & Co., Inc., 1935.

Barzun, J. *Berlioz and the Romantic Century.* 2 vols. Boston: Little, Brown & Co., 1950.

Blum, J. *Noble Landowners and Agriculture in Austria, 1814-1848: a Study in the Origins of the Peasant Emancipation of 1848.* Baltimore: The Johns Hopkins Press, 1948.

Cecil, A. *Queen Victoria and Her Prime Ministers.* New York: Oxford University Press, 1953.

Clapham, J. H. *The Early Railway Age, 1820-1850. (An Economic History of Modern Britain,* Vol. I.) London: Cambridge University Press, 1926.

Clough, S. B. *France, a History of National Economics, 1789-1939.* New York: Charles Scribner's Sons, 1939.

Dietz, F. C. *The Industrial Revolution.* New York: Henry Holt & Co., Inc., 1927.

Dyboski, R. *Outlines of Polish History.* London: University of London, 1925.

Elton, G. *The Revolutionary Idea in France, 1789-1871.* 2d ed. London: E. Arnold & Co., 1937.

Guérard, A. L. *Napoleon III.* Cambridge: Harvard University Press, 1943.

Hall, W. P., and Beller, E. A. *Historical Readings in Nineteenth Century Thought.* New York: D. Appleton-Century Co., 1928.

Hayes, C. J. H. *The Historical Evolution of Modern Nationalism.* New York: Richard R. Smith, Inc., 1931.

Hearnshaw, F. J. C. (ed.). *The Social and Political Ideas of Some Representative Thinkers of the Age of Reaction and Reconstruction, 1816-1865.* New York: Barnes & Noble, Inc., 1950.

Hook, S. *Towards the Understanding of Karl Marx.* New York: The John Day Co., 1933.

Knowles, L. C. A. *Economic Development in the Nineteenth Century: France, Germany, Russia, and the United States.* London: G. Routledge & Sons, 1932.

Kohn, H. *Pan-Slavism, its History and Ideology.* Notre Dame: University of Notre Dame, 1953.

———. *Prophets and People: Studies in 19th Century Nationalism.* New York: The Macmillan Co., 1946.

Lucas-Dubreton, J. *The Restoration and the July Monarchy.* New York: G. P. Putnam's Sons, 1929.

McKay, D. *The National Workshops: a Study in the French Revolution of 1848.* Cambridge: Harvard University Press, 1933.

May, A. *The Age of Metternich, 1814-1848.* New York: Henry Holt & Co., Inc., 1933.

Muret, C. T. *French Royalist Doctrines since the Revolution.* New York: Columbia University Press, 1933.

Namier, L. B. *1848: the Revolution of the Intellectuals.* Oxford: Oxford University Press, 1946.

New, C. W. *Lord Durham, a Biography.* New York: Oxford University Press, 1929.

Parry, A. *Whistler's Father.* Indianapolis: The Bobbs-Merrill Co., 1939.

Pierson, G. W. *Tocqueville and Beaumont in America.* New York: Oxford University Press, 1938.

Price, A. H. *The Evolution of the Zollverein.* Ann Arbor: University of Michigan Press, 1949.

Robertson, P. *Revolutions of 1848: a Social History.* Princeton: Princeton University Press, 1952.

Schapiro, J. S. *Liberalism and the Challenge of Fascism: Social Forces in England and France, 1815-1870.* New York: The McGraw-Hill Book Co., 1949.

Simpson, F. A. *The Rise of Louis Napoleon, 1808-1848.* New York: Longmans, Green & Co., 1925.

Soltau, R. H. *French Political Thought in the Nineteenth Century.* New Haven: Yale University Press, 1931.

Webster, C. K. *The Foreign Policy of Palmerston, 1830-1841.* 2 vols. London: George Bell & Sons, Ltd., 1951.

Woodward, E. L. *French Revolutions.* Oxford: Oxford University Press, 1934.

Chapter 3

Arendt, H. *The Origins of Totalitarianism.* New York: Harcourt, Brace & Co., 1951.

Barzun, J. *Wagner, Marx, Darwin; Critique of a Heritage.* Boston: Little, Brown & Co., 1941.

Baxter, J. P. *The Introduction of the Iron-clad Warship.* Cambridge: Harvard University Press, 1933.

Binkley, R. C. *Realism and Nationalism, 1852-1871.* New York: Harper & Bros., 1935.

Bourgeois, E. *History of Modern France, 1815-1913.* Vol. II. Cambridge: The University Press, 1922.

Case, L. M. *Franco-Italian Relations, 1860-1865; the Roman Question and the Convention of September.* Philadelphia: University of Pennsylvania Press, 1932.

Clark, C. W. *Franz Joseph and Bismarck: the Diplomacy of Austria before the War of 1866.* Cambridge: Harvard University Press, 1934.

Eyck, E. *Bismarck and the German Empire.* London: George Allen & Unwin, Ltd., 1950.

Gillespie, C. C. *Genesis and Geology, a Study in the Relation of Scientific Thought, Natural Theology, and Social Opinion in Great Britain, 1790-1850.* Cambridge: Harvard University Press, 1951.

Guedalla, P. *The Second Empire.* New York: G. P. Putnam's Sons, 1922.

Headlam, J. W. *Bismarck and the Foundation of the German Empire.* New York: G. P. Putnam's Sons, 1901.

Hearnshaw, F. J. C. (ed.). *The Social and Political Ideas of Some Representative Thinkers of the Victorian Age.* New York: Barnes & Noble, Inc., 1950.

Himmelfarb, G. *Lord Acton, a Study in Conscience and Politics.* Chicago: The University of Chicago Press, 1952.

Jászi, O. *Dissolution of the Habsburg Monarchy; a Failure in Civic Training.* Chicago: The University of Chicago Press, 1929.

Kohn, H. *The Twentieth Century.* New York: The Macmillan Co., 1949.

Lord, R. H. *The Origins of the War of 1870; New Documents from the German Archives.* Cambridge: Harvard University Press, 1924.

Mavor, J. *Economic History of Russia.* 2 vols. Rev. ed. New York: E. P. Dutton & Sons, 1925.

Monypenny, W. F., and Buckle, G. E. *The Life of Benjamin Disraeli, Earl of Beaconsfield.* 6 vols. Rev. ed. New York: The Macmillan Co., 1929.

Oncken, H. *Napoleon III and the Rhine: the Origin of the War of 1870-71.* Translated by E. H. Zeydel. New York: Alfred A. Knopf, Inc., 1928.

Paléologue, M. *Cavour.* New York: Harper & Bros., 1927.

Palm, F. C. *England and Napoleon III: a Study of the Rise of a Utopian Dictator.* Durham: Duke University Press, 1948.

Plamenatz, J. *The Revolutionary Movement in France, 1815-1871.* London: Longmans, Green & Co., 1952.

Postgate, R. W. *Revolution from 1789 to 1906.* Rev. ed. Boston: Houghton Mifflin Co., 1921.

Puryear, V. J. *England, Russia, and the Straits Question, 1844-1856.* Berkeley: University of California Press, 1931.

Riker, T. W. *The Making of Roumania: a Study of an International Problem, 1856-1866.* New York: Oxford University Press, 1931.

Robertson, C. G. *Bismarck.* New York: Barnes & Noble, Inc., 1947.

Robinson, G. T. *Rural Russia under the Old Regime: a History of the Landlord-Peasant World and a Prologue to the Peasant Revolution of 1917.* New York: The Macmillan Co., 1949.

Schmitt, B. E. *England and Germany.* Princeton: Princeton University Press, 1916.

Sencourt, R. *Napoleon III: the Modern Emperor.* New York: D. Appleton-Century Co., 1933.

Seton-Watson, H. *The Decline of Imperial Russia, 1855-1914.* New York: Frederick A. Praeger, Inc., 1952.

Steefel, L. D. *The Schleswig-Holstein Question.* Cambridge: Harvard University Press, 1932.

Thayer, W. R. *The Dawn of Italian Independence.* Boston: Houghton Mifflin Co., 1893.

——. *The Life and Times of Cavour.* 2 vols. Boston: Houghton Mifflin Co., 1914.

Trevelyan, G. M. *Garibaldi and the Thousand.* London: Longmans, Green & Co., 1909.

Wallace, D. M. *Russia.* New York: Henry Holt & Co., 1877.

Woodham-Smith, C. *Florence Nightingale.* New York: The McGraw-Hill Book Co., 1951.

Yarmolinsky, A. *Turgenev: the Man in His Art and His Age.* London: Hodder & Stoughton, 1926.

Chapter 4

Adams, E. D. *Great Britain and the American Civil War.* 2 vols. London: Longmans, Green & Co., 1925.

Bernstein, H. *Modern and Contemporary Latin America.* Philadelphia: J. B. Lippincott Co., 1952.

Billington, R. A. *The Protestant Crusade, 1800-1860.* New York: Rinehart & Co., 1952.

——, and Hedges, J. B. *Westward Expansion, a History of the American Frontier.* New York: The Macmillan Co., 1953.

Brebner, J. B. *North Atlantic Triangle, the Interplay of Canada, the United States, and Great Britain.* New Haven: Yale University Press, 1945.

Buley, R. C. *The Old Northwest: Pioneer Period, 1815-1840.* Bloomington: Indiana University Press, 1951.

Commons, J. R., et al. *History of Labour in the U.S.* Vol. I. New York: The Macmillan Co., 1921.

Craven, A. O. *The Coming of the Civil War.* New York: Charles Scribner's Sons, 1942.

——. *The Growth of Southern Nationalism, 1848-1861.* Baton Rouge: Louisiana State University Press, 1953.

Creighton, D. *John A. MacDonald: the Young Politician.* Boston: Houghton Mifflin Co., 1953.

Dangerfield, G. B. *The Era of Good Feelings.* New York: Harcourt, Brace & Co., 1952.

Davis, H. E. *The Americas in History.* New York: Ronald Press Co., 1953.

Handlin, O. *The Uprooted.* Boston: Little, Brown & Co., 1951.

Hansen, M. L. *The Atlantic Migration: 1607-1860, a History of the Continuing Settlement of the United States.* Cambridge: Harvard University Press, 1940.

Henderson, D. *The Hidden Coasts: a Biography of Admiral Charles Wilkes.* New York: William Sloane Associates, 1953.

Hutchinson, W. T. *Cyrus Hall McCormick.* 2 vols. New York: D. Appleton-Century Co., 1930-1935.

Jordan, D., and Pratt, E. J. *Europe and the American Civil War.* Boston: Houghton Mifflin Co., 1931.

McLemore, R. A. *Franco-American Diplomatic Relations, 1816-1836.* Baton Rouge: Louisiana State University Press, 1941.

Matthiessen, F. O. *American Renaissance.* New York: Oxford University Press, 1941.

Nevins, A. *The Statesmanship of the Civil War.* New York: The Macmillan Co., 1953.

Pierce, B. L. *From Town to City, 1848-1871. (A History of Chicago, Vol. II.)* New York: Alfred A. Knopf, Inc., 1940.

Randall, J. G. *Civil War and Reconstruction.* Boston: D. C. Heath & Co., 1937.

Rippy, J. F. *The United States and Mexico.* Rev. ed. New York: F. S. Crofts Co., 1931.

Sandburg, C. *Abraham Lincoln.* 6 vols. New York: Harcourt, Brace & Co., 1926-1939.

Smith, T. C. *The United States as a Factor in World History.* New York: Henry Holt & Co., Inc., 1941.

Socialism and American Life. 2 vols. Edited by D. D. Egbert and S. Persons. Princeton: Princeton University Press, 1952.

Taylor, G. R. *The Transportation Revolution: Industry, 1815-1816.* New York: Rinehart & Co., 1951.

White, E. B. *American Opinion of France from Lafayette to Poincaré.* New York: Alfred A. Knopf, Inc., 1927.

Williams, H. T. *Lincoln and His Generals.* New York: Alfred A. Knopf, Inc., 1952.

Willson, B. *American Ambassadors to France (1777-1927).* London: John Murray, 1928.

Wilson, W. *Division and Reunion, 1829-1909.* Rev. ed. New York: Longmans, Green & Co., 1912.

Chapter 5

Dulles, F. R. *China and America: the Story of Their Relations since 1784.* Princeton: Princeton University Press, 1946.

Ennis T. E. *Eastern Asia.* Philadelphia: J. B. Lippincott Co., 1948.

———, *French Policy and Developments in Indo-China.* Chicago: The University of Chicago Press, 1936.

Fairbank, J. K. *The United States and China.* Cambridge: Harvard University Press, 1948.

Hazard, H. W., and Cooke, H. L., Jr. *Atlas of Islamic History.* Princeton: Princeton University Press, 1951.

Hoskins, H. L. *British Routes to India.* New York: Longmans, Green & Co., 1928.

Lattimore, O., and Lattimore, E. *China: a Short History.* Rev. ed. New York: W. W. Norton & Co., Inc., 1947.

Lobanov-Rostovsky, A. A. *Russia and Asia.* Ann Arbor: Wahr Publishing Co., 1933.

Owen, D. E. *Imperialism and Nationalism in the Far East.* New York: Henry Holt & Co., Inc., 1929.

Sansom, G. B. *Japan in World History.* New York: Institute of Pacific Relations, 1951.

Treat, P. J. *Japan and the United States, 1853-1921, Revised and Continued to 1928.* Boston: Houghton Mifflin Co., 1928.

Trotter, R. G. *The British Empire-Commonwealth, a Study in Political Evolution.* New York: Henry Holt & Co., Inc., 1932.

Yanaga, C. *Japan since Perry.* New York: The McGraw-Hill Book Co., 1944.

Chapter 6

Beatty, R. C., *et al. The Literature of the South.* Chicago: Scott, Foresman and Company, 1952.

Bismarck, O. von. *Bismarck, the Man and the Statesman.* Translated by A. J. Butler. New York: Harper & Bros., 1899.

Brogan, D. W. *France under the Republic.* New York: Harper & Bros., 1940.

Condit, C. W. *The Rise of the Skyscraper.* Chicago: The University of Chicago Press, 1952.

Croce, B. *A History of Italy, 1871-1915.* Translated by C. M. Ady. Oxford: The Clarendon Press, 1929.

Dawson, W. H. *The German Empire, 1867-1914, and the Unity Movement.* 2 vols, New York: The Macmillan Co., 1919.

Ensor, R. C. K. *England, 1870-1914.* New ed. New York: Oxford University Press, 1949.

Feis, H. *Europe, the World's Banker, 1870-1914: an Account of European Foreign Investments and the Connection of World Finance with Diplomacy Before the War.* New Haven: Yale University Press, 1930.

Gooch, G. P. *History and Historians in the 19th Century.* New ed. New York: Longmans, Green & Co., 1952.

Halperin, S. W. *Italy and the Vatican at War: a Study of Their Relations from the Outbreak of the Franco-Prussian War to the Death of Pius IX.* Chicago: The University of Chicago Press, 1939.

1027

Hayes, C. J. H. *Contemporary Europe since 1870.* New York: The Macmillan Co., 1953.
——. *A Generation of Materialism, 1871-1900.* New York: Harper & Bros., 1941.
Hofstadter, R. *Social Darwinism in American Thought (1860-1915).* Philadelphia: University of Pennsylvania Press, 1944.
Jenks, L. H. *The Migration of British Capital to 1875.* New York: Alfred A. Knopf, Inc., 1938.
Karpovich, M. *Imperial Russia, 1801-1917.* New York: Henry Holt & Co., Inc., 1932.
Langer, W. L. *European Alliances and Alignments 1871-1890.* New York: Alfred A. Knopf, Inc., 1931.
Mason, E. S. *The Paris Commune: an Episode in the History of the Socialist Movement.* New York: The Macmillan Co., 1930.
May, A. J. *The Habsburg Monarchy, 1867-1914.* Cambridge: Harvard University Press, 1951.
Morley, J. *Life of William Ewart Gladstone.* 3 vols. New York: The Macmillan Co., 1903.
Schlesinger, A. M. *The Rise of Modern America, 1865-1951.* New ed. New York: The Macmillan Co., 1951.
Simmons, E. J. *Leo Tolstoy.* Boston: Little, Brown & Co., 1946.
Strachey, L. *Queen Victoria.* New York: Harcourt, Brace & Co., 1921.
Sumner, B. H. *Russia and the Balkans, 1870-1880.* Oxford: The Clarendon Press, 1937.
Thomson, D. *Democracy in France: the Third and Fourth Republic.* 2d ed. New York: Oxford University Press, 1952.

Chapter 7

Acomb, E. M. *The French Laic Laws (1879-1889), the First Anticlerical Campaign of the Third French Republic.* New York: Columbia University Press, 1941.
Adams, H. *The Education of Henry Adams.* Boston: Houghton Mifflin Co., 1927.
Barker, E. *Political Thought in England from Herbert Spencer to the Present Day.* New ed. New York: Oxford University Press, 1947.
Black, C. E. *The Establishment of Constitutional Government in Bulgaria.* Princeton: Princeton University Press, 1944.
Bowers, D. F. (ed.). *Foreign Influences in American Life, Essays and Critical Bibliographies.* Princeton: Princeton University Press, 1944.
Boynton, P. H. *Literature and American Life.* Boston: Ginn & Co., 1936.
Dubos, R. J. *Louis Pasteur, Free Lance of Science.* Boston: Little, Brown & Co., 1950.
Halperin, S. W. *The Separation of Church and State in Italian Thought from Cavour to*

Mussolini. Chicago: The University of Chicago Press, 1937.
Hemmings, F. W. J. *Emile Zola.* Oxford: The Clarendon Press, 1953.
Hoffman, R. J. S. *Great Britain and the German Trade Rivalry, 1875-1914.* Philadelphia: University of Pennsylvania Press, 1933.
Hoskins, H. L. *European Imperialism in Africa.* New York: Henry Holt & Co., Inc., 1930.
Josephson, M. *Zola and His Times: the History of His Martial Career in Letters.* London: Victor Gollancz, Ltd., 1928.
Kaufman, W. A. *Nietzsche: Philosopher, Psychologist, Antichrist.* Princeton: Princeton University Press, 1951.
Massing, P. *Rehearsal for Destruction: a Study of Political Anti-Semitism in Imperial Germany.* New York: Harper & Bros., 1949.
Pease, E. R. *The History of the Fabian Society.* London: A. C. Fifield, 1916.
Pribram, A. F. *England and the International Policy of the European Great Powers, 1871-1914.* Oxford: The Clarendon Press, 1931.
Priestley, H. I. *France Overseas: a Study of Modern Imperialism.* New York: D. Appleton-Century Co., 1939.
Rosenberg, A. *The Birth of the German Republic, 1871-1918.* Translated by I. F. D. Morrow. New York: Oxford University Press, 1931.
Russell, B. *Proposed Roads to Freedom: Socialism, Anarchism, and Syndicalism.* New York: Henry Holt & Co., Inc., 1919.
Saveth, E. N. *American Historians and European Immigrants, 1875-1925.* New York: Columbia University Press, 1948.
Sontag, R. J. *European Diplomatic History (1871-1932).* New York: D. Appleton-Century Co., 1933.
——. *Germany and England: Background of Conflict, 1848-1894.* New York: D. Appleton-Century Co., 1938.
Strachey, L. *Eminent Victorians.* New ed. New York: Modern Library, Inc., 1933.
Sweet, F. A. *Sargent, Whistler, and Mary Cassatt.* Chicago: The Art Institute, 1954.
Townsend, M. E., and Peake, C. H. *European Colonial Expansion since 1871.* Philadelphia: J. B. Lippincott Co., 1941.

Chapter 8

Anderson, P. R. *Background of Anti-English Feeling in Germany, 1890-1902.* Washington: American University Press, 1939.
Bodde, D. *Tolstoy and China.* Princeton: Princeton University Press, 1950.
Brandenburg, E. *From Bismarck to the World War: a History of German Foreign Policy, 1870-1914.* Translated by A. E. Adams. New York: Oxford University Press, 1927.

Bruun, G. *The World in the 20th Century.* Rev. ed. New York: D. C. Heath & Co., 1952.

Bülow, Prince B. von. *Memoirs.* Vol. I, 1897-1903. Translated by F. A. Voigt. Boston: Little, Brown & Co., 1931-1932.

Cameron, M. E., *et al. China, Japan, and the Powers.* New York: Ronald Press Co., 1952.

Churchill, W. S. *The River War; an Historical Account of the Reconquest of the Soudan.* New and rev. ed. London: Longmans, Green & Co., 1902.

Destler, C. M. *American Radicalism 1865-1901, Essays and Documents.* New London: Connecticut College, 1946.

The Dreyfus Case, by the Man—Alfred Dreyfus —and His Son Pierre Dreyfus. Translated and edited by D. C. McKay. New Haven: Yale University Press, 1937.

Faulkner, H. U. *The Decline of Laissez Faire: 1897-1917.* New York: Rinehart & Co., 1951.

Garvin, J. L., and Amery, J. *The Life of Joseph Chamberlain.* 4 vols. London: Macmillan & Co., Ltd., 1932-1951.

Langer, W. L. *The Diplomacy of Imperialism, 1890-1902.* 2d ed. New York: Alfred A. Knopf, Inc., 1951.

Moon, P. T. *Imperialism and World Politics.* New York: The Macmillan Co., 1926.

Muncy, L. W. *The Junker in the Prussian Administration under William II, 1888-1914.* Providence: Brown University, 1944.

Nevins, A. *Grover Cleveland.* New York: Dodd, Mead & Co., 1932.

Nobel, the Man and His Prizes. Edited by the Nobel Foundation. New York and Stockholm: Bonniers, Inc., 1950.

Pratt, J. W. *Expansionists of 1898: the Acquisition of Hawaii and the Spanish Islands.* Baltimore: The Johns Hopkins Press, 1936.

Schmitt, B. E. *Triple Alliance and Triple Entente.* New York: Henry Holt & Co., Inc., 1934.

Townsend, M. E. *The Rise and Fall of Germany's Colonial Empire, 1884-1918.* New York: The Macmillan Co., 1930.

Vucinich, W. S. *Serbia Between East and West: the Events of 1903-1908.* Stanford: Stanford University Press, 1954.

Weinberg, A. K. *Manifest Destiny; a Study of Nationalist Expansion in American History.* Baltimore: The Johns Hopkins Press, 1935.

Wiener, P. P. *Evolution and the Founders of Pragmatism.* Cambridge: Harvard University Press, 1951.

Chapter 9

Albertini, L. *The Origins of the War of 1914.* 2 vols. Rev. and translated by I. M. Massey. New York: Oxford University Press, 1952-1953.

Anderson, E. N. *The First Moroccan Crisis, 1904-1906.* Chicago: The University of Chicago Press, 1930.

Bemis, S. F. *The United States as a World Power, 1900-1950.* New York: Henry Holt & Co., Inc., 1950.

Churchill, R. P. *The Anglo-Russian Convention of 1907.* Cedar Rapids: The Torch Press, 1939.

Cline, H. F. *The United States and Mexico.* Cambridge: Harvard University Press, 1953.

Dubnow, S. M. *History of the Jews in Russia and Poland.* Vol. III. Philadelphia: The Jewish Publication Society of America, 1920.

Dumond, D. L. *America in Our Time, 1896-1946.* New York: Henry Holt & Co., Inc., 1947.

Earle, E. M. *Turkey, the Great Powers, and the Bagdad Railway: a Study in Imperialism.* New York: The Macmillan Co., 1923.

Fay, S. B. *The Origins of the World War.* 2d ed. New York: The Macmillan Co., 1930.

Gooch, G. P. *History of Modern Europe, 1878-1919.* New York: Henry Holt & Co., Inc., 1923.

Hacker, L. M., and Zahler, H. S. *The United States in the 20th Century.* New York: Appleton-Century-Crofts, Inc., 1952.

Link, A. S. *Woodrow Wilson and the Progressive Era.* New York: Harper & Bros., 1953.

Marriott, J. A. R. *The Eastern Question: an Historical Study in European Diplomacy.* 4th ed. New York: Oxford University Press, 1940.

Miller, W. *The Ottoman Empire and Its Successors, 1801-1927, with an Appendix, 1927-1936.* London: Cambridge University Press, 1936.

Nicolson, H. G. *King George the Fifth: His Life and Reign.* Garden City: Doubleday & Co., 1953.

Phillips, C. S. *The Church in France.* 2 vols. New York: The Macmillan Co., 1936.

Riesman, D. *Thorstein Veblen, a Critical Interpretation.* New York: Charles Scribner's Sons, 1953.

Rippy, J. F. *Latin America and the Industrial Age.* New York: G. P. Putnam's Sons, 1944.

Schmitt, B. E. *The Annexation of Bosnia, 1908-1909.* Cambridge: Harvard University Press, 1937.

——. *The Coming of the War, 1914.* 2 vols. New York: Charles Scribner's Sons, 1930.

Staley, E. *War and the Private Investor: a Study in the Relations of International Politics and International Investment.* Chicago: The University of Chicago Press, 1935.

Tannenbaum, F. *Mexico: the Struggle for Peace and Bread.* New York: Alfred A. Knopf, Inc., 1950.

Chapter 10

Baker, R. S. *Woodrow Wilson: Life and Letters.* 7 vols. Garden City: Doubleday, Page & Co., 1927-1929.

Baltzly, A., and Salomone, A. W. (eds.). *Readings in Twentieth-Century European History.* New York: Appleton-Century-Crofts, Inc., 1950.

Benns, F. L. *Europe since 1914.* 8th ed. New York: Appleton-Century-Crofts, Inc., 1954.

Bruun, G. *Clemenceau.* Cambridge: Harvard University Press, 1943.

Chamberlin, W. H. *The Russian Revolution, 1917-1921.* 2 vols. New York: The Macmillan Co., 1935.

Churchill, W. S. *The World Crisis.* 4 vols. 1911-1914. New York: Charles Scribner's Sons, 1923-1929.

Cruttwell, C. R. M. F. *A History of the Great War, 1914-1918.* Oxford: The Clarendon Press, 1934.

Curtiss, J. S. *Church and State in Russia: the Last Years of the Empire, 1900-1917.* New York: Columbia University Press, 1940.

Economic and Social History of the World War. Edited by J. T. Shotwell. About 58 vols. in English, in several series. New York: Carnegie Endowment for International Peace, 1921-1940.

Ergang, R. *Europe in Our Time.* Rev. ed. Boston: D. C. Heath & Co., 1953.

Gatzke, H. W. *Germany's Drive to the West—a Study of Germany's Western War Aims during the First World War.* Baltimore: The Johns Hopkins Press, 1950.

Hayes, C. J. H. *A Brief History of the Great War.* New York: The Macmillan Co., 1921.

———. *France: a Nation of Patriots.* New York: Columbia University Press, 1930.

Langsam, W. C. *The World Since 1914.* 6th ed. New York: The Macmillan Co., 1948.

Lawrence, T. E. *Seven Pillars of Wisdom: a Triumph.* New York: Doubleday & Co., Inc., 1947.

Margutti, A. A. V. *The Emperor Francis Joseph and His Times.* London: Hutchinson & Co., 1921.

May, A. J. *Europe and Two World Wars.* New York: Charles Scribner's Sons, 1947.

Nowak, K. F. *The Collapse of Central Europe.* Translated by P. Lochner and E. W. Dickes. New York: E. P. Dutton & Co., Inc., 1924.

Renouvin, P. *The Immediate Origins of the War (28th June-4th August, 1914).* New Haven: Yale University Press, 1928.

Rudin, H. R. *Armistice, 1918.* New Haven: Yale University Press, 1944.

Seton-Watson, R. W. *Sarajevo, a Study in the Origins of the Great War.* London: Hutchinson & Co., Ltd., 1926.

Thomson, M. *David Lloyd George: the Official Biography.* London: Hutchinson & Co., Ltd., 1948.

Trotsky, L. *The History of the Russian Revolution.* New York: Simon & Schuster, 1937.

Vernadsky, G. *The Russian Revolution, 1917-1931.* New York: Henry Holt & Co., Inc., 1932.

Warth, R. D. *The Allies and the Russian Revolution from the Fall of the Monarchy to the Peace of Brest-Litovsk.* Durham: Duke University Press, 1954.

Willis, I. C. *England's Holy War: a Study of English Liberal Idealism During the Great War.* New York: Alfred A. Knopf, Inc., 1928.

Winkler, H. R. *The League of Nations Movement in Great Britain, 1914-1919.* New Brunswick: Rutgers University Press, 1952.

Wolfe, B. D. *Three Who Made a Revolution: a Biographical History.* New York: Dial Press, Inc., 1948.

Chapter 11

Birdsall, P. *Versailles Twenty Years After.* New York: Reynal & Hitchcock, 1941.

Black, C. E., and Helmreich, E. C. *Twentieth Century Europe: a History.* New York: Alfred A. Knopf, Inc., 1950.

Borgese, G. A. *Goliath: the March of Fascism.* New York: The Viking Press, 1938.

Carr, E. H. *The Bolshevik Revolution, 1917-1923.* New York: The Macmillan Co., 1953.

———. *German-Soviet Relations Between the Two World Wars: 1919-1938.* Baltimore: The Johns Hopkins Press, 1951.

Cobban, A. *National Self-determination.* Chicago: The University of Chicago Press, 1948.

Deutscher, I. *The Prophet Armed: Trotsky: 1879-1921.* New York: Oxford University Press, 1954.

Easum, C. V. *Half-century of Conflict.* New York: Harper & Bros., 1952.

Fischer, L. *The Soviets in World Affairs.* 2 vols. Princeton: Princeton University Press, 1952.

Funk, A. L. *Source Problems in Twentieth Century History.* New York: American Book Co., 1953.

Haskins, C. H., and Lord, R. H. *Some Problems of the Peace Conference.* Cambridge: Harvard University Press, 1922.

Keynes, J. M. *The Economic Consequences of the Peace.* New York: Harcourt, Brace & Howe, 1920.

Knapton, E. J. *France since Versailles.* New York: Henry Holt & Co., Inc., 1952.

Langsam, W. C. *Documents and Readings in the History of Europe since 1918.* New ed. Philadelphia: J. B. Lippincott Co., 1951.

Mantoux, E. *The Carthaginian Peace—or the*

Economic Consequences of Mr. Keynes. New York: Charles Scribner's Sons, 1946.

Nicolson, H. G. *Peacemaking, 1919.* Boston: Houghton Mifflin Co., 1933.

The Russia I Believe In: the Memoirs of Samuel N. Harper, 1902-1941. Edited by P. V. Harper and R. Thompson. Chicago: The University of Chicago Press, 1945.

Salvadori, M. *The Rise of Modern Communism, a Brief History of the Communist Movement in the Twentieth Century.* New York: Henry Holt & Co., Inc., 1952.

Schuman, F. L. *Europe on the Eve: the Crises of Diplomacy, 1933-1939.* New York: Alfred A. Knopf, Inc., 1939.

———. *Soviet Politics at Home and Abroad.* New York: Alfred A. Knopf, Inc., 1946.

Seton-Watson, H. *From Lenin to Malenkov—the History of World Communism.* New York: Frederick A. Praeger, 1953.

Sullivan, M. *The Twenties. (Our Times, The United States, 1900-1925,* Vol. VI.) New York: Charles Scribner's Sons, 1935.

Temperley, H. W. V. (ed.). *A History of the Peace Conference of Paris.* 6 vols. New York: Oxford University Press, 1920-1924.

Welles, S. *An Intelligent American's Guide to the Peace.* New York: The Dryden Press, 1945.

Wish, H. *Society and Thought in Modern America.* New York: Longmans, Green & Co., 1952.

Zimmern, A. E. *The League of Nations and the Rule of Law, 1918-1935.* New York: The Macmillan Co., 1936.

Chapter 12

Albjerg, M. H., and Albjerg, V. L. *Europe from 1914 to the Present.* New York: The McGraw-Hill Book Co., 1951.

Beloff, M. *The Foreign Policy of Soviet Russia, 1929-1941.* 2 vols. New York: Oxford University Press, 1947-1949.

Berge, W. *Cartels, Challenge to a Free World.* Washington: Public Affairs Press, 1944.

Carr, E. H. *The Twenty Years' Crisis, 1919-1939: an Introduction to the Study of International Relations.* 2d ed. New York: St. Martin's Press, Inc., 1946.

Chambers, F. P., et al. *This Age of Conflict.* New York: Harcourt, Brace & Co., 1945.

Cobban, A. *Dictatorship: Its History and Theory.* London: Jonathan Cape, Ltd., 1939.

Current, R. N. *Secretary Stimson: a Study in Statecraft.* New Brunswick: Rutgers University Press, 1954.

Deutscher, I. *Stalin: a Political Biography.* New York: Oxford University Press, 1949.

Finer, H. *Mussolini's Italy.* New York: Henry Holt & Co., Inc., 1935.

Goerlitz, W. *History of the German General Staff, 1657 to 1945.* Translated by B. Battershaw. New York: Frederick A. Praeger, 1953.

Groseclose, E. *Money: the Human Conflict.* Norman: University of Oklahoma Press, 1934.

Halperin, S. W. *Germany Tried Democracy: a Political History of the Reich from 1918 to 1933.* New York: Thomas Y. Crowell Co., 1946.

Harper, S. N., and Thompson, R. *The Government of the Soviet Union.* 2d ed. New York: D. Van Nostrand Co., Inc., 1949.

Heiden, K. *Der Fuehrer: Hitler's Rise to Power.* Boston: Houghton Mifflin Co., 1944.

Hermens, F. A. *The Tyrants' War and the Peoples' Peace.* Chicago: The University of Chicago Press, 1944.

Lichtenberger, H. *The Third Reich.* Translated and edited by K. S. Pinson. New York: The Greystone Press, 1937.

Maynard, J. *Russia in Flux.* New York: The Macmillan Co., 1948.

Olden, R. *Hitler.* Translated by W. Ettinghausen. New York: Covici, Friede, Inc., 1936.

Reischauer, R. K. *Japan, Government—Politics.* New York: Thomas Nelson & Sons, 1939.

Rosenfeld, P. *Musical Chronicle, 1917-1923.* New York: Harcourt, Brace & Co., 1923.

Salvemini, G. *Prelude to World War II.* Garden City: Doubleday and Co., 1954.

Taylor, J. *The Economic Development of Poland: 1919-1950.* Ithaca: Cornell University Press, 1952.

Throm, E. L. (ed.). *Popular Mechanics' Picture History of American Transportation.* New York: Simon and Schuster, Inc., 1952.

Throm, E. L., and Crenshaw, J. *Popular Mechanics' Aviation Album.* Chicago: Popular Mechanics Press, 1953.

Towster, J. *Political Power in the U.S.S.R., 1917-1947; the Theory and Structure of Government in the Soviet State.* New York: Oxford University Press, 1948.

Viereck, P. R. *Metapolitics, from the Romantics to Hitler.* New York: Alfred A. Knopf, Inc., 1941.

Walters, F. P. *A History of the League of Nations.* 2 vols. New York: Oxford University Press, 1952.

Wolfe, M. *The French Franc Between the Wars, 1919-1939.* New York: Columbia University Press, 1951.

Chapter 13

Browder, R. P. *The Origins of Soviet-American Diplomacy.* Princeton: Princeton University Press, 1953.

Christy, A. E. *The Asian Legacy and American Life*. New York: The John Day Co., 1945.

The Diplomats, 1919-1939. Edited by G. A. Craig and F. Gilbert. Princeton: Princeton University Press, 1953.

Ehrmann, H. W. *French Labor from Popular Front to Liberation*. Ithaca: Cornell University Press, 1947.

Esch, P. A. M. van der. *Prelude to War: the International Repercussions of the Spanish Civil War*. The Hague: Martenius Nijhoff, 1951.

Gibb, H. A. R. *Modern Trends in Islam*. Chicago: The University of Chicago Press, 1947.

Grew, J. C. *Turbulent Era, a Diplomatic Record of Forty Years, 1904-1945*. Edited by Walter Johnson. 2 vols. Boston: Houghton Mifflin Co., 1952.

Gulick, C. A. *Austria from Habsburg to Hitler*. 2 vols. Berkeley: University of California Press, 1948.

Johnson, W. *William Allen White's America*. New York: Henry Holt & Co., Inc., 1947.

Langer, W. L., and Gleason, S. E. *The Challenge to Isolation: 1937-1940*. New York: Harper & Bros., 1952.

Majumdar, H. T. *Mahatma Gandhi, Peaceful Revolutionary*. New York: Charles Scribner's Sons, 1952.

Meinecke, F. *The German Catastrophe: Reflections and Recollections*. Translated by S. B. Fay. Cambridge: Harvard University Press, 1950.

Micaud, C. A. *The French Right and Nazi Germany, 1933-1939: a Study of Public Opinion*. Durham: Duke University Press, 1943.

Millis, H. A., and Brown, E. C. *From the Wagner Act to Taft-Hartley*. Chicago: The University of Chicago Press, 1950.

Namier, L. B. *Diplomatic Prelude, 1938-1939*. New York: St. Martin's Press, Inc., 1948.

Roosevelt, F. D. *The Public Papers and Addresses of Franklin D. Roosevelt, 1941-1945*. 4 vols. Edited by S. I. Rosenman. New York: The Macmillan Co., 1950.

Rothfels, H. *The German Opposition to Hitler*. Chicago: Henry Regnery Co., 1948.

Roucek, J. S. *Balkan Politics: International Relations in No Man's Land*. Stanford: Stanford University Press, 1948.

Schwartz, B. I. *Chinese Communism and the Rise of Mao*. Cambridge: Harvard University Press, 1951.

Seton-Watson, H. *Eastern Europe between the Wars, 1918-1941*. New York: The Macmillan Co., 1945.

Sharp, W. R. *The Government of the French Republic*. New York: D. Van Nostrand Co., Inc., 1938.

Sherwood, R. E. *Roosevelt and Hopkins: an Intimate History*. Rev. ed. New York: Harper & Bros., 1950.

Van Alstyne, R. W. *American Crisis Diplomacy: the Quest for Collective Security, 1918-1952*. Stanford: Stanford University Press, 1952.

Werth, A. *The Twilight of France, 1933-1940*. Edited by D. W. Brogan. New York: Harper & Bros., 1942.

Chapter 14

Belot, R. de. *The Struggle for the Mediterranean, 1939-1945*. Translated by J. A. Field, Jr. Princeton: Princeton University Press, 1951.

Brown, F., and Herlin, E. *The War in Maps, an Atlas of The New York Times Maps*. New York: Oxford University Press, 1946.

Bush, V. *Modern Arms and Free Men; a Discussion of the Role of Science in Preserving Democracy*. New York: Simon & Schuster, 1949.

Churchill, W. S. *The Second World War*. 6 vols. Boston: Houghton Mifflin Co., 1948-1954.

Craven, W. F., and Cate, J. L. (eds.). *The Army Air Forces in World War II*. 7 vols. Chicago: The University of Chicago Press, 1948-1953.

Feis, H. *The China Tangle, the American Effort in China from Pearl Harbor to the Marshall Mission*. Princeton: Princeton University Press, 1953.

———. *The Road to Pearl Harbor*. Princeton: Princeton University Press, 1950.

Fisher, H. H. *America and Russia in the World Community*. Claremont, Calif.: Claremont College, 1946.

Historical Division, Department of the Army. *American Forces in Action*. 14 vols. Washington: Government Printing Office, 1943-1947.

Langer, W. L. *Our Vichy Gamble*. New York: Alfred A. Knopf, Inc., 1947.

McInnis, E. *The War*. 6 vols. New York: Oxford University Press, 1940-1946.

McNiell, W. H. *America, Britain, and Russia: Their Co-operation and Conflict, 1941-6*. London: Royal Institute of International Affairs, 1954.

Miller, H. H. *France: Crossroads of a Continent*. New York: Foreign Policy Association, Inc., 1944.

Morison, S. E. *History of United States Naval Operations in World War II*. 8 vols. to date. Boston: Little, Brown & Co., 1947 to date.

The New Yorker Book of War Pieces. New York: Reynal & Hitchcock, 1947.

Office of the Chief of Military History. *United States Army in World War II*. About 20 parts to date. Washington: Government Printing Office, 1947 to date.

O'Neill, H. C. *A Short History of the Second*

World War and Its Social and Political Significance. New York: Frederick A. Praeger, 1950.

Rosinger, L. K. Restless India. New York: Foreign Policy Association, Inc., 1946.

Schmidt, P. Hitler's Interpreter. Edited by R. H. C. Steed. London: William Heineman, Ltd., 1951.

Shugg, R. W., and De Weerd, H. A. World War II, a Concise History. Washington, D.C.: Infantry Journal Press, 1946.

Sontag, R. J., and Beddie, J. S. (eds.). Nazi-Soviet Relations, 1939-1944; Documents from the Archives of German Foreign Office. Washington: Department of State, 1948.

Stettinius, E. Roosevelt and the Russians: the Yalta Conference. Edited by W. Johnson. New York: Doubleday & Co., 1949.

Wilmot, C. The Struggle for Europe: History, World War II. New York: Harper & Bros., 1952.

Young, D. The Desert Fox. New York: Harper & Bros., 1950.

Chapter 15

Beloff, M. Soviet Policy in the Far East, 1944-1951. New York: Oxford University Press, 1953.

Brown, W. N. India, Pakistan, Ceylon. Ithaca: Cornell University Press, 1951.

——. The United States and India and Pakistan. Cambridge: Harvard University Press, 1953.

Crane, R. I., and Stein, B. Aspects of Economic Development in South Asia. New York: Institute of Pacific Relations, 1954.

Dallin, D. J. The New Soviet Empire. New Haven: Yale University Press, 1951.

Dean, V. M. The United States and Russia. Cambridge: Harvard University Press, 1947.

Earle, E. M. (ed.). Modern France: Problems of the Third and Fourth Republics. Princeton: Princeton University Press, 1951.

Einaudi, M., et al. Communism in Western Europe. Ithaca: Cornell University Press, 1951.

Fitzgerald, C. P. Revolution in China. New York: Frederick A. Praeger, 1952.

Goguel-Nyegaard, F. France under the Fourth Republic. Translated by R. Pierce. Ithaca: Cornell University Press, 1952.

Harrison, J. B. This Age of Global Strife. Philadelphia: J. B. Lippincott Co., 1952.

Hughes, S. H. The United States and Italy. Cambridge: Harvard University Press, 1953.

In Quest of Peace and Security, selected documents in American Foreign Policy, 1941-1951. Washington: Dept. of State Publication 4245, 1951.

Knappen, M. And Call It Peace. Chicago: The University of Chicago Press, 1947.

Latourette, K. S. The American Record in the Far East, 1945-1951. New York: The Macmillan Co., 1952.

Lenczowski, G. The Middle East in World Affairs. Ithaca: Cornell University Press, 1952.

Morgenthau, H. J. Politics among Nations. Rev. ed. New York: Alfred A. Knopf, Inc., 1953.

Ogg, F. A., and Zink, H. Modern Foreign Governments. Rev. ed. New York: The Macmillan Co., 1953.

Pickles, D. M. French Politics, the First Years of the Fourth Republic. London: Royal Institute of International Affairs, 1953.

Rosinger, L. K., et al. The State of Asia. New York: Alfred A. Knopf, Inc., 1951.

Schuman, F. L. International Politics, the Western State System in Mid-century. Rev. ed. New York: The McGraw-Hill Book Co., 1953.

Seton-Watson, H. The East European Revolution. London: Methuen & Co., Ltd., 1950.

Taylor, O. R. The Fourth Republic of France, Constitution and Political Parties. London: Royal Institute of International Affairs, 1951.

Vinacke, H. M. The United States and the Far East 1945-1951. Stanford: Stanford University Press, 1952.

Williams, F. Socialist Britain, Its Background, Its Present, and an Estimate of Its Future. New York: The Viking Press, 1949.

Windrich, E. British Labour's Foreign Policy. Stanford: Stanford University Press, 1952.

Wright, G. The Reshaping of French Democracy. New York: Reynal & Hitchcock, 1948.

LIST OF ILLUSTRATIONS

INDEX

Key to Pronunciation

a	hat, cap	ng	long, bring	z	zero, breeze
ā	age, face	o	hot, rock	zh	measure, seizure
ã	care, air	ō	open, go		
ä	father, far	ô	order, all	ə	represents:
b	bad, rob	oi	oil, voice		a in about
ch	child, much	ou	house, out		e in taken
d	did, red	p	paper, cup		i in pencil
e	let, best	r	run, try		o in lemon
ē	equal, see	s	say, yes		u in circus
èr	term, learn	sh	she, rush		
f	fat, if	t	tell, it		
g	go, bag	th	thin, both		FOREIGN SOUNDS
h	he, how	ᵺ	then, smooth	Y	as in French du. Pronounce ē with the lips
i	it, pin	u	cup, butter		rounded as for English ü in **rule.**
ī	ice, five	ù	full, put	œ	as in French peu. Pronounce ā with the lips
j	jam, enjoy	ü	rule, move		rounded as for ō.
k	kind, seek	ū	use, music	N	as in French bon. The N is not pronounced,
l	land, coal	v	very, save		but shows that the vowel before it is nasal.
m	me, am	w	will, woman	H	as in German ach. Pronounce k without
n	no, in	y	you, yet		closing the breath passage.

Abbreviations

c.=chart m.=map p.=picture.
Bold face figures indicate the more important references.

Anson, Admiral George, 264
Anthropology, **458-459**, 462
Antibiotics, 796, 965
Anti-Bolsheviks. See White Russians.
Anticlericalism, **398**
Anti-Comintern Pact, **818-819**, 821-822, 824
Anti-Corn-Law League, 87, 111
Antietam, Battle of, 248-249
Antigua, 875
Anti-Masonic Party, 214
Antirealism, **396-397**
Anti-Semitism, 336, 358, **398-399**, 1003; in France, 436; in Germany, 705; literature of, 462-463; in the United States, 786. See also Dreyfus Affair and Jews.
Anti-Socialist Law, 338, 378
Antonescu, Marshal Ion (än'to nës kü, **yon**), 871
Anzio Beach, 894
Anzus Pact, m. 981
Apologia pro Vita Sua (Newman), **397**
Appomattox Court House, 250
Arab alphabet, 726
Arab League, 958, 960, 961
Arabs, 535, 604, 611-612, **696-699**, 737, 809, **959-962**
Aragon, Louis, 968
Araucanians, 412
Arch of Triumph, 94
Archaeology, 458-459
Archangel, 606
Archipenko, Aleksandr, 974
Architecture, 110, **404**, 480, 543-544, 721-722, 802, **838-840**
Ardennes Forest, 897
Argentina, 59, 72, 342, 501-502, 658, 783; and boundary dispute with Chile, 484; Indian problem in, 411; slavery abolished in, 183; suffrage in, 545; and the Second World War, 900, 982
Arizona, 224
Arkansas, 247, 250
Armament race, 560-561, 569, **707**
Armenia, 505-506, 691
Armenian massacres, 535
Armistice of 1918, 614-615, 624
Arms and the Man (Shaw), 431, 456
Army of the Future, The (De Gaulle), 808
Arnold, Matthew, 161, 162
Arrowsmith (Lewis), 834
Art, 47-48, 110, **396-397**, 969, 1011. See also Classicism, Impressionism, etc., and Literature, Music, and other specific arts.
Artisans' Dwelling Act, 334
"Ash-can school" of painting, 840
Ashbourne Act, 438
Ashburton, Lord, 219
Asia, 302, 303, 307, 367, 422, 716, m. 822-823; Anglo-Russian hostility in, 418; anticolonial revolution in, 632; antiforeignism in, 306; boundary between China and Russia in, 289; and Eastern Europe in 1800's, **19-26**; French

in, 286-289; imperialism in, **61-64**, 263-264, **301-302**, **413-423**, 429; influence on American letters and farming of, **306**; interest of West in culture of, **349-350**, **423**, **824-833**; in interwar period, 793-794; Japan's rise in, 551; nationalism in, **351-356**; Russians in, 22, **63-64**, 275, 286, 289, 290, 292, **293-294**, 298; as threat to West, 490; in First World War, 591-592, 616. See also China, Japan, and other individual countries, and Far East.
Asia Minor, 612, 642
Asiatic Society, 305
Asiatics, 300, 307; discrimination against, 408, 490, 520
Asquith, Herbert, prime minister of England, 537, 582, 725
Association for a United Church for America, 971
Associations Law, 469
Assommoir, L', (Zola), 338
Astor, John Jacob, 221, 343
Astronomy. See Physical sciences.
Ataturk, Mustafa Kemal (ä' tä tʏrk', mûs'tä fä kə mäl'), 631
Atlanta, Sherman's occupation of, 250
Atlantic, battle of the, **879-880**
Atlantic cable, 207
Atlantic Charter, 880, 886
Atlantic Wall, 896
Atomic bombs, 898, **904**, 940, 976
Atomic energy, 889, **962-965**, 967; theory of, 461, 795
Atomic Energy Commission (UN), 963
Attlee, Clement, 861, 903, 932, 933, 951
Auckland, Lord, 296, **297-298**
Auden, W. H., 972
Audubon, John J., 233
Augusta, empress of Germany, 331
Auriol, Vincent (ō ryô, vaɴ sän'), 935
Ausgleich, of 1867 (ous'glīн), 194, **328**
Austin, Moses, 219, 224
Australasia, 296, 307, 367
Australia, 147-149, 281, 307, **519-520**, 538, 643, 658, 883, 901; colonization of, 92, 265-266, 294-295; constitution of, **295**; and danger from European imperialism, 354, 417, 418; as a mandatory, 696; self-government in, **294-295**, 301; trade in, 413; unification of, **421-422**
Australian Colonies Government Act, 295
Austria, 92, 138, 144, 145, 152, 363, 364, 366, 367, 471-472, 564, 611, m. 174-175, m. 191; and Balkan War, 567-568; banking in, 149; Communism in, 688; at Congress of Vienna, 39-41; after Crimean War, 171; effect of 1929 depression on, 746-747; Fascists in, 758; under Ferdinand I, 121; and France, 172, 173-174, 200; and Germany, 9, 187, 432, 440; in war with Germany, 190, 192, **194**, 199; revolts against Habsburgs in, 75; made administrator of Holstein, 188-189; industry in, 197, 372, 374; in war with Italy, 187; and decline of

Channing, William Ellery, 235
Chaplin, Charlie, 720, 752
Charcot, Jean Martin (shär kō′, zhäN mär-taN′), 384
"Charge of the Light Brigade" (Tennyson), 152
Charivari, Le, 94
Charles I, emperor of Austria, 598
Charles IV, king of Hungary. See Charles I.
Charles X, king of France, 49, 65, 73, p. 64
Charles XIV, king of Sweden, 123
Charles Albert, king of Sardinia, 68, 122, 127, 133, 134, 137
Charleston, S.C., 227, 245
Charter Oath of 1869 (Japan), 352-353
Chartist movement, 89, 129, 194, 209, p. 130
Château-Thierry, 610
Chateaubriand, François René de (shä tō brē-äN′ frän swä′ rə nā′ də), 50-51
Châtiments, Les (Hugo), 164
Chavannes, Édouard (shä vän′, ā dwär′), 515
Chávez, Carlos, 838
Chekhov, Anton, 455, 541
Chelmsford, Lord, viceroy of India, 617
Chemistry, 156, 341, 374, 384
Cherokees, 213
Cherry Orchard (Chekhov), 455
Chevalier, Guillaume Sulpice (shə vä lyā′, gē yōm′ sYl pēs′), 98
Chevalier, Michel (shə vä lyā′, mē shel′), 178
Cheyney, Edward P., 790
Chiang Kai-shek, 741-742, 743, 770, 773, 829, 831-832, 882, 901, 945, 948
Chiang Kai-shek, Madame, 773
Chicago, 341, 344, 375, 543; fire (1871), 404
Chicago Daily Tribune, 883
Chicago Exposition of 1893. See World's Columbian Exposition.
Child labor, 228
Chile, 342, 411, 412, 484, 653, 783
China, 267, 289, 300, 367, 515, 912, p. 270; Boxer Rebellion in, 512-513; and British, 62, 267, 268, 269, 271-272, 274, 293; Chiang Kai-shek and, 741-742; civil war in, 292-293, 601; Communism in, 742-743; "dollar diplomacy" in, 547; in the Franco-Chinese War of 1884, 414, p. 415; and Japan, 283, 354, 414, 416, 487, 488-489, 645; and Korea, 356; under the Manchu dynasty, 277, 278, 279, 289, 290, 292, 355; and Manchuria, 552, 743-746; Middle Kingdom in, 269, 271; opening of, 268-281, 284, 306, m. 272 and m. 778; at Paris Conference, 643-644; partition of, 489-494, m. 492; "Popular Front" in, 829; reform in, 512-513, 554-555; Republic of, 555, 742; revolution in, 554-556; and Russia, 289, 290, 291-292, 294, 422, 662, 945-946; Second Western War in, 274-275, 287, 291; in Siberia, 644; Taiping Rebellion in, 272; in Tibet, 420, 518, 563; and Tientsin treaties of 1858, 275-277, 291; and Treaty of Nanking, 272, 288; and Treaty of Portsmouth, 524-525; at war with Japan (1932), 764-765,

767-768; (1937-1938), 830-833; at Washington Conference, 646, 647-649; early relations of, with West, 20, 21; in the First World War, 592, 597, 600-602, 616. See also Communism, Communist China, and Kuomintang.
China (von Richthofen), 422
"China Incident, the," 830-831
Chinese Dictionary (Morrison), 302
Chinese Eastern Railway, 743-745
Chinese Exclusion Act, 408, 475-476
"Chinese" Gordon. See Charles George Gordon.
Chinese Passenger Act, 280
Chinese Soviet Republic, 770-774. See also Communist China.
Ch'ing dynasty, 554, 555. See also Manchu dynasty.
Chinkiang, 271
Chocolate Soldier, The (Straus), 431
Chopin, Frédéric François, 53, 96, 100, 104
Chosen. See Korea.
Choshu, 416
Christ of the Andes, 484
Christian Doctrines (Strauss), 103
Christian Socialist movement, 108
Christianity, 272, 279, 287-288, 300, 513, 535, 558, 1002-1003
Christina of Naples, queen-regent of Spain, 123
Chronicle of the Great War (Barrès), 624
Chrysler Building, 721
Chungking government, 832-833
Church of England, 90-91, 195, 473
Church, Protestant. See Protestant churches.
Church, Roman Catholic, 5, 91, 286, 397-398, 453-454, 455, 469, 757, 969-970, 971, 1003. Bismarck's attack upon in Kulturkampf, 330; in Britain, 71; and Crimean War, 151; France as protectors of, in Asia, 286; in French North America, 15; in French politics, 327; influence on French literature, 50; in Italy, 729-730; Leo XIII and the French Ralliement, 436-437; loss of recognition as state religion in France, 74; missionary activity in the Orient, 303; in New Spain, 14; in the Philippines, 353-354; in Poland, churches and monasteries destroyed, 185; in Spain, 760; temporary disestablishment of by the French Revolution, 11; ultramontanism, 96; and the unification of Italy, 176-177. See also Catholics and Religion.
Church and state, problem of: in Europe in the 1850's, 144; in France, 540; in Italy, 729-731; separation of, 470; in Spain, 760
Church of the Sacred Heart (Paris), 327
Churchill, Winston, 808, 861, 864, 866, 879, 880, 892, 894, 895, 901, 903, 932, 933, 944, 976, 982, p. 978
Chusan archipelago, 271
Ciano, Count Galeazzo (chä′ nō, gä′lä ät′ sō), 893
"Citizen Army" (Irish), 597
Civil Rights Bill, 322

1043

Civilian Conservation Corps, 779
Civilization and Its Discontents (Freud), **798**
Classicism, 50, 391, 542
Claudel, Paul, 457
Clausewitz, General Karl von, 906
Clay, Henry, 71, 212, 214, 217, 218, 221, **224**; and Compromise of 1850, 241
Clayton Anti-Trust Act, 549
Clemenceau, Georges (kla mäN sō′, zhôrzh), premier of France, 429, 430, 634, *p.* 635
Clemens, Samuel Langhorn. *See* Mark Twain.
Clericalism, **327**, 331
Cleveland, Grover, 340, 400, 495-496
Cloister and the Hearth, The (Reade), 161
Clotilda, Princess, 172
Coal, **372-373**, 374, 726
Coal and Steel Community, 980, 982. *See also* Schuman Plan.
Cobbett, William, 48, 209
Cobden, Richard, 111, 178, 251
Cobden-Chevalier Treaty, **178**
Cochin China, 286, 288, 289, 355
Cocteau, Jean, 972
Co-hong, 268-269
"Cold war," **957-959, 974-984,** 1006
Coleridge, Samuel Taylor, 47, 235
Collective security policy, **806-807**
Collectivization, 727-728, 761, 945
Collège de France, 305
Collier's, 480
Cologne zone, 709-710
Colombia, 72, 501
Colombo Plan, 983
"Colonel Blimp" (Low), 804
Colonial Conference, 439
Colonialism: Soviet opposition to, **668**; Wakefield's theories of, 265-266; after the First World War, 616, 666-667; collapse of after the Second World War, **949-962**
Colonization, 13-16, 297
Colt, Samuel, 213
Columbia River, 221
Columbia University, 227
Combes, Émile (kôNb, ā mēl′), 469-470
Combination Acts, 71
Cominform, 944
Commentaries on the Law of England (Blackstone), 207
Commerce, 284-285, 288, **409.** *See also* Trade.
Common Law, The (Holmes), 406
Commune of Paris, 115, 203, 326, 338, 339, 379
Communications: in Britain, 87-89; Indian, 300; revolution in, **718;** telegraphic, 180-181; wireless, 385
Communism, 146, 603, 606, 619, **687-691,** 716, 787, *m.* 762; appeal to intellectuals of, 968; in Asia, 668, **742-743,** 827, **941-949;** in Austria, 688; Catholic response to, **969-970;** in China, 661-662, 770-774, 829; in Czechoslovakia, 983; defenses against, 982-983, *m.* 980, *m.* 981; in East Indies, 828; in France,

193, 197, 203, 379, 725, 936; in Germany, 196, 633, 640, 680, 687-688, 703, 705, 711, 723, 752, 755; in Hungary, 684, 688; in India, 954; in Indochina, 956; in Iran, 959; in Italy, 677-678, 917, 918; in Latin America, 783; in Siam, 775; in Siberia, 644-655; in Spain, 814; in the United States, 231-232, 655, 658, 722, **786,** 833, 874; after the Second World War, **895, 944, 976, 985,** 992-993, **997-998,** 1007, 1016. *See also* Bolshevism.
Communist China, **945-948,** 984-985
Communist International, 662
Communist League, 116
Communist Manifesto (Marx and Engels), 115-116, 129, 131, 159
Communist Party (in Russia), 670, 690, 726-728, 755, **806-807,** 942
Comparative Grammar of Indo-German Languages (Brugmann), 349
Compiègne, forest of, 614, 685
"Complaint of Job, The" (Blake), *p.* 48
Compromise of 1850, **241-242,** 244
Compton, Arthur H., 796
Comte, Auguste (kōNt, ō gvst′), 114
Concentration camps, **887**
Concert of Europe, 45, 52, 54, 59, 67, 108, 153, 204, 258, 571, 588. *See also* Vienna, Congress of, *etc.*
"Concord Group," 235-236
Concordat: of 1801, 470, 540; of 1851, 760
Conditions of the Working Class in England (Engels), 116
Confederate States of America, **245-246,** 247-248, **249,** 254-256, *m.* 254
Confederation of the Rhine, 33, 41
Confucianism, 460
Congo basin, 346, 425, 426
Congo Free State, 426
Congress of Industrial Organization, 782, 841-842
"Congress system." *See* Concert of Europe.
Coningsby (Disraeli), 108
Connecticut Yankee at King Arthur's Court, A (Twain), 402
Conrad von Hötzendorf, Count, 577, 578
Conrad, Joseph, 456, 581
Conservatism: clerical influence on, **144;** in France, 50-51; in the United States, 722
Conservative Party in Canada, 783; in England, 195, 333, 438, 861, 933 (*see also* Tory Party); in Germany, 337, 382, 532-534; in Mexico, 252; in Spain, 123
Constable, John, 47
Constant, Benjamin, 73
Constantine, grand duke of Russia, 66, 433
Constantine, king of Greece, 604
Constantinople, 362-363, 432, 566, 567, 568, 593, 642, 686. *See also* Istanbul.
Constitution Act of 1852 (New Zealand), 296
Constitution (Japanese), 415
Constitution of 1812 (Spain), 54, 55, 58
Constitution of 1850 (Prussia), 145

1046

1832, 194-195; "splendid isolation" of, 427; degree of guilt for the First World War, 587-588. *See also* Great Britain *and* United Kingdom.

English Channel, 609, 894
English language, 297, 538
Enim Pasha, 347
Enlightenment, the, 8-9, 31, **47**
Entente Cordiale, 92, 108, 123, **521-522**, **565**, 569
Epirus, 359
Episcopalian Church of America, 91
Epstein, Jacob, 974
Erfurt parliament, 138
Erfurt Program, 470
Erickson, Captain John, *p.* 249
Erie Canal, 229
Eritrea, 425, 871, 916
Ernest Augustus, king of Hanover, 91, 119
Essay on the Inequality of the Human Races (Gobineau), 399
Estates General, 10
Esterhazy, Count Marie Charles Walsin-, 467, 468
Estheticism, **395-396**
Estonia, 606, 691, 814, 858, 943
Ethiopia, 426, 506, **811-812**, 871, 916, **985**. *See also* Abyssinia.
Eugene Onegin (Pushkin), 106
Eugenics, 158
Eugénie, empress of France, 148
European Defense Community, 956, 982
European Recovery Program, 977-979
Evans, Mary Ann. *See* George Eliot.
Evans, Powys, *p.* 835
Evening Post (New York), 234
Everybody's, 480
Evolution, theory of, 157-158, 265, 405-407. *See also* Darwinism.
Exchange, The (Claudel), 457
Existence and the Existent (Maritain), 969
Existentialism, 968-969
Existentialism (Sartre), 969
Expansion of England, The (Seeley), 346
Experience and Nature (Dewey), 836
Experiments and Observations on the Gastric Juice and the Physiology of Digestion (Beaumont), 234
Explosives, 341, 384, 541. *See also* Atomic bombs.
"Expressionism," 542
Extraterritoriality, **272**, 277, 285, 291, 648, 775
Eyeless in Gaza (Huxley), 825

F

Fabian Society, **379-380**, 454-455
"Fable for Critics, A" (Lowell), 236
Facta, Luigi, prime minister of Italy, 678
Factory Act: of 1833, 86; of 1874, 112, 334
Fair Deal, 940
Fair Labor Standards Act of 1938, 841
1048 Falkenhayn, Erich von (fäl′kən hīn, ā′riн fən),

German chief of staff, 595
Falkland Islands, Battle of the, **591**
Falla, Manuel de, 804
Falloux, Vicomte de (fä lü′), 145
Falstaff (Verdi), 391
Fantastic Symphony (Berlioz), 99
Far East, the, 281, **351-356**, **763-776**, *m.* 152; balance of power in, 607, 644; British policy in, 93, 649; "dollar diplomacy" and, 554; relations of, with Europeans, 263-264; French policy in, 286-289; influence of, on Europe and America, **302-306**, 632, **967-968**; Japanese position in, 306; Russian aggression in, 289-291; on eve of the First World War, **551-560**; post-First World War structure of, 646-649; Yalta agreements on, 898. *See also* Orient, China, Japan, *and other individual countries.*
"Far Eastern Republic," **644-645**, 740. *See also* Siberia.
Faraday, Michael, 110, 155, 385
Farben, I. G. *See* Interessengemeinschaft Farbenindustrie.
Farewell to Arms (Hemingway), 833-834
Faroe Islands, 874
Farouk, king of Egypt, 810, 961
Farmers' Alliances, **409**, 477
Farrell, James T., 837
Fascism, 146, 204, 457, 670, 675, 676-679, **814**; 993, 1017, *m.* 823, 910; compared with Bolshevism, 730; in Italy, 728; in Latin America, 783, 982; in southeastern Europe, 758; in Spain, **813-814**; in the United States, **785-786**, 833
Fascisti Exposed, The (Matteotti), 679
Fashoda Incident, 509-510
Fast, Howard, 968
Fathers and Sons (Turgenev), 168-169
Faulkner, William, 833, 834, 972
Faure, Félix (fōr, fä lēks′), president of France, 467
Faust (Gounod), 167
Fauves, 542
February Patent of 1861, 179, 194
Fechner, Gustav, 156
Federal Bureau of Investigation, 972
Federal Farm Board, 722
Federal Farm Loan Act, 549
Federal Reserve Act of 1913, 549
Federal Trade Commission, 549, 653
Feisal (fī′səl): as king of Iraq, 697, 698, 737, 809; as king of Syria, 698
"Fellow travelers," 688, 786, 943
Feme, the, 701
Fenian Movement, 195, 318, 359, *m.* 319
Ferdinand, prince of Saxe-Coburg, 431
Ferdinand, prince (czar) of Bulgaria, 564
Ferdinand I, emperor of Austria, 103, 105, 121, 126, 134
Ferdinand II, king of Naples, 133, 137
Ferdinand VII, king of Spain, 54, 55, 58, 59, 123
Fermi, Enrico, 795, 840

1056

O

Oberlin Collegiate Institute (Ohio), 232
Obregon, General Alvaro, president of Mexico, 658
O'Casey, Sean, 798
Oceania, 61, **264-268**, 289, 302, 306-307, 354, 367, 417, 666-667, 716, 901, 950
October Diploma (Austria), 179
October Manifesto (Russia), 465-466, 531
Octopus, The (Norris), 481
"Ode to Liberty" (Shelley), 55
Of Time and the River (Wolfe), 837
Offenbach, Jacques, 167
O'Flaherty, Liam, 798
Ogdenburg Agreement, 900
"Oh! Susanna" (Foster), 207, 237
Okhotsk, 290
Ohio, 228
Oil for the Lamps of China (Hobart), 825
O'Keeffe, Georgia, 840
Okinawa, Battle of, 901
"Old Black Joe" (Foster), 257
Olney, Richard, 495
Olympic games, 510
Omar Khayyám, 170
Omdurman, Battle of, 509
Omnibus Bill, 241
Omoo (Melville), 306
On Liberty (Mill), 159
On the Criticism of Political Economy (Marx), 159
"On the Death of the Poet" (Lermontov), 106
On the Origin of Species by Means of Natural Selection (Darwin), 157, 159
On War (Clausewitz), 906
"One World," concept of, 1015-1016
O'Neill, Eugene, 833, 834
Ontario, 318
"Open door" policy, 272, 293, 494, 499, **504**, 514, 647
Opera. *See* Music.
Opéra, L' (Paris), 167
Opium, 269-271
"Opium War," 271-272, 274, 292, *p. 282*
Optatissima pax (Pius XII), 969-970
Oran, Battle of, 865
Orange Free State, 347, 426, 511, 538
Ordeal of Richard Feverel, The (Meredith), 161
Ordinance of Nullification, 212
Oregon, **220-223**, 317
Oregon (battleship), 500
Organization for European Economic Cooperation (OEEC), 977-979
Organization of American States, **982-983**
Organization of Labor (Blanc), 95, 130
Orientalism, **345-351**
Orient, the, **281-282**, 288, 289, 303-304, **305-306**, **349-350**, 458-460. *See also* the Far East.
Origins of Contemporary France, The (Taine), 385

Orlando, Victor Emanuele, premier of Italy, 634
Orléans, house of, 326, 430. *See also* France.
Orozco, José, 973
Orthodox Church (Russian), 434, 763
Oscar I, king of Sweden, 123
Otello (Verdi), 391
Ottoman Empire, 22-25, 55, 151, 153, 289, 293, 298, 362, 427, 505, 535-536, 604, 609, 641, 643, *m.* 67. *See also* Turkey.
Oudh, 300
Outer Mongolia, 552, 601, 946
Outline of History (Wells), 797, 824
Overland Monthly, 496
Overseas (Bourget), 457-458
Overture 1812 (Tchaikovsky), 170
Owen, Robert, 48, 65, 89, 231-232
Owen, Wilfred, 623
Owenites, 115, 231-232
Oxford Movement, **90-91**
Oxford University, 90
Ozanam, Antoine Frédéric, 95-96

P

Pacific Islands, Trust Territory of, 950
Pacific Ocean, 268, 289, 290, 303-304, 421, *m.* 283; annexations of islands of, 305, **354**; British Empire in, 301-302; European imperialism in, 417-418; exploration in, 266-267; Russo-American relations in, **293-294**; Second World War in, **883-884**
Pacifists, 817
Paderewski, Ignace Jan (pä'de ref'skē, ē nyäs' yän), 686
Paganini, Nicolò, 53, 99
Pagliacci, I (Leoncavallo), 392
Pagopago, 354, 413, 499
Pahlavi. *See* Reza Shah Pahlaví.
Painting, **305-306**, **389-390**, 403-404, 459-460, 480, 542-543, **802-804**, 840, **972-973**, 1011. *See also* Art; Impressionism, Realism, *etc.*; and Picasso, Whistler, *and names of other artists.*
Pakistan, 828, 951-953
Palacky, Frantisek, 121, 129, 171
Palau Islands, 827
Palestine, 151, 612, **695-698**, 737, **755-757**, 809, 956, **959-960**
Palmer raids, 656-657
Palmerston, Lord, prime minister of England, 194, 298
Pan-American Conferences: of 1889, 412; of 1901, 484; of 1906, 502; of 1910, 544; of 1923 and 1928, 738; of 1933, 758; of 1936, 844
Pan American Union, 412, 484, 738
Pan-Americanism, 72, **412-413**, 544
Panama, 413, 500-501, 600, 738, 785
Panama Canal, 411, 500-501, 547, 550, 559, 659
Panama Canal Zone, 544
Panama scandal, **436**, 466
Pan-Arab Congress, 809

Picasso, Pablo, 542, 802, 968, 973
Picquart, Colonel Georges (pē kär', zhôrzh), 467
Picture of Dorian Gray, The (Wilde), 396
Piedmont, 56, 133, 172-173, 175-178. *See also* Sardinia.
Pierce, Franklin, 242
Pig War, 562
Pilsudski, General Joseph, 686, 845
Pinkerton Detective Agency, 476
Pirandello, Luigi, 801
Pishevari, Jaafar, 959
Pissaro, Camille, 166, 389, *p.* 350
Piston, Walter, 838
Pit, The (Norris), 481
Pitt, William, 268
Pittsburgh, 211, 230, 340, 344
Pius VII, pope, 44
Pius IX, pope, 122, 127, 133, 137, 145, 197-198, 328, 329, 331, 398
Pius XI, pope, 453-455, 469, **729-730,** 814
Pius XII, pope, 814, 970
Planck, Max, 461
Planned economy, 727-728, 749-750, **761**
Plantation system, 321
Plastics, 717, **721,** 806. *See also* Synthetics.
Platt Amendment, 499, 785
Plekhanov, Georgi V., 435, 464
Plombières meetings, 172-173
Plough and the Stars, The (O'Casey), 798
Pobyedonostzev, Konstantin Petrovich (pô byə də nôs'tsəf, kôn stän tēn' pə trô'vich), **434,** 463, 465
Poe, Edgar Allan, 166, 235
Poetry, **165-166,** 235, 403, **835-836,** 972. *See also* Literature.
Poetry: A Magazine of Verse, 835
Poincaré, Raymond, president of France, **578,** 699, 702, 705, 725, 789, *p.* 726
Point Four, **983**
Poison gas, 592, 605, 812
Poland, **24-25,** 185-186, 199, 253-254, 375, 381, 383, 606, 609, 612, 620; and Congress of Vienna settlements, 42-43, 74-75, 121, *m.* 75; and Locarno agreements, 710-711; after First World War, 637, 640, 686, 688, 691; in Second World War, 820, **821-823, 856-858, 889,** 898, *m.* 857; after Second World War, 903-904, 919, 943, 944
Poles, 185, 357, 532, 685
Polish Corridor, 637, 821, 822
Political Economy (Mill), 109
Politics (Dahlmann), 101
Polk, James K., 221, **223-224**
Polynesian Islands, 266-267
Poor Law of 1834, 86-87
Poor White (Anderson), 834
Pope, John, 840
Popolo d'Italia, 676
Popular Fronts, 806-808, **813,** 820, **829**
"Popular sovereignty" principle, **242**
Populist Party, 409, 477, 480

Porgy and Bess (Gershwin), 838, 974
Port Arthur, 491-493
Port Said naval base, 810
Porte, The, 23, 56
Porter Proposition, 502
Portsmouth, Treaty of, 524-525
Portugal, 55, 58, 92-93, 280-281, **759, 814, 412,** 426, 596, 646, *p.* 376
Posen, 637
Posen revolt, 135
Positive philosophy. *See* Auguste Comte.
Post, Wiley, 805-806
Post-impressionism, 396
Postal Union, 181
Potemkin (battleship), 465
Potsdam Conference, **902-904,** 919, 924, 949
Pound, Ezra, 826, 833, 836
Pragmatism, **405-406,** 836
Pragmatism: A New Name for Some Old Ways of Thinking (James), 406
Prague, Treaty of, 360
Prajadhipok, king of Siam, 775
Pre-Raphaelites, 161, **162-164,** 166
Prescott, William H., 236
Prevention of Crimes Act (Britain), 437
Prim, General Juan, 329
Prince Edward Island, 319
Principles of Geology (Lyell), 157
Principles of Psychology (James), 406
Printing, 374-375, 717
Profit sharing, 655
Progress and Poverty (George), 379, 407
Progressive Party. *See* Bull Moose Party.
Progressivism (U.S., 1912), 548
Prohibition, 659, 780
Prokofiev, Sergei S., 804, 967
Proletarian revolutions, 618. *See also* Russian Revolution
Protestant churches, 5, 71, 303, 455, 498, **970-971,** 1002
Proudhon, Pierre Joseph, 115, 197
Prussia, **52,** 92, 101-103, 119-120, 138, 144, **145,** 152, 174, 178, 196, 330, 366, 382, 440, 532-534, 613, 681, 753, *m.* 191, *p.* 202; attitude toward American Civil War, 185, 252; in Franco-Prussian War, **199,** 200-202; and German unification, 186-187, 358, 441; in Prussian-Danish War, 135, 188-189; Revolution of 1848 in, 129, 134-136; in Seven Weeks' War, 190, 192, 194; and Treaty of Versailles, 637
Psychiatry, 384, 462
Psychology, 156, 384, 837, **971,** 1010-1011
Pu Yi, Henry, 555, 768
Public school system (U.S.), 232-233
Puccini, Giacomo (püt chē'nē, jä'kō mō), **392,** 826
Puerto Rico, 497, 950
Pugin, A. W. N., 163
Pulitzer, Joseph, 496
Pullman strike, 476
Punch, 108

Pure Food and Drugs Act, 545
Pure in Heart, The (Werfel), 800
Pushkin, Alexander (push′kin), 66, 105, 106
Putiatin, Count, 291

Q

Quadragesimo Anno (Pius XI), 814
Quadruple Alliance, **44-45**, 51
Quanta Cura, 197-198
Quebec meetings (1943), 894
Queensland, 519
Quintuple Alliance, 51, 55, 56, **67-68**
Quisling, Major Vidkun, 818, 860

R

Rachmaninov, Sergei, 804
Radar, 869, 889, **965-966**
Radetzky, Count Joseph, 125, 133
Radio, 385, 717, 718
Raemaekers, Louis, *p.* 584
Railroads, 101, 106, 150, 299, 317, 328, 334,
    p. 335; in Europe, 112, 149, **334-335**, 375; in
    France, 112, 147, *p.* 148; in Great Britain, 87,
    112; in the United States, 214, 230, 281, 320,
    339-340, 344, 351-352, 409
Ralliement, **436-437**
Rama IV, king of Siam, 288
Ranke, Leopold von, 5, 69, 103, 109
Rapallo, Treaty of, 691, **640-641**, 703
Rarahu (Loti), 423
Rasin, Alois, 706
Rasputin, Grigori, 532, 603
Rathenau, Emil, 374
Rationalism, 8-9, 383
"Rationalization" of business and industry, **999**
Ravel, Maurice, 804
Rayon, 622, 721
Reade, Charles, 161
Realism, in science and arts, 98-99, **160, 164-
    166, 168-169, 383-399, 407,** 455-457, 458,
    478-479
Realpolitik, 139, **186-187,** 198, 204, 316, 441,
    m. 428
"Recessional" (Kipling), 519
Reciprocal Trade Agreements Act (1934), 785
Reciprocity Treaty of 1854 (U.S.-Canada), 318
Reconstruction (of the South), 257, 321-323
Reconstruction Finance Corporation (U.S.), 777,
    780
Reconstruction in Philosophy (Dewey), 836
Red and the Black, The (Stendhal), 98
Red Cross. *See* International Red Cross.
Red River Rebellion, 343, *m.* 319
"Red Shirts" (Garibaldi's), 176-177
Redistribution Bill of 1885 (Britain), 437
Reed, Walter, 550
Reed, William B., 275
Reflections on Violence (Sorel), 539
Reform Bill: of 1832, 77, 86, 89, 195, 209; of
    1867, 195
1066 Reformation, 7, 9, 17

Réforme, La (newspaper), **114, 118**
Refugees, political, 805
Regamy, Felix, *p.* 201
Reichsbank, 336
Reichstag building fire, 755
Reinach, Baron Jacques de, 436
Reinhardt, Max, 451, 541
Reinsurance Treaty, **426-433, 440,** *m.* 428
Religion, 455, 763. *See also* Church and state;
    and names of churches
"Relocation camps," 883
Remarque, Erich Maria, 800
Renan, Ernest, 165, 170
Renner, Karl, 683, 924
Renoir, Pierre Auguste (rə nwär′, pyär ō gyst′),
    350, 389
Reparations, 636, **638-640,** 658, 699-702, 738-
    739, 747-748, **749**
Report on the Affairs of British North America
    (Durham), 92
Representation of the People Act (Britain,
    1928), 725
Republic Steel Corporation, 842
Republican Party (U.S.), 214, 244, 249, 256,
    322, 400, 410, 480, 650, 949, *p.* 130; formation
    of, 242-243; in election of 1912, 548; of 1928,
    722; of 1940, 875-876; of 1948, 939; of 1952,
    940-941
Republicanism, **58-61,** 145, 193, **327,** 329
Rerum novarum (Leo XIII), 453-454
Resistance movements, **887-888,** 894
Retour de l'U.R.S.S. (Gide), 800
Return to Life (Berlioz), 99
Reuter, Julius, 89
Revolution, tradition of, **9-10,** 85. *See also*
    French Revolution, *etc.*
Rexists, 789, 814
Reza Shah Pahlavi (Iran), 879
Rhapsody in Blue (Gershwin), 838
Rheims, 899
Rheinisch-Westfälisches Kohlensyndikat, 452
Rhineland, 638, 705, 739
Rhode Island, 209, 232
Rhodes, Cecil, 506-507
Ribbentrop, Joachim von, 877, 920
Richardson, Henry Hobson, 404, 840
Richer by Asia (Taylor), 968
Richmond, Va., 248, 250, *p.* 257
Richthofen, Baron Ferdinand von, 422, 490
Riddle of the Universe, The (Haeckel), 455
Riel, Louis, 343
Righteous Harmony Fists. *See* Boxer Rebellion
Rigoletto (Verdi), 170
Rig-Veda, 303
Riis, Jacob August (rēs, yä′kôp ou′gùst), 478
Rilke, Rainer Maria (ril′kə, rī′nər mä re′ä),
    799-800
Rimbaud, Arthur (raN bō′, är tyr′), 395
Rimsky-Korsakoff, Nicholas, 169
Ring and the Book, The (Browning), 161
Rio Pact, *m.* 981

Ripon, Lord, 418
Risorgimento, the, 122-123
Rivera, Diego, 968, 973
Rivera, General Miguel Primo de, 687
Robert le Diable (Meyerbeer), 99
Roberts, Lord, 511
Robinson, Edward Arlington, 836
Rochdale Society, 112-113, 452
Rockefeller, John D., 400, 441, 482, **544**
Rockefeller, John D., Jr., 914
Rockefeller Center, 778, 838
Rockhill, W. W., 422
Rodin, Auguste, 390-391, 441, 799, *p.* 390
Rodin Museum, 391
Roebling (engineering family), 721
Röntgen, Konrad, 461
Rolland, Romain, 624
Romagna, 174
Roman History (Niebuhr), 53
"Roman Question, the," 176-178, 729-730
Roman Republic, 136
Romantic movement, 9, 104, **164,** 204, 237, 391; in British arts and letters, 47-48, 235; in France, **96-100,** 113, **164**
Rome, 176, 177, 201-202, 893, *m.* 174-175, *m.* 192
Rome-Berlin Axis, 818
Romeo and Juliet (Gounod), 167
Rommel, Marshal Erwin, 892-893, 896
Roon, General Albert von, 187
Roosevelt, Franklin Delano: first administration of, **778-779,** 780-783, 784-785; second administration of, 786, **841, 843-844;** third administration of, **875-876,** 880, 883, 886, 889, 905; fourth administration of, 892, 894, 895, 901; death of, 899
Roosevelt, Theodore, 480-482, 496, 497, 499-504, 516, 521, 524, 545-547, 560
Roosevelt (Theodore) Corollary, 502-504, **545, 738.**
Root-Takahira notes, 553
Rosenberg, Alfred, 816
Rosenkavalier, Der (Strauss), 458
Rossetti, Christina, 162
Rossetti, Dante Gabriel, 162, 163, *p.* 163
Rossetti, William Michael, 162-163
Rossini, Gioachino Antonio (rôs sē′nē, jō′äk-kē′nō än tō′nyō), 69, 73, 99
Rothschild (banking family), 149, 336
Rothschild, Lionel, 195
Rothschild, Lord, 697
Rotterdam, 862, 931
Rouault, Georges, 803, 972
Rougon-Macquart novels (Zola), 388
Rousseau, Jean-Jacques (rü sō′, zhän zhäk), 9
Rousseau, Theodore, 166
Rowlatt Act of 1919, 663-664
Royal Academy (Britain), 47
Royal Air Force, 864, 867, 869
Royal Charter of 1814 (France), **38, 49, 65,** 73, 74

Ruanda-Urundi, 696
Rubáiyát of Omar Khayyám, The (FitzGerald), 162
Rubenstein, Anton, 170
"Rue St. Vincent at Montmartre" (Pissaro), *p.* 350
Ruhr, 700, **702-705,** 707, 869
Rumania, 152, 362-364, 381-382, 429, 473, 561, 568, 686, 691, 943; established as a nation, 154, 203; fascism in, 758, 814; and the First World War, 596, 608, 611, 614, 640, 641; and the Second World War, 870-871, 878, 897, 916
Rumanians, 121, 137, 154, 684
Runyon, Damon, 834
Rush-Bagot agreement, 59
Ruskin, John, 110, 162, 170
Russell, George W., 536
Russell, William Howard, 151
Russia, 35, 40, **53-54,** 56, **66-67,** 92, 100, 105-107, **168-170,** 173, 192, 195, 199, 252, 297, **303-304,** 335, 338, 366, **375,** 382, 393, 399, 460, 486, 524, **531-532,** 552, 563-566, 691, 703, *m.* 67, *m.* 365, *p.* 376; under Czar Alexander II, 181-186, 377-378; under Czar Alexander III, **433-435;** Afghanistan conflict with Great Britain and, **298,** 348, **418,** 429; advance into Asia of, 22, **25-26,** 63-64, 286, **289-294,** 299, *m.* 553; and Balkan Wars, 362-368, 567-568; relations of, with Bismarck, 361, 427, 429, **432,** *m.* 428; relations of, with China, 274-275, 289, **291-292, 422,** 491-493, 515, **743-746,** *m.* 278; and Crimean War, 151-152, 171, 291, *m.* 152; relations of, with Japan (prior to the Second World War), 283-284, **290, 292,** 356, 489, 491-493, 525, *m.* 283; relations of, with Korea (1890's), 488, 491-492; Nazism opposed by, **789-790;** revolution of 1905 in, **463-466;** revolution of 1917-1918 in, **603, 606-607, 618-619, 687-691,** 727; in the Serbo-Bulgarian War, 430, 431; Stalin's victory in, **726-728;** and Tibet, 420, 518; *V Narod* movement in, **324-326;** and the First World War, 569, 578, 579, **580-581,** 583, 604-606, 614, 688; and the Second World War, 585-586, 806, **821-822, 856-858,** 870, **877-879,** 881, 886, **894-895,** 904-905, *m.* 744; after the Second World War, 912, 959, 963, 976. *See also* Communism, Stalin, *and* USSR.
Russian Geographical Society, 422
Russian Revolution: of 1905, **463-466;** of 1917-1918, **603, 606-607, 618-619, 687-691,** 727
Russification, 358, 434
Russo-German Reinsurance Treaty, 485
Russo-Japanese War, 464, **521-524.**
Ruthenians. *See* Czechoslovakia *and* Ukrainian People's Republic.
Rutherford, Ernest, 461, 795
Ruwenzori Mountains, 347
Rydz-Smigly, Marshal Edward (rits′smēg′li, ed′värt), 845
Ryukyu Islands, 354, 356, 928

S

Saar region, 637, 694, 700, **735**
Sacco-Vanzetti case, 722
Sacramento Valley, 224
Sacre-Coeur (Paris), 327
Sacred Books of the East, The (Müller, ed.), 350
Sadowa, Battle of, 190, 192, 199
Saigon, Treaty of, **287-288**, 355, 356
Sainte-Beuve, Charles Augustin (saɴt bœvʹ, shärl
  ō gʏs taɴʹ), 165
Saint-Gaudens, Augustus, 404, 542
Saint-Germain, Treaty of, **640-641**
St. Helena, 36, 37
Saint-Hilaire. *See* Geoffrey Saint-Hilaire.
Saint Joan (Shaw), 802
St. Lawrence Seaway, 783
St. Louis Exhibition of 1904, **543**
Saint Lucia, 875
St. Paul's Cathedral, 868
Saint Petersburg (Russia), 66, 106, 187, 290,
  303, 304; revolutions in (1917), **603**
St. Petersburg Academy, 304
Saint-Simon, Claude Henrí, Comte de, 65
Saint-Simonianism, 89, 95, 118
Saipan, 901
Saito, Admiral Makoto, premier of Japan, 768
Sakhalin Island, 283, 290, 524, 607, 644, 645,
  928, 943
Sakuma Shōzan, 281
Salazar, Antonio de Oliveira, prime minister of
  Portugal, **759**, 814
Salisbury, Edward, 306
Salisbury, Lord, prime minister of England,
  438, **439**, 505, 507
Salome (Strauss), 458
Salomé (Wilde), 396
Salomons, David, 195
Salonika, 535, 611
Samara. *See* Kuibyshev.
Samoa, 267, 354, **413**, 495, **498-499**
Samuel, Sir Herbert, 697
Sandburg, Carl, 836
San Francisco Bridge, 779
San Francisco conferences, 905, 910, **928-929**
San Martin, José de, 59
San Min Chu I (Sun Yat-sen), 661, 774
San Remo, Conference of, 698
San Stefano, Treaty of, 363, 364, **430**
Sand, George, 96, 113, 164
Sanders. *See* Liman von Sanders.
Sanskrit, **303**, 306, 349, 824
Sanskrit Grammar (Whitney), 349
Santa Anna, Antonio de, president of Mexico,
  219-220, 224, 252
Santa Fe, 224
Santo Domingo, 659
Sarajevo, 571, 576
Sarawak, 418
Sardinia, 127, 133, 137, 145, **171-172**, 174, 186-
  187, 358, 364, *m.* 174-175; and Crimean War,
  151, 153. *See also* Piedmont *and* Savoy.

Sargent, John Singer, 403, 480
Sartre, Jean-Paul, 968-969, 972
Saseno Island, 916
Saskatchewan, 319
Sassoon, Siegfried, 623
Satsuma clan, 416
Saudi Arabia, 958, 961
Savage Island, 499
Savigny, Friedrich Karl von, 69
Savoy, **42-43**, 172, 177, 187; house of, 122, 137,
  145, 175, 186, 729, 917
Saxony, 76, 135
Scandinavia, 252, 340, 393. *See also* Denmark,
  Norway, *and* Sweden.
SCAP (Supreme Commander of the Allied
  Powers), 925-927
Scapa Flow, 582, 638
Schacht, Hjalmar (shäɴt, yälʹmär), 706
Scheidemann, Philip, 680, 724
Schleicher, General Kurt von, chancellor of
  Germany, **753-754**
Schleiden, Matthias Jakob, 103
Schleswig, 188-189, 637
Schleswig-Holstein, 135, 185, **188-189**, 194. *See
  also* Holstein *and* Schleswig.
Schlieffen Plan, 581, 582, 589, *m.* 590
Schmidt, I. J., 304
Schnaebelé, Guillaume (shneb läʹ, gē yōmʹ), 430,
  431, 435
Schnitzer, Eduard (Emin Pasha), 347
Schönberg, Arnold, 542, 804, 974
School and Society, The (Dewey), 836
Schopenhauer, Arthur, 69
Schroeder, Baron Kurt von, 754
Schubert, Franz, 53
Schuman, Robert, 979, *p.* 979
Schuman Plan, 373, 979-980, *m.* 980. *See also*
  Coal and Steel Community.
Schumann, Robert, 99, 104
Schurz, Karl, 144
Schuschnigg, Kurt von, 811, 819
Schwann, Theodor, 103
Schwartzkoppen, Colonel L. C. von, 466
Schwarzenberg, Felix, Prince von, 134, 135, 138,
  144
Schweinfurth, Georg, 347
Schweitzer, Albert, 974
Science, 264-265, 341, **385**, 455-456; advances
  of: in the 1850's, **154-158**; in 1905-1914, 541-
  542; during the First World War, 621; after
  the Second World War, **1008-1012**; cosmo-
  politanism in, **170**; in German universities,
  103, 119; in Great Britain, 110; realism in,
  383-386; in Russia, **966-967**; in the United
  States, **233-234**, 267, **840**. *See also* Medical
  science, Physical sciences, Technology, *etc.*
Scientism, 316, **385**
"Scorched earth" policy, 879
Scott, Dred, 243-244
Scott, Walter, 105, 110
Scott, General Winfield, 224
Scottish Burgh Act of 1833, 86

Thiers, Adolphe (tyär, ä dôlf′), 73, 93, 95, 107, 118, 144, 200, 202
Thirteenth Amendment, 321
This Side of Paradise (Fitzgerald), 833
Thoiry, 735
Thomas, Sidney G., 372
Thomas, Theodore, 480
Thomism, 397, 969
Thomson, J. J., 461, 541
Thomson, William (Lord Kelvin), 155, 341
Thoreau, Henry, 236
Thrace, 641, 642
Three Emperors' League, 363, **427**, 429
Three Musketeers, The (Dumas), 97
Three Soldiers (Dos Passos), 834
Thus Spake Zarathustra (Nietzsche), 393
Thyssen, Fritz, 683
Tibet, 64, 302, **419-420**, 422, 518-519, 563, 954
Tieck, Ludwig (tēk, lüt′vin), 53
Tientsin, 274, 291, 514, 662
Tientsin treaties, **275-277**, 291, *p.* 275
Tilak, B. G., 617
Till Eulenspiegel's Merry Pranks (Strauss), 458
Tilsit, Treaty of, 33-34
Times (London), 151
Tipperary, 128
Tirpitz, Admiral von, 508, 569, 593
Tiso, Joseph, 821
Tisza, Count Stephen, prime minister of Hungary, 578
Titan, The (Dreiser), 543
Tito, Marshal, 945
To Have and Have Not (Hemingway), 838
Tocqueville, Alexis de (tôk vēl′, ä lek sē′ də), 209, 231, 1006
Togoland, 425, 696
Tojo, General Hideki, 882, 925
Tokugawa shogunate (tō kü gä wä), 20, 282-283, **284**, 285-286
Tokyo, 282, 285, 286
Tokyo-Berlin Axis, 818-819
Tolstoy, Count Leo, 168-169, 170, 182, 325, 388, 392, 407, 440, 460
Tom Sawyer (Mark Twain), 402
Tonga Islands, 499
Tonkin, **288-289**, 414
Tory Party, 45, 46, 48, 58, 70, 111, 194
Tosca, La (Puccini), 392
Townsend Harris Treaty, 285
Toynbee, Arnold J., 797, 971
Toynbee Hall, 478
Tracts for the Times, 90
Trade, 267-270, 272, 284-286, 289, 291, 298-300, 382, 400-401, 410, 482, 517, 620, 657, 750, 716, 776, 785. *See also* Commerce.
Trade Disputes Bill of 1906 (Britain), 538
Trade Union Act (Britain, 1913), 538
Trade unions, 453-454, 481; in Canada, 483; in France, 150, 379; in Germany, 332, 681; in Great Britain, 89, 112. *See also* Labor unions.
1072 Trades Disputes and Trades Union Act (Britain,

1927), 725
Trades Union Congress, 538-539, **724**
Transatlantic cable, 341
Transcaucasia, 606, 612
Transcendentalism, 232, **235-236,** 237, 306
Trans-Jordan, 695, 698, 958. *See also* Jordan.
Transportation, 87-89, 106, 181, 334-335, 351, 375; in the United States, 214, 229-230, 409
Transportation Building (Chicago), 543
Trans-Siberian Railroad, 375, 491, 606, 607
Transvaal, 347, 426, 511, 538
Transylvania, 561, 596, 641, 871
Traveler from Altruria, A (Howells), 479
Treason of the Intellectuals, The (Benda), 798
Treaties of 1947, *m.* 929
Tree, Sir Herbert Beerbohm, 451
Treitschke, Heinrich von (trīch′kə, hīn rin fən), 385, 487
Trench warfare, **589-590,** 606
Trent Affair, **252-253**
Trentino, 641
Trial, The (Kafka), 800
Trial Monarchy, 561
Trianon, Treaty of, **641**
Trieste, 428, 561, 641, 916
Trinidad, 875
Tripartite Pact, 870, 877
Triple Alliance, **426-432,** 486, 516, 561, 565, 566, 570. *See also* Germany, Austria, *and* Italy.
Triple Entente, 552, **563,** 564, 570. *See also* France, Russia, *and* England.
Tripoli, 347, 429, 565, 566, 892
Tripolitan War, 720
"Trizonia," 922. *See also* West Germany.
Trollope, Mrs. Frances, 209
Troppau Conference, 55, 56
Trotsky, Leon, 465, 605, 619, 690, 726-727, 762
Truman, Harry S., **902-904, 939-940,** 977, 983
"Truman Doctrine," 944, **976-977**
Trusteeship Council (UN), 695, 913
Trust-busting, 481-482
Trusts, 336, **400,** 410, 682, 722; vertical, 682. *See also* Business combinations.
Tsarskoye Selo, 106
Tsêng Kuo-fan (tseng′kwō′fän′), 279
Tsingtao, 649
Tu Duc, emperor of Annam, 286, 287, 288, **355**
Tunis, 426
Tunisia, 364, 427, 892-893, 936
Turgenev, Ivan Sergeyevich, 168-169, 182, 184, 388
Turkey, 23-24, 153, 154, 362-364, 426, 432, 433, **505,** 509, 564, 566-568, 614, 662, 814; in Crimean War, 151; dispute with Egypt in the 1820's and 1830's, 107; and Greek War of Independence, 66-67; political and social revolution in, **534-536, 686, 726;** and First World War, 592, 606, 611, 612, 614; after First World War, 641-643; and Second World

War, 859, 881; after Second World War, 976-977
Turkish language, 304, 422
Turkish Republic, 686. *See also* Turkey.
Turkistan-Siberia Railroad, 761
Turner, J. M. W., 47, 110
Turner, Nat, 240
Tuscany, 137, 145, 174, *m.* 174-175
Twain, Mark, 402, 457-458
"Twenty-one Demands," 600-601, 647, 649
Twenty-first Amendment, 780
Twenty-second Amendment, 875
Two Years before the Mast (Dana), 236
Tydings-McDuffie Act (1934), 784, 829
Tyler, John, **218**, 220, 221
Typee (Melville), 306
Tz'u Hsi, empress (tsü′ shē′), 513, 554

U

U-boats, 879, 880-881
Uitlanders, 507, 511
Ukraine, 606, 685, 688, 691, 761, 878
Ukrainian People's Republic, 606
Ulster, 438, 536-538, 583, 671, 672
Ultramontanism, 95, 96
Ulyanov, Nikolai. *See* Lenin.
Ulysses (Joyce), 798-799
Umbria, 177
Uncle Tom's Cabin (Stowe), 168, 240
"Unconditional surrender," 892, 898-901, 905, 919, 931
"Undeclared War" (France and U.S.), 599
Under Fire (Barbusse), 623
Underground (London), 543
Underground movements, **887-888**
"Underground railway," 240
Underwood Tariff, 549
UNESCO, 1007
Union Act of 1840, 92
Union of India, **952-953**. *See also* India.
Union Pacific Railroad, 256, 351, 408
Union of South Africa, **538**, 696
Union of Soviet Socialist Republics. *See* USSR.
"Union or Death" society, 576
Unitarianism, 235
United Kingdom, 194, *m.* 428. *See also* England, Great Britain, *etc.*
United Landtag of 1847, 120
United Mine Workers, 256, 481
United Nations (organization), **885-886**, 905, **910-914**, 953, 954, 958, 959, 984, *c.* 915; compared with League of Nations, *c.* 693
United Nations Charter, 905, **910-911**
United States of America, 59-60, **293-294, 340-341**, 366, 367, **401-403**; literary renaissance in, **225-237**; anti-German sentiment in, 560, 594, 599-600; and atomic energy control, 962-964; attitude toward Boer War of, 512; boom in, after 1922, **721-722**; relations of, with Canada, 218-219, 317, 318, 320; relations of, with China, 275, 293, 767, 946-947; aftermath of Civil War in, 255-256, **317-324, 339-345;**

communist and socialist experiments in, 231-232; and Crimean War, 153; in Cuba, 496, 497, 499; democratic ideal in, **209-210;** domestic problems in (1890's), **474-482;** in Dominican Republic, 502-504; economic sectionalism in, **239;** election procedure and suffrage in, 209-210, 214; and Europe, 18, 144, **209**, 215, **341-342, 374**, 457-458, 542, 543, **732;** European Recovery Program of, 977; decline of expansionism in, **319-320;** and Far East, 293, **302-306**, 552, 645; farmers in, 343, 657-658, 722, 780; foreign policy of, under Truman, 940; foreign policy of, under Wilson, **550-551;** and France, 179, 189, 215; Gilded Age in, **399-413;** relations of, with Great Britain, **59-60**, 218-219, 320; immigration to, 340, **376-377**, 381, 655-656, *m.* 376; income tax, first in, 254; inflation and "boom" of 1835-1836 in, **215-216;** interventionism, growth of, in, **844-845;** isolationism in, 632, 650, **784**, 785, **842-843**, 873-874, 876, 883; relations of, with Japan (pre-Pearl Harbor), 55, 285-286, 293, 416, 515-516, 525, 552-553, **558-559**, 600, 643, 646, **882**, *m.* 283; in Korea, 984; labor *vs.* laissez faire system in, **343-345;** in Latin America, 542, 544-545, 658; and Locarno agreements, 710-711; and Manchuria, 554, **766-767;** national supremacy *vs.* state sovereignty issue in, 211-212; nationalism in, 655-656; neutrality of, before world wars, 597-598, **842-843**, 859; in the Pacific, **267**, 320; in Panama, 499-500, 659; Pan-Americanism and, **738, 844;** at Paris Peace Conference, 634; and the Philippines, 498, 828, 829; population growth of, in, **225-228;** investments of, abroad, *c.* 733; New Deal in, **776-786;** political reform in, 478; public-works program in, 777, 779; reparations and, 701, 749; revolutionary tradition in, **17-19;** in Russo-Japanese War, 521; in Samoa, 354, **413**, 418; and Siam, 288; and the United Nations, 912; urbanization in, **227-228;** waterways, in, 229-230; and Western Hemisphere defense by, **874-875;** and Venezuela, 495-496, 500; at Washington Conference, 646-647; as a world power, **494-504**, *m.* 503; in First World War, 598, 599-600, 609-611, **615;** post-First World War period in, **650-659, 716-723;** and Second World War, 856, **873-875**, 927; after Second World War, 931, **937-941, 950.**
U.S. Bureau of Corporations, 482
U.S. Department of Commerce and Labor, 482
U.S. Office of Production Management, 875
U.S. Supreme Court, 243-244, 344, 400, 547, 655, 780, 786, 841
U.S.A. (Dos Passos), 837
United States Steel Corp., 482, 721, 778
Universal German Workingmen's Association, 196
University of Chicago, 544
University of Kazan, 304
University of Munich, 302

1073

Wuthering Heights (Brontë), 109
Wyndham Act, 472

X

Xenophobia, 655-656, 704

Y

Yakub Beg (yä küb′ beg′), Moslem leader, 292
Yale University, 306
Yangtze River, 277, 414
Yangtze Valley, 493, 742, 767
Yeast (Kingsley), 108
Yeats, William Butler, 395, 536, 798, 825
Yedo. *See* Tokyo.
"Yellow Peril," **422,** 490, 576
"Yellow press," 375
Yemen, 958, 961
Yenan, 772
Yerkes, Charles T., 543-544
Yerkes Observatory, 544
Yersin, Alexander, 460
Yoshida Shigeru, 927
Young, Brigham, 224
Young, Owen D., 707, 739
Young Germany movement, 102, 104
Young Italy movement, 104, 122
Young Ireland movement, 112, 129
Young Norway party, 123

Young Plan, **738-739,** 749
Young Turk Party, **534-536,** 564, 568
Ypres, First Battle of, 589
Yüan Shih-kai, 513, 555, 592
Yuen-ming-yuen, 277
Yugoslavia, 633-634, 640, 641, 686, 758, 814, 872, 916, 943, 944, **945**
Yugoslavs 561, 562, 612
Yünnan, 415

Z

Zaibatsu, 740
Zamora, Niceto Alcalá, president of Spain, **759**
Zanzibar, 485
Zemstvo Congress, 464-466
Zemstvo laws, 184
Zeppelin, Count Ferdinand von, 452
Zeppelins, 720
Zimmermann note, 599-600
Zinoviev, Grigori, 690, 726-727, 762
Zionism, 359, 473-474, **696-698,** 959, 1003
Zola, Émile, 98, 338, 371, 387, 394, 440, **467-468,** *p.* 468
Zollverein, 52, 69, 101, 103, 178, 186, 192, 412, *m.* 191
Zollvereinblatt (List), 119
Zulu War, 347
Zurich, Treaty of, 175
Zweig, Arnold, 800